TELEVISION'S GREATEST HITS

Every hit television programme since 1960

PAUL GAMBACCINI ■ ROD TAYLOR

D1337376

Network Books

Network Books is an imprint of BBC Books,
a division of BBC Enterprises Limited,
Woodlands, 80 Wood Lane, London W12 0TT
First published 1993
© Paul Gambaccini and Rod Taylor 1993
ISBN 0 563 36247 2
The moral rights of the authors have been asserted
Designed by Grahame Dudley

Set in Helvetica and Bodoni by Ace Filmsetting Ltd, Frome
Printed and bound in Great Britain by Butler and Tanner Ltd, Frome
Cover printed by Clays Ltd, St Ives plc

CONTENTS

PAUL GAMBACCINI

Paul Gambaccini has at some point been a regular on all four British terrestrial television networks. He has also been co-author of a number of best-selling books, including the Guinness Book of *British Hit Singles*.

ROD TAYLOR

Rod Taylor began his career at Granada Television in 1964 as a producer specializing in children's shows, comedy and light entertainment. During his time at Granada he met drama and documentary maker Michael Darlow with whom he still has a partnership. It was Darlow who first brought Rod and Paul Gambaccini together to make a series called 'The Other Side Of The Tracks' for Channel 4. This seminal popular music series ran for three seasons and was filmed all over the world. It was during one of Rod and Paul's many transatlantic flights that the idea of *Television's Greatest Hits* was born. Again for Channel 4 the pair went on to produce the award-winning 'Motown Story'.

Over the last ten years Rod has produced and directed shows for all four channels. He has an encyclopaedic knowledge of the variety theatre and television light entertainment and is in much demand as an after dinner speaker. He lives in Cheshire and has three children.

INTRODUCTION

Although some of us can remember life before television, most of us can't imagine life without it. The number of people in the first category gets smaller every day. Like Mickey Mouse, fast food and the song 'Happy Birthday', television is an invention of the twentieth century that seems like it must always have been there. What would it be like to hold a birthday party and not be able to sing 'Happy Birthday'? What would you do if you only had time for a quick snack and found that no snacks were quick? What did children laugh at before Mickey Mouse and Donald Duck? How did people spend their evenings before television?

'We talked to each other and we read,' one 70-year-old woman shrugged, as if life without television were a perfectly normal existence – which, of course, it is. You don't miss what you've never known. But to many people of later generations, the idea of spending an evening chatting or poring over books seems either romantically quaint or socially disastrous. To deprive the majority of young people their several daily hours of television viewing would leave a massive gap in their lives.

A rock 'n' roll single in the late 1950s or a punk record in the late 1970s made a social statement regardless of its lyrical content. Television in itself says nothing. It can be used for various purposes, depending on the motivation of the powers that control it. For example, you often hear elegies for the high culture programmes of the 1950s, as if the imposition of quality standards on broadcasting could lift the intellectual tone of the population. In many dictatorships television has existed primarily to disseminate party doctrine and praise the country's leaders. In the United States television exists to fill the time between commercials in a way that maximizes the viewing and effectiveness of the ads.

In Britain there is a balance between the state-chartered BBC and the commercial companies. Their co-existence affects the type of programmes that each one broadcasts. The BBC has found that to validate the method by which it is funded, the licence fee, it has to demonstrate its programmes are actually popular. The commercial franchises, on the other hand, must maintain some dignity and quality control to justify their position alongside the BBC. This is the conflict that results in the BBC presenting the Australian soap opera *Neighbours* and ITV producing some of the most acclaimed drama of the 1980s.

Television supplies reference points for conversation and role models for young people. It popularizes some vocations at the expense of others. The amount of airtime devoted to pop music, for example, communicates the idea that achieving this kind of glamorous life is open to all, though in fact there will only ever be ten places in the Top Ten. Perhaps if television companies devoted three hours per day to botany, there would be more botanists.

The medium has also altered the way in which professionals communicate with the general public. Celebrities, who might once have granted interviews at any time of year, now focus on major talk shows when they have a new product to promote. Politicians tailor their public remarks to include the 10-second 'sound bite' that will look good on the evening news. They pay attention to their visual image to appeal to voters. A classic example of this is Margaret Thatcher, who altered the way she looked and the manner in which she spoke so viewers would be more likely to support her. When Walter Mondale was trounced by Ronald Reagan in 1984, his first explanation was that he wasn't good on TV – an implicit reminder that his foe was.

The effects that television advertising have had on consumer spending and acquisitiveness could be the study of an entire volume. An excellent example, however, is that of children's toys. Before the advent of mass production and mass marketing, toys were limited in range and number, but children were at least likely to have *different* dolls and books. Today's production techniques and promotions on television result in lemming-like crazes that have youngsters demanding the same toys throughout an entire country or even the world. In fact many children's animated programmes are commissioned with toy tie-ins in mind.

It is clear from this example that the influence and power of television has grown dramatically in the last thirty years. There is now enough television history to want to know what the most-viewed programmes have been on a week-to-week basis, what was the attraction of the most-popular episode of each charted show, what kind of programme each was, and who starred in it. For anyone who wants to gauge the influence of television in Great Britain, the information starts here.

Television's Greatest Hits isn't just for reference. You can spend hours reading this book, watching the rise and fall of your own favourite programmes and wondering how on earth anyone could have found something of interest in others. Photographs will show you what every number one programme looked like during its peak period of popularity.

When we first considered compiling this book five years ago some people said that no one would be interested. Television isn't like popular music, we were told; there were no golden oldies and you couldn't walk into a store and buy an old Number One you hadn't heard. This underestimates the popularity of television and the growth of the video market. Enter any well-stocked video shop and you can buy any episode of *Monty Python's Flying Circus*, any number of Cup Finals, and a huge range of drama. Speak to any lifelong television viewer and they'll talk your ear off about *Crossroads*, *This Is Your Life* and *Top of the Pops*. Television contributes to our impressions of life, whether they be from *Armchair Theatre* or *Dallas*, and brings live events into the home, whether it's Wimbledon or the Gulf War. It is this all-embracing mix that makes television so formidable. It gives us the Coronation, *Coronation Street*, and a chef preparing Coronation Chicken, all without batting its single eye.

We've written this book because we want to add to an understanding of the medium that dominates our age. Before we can figure out why people have watched what they have, we have got to know what it is they've watched. We hope you'll want to know, too.

We also hope popular demand will allow us to publish updated editions on a regular basis. If there are features you would like to see in subsequent versions, let us know. We always want to improve our ratings.

A brief history of television broadcasting in the UK

On 2 October 1925, John Logie Baird transmitted the first recognizable image of a human face into a television screen in his Soho laboratory. The face belonged to his office boy William Taynton. Just less than two years later the Television Society was formed with the aim of studying the possibilities of the development of television.

The BBC began the first public service on 22 August 1932 from a Baird-equipped studio in Broadcasting House, London. The system used a low-definition 30 lines. By the time the BBC Television service was officially inaugurated by the Postmaster General, Major G.C. Tryon, on 2 November 1936, two systems were in operation. From London's Alexandra Palace the Baird 240-line system alternated on a weekly basis with the Marconi-EMI 405-line system. The service was available in the London area only and covered the Coronation of King George VI in May 1937. Earlier that year the Baird system was dropped altogether. The BBC continued to transmit on 405 lines until the service was closed down on 1 September 1939 because of the imminent out-break of war.

The television service resumed from Alexandra Palace on 7 June 1946 and covered the victory parades in London the following day. It was still only available in the London area. TV licences numbered a mere 14,560 in 1947, rising to 125,567 the following year.

New transmitters slowly brought television to other areas of the country. The single event that most stimulated public interest in owning a set was the Coronation of Her Majesty Queen Elizabeth II on 2 June 1953. From then on there was no looking back. Parliamentary debate ensued on the introduction of a competitor to the BBC.

The Television Act of 1954 received Royal Assent on 30 July the same year and provided for the establishment of the Independent Television Authority (ITA). This body was to be responsible to Parliament, would own and operate the necessary transmitters, appoint the programme companies, supervise programme planning and control the advertisements. The ITA, with Sir Kenneth Clark in the chair, held its first meeting on 4 August 1954 and appointed Sir Robert Fraser as its first director-general. The franchise framework was devised, splitting the major population areas into weekday and weekend slots. On 24 August 1954 an advertisement appeared in the press inviting applications to become Independent Television contractors for London, the Midlands and the North of England. ITV began in the London area on 22 September 1955 with a live transmission of its inaugural banquet at the Guildhall in the City of London. This was mounted by the two successful applicants for the weekday and weekend broadcasting slots for the London area: Associated Rediffusion (AR) and the Associated Broadcasting Company (later renamed Associated Television, or ATV). They were joined in this broadcast by Independent Television News (ITN), set up by the successful applicants to provide their own news service.

The ITV map grew over the years and has changed as follows:

AREA	COMPANY	First Transmission	Last Transmission
London (weekday)	Associated Rediffusion (AR)	22.9.55	29.7.68
	Thames	30.7.68	31.12.92
	Carlton	1.1.93	
London (weekend)	Associated Television (ATV)	24.9.55	28.7.68
	London Weekend (LWT)	2.8.68	
Midlands (weekday)	ATV	17.2.56	31.12.81
	Central	1.1.82	
Midlands (weekend)	ABC	18.2.56	28.7.68
	ATV	2.8.68	30.12.81
	Central	5.1.82	
North (weekday)	Granada (incl. Yorkshire)	3.5.56	26.7.68
North (weekend)	ABC	5.5.56	28.7.68
North-West	Granada	29.7.68	
Central Scotland	Scottish Television (STV)	31.8.57	
North Scotland	Grampian Television	30.9.61	
Wales and West of England	TWW	14.1.58	3.3.68
	Harlech Television (HTV)	4.3.68	
South of England	Southern Television	30.8.58	31.12.81
	TVS	1.1.82	31.12.92
	Meridian	1.1.93	
East of England	Anglia Television	27.10.59	
North-East England	Tyne Tees Television (TTT)	15.1.59	
Northern Ireland	Ulster Television	31.10.59	
South-West England	Westward Television	29.4.61	11.8.81
	Television South-West (TSW)	12.8.81	31.12.92
	Westcountry Television	1.1.93	
The Borders	Border Television	1.1.61	
Channel Islands	Channel Television	1.9.62	
West and North Wales	Wales (West and North)	14.9.62	26.1.64
(This area was later absorbed by Wales and West of England)			
Yorkshire	Yorkshire Television (YTV)	29.7.68	
Breakfast	TV-am	1.2.83	31.12.92
	Good Morning Television (GMTV)	1.1.93	

The Pilkington Committee of Broadcasting was set up in July 1960, under the chairmanship of Sir Harry Pilkington, to consider the future of broadcasting in the UK. It reported in June 1962. Although it was highly critical of ITV, the government largely rejected its recommendations with the notable exception that the BBC should begin an additional television service on 625 lines UHF. As a result BBC2 began broadcasting on 20 April 1964.

The launch of the telecommunications satellite Telstar in 1962 opened the world to the possibilities of global television. The first live pictures from the USA were beamed across the Atlantic on 11 July 1962 and were seen by an estimated 200 million viewers in European countries.

The first regular colour television service in the UK began on BBC2 on 1 July 1967. The colour service was extended to BBC1 and ITV using the same system and UHF on 15 November 1969.

The Ministry of Posts and Telecommunications was wound up in May 1974 and government responsibility for broadcasting passed to the Home Office. In April of that year the Annan Committee on Broadcasting was set up under the chairmanship of Lord Annan. It reported on 24 March 1977, recommending that broadcasting be preserved as a public service accountable to Parliament but free from political pressure and that a structure be devised to enable the expansion of the industry over a 15-year period.

In May 1979 it was proposed that a new channel should be operated by the Independent Broadcasting Authority (IBA). In January 1981 Channel 4 began to broadcast with the remit to innovate and experiment with programmes appealing to tastes not generally catered for by ITV. Channel 4 was the first UK broadcaster not to be a programme maker: its method of commissioning programmes spawned a whole generation of independent producers.

In the meantime a deterioration of labour relations between ITV programme contractors and the technicians union ACTT resulted in an 11-week stoppage from 10 August to 19 October 1979. It is estimated that more than £100 million in advertising revenue was lost. As a result of this and other continuing disputes, the government of Margaret Thatcher determined to deregulate television and increase competition, encouraging the growth of the independent production and technical facilities sectors of the industry.

The BBC began a breakfast service on 17 January 1983, followed on 1 February by the new ITV franchise contractor TV-am. Yorkshire Television launched the first 24-hour-a-day service in 1986 and the BBC started a daytime service on 27 October, 1986.

Satellite television meanwhile had made great advances since Telstar in 1962, and Sky Television began on 16 January 1984. Initially it was available on a cable service only in Swindon, Milton Keynes and Greenwich. The right to operate Britain's first direct broadcasting by satellite was awarded to BSB, a consortium set up by Granada, Anglia, the Virgin group, Amstrad Electronics and the Pearson group. With both Sky and BSB registering heavy operating losses, the two merged into BSkyB at the end of 1990. Today BSkyB shows signs of public acceptance, principally through its aggressive policy of bidding for the exclusive rights to major sporting events and films.

With the new ITV franchises in position from January 1993, the BBC's charter obligation to continue public service broadcasting, Channel 4's on-going remit, the growth of satellite accessibility and the possibility of a terrestrial Channel 5, there seems no stopping the voracious public appetite for television. It is an industry which generates and consumes vast amounts of money. There is, today, a great deal more than pride at stake in producing *Television's Greatest Hits*.

The ratings

The first edition of the TV show *Television's Greatest Hits* was transmitted on BBC1 on 6 April 1992. We were told the following morning that it had been seen by 12.2 million viewers. How did anybody know? That is the question most often asked about television ratings. We cannot claim to fully understand the sophisticated data-gathering processes from which the figures are produced. Suffice it to say that they are considered to be so accurate that the advertising industry disposes of its vast budgets according to the ratings. Producers' programmes survive or face the axe according to their ratings performance.

The BBC conducted the first broadcasting research in 1936. Its Audience Research Department was established in 1938. The Daily Survey of Listening began in 1939 and was extended to cover television in 1952. The method employed used an aided-recall (i.e. based on memory) system of interviews with a varying number of representative individuals. The BBC used its findings to respond to the requirements of its viewers, but with the advent of ITV in 1955, the research was of greater importance to advertisers who wished to assess the selling potential of the new commercial channel.

Several organizations and systems of audience measurement were tried at first. The giant American company A.C. Nielsen started the Nielsen Television Index using its 'audimeter' system. They were retained by Granada Television only until 1959. Occasional reports based on aided-recall interviews were produced by Gallup, while another aided-recall company, Pulse, provided ratings for the London and Midlands areas. The first official company to represent the ITV contractors was Television Audience Measurement (TAM), which installed meters in 2300 homes throughout the UK in 1956. The BBC continued to produce its own ratings.

In 1967 a breakaway group of four TAM executives formed a new company in 1967, Audits of Great Britain (AGB), and won the contract to provide the official service to the Joint Industry Committee for Television Audience Research (JICTAR). This committee had been set up by the Independent Television Companies Association (ITCA), the Institute of Practitioners in Advertising (IPA) and the Incorporated Society of British Advertisers (ISBA). The JICTAR ratings were produced through a mixed system of meters, interviews and diaries. The BBC figures and those produced for JICTAR were often in considerable conflict. In 1977 the Annan Committee recommended the establishment of an audience measurement system to be shared by the BBC and ITV. In the interim three years before this recommendation became practice, JICTAR moved away from measuring the number of homes tuned in to a programme to an assessment of the number of individual viewers who watched. This important change is reflected in this book in the dramatic rise in viewing figures from 1 August 1977.

Following protracted discussions between the BBC and the ITCA, whose requirements from audience research data are very different, the Broadcasters' Audience Research Board (BARB) was set up in 1980 and began to provide the results of quantitative research in August 1981. The modern ratings are produced by selecting samples of the population according to age, sex, social and economic status. Each selected household has a meter directly connected to a computer, so the data is received automatically. A cross-section of households are used, with varying numbers of residents. The figures now include those programmes recorded on video. The aided-

recall interview and the diaries given to selected households are still in use to supplement the electronic data, while a variety of special audience surveys is undertaken for specific market research. As well as audience measurement, BARB, through the BBC Research Department, also gauges audience reaction in terms of response and appreciation. For the purposes of this book, however, we have restricted entries to audience measurement.

A programme qualifies for entry in *Television's Greatest Hits* if it made the weekly Top Twenty of the national ratings. There are certain anomalies. In the first few months of 1960 data was only available to establish a Top Ten. For the weeks commencing 3 and 10 September 1979 it was decided not to publish any figures whatsoever because of the ITV strike. For a period in the mid-eighties soaps which were screened more than once a week were given a cumulative rather than an average rating, thus providing an unrealistically high figure.

EastEnders benefited controversially from the amalgamation of viewing figures for multiple episodes shown in the same week.

The data

In *Television's Greatest Hits* the programmes are listed alphabetically. If 'A' or 'The' is the first word in the title, then the second word determines the ordering. In the case of an individual beginning the show's title it is his or her name that determines the alphabetical position.
For example:

The Paul Daniels Magic Show is listed under 'P'

Total number of weeks spent in the Top Twenty between 1960 and 1991

Broadcasting company, category of show

Paul Daniels Magic Show, The   **59 wks**

BBC, magic

Paul Daniels came from the north-east of England, practising his magical skills in working men's clubs and stopping off for a couple of series at Granada in 1977 and 1978. He arrived at the BBC in London in 1979 and became the most successful magician in the history of British television. From 1982 Paul was assisted by Debbie McGee, who was also Mrs Daniels.
Directors: *included etc.*

A brief explanation of the programme or series

Highest viewing figure achieved, to the nearest 100,000

Exact date and time of the most watched edition

Highest position achieved by this programme in charts

Year shown

Total number of weeks in chart during the year

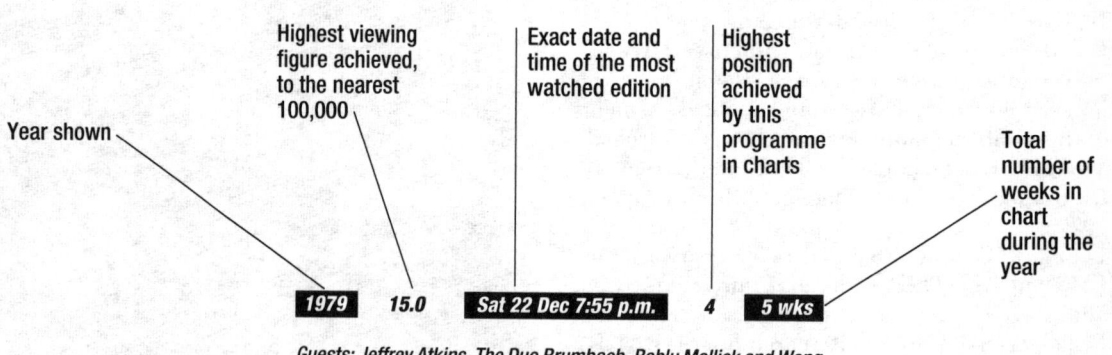

1979   **15.0**   **Sat 22 Dec 7:55 p.m.**   4   **5 wks**

Guests: Jeffrey Atkins, The Duo Brumbach, Bablu Mallick and Wong Mow Ting.

Details of actual show

We have listed individual sports, such as boxing, football and snooker, under the name of the sport and limited the text to the top rated event for each year. Programme strands such as *Sportsnight* do receive their own entries, as do the quadrennial special event programmes like *Olympic Grandstand* and the *World Cup*. The BBC and ITV get one *News* listing each per year covering their various regular newscasts, but special news events get their own individual listings.

Credits

Where possible production credits for all British-originated programmes are given. Set designers are credited for major dramas, and writers for programmes to which they contributed significantly. Where a producer is listed without a separate director it is assumed the producer also directed. In the case of feature films we have restricted the credit to that of the director. When someone has performed his or her task for the entire chart run of the programme his or her name is listed in the general descriptive information below the title and above the annual breakdown. If the contributor has performed his or her job for the bulk but not all of the peak programmes, his

or her name is still listed in the general descriptive information, but with the relevant years in parentheses.

Sadly television was not always aware that it would be of historic significance, and numerous documents and indeed programmes of value have been lost or destroyed. We would very much welcome proposed additions and corrections for future editions.

Acknowledgments

The authors would like to thank all those who have helped in the collation of the data contained in this book. This volume would not have existed without the generous co-operation of Manchester Central Libraries, the Picton Library, Liverpool, the Westminster Library, the IBA (ITC) Library and the ITVA Library. We are personally grateful to Sylvia Reeves, Graeme White, Ian Campbell, Laura Peaple, Alex Galvin, Nigel Hill, Robert Heading, Rory Sheehan and Terry Gibbens.

The authors also wish to extend special thanks and appreciation to their long-suffering editor Julian Flanders and to commissioning editor Heather Holden-Brown for her unrelenting patience and encouragement.

'A' for Andromeda — 1 wk

BBC, drama

In this sci-fi thriller serial in seven parts by writer John Elliot and Cambridge Professor of Astronomy Fred Hoyle, earthlings followed instructions from outer space to build a computer to master the world. Set in 1970, the serial was produced by Michael Hayes and Norman James and introduced Julie Christie as Andromeda.

Hayes had spotted Christie at the Central School of Drama in the summer of 1960. When Hoyle and Elliot came up with the scripts for the serial he knew he needed a stunning, unusual girl for the central character. He had not considered Christie outstanding in 1960, but when he saw her as Anne Frank at an end-of-term matinee he knew he had his Andromeda.

The series starred Esmond Knight and Mary Morris with Peter Halliday, Noel Johnson and Patricia Kneale.

| 1961 | 5.4 | Tue 14 Nov 8:30 p.m. | 12 | 1 wk |

'The Last Mystery'
In this final part of the serial, the computer provides the government with a rocket capable of destroying any space satellite. John Fleming (Peter Halliday) tries to sabotage the computer, but it takes its revenge.

A-Team, The — 90 wks

USA presented by ITV, drama

This series starred George Peppard as Colonel 'Hannibal' Smith, leader of a band of soldiers of fortune. They were all Vietnam war veterans who were convicted of a military crime allegedly committed at the end of that war. The men existed as outlaws in the ghettos of Los Angeles. The show also starred Melinda Culea as Amy Allen, Dirk Benedict as Peck, Dwight Schultz as Murdock and Mr T as Baracus.

| 1983 | 14.6 | Fri 4 Nov 7:30 p.m. | 2 | 20 wks |

'The Only Church in Town'
The team goes on a rescue mission to save an orphanage in South America.

| 1984 | 16.6 | Sat 29 Dec 6:05 p.m. | 2 | 24 wks |

'Showdown'
Hannibal leads his soldiers into one of their most dangerous assignments.

| 1985 | 14.0 | Sat 16 Feb 5:35 p.m. | 10 | 11 wks |

'The Big Squeeze'
A corrupt money lender and his hit man terrorize a small-time businessman.

| 1986 | 13.8 | Sat 22 Nov 5:35 p.m. | 5 | 22 wks |

'Trial by Fire'
Team members are arrested and charged with murder. Guest star: Robert Vaughn.

| 1987 | 13.9 | Sat 17 Jan 5:45 p.m. | 6 | 13 wks |

'Semi-Friendly Persuasion'
The team tries to protect a peace-loving group from a gang of ruffians.

A. J. Wentworth BA — 6 wks

Thames, situation comedy

This series by Basil Boothroyd was adapted from stories by H. F. Ellis set in a 1940s school. Arthur Lowe starred in the title role as a maths master obsessed by the honour of the school, the high cost of pen nibs and the sneaky tactics of his arch enemy, Matron (Marion Mathie). Harry Andrews played the headmaster. The series was recorded just a few weeks before Lowe died on 15 April, 1982.

| 1982 | 12.9 | Mon 12 Jul 8:00 p.m. | 3 | 6 wks |

Matron suggests to the headmaster that Wentworth is not being totally reasonable in his attitude towards the rest of the staff.
Producer: Michael Mills.

ASA National Swimming Championships — 1 wk

BBC, sport

| 1966 | 5.1 | Sat 10 Sep 9:10 p.m. | 18 | 1 wk |

Max Robertson and Harry Carpenter introduce the finals from the Derby Baths, Blackpool.
Television Presentation: Nick Hunter.

ABBA in Concert — 1 wk

BBC, music

The group from Sweden (Benny Andersson, Agnetha Faltskog, Annifrid 'Frida' Lyngstand and Bjorn Ulvaeus) came to fame winning THE EUROVISION SONG CONTEST in 1974. 'ABBA' was an acronym of their initials.

| 1980 | 10.4 | Sun 7 Sep 8:35 p.m. | 20 | 1 wk |

Director: Urban Lasson.

....

Abracadabra — 20 wks

AR, game show

Roy Ward Dickson hosted a game show of his own devising. 'Word Magic' tested and improved vocabulary.
Director: Eric Croall.

| 1961 | 5.1 | Thu 3 Aug 7:30 p.m. | 5 | 8 wks |

Assisted by Shirley Ward Dickson.

| 1962 | 4.9 | Thu 23 Aug 7:00 p.m. | 8 | 12 wks |

Assisted by Gaynor Jones.

....

According to Dora — 7 wks

BBC, comedy

In this series starring Dora Bryan, a theme was explored each week.
Producer: Robin Nash.

| 1968 | 5.3 | Tue 23 Jul 9:05 p.m. | 6 | 5 wks |

'Entertainment'

| | | Tue 6 Aug 9:05 p.m. | | |

'Holidays And Leisure'
These two programmes achieved identical viewing figures and chart positions. They both featured Terence Brady and Diana King.
Musical Director: Geoff Love.

| 1969 | 6.1 | Fri 2 May 7:55 p.m. | 10 | 2 wks |

'A Bryan's Eye View of the World'
With Doug Fisher, Rex Garner, John Junkin, Ronnie Stevens and Mark Wynter.
Musical Director: Malcolm Lockyer.

According to Dora Special — 1 wk

BBC, comedy

| 1968 | 6.1 | Tue 31 Dec 7:30 p.m. | 20 | 1 wk |

'Past, Present and Future'
A New Year's Eve special starring Dora Bryan with Tim Barrett, Barbara New, Hugh Paddick and Michael Stainton.
Writers: John Junkin, Lew Schwarz, Ronald Chesney and Ronald Wolfe.
Musical Director: Dennis Wilson. **Producer:** Robin Nash.

....

Achille Lauro Affair, The — 2 wks

USA presented by ITV, drama

| 1991 | 11.4 | Mon 9 Sep 8:00 p.m. | 13 | 2 wks |

The second and final part of a true story. In 1985 four Palestinians hijacked the Italian luxury liner Achille Lauro as it cruised in the Mediterranean. Burt Lancaster stars with Robert Culp and Eva Marie Saint.
Director: Alberto Negrin.

....

Act of Separation — 1 wk

LWT, drama

| 1970 | 4.9 | Sun 9 Aug 10:15 p.m. | 18 | 1 wk |

This adaptation by Ilona Ference of Guy de Maupassant's story 'Monsieur Parent' stars Keith Bell, Lisa Daniel, Gwen Nelson and Jack Watling. A man turns his housekeeper out of the house because of her insinuations about the unfaithfulness of his wife.
Designer: Don Fisher. **Director:** Anthony Kearey. **Executive Producer:** Cecil Clarke.

....

Adam Adamant Lives — 1 wk

BBC, drama

Gerald Harper starred as Adam, a Victorian gentleman dedicated to the fight against evil. In 1902 he was trapped and entombed in a block of ice by his deadliest enemy, The Face. He thawed out to live again in 1966.

| 1966 | 5.3 | Thu 23 Jun 8:00 p.m. | 15 | 1 wk |

'A Vintage Year for Scoundrels' by Tony Williamson.
Adam Adamant emerges into the swinging Sixties.
Designer: Darrol Blake. **Director:** David Proudfoot. **Producer:** Verity Lambert.

Adam Faith Show, The | 1 wk

AR, music

| 1961 | 5.6 | Wed 21 Jun 8:00 p.m. | 7 | 1 wk |

Adam Faith, aged twenty, has his first prime-time special. Guests include Adele Leigh, Richard Wattis and trad band Dick Charlesworth and his City Gents. Special guest star: Tony Bennett. With Tony Osborne and his Orchestra.
Director: Grahame Turner.

Adult Movie, The | 8 wks

Presented by ITV, film

| 1983 | 12.0 | Sat 10 Sep 9:15 p.m. | 6 | 5 wks |

'Escape from Alcatraz'
Clint Eastwood stars in this tale of a break out from the supposedly escape-proof prison on an island off San Francisco.
Director: Don Siegel.

| 1984 | 11.1 | Sat 10 Mar 9:15 p.m. | 15 | 3 wks |

'Nine to Five'
Jane Fonda, Dolly Parton and Lily Tomlin star as three office girls who plot to get rid of their boss.
Director: Colin Higgins.

Adventures of Black Beauty, The | 8 wks

LWT, drama

This twenty-six week series was adapted by seven different writers and several directors from Anna Sewell's novel Black Beauty. The star was Black Jet, a seven-year-old American-bred horse, with William Lucas as the widower Dr Gordon and Charlotte Mitchell as the housekeeper Amy. Two children, Kevin and Vicky, were played by Roderick Shaw and Judi Bowker.
Producer (1972–74): Sidney Cole. **Executive Producer:** Paul Knight.

| 1972 | 6.4 | Sun 10 Dec 5:35 p.m. | 17 | 1 wk |

'Clown on Horseback' by David Butler.
Vicky and Black Beauty meet Thunder, a wild chestnut being broken in by Dan Collins (Len Jones), the son of the owner of the livery stable (John Nettleton). Kevin meets a clown from the nearby circus and brings him home to York Cottage.
Director: Alan Gibson.

| 1973 | 6.3 | Sun 11 Feb 5:35 p.m. | 19 | 3 wks |

'Two of a Kind' by David Hopkins.
Two orphaned children try to escape on Black Beauty. Kevin and Vicky get to hear of their plight and do what they can to help them.
Director: Charles Crichton.

| 1974 | 6.7 | Sun 10 Mar 5:35 p.m. | 17 | 4 wks |

'Game of Chance' by Richard Carpenter.
Dr Gordon and Amy go to London for the day leaving Jenny (Stacy Dorning) in charge.

Adventures of Sherlock Holmes, The | 2 wks

Granada, drama

Stories by Sir Arthur Conan Doyle were developed for television by John Hawkesworth. The series starred Jeremy Brett as Holmes and David Burke as Dr Watson.
Designer: Michael Grimes. **Producer:** Michael Cox.

| 1985 | 11.3 | Sun 25 Aug 9:45 p.m. | 6 | 1 wk |

'The Copper Beeches' dramatized by Bill Craig.
Violet Hunter (Natasha Richardson) consults Holmes after her employer (Joss Ackland) insists she cut off all her hair.

| 1989 | 9.2 | Wed 24 May 9:00 p.m. | 11 | 1 wk |

'The Speckled Band' dramatized by Jeremy Paul.
Julia Stoner (Denise Armon) is haunted by the strange death of her sister. Also starring Jeremy Kemp and Rosalyn Landor.
Director: John Bruce.

Affairs of the Heart | 4 wks

Granada, drama

This light comedy series was about heart attack victim Peter Bonamy (Derek Fowlds) picking up the threads of his life with help from his wife Jane (Sarah Badel) and in spite of his teenage daughter Rosemary (Elizabeth Anson, later Holly Aird). The series was written by actor Paul Daneman and based on his own experiences following a heart attack.
Producer: Brian Armstrong.

| 1983 | 7.0 | Tue 23 Aug 8:30 p.m. | 17 | 1 wk |

Peter is due home from hospital after recovering from a heart attack. Jane hopes for a quiet reception, but their daughter Rosemary has organized a big party.
Director: Richard Holthouse.

| 1985 | 10.0 | Mon 29 Jul 8:00 p.m. | 18 | 3 wks |

Just as Peter and Jane think they have found peace and tranquility, Rosemary and her friends arrive.
Director: Charles Kitchen.

After All I've Been Through
1 wk

ATV, documentary

| 1974 | 5.5 | Mon 12 Aug 8:00 p.m. | 10 | 1 wk |

The programme follows the progress, or lack of same, of NEW FACES contestant Francis Mallon, a schoolteacher trying to make the grade as a folk singer.
Producer: John Robins.

After Henry
8 wks

Thames, situation comedy

This series followed the lives of three women after the death of Henry. They were his widow Sarah (Prunella Scales), his mother Eleanor (Joan Sanderson) and his daughter Clare (Janine Wood). Sarah worked in a bookshop run by Russell (Jonathan Newth).
Writer: Simon Brett. **Producer:** Peter Frazer-Jones.

| 1988 | 13.9 | Mon 1 Feb 9:00 p.m. | 6 | 5 wks |

'Romantic Complications'
Sarah has to listen to the love-life problems of both her daughter and her mother.

| 1989 | 12.3 | Tue 25 Apr 8:30 p.m. | 8 | 3 wks |

'Security'
Sarah installs a burglar alarm but Eleanor has other ideas to protect their property.

After Ten with Tarbuck
1 wk

LWT, entertainment

Music, comedy and chat with Liverpudlian Jimmy Tarbuck.

| 1988 | 8.7 | Sat 14 May 10:20 p.m. | 19 | 1 wk |

Guests: John Denver, Richard Digance, Fatima Whitbread and Kim Wilde. With the Alyn Ainsworth orchestra.
Director: Nick Vaughan-Barratt. **Producer:** Paul Lewis. **Executive Producer:** Marcus Plantin.

Agatha Christie Hour, The
5 wks

Thames, drama

A series of ten dramatizations of the author's stories.

| 1982 | 11.6 | Tue 7 Sep 9:00 p.m. | 5 | 5 wks |

'The Case of the Middle-Aged Wife' dramatized by Freda Kelsall. Starring Maurice Denham, Peter Jones, Linda Robson and Gwen Watford.

Designer: Patrick Downing. **Director:** Michael Simpson. **Producer:** Pat Sandys. **Executive Producer:** John Frankau.

Airline
4 wks

YTV, drama

This series created by Wilfred Greatorex starred Roy Marsden as Jack Ruskin. This wartime pilot with ruthless ambition began his own airline in peacetime. Polly Hemingway played his girlfriend Jenny.

| 1982 | 14.6 | Sun 10 Jan 9:15 p.m. | 12 | 4 wks |

'Brave New World'
In the summer of 1946 Ruskin only has his demob suit and £70.
Producer: Michael Ferguson. **Executive Producer:** David Cunliffe.

Airplane
2 wks

Presented by ITV, film

| 1984 | 18.1 | Wed 26 Dec 9:15 p.m. | 4 | 1 wk |

Flight 209 takes off from Los Angeles for Chicago. A weird collection of passengers and crew are on board. Starring Lloyd Bridges, Julie Hagerty, Robert Hays, Ethel Merman and Robert Stack.
Directors: Jim Abrahams, David Zucker and Jerry Zucker.

| 1988 | 11.6 | Tue 4 Oct 8:30 p.m. | 15 | 1 wk |

Repeat showing of the above film.

Airplane II: The Sequel
1 wk

Presented by ITV, film

| 1989 | 9.4 | Tue 4 Jul 8:30 p.m. | 16 | 1 wk |

The first lunar shuttle from a commercial terminal hits trouble right from the launch. Starring Sonny Bono, Lloyd Bridges, Raymond Burr, Chuck Connors, Peter Graves, Julie Hagerty, Robert Hays and William Shatner.
Director: Ken Finkleman.

Airport
1 wk

AR, documentary

| 1964 | 5.3 | Wed 23 Sep 9:40 p.m. | 18 | 1 wk |

A dawn-to-dusk visit to London Airport meeting VIPs and ordinary people waving hello and goodbye.
Director: Charles Squires.

Airport | 1 wk

Presented by BBC, film

| 1978 | 11.9 | Mon 28 Aug 8:00 p.m. | 9 | 1 wk |

Arthur Hailey's story of the events at a midwestern airport one snowy night. Starring Burt Lancaster and Dean Martin with Jacqueline Bisset, Helen Hayes and Jean Seberg.
Director: George Seaton.

Airport '75 | 2 wks

Presented by ITV, film

| 1986 | 9.7 | Wed 28 May 8:00 p.m. | 15 | 1 wk |

Charlton Heston stars in the story of a stricken 747 trying to land at Salt Lake City. A mid-air collision has blinded the pilot and killed the co-pilot. Also starring Dana Andrews, Karen Black, Sid Caesar, Myrna Loy, Helen Reddy, Gloria Swanson, Roy Thinnes and Efrem Zimbalist Jr.
Director: Jack Smight.

| 1988 | 10.3 | Sun 27 Mar 7:15 p.m. | 19 | 1 wk |

Repeat showing of the above film.

Airport '77 | 1 wk

Presented by BBC, film

| 1986 | 9.3 | Sat 7 Jun 7:20 p.m. | 13 | 1 wk |

Hijackers take control of a 747 and crash into an offshore oil platform. The passengers fight to escape. Starring Joseph Cotten, Lee Grant, Olivia de Havilland, Christopher Lee, Jack Lemmon, Darren McGavin and Brenda Vaccaro.
Director: Jerry Jameson.

Airport '80: The Concorde | 2 wks

Presented by ITV, film

| 1982 | 10.9 | Sat 2 Oct 7:00 p.m. | 9 | 1 wk |

This sequel, released in America as AIRPORT '79, transposes the difficulties that can befall an aeroplane onto the grandest of them all, Concorde. Starring Eddie Albert, Alain Delon, Sylvia Kristel and Robert Wagner.
Director: David Lowell Rich.

| 1983 | 12.6 | Thu 13 Oct 7:30 p.m. | 7 | 1 wk |

Repeat showing of the above film.

Airwolf | 3 wks

USA presented by ITV, drama

This series featured combat helicopter pilot Stringfellow Hawke (Jan-Michael Vincent). It also starred Ernest Borgnine and Alex Cord.
Producer: Donald P. Bellisarius

| 1984 | 12.3 | Fri 2 Nov 7:00 p.m. | 12 | 3 wks |

'Daddy's Gone A-Hunt'n'
An old friend of Hawke's is poised to commit an act of treason.

Alamo, The | 1 wk

Presented by BBC, film

| 1972 | 6.3 | Fri 7 Jan 6:20 p.m. | 17 | 1 wk |

Outnumbered men defend a Texas mission from the Mexicans in 1836. Starring Frankie Avalon, Richard Boone, Laurence Harvey, John Wayne and Richard Widmark.
Director: John Wayne.

Alan King Show, The | 1 wk

ATV, comedy

This American comedian, a fixture on The Ed Sullivan Show in the United States, was brought to Britain by ATV boss Lew Grade for this one-off special.

| 1963 | 4.2 | Sun 4 Aug 8:25 p.m. | 16 | 1 wk |

Special guest star: Sophie Tucker. With Adele Leigh, the Pamela Devis Dancers and Jack Parnell's orchestra.
Producer: Albert Locke.

Albert | 6 wks

YTV, situation comedy

This series was written and produced by its star, Rodney Bewes. The character of Albert Courtney was carried over from DEAR MOTHER – LOVE ALBERT. The north-country innocent had moved to London.

| 1972 | 6.5 | Tue 2 May 8:30 p.m. | 10 | 6 wks |

'A Ghost Story'
As Albert sits morosely in his flat, suffering from flu and reading his Mum's latest letter, the ghost of his boss appears through the wall announcing his intention to teach Albert a lesson.
Director: Bill Hitchcock.

Albert and Victoria | 1 wk

YTV, comedy

This series was created by Reuben Ship. Great Aunt Agatha left all her wealth to her niece, Mrs Victoria Hackett (Frances Bennett), but with certain strings attached before she and her husband Albert (Alfred Marks) could lay their hands on the legacy. The situations involved the whole family, including Emma (Gay Hamilton), Lydia (Petra Markham) and George (John Alkin).

| 1971 | 5.5 | Fri 17 Sep 8:25 p.m. | 20 | 1 wk |

'Rise, Sir Albert'
If Albert values one thing more than money it's a title. He gets his title all right – but not the one he expects.
Producer: Quentin Lawrence.

Alcock and Gander | 5 wks

Thames, situation comedy

This series, written by Johnnie Mortimer and Brian Cooke, was set in a small office in Soho from which Mrs Alcock (Beryl Reid) ran her late husband's small business empire. His ashes stood on the mantelpiece facing the window. Mrs Alcock's partner Richard Gander (Richard O'Sullivan) and employee Ernest (John Cater) helped her supply the world with such desirables as Alcock's Swiss Elixir and the Tom O'Thimble Lucky Pixie.

| 1972 | 7.3 | Mon 5 Jan 8:25 p.m. | 3 | 5 wks |

An office crisis arises and Mrs Alcock has need of the services of a safebreaker. 'Fingers' (J. G. Devlin) comes to her aid.
Producer: Alan Tarrant.

Alexander the Greatest | 6 wks

ATV, situation comedy

This series created and written by Bernard Kops was about Alexander Green (Gary Warren), a sixteen-year-old rebel who thought himself ready to leave home, school and middle-class society. His parents Joe (Sydney Tafler) and Fay (Libby Morris) moved mountains to make him happy, so he stayed. Alexander also had a sister, Renata (Adrienne Posta), and she a boyfriend, Murray (Peter Birrel).

| 1971 | 5.8 | Thu 19 Aug 9:00 p.m. | 8 | 6 wks |

'Happy Anniversary'
Joe has bought a sexy present for Fay on their twenty-fourth wedding anniversary. With Murray's help, he hides it until later in the evening when he will be alone with Fay. Things don't work out as romantically as he'd planned.
Producer: Shaun O'Riordan.

Alfie | 1 wk

BBC, film

| 1973 | 6.2 | Sun 22 Apr 9:25 p.m. | 13 | 1 wk |

Screened on Easter Sunday. Bill Naughton's creation Alfie (Michael Caine) is a swinging lover who moves from one conquest to the next without ever stopping to consider the cost to himself or others. Also starring Jane Asher, Eleanor Bron, Denholm Elliott, Shirley Anne Field, Julia Foster, Millicent Martin, Vivien Merchant and Shelley Winters.
Director: Lewis Gilbert.

Alfred Hitchcock Hour, The | 18 wks

USA presented by ITV, drama

This long-running series of suspense-filled whodunits often had a touch of comedy. Hitchcock himself introduced each episode, walking into shot menacingly to the sound of his signature music. He invariably signed off in person with a throwaway moral ending.

| 1963 | 5.6 | Thu 29 Aug 8:00 p.m. | 9 | 18 wks |

'Final Vow' by Henry Slesar.
Sister Pamela is deeply troubled. In the year since she took her first vows she has yet to feel worthy of renewing them. Assailed by doubts, she wonders if she truly belongs to the convent. She's about to find out – from the outside! Starring Clu Gulager and Carol Lynley.

Alice – A Fight for Life | 1 wk

YTV, documentary

| 1982 | 8.1 | Tue 20 Jul 9:00 p.m. | 16 | 1 wk |

Forty-seven-year-old Alice once spent nine months working in an asbestos factory. She now suffers from mesothelioma, cancer of the lung lining.
Producer: John Willis.

Alien | 1 wk

Presented by ITV, film

| 1982 | 9.7 | Sun 11 Jul 9:30 p.m. | 13 | 1 wk |

A spaceship returning to Earth carries a horrible infection. Something is eating John Hurt. Also starring Ian Holm, Tom Skerritt and Sigourney Weaver.
Director: Ridley Scott.

All About You — 8 wks

AR, game show

Host Barry Westwood asked viewers ten questions on a chosen theme. Their answers were then compared with answers to the same questions from a national Gallup poll.
Producer: Elkan Allan.

| 1966 | 5.1 | Tue 14 Jun 7:00 p.m. | 14 | 8 wks |

'Honesty'
Director: Bimbi Harris.

| | | Thu 7 Jul 7:00 p.m. |

'Ambition'
Director: Robert Fleming.
These programmes achieved the same ratings and chart position.

....

All at No. 20 — 6 wks

Thames, situation comedy

This series by Richard Ommanney starred Maureen Lipman as Sheila Haddon. She struggled to make ends meet after her husband died leaving her with a large mortgage and daughter Monica (Lisa Jacobs). Gary Waldhorn played old family friend Richard Beamish.

| 1986 | 13.7 | Mon 10 Mar 8:00 p.m. | 7 | 6 wks |

Sheila is typing out a manuscript for writer Millicent Bates (Patsy Smart). It is called 'Frozen Dreams', and proves prophetic.
Producer: Peter Frazer-Jones.

....

All Creatures Great and Small — 82 wks

BBC, drama

This series was based on James Herriott's books about a country veterinary practice in the North Riding of Yorkshire. Christopher Timothy played Herriott, Robert Hardy was Siegfried Farnon, Peter Davison was Tristan Farnon and the part of Helen was played first by Carol Drinkwater and later by Lynda Bellingham.
Directors included Christopher Barry (1971, 1979) and Peter Moffatt (1985, 1988).
Producer: Bill Sellars.

| 1971 | 18.1 | Sat 11 Nov 7:40 p.m. | 1 | 23 wks |

'Pride of Possession' adapted by Anthony Steven.
When James tries out a new hormonal treatment, the cows of Farmer Ogilvie (Paul Dawkins) want nothing to do with his bull.

| 1979 | 15.3 | Tue 25 Dec 6:30 p.m. | 6 | 1 wk |

'Plenty to Grouse About' adapted by Terence Dudley.
Siegfried takes a dislike to Mr Murray (Andrew Robertson), who treats a dog badly.

| 1980 | 18.7 | Sat 2 Feb 7:10 p.m. | 1 | 14 wks |

'Pig in the Middle' adapted by Johnny Byrne.
There are complications as James, Tristan and Siegfried all want the same night off.
Director: Michael Hayes.

| 1983 | 12.2 | Sun 25 Dec 8:05 p.m. | 10 | 1 wk |

'The Lord God Made Them All' adapted by Brian Finch.
A special feature-length Christmas Day edition set in 1947. James Herriott returns to Yorkshire after demobilization.
Director: Terence Dudley.

| 1985 | 15.4 | Wed 25 Dec 4:55 p.m. | 9 | 1 wk |

A special edition based on 'The Lord God Made Them All', adapted by Johnny Byrne.
Tristan now works for the Ministry and has picked up the remains of an old romance. James and Siegfried prepare for the inevitable progress brought by modern veterinary science.

| 1988 | 14.2 | Sun 17 Jan 7:15 p.m. | 5 | 22 wks |

'One of Nature's Little Miracles' adapted by Johnny Byrne.
Tristan fears his bachelor days may be numbered.

| 1989 | 11.7 | Sat 7 Oct 8:00 p.m. | 9 | 17 wks |

'Where Sheep May Safely Graze' adapted by Michael Russell.
James struggles to identify the cause of a mysterious cat illness.
Director: Michael Brayshaw.

| 1990 | 9.3 | Sun 19 Aug 7:15 p.m. | 17 | 3 wks |

'Big Fish, Little Fish' adapted by Michael Russell.
Siegfried befriends a ten-year-old boy when his goldfish dies. (Repeat.)
Director: Tony Virgo.

....

All Creatures Great and Small — 1 wk

Presented by BBC, film

| 1986 | 10.2 | Sun 1 Jun 7:15 p.m. | 12 | 1 wk |

A newly-qualified vet begins working in the Yorkshire Dales during the 1930s. Simon Ward stars as James Herriott and Anthony Hopkins is Siegfried Farnon.
Director: Claude Whatham.

....

All Gas and Gaiters — 3 wks

BBC, situation comedy

Created by Edwin Apps and Pauline Devaney, this series poked gentle fun at the clergy. Starring Robertson Hare as the Archdeacon, William Mervyn as the Bishop and Derek Nimmo as the Curate, with Ernest Clark as the Dean.

| 1967 | 6.6 | Fri 29 Dec 8:20 p.m. | 6 | 3 wks |

'The Bishop Gives a Shove'
Mr Dobson (Frank Williams), the workman (Hamish Roughead) and the butler (Johnson Bayly) all feel the shove.
Producer: Stuart Allen.

All in Good Faith · 6 wks

Thames, situation comedy

This series by John Kane starred Richard Briers as the Reverend Philip Lambe, a vicar with a crisis of conscience brought on by middle age. Barbara Ferris played his wife Emma.
Producer: John Howard Davies.

| 1985 | 12.5 | Mon 30 Dec 8:00 p.m. | 20 | 1 wk |

'In the Beginning'
Reverend Lambe transfers from his rich rural parish to a tough Midlands city.

| 1986 | 14.6 | Mon 27 Jan 8:00 p.m. | 3 | 5 wks |

'An Eye For An Eye'
Open hostilities are declared between Philip and his parishoners.

All in the Game · 3 wks

ITV, sport

Footballers pitted their individual skills against each other in the name of their club in a series of games devised by the then-Bristol City manager Alan Dicks.

| 1976 | 6.2 | Wed 1 Sep 7:00 p.m. | 11 | 3 wks |

From Bristol City's ground, Dickie Davies and Brian Moore introduce the final between Derby County and Norwich City.
Director: Bob Gardam. **Producer:** John Mead. **Executive Producer:** John Bromley.

All Kinds of Dana · 1 wk

Thames, music

This special starred the Irish singer who won THE EUROVISION SONG CONTEST in 1970.

| 1980 | 13.1 | Wed 28 May 9:30 p.m. | 5 | 1 wk |

With the Nigel Lythgoe dancers and the Alyn Ainsworth orchestra.
Executive Producer: Philip Jones.

All Kinds of Music · 1 wk

ATV, music

This series of music shows was put together by impresario Val Parnell.

| 1961 | 5.0 | Tue 3 Oct 8:00 p.m. | 17 | 1 wk |

With Kenny Ball's Jazzmen, Adele Leigh, Janie Marden, Nina and Frederik, Lynn Seymour and John Gilpin. With the Jack Parnell orchestra.
Producer: Francis Essex.

All Our Saturdays · 6 wks

YTV, situation comedy

This series starred Diana Dors as Di Dorkins, known as 'Big D', who ran a large textile business called Garsley Garments somewhere in the West Riding of Yorkshire. The firm had an amateur rugby league team which regularly propped up the foot of the local league until Di took over the management and proved herself rougher, tougher and fitter than the lads.

| 1973 | 7.0 | Wed 21 Feb 8:30 p.m. | 12 | 6 wks |

'The Unhappy Hooker' by Oliver Free.
Big D has renamed the team 'The Frilly Things' in the belief that they will be forced to win matches to prove their manhood. The lads find the local reporter's account of their new name embarrassing.
Director: Roger Cheveley. **Producer:** Ian Davidson.

All Our Yesterdays · 140 wks

Granada, documentary

Brian Inglis presented this series, which ran from 1960 to 1973. Each week he recalled the events of twenty-five years ago, mainly by the use of cinema newsreels.
Director (1961–62 and 1965): Peter Plummer. **Producers** included Jeremy Isaacs (1961–62) and Bill Grundy (1964–67).

| 1961 | 4.5 | Mon 13 Nov 7:00 p.m. | 20 | 1 wk |

The Spanish rebel forces approach Madrid. Fred Perry, three times Wimbledon champion (1934–36), turns professional.

| 1962 | 5.2 | Mon 15 Jan 7:00 p.m. | 11 | 21 wks |

Chiang Kai-Shek and Colonel Batista are in the news. In Holland, Princess Juliana marries Prince Bernhard.

| 1963 | 5.7 | Mon 30 Dec 7:00 p.m. | 19 | 2 wks |

A portrait of 1938 - the resignation of Anthony Eden, the Anschluss, Munich, the Test Matches, the Derby and the Chelsea Arts Ball.
Director: Michael Cox. **Producer:** David Plowright.

| 1964 | 7.1 | Mon 14 Dec 7:00 p.m. | 6 | 15 wks |

The German pocket battleship Graf Spey cowers in Montevideo harbour following a running battle with the cruisers Exeter, Ajax and Achilles. These wait at the mouth of the River Plate for the Graf Spey to emerge.
Director: Michael Cox.

| 1965 | 7.1 | Mon 1 Feb 7:00 p.m. | 6 | 49 wks |

Brian Inglis recalls the life and times of Lord Haw-Haw (William Joyce).

| 1966 | 7.0 | Mon 10 Jan 7:00 p.m. | 10 | 45 wks |

President Roosevelt's personal representative Harry Hopkins comes to visit Winston Churchill as America's participation in the war seems increasingly inevitable.
Director: Richard Guinea.

| 1967 | 6.0 | Mon 9 Jan 7:00 p.m. | 10 | 7 wks |

Soviet troops push back the Germans in the Crimea. Japanese troops land on Borneo and other islands in Southeast Asia.
Director: Les Chatfield.

All Square   3 wks

ATV, situation comedy

This series starred Michael Bentine as head of the fictitious country Ozonia and was set in the capital city of Filthnik.

| 1966 | 6.1 | Sat 8 Oct 8:30 p.m. | 14 | 3 wks |

Assisted by Deryck Guyler, Benny Lee and Leon Thau, Bentine sets out to turn Ozonia into a mecca for tourists. With the Jack Parnell orchestra.
Producer: Jon Scoffield.

All Star Secrets   12 wks

LWT, game show

Michael Parkinson hosted this game in which celebrities revealed their most trivial secrets.
Producer: Gill Stribling-Wright.

| 1985 | 15.3 | Sat 19 Jan 7:15 p.m. | 5 | 7 wks |

Guests: Christopher Biggins, Marti Caine, Billy Dainty, Kenny Lynch and Libby Morris.
Director: Noel D. Green.

| 1986 | 10.3 | Sat 12 Jul 8:30 p.m. | 5 | 5 wks |

Guests: Michael Barrymore, Pat Coombs, Jeffrey Holland, Ronnie Scott and Barbara Windsor.
Director: John Gorman.

All Star Show, The   1 wk

ATV, entertainment

| 1963 | 5.1 | Sun 21 Jul 8:25 p.m. | 6 | 1 wk |

Presented by the Stars' Organisation for Spastics in a specially-built night-club at Elstree Studios. Stars included Eve Boswell, Jill Browne, Patrick Cargill, Alma Cogan, Hy Hazell, Dennis Lotis, Libby Morris, Mary Peach, Wilfred Pickles, Brian Rix, Harry Secombe, Ronald Shiner, Graham Stark and Bert Weedon. With the Pamela Devis dancers.
Producer: Albert Locke.

All That Jazz   21 wks

ATV, music

A series of half-hour music programmes with various bands and singers, many of whom had little to do with jazz.

| 1962 | 5.3 | Fri 9 Feb 10:00 p.m. | 12 | 21 wks |

In this edition are the Karl Denver Trio, Frank Ilfield, Lorrie Mann, Bob Miller and the Millermen and Mick Mulligan and his Band. With the Jack Parnell orchestra.
Producer: Dicky Leeman.

All the Best – Dave Allen   1 wk

BBC, comedy

| 1986 | 12.6 | Thu 6 Nov 9:30 p.m. | 9 | 1 wk |

A selection of extracts from DAVE ALLEN AT LARGE.
Producer: Peter Whitmore.

All This and Christmas Too   1 wk

YTV, comedy

| 1971 | 5.8 | Fri 24 Dec 10:15 p.m. | 20 | 1 wk |

Christmas Eve special written by Sam Cree. Three neighbouring families, the Joneses (headed by Sid James), the Beatties (by Kenneth Connor) and the Halls (by Joe Gladwin), are at loggerheads this Christmas. There's a baby due, an unwanted visiting aunt and a paucity of good will.
Producer: Bill Hitchcock.

All We Want is Everything | 1 wk

Granada, documentary

| 1968, | 4.7 | Tue 2 Jul 9:15 p.m. | 19 | 1 wk |

This programme examines the barometer of world change as measured by the opinions and protests of students.
Producer: Denis Mitchell.

Allan Stewart Show, The | 1 wk

Thames, entertainment

This series starred the Scottish singer and impressionist.

| 1980 | 16.1 | Mon 29 Dec 8:30 p.m. | 7 | 1 wk |

Guests: Terence Alexander, Anna Dawson and Bob Todd.
Producer: Stuart Hall.

Alligator | 1 wk

Presented by ITV, film

| 1985 | 13.3 | Mon 27 May 9:15 p.m. | 2 | 1 wk |

Robert Foster and Robin Ryker star in the story of an alligator flushed down a toilet. It grows to an enormous size and goes on the rampage killing a police officer.
Director: Lewis Teague.

'Allo 'Allo! | 63 wks

BBC, situation comedy

This series by Jeremy Lloyd and David Croft dealt with the French Resistance in World War II. It centred on a café owned by René Artois (Gorden Kaye) and his wife Edith (Carmen Silvera). The running plot concerned the plight of two British airmen, Fairfax (John D. Collins) and Carstairs (Nicholas Frankau), who had to be concealed from the occupying Germans. The servicemen hoped to be repatriated. Characters included Yvette (Vicki Michelle), Herr Flick (Richard Gibson), General von Klinkerhoffen (Hilary Minster), Lieutenant Gruber (Guy Siner), Maria (Francesca Gonshaw), Michelle (Kirsten Cooke), Von Smallhausen (John Louis Mansi), Crabtree (Arthur Bostrom), Colonel Von Strohm (Richard Marner), Fanny (Rose Hill), Helga (Kim Hartman), Leclerc (Jack Haig) and Alfonse (Kenneth Connor).
Directors included Robin Carr (1986–87) and Martin Dennis (1988 and 1990). **Producer** (1985–90): David Croft.

| 1985 | 16.7 | Thu 26 Dec 7:40 p.m. | 3 | 7 wks |

General von Klinkerhoffen has assumed control of the district. The Resistance is determined to blow him up. Herr Flick is equally disenchanted with the General and prepares a poisoned dart for him.

| 1986 | 14.8 | Fri 26 Dec 7:45 p.m. | 5 | 11 wks |

René and the others disguise themselves as roadworkers in a plan to get the airmen home.

| 1987 | 13.1 | Fri 9 Jan 7:25 p.m. | 10 | 4 wks |

René is knee-deep in a tunnel looking for uniforms for the British airmen.

| 1988 | 17.1 | Sat 24 Dec 7:30 p.m. | 6 | 19 wks |

Michelle and Crabtree hatch a bold if hare-brained scheme to return the British airmen to England.

| 1989 | 14.7 | Sat 25 Feb 7:15 p.m. | 8 | 11 wks |

René's café is filled with his hoardings, including the two British airmen, four bars of gold, a German coding machine, the painting of The Fallen Madonna, The Cracked Vase by Van Gogh and other bric-a-brac.
Director: Richard Boden.

| 1990 | 14.2 | Fri 8 Jun 7:45 p.m. | 7 | 8 wks |

Michelle has to hide 1000 kilos of stolen high explosives. She decides to conceal them in 500 Christmas puddings. (Repeat.)

| 1991 | 12.9 | Tue 24 Dec 8:20 p.m. | 14 | 3 wks |

René is planning to fly to England after learning that Yvette is pregnant.
Producer: John B. Hobbs.

Amazing Spiderman, The | 6 wks

USA presented by ITV, drama

Nicholas Hammond starred as Peter Parker, a science student with ambitions to become a news photographer. After being bitten by a radioactive spider he found himself able to climb walls and spin webs. This show was based on the comic book character created by Stanley and Steve Ditko.
Producers: Charles Fries and Edward J. Montagne.

| 1981 | 14.1 | Fri 4 Sep 7:00 p.m. | 4 | 6 wks |

The writer of an anonymous letter makes a massive ransom demand, claiming that ten eminent people have been programmed to self-destruct.
Director: E. W. Swackhamer.

America — 1 wk

AR for Intertel, documentary

| 1965 | 5.9 | Wed 27 Jan 9:40 p.m. | 16 | 1 wk |

'On the Edge of Abundance'
The first of two programmes assessing how America will cope with less work in the age of increased technology and machinery.
Writer: Jack Hargreaves. **Narrator:** James Cameron. **Producer:** Bill Morton.

America Abroad — 1 wk

AR for Intertel, documentary

| 1962 | 4.5 | Wed 30 May 9:45 p.m. | 17 | 1 wk |

America has aid projects in seventy countries resulting in two million Americans living abroad. This film visits Cambodia, South Vietnam, Ghana and Pakistan to assess the progress of these projects.
Narrators: Peter Dyneley and Michael Ingrams. **Camera:** Ron Osborn. **Director:** Michael Ingrams. **Writer** and **Producer:** Peter Hunt. **Editor:** Aidan Crawley.

American Man Shoot — 1 wk

ITN, news

| 1962 | 5.3 | Thu 24 May 10:00 p.m. | 12 | 1 wk |

The dramatic last hour of Aurora 7. Astronaut Scott Carpenter overshot his landing by 250 miles and was lost for an agonizing 53 minutes, having re-entered the Earth's atmosphere just after 6:45 p.m. BST. All ships and planes began an immediate emergency search of the area. He was eventually located between Puerto Rico and Turk Island thanks to a British-made radio beacon codenamed 'Sarah'. He had to spend three hours in his life raft before being winched on board a helicopter and flown to the carrier Intrepid. The BBC covered the events live but it was ITN's edited highlights which scored the highest viewing figure.

Anastasia — 2 wks

Presented by BBC, film

| 1988 | 9.6 | Sun 17 Jul 8:15 p.m. | 14 | 2 wks |

This epic, screened in two parts on consecutive Sundays, stars Rex Harrison as Grand Duke Cyril Romanov, Olivia de Havilland as the Dowager Empress, Omar Sharif as Tsar Nicholas II, Claire Bloom as Tsarina Alexandra and Amy Irving as Anna Anderson, who claims to be the Grand Duchess Anastasia. If her claim is true, she is the youngest daughter of the Tsar and the only survivor of the 1918 massacre.
Director: Martin Chomsky.

And Mother Makes Five — 21 wks

Thames, situation comedy

With Sally and David married in the 1973 series of AND MOTHER MAKES THREE (see below), three increased to five.
Writer: Richard Waring. **Producer:** Peter Frazer-Jones.

| 1974 | 8.6 | Wed 1 May 8:00 p.m. | 1 | 12 wks |

'Where Our Caravan is Resting'
The whole family is looking forward to a holiday in a caravan loaned by a neighbour. When it arrives it is obvious it has seen far better days.

| 1975 | 6.9 | Wed 18 Jun 8:00 p.m. | 2 | 5 wks |

'Friends and Neighbours'
The Spicers (Tony Britton and Charlotte Mitchell) have moved in next door. Sally invites them round to a welcoming drink, but everything goes wrong.

| 1976 | 7.3 | Wed 4 Feb 8:00 p.m. | 11 | 4 wks |

'Sally's Diary'
Bored with life as a housewife, Sally decides to spice up her diary in the hopes it might be published.

And Mother Makes Three — 25 wks

Thames, situation comedy

This series created by Richard Waring starred Wendy Craig as an attractive young widow coping with the problems of bringing up two sons, a cat and a goldfish.
Producer: Peter Frazer-Jones.

| 1971 | 7.4 | Tue 27 Apr 8:30 p.m. | 5 | 11 wks |

In this untitled first episode, Mother gets a job with the local vet and asks Auntie (Valerie Lush) to come and live with the family to help with the children, Simon (Robin Davies) and Peter (David Parfitt).

| 1972 | 7.3 | Thu 5 Oct 9:00 p.m. | 3 | 7 wks |

'Thank Heaven for Little Girls'
David Redway (Richard Coleman) wants his daughter Jane (Miriam Mann) to meet Sally's sons, but Sally is initially reluctant. He asks Sally to join him as he takes Jane back to school. It gets too complicated for her liking.

| 1973 | 8.5 | Wed 20 Jun 8:00 p.m. | 1 | 7 wks |

'Starting Trouble'
Sally has married David, but as they set off on honeymoon they are told there is only one seat left on the plane. Reluctantly they agree to fly separately, but when Sally arrives in Paris she hears that David's flight has been delayed – indefinitely!

And There's More Cricket — 2 wks

Central, comedy

Irish comedian Jimmy Cricket starred in his own series.

| 1986 | 8.8 | Sat 16 Aug 6:30 p.m. | 15 | 2 wks |

Guests: Brian Conley, David Jacobs and Bob Todd. With the Nigel Lythgoe dancers.
Producer: Tony Wolfe.

....

Andromeda Strain, The — 1 wk

Presented by ITV, film

| 1977 | 14.6 | Sun 27 Nov 7:45 p.m. | 16 | 1 wk |

A space satellite falls to Earth and is traced to a remote township in New Mexico.
Director: Robert Wise.

....

Andy Capp — 1 wk

Thames, situation comedy

This series by Keith Waterhouse starred James Bolam in the title role, the work-shy chauvinist comic-strip creation of Reg Smythe. Paula Tilbrook played his wife Flo.

| 1988 | 12.5 | Mon 22 Feb 8:00 p.m. | 10 | 1 wk |

'New Leaf'
Andy decides it is time to mend his ways – with a little help from Flo's rolling pin.
Producer: John Howard Davies.

....

Angels — 11 wks

BBC, soap

This twice-weekly serial was created by Paula Milne about the staff of St Angela's Hospital, Battersea.
Producer: Julia Smith.

| 1979 | 20.9 | Mon 15 Oct 6:55 p.m. | 4 | 10 wks |

Anna Newcross (Joanna Monro) returns to face the music following her party.
Writer: Janey Preger. **Director:** Michael Custance.

| 1982 | 10.5 | Mon 13 Dec 7:00 p.m. | 12 | 1 wk |

The nurses deal with the victims of a motorway pile-up.
Writer: Glenn Chandler. **Director:** Graeme Harper.

Animal Squad — 3 wks

BBC, documentary

This series followed an RSPCA squad led by Sid Jenkins as it investigated cruelty and lawbreaking by animal owners and hunters.

| 1986 | 10.4 | Wed 1 Oct 9:30 p.m. | 17 | 3 wks |

'We Win Some – We Lose Some'
The RSPCA examines dogfighting.
Producer: Paul Berriff. **Executive Producer:** Roger Mills.

....

Animal War, The — 1 wk

ATV, documentary

| 1971 | 6.0 | Mon 12 Dec 8:00 p.m. | 19 | 1 wk |

In the Serengeti Game Reserve, armed bands of poachers slaughter many animals to feed the trophy racket. To check them the Tanzanian government has established a paramilitary force of rangers.
Camera: Michael Whittaker. **Sound:** Colin Richards. **Producer:** Robin Brown.

....

Annika — 3 wks

Central/Sweden, drama

This three-part drama was written and produced by Colin Nutley and Sven-Gosta Holst.

| 1984 | 7.8 | Fri 24 Aug 9:00 p.m. | 17 | 3 wks |

English teenager Pete (Jesse Birdsall) is spending summer on the Isle of Wight. He meets Swedish language student Annika (Christina Rigner) and follows her home to Stockholm. A shocking accident brings the pressures of their love affair to a head.
Executive Producers: Lewis Rudd and Ingrid Edström.

....

Another Bouquet — 6 wks

LWT, drama

Andrea Newman's seven-part sequel to BOUQUET OF BARBED WIRE continued the saga of sexual intrigue involving Peter Manson (Frank Finlay), his family and his secretary.

| 1977 | 7.7 | Fri 11 Feb 9:00 p.m. | 14 | 6 wks |

'Emergencies'
Following his attempted suicide, after the loss of his daughter Prue, Manson is determined to leave the clinic and return to normal life.
Designer: Gordon Melhuish. **Producer:** John Frankau. **Executive Producer:** Tony Wharmby.

(Top) Wendy Craig looks unhappy at her prospects in **And Mother Makes Three**.

(Bottom) Things have obviously improved for her in **And Mother Makes Five**.

Anthony Adverse — 1 wk

ITV, film

1961	5.1	Thu 14 Dec 8:00 p.m.	9	1 wk

Based on the novel by Harvey Allen, this is the story of a convent-raised boy, the son of an Englishwoman and a young officer with whom she ran off while on honeymoon with her Spanish Marquis husband. Starring Frederick March, Olivia de Havilland and Claude Rains.
Director: Mervyn Leroy.

Antiques Roadshow, The — 63 wks

BBC, documentary

The BBC's first antiques expert, Arthur Negus, began this series, which toured Britain encouraging the public to produce their treasures for expert appraisal and valuation. Negus died in 1985. **Producers** included Robin Drake (1981, 1983, 1986) and Christopher Lewis (1985, 1988–91). He was succeeded as presenter by Hugh Scully.

1981	13.3	Sun 3 May 6:00 p.m.	4	6 wks

Introduced by Angela Rippon with Arthur Negus from Bognor Regis.
Director: Roy Chapman.

1983	10.0	Sun 22 May 6:00 p.m.	13	1 wk

Co-presented by Arthur Negus and Hugh Scully from Folkestone.
Directors: Dave Mitchell and Chris Hunt.

1985	10.5	Sun 19 May 5:45 p.m.	19	1 wk

From the Isle of Man.
Director: David Mitchell.

1986	13.2	Sun 6 Apr 5:45 p.m.	7	8 wks

From Llandudno.
Director: Roy Chapman.

1987	14.6	Sun 22 Mar 5:30 p.m.	5	9 wks

From Margate.
Directors: Andy Batten-Foster and Ian Paul.

1988	14.2	Sun 13 Mar 5:30 p.m.	5	7 wks

From Maidenhead.
Directors: Andy Batten-Foster and Diane Reid.

1989	14.3	Sun 26 Feb 5:30 p.m.	6	10 wks

From Newark.
Directors: Nick Bamford, Ian Paul and Diane Reid.

1990	13.1	Sun 30 Dec 5:40 p.m.	11	11 wks

From Islington.
Directors: Michèle Burgess, Louise Capell and Brian Hawkins.

1991	15.3	Sun 17 Feb 5:30 p.m.	7	10 wks

From Salisbury.
Directors: Michèle Burgess and Brian Hawkins.

Any Old Thing — 1 wk

ATV, documentary

1965	5.6	Wed 2 Jun 9:40 p.m.	11	1 wk

A lighthearted guide to what treasures may be discovered in the attic. Britain gives the appearance of turning itself into one huge bazaar with people offering their wares from street stalls.
Narrator: Eddy Gilmore. **Writer** and **Producer:** Leslie Mallory.
Director: Derek Stewart.

Any Which Way You Can — 3 wks

Presented by ITV, film

1984	16.2	Tue 9 Oct 8:00 p.m.	3	1 wk

Clint Eastwood stars as bare knuckle fighter Philo Beddoe in this sequel to EVERY WHICH WAY BUT LOOSE. Harry Guardino, Geoffrey Lewis and Sondra Locke also star.
Director: Buddy Van Horn.

1985	11.5	Fri 20 Dec 8:00 p.m.	16	1 wk
1987	12.6	Tue 3 Feb 8:00 p.m.	14	1 wk

Repeat showings of the above film.

Aphrodite Inheritance, The — 1 wk

BBC, drama

This eight-part series by Michael Bird was set in Cyprus.

1979	14.4	Wed 3 Jan 8:05 p.m.	20	1 wk

'A Death in the Family'
David Collier (Peter McEnery) is urgently summoned to Cyprus. He receives disturbing news from the mysterious Helène (Alexandra Bastedo).
Designer: John Pusey. **Producer:** Andrew Osborn.

Apollo 8   1 wk

BBC, news

| 1968 | 7.0 | Fri 27 Dec 6:04 p.m. | 3 | 1 wk |

After sending the first live pictures to Earth from space and spending Christmas making ten orbits of the moon, astronauts Borman, Lovell and Anders are scheduled to splash down in the Pacific. They will board the recovery vessel USS Yorktown in the late afternoon.

Apollo 8 Special   1 wk

BBC, news

| 1968 | 6.6 | Tue 24 Dec (see below) | 7 | 1 wk |

Transmissions are made on BBC1 and BBC2 throughout the day. Apollo 8 sends live television pictures during ten orbits of the moon from a height of sixty miles. Commentary in the London Space Studio is by James Burke and Patrick Moore. Charles Wheeler is at Mission Control, Houston.
Executive Producer: Richard Francis.

Apollo 10 Splashdown   1 wk

BBC, news

| 1969 | 5.0 | Mon 26 May 5:35 p.m. | 13 | 1 wk |

Apollo 10 was a dress rehearsal for the moon landing of Apollo 11 later in 1969. Astronauts Tom Stafford, John Young and Eugene Cernan's mission was to orbit the moon as close as 10 miles from the surface. The splashdown occurred at 5:52 p.m. BST.

Apollo 11 Report   2 wks

BBC, news

| 1969 | 5.2 | Mon 21 Jul 10:30 p.m. | 10 | 2 wks |

After Neil Armstrong's historic first steps on the moon he and fellow astronaut Edwin 'Buzz' Aldrin took off in the lunar module to rejoin Michael Collins in the command module at 6:45 p.m. BST.

Apollo 13 Splashdown   1 wk

BBC, news

| 1970 | 8.4 | Tue 21 Apr 9:00 p.m. | 2 | 1 wk |

Apollo 13 was launched on 11 April and is scheduled to splash down in the South Pacific, 200 miles off Christmas Island. The expected programme is: re-entry 9:02 p.m., parachutes open 9:11 p.m., splashdown 9:16 p.m. (This third lunar landing mission almost ended in disaster. Just two days out and 2056 miles up a faulty heater system in the main oxygen tank exploded leaving Commander James Lovell and astronauts James Schweigert and Fred Hayes without oxygen, electricity and propulsion. For four days their fate was uncertain. By improvisation and skill they left the command module and used the lunar module as a lifeboat to return safely to Earth.)
Studio Director: Tam Fry. **Executive Producer:** Richard Francis.

Apollo 15   1 wk

BBC, news

| 1971 | 5.4 | Mon 2 Aug 7:55 p.m. | 11 | 1 wk |

Live pictures from space as the lunar module Falcon flies up from the moon to dock in space with command module Endeavor, orbiting 60 miles above the moon.

Apollo 16   1 wk

ITN, news

| 1972 | 6.8 | Thu 20 Apr 9:31 p.m. | 12 | 1 wk |

Orion touches down on the moon in an area known as Descartes. Astronauts John Young and Charles Duke will be the first men to visit the moon's central highlands. Their moon-car will send back colour pictures. Alastair Burnet and Peter Fairley comment from the studio and Robert Hargreaves is at Mission Control, Houston.

Applause Applause   4 wks

Thames, entertainment

This series profiled entertainers from the days of music hall and variety.

| 1969 | 5.1 | Wed 20 Aug 10:30 p.m. | 13 | 4 wks |

'Gracie Fields'
John Stone narrates the story of Gracie with clips from her films.
Producer: Margery Baker.

Appointment With Death   1 wk

Presented by BBC, film

| 1990 | 13.9 | Sun 30 Dec 8:05 p.m. | 13 | 1 wk |

In Agatha Christie's story Hercule Poirot (Peter Ustinov) finds murder while on holiday in 1930s Palestine. Also starring Lauren Bacall, Carrie Fisher, John Gielgud, Piper Laurie, Hayley Mills, Jenny Seagrove and David Soul.
Director: Michael Winner.

April Fool's Day Cinema — 1 wk

Granada, entertainment

| 1966 | 6.8 | Fri 1 Apr 9:10 p.m. | 7 | 1 wk |

A special edition of CINEMA in which Mike Scott selects his favourite clips from CARRY ON, DOCTOR and ST TRINIAN'S films.
Director: Philip Casson. **Producer:** Graeme McDonald.

Arabian Knight, An — 1 wk

AR, drama

| 1960 | 5.5 | Thu 9 Jun 8:00 p.m. | 5 | 1 wk |

This 85-minute play marked the opening of AR's Wembley studio, the largest in Europe to date. The story is taken from The Thousand and One Nights and supplemented with music and dancing.

Orson Welles is the storyteller. Starring Stanley Holloway and Martin Benson, Robert Loggia, Henry Kendall, Avice Landon, Joseph O'Connor, Susan Stranks, Sydney Tafler and Alan Wheatley.
Music: Muir Mathieson. **Choreographer:** Philippe Perrottet. **Designer:** John Clements. **Director:** Mark Lawton. **Producer:** John McMillan.

Arch of Triumph — 1 wk

HTV, drama

This single drama was adapted by Charles Israel from the novel by Erich Maria Remarque. It was set in Paris just before the Second World War.

| 1984 | 12.4 | Wed 19 Dec 9:00 p.m. | 17 | 1 wk |

Anthony Hopkins stars as Ravic, a refugee surgeon from Hitler's Germany. He remains haunted by his experiences at the hands of the Gestapo. When he sees his torturer in a Paris street, he devises a plan to kill him. Also starring Lesley-Anne Down, Frank Finlay, Richard Pasco and Donald Pleasence.
Designer: Jane Martin. **Director:** Waris Hussein. **Executive Producers:** Patrick Dromgoole and Milton T. Raynor.

Are We Being Served — 1 wk

BBC, documentary

In this series members of the public were invited behind the scenes to view and question the work of public authorities.

| 1981 | 11.2 | Wed 15 Apr 9:25 p.m. | 18 | 1 wk |

'The Age of the Strain'
Commuters come face to face with the Chairman of British Rail, Sir Peter Parker.
Producer: John Pettman. **Series Producer:** Maryse Addison.

Are You Being Served? — 60 wks

BBC, situation comedy

Created by Jeremy Lloyd and David Croft, this series was set in Grace Brothers, an old-fashioned department store. Principal characters: Mr Humphries (John Inman), Mrs Slocombe (Mollie Sugden), Captain Peacock (Frank Thornton), Mr Lucas (Trevor Bannister), Miss Brahms (Wendy Richard), Mr Grainger (Arthur Brough), Mr Rumbold (Nicholas Smith), young Mr Grace (Harold Bennett) and Mr Harman (Arthur English).
Director (1975–78): Ray Butt. **Producer** (1975–79, 1981) and **Executive Producer** (1983, 1985): David Croft.

| 1975 | 7.9 | Thu 17 Apr 8:30 p.m. | 2 | 11 wks |

'New Look'
The decision is taken to give Grace Brothers a 'Great Gatsby' look.

| 1976 | 7.9 | Fri 24 Dec 7:30 p.m. | 5 | 11 wks |

'The Father Christmas Affair'
Grace Brothers offer a bonus for the member of staff who will play the role of Father Christmas in the store.

| 1977 | 7.6 | Fri 25 Feb 8:00 p.m. | 8 | 6 wks |

'Mrs Slocombe Expects'
Mrs Slocombe faces a family crisis.

| 1978 | 10 | Sat 24 Jun 6:10 p.m. | 19 | 1 wk |

'A Change is as Good as a Rest'
Captain Peacock decides the climate is right to change the staffing arrangements at the store.

| 1979 | 22.6 | Fri 19 Oct 7:05 p.m. | 3 | 8 wks |

'The Junior'
Grace Brothers have placed an advertisement in the local papers for a junior staff vacancy.

| 1981 | 15.7 | Thu 9 Apr 8:00 p.m. | 2 | 8 wks |

'Is It Catching?'
The department has to be isolated when Mr Humphries catches a tropical disease.
Director: John Kilby.

| 1983 | 11.7 | Fri 29 Apr 8:30 p.m. | 8 | 4 wks |

'Conduct Unbecoming'
Money is missing from the till. The finger of suspicion points at Mr Humphries.
Producer: Bob Spiers.

| 1985 | 14.5 | Mon 18 Feb 8:30 p.m. | 8 | 11 wks |

'Goodbye Mrs Slocombe'
Mrs Slocombe returns from sick leave to learn of the new early retirement plan initiated by Grace Brothers. She intends to be first in line.
Producer: Michael Shardlow.

Are You Being Served? `1 wk`

Presented by BBC, film

| 1980 | 11.7 | Mon 22 Dec 9:55 p.m. | 10 | 1 wk |

In this full-length film version the staff of Grace Brothers take a package holiday on the Costa Plonka.
Director: Bob Kellett.

Armchair Cinema `2 wks`

Thames, drama

ARMCHAIR THEATRE moved out of the studio and onto film locations.

| 1974 | 7.9 | Tue 28 May 8:30 p.m. | 1 | 2 wks |

'The Prison' by Georges Simenon, adapted for television by Geoffrey Gilbert.
Filmed in Paris. Alain Poitaud (James Laurenson) is the owner of a French sex magazine. His is a rags-to-riches story punctuated by numerous affairs, including one with his sister-in-law. His wealth and dalliances lead to jealousy and murder. Also starring Kenneth Griffith, James Maxwell and André Morell with Diane Keen, Philip Madoc and Peter Sallis.
Director: David Wickes. **Producer:** Geoffrey Gilbert. **Executive Producers:** Lloyd Shirley and George Taylor.

Armchair Mystery Theatre `24 wks`

ABC, drama

From the same production team as ARMCHAIR THEATRE, these plays were unified by the theme of 'mystery'.
Producer: Leonard White.

| 1960 | 5.4 | Sun 26 Jun 10:00 p.m. | 3 | 8 wks |

'Flag Fall' by Royston Morley.
Introduced by Donald Pleasence. Patrick Barr stars as the police officer in charge of investigations into a series of motiveless murders of taxi drivers in Sydney. The only clue is to be found in a café. Millicent Martin plays the café proprietress and Madge Ryan the radio taxi switch operator.
Designer: Roy Stannard. **Director:** Royston Morley.

| 1964 | 7.1 | Sun 6 Sep 9:35 p.m. | 3 | 7 wks |

'You Must Be Virginia' by Richard Harris.
An entry in a diary and a visit from a stranger – suddenly the marriage of an attractive young couple is in serious jeopardy. Starring Richard Johnson, Toby Robins and Nigel Stock.
Designer: David Marshall. **Director:** Don Leaver.

| 1965 | 6.0 | Sun 27 Jun 10:05 p.m. | 5 | 9 wks |

'Time and Mr Madingley' by Richard Harris.
The discovery of a body relieves Prescott of a blackmail threat but involves him in a murder. Starring Charles Gray and Peter Jeffrey with John Barron.
Designer: Assheton Gordon. **Director:** Raymond Menmuir.

Armchair Theatre `156 wks`

ABC (1960–68) and Thames (1969–73), drama

This series launched in 1956 found its own personality with the arrival of Canadian producer Sydney Newman in 1958. Until his departure in 1963, he pursued a deliberate policy of examining contemporary themes and assembling a stable of young writers including Ray Rigby, Alun Owen and Robert Muller. The series later moved to Thames.
Producers included Sydney Newman (1961–62), Leonard White and Lloyd Shirley (1970-72).

| 1960 | 7.7 | Sun 11 Dec 9:05 p.m. | 1 | 12 wks |

'The Cupboard' by Ray Rigby.
The police are called when Fred Watson (Donald Pleasence) papers over two cupboards in his bedroom and both his wife and landlady mysteriously disappear.
Designer: Roy Stannard. **Director:** David Greene.

| 1961 | 6.5 | Sun 29 Jan 10:00 p.m. | 20 | 12 wks |

'Honeymoon Postponed' by Bill Naughton.
Violet and Arthur Fitton (Lois Dane and Trevor Bannister) are Lancashire newlyweds who, for reasons of work, have to delay their honeymoon and temporarily live with Arthur's parents. Only then do their problems begin. Also starring Patience Collier, Jack Howarth, Derren Nesbitt and Paul Rogers.
Designer: Tom Spaulding. **Director:** John Knight.

| 1962 | 7.3 | Sun 14 Oct 9:35 p.m. | 3 | 17 wks |

'Dead Letter' by Robert Storey.
At a gathering for tea following a funeral, relatives discover they have an inheritance problem on their hands.
Designer: Timothy O'Brien. **Director:** William T. Kotcheff.

| 1963 | 7.9 | Sun 1 Dec 9:35 p.m. | 3 | 23 wks |

'The Higher They Fly' by Christopher Hodder-Williams.
The judgment of test pilot Fleming (Michael Goodliffe) is vindicated when the Jet Four develops an undercarriage fault on a passenger flight. Can he direct mid-air repairs from the ground? Also starring Jill Dixon, Mark Eden, Frederick Jaeger, John Paul and June Thorburn.
Director: Guy Verney.

| 1964 | 8.3 | Sun 13 Dec 10:05 p.m. | 3 | 23 wks |

'The Hothouse' by Donald Churchill.
A shrivelling mango, two wives and an ambitious employee all help to upset a young supermarket tycoon's quiet weekend in the hothouse. Starring Harry H. Corbett with Donald Churchill, Miranda Connell and Diana Rigg.
Designer: Assheton Gordon. **Director:** Guy Verney.

| 1965 | 6.7 | Sun 27 Jun 10:05 p.m. | 10 | 12 wks |

'I've Got A System' by Allan Prior.
This last play in a trilogy about people on Blackpool's Golden Mile stars Derek Francis as Dr Walter Williams. He has developed a system for picking horses based on the errors of the handicappers. His wife, Martha (Avis Bunnage) is preoccupied with her boarding house, lodger Val (Kika Markham) is a sociology student trying to find herself, and wide-boy Harry (Keith Baxter) just wants some cash.
Designer: Voytek. **Director:** Alvin Rakoff.

| 1966 | 6.6 | Sat 22 Jan 10:05 p.m. | 16 | 5 wks |

'The Pity Of It All' by Stan Barstow.
Young miner's widow Nancy Harper (Billie Whitelaw) works in a sweet shop to support her daughter. The child is killed in an accident by a car driven by Walter Daymer (Nigel Stock). Daymer innocently calls on Nancy and slowly they fall in love. However, he is already married and a different kind of tragedy looms.
Designer: David Marshall. **Director:** Patrick Dromgoole.

| 1967 | 6.1 | Sat 28 Jan 10:05 p.m. | 9 | 7 wks |

'The Floating Population' by Donald Churchill.
Nurse Marjorie Padfield (Wendy Craig) meets young tycoon Bernard Thompson (Ian Bannen). They play an unusual game of cards.
Designer: Michael Knight. **Director:** Jonathan Alwyn.

| 1968 | 4.8 | Sat 8 Jun 10:15 p.m. | 19 | 2 wks |

'The Three Wives of Felix Hull' by Fay Weldon.
Felix (Charles Gray) visits a health farm with his third wife. Unexpectedly, his second wife is also there. His daughter by his first marriage and a stepdaughter are present, too. Also starring Elvi Hale, Dilys Laye and Fulton Mackay.
Designer: Eddie Wolfram. **Director:** Alan Cooke.

| 1969 | 7.0 | Mon 6 Jan 8:30 p.m. | 5 | 9 wks |

'The Frobisher Game' by David Perry.
The owners of a splendid country house are off on holiday. Their departure is the signal for the servants to begin a game in which the gardener and the housekeeper impersonate the master and mistress. Starring Bill Fraser, Peter Graves, Avice Landon, Vanessa Lee, Dandy Nichols and Richard Pearson.
Designer: Eddie Wolfram. **Director:** Patrick Dromgoole.

| 1970 | 7.2 | Tue 13 Oct 9:00 p.m. | 3 | 13 wks |

'Poor Mother' by Fay Weldon.
Bambi (Amanda Reiss) is only nineteen and has just had a baby. Her happiness is short-lived when her husband is late for visiting and she discovers the wine he has brought is not for her!
Designer: Fred Pusey. **Director:** James Goddard.

| 1971 | 6.4 | Tue 21 Sep 9:00 p.m. | 8 | 7 wks |

'The Girl On The M1' by Katy Gardiner.
Veronica earns her daily bread fraternizing with lorry drivers up and down the M1. She gets a chance to escape from the endless pick-ups. Can she overcome her past and start again? Starring Sharon Duce, Roddy McMillan and Terence Rigby.
Designer: Stan Woodward. **Director:** Peter Duguid.

| 1972 | 7.3 | Tue 31 Oct 9:00 p.m. | 3 | 7 wks |

'Anywhere But England' by John Hale.
Jennifer (Denise Buckley) goes to stay with her father Miles (Denholm Elliott) on a small island in the Mediterranean where he and his pal Freddie (John Le Mesurier) live out an English way of life under the sun. Their cosy existence is soon threatened by local politics.
Designer: Fred Pusey. **Director:** Mike Vardy. **Producer:** Kim Mills.

| 1973 | 7.1 | Tue 9 Oct 9:00 p.m. | 3 | 7 wks |

'Red Riding Hood' by John Peacock.
A young girl's visit to her grandmother turns into a terrible nightmare with macabre events taking place in the house. Keith Barron and Rita Tushingham star.
Designer: Ray Simm. **Producer:** Joan Kemp-Welch.

Armchair Thriller   31 wks

Southern, drama

| 1978 | 17.2 | Tue 2 May 8:30 p.m. | 1 | 20 wks |

'The Limbo Connection' dramatized by Philip Mackie from the novel by Derry Quinn.
Mark Omney (James Bolam) is a film writer whose life is falling apart. He is drinking to excess and having rows with his wife Clare (Suzanne Bertish). He is also failing to make a living.
Designer: David Marshall. **Director:** Robert Tronson. **Producer:** Jacqueline Davis.

| 1980 | 14.7 | Tue 5 Feb 8:00 p.m. | 8 | 11 wks |

'Dead Man's Kit' by Tom McClenaghan.
The Master at Arms of a British ship is knocked unconscious and thrown overboard. Chief Petty Officer White (Larry Lamb) seeks the key to the crime but is himself pursued by two hired killers. Also stars Maurice Colbourne, Philip Locke and Cherie Lunghi.
Director: Colin Bucksey. **Producer:** Andrew Brown.

Army Game, The   35 wks

Granada, situation comedy

This archetypal Army farce was created by Sid Colin and ran from 1957 to 1962. William Hartnell was the original Sergeant-Major, R.S.M. Bullimore. Bill Fraser played Sergeant Snudge, Alfie Bass was 'excused boots' Bisley (known as Bootsie since he walked around in unlaced plimsolls) and Norman Rossington played 'Cupcake'. Other stars included Bernard Bresslaw, Charles Hawtrey and Michael Medwin.

| 1960 | 7.2 | Tue 27 Sep 8:00 p.m. | 1 | 17 wks |

William Hartnell returns after an absence of almost two years. Also starring Geoffrey Sumner as Major Upshot-Bagley with Mario Fabrizi, Harry Fowler, Ted Lune, Frank Williams and Dick Emery as Private Chubby Catchpole.
Writer: Maurice Wiltshire. **Director:** Max Morgan-Witts. **Producer:** Peter Eton.

1961	7.4	Tue 11 Apr 8:55 p.m.	1	18 wks

R.S.M. Bullimore finds that discipline falls below the standards he thought he had established at Netherhopping.
Writers: Derek Collyer and David Cumming. **Director:** Graeme McDonald. **Producer:** Eric Fawcett.

....

Around the Beatles   1 wk

AR, music

1964	7.6	Wed 5 May 9:45 p.m.	6	1 wk

Starring John, Paul, George and Ringo with Long John Baldry, Cilla Black, Millie, Murray the 'K', P. J. Proby, Sounds Incorporated and the Vernons Girls.
Director: Rita Gillespie. **Producer:** Jack Good.

....

Around the World in 80 Days   1 wk

BBC, documentary

Michael Palin attempted to emulate Jules Verne's character Phileas Fogg, who accomplished the title feat accompanied by his valet. Palin took seven programmes to make it back to London.

1989	12.8	Wed 22 Nov 9:30 p.m.	12	1 wk

'Dateline To Deadline'
The home stretch. Will Palin get back in time?
Director: Roger Mills. **Producer:** Clem Vallance.

....

Arthur Askey Show, The   1 wk

ATV, comedy

Arthur Askey was one of the few radio comedians to make a successful transition to television. He made countless TV appearances prior to his death on 16 November 1982.

1960	5.0	Sat 23 Jul 7:55 p.m.	5	1 wk

Arthur presents his 'Company of Talented Players' with the Jack Parnell orchestra.
Writers: Sid Green and Dick Hills. **Producer:** Francis Essex.

....

Arthur C. Clarke's World of Strange Powers   7 wks

YTV, documentary

This series explored psychic phenomena.

1985	12.0	Wed 1 May 7:00 p.m.	14	7 wks

'Ghosts, Apparitions and Haunted Houses'
Narrator: Anna Ford. **Director:** Charles Flynn. **Producer:** Adam Hart-Davis. **Executive Producer:** Simon Welfare.

....

Arthur Hailey's Strong Medicine   1 wk

TVS, drama

Rita Lakin and Lisa McKenzie adapted a Hailey story in two parts.

1986	10.1	Thu 21 Aug 8:00 p.m. Fri 22 Aug 7:30 p.m.	6	1 wk

The episodes were listed together in the ratings.

Pamela Sue Martin plays Celia Gray, who fights corruption and male domination to reach the top in big business. Also starring Ben Cross, Patrick Duffy, Douglas Fairbanks Jr., Gayle Hunnicutt, Sam Neill, Anette O'Toole and Dick Van Dyke.
Designer: Allan Cameron. **Director:** Guy Green. **Producer:** Dickie Bamber.

....

Arthur Haynes Show, The   62 wks

ATV, comedy

Arthur Haynes played a lovable social menace whose cocky self-assurance was set against the erudite charm, authority and learning of Nicholas Parsons. Dermot Kelly also gave regular support. Many of Haynes' characters were the creations of writer Johnny Speight, including 'the tramp' inspired by a real tramp who climbed into Speight's Rolls Royce while it was stopped at a traffic light. Haynes died of a heart attack at the age of 52 in 1966.
Producers included Colin Clews (1960, 1962–63) and Dicky Leeman (1961, 1964–65). With the Jack Parnell Orchestra.

1960	6.9	Thu 27 Oct 8:00 p.m.	2	18 wks

Guests: Aileen Cochrane and Dorothy Dampier.

1961	6.6	Thu 27 Apr 8:00 p.m.	4	4 wks

Guests: Teddy Johnson and Pearl Carr.

1962	5.7	Sat 29 Dec 8:25 p.m.	9	6 wks

Guests: Joe 'Mr Piano' Henderson and Janie Marden.

1963	6.2	Sat 26 Jan 8:25 p.m.	7	8 wks

Guests: The Springfields.

1964	6.6	Sat 5 Dec 8:25 p.m.	7	21 wks

Guests: Kenny Ball and his Jazzmen and the Raindrops.

'The Limbo Connection' starring James Bolam was Number One with two of its six episodes of **Armchair Thriller**.

| 1965 | 6.5 | Sat 2 Jan 8:25 p.m. | 14 | 2 wks |

Guests: Joe Brown and the Bruvvers, Teddy Johnson and Pearl Carr, and Billy Walker.

| 1966 | 7.6 | Sat 26 Mar 8:20 p.m. | 4 | 3 wks |

Guests: The Fortunes, Elizabeth Larner, The Morgan-James Duo and Graham Stark.
Director: *Dicky Leeman.* **Producer:** *Alan Tarrant.*

Arthur's Treasured Volumes · 4 wks

ATV, comedy

This series starred Arthur Askey in comedy sketches and situations.

| 1960 | 5.8 | Mon 2 May 8:00 p.m. | 5 | 4 wks |

'A Blow in Anger'
Cast includes Wilfrid Brambell, Sam Kydd, Arthur Mullard and June Whitfield.
Writer: *Dave Freeman.* **Producer:** *Bill Ward.*

As You Like It · 1 wk

Southern, music

This series of pop shows was hosted by Don Moss and produced by Mike Mansfield.

| 1967 | 4.5 | Tue 27 Jun 6:30 p.m. | 19 | 1 wk |

Guests: Billy Fury, Jonathan King, The Monkees, Paul and Barry Ryan, and Sandie Shaw.

Ashanti · 2 wks

Presented by ITV, film

| 1982 | 9.3 | Mon 30 Aug 9:00 p.m. | 14 | 1 wk |

A woman is seized by slave traders in West Africa. Starring Michael Caine, Rex Harrison, William Holden, Omar Sharif and Peter Ustinov.
Director: *Richard Fleischer.*

| 1990 | 8.9 | Sat 23 Jun 8:00 p.m. | 18 | 1 wk |

Repeat showing of the above film.

Ask The Family · 4 wks

BBC, game show

In this long-running quiz show hosted by Robert Robinson, two families competed to answer questions requiring a high standard of general knowledge.

| 1979 | 17.1 | Mon 13 Aug 6:50 p.m. | 2 | 3 wks |

Director: *Rosalind Gold.* **Producer:** *Mark Patterson.*

| 1981 | 11.6 | Mon 6 Apr 6:55 p.m. | 19 | 1 wk |

Producer: *Rosalind Gold.*

Aspel and Company · 6 wks

LWT, talk show

Michael Aspel interviewed leading celebrities, most of them from show business.
Director: *Nicholas Vaughan-Barratt.* **Producer** *(1984–85):* *Helen Fraser.*

| 1984 | 9.1 | Sat 9 Jun 9:30 p.m. | 12 | 3 wks |

Guests: Richard Clayderman, Paul McCartney and Tracey Ullman.

| 1985 | 14.3 | Sat 19 Jan 9:00 p.m. | 16 | 1 wk |

Guests: Clint Eastwood and Dennis Waterman.

| 1987 | 14.9 | Sat 7 Mar 9:05 p.m. | 3 | 1 wk |

Guests: Julie Andrews, Leslie Crowther and Tom Jones.
Director: *Alasdair Macmillan.* **Producer:** *Gill Stribling-Wright.*

| 1988 | 10.1 | Sat 2 Apr 9:35 p.m. | 16 | 1 wk |

Guests: Dolly Parton and Victoria Wood.
Producer: *Judith Holder.*

Aspen Murder, The · 3 wks

USA presented by ITV, drama

Douglas Heyes wrote and directed this three-part murder trial.

| 1978 | 13.3 | Wed 30 Aug 9:10 p.m. | 2 | 3 wks |

Lee Bishop (Perry King) has been convicted of murder in Colorado. He files his eleventh appeal from Death Row. Also starring Gene Barry, Sam Elliott, Anthony Franciosa, John Houseman, John McIntyre and Michelle Phillips.

At Home With Jimmy and Ben   1 wk

AR, comedy

Jimmy Jewel and Ben Warriss were Britain's top comedy double act of the forties and fifties. Warriss died 14 January 1993.

| 1962 | 4.7 | Wed 24 Jan 9:40 p.m. | 16 | 1 wk |

Jewel and Warriss have eaten their way through Christmas and the New Year and now have nothing but their television set to sustain them through 1962.
Writers: Sid Green and Dick Hills. **Producer:** Peter Croft.

Athletics   12 wks

BBC (1962, 1980, 1982 and 1984) and ITV (1978, 1985–6), sport

| 1962 | 4.2 | Sun 16 Sep 6:10 p.m. | 18 | 1 wk |

The European Championships held at the Yugoslav National Army Stadium in Belgrade.
Commentators: David Coleman and Norris McWhirter. **Television presentation:** Bryan Cowgill.

| 1978 | 11.1 | Fri 1 Sep 7:00 p.m. | 15 | 1 wk |

Events were shown from the fourth day of the European Championships in Prague.
Commentator: Adrian Metcalfe. **Television presentation:** Ted Ayling.

| 1980 | 11.0 | Fri 8 Aug 8:30 p.m. | 9 | 1 wk |

International athletics from Crystal Palace.
Commentators: David Coleman, Ron Pickering and Stuart Storey. **Television presentation:** John Shrewsbury.

| 1982 | 9.7 | Sat 26 Jun 9:45 p.m. | 12 | 3 wks |

Introduced from Oslo by Frank Bough.
Commentators: David Coleman and Ron Pickering. **Television presentation:** Norwegian Television Service.

| 1984 | 7.9 | Wed 22 Aug 8:40 p.m. | 17 | 2 wks |

International athletics meeting in Zurich.
Commentators: David Coleman, Ron Pickering and Stuart Storey. **Television presentation:** Swiss Television Service.

| 1985 | 10.2 | Fri 9 Aug 8:00 p.m. | 13 | 3 wks |

Jim Rosenthal introduces the events from Gateshead.
Commentators: Alan Parry and Adrian Metcalfe. **Television presentation:** Richard Russell.

| 1986 | 8.9 | Wed 13 Aug 8:00 p.m. | 14 | 1 wk |

Introduced by Jim Rosenthal from Zurich.
Commentators: Peter Matthews and Alan Parry. **Television presentation:** John Davis.

Auf Wiedersehen Pet   21 wks

Central, situation comedy

Dick Clement and Ian La Frenais created this series from an idea by Franc Roddam. A gang of Geordie brickies unable to find work in Newcastle went to Germany. The programme starred Tim Healy as Dennis, Gary Holton as Wayne, Jimmy Nail as Oz, Pat Roach as Bomber, Timothy Spall as Barry and Kevin Whately as Neville.
Director: Roger Bamford. **Producer:** Martin McKeand. **Executive Producer:** Allan McKeown.

| 1983 | 10.9 | Fri 16 Dec 9:00 p.m | 19 | 2 wks |

'The Accused'
Dennis faces an impending divorce. Neville is suspected by his wife of living it up behind her back.

| 1984 | 13.4 | Fri 10 Feb 9:00 p.m. | 9 | 6 wks |

'When the Boat Goes Out'
Will Dennis stay with his German girlfriend Dagmar (Brigitte Kahn) or return to Vera (Caroline Hutchison)? Can Wayne remain faithful to Christa (Lysette Anthony)?
Writer: Stan Key.

| 1986 | 16.0 | Fri 11 Apr 9:00 p.m. | 2 | 13 wks |

'Marjorie Doesn't Live Here Anymore'
The lads go home on a visit, but Oz has a shock when he calls on his wife Marjorie (Su Elliott).

Auntie's Bloomers   1 wk

BBC, comedy

| 1991 | 18.2 | Sun 29 Dec 7:15 p.m. | 2 | 1 wk |

Terry Wogan presents a selection of out-takes.
Director: Patricia Mordecai. **Producer:** Paul Smith.
(A Celador production.)

Avalanche Express   1 wk

Presented by ITV, film

| 1982 | 12.6 | Tue 14 Dec 7:30 p.m. | 5 | 1 wk |

Spies from many countries take a train journey from Milan to Rotterdam. The star of the movie, Robert Shaw, died during the filming on 28 August 1978. Other stars include Horst Buchholz, Linda Evans, Lee Marvin, Joe Namath and Maximillian Schell.
Director: Mark Robson.

Avengers, The — 103 wks

ABC, drama

The original series starred Ian Hendry as Dr David Keel, whose goal was to avenge the murder of his fiancée, and Patrick Macnee as the bowler-hatted secret service agent Steed. After the first season and following an actor's strike Hendry did not continue. Steed became the main character and Honor Blackman was introduced as Catherine Gale, a widowed anthropologist. Macnee's subsequent partners were Diana Rigg as Emma Peel and Linda Thorson as Tara King. He was later joined in THE NEW AVENGERS by Joanna Lumley as Purdey and Gareth Hunt as former army major, Mike Gambit. The theme music was by Johnny Dankworth.

Producers included Leonard White (1961–62), John Bryce (1963–64), Julian Wintle (1965–66) and the team of Albert Fennell and Brian Clemens (1967–69).

| 1961 | 5.1 | Sat 16 Dec 10:00 p.m. | 5 | 8 wks |

'The Deadly Air' by Lester Powell.
Keel and Steed face a murder weapon which cannot be detected until it has struck.
Director: John Knight.

| 1962 | 5.8 | Sat 29 Dec 10:05 p.m. | 8 | 6 wks |

'Dead on Course' by Eric Pace.
Steed finds unexpected adventure when he goes to a remote convent following a mysterious plane crash.
Director: Richmond Harding.

| 1963 | 7.3 | Sat 21 Dec 8:55 p.m. | 7 | 11 wks |

'Death à la Carte' by John Lucarotti.
Steed becomes a chef and Cathy strives to prevent a murder.
Director: Kim Mills.

| 1964 | 7.6 | Sat 8 Feb 9:10 p.m. | 9 | 12 wks |

'Trojan Horse' by Malcolm Hulke.
Steed goes horse racing and Cathy becomes the favourite for murder.
Director: Laurence Bourne.

| 1965 | 7.5 | Sat 20 Nov 9:05 p.m. | 6 | 12 wks |

'A Surfeit of H2O' by Colin Finbow.
Steed plans a boat trip and Emma gets very wet.
Director: Sidney Hayers.

| 1966 | 8.4 | Sat 19 Feb 9:05 p.m. | 4 | 12 wks |

'A Touch of Brimstone' by Brian Clemens.
Steed joins the Hellfire Club and Emma becomes Queen of Sin.
Director: James Hill.

| 1967 | 8.0 | Sat 21 Jan 9:10 p.m | 3 | 23 wks |

'The Fear Merchants' by Philip Levene.
Emma Peel is given the fright of her life.
Director: Gordon Flemyng.

| 1968 | 5.5 | Wed 16 Oct 8:00 p.m. | 12 | 4 wks |

'You'll Catch Your Death' by Jeremy Burnham.
Tara is imprisoned in a deep-freeze room in a cold-cure research centre where a doctor has sneezed to death.
Director: Paul Dickson.

| 1969 | 6.8 | Sun 12 Jan 8:25 p.m. | 8 | 15 wks |

'The Forget-Me-Not' by Brian Clemens.
Exit Emma and enter Tara as two Avengers are paralysed by memory-killing darts. (Repeat.)
Director: James Hill.

Award Show, The — 1 wk

ATV, entertainment

| 1962 | 6.8 | Sun 29 Jul 8:25 p.m. | 2 | 1 wk |

Bruce Forsyth hosts the Daily Mirror's presentation of awards to entertainers selected by its readers. Among the recipients are Lady Barnett, Jeremy Brett, Violet Carson, Raymond Francis, Margaret Lockwood, Cliff Richard and the Shadows, Barry Took and Marty Feldman.
Producer: Alan Tarrant.

Aweful Mr Goodall — 5 wks

LWT, drama

After fifteen years as a Colonel in MI5, widower Jack Goodall (Robert Urquhart) retired to Eastbourne in search of a quiet life. His nose for trouble precluded such a life.

| 1974 | 7.2 | Fri 12 Apr 9:00 p.m. | 9 | 5 wks |

'Indiscretion' by Trevor Preston.
Mr Goodall goes in search of the answers to a set of problems that no one else admits exist.
Designer: Frank Nerini. **Director:** Jim Goddard. **Producer:** Richard Bates.

B

Baby M	1 wk

Presented by BBC, film

1990	9.4	Tue–Wed 7–8 Aug 9:30 p.m.	12	1 wk

These episodes were listed together in the ratings.
John Shea, Robin Strasser and JoBeth Williams star in the story of a surrogate mother's battle to keep the baby she bore for another couple.
Director: James Steven Sadwith.

Bacharach Sound, The	1 wk

Granada, music

1965	6.8	Wed 14 Apr 9:40 p.m.	6	1 wk

Starring Burt Bacharach with his orchestra in a special featuring his own music recorded at Granada's Chelsea Palace studios. Guests: Chuck Jackson, the Merseybeats, the Searchers, Dusty Springfield and Dionne Warwick.
Director: Philip Casson. **Producer:** John Hamp.

Bachelor Father	5 wks

BBC, situation comedy

This series was created and written by Richard Waring. Wealthy bachelor Peter Lamb (Ian Carmichael) was jaded after a succession of romantic failures. He found new meaning in life after becoming a full-time foster father, thus acquiring the family he had always wanted without the bother of a woman.

1970	6.4	Thu 26 Nov 7:45 p.m.	15	5 wks

'Time To Go Home'
The children conspire to prevent one of them, Freddie, from returning to his real mother.
Producer: Graeme Muir.

Back To The Future	1 wk

Presented by BBC, film

1988	14.9	Sun 25 Dec 3:10 p.m.	11	1 wk

Michael J. Fox stars as Marty McFly, who tries out the time machine of an eccentric scientist (Christopher Lloyd) and finds he is responsible for his parents' romance and hence his own existence.
Director: Robert Zemeckis.

Backs To The Land	3 wks

Anglia, drama

This series by David Climie was set during the Second World War and revolved around the lives of farmer Tom Whitlow (John Stratton) and three girls who worked on his farm, Jenny (Teresa Stevens), Shirley (Philippa Howell) and Bunny (Pippa Page).

1978	11.1	Fri 4 Aug 7:30 p.m.	8	3 wks

'Let's Talk Turkey'
Miss Rainbow (Geraldine Newman) has moved into Crabtree Farm to protect the girls from Tom – but it is actually Tom who needs protection from Miss Rainbow.
Director: John Davies. **Producer:** John Rosenburg.

Badger's Set	1 wk

YTV, drama

1974	6.2	Mon 23 Sep 8:00 p.m.	16	1 wk

In this single comedy play Julian Orchard stars as ballet critic Eric Badger, who runs into trouble over a particularly scathing review.
Designer: Colin Pigott. **Music Director:** Ken Jones. **Producer:** Paddy Russell.

Bangkok Hilton `1 wk`

Australia presented by BBC, drama

This mini-series starred Nicole Kidman as heroin addict Katrina Stanton, who embarked on a search for her father Hal (Denholm Elliott) and was arrested in Thailand for drug smuggling. She was locked in the notorious prison known as the 'Bangkok Hilton'.

`1990`	9.0	`Fri 4 May 9:30 p.m.`	15	`1 wk`

The day of Katrina's trial approaches.
Writer: Terry Hayes. **Director:** Ken Cameron. (A Kennedy Miller production.)

Barbara in Black `1 wk`

BBC, drama

This thriller serial in six parts was written by Elaine Morgan and produced by David J. Thomas. A crash in the Welsh mountains involving a van and a heavy lorry on a lonely road started off a mysterious chain of events. John Cairney played Dr Dave Sharland and Tracey Lloyd played Barbara Griffiths.

`1962`	5.0	`Mon 26 Feb 8:00 p.m.`	16	`1 wk`

Episode Two
A strange man turns up at Abereithin police station and an unusual substance is hidden down a mine.
Designer: Alan Taylor.

Barbara Woodhouse Goes to Beverly Hills `1 wk`

YTV, documentary

`1981`	13.2	`Wed 30 Dec 9:00 p.m.`	12	`1 wk`

Dog training expert Barbara takes her 'walkies' to the land of talkies. She meets the canine culture of California and the pampered pets of Britt Ekland, Zsa Zsa Gabor, Lorne Greene, Tippi Hedren, Dorothy Lamour, Stefanie Powers, William Shatner, Elke Sommer and Wilfrid Hyde White.
Director: David Gerrard. **Producer:** Nigel Turner. **Executive Producers:** Michael Deakin and Frank Smith.

Barlow at Large `1 wk`

BBC, drama

Another spinoff for Charlie Barlow (Stratford Johns) followed Z CARS and SOFTLY SOFTLY. This time Barlow had moved to Whitehall to work with the Police Research Services Branch, co-ordinating enquiries. The series also featured Norman Comer as Detective Sergeant Rees and Neil Stacy as A. G. Fenton. Created by Elwyn Jones.

`1973`	6.6	`Wed 28 Feb 8:00 p.m.`	16	`1 wk`

'Publicity' by Allan Prior.
A girl has been murdered in the West Country. Routine police methods have failed to provide any leads. Barlow is asked to try something different.
Director: Michael Hayes. **Producer:** Keith Williams.

Barrymore `1 wk`

LWT, entertainment

This series starred Michael Barrymore with members of the public in unusual or unexpected situations or performing their party pieces.

`1991`	13.4	`Sat 21 Dec 8:00 p.m.`	12	`1 wk`

Producer: Ian Hamilton.

Basil Brush Show, The `1 wk`

BBC, children's

A glove puppet of a fox with an upper class voice and catchphrase 'boom boom' was created and manipulated by Ivan Owen.

`1976`	6.5	`Sat 27 Nov 5:20 p.m.`	18	`1 wk`

Introduced by Roy North with guests Dennis Waterman and the 'G' Men.
Writer: George Martin. **Producer:** Brian Penders.

Basil in Neverland `1 wk`

BBC, children's

`1976`	6.8	`Sat 18 Dec 5:20 p.m.`	18	`1 wk`

A Christmas fantasy with Basil Brush and Roy North with guests Brian Blessed and Jan Hunt.
Writer: George Martin. **Producer:** Brian Penders.

Bass Player and the Blonde, The `2 wks`

ATV, drama

`1978`	10.7	`Tue 22 Aug 9:00 p.m.`	16	`2 wks`

Three-part story by Ian Lindsay about romantic runaways Mangham and Terry (Edward Woodward and Jane Wymark). Also starring Ronald Fraser, Sam Kydd and Betty McDowell.
Designer: Michael Eve. **Producer:** Dennis Vance.

Batteries Not Included `1 wk`

Presented by BBC, film

| 1991 | 11.7 | Mon 1 Apr 6:15 p.m. | 15 | 1 wk |

Alien visitors to New York make everybody's life easier. Hume Cronyn and Jessica Tandy are among those who benefit.
Director: Matthew Robbins.

Battle Beyond the Stars `1 wk`

Presented by ITV, film

| 1983 | 10.5 | Thu 6 Oct 7:30 p.m. | 15 | 1 wk |

A small planet fights for survival against unwelcome invaders. Starring John Saxon, Richard Thomas and Robert Vaughn.
Director: Jimmy T. Murakami.

Battle for the Desert `1 wk`

ATV, documentary

| 1967 | 6.2 | Tue 24 Oct 9:00 p.m. | 13 | 1 wk |

This account of the war in the Western Desert coincides with the twenty-fifth anniversary of the victory at El Alamein, 23 October to 4 November 1942.
Narrator: Bernard Archard. **Writer** and **Producer:** Peter Batty.

Battle of Britain `1 wk`

Presented by BBC, film

| 1974 | 7.6 | Sun 15 Sep 8:15 p.m. | 1 | 1 wk |

First television screening for this war film starring Harry Andrews, Michael Bates, Isla Blair, Michael Caine, Robert Flemyng, Barry Foster, Edward Fox, Trevor Howard, Curt Jurgens, Ian McShane, Kenneth More, Laurence Olivier, Nigel Patrick, Christopher Plummer, Michael Redgrave, Robert Shaw, Patrick Wymark and Susannah York.
Director: Guy Hamilton.

Battle of the Bulge, The `2 wks`

Presented by ITV, film

| 1975 | 6.1 | Mon 31 Mar 8:00 p.m. | 17 | 1 wk |

The story of this crucial Second World War battle in the Ardennes is recounted. Starring Henry Fonda with Dana Andrews, Pier Angeli, Charles Bronson, Ty Hardin, Robert Ryan, Telly Savalas and Robert Shaw.
Director: Ken Annakin.

| 1982 | 8.6 | Sat 3 Jul 7:15 p.m. | 14 | 1 wk |

Repeat showing of the above film.

Battle of the Midway `1 wk`

Presented by BBC, film

| 1986 | 9.8 | Sat 10 May 7:30 p.m. | 18 | 1 wk |

The story of the sea battle between American and Japanese forces that proved crucial in the Pacific theatre of the Second World War. Starring James Coburn, Henry Fonda, Glenn Ford, Charlton Heston, Hal Holbrook, Robert Mitchum, Cliff Robertson and Robert Wagner.
Director: Jack Smight.

Batman `1 wk`

Presented by ITV, film

| 1991 | 14.3 | Wed 25 Dec 6:00 p.m. | 9 | 1 wk |

Bob Kane's comic-book hero is played by Michael Keaton. In this film he faces his nemesis The Joker (Jack Nicholson). With Kim Basinger as Vicki Vale and Jack Palance as Carl Grissom.
Director: Tim Burton.

Bay of Saint Michel, The `1 wk`

Presented by BBC, film

| 1971 | 4.8 | Tue 29 Jun 7:50 p.m. | 20 | 1 wk |

Three ex-naval commanders receive orders to re-form their group for a secret operation in search of Nazi loot. The exploit takes them to the abbey of Mont Saint Michel. Starring Keenan Wynn and Mai Zetterling with Rona Anderson, Trader Faulkner and Ronald Howard.
Director: John Ainsworth.

Baywatch `3 wks`

USA presented by ITV, drama

The beach lifeguards on duty at Malibu were celebrated in this series. David Hasselhoff and Parker Stevenson starred with a bevy of scantily clad starlets.

| 1990 | 13.7 | Sat 6 Jan 6:50 p.m. | 10 | 3 wks |

'Panic on Malibu Pier'
An attorney who moonlights as a lifeguard in his spare time is the victim of a young girl's obsessive passion.

Beadle's About — 52 wks

LWT, comedy

Jeremy Beadle reworked the idea of CANDID CAMERA by trapping the public in situations with hidden cameras.
Directors included Terry Kinane (1986, 1988), Sue McMahon (1988–89) and Chris Fox (1989–90). **Producer** (1987–91): Robert Randell (1987–91).

| 1986 | 14.8 | Sat 22 Nov 7:15 p.m. | 5 | 5 wks |

Producer: Trevor Hopkins.

| 1987 | 12.4 | Sat 10 Oct 7:15 p.m. | 8 | 8 wks |

Directors: Vic Finch and Richard Hearsey.

1988	13.4	Sat 19 Nov 7:20 p.m.	9	8 wks
1989	15.2	Sat 18 Nov 7:35 p.m.	8	12 wks
1990	14.1	Sat 24 Nov 7:25 p.m.	7	13 wks

Director: Simon Cochrane.

| 1991 | 13.6 | Sun 17 Nov 7:15 p.m. | 16 | 6 wks |

Bear Island — 3 wks

Presented by ITV, film

| 1982 | 9.8 | Sun 26 Dec 7:15 p.m. | 20 | 1 wk |

A United Nations scientific team goes to the Arctic to research global weather changes. Starring Vanessa Redgrave and Donald Sutherland.
Director: Don Sharp.

| 1984 | 13.1 | Thu 5 Apr 7:25 p.m. | 8 | 1 wk |
| 1988 | 10.1 | Fri 26 Aug 8:00 p.m. | 12 | 1 wk |

Repeat showing of the above film.

Beat City — 1 wk

AR, documentary

| 1963 | 5.6 | Tue 24 Dec 9:10 p.m. | 14 | 1 wk |

Daniel Farson examines why Liverpool has found new fame with the emergence of so many beat groups. Contributions from Gerry and the Pacemakers, Rory Storm and the Hurricanes, Faron's Flamingos, the Chants, and the Spinners.
Director: Charles Squires.

Beat the Cheat — 1 wk

Thames, documentary

This series concentrated on how to avoid being conned in everyday life. Presented by John Stalker and Trish Williamson.

| 1991 | 8.9 | Mon 29 Jul 8:00 p.m. | 10 | 1 wk |

Guests: Loyd Grossman, Fred Housego and Peter Stringfellow.
Producer: Alastair Pirrie.

Beatles on Tour — 1 wk

Granada, documentary

| 1964 | 6.1 | Tue 23 Jun 10:07 p.m. | 6 | 1 wk |

Bill Grundy introduces this film of life on the road with the Fab Four.
Producer: Dick Fontaine.

Beauty and the Beast — 3 wks

USA presented by ITV, drama

Linda Hamilton starred as New York attorney Catherine Chandler. She was attacked by a gang of thugs and rescued by a powerful but grotesque man played by Ron Perlman. He lived in the tunnels beneath Manhattan. Roy Dotrice portrayed Catherine's father.

| 1988 | 11.0 | Fri 30 Sep 8:00 p.m. | 18 | 3 wks |

'The Beast Within' by Andrew Laskes.
Cathy's life is endangered when she investigates the death of a longshoreman.
Director: Paul Lynch.

Beauty, Bonny, Daisy, Violet, Grace, and Geoffrey Morton — 1 wk

Thames, documentary

| 1974 | 6.0 | Tue 1 Oct 9:10 p.m. | 19 | 1 wk |

Geoffrey Morton is a Yorkshireman who farms his one hundred and forty acres using shire horses (names as in the title). He has managed to make a success by using farming ideas abandoned many years ago.
Camera: Mike Fash. **Producer:** Frank Cvitanovich. **Executive Producer:** Jolyon Wimhurst.

Bed-Sit Girl, The   5 wks

BBC, situation comedy

This series, created by Ronald Chesney and Ronald Wolfe, starred Sheila Hancock and Dilys Laye as two unmarried girls sharing both a bed-sit and a procession of men.

| 1965 | 6.3 | Tue 27 Apr 8:00 p.m. | 10 | 5 wks |

'The Medical Stud'
Sheila and Dilys, both unhappily unmarried, set their sights on the same medical student. Guests include George A. Cooper, Derrick Sherwin and Ronnie Stevens.
Producer: Duncan Wood.

Beetlejuice   1 wk

Presented by ITV, film

| 1991 | 14.9 | Mon 30 Dec 9:00 p.m. | 12 | 1 wk |

Michael Keaton stars in this supernatural comedy with ghosts and a bio-exorcist. Also starring Alec Baldwin and Geena Davis.
Director: Tim Burton.

Befrienders, The   1 wk

BBC, drama

This series was based on the work of the Samaritans, the organization founded by Chad Varah. Series created by Harry W. Junkin.

| 1972 | 6.1 | Sat 25 Mar 8:30 p.m. | 18 | 1 wk |

'Nobody Understands Miranda' by Chad Varah.
Starring, as Samaritans, Peter Armitage (Chuck), Michael Culver (Jerry), Megs Jenkins (Janet) and Jenny Till (Frances), with guest star Jean Marsh as Miranda.
Director: Raymond Menmuir. **Producers:** John Henderson and Harry W. Junkin.

Beggar My Neighbour   6 wks

BBC, situation comedy

This series by Ken Hoare and Mike Sharland originated from a 1966 episode of COMEDY PLAYHOUSE. The Garveys and the Butts lived next door to each other in Muswell Hill. The Garveys had considerably less money than the Butts. The two wives were sisters. Peter Jones and June Whitfield starred as Gerald and Rose Garvey, with Reg Varney and Pat Coombs as Harry and Lana Butt.

| 1967 | 6.0 | Mon 13 Mar 7:30 p.m. | 14 | 4 wks |

The ownership of a motor car is a serious affair for the Garveys and creates the usual conflict with the Butts.
Producer: David Croft.

| 1968 | 6.5 | Tue 6 Feb 7.30 p.m. | 16 | 2 wks |

'Ask Me No Questions'
Guest stars Rosemary Faith and Joyce Grant appear as Deirdre Garvey and the headmistress, respectively. In this series Desmond Walter-Ellis takes over from Peter Jones as Gerald Garvey.
Producer: Eric Fawcett.

Beiderbecke Affair, The   2 wks

YTV, drama

This thriller series by Alan Plater was set in northeast England and made extensive use of the music of jazz legend Bix Beiderbecke. All Trevor Chaplin (James Bolam) wanted was a set of Beiderbecke's records and all Jill (Barbara Flynn) wanted was to stand for the local council. The music was supervised by Frank Ricotti with Kenny Baker playing for Beiderbecke.

| 1985 | 13.4 | Sun 13 Jan 8:45 p.m. | 15 | 2 wks |

'Can Anybody Join In?'
Jill is detained for police questioning while Trevor chases a beautiful blonde. Big Al (Terence Rigby) reveals a few secrets about his dubious empire. Detective Sergeant Hobson (Dominic Jephcott) tries to make sense of them all.
Designer: Mike Long. **Director:** David Reynolds. **Producer:** Anne W. Gibbons. **Executive Producer:** David Cunliffe.

Ben Hur   1 wk

Presented by ITV, film

| 1978 | 15.0 | Sun 7 May 7:15 p.m. | 6 | 1 wk |

Two boys (Charlton Heston and Stephen Boyd) born in the Roman Empire during the reign of Augustus Caesar grow up together as friends but end up sworn enemies. Also starring Jack Hawkins.
Director: William Wyler.

Beneath the Planet of the Apes   1 wk

Presented by ITV, film

| 1982 | 9.4 | Sat 5 Jun 8:00 p.m. | 14 | 1 wk |

James Franciscus and Charlton Heston star as the astronauts who discover that the Simian planet is really Earth.
Director: Ted Post.

Benny Hill Down Under — 2 wks

Australia presented by ITV, comedy

| 1978 | 17.2 | Wed 12 Apr 8:00 p.m. | 2 | 2 wks |

This programme was recorded during the comedian's visit to Australia in 1977.

....

Benny Hill Show, The — 126 wks

BBC (later Thames), comedy

Perennial naughty schoolboy Hill pursued a hugely successful policy of broad humour for more than three decades and was one of the few British comedians to succeed in the United States. He died 20 April 1992.

Producers included Duncan Wood (1962–3), Kenneth Carter (1964–68), John Robins (1969–74), Mark Stuart (1975–77) and Dennis Kirkland (1979–86, 1988–89). Long-serving billed performers included Patricia Hayes (1964, 1966–67, 1970, 1979), Bella Emberg (1966, 1981–82), Henry McGee (1968–69, 1973–89), Jack Wright (1968–73, 1975–84, 1987), Jenny Lee-Wright (1968, 1971–72, 1979, 1983–84), Nicholas Parsons (1970–72), Bob Todd (1971–74, 1980–89), Hill's Angels (1980–89), Sue Upton (1980–81, 1986–89), Louise English (1981, 1983–85), Jon Jon Keefe (1982–83, 1985–89), Lorraine Doyle (1985, 1988–89), Anna Dawson (1986, 1988–89); The Ronnie Aldrich orchestra played throughout the period 1969–89 with vocal backing from the Ladybirds.

| 1962 | 4.6 | Fri 23 Mar 8:45 p.m. | 19 | 1 wk |

'The Before Man' with Edwin Apps, Priscilla Morgan, Ken Roberts and the Campbell Singers.

| 1963 | 6.0 | Fri 4 Jan 8:50 p.m. | 16 | 1 wk |

'The Shooting of Willie The Kid' with John Bluthall, Maggie Fitzgibbon, Bill Kerr and Graham Stark.

| 1964 | 5.4 | Fri 6 Nov 8:25 p.m. | 18 | 1 wk |

With Alex MacIntosh, Mark Murphy, Julie Rogers and the Burt Rhodes orchestra.

| 1966 | 6.3 | Sat 8 Jan 8:50 p.m. | 18 | 1 wk |

With Jeremy Hawk, Patsy Ann Noble and the Burt Rhodes orchestra.

| 1967 | 6.3 | Sat 6 May 8:30 p.m | 12 | 1 wk |

With Jeremy Hawk, Julie Rogers, and the Harry Rabinowicz orchestra.

| 1968 | 5.6 | Thu 26 Dec 7:15 p.m. | 17 | 1 wk |

With Tammy Jones, Doris Rogers, June Whitfield and the Burt Rhodes orchestra.

| 1969 | 8.3 | Wed 19 Nov 8:00 p.m. | 1 | 1 wk |

With David Battley, Eira Heath and Ken Parry. (In 1969 the show moved from the BBC to Thames Television.)

| 1970 | 9.3 | Wed 11 Mar 8:00 p.m. | 1 | 7 wks |

With Eira Heath, Michael Sharvell-Martin, Nicole Shelby and Jimmy Thompson.

| 1971 | 9.9 | Wed 24 Mar 8:00 p.m. | 1 | 5 wks |

With Andrée Melly.

| 1972 | 8.1 | Wed 22 Mar 8:00 p.m. | 1 | 4 wks |

With Zienia Merton.

| 1973 | 9.2 | Thu 27 Dec 9:00 p.m. | 1 | 4 wks |

With Anne Shelton and Lesley Goldie.

| 1974 | 8.9 | Thu 7 Feb 8:25 p.m. | 2 | 5 wks |

With Diane Darvey, Design, Lesley Goldie and David Hamilton.

| 1975 | 9.5 | Wed 17 Dec 8:00 p.m. | 1 | 5 wks |

With Eddie Buchanan, Clare Ruane, Dilys Watling and Jenny Westbrook.

| 1976 | 9.1 | Wed 18 Feb 8:00 p.m. | 1 | 8 wks |

With Eddie Buchanan, Moira Foot and Love Machine.

| 1977 | 15.8 | Wed 2 Nov 8:00 p.m. | 1 | 5 wks |

With Dilys Watling and Rita Webb.

| 1978 | 15.0 | Wed 13 Sep 8:00 p.m. | 2 | 2 wks |

With the Cotton Mill Boys, Dee Dee Darlington and Charles Stapley. **Producer:** Keith Beckett.

| 1979 | 20.9 | Wed 14 Mar 8:00 p.m. | 1 | 4 wks |

With Geraldine and Johnny Vyvyan.

1980	18.1	Wed 6 Feb 8:00 p.m.	2	4 wks
1981	20.0	Wed 7 Jan 8:00 p.m.	1	13 wks
1982	17.9	Wed 6 Jan 8:00 p.m.	2	11 wks
1983	14.1	Wed 5 Jan 8:00 p.m.	3	8 wks

With Kathy Staff.

| 1984 | 14.8 | Tue 31 Jan 8:00 p.m. | 2 | 9 wks |

With Pat Ashton, Helen Horton and Kathy Staff.

1985	14.3	Wed 2 Jan 8:00 p.m.	4	10 wks

With Carl Wayne.

1986	13.6	Mon 31 Mar 8:00 p.m.	7	10 wks

With Alison and Rebecca Marsh.

1987	11.3	Mon 14 Sep 9:30 p.m.	9	2 wks

Producers: Keith Beckett and John Robins.

1988	10.3	Wed 27 Apr 8:00 p.m.	14	2 wks

With Derek Deadman, Johnny Hutch and Christine Pilgrim.

1989	9.6	Mon 1 May 8:00 p.m.	16	1 wk

With Derek Deadman and Johnny Hutch.

Bergerac — 68 wks

BBC, drama

This series created by Robert Banks Stewart was set on the Channel Island of Jersey and starred John Nettles as Detective Sergeant Jim Bergerac and Terence Alexander as Charles Hungerford.
Producers included Robert Banks Stewart (1981 and 1983), Jonathan Alwyn (1984–87) and George Gallaccio (1988–90).

1981	17.4	Sun 6 Dec 8:15 p.m.	1	9 wks

'Late For a Funeral' by Dennis Spooner.
Two bodies are washed up on a beach. One has been dead a few hours, the other for more than forty years.
Director: Henry Herbert.

1983	13.0	Sun 13 Mar 9:10 p.m.	7	8 wks

'Relative Values' by Peter Miller.
The meanest millionaire on the island will do anything to save a few pence – even when his own life is at stake. (Repeat.)
Director: Martin Campbell.

1984	14.5	Sat 14 Jan 8:50 p.m.	4	3 wks

'A Cry in the Night' by Robert Holmes.
Many people have good reason to treat the death of an islander as an accident. Jim Bergerac is not among them.
Director: Oliver Horsbrugh.

1985	15.2	Fri 18 Oct 9:25 p.m.	4	8 wks

'Offshore Trades' by Nick McCarty.
The death of a scuba diver and the disappearance of the wife of a film star appear to be connected.
Director: Robert Tronson.

1986	13.2	Fri 26 Dec 8:30 p.m.	16	1 wk

'Fires in the Fall' by Chris Boucher.
A message from beyond the grave leads Bergerac to a pattern of corruption and insanity.
Director: Tom Clegg.

1987	15.8	Sat 17 Jan 8:10 p.m.	3	19 wks

'Root and Branch' by Brian Finch.
Jim Bergerac risks his job trying to establish whether or not Deborah (Deborah Grant) has real fears or is hallucinating.
Director: Baz Taylor.

1988	14.6	Sat 2 Jan 8:15 p.m.	6	5 wks

'Whatever Lola Wants' by Brian Finch.
The relationship between Jim and Susan (Louise Jameson) is not going too well. It is made worse by Lola Betts (Ann Mitchell), the mother of a supergrass.
Director: Nigel Finch.

1989	14.0	Sat 18 Mar 8:05 p.m.	7	8 wks

'Trenchard's Last Case' by Brian Finch.
A former Scotland Yard detective, Trenchard (Alec McCowen), turns up in Jersey, ostensibly on a fishing trip. Bergerac wonders just what he is trying to catch.
Director: Mike Barnes.

1990	14.2	Sun 4 Feb 8:05 p.m.	10	7 wks

'Roots of Evil' by Brian Finch.
Nigel Carter (Geoffrey Palmer) is terrorized, but he refuses to help the police find those responsible. Only when his daughter Joanna Carter (Lynsey Baxter) becomes their target does Bergerac begin to unravel the mystery.
Director: Richard Spence.

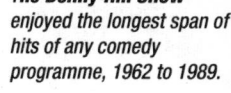

The Benny Hill Show enjoyed the longest span of hits of any comedy programme, 1962 to 1989.

John Nettles starred as Channel Island detective **Bergerac.**

Bernard Delfont's Sunday Show · 30 wks

ATV, entertainment

Lord Delfont, impresario brother of former ATV chairman Lord Grade, was the most powerful controller of light entertainment talent in Britain for more than three decades. He presented the ROYAL VARIETY PERFORMANCE for twenty-one consecutive years from 1958. This variety series was presented in his own theatre, the Prince of Wales in London.

| 1960 | 6.9 | Sun 3 Apr 8:00 p.m. | 2 | 12 wks |

Robert Morley introduces Yma Sumac with John Hanson, The King Brothers, Morecambe and Wise, Des O'Connor, Dennis Spicer and The Tiller Girls. With the Harold Collins orchestra.
Producer: Albert Locke.

| 1961 | 5.8 | Sun 13 Aug 8:55 p.m. | 2 | 8 wks |

Eartha Kitt stars with Billy Dainty, Edmund Hockridge and the Jack Parnell orchestra.
Producer: Kenneth Carter.

| 1962 | 7.1 | Sun 2 Sep 8:25 p.m. | 2 | 10 wks |

This special edition stars Tommy Steele, who takes over the whole show.
Writer: Eric Merriman. **Producer:** Jon Scoffield.

Bernard Manning in Las Vegas · 1 wk

Granada, documentary

| 1978 | 16.0 | Wed 8 Feb 8:00 p.m. | 19 | 1 wk |

Cameras follow comedian Bernard Manning from his own nightclub, the Embassy in Manchester, to the MGM Grand Hotel, Las Vegas, where he achieves a lifetime ambition by playing one of the hotel's lounges.
Director: Baz Taylor. **Producer:** John Hamp.

Bernie · 5 wks

Thames, comedy

Following the break-up of Mike and Bernie Winters' double act in 1978, Bernie pursued a solo career as a comedian.

| 1978 | 15.0 | Mon 27 Nov 7:00 p.m. | 10 | 5 wks |

Guests: Tim Barrett, Anna Dawson, Donald Houston, John Quayle and Jimmy Thompson.
Writers: Johnnie Mortimer, Brian Cooke, Dave Freeman and Eric Merriman. **Director:** Leon Thau. **Producer:** John Ammonds.

Bernie Clifton on Stage · 1 wk

ATV, comedy

Bernie Clifton began his career as a singer in Chesterfield before specializing in comedy. He used outrageous and ingenious props, wore an ostrich suit and danced 'The Skater's Waltz' wearing biscuit tins on his feet.

| 1980 | 9.7 | Sun 6 Jul 9:15 p.m. | 19 | 1 wk |

Guests: Dickie Davies, Aiden J. Harvey and Rusty Goffe.
Producer: Royston Mayoh.

Beryl's Lot · 25 wks

YTV, situation comedy

This series was inspired by author Margaret Powell, a cook who married a milkman, took her 'O' and 'A' levels from the age of fifty-eight and had her first book published at the age of sixty-one. Beryl, played by Carmel McSharry, was a charlady, nearly forty years of age and, like Margaret Powell, married to a milkman and determined to improve herself. Husband Tom was played by Mark Kingston (later by George Selway).
Writer (1973, 1975, 1977): Kevin Laffan. **Producer** (1973–74): John Frankau. **Executive producers** included Peter Willes (1973–74) and David Cunliffe (1975 and 1977).

| 1973 | 6.7 | Thu 1 Nov 8:25 p.m. | 10 | 3 wks |

'Getting Up'
Beryl contemplates what she has to show for her forty years and decides to break the pattern of her life before it passes her by.

| 1974 | 7.5 | Thu 10 Jan 8:25 p.m. | 4 | 4 wks |

'A Bit of Culture'
Beryl tries to help with the problems of a neighbour and ends up with no thanks and problems of her own.
Writer: Bill MacIlwraith. **Director:** Moira Armstrong.

| 1975 | 7.0 | Fri 21 Nov 9:00 p.m. | 15 | 12 wks |

'Stool Pigeon'
Tom and Beryl find themselves sleeping in separate rooms.
Director: David Reynolds. **Producer:** Jacky Stoller.

| 1977 | 7.0 | Fri 21 Jan 7:00 p.m. | 14 | 6 wks |

'Guilty Secrets'
Beryl and Tom need extra money and are prepared to economize – unlike some of their acquaintances who are on the fiddle!
Producer: Derek Bennett.

Best of Blind Date, The   2 wks

LWT, game show

Cilla Black introduces some of the funniest segments from previous series of BLIND DATE.
Director: Martin Scott.

| 1990 | 13.1 | Sat 29 Dec 8:00 p.m. | 18 | 1 wk |

Producer: Colman Hutchinson.

| 1991 | 16.4 | Sat 9 Feb 6:40 p.m. | 9 | 1 wk |

Producer: Michael Longmire.

Best of Cannon and Ball, The   2 wks

LWT, comedy

| 1982 | 11.3 | Sat 11 Dec 6:10 p.m. | 14 | 1 wk |

Highlights from the recent series feature Adam Ant, Steve Davis, Leo Sayer and Iris Williams.
Director: Alasdair Macmillan. **Writer** and **Producer:** Sid Green.
Executive Producer: David Bell.

| 1985 | 13.2 | Sun 7 Apr 8:45 p.m. | 7 | 1 wk |

Highlights from the recent series feature Fred Evans, Status Quo and Jocky Wilson.
Writers: Geoff Atkinson, Rob Grant, Sid Green, Doug Naylor and Geoff Lister. **Director:** Terry Kinane. **Producer:** Paul Jackson.

Best of Carrott Confidential   1 wk

BBC, comedy

| 1989 | 8.1 | Sat 26 Aug 10:10 p.m. | 20 | 1 wk |

Highlights from the recent series starring Jasper Carrott.
Director: Geoff Miles. **Producer:** Bill Wilson.

Best of Dick Emery, The   2 wks

BBC, comedy

Producer: Harold Snoad.

| 1976 | 7.8 | Sat 11 Dec 8:35 p.m. | 9 | 1 wk |

Guests: Alfie Bass, Arthur English, Francis Matthews, Mollie Sugden, Josephine Tewson and Frank Thornton.

| 1977 | 14.2 | Sat 29 Oct 8:25 p.m. | 8 | 1 wk |

A selection of items from the recent series. With Erik Chitty, Roy Kinnear and Henry McGee.

Best of Enemies   2 wks

Thames, situation comedy

This series by Vince Powell and Harry Driver about rival Members of Parliament starred Tim Barrett (Geoffrey Broom MP), Robert Coote (Willie Gordon MP) and Deryck Guyler (Wilkins).

| 1968 | 4.6 | Tue 6 Aug 8:45 p.m. | 17 | 1 wk |

Wilkins and Johnson (Geoffrey Palmer) struggle to keep the peace.
Producer: Malcolm Morris.

| 1969 | 4.6 | Wed 16 Jul 10:30 p.m. | 17 | 1 wk |

Geoffrey Broom MP gets himself in a tangle over the Divorce Law Reform Bill with little understanding from his wife (Jan Butlin).
Producer: Alan Tarrant.

Best of Fred, The   1 wk

AR, comedy

| 1963 | 5.0 | Wed 18 Sep 9:15 p.m. | 17 | 1 wk |

From the archives of Associated Rediffusion come choice extracts from the 1950s series A SHOW CALLED FRED and SON OF FRED written by Spike Milligan, John Antrobus, Maurice Wiltshire and Dave Freeman. Starring Spike Milligan and Peter Sellers with The Alberts, Kenneth Connor, Valentine Dyall, Graham Stark and Johnny Vyvyan. Original productions were directed by Dick Lester.
Compilation Producer: Robert Fleming.

Best of Game for a Laugh, The   3 wks

LWT, comedy

| 1984 | 9.3 | Sat 18 Aug 6:30 p.m. | 7 | 3 wks |

Jeremy Beadle, Henry Kelly, Matthew Kelly and Sarah Kennedy present a selection of the best stunts and games from the previous series.
Director: Terry Kinane. **Producer:** Alan Boyd.

1

2

3

4

1 *Kylie Minogue and Jason Donovan captured the nation's heart as Charlene and Scott in* **Neighbours.**

2 *Meg Richardson (Noele Gordon) ran the* **Crossroads** *Motel with her son Sandy (Roger Tonge).*

3 *The original leading ladies of* **Coronation Street** *gather in the snug of the Rover's Return. From left to right are Minnie Caldwell (Margot Bryant), Ena Sharples (Violet Carson) and Martha Longhurst (Lynne Carol).*

4 *The matriarch of* **Dallas**, *Miss Ellie Ewing (Barbara Bel Geddes), is pictured outside Southfork with her two sons J.R. (Larry Hagman) and Bobby (Patrick Duffy).*

5 **EastEnders** *is the only programme to be Number One for an entire calendar year. In the year in question, 1986, the stars included Anita Dobson as Angie, Leslie Grantham as Den and Letitia Dean as their daughter Sharon.*

Best of Just Amazing, The — 1 wk

YTV, entertainment

| 1985 | 10.3 | Sat 22 Jun 7:30 p.m. | 14 | 1 wk |

Presented by Barry Sheene.
Director: Graham Wetherell. **Producer:** Ian Bolt.

Best of Maigret, The — 3 wks

BBC, drama

| 1964 | 7.0 | Mon 27 Jan 9:25 p.m. | 9 | 3 wks |

A repeat showing of 'Love From Félicie'.

Best of Morecambe and Wise, The — 1 wk

BBC, entertainment

| 1969 | 7.0 | Sat 22 Feb 7:00 p.m. | 8 | 1 wk |

An edited compilation of highlights from Eric and Ernie's last series.
Producer: John Ammonds.

Best of the Two Ronnies, The — 2 wks

BBC, comedy

A compilation of highlights from recent series.

| 1977 | 13.1 | Mon 29 Aug 8:20 p.m. | 8 | 1 wk |

Producer: Terry Hughes.

| 1978 | 14.0 | Sat 23 Sep 8:30 p.m. | 5 | 1 wk |

Producer: Peter Whitmore.

Best of Three of a Kind, The — 1 wk

BBC, comedy

| 1983 | 11.0 | Wed 28 Dec 9:00 p.m. | 13 | 1 wk |

Highlights from the recent series starring David Copperfield, Lenny Henry and Tracey Ullman.
Producer: Paul Jackson.

Best of Tommy Cooper, The — 4 wks

Thames, comedy

| 1991 | 9.7 | Tue 6 Aug 8:30 p.m. | 12 | 4 wks |

Edited highlights from the many shows which Cooper recorded for Thames.
Executive Producer: John Fisher.

Best of Yarwood, The — 1 wk

BBC, comedy

| 1978 | 11.0 | Sun 3 Sep 8:05 p.m. | 16 | 1 wk |

Highlights from his previous series starring Mike Yarwood with guests including Janet Brown, Petula Clark and Twiggy.
Producer: Alan Boyd. **Executive Producer:** John Ammonds.

Best Sellers — 30 wks

USA presented by ITV, drama

Series of adaptations of best-selling novels by American writers.

| 1977 | 10.8 | Thu 4 Aug 9:00 p.m. | 4 | 4 wks |

'Captains and Kings' by Taylor Caldwell.
Adapted in five parts, this is the story of Joseph Armagh (Richard Jordan), an Irish immigrant in nineteenth-century America, who sees his dream come true when his son Rory (Perry King) becomes the first Irish Catholic President. Also starring Jane Seymour and Robert Vaughn.

| 1978 | 13.9 | Fri 2 Jun 9:00 p.m. | 1 | 5 wks |

'79 Park Avenue'
Three-part mini-series adaptation of Harold Robbins' novel screened on consecutive nights. Because two transmissions were split by the news, it was credited with five chart entries.
   Raymond Burr, Polly Bergen and Lesley Ann Warren star in the story of a girl's decline from innocent teenager to prostitute. An infamous madam faces a murder charge.

| 1979 | 14.4 | Mon 9 Apr 9:00 p.m. | 5 | 6 wks |

'From Here To Eternity' by James Jones.
Dramatized in three parts, Natalie Wood stars as Karen Holmes and William Devane as Sergeant Milt Warden in the story of US army men and women with highly charged emotions. Kim Basinger, Joe Pantoliano, Steve Railsback and Roy Thinnes also star.

1980	14.3	Thu 3 Apr 9:00 p.m.	8	4 wks

'A Man Called Intrepid'
Adapted by William Blinn from the book by Canadian William Stephenson, who set up a wartime British espionage ring in 1938 called Intrepid at the request of Winston Churchill. Starring David Niven as Stephenson and Nigel Stock as Churchill, with Peter Gilmore, Barbara Hershey, Gayle Hunnicutt, Flora Robson and Michael York. Dramatized by David Ambrose.

1981	14.7	Tue 6 Jan 9:00 p.m.	6	5 wks

'Beulah Land'
This three-part mini-series based on the novel by Lonnie Coleman is set on a plantation before and during the American Civil War. It is the story of two sisters, Sarah and Laura Pennington (Lesley Ann Warren and Meredity Baxter Birney). Also starring Jenny Agutter, Eddie Albert, Don Johnson and Hope Lange.

1982	13.3	Mon 23 Aug 9:00 p.m.	1	5 wks

'Valley of the Dolls'
This three-part mini-series is based on the novel by Jacqueline Susann. It tells the story of sex, drugs and fame among the Hollywood jet set. Starring David Birney, James Coburn, Britt Ekland, Veronica Hamel, Lisa Hartman, Catherine Hicks and Jean Simmons.

1984	9.7	Sun 29 Apr 9:00 p.m.	10	1 wk

'Valley of the Dolls' (Repeat.)

Best Things in Life, The				13 wks

ATV, situation comedy

This series was created by Bernard Botting and featured the Pollard household: Mrs Pollard (Pearl Hackney), Mr Pollard (Bob Todd), Mabel Pollard (June Whitfield) and lodger Alfred Wilcox (Harry H. Corbett). The hang-dog Wilcox learned that life had not much to offer him, although Mabel was quite determined to offer herself in marriage. They had been engaged for eleven years and both worked at the same plastics factory.
Producer: Shaun O'Riordan.

1969	7.8	Tue 16 Sep 8:30 p.m.	1	6 wks

Mabel looks for new ways to provide the necessary stimulus to her romance with Alfred following a recent day-trip to France.

1970	6.2	Mon 13 Jul 9:30 p.m.	4	7 wks

'The Emigrant'
It's election night and all over the country people wait with excitement and anticipation for the results to come through, but not in the Pollard household. Alfred has proclaimed that it will be just as bad whichever side wins – his lot won't improve. With Carmel McSharry, Diana Quick, Madge Ryan and Bob Todd.
Writer: Jack Trevor Storey. **Director:** John Robins.

Beverly Hills Connection				1 wk

Presented by BBC, film

1989	9.4	Tue 13 Jun 9:35 p.m.	11	1 wk

A murder in Hollywood brings the victim's friend Amanda Ryder (Lisa Hartman) to Los Angeles to investigate. Also starring James Brolin, David Hemmings and Stuart Whitman.
Director: Corey Allen.

Beverly Hills Cop				2 wks

Presented by BBC, film

1988	12.8	Mon 26 Dec 8:20 p.m.	10	1 wk

Eddie Murphy stars as Detroit policeman Axel Foley. He seeks the murderer of his friend and travels to California against the orders of his boss. Judge Reinhold plays Billy Rosewood.
Director: Martin Brest.

1990	11.9	Mon 28 May 8:00 p.m.	6	1 wk

Repeat showing of the above film.

Beverly Hills Cop 2				2 wks

Presented by ITV, film

1990	13.1	Tue 25 Dec 8:00 p.m.	20	1 wk

Axel Foley (Eddie Murphy) travels from Detroit to Los Angeles again, this time after his friend Captain Bogomil (Ronny Cox) has been wounded by a gang of jewel thieves. Judge Reinhold reappears as Billy Rosewood.
Director: Tony Scott.

1991	13.9	Sat 5 Oct 7:15 p.m.	10	1 wk

Repeat showing of the above film.

Beyond the Poseidon Adventure				3 wks

Presented by ITV, film

1982	12.0	Sun 19 Sep 7:15 p.m.	4	1 wk

In this sequel to THE POSEIDON ADVENTURE the giant liner lies upside down in the sea. A salvage vessel arrives with a medical team three days after the boat capsized. Starring Michael Caine, Sally Field, Shirley Jones, Karl Malden and Telly Savalas.
Director: Irwin Allen.

1983	11.8	Thu 29 Sep 7:30 p.m.	8	1 wk
1985	10.00	Thu 8 Aug 7:30 p.m.	16	1 wk

Repeat showings of the above film.

Lesley Ann Warren contemplates her loss of innocence at '79 Park Avenue', one of Harold Robbins' **Best Sellers**.

Big — 1 wk

Presented by ITV, film

| 1991 | 16.5 | Wed 4 Dec 8:00 p.m. | 8 | 1 wk |

A twelve-year-old's wish to be 'big' comes true. He soon learns that being grown up isn't all it's cracked up to be. Tom Hanks stars with Elizabeth Perkins.
Director: Penny Marshall.

Big Beat '64 — 1 wk

ABC, music

| 1964 | 5.8 | Sun 3 May 4:05 p.m. | 17 | 1 wk |

The New Musical Express poll winners for 1963–64 in concert from the Empire Pool, Wembley. David Jacobs and Jimmy Savile introduce the Beatles, Joe Brown, the Dave Clark Five, Freddie and the Dreamers, Gerry and the Pacemakers, the Hollies, Big Dee Irwin, Kathy Kirby, Billy J. Kramer and the Dakotas, Joe Loss, Manfred Mann, The Merseybeats, Brian Poole and the Tremeloes, Cliff Richard, the Rolling Stones, the Shadows, and the Swinging Blue Jeans.
Director: Mark Stuart.

Big Boy Now — 3 wks

ATV, situation comedy

This series by Ronnie Taylor starred Fabia Drake as Heather Merchant and Leslie Crowther as mother's boy Tony.

| 1977 | 7.4 | Thu 17 Feb 6:40 p.m. | 17 | 3 wks |

'She Was Only a Bookie's Daughter'
Tony hides behind his mother when his girlfriend's bookmaker father calls in anger.
Producer: Les Chatfield.

Big Break — 13 wks

BBC, game show

This game show, incorporating general knowledge and snooker, was hosted by Jim Davidson, with John Virgo as referee.

| 1991 | 16.5 | Tue 30 Apr 8:30 p.m. | 7 | 13 wks |

Guests: Mike Hallett, Stephen Hendry and Joe Johnson.
Director: Nick Hurran. **Producer:** John Burrowes.

Big Fight Preview, The — 1 wk

ITV, sport

| 1986 | 12.2 | Sat 22 Nov 8:45 p.m. | 17 | 1 wk |

From the Las Vegas Hilton, Dickie Davies previews the World Heavyweight Championship fight between Trevor Berbick and Mike Tyson, which is to be shown live on ITV at 3:15 a.m. tomorrow morning.

Big Film, The — 4 wks

ITV, film

| 1976 | 7.3 | Sat 28 Feb 7:15 p.m. | 10 | 2 wks |

'Gunfight at the OK Corral'
This feature film tells the story of the conflict between Wyatt Earp and the Clantons, starring Burt Lancaster as Earp and Kirk Douglas as Doc Holliday.
Director: John Sturges.

| 1981 | 16.0 | Sat 16 May 9:20 p.m. | 1 | 2 wks |

'Death Wish'
A New York businessman (Charles Bronson) becomes a vigilante when his daughter becomes a vegetable and his wife is killed in a vicious attack.
Director: Michael Winner.

Big Night Out — 7 wks

ABC, entertainment

After 1961 this series originated from seaside resorts and featured entertainers playing summer seasons in these coastal towns. With Bob Sharples and the ABC Showband.
Producer: Philip Jones.

| 1961 | 4.1 | Sat 26 Aug 8:00 p.m. | 18 | 2 wks |

Starring Peggy Lee in her first British television show with special guests Bing Crosby, Sammy Cahn and Jimmy Van Heusen, the Victor Feldman Quartet and David Kossoff.

| 1962 | 4.0 | Sat 21 Jul 8:00 p.m. | 18 | 1 wk |

From the Pavilion Theatre, Rhyl, Paul Andrews introduces Freddie Frinton, The Kaye Sisters and Jimmy Wheeler.
Director: Helen Standage.

| 1964 | 6.7 | Sat 14 Mar 6:35 p.m. | 13 | 4 wks |

Mike and Bernie Winters are the regular hosts for the 1964 season. This week they introduce Adam Faith, Margo Henderson and Patsy Ann Noble. Also appearing are the Lionel Blair dancers.

Big Picture Show, The   2 wks

Presented by ITV, film

| 1981 | 23.3 | Thu 8 Oct 7:30 p.m. | 1 | 2 wks |

'Jaws' (See separate entry.)

Big Send Up, The   1 wk

Granada, entertainment

| 1977 | 13.2 | Wed 26 Oct 8:00 p.m. | 19 | 1 wk |

Variety show starring Bernard Manning and Paul Daniels with Tony Brutus, the Cherokees, David Copperfield, Mark Raffles and the Ukrainian Black Sea Cossacks.
Musical Director: Derek Hilton. **Director:** Nicholas Ferguson. **Producer:** John Hamp.

Big Show, The   11 wks

ATV, entertainment

| 1968 | 7.2 | Sun 21 Apr 10:05 p.m. | 1 | 11 wks |

Dave Allen introduces Frankie Fontaine, Frank Ifield, the Ted Kavanagh Irish Dancers, the Kladagh Ceilidh Band, Dusty Springfield and Max Wall with the Mike Sammes Singers and the Jack Parnell orchestra.
Director: Philip Casson. **Producer:** Jon Scoffield.

Big Top Variety Show, The   11 wks

Thames, entertainment

This mix of circus and variety performers was staged in the tent of Billy Smart's Circus. Bernie Winters hosted the shows from 1979 to 1981. With the Alan Braden orchestra.
Producer: Christopher Palmer. **Choreographer** (1980–82): Anthony Van Laast

| 1979 | 14.0 | Wed 5 Dec 8:00 p.m. | 13 | 2 wks |

Starring Champagne, Ray Dondy, the Brother Lees, Lulu, Reflections and the Santus Family.

| 1980 | 12.3 | Wed 13 Aug 8:00 p.m. | 2 | 3 wks |

Starring Gladys Knight and the Pips, the Krankies, the Laner Brothers, Little John and Partner, Trio Bogino, and The Wurzels.

| 1981 | 14.3 | Wed 19 Aug 8:00 p.m. | 2 | 3 wks |

Starring David Essex with Bucks Fizz, the Dingbats, the Krankies and Duo Zalewski.

| 1982 | 10.5 | Wed 28 Jul 8:00 p.m. | 3 | 3 wks |

Bernie Clifton introduces Lulu with The Dooleys, Aiden J. Harvey, The Kehajovi Troupe and The Trio Biarge.

Big Trouble in Little China   1 wk

Presented by ITV, film

| 1991 | 14.4 | Wed 4 Sep 8:00 p.m. | 6 | 1 wk |

Kurt Russell and Dennis Dun star in an adventure which takes them in search of an abducted woman. The trail leads them deep into the underworld of Chinatown in San Francisco.
Director: John Carpenter.

Big Valley, The   4 wks

USA presented by ITV, drama

The story of a family of cattle ranchers in the San Joaquin Valley of California around 1870. The family head was widowed Victoria Barkley (Barbara Stanwyck) and her family were lawyer Jarrod (Richard Long), her second son and ranch foreman Nick (Peter Breck), youngest son Eugene (Charles Briles), daughter Audra (Linda Evans) and Heath (Lee Majors), her late husband's illegitimate son by an Indian girl.

| 1965 | 6.6 | Thu 28 Oct 9:40 p.m. | 12 | 4 wks |

'The Odyssey of Jubal Tanner'
Land bought by an old man and his grandson is wanted by the government as a site for a dam of great benefit to the entire valley. The Barkleys come to the aid of the old man after a skirmish with some of the townspeople.
Director: Arnold Laven.

Biggest Bank Robbery, The   2 wks

Presented by ITV, film

| 1981 | 15.4 | Fri 23 Jan 7:00 p.m. | 6 | 1 wk |

When Pinky Green (Richard Jordan) is released from prison his friends conspire to keep him out of further trouble and out of the clutches of Ivan The Terrible (David Niven), one of London's biggest gang bosses. Also starring Joss Ackland, Gloria Grahame, Richard Johnson, Elke Sommer and Oliver Tobias.
Director: Ralph Thomas.

| 1982 | 11.3 | Wed 18 Aug 8:00 p.m. | 3 | 1 wk |

Repeat showing of the above film.

Dave Allen was the host of the top-rated edition of **The Big Show**.

Bill, The — 349 wks

Thames, drama

This series of everyday stories in the life of Sun Hill police station in London's East End was devised by Geoff McQueen.
Writer (1984–86, 1988): Barry Appleton. **Producers** included Michael Chapman (1984–85) and Peter Cregeen (1986–87). **Executive Producers:** included Lloyd Shirley (1984–87), Peter Cregeen (1988–89) and Michael Chapman (1990-91).

| 1984 | 13.9 | Tue 13 Nov 9:00 p.m. | 12 | 4 wks |

'It's Not Such a Bad Job After All'
The life of a young girl is at stake.
Director: John Woods.

| 1985 | 12.8 | Tue 22 Jan 9:00 p.m. | 11 | 4 wks |

'The Sweet Smell of Failure'
An elderly couple of thieves cause problems for PC Carver and WPC Ackland (Mark Wingett and Trudie Goodwin).
Director: John Michael Phillips.

| 1986 | 14.9 | Mon 10 Feb 9:00 p.m. | 6 | 5 wks |

'The Chief Super's Party'
A celebration turns dangerous.

| 1987 | 15.4 | Mon 23 Nov 9:00 p.m. | 6 | 15 wks |

'Skipper' by Christopher Russell.
Sergeant Cryer (Eric Richard) tells PCs Shaw and Edwards (Chris Walker and Colin Blumenau) that the most practical way to police the area is by bicycle.
Director: Richard Bramall.

| 1988 | 13.5 | Thu 10 Nov 8:00 p.m. | 7 | 40 wks |

'Paper Chase'
Detective Inspector Burnside (Christopher Ellison) is in pursuit of a kidnapper holding a schoolgirl to ransom.
Director: Niall Leonard. **Producer:** Michael Ferguson.

| 1989 | 14.9 | Tue 25 Apr 8:00 p.m. | 6 | 97 wks |

'Out To Lunch' by Julian Jones.
Detective Inspector Burnside is bewildered, but WPC Brind (Kelly Lawrence) saves the day.
Director: Brian Parker. **Producer:** Pat Sandys.

| 1990 | 15.3 | Thu 11 Jan 8:00 p.m. | 7 | 84 wks |

'I Thought You'd Gone' by J. C. Wilsher.
Inspector Frazer (Barbara Thorn) and Taffy Edwards are about to discover there is life after Sun Hill.
Director: Nicholas Laughland. **Producer:** Michael Simpson.

| 1991 | 15.9 | Tue 12 Nov 8:00 p.m. | 8 | 100 wks |

'The Taste' by Julian Jones.
Smollett (Nick Stringer) discovers he still has the taste for action.
Director: Alan Bell. **Producer:** Peter Wolfes.

Billy Cotton Band Show, The — 4 wks

BBC, entertainment

Billy Cotton was a national institution both on radio and television with his catchphrase 'Wakey-Wakey'. The roly-poly bandleader would have a go at anything, even allowing his show to be produced by his own son, Bill Cotton Jnr., who in turn went on to become Managing Director of BBC Television. Series regulars included Alan Breeze, Kathie Kay, Leslie Roberts' Silhouettes and the High-Lights.
Writer: Jimmy Grafton.

| 1961 | 5.4 | Sat 2 Dec 7:15 p.m. | 11 | 1 wk |

Guests: Craig Douglas and Mrs Mills.
Producer: Bill Cotton Jr.

| 1962 | 5.0 | Sat 3 Nov 7:15 p.m. | 14 | 3 wks |

Guests: Michael Bentine, Russ Conway and Craig Douglas.
Producer: Johnnie Stewart.

Billy Cotton's Music Hall — 3 wks

BBC, entertainment

| 1967 | 5.1 | Sat 29 Jul 8:35 p.m. | 12 | 3 wks |

With Leslie Crowther, Lulu, Ralph Reader and the Scout Gang Show, Terry Scott and the Tiller Girls.
Writer: Eric Davidson. **Choreographer:** Barbara Aitken. **Producer:** Michael Hurll.

Billy Dainty Esq — 4 wks

Thames, comedy

Billy Dainty, buck-toothed comedian, eccentric dancer and pantomime dame had spent a career as everyone's guest before being rewarded with his own series. He died in 1987.
Producer: Dennis Kirkland.

| 1976 | 6.1 | Mon 17 May 6:40 p.m. | 10 | 2 wks |

With Graham Crowden, Derek Deadman and Sheila White.

| 1977 | 6.4 | Mon 13 Jun 6:45 p.m. | 12 | 2 wks |

A repeat of one of the shows from the last series.

Billy Fury Show, The — 1 wk

ATV, entertainment

Fury was one of Britain's leading homegrown rock 'n' roll stars. After suffering heart disease for years, he died 28 January 1983.

| 1964 | 6.4 | Wed 9 Nov 9:40 p.m. | 11 | 1 wk |

With the Ross Taylor dancers and the Jack Parnell orchestra.
Producer: Colin Clews.

....

Billy Liar — 7 wks

LWT, situation comedy

The creation of Keith Waterhouse and Willis Hall had already appeared as a successful novel, stage play and film. This TV series starred Jeff Rawle in the title role of the famous dreamer. His parents were played by George A. Cooper and Pamela Vezey.
Producer: Stuart Allen.

| 1973 | 6.4 | Fri 21 Dec 8:25 p.m. | 14 | 4 wks |

'Billy and the Gift of the Magi'
Billy has set his heart on a pair of bright-yellow trousers, but as usual he has no money. One solution would be for his parents to buy them as a Christmas present, but his dad is determined Billy will not be seen in such ridiculous pants.

| 1974 | 6.7 | Fri 11 Jan 8:30 p.m. | 18 | 3 wks |

'Billy and Pandora's Box'
Billy's family find the key to his secret store cupboard and discover the peculiar contents locked away by its magpie owner.
Director: Alan Wallis.

....

Billy Smart's Circus — 4 wks

BBC, circus

Billy Smart began his career at the age of 15 in charge of a hand roundabout at a fairground in Slough. In 1914 he set himself up as a fairground proprietor and in 1946 he established his own circus. The master showman died at the age of 73 on 26 September 1968.
Producer (1962–63, 1968): Derek Burrell-Davis.

| 1962 | 4.6 | Tue 25 Dec 3:10 p.m. | 20 | 1 wk |

Ringmaster Alfred Delboscq introduces more than two hundred performers including Captain Decker's California Sealions, Roger Debille's Polar Bears, the Flying Falcos, the Papazov Troupe and the Paulos.

| 1963 | 4.7 | Wed 25 Dec 3:00 p.m. | 20 | 1 wk |

Harry Towb introduces Ringmaster Ares de Wit, who presents performers including the Cycling Czechmates, The Stawickis, Arturo Segura, Los Najarros, and Billy Smart Junior's elephants.

| 1968 | 5.6 | Wed 25 Dec 3:05 p.m. | 17 | 1 wk |

John Witty introduces Ringmaster Dick Barton, Berosini, the Caroli Riders, the Francesco Clowns, El Grupo Rodriguez, Krenzola's Animal Revue and Billy Smart Junior's elephants.

| 1971 | 5.5 | Mon 30 Aug 6:15 p.m. | 18 | 1 wk |

Ringmaster Yasmin Smart introduces the Amaros, the Astoris, the Cardinals, the Castors, the Herculeans, Don Saunders and Toly M.
Producer: Mary Davis.

Bing Crosby Show, The — 1 wk

AR, entertainment

The 'Old Groaner' came to London to star in his first British television special.

| 1963 | 6.6 | Wed 27 Feb 9:40 p.m. | 9 | 1 wk |

Bing roves around London meeting up with friends Shirley Bassey, Terry-Thomas, Dave King, Miriam Karlin, Marion Ryan and Bob Hope. With the Peter Knight orchestra.
Writers: Howard Leeds, Bill Morrow, Sid Green and Dick Hills.
Director: Peter Croft.

....

Bionic Woman, The — 19 wks

USA presented by ITV, drama

Spin-off series from THE SIX MILLION DOLLAR MAN establishing Jaime Sommers (Lindsay Wagner) as the heroine. She had been rebuilt following serious injury in a sky-diving accident while on active duty for the CIA. Richard Anderson played Oscar Goldman.

| 1976 | 7.0 | Thu 8 Jul 7:00 p.m. | 1 | 12 wks |

'Welcome Home Jaime'
As Jaime begins a new life as a school teacher, she restricts her top secret missions to weekends. She soon needs all her bionic powers to survive a car accident which is not an accident!

| 1977 | 7.4 | Thu 12 May 6:40 p.m. | 8 | 7 wks |

'The Vega Influence'
A meteorite has the potential to overpower human will. It requires bionic strength to repel it.

....

Bird Brain of Britain — 1 wk

BBC, documentary

| 1985 | 13.1 | Sun 7 Apr 7:45 p.m. | 10 | 1 wk |

Cameraman Simon King explores the brain power of garden birds.
Director: Alastair Fothergill. **Producer:** Mike Beynon.

Lindsay Wagner played the title role in **The Bionic Woman**.

Birds of a Feather — 46 wks

BBC, situation comedy

This series by Maurice Gran and Laurence Marks starred Pauline Quirke as Sharon and Linda Robson as Tracey. Both their husbands were in prison. Lesley Joseph played man-mad neighbour Dorien. An Alomo production.

| 1989 | 13.0 | Mon 23 Oct 8:30 p.m. | 10 | 6 wks |

'Just Visiting'
Sharon and Tracey try to come to terms with their husbands' imprisonment. They attempt to explain the situation to Tracey's son Garth (Simon Nash).
Director: Tony Dow. **Producer:** Esta Charkham.

| 1990 | 13.4 | Thu 22 Nov 8:30 p.m. | 9 | 15 wks |

'Old Friends'
Sharon fears that blood is truly thicker than water.
Writer: John Ross. **Director:** Sue Bysh. **Producer:** Nic Phillips.

| 1991 | 14.4 | Sat 16 Nov 8:05 p.m. | 7 | 25 wks |

'Business'
Sharon and Tracey fall out over an inheritance.
Writers: Gary Lawson and John Phelps. **Producer:** Nic Phillips.

Birds of Prey — 1 wk

USA presented by ITV, film

| 1983 | 10.9 | Tue 29 Mar 7:35 p.m. | 14 | 1 wk |

In this film made for television David Janssen stars as a helicopter pilot who witnesses a bank robbery. The criminals take to their own helicopter and an airborne chase ensues.

Birth — 1 wk

AR, documentary

| 1962 | 4.8 | Wed 25 Jul 9:45 p.m. | 8 | 1 wk |

Daniel Farson looks at the changing attitudes to childbirth and examines the role a father can play.
Camera: Ricky Briggs. **Director:** Rollo Gamble.

Birthday Show, The — 1 wk

Thames, entertainment

| 1989 | 9.9 | Thu 27 Jul 8:30 p.m. | 10 | 1 wk |

Edward Woodward presents highlights from twenty-one years of Thames Television's variety shows.
Producer: Philip Jones.

Bit of a Do, A — 6 wks

YTV, situation comedy

This series by David Nobbs followed the financial and romantic fortunes of Ted and Rita Simcock (David Jason and Gwen Taylor). Ever present through their trials and making up the incestuous society of a small Yorkshire town were Liz Rodenhurst (Nicola Pagett), Neville Badger (Michael Jayston), Rodney and Betty Sillitoe (Tim Wylton and Stephanie Cole), Paul, Jenny and Elvis Simcock (David Thewlis, Sarah-Jane Holm and Wayne Foskett), Simon Rodenhurst (Nigel Hastings) and Carol Fordingbridge (Karen Drury). Barman Eric was played by Malcolm Hebden and waitress Sandra by Tracy Brabin.

| 1989 | 14.8 | Fri 17 Feb 9:00 p.m. | 6 | 6 wks |

'The Registry Office Wedding'
The recently widowed Liz Rodenhurst, who is pregnant with Ted Simcock's child, marries widower Neville Badger.
Director: Ian Fisher. **Producer:** David Reynolds. **Executive Producer:** Vernon Lawrence.

Bit of an Experience, A — 1 wk

BBC, documentary

| 1967 | 5.2 | Thu 7 Sep 9:05 p.m. | 15 | 1 wk |

The Kent family live in a London suburb. Heather Kent has a tumour. The cameras have followed events from diagnosis to the moment when Granny comes to take charge of the children as mum goes into hospital. We now look at the future in store for the family.
Producers: Michael Latham and Gordon Thomas.

Black Abbots, The — 4 wks

YTV, comedy

This Liverpool cabaret group (Russ Abbot, Clive Jones, Lennie Reynolds and Bobby Turner) found great club success in the 1970s. After this series drummer Russ Abbot left to pursue a solo career.
Director: Ian Bolt.

| 1979 | 11.4 | Wed 13 Jun 9:30 p.m. | 13 | 1 wk |

Musical Director: Johnny Pearson. **Producer:** Ronnie Baxter.

| 1980 | 15.2 | Thu 6 Nov 8:30 p.m. | 6 | 3 wks |

Musical Director: Laurie Holloway. **Producer:** Alan Tarrant.

Black Adder, The

2 wks

BBC, situation comedy

The Radio Times *introduced the first series, created by Richard Curtis and Ben Elton, as 'the thoroughly unwholesome adventures of the scummiest toe-rags in the great laundry basket of English history'. The programme began to celebrate the five hundredth anniversary of the accession of Richard III with Peter Cook in that role. He was swiftly replaced by Brian Blessed as Richard IV. Rowan Atkinson starred as the Black Adder, a lone horseman from the Dark Ages cursed with a deformed haircut and an evil pair of tights. Tony Robinson played the part of Baldrick.*

| **1983** | **6.7** | **Wed 20 Jul 9:30 p.m.** | **17** | **2 wks** |

'The Black Seal'
The Black Adder rides forth in search of the seven most evil men in the land. The only man who can now stop him is The Moorhen (Patrick Allen).
Writers: *Richard Curtis and Rowan Atkinson.* **Director:** *Martin Shardlow.* **Producer:** *John Lloyd.*

....

Black and White Minstrel Show, The

47 wks

BBC, entertainment

This series created by George Inns in 1958 ran for twenty-one seasons before changes in racial attitudes decreed that white men blacking up in the tradition of Al Jolson was no longer acceptable. The Minstrels' musical director was George Mitchell and the best-remembered principal singers were John Boulter (until 1971), Dai Francis (until 1972) and Tony Mercer (until 1968). Other regulars included Benny Garcia (1962, 1963 and 1969), Andy Cole (1969–72), Les Rawlings (1967–72 and 1975), Margaret Savage (1966–72 and 1975), Penny Jewkes (1966-71), Delia Wicks (1966-71) and Les Waut (1969-72, 1975). The Television Toppers appeared in every show.
Choreographers *included Larry Gordon (1962–63) and Roy Gunson (1966–68 and 1971–72).* **Producers** *included George Inns (until 1970), Ernest Maxin (1971–72) and Brian Whitehouse (1975).*

| **1962** | **5.5** | **Sun 21 Oct 7:25 p.m.** | **8** | **8 wks** |

With Eddie Calvert, George Chisholm, Stan Stennett and Johnny Vyvyan.

| **1963** | **6.4** | **Sun 20 Jan 7:25 p.m.** | **10** | **2 wks** |

With George Chisholm, Tolchard Evans and Stan Stennett.

| **1966** | **6.7** | **Sat 15 Jan 8:30 p.m.** | **15** | **4 wks** |

With Ted Ray.

| **1967** | **6.3** | **Sat 15 Apr 8:45 p.m.** | **11** | **7 wks** |

With Don Arrol and Lyn and Graham McCarthy.

| **1968** | **6.2** | **Sat 28 Sep 7:30 p.m.** | **5** | **7 wks** |

With Sheila Bernette and Leslie Crowther.

| **1969** | **5.7** | **Mon 26 May 8:20 p.m** | **9** | **3 wks** |

Special Bank Holiday edition.
Choreographer: *Elspeth Hands.*

| **1970** | **7.2** | **Sat 14 Mar 8:15 p.m.** | **7** | **9 wks** |

With Peter Kaye.
Choreographer: *Ralph Tobert.*

| **1971** | **6.5** | **Sat 5 Jun 8:05 p.m.** | **1** | **3 wks** |

With Neville King and The Monarchs.

| **1972** | **5.4** | **Sat 17 Jun 8:30 p.m.** | **16** | **3 wks** |

With Ted Darling, Johnny Hutch and The Apaches.

| **1975** | **8.0** | **Sat 24 May 6:30 p.m.** | **2** | **1 wk** |

With Ted Darling, Elspeth Hands and Don Maclean.
Choreographer: *Richard Gough.*

B

*Dai Francis and John Boulter were two of the stalwarts of the long-running **Black and White Minstrel Show.***

Black and White Minstrel Christmas Show, The — 3 wks

BBC, entertainment

Choreographer (1969, 1975): Roy Gunson. **Producer** (1975–76): Brian Whitehouse.

| 1969 | 6.2 | Tue 23 Dec 7:15 p.m. | 8 | 1 wk |

Leslie Crowther introduces the George Mitchell Minstrels starring John Boulter, Dai Francis and Tony Mercer with special guest Semprini.
Producer: George Inns.

| 1975 | 7.2 | Sat 20 Dec 8:15 p.m. | 17 | 1 wk |

With the Mitchell Minstrels, Ted Darling, Lenny Henry, Jan Hunt, Elspeth Hands, Don Maclean, Les Rawlings, Margaret Savage and Les Want.

| 1976 | 8.0 | Sat 18 Dec 8:15 p.m. | 5 | 1 wk |

The Mitchell Minstrels with Ted Darling, Rita Morris, Les Rawlings, Margaret Savage and Les Want with guests Brooks Aehron, Pam Ayres and Keith Harris.
Choreographer: Flick Colby. **Producer:** Brian Whitehouse.

Black Candle, The — 1 wk

Tyne Tees, drama

| 1991 | 10.8 | Sun 26 May 7:50 p.m. | 8 | 1 wk |

In this adaptation of Catherine Cookson's novel, the world of wealthy factory owner Bridget Mordaunt (Samantha Bond) begins to crumble when her work's manager is accused of murder. Also starring Denholm Elliott, Tara Fitzgerald, Nathaniel Parker and Sian Phillips.
Director: Roy Battersby. **Producer:** Ray Marshall.

Black Marries White — 1 wk

AR, documentary

| 1964 | 7.6 | Wed 29 Apr 9:40 p.m. | 3 | 1 wk |

A study of the elements which make or break a marriage already complicated beyond measure by racial prejudice. Mixed couples share their experiences and invite the television audience to re-examine their attitudes.
Director: Peter Morley.

Black Velvet Gown, The — 1 wk

Tyne Tees, drama

| 1991 | 12.8 | Sun 2 Jun 7:50 p.m. | 5 | 1 wk |

This adaptation of Catherine Cookson's novel is set in rural Northumberland in 1830. A family endures tragic consequences when a penniless widow allows her children to be educated beyond their class. Starring Jean Anderson, Janet McTeer and Bob Peck.
Director: Norman Stone. **Producer:** Ray Marshall.

Black Widow — 1 wk

Presented by ITV, film

| 1991 | 12.2 | Sat 23 Nov 9:05 p.m. | 18 | 1 wk |

A series of deaths of recently married millionaires convinces Justice Department agent Alexandra Barnes (Debra Winger) that a 'black widow' is on the loose. Also starring Dennis Hopper, Diane Ladd, Theresa Russell and Nicol Williamson.
Director: Bob Rafelson.

Blackadder II — 3 wks

BBC, situation comedy

This second series, featuring Rowan Atkinson as Lord Edmund Blackadder, also starred Tony Robinson as Baldrick, Tim McInnery as Lord Percy, Miranda Richardson as Queen Elizabeth, Stephen Fry as Lord Melchett, Tom Baker as Captain Rum and Simon Jones as Sir Walter Raleigh.

| 1990 | 9.1 | Sun 3 Jun 8:05 p.m. | 17 | 3 wks |

'**Potato**' by Richard Curtis and Ben Elton.
Set in New Zealand, this episode features Lord Edmund's two-year mission to find new potatoes. (Repeat.)
Director: Mandie Fletcher. **Producer:** John Lloyd.

Blackadder the Third — 6 wks

BBC, situation comedy

The third Blackadder series with Rowan Atkinson in the leading role, also starring Tony Robinson as Baldrick, Hugh Laurie as the Prince Regent, Helen Atkinson Wood as Mrs Miggins, Stephen Fry as the Duke of Wellington and Gertan Klauber as King George III.

| 1990 | 10.5 | Sun 19 Aug 8:05 p.m. | 9 | 6 wks |

'**Duel and Duality**' By Richard Curtis and Ben Elton.
Set between 1760 and 1815 this episode features Blackadder as butler to the Prince Regent veering from calamity to disaster in Regency England. (Repeat.)
Director: Mandie Fletcher. **Producer:** John Lloyd.

Blackadder Goes Forth — 6 wks

BBC, situation comedy

In this fourth series Blackadder (Rowan Atkinson) progressed through history taking advantage of everything and everyone. Also starred Tony Robinson as Private Baldrick, Hugh Laurie as Colthurst St Barleigh, Tim McInnery as Captain Darling and Stephen Fry as General Melchett.

| 1989 | 13.1 | Thu 5 Oct 9:30 p.m. | 8 | 6 wks |

'Plan B: Corporal Punishment' by Richard Curtis and Ben Elton. It is 1917, and two million men are doomed to die horribly in the trenches of northern France. Orders arrive for Operation Insanity. Blackadder responds by eating the messenger.
Director: Richard Boden. **Producer:** John Lloyd.

Blackmail   25 wks

AR, drama

This series on the title subject produced by Stella Richman.

| 1965 | 7.6 | Fri 22 Oct 9:40 p.m. | 6 | 12 wks |

'Call Me Friend' by John Whitney and Geoffrey Bellman. Architect Lucien (John Slater) and his wife Maxine (Helen Cherry) accept a dinner invitation from Patek (Ray Barrett) at the embassy of a mythical Latin American country. A terrifying ordeal with tragic consequences awaits them.
Designer: Frank Nerini. **Director:** Quentin Lawrence.

| 1966 | 7.6 | Fri 28 Oct 9:10 p.m. | 5 | 13 wks |

'A Man of Reputation' by Alexander Bacon. Sir James Belmont (David Langton) is a distinguished doctor and occupies an elevated position in public life. He is threatened with the exposure of an affair with Marianne (Jennifer Jayne), the sister of his wife Rosalind (Isabel Dean).
Designer: Bernard Goodwin. **Director:** Joan Kemp-Welch.

Blackpool Night Out   24 wks

ABC, entertainment

This series of summer variety shows hosted by Mike and Bernie Winters came from the ABC Theatre, Blackpool. With the Lionel Blair dancers and the ABC showband.

| 1964 | 7.7 | Sun 30 Aug 8:25 p.m. | 2 | 11 wks |

Guests: Ray Alan, Dave King, Peter and Gordon, and Jackie Trent.
Producer: Philip Jones.

| 1965 | 6.8 | Sun 27 Jun 9:00 p.m. | 3 | 13 wks |

Guests: the Bachelors, Jimmy Edwards, Barbara Evans and Peter Goodwright.
Producer: Pat Johns.

Blackpool Show, The   8 wks

ABC, entertainment

| 1966 | 7.7 | Sun 10 Jul 10:05 p.m. | 1 | 8 wks |

From the ABC Theatre, Blackpool, Tony Hancock introduces Frankie Howerd with Terry Hall and Lenny the Lion, John Junkin, the Kaye Sisters and the Peter Gordeno dancers.
Producer: Mark Stuart.

Blackpool Tower Circus   4 wks

ATV, circus

| 1961 | 6.5 | Sun 3 Sep 8:55 p.m. | 1 | 1 wk |

Ringmasters Henry Lytton and Harold Holt introduce the Berosinis, Charlie Cairoli and Paul, Circus Knie's Ponies and Mules and the Three Lorandos.
Television presentation: Bill Ward.

| 1962 | 6.4 | Sun 28 Oct 8:25 p.m. | 7 | 2 wks |

Compered by Shaw Taylor, with ringmaster Henry Lytton introducing Circus Knie's Legion Horses, Dic and Doc, the Two Dominics, Tibor Alexander's Canine Revue, the Trio Reyros and Charlie Cairoli and Company.
Television presentation: Stephen Wade.

| 1968 | 5.5 | Fri 18 Oct 7:05 p.m. | 14 | 1 wk |

Geoffrey Wheeler introduces the seventy-fifth anniversary show with Chy Bao Guy Troupe, Ivan Bratuchin Cossack Troupe, Charlie Cairoli, Concha and Concha, the Rodriguez and Gerd Siemoneit. The ringmasters are Norman Barrett and Harold Holt.
Television presentation: Barrie Edgar.

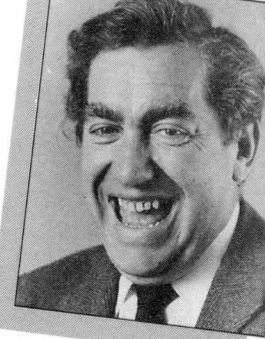

Tony Hancock was still a chart-topper in his final British series **The Blackpool Show**.

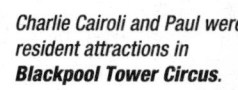

Charlie Cairoli and Paul were resident attractions in **Blackpool Tower Circus**.

Blankety Blank — 99 wks

BBC, game show

Hosted by Terry Wogan (1979-83) and Les Dawson (1984-87). Contestants were given an incomplete sentence and tried to fill the blanks to match the selections of a celebrity panel.
Directors included David Taylor (1983–84) and Bruce Millar (1986–87). **Producers** included Marcus Plantin (1979–84) and Stanley Appel (1985–87).

| 1979 | 23.3 | Tue 4 Oct 7:55 p.m. | 1 | 32 wks |

With Lorraine Chase, Barry Cryer, Russell Harty, Lulu, Michael Parkinson and Beryl Reid.

| 1980 | 19.1 | Fri 26 Dec 6:45 p.m. | 1 | 16 wks |

A special Christmas edition hosted by Wogan with a larger than usual list of guests: Katie Boyle, Windsor Davies, Les Dawson, Sandra Dickinson, Kenny Everett, Shirley Anne Field, David Hamilton, Roy Hudd, the Krankies, Rula Lenska, Patrick Moore, Beryl Reid, Madeline Smith and Jimmy Tarbuck.

| 1981 | 15.3 | Thu 19 Nov 7:55 p.m. | 6 | 13 wks |

With Patricia Brake, Billy Dainty, Shirley Anne Field, Fred Housego, Roy Hudd and Beryl Reid.
Director: Geoffrey Posner.

| 1982 | 12.3 | Sat 27 Nov 6:55 p.m. | 9 | 9 wks |

With Pat Coombs, Ken Dodd, Stu Francis, Nerys Hughes, Roy Kinnear and Tessa Wyatt.
Director: Dave Perrottet.

| 1983 | 11.1 | Sat 19 Nov 6:35 p.m. | 6 | 8 wks |

With Nerys Hughes, Jonathan King, Anneka Rice, Ted Rogers, Wayne Sleep and Sheila Steafel.

| 1984 | 11.2 | Fri 5 Oct 6:55 p.m. | 20 | 1 wk |

With Lorraine Chase, Les Dennis, Sabina Franklyn, Dustin Gee, Kelly Monteith and Anneka Rice.

| 1985 | 13.3 | Fri 11 Oct 7:40 p.m. | 8 | 13 wks |

With Bella Emberg, Pete Murray, Linda Nolan, Bill Pertwee, Fiona Richmond and Frankie Vaughan.
Director: Tony Newman.

| 1986 | 13.2 | Fri 10 Jan 7:40 p.m. | 11 | 4 wks |

With Leslie Ash, Lynda Baron, Tracey Childs, Bernie Clifton, Jack Douglas and John Dunn.

| 1987 | 14.1 | Fri 13 Mar 7:35 p.m. | 7 | 3 wks |

With Cheryl Baker, Lynda Baron, Joe Brown, Norman Collier, Belinda Lang and Chris Serle.

Blazing Saddles — 1 wk

Presented by BBC, film

| 1985 | 14.1 | Sat 6 Apr 9:00 p.m. | 5 | 1 wk |

Gene Wilder stars with Mel Brooks, writer and director of this Western parody featuring a black sheriff and a Kosher indian chief.

Bless Me Father — 8 wks

LWT, situation comedy

This clerical comedy by Peter de Rosa set in a London suburb starred Arthur Lowe as parish priest Father Duddleswell with Daniel Abineri as young curate Father Neil and Gabrielle Daye as housekeeper Mrs Pring.
Producer (1978–81): David Askey.

| 1978 | 12.6 | Sun 24 Sep 9:15 p.m. | 12 | 1 wk |

'Baptism of Fire'
Father Duddleswell is expecting a new curate, the recently ordained Father Neil.

| 1979 | 15.8 | Sun 25 Nov 9:00 p.m. | 5 | 1 wk |

'Fatal Lady'
Father Neil receives embarrassing attentions from Miss Davenport (Barbara Young). He must tolerate it because she is a generous benefactor of the Parish.

| 1980 | 15.0 | Sun 6 Jan 9:15 p.m. | 14 | 1 wk |

'A Back to Front Wedding'
Father Duddleswell gets confused during a marriage ceremony.

| 1981 | 12.5 | Sun 5 Jul 8:45 p.m. | 4 | 5 wks |

'Things Are Not What They Seem'
Father Neil offers advice to a woman with marital problems and thereby provides a field day for gossips.

Bless This House — 77 wks

Thames, situation comedy

The Abbotts were a family divided by a generation gap. Sid (Sid James) was a representative for a stationery firm. His interests were as simple as ABC – ale, birds and Chelsea FC. He erroneously considered himself to be 'with it'. Jean (Diana Coupland) was the usual winner of the battle of the sexes. Son Mike (Robin Stewart) had just left school but was too preoccupied with the affairs of the world to get a job. Daughter Sally (Sally Geeson), in her last year at grammar school, was Daddy's girl – or so he thought.
Writers included Vince Powell and Harry Driver (1971 and 1973), Carla Lane (1972, 1975 and 1977) and Dave Freeman (1974 and 1982). **Producer:** William G. Stewart.

| 1971 | 8.9 | Tue 9 Mar 8:30 p.m. | 2 | 12 wks |

'For Whom the Bell Tolls'
Will Mike go off and secretly marry his fiancée? Not if Sid has anything to do with it. The bride's parents pay for a wedding and he's not missing out on a free do.

| 1972 | 8.1 | Mon 1 May 8:25 p.m. | 2 | 12 wks |

'People in Glass Houses'
Sid plans to present Mike with a gold watch for his birthday, but Mike doesn't want one.

| 1973 | 8.2 | Mon 30 Apr 8:00 p.m. | 1 | 12 wks |

'Will the Real Sid Abbott Stand Up Please'
Sid takes on a new lease of life when he tangles with office secretary 'Sexy Sandra' (Charlotte Howard). Jean decides it's time to go home to mother.

| 1974 | 9.0 | Wed 10 Apr 8:00 p.m. | 1 | 18 wks |

'The First Twenty-five Years are the Worst'
Sid forgets his silver wedding anniversary party.

| 1975 | 8.7 | Wed 7 May 8:00 p.m. | 3 | 3 wks |

'Atishoo! Atishoo! We All Fall Down'
Jean, Sally and Mike are all going down with flu, but Sid can cope – until Betty's (Patsy Rowland) pregnant twinges break the sofa.

| 1976 | 7.2 | Thu 1 Apr 8:00 p.m. | 12 | 13 wks |

'Well, Well, Well'
What starts as a damp patch on the carpet with Sid investigating behind the skirting board becomes a major incident involving the Water Board and the Archaeological Society.
Writer: Bernie Sharp.

| 1977 | 7.8 | Mon 1 Aug 8:00 p.m. | 7 | 6 wks |

'Men of Consequence'
The Abbotts wake up to discover a midnight intruder.

| 1982 | 11.2 | Tue 15 Jun 7:00 p.m. | 6 | 1 wk |

'The Frozen Limit'
Jean wants a new deep freeze. (Repeat.)

Bless This House — 1 wk

Presented by ITV, film

| 1978 | 15.8 | Thu 31 Aug 7:45 p.m. | 1 | 1 wk |

Full length film version in which the Abbott family has new next-door neighbours, the Baines (Terry Scott and June Whitfield), with whom they get off to a bad start.
Writer: Dave Freeman. **Director:** Gerald Thomas.

Blind Date — 94 wks

LWT, game show

One unmarried and available person posed three scripted questions to three unseen members of the opposite sex who delivered scripted answers. On the basis of these replies the questioner selected one panellist to become his or her BLIND DATE. Cameras accompanied them on their day out. Cilla Black hosted.
Director (1985–86, 1989–90): John Gorman. **Producers** included Gill Stribling-Wright (1985–87) and Kevin Roast (1988–90).

1985	13.3	Sat 14 Dec 6:30 p.m.	5	3 wks
1986	18.2	Sat 22 Nov 6:30 p.m.	2	17 wks
1987	15.6	Sat 12 Dec 6:45 p.m.	4	15 wks

Director: Terry Kinane.

| 1988 | 14.9 | Sat 19 Nov 6:35 p.m. | 7 | 16 wks |

Director: Noel D. Green.

1989	16.9	Sat 18 Nov 6:45 p.m.	7	17 wks
1990	15.8	Sat 3 Feb 7:10 p.m.	7	19 wks
1991	15.6	Sat 19 Jan 6:40 p.m.	9	7 wks

Director: Martin Scott. **Producer:** Michael Longmire.

Blind Date Christmas Cracker — 1 wk

LWT, game show

| 1991 | 12.0 | Sat 21 Dec 7:00 p.m. | 18 | 1 wk |

Cilla Black looks back at highlights from past shows.
Producer: Michael Longmire. **Executive Producer:** Kevin Roast.

Blind Date Wedding of the Year — 1 wk

LWT, documentary

| 1991 | 16.9 | Sun 20 Oct 7:15 p.m. | 6 | 1 wk |

The first couple to marry after meeting on BLIND DATE are Sue Middleton and Alex Tatham. They met on the show three years ago. Cilla Black and a film crew were at yesterday's wedding.
Directors: John Gorman and Martin Scott. **Producer:** Kevin Roast.

Diana Coupland and Sid James tried to bridge the generation gap in **Bless This House**.

Blockbusters   2 wks

Central, game show

Bob Holness hosted this general knowledge game for sixteen to eighteen-year-olds. A player needed to complete a row of four against a couple who had to complete a row of five squares. A square was won by answering a question, the correct answer to which began with a given letter.

| 1984 | 10.4 | Sat 15 Sep 5:35 p.m. | 19 | 2 wks |

Producer: Graham C. Williams.

Blood and Orchids   1 wk

USA presented by ITV, drama

| 1987 | 11.2 | Tue–Wed 8–9 Dec 9:00 p.m. | 6 | 1 wk |

Both episodes of this mini-series were listed together in the ratings. Kris Kristofferson plays Captain Maddox, who is assigned to a case in which four Hawaiian youths are accused of assault and rape against the wife of a Lieutenant.

Blood Vows   1 wk

Presented by BBC, film

| 1989 | 8.8 | Tue 1 Aug 9:30 p.m. | 14 | 1 wk |

Melissa Gilbert stars as Marian and Joe Penny as Edward Moran, fall in love and marry. Marian has no idea she has joined a Mafia family. **Director:** Paul Wendkos.

Bloodline   2 wks

Presented by ITV, film

| 1982 | 11.4 | Tue 21 Dec 9:00 p.m. | 10 | 1 wk |

In this adaptation of Sidney Sheldon's novel an international pharmaceutical tycoon is murdered and his daughter seems to be next on the hit list. Stars include Ben Gazzara, Audrey Hepburn, James Mason, Romy Schneider and Omar Sharif. **Director:** Terence Young.

| 1985 | 11.7 | Sun 12 May 7:45 p.m. | 12 | 1 wk |

Repeat showing of the above film.

Blue Lagoon, The   1 wk

Presented by BBC, film

| 1985 | 12.2 | Sat 5 Oct 9:30 p.m. | 14 | 1 wk |

Emmeline and Richard (Brooke Shields and Christopher Atkins) are shipwrecked on a Pacific island with ship's cook Paddy (Leo McKern). He teaches them survival techniques but then dies, leaving them to cope with adolescence by themselves. **Director:** Randal Kleiser.

Blue Peter Special Assignment   1 wk

BBC, documentary

This series of films by the makers of the award-winning children's show BLUE PETER recreated history on location. They were introduced by Peter Purves.

| 1979 | 15.1 | Tue 14 Aug 6:20 p.m. | 12 | 1 wk |

'The Duke of Wellington at Stratfield Saye'
Tom Bell stars as the Duke and Cheryl Campbell as the Duchess. **Director:** Hugh David. **Producer:** Edward Barnes.

Bluebell   2 wks

BBC, drama

This eight-part serial by Paul Wheeler starred Carolyn Pickles as Margaret Kelly, who rose from poverty in Dublin and Liverpool to become Miss Bluebell, founder of the Bluebell Girls.

| 1986 | 13.0 | Sun 2 Mar 7:45 p.m. | 19 | 2 wks |

In this final episode Bluebell has kept Marcel (Philip Sayer) in hiding in German-occupied Paris for two years, knowing her own life is in danger. **Choreographer:** Anthony Van Laast. **Designer:** Jan Spoczynski. **Director:** Moira Armstrong. **Producer:** Brian Spiby. **Executive Producer:** Richard Bates.

Boat Race, The   1 wk

BBC, sport

The annual race on the Thames from Putney to Mortlake between crews from Oxford and Cambridge universities. The contest began at Henley in 1829 and moved to London in 1845.

| 1968 | 8.8 | Sat 30 Mar 1:50 p.m. | 2 | 1 wk |

Commentators: Harry Carpenter and Desmond Hill. **Television presentation:** Philip S. Gilbert, Ian Smith and John Vernon.

Bob Hope at the London Palladium   1 wk

ATV, entertainment

| 1979 | 10.7 | Mon 28 May 8:00 p.m. | 18 | 1 wk |

Guests: Richard Burton, Leif Garrett, Leslie Uggams and Raquel Welch. With the Norman Maen dancers and Peter Knight orchestra. **Producer:** Syd Vinnedge.

....

Bob Hope Classic Cabaret, The   1 wk

LWT, entertainment

| 1981 | 11.8 | Sat 26 Dec 9:00 p.m. | 17 | 1 wk |

Following the pro-am golf at Moor Park, the stars gathered at Grosvenor House Hotel in the presence of HRH The Princess Margaret for a cabaret benefit for the Stars' Organisation for Spastics. In this recorded programme Dickie Henderson introduces Bob Hope, Lennie Bennett, Vic Damone, John Mills, David Soul, Jimmy Tarbuck and Iris Williams.
Director: Alasdair Macmillan. **Producer:** David Bell.

....

Bob Hope Show, The   5 wks

USA presented by BBC (1961) and ITV (1962-63), entertainment

| 1961 | 4.5 | Wed 8 Nov 9:45 p.m. | 13 | 1 wk |

Guests: James Garner, Julie London and Juliet Prowse.

| 1962 | 6.3 | Wed 7 Nov 9:45 p.m. | 9 | 1 wk |

Guests: Lucille Ball, Les Brown and his Band of Renown, Bing Crosby and Juliet Prowse.

| 1963 | 5.8 | Wed 22 May 9:45 p.m. | 8 | 3 wks |

Guests: Robert Goulet, Brenda Lee and Frank Sinatra.

....

Bob Hope's Royal Birthday Party   1 wk

ITV, entertainment

| 1985 | 12.4 | Thu 6 Jun 7:30 p.m. | 4 | 1 wk |

From the Lyric Theatre, London, in the presence of HRH The Duke of Edinburgh, Bob Hope celebrates his eighty-second birthday with help from Ray Alan, Rowan Atkinson, Michael Caine, Chevy Chase, Phyllis Diller, Duran Duran, Charlton Heston, Julio Iglesias, Ben Kingsley, Spike Milligan, The Muppets, Debbie Reynolds and Mike Yarwood.

....

Bob Monkhouse Comedy Hour, The   1 wk

Thames, entertainment

Bob Monkhouse became a television star as both writer and performer in the 1950s with his then-partner Dennis Goodwin.

| 1972 | 7.1 | Wed 19 Apr 8:00 p.m. | 8 | 1 wk |

Guests: Moira Anderson, Clive Dunn and David Nixon, with the Mike Sammes singers and the Johnnie Greenland dancers.
Writers: Eric Davidson, Wally Malston and Bob Monkhouse. **Musical Director:** Ronnie Aldrich. **Producer:** Stuart Allen.

....

Bob Monkhouse Show, The   3 wks

BBC, comedy

A series of shows with comedy guests.
Producer: John Fisher.

| 1984 | 8.1 | Wed 4 Jul 9:25 p.m. | 14 | 1 wk |

Guests: Tommy Cooper, Karen Kay and Steven Wright.
Director: Geoff Miles. (First shown on BBC2.)

| 1986 | 9.7 | Sat 21 Jun 8:50 p.m. | 11 | 2 wks |

Guests: Les Dawson and the Roly Polys, with the Harry Stoneham Band.
Director: David Taylor.

....

Bob Says 'Opportunity Knocks'   15 wks

BBC, entertainment

Bob Monkhouse hosted the familiar talent show format Hughie Green had pioneered. Green was the consultant on this show.
Producer: Stewart Morris.

| 1987 | 14.0 | Sat 21 Mar 7:45 p.m. | 6 | 12 wks |

Eventual Winners: Rosser and Davies.

| 1988 | 9.6 | Sat 4 Jun 7:05 p.m. | 11 | 1 wk |

The final. Winner: Jane Harrison.

| 1989 | 11.6 | Sat 3 Jun 7:05 p.m. | 10 | 2 wks |

The final. Winner: Brenda Cochrane.

....

Bobby Davro on the Box   6 wks

TVS, comedy

Impressionist Davro first came to notice on the TV show COPY CATS.

| 1986 | 12.5 | Sat 15 Mar 6:30 p.m. | 11 | 6 wks |

With Jessica Martin and the Alyn Ainsworth orchestra.
Producer: John Kaye Cooper.

Bobby Davro's Television Weekly — 9 wks

TVS, comedy

| 1987 | 11.9 | Sat 7 Mar 6:45 p.m. | 17 | 3 wks |

With Jessica Martin and the Alyn Ainsworth orchestra.
Director: Nigel Lythgoe. **Producer:** John Kaye Cooper.

| 1988 | 12.5 | Sat 12 Mar 6:35 p.m. | 11 | 6 wks |

With Ray Alan, Terence Alexander, Belinda Carlisle, Jack Hedley and Anneka Rice.
Producer: Nigel Lythgoe.

Bob's Christmas Full House — 2 wks

BBC, game show

A charity edition of BOB'S FULL HOUSE hosted by Bob Monkhouse.

| 1985 | 14.0 | Thu 26 Dec 5:45 p.m. | 17 | 1 wk |

Director: David Taylor. **Producer:** John Bishop.

| 1987 | 13.0 | Sat 26 Dec 6:45 p.m. | 17 | 1 wk |

Producer: Geoff Miles.

Bob's Full House — 24 wks

BBC, game show

Bob Monkhouse hosted this show based on bingo in which the winner had a chance to hit the jackpot prize of a holiday.
Producer (1984–85, 1988): John Bishop.

| 1984 | 13.3 | Sat 24 Nov 6:35 p.m. | 13 | 3 wks |

Director: David Taylor.

| 1985 | 13.8 | Sat 16 Nov 7:05 p.m. | 9 | 5 wks |

Director: Tony Newman.

| 1987 | 13.4 | Sat 17 Jan 6:50 p.m. | 7 | 12 wks |

Director: Geoff Miles. **Producer:** Brian Whitehouse.

| 1988 | 12.8 | Sat 2 Jan 6:50 p.m. | 12 | 3 wks |

Producer: Geoff Miles.

| 1989 | 9.7 | Sat 16 Sep 6:45 p.m. | 18 | 1 wk |

Director: Bill Morton. **Producer:** Geoff Miles.

Bob's Your Uncle — 1 wk

Central, game show

Bob Monkhouse hosted games in which newly wed couples competed for big prizes, and, in full wedding regalia, often ended up submerged in a tank of water.

| 1991 | 9.3 | Sat 8 Jun 6:45 p.m. | 19 | 1 wk |

Producer: Nigel Lythgoe. **Executive Producer:** Tony Wolfe.

Body Matters — 3 wks

BBC, documentary

This series was presented by Doctors Alan Maryon Davis, Graeme Garden and Gillian Rice.
Series Editor: David Filkin. **Director:** Stuart McDonald. **Producer:** Caroline Van Den Brul.

| 1986 | 8.4 | Thu 21 Aug 8:00 p.m. | 18 | 1 wk |

'Hair Today, Gone Tomorrow'
Why do some people lose their hair?

| 1987 | 9.8 | Thu 27 Aug 8:00 p.m. | 9 | 2 wks |

'Wake Up To Sleep'
How much sleep do we require?

Boon — 34 wks

Central, drama

This series created by Jim Hill and Bill Stair starred Michael Elphick as urban cowboy Ken Boon, who had been forced to retire from the fire sevice after suffering lung damage in a rescue attempt. In retirement he became a freelance trouble shooter. Also starred David Daker as n'er-do-well Harry Crawford.
Directors included Laurence Moody (1986 and 1989). **Producers** included Esta Charkham (1987–89) and Simon Lewis (1990–91). **Executive Producers** included Ted Childs (1986–87) and William Smethurst (1988–89).

| 1986 | 14.6 | Tue 8 Apr 9:00 p.m. | 5 | 8 wks |

'Full Circle'
Harry Crawford tries to buy a hotel. He over-reaches himself with tragic consequences.
Producer: Kenny McBain.

| 1987 | 13.3 | Tue 31 Mar 9:00 p.m. | 8 | 12 wks |

'A Ride on the Wild Side' by Billy Hamon.
Boon has made a delivery to a dubious film crew but has not been paid.
Director: Moira Armstrong.

1988	12.7	Tue 1 Nov 9:00 p.m.	10	9 wks

'Charity Begins at Home' by Tony McHale.
Boon and Harry Crawford have a disagreement over a charity event to be held at Crawford's Plaza Suite.
Director: Baz Taylor.

1989	13.0	Tue 24 Jan 9:00 p.m.	15	3 wks

'The Not So Lone Ranger' by Douglas Watkinson.
As a result of a chance meeting Ken is able to help a friend in need.

1990	11.0	Tue 18 Dec 9:00 p.m.	19	1 wk

'The Tender Trap' by Veronica Henry.
It's all routine to Boon when he simultaneously encounters a beautiful woman, adultery and blackmail.
Director: John Woods.

1991	12.1	Tue 22 Oct 9:00 p.m.	19	1 wk

'The Barefaced Contessa' by Helen Slavin.
Ken Boon meets up with an old flame.
Director: Nicholas Laughland.

Bootsie and Snudge — 103 wks

Granada, situation comedy

This series was devised and written by Barry Took and Marty Feldman. Bootsie (Alfie Bass) and Snudge (Bill Fraser) were taken from THE ARMY GAME and redeployed into civilian life as boots boy and major-domo in a seedy gentleman's club, The Imperial, in London. Robert Dorning was the Rt. Hon. Sec. Hesketh Pendleton and Clive Dunn played the fourth member of the staff, Old Johnson. **Director** (1960–61, 1963): Milo Lewis. **Producer** (1960–62): Peter Eton.

1960	7.2	Fri 11 Nov 8:55 p.m.	1	14 wks

Bootsie and Snudge are appointed to their posts at the Imperial Club.

1961	7.5	Sat 27 May 8:55 p.m.	1	35 wks

Snudge lays down the law to Bootsie and Old Johnson saying 'Hi ham not 'aving hany more hexcuses for bone hidleness, not no way, not no 'ow!'

1962	6.5	Thu 13 Dec 7:30 p.m.	5	28 wks

'The Toerag'
Bootsie and Snudge have an encounter with a policeman (Geoffrey Palmer) as a result of meeting a toerag (Peter McAlinney).
Director: Eric Fawcett.

1963	6.1	Thu 21 Mar 7:30 p.m.	10	20 wks

'He's Got to Go'
Old Johnson is too elderly and inefficient to be kept on at the club. The decision is made that he'll have to go – but who's going to tell him?
Writers: Peter Miller and James Kelly. **Producer:** Eric Fawcett

1974	7.4	Wed 16 Oct 8:30 p.m.	4	4 wks

'Two in a Million'
Returning to the screen after an eleven-year absence, the two characters have their roles reversed. Bootsie has become the world's first £1,000,000 pools winner and Snudge has to do the creeping. He gives up his job to help Bootsie spend it.
Writers: David Climie and Ronnie Cass. **Producer:** Bill Podmore.

Born and Bred — 1 wk

Thames, situation comedy

This series by Douglas Livingstone concerned a South London family and the events which brought the different members together. The cast included Pat Ashton, Christopher Driscoll, James Grout, Rose Hill, Derek James, Gorden Kaye, Niall Padden, Trevor Peacock, Gillian Raine, Joan Sims, Max Wall and Kate Williams.

1978	12.1	Wed 13 Sep 9:10 p.m.	17	1 wk

'Together Again'
Annie Benge (Rose Hill) is the oldest member of the family. She has spent most of her life caring for stray and sick animals. To recognise her work the local newspaper organises a reunion of all her family members.
Director: Baz Taylor. **Producer:** Peter Duguid.

Born to be Small — 1 wk

ATV, documentary

1971	7.1	Mon 6 Dec 8:00 p.m.	8	1 wk

A film exploring the lives and difficulties of people often described as dwarfs or midgets.
Narrator and **Producer:** Derek Hart. **Director:** Lord Snowdon.

Both Ends Meet — 2 wks

LWT, situation comedy

This series written by Brian Chaser, Len Downs, Mike Firman and Patrick Radcliffe starred Dora Bryan as Dora Page, who supported both her teenage son Ronnie (David Howe) and father-in-law (Meadows White) by working in a factory. Her workmates were Flo (Deddie Davies), Glad (Pat Ashton) and Maudie (Wendy Richard).

1972	6.3	Sat 11 Mar 5:10 p.m.	14	2 wks

'Party Piece'
Mr Cannon (Ivor Dean) the factory owner sees a chance for a free commercial when a TV quiz show visits the factory.
Producer: Philip Casson. **Executive Producer:** Mark Stuart.

Bottle Boys — 1 wk

LWT, situation comedy

This series by Vince Powell starred Robin Askwith as milkman Dave Deacon who risked all to serve his public.

| 1984 | 9.3 | Sat 1 Sep 7:30 p.m. | 16 | 1 wk |

'Fools Rush In'
Dave finds one of his customers poised to commit suicide.
Producer: Stuart Allen.

Bounder, The — 15 wks

YTV, situation comedy

This series by Eric Chappell starred Peter Bowles as suave and sophisticated conman Howard, recently released from prison after a two-year sentence for embezzlement. He lodged next door to rich young widow Laura (Isla Blair), on whom he had designs. Humourless estate agent Trevor was portrayed by George Cole. Trevor's wife Mary, who was Howard's sister, was played by Rosalind Ayres.
Producer: Vernon Lawrence.

| 1982 | 14.1 | Fri 23 Apr 8:30 p.m. | 5 | 6 wks |

'Howard At The Majestic'
Howard takes Trevor and Mary to a night club but can't pay the bill.

| 1983 | 11.9 | Fri 12 Oct 8:30 p.m. | 7 | 9 wks |

'A Genuine Simpson'
Howard meets Simpson (Nicholas Le Prevost), another ex-con and a first-class forger of paintings.

Bounty, The — 1 wk

Presented by BBC, film

| 1988 | 11.6 | Fri 1 Jan 7:35 p.m. | 17 | 1 wk |

The most famous mutiny in naval history is recreated with Anthony Hopkins as Captain Bligh, Mel Gibson as Fletcher Christian, Laurence Olivier as Admiral Hood, Edward Fox as Captain Greetham and Daniel Day Lewis as John Fryer.
Director: Roger Donaldson.

Bouquet of Barbed Wire — 7 wks

LWT, drama

Andrea Newman created this seven-part series about a crumbling middle-class marriage. Peter Manson (Frank Finlay) developed an obsessive love for his married daughter Prue Sorenson (Susan Penhaligon). Other principal characters were Gavin Sorenson (James Aubrey), Cassie Manson (Sheila Allen) and secretary Sarah Francis (Deborah Grant).

| 1976 | 7.5 | Fri 13 Feb 9:00 p.m. | 9 | 7 wks |

'Premonitions'
Prue returns from hospital to find her relationships ever more complicated.
Designer: Richard Dunn. **Producer:** Tony Wharmby. **Executive Producer:** Rex Firkin.

Bowler — 1 wk

LWT, situation comedy

This series by John Esmonde and Bob Larbey took the character Stanley Bowler (George Baker) out of THE FENN STREET GANG, where he had been Craven's rather dodgy boss. Bowler was a villain with a finger in every profitable pie, but while his money could dress him elegantly and provide material things, it could not buy the one thing he sought more than all others – class.

| 1973 | 5.7 | Sun 30 Sep 7:25 p.m. | 18 | 1 wk |

'R.I.P.'
One of Bowler's personal codes is 'It's not what you do, it's the way that you do it.' He applies it, even to a funeral.
Producer: Philip Casson.

Boxing — 66 wks

Various, sport

| 1960 | 5.8 | Thu 22 Sep 9:35 p.m. | 7 | 1 wk |

From the Sophia Gardens, Cardiff, a double bill with a heavyweight contest between Jose Gonzales (Spain) and Joe Erskine (UK), and a featherweight match between Howard Winstone (UK) and Jean Renard (Belgium). Commentary is by Fred Verlander.
TWW television presentation: John Wynn-Jones.

| 1961 | 6.0 | Mon 9 Oct 8:30 p.m. | 10 | 3 wks |

A heavyweight contest between Ray Shiel (St Helens) and Henry Cooper's twin brother Jim (Birmingham) from the Free Trade Hall, Manchester. Commentary is by Fred Verlander and Gerry Loftus.
Granada television presentation: David Warwick.

| 1962 | 6.1 | Tue 6 Nov 9:25 p.m. | 5 | 9 wks |

A lightweight bout from the Town Hall, Shoreditch between Vic Andreeti and Johnny Cooke. Commentary is by Harry Carpenter.
BBC television presentation: Andy Wiseman.

| 1963 | 6.3 | Tue 5 Mar 8:00 p.m. | 5 | 4 wks |

From the Seymour Hall, London, a ten-round middleweight contest between Terry Downes (UK) and Jimmy Beecham (USA). Commentary is by Fred Verlander.
AR television presentation: Grahame Turner.

1964   7.1   **Tue 10 Mar 9:25 p.m.**   6   **9 wks**

From the Royal Albert Hall, Harry Carpenter introduces an international heavyweight contest between Billy Walker (UK) and Bill Nielsen (USA).
BBC television presentation: A. P. Wilkinson.

1965   7.3   **Wed 26 May 9:00 p.m.**   6   **6 wks**

A recording of the World Heavyweight Championship fight in Lewiston, Maine between Cassius Clay and Sonny Liston, which took place early this morning. Commentary is by Harry Carpenter.
BBC television presentation: Fred Viner.

1966   8.2   **Sat 10 Sep 7:50 p.m.**   1   **3 wks**

From Frankfurt, Harry Carpenter introduces the World Heavyweight Championship fight between the holder Cassius Clay and Karl Mildenberger of West Germany, the European Champion.
BBC television presentation: Fred Viner.

1968   6.4   **Tue 6 Feb 8:00 p.m.**   13   **3 wks**

Heavyweight bout between Johnny Prescott and Jack Bodell. The winner is in line for a match with Henry Cooper for the British title. Commentary is by Reg Gutteridge.
ATV television presentation: Anthony Flanagan.

1971   9.6   **Tue 9 Mar 9:20 p.m.**   1   **3 wks**

Coverage of Muhammad Ali v Joe Frazier for the World Heavyweight Championship from Madison Square Garden, New York. Commentary is by Harry Carpenter.
BBC television presentation: Ted Ayling.

1972   7.0   **Wed 22 Nov 9:00 p.m.**   6   **5 wks**

From Stateline, Nevada, Reg Gutteridge introduces coverage of the fight between Heavyweight Muhammad Ali and World Light-Heavyweight Champion Bob Foster.
Thames television presentation: Grahame Turner and Steve Minchin.

1973   8.0   **Thu 15 Feb 9:00 p.m.**   2   **2 wks**

Reg Gutteridge introduces from the Convention Centre, Las Vegas the fight between Britain's Joe Bugner and Muhammad Ali.
Thames television presentation: Grahame Turner and Steve Minchin.

1974   7.7   **Wed 30 Oct 8:00 p.m.**   2   **2 wks**

By satellite from Kinshasa, Zaire, the World Heavyweight Championship fight between George Foreman and Muhammad Ali. Commentary is by Harry Carpenter.
BBC television presentation: Bob Duncan.

1976   6.9   **Tue 25 May 8:00 p.m.**   5   **1 wk**

Reg Gutteridge introduces the World Heavyweight Boxing Championship from the Olympic Hall, Munich between holder Muhammad Ali and challenger Richard Dunn, the southpaw ex-scaffolder from Bradford.
Thames television presentation: Steve Minchin.

1978   13.3   **Wed 13 Sep 10:25 p.m.**   8   **2 wks**

From Wembley Conference Centre, Harry Carpenter introduces the flyweight contest between Charlie Magri and Sabatino de Fillipo.
BBC television presentation: Bob Duncan.

1980   14.1   **Sun 16 Mar 9:15 p.m.**   16   **1 wk**

From Las Vegas, Dickie Davies introduces the Middleweight Championship of the World between Vita Antuofermo and Alan Minter. Commentary is by Reg Gutteridge.
ITS television presentation: Patricia Mordecai.

1983   9.5   **Sat 4 Jun 9:45 p.m.**   12   **1 wk**

From the Sands Hotel in Atlantic City, Dickie Davies introduces the bout between Joe Bugner and Marvis Frazier (son of Joe Frazier). Commentary is by Reg Gutteridge with Frank Bruno and Henry Cooper.
ITS television presentation: Patricia Mordecai.

1985   18.0   **Sat 8 Jun 9:40 p.m.**   1   **3 wks**

From Loftus Road, Harry Carpenter introduces the World Featherweight Championship bout between challenger Barry McGuigan and titleholder Eusebio Pedroza.
BBC television presentation: Bob Duncan.

1986   18.3   **Sat 15 Feb 9:25 p.m.**   2   **1 wk**

From Dublin, Desmond Lynam introduces the World Featherweight Championship fight between challenger Denilo Cabrera and titleholder Barry McGuigan. Commentary is by Harry Carpenter with Terry Lawless.
BBC television presentation: John Rowlinson.

1987   16.3   **Sat 24 Oct 10:30 p.m.**   3   **4 wks**

From White Hart Lane, Frank Bruno faces Joe Bugner. Commentary is by Reg Gutteridge.
ITS television presentation: Ted Ayling.

1988   8.4   **Sat 25 Jun 10:20 p.m.**   16   **1 wk**

From Luton Town Football Club, Dickie Davies introduces the bout between Barry McGuigan and Tomas Da Cruz. Commentary is by Reg Gutteridge and Jim Watt.
ITS television presentation: Ted Ayling.

1989   17.9   **Sun 26 Feb 3:00 p.m.**   6   **1 wk**

Des Lynam introduces a recording of the fight which was shown live from Las Vegas at 4:00 a.m. in the morning. Champion Mike Tyson and challenger Frank Bruno meet in a heavyweight title bout. Commentary is by Harry Carpenter.

1991   12.7   **Sat 21 Sep 9:50 p.m.**   10   **1 wk**

From White Hart Lane, Jim Rosenthal introduces live coverage of the WBO Super Middleweight Championship between Chris Eubank and Michael Watson. Commentary is by Reg Gutteridge and Jim Watt.
ITS television presentation: Ted Ayling.

B

Boy Meets Girl | 6 wks

BBC, drama

This series of single dramas explored the eternal theme of young love.

| 1969 | 5.3 | Mon 25 Aug 9:05 p.m. | 13 | 6 wks |

'Once in Every Lifetime' dramatized by John Wilson from a story by Tom Hamlin.
Frank and Jenny (Tom Conti and Kara Wilson) first met at school and swore to marry each other when they grew up. However, fate has a habit of keeping them far apart.
Designer: Malcolm Middleton. **Director:** Brian Hulme. **Producer:** George Spenton-Foster.

Boy Dominic, The | 1 wk

YTV, drama

This series was set in 1820. Captain Charles Bulman (Richard Todd) was shipwrecked off the coast of Africa. A succession of adventures landed him in prison. Meanwhile his wife Emma (Hildegard Neil) and son Dominic (Murray Dale) lived in Boston, Lincolnshire. Brian Blessed co-starred as William Woodcock.

| 1975 | 6.2 | Wed 31 Dec 4:50 p.m. | 17 | 1 wk |

'Friends of the Family' by Penelope Lively.
Charles awakes to discover he is no longer in prison but in the home of an English lady (Maxine Audley) living in Tunis. In England, Emma and Dominic are uncertain whether to trust Mr Jackson (Julian Glover).
Designer: Roger Andrews. **Producer:** Terence Williams. **Executive Producer:** Jess Yates.

Boyd QC | 12 wks

AR, drama

This series began in 1956 and starred Michael Dennison as Richard Boyd QC and Charles Leno as Jack, his clerk. Boyd always won his case.

| 1961 | 6.3 | Wed 14 Jun 8:55 p.m. | 2 | 9 wks |

'Out of the Frying Pan' by Jack Roffey.
Acting as Commissioner at the County Assizes, Boyd gives a junior an opportunity to act for the defence in a case of bigamy.
Director: Richard Gilbert.

| 1963 | 4.4 | Fri 12 Jul 10:05 p.m. | 20 | 1 wk |

'By Gas – That's Murder' by Jack Roffey.
Boyd struggles to crack the alibi of Frederick Smee (John Barrard), a man of previous respectability, accused of murdering his wife.
Director: Pat Baker.

| 1964 | 6.0 | Wed 23 Sep 9:10 p.m. | 12 | 2 wks |

'The Case of the Lazy Eye' by Jack Roffey.
Boyd defends Halfern's Holiday Camps in a claim for damages against them. He thinks the company is clearly in the wrong until one witness makes a slip.
Director: Raymond Menmuir.

Boys from Brazil, The | 1 wk

Presented by ITV, film

| 1982 | 11.9 | Mon 12 Apr 7:30 p.m. | 14 | 1 wk |

Laurence Olivier stars as Nazi hunter Ezra Lieberman. Former Auschwitz experimental biologist Dr Joseph Mengele (Gregory Peck) has been sighted in Paraguay. Also starring Denholm Elliott, Steven Guttenberg, Uta Hagen, James Mason and Lilli Palmer.
Director: Franklin J. Schaffner.

Boys in Blue, The | 1 wk

Presented by ITV, film

| 1986 | 8.9 | Fri 6 Jun 7:30 p.m. | 15 | 1 wk |

Tom Cannon and Bobby Ball star as local policemen in an English village. Also appearing are Suzanne Danielle, Jack Douglas, Arthur English, Roy Kinnear, Jon Pertwee and Eric Sykes.
Director: Val Guest.

Brass | 5 wks

Granada, situation comedy

This series by John Stevenson and Julian Roach was set in the Northern town of Utterley during the 1930s. It intertwined the lives of two families, the rich Hardacres and the poor Fairchilds. Timothy West played Bradley Hardacre, master of all he surveyed, and Caroline Blakiston played his dipsomaniac wheelchair-bound wife Patience. Barbara Ewing and Geoffrey Hinsliff played Agnes and George Fairchild.

| 1983 | 13.0 | Mon 21 Feb 8:00 p.m. | 8 | 3 wks |

Bradley unveils a monument which meets with mixed reactions.
Director: Gareth Jones. **Producer:** Bill Podmore.

| 1984 | 8.4 | Mon 9 Jul 8:00 p.m. | 12 | 2 wks |

Jack Fairchild (Shaun Scott) proposes to Charlotte Hardacre (Emily Morgan), but all he gets in return is a feminist earful.
Producer: Gareth Jones. **Executive Producer:** Bill Podmore.

Bread — 93 wks

BBC, situation comedy

Created and written by Carla Lane, this series was about the Boswell family's struggle for existence in contemporary Liverpool. The cast included Jean Boht as Mrs Boswell, Peter Howitt (later Graham Bickley) as Joey, Victor McGuire as Jack, Nick Conway as Billy, Gilly Coman (later Melanie Hall) as Aveline, Jonathon Morris as Adrian, Ronald Forfar as Mr Boswell, Giles Watling as Oswald, Rita Tushingham as Celia, Kenneth Waller as Grandad and Eileen Pollock as Lilo Lill. **Producers** included Robin Nash (1986–89) and John B. Hobbs (1990–91).

1986	13.0	Thu 8 May 9:30 p.m.	4	5 wks

Grandad is grumpy because his canary has disappeared, cage and all.
Director: Susan Belbin.

1987	16.0	Sun 22 Nov 8:35 p.m.	4	27 wks

Two things the family members don't like, police and hospitals, enter their lives.

1988	21.0	Sun 11 Dec 8:45 p.m.	1	27 wks

Family and friends celebrate as Aveline and Oswald get married.

1989	16.5	Mon 25 Dec 3:15 p.m.	6	22 wks

The Boswells decide on a quiet Christmas to help save the planet.

1990	13.0	Sun 4 Nov 8:35 p.m.	7	10 wks

Adrian is struggling with love problems without much sympathy from the other Boswells.

1991	10.5	Sun 1 Sep 7:45 p.m.	14	2 wks

Billy is in trouble with the law. He meets a girl called Connie (Katy Carmichael).

Breakheart Pass — 1 wk

Presented by BBC, film

1981	15.6	Fri 2 Jan 9:45 p.m.	10	1 wk

Charles Bronson, Richard Crenna, Jill Ireland and Ben Johnson star in Alistair Maclean's story of a US Cavalry group crossing the Rockies by train.
Director: Tom Gries.

Breakout — 1 wk

Presented by ITV, film

1980	11.0	Sun 22 Jun 9:45 p.m.	12	1 wk

Harris Wagner (John Huston) frames his grandson Jay (Robert Duvall) for murder. Jay's wife (Jill Ireland) plots with pilot Nick Colton (Charles Bronson) to spring Jay from his Mexican prison.
Director: Tom Gries.

Brewster's Millions — 1 wk

Presented by BBC, film

1989	10.9	Sat 7 Oct 9:05 p.m.	18	1 wk

Richard Pryor stars in this story of a baseball player who must spend one million dollars per day for thirty days in order to inherit thirty million more.
Director: Walter Hill.

Bridge Too Far, A — 1 wk

Presented by ITV, film

1982	12.2	Thu 9 Sep 7:15 p.m.	2	1 wk

Operation Market Garden was an attempt by Eisenhower and Montgomery to terminate the Second World War in one single thrust. It failed. The Allies lost at Arnhem. Starring Dirk Bogarde, Sean Connery, Michael Caine, James Caan, Ben Cross, Denholm Elliott, Edward Fox, Elliott Gould, Gene Hackman, Anthony Hopkins, Jeremy Kemp, Hardy Kruger, Laurence Olivier, Ryan O'Neal, Robert Redford, Maximilian Schell, John Stride and Liv Ullman.
Director: Richard Attenborough.

Brief, The — 3 wks

TVS, drama

This thirteen-part series by Ray Jenkins starred Ray Lonnen as barrister Lucas Hellier and Isobel Black as his wife Samantha. When Hellier went to Germany to defend a British soldier accused of defecting to the East, he had an affair with court officer Annika Newman (Sabine Postel) and involved himself in a web of deceit and international intrigue.

1984	8.6	Tue 26 Jun 9:00 p.m.	13	3 wks

'People'
The death of a colleague sends Lucas Hellier to Germany as a replacement.
Director: John Frankau. **Producer:** Rex Firkin. **Executive Producer:** James Gatward.

Bring 'Em Back Alive — 2 wks

USA presented by ITV, drama

This series set in Singapore in 1938 starred Bruce Boxleitner as Frank Buck, a big game hunter from Texas. Buck had started trapping wild animals in South America in 1911, but never shot to kill. Cindy Morgan as American diplomat Gloria Marlowe provided the romantic interest.

1982	10.6	Fri 22 Oct 7:30 p.m.	17	2 wks

In a 90-minute pilot for the series Buck finds himself trapped in the pre-war politics of Singapore.
Writers and **Producers:** Frank Cardea and George Scherik

Bring on the Girls — 1 wk

AR, music

This series of music programmes featured a different female vocalist in each show.

1964	6.7	Mon 28 Sep 9:10 p.m.	8	1 wk

Dana Valery sings a selection of songs about women who have loved and lost.
Director: Robert Fleming.

Bring on the Girls — 1 wk

Thames, entertainment

1976	6.5	Wed 28 Jul 8:00 p.m.	1	1 wk

This musical special starred Bruce Forsyth with Honor Blackman, the Three Degrees, Twiggy, Lena Zavaroni and the Lionel Blair dancers with the Peter Knight orchestra.
Producer: Keith Beckett. **Executive Producer:** Philip Jones.

Britain's Strongest Man — 4 wks

Thames, entertainment

This contest of strength was co-produced with Trans World International. Derek Hobson was always one of the hosts.

1979	13.9	Thu 29 Nov 7:00 p.m.	20	2 wks

Co-host: Barbara Windsor.
Director: Bob Service. **Executive Producer:** Ken Hawkes.

1980	13.5	Tue 28 Oct 7:30 p.m.	18	1 wk

Co-hosts: Henry Cooper and Geoff Capes.
Director: George Sawford. **Producer:** Brian Venner.

1981	13.1	Tue 27 Oct 7:30 p.m.	9	1 wk

Co-host: Henry Cooper.
Producer: George Sawford. **Executive Producer:** Brian Venner.

British Academy Awards, The — 4 wks

Thames (1978, 1980), BBC (1983) and LWT (1986), entertainment

1978	14.5	Thu 16 Mar 9:30 p.m.	18	1 wk

From Wembley Royal Hall, Andrew Gardner and Susannah York introduce the nominees for awards. HRH The Princess Anne presents the trophies.
Director: Dave Rogers. **Producer:** Steve Minchin.

1980	14.1	Thu 20 Mar 9:30 p.m.	12	1 wk

Anna Ford and Edward Fox introduce the nominations and HRH The Princess Anne presents the awards at the Royal Albert Hall.
Producer: Steve Minchin.

1983	11.6	Sun 20 Mar 9:00 p.m.	11	1 wk

Frank Bough and Selina Scott introduce the ceremonies from Grosvenor House. HRH The Princess Anne presents the awards.
Director: Rick Gardner. **Producer:** Ian Smith.

1986	13.9	Sun 16 Mar 8:00 p.m.	4	1 wk

Michael Aspel introduces the nominees from Grosvenor House where celebrities present the awards.
Director: Alan Boyd. **Producers:** Richard Drewett and Nicholas Barrett. **Executive Producer:** David Bell.

British Academy Craft Awards, The — 1 wk

Granada, entertainment

1987	12.2	Sun 15 Mar 9:30 p.m.	14	1 wk

The awards are introduced by Gordon Burns and Nick Ross and presented by HRH The Princess Royal.
Director: David Liddiment. **Producer:** Geoff Moore.

British Beauty Championships, The — 3 wks

Thames, entertainment

Judith Chalmers and Peter Marshall host as Misses England, Scotland and Wales are selected. With the Phil Tate orchestra.
Producer: Steve Minchin.

1980	11.9	Thu 29 May 7:45 p.m.	8	1 wk

From Wembley Grand Hall. Cabaret: Dave Blakeley.

| 1982 | 11.1 | Wed 19 May 8:00 p.m. | 16 | 1 wk |

From Wembley Grand Hall. Cabaret: The Three Degrees.

| 1983 | 11.0 | Wed 18 May 8:00 p.m. | 7 | 1 wk |

From Agadir and the Dome in Brighton. Cabaret: Casablanca.

British Comedy Awards, The · 2 wks

LWT, entertainment

| 1990 | 11.3 | Sun 16 Dec 7:45 p.m. | 19 | 1 wk |

Michael Parkinson hosts from the London Palladium.
Producer: Michael Hurll.

| 1991 | 13.0 | Sun 22 Dec 8:15 p.m. | 15 | 1 wk |

Jonathan Ross is this year's host from LWT's Studio One in London.
Director: Alasdair Macmillan. **Producer:** Michael Hurll.

British Commonwealth Games, The · 1 wk

BBC, sport

| 1970 | 5.1 | Sat 25 Jul 10:35 p.m. | 17 | 1 wk |

After ten days of coverage, highlights of the final day and the closing ceremony from Edinburgh.
Commentators: David Coleman, Norris McWhirter and Ron Pickering.
Outside broadcast presentation: Alan Mouncer, Richard Tilling, Brian Venner and Fred Viner. **Editor:** Alan Hart. **Executive Producer:** Bryan Cowgill.

British Film Academy Awards, The · 1 wk

Granada, entertainment

| 1966 | 6.8 | Wed 23 Mar 9:45 p.m. | 10 | 1 wk |

Mike Scott introduces the ceremony from the Grosvenor House Hotel, London. Hosted by Leslie Caron and James Mason.
Director: Philip Casson. **Producer:** John Hamp.

British Film Comedy · 21 wks

Presented by BBC, film

| 1968 | 7.6 | Tue 9 Jan 7:30 p.m. | 7 | 13 wks |

'The Green Man'
George Cole, Alastair Sim and Terry-Thomas star in the story of a vacuum cleaner salesman who turns the plans of a professional assassin into farce.
Director: Robert Day.

| 1969 | 7.3 | Tue 28 Jan 7:25 p.m. | 3 | 8 wks |

'What A Carve Up'
Ray Cooney and Tony Hilton wrote the screenplay from the novel The Ghoul by Frank King. Following his death, the relatives of the owner of a country mansion gather for the reading of his will. The stars are Kenneth Connor, Shirley Eaton, Sidney James, Donald Pleasence and Dennis Price.
Director: Pat Jackson.

British Film Night · 4 wks

Presented by BBC, film

| 1969 | 7.1 | Sun 9 Nov 8:15 p.m. | 6 | 4 wks |

'The Password Is Courage'
The wartime adventures of Sergeant Major Charles Coward (Dirk Bogarde), who waged a one-man battle against the Germans.
Director: Andrew L. Stone.

British Screen Awards, The · 4 wks

BBC (1971) and Thames (1972, 1974, 1976), entertainment

The film and television industry's annual pat on the back rewarding actors, writers, directors et al became the BRITISH ACADEMY AWARDS from 1978.
Television presentation (1972, 1974, 1976): Steve Minchin.
Executive producer (1972, 1974 and 1976): Philip Jones.

| 1971 | 7.1 | Thu 4 Mar 9:20 p.m. | 8 | 1 wk |

Richard Attenborough hosts the ceremony from the Royal Albert Hall in the presence of HRH The Princess Anne. Cabaret: Sacha Distel and the Young Generation.
Television presentation: Philip Lewis.

| 1972 | 6.8 | Wed 23 Feb 9:00 p.m. | 8 | 1 wk |

Richard Attenborough introduces the winners, who are presented with their awards by HRH The Princess Alexandra at the Royal Albert Hall. Cabaret: Eric Sykes and Dougie Squires' Second Generation.

| 1974 | 8.8 | Wed 6 Mar 8:00 p.m. | 2 | 1 wk |

Introduced by Eamonn Andrews and Petula Clark from the Royal Albert Hall. The awards are presented by HRH The Princess Anne and Captain Mark Phillips. Cabaret: Norman Vaughan, Harry Secombe and Harry Worth with Dougie Squires' Second Generation and the team from WHO DO YOU DO?

| 1976 | 7.2 | Wed 17 Mar 8:30 p.m. | 9 | 1 wk |

Introduced by Eamonn Andrews and Diana Rigg from the Royal Albert Hall. The awards are presented by HRH The Princess Anne. Cabaret: Geoff Love and his orchestra.

British Song Contest, The | 4 wks

AR, music

This contest ran heats culminating in the final.

| 1961 | 6.7 | Fri 17 Feb 10:30 p.m. | 5 | 1 wk |

Huw Thomas introduces the finals from the Royal Festival Hall with the Peter Knight orchestra. (The winning song was 'My Kind of Girl', written by Leslie Bricusse and sung by Matt Monro. It reached number five in the charts.)
Producer: Grahame Turner.

| 1965 | 7.0 | Wed 26 May 9:10 p.m. | 7 | 3 wks |

The final of the competition for the Golden Manuscript Trophy. Keith Fordyce and Anne Nightingale introduce from the Dome in Brighton, with Bob Miller and the Millermen. The trophy was won by Kenny Lynch for singing 'I'll Stand By You'. The song was written by Kenny Lynch and Hal Shaper.
Director: Peter Croft. **Executive Producer:** Elkan Allan.

Bronco | 21 wks

USA presented by BBC, western

Ty Hardin starred as roving cowboy adventurer Bronco Layne, former Confederate army captain.

| 1961 | 4.4 | Sun 31 Dec 5:20 p.m. | 17 | 1 wk |

'The Mustangers'
Bronco is charged with murder on the evidence of a jealous foreman.

| 1962 | 6.3 | Sun 18 Nov 5:25 p.m. | 8 | 18 wks |

'One Evening in Abilene'
Bronco meets a beautiful woman and some gamblers.

| 1963 | 6.8 | Sun 13 Jan 5:25 p.m. | 8 | 2 wks |

'Then the Mountains'
Bronco is responsible for a wagon train which is under threat from a gang of outlaws.

Bronco Billy | 1 wk

Presented by ITV, film

| 1984 | 11.1 | Tue 3 Jan 6:45 p.m. | 16 | 1 wk |

Clint Eastwood stars as Bronco Billy McCoy, who tours in a Wild West show as a sharpshooter and knife thrower. His assistant, Antoinette Lilly (Sondra Locke), is a New York heiress on the run from her husband.
Director: Clint Eastwood.

Brotherhood of the Rose, The | 1 wk

USA presented by ITV, drama

| 1990 | 9.3 | Mon 21 May 9:00 p.m. | 15 | 1 wk |
| | | Wed 23 May 9:00 p.m. | | |

These episodes were listed together in the ratings.
Robert Mitchum stars as John Eliot, a top CIA agent. He raised two orphans, Saul Grisman (Peter Strauss) and Chris Kilmoonie (David Morse), training them to be skilled agents. During an assignment a story of betrayal develops starting an international game of cat and mouse between all three of them.

Brotherly Love | 1 wk

YTV, comedy

| 1974 | 5.8 | Mon 16 Sep 8:00 p.m. | 19 | 1 wk |

Single comedy by Tom Brennand and Roy Bottomley starring Keith Barron as Mike Hanson, a self-made success for whom the good times are here to stay. So, too, is his brother Eddie (David Swift).
Producer: Derrick Goodwin.

Brothers, The | 3 wks

BBC, drama

This serial in ten parts was created and produced by Gerard Glaister and N.J. Crisp. Robert Hammond had built up a very successful haulage company. On his death he left his widow Mary (Jean Anderson) and three sons. The eldest, Edward (Glyn Owen), had helped build the business and expected to take it over. But on the reading of the will he discovered that his brothers shared the inherited responsibility. They were David (Robin Chadwick), the youngest, a graduate who had never settled to a proper job, and Brian (Richard Eastman), an accountant. The three were in conflict, yet all were dominated by their mother. Other regular characters were played by Julia Goodman, Hilary Tindall and Jennifer Wilson.

| 1972 | 5.9 | Fri 7 Apr 8:10 p.m. | 15 | 3 wks |

'The Party' by N. J. Crisp.
The Hammonds are invited to a party hosted by an old friend of their late father.
Director: Ronald Wilson.

Brothers McGregor, The · 7 wks

Granada, situation comedy

This series by John Stevenson and Julian Roach concerned two half-brothers. Black brother Wesley (Paul Barber) had dreams of being a business tycoon, while white Cyril (Philip Whitchurch) saw himself as the next Frank Sinatra. Together they ran a second-hand car lot in Liverpool. Jean Heywood played their mother Dolly, who yearned to see Wesley's father, a West African missionary, once more. Jackie Downey portrayed Cyril's fiancée Glenys Pike.

| 1985 | 15.2 | Wed 4 Sep 8:30 p.m. | 5 | 7 wks |

Wesley fancies himself as a politician, and writes letters to world leaders in order to introduce himself.
Producer: Bernard Thompson. **Executive Producer:** Bill Podmore.

Bruce and More Girls · 1 wk

Thames, entertainment

| 1977 | 8.8 | Wed 13 Apr 8:00 p.m. | 1 | 1 wk |

This follow-up to the 1976 show BRING ON THE GIRLS stars Bruce Forsyth with Dana, Lesley-Anne Down and Nanette Newman.
Writers: Barry Cryer and Eric Merriman. **Producer:** David Bell.

Bruce Forsyth Show, The · 6 wks

ATV, entertainment

After Bruce Forsyth took over the compere duties on SUNDAY NIGHT AT THE LONDON PALLADIUM from Tommy Trinder in 1958 he became the most durable of all British television personalities.

| 1962 | 6.6 | Sat 1 Dec 8:25 p.m. | 5 | 6 wks |

Guests: Bud Flanagan and the Alyn Ainsworth orchestra.
Producer: Francis Essex.

Bruce Forsyth Show, The · 12 wks

ABC, entertainment

Bruce Forsyth starred in a series of Sunday night specials. With the Lionel Blair dancers.

| 1966 | 7.4 | Sun 18 Sep 10:05 p.m. | 1 | 6 wks |

Guests: Roy Castle and Aleta Morrison.
Producer: Philip Jones.

| 1967 | 7.3 | Sun 24 Sep 10:05 p.m. | 2 | 6 wks |

Guests: Engelbert Humperdinck, the King Brothers, Aleta Morrison and Beryl Reid.
Producer: Keith Beckett.

Bruce Forsyth Show, The · 1 wk

YTV, entertainment

Bruce Forsyth starred in this one-off variety special.

| 1969 | 4.6 | Fri 18 Jul 7:00 p.m. | 15 | 1 wk |

Guest: Harry Secombe.
Producer: Gordon Reece.

Bruce Forsyth's Big Night Out · 2 wks

LWT, entertainment

This series of Saturday night marathons lasted almost two hours with guests, games and re-creations of old radio and TV shows.

| 1978 | 14.6 | Sat 7 Oct 7:25 p.m. | 6 | 2 wks |

With Jimmy Edwards, Ian Lavender and Patricia Brake in THE GLUMS, Charlie Drake and Henry McGee in THE WORKER, Liza Goddard and Russell Harty in THE PYRAMID GAME and guests Rod Hull and Emu and Bette Midler with the Alyn Ainsworth orchestra.
Directors: John Kaye Cooper, Stuart Allen, and Paul Smith. **Producer:** Richard Drewett. **Executive Producer:** David Bell.

Bruce Meets the Girls · 1 wk

Thames, entertainment

| 1981 | 14.3 | Wed 2 Dec 8:00 p.m. | 15 | 1 wk |

This one-hour special stars Bruce Forsyth with Anita Harris, Diane Keen, Ruth Madoc and Bruce's daughters Julie and Laura.
Producer: Keith Beckett.

Bruce's Choice	3 wks

BBC, entertainment

Bruce Forsyth presented his own favourite moments from the most recent series of THE GENERATION GAME.
Director: Alan Boyd. **Producer:** James Moir.

1976	6.2	Fri 31 Dec 7:00 p.m.	17	1 wk
1977	16.3	Sat 22 Oct 6:30 p.m.	1	2 wks

Brush Strokes	27 wks

BBC, situation comedy

This series by John Esmonde and Bob Larbey focused on the relationship between Jacko (Karl Howman) and the opposite sex. It also starred Jackie Lye as Sandra, Gary Waldhorn as Lionel, Mike Walling as Eric and Elizabeth Counsell as Veronica.
Producer (1990–91): John B. Hobbs.

1986	13.4	Mon 17 Nov 8:30 p.m.	9	8 wks

Sandra has a new boyfriend, Roy Hooper (Ron Emslie). Jacko knows all about his dubious past.
Director: Mandie Fletcher. **Producer:** Sydney Lotterby.

1988	12.2	Mon 28 Nov 8:00 p.m.	11	9 wks

Jacko senses a terrible mistake as Sandra walks up the aisle on her father's arm.
Producer: Harold Snoad.

1990	12.7	Thu 22 Feb 8:30 p.m.	11	6 wks

Jacko gets a few surprises from his workmates.

1991	11.5	Sun 3 Mar 7:15 p.m.	15	4 wks

Jacko continues the search for Miss Perfect.

Buck Rogers in the 25th Century	5 wks

USA presented by ITV, drama

The first science-fiction character with his own comic strip, Buck Rogers began life in an American newspaper in 1929. In this series, he was launched into space, frozen for five hundred years and returned to Earth to attend a peace conference. Gil Gerard starred as Rogers.
Producer: John Mantley.

1980	13.5	Sat 6 Dec 5:45 p.m.	17	2 wks

'Escape From Wedded Bliss'
Buck investigates a mysterious rotating pyramid which turns out to be a weapon capable of wiping out every city on Earth.

1981	13.5	Sat 21 Mar 5:40 p.m.	17	3 wks

'The Guardians'
A fevered Buck hallucinates. He believes an ambassador is a lizard plotting to destroy Starship Searcher.

Buck Rogers – The Movie	1 wk

Presented by ITV, film

1982	10.3	Sat 25 Sep 7:00 p.m.	13	1 wk

Gil Gerard stars as a cheerful Buck Rogers who foils the evil Princess Ardela (Pamela Hensley).
Director: Daniel Haller.

Buckman Treatment, The	1 wk

YTV, documentary

1989	8.6	Mon 17 Jul 7:00 p.m.	20	1 wk

On a tour of Los Angeles, Dr Robert Buckman attempts to separate reality from fantasy.
Camera: Mostafa Hammuri. **Director:** Charles Flynn. **Producer:** Paul Dunston. **Executive Producer:** Duncan Dallas.

Bud	1 wk

ATV, situation comedy

This series aimed at finding Bud Flanagan a new job after the Crazy Gang disbanded.

1963	4.2	Fri 26 Jul 10:15 p.m.	17	1 wk

'A Funny Thing Happened as I Left the Theatre'
In this, the first show of the series, Bud is running a betting shop. (In real life he was a partner in three London betting shops with boxing promoter Jack Solomons.) Also starring Chesney Allen, Jerry Desmonde, Jack Hylton and Charlie Naughton.
Writer: Barry Laffen. **Director:** Philip Barker.

Budget, The — 10 wks

BBC/ITV, politics

As with early PARTY POLITICAL BROADCASTs, the Budget and the opposition's reply the following evening were shown on both channels at the same time, consequently scoring high ratings. The Chancellors were questioned by Kenneth Harris (1960–61) and Robin Day (1962–64).

| 1960 | 7.6 | Mon 4 Apr 9:30 p.m. | 1 | 2 wks |

The Chancellor of the Exchequer The Rt. Hon. Derick Heathcoat Amory MP.

| 1961 | 8.6 | Mon 17 Apr 9:30 p.m. | 1 | 2 wks |

The Chancellor of the Exchequer The Rt. Hon. Selwyn Lloyd CBE, MP.

| 1962 | 9.1 | Mon 9 Apr 9:30 p.m. | 1 | 2 wks |

The Chancellor of the Exchequer The Rt. Hon. Selwyn Lloyd CBE, MP.

| 1963 | 9.6 | Tue 2 Apr 9:30 p.m. | 1 | 2 wks |

The Chancellor of the Exchequer The Rt. Hon. Reginald Maudling MP.

| 1964 | 10.1 | Tue 14 Apr 9:30 p.m. | 1 | 2 wks |

The Chancellor of the Exchequer The Rt. Hon. Reginald Maudling MP.

Budgie — 16 wks

LWT, drama

This series starred Adam Faith as Budgie Bird, a petty crook clinging to the fringe of corrupt society in Soho and South London, with Iain Cuthbertson as Charlie Endell, the Mr Big of Budgie's scene. Created by Keith Waterhouse and Willis Hall.
Producer: Verity Lambert.

| 1971 | 6.9 | Fri 9 Apr 9:00 p.m. | 6 | 11 wks |

'Out'
Budgie is out on the streets, but not looking for work. His wife has left him and his girlfriend Hazel (Lynn Dalby) has just had a baby. He's looking for an easy deal to get some easy money.
Designer: John Emery. **Director:** James Goddard. **Executive Producer:** Rex Firkin.

| 1972 | 6.0 | Fri 5 May 9:00 p.m. | 16 | 5 wks |

'Louie "The Ring" is Dead and Buried in Kensal Green Cemetery'
Following a meeting with old flame Hazel, Budgie decides it's time he made some quick money. He senses his worries may be over when Charlie receives a small legacy.
Designer: Frank Nerini. **Director:** Michael Lindsay-Hogg.

Bulldog Breed — 1 wk

Granada, situation comedy

The series was devised and produced by Derek Granger and starred Donald Churchill as Tom Bowler, an amiable young man who managed to provoke chaos. Amanda Barrie played his girlfriend Sandra and his friend Billy was portrayed by Geoffrey Whitehead. Peter Butterworth and Betty Huntley-Wright played Billy's despairing parents.

| 1962 | 6.4 | Wed 19 Sep 9:15 p.m. | 7 | 1 wk |

'The New Digs' by Jack Rosenthal from a story by Harry Driver. Tom has been fired, his landlady has shown him the door and his girlfriend has told him to get lost.
Director: Graeme McDonald.

Bullitt — 1 wk

Presented by ITV, film

| 1979 | 15.5 | Sun 7 Jan 9:15 p.m. | 11 | 1 wk |

Steve McQueen stars as Detective Frank Bullitt. Jacqueline Bissett, Robert Duvall and Robert Vaughn also appear in a film famous for a car chase through the streets of San Francisco.
Director: Peter Yates.

Bullseye — 64 wks

ATV (later Central), game show

Jim Bowen played host to professional darts players and contestants. Skill at darts and an average general knowledge were required to win prizes both for contestants and for charity.
Producers included Peter Holmans (1981–82) and Bob Cousins (1984–88, 1991).

1981	14.7	Mon 14 Dec 7:00 p.m.	6	13 wks
1982	9.8	Sun 19 Dec 5:00 p.m.	18	1 wk
1984	17.6	Sun 23 Dec 5:30 p.m.	2	11 wks
1985	14.5	Sun 6 Jan 6:00 p.m.	8	6 wks
1986	14.5	Sun 23 Nov 6:00 p.m.	5	15 wks
1987	13.4	Sun 1 Nov 5:30 p.m.	8	10 wks
1988	12.6	Sun 10 Jan 6:00 p.m.	12	4 wks
1991	13.5	Sun 17 Nov 5:00 p.m.	15	4 wks

The Rt. Hon. Derick Heathcote Amory MP was the first Chancellor to top the charts with his 1960 show **The Budget**.

Bullseye Special — 1 wk

Central, game show

| 1986 | 13.6 | Sun 28 Dec 4:45 p.m. | 13 | 1 wk |

Jim Bowen introduces Ray Alan, Eric Bristow, Frank Carson, Sarah Greene, John Lowe and Fatima Whitbread.
Producer: Bob Cousins.

Bulman — 14 wks

Granada, drama

Don Henderson starred as George Bulman, retired from the police force where he had been a Detective Chief Inspector in STRANGERS. In retirement he worked as a clock mender, but life refused to leave him in peace and quiet.

| 1985 | 13.1 | Wed 28 Aug 9:00 p.m. | 6 | 11 wks |

'A Man of Conviction' by Murray Smith.
Bulman enters prison to try to trap a gang of armed robbers operating from inside. His life is threatened and his assistant Lucy McGinty (Siobhan Redmond) comes to his aid.
Designer: Taff Batley. **Director:** Tom Cotter. **Producer:** Steve Hawes.

| 1987 | 10.2 | Sat 8 Aug 9:30 p.m. | 10 | 3 wks |

'Ministry of Accidents' by Murray Smith.
Bulman and Lucy McGinty are pawns in a game between civil servants. It could wipe them out.
Designer: Alan Pickford. **Director:** Brian Mills. **Producer:** Sita Williams.

Burke Special, The — 5 wks

BBC, documentary

James Burke presented this series dealing with developments in science and research that will sooner or later change our lives.

| 1973 | 6.8 | Thu 15 Mar 8:30 p.m. | 9 | 4 wks |

James Burke looks at the changing pace of life, and the problems that people have keeping up.
Director: Robin Bates. **Producer:** Michael Blakstad.

| 1976 | 6.4 | Thu 22 Apr 8:30 p.m. | 14 | 1 wk |

James Burke explores the possibility of us seeing ourselves as others see us.
Director: John Gorman. **Producer:** Martin Freeth. **Editor:** Michael Blakstad.

Burke's Law — 1 wk

USA presented by ITV, drama

This series of murder stories created by Ivan Goff and Ben Roberts starred Gene Barry as wealthy Los Angeles police captain Amos Burke, who dealt with homicide from the comfort of his Rolls Royce. The title of each episode began 'Who Killed . . .'. Producer Aaron Spelling made much use of guest stars.

| 1964 | 5.4 | Wed 4 Nov 8:00 p.m. | 17 | 1 wk |

'Who Killed Vaudeville?'
Rags McGuire, a vaudeville entertainer, is poisoned by cyanide. All the other members of the show are suspects. Guest stars: Jim Backus, William Demarest, Eddie Foy Jr., Phil Harris, Gypsy Rose Lee, Gene Nelson and Gloria Swanson.

Busman's Holiday — 31 wks

Granada, game show

Teams from different professions compete for travel prizes connected with their jobs. Presented by Sarah Kennedy (1989–91).
Producer: (1985) and **Executive Producer** (1989-90): Stephen Leahy. An Action Time production (1989–91).

| 1985 | 14.1 | Tue 26 Feb 7:30 p.m. | 3 | 13 wks |

Midwives, police officers and hoteliers compete.
Presenter: Julian Pettifer. **Director:** Frank Hayes.

| 1989 | 12.5 | Wed 15 Mar 7:00 p.m. | 1 | 10 wks |

Farmers, holiday park managers and an air cabin crew compete.
Director: Jonathan Bullen. **Producer:** Patricia Pearson.

| 1990 | 10.3 | Wed 6 Jun 7:00 p.m. | 13 | 4 wks |

Car salesmen, fingerprint officers and hovercraft pilots compete.
Director: Terry Kinane. **Producer:** Richard Bradley.

| 1991 | 9.6 | Wed 7 Aug 7:00 p.m. | 13 | 4 wks |

Teams of music directors, osteopaths and stately home wardens compete.
Producer: Jenny Dodd. **Executive Producer:** Dianne Nelmes.

Busman's Holiday Celebrity Special — 1 wk

Granada, game show

| 1991 | 10.1 | Wed 12 Jun 7:00 p.m. | 14 | 1 wk |

Sarah Kennedy promotes Michael Elphick, Jill Gascoine and Don Henderson versus Dickie Bird, John McCririck and Tessa Sanderson versus Greg Benson, Mouche Phillips and Adam Willits. **Producer:** Jenny Dodd. **Executive Producer:** Dianne Nelmes. An Action Time production.

Bust   2 wks

LWT, situation comedy

This series created by Philip Hinchcliffe and Simon Passmore starred Paul Nicholas as unsuccessful wheeler-dealer Neil Walsh, who faced both divorce and bankruptcy. The show also starred Phyllis Logan as his wife Sheila and Geraldine Alexander as Janet Summers, his trustee in bankruptcy.

| 1987 | 10.6 | Fri 11 Sep 9:00 p.m. | 16 | 2 wks |

'Hidden Assets'
Neil is part-owner of a forgotten piece of land. He would like to turn it into cash.
Director: Don Laver. **Producer:** Philip Hinchcliffe. **Executive Producer:** Nick Elliott.

Buster   1 wk

Presented by ITV, film

| 1991 | 13.7 | Sat 28 Sep 9:35 p.m. | 7 | 1 wk |

Phil Collins stars as Great Train Robber 'Buster' Edwards. Julie Walters plays his wife June.
Director: David Green.

Butch and Sundance – the Early Days   1 wk

Presented by ITV, film

| 1982 | 9.5 | Sat 19 Jun 7:45 p.m. | 15 | 1 wk |

Harry Longbaum alias the Sundance Kid (William Katt) and Robert Parker alias Butch Cassidy (Tom Berenger) become partners in crime.
Director: Richard Lester.

Butch Cassidy and the Sundance Kid   1 wk

Presented by BBC, film

| 1975 | 6.7 | Thu 25 Dec 8:45 p.m. | 4 | 1 wk |

Christmas Day world television premiere of George Roy Hill's film about outlaws Robert Parker and Harry Longbaum, otherwise known as Butch Cassidy (Paul Newman) and the Sundance Kid (Robert Redford). Also starring Katharine Ross with Jeff Corey, Henry Jones and Strother Martin.

Butterflies   18 wks

BBC, situation comedy

This series created by Carla Lane starred Wendy Craig as Ria and Geoffrey Palmer as her boring dentist husband Ben. Their two sons Adam and Russell were played by Nicholas Lyndhurst and Andrew Hall. Bruce Montague as Leonard was the object of Ria's very chaste escapist attentions. The series was first shown on BBC2 and was repeated in 1991.
Producers included Gareth Gwenlan (1979–80, 1991) and Sydney Lotterby (1981 and 1984).

| 1979 | 15.2 | Thu 25 Jan 8:30 p.m. | 12 | 4 wks |

Ria knows it is time to break away from her humdrum routine.

| 1980 | 13.4 | Fri 21 Mar 7:50 p.m. | 17 | 1 wk |

Ria wonders if the butterflies she has tonight are real or imaginary.

| 1981 | 14.5 | Thu 7 May 8:30 p.m. | 3 | 7 wks |

Russell is keeping something from Ria and Ben, but they don't know what.
Director: John B. Hobbs.

| 1984 | 10.7 | Tue 28 Aug 8:30 p.m. | 7 | 1 wk |

Ria wonders why her family fails to understand her.

| 1991 | 12.9 | Sun 17 Feb 8:35 p.m. | 11 | 5 wks |

A repeat of the episode in which Ria first meets Leonard.

By Royal Command   1 wk

BBC, documentary

| 1986 | 12.6 | Fri 28 Nov 9:30 p.m. | 10 | 1 wk |

More than forty stars make special film contributions to tell stories from THE ROYAL VARIETY PERFORMANCE, which began in 1912.
Producer: Rod Taylor.

By the Sea   2 wks

BBC, comedy

| 1982 | 15.0 | Mon 12 Apr 7:40 p.m. | 3 | 1 wk |

Ronnie Barker and Ronnie Corbett enjoy a weekend in an old-fashioned English resort as members of the family first seen in THE PICNIC. Also featured are Debbi Blythe, John Brewer, Madge Hindle, Rikki Howard and Barbara New.
Director: Bill Wilson. **Executive Producer:** Michael Hurll.

| 1984 | 10.9 | Tue 10 Apr 6:45 p.m. | 17 | 1 wk |

Repeat of the above programme.

C

Cabaret Showtime — 1 wk

BBC, entertainment

| 1978 | 10.5 | Tue 17 Jul 9:25 p.m. | 15 | 1 wk |

Variety show from Scotland hosted by Jimmy Logan with Baccara, Sydney Devine, Stu Francis, Josephine McQueen and Annie Ross, with Brian Fahey and the Scottish Radio orchestra.
Director: James W. Goulding. **Producer:** Iain Macfadyen.

Cabbage Patch, The — 2 wks

Central, situation comedy

This series by Joan Greening was about family life as seen from a mother's point of view. It starred Julia Foster as Janet and Emlyn Price as Tony.

| 1983 | 9.6 | Fri 2 Sep 8:30 p.m. | 7 | 2 wks |

'The School Play'
Tony misses the school play, much to Janet's annoyance.
Director: Paul Harrison. **Producer:** Shaun O'Riordan.

Cade's County — 10 wks

USA presented by ITV, western

This modern western series starred Glenn Ford as Marshal Sam Cade, who ruled Madrid County in New Mexico with his own brand of law.

| 1972 | 7.4 | Wed 26 Apr 8:00 p.m. | 3 | 10 wks |

'The Alien Land'
Sam gets involved with a girl, her possessive father, politics and a murder.

Cagney and Lacey — 2 wks

Presented by BBC, film

| 1982 | 11.7 | Mon 29 Mar 9:25 p.m. | 20 | 1 wk |

The pilot film to establish the series stars Loretta Swit as Chris Cagney and Tyne Daly as Mary Beth Lacey. They struggle against violence on the streets of New York while also battling against sexual prejudice. They decide to earn respect as detectives the hard way – on their own.
Director: Ted Post.

| 1989 | 11.0 | Tue 30 May 9:30 p.m. | 13 | 1 wk |

Repeat showing of the above film.

Cagney and Lacey — 22 wks

USA presented by BBC, drama

In the series that followed the above pilot film Meg Foster played Cagney for the first season. She was succeeded by Sharon Gless. Tyne Daly continued as Lacey.

| 1982 | 10.2 | Fri 9 Jul 9:25 p.m. | 8 | 6 wks |

'Street Scene'
Cagney and Lacey are called to the scene where an old man is accused of shooting a member of a gang of Puerto Rican youths.

| 1983 | 10.3 | Fri 18 Mar 9:25 p.m. | 8 | 6 wks |

'Recreational Use'
Cagney is delighted when her boyfriend, Detective Sergeant McKenna, is assigned to work with her. They soon find that working closely together is not such a good idea.

| 1984 | 10.2 | Sat 21 Apr 9:45 p.m. | 13 | 1 wk |

'Matinée'
A suburban housewife vanishes. Cagney and Lacey embark on a murder hunt.

| 1986 | 10.6 | Sat 31 May 9:00 p.m. | 9 | 3 wks |

'Post-Partum'
A West Point cadet held on a narcotics charge finds his inflexible sense of honour is an obstacle in establishing his innocence.

| 1987 | 12.1 | Sat 3 Jan 9:55 p.m. | 12 | 4 wks |

'Schedule One'
An informant names a fourteenth precinct cop as the thief of heroin taken from police drug busts.

1988	12.2	Sat 16 Jan 9:20 p.m.	15	2 wks

'Don't I Know You?'
Cagney is raped after a date with a seemingly charming man.

Cagney Cavalcade — 1 wk

Presented by BBC, film

Season of films starring James Cagney.

1969	4.2	Sat 2 Aug 8:15 p.m.	18	1 wk

'The Gallant Hours'
Cagney plays Admiral William 'Bull' Halsey who, in October 1942, took on the assignment of trying to stop the Japanese naval advance in the South Pacific.
Director: Robert Montgomery.

Call in on Carroll — 3 wks

ATV, music

This series starred Irish singer Ronnie Carroll.

1964	5.8	Tue 29 Sep 9:10 p.m.	16	3 wks

With Janie Marden, the Seekers and the Jack Parnell orchestra.
Producer: Jon Scoffield.

Call in on Tom — 1 wk

ATV, music

1965	7.1	Wed 17 Nov 9:10 p.m.	8	1 wk

Starring Tom Jones with Mia Lewis in this one-off special.
Director: Alan Tarrant. **Producer:** Victor Rudolf.

Call in on Valentine — 4 wks

ATV, music

Dickie Valentine Britain's number one crooner of the 1950s.

1965	6.1	Tue 6 Apr 9:10 p.m.	12	4 wks

With Kenny Baker, Patsy Ann Noble and the Jack Parnell orchestra.
Producer: Victor Rudolf.

Call in on Wynter — 2 wks

ATV, music

Singer and actor Mark Wynter first hit the pop charts in 1960.

1965	7.1	Wed 10 Nov 9:10 p.m.	9	2 wks

With Susan Maughan, the Morgan-James Duo and the Jack Parnell orchestra.
Producer: Albert Locke.

Call of the Wild — 1 wk

Presented by BBC, film

1978	14.7	Thu 28 Dec 6:00 p.m.	11	1 wk

Charlton Heston and Michelle Mercier star in the story of Buck, an Alsatian stolen from his California home and sold in Alaska.
Director: Ken Annakin.

Callan — 29 wks

Thames, drama

This series, created by James Mitchell, starred Edward Woodward as the title character, a secret service agent with his own ruthless ethics. Writing in the Sunday Telegraph, Philip Purser said 'Callan is what Ian Fleming set out to make Bond – a blunt instrument.' Russell Hunter appeared as Lonely. Anthony Valentine played Callan's fellow agent Meres. Their boss, Hunter, was first played by Michael Goodliffe, then by Derek Bond and finally by William Squire. Patrick Mower portrayed agent Cross.
Producer (1969–70, 1972): Reginald Collin.

1969	7.0	Wed 16 Apr 9:00 p.m.	1	6 wks

'Death of a Hunter' by Michael Winder.
Death is the ever-present possibility in the life of an agent. It is coming to one of them tonight.
Designer: Neville Green.

1970	7.8	Wed 8 Apr 9:15 p.m.	1	9 wks

'Where Else Could I Go?' by James Mitchell.
Having ended the previous series with doubt as to whether or not Callan had been killed, this first programme of the new series dispels all doubts. Callan lives!
Designer: Mike Hall. **Director:** James Goddard.

1972	7.4	Wed 24 May 9:00 p.m.	3	13 wks

'A Man Like Me' by James Mitchell.
The last show of the 1972 series brings a conclusion to the running battle between Callan and Richmond (T.P. McKenna).
Designer: Bill Palmer. **Producer:** Reginald Collin.

1981	12.8	Wed 2 Sep 8:30 p.m.	6	1 wk

'Wet Job' by James Mitchell.
It's ten years since Callan's last secret mission. He is now a dealer in militaria with his own shop. He is drawn out of retirement by the potential embarrassment of an ex-MP's memoirs and the disappearance of a dissident Czech professor.
Designer: David Chandler. **Producer:** Shaun O'Riordan.

Edward Woodward starred as the ruthless secret service agent **Callan**.

Callan | 2 wks

Presented by ITV, film

| 1981 | 13.0 | Tue 12 May 7:30 p.m. | 11 | 1 wk |

In this full-length film version Callan (Edward Woodward) is requested by his boss Hunter (Eric Porter) to kill a German businessman – quickly.
Director: Don Sharp.

| 1984 | 11.2 | Sun 5 Feb 7:45 p.m. | 19 | 1 wk |

Repeat showing of this film.

Calling Dickie Valentine | 7 wks

ATV, music

Dickie Valentine began his career as a band singer with Ted Heath. He made frequent television appearances after his first hit record in 1953. His life was brought to a premature end in a car crash in South Wales on 6 May 1971.

| 1961 | 4.4 | Wed 16 Aug 8:00 p.m. | 13 | 7 wks |

Guests: Sheila Buxton and Ronnie Carroll with the Jack Parnell Dance Band and the Malcolm Goddard dancers.
Producer: Colin Clews.

Camera in Action | 2 wks

Granada, documentary

A series of four programmes using photographic studies of the past. The other titles were 'A Prospect of Whitby', 'Photographer' and 'War of the Brothers'.

| 1965 | 5.6 | Tue 10 Aug 10:05 p.m. | 9 | 2 wks |

'The Uprooted'
Thirty-five million Europeans emigrated to the USA between 1820 and 1920. Their story is shown in a series of photographs taken at the turn of the century by Jacob Riss and Lewis Hine.
Writer and **Narrator:** James Cameron. **Camera:** Ray Goode. **Director:** Peter Jones. **Producer:** Mike Wooller.

Can We Get on Now, Please? | 4 wks

Granada, situation comedy

This series by Dennis Woolf was set in a magistrates' court and starred Hugh Paddick as Clerk to the Justices Mr Pettigrew, Robert Dorning as Chairman of the Bench Mr Butterfield, Sheila Steafel as magistrate Mrs Pryor and Michael Barrington as fellow magistrate Mr Skinner. The court usher Mr Bailey was played by Charles Lamb and the assistant clerk Miss Teasdale by Valerie Phillips.

| 1980 | 12.6 | Mon 23 Jun 8:00 p.m. | 6 | 4 wks |

'Pettigrew's Last Stand'
Mr Dedrick (Angus Mackay) is a lawyer who appears to wangle legal aid cases. Mr Pettigrew tackles this corruption.
Director: Eric Prytherch. **Producer:** Brian Armstrong.

Candid Camera | 20 wks

ABC, comedy

The original American format was devised by Allen Funt in the 1950s. The British series, presented from the studio by Bob Monkhouse, featured Jonathan Routh with the candid camera. Members of the general public demonstrated their own gullibility in impossible situations.
Directors included Geoffrey Ramsay (1961–62).

| 1960 | 6.2 | Sat 10 Dec 9:30 p.m. | 5 | 1 wk |

Director: Ronnie Taylor.

1961	4.6	Sat 30 Dec 9:30 p.m.	11	2 wks
1962	5.2	Sat 3 Feb 9:30 p.m.	11	8 wks
1974	7.4	Sat 2 Feb 6:25 p.m.	6	9 wks

The series is revived on LWT. Presented by Peter Dulay and Arthur Atkins with guest Sheila Burnette.
Director: Denys Palmer. **Producer:** Peter Dulay.

Candid Camera | 2 wks

USA presented by ITV, comedy

| 1984 | 11.3 | Sat 14 Apr 7:00 p.m. | 13 | 2 wks |

Allen Funt presents clips from the latest US series.

Candid Camera Now and Then | 2 wks

USA presented by ITV, comedy

| 1983 | 10.4 | Sun 10 Jul 8:45 p.m. | 2 | 2 wks |

Highlights from the past and present series are presented by Angie Dickinson and Allen Funt.

Candid Camera's 35th Birthday Party | 1 wk

USA presented by ITV, comedy

| 1983 | 10.1 | Fri 22 Jul 7:30 p.m. | 3 | 1 wk |

Allen Funt fronts the celebration.

Canned Carrott				**1 wk**

BBC, comedy

1991	**12.5**	**Thu 5 Dec 9:30 p.m.**	**18**	**1 wk**

Jasper Carrott is joined by Hugh Dennis, Tony Blackburn, Steve Punt and Ruby Wax.
Producer: Ed Bye. (A Celador production.)

....

Cannon				**31 wks**

USA presented by BBC, drama

This series created by Quinn Martin starred William Conrad as Frank Cannon, a middle-aged, overweight and balding West Coast private eye.

1973	**7.3**	**Thu 13 Sep 9:25 p.m.**	**1**	**5 wks**

'The Girl in the Electric Coffin'
Cannon hands over a simple case of finding a man's missing daughter to his friend Harry Somers. It's a routine enquiry until Harry is murdered.

1974	**6.0**	**Thu 13 Jun 9:25 p.m.**	**4**	**5 wks**

'Bad Cats and Sudden Death'
A young district attorney is investigating a gang of car thieves. In return they frame him for the murder of his own wife.

1975	**7.3**	**Sat 24 May 10:00 p.m.**	**2**	**7 wks**

'Triangle of Terror'
Cannon has some tricky investigations following the mysterious death of an English resident in the Caribbean. With guests Lloyd Buchner and Dana Wynter.

1976	**6.7**	**Sat 20 Mar 9:00 p.m.**	**16**	**6 wks**

'Photo Finish'
Cannon becomes the target of a sniper's gunfire when he takes on a murder enquiry on behalf of an international mercenary soldier. With guest stars Jack Cassidy and Herb Edelman.

1977	**11.7**	**Sat 27 Aug 9:15 p.m.**	**9**	**7 wks**

'The Ice Man'
A former district attorney is in prison for murder. When he refuses parole his old friend Cannon begins to scrutinize his case.

1978	**15.0**	**Thu 30 Mar 9:25 p.m.**	**6**	**1 wk**

'Quasar Kill'
A doctor studying signals from outer space is killed by a laser beam.

....

Cannon and Ball Show, The				**31 wks**

LWT, comedy

Lancashire comedians Tommy Cannon and Bobby Ball worked their way up through the northern clubs but had to go to London Weekend for television stardom. They were supported by the Alyn Ainsworth orchestra (1980-86). Written by Sid Green.
Writer: Sid Green. **Producers** included Sid Green (1980–82) and Paul Jackson (1983–84). **Director** (1980–81): David Crossman.

1980	**13.5**	**Fri 11 Apr 7:30 p.m.**	**10**	**6 wks**

Guests: Ritz.

1981	**14.4**	**Sat 2 May 7:35 p.m.**	**7**	**5 wks**

Guest: Anne Murray.

1982	**14.0**	**Sat 2 Jan 7:00 p.m.**	**8**	**3 wks**

From the Theatre Royal, Drury Lane, this special stars Jack Jones and Zee and Co. With the Brian Rogers dancers.
Stage Director: David Bell. **Television Director:** Alasdair Macmillan.

1983	**14.3**	**Sat 17 Dec 7:00 p.m.**	**2**	**3 wks**

Guests: Sarah Brightman, Shakin' Stevens and Jocky Wilson.

1984	**13.0**	**Sat 13 Oct 7:00 p.m.**	**9**	**7 wks**

Guests: the Beverley Sisters, Engelbert Humperdinck, the Little Foxes and Billy Wright.
Director: Terry Kinane.

1986	**11.4**	**Sat 26 Apr 7:00 p.m.**	**7**	**6 wks**

Guest: Michael Aspel.
Writers: Geoff Atkinson, Bryan Blackburn and David McKellar.
Producer: Marcus Plantin.

1988	**9.0**	**Sat 28 May 7:00 p.m.**	**16**	**1 wk**

Guests: Marti Caine and Kenny Lynch. With the Ray Monk orchestra.
Writer: Bryan Blackburn. **Producer:** Michael Hurll.

William Conrad as Frank Cannon found 'The Girl in the Electric Coffin' in the only Number One episode of **Cannon**.

Cannon and Ball Easter Show, The — 1 wk

LWT, comedy

| 1983 | 11.5 | Sat 2 Apr 7:00 p.m. | 11 | 1 wk |

Guests: Jill Gascoine, Renée and Renato, Eric Sykes and Mari Wilson. **Director:** Alasdair Macmillan. **Producer:** Sid Green.

Cannonball Run, The — 3 wks

Presented by BBC, film

| 1985 | 14.4 | Mon 8 Apr 8:10 p.m. | 4 | 1 wk |

Easter Monday showing of a race across America from Connecticut to California in vehicles ranging from a Ferrari to an ambulance. Starring Sammy Davis Jr., Dom DeLuise, Farrah Fawcett, Peter Fonda, Dean Martin, Roger Moore and Burt Reynolds. **Director:** Hal Needham.

| 1987 | 10.6 | Mon 31 Aug 8:35 p.m. | 10 | 1 wk |
| 1989 | 8.4 | Wed 23 Aug 10:10 p.m. | 18 | 1 wk |

Repeat showings of the above film.

Capstick's Law — 1 wk

Granada, drama

This family saga by John Finch was set in the Yorkshire Dales in the 1950s. The head of the family was solicitor Edward Capstick (William Gaunt), married to Madge (Wanda Ventham). Their eldest son Jonty (Christopher Villiers) had his own legal practice. Younger son Tony (Guy Scantlebury) was an articled clerk in London. Edward's brother Henry was played by Robin Ellis.

| 1989 | 11.8 | Sun 9 Apr 7:45 p.m. | 14 | 1 wk |

Edward and Madge, like all their neighbours, are looking forward to the Coronation of Queen Elizabeth II, but an open window at Colnay Hall stirs up memories of the past. **Designers:** Mike Joyce and Tim Wilding. **Director:** John Michael Phillips. **Producer:** Roderick Graham. **Executive Producer:** June Howson. (A Messenger Television production.)

Cargo to Capetown — 1 wk

Presented by ITV, film

| 1968 | 4.7 | Wed 14 Aug 6:05 p.m. | 13 | 1 wk |

Broderick Crawford stars as a merchant sea captain on a long voyage of adventure. **Director:** Earl McEvoy.

Caribbean Mystery, A — 2 wks

Presented by ITV, film

| 1984 | 11.4 | Sun 25 Mar 7:15 p.m. | 14 | 1 wk |

Helen Hayes stars as Miss Marple in this Agatha Christie story. Marple is staying at a hotel where two murders are committed. Her relaxing holiday turns into a race against the clock to prevent a third murder. **Director:** Robert Lewis.

| 1989 | 11.7 | Sun 10 Dec 7:15 p.m. | 19 | 1 wk |

Repeat showing of the above film.

Caribbean Mystery, The — 1 wk

Presented by ITV, film

| 1988 | 11.0 | Sat 17 Sep 8:00 p.m. | 14 | 1 wk |

Several geologists disappear while working for an oil company. **Director:** Robert Webb.

Carquake — 1 wk

Presented by ITV, film

| 1982 | 12.5 | Sat 2 Jan 9:15 p.m. | 16 | 1 wk |

The Trans-America Grand Prix Road Race from the Pacific to Manhattan has no rules. Starring David Carradine, Veronica Hamel and Bill McKinney. **Director:** Paul Bartel.

Carroll Calling — 5 wks

ATV, music

A switch of ATV titling has Ronnie Carroll calling as opposed to inviting us to 'Call in . . .'.

| 1965 | 6.3 | Wed 14 Apr 9:10 p.m. | 10 | 5 wks |

With Janie Marden, Topo Gigio and the Seekers. **Producer:** Albert Locke.

Carrott's Commercial Breakdown — 1 wk

BBC, comedy

| 1991 | 14.2 | Fri 27 Dec 10:00 p.m. | 10 | 1 wk |

Jasper Carrott reviews some of the world's weirdest and most outrageous television adverts.
Producer: Paul Smith. (A Celador production.)

| Carrott's Lib | | | | 1 wk |

BBC, comedy

| 1983 | 8.1 | Thu 9 Jun 10:00 p.m. | 17 | 1 wk |

Jasper Carrott stars in this Election Night Special live from the Television Theatre with Chris Barrie, Emma Thompson and Nick Wilton.
Producer: Paul Jackson.

| Carry On | | | | 2 wks |

Presented by ITV, film

The first CARRY ON film was **'Carry On Sergeant'** made in 1958. For almost 20 years afterwards writer Talbot Rothwell, director Gerald Thomas and producer Peter Rogers churned out these light blue farces at the rate of two a year. The repertory company of CARRY ON players comprised a stalwart group of regulars led by Sid James and Kenneth Williams.

| 1978 | 18.5 | Sun 8 Jan 7:45 p.m. | 3 | 2 wks |

'Carry On Abroad' (See separate entry for this film.)

| Carry On | | | | 1 wk |

Presented by BBC, film

| 1978 | 13.7 | Wed 27 Dec 9:15 p.m. | 16 | 1 wk |

'Carry On Girls'
Sid James stars as Sidney Fiddler, who persuades the Fircome council to stage a seaside beauty contest. Barbara Windsor co-stars as Hope Springs. With Robin Asquith, Bernard Bresslaw, Peter Butterworth, Kenneth Connor, Jack Douglas, Sally Geeson, Joan Hickson, Valerie Leon, David Lodge, Jimmy Logan, Wendy Richard, Arnold Ridley, Joan Sims and June Whitfield.

| Carry On Abroad | | | | 1 wk |

Presented by ITV, film

| 1982 | 9.4 | Tue 1 Jun 7:30 p.m. | 14 | 1 wk |

Kenneth Williams plays a courier shepherding a group of British tourists to a half-built hotel on the Mediterranean island of Elsbels. Also starring Peter Butterworth, Kenneth Connor, Sally Geeson, Charles Hawtrey, Hattie Jacques, Sid James, Jimmy Logan, Joan Sims, June Whitfield and Barbara Windsor.

| Carry On Again Christmas | | | | 1 wk |

Thames, comedy

| 1970 | 6.8 | Thu 24 Dec 9:10 p.m. | 8 | 1 wk |

Following the success of CARRY ON CHRISTMAS in 1969, the team now offer **'Carry On Long John'** by Sid Colin and Dave Freeman as a Christmas special, featuring the following characters: Long John Silver (Sid James), Squire Treyhornay (Terry Scott), Old Pew (Charles Hawtrey), Dr Livershake (Kenneth Connor), Jim Hawkins (Barbara Windsor), Rollicky Bill (Bernard Bresslaw), Ben Gunn (Bob Todd) and Kate (Wendy Richard).
Designer: Roger Allan. **Producer:** Alan Tarrant. **Executive Producer:** Peter Eton.

| Carry On Behind | | | | 1 wk |

Presented by ITV, film

| 1982 | 14.0 | Tue 25 May 7:30 p.m. | 3 | 1 wk |

Kenneth Williams stars as Professor Roland Crump who enlists a bunch of students to dig the remains of a Roman camp at the back of a caravan site populated by a motley crew of holidaymakers. Also starring Bernard Bresslaw, Peter Butterworth, Kenneth Connor, Windsor Davies, Jack Douglas, Liz Fraser, Adrienne Posta, Joan Sims and Elke Sommer.

| Carry On Camping | | | | 1 wk |

Presented by ITV, film

| 1975 | 6.9 | Sat 15 Feb 7:05 p.m. | 18 | 1 wk |

Sid (James) and Bernie (Bresslaw) decide to spend their holiday at a nudist camp, but they have yet to tell their girlfriends. Also starring Peter Butterworth, Hattie Jacques, Charles Hawtrey, Julian Holloway, Dilys Laye, Betty Marsden, Terry Scott, Joan Sims, Kenneth Williams and Barbara Windsor.

Carry On Christmas — 5 wks

Thames, comedy

Writer: *Talbot Rothwell.* **Directors** *(1969, 1971–72, 1974): Ronnie Baxter.* **Producers** *included Peter Eton (1969, 1971) and Gerald Thomas (1972, 1974–75).* **Executive Producer:** *Peter Rogers.*

| 1969 | 7.4 | Wed 24 Dec 9:15 p.m. | 1 | 1 wk |

'Ghosts Of Christmas'
The characters are Scrooge (Sid James), Dr Frank N. Stein (Terry Scott), The Spirit of Christmas Past (Charles Hawtrey), Elizabeth Barrett (Hattie Jacques), Cinderella (Barbara Windsor), Cissie (Bernard Bresslaw) and Dracula (Peter Butterworth). With guest star Frankie Howerd as Robert Browning.

| 1971 | 8.1 | Mon 20 Dec 9:00 p.m. | 3 | 1 wk |

A repeat of **'Ghosts Of Christmas'**.

| 1972 | 7.7 | Wed 20 Dec 8:00 p.m. | 5 | 1 wk |

The CARRY ON team enjoy a Christmas banquet in an eighteenth-century house. Starring Peter Butterworth, Kenneth Connor, Jack Douglas, Hattie Jacques, Norman Rossington, Joan Sims and Barbara Windsor.
Co-writer: *Dave Freeman.*

| 1974 | 6.1 | Mon 16 Dec 9:00 p.m. | 15 | 1 wk |

Repeat of the 1972 programme.

| 1975 | 8.1 | Thu 18 Dec 9:00 p.m. | 5 | 1 wk |

A repeat in which the CARRY ON team explore how our ancestors have celebrated Christmas through the ages, from the Stone Age to the trenches of the First World War. Stars Sid James as Santa, with Peter Butterworth, Bernard Bresslaw, Kenneth Connor, Julian Holloway, Jack Douglas, Joan Sims and Barbara Windsor.

Carry On Cleo — 1 wk

Presented by BBC, film

| 1985 | 10.5 | Tue 27 Aug 7:30 p.m. | 17 | 1 wk |

Sid James stars as Mark Anthony, Kenneth Williams as Julius Caesar and Amanda Barrie as Cleopatra in the CARRY ON team's version of Shakespeare's rendition of Roman history. Also starring Kenneth Connor, Jim Dale, Sheila Hancock, Charles Hawtrey, Warren Mitchell, Jon Pertwee and Joan Sims.

Carry On Cowboy — 1 wk

Presented by BBC, film

| 1981 | 15.2 | Fri 24 Apr 7:30 p.m. | 4 | 1 wk |

The feared Rumpo Kid (Sid James) rides in to disrupt the peace of the frontier town Stodge City. But he comes up against an Englishman Marshal P. Knutt (Jim Dale). Also starring Kenneth Williams with Bernard Bresslaw, Peter Butterworth, Angela Douglas, Peter Gilmore, Charles Hawtrey, Davy Kaye, Jon Pertwee and Joan Sims. (Edina Ronay, later a top fashion designer, plays the part of Dolores.)

Carry On Doctor — 1 wk

Presented by BBC, film

| 1988 | 10.5 | Sat 13 Aug 8:00 p.m. | 8 | 1 wk |

Francis Bigger (Frankie Howerd) is a notorious charlatan who lectures on mind over matter. One day, in mid-flow, he slips off the lecture platform and ends up in hospital in the care of Dr Tinkle (Kenneth Williams) and Doctor Kilmore (Jim Dale). Also starring Sid James and Barbara Windsor with Bernard Bresslaw, Peter Butterworth, Hattie Jacques, Anita Harris, Charles Hawtrey and Joan Sims.

Carry On . . . Don't Lose Your Head — 1 wk

Presented by BBC, film

| 1984 | 13.0 | Sat 15 Dec 6:45 p.m. | 15 | 1 wk |

Sid James stars as Sir Roger Ffing and Jim Dale as Lord Darcy. They rescue several nobles from the guillotine during the French Revolution. Citizen Camembert (Kenneth Williams) and Citizen Bidet (Peter Butterworth) are soon on their tails. Also starring Peter Gilmore, Charles Hawtrey, Dany Robin and Joan Sims.

Carry On England — 1 wk

Presented by BBC, film

| 1983 | 9.6 | Wed 25 May 9:50 p.m. | 14 | 1 wk |

Members of a mixed male and female aircraft unit mingle. Starring Peter Butterworth, Kenneth Connor, Windsor Davies, Jack Douglas, Judy Geeson, Melvyn Hayes, Peter Jones, David Lodge, Patrick Mower, and Joan Sims.

Carry On Follow That Camel — 1 wk

Presented by BBC, film

| 1985 | 11.6 | Sat 21 Dec 6:25 p.m. | 15 | 1 wk |

True Englishman Bertram Oliphant West (Jim Dale) and his manservant (Peter Butterworth) join the French Foreign Legion in the Oasis El Nooki. They report to the Commandant (Kenneth Williams) and Sergeant Nocker (Phil Silvers). Also starring Bernard Bresslaw, Angela Douglas, Anita Harris, Charles Hawtrey and Joan Sims.

Carry On Girls

1 wk

Presented by BBC, film

1988	11.1	Sat 20 Aug 6:40 p.m.	9	1 wk

See CARRY ON (BBC).

Carry On Henry

2 wks

Presented by ITV, film

1979	16.5	Thu 4 Jan 7:30 p.m.	5	1 wk

Sid James stars as Henry VIII and Kenneth Williams as Sir Thomas Cromwell. With Peter Butterworth, Kenneth Connor, Charles Hawtrey, Bill Maynard, Terry Scott, Joan Sims and Barbara Windsor.

1981	14.1	Sat 17 Jan 7:35 p.m.	14	1 wk

Repeat showing of the above film.

Carry On Laughing

1 wk

ATV, situation comedy

This series of specially written half hours by different writers had various permutations of the CARRY ON team in the cast.
Executive Producer: Peter Rogers.

1975	6.8	Sun 9 Nov 7:25 p.m.	14	1 wk

'And in My Lady's Chamber'
A send-up of UPSTAIRS DOWNSTAIRS in which the butler Hudson becomes Clodson and so forth. Starring Bernard Bresslaw, Peter Butterworth, Kenneth Connor, Jack Douglas, Joan Sims and Barbara Windsor.
Writer: Lew Schwarz. **Director:** Alan Tarrant.

Carry On Laughing

15 wks

Presented by ITV, film

Classic comedy moments from the CARRY ON films compiled by producers Gerald Thomas and Peter Rogers.

1981	16.5	Thu 31 Dec 7:30 p.m.	2	1 wk
1982	12.1	Wed 8 Dec 8:00 p.m.	10	8 wks
1983	14.4	Wed 3 Apr 7:00 p.m.	2	5 wks
1985	11.1	Tue 17 Sep 8:00 p.m.	15	1 wk

Carry On Season, A

10 wks

Presented by BBC, film

1974	6.1	Wed 11 Sep 6:40 p.m.	15	4 wks

'Carry On Doctor'
(See separate entry.)

1976	6.2	Wed 20 Oct 6:45 p.m.	17	1 wk

'Carry On Cruising'
Sid James stars as Captain Crowther of the SS Happy Wanderer on a Mediterranean Cruise with a brand new crew. Also stars Esme Cannon, Kenneth Connor, Liz Fraser, Dilys Laye, Lance Percival and Kenneth Williams.

1987	11.1	Sat 22 Aug 6:30 p.m.	6	5 wks

'Carry On At Your Convenience'
Sid James stars as Sid Plummer and Kenneth Williams as W.C. Boggs. With Bernard Bresslaw, Kenneth Cope, Charles Hawtrey, Renée Houston, Hattie Jacques, Davy Kaye, Bill Maynard and Joan Sims.

Carry On Spying

1 wk

Presented by BBC, film.

1972	6.0	Mon 3 Apr 8:00 p.m.	14	1 wk

Easter Monday showing of the spy spoof in which Barbara Windsor makes her CARRY ON debut. Joining her in the service of the nation are Eric Barker, Bernard Cribbins, Jim Dale, Charles Hawtrey, Dilys Laye, Richard Wattis and Kenneth Williams.

Casanova '73

2 wks

BBC, comedy

This series by Ray Galton and Alan Simpson starred Leslie Phillips as womaniser Henry Newhouse, a married man who worked in public relations. His wife Carol was played by Jan Holden.

1973	5.8	Thu 13 Sep 8:00 p.m.	17	2 wks

'The Adventures of a Twentieth-Century Libertine'
Henry receives an unwanted letter from a girl named Valerie. What is more, she says she is going to write every day.
Producer: Harold Snoad.

Case, The 1 wk

BBC (with Scandinavian companies SR, NRK and YLE), comedy

| 1972 | 5.0 | Sat 2 Sep 8:15 p.m. | 14 | 1 wk |

A one-hour film comedy by Eric Davidson starring Cliff Richard and Tim Brooke-Taylor with Olivia Newton-John. The action takes place in Sweden, Norway and Finland. Cliff and Tim get involved with a gang of crooks at a railway station when Cliff inadvertently picks up the wrong suitcase and finds it contains the haul from a bank robbery.
Producer: Michael Hurll.

Cassandra Crossing, The 3 wks

Presented by ITV, film

| 1981 | 14.4 | Thu 1 Oct 7:30 p.m. | 5 | 1 wk |

A train has to go from Geneva to a decontamination plant in Poland after coming into contact with a plague virus. The trip requires negotiating the Cassandra crossing, an unsafe trestle bridge. Starring Ava Gardner, Richard Harris, Burt Lancaster, Sophia Loren and Martin Sheen.
Director: George Pan Cosmatos.

| 1982 | 10.7 | Sat 13 Nov 7:05 p.m. | 18 | 1 wk |

Repeat showing of the above film.

| 1989 | 10.7 | Wed 9 Aug 9:30 p.m. | 9 | 1 wk |

The BBC shows the above film.

Casualty 54 wks

BBC, drama

This series, set in the casualty unit of a British hospital, was created by Jeremy Brock and Paul Unwin.
Producers included Geraint Morris (1987–88, 1991) and Peter Norris (1989–90).

| 1987 | 10.9 | Sat 12 Dec 7:50 p.m. | 19 | 2 wks |

'Burning Cases' by Jeremy Brock.
Consultant Ewart Plimmer (Bernard Gallagher) deals with a serious burns case.
Director: Christopher Menaul.

| 1988 | 11.4 | Fri 28 Oct 9:30 p.m. | 17 | 3 wks |

'Living Memories' by Sam Snape.
A mother faces the truth when her son's brain scan shows damage.
Director: Keith Washington.

| 1989 | 13.1 | Fri 1 Dec 9:30 p.m. | 8 | 20 wks |

'Hanging On' by Sam Snape.
A candlelit dinner for two is cancelled as the hospital goes on yellow alert.
Director: Steve Goldie.

| 1990 | 13.4 | Fri 7 Dec 9:30 p.m. | 7 | 14 wks |

'A Reasonable Man' by Barbara Machin.
Megan Roach (Brenda Fricker) decides to give up her career as a nurse. She must also deal with the jealousy of Charlie Fairhead (Derek Thompson).
Director: Andrew Morgan.

| 1991 | 16.1 | Fri 29 Nov 9:30 p.m. | 7 | 15 wks |

'Pressure! What Pressure?' by Arthur Mackenzie.
A battered wife creates problems when her husband turns up at the hospital. She threatens to meet violence with violence.
Director: Michael Brayshaw.

Catch Hand 1 wk

BBC, drama

In this series Mark Eden starred as Johnny Rich, a drifter and itinerant labourer who was always itching to be up and away to another town, another job. Anthony Booth also starred as Finn Brodie, a brash exuberant labourer who lived from hand to mouth spending money on drink and women.

| 1964 | 7.2 | Wed 1 Jul 8:00 p.m. | 9 | 1 wk |

'Stop Counting at Once' by H.V. Kershaw.
Johnny and Finn try to sort out trouble on a construction site. It is dangerous because it involves thwarting a man with a keen interest in ensuring that the job does not get finished.
Director: Bill Hays. **Producer:** Terence Williams.

Catchphrase 47 wks

TVS, game show

In this game hosted by Roy Walker, contestants identified a well-known catchphrase from a build-up of computer graphics.
Directors: included Bob Collins (1986–87) and Liddy Oldroyd (1988–90). **Producer** (1986–88, 1990): Graham C. Williams. **Executive producer** (1986–88): John Kaye Cooper.

1986	13.0	Sun 9 Mar 7:15 p.m.	8	12 wks
1987	11.7	Sun 8 Mar 7:15 p.m.	16	5 wks
1988	13.8	Sat 13 Feb 6:45 p.m.	7	13 wks
1989	13.9	Sun 19 Mar 7:15 p.m.	8	12 wks

Producer: Frank Hayes.

| 1990 | 12.5 | Sat 27 Jan 6:10 p.m. | 14 | 3 wks |
| 1991 | 11.8 | Sat 26 Jan 6:10 p.m. | 18 | 2 wks |

Catchphrase Celebrity Special   1 wk

TVS, game show

| 1988 | 11.0 | Sat 2 Apr 6:35 p.m. | 13 | 1 wk |

Roy Walker introduces Debbie Greenwood, Bob Holness, Matthew Kelly and Jessica Martin.
Director: Liddy Oldroyd. **Producer:** Graham C. Williams. **Executive Producer:** John Kaye Cooper.

C.A.T.S. Eyes   17 wks

TVS, drama

In this thriller series by Terence Feely CATS stood for Covert Activities Thames Section. Jill Gascoine took her character Maggie Forbes from THE GENTLE TOUCH to join CATS. Leslie Ash played Fred Smith. Rosalyn Landor and Don Warrington also starred.
Producer (1986–88): Raymond Menmuir. **Executive Producer:** Rex Firkin.

| 1985 | 13.4 | Fri 12 Apr 8:30 p.m. | 10 | 9 wks |

'Goodbye Jenny Wren' by Terence Feely.
In this feature-length first episode, a tragic death occurs just as Maggie begins her new job.
Director: William Brayne. **Producers:** Dickie Bamber and Frank Cox.

| 1986 | 9.9 | Sat 31 May 9:15 p.m. | 8 | 3 wks |

'Honeytrap' by Terence Feely.
A KGB agent has been seeking out Whitehall spinsters and offering his services as a gigolo.
Director: Bob Fuest.

| 1987 | 10.6 | Sat 9 May 9:00 p.m. | 10 | 4 wks |

'Country Weekend' by Paul Wheeler.
Tessa (Tracy-Louise Ward) invites Fred to a peaceful weekend at her mother's country house.

| 1988 | 9.5 | Fri 22 Jul 9:00 p.m. | 15 | 1 wk |

'Fit' by Reg Ford.
Fred and Tessa go on a gruelling refresher course at a top secret spy school.
Director: Terry Marcel.

Celebrity   2 wks

USA presented by ITV, drama

| 1985 | 12.6 | Sat 13 Apr 9:20 p.m. | 12 | 2 wks |

Part one of a three-part mini-series about three Texas high school seniors who attain fame in different fields. They share a secret of rape and murder that will destroy their careers. Starring Michael Beck, Joseph Bottoms and Ben Masters.
Writer: Thomas Thompson.

Celebrity Game, The   14 wks

AR, game show

Viewers submitted questions to a panel of celebrities and received a one pound premium bond for each question used. Hosted by Clive Goodwin.

| 1964 | 6.4 | Fri 19 Jun 7:00 p.m. | 4 | 14 wks |

Panellists: Jane Asher, Zsa Zsa Gabor, Miriam Karlin, Stirling Moss, Tommy Trinder and Lord Willis.
Director: Marc Miller.

Celebrity Play Your Cards Right   1 wk

LWT, game show

| 1986 | 11.7 | Fri 19 Dec 7:00 p.m. | 12 | 1 wk |

Bruce Forsyth plays host to competing couples Dickie and Liz Davies and Des and Claire Rayner. They play for charity.
Producer: Alasdair Macmillan.

Celebrity Sale of the Century   1 wk

Anglia, game show

| 1981 | 17.1 | Fri 2 Jan 8:30 p.m. | 3 | 1 wk |

Presented by Nicholas Parsons with Derek Batey, Steve Jones and Tom O'Connor.
Producer: Bill Perry.

Celebrity Squares   37 wks

ATV, quiz

In this series hosted by Bob Monkhouse nine celebrities occupied squares on a giant noughts and crosses board. The two competing contestants nominated the celebrities to answer general knowledge questions and then had to confirm whether or not that answer was correct, winning ten pounds for each successful confirmation. Kenny Everett provided voiceover introductions from 1975 to 1978. **Producer** (1975–78): Paul Stewart Laing.

| 1975 | 7.1 | Sun 16 Nov 4:50 p.m. | 14 | 3 wks |

With Anne Aston, Pat Coombs, Charlie Drake, Noele Gordon, Gordon Jackson, John Inman, Arthur Mullard, Jimmy Tarbuck and William Rushton.

| 1976 | 7.6 | Sat 31 Jan 7:00 p.m. | 6 | 12 wks |

With Pat Coombs, Fanny and Johnnie Craddock, Charlie Drake, Gordon Jackson, Diane Keen, Barbara Mitchell, Patrick Mower, Arthur Mullard and Ted Ray.

| 1977 | 7.4 | Sat 26 Mar 7:15 p.m. | 15 | 6 wks |

With Keith Chegwin, Pat Coombs, Peter Goodwright, Elizabeth Harrison, Dickie Henderson, Hinge and Bracket, Tom O'Connor, Jean Rook and Willie Rushton.

| 1978 | 14.6 | Sat 8 Apr 6:45 p.m. | 10 | 8 wks |

With Katie Boyle, Frank Carson, Charlie Drake, Barry Evans, Pearly Gates, Stacey Gregg, Don Maclean, Willie Rushton and Barbara Windsor.

| 1979 | 16.3 | Sat 6 Jan 7:00 p.m. | 5 | 8 wks |

With Frank Carson, Barry Cryer, Sacha Distel, Diana Dors, Jenny Hanley, Don Maclean, Françoise Pascal, Willie Rushton, Percy Thrower and the voice of Lance Percival. **Producer:** Glyn Edwards.

Centennial   1 wk

USA presented by BBC, drama

This twelve-part series was adapted by John Wilder from the novel by James A. Michener. It told of the settlement of the American West. The stars included Raymond Burr, Richard Chamberlain, Robert Conrad, David Janssen and Sally Kellerman.

| 1979 | 10.9 | Mon 28 May 7:25 p.m. | 15 | 1 wk |

'Only the Rocks Live Forever'
The forerunners of doom for the Indians arrive in Colorado.
Director: Virgil Vogel. **Producer:** Howard Alston.

Chalk and Cheese   5 wks

Thames, situation comedy

This series by Alex Shearer starred Michael Crawford and Gillian Martell as Dave and Rose Finn, Cockneys living in an otherwise gentrified street. They didn't get on with neighbours Roger and Amanda Scott (Robin Hawdon and Julia Goodman).
Producer: Michael Mills.

| 1979 | 16.7 | Mon 2 Apr 8:00 p.m. | 3 | 5 wks |

'Spasms'
Two expectant fathers wait outside the delivery room in the early hours of the morning.

Challenge Anneka   5 wks

BBC, entertainment

Anneka Rice set out to accomplish seemingly impossible tasks within a set time limit.

| 1989 | 11.1 | Fri 6 Oct 8:20 p.m. | 13 | 5 wks |

Directors: Tom Gutteridge and Juliet May. **Producer:** Tom Gutteridge. (A Mentorn Films production.)

Chance in a Million   3 wks

Thames, situation comedy

This series by Andrew Norris and Richard Fegen starred Simon Callow as Tom Chance, who began his sentences with verbs and omitted all definite and indefinite articles. Brenda Blethyn played his girlfriend Alison Little, who inadvertently became involved in his misfortunes.

| 1985 | 12.5 | Tue 9 Apr 8:30 p.m. | 17 | 3 wks |

'Stuff of Dreams'
A television news crew arrives in the mistaken belief that a gangland boss is holed up in Tom's house.
Producer: Michael Mills.

Chaos Supercedes ENSA   1 wk

Southern, documentary

| 1980 | 10.9 | Wed 27 Aug 9:00 p.m. | 11 | 1 wk |

The title comes from Tommy Trinder who, during the Second World War, gave a new meaning to ENSA, the Entertainments National Services Association, calling it Every Night Something Awful. When ENSA was replaced by the CSE, the Combined Services Entertainments, Trinder called it CHAOS SUPERCEDES ENSA. Patrick Garland narrates the story with contributions from Larry Adler, Ingrid Bergman, Ian Carmichael, Charlie Chester, Joyce Grenfell, Frankie Howerd, Arthur Marshall, Spike Milligan, Denis Norden, Ralph Richardson, John Schlesinger, Anne Shelton, Peter Ustinov and Kenneth Williams. **Producer:** Patrick Garland.

....

Chariots of Fire   2 wks

Presented by BBC, film

| 1984 | 14.3 | Sun 22 Apr 7:15 p.m. | 3 | 1 wk |

The true story of Harold Abrahams (Ben Cross) and Eric Liddell (Ian Charleson), who win honour for Britain in the 1924 Paris Olympic Games. Also starring Nigel Davenport, John Gielgud, Nigel Havers, Ian Holm, Alice Krige and Patrick Magee. **Director:** Hugh Hudson.

| 1988 | 10.3 | 21 Aug 7:45 p.m. | 10 | 1 wk |

Repeat showing of the above film.

....

Charlie and Julie   1 wk

YTV, drama

This two-part love story by Charles Humphreys starred Nicholas Clay as Charlie and Tina Marian as Julie.

| 1978 | 9.7 | Tue 25 Jul 9:00 p.m. | 17 | 1 wk |

'The Meeting'
After an unconventional meeting, Julie seems to be playing hard to get.
Designer: Alan Pickford. **Producer:** Marc Miller. **Executive Producer:** Peter Willes.

....

Charlie Drake Show, The   10 wks

BBC (1960–61) and ATV (1963), comedy

Diminutive East Ender Charlie Drake began his slapstick career in children's television as one half of the duo Mick and Montmorency. He went on to win two Golden Rose of Montreux comedy awards.

| 1960 | 5.3 | Mon 26 Dec 6:30 p.m. | 10 | 1 wk |

A compilation of highlights from Charlie's recent series which involved him in various situations in the world of high finance. Also starring Sam Kydd, Roger Maxwell and Betty Turner. The original series was produced by Ernest Maxin.
Compilation Producer: Ronald Marsh.

| 1961 | 6.4 | Tue 24 Oct 8:00 p.m. | 5 | 3 wks |

'Bingo Madness'
The first of a series of six programmes transmitted live. Subtitled 'Somewhere a Voice is Calling', this episode features Charlie going to Bingo and getting involved in some complicated knockabout sequences.
Writers: Charlie Drake and Richard Waring. **Producer:** Ronald Marsh.

| 1963 | 6.0 | Sat 26 Oct 8:25 p.m. | 13 | 6 wks |

Featuring sketches and sequences with guests The Skylons, Wanda Ventham and Albert and Les Ward with the Jack Parnell orchestra.
Writers: Charlie Drake and Lew Schwarz. **Producer:** Colin Clews.

....

Charlie Muffin   1 wk

Presented by ITV, film

| 1983 | 10.1 | Wed 31 Aug 8:00 p.m. | 8 | 1 wk |

David Hemmings stars as Charlie Muffin, a British intelligence agent seeking evidence to convict the captured head of a Soviet spy network in Europe. Also starring Ralph Richardson and Sam Wanamaker.
Director: Jack Gold.

....

Charlie's Angels   48 wks

USA presented by ITV, drama

Charlie (the voice of John Forsythe) was the unseen boss of Townsend Investigations in Los Angeles. The Angels were three former police-women whose assignments were often dangerous. The original three were Sabrina Duncan (Kate Jackson), Jill Munroe (Farrah Fawcett-Majors) and Kelly Garrett (Jaclyn Smith). When Farrah Fawcett-Majors left the show she was replaced by Cheryl Ladd as Kris Munroe. Further replacements were played by Tanya Roberts and Shelley Hack.
Executive producer: Aaron Spelling.

| 1977 | 15.5 | Tue 25 Oct 7:30 p.m. | 2 | 30 wks |

'Angels in Paradise'
Charlie has been kidnapped. Perhaps the Angels (Kate Jackson, Cheryl Ladd and Jaclyn Smith) will finally get to meet him?

| 1978 | 14.0 | Tue 13 Jun 7:30 p.m. | 2 | 5 wks |

'Angels on the Run'
Sabrina, Kelly and Kris are confronted by a philandering truck driver, a package of diamonds and a kidnapping.

| 1979 | 16.9 | Tue 23 Jan 7:30 p.m. | 4 | 13 wks |

'Angels Ahoy'
Sabrina, Kelly and Kris pursue a gang of smugglers on board a luxury liner.

84

5

1 *Charles Hawtrey gets the bird in* **Carry On Christmas**.

7

2 *Captain Shepard (Kenneth More) and Anne Davis (Dana Wynter) discuss how best to* **Sink the Bismark**.

3 *Robert Shaw as Squadron Leader 'Skipper' prepares to take to the air in* **The Battle of Britain**.

4 *Michael Caine and Janet Suzman starred in 'The Black Windmill', the top-rated film shown in the series* **Saturday Night at the Movies**.

5 *Christopher Malcolm, Ian McShane and Warren Clarke burrowed for riches in* **Dirty Money**, *a film also knows as 'Sewers of Gold'.*

6 *Mike Scott hosts the highest charting edition of* **Cinema**.

7 *The presence of Michael Caine regularly boosted the ratings of televised screenings of films in which he appeared, including* **The Italian Job**.

Charmer, The — 5 wks

LWT, drama

This series by Allan Prior starred Nigel Havers as Ralph Ernest Gorse, a social climber and seducer of women. It also starred Bernard Hepton as Donald Stimpson, Fiona Fullerton as Clarice Mannors and Rosemary Leach as Joan Plumleigh Bruce.

| 1987 | 13.4 | Sun 22 Nov 9:00 p.m. | 9 | 5 wks |

'Gorse at the End'
Joan and Donald travel to Brighton only to discover that the body in the mortuary is not that of Gorse. He is in a hotel with a girlfriend.
Designer: Bryan Bagge. **Director:** Alan Gibson. **Producer:** Philip Hinchcliffe. **Executive Producer:** Nick Elliott.

Chas and Dave's Knees-up — 1 wk

LWT, music

This series starred Cockney musicians Chas Hodges and Dave Peacock.

| 1983 | 8.4 | Sat 2 Jul 7:45 p.m. | 13 | 1 wk |

Guests: Lonnie Donegan and Gary Wilmot.
Director: Alasdair Macmillan. **Producer:** David Bell.

Chase Me Comrade — 1 wk

BBC, comedy

| 1964 | 4.7 | Fri 28 Aug 9:25 p.m. | 19 | 1 wk |

The first act from Ray Cooney's farce playing at the Whitehall Theatre. A Russian ballet dancer defects to the West having been passed off as a woodworm expert. He comes to the house of a naval officer whose pretty daughter pretends to be an au pair so her fiancé can pretend to be all sorts of farcical characters. Starring Brian Rix with Jacqueline Ellis, Leo Franklyn, Peter Gray, Helen Jessop, Kerry Gardner and Dennis Ramsden.
Stage Director: Wallace Douglas. **Television presentation:** Derek Burrell-Davis.

Cheap at Half the Price — 1 wk

Thames, comedy

This series by Vince Powell and Harry Driver starred Roy Kinnear as the proprietor of the Treasure House antiques shop in Chelsea.

| 1972 | 7.1 | Mon 22 May 8:25 p.m. | 4 | 1 wk |

Roy's ambitions are thwarted by the dimwittedness of his assistant Charlie (Doug Fisher) and his own incompetence. Long-suffering wife Madge (Marjie Lawrence) looks on without amazement.
Producer: Les Chatfield.

Check-Mates — 1 wk

ATV, comedy

This series starred ventriloquist Ray Alan with his dummy Lord Charles.

| 1966 | 6.8 | Wed 18 May 9:40 p.m. | 8 | 1 wk |

Guests: Lynda Baron, Roy Castle, Jack Haig and the King Brothers with the Jack Parnell orchestra.
Producer: Jon Scoffield.

Chessgame — 1 wk

Granada, drama

This spy serial was based on the novels by Anthony Price about the discovery of a twenty-seven-year-old plane wreck in a lake drained for motorway construction.

| 1983 | 11.7 | Wed 23 Nov 9:00 p.m. | 13 | 1 wk |

'Flying Blind'
When the Russians show interest in the wreckage, so too do British intelligence, led by David Audley (Terence Stamp).
Designer: James Weatherup. **Director:** William Brayne. **Producer:** Richard Everitt.

Chester: Portrait of a City — 1 wk

Granada, documentary

| 1973 | 5.2 | Mon 3 Sep 8:30 p.m. | 18 | 1 wk |

Ray Gosling examines Chester's way of life and finds it more or less changeless.
Director: Jim Clark. **Executive Producer:** Mike Scott.

Chief of Detectives — 9 wks

USA presented by ITV, drama

Joe Don Baker starred as Police Chief Eischied in this series set on the streets of New York.

| 1980 | 15.1 | Thu 7 Feb 9:00 p.m. | 11 | 9 wks |

'Friday's Child'
Eischied finds that hardened criminals will stop at nothing, even when a child is involved.

Children in Need — 3 wks

BBC, charity

Sue Cook and Terry Wogan presented a night of fund-raising.

| **1987** | **17.2** | **Fri 27 Nov 9:30 p.m.** | **3** | **2 wks** |

The second part of the evening.

| **1989** | **11.4** | **Fri 17 Nov 7:00 p.m.** | **19** | **1 wk** |

The first part of the show.

....

Children of Courage   4 wks

BBC, documentary

As part of the CHILDREN IN NEED appeal hosted by Terry Wogan and Sue Cook, Esther Rantzen told remarkable stories of young people who had demonstrated extraordinary courage.

1985	**12.9**	**Fri 22 Nov 9:45 p.m.**	**13**	**1 wk**
1987	**14.6**	**Fri 27 Nov 9:45 p.m.**	**8**	**1 wk**
1988	**13.8**	**Fri 18 Nov 9:45 p.m.**	**8**	**1 wk**

Gavin Campbell appears with Esther Rantzen.

| **1989** | **11.1** | **Fri 17 Nov 9:45 p.m.** | **20** | **1 wk** |

Gavin Campbell again helps Esther Rantzen present the inspiring tales.

....

Children of Revolution   1 wk

AR, documentary

| **1965** | **4.6** | **Wed 21 Jul 9:40 p.m.** | **20** | **1 wk** |

A report written and narrated by Robert Kee on the youth of Czecho-slovakia as the first children of the revolution reach maturity.
Director: Randal Beattie. **Executive Producer:** David Windlesham.

....

Children's Royal Variety Performance, The   5 wks

LWT, entertainment

The idea to stage this annual show came from Australian entertainer Rod Hull, who realized the potential to raise considerable amounts of money for a variety of children's hospitals and other charities. HRH The Princess Margaret helped turn Hull's idea into reality.
Stage Director (1982–84): Norman Maen. **Director** (1982–84): Alan Boyd. **Producer** (1982–84): David Bell.

| **1982** | **10.3** | **Sat 28 Aug 6:15 p.m.** | **11** | **1 wk** |

From the Dominion Theatre, London in the presence of HRH The Princess Margaret. Artists include Russ Abbot, Altered Images, Cannon and Ball, Chas and Dave, Petula Clark, Bernie Clifton, Keith Harris, the Krankies, Bonnie Langford, Jon Pertwee, the National Children's orchestra, Shakin' Stevens and the Alyn Ainsworth orchestra.

| **1983** | **11.1** | **Sat 16 Apr 6:45 p.m.** | **9** | **1 wk** |

Presented from Her Majesty's Theatre in the presence of HRH The Princess Margaret in aid of the NSPCC. Artists include Russ Abbot, Keith Chegwin, Jimmy Cricket, Martin Daniels, Roger de Courcey and Nookie Bear, Stu Francis, Dustin Gee, Rod Hull and Emu, and Kajagoogoo, with the Alyn Ainsworth orchestra.

| **1984** | **12.2** | **Sat 23 Jun 6:30 p.m.** | **1** | **1 wk** |

From Her Majesty's Theatre in the presence of HRH The Princess Anne. Artists include Stanley Baxter, Jimmy Cricket, Bucks Fizz, the Grumbleweeds, Rod Hull, Donny Osmond and Gary Wilmot, with the Alyn Ainsworth orchestra.

| **1987** | **9.5** | **Sat 18 Apr 5:55 p.m.** | **18** | **1 wk** |

The BBC presents this year's show. It comes from the London Palladium in the presence of HRH The Princess Margaret, in aid of the NSPCC. Artists include Russ Abbot, Cheryl Baker, Curiosity Killed the Cat, Mark Curry, Martin Daniels, Les Dennis, Wayne Dobson, Five Star, Tim Flavin, Rod Hull, Aled Jones, Little and Large, Joe Longthorne, Lulu, Elaine Paige, Roland Rat, Angela Rippon, Gian Sammarco and Phillip Schofield, with the Ronnie Hazlehurst orchestra.
Producer: Yvonne Littlewood.

| **1989** | **11.9** | **Mon 1 May 5:45 p.m.** | **8** | **1 wk** |

Introduced by Sue Cook for the BBC from the Dominion Theatre, London in the presence of HRH The Princess Margaret. With Andy Crane, Jimmy Cricket, Dana, Martin Daniels, Jason Donovan, Mike Doyle, Tim Flavin, Derek Griffiths, Caron Keating, Rula Lenska, Jessica Martin, Kylie Minogue, Billy Pearce, Su Pollard, Kate Robbins and Gary Wilmot, with the Ronnie Hazlehurst orchestra.
Producer: Brian Whitehouse. **Executive Producer:** Yvonne Littlewood.

....

Child's Play   29 wks

LWT, game show

Host Michael Aspel asked contestants and their celebrity partners to identify a word from a child's description of that word.

| **1984** | **15.3** | **Sat 25 Feb 6:30 p.m.** | **4** | **27 wks** |

Guests: Patricia Brake and David Hamilton.
Directors: John Gorman and Tom Poole. **Producer:** Keith Stewart.
Executive Producer: Alan Boyd.

| **1985** | **11.7** | **Sat 31 Aug 6:30 p.m.** | **13** | **2 wks** |

Guests: Colin Baker and Fiona Hendley.
Director: John Gorman. **Producer:** Richard Hearsey.

Chimera ⬛ 4 wks

Anglia, drama

This four-part thriller set in the world of genetic engineering was adapted by Stephen Gallagher from his own novel. John Lynch and Kenneth Cranham starred.

1991 **9.7** **Sun 14 Jul 9:05 p.m.** **11** **4 wks**

In this second part, a maniac is on the run following a massacre at the Chimera research clinic in North Yorkshire.
Director: Nick Gillott. **Producer:** Lawrence Gordon-Clark.

Chinatown ⬛ 1 wk

Presented by ITV, film

1981 **11.1** **Sat 13 Jun 9:25 p.m.** **18** **1 wk**

This film is set in Los Angeles in 1937. Jack Nicholson plays private investigator J. J. Gittes, who is hired by a woman to research her husband's adultery. Shortly afterwards the suspect's body is fished out of a reservoir and Gittes discovers the woman was not his real wife. Also starring Faye Dunaway and John Huston.
Director: Roman Polanski.

Chintz ⬛ 1 wk

Granada, situation comedy

This series by Alex Adams, Dilys Laye and Peg Lynch concerned a middle-class Cheshire couple, Kate and Richard Carter (Michele Dotrice and Richard Easton), and their neighbours Dottie and Fred Nelson (Dilys Laye and Christopher Benjamin).

1981 **12.2** **Mon 27 Apr 8:00 p.m.** **20** **1 wk**

The first episode, in which an evening playing bridge turns out to be more stimulating than expected.
Director: Eric Prytherch. **Producer:** Brian Armstrong.

Chipperfield's Circus ⬛ 1 wk

ATV, circus

1963 **5.4** **Wed 4 Sep 9:45 p.m.** **10** **1 wk**

Ringmaster Shaw Taylor, assisted by Noele Gordon, introduces highlights from Dick Chipperfield's summer circus.
Director: Stephen Wade.

Chisum ⬛ 1 wk

Presented by BBC, film

1981 **12.2** **Sun 27 Sep 8:20 p.m.** **14** **1 wk**

John Wayne stars in a story of corrupt cattlemen.
Director: Andrew V. McLaglen.

Chitty Chitty Bang Bang ⬛ 1 wk

Presented by BBC, film

1982 **11.5** **Fri 9 Apr 6:20 p.m.** **17** **1 wk**

A musical fantasy about a car with magical powers. Starring Dick Van Dyke and Sally Ann Howes with Gert Frobe, Robert Helpmann, Benny Hill, Lionel Jeffries, James Robertson Justice, Anna Quayle and Barbara Windsor.
Director: Ken Hughes.

Choice of Coward, A ⬛ 2 wks

Granada, drama

A season of four Noël Coward plays, each introduced by the author from his home in Les Avants sur Montreux, Switzerland.

1964 **5.8** **Mon 17 Aug 9:10 p.m.** **8** **2 wks**

'Blithe Spirit' adapted for television by Gerald Savory.
Coward wrote this play at Portmeirion in 1941. It took him just six days from start to completed manuscript. It tells the story of Charles Condomine, an author henpecked and mercilessly tormented by wives both living and dead. He requires help from the improbable, outrageous, bicycling Madame Arcati. Starring Helen Cherry, Joanna Dunham, Hattie Jacques and Griffith Jones.
Director: Joan Kemp-Welch.

Christmas at Robin's Nest ⬛ 1 wk

Thames, situation comedy

The characters from ROBIN'S NEST appeared in a special Christmas edition.

1980 **15.0** **Wed 24 Dec 7:00 p.m.** **13** **1 wk**

'No Room At The Inn'
Robin faces Christmas dinner alone, with Vicky still in hospital after having twins.
Producer: Peter Frazer-Jones.

Christmas Blankety Blank ⬛ 1 wk

BBC, game show

1984 **15.4** **Tue 25 Dec 5:30 p.m.** **11** **1 wk**

Les Dawson introduces Lorraine Chase, Suzanne Danielle, Ken Dodd, Russell Harty, Ruth Madoc and Derek Nimmo. **Director:** David Taylor. **Producer:** John Bishop.

Christmas Blind Date | 1 wk

LWT, game show

| 1987 | 14.5 | Fri 25 Dec 6:45 p.m. | 14 | 1 wk |

Cilla Black hosts a special Christmas edition of the flirtatious game show.
Director: Terry Kinane. **Producer:** Gill Stribling-Wright.

Christmas Cannon and Ball | 1 wk

LWT, comedy

| 1985 | 12.3 | Sat 21 Dec 7:45 p.m. | 9 | 1 wk |

Tommy Cannon and Bobby Ball star in this seasonal special. Guests: Ruth Madoc and Paul Nicholas.
Producer: Marcus Plantin.

Christmas Carry On | 1 wk

Presented by BBC, film

| 1975 | 6.2 | Tue 23 Dec 7:00 p.m. | 11 | 1 wk |

Special Christmas presentation of **'Carry On Up The Khyber'**. It is set in India in 1845. Sid James plays Sir Sidney Ruff-Diamond. With Bernard Bresslaw, Roy Castle, Angela Douglas, Peter Gilmore, Charles Hawtrey, Terry Scott, Joan Sims, Cardew Robinson, Wanda Ventham and Kenneth Williams.
Director: Gerald Thomas.

Christmas Comedy | 1 wk

AR, comedy

| 1964 | 7.5 | Mon 21 Dec 9:10 p.m. | 4 | 1 wk |

'Deep and Crisp and Stolen'
This comedy thriller is set in Tarringes' department store, where there is a plot afoot to rob the store of its Christmas Eve takings. Raymond Francis plays two roles, Detective Chief-Superintendent Lockhart and Percy, a petty conman with a weakness for booze, who happens to be the double of Lockhart. Also starring Maggie Fitzgibbon and Dennis Price with Robert Dorning, Joan Hickson, George Moon, Arthur Mullard and Dennis Lotis. Guest stars: Patrick Allen, Gerald

Flood, Keith Fordyce, Jimmy Hanley, Sam Kydd, Cathy McGowan and Michael Miles.
Writer: Dave Freeman. **Director:** Ronald Marriott. **Executive Producer:** Antony Kearey.

Christmas Eve at the Golden Garter | 1 wk

Granada, entertainment

| 1970 | 5.7 | Thu 24 Dec 10:25 p.m. | 19 | 1 wk |

From the Golden Garter Club in Wythenshaw, Manchester, Peter Noone (Herman of Herman's Hermits) introduces party pieces from Arthur Askey, Lonnie Donegan, Johnny Hackett, Joe 'Mr Piano' Henderson, Edmund Hockridge, Frank Ifield, Shep's Banjo Boys and Joan Turner.
Director: Eric Prytherch. **Producer:** John Hamp.

Christmas Family Fortunes | 1 wk

Central, game show

| 1983 | 12.6 | Fri 23 Dec 7:00 p.m. | 7 | 1 wk |

Max Bygraves presents a celebrity edition with a team from TV-am (Anne Diamond, Nick Owen, John Stapleton, Lizzie Webb and Wincey Willis) competing against a team of Agony Aunts (Katie Boyle, Virginia Ironside, Marjorie Proops, Deirdre Sanders and Claire Rayner).
Director: David Millard. **Producer:** William G. Stewart.

Christmas Generation Game, The | 1 wk

BBC, game show

| 1990 | 16.7 | Tue 25 Dec 6:25 p.m. | 9 | 1 wk |

Bruce Forsyth stars with Rosemarie Ford.
Director: Sylvie Boden. **Producer:** David Taylor.

Christmas in Coronation Street | 1 wk

Granada, drama

| 1968 | 5.9 | Sat 28 Dec 6:15 p.m. | 15 | 1 wk |

While Jack and Annie Walker (Arthur Leslie and Doris Speed) clear the Rover's Return of the aftermath of the holiday season, they conjure up memories of Christmases past.
Writers: H.V. Kershaw, Geoffrey Lancashire, Jack Rosenthal and Tony Warren. **Director:** Tim Jones. **Producer:** H.V. Kershaw.

Christmas Night with the Stars — 5 wks

BBC, entertainment

Producers included Graeme Muir (1962–64) and Stewart Morris (1967–68).

| 1962 | 4.6 | Tue 25 Dec 7:15 p.m. | 20 | 1 wk |

Eamonn Andrews introduces specially recorded Christmas contribu-- tions from the casts of BBC shows including THE BILLY COTTON BAND SHOW, THE BLACK AND WHITE MINSTRELS, DIXON OF DOCK GREEN, THE RAG TRADE and THE WHITE HEATHER CLUB.

| 1963 | 5.4 | Wed 25 Dec 8:05 p.m. | 11 | 1 wk |

Introduced by Eamonn Andrews with contributions from Stanley Baxter, Michael Bentine, the Black and White Minstrels, MARRIAGE LINES (Richard Briers and Prunella Scales), Russ Conway, Billy Cotton, the cast of DIXON OF DOCK GREEN, Dick Emery, Kenneth McKellar, Nina and Frederik, Terry Scott and Hugh Lloyd and Andy Stewart. With the Harry Rabinowitz orchestra.

| 1964 | 4.6 | Fri 25 Dec 7:15 p.m. | 19 | 1 wk |

Jack Warner introduces the Barron Knights, the Black and White Minstrels, Roy Castle, Billy Cotton, Dick Emery, Benny Hill, Kathy Kirby, THE LIKELY LADS (Rodney Bewes and James Bolam), MARRIAGE LINES (Richard Briers and Prunella Scales), MEET THE WIFE (Freddie Frinton and Thora Hird), Terry Scott and Hugh Lloyd, and Andy Stewart with the Harry Rabinowitz orchestra.

| 1967 | 6.2 | Mon 25 Dec 6:40 p.m. | 12 | 1 wk |

Introduced by Rolf Harris with Cilla Black, Billy Cotton, Val Doonican, Roy Hudd, Lulu, David Nixon, Beryl Reid, Sandie Shaw, Kenneth Williams and Harry Worth with the casts of BEGGAR MY NEIGHBOUR, STEPTOE AND SON and TILL DEATH US DO PART. With the Alyn Ainsworth orchestra.

| 1968 | 5.4 | Wed 25 Dec 6:40 p.m. | 20 | 1 wk |

Eric Morecambe and Ernie Wise introduce Louis Armstrong, Petula Clark, Rolf Harris, Jimmy Logan, Lulu, Kenneth McKellar, Nana Mouskouri, Cliff Richard, the Seekers and the Young Generation with excerpts from RAY ALAN'S ICE CABARET, MARTY FELDMAN, OH BROTHER, NOT IN FRONT OF THE CHILDREN, DAD'S ARMY and HARRY WORTH. With the Alyn Ainsworth orchestra.

Christmas Punchlines — 1 wk

LWT, game show

| 1984 | 12.8 | Sat 22 Dec 6:10 p.m. | 15 | 1 wk |

Lennie Bennett introduces Patti Boulaye, Faith Brown, Freddie Davis, Jayne Irving, Dave Lee Travis, Kenny Lynch, Bernard Manning, Mike Reid, Isla St Clair and June Whitfield.
Director: Vic Finch. **Producer:** Noel D. Greene. **Executive Producer:** Alan Boyd.

Christmas Surprise Surprise — 1 wk

LWT, entertainment

| 1984 | 12.4 | Sun 23 Dec 8:15 p.m. | 18 | 1 wk |

Cilla Black stars with Christopher Biggins.
Directors: Phil Bishop, John Gorman and Tom Poole. **Producers:** Bob Merrilees and Brian Wesley. **Executive Producer:** Alan Boyd.

Christmas Telly Addicts — 1 wk

BBC, game show

| 1988 | 13.4 | Fri 23 Dec 7:00 p.m. | 14 | 1 wk |

Noel Edmonds introduces Bill Cotton's Brigade versus Michael Grade's All Stars.
Director: Nick Hurran. **Producers:** Richard Lewis and Tim Manning. **Executive Producer:** John King.

Christmas Who Do You Do? — 1 wk

LWT, entertainment

The mimics from WHO DO YOU DO? presented their seasonal special edition.

| 1974 | 6.4 | Sun 29 Dec 7:25 p.m. | 8 | 1 wk |

Freddie Starr leads the impressionists' Christmas party, with Janet Brown, Mike Goddard, Peter Goodwright, Aiden J. Harvey, Johnny More and Paula Scott.
Producer: John Scoffield.

Christmas with Kojak — 1 wk

Presented by BBC, drama

| 1975 | 6.1 | Wed 24 Dec 9:10 p.m. | 15 | 1 wk |

'A Question of Answers'
A full-length film with guest star Eli Wallach. A desperate man tries to clear his name and escape imprisonment by helping Kojak (Telly Savalas) trap a ruthless loan shark.

Christmas with Shelley
1 wk

Thames, situation comedy

1980	16.8	Mon 22 Dec 8:00 p.m.	5	1 wk

Shelley (Hywel Bennett) and Fran (Belinda Sinclair) have an early Christmas dinner before the real one with their parents. Some unexpected guests arrive.
Writer: Peter Tilbury. **Producer:** Anthony Parker.

Christmas with Terry and June
1 wk

BBC, situation comedy

1982	10.6	Fri 24 Dec 8:40 p.m.	14	1 wk

Terry Scott and June Whitfield sit down for Christmas dinner with Sir Dennis Hodge (Reginald Marsh), Malcolm and Beattie (Tim Barrett and Rosemary Frankau) and Miss Fennel (Joanna Henderson).
Writer: John Kane. **Producer:** Peter Whitmore.

Chubby Checker Show, The
1 wk

ATV, music

1962	4.2	Fri 7 Sep 10:10 p.m.	15	1 wk

The 'King of the Twist' arrives for his first British special with guests including the Brook Brothers, Valerie Masters and the Red Price orchestra.
Producer: Dicky Leeman.

Cilla
30 wks

BBC, entertainment

Cilla Black first came to notice in October 1963 with her recording of the Lennon-McCartney song 'The Love of the Loved'. She became the country's top female television entertainment personality. In this series, transmitted live, Cilla talked to members of the public using outside broadcast units. She also helped some of them to realize their unusual ambitions.
Choreographer (1971, 1973, 1976): Irving Davies. **Musical Director** (1971, 1973, 1976): Ronnie Hazlehurst. **Producer** (1968, 1971, 1973): Michael Hurll.

1968	7.0	Tue 5 Mar 8:00 p.m.	9	8 wks

Cilla's series features Cliff Richard singing a contender for 'A Song For Europe' each week. ('Congratulations' was chosen.) Also includes guests Terry Scott, Hugh Lloyd and Mike Yarwood.
Musical Director: Harry Rabinowitz.

1971	7.4	Sat 13 Feb 7:40 p.m.	7	12 wks

Guests: Noel Harrison, Stanley Holloway and Ringo Starr.

1973	7.9	Sat 3 Mar 8:15 p.m.	2	9 wks

Cliff Richard sings one of the songs competing to represent the United Kingdom in the 1973 EUROVISION SONG CONTEST. ('Power to All Our Friends' was chosen.)

1976	7.3	Sat 21 Feb 8:15 p.m.	10	1 wk

Guests: Dana, Diana Dors and Roy Hudd.
Producer: James Moir.

Cilla
1 wk

Thames, entertainment

1978	12.3	Wed 24 May 8:00 p.m.	9	1 wk

This one-hour special stars Cilla Black with guests Frankie Howerd, Lewis Collins, Irene Handl, Nicholas Parsons, Joan Sims and the Irving Davies dancers.
Producer: Dennis Kirkland.

Cilla at the Savoy
1 wk

AR, music

1966	6.9	Wed 6 Jul 9:40 p.m.	3	1 wk

Cilla Black stars in her own spectacular from the Savoy Hotel, London, with the Peter Gordeno dancers and the George Martin orchestra.
Producer: John Robins.

Cilla Black
1 wk

BBC, entertainment

1970	5.8	Thu 10 Sep 9:10 p.m.	12	1 wk

Cilla has just won the Female Personality of the Year in the Sun newspaper's television awards. This programme is a compilation of highlights from her last series. Guests: Peter Cook, Ronnie Corbett, The Hollies and Des O'Connor with the Irving Davies dancers.
Producer: Michael Hurll.

Cilla's Comedy Six · 6 wks

ATV, comedy

This series of six half-hour comedies was written by Ronnie Taylor, each starring Cilla Black in a different role with different supporting casts.

1975 · **8.8** · **Wed 29 Jan 8:00 p.m.** · **3** · **6 wks**

'Sea View'
Fun and games for Thelma (Cilla) and Barry Fosset (Alan Rothwell) when they take the kids for a seaside break.
Producer: Les Chatfield.

....

Cilla's World of Comedy · 1 wk

ATV, comedy

Following the success of CILLA'S COMEDY SIX Cilla again teamed up with writer Ronnie Taylor for another series.

1976 · **5.9** · **Tue 31 Aug 8:00 p.m.** · **19** · **1 wk**

'She'll Have To Go'
Linda (Cilla Black) is married to Henry (Keith Barron) is waging a war of silence with her mother-in-law (Dorothy Reynolds).
Producer: Les Chatfield.

....

Cimarron Strip · 1 wk

USA presented by ITV, western

This series was set in the 1880s. The US government had given ten million acres to Indian tribes west of the Cimarron river. To the other side lay a 100,000 square mile strip of land, where settlers and cattlemen resented the presence of the Indians. Stuart Whitman played Marshal Jim Crown, whose job was to keep the peace. He was aided by deputies Macgregor (Percy Herbert) and Francis (Randy Boone). Jill Townsend appeared as Dulcey, a close friend of Marshal Crown.
Producer: Phillip Leacock.

1967 · **6.3** · **Sat 11 Nov 10:05 p.m.** · **16** · **1 wk**

'Whitey'
A young bandit kidnaps Dulcey and threatens to kill her unless Crown agrees to try to convict his former outlaw boss for murder.

....

Cinema · 186 wks

Granada, entertainment

This programme linked film clips to the star, director or theme of new releases. Leslie Halliwell was advisor throughout. Presenters: Mike Scott (1965–68) and Michael Parkinson (1969–71).
Directors (1969-71): Mike Becker. **Producer** (1965, 1969–71): John Hamp.

1964 · **6.5** · **Wed 7 Oct 7:00 p.m.** · **8** · **14 wks**

Bamber Gascoigne looks at films from today and yesterday including Carl Foreman's anti-war film THE VICTORS and the new Italian comedy YESTERDAY, TODAY AND TOMORROW.
Director: Peter Jones. **Producer:** Derek Granger (who became the presenter from 4 November 1964).

1965 · **7.7** · **Fri 17 Dec 9:10 p.m.** · **5** · **42 wks**

The spotlight shines on the films of Norman Wisdom and Jerry Lewis.
Director: Philip Casson.

1966 · **8.3** · **Wed 26 Oct 9:10 p.m.** · **2** · **48 wks**

Director: Mike Beckham. **Producer:** Peter Wildeblood.

1967 · **8.0** · **Wed 15 Mar 9:10 p.m.** · **2** · **40 wks**

Director: Richard Guinea. **Producer:** Peter Wildeblood.

1968 · **7.6** · **Wed 31 Jan 9:30 p.m.** · **1** · **23 wks**

Director: Bill Podmore. **Producer:** Mark Shivas.

1969 · **5.3** · **Thu 26 Jun 10:30 p.m.** · **16** · **11 wks**

The feature is on comedy westerns.

1970 · **5.5** · **Thu 17 Aug 9:30 p.m.** · **12** · **7 wks**

Michael Parkinson talks to Sir Alec Guinness and shows clips from many of Sir Alec's films, including the latest, CROMWELL, in which he plays Charles I.

1971 · **4.8** · **Thu 3 Jun 10:30 p.m.** · **20** · **1 wk**

....

Circus Comes to Town, The · 6 wks

Granada, circus

From the late 1950s until 1966 Granada recorded highlights of the annual winter circus from King's Hall, Belle Vue Pleasure Gardens in Manchester. George Lockhart, 80 years old in 1960, was ringmaster for all but the final broadcast.
Directors included David Warwick (1960–62, 1966) and Eric Harrison (1964–65). **Producers** included Barrie Heads (1960–62) and John Hamp (1964–66).

1960 · **6.1** · **Wed 5 Oct 8:30 p.m.** · **9** · **1 wk**

Performers include Rudi Lenz and his chimpanzees, Nadia Houckes and her Liberty Horses, the Two Primlettys performing the Dive of Death and all the clowns and acrobats of the circus.

| 1961 | 6.6 | Tue 10 Oct 8:00 p.m. | 6 | 1 wk |

Performers include the Four Prietos, Moritz Bhulman's Lions, Nock and Max, and Phyllis Allen's Poodles.

| 1962 | 4.8 | Wed 22 Aug 9:45 p.m. | 9 | 1 wk |

The Belle Vue Circus includes an act new to Britain, Karah Khavak's crocodiles, with Arturo Segura, King's Sea Lions, Robert's Five Baby Elephants and The Brandt Troupe.

| 1964 | 5.4 | Wed 7 Oct 9:50 p.m. | 20 | 1 wk |

Performers include the Austins, Robert's Baby Elephants, the Two Wolmedays, Nadia's Horses and the Alcarez Troupe.

| 1965 | 5.9 | Wed 24 Mar 9:40 p.m. | 16 | 1 wk |

Featuring international circus acts.

| 1966 | 6.7 | Fri 30 Dec 7:30 p.m. | 7 | 1 wk |

With a star-studded international cast.

Circus from Paris | 1 wk

BBC, circus

| 1962 | 3.5 | Mon 6 Aug 5:00 p.m. | 17 | 1 wk |

'From France's Gay Capital' comes a holiday circus with the accent on youth, recorded on the Eurovision link direct from the Cirque d'Hiver, Paris, and introduced by Robin Scott.
Television presentation: Derek Burrell-Davis.

Citadel, The | 1 wk

AR, drama

A.J. Cronin's story was adapted for television in nine parts by Kenneth Hyde. Set in the 1920s and 1930s, the drama spanned ten years in the life of Dr Andrew Manson (Eric Lander), who began his professional life with high ideals and determination but soon became disillusioned in his first practice in South Wales and moved to Harley Street. Also starred Zena Walker as Christine Barlow and Jack May as Philip Denny.

| 1960 | 5.5 | Wed 28 Dec 8:55 p.m. | 8 | 1 wk |

As the practice becomes more and more fashionable, Dr Manson finds his time occupied by his rich patients, leaving little time for those really in need.
Designer: Frank Nerini. **Director:** John Frankau. **Producer:** Peter Graham Scott.

Citadel, The | 9 wks

BBC, drama

Re-make of the above A.J. Cronin story. The ten-part dramatization by Don Shaw starred Ben Cross as Dr Andrew Manson.

| 1983 | 13.4 | Thu 17 Mar 9:25 p.m. | 4 | 9 wks |

Episode Ten
Andrew is assisting Charles Ivory (John Nettleton) in an operation and begins to see all the rich patients in a new light.
Designer: Chris Edwards. **Director:** Mike Vardy. **Producer:** Ken Riddington.

Citizen James | 5 wks

BBC, situation comedy

TV's favourite Cockney, Sid James, was born in South Africa and only came to London in 1946. He played the stooge to Tony Hancock in HANCOCK'S HALF HOUR and starred in most of the CARRY ON films. He also starred in BLESS THIS HOUSE. He died in 1976. In CITIZEN JAMES he played a public-spirited doer of good deeds, battler for lost causes and champion of the underdog who invariably got bitten himself.

| 1962 | 5.4 | Fri 2 Nov 9:25 p.m. | 15 | 5 wks |

'The Watchdog'
Also starring Irene Handl and Sydney Tafler.
Writers: Sid Green and Dick Hills. **Producer:** Ronald Marsh.

Citizen Smith | 10 wks

BBC, situation comedy

This series by John Sullivan starred Robert Lindsay as Wolfie Smith, a drop-out and would-be revolutionary leader of the Tooting Popular Front. Cheryl Hall played his long-suffering girlfriend Shirley. Her parents were played by Hilda Braid and Peter Vaughan.

| 1979 | 21.8 | Thu 4 Oct 8:25 p.m. | 6 | 9 wks |

'The Big Job'
Smith comes face to face with a car salesman (Derek Newmark).
Director: Ray Butt. **Producer:** Dennis Main Wilson.

| 1981 | 9.4 | Thu 27 Aug 8:00 p.m. | 13 | 1 wk |

'Sweet Sorrow'
Repeat of the episode in which Wolfie finds trouble while trying to save Tooting single-handed.
Producer: Ray Butt.

C

City, The

`1 wk`

ATV, documentary

| 1963 | 4.3 | Wed 17 Jul 9:45 p.m. | 20 | 1 wk |

Fewer than five thousand people live within the City of London, yet more than four hundred thousand come to work there every day. The programme questions whether the City works as well as it might in the second half of the twentieth century. Written and narrated by Paul Ferris.
Producer: James Bredin.

City '68

`1 wk`

Granada, drama

Series of single plays.

| 1968 | 6.2 | Fri 2 Feb 9:00 p.m. | 20 | 1 wk |

'Love Thy Neighbour' by Anthony Skene, based on an idea by John Finch.
This story of a particularly un-English outbreak of good neighbourliness stars John Barrett, A.J. Brown, Bernard Hepton, Yootha Joyce, Reginald Marsh, Charlotte Mitchell, June Ritchie and Wanda Ventham. Julie Goodyear appears as a serving lady.
Designer: Denis Parkin. **Director:** Cyril Coke. **Producer:** H.V. Kershaw.

Claire

`3 wks`

BBC, drama

This six-part series by Alick Rowe concerned the child Claire (Caroline Embling) who was fostered with the hope of adoption. William Gaunt and Lynn Farleigh played foster parents Tony and Pam Hunter. Neil Nisbet portrayed their natural son Robert.

| 1982 | 11.0 | Thu 7 Oct 9:25 p.m. | 13 | 3 wks |

Part Five
Claire has run away following an uneasy sexual encounter with Robert and a suggestion from Pam that she may prefer to return to the children's home.
Designer: Sally Engelbach. **Director:** John Gorrie. **Producer:** Ron Craddock.

Clash of the Titans

`1 wk`

Presented by BBC, film

| 1986 | 15.9 | Wed 1 Jan 6:20 p.m. | 4 | 1 wk |

Perseus (Harry Hamlin), son of Zeus (Laurence Olivier), sets out to overcome the terrifying obstacles placed in his path by the Gods on Mount Olympus to win the love of Andromeda (Judi Bowker). Also starring Ursula Andress, Claire Bloom, Burgess Meredith, Sian Phillips, Flora Robson and Maggie Smith.
Director: Desmond Davis.

Clayhanger

`1 wk`

ATV, drama

Arnold Beckett's epic saga of two generations of a Potteries family in the nineteenth century, adapted by Douglas Livingstone in twenty-six parts. Principal players included Harry Andrews, Peter McEnery, Denholm Elliott, Joyce Redman and Janet Suzman.

| 1976 | 4.8 | Thu 24 Jun 8:30 p.m. | 20 | 1 wk |

'The Discovery'
Hilda Clayhanger (Janet Suzman) has decided she and Edwin (Peter McEnery) will live in the country.
Designer: Michael Bailey. **Director:** John Davies. **Producers:** David Reid and Douglas Livingstone. **Executive Producer:** Stella Richman.

Cliff

`3 wks`

ATV, music

| 1961 | 6.1 | Thu 16 Feb 8:10 p.m. | 8 | 1 wk |

With his new record, 'Theme for a Dream', about to enter the charts, Cliff Richard stars in his own show with the Shadows and the Vernons Girls. Guest: Petula Clark.
Producer: Dinah Thetford.

| 1964 | 5.8 | Wed 1 Jul 9:40 p.m. | 7 | 1 wk |

Guest: Liza Minnelli.
Producer: Jon Scoffield.

| 1967 | 6.0 | Wed 24 May 9:40 p.m. | 10 | 1 wk |

Producer: Dicky Leeman.

Cliff and the Shadows

`3 wks`

ATV, music

This series featured Cliff Richard and his backing band.

| 1965 | 7.6 | Wed 13 Oct 9:15 p.m. | 6 | 3 wks |

With the Malcolm Clare dancers, the Mike Sammes singers and the Jack Parnell orchestra.
Producer: Colin Clews.

Cliff Richard Show, The — 2 wks

ATV, music

With his first solo series, Cliff began to move away from the image of the pouting, moody rock star which had been created for him by Jack Good on ABC's OH BOY. The emerging all-round entertainer was given the ATV gloss, surrounded by dancers and a large orchestra.

| 1960 | 4.5 | Sat 30 Jul 8:00 p.m. | 6 | 1 wk |

Guests: Cherry Wainer, Barbara Windsor and Mike and Bernie Winters with the George Carden dancers and the Jack Parnell orchestra.
Producer: Albert Locke.

| 1963 | 5.8 | Sun 28 Apr 7:25 p.m. | 9 | 1 wk |

Guests: The Shadows, Daley and Wayne, Sid James and Millicent Martin.
Choreographer: Douglas Squires. **Musical Director:** Harry Rabinowitz. **Producer:** Neville Wortman.

Clint Eastwood Movie, The — 6 wks

Presented by ITV, film

A season of films starring Clint Eastwood.

| 1986 | 9.9 | Sat 23 Aug 9:15 p.m. | 7 | 3 wks |

'The Outlaw Josey Wales' (See separate entry.)

| 1987 | 14.7 | Thu 8 Jan 8:00 p.m. | 4 | 3 wks |

'Joe Kidd'
A bounty hunter goes in search of the leader of a gang of Mexican bandits.
Director: John Sturges.

Clive James Finally Meets Frank Sinatra — 1 wk

BBC, documentary

| 1988 | 9.8 | Wed 31 Aug 9:30 p.m. | 20 | 1 wk |

Clive James travels to his native Australia to host the first Frank Sinatra concert there since the singer and the nation's press went to war in 1974. Ol' Blue Eyes had said he would never set foot there again. An eccentric millionaire has persuaded him to reconsider. After an extraordinary week, James meets the singer for just a few minutes.
Director: Paul Ransley. **Producer:** Richard Drewett.

Clive James on Television — 12 wks

LWT, entertainment

In this series Clive James presented amusing and bizarre selections from other nations' television programmes.
Directors included Peter Swain (1984, 1987) and Nick Vaughan-Barratt (1986, 1988). **Producer** (1986–88): Nicholas Barratt. **Executive producer:** Richard Drewett.

| 1984 | 14.0 | Sun 18 Nov 10:00 p.m. | 11 | 3 wks |

The themes are Japanese game shows and the underwear advertising war.
Producer: Nick Vaughan-Barratt.

| 1986 | 12.7 | Sun 28 Dec 9:15 p.m. | 19 | 2 wks |

A look at the proliferation of strippers and nude performers on French and European satellite television.

| 1987 | 15.1 | Sun 15 Mar 9:00 p.m. | 3 | 5 wks |

A worldwide examination of the reactions of contestants on game shows.

| 1988 | 9.8 | Sun 21 Aug 8:15 p.m. | 12 | 2 wks |

Repeat showing of the top 1986 show.

Clive James – Postcard from Miami — 2 wks

BBC, documentary

In this series Clive James went to discover if the vice capital lived down to its reputation.

| 1990 | 9.1 | Thu 17 May 9:30 p.m. | 16 | 2 wks |

James explores the underworld and then meets Don Johnson and Gloria Estefan.
Director: Alan Lewens. **Producer:** Beatrice Ballard.

Clive James's Postcard from Sydney — 2 wks

BBC, documentary

| 1991 | 9.1 | Thu 30 May 9:35 p.m. | 18 | 2 wks |

James examines the changes in his home town since he left thirty years ago.
Producer: Elaine Bedell. **Executive Producer:** Richard Drewett.

C

Close Encounters of the Third Kind				2 wks

Presented by ITV, film

1981	14.8	Mon 28 Dec 7:30 p.m.	4	1 wk

Richard Dreyfuss stars as Ray Neary, an electrical repairman in Indiana who sees UFOs, thus setting off a startling chain of events. **Director:** Steven Spielberg.

1983	10.0	Sat 3 Sep 7:20 p.m.	9	1 wk

Repeat showing of the above film.

Club Night		1 wk

BBC, entertainment

The mid-sixties saw the boom of the northern working-men's clubs and cabarets. This series, hosted by crooner Donald Peers, came from the Palace Theatre Club, Offerton, near Stockport.

1964	8.0	Fri 3 Jul 9:25 p.m.	1	1 wk

With the Clark Brothers, Hope and Keen, Kevin Kent, Johnny Laycock, Anne Shelton and the Harry Hayward orchestra.
Director: Douglas Argent. **Producer:** Albert Stevenson.

Clue		1 wk

Presented by BBC, film

1989	9.1	Tue 20 Jun 9:30 p.m.	13	1 wk

This adaptation of the board game Cluedo stars Eileen Brennan as Mrs Peacock, Tim Curry as Wadsworth, Madeline Kahn as Mrs White, Christopher Lloyd as Professor Plum, Michael McKean as Mr Green, Martin Mull as Colonel Mustard and Lesley Ann Warren as Miss Scarlet.
Writer and **Director:** Jonathan Lynn.

Cluedo		4 wks

Granada, game show

This programme based on the board game of the same name had a high content of drama. A murder was acted out and guest panellists questioned the characters to ascertain the identity of the killer.

1990	9.2	Wed 15 Aug 7:00 p.m.	20	2 wks

James Bellini presents. Suspects: Mrs Peacock (Stephanie Beacham), Colonel Mustard (Robin Ellis), Reverend Green (Robin Nedwell), Professor Plum (Kristoffer Tabori), Miss Scarlet (Tracy-Louise Ward), Mrs White (June Whitfield), Mrs Hope (Joanna Van Gyseghem) and Mr Hope (Paul Darrow). Sleuths include Thelma Barlow and Ned Sherrin.

Director: John Kaye Cooper. **Producer:** Stephen Leahy. **Executive Producer:** Dianne Nelmes.

1991	10.1	Wed 24 Apr 7:00 p.m.	17	2 wks

Chris Tarrant presents. Suspects: Colonel Mustard (Michael Jayston), Mrs Peacock (Rula Lenska), Professor Plum (David McCallum), Miss Scarlett (Koo Stark), Mrs White (Mollie Sugden) and Reverend Green (Richard Wilson). Sleuths: Matthew Kelly, John McArdle, Michaela Strachan and Sally Whittaker.
Producer: Kieran Roberts. **Executive producer:** Dianne Nelmes.

Cluff		2 wks

BBC, drama

This six-part series created by Gil North starred Leslie Sands as Sergeant Cluff, a character created by the same writer in his earlier series DETECTIVE. Cluff set about fighting crime in the Yorkshire town of Gummershaw armed with a stick, a pipe and a black-and-tan dog named Clive. Cluff's colleague Inspector Mole was played by Eric Barker.

1964	5.9	Mon 31 Aug 9:25 p.m.	11	2 wks

'The Daughter-In-Law'
Cautiously and methodically Cluff probes the problems created by Miriam Bateson (Alethea Charlton). Guest star Wilfrid Lawson with James Bolam, Maggie Fitzgibbon and Eileen Way.
Designer: Geoff Kirkland. **Director:** Paul Bernard. **Producer:** Terence Dudley.

Cocoon		1 wk

Presented by ITV, film

1989	12.9	Mon 28 Aug 8:00 p.m.	7	1 wk

Aliens leave giant pods in a swimming pool where the residents of a Florida old people's home are rejuvenated. Some of the old folk choose to enjoy eternal youth in another galaxy. Starring Don Ameche, Wilford Brimley, Hume Cronyn, Jack Gilford, Steve Guttenberg, Maureen Stapleton, Jessica Tandy and Gwen Verdon. **Director:** Ron Howard.

Colbys, The		3 wks

USA presented by BBC, soap

This spinoff series from DYNASTY dealt with one branch of the Carrington family. The leading characters were Jason Colby (Charlton Heston), Constance Colby Patterson (Barbara Stanwyck), Jeff Colby (John James), Francesca Scott Colby Hamilton (Katharine Ross), Sable Colby (Stephanie Beacham), Fallon Colby (Emma Samms), Miles Colby (Maxwell Caulfield), Zack Powers (Ricardo Montalban), Monica Colby (Tracy Scoggins) and Garrett Boydston (Ken Howard).

| 1986 | 10.4 | Fri 30 May 8:10 p.m. | 7 | 3 wks |

'Fallon's Choice' by Doris Silverton.
Jeff and Fallon's son fights for his life in hospital.
Director: Curtis Harrington.

....

Colditz — 17 wks

BBC (co-production with Universal), drama

This series was based on THE COLDITZ STORY and set in Colditz castle in eastern Germany, where Allied officers were held after capture during the Second World War. Devised by Brian Degas and Gerard Glaister and starring David McCallum, Edward Hardwicke, Jack Hedley, Bernard Hepton, Christopher Neame and Hans Meyer.
Director (1972 and 1974): Viktors Ritelis. **Producer:** Gerard Glaister.

| 1972 | 7.5 | Thu 16 Nov 9:25 p.m. | 3 | 11 wks |

'Maximum Security' by John Kruse.
Security is intensified as the SS threaten to take over control of Colditz.

| 1973 | 8.4 | Thu 18 Jan 9:25 p.m. | 2 | 4 wks |

'Gone Away' by John Brason.
Valuable inside knowledge of a German garrison makes an ingenious escape plan possible.
Director: William Slater.

| 1974 | 7.0 | Mon 1 Apr 9:25 p.m. | 12 | 2 wks |

'Liberation' by Ivan Moffatt.
The prisoners fear for their own safety as American tanks are spotted advancing on the town. Major Carrington tries to get through to American lines. With special guest appearance by Robert Wagner as Major Carrington.

....

Colditz Story, The — 1 wk

Presented by BBC, film

| 1970 | 6.0 | Mon 30 Mar 9:35 p.m. | 15 | 1 wk |

Bank Holiday Monday screening. During the war the heavily guarded Colditz castle in Saxony was used as a prison for Allied officers who had already escaped from other camps. They made even more ingenious plans to get out of Colditz. Starring John Mills and Eric Portman with Ian Carmichael, Bryan Forbes, Lionel Jeffries and Christopher Rhodes.
Writer and **Director:** Guy Hamilton.

....

Colonel Trumper's Private War — 3 wks

Granada, situation comedy

In the summer of 1940 Britain stood alone with Colonel Trumper (Dennis Price) her secret weapon. He was assisted on dangerous missions for counter intelligence by Pan Malcov (Warren Mitchell), Lt. Hasting (William Gaunt) and Hicks (George Tovey).

| 1961 | 5.3 | Fri 15 Sep 8:55 p.m. | 12 | 3 wks |

'Operation Lubenski'
Colonel Trumper is chosen to lead a mission to rescue a Polish professor.
Writers: Bill Craig, Barry Took, Dick Vosburgh and Hugh Woodhouse.
Director: Stuart Latham. **Producer:** Peter Eton.

....

Columbo — 24 wks

USA presented by BBC, drama

Peter Falk starred as scruffy Los Angeles homicide detective Lieutenant Columbo, who always wore a grubby raincoat and rumpled suit. His tenacity as an interrogator always led to the successful conclusion of his investigations. Created and produced by Richard Levinson and William Link.

| 1979 | 14.1 | Sun 15 Apr 8:15 p.m. | 10 | 2 wks |

'Murder Under Glass'
Food critic Paul Gerard (Louis Jourdan) blackmails restaurateurs in exchange for good reviews in his column.

| 1988 | 10.2 | Sat 23 Jul 8:40 p.m. | 8 | 3 wks |

'Candidate for Crime'
Lieutenant Columbo investigates murder on the political campaign trail.

| 1989 | 11.9 | Sat 3 Jun 8:15 p.m. | 7 | 16 wks |

'Troubled Waters'
The passenger list of a sunshine pleasure cruise contains a murderer. With guest star Robert Vaughn and veteran actor Ben Gazzara as director of this episode.

| 1991 | 11.7 | Sat 23 Feb 7:40 p.m. | 17 | 3 wks |

'Murder, Smoke and Shadows'
In this feature-length episode a book about a famous film director is the only clue in the death of a man whose body is found on Malibu Beach.

....

Donald Peers leads the singalong in **Club Night**.

Comancheros, The   1 wk

Presented by BBC, film

| 1966 | 5.3 | Sun 25 Dec 8:45 p.m. | 19 | 1 wk |

John Wayne and Lee Marvin star in the story of a Ranger and his prisoner who join forces to fight renegade gunmen.
Director: Michael Curtiz.

....

Come and Get Your Money   1 wk

Granada, documentary

| 1967 | 6.4 | Wed 25 Jan 9:40 p.m. | 13 | 1 wk |

Ten years after Tommy Steele's debut as a rock 'n' roll star, he is seen on the film set of HALF A SIXPENCE. What fates befell his contemporary rockers? The programme meets Steele, Lionel Bart, Terry Dene, Wee Willie Harris, Mickie Most and Screaming Lord Sutch.
Director: Philip Casson. **Producer:** John Hamp.

....

Come Dancing   8 wks

BBC, entertainment

Long-running series featuring amateur and professional ballroom dancers, sometimes in exhibition, sometimes in competition.

| 1961 | 4.2 | Mon 18 Dec 10:15 p.m. | 20 | 1 wk |

Peter West introduces the sixth heat in the nationwide amateur contest for the BBC Television Award and the Formation Team Cup. The North West competes against East Scotland. In the North West at the Ritz Ballroom, Manchester, are Phil Moss and his orchestra with compere Geoffrey Wheeler. (Producer: Ray Lakeland.) In East Scotland from the Palais, Edinburgh are Nat Allen and his orchestra with compere Leonard Maguire. (Producer: Robert Stewart.)
Series Director: Reg Perrin. **Executive Producer:** Barrie Edgar.

| 1962 | 5.0 | Mon 26 Feb 10:20 p.m. | 16 | 2 wks |

Peter West presents the final of the inter-regional contest between the North West and South London. In the North West at the Ritz Ballroom, Manchester are compere Geoffrey Wheeler and the Phil Moss orchestra (Producer: Ray Lakeland) and in South London at the Streatham Locarno are compere Keith Fordyce and the Denny Boyce orchestra (Producer: Barrie Edgar).

| 1965 | 6.7 | Mon 22 Nov 9:50 p.m. | 13 | 1 wk |

The West Midlands' team, from the ballroom in Coventry, with music by the Colin Hulme orchestra and compere James Lloyd (Producer: Barrie Edgar), compete against the North West team in Manchester, with music by the Phil Moss orchestra and compere Geoffrey Wheeler (Producer: Ray Lakelend). Introduced by Peter West.
Series Producer: Philip Lewis.

| 1968 | 6.9 | Mon 25 Mar 9:55 p.m. | 7 | 1 wk |

Peter West introduces the grand final with compere Keith Fordyce and the Johnny Howard band in Purley with the Home Counties competitors (Producers: Douglas Hespe and Reg Perrin). Alex MacIntosh and the Ken Mackintosh orchestra are in Glasgow with the West Scotland competitors (Producer: Charles Clifford).
Executive Producer: Philip Lewis.

| 1969 | 5.7 | Fri 25 Apr 9:05 p.m. | 16 | 1 wk |

Peter West introduces the final between Home Counties North, compere Don Moss with Ray McVay and his orchestra (Producers: Douglas Hespe and Reg Perrin), and the North West, compere Stuart Hall with Phil Moss and his orchestra (Producer: Ray Lakeland).
Executive Producer: Philip Lewis.

| 1979 | 16.3 | Wed 29 Aug 9:25 p.m. | 11 | 1 wk |

From the Assembly Rooms in Derby Terry Wogan introduces the second of this year's semi-finals between Northern Ireland and the North West. Ray Moore is the commentator and the music is by Andy Ross, his orchestra and chorus.
Director: Simon Betts. **Producer:** Ken Griffin.

| 1985 | 9.6 | Thu 22 Aug 9:25 p.m. | 12 | 1 wk |

David Jacobs introduces the final of the thirty-fifth series from the Hammersmith Palais. The North West and the Midlands compete.
Director: David Pickthall. **Producer:** Simon Betts.

....

Come Home Charlie and Face Them   1 wk

LWT, drama

This three-part series by Alun Owen was based on R.F. Delderfield's novel set in North Wales in the 1930s. Charlie Pritchard (Tom Radcliffe) was a bored bank clerk lodging with the manager (Peter Sallis) and his wife (Sylvia Kay). Their daughter Ida (Mossie Smith) diverted Pritchard until he met Delphine (Jennifer Calvert).

| 1990 | 10.8 | Sun 25 Nov 9:05 p.m. | 18 | 1 wk |

Under Delphine's domination, Charlie helps rob his own bank for fun.
Director: Roger Bamford. **Producer:** Sue Whatmough.

....

Come Laughing Home   1 wk

ATV, drama

| 1966 | 7.9 | Tue 20 Dec 9:10 p.m. | 3 | 1 wk |

A north country family living on a council estate receives a startling announcement. Eric and Edith Fawcett (Reginald Marsh and Avis Bunnage) learn their daughter Vera (Gemma Jones) is pregnant by bus driver Brian Hudson (Keith Barron). Seeing a bleak future ahead, Vera decides to leave home.
Designer: Michael Eve. **Director:** John Moxey. **Producer:** Cecil Clarke.

Come On Cousins | 1 wk

BBC, sport

| 1980 | 16.1 | Thu 13 Mar 8:30 p.m. | 7 | 1 wk |

Olympic gold medallist Robin Cousins bids for the title at the World Figure Skating Championships in Dortmund.
Commentator: Alan Weeks.

Come Spy With Me | 1 wk

LWT, comedy

| 1977 | 12.3 | Sun 11 Sep 7:45 p.m. | 18 | 1 wk |

Television adaptation of the West End musical farce by Bryan Blackburn. Danny La Rue stars as a secret agent, with Patrick Cargill, Irene Handl, Alfred Marks, Kenneth Waller and Barbara Windsor.
Designer: Bill McPherson. **Director:** Philip Casson. **Producer:** Jack Williams.

Comedians, The | 24 wks

Granada, comedy

Non-stop gags, edited so that stand-up comedians followed each other often as fast as one gag at a time. The series provided a television springboard for numerous comics of vast stage and club experience, including Russ Abbot, Lennie Bennett, Jim Bowen, Duggie Brown, Mike Burton, Frank Carson, Colin Crompton, Ken Goodwin, Bernard Manning, Tom O'Connor, Mike Reid, George Roper and Charlie Williams. With Shep's Banjo Boys (1971–73).
Directors: included Walter Butler (1971–72) and David Warwick (1973, 1979 and 1985). **Producer:** John Hamp.

1971	6.7	Sat 16 Oct 8:55 p.m.	11	7 wks
1972	7.2	Sat 11 Mar 6:10 p.m.	5	10 wks
1973	6.2	Sat 22 Dec 9:00 p.m.	20	1 wk

A Christmas Music Hall with the Bel Canto singers and the Pamela Devis dancers.

| 1979 | 13.8 | Fri 7 Dec 8:30 p.m. | 3 | 4 wks |

The series returns with a new batch of comics, including Stan Boardman, Johnny Carroll, George King, Mick Miller, Harry Scott, Roy Walker and Lee Wilson.

| 1985 | 11.0 | Sat 8 Jun 6:50 p.m. | 15 | 2 wks |

Comedians' Christmas Party, The | 1 wk

Granada, comedy

| 1971 | 7.4 | Fri 24 Dec 7:00 p.m. | 5 | 1 wk |

Christmas special with THE COMEDIANS team, including Duggie Brown, Frank Carson, Ken Goodwin, Bernard Manning, Tom O'Connor and Charlie Williams.
Director: Baz Taylor. **Producer:** John Hamp.

Comedy Bandbox | 1 wk

ABC, entertainment

| 1963 | 6.1 | Sat 23 Nov 6:35 p.m. | 18 | 1 wk |

Ted Durante introduces Les Dawson, Clive Dunn, Syd and Max Harrison, Neville King and Des Lane with the ABC Showband.
Director: Ronnie Baxter. **Producer:** Peter Dulay.

Comedy Four | 3 wks

Granada, comedy

A series of four one-off comedies by the same writers, Barry Took, Peter Miller and James Kelly, with a different cast each week.

| 1963 | 4.8 | Thu 13 Jun 7:30 p.m. | 15 | 3 wks |

'Fit for Heroes'
Major Hepplewhite (Deryck Guyler) and Corporal Rust (Kenneth Connor) decide to teach the Ministry of Pensions a lesson . . . with unexpected consequences.
Director: Graeme McDonald. **Producer:** Peter Eton.

Comedy Playhouse | 6 wks

BBC, comedy

This strand of half-hour plays spawned several series, most notably STEPTOE AND SON (from a 1962 programme entitled 'The Offer') and TILL DEATH US DO PART (from 1966).

| 1965 | 4.7 | Thu 19 Aug 8:50 p.m. | 17 | 3 wks |

'Betsy Mae' by Mike Sharland.
Starring Hermione Gingold with Peter Elliott, Michael Newport and Nicholas Phipps.
A twelve-year-old schoolboy has written a winning essay on the works of children's author Betsy Mae Meadows (Hermione Gingold). His prize is a visit to her home.
Producer: Douglas Moodie. **Executive Producer:** Graeme Muir.

| 1966 | 4.8 | Tue 28 Jun 7:30 p.m. | 17 | 1 wk |

'Seven Year Hitch' by Fred Robinson.
Starring Harry H. Corbett as Ern and Joan Sims as Is, proprietors of an unsuccessful dancing school. Ern forgets their seventh wedding anniversary.
Producer: Vere Lorrimer.

| 1967 | 5.5 | Thu 29 Jun 9:30 p.m. | 7 | 1 wk |

'To Lucifer a Son' by Johnny Speight.
Jimmy Tarbuck plays the son of the Devil, with John Le Mesurier and Pat Coombs, Arthur English, Tommy Godfrey, Dermot Kelly and Rita Webb.
Producer: Dennis Main Wilson.

| 1968 | 6.6 | Fri 10 May 8:20 p.m. | 10 | 1 wk |

'The Family of Fred' by Peter Robinson.
Fred Holmes (Freddie Frinton) has been a widower for twelve years, dominated by his three daughters. Next-door neighbour Aggie Plunkett (Jean Kent) has her marriage sights set on Fred.
Producer: Douglas Argent.

....

Comedy Premiere   4 wks

ATV, comedy

Series for trying out comedy formats.

| 1975 | 7.3 | Wed 26 Nov 8:00 p.m. | 16 | 4 wks |

'Milk-O'
Milkman Jim (Bob Grant) oversleeps, throwing many households into confusion. Also starring Alan Curtis, Leslie Dwyer and Anna Karen.
Writers: Anthony Marriott and Bob Grant. **Producer:** John Scholz-Conway.

....

Comedy Tonight   10 wks

Presented by BBC, film

Season of comedy films.

| 1968 | 7.9 | Tue 8 Oct 7:25 p.m. | 2 | 10 wks |

'Up in the World'
Norman Wisdom stars as a window cleaner who meets a young millionaire and becomes the centre of a kidnapping plot. Also starring Jerry Desmonde, Ambrosine Philpotts and Maureen Swanson.
Director: John Paddy Carstairs.

Comedy Tonight   1 wk

LWT, comedy

| 1980 | 13.9 | Sun 23 Mar 8:45 p.m. | 13 | 1 wk |

'Tell It to the Judge' by Sid Green.
Single comedy play starring Dave King as Detective Inspector Saggers of Catley CID, where everything is going badly on a particularly hateful Friday.
Producer: Derrick Goodwin.

....

Coming to America   1 wk

Presented by BBC, film

| 1991 | 13.0 | Wed 25 Dec 9:30 p.m. | 16 | 1 wk |

Eddie Murphy stars as Prince Akeem of Zamunda. He travels to New York to escape an arranged marriage and find his own woman. Also starring Don Ameche, Ralph Bellamy, Arsenio Hall and James Earl Jones.
Director: John Landis.

....

Common Lot, The   1 wk

ATV, drama

| 1977 | 6.8 | Tue 5 Apr 7:00 p.m. | 17 | 1 wk |

This single comedy by Caroline Graham stars Leslie Dwyer, Bernard Kay and John Savident as council gardeners who secretly grow a hybrid plant in spite of the bureaucracy which attempts to stop them.
Producer: Alan Tarrant.

....

Commonwealth Entertains, The   1 wk

ATV, entertainment

| 1965 | 6.0 | Wed 15 Sep 9:40 p.m. | 14 | 1 wk |

Artists include the Australian Ballet, the Kandyan Dancers from Ceylon, the National Dance Theatre of Jamaica, the Merry Men from Barbados, the Royal Winnipeg Ballet, the Musicians of Ghana, the National Dance Troupe of Sierra Leone and the Trinidad Steel Band and Limbo Dancers. With the Jack Parnell orchestra.
Director: Albert Locke. **Producer:** Alan Tarrant.

....

Commonwealth Games, The   2 wks

BBC, sport

| 1978 | 10.2 | Sat 12 Aug 9:30 p.m. | 16 | 1 wk |

Frank Bough introduces events from Edmonton, Canada. **Commentators:** David Coleman, Ron Pickering and Stuart Storey.

| 1986 | 9.5 | Thu 24 Jul 6:30 p.m. | 8 | 1 wk |

The opening ceremony of the thirteenth games in Edinburgh is held in the presence of HRH The Duke of Edinburgh. David Coleman commentates.
Television presentation: Stewart Morris.

Compact   24 wks

BBC, soap

This twice-weekly soap opera was created by Hazel Adair and Peter Ling and set in the offices and homes of the staff of a women's magazine.

| 1962 | 5.3 | Tue 20 Feb 7:30 p.m. | 9 | 23 wks |

'Something to Celebrate'
Joanne (Jean Harvey) returns from an international conference in Paris to learn that the identity of the office thief has been discovered.
Writers: Hazel Adair and Peter Ling. **Director:** Vere Lorrimer. **Producer:** Alan Bromley.

| 1965 | 5.2 | Tue 18 May 7:35 p.m. | 20 | 1 wk |

'Wild Goose Chase'
After an uncomfortable night in a remote cottage on the Welsh mountains, David Rome (Vincent Ball) and Tessa March (Bridget Armstrong) feel rather miserable. Their plight is not eased by the arrival of an angry farmer.
Writer: Janet Dunbar. **Director:** Michael Hart. **Producer:** William Sterling.

Concentration   5 wks

Granada, game show

This UK version of a popular American programme required keen observation and good memory. It was based on the old parlour game of Pelmanism, remembering where two cards of identical value lay. David Gell hosted.

| 1960 | 6.0 | Tue 8 Mar 8:00 p.m. | 6 | 5 wks |

Director: Peter Mullings.

Condorman   1 wk

Presented by ITV, film

| 1986 | 12.7 | Mon 31 Mar 5:20 p.m. | 12 | 1 wk |

Michael Crawford as Woody Wilkins gets mixed up with both CIA and KGB agents when he pretends to be an American spy codenamed 'Condorman'. Barbara Carrera and Oliver Reed also star.
Director: Charles Jarrott.

Confession   2 wks

Granada, drama

This series of plays, connected by the title theme, concerned confessions of many kinds, from those which break up marriages and destroy lives to those about little secrets people prefer to conceal.

| 1970 | 6.1 | Fri 3 Jul 9:00 p.m. | 10 | 2 wks |

'The Python Method' by John Kruse.
Professor Alan Whitelaw (Keith Barron) is a young scientist off on a mission behind the Iron Curtain. Is he safe? Will he talk and confess under pressure – particularly when the nightmare begins? Also starring James Donnelly.
Designer: Peter Phillips. **Director:** Barry Davis. **Producer:** Richard Everitt.

Conjugal Rights   1 wk

YTV, drama

This trilogy of plays by Philip Mackie was based on the emotional entanglements of six people: Michael (Ian Holm), Jenny (Barbara Ferris), Alan (Julian Holloway), Rosamund (Ann Bell), Charles (Julian Glover) and Paula (Sarah Badel).

| 1973 | 6.7 | Mon 8 Jan 9:00 p.m. | 14 | 1 wk |

'Alan and Rosamund'
Alan is happily married to Rosamund, but is she happy with him?
Designer: Vic Symonds. **Director:** Marc Miller. **Executive Producer:** Peter Willes.

Connie   3 wks

Central, drama

This series by Ron Hutchinson starred Stephanie Beacham as Connie, the former owner of a chain of fashion shops who felt cheated out of them. After eight years in the Greek Islands she returned penniless but resolute to reclaim her position in the world of high fashion by whatever means she chose. Brenda Bruce, Pam Ferris, Richard Morant and Paul Rogers also starred.

| 1985 | 10.6 | Sun 23 Jun 9:00 p.m. | 16 | 3 wks |

Young new employee Lisa (Georgia Allen) receives distracting attention from Hector (Paul Rogers). Connie walks out of a meeting after a row about plans for the company's expansion.
Designer: Michael Eve. **Director:** Alan Dossor. **Producer:** Nicholas Palmer.

Conversations with David Niven — 1 wk

ITV, news

| 1983 | 6.4 | Fri 29 Jul 10:30 p.m. | 19 | 1 wk |

The actor David Niven died earlier in the day. This tribute presents extracts from past interviews.

....

Cook Report, The — 17 wks

Central, documentary

After several years of acclaim on radio, investigative journalist Roger Cook brought his show to television. His methods were fearless and often dangerous.
Editor: Mike Townson. **Series Producer:** Mark Gottschalk.

| 1987 | 9.9 | Wed 22 Jul 8:30 p.m. | 10 | 3 wks |

'Costa Del Crime'
As Britain and Spain discuss an extradition treaty, Roger Cook confronts some of Britain's most wanted men living in luxury on the Costa del Sol. He is physically attacked while flushing out the reluctant subjects.

| 1989 | 9.8 | Mon 12 Jun 7:00 p.m. | 18 | 2 wks |

'Blood Money'
Cook investigates protection rackets and other corruption operated by terrorists on both sides in Northern Ireland alleging that the profits are used to purchase weapons.

| 1990 | 9.4 | Mon 13 Aug 7:00 p.m. | 13 | 7 wks |

'Heroin Highway'
As two Birmingham girls begin long prison sentences in Bangkok for drugs offences, Cook traces the route of the suppliers to the Golden Triangle in Burma where he confronts the man responsible for the girls' incarceration.

| 1991 | 12.1 | Mon 8 Apr 7:00 p.m. | 9 | 5 wks |

'Hot Dog Wars'
A man running a hot dog stand was murdered. He had £75,000 in his pocket. Cook uncovers a network of corruption in which innocent franchisees get turned over.

....

Cook Report (Update), The — 2 wks

Central, documentary

Roger Cook reports progress on stories covered during the last series. **Series Editor:** Mike Townson.

| 1989 | 9.9 | Mon 14 Aug 7:00 p.m. | 16 | 1 wk |
| 1991 | 8.2 | Mon 8 Apr 7:00 p.m. | 17 | 1 wk |

Cooper — 2 wks

Thames, comedy

This series starred Tommy Cooper with guests.

| 1975 | 6.4 | Wed 15 Oct 8:30 p.m. | 19 | 2 wks |

Guests: David Hamilton, Lynsey de Paul, Norman Rossington and Victor Spinetti.
Producer: Royston Mayoh.

....

Cooper at Large — 1 wk

Thames, comedy

| 1968 | 6.7 | Wed 6 Nov 9:15 p.m. | 6 | 1 wk |

A special in which Tommy Cooper finds himself in a deserted studio where his fantasies are given free rein. With the Irving Davies dancers and the Bob Sharples orchestra.
Producer: Mark Stuart.

....

Cooper – Just Like That! — 5 wks

Thames, comedy

This series starred Tommy Cooper and used his catchphrase as its title.

| 1978 | 14.2 | Mon 2 Oct 7:00 p.m. | 12 | 5 wks |

With Chaz Chase and the Sisters Duane.
Director: Stuart Hall. **Producer:** Peter Dulay.

....

Cooper King Size — 1 wk

Thames, comedy

| 1968 | 5.0 | Tue 27 Aug 9:00 p.m. | 5 | 1 wk |

Tommy Cooper welcomes guests Deryck Guyler, Julie Rogers and Frankie Vaughan to his hour-long special.
Producer: Mark Stuart.

....

Copper's End — 3 wks

ATV, situation comedy

The police staff at Copper's End worked very hard to avoid work, everything from form-filling to plodding the beat. The one and only squad car was available for hire for weddings, funerals, driving lessons, and such. The chief personnel were Sergeant Sam Short (Bill Owen), PC Eddie Edwards (Richard Wattis) and PC Chipper Collins (George Moon). Series created by Ted Willis.

1971	7.1	Fri 19 Feb 8:25 p.m.	13	3 wks

Life will never be as cushy again after the arrival of the most enthusiastic and efficient sergeant the force has ever known, WPS Penny Pringle (Josephine Tewson).
Writers: David Cumming and Derek Collyer. **Director:** John Sichel. **Producer:** Shaun O'Riordan.

Cops and Robbers — 1 wk

Presented by BBC, film

A season of films with the theme of police and thieves.

1984	8.0	Mon 18 Jun 9:25 p.m.	20	1 wk

'Dirty Mary, Crazy Larry'
Susan George as Mary and Peter Fonda as Larry star in a sequence of stunts and car chases following a supermarket robbery.
Director: John Hough.

Copy Cats — 13 wks

LWT, comedy

A change of name for WHO DO YOU DO.
Director (1985–86): Vic Finch. **Producer** (1985–86): David Bell.

1985	12.9	Sat 7 Dec 7:15 p.m.	7	4 wks

With Bobby Davro, Dave Evans, Aiden J. Harvey, Jessica Martin, Johnny More, Andrew O'Connor and Gary Wilmot.

1986	12.7	Sat 4 Jan 6:30 p.m.	8	6 wks

With Bobby Davro, Dave Evans, Aiden J. Harvey, Jessica Martin, Johnny More, Andrew O'Connor, Allan Stewart and Gary Wilmot.

1987	11.6	Sat 5 Dec 6:45 p.m.	17	3 wks

With Pauline Hannah, Aiden J. Harvey, Andrew O'Connor, Hilary O'Neil, Mike Osman, Allan Stewart and Mark Walker.
Producer: Vic Finch. **Executive Producer:** John Ammonds.

Corbett, Palin, Garnett and Cool — 1 wk

BBC, comedy

1988	12.8	Fri 5 Feb 10:30 p.m.	19	1 wk

Ronnie Corbett, Michael Palin, Alf Garnett (Warren Mitchell) and Phil Cool unite to raise laughter and money for the Comic Relief appeal.

Coronation Street — 3030 wks

Granada, soap

Britain's best-loved soap opera began in December 1960 from an original idea by Tony Warren. It was set in the fictitious area of Weatherfield in Salford. The theme music was composed by Eric Spear. As well as the characters and actors listed in individual episodes the cast also included the following: Des Barnes (Philip Middlemass), Ivy Brennan (Lynne Perrie), Gordon Clegg (Bill Kenwright), Jack and Vera Duckworth (William Tarmey and Elizabeth Dawn), Terry Duckworth (Nigel Pivaro), Christine Hardman (Christine Hargreaves), Reg Holdsworth (Ken Morley), Ray Langton (Neville Buswell), Doreen Lostock (Angela Crowe), Jim and Liz McDonald (Charles Lawson and Beverley Callard), Martin Platt (Sean Wilson), Audrey Roberts (Sue Nicholls), Renee Roberts (Madge Hindle), Alma Sedgewick (Amanda Barrie), Jed Stone (Kenneth Cope), Percy Sugden (Bill Waddington), Sally Webster (Sally Whittaker), Rachel Wolstenholme (Sarah Lancashire) and Eddie Yeats (Geoffrey Hughes).
Writers included Jack Rosenthal (1961 and 1964), John Finch (1962–63), Adele Rose (1965–66, 1969, 1989 and 1990), Brian Finch (1971, 1974, 1977), Leslie Duxbury (1972–73, 1976, 1981 and 1983), and H.V. Kershaw (1979, 1982, 1984 and 1986).
Directors included Christopher McMaster (1962–65) and Eric Prytherch (1971–72). **Producers** included H.V. Kershaw (1962, 1964–66 and 1970), Eric Prytherch (1973–74), Bill Podmore (1976–82, 1987–88) and Mervyn Watson (1983–85, 1989–91).

1961	7.5	Wed 29 Nov 7:30 p.m.	1	70 wks

Minnie Caldwell (Margot Bryant) has an unexpected visitor. Dennis Tanner (Philip Lowrie) offers a helping hand to Ena Sharples (Violet Carson). Miss Nugent (Eileen Derbyshire) makes a sacrifice for Mr Swindley (Arthur Lowe) and Annie Walker (Doris Speed) reaches boiling point in the Rover's Return.
Director: Howard Baker. **Producer:** Derek Granger.

1962	8.9	Mon 8 Oct 7:30 p.m.	1	105 wks

The search continues for the missing Hewitt baby, Christopher. The neighbours gather to support the Hewitt family: Concepta (Doreen Keogh), Harry (Ivan Beavis) and Lucille (Jennifer Moss).

1963	9.2	Mon 18 Nov 7:30 p.m.	1	103 wks

This is the big week for Walter Potts (Christopher Sandford). The Street's swinging window cleaner's first record, 'Not Too Little, Not Too Much', is launched. (It reached number 17 in the charts.)
Producer: Margaret Morris.

1964	9.7	Mon 12 Oct 7:30 p.m.	1	103 wks

Miss Nugent learns of an embarrassing secret. Len Fairclough (Peter Adamson) hears that his former wife, Nellie, has died. He builds up to proposing again to Elsie Tanner (Pat Phoenix).

1965	9.7	Wed 20 Jan 7:30 p.m.	1	98 wks

Elsie Tanner engages in a little marriage guidance, but it doesn't really help Jerry and Myra Booth (Graham Haberfield and Susan Jameson).

| **1966** | **9.1** | **Mon 24 Oct 7:30 p.m.** | **1** | **105 wks** |

Elsie reaches the end of her tether and confronts the person who has been tormenting her with anonymous phone calls.
Director: Bob Hird.

| **1967** | **9.5** | **Mon 4 Sep 7:30 p.m.** | **1** | **101 wks** |

Elsie marries US Sergeant Steve Tanner (Paul Maxwell). Dennis Tanner, Elsie's son, comes home for the big day.
Writer: Geoffrey Lancashire. **Director:** Richard Doubleday. **Producer:** Jack Rosenthal.

| **1968** | **8.7** | **Mon 8 Jan 7:30 p.m.** | **1** | **104 wks** |

As the bulldozers prepare to enter, Ena Sharples is evicted from the Mission. She is to retire to St Anne's, where she will be a housekeeper for a gentleman.
Writer: John Linter. **Director:** Les Chatfield. **Producer:** Michael Cox.

| **1969** | **8.4** | **Wed 26 Feb 7:30 p.m.** | **1** | **104 wks** |

'Found'
In Monday's episode (entitled 'Lost') Minnie Caldwell disappeared leaving a note saying 'Look after the cat'. She has been gambling secretly and owes Dave Smith (Reginald Marsh) £10. She is found in hospital after collapsing in the street.
Director: Tim Jones. **Producer:** John Finch.

| **1970** | **8.9** | **Wed 18 Feb 7:30 p.m.** | **1** | **96 wks** |

Albert Tatlock (Jack Howarth) meets his Waterloo but Annie Walker romantically meets her Valentine.
Writer: Ron McDonnell. **Director:** Joy Boyer.

| **1971** | **8.7** | **Mon 8 Feb 7:30 p.m.** | **1** | **104 wks** |

Following the funeral of his wife Valerie (Anne Reid) Ken Barlow (William Roache) has retired to the Bay Tree Hotel, where a receptionist comforts him.
Producer: Leslie Duxbury.

| **1972** | **8.3** | **Wed 5 Apr 7:30 p.m.** | **2** | **103 wks** |

As Ernest Bishop (Stephen Hancock) and Emily Nugent build up to their wedding day, Stan Ogden (Bernard Youens) worries that he won't get Ernest to the church on time.
Producer: Brian Armstrong.

| **1973** | **8.3** | **Wed 17 Oct 7:30 p.m.** | **1** | **101 wks** |

Hilda Ogden (Jean Alexander) is holding a party. Who will be invited?
Director: Alan Grint.

| **1974** | **8.3** | **Wed 20 Mar 7:30 p.m.** | **1** | **100 wks** |

Lucille Hewitt has a new love life which Rita Fairclough (Barbara Knox) knows about. Annie Walker strives hard to become a real 'lady'.
Director: Nick Burrell-Davis.

| **1975** | **8.8** | **Mon 27 Jan 7:30 p.m.** | **1** | **104 wks** |

Len Fairclough has been visited by an unknown lady wearing dark glasses. She's now dead, and Len is grilled about her death.
Writer: Barry Hill. **Director:** Ken Grieve. **Producer:** Susi Hush.

| **1976** | **8.8** | **Mon 5 Apr 7:30 p.m.** | **1** | **97 wks** |

Elsie Tanner returns to the street after three years. Why has she come back and where is her husband Alan Howard (Alan Browning)?
Director: Bill Gilmour.

| **1977** | **16.6** | **Mon 28 Nov 7:30 p.m.** | **1** | **96 wks** |

Suzie Birchall (Cheryl Murray) has a date with Mike Baldwin (Johnny Briggs). Derek Wilton (Peter Baldwin) goes househunting with Mavis Riley (Thelma Barlow).
Director: Colin Richards.

| **1978** | **20.5** | **Wed 21 Dec 7:30 p.m.** | **1** | **100 wks** |

One of the girls at Mike Baldwin's factory has disappeared with the Christmas club money.

| **1979** | **19.5** | **Wed 14 Mar 7:30 p.m.** | **1** | **80 wks** |

Mike Baldwin, Len Fairclough and Alf Roberts (Bryan Mosley) are in hospital after a lorry, whose driver had died of a heart attack, ploughed into the Rovers Return. Police mount a search for Deirdre Langton (Anne Kirkbride) and daughter Tracy (Christabel Finch). Tracy's pram was seen parked outside the Rovers shortly before the accident. Believing her baby killed, Deirdre has vanished in hysterics.
Director: Jeremy Summers.

| **1980** | **19.0** | **Wed 3 Dec 7:30 p.m.** | **1** | **104 wks** |

Emily Swain (Eileen Derbyshire) receives dramatic news about her new husband Arnold (George Waring). He is exposed as a bigamist. Stan finally goes to the doctor and is given advice that rocks him on his heels. He is told he is allergic to beer!
Writer: Peter Whalley. **Director:** Richard Holthouse.

| **1981** | **20.8** | **Wed 18 Feb 7:30 p.m.** | **1** | **99 wks** |

Ken Barlow realizes he has a rival in his pursuit of Deirdre.
Director: Nicholas Ferguson.

| **1982** | **18.9** | **Wed 6 Jan 7:30 p.m.** | **1** | **104 wks** |

Mike Baldwin's dad Frankie (Sam Kydd) tries to bribe him for a loan.
Director: Brian Mills.

| 1983 | 19.3 | Mon 14 Feb 7:30 p.m. | 1 | 54 wks |
| | | Wed 16 Feb 7:30 p.m. | | |

The above two programmes were listed together in the ratings.
In the first programme, it's Valentine's Night, and Mike Baldwin pressurizes Deirdre Barlow (Anne Kirkbride) to make a decision on their future together.
Writer: Barry Hill.
In the second, Ken Barlow has a bad day. All his illusions about marriage are shattered.
Director: Jeremy Summers.

| 1984 | 21.1 | Mon 12 Nov 7:30 p.m. | 1 | 53 wks |
| | | Wed 14 Nov 7:30 p.m. | | |

The above two episodes were listed together in the ratings.
In the first programme, Bet Lynch (Julie Goodyear) has a new man in her life, Tony Cunliffe (Jack Carr).
In the second, Betty Turpin (Betty Driver) tries to persuade Billy Walker (Kenneth Farrington) that his wild nights at the Rover's Return will get him into trouble.
Writer: Peter Whalley. **Director:** Ric Mellis.

| 1985 | 20.6 | Wed 16 Jan 7:30 p.m. | 1 | 59 wks |

Mike Baldwin lures Christina Millward (Julie Shipley) round to his flat. Curly Watts (Kevin Kennedy) tells Hilda Ogden some disturbing news about her lodger Henry Wakefield (Finetime Fontayne).
Writer: John Stevenson. **Director:** John Michael Phillips.

| 1986 | 18.6 | Mon 24 Feb 7:30 p.m. | 2 | 52 wks |
| | | Wed 26 Feb 7:30 p.m. | | |

The above two episodes were listed together in the ratings.
In the first, Ken realizes what all the conflict with Deirdre is doing to Tracy (Holly Chamarette) and in the second Phyllis Pearce (Jill Summers) uses her special technique to get rid of unwanted men.
Writer: John Stevenson. **Director:** Ron Francis. **Producer:** John G. Temple.

| 1987 | 26.6 | Fri 25 Dec 7:30 p.m. | 1 | 95 wks |

Hilda Ogden has left hospital following the attack by burglars at the home of Dr and Mrs Lowther. Mrs Lowther has died as a result of the violence and Hilda puts away her pinny and curlers for the last time as she retires to become housekeeper to Dr Lowther in an idyllic Derbyshire village.
Director: Ric Mellis.

| 1988 | 18.1 | Mon 4 Jan 7:30 p.m. | 2 | 106 wks |

Jenny Bradley (Sally Ann Matthews) looks forward to seeing her French boyfriend Patrick Podevin (Franc du Bosc).
Writer: Barry Hill. **Director:** Tim Sullivan.

| 1989 | 24.4 | Mon 13 Mar 7:30 p.m. | 1 | 117 wks |

| | | Wed 15 Mar 7:30 p.m. | | |

The above two episodes were listed together in the ratings.
Percy becomes protective towards Emily, who has a new man in her life. Gossip at the Rovers speculates on who Bet will choose as the new barmaid.
Writers: Tony Perrin and John Stevenson. **Director:** Sarah Harding.

| 1990 | 22.8 | Wed 3 Jan 7:30 p.m. | 1 | 158 wks |

Tracy Barlow (Dawn Acton) has her illusions about her father shattered. Don Brennan (Geoff Hinsliff) visits the betting shop and soon regrets it.
Director: Richard Holthouse.

| 1991 | 21.6 | Wed 20 Nov 7:30 p.m. | 1 | 155 wks |

Christmas comes twice a year if you're Alec Gilroy (Roy Barraclough).
Writer: John Stevenson. **Director:** Ken Horn.

| Coronation Street – The First Episode | | | | 1 wk |

Granada, soap

| 1990 | 12.1 | Sun 2 Dec 7:15 p.m. | 18 | 1 wk |

Thirty years to the month since the serial began this first episode, written by its creator, Tony Warren, is repeated. It began with Elsie Lappin (Maudie Edwards) handing over the corner shop to Florrie Lindley (Betty Alberge). Other characters in at the outset included Linda Cheveski (Anne Cunningham), Elsie Tanner (Patricia Phoenix), Dennis Tanner (Philip Lowrie), Frank Barlow (Frank Pemberton), Ida Barlow (Noel Dyson), Kenneth Barlow (William Roache), David Barlow (Alan Rothwell), Annie Walker (Doris Speed), Jack Walker (Arthur Leslie), Albert Tatlock (Jack Howarth), Ena Sharples (Violet Carson) and Susan Cunningham (Patricia Shakesby).
Director: Derek Bennett. **Producer:** Stuart Latham.

| Corridor People, The | | | | 5 wks |

Granada, drama

This offbeat thriller series created by Edward Boyd starred Gary Cockrell as private eye Scotty, John Sharp as Kronk of the CID, Alan Curtis and William Maxwell as Kronk's unwilling assistants Inspector Blood and Sergeant Hound, and Elizabeth Shepherd as the villainous Persian, Syrie Van Epp.

| 1966 | 4.8 | Fri 9 Sep 9:40 p.m. | 16 | 3 wks |

'Victim in Red'
A stroll along memory lane ends in death.
Director: David Boisseau. **Producer:** Richard Everitt.

Cost of Loving, The   2 wks

YTV, drama

These seven plays by Stan Barstow are set in a fictitious northern town.

| 1977 | 14.5 | Sun 30 Oct 9:30 p.m. | 5 | 2 wks |

'Flesh Pink and Black'
Luther Holroyd (Jack Watson) has a mistress who works in the local lingerie shop. The rest of his family is displeased. Also starring Rosemary Martin, Carolyn Pickles and Diana Rayworth.
Designer: Chris George. **Producer:** James Ormerod. **Executive Producer:** David Cunliffe.

Cottage To Let   5 wks

ATV, drama

These stories by a variety of writers, each one with a different cast, dealt with the people who rented a quiet country cottage.

| 1977 | 13.2 | Tue 30 Aug 9:00 p.m. | 2 | 5 wks |

'Second Opinion' by Alan Hackney.
Dr Weston (Timothy West) rents a Devon cottage with his fiancée (Lynda Bellingham). He's contemplating marriage but takes his daughter Tina (Lynn Dalby) along for a second opinion.
Designer: Richard Lake. **Director:** John Sichel. **Producer:** John Cooper.

Could Your Street Be Next?   1 wk

ATV, documentary

| 1973 | 5.6 | Mon 20 Aug 8:30 p.m. | 16 | 1 wk |

An examination of the planners and workers who dig up, widen and demolish streets without thought for people. Is this the ultimate triumph of the motor car?
Camera: Ivan Strasbury. **Producer:** Charles Stewart.

Count of Monte Cristo, The   1 wk

Presented by ITV, film

| 1981 | 14.8 | Wed 20 May 8:00 p.m. | 3 | 1 wk |

Film version of the story by Alexandre Dumas. Secret treasure hidden on the Spanish island of Monte Cristo in Napoleonic times inspires betrayal and vengeance. Starring Richard Chamberlain, Tony Curtis, Trevor Howard, Louis Jourdan and Donald Pleasence.
Director: David Greene.

Counterstrike   1 wk

BBC, drama

This series created by Tony Williamson starred Jon Finch as Simon King and Sarah Brackett as Mary in weekly self-contained stories by various writers.

| 1969 | 6.0 | Mon 10 Nov 9:10 p.m. | 19 | 1 wk |

'The Mutant' by Dick Sharples.
A deadly new germ escapes in a biological warfare laboratory and there is no known antidote. The race is on to find one before the germ produces a killer plague.
Designer: John Hurst. **Director:** William Sterling. **Producer:** Patrick Alexander.

Country Diary of an Edwardian Lady   4 wks

Central, drama

Elaine Feinstein and Dirk Campbell adapted the 1906 diary compiled by Warwickshire schoolteacher Edith Holden. Pippa Guard starred as Edith.

| 1984 | 13.6 | Wed 22 Feb 7:00 p.m. | 10 | 4 wks |

'January'
Edith wanders along the country lanes around her home discovering winter flowers, hungry rabbits and territorial robins all surviving the January freeze-up.
Director: Dirk Campbell. **Producer:** Patrick Gamble. **Executive Producer:** Brian Lewis.

Country Matters   3 wks

Granada, drama

This series was adapted from seven short stories by H.E. Bates and six by A.E. Coppard, all set in the English countryside. With music by Derek Hilton.
Producer: Derek Granger.

| 1972 | 5.8 | Sun 17 Sep 10:15 p.m. | 15 | 1 wk |

'The Watercress Girl' by A.E. Coppard, adapted by Hugh Leonard.
Mary (Susan Fleetwood) stands trial for throwing vitriol in the face of Elizabeth (Susan Tebbs), her rival for the love of Frank (Gareth Thomas). Mary has previously refused to marry Frank. He gives evidence against her which sends her to prison.
Designer: Roy Stonehouse. **Director:** Barry Davis.

| 1973 | 6.7 | Sun 28 Jan 10:15 p.m. | 14 | 2 wks |

'The Little Farm' by H.E. Bates, adapted by Hugh Leonard.
Tom Richards (Bryan Marshall) is a lonely and illiterate young farmer. He advertises for someone to look after him on his remote, cheerless farm. Edna Johnson (Barbara Ewing) takes on the job. Affections develop, but the destructive forces of jealousy enter the story. Also starring Michael Elphick as Jack and Diane Keen as the girl in the office.
Director: Silvio Narizzano.

Cover Her Face   6 wks

Anglia, drama

This dramatization of a story by P.D. James starred Roy Marsden as Scotland Yard sleuth Adam Dalgliesh, who suspected a murder victim was a drugs racketeer.

| 1985 | 15.3 | Sun 24 Mar 8:45 p.m. | 6 | 6 wks |

Dalgliesh engineers the vital confession.
Designer: Jon Pusey. **Director:** John Davies. **Producer:** John Rosenberg.

Cover Up   1 wk

USA presented by BBC, drama

This series spotlighted fashion photographers, models and spies on foreign assignments.

| 1985 | 8.6 | Fri 23 Aug 7:40 p.m. | 18 | 1 wk |

'Passions' by Doug Heyes Jr.
Glamorous duo Jack and Dani (Antony Hamilton and Jennifer O'Neill) are trapped when the 'Black Widow' (Martine Beswick) escapes from jail determined to seek revenge for her incarceration.
Director: Don Carlos Dunaway.

Cowboys   6 wks

Thames, situation comedy

This series by Peter Learmouth was about a small building firm mismanaged by Joe Jones (Roy Kinnear) with a number of cowboy workers including Geyser (Colin Welland) and Wobbly Ron (Dermot Kelly).

| 1980 | 16.5 | Wed 8 Oct 8:30 p.m. | 2 | 6 wks |

'Two Right Casanovas'
Geyser and Joe run into woman trouble on the firm's annual outing.
Producer: Michael Mills.

Crane   39 wks

AR, drama

This adventure series was about a smuggler called Crane (Patrick Allen), who swapped his bowler hat and smart suburban home for a battered panama and a rundown cafe on a beach near Casablanca. He bought a boat and let it be known he was available for 'import-export' assignments. Sam Kydd played his right-hand man Orlando. Laya Raki was the barmaid and Gerald Flood the fastidious police officer, Mahmoud.
Producer: Jordan Lawrence.

| 1963 | 6.2 | Tue 2 Apr 8:00 p.m. | 4 | 13 wks |

'A Death of No Importance' by Terence Feely.
A murderer is hiding in Casablanca. Crane hunts him relentlessly with a very special reason to find him.
Director: Raymond Menmuir.

| 1964 | 8.3 | Mon 13 Jan 8:00 p.m. | 3 | 22 wks |

'The Death of Marie Vetier' by Patrick Tilley.
Marie (Patricia Haines) is a desperate woman. Crane helps her to tackle her fears.
Director: Richard Doubleday.

| 1965 | 8.1 | Mon 25 Jan 8:00 p.m. | 4 | 4 wks |

'The Man in the Gold Waistcoat' by James Mitchell.
A murder in the desert would not have involved Crane had it not been for the waistcoat.
Director: Christopher Hodson.

Crazy Like a Fox   7 wks

USA presented by ITV, drama

This series concerned San Francisco private investigator Harry Fox (Jack Warden) and his lawyer son Harrison (John Rubinstein).

| 1986 | 14.0 | Sun 23 Feb 8:45 p.m. | 7 | 7 wks |

'Motor Homicide'
Harry witnesses a murder while looking for a campsite in the woods.

Crazy Like a Fox   1 wk

Presented by ITV, film

| 1987 | 9.7 | Sat 29 Aug 9:15 p.m. | 11 | 1 wk |

While on holiday in London, private eye Harry Fox (Jack Warden) surprises a man going through his belongings in his hotel room. He chases him and roughs him up. The man turns out to be the Duke of Trent (James Faulkner). When the Duke is murdered, Harry is accused. Also starring Allan Cuthbertson, Michael Jayston, Rosemary Leach, Catherine Oxenberg, Penny Peyser and John Rubinstein.
Director: Paul Krasny.

1

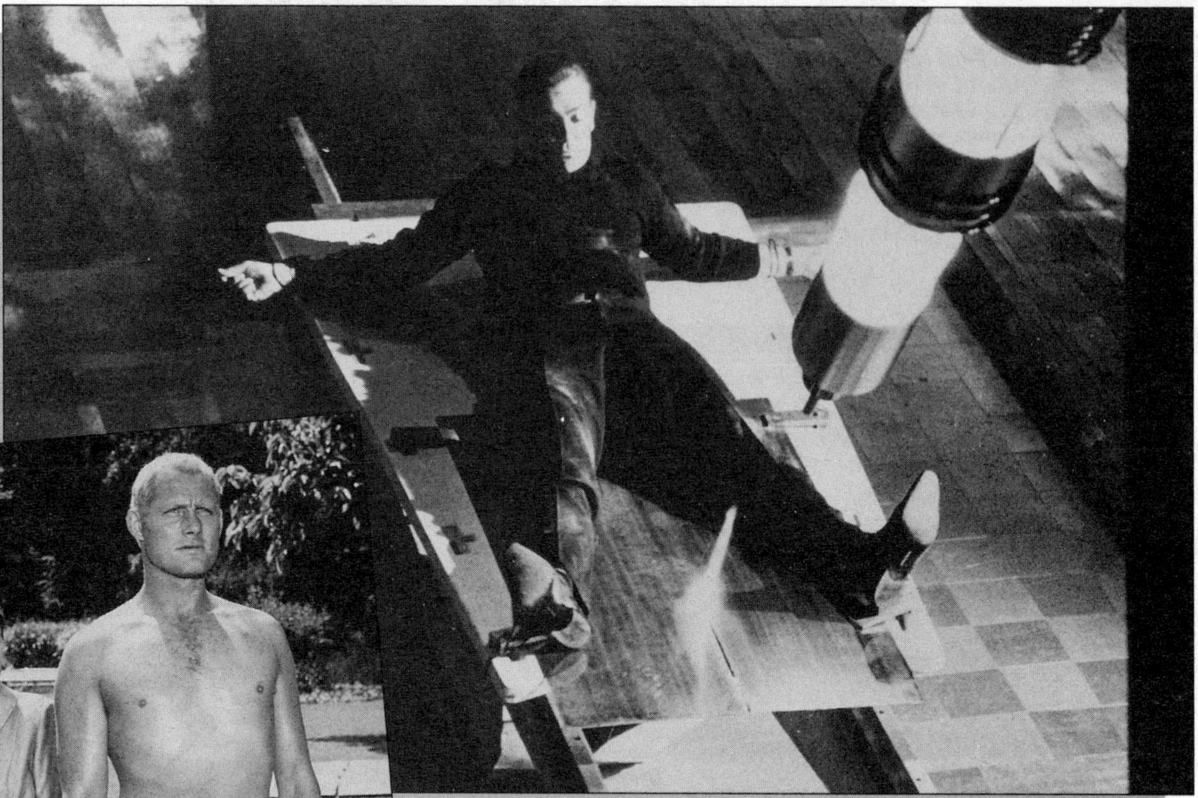

2

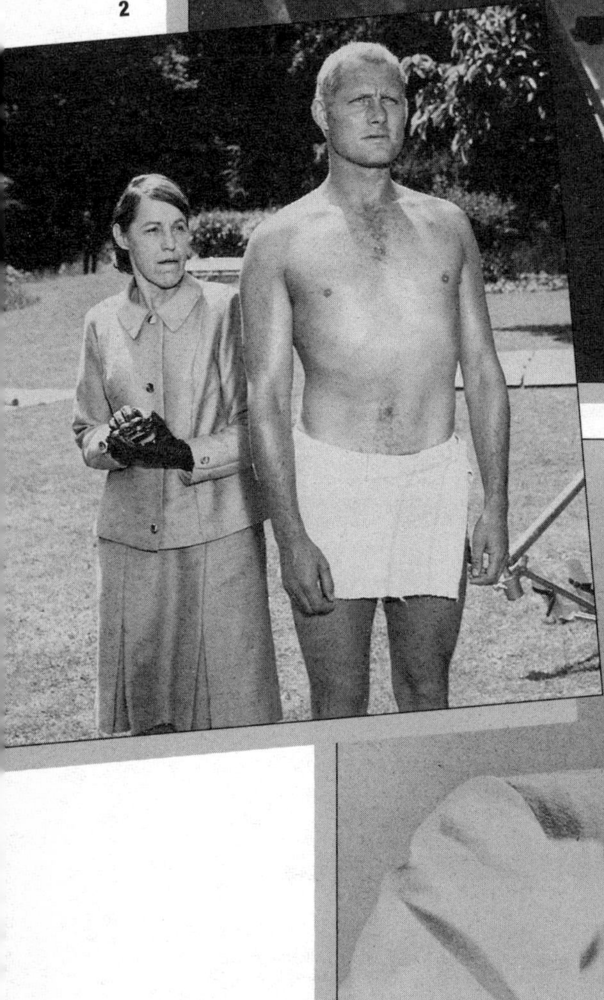

3

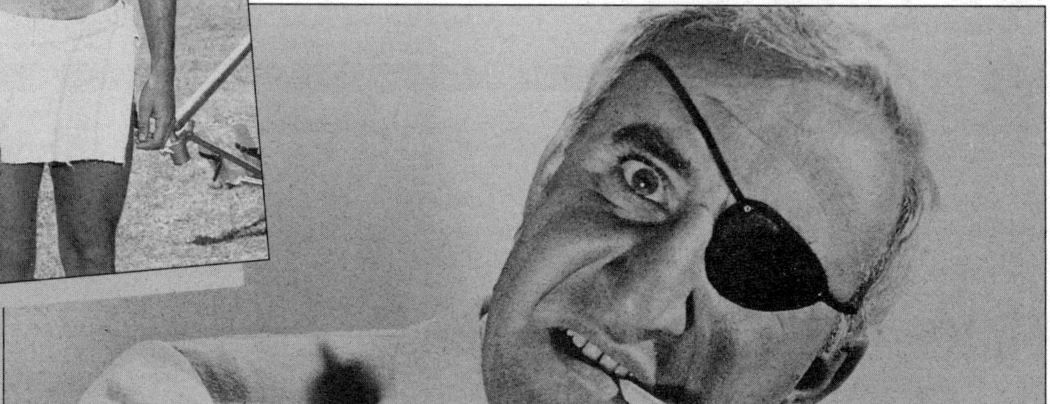

4

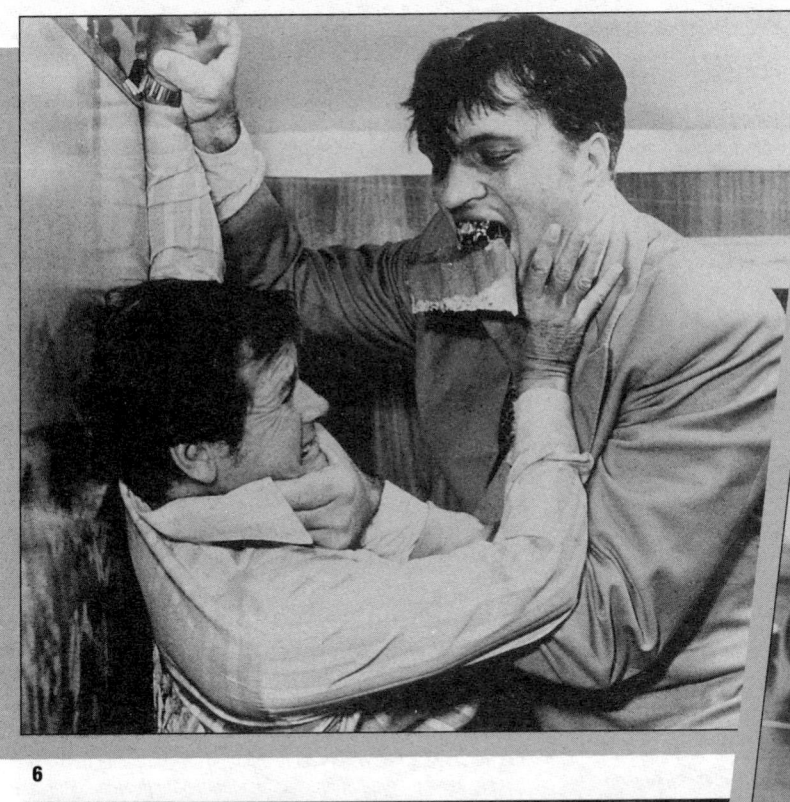

5

6

1 *James is in bondage in* **Goldfinger**.

2 *Lotte Lenya ogles a lotta Robert Shaw in* **From Russia with Love**.

3 *Adolfo Celi was the villain Emilio Largo in the James Bond film* **Thunderball**.

4 *The 7'2" 'Jaws' (Richard Kiel) tries to get his teeth into James Bond in* **The Spy Who Loved Me**.

5 *George Lazenby portrayed James Bond in just one film,* **On Her Majesty's Secret Service**.

6 *Jane Seymour came to fame as the Bond girl Solitaire and Roger Moore made his 007 debut in* **Live and Let Die**.

Cribb
2 wks

Granada, drama

These seven self-contained adventures from the novels of Peter Lovesey were adapted by Brian Thompson and starred Alan Dobie as Detective Sergeant Cribb and William Simons as Detective Constable Thackeray.

1980 **13.9** **Sun 13 Apr 9:00 p.m.** **9** **2 wks**

'Swing, Swing Together'
A murder appears to have been committed by three men and a dog in a boat.
Designer: Alan Price. **Producer:** June Wyndham-Davies.

Cribbins
12 wks

Thames, comedy

Bernard Cribbins was a stalwart of British comedy both as an actor and singer for many years. This series was an amalgam of sketches and comic songs written by Johnnie Mortimer and Brian Cooke with the resident team of Tim Barrett, Sheila Steafel, Bob Todd and with Geoff Love's orchestra.

1969 **6.6** **Tue 18 Nov 8:25 p.m.** **11** **6 wks**

Joining in the sketches are Terence Brady, Carmel McSharry, Maddie Smith and Laura Thurlow.
Producer: Alan Tarrant.

1970 **6.9** **Tue 13 Oct 8:30 p.m.** **4** **6 wks**

Bernard plays a bank clerk, the manager of a cross-channel swimmer and, among other things, a librarian. He also finds a lodger in the kitchen.
Producer: Alan Tarrant.

Cricket
1 wk

BBC, sport

1964 **4.7** **Mon 6 Jul 6:10 p.m.** **18** **1 wk**

Coverage of the fourth day's play from Headingley, Leeds, of the third test match in the series between England and Australia. Commentators: Brian Johnston, Robert Hudson, Denis Compton and Ritchie Benaud.
Television presentation: Ray Lakeland.

Crime Buster
6 wks

ATV, drama

This series concerned sportswriter Ray Saxon (Mark Eden) and his campaigns to clean up sport.

1968 **5.7** **Thu 31 Oct 8:30 p.m.** **3** **6 wks**

'The Loser' by Joshua Adam.
Ray discovers a winner whose conscience won't let him forget that he should have lost.
Director: Hugh Munro. **Producer:** Jack Williams.

Crime Inc.
1 wk

Thames, documentary

This series of seven programmes explored the secrets of Mafia crime families.

1984 **7.6** **Wed 25 Jul 9:00 p.m.** **18** **1 wk**

An investigation into the alliance between politicians, police and hoodlums in Chicago.
Writer, Narrator and **Producer:** Martin Short. **Directors:** Ken Craig and Ian Stuttard. **Series Producer:** John Edwards.

Crime of Passion
31 wks

ATV, drama

Series creator Ted Willis reconstructed real-life cases from French courts, where Crime of Passion is a legitimate defence. The series featured Anthony Newlands as President of the Court, John Phillips as Maître Lacan and Daniel Moynihan as Maître Savel.

1970 **7.7** **Mon 16 Mar 8:30 p.m.** **4** **6 wks**

'Catherine' by Ted Willis.
Felicity Kendal stars as a country girl who has married into a distinguished London family. She is charged with murder.
Director: Valerie Hanson. **Producers:** Cecil Clarke and Robert D. Cardona.

1971 **6.5** **Tue 20 Jul 9:00 p.m.** **1** **7 wks**

'Louis' by Eric Paice.
Louis (Johnny Briggs) is ambitious to be a competitive cyclist, but he receives nothing but opposition from his wife (Tessa Wyatt) and mother-in-law (Vanda Godsell). One day he decides to do something about it.
Director: Ian Fordyce. **Executive Producer:** Cecil Clarke.

1972 **7.6** **Tue 2 May 9:00 p.m.** **1** **13 wks**

'Lina' by Ted Willis.
Lina (Cyd Hayman) has just tried to murder her artist lover Guy (Ralph Bates). Maître Savel accepts her as a client but is puzzled by the silence of both Lina and Guy.
Director: Michael Eve. **Producer:** Ian Fordyce.

| 1973 | 6.2 | Mon 8 Oct 9:00 p.m. | 11 | 5 wks |

'Claudine' by Nicholas Palmer.
Claudine (Helen Ryan) is the daughter of impoverished aristocrats Comte and Comtesse De Rouart (Cyril Luckham and Lally Bowers). She marries Gui Vanier (Ben Howard) who wants vengeance for the fate of his own parents and sees his wife's gullibility as the chance to exact that revenge.
Director: Peter Jeffries. **Producer:** Robert D. Cardona.

Crime Sheet   1 wk

AR, drama

| 1961 | 6.7 | Wed 8 Nov 7:55 p.m. | 6 | 1 wk |

This story by Raymond Marshall stars Gerald Case as Chief Superintendent Carr and Reginald Marsh as Inspector Nicholson. They follow the trail of a sandwichboard man. Also starring Paddy Joyce, Warren Mitchell and Ewen Solon.
Producer: Daphne Shadwell.

Crime Squad   1 wk

ATV, documentary

| 1973 | 6.1 | Tue 10 Apr 9:00 p.m. | | 1 wk |

A look at the everyday work of the Birmingham-based No. 4 Regional Crime Squad.
Camera: Jack Hazan. **Narrator:** Peter Williams. **Writer** and **Producer:** David C. Rea.

Crimewatch File   6 wks

BBC, documentary

This occasional series of crime reports was presented by Nick Ross.

| 1989 | 14.0 | Wed 23 Aug 9:30 p.m. | 6 | 2 wks |

Nick Ross reports on Operation Osprey, the eventually successful seven-year hunt for a rapist by Greater Manchester Police.
Producer: Tracy Cook. **Series Producer:** Anne Morrison.

| 1990 | 10.9 | Wed 22 Aug 9:30 p.m. | 7 | 2 wks |

Nick Ross presents a reconstruction of a 1986 murder near Ashdown Forest, Sussex.
Producer: Jo Johnson.

| 1991 | 10.2 | Wed 24 Jul 9:30 p.m. | 10 | 2 wks |

Nick Ross examines Operation Trigger, in which a small enquiry into a spate of burglaries on the Isle of Wight led to the country's combined forces cornering a reckless gang of armed robbers.
Producer: Robert Del Maestro. **Executive Producer:** Nikki Cheetham.

Crimewatch UK   44 wks

BBC, documentary

Sue Cook and Nick Ross presented occasional programmes in association with the police. The shows reconstructed crimes and used other means that might jog the memories of members of the public who witnessed the offences. The goal was to bring the cases presented to a successful conclusion.
Directors (1985–88, 1991): Pieter Morpurgo. **Producers** included Ritchie Cogan (1984–85) and Sam Organ (1985–87). **Editors** included Peter Chafer (1984–87) and Ritchie Cogan (1988–89).

1984	10.5	Thu 16 Aug 9:25 p.m.	2	3 wks
1985	13.4	Thu 29 Aug 9:25 p.m.	2	3 wks
1986	15.1	Thu 24 Apr 9:30 p.m.	3	9 wks
1987	13.6	Thu 29 Jan 9:30 p.m.	8	6 wks
1988	12.2	Thu 18 Feb 9:30 p.m.	8	7 wks

Producer: Peter Grimsdale.

| 1989 | 12.0 | Thu 9 Feb 9:30 p.m. | 8 | 7 wks |

Director: Rob Hopkin. **Producer:** Anne Morrison.

| 1990 | 12.3 | Thu 1 Nov 9:30 p.m. | 11 | 4 wks |

Producer: Nikki Cheetham.

| 1991 | 11.3 | Thu 12 Sep 9:30 p.m. | 12 | 5 wks |

Producer: Linda Cleeve.

Crisis on Wheels   1 wk

ATV, documentary

| 1966 | 4.9 | Wed 29 Jun 9:40 p.m. | 15 | 1 wk |

Derek Hart examines the role of the car in today's world and questions whether we could manage without it.
Camera: Chris Menges. **Director:** Kevin Brownlow. **Writer** and **Producer:** Stuart Hood.

Crisis Over Cuba   1 wk

ITN, news

| 1962 | 6.1 | Tue 23 Oct 9:15 p.m. | 10 | 1 wk |

The world holds its breath as President Kennedy announces a blockade of Cuba and twenty-five Russian ships continue their collision course towards that blockade.

Criss-Cross Quiz
3 wks

Granada, game show

General knowledge game based on noughts and crosses, taken from the American format TIC TAC DOUGH. The show was hosted by Jeremy Hawk.

| **1960** | **4.9** | **Tue 21 Jun 8:00 p.m.** | **6** | **1 wk** |

Director: Graeme McDonald.

| **1961** | **4.9** | **Wed 8 Nov 7:00 p.m.** | **18** | **2 wks** |

Director: Philip Casson.

Crocodile Dundee
2 wks

Presented by BBC, film

| **1989** | **21.8** | **Mon 25 Dec 6:15 p.m.** | **1** | **1 wk** |

Paul Hogan stars in this story of a crocodile hunter from the Australian outback caught in the mad whirl of Manhattan. Linda Kozlowski also stars.
Director: Peter Faiman.

| **1991** | **12.0** | **Sat 7 Sep 6:30 p.m.** | **9** | **1 wk** |

Repeat showing of the above film.

Crossfire, The
1 wk

Anglia, drama

| **1967** | **6.0** | **Thu 9 Feb 9:40 p.m.** | **20** | **1 wk** |

Single drama by Maurice Edelman set in Algeria during the civil war, which ended in 1962. Eric Portman stars as a distinguished physician caught up in the crossfire between European and Moslem extremists. Also starring Patrick Barr, Ian Hendry, Jeanette Sterke and Peter Wyngarde.
Designer: Reece Pemberton. **Producer:** John Jacobs.

Crossroads
1721 wks

ATV, soap

Having run for seven years in the Midlands and a few other regions, ATV's soap set in a motel in King's Oak near Birmingham finally made the network in 1972. Up until 1981 the motel was run by widow Meg Richardson, played by Noele Gordon. Created by Peter Ling and Hazel Adair.
Producers included Reg Watson (1972–74), Jack Barton (1975–85) and Philip Bowman (1985–86).

| **1972** | **6.9** | **Wed 29 Nov 5:15 p.m.** | **13** | **24 wks** |

Sheila (Sonia Fox) goes against the flow of opinion on Harry Wade (David Rose). She likes him and finds him honest.
Director: Eric Price.

| **1973** | **7.6** | **Wed 19 Dec 5:20 p.m.** | **2** | **156 wks** |

Cynthia Cunningham (Jean Bayliss) has returned to King's Oak at a time when Ted Hope (Charles Stapley) needs a sympathetic ear.
Director: Michael Hart.

| **1974** | **7.8** | **Tue 19 Feb 1:30 p.m.** | **4** | **190 wks** |

The reputation of Vince Parker (Peter Brookes) is almost ruined.
Director: Malcolm Taylor.

| **1975** | **8.3** | **Thu 14 Nov 5:20 p.m.** | **2** | **191 wks** |

Carole Hewson (Patricia Denys) makes a decision which comes as a bombshell to David Hunter (Ronald Allen).
Director: Sid Kilbey.

| **1976** | **8.1** | **Tue 20 Jan 5:20 p.m.** | **1** | **203 wks** |

Tina Webb (Rosie Collins) has a tearful experience hitchhiking.
Director: Sid Kilbey.

| **1977** | **17.0** | **Tue 6 Dec 5:15 p.m.** | **2** | **200 wks** |

The love of Maureen Flynn (Nell Curran) for Benny (Paul Henry) is questioned. Meg Mortimer needs great tact when Sandy Richardson (Roger Tonge) asks about Jill Harvey (Jane Rossington).
Director: David Dunn.

| **1978** | **17.7** | **Wed 11 Jan 5:15 p.m.** | **4** | **182 wks** |

Con man Philip Warner-Bligh (Anthony Steel) arrives at the motel in a hired Rolls Royce. He is fleeing from his creditors.
Director: Alan Bromly.

| **1979** | **16.6** | **Wed 14 Feb 5:15 p.m.** | **2** | **135 wks** |

David Hunter's anxiety about his missing son grows.
Director: John Scholz-Conway.

| **1980** | **15.8** | **Wed 19 Nov 6:30 p.m.** | **2** | **121 wks** |

Iris Scott (Angela Webb) makes a candid confession to Marian Owen (Margaret John).
Director: Michael Hart.

| **1981** | **16.8** | **Wed 28 Jan 6:30 p.m.** | **3** | **63 wks** |

Meg Mortimer tries to console Kathy Brownlow (Pamela Vezey) after her visit from the police.
Director: Michael Hart.

| **1982** | **11.0** | **Thu 8 Jul 7:00 p.m.** | **4** | **4 wks** |

Benny can't understand why some people refuse his offer of money.
Directors: David Dunn and Malcolm Taylor.

1983	**16.6**	**Tue 24 May 6:05 p.m.** **Thu 26 May 6:05 p.m.**	**1**	**50 wks**

These episodes were listed together in the ratings.
Paul Ross (Sandor Elès) is angry over an indiscreet telephone call. Richard Lord (Jeremy Mason) tells Lucy Hamilton (Jan Todd) some home truths. David Hunter announces an explosive new idea.
Director: John Scholz-Conway.

1984	**15.3**	**Tue 4 Dec 6:05 p.m.** **Thu 6 Dec 6:05 p.m.**	**2**	**51 wks**

These episodes were listed together in the ratings.
Kevin Banks (David Moran) is finding it hard to be both father and mother to his daughter Katy Louise (Emily Albu). Edna Tilling (Mary Kenton) quarrels with her daughter Gloria (Kate Binchy). Iris Scott plots against Cliff Ryan (John Alkin).
Director: Brian Morgan.

1985	**18.1**	**Tue 1 Jan 5:15 p.m.** **Wed 2 Jan 6:00 p.m.** **Thu 3 Jan 6:05 p.m.**	**5**	**46 wks**

These episodes were listed together in the ratings.
J. Henry Pollard (Michael Turner) is led to believe that his daughter Miranda (Claire Faulkenbridge) will not marry Douglas Brady (Nigel Williams). Gloria Tilling decides to leave her mother Edna (Mary Kenton). Sid Hooper (Stan Stennett) helps Benny find a room.
Director: Brian Morgan.

1986	**14.0**	**Tue 7 Jan 6:35 p.m.** **Thu 9 Jan 6:35 p.m.**	**3**	**50 wks**

These episodes were listed together in the ratings.
Mavis Hooper (Charmian Eyre) explains her feelings for Sid. Jo (Mary Lincoln) mysteriously vanishes. Police investigate her disappearance.
Directors: Lyn Webster and Tony Virgo. **Producer:** Marian Nelson.

1987	**13.1**	**Tue 13 Jan 6:30 p.m.** **Thu 15 Jan 6:30 p.m.**	**10**	**54 wks**

These episodes were listed together in the ratings.
There has been a kidnapping at the motel. Charlie Mycroft (Graham Seed) is frantic with worry. Benny has spotted a removal van outside the village shop. A note is found in the motel saying 'I've gone back to Birmingham.' But who is it from?
Directors: Brian Lighthill and Mervyn Cumming. **Producer:** William Smethurst.

1988	**12.6**	**Mon 4 Jan 6:15 p.m.**	**8**	**1 wk**

The last of more than 4,500 editions leaves the staff of King's Oak Country Motel pondering the future.
Director: Nicholas Prosser. **Producer:** Michele Buck.

Crowther Collection, The   1 wk

ATV, comedy

This series of sketches by Barry Cryer and John Junkin starred Leslie Crowther with Anna Dawson and Francis Matthews.

1981	**11.3**	**Mon 24 Aug 8:00 p.m.**	**6**	**1 wk**

Producer: Colin Clews.

Crowther's in Town   3 wks

LWT, entertainment

This was the first series to feature Leslie Crowther's name in the title, although he already had many years of credits to his name, notably with the children's show CRACKERJACK and as a sometime resident on THE BLACK AND WHITE MINSTREL SHOW. This series from the Palace Theatre, London was a straightforward variety show.

1970	**6.3**	**Sat 3 Oct 6:15 p.m.**	**16**	**3 wks**

Guests: Ray Alan and Lord Charles, Chris Barber and his Band, Joe Henderson, Trisha Noble and Edward Woodward.
Musical Director: Harry Rabinowitz. **Producer:** Gordon Hesketh.

Cry from the Streets   1 wk

Presented by BBC, film

1967	**6.4**	**Sun 15 Jan 7:25 p.m.**	**15**	**1 wk**

The story of a little girl and her two brothers (Dana Wilson, Colin Peterson and Sean Barrett) from the slums behind King's Cross in London. They are befriended by Bill Lowther (Max Bygraves). Also starring Kathleen Harrison, Barbara Murray and Eleanor Summerfield.
Director: Lewis Gilbert.

Cry of the Innocent   1 wk

Presented by ITV, film

1981	**10.1**	**Sat 8 Aug 7:35 p.m.**	**11**	**1 wk**

A plane crashes in mysterious circumstances on a holiday cottage in Ireland. Starring Cyril Cusack, Nigel Davenport, Joanna Pettet and Rod Taylor.
Director: Michael O'Herlihy.

Paul Hogan hangs out in New York in **Crocodile Dundee**.

Cuckoo Waltz, The — 23 wks

Granada, situation comedy

Written by Geoffrey Lancashire (some episodes by John G. Temple). Chris and Fliss (short for Felicity) Hawthorne (David Roper and Diane Keen) were poor but happy and lived in a rundown house with their twins, a deckchair marked 'Property of Prestatyn UDC' and little else. Chris's rich friend Gavin Rumsey (Lewis Collins) arrived, fresh from a broken marriage, with a vanload of posh furniture. He became the lodger and the effect of his affluence and liberal sexual attitude was unsettling, to say the least!

1975   **7.5**   **Mon 17 Nov 8:00 p.m.**   **12**   **7 wks**

Chris and Fliss celebrate their wedding anniversary – with Gavin.
Producer: Bill Gilmour.

1976   **6.6**   **Thu 15 Jul 8:00 p.m.**   **3**   **6 wks**

Fliss needs a new washing machine but can't afford one. Gavin affords a new car but doesn't need one.
Director: Brian Mills. **Producer:** Brian Armstrong.

1977   **9.4**   **Mon 10 Jan 8:00 p.m.**   **2**   **6 wks**

Chris and Fliss are harder up for money than ever. Gavin is in Athens with Ariana (Stassia Stakis).
Director: Brian Mills. **Producer:** John G. Temple.

1980   **11.6**   **Thu 17 Jul 8:00 p.m.**   **7**   **4 wks**

Chris thinks it's all a big laugh, but has new lodger Adrian Lockett (Ian Saynor) really fallen for Fliss?
Director: Douglas Argent. **Producer:** John G. Temple.

Cue Gary — 1 wk

Central, entertainment

1987   **10.2**   **Sat 18 Jul 6:00 p.m.**   **9**   **1 wk**

Singer and impressionist Gary Wilmot mixed the worlds of fact and fantasy in song and comedy. Martin Beaumont and Nikki Boughton supported.
Director: Dennis Liddington. **Producer:** Brian Wesley. **Executive Producer:** Tony Wolfe.

Curry and Chips — 5 wks

LWT, situation comedy

This series by Johnny Speight was set in a factory where Eric Sykes was the liberal-minded foreman and Spike Milligan played Pakistani immigrant Kevin O'Grady (nicknamed Paki-Paddy). The other regulars were Fanny Carby, Geoffrey Hughes, Kenny Lynch and Norman Rossington.

1969   **7.2**   **Fri 5 Dec 7:30 p.m.**   **7**   **5 wks**

Kevin O'Grady is suddenly very popular when he gets eight draws on the treble chance.
Producer: Keith Beckett.

Curse of Mr Bean, The — 1 wk

Thames, comedy

1991   **14.0**   **Tue 22 Oct 8:30 p.m.**   **11**   **1 wk**

Repeat showing of the film billed as MR BEAN in 1990.

D

Dad's Army			64 wks

BBC, comedy

Jimmy Perry and David Croft created this series about a grossly inadequate group of local defence volunteers (The Home Guard) in the southern coastal town of Walmington-on-Sea. The characters were introduced each week by the signature tune 'Who Do You Think You Are Kiddin' Mr Hitler' played by the Band of the Coldstream Guards with the voice of Bud Flanagan. Those characters were Captain Mainwaring, the bank manager (Arthur Lowe), Sergeant Wilson, assistant bank manager (John Le Mesurier), and Corporal Jones, the butcher (Clive Dunn), with Private Frazer (John Laurie), Private Walker (James Beck), Private Godfrey (Arnold Ridley), Private Pike (Ian Lavender), Hodges the ARP warden (Bill Pertwee), the parish vicar (Frank Williams), the verger (Edward Sinclair) and Private Cheesman (Talfryn Thomas).
Series Producer: David Croft.

1968	4.9	Wed 11 Sep 8:20 p.m.	15	1 wk

'Shooting Pains'
A VIP has to be protected and Mainwaring is determined his platoon will have the honour.

1969	7.1	Sat 1 Mar 7:00 p.m.	7	19 wks

'Operation Kilt'
Mainwaring's platoon engages in a trial of strength with the regular army. A Scottish regiment is to try to capture the Home Guard HQ.

1970	7.4	Fri 20 Nov 8:00 p.m.	6	15 wks

'Mum's Army'
Mrs Gray (Carmen Silvera) organizes the ladies of Walmington-on-Sea to fight their own battle. Joining her are Mrs Pike (Janet Davies), Edith Parish (Wendy Richard), Mrs Fox (Pamela Cundell), Ivy Samways (Rosemary Faith) and Mrs Prosser (Eleanor Smale).

1971	6.4	Tue 16 Mar 7:30 p.m.	15	1 wk

'Something Nasty in the Vault'
Mainwaring's men discover an unexploded bomb.

1972	7.5	Fri 1 Dec 8:30 p.m.	2	12 wks

'When Did You Last See Your Money?'
Jones can't remember where he put the five hundred pounds collected for the canteen fund. The platoon tries to jog his memory.

1973	6.5	Wed 31 Oct 6:50 p.m.	12	2 wks

'The Deadly Detachment'
Mainwaring's platoon is detailed to guard a captured U-boat crew landed from a fishing vessel. Philip Madoc plays the U-boat captain.

1974	7.1	Mon 23 Dec 8:00 p.m.	14	3 wks

'Turkey Dinner'
After visiting several pubs with the platoon Corporal Jones shoots a turkey. Captain Mainwaring fails to establish the rightful owner of the bird so they decide to give a Christmas dinner for all the pensioners of Walmington-on-Sea.

1975	8.9	Thu 29 May 7:40 p.m.	2	5 wks

'Gorilla Warfare'
During exercises Captain Mainwaring casts himself in the role of a 'Highly Important Secret Agent'. The regular army tries to stop him.

1988	16.4	Fri 5 Feb 10:00 p.m.	7	1 wk

'The Royal Train'
Due to wrongly coded sealed orders Captain Mainwaring thinks that the Royal Train will pass through Walmington-on-Sea. He lines up an escort platoon, boards the train at the station . . . and discovers that it is not the Royal Train at all. (Repeat.)

1991	9.4	Mon 9 Apr 8:00 p.m.	14	5 wks

'Things That Go Bump in the Night'
Corporal Jones's butcher's van breaks down outside a house from which they hear strange noises. The sounds continue and the soldiers become convinced that the house is haunted. (Repeat.)

Dad's Army			3 wks

Presented by BBC, film

1976	6.2	Mon 19 Apr 7:00 p.m.	20	1 wk

It is 1940, and Walmington-on-Sea is threatened with invasion.
Director: Norman Cohen.

1979	12.5	Sat 5 May 6:45 p.m.	15	1 wk
1983	10.6	Sat 5 Mar 6:50 p.m.	20	1 wk

Repeat showings of the above film.

Daily Express Nurse of the Year — 1 wk

ATV, entertainment

This was a nationwide contest.

| 1976 | 6.0 | Wed 5 May 8:00 p.m. | 19 | 1 wk |

The ten finalists from all over the country are introduced by Leslie Crowther, who was once a hospital orderly himself. They are judged by a panel of medical experts.
Director: *Peter Harris.* **Producer:** *Jean Morton.*

Daktari — 14 wks

USA presented by BBC, drama

This series set in an African wildlife reserve starred Marshall Thompson as Dr Marsh Tracy and Cheryl Miller as Paula Tracy. Yale Summers played Dr Tracy's assistant Jack Dane, aided and abetted by Clarence the cross-eyed lion and Judy the chimp. Hedley Mattingly portrayed District Officer Hedley. The series was filmed in 200 acres of land about 50 miles from Hollywood known as Africa USA. This safari park was founded by the Executive Producer of Daktari, Ivan Tors, and animal trainer Ralph Helfer.

| 1966 | 5.6 | Mon 5 Dec 6:15 p.m. | 17 | 2 wks |

'Killer Dog'
A dog named Prince is accused of killing sheep.

| 1967 | 6.4 | Mon 6 Mar 6:15 p.m. | 5 | 12 wks |

'Daktari's Last Hunt'
A big game hunter sets out to prove that men and animals are born killers.

Dallas — 146 wks

USA presented by BBC, soap

In 1978 David Jacobs created a three-part mini-series that turned into the modern saga of a rich Texas family, the Ewings of Southfork Ranch. Daily Variety described it as 'a limited series with a limited future'. The principal stars included Larry Hagman as J.R. Ewing, ruthless in his quest for money and power, Patrick Duffy as Bobby Ewing, Barbara Bel Geddes (briefly replaced by Donna Reed) as their mother Miss Ellie, Linda Gray as Sue Ellen, Victoria Principal as Pamela Barnes and Ken Kercheval as Cliff Barnes. The Ewings and the Barnes continued a feud which began when their fathers had been drilling for oil together. One cheated on the other. The feud was further complicated when Bobby Ewing married Pamela Barnes. Other principal characters were Howard Keel as Clayton Farlow, Priscilla Presley as Jenna, Charlene Tilton as Lucy and Mary Crosby as Kristin Shepard, who tried to murder J.R.

| 1980 | 21.6 | Sat 22 Nov 9:10 p.m. | 1 | 23 wks |

'Who Dun It?'
The moment of truth arrives as we discover who shot J.R.

| 1981 | 15.2 | Sun 20 Dec 9:15 p.m. | 4 | 14 wks |

'Starting Over'
Bobby is shocked to find that J.R. is the father of Kristin's baby.

| 1982 | 14.5 | Sat 9 Jan 8:50 p.m. | 4 | 18 wks |

'The Search'
Shocking news disrupts the annual Ewing barbecue.

| 1983 | 12.7 | Wed 4 May 8:10 p.m. | 3 | 16 wks |

'Penultimate'
Sue Ellen has been taken to hospital after a car crash.

| 1984 | 14.9 | Tue 22 May 8:10 p.m. | 1 | 23 wks |

'End Game'
Cliff Barnes wonders whether Katherine (Morgan Brittany) has saved the family fortune. Clayton and Miss Ellie head for the altar.

| 1985 | 15.0 | Wed 17 Jul 7:40 p.m. | 1 | 23 wks |

'Swan Song'
Bobby Ewing embarks on a journey that will change life at Southfork.

| 1986 | 14.0 | Wed 5 Mar 7:30 p.m. | 3 | 27 wks |

'The Family Ewing'
This feature-length edition launches the new series. The clan gathers for Bobby's funeral.

| 1987 | 11.3 | Wed 2 Dec 8:00 p.m. | 19 | 2 wks |

'Ewing Rise'
Pam lies in a Dallas hospital, severely burned. She is hanging on to life by a thread.

Dame of Sark, The — 1 wk

Anglia, drama

| 1976 | 8.0 | Wed 29 Dec 9:10 p.m. | 1 | 1 wk |

Play by William Douglas-Home, adapted by David Butler. The Dame of Sark, Sybil Hathaway (Celia Johnson), fights for the survival of the islanders during German occupation. Also starring Tony Britton.
Designer: *James Weatherup.* **Director:** *Alvin Rakoff.* **Producer:** *John Jacobs.*

Damien: Omen II — 1 wk

Presented by ITV, film

| 1982 | 10.7 | Wed 26 May 9:45 p.m. | 11 | 1 wk |

A sinister teenager turns on his foster parents. This sequel to THE OMEN had a complete change of cast. Starring William Holden, Lee Grant and Jonathan Scott-Taylor.
Director: *Don Taylor.*

Dan Farson Meets . . . — 2 wks

AR, documentary

Daniel Farson, journalist and television reporter, interviewed personalities about their life and work.

| 1962 | 5.7 | Wed 21 Mar 9:15 p.m. | 9 | 2 wks |

'The Shadows'
Cliff Richard's backing group developed their own identity when 'Apache' hit number one in the summer of 1960. Now they come under the spotlight with Dan Farson probing their past, present and future.
Producer: Daphne Shadwell.

....

Danger UXB — 4 wks

Thames, drama

John Hawkesworth created this series about a squad of bomb disposal experts, or sappers, in wartime London. Anthony Andrews and Judy Geeson starred as Brian and Susan Ash.

| 1979 | 16.1 | Mon 2 Apr 9:00 p.m. | 5 | 4 wks |

'With Love From Adolf'
Even after four years of war, the squad finds little respite.
Producer: John Hawkesworth. **Executive Producer:** Johnny Goodman.
(Produced by Euston Films.)

....

Dangerous Knowledge — 5 wks

Southern, drama

Mystery thriller in six parts by N.J. Crisp. The 'dangerous knowledge' of the title belonged to Kirby (John Gregson), an insurance agent who took big risks for high stakes. Also starred Patrick Allen, Ralph Bates, Prunella Ransome and Ruth Trouncer.

| 1976 | 6.6 | Wed 19 May 8:30 p.m. | 9 | 5 wks |

'Comprehensive Cover'
It all begins with a chance meeting on a cross-channel ferry and the discovery of a body in the car.
Designer: John Dilly. **Producer:** Alan Gibson. **Executive Producer:** Lewis Rudd.

....

Danny Kaye Show, The — 1 wk

USA presented by BBC, entertainment

| 1965 | 5.4 | Tue 27 Apr 8:25 p.m. | 16 | 1 wk |

Guests: Buddy Ebsen, Marilyn Lovell and Howard Morris with the Paul Weston orchestra. (Series first shown on BBC2.)

Danny La Rue at the Palace — 1 wk

Thames, entertainment

The Irish drag artist cleaned up his nightclub act for television and became one of the medium's most-loved stars.

| 1972 | 7.3 | Thu 22 Jun 8:00 p.m. | 1 | 1 wk |

A recording of a performance of Danny's long-running show at the Palace Theatre, London with Joe Church, David Ellen, Toni Palmer, Jackie Sands and the Black Theatre of Prague.
Theatre Director: Freddie Carpenter. **Choreographer:** Lionel Blair. **Television presentation:** Steve Minchin.

....

Danny La Rue – The Ladies I Love — 1 wk

LWT, entertainment

| 1974 | 6.2 | Sat 14 Dec 7:30 p.m. | 8 | 1 wk |

A one-hour special in which Danny impersonates Lucille Ball, Shirley Temple, Marlene Dietrich, Zsa Zsa Gabor, Liza Minnelli and Dorothy Squires. Danny plays Kitty McShane with Roy Rolland as 'Old Mother Riley'. In a musical version of GONE WITH THE WIND, Gene Barry is Rhett Butler with Danny cast in the role of Scarlet O'Horror.
Producer: David Bell.

....

Dare I Weep – Dare I Mourn? — 1 wk

Presented by ITV, film

| 1966 | 8.1 | Wed 28 Sep 9:40 p.m. | 4 | 1 wk |

Otto Hoffman (James Mason) tries to bring his father's body back from East to West Berlin for burial. Also starring Jill Bennett and Hugh Griffith.
Director: Ted Kotcheff.

....

Dark Number, The — 5 wks

BBC, drama

This serial in five episodes was written by Edward Boyd. Set in Scotland, the Dark Number was the number of unknown crimes committed each year. Roddy McMillan played Inspector Wardlaw, who led the search for a missing woman. A crime may or may not have been involved. Her estranged husband Johnny Maxen (Patrick Allen) joined the search with some reluctance and irritation since he had made a new life for himself. (Series first shown on BBC2.)
Director: Michael Ferguson. **Producer:** Alan Bromley.

| 1968 | 7.7 | Tue 5 Mar 9:05 p.m. | 4 | 5 wks |

Episode 2
On his return to Glasgow after five years, Johnny Maxen goes to the flat of his estranged wife. He discovers a suicide.

D

The Irish drag artist impersonates Carol Channing in **Danny La Rue at the Palace**.

Darling Buds of May, The — 7 wks

YTV, drama

Bob Larbey adapted the novels of H.E. Bates about the Larkin family. David Jason starred as Pop Larkin with Pam Ferris as Ma, Philip Franks as Charley Charlton and Catherine Zeta Jones as Mariette. **Executive Producers:** Richard Bates and Vernon Lawrence.

| 1991 | 18.3 | Sun 21 Apr 7:45 p.m. | 1 | 7 wks |

'When The Greenwoods Laugh'
Mariette is set to marry tax inspector Charley.
Director: Robert Tronson. **Producer:** Robert Banks Stewart.

Date With Danger — 3 wks

Presented by BBC, film

A series of adventure films.

| 1983 | 9.6 | Sat 21 May 7:20 p.m. | 9 | 3 wks |

'Crisis in Mid-Air'
George Peppard stars as air-traffic controller Nick Culver. He is haunted by a recent mid-air collision and his marriage is on the rocks. Also starring Desi Arnaz Jr and Karen Grassle.
Director: Walter Grauman.

Dave Allen — 13 wks

ATV, comedy

| 1978 | 17.5 | Tue 3 Jan 7:00 p.m. | 5 | 13 wks |

Dave Allen pursues extraordinary people in America.
Producer: Robin Brown.

Dave Allen — 1 wk

BBC, comedy

| 1981 | 14.2 | Mon 20 Apr 10:00 p.m. | 8 | 1 wk |

Holiday special with Peter Bland, Jacqueline Clarke, Keith Drinkel, Sabina Franklyn, Paul McDowell and Michael Sharvell-Martin.
Director: Bill Wilson. **Producer:** James Moir.

Dave Allen and Friends — 13 wks

ATV, comedy

| 1977 | 8.6 | Tue 1 Feb 7:00 p.m. | 4 | 13 wks |

Dave Allen starts his search for the unusual and the exotic.

Dave Allen at Large — 8 wks

BBC, comedy

This Irish stand-up, or rather sit-down-on-a-stool, comedian, had a fearless approach to topics once considered taboo, most notably sex and religion.
Writers: Dave Allen, Austin Steele and Peter Vincent. **Producer:** Peter Whitmore. (The 1971–73 programmes were first shown on BBC2.)

1971	5.1	Wed 2 Jun 9:55 p.m.	15	1 wk
1972	5.0	Fri 1 Sep 8:15 p.m.	13	1 wk
1973	6.0	Fri 19 Oct 8:15 p.m.	12	3 wks
1976	6.3	Wed 14 Jan 8:15 p.m.	20	1 wk
1977	12.4	Tue 4 Oct 9:25 p.m.	19	2 wks

Dave Allen in Search of the Great English Eccentric — 1 wk

ATV, documentary

| 1974 | 7.2 | Tue 8 Oct 9:10 p.m. | 2 | 1 wk |

Dave Allen meets, among other eccentrics, a man who has lived for twenty-five years in a four-foot box and a couple who live in a shed using steam power.

Dave Allen Show, The — 1 wk

BBC, entertainment

| 1969 | 5.6 | Sat 26 Apr 7:30 p.m. | 19 | 1 wk |

Guests: Ray Barrett, Peter Gordeno, Matt Monro and Trisha Noble with the George Mitchell singers and the Alyn Ainsworth orchestra. **Producer:** Ernest Maxin.

Dave King Show, The — 5 wks

ABC, entertainment

This Cockney comedian hit the pop charts in the mid-1950s but faded away before returning as a successful character actor in the 1970s.

| 1963 | 5.1 | Sat 18 May 8:30 p.m. | 18 | 1 wk |

Guests: Patrick Macnee and Patsy Ann Noble with the Norman Percival orchestra.
Writers: Brad Ashton, Bob Block and Gerry Maxin. **Producer:** Ernest Maxin.

| 1969 | 6.9 | Thu 20 Nov 9:00 p.m. | 10 | 1 wk |

Guest: Trisha Noble with the Jack Parnell orchestra and the Pamela Devis dancers.
Producer: Pat Johns.

| 1970 | 6.5 | Thu 15 Jan 9:00 p.m. | 14 | 3 wks |

Guest: Barbara Windsor with the Jack Parnell orchestra and the Pamela Devis dancers.
Director: John Scholz-Conway. **Producer:** Dick Hills.

....

Dave's Kingdom   6 wks

ATV, entertainment

Series starring Dave King.

| 1964 | 6.8 | Wed 2 Dec 9:10 p.m. | 8 | 6 wks |

Guests: Nicholas Brent, Jack Douglas, John Hewer and Victor Maddern with the Jack Parnell orchestra.
Writers: John Warren and John Singer. **Director:** Francis Essex.

....

David Copperfield   2 wks

BBC, drama

Six-part dramatization by Hugh Whitemore of the novel by Charles Dickens.

| 1974 | 6.2 | Sun 15 Dec 5:10 p.m. | 18 | 2 wks |

David (David Yelland) has been adopted by Aunt Betsey (Patience Collier) and educated at her expense. At a coach station he meets his old friend and protector Steerforth (Anthony Andrews). Others in the cast include Martin Jarvis as Uriah Heep and Arthur Lowe and Patricia Routledge as Mr and Mrs Micawber.
Designer: Paul Joel. **Director:** Joan Craft. **Producer:** John McRae.

....

David Nixon Magic Hour, The   1 wk

Thames, magic

| 1975 | 6.4 | Tue 23 Dec 7:15 p.m. | 10 | 1 wk |

A special with guests George Carl, Dash's chimpanzees, Rolf Harris and Caterina Valente, with the Ronnie Aldrich orchestra.
Producer: Peter Frazer-Jones.

....

David Nixon Show, The   37 wks

Thames, magic

With the Ronnie Aldrich orchestra.
Producer (1973, 1975–77): Royston Mayoh.

| 1972 | 6.7 | Mon 8 May 6:40 p.m. | 6 | 12 wks |

Guests: Freddie Davies, Rita Morris and Lovelace Watkins.
Director: Daphne Shadwell. **Producer:** David Clark.

| 1973 | 6.2 | Mon 7 May 6:40 p.m. | 8 | 6 wks |

Guests: Shag Connor and the Carrot Scrunchers, Les Dawson, Finn Jon, Anita Harris and Bevan Raynor.

| 1974 | 6.6 | Mon 6 May 6:40 p.m. | 5 | 6 wks |

Guests: Anita Harris, Rolf Harris and Des Lane.
Director: Royston Mayoh. **Producer:** Eddie Joffe.

| 1975 | 7.0 | Mon 12 May 6:40 p.m. | 13 | 5 wks |

Guests: Janet Brown, Fivepenny Piece, The Great Kovari and Little and Large.

| 1976 | 7.1 | Mon 26 Apr 6:40 p.m. | 11 | 6 wks |

Guests: Michael Allport and Jennifer, Ali Baba, Barbara Hanna and John Inman.

| 1977 | 11.2 | Mon 22 Aug 6:45 p.m. | 8 | 2 wks |

Guests: Ray Alan and Lord Charles, Robert Danau, Fred Kaps and Reflections.

....

David Nixon's Magic Box   20 wks

Thames, magic

Bald-headed magician David Nixon was a favourite television personality from the 1950s, when he had been a regular panellist on WHAT'S MY LINE. He was the first British magician to become a television star. This series was a variety show with magic. With the Ronnie Aldrich orchestra.

| 1970 | 7.0 | Mon 9 March 6:40 p.m. | 9 | 7 wks |

Guests: Ray Fell, Anita Harris and Ritani.
Producer: Peter Frazer-Jones.

| 1971 | 6.8 | Mon 8 Feb 6:40 p.m. | 15 | 13 wks |

Guests: Norman Barrett's Performing Budgerigars, Joe Castor, Anita Harris and Roger Whittaker.
Producer: Peter Frazer-Jones.

Davro's Sketch Pad — 1 wk

TVS, comedy

Series of sketches and impressions starring Bobby Davro.

1989 | **10.2** | **Sat 29 Apr 7:30 p.m.** | **19** | **1 wk**

Guests: Fred Evans, Harry Fowler and Anneka Rice.
Producer: Nigel Lythgoe.

Dawson and Friends — 3 wks

YTV, comedy

Series starring Les Dawson with the Syd Lawrence orchestra.

1977 | **8.1** | **Wed 20 Apr 8:00 p.m.** | **7** | **3 wks**

Guests: Lulu, Guys and Dolls with Roy Barraclough, Norman Chappell, Humphrey Lyttelton, Julian Orchard, Willie Rushton and Kathy Staff. **Writers:** Barry Cryer, Les Dawson and David Nobbs. **Director:** Len Lurcuck. **Producer:** Vernon Lawrence.

Dawson Watch, The — 4 wks

BBC, comedy

This series starred Les Dawson with Roy Barraclough, Vicki Michelle, Daphne Oxenford and Gordon Peters.
Producer: Peter Whitmore.

1979 | **16.8** | **Thu 29 Nov 8:30 p.m.** | **4** | **4 wks**

Day After, The — 1 wk

Presented by ITV, film

1983 | **11.3** | **Sat 10 Dec 9:30 p.m.** | **14** | **1 wk**

American citizens are advised to take to nuclear shelters as NATO and Soviet forces engage in Europe. Starring Jason Robards, Steve Guttenberg and JoBeth Williams.
Director: Nicholas Meyer.

Day of Celebration, A — 2 wks

BBC, news

1977 | **7.2** | **Tue 7 Jun 10:10 a.m.** | **3** | **2 wks**

The Nation and the Commonwealth honour Her Majesty Queen Elizabeth II on her Silver Jubilee. Tom Fleming commentates.
Executive Producer: Antony Craxton.

Day of the Jackal, The — 1 wk

Presented by ITV, film

1980 | **11.9** | **Sat 19 Apr 8:00 p.m.** | **18** | **1 wk**

Adaptation of Frederick Forsyth's novel. Starring Edward Fox as the Jackal, an assassin hired by French Secret Army chief Colonel Rodin (Eric Porter) to kill President de Gaulle. Also starring Alan Badel, Tony Britton, Cyril Cusack, Maurice Denham, Michel Lonsdale, Anton Rodgers, Donald Sinden, Jean Sorel and Timothy West.
Director: Fred Zinnemann.

Day War Broke Out, The — 1 wk

Thames, documentary

1975 | **6.1** | **Tue 15 Jul 9:00 p.m.** | **7** | **1 wk**

Archive footage of artists who entertained the Allied troops through World War Two including Fred Astaire, Bing Crosby, George Formby, Bob Hope, Vera Lynn, Tommy Trinder, Jack Warner and Robb Wilton, whose catchphrase provides the show's title.
Producer: John Robins.

D-Day, The Sixth of June — 1 wk

Presented by BBC, film

1980 | **10.9** | **Fri 6 Jun 9:25 p.m.** | **11** | **1 wk**

It is the dawn of D-Day, 1944. British Lieutenant-Colonel John Wynter (Richard Todd) and American Captain Brad Parker (Robert Taylor) stand on the deck of their assault craft as they near the Normandy beach. They are both thinking of the same girl.
Director: Henry Koster.

D-Day 25 Years On — 1 wk

Granada, documentary

1969 | **4.8** | **Tue 3 Jun 10:30 p.m.** | **19** | **1 wk**

Brian Inglis commemorates the Normandy landing of 1944.
Director: Richard Guinea. **Producer:** James Butler.

Dead End Lads, The — 1 wk

ATV, documentary

1972 | **5.7** | **Thu 10 Aug 9:15 p.m.** | **13** | **1 wk**

Thousands of fifteen to eighteen-year-olds are on the scrapheap before they have even started work. This programme examines how they pass their days and what they themselves think of society.

Narrator: Ashley Bruce. *Camera:* Nic Knowland. *Producer:* John Goldschmidt.

....

Dead Ernest   5 wks

Central, situation comedy

This series by John Stevenson and Julian Roach starred Andrew Sachs as Ernest Springer. He won the pools, got hit in the eye with a champagne cork and woke up in Heaven. Ken Jones appeared as Archangel Derek and Harry Fowler played Cherub Fred.
Director: Alan Wallis. *Producer:* Tony Charles. **Executive Producer:** Allan McKeown.

| 1982 | 14.9 | Mon 15 Jan 8:00 p.m. | 7 | 5 wks |

....

Dead Man's Folly   1 wk

Presented by ITV, film

| 1988 | 11.5 | Sun 12 Jun 7:45 p.m. | 8 | 1 wk |

Peter Ustinov is Hercule Poirot in Agatha Christie's story of the murder of a young girl at a country estate. As the hunt begins, more deaths occur.
Director: Clive Donner.

....

Deadline Midnight   10 wks

ATV, drama

This series set out to represent life on a fictitious national newspaper, the Daily Globe. The actors were deliberately chosen because they were not well-known television faces, thus adding to the feel of authenticity. Arthur Christiansen, former editor of the Daily Express, was retained as series advisor.

| 1960 | 5.2 | Mon 15 Aug 9:35 p.m. | 2 | 7 wks |

A young girl (Wendy Williams) goes pot-holing in North Wales with disastrous consequences. Cast also includes Ray Barrett, Barbara Clegg, Shay Gorman and Peter Vaughan.
Writer: L.F. Lampitt. *Producer:* Hugh Rennie.

| 1961 | 4.9 | Sat 21 Oct 10:00 p.m. | 17 | 3 wks |

'Before The Cock Crows' by Bill Craig.
Matt Stewart (Bruce Beeby) is in Wallgreen to write a feature for the Daily Globe. While he is there, a mission hall is wrecked by a gang of thugs.
Director: John Knight. *Producer:* Rex Firkin.

Deadly Encounter   1 wk

Presented by BBC, film

| 1986 | 11.4 | Tue 26 Aug 9:30 p.m. | 11 | 1 wk |

Larry Hagman stars as a pilot running a helicopter charter service in Mexico. He gets involved in a very dangerous race when an old girlfriend (Susan Anspach) is kidnapped by gangsters.
Director: William A. Graham.

....

Deadly Puzzle, A   1 wk

Presented by BBC, film

| 1986 | 9.3 | Sun 6 Jul 7:15 p.m. | 5 | 1 wk |

A man is reported killed in a plane crash. His wife finds the official explanation unsatisfactory. When she digs deeper she finds he was not the man she believed him to be. Ben Masters and Karen Valentine star.
Director: Walter Grauman.

....

Deadly Stranger   1 wk

Presented by ITV, film

| 1981 | 13.0 | Sat 10 Oct 9:15 p.m. | 12 | 1 wk |

Belle Adams (Hayley Mills) is brutally attacked by a lorry driver after her car breaks down. She is rescued by Stephen Slade (Simon Ward).
Director: Sidney Hayers.

....

Dear John   9 wks

BBC, situation comedy

This series by John Sullivan starred Ralph Bates as the recently and reluctantly divorced John.

| 1986 | 15.6 | Mon 17 Feb 8:30 p.m. | 5 | 5 wks |

'The 1–2–1 Club'
Schoolteacher John arrives home to find his wife has left him. She's been having an affair with his best friend.
Producer: Ray Butt.

| 1987 | 13.0 | Mon 12 Oct 8:30 p.m. | 8 | 4 wks |

'Once Bitten'
John embarks on yet another romantic association.
Director: Sue Bysh. *Producer:* Ray Butt.

Dear Mother – Love Albert | 12 wks

YTV, comedy

This series was written by Rodney Bewes and Derrick Goodwin and starred Bewes as incurable bachelor Albert Courtnay, a confectionery salesman. Each week Albert wrote a letter home to mother.
Executive Producer: John Duncan.

| 1969 | 7.1 | Mon 20 Oct 9:30 p.m. | 5 | 6 wks |

'The Verge of Stardom'
Albert's firm is planning a new TV commercial and Albert believes he should be the star.

| 1971 | 7.5 | Mon 22 Feb 8:30 p.m. | 9 | 6 wks |

'De Profundis'
Albert is arrested and locked up. He asks for paper to write **'The Ballad of Reading Jail'**, his de profundis. His boss arrives, but instead of bailing him out suggests leaving him there for ten years! And where is girlfriend Doreen Bissel? With Liz Gebhardt, Garfield Morgan and Michael Robbins.

Death by Misadventure | 3 wks

Granada, documentary

This series recalled mysterious real-life disasters.

| 1967 | 8.0 | Tue 21 Nov 9:00 p.m. | 3 | 3 wks |

HM Airship-R101 set out on 4 October 1930 and crashed in a storm near Beauvais, France. Thirty-seven years later, the people most closely associated with the project give their testimony.
Narrator: Frank Duncan. **Writer:** John Chandos. **Director:** Michael Cox. **Producer:** Mike Wooller.

Death Car on the Freeway | 1 wk

Presented by ITV, film

| 1982 | 9.0 | Thu 29 Jul 7:45 p.m. | 10 | 1 wk |

Several attractive female drivers have been killed on the Los Angeles freeway in suspicious collisions. Television reporter Jan Clausen (Shelley Hack) establishes a pattern and relentlessly pursues the culprit. Also starring Frank Gorshin, Peter Graves, George Hamilton, Barbara Rush and Dinah Shore.
Director: Hal Needham.

Death in California, A | 2 wks

Presented by BBC, film

| 1991 | 9.9 | Tue 20 Aug 9:42 p.m. | 11 | 2 wks |

Sam Elliott and Cheryl Ladd star in the true story of an innocent victim held under the spell of a murderer.
Director: Delbert Mann.
This film was shown on two consecutive evenings. Both episodes charted.

Death of a Rebel | 1 wk

Granada, documentary

| 1967 | 5.7 | Tue 12 Sep 8:45 p.m. | 9 | 1 wk |

This allegorical documentary reflects a depressing view of the contemporary abuse of nature as seen through the eyes and voice of a dog, Panzer.
Writer and **producer:** Ronald Eyre. **Executive Producer:** Denis Mitchell.

Death of Adolf Hitler, The | 1 wk

LWT, drama

| 1973 | 6.6 | Sun 7 Jan 7:55 p.m. | 13 | 1 wk |

Vincent Tilsley's story of the last ten days of Hitler's life. A cast of more than fifty and a crew in excess of two hundred spent a year making this programme. The cast includes Frank Finlay as Hitler, Caroline Mortimer as Eva Braun, Ed Devereaux as Martin Borman, Oscar Quitak as Josef Goebbels, Robert Cawdron as Hermann Goering and Michael Sheard as Heinrich Himmler.
Designer: Michael Yates. **Producer:** Rex Firkin.

Death of an Expert Witness | 4 wks

Anglia, drama

This seven-part thriller by P.D. James was set in Norfolk. A nineteen-year-old girl was murdered and found in the back seat of an old car near a quarry. She was the latest of five victims of the notorious 'Back Seat Strangler'. Det. Chief Supt. Adam Dalgliesh (Roy Marsden) led the hunt, with police pathologist Henry Kerrison (Ray Brooks). Also starred Barry Foster, Geoffrey Palmer and Andrew Ray.

| 1983 | 10.6 | Fri 8 Apr 9:00 p.m. | 13 | 4 wks |

Episode 1
Kerrison is called to the scene of the murder. The victim has been strangled and the first links with the other murders are established.
Designer: Leo Austin. **Director:** Herbert Wise. **Producer:** John Rosenberg.

Death on the Nile | 2 wks

Presented by BBC, film

| 1982 | 10.3 | Sat 25 Dec 8:15 p.m. | 15 | 1 wk |

Peter Ustinov stars as Hercule Poirot in Agatha Christie's story of murder aboard a Nile steam cruiser. Also starring Harry Andrews, Jane Birkin, Lois Chiles, Bette Davis, Mia Farrow, Jon Finch, Olivia Hussey, I.S. Johar, George Kennedy, Angela Lansbury, Simon MacCorkindale, David Niven, Maggie Smith and Sam Wanamaker. **Director:** John Guillermin.

| 1985 | 15.2 | Sat 28 Dec 7:55 p.m. | 10 | 1 wk |

Repeat showing of the above film.

Death of Ocean View Park, The | 1 wk

Presented by ITV, film

| 1982 | 10.6 | Thu 7 Oct 7:40 p.m. | 16 | 1 wk |

A massive storm over the Fourth of July weekend cuts power in an amusement park. A gas explosion follows and the roller coaster collapses. Everyone panics and tries to flee. **Director:** E.W. Swackhamer.

Deceptions | 1 wk

USA presented by BBC, drama

Judith Michael's bestseller, adapted for television in 2 parts by Melville Shavelson, starred Stefanie Powers in dual roles. She played Stephanie, married with 2 children and living in suburbia, and identical twin-sister Sabrina, who had a country estate, a chauffeur and a wealthy lover. They swapped lives for a week with terrible consequences. Barry Bostwick, Jeremy Brett, Tracey Childs, James Faulkner, Gina Lollobrigida, Joan Sims, Fabio Testi, Brenda Vacarro, Sam Wanamaker and John Woodvine also starred. **Directors:** Robert Cherault and Melville Shavelson.

| 1990 | 8.5 | Tue 21 Aug 9:30 p.m.
Wed 22 Aug 9:30 p.m. | 19 | 1 wk |

(These repeat episodes were listed together in the ratings.)
Episode One: A jet set party comes to a tragic end when a yacht in the Mediterranean explodes in a fireball.
Episode Two: Sabrina is injured in a car crash bringing a sinister new twist to the sisters' deception.

Deckie Learner | 1 wk

Granada, documentary

| 1965 | 4.7 | Wed 16 Jun 9:40 p.m. | 19 | 1 wk |

A fly-on-the-wall film of John Bratley, a fifteen-year-old lad from Grimsby, as he faces his first trip, twenty-two days at sea as a trainee 'deckie' on a North Sea trawler.
Camera: Terry Gould. **Sound:** John Purchese. **Producer:** Mike Grigsby.

Dee Time | 1 wk

BBC, entertainment

Former pirate radio disc jockey Simon Dee enjoyed brief success as a television host.

| 1967 | 5.4 | Tue 11 Apr 6:25 p.m. | 19 | 1 wk |

Guests: Vikki Carr, Ray Fell, Paul Jones, Lulu, Manfred Mann and Ted Ray with Bernard Hermann and the Northern Dance orchestra.
Director: Sydney Lotterby. **Producer:** Terry Henebery.

Deep, The | 3 wks

Presented by ITV, film

| 1982 | 10.3 | Sat 18 Sep 7:00 p.m. | 12 | 1 wk |

Scuba divers Gail Berke (Jacqueline Bissett) and David Sanders (Nick Nolte) discover the wreck of a Second World War freighter off Bermuda. Robert Shaw and Eli Wallach also star.
Director: Peter Yates.

| 1986 | 13.8 | Sun 11 May 7:45 p.m. | 3 | 1 wk |
| 1990 | 9.2 | Mon 27 Aug 8:00 p.m. | 19 | 1 wk |

Repeat showings of the above film.

Defeat in the West | 1 wk

AR, documentary

| 1963 | 5.0 | Wed 29 May 9:45 p.m. | 19 | 1 wk |

This programme examines how Hitler's army lost the war. Much use is made of German wartime footage, the filming of which cost the lives of more than six hundred cameramen.
Writer and **Narrator:** Paul Johnson. **Producer:** Peter Morley.

Defenders, The | 5 wks

USA presented by BBC, drama

This highly respected series of courtroom dramas created by Reginald Rose starred E.G. Marshall and Robert Reed as the father and son legal team Lawrence and Kenneth Preston. Each episode tackled a serious issue such as civil disobedience, abortion, racial violence and euthanasia. The Prestons did not always win.
Producers: Herb Brodkin and Robert Markell.

| 1963 | 7.6 | Tue 26 Mar 8:25 p.m. | 3 | 3 wks |

'The Hidden Jungle'
Lawrence Preston is defending a man charged with the brutal murder of a young girl. He is tormented by doubts of his client's innocence and the possible consequences of an acquittal. With guest star Carrol O'Connor.

| 1964 | 7.0 | Fri 3 Jul 8:25 p.m. | 12 | 1 wk |

'The Non-Violent'
A simple court hearing develops into a dramatic trial concerned with civil rights and the issues of free speech and assembly. Guest appearances by Ivan Dixon, James Earl Jones and Gene Raymond.

| 1966 | 4.5 | Mon 25 Jul 9:30 p.m. | 16 | 1 wk |

'No Knock'
Willie Drucker (Jack Gilford) shoots an intruder in his home. The stranger turns out to be a policeman. The law shows little mercy towards a cop killer.

Deliberate Stranger, The | 2 wks

Presented by BBC, film

| 1991 | 14.8 | Wed 7 Aug 9:30 p.m. | 6 | 2 wks |

The re-enactment of a real-life manhunt for serial killer Theodore 'Ted' Bundy (Mark Harmon) in 1974. Also stars Frederic Forrest and M. Emmet Walsh. This is the second of two parts.
Director: Marvin Chomsky.

Delivery Man, The | 2 wks

Granada, documentary

| 1967 | 6.4 | Wed 3 May 9:40 p.m. | 11 | 2 wks |

One of two programmes about the life of a young surgeon in a Yorkshire women's hospital, using real life cases as well as some re-construction with actors.
Camera: Norman Langley. **Director:** James Clark. **Producer:** Denis Mitchell.

Dempsey and Makepeace | 33 wks

LWT, drama

This crime series set in London paired English policewoman and Cambridge graduate Det Sgt Harriet Makepeace (Glynis Barber) with Lieutenant James Dempsey (Michael Brandon), a New York cop on attachment. They are assigned to SI 10, a department of Scotland Yard, under the command of the irascible Gordon Spikings (Ray Smith).

| 1985 | 16.1 | Fri 18 Jan 8:30 p.m. | 5 | 20 wks |

'The Squeeze' by Jesse Carr-Martindale.
A security officer is murdered as a van containing half a million pounds is hijacked.
Designers: Gordon Melhuish and Colin Monk. **Producer:** Tony Wharmby. **Executive Producer:** Nick Elliott.

| 1986 | 12.8 | Sat 13 Sep 9:00 p.m. | 4 | 9 wks |

'Jericho Scam' by Jeffrey Caine.
Dempsey is framed for a robbery.
Designer: Mike Oxley. **Director:** Robert Tronson. **Producer:** Ranald Graham. **Executive Producer:** Nick Elliott.

| 1987 | 12.3 | Sat 21 Feb 9:00 p.m. | 14 | 4 wks |

'Blind Eye' by Jesse Carr-Martindale.
Spikings discovers something rotten at the core of SI 10 which endangers his life.
Designer: Gordon Melhuish. **Director:** Gerry Mill. **Producer:** Tony Wharmby. **Executive Producer:** Nick Elliott.

Denis Norden's Laughter File | 1 wk

LWT, comedy

| 1991 | 17.4 | Sun 21 Sep 7:45 p.m. | 3 | 1 wk |

Norden presents a collection of stunts and pranks television personalities played on each other.
Director: Keith Haley. **Producer:** Paul Lewis.

Denis Norden's World of Television | 1 wk

LWT, comedy

| 1980 | 14.1 | Sun 28 Dec 7:15 p.m. | 20 | 1 wk |

Denis Norden presents odd clips from around the world.
Director: Ken O'Neill. **Producer:** Nicholas Barrett. **Executive Producer:** Richard Drewett.

Des | 14 wks

ATV, entertainment

This series starred entertainer Des O'Connor.

| 1972 | 7.5 | Tue 18 Apr 8:30 p.m. | 3 | 14 wks |

With Johnny Vyvyan, the Mike Sammes singers and the Jack Parnell orchestra.
Producer: Albert Locke.

Des and the Best of Guests | 2 wks

Thames, entertainment

| 1986 | 8.8 | Wed 6 Aug 8:00 p.m. | 12 | 2 wks |

Highlights from the recent series of DES O'CONNOR TONIGHT.
Producer: Brian Penders.

Des O'Connor Entertains | 16 wks

ATV, entertainment

Producer: Colin Clewes.

| 1974 | 9.0 | Tue 19 Feb 7:10 p.m. | 2 | 7 wks |

Guests: Charlie Drake and Peters and Lee, with the Mike Sammes singers and the Jack Parnell orchestra.

| 1975 | 7.5 | Fri 11 Apr 7:30 p.m. | 10 | 7 wks |

Guests: Peters and Lee. With Mike Burton, Sandra Dickinson, Colin Keyes, Johnny Vyvyan, Eli Woods, the Mike Sammes singers and the Jack Parnell orchestra.

| 1976 | 6.8 | Fri 27 Feb 9:00 p.m. | 15 | 2 wks |

Guests: Marti Caine, Rod Hull and Emu, John Inman and the Muppets, with the Tony Mansell singers and the Jack Parnell orchestra.

Des O'Connor on Reflection | 6 wks

ATV, entertainment

| 1969 | 6.3 | Sat 26 Apr 6:15 p.m. | 5 | 6 wks |

Highlights of the last series of THE DES O'CONNOR SHOW with Roy Hudd, Matt Monro, Esther and Abi Ofarim, Una Stubbs and Frankie Vaughan.
Producer: Albert Locke.

Des O'Connor Show, The | 45 wks

ATV, entertainment

Des, the comedian who sang, became the singer who was occasionally a comedian after scoring in the pop charts in 1967. His singing became the butt of many Morecambe and Wise jokes and, later, Russ Abbot jabs, but his television career is one of the longest and most successful of all time. With the Jack Parnell orchestra and the Mike Sammes singers.
Producers included Albert Locke (1963, 1967–68, 1970) and Alan Tarrant (1966, 1971).

| 1963 | 5.1 | Wed 29 May 9:15 p.m. | 15 | 1 wk |

Guests: Jack Douglas, Terry Lightfoot's Jazzmen and the Raindrops with the Irving Davies dancers.
Director: Brian Bartholomew.

| 1965 | 5.9 | Thur 15 Jul 7:00 p.m. | 7 | 5 wks |

Guests: Jack Douglas and Barbara Law with the Norman Maen dancers.
Producer: Dicky Leeman.

| 1966 | 7.0 | Wed 18 May 9:10 p.m. | 6 | 11 wks |

Guests: Jack Douglas, William Franklyn and the Korean Kittens with the Norman Maen dancers.

| 1967 | 6.5 | Sat 11 Nov 7:00 p.m. | 4 | 6 wks |

Guests: Jack Douglas and Kenneth McKellar.

| 1968 | 8.1 | Sat 27 Apr 7:00 p.m. | 1 | 9 wks |

Guests: Chaz Chase, Clinton Ford and Frankie Vaughan.

| 1970 | 5.4 | Sat 25 Jul 9:00 p.m. | 14 | 7 wks |

Guests: Jim Couton and Rex, Jimmy Edwards, Jimmie Rodgers and Connie Stevens.
Director: John Robins.

| 1971 | 5.7 | Sat 18 Sep 9:25 p.m. | 15 | 5 wks |

Guests: Joe Baker, Jack Douglas, Buddy Greco, Connie Stevens and Johnny Vyvyan. With the Paddy Stone dancers.
Director: Jon Scoffield.

| 1973 | 6.8 | Fri 28 Dec 9:00 p.m. | 4 | 1 wk |

Guests: Jim Couton and Rex, Rod Hull and Emu.
Producer: Colin Clews.

Des and Dusty duet on **The Des O'Connor Show**.

Des O'Connor Tonight — 5 wks

BBC, entertainment

Des O'Connor hosted a show of chat and performance.

1979 — 17.0 — Fri 17 Aug 8:10 p.m. — 2 — 5 wks

Guests: Lennie Bennett, Hank Garcia, Jerry Stevens and The Three Degrees.
Producer: James Moir. (First shown on BBC2.)

Des O'Connor Tonight — 13 wks

Thames, entertainment

Producer: Brian Penders.

1983 — 10.8 — Tue 15 Nov 8:00 p.m. — 19 — 1 wk

Guests: Sheila Ferguson, Ronnie Schell and Freddie Starr.

1984 — 12.7 — Tue 20 Nov 8:00 p.m. — 14 — 3 wks

Guests: Roger de Courcey, Elaine Paige, the Flying Pickets and Miss World.

1985 — 12.1 — Tue 10 Dec 8:00 p.m. — 17 — 2 wks

Guests: Michael Barrymore, Dom DeLuise, Paul Nicholas, Shakin' Stevens and Mike Yarwood.

1987 — 11.2 — Wed 21 Oct 8:00 p.m. — 19 — 2 wks

Guests: Anne Diamond, Rita Rudner and Freddie Starr.

1988 — 12.6 — Wed 28 Dec 8:00 p.m. — 12 — 1 wk

Guests: Tony Curtis, Jason Donovan, Vince Hill and Kylie Minogue.

1990 — 12.1 — Wed 28 Nov 8:00 p.m. — 15 — 2 wks

Guests: Kim Appleby, Mike Doyle, Gary Lineker, Kenny Rogers and Freddie Starr.

1991 — 12.7 — Wed 11 Dec 8:00 p.m. — 17 — 2 wks

Guests: Cher, Jim Davidson, Jason Donovan and Cliff Richard.

Desert Fox, The — 1 wk

Presented by BBC, film

1971 — 6.2 — Sun 5 Dec 8:10 p.m. — 20 — 1 wk

After the defeat at El Alamein, Rommel 'The Desert Fox' (James Mason) is relieved of command and goes back to Germany. Co-starring Cedric Hardwicke and Jessica Tandy.
Director: Henry Hathaway.

Desperately Seeking Susan — 1 wk

Presented by BBC, film

1990 — 8.5 — Tue 10 Jul 9:30 p.m. — 15 — 1 wk

Intriguing advertisements in a personal column lead a bored housewife (Rosanna Arquette) into a world of mayhem, night clubs, magic and murder. Madonna stars as Susan.
Director: Susan Seidelman.

Detective — 5 wks

BBC, drama

In this series the great sleuths of crime fiction were featured. The 1964 programmes were introduced by Rupert Davies as MAIGRET.

1964 — 6.3 — Mon 30 Mar 9:25 p.m. — 7 — 2 wks

'The Moving Toy Shop' by Edmund Crispin, adapted by John Hopkins.
A poet finds a body in a toy shop, but when he returns with the police the next morning the body has disappeared – and so has the toy shop. Shortly afterwards a cryptic advertisement appears in the local paper which seems to refer to the nonsense poems of Edward Lear. There is none better at nailing literary allusion than the slightly dotty Professor Gervase Fen (Richard Wordsworth).
Designer: Margaret Peacock. **Director:** Shaun Sutton. **Producer:** David Goddard.

1968 — 5.0 — Fri 21 Jun 9:05 p.m. — 17 — 3 wks

'The Beast Must Die' by Nicholas Blake (alias C. Day Lewis), adapted by Pip and Jane Baker.
A murder attempt is foiled and the would-be murderer is arrested. Later in the day the would-be victim dies. Starring Bernard Horsfall as private detective Nigel Strangeways.
Designer: Raymond London. **Director:** Tina Wakerell. **Producer:** Verity Lambert.

Diamond Crack Diamond — 3 wks

LWT, drama

In this six-part series reporter John Diamond (Alan Dobie) escaped from an African jail and returned to London. He lived dangerously exposing the corruption behind big business attempts to exploit emerging African countries. Also starred Judy Parfitt as his wife Joyce and Iain Cuthbertson as lawyer Mark Terson.

1970 — 6.7 — Fri 2 Oct 9:00 p.m. — 11 — 3 wks

'Diamond c/o Terson' by Robin Chapman.
Diamond and Terson prepare for the next move by unknown assassins out to silence Diamond before he can reveal the corruption surrounding a new African state.
Director: James Goddard. **Producer:** Andrew Brown. **Executive Producer:** Rex Firkin.

Diamonds — 8 wks

ATV, drama

This thirteen-part series by John Brason concerned Coleman and Sons, a family firm of diamond merchants. It starred John Stride as Frank Coleman, Norman Wooland as Joseph Coleman, Hildegard Neil as Margaret Coleman, Doris Hare as Dora Coleman and Simon Ward as Bernard de Haan.

| 1981 | 13.3 | Wed 25 Nov 9:00 p.m. | 15 | 8 wks |

'House of Cards'
Too late, Frank realizes he is the victim of a confidence trick.
Producer: John Cooper. **Executive Producer:** David Reid.

Diamonds — 8 wks

Presented by ITV, film

| 1982 | 8.7 | Sat 31 Jul 7:45 p.m. | 15 | 7 wks |

Robert Shaw stars as a London diamond merchant who schemes to blackmail a master safecracker (Richard Roundtree) to help raid the Tel Aviv diamond repository. Also starring Barbara Seagull and Shelley Winters.
Director: Menahem Golan.

| 1988 | 9.8 | Sat 23 Apr 8:00 p.m. | 16 | 1 wk |

Repeat showing of the above film.

All of Sean Connery's original James Bond films became Number One television hits, including **Diamonds Are Forever**.

Diamonds are Forever — 6 wks

Presented by ITV, film

| 1978 | 14.4 | Mon 25 Dec 6:45 p.m. | 12 | 1 wk |

Christmas showing of the James Bond film starring Sean Connery in pursuit of a racketeer smuggling diamonds out of South Africa. Also starring Charles Gray as Blofeld and Jill St John as Tiffany Case.
Director: Guy Hamilton.

1981	22.2	Sun 15 Mar 7:45 p.m.	1	1 wk
1984	14.9	Thu 28 Mar 7:20 p.m.	3	1 wk
1986	15.5	Sun 4 May 7:45 p.m.	2	1 wk
1988	12.7	Mon 2 May 8:00 p.m.	7	1 wk
1990	9.6	Sat 8 Sep 7:40 p.m.	16	1 wk

Repeat showings of the above film.

Diana: Progress of a Princess — 1 wk

ITN, documentary

| 1991 | 10.0 | Sun 28 Jul 9:05 p.m. | 11 | 1 wk |

Carol Barnes reports on the last ten years in the life of the Princess of Wales.
Editor: Mike Sheppard.

Diary of the Cannes Film Festival — 1 wk

ATV, documentary

| 1980 | 11.2 | Fri 18 Jul 9:00 p.m. | 9 | 1 wk |

American columnist Rex Reed attends the 33rd Festival.
Director: Iain Johnstone. **Producer:** Billy Baxter.

Dick Emery Christmas Show, The — 2 wks

BBC, comedy

| 1974 | 6.7 | Tue 24 Dec 7:10 p.m. | 5 | 1 wk |

With Geoffrey Chater, Pat Coombs, Robert Dorning, Helen Fraser and Victor Maddern.
Producer: Harold Snoad. **Executive Producer:** John Ammonds.

| 1977 | 14.0 | Sat 24 Dec 9:05 p.m. | 17 | 1 wk |

Guests: Judy Cornwell, Roy Kinnear, Patrick Troughton and June Whitfield.
Producer: Harold Snoad.

Dick Emery Comedy Hour, The   1 wk

Thames, comedy

| 1979 | 15.5 | Wed 6 Jun 8:00 p.m. | 1 | 1 wk |

Dick Emery's first show for ITV, with guests Tim Barrett, Lulu, Beryl Reid and John Rutland, with the Irving Davies dancers and the Peter Knight orchestra.
Writers: Eric Merriman, Freddie Sales, John Singer, Mike Waiters. **Producer:** Keith Beckett.

....

Dick Emery Show, The   88 wks

BBC, comedy

Dick Emery was a character comedian whose creations included the toothy vicar, the bovver boy, Mandy (she of dubious virtue), a gentleman tramp and the creaking grandad. He died in 1984. **Writers** included John Singer (1971–80) and John Warren (1971–76). **Producers** included Ernest Maxin (1969–70), Colin Charman (1971–73), and Harold Snoad (1974–80).

| 1969 | 7.1 | Fri 7 Feb 7:55 p.m. | 7 | 9 wks |

Guests: The Satin Bells with the Norman Percival orchestra.

| 1970 | 6.3 | Fri 10 Apr 8:25 p.m. | 10 | 3 wks |

Guests: Tim Barrett, Josephine Blake, Samantha Jones, Joy Stewart and Jo Warne.

| 1971 | 6.6 | Fri 5 Mar 8:30 p.m. | 8 | 9 wks |

'The Army'
Each of this year's ten shows was built around one theme. Dick plays the Colonel, the recruiting sergeant, the old corporal in charge of the regimental museum and a strapping WRAC.

| 1972 | 7.4 | Sat 8 Jan 9:20 p.m. | 5 | 15 wks |

Guests: Gordon Clyde, Pat Coombs, David Healy and Bob Todd.

| 1973 | 7.5 | Sat 10 Mar 8:30 p.m. | 4 | 14 wks |

Guests: Norman Chappell, Pat Coombs, Gillian Lind, Reg Lye and Michael Ward.

| 1974 | 6.8 | Sat 23 Nov 8:10 p.m. | 7 | 6 wks |

Guests: Pat Coombs, Royce Mills, Josephine Tewson and Jonathan Lynn.

| 1975 | 7.1 | Wed 24 Dec 7:55 p.m. | 1 | 10 wks |

Guests: Helen Fraser, Victor Maddern, George Moon and Josephine Tewson.

| 1976 | 6.6 | Tue 14 Sep 8:00 p.m. | 17 | 5 wks |

Special guest Ian Hendry, with Patrick Newell and David Stoll.

| 1977 | 13.9 | Sat 1 Oct 8:30 p.m. | 9 | 7 wks |

Guests: Ronald Fraser and Roy Kinnear, with Helen Fraser, Michael Knowles, Victor Maddern and Vivienne Martin.

| | | Sat 22 Oct 8:20 p.m. | | |

Guests: Pat Coombs, Frederick Jaeger and Roy Kinnear with Anna Karen, Jenny McCracken and Johnny Shannon.
These episodes achieved identical viewing figures and chart positions.

| 1978 | 13.8 | Wed 3 May 9:35 p.m. | 11 | 3 wks |

Repeat showing from the previous series with Roy Kinnear and Francis Matthews.

| 1979 | 15.3 | Sat 3 Mar 8:30 p.m. | 6 | 5 wks |

Guests: Gretchen Franklin, Helen Fraser, Henry McGee, Victor Maddern, Josephine Tewson and Queenie Watts.

| 1980 | 18.9 | Sat 9 Feb 8:05 p.m. | 2 | 2 wks |

Guests: Pat Coombs, Helen Fraser, David Healy, Vivienne Martin and Larry Martyn.

....

Dick Emery's Grand Prix   1 wk

BBC, comedy

| 1970 | 5.0 | Thu 2 Jul 9:10 p.m. | 17 | 1 wk |

A fifty-minute special in which Dick plays a veteran driving ace in a comeback against the world's top drivers, with a special guest appearance by Graham Hill.
Writers: Peter Buchanan and Peter Robinson. **Producer:** Ernest Maxin.

....

Dick Powell Show, The   17 wks

USA presented by BBC, drama

Powell was one of Hollywood's leading men of the 1930s and 1940s. In the 1950s he founded Four Star Television with David Niven and Charles Boyer (there was no fourth star). He hosted and appeared in this series of dramas, which was sometimes known as THE DICK POWELL THEATRE.

| 1962 | 5.5 | Tue 16 Oct 8:25 p.m. | 13 | 1 wk |

'The Legend'
Sammy Davis Jr. stars in a tale about a newspaper's fight with a crooked boxing promoter.
Writer and **Director:** Aaron Spelling.

| 1963 | 5.5 | Mon 7 Oct 8:10 p.m. | 15 | 1 wk |

'In Search of a Son'
Introduced by David Niven. Gary Harper (Dean Stockwell), the son of wealthy business executive Alex Harper (Dick Powell), has been living somewhere in Europe, ignoring his father's letters asking him to return and join the family business. Alex employs a private detective who finds Gary living in a beach shack in Spain. He's fallen in love with Mary (Yvonne Craig). Alex flies over to confront Gary but his attitude changes when he meets Mary and her mother (Gladys Cooper).
Director: Buzz Kulik.

| 1964 | 8.5 | Tue 28 Jan 8:25 p.m. | 4 | 15 wks |

'Colossus'
Set in the San Fernando Valley in 1912, this is the story of two young immigrants struggling to establish themselves in America, the Swede, Eric Tegman (William Shatner), and the Irishman John Michael Rearden (Robert A. Brown). They buy a piece of land, but their tyrannical neighbour Corbett (Frank Overton) tries to drive them away. Corbett's hostility is extended when his daughter Ruth (Geraldine Brooks) falls in love with Tegman.
Writer and **Producer:** Alan Simmons.

Dick Turpin 2 wks

LWT, drama

In this thirteen-part series Richard O'Sullivan starred as the eighteenth-century English highwayman.

| 1979 | 14.6 | Sat 6 Jan 7:30 p.m. | 18 | 2 wks |

'Swiftnick' by Richard Carpenter.
Turpin comes to the aid of a woman and her son who are being evicted from their inn.
Designer: John Bleyard. **Director:** Charles Chrichton. **Producers:** Sidney Cole and Paul Knight.

Dick Van Dyke Show, The 3 wks

USA presented by BBC, situation comedy

Created by Carl Reiner, this series picked up Emmy awards in both 1964 and 1965. Van Dyke played the role of Rob Petrie, head scriptwriter of 'The Alan Brady Show', living at home in New York with his wife Laura (Mary Tyler Moore), a former dancer, and their young son Richie (Larry Matthews). Rob worked with two writing partners, Buddy Sorrel and Sally Rogers (Morey Amsterdam and Rose Marie). Carl Reiner played their boss.

| 1963 | 5.2 | Fri 11 Oct 9:10 p.m. | 19 | 1 wk |

'The Return of Happy Spangler'
The cast proves that many hands do not necessarily make light work.

| 1966 | 4.1 | Sat 30 Jul 7:05 p.m. | 20 | 1 wk |

'Odd But True'
Bells and clapper boards are part of a scriptwriter's everyday life, but when used by the wrong people at the wrong time they can cause problems.

| 1969 | 5.2 | Fri 12 Sep 9:10 p.m. | 18 | 1 wk |

A reunion programme with Mary Tyler Moore. Van Dyke and Moore appear not as Mr and Mrs Petrie but as themselves in a show of song, dance and comedy.

Dickie Henderson Show, The 83 wks

AR, situation comedy

One-time child star Dickie Henderson, son of Yorkshire comedian Dick Henderson, achieved much popularity with this domestic situation comedy, which also starred June Laverick as his wife, John Parsons as their son and Lionel Murton as Richard, Dickie's friend and go-between. The script editor was Jimmy Gratton.
Producer (1960–65): Bill Hitchcock.

| 1960 | 6.2 | Mon 19 Dec 8:00 p.m. | 3 | 5 wks |

Guest star: Richard Wattis.

| 1961 | 7.0 | Mon 20 Mar 8:00 p.m. | 1 | 23 wks |

Guest star: Naunton Wayne.

| 1962 | 6.1 | Wed 5 Dec 9:15 p.m. | 4 | 12 wks |

Guest stars: Peter Barkworth and Carole Shelley.

| 1963 | 7.6 | Thu 17 Oct 7:30 p.m. | 3 | 22 wks |

Dickie pooh-poohs the idea of June paying for driving lessons and insists on instructing her himself. The result is not harmonious.

| 1964 | 7.0 | Wed 29 Apr 9:10 p.m. | 4 | 10 wks |

Dickie lectures his pal Richard on the evils of jealousy, but when an old boyfriend of June's comes to call he finds it hard to practise what he preaches.

| 1965 | 6.9 | Mon 6 Sep 9:10 p.m. | 4 | 11 wks |

Dickie sets out to prove to June that men are quicker and better shoppers than women.

The Dick Emery Comedy Hour, and his very first ITV show, was a Number One. His most famous character creation, Mandy, was featured in the programme.

The Dick Emery Show on the BBC reached Number One in its seventh series.

The variety entertainer Dickie Henderson achieved his only Number One with a domestic sit-com called The Dickie Henderson Show.

Dickie Henderson Show, The — 1 wk

LWT, entertainment

Henderson starred in his own series, in his best-known guise as a song-and-dance man.

| 1971 | 6.1 | Sat 3 Apr 8:05 p.m. | 19 | 1 wk |

Guests: Roy Castle, William Franklyn, Johnny Mathis, Teddy Peiro and Dilys Watling with the Harry Rabinowitz orchestra and the Lionel Blair dancers.
Director: Philip Casson. **Producer:** Terry Henebery.

Dickie Valentine Show, The — 7 wks

ATV, music

Producer: Dicky Leeman.

| 1966 | 6.1 | Wed 6 Jul 9:10 p.m. | 6 | 6 wks |

Guests: Johnny Dankworth, Cleo Laine, Norman Vaughan and the Jack Parnell orchestra.
Choreographer: Gary Cockrell.

| 1967 | 4.5 | Fri 18 Aug 8:25 p.m. | 19 | 1 wk |

Guests: Billy Daniels with the Breakaways, Pan's People and the Jack Parnell orchestra.
Choreographer: Flick Colby.

Digby, The Biggest Dog in the World — 1 wk

Presented by ITV, film

| 1979 | 14.4 | Sat 22 Dec 6:00 p.m. | 11 | 1 wk |

Digby accidentally acquires his size by eating a chemical which has been developed for use on vegetables. Jim Dale stars with Angela Douglas, Dinsdale Landen, Spike Milligan, Milo O'Shea and Norman Rossington.
Director: Joseph McGrath.

Dimbleby Talk-in, The — 1 wk

BBC, talk

In this series David Dimbleby discussed issues and arguments of the moment with guests and a studio audience.

| 1973 | 7.1 | Fri 23 Nov 10:30 p.m. | 12 | 1 wk |

Tonight's subject is telepathy and other strange mental powers. Dimbleby pits sceptics and believers against one another.
Producer: Antony Rouse.

Dirtwater Dynasty — 3 wks

Australia presented by BBC, drama

This four-part saga spanned three generations of greed, rivalry and ambition.
Producers: Terry Hayes, George Miller and Doug Mitchell.

| 1989 | 10.3 | Tue 15 Aug 9:30 p.m. | 12 | 3 wks |

Episode Two
Richard Eastwick (Hugo Weaving) begins to build his empire. His determination to find water under the ground pays off, but soon he is engulfed by personal tragedy.

Dirty Dozen: The Deadly Mission, The — 1 wk

Presented by ITV, film

| 1989 | 11.7 | Sun 3 Dec 7:15 p.m. | 20 | 1 wk |

Major Wright (Telly Savalas) leads twelve military convicts to rescue a group of scientists coerced into making nerve gas. The dozen receive their orders from General Worden (Ernest Borgnine).
Director: Lee H. Katzin.

Dirty Dozen: The Next Mission, The — 1 wk

Presented by BBC, film

| 1986 | 10.2 | Fri 29 Aug 8:15 p.m. | 19 | 1 wk |

Major Reisman (Lee Marvin) faces a court martial in 1944. As an alternative he is offered a dangerous mission behind enemy lines. He picks and trains the new Dirty Dozen, all convicted GIs sentenced to death or hard labour. Ernest Borgnine, Richard Jaeckel and Ken Wahl also star.
Director: Andrew V. McLaglen.

Dirty Harry — 2 wks

Presented by BBC, film

| 1986 | 11.8 | Thu 24 Jul 10:00 p.m. | 5 | 1 wk |

Clint Eastwood stars as Inspector Harry Callahan, a police officer who gets all the tough or dirty jobs and is ruthlessly determined in the execution of his task. When a sniper murders a young girl and holds the city of San Francisco to ransom, Harry is put on the case with Lieutenant Bressier (Harry Guardino).
Director: Don Siegel.

| 1990 | 11.1 | Sat 1 Sep 9:30 p.m. | 10 | 1 wk |

Repeat showing of the above film.

Dirty Money `1 wk`

ATV, drama

| 1979 | 19.1 | Wed 21 Mar 8:00 p.m. | 1 | 1 wk |

Ian McShane stars as Bert 'The Brain', who plans to organize a fascist takeover of France financed by a bank robbery in Nice. The story is based on the real-life exploits of Albert Spaggiari. Also stars Warren Clarke, Stephen Greif and Christopher Malcolm.
Writer and **Director:** Francis Megahy.

Disappearing World `3 wks`

Granada, documentary

This series created by Brian Moser reported from the farthest corners of the Earth on its flora, fauna and human inhabitants.

| 1974 | 7.6 | Wed 20 Nov 9:00 p.m. | 9 | 3 wks |

'The Mehinacu'
The Mehinacu people live near the head of the Xingu river in the national park of central Brazil. The rituals of the people centre around the Piqui tree, both for its highly valued fruit and its sexual implications.
Camera: Stephen Goldblatt. **Sound:** Bruce White. **Director:** Carlos Pasini. **Editor:** Brian Moser.

Disaster in the Sky `1 wk`

Presented by ITV, film

| 1982 | 10.2 | Sat 24 Jul 7:45 p.m. | 4 | 1 wk |

The USA's first supersonic flight between New York and Paris takes off. Unknown to the two hundred and fifty passengers and crew, the hydraulic system has been tampered with. Starring Peter Graves, Lorne Greene, Doug McClure, George Maharis, Burgess Meredith, Robert Reed and Susan Strasberg.
Director: David Lowell Rich.

Disaster on the Coastliner `2 wks`

Presented by ITV, film

| 1980 | 14.9 | Wed 23 Jan 9:00 p.m. | 13 | 1 wk |

A computer genius programmes two trains on a collision course on the San Francisco to Los Angeles line. Starring Lloyd Bridges, Raymond Burr and Yvette Mimieux.
Director: Richard Sarafian.

| 1982 | 11.7 | Thu 11 Feb 7:30 p.m. | 19 | 1 wk |

Repeat showing of the above film.

Disney Special, The `2 wks`

BBC, entertainment

| 1973 | 5.9 | Sat 20 Oct 5:40 p.m. | 15 | 2 wks |

A special showing of film clips to celebrate the fiftieth anniversary of Walt Disney Productions. Introduced and narrated by Roy Castle.
Television presentation: Richard Evans.

Disney Time `15 wks`

BBC, entertainment

Producer: Richard Evans.

| 1964 | 4.8 | Fri 25 Dec 4:10 p.m. | 17 | 1 wk |

Julie Andrews introduces favourite clips from Walt Disney films, with the emphasis on comedy, including PLUTO'S CHRISTMAS TREE, PETER PAN, PINOCCHIO, LADY AND THE TRAMP, MARY POPPINS, SNOW WHITE AND THE SEVEN DWARFS and VANISHING PRAIRIE.

| 1966 | 5.6 | Mon 11 Apr 5:05 p.m. | 20 | 1 wk |

Easter Monday presentation of clips from Disney films, introduced by Nancy Kwan, including ALICE IN WONDERLAND, CINDERELLA, THE INCREDIBLE JOURNEY, TENDERFOOT, THE UGLY DACHSHUND and WINNIE THE POOH AND THE HONEY TREE.

| 1967 | 5.7 | Mon 27 Mar 6:15 p.m. | 19 | 1 wk |

Easter Monday presentation by Leslie Crowther and Peter Glaze with Maurice Chevalier in Paris. Films featured are FANTASIA, BAMBI, THE WIND IN THE WILLOWS, THE GNOME-MOBILE and SONG OF THE SOUTH.

| 1968 | 6.1 | Wed 25 Dec 4:10 p.m. | 14 | 1 wk |

Val Doonican introduces clips from BAMBI, PETER PAN, MARY POPPINS and THE HAPPIEST MILLIONAIRE.

| 1969 | 5.0 | Mon 26 May 7:30 p.m. | 17 | 2 wks |

Petula Clark introduces scenes from THE ABSENT MINDED PROFESSOR, ALICE IN WONDERLAND, CINDERELLA and THE LOVE BUG.

| 1970 | 5.8 | Mon 29 Mar 6:15 p.m. | 18 | 1 wk |

Easter Monday programme. Jimmy Tarbuck introduces clips from ALICE IN WONDERLAND, SNOW WHITE AND THE SEVEN DWARFS and IN SEARCH OF THE CASTAWAYS.

| 1971 | 5.1 | Mon 30 Aug 5:15 p.m. | 16 | 1 wk |

Derek Nimmo introduces clips from the Disney catalogue including THE ARISTOCATS, BEDKNOBS AND BROOMSTICKS and SLEEPING BEAUTY.

| 1972 | 4.7 | Mon 28 Aug 5:15 p.m. | 17 | 1 wk |

Dick Emery introduces clips from THE ARISTOCATS, THE GNOME-MOBILE, NAPOLEON AND SAMANTHA and other Disney films. Mickey Mouse also appears.

| 1974 | 6.9 | Sat 21 Dec 5:30 p.m. | 15 | 1 wk |

Derek Nimmo introduces clips from PETER PAN, MARY POPPINS, THE CASTAWAY COWBOY and ONE OF OUR DINOSAURS IS MISSING.

| 1977 | 15.2 | Tue 27 Dec 5:25 p.m. | 9 | 1 wk |

David Jacobs, who presented the BBC's first edition of DISNEY TIME, hosts today's fiftieth show with clips from, among others, MARY POPPINS, HERBIE GOES TO MONTE CARLO, THE SWISS FAMILY ROBINSON and PETE'S DRAGON.

| 1978 | 13.5 | Mon 27 Mar 6:15 p.m. | 19 | 1 wk |

Cliff Richard introduces clips including 20,000 LEAGUES UNDER THE SEA, MARY POPPINS, THAT DARN CAT and HERBIE GOES TO MONTE CARLO.

| 1980 | 16.1 | Fri 26 Dec 5:10 p.m. | 7 | 1 wk |

Marti Caine introduces clips from DUMBO, PINOCCHIO, THE LADY AND THE TRAMP and SNOW WHITE.

| 1981 | 14.9 | Sun 27 Dec 6:00 p.m. | 12 | 1 wk |

Windsor Davies introduces excerpts from DUMBO, THE FOX AND THE HOUND, THE FIGHTING PRINCE OF DONEGAL and SLEEPING BEAUTY.

| 1985 | 14.4 | Tue 1 Jan 5:20 p.m. | 9 | 1 wk |

Paul Nicholas presents excerpts from 101 DALMATIANS, PETER AND THE WOLF, SUPERDAD, LONESOME GHOSTS, THE JUNGLE BOOK and others.

Dive to Midnight Waters — 1 wk

BBC, documentary

| 1986 | 9.7 | Thu 22 May 8:30 p.m. | 13 | 1 wk |

Ian Holm narrates a film shot by night in the depths of the Pacific Ocean. The lights reveal a galaxy of soft-bodied creatures, many of which light up like fireworks.
Camera: Hugh Maynard and Mark Shelley. **Producer:** Adrian Warren.

Division, The — 1 wk

Granada, drama

| 1967 | 5.8 | Thu 25 May 9:40 p.m. | 13 | 1 wk |

This single drama by Bill Meilen was based on his own experiences of approved schools. Set on a ship where the discipline is the order of the fist, the play stars Roddy McMillan and Alan MacNaughton, with Ivan Beavis and Ivor Dean.
Designer: Roy Stonehouse. **Producer:** Derek Bennett.

Dixon of Dock Green — 75 wks

BBC, drama

Policeman George Dixon was killed in the movie THE BLUE LAMP. He was revived for the BBC in 1955 and was still there twenty-one years later when Jack Warner, the actor who played him, was eighty years of age. The series was created by Ted Willis and told stories of a London constable who was eventually promoted to desk sergeant. Dixon's son-in-law, Detective Sergeant Andy Crawford, was played by Peter Byrne.

| 1961 | 4.5 | Sat 16 Dec 6:30 p.m. | 17 | 2 wks |

'The Lifters and the Leaners' by Ted Willis.
When there's work to be done, George Dixon finds that people fall into one of these two categories.
Director: Michael Goodwin. **Producer:** Douglas Moodie.

| 1962 | 4.4 | Sat 6 Jan 6:30 p.m. | 18 | 1 wk |

'Counsel for the Defence' by Ted Willis.
Prosecuting counsel (John Boxer) has a difficult job convincing the magistrate (Ivan Samson) to see the police point of view.
Producer: Douglas Moodie.

| 1963 | 5.4 | Sat 7 Dec 6:35 p.m. | 20 | 1 wk |

'The Gunman' by Gerald Kelsey.
A young man lands in hospital having been shot in the eye with an airgun. Dixon is determined to find the culprit while Andy Crawford investigates a case involving trading stamps.
Director: David Askey. **Producer:** Ronald Marsh.

| 1966 | 5.9 | Sat 19 Feb 6:15 p.m. | 18 | 3 wks |

'Touch and Go' by Gerald Kelsey.
Sergeant Dixon's life hangs by a thread.
Director: Vere Lorrimer. **Producer:** Ronald Marsh.

| 1967 | 6.8 | Sat 9 Dec 7:10 p.m. | 11 | 6 wks |

'The Stepbrother' by Eric Paice.
Tommy Carpenter (Patrick Newell) returns home but is unwelcome.
Director: David Askey. **Producer:** Ronald Marsh.

1968 6.6 **Sat 23 Nov 6:45 p.m.** 5 **16 wks**

'High Finance' by N.J. Crisp.
A little old lady buys and sells. Unfortunately she doesn't always own what she sells.
Director: Eric Fawcett. Producer: Ronald Marsh.

1969 6.5 **Sat 20 Dec 8:25 p.m.** 16 **3 wks**

'Bobby' by N.J. Crisp.
Bobby Brown (Barry Jackson) is a criminal for whom even the police feel sorry.
Producer: Robin Nash.

1970 7.0 **Sat 28 Nov 6:45 p.m.** 7 **7 wks**

'The House in Albert Street' by Gerald Kelsey.
A man who has been reluctantly drawn into crime finds himself driven to lengths beyond his own imaginings.
Director: Robin Nash. Producer: Joe Waters.

1971 8.0 **Sat 13 Feb 6:55 p.m.** 5 **14 wks**

'Nightmare Hours' by Eric Paice.
Dixon's experience has taught him to be dismissive of the accused who says 'I don't remember a thing – I had a blackout'. But in this case he discovers it really can happen.
Producer: Joe Waters.

1972 7.4 **Sat 29 Jan 7:00 p.m.** 2 **19 wks**

'The Bad Debt Men' by Derek Ingrey.
A man is put behind bars on the evidence of a mistaken witness and a vindictive woman.
Director: Vere Lorrimer. Producer: Joe Waters.

1973 6.2 **Sat 29 Dec 6:30 p.m.** 8 **1 wk**

'Eye Witness' by Derek Ingrey.
Dixon takes an unexpected holiday in the company of the only witness to a gangland murder.
Producer: Joe Waters.

1974 6.6 **Sat 19 Jan 6:45 p.m.** 18 **2 wks**

'Question in the House' by Ben Bassett.
An old murder case rears its head and Dixon is forced to wonder whether there has been a miscarriage of justice.
Director: Ian Wyatt. Producer: Joe Waters.

Do You Come Here Often? 1 wk

AR, documentary

1962 4.4 **Wed 12 Sep 9:45 p.m.** 16 **1 wk**

Mike Sarne tells the story of dancing from the waltz to the twist. With the Frank and Peggy Spencer formation dancers, the Malcolm Goddard dancers and the Alan Braden orchestra.
Producer: Bill Turner.

Doctor, The 2 wks

BBC, documentary

Six programmes about the lives of Dr Barry Brewster and his four GP partners in the Yorkshire Dales.

1991 8.6 **Tue 20 Aug 8:30 p.m.** 17 **2 wks**

A ninety-four-year-old has breathing problems and there is a death at the local hospital.
Producer: Jeremy Mills. Executive Producer: Paul Hamann.

Doctor at Large 21 wks

LWT, situation comedy

The medical students from DOCTOR IN THE HOUSE, now qualified, had to find jobs!

1971 7.5 **Sun 25 Apr 7:20 p.m.** 2 **21 wks**

'Lock, Stock and Beryl'
Michael Upton (Barry Evans) is on the lookout for a better job. When Paul Collier (George Layton) grabs the first one to come up, it's war.
Writers: Graham Chapman and Bernard McKenna. Director: Bill Turner. Executive Producer: Humphrey Barclay.

Doctor at Sea 7 wks

LWT, situation comedy

Duncan Waring (Robin Nedwell) resigned from St Swithin's following the sacking of Dick Stuart-Clark (Geoffrey Davies). They became ship's doctors on a cruise liner.

1974 6.1 **Sun 9 Jun 7:30 p.m.** 12 **7 wks**

'The VIP'
Duncan gets on the wrong side of an attractive female passenger. He is unaware that she is a journalist writing an article about the cruise.
Writers: George Layton and Jonathan Lynn. Director: David Askey. Producer: Humphrey Barclay.

Doctor at the Top 1 wk

BBC, situation comedy

This series starred Robin Nedwell as Duncan Waring, George Layton as Paul Collier, Jill Benedict as Emma Stuart-Clark and Geoffrey Davies as Professor Stuart-Clark.

1991 12.6 **Thu 21 Feb 8:30 p.m.** 11 **1 wk**

'Sins of the Father'
The 1990s are very different for the doctors who were medical students in the 1960s, but there are skeletons in the cupboard.
Writer: George Layton. Producer: Susan Belbin.

1

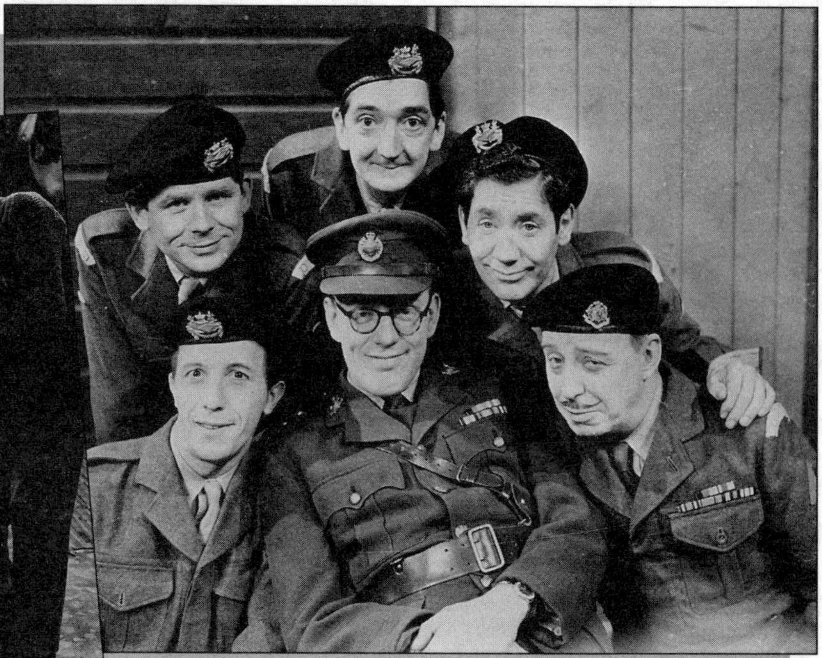

2

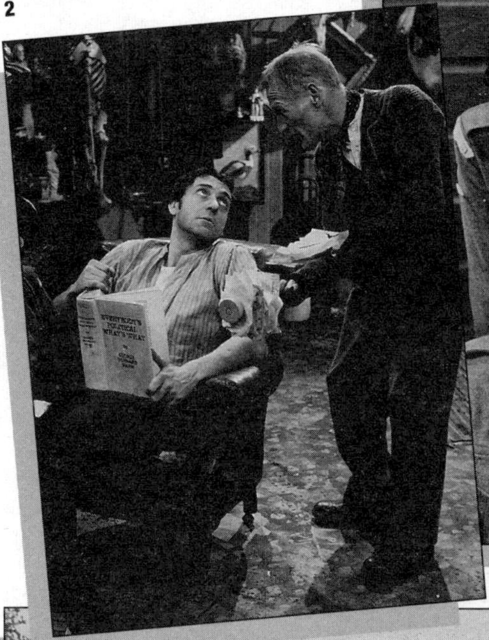

3

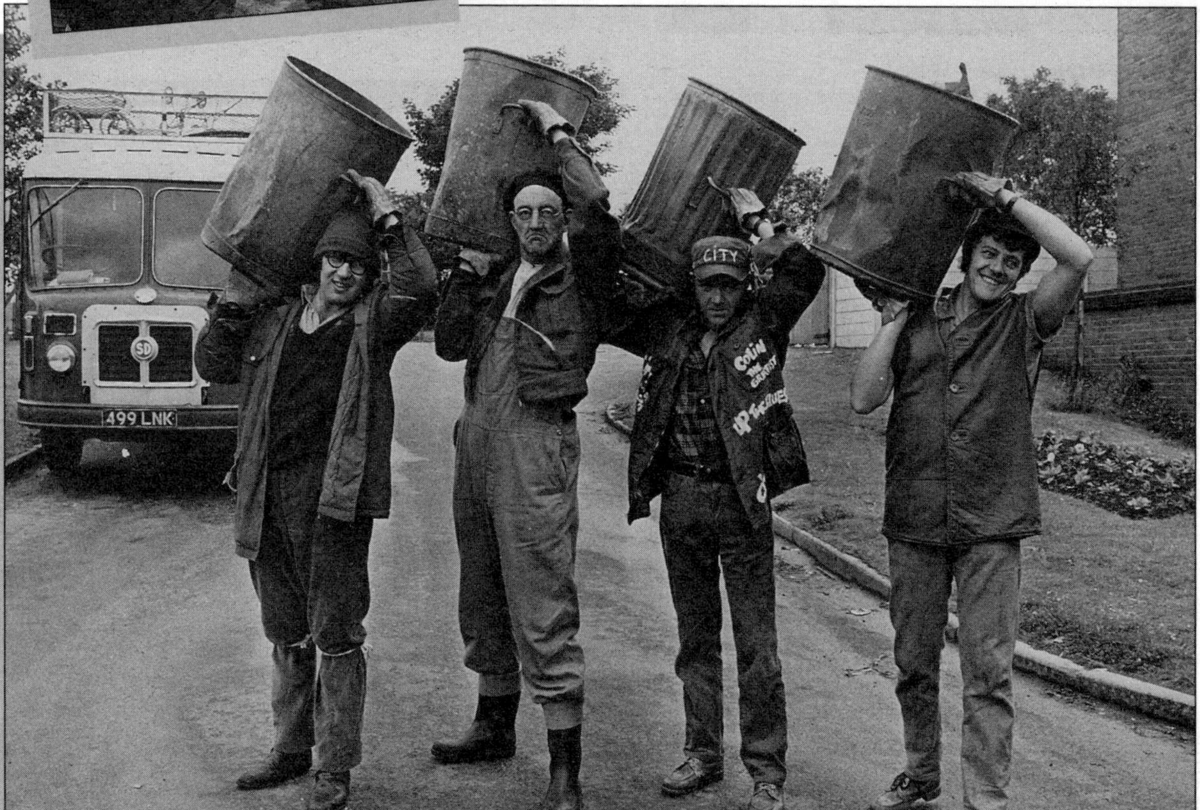

4

5

6

7

1 **The Army Game**, already a hit before the period covered in this book, was still a Number One in its final two years.

2 Alfred (Wilfrid Brambell) interrupts the self-education of Harold (Harry H. Corbett) in **Steptoe and Son**.

3 All six episodes of the first series of **The Dustbinmen** reached Number One. Beneath the bins are (left to right) Tim Wylton, Bryan Pringle, Graham Habberfield and Trevor Bannister.

4 The tramp, the most popular character from **The Arthur Haynes Show**, offers his foot to Dr Nicholas Parsons.

5 Members of **The Larkins** cast included (left to right) Ronan O'Casey, Peggy Mount and David Kossoff.

6 Bill Fraser (right) keeps his beady eye on Alfie Bass in **Bootsie and Snudge**.

7 Alf Garnett harangues son-in-law Mike in **Till Death Us Do Part**.

Doctor in Charge — 22 wks

LWT, situation comedy

A further twenty-six episodes of the St Swithin's medics from DOCTOR IN THE HOUSE, starred Robin Nedwell, George Layton and Geoffrey Davies.

1972 | **7.2** | **Sun 23 Apr 7:25 p.m.** | **6** | **22 wks**

'The Minister's Health' by Graham Chapman and Bernard McKenna. A VIP is admitted to the hospital and puts everyone in a flap, especially a professor who has new hopes of receiving a knighthood. The Minister of Health is played by Basil Henson. Also starring Richard O'Sullivan as Lawrence Bingham.
Director: Alan Wallis. **Producer:** Humphrey Barclay.

Doctor in Clover — 1 wk

Presented by BBC, film

1974 | **7.1** | **Sat 21 Dec 7:10 p.m.** | **12** | **1 wk**

Film based on Richard Gordon's novel of the same name. Starring Leslie Phillips and James Robertson Justice with Eric Barker, Alfie Bass, Elisabeth Ercy, Shirley Anne Field, John Fraser, Fenella Fielding, Arthur Haynes, Jeremy Lloyd, Noel Purcell, Joan Sims, Terry Scott and Norman Vaughan.
Director: Ralph Thomas.

Doctor in the House — 1 wk

Presented by ITV, film

1969 | **7.1** | **Wed 24 Dec 7:30 p.m.** | **4** | **1 wk**

Dirk Bogarde stars as medical student Simon Sparrow in the first of the 'Doctor' series based on the book by Richard Gordon. The cast also includes Donald Houston, James Robertson Justice, Kay Kendall, Kenneth More, Muriel Pavlow and Donald Sinden.
Director: Ralph Thomas.

Doctor in the House — 23 wks

LWT, situation comedy

The riotous medical students from the films based on Richard Gordon's DOCTOR books settled into television with great success. The series starred Robin Nedwell with Ernest Clark, Simon Cuff, Geoffrey Davies, Barry Evans, George Layton and Jonathan Lynn.
Producer: Humphrey Barclay.

1969 | **6.1** | **Fri 3 Oct 8:30 p.m.** | **7** | **11 wks**

'Pass or Fail'
It's exam time at St Swithins, and last-minute panic for the students.
Director: Bill Turner.

1970 | **7.1** | **Fri 24 Apr 8:25 p.m.** | **4** | **12 wks**

'Take Off Your Clothes and Hide'
The medics take a night off and visit a strip club. Unforeseen events interrupt the show.
Writers: Graeme Garden and Bill Oddie. **Director:** David Askey.

Doctor in the House — 1 wk

Presented by ITV, film

1983 | **11.3** | **Thu 6 Jan 6:55 p.m.** | **18** | **1 wk**

A compilation of clips from fifteen years of the DOCTOR films.

Doctor in Trouble — 1 wk

Presented by ITV, film

1978 | **14.9** | **Sun 1 Jan 7:45 p.m.** | **11** | **1 wk**

This adaptation of Richard Gordon's novel DOCTOR ON TOAST stars Leslie Phillips as Dr Simon Burke. He is called to a patient who turns out to be his old school enemy Basil (Simon Dee), who has become a TV star. Also starring Graham Chapman, Fred Emney, Freddie Jones, James Robertson Justice, Irene Handl, John Le Mesurier, Robert Morley, Angela Scoular, Harry Secombe and Joan Sims.
Director: Ralph Thomas.

Doctor on the Go — 10 wks

LWT, situation comedy

Another series of Richard Gordon stories which starred Robin Nedwell, Ernest Clark and Geoffrey Davies.

1977 | **9.4** | **Sun 13 Mar 8:20 p.m.** | **3** | **10 wks**

'A Turn for the Nurse'
The entertainment committee tries to account for missing funds.
Writers: Gail Renard and Brenda Crankmen. **Director:** Bryan Izzard.
Producer: Humphrey Barclay.

Doctor's Daughters — 1 wk

ATV, situation comedy

This series by Richard Gordon and Ralph Thomas concerned three family doctors (Bill Fraser, Richard Murdoch and Jack Watling), who had been in practice for thirty-five years. Professional colleagues told them they were out of date, so two young female doctors named Fay and Lucy (Victoria Burgoyne and Lesley Duff) were brought in.

1981	13.4	Sun 22 Feb 7:15 p.m.	18	1 wk

'A Change of Sex'
The new face of medicine is much prettier than the old when Fay and Lucy arrive at the Old Chapterhouse Surgery.
Producer: Stuart Allen.

Dr Finlay's Casebook | 12 wks

BBC, drama

This series created by A.J. Cronin was set in a Scottish village in the 1920s. The stories revolved around the elderly Dr Cameron (Andrew Cruickshank), the young Dr Finlay (Bill Simpson) and their canny housekeeper Janet (Barbara Mullen) in their Tannochbrae practice.
Producer (1967, 1969): Royston Morley.

1963	8.4	Fri 22 Nov 8:10 p.m.	4	1 wk

'The Face Saver'
Brenda Bruce and Alex McCrindle make guest appearances as Bridie and Colin Bell, who find themselves in the waiting room of the Tannochbrae surgery.
Designer: Lawrence Broadhouse. **Writer:** Elaine Morgan. **Director:** Julia Smith. **Producer:** Campbell Logan.

1965	6.5	Sun 31 Jan 9:50 p.m.	12	2 wks

'The Bull Calf'
Tannochbrae is in an uproar after Dr Finlay is persuaded in an emergency to act as midwife to a prize cow. There is open war between the human doctors and the veterinary surgeons.
Designer: Lawrence Broadhouse. **Writer:** Stewart Farrer. **Director:** William Slater. **Producer:** Andrew Osborn.

1967	8.5	Mon 11 Dec 9:05 p.m.	2	8 wks

'Death is a Colony'
Mr Usher (Ewan Hooper) brings hospital problems for Matron (Molly Urquhart) and Dr White (Brook Williams).
Designer: Gwen Evans. **Writer:** John Pennington. **Director:** Richard Argent.

1969	6.5	Sun 9 Mar 7:25 p.m.	11	1 wk

'The Visitation'
Dr Finlay clashes with Miss Seymour (Patricia Jessel), the headmistress of a Tannochbrae girls' school. Her Victorian ideals lead her to object to the doctor's influence on the pupils when he is called to treat a girl with a dislocated shoulder.
Designer: Cynthia Hood. **Writer:** Donald Bull. **Director:** Tina Wakerell.

Dr Jekyll and Mr Hyde | 1 wk

LWT, drama

1990	11.8	Sat 6 Jan 9:00 p.m.	18	1 wk

Michael Caine stars in Robert Louis Stevenson's story of the London physician who, through experimentation, separated the good and bad sides of his soul. The evil incarnation was the monstrous Mr Hyde. Joss Ackland, Lionel Jeffries, Diane Keen, Cheryl Ladd, Lee Montague and Ronald Pickup also star.
Writer and **Director:** David Wickes. **Producer:** Patricia Carr. **Executive Producer:** Nick Elliott.

Dr Kildare | 18 wks

USA presented by BBC, drama

This series was based on the 1940s stories by Max Brand in which young intern Dr Kildare (Richard Chamberlain) learned the practice of medicine at Blair Hospital under kindly mentor Dr Leonard Gillespie (Raymond Massey). Music by Jerry Goldsmith.
Producer: David Victor.

1961	5.5	Fri 29 Dec 8:00 p.m.	6	8 wks

'The Patient'
Dr Kildare has a fall and finds himself a patient in his own hospital.

1962	5.8	Wed 17 Jan 8:00 p.m.	7	7 wks

'Hit and Run'
A father's phobia of doctors leads him to attempt to halt his son's vital operation.

1964	5.8	Thu 17 Dec 8:25 p.m.	15	3 wks

'Rome Will Never Leave You'
Kildare and Gillespie have been in Rome for three weeks finding out about an important new medical breakthrough. They have also fallen in love, Kildare with Francesca (Daniela Bianchi) and Gillespie with Countess Luisa Brabante (Alida Valli). They face the inevitable as they prepare to return to the USA.

Ursula Andress in **Dr No** (overleaf) was the first Bond girl.

Dr No · 5 wks

Presented by ITV, film

| 1975 | 10.5 | Tue 28 Oct 8:00 p.m. | 1 | 1 wk |

Starring Sean Connery as James Bond, who goes to Jamaica to investigate the death of a British secret agent. With Ursula Andress as Honey, Bernard Lee as M, Lois Maxwell as Miss Moneypenny, and Joseph Wiseman as Dr No.
Director: Terence Young.

1985	17.5	Tue 1 Jan 6:30 p.m.	5	1 wk
1987	14.8	Sat 22 Mar 7:45 p.m.	5	1 wk
1988	11.6	Wed 19 Oct 8:00 p.m.	13	1 wk
1991	12.9	Sat 28 Sep 7:15 p.m.	11	1 wk

Repeat showings of the above film.

Dr Who · 22 wks

BBC, drama

Science fiction series in which the Doctor travelled through time and space in his Tardis (Time and Relative Dimension in Space) – a converted police box. The series began in 1963 and the leading role has been played by William Hartnell, Patrick Troughton, Jon Pertwee, Tom Baker, Peter Davison, Colin Baker and Sylvester McCoy.
Title music: Ron Grainer.

| 1964 | 5.4 | Sat 19 Dec 5:40 p.m. | 18 | 1 wk |

'The Waking Ally' by Terry Nation.
The reason for the presence of the Daleks at last becomes clear as the travellers build up to the final battle.
Director: Richard Martin. **Producer:** Verity Lambert.

| 1965 | 5.5 | Sat 13 Feb 5:40 p.m. | 18 | 2 wks |

'The Web Planet' by Bill Strutton.
Dr Who (William Hartnell) and Ian Chesterton (William Russell) investigate an unknown force, leaving Barbara Wright (Jacqueline Hill) and Vicki (Maureen O'Brien) behind.
Director: Richard Martin. **Producer:** Verity Lambert.

| 1975 | 7.0 | Sat 13 Dec 5:55 p.m. | 15 | 4 wks |

'The Android Invasion' by Terry Nation.
Only Dr Who (Tom Baker) can foil the Kraal invasion – and he's millions of miles away.
Director: Barry Letts. **Producer:** Philip Hinchcliffe.

| 1976 | 7.2 | Sat 23 Oct 6:00 p.m. | 12 | 8 wks |

'The Hand of Fear' by Bob Baker and Dave Martin.
In the fourth and final part of this adventure, the Doctor (Tom Baker) and Sarah Jane (Elizabeth Sladen) return to the twentieth century to avert a holocaust at a nuclear power station.
Director: Lennie Mayne. **Producer:** Philip Hinchcliffe.

| 1977 | 13.8 | Sat 19 Nov 6:10 p.m. | 18 | 1 wk |

'Image of the Fendahl' by Chris Boucher.
The final part of a four-part story in which the Doctor (Tom Baker) tries to defeat the Fendahl and save mankind. Also starring Louise Jameson as Leela and Wanda Ventham as Thea Ransome.
Director: George Spenton-Foster. **Producer:** Graham Williams.

| 1979 | 19.6 | Sat 20 Oct 6:15 p.m. | 16 | 6 wks |

'City of Death' by David Agnew.
Tom Baker stars in the final part of one of the strangest adventures of Dr Who's career. He goes to Paris where an alien creature is trying to steal the Mona Lisa.
Director: Michael Hayes. **Producer:** Graham Williams.

Doddy for Christmas · 1 wk

BBC, comedy

| 1968 | 5.4 | Wed 25 Dec 8:45 p.m. | 20 | 1 wk |

Ken Dodd's guests are Judith Chalmers, Patricia Hayes, Dermot Kelly, Jennifer Lowe, the New Faces, Graham Stark and Señor Wences.
Writers: Eddie Braben and Ken Dodd. **Producer:** Michael Hurll.

Doddy's Music Box · 19 wks

ABC, entertainment

This series starred Ken Dodd with David Hamilton and guests. With the ABC Showband.

| 1967 | 7.6 | Sat 7 Jan 6:20 p.m. | 6 | 11 wks |

Guests: Tom Jones, Peter and Gordon, and Julie Rogers.
Director: Peter Frazer-Jones. **Producer:** Philip Jones.

| 1968 | 7.6 | Sat 2 Mar 6:15 p.m. | 5 | 8 wks |

Guests: Adam Faith, Anita Harris, Vince Hill and Nigel Hopkins.
Producer: Peter Frazer-Jones.

Dolly Parton in London · 1 wk

BBC (with Home Box Office), music

| 1984 | 8.8 | Wed 13 Jun 10:00 p.m. | 18 | 1 wk |

This recording of Dolly Parton's concert at the Dominion Theatre features guests Tom Rutledge and Jim Salestrom.
Producer: Stan Harris.

Don't Ask Me — 35 wks

YTV, documentary

In this series three experts answered questions from viewers on matters of science and the everyday world.
Director (1974–75, 1977–78): Peter Jones. **Producer:** Duncan Dallas.

| 1974 | 6.4 | Wed 10 Jul 7:00 p.m. | 3 | 9 wks |

Experts: David Bellamy, Magnus Pyke and Miriam Stoppard.

| 1975 | 7.0 | Wed 14 May 7:00 p.m. | 10 | 9 wks |

Experts: David Bellamy, Magnus Pyke and Miriam Stoppard.

| 1976 | 6.3 | Wed 19 May 7:00 p.m. | 11 | 7 wks |

Experts: David Bellamy, Magnus Pyke and Miriam Stoppard.
Director: David Millard.

| 1977 | 6.2 | Wed 15 Jun 7:00 p.m. | 16 | 1 wk |

Experts: Robert Buckman, Maggie Makepeace, Austin Mitchell and Magnus Pyke.

| 1978 | 12.0 | Wed 5 Jul 7:00 p.m. | 10 | 9 wks |

Experts: Robert Buckman, Austin Mitchell and Magnus Pyke.

Don't Bring Libby, She'll Come By Herself — 1 wk

AR, music

| 1965 | 6.1 | Wed 24 Feb 9:10 p.m. | 15 | 1 wk |

This title, a parody of the song 'Don't Bring Lulu', refers to singer, dancer and actress Libby Morris, who enjoyed much television success from the mid-1950s.
Producer: Peter Croft.

Don't Drink the Water — 2 wks

LWT, comedy

Writers Ronald Wolfe and Ronald Chesney took the character Blakey (Stephen Lewis) from ON THE BUSES and moved him to Spain, where he bought a retirement flat with his spinster sister Dorothy (Pat Coombs).

| 1974 | 5.9 | Sat 7 Sep 7:05 p.m. | 14 | 2 wks |

'The Smell'
There is a terrible smell from the drains. Spanish plumbing is just one reason why Dorothy wants to go home. Carlos the porter (Derek Griffiths) does his best to divert the odour.
Producer: Mark Stuart.

Don't Just Sit There — 16 wks

YTV, documentary

Viewers were invited to discuss science with David Bellamy, Robert Buckman, Magnus Pyke and Miriam Stoppard.

| 1979 | 13.6 | Wed 2 May 7:00 p.m. | 9 | 10 wks |

Director: Nick Gray. **Producers:** Paul Dunstan, Hilary Lawson and David Taylor. **Executive Producer:** Duncan Dallas.

| 1980 | 12.1 | Wed 25 Jun 7:00 p.m. | 8 | 6 wks |

Director: Peter Jones. **Producers:** Hilary Lawson and David Taylor. **Executive Producer:** Duncan Dallas.

Don't Rock the Boat — 6 wks

Thames, situation comedy

This series by John Esmonde and Bob Larbey dealt with the Hoxton family, Jack (Nigel Davenport), Dixie (Sheila White), Les (John Price) and Billy (David Janson).

| 1983 | 7.9 | Tue 2 Aug 8:30 p.m. | 11 | 6 wks |

'The Flesh is Weak'
Billy suddenly begins to fancy his stepmother Dixie.
Producer: Mark Stuart.

Don't Say a Word — 19 wks

AR, quiz

Series devised by Mike Stokey derived from the parlour game Charades in which two teams of regulars (Jill Browne, Libby Morris and Harry Fowler versus Kenneth Connor, Glen Mason and Una Stubbs) mimed their clues so their opponents could guess the object of the mime. Known in the USA as PANTOMIME QUIZ. Hosted by Ronan O'Casey.

| 1963 | 5.0 | Thu 5 Sep 7:00 p.m. | 10 | 9 wks |

Director: Robert Fleming.

| 1964 | 5.8 | Thu 18 Jun 7:00 p.m. | 9 | 10 wks |

Director: Daphne Shadwell.

Reg Varney conceived as well as starred in **Down the Gate.**

Don't Wait Up | 20 wks

BBC, situation comedy

Tony Britton and Nigel Havers starred as father and son doctors Toby and Tom Latimer, respectively. They lived together after both their marriages had failed.
Writer: George Layton. **Producer:** Harold Snoad.

| 1985 | 12.9 | Mon 2 Dec 8:30 p.m. | 7 | 3 wks |

With Toby and Angela (Dinah Sheridan) on a reconciliation cruise that is far from plain sailing, Tom and Madeline (Susan Skipper) plan a weekend in the country.

| 1986 | 14.0 | Mon 3 Feb 8:30 p.m. | 6 | 5 wks |

A repeat in which Tom is only recently divorced.

| 1987 | 16.7 | Mon 30 Mar 8:30 p.m. | 3 | 7 wks |

Tom gets the chance to buy an old flat at a bargain price.

| 1988 | 9.8 | Mon 11 Jul 8:00 p.m. | 11 | 5 wks |

The differences between the NHS and private practice are brought home to Tom by a sequence of events.

Doomwatch | 2 wks

BBC, drama

This series of sci-fi stories, anchored in reality, speculated on what might happen if a particular experiment or technology got out of hand. Much of what the series dramatized came to pass later. Devised by Kit Pedler, a scientist, and Gerry Davis, a dramatist. Kit's father, Dr C.M.H. Pedler, acted as scientific advisor. The Doomwatch team was led by Dr Spencer Quist (John Paul) with Dr John Ridge (Simon Oates).

| 1970 | 5.7 | Mon 21 Dec 9:50 p.m. | 18 | 1 wk |

'Invasion' by Martin Worth.
In a remote Yorkshire village a mystery army unit has orders to kill everything that emerges from the ground.
Designer: Jeremy Davies. **Director:** Jonathan Alwyn. **Producer:** Terence Dudley.

| 1971 | 5.9 | Mon 15 Mar 9:20 p.m. | 19 | 1 wk |

'The Logicians' by Dennis Spooner.
A story exploring the theory that logic in a child is in many ways superior to that in an adult. Industrial spies are blamed for a mysterious break-in at Beresford Chemicals. Police have no clues as to how the sophisticated electronic security system was breached.
Designer: Graham Oakley. **Director:** David Proudfoot. **Producer:** Terence Dudley.

Double Blind, The | 1 wk

BBC, drama

| 1962 | 3.5 | Fri 10 Aug 9:25 p.m. | 17 | 1 wk |

Single drama from the novel by John Rowan Wilson, adapted for television by Vincent Tilsley.
Dr Farrell (Lyndon Brook) and Father de Freitas (Peter Illing) are in conflict on a small island off the west coast of Africa. Farrell's experiments with a vaccine to treat a centuries-old disease has resulted in several deaths. Dr Peter Mayne (Richard Leech) is sent from London by the Ministry of Health to decide whether the experiment should continue.
Designer: John Cooper. **Producer:** John Elliot.

Double Your Money | 269 wks

AR, game show

Based on the American quiz of THE $64,000 QUESTION. Contestants doubled their money for correct answers given to general knowledge questions, posed by Hughie Green, until they hit the Treasure Trail. At this point the lighthearted banter turned deadly serious as the contestant entered 'the soundproof booth'. The series began in 1955 and ran for almost twenty years. Hostesses included Nancy Roberts (1961–65), Monica Rose (1963–68) and Julie de Marco (1963–65). Also starred organist Robin Richmond (1960–67).
Directors included Eric Croall (1960–62) and Don Gale (1963 and 1965).

1960	6.6	Fri 4 Nov 7:30 p.m.	2	15 wks
1961	6.9	Thu 19 Oct 7:30 p.m.	2	23 wks
1962	7.0	Thu 22 Nov 7:30 p.m.	3	40 wks
1963	7.4	Thu 5 Dec 7:00 p.m.	2	37 wks
1964	7.8	Thu 30 Jan 7:00 p.m.	2	38 wks

Director: Jim Pople.

| 1965 | 8.3 | Thu 18 Feb 7:00 p.m. | 2 | 32 wks |
| 1966 | 8.9 | Tue 8 Nov 7:00 p.m. | 1 | 37 wks |

Hughie Green presents the show from the House of Friendship, Moscow with his assistants Monica Rose and Natasha Vasylyeva and contestants from the USSR. Because of Communist Party rules the show could not award money as a prize. The top prize was a television set.
Director: Peter Croft.

| 1967 | 8.1 | Tue 28 Feb 7:00 p.m. | 2 | 18 wks |
| 1968 | 7.8 | Wed 10 Jan 7:00 p.m. | 5 | 29 wks |

Doubletake

1 wk

USA presented by ITV, drama

| **1987** | **13.2** | **Sun 1 Mar 9:00 p.m.** | **8** | **1 wk** |

The first part of a two-part drama stars Richard Crenna as Detective Frank Janek of the New York Crime Department. He leads the hunt for the killer of two women.

Dowager in Hot Pants

1 wk

Thames, documentary

| **1971** | **5.6** | **Tue 17 Aug 9:00 p.m.** | **15** | **1 wk** |

A film involving some of the earliest Hollywood personalities, including Betty Blythe (the first Queen of Sheba), Babe London (a comedy star of the Buster Keaton era) and Ben Lane ('the best make-up artist in the world').
Producer: Jack Gold. **Executive Producer:** Jeremy Isaacs.

Down and Out in Beverly Hills

1 wk

Presented by ITV, film

| **1989** | **12.4** | **Mon 25 Dec 9:00 p.m.** | **15** | **1 wk** |

In this Hollywood remake of Renoir's BOUDU SAUVÉ DES EAUX a tramp tries to drown in the swimming pool of a Beverly Hills mansion. He takes over the home and lives off his rescuers. Starring Richard Dreyfuss, Bette Midler, Nick Nolte and Little Richard.
Director: Paul Mazursky.

Down the Gate

5 wks

ATV, situation comedy

This series by Maurice Sellar and Roy Tuvey was based on an idea by Reg Varney. Reg used to buy fish at Billingsgate Market, where he met people who inspired the characters in this series. Varney played a porter, Reg Furnell, and Dilys Laye portrayed his wife Irene. Tony Melody played his antagonist Len Peacock.
Producer: William G. Stewart.

| **1975** | **6.9** | **Wed 23 Jul 8:00 p.m.** | **1** | **5 wks** |

The fastest eel cutters in the trade top and tail – and the language is as ripe as the fish is fresh. Reg pulls his trolley and carries boxes on his head.

Dragnet

1 wk

Presented by BBC, film

| **1991** | **10.2** | **Mon 27 May 9:20 p.m.** | **11** | **1 wk** |

Dan Aykroyd plays Detective Sergeant Joe Friday in this film based on the 1950s US television series of the same title. Friday and his partner Pep Streebeck (Tom Hanks) tackle some bizarre crimes.
Director: Tom Mankiewicz.

Dragon Slayer

1 wk

Presented by ITV, film

| **1991** | **9.9** | **Wed 8 May 8:00 p.m.** | **15** | **1 wk** |

During the Dark Ages a wizard and his apprentice take on a dragon to rescue a princess. Peter MacNicol and Ralph Richardson star.
Director: Matthew Robbins.

Drama

61 wks

ATV, drama

This series was named by production year (e.g. DRAMA '61).

| **1961** | **6.6** | **Sun 26 Nov 9:00 p.m.** | **7** | **9 wks** |

'Torment' by Philip Levene.
A young law student confesses to the murder of a girl he claims to have killed a year ago. However, there are doubts as to whether the murder ever took place. It could be a figment of his tormented mind. Starring Peter Dyneley, Betty McDowell and Douglas Wilmer.
Designer: Eric Shedden. **Producer:** Quentin Lawrence.

| **1962** | **7.1** | **Sun 21 Oct 9:00 p.m.** | **3** | **20 wks** |

'A Chance in Life' by Bill Naughton.
A normal family wins the pools and waves goodbye to normality. Starring Maurice Denham, Hilda Fenemore, Dudley Foster, Arthur Mullard, Andrew Ray and Marjorie Rhodes.
Designer: Anthony Waller. **Producer:** Cliff Owen.

| **1963** | **8.3** | **Sun 8 Dec 9:35 p.m.** | **3** | **23 wks** |

'Leave All Hope Behind' by Jacques Gillies.
'Having a wonderful time,' wrote Kemp (Mark Eden) from Dublin. But Kemp has never been to Dublin. He tries to leave his life behind and abandons his future. Also starring Patrick Barr and David Garth.
Designer: Henry Graveney. **Producer:** Royston Morley.

| **1964** | **6.9** | **Sun 20 Dec 10:05 p.m.** | **6** | **9 wks** |

'It's Sad About Eddie' by Philip Levene.
Max Bygraves stars as Eddie Stanway, a songwriter who has run out of hits. He tells a disc jockey (Pete Murray) that music is being stolen from his mind and that he might just have seen a murder.
Designer: Vic Symonds. **Producer:** Josephine Douglas.

D

Drama Playhouse | 2 wks

BBC, drama

An occasional series of plays.

| 1972 | 6.0 | Wed 6 Sep 8:10 p.m. | 8 | 2 wks |

'The Incredible Robert Baldick' by Terry Nation.
Robert Baldick (Robert Hardy) lives with a horrifying fear that encloses him. If he is to avoid being totally smothered by terror, he must overcome this fear. With Julian Holloway, John Rhys-Davies and Reginald Marsh.
Designer: John Burrowes. **Director:** Cyril Coke. **Producer:** Anthony Coburn.

Dream Machine, The | 1 wk

ATV, documentary

| 1964 | 5.4 | Wed 11 Nov 9:10 p.m. | 19 | 1 wk |

A programme about TV featuring the work of two men. Producer Francis Essex plans, rehearses and records a show called SIX WONDERFUL GIRLS (Honor Blackman, Dora Bryan, Cleo Laine, Adele Leigh, Millicent Martin and Nadia Nerina). Roy Knight, lecturer in film and television at Durham University, begins teaching a new course.
Director: Denis Mitchell.

Dream Singing, A | 1 wk

AR, music

| 1964 | 5.4 | Wed 22 Jul 9:10 p.m. | 9 | 1 wk |

A one-off programme featuring songs about dreams. Starring Adam Faith with Patsy Ann Noble.
Director: Robert Fleming.

Driving Ambition | 1 wk

BBC, drama

This eight-part drama by Paula Milne concerned middle-aged house-wife Donna Hewitt (Rosemary Martin), who was obsessed with carving a niche in the male-dominated world of fast cars. She had her clapped-out Mini adapted by expert Ken Lark (Gavin Richards) to compete in saloon car races. Her friend, Jen Robinson (Anne Carroll), acted as mechanic, and their husbands Ray (Mark Kingston) and Mick (Donald Gee) grudgingly completed the team.

| 1984 | 9.4 | Sat 21 Apr 8:55 p.m. | 18 | 1 wk |

'A Class of Their Own'
The big day arrives and both families head for Brands Hatch. Donna panics when there's no sign of Ken Lark.

Designer: Bob Smart. **Director:** Michael Simpson. **Producer:** Carol Robertson.

Driving Force | 1 wk

BBC, sport

| 1989 | 9.5 | Fri 30 Jun 8:10 p.m. | 14 | 1 wk |

From the Channel Islands, Mike Smith and Murray Walker introduce a pro-celebrity driving competition. Teams: Joey Dunlop and Barry McGuigan, Jonathan Palmer and Mark King, Stefan Johansson and Kathy Tayler, and Juha Kankkunen and Phillip Schofield.
Television presentation: Peter Hylton Cleaver.

Drug Takers, The | 1 wk

ATV, documentary

| 1963 | 6.0 | Wed 30 Oct 9:48 p.m. | 16 | 1 wk |

Brian Abel-Smith investigates drug traffic in Britain.
Writer: John Deane Potter. **Producer:** Tony Firth.

Duchess of Duke Street, The | 25 wks

BBC, drama

Created and produced by John Hawkesworth. Set in the London of Edward VII, the fifteen-part series told the story of Louisa Trotter (Gemma Jones), a cook who rose to become proprietress of the Bentinck Hotel, Duke Street. It was based on the true story of Rosa Lewis, a cockney girl who began scrubbing floors at the age of twelve and became the owner of the Cavendish Hotel in Jermyn Street. Other principal characters included head porter Starr (John Cater), Lizzie (Maureen O'Brien), Major Smith-Barton (Richard Vernon), head waiter Merriman (John Welsh), Mary the maid (Victoria Plucknett), Charlie Tyrrell (Christopher Cazenove) and Starr's fox terrier, Fred.

| 1976 | 8.0 | Sat 23 Oct 7:25 p.m. | 5 | 15 wks |

'Trouble and Strife' by Jeremy Paul.
Starr and Fred receive a visitor who knows much more about Starr's past than Louisa does.
Designer: Paul Joel. **Director:** Raymond Menmuir.

| 1977 | 14.6 | Sat 3 Dec 7:25 p.m. | 10 | 10 wks |

The 1977 series takes up the story in 1911 with Louisa Trotter the mistress of the Prince of Wales and owner of the Bentinck Hotel.
'Lottie' by Jeremy Paul.
Louisa and Major Smith-Barton return to the Bentinck, bringing with them the young Lottie (Lalla Ward). Louisa has failed before when she tried to mix hotel and family business. Can she succeed this time?
Designer: Raymond Cusick. **Director:** Bill Bain.

D

Duchy of Cornwall, The — 1 wk

BBC, documentary

| 1986 | 8.7 | Tue 19 Aug 9:30 p.m. | 14 | 1 wk |

HRH The Prince of Wales is the 24th Duke of Cornwall. As such he controls and derives income from the 130,000-acre estate. **Reporter:** Jenni Murray. **Producer:** Dennis Adams.

Dudh Kosi – The Relentless River of Everest — 1 wk

HTV, documentary

| 1977 | 14.5 | Wed 28 Dec 9:00 p.m. | 13 | 1 wk |

Ian McNaught Davies narrates the story of Dr Mike Jones and his team, who canoed down the world's most dangerous river. **Camera:** Leo Dickinson and Mike Reynolds. **Producer:** Aled Vaughan.

Duel at Diablo — 1 wk

Presented by BBC, film

| 1976 | 6.3 | Mon 14 Jun 9:25 p.m. | 10 | 1 wk |

The US Cavalry rescues a woman from the Apaches and launches a new assault on Chief Chata and Fort Concho. Starring James Garner, Sidney Poitier, Bill Travers and Dennis Weaver. **Director:** Ralph Nelson.

Dukes of Hazzard, The — 2 wks

USA presented by BBC, drama

Hazzard County good guys became outlaws baiting the Sheriff. Starred Catherine Bach as Daisy, James Best as Sheriff Rosco Coltrane, Sorrell Booke as Boss Hogg, Denver Pyle as Uncle Jesse, John Schneider as Bo Duke and Tom Wopat as Luke Duke. **Producers:** Joseph Gantman and Paul Picard.

| 1982 | 12.0 | Sat 6 Mar 5:45 p.m. | 20 | 2 wks |

'The Legacy'
Boss Hogg refuses to pay up on a forty-year-old IOU. **Director:** Hollingsworth Morse.

Dumbo — 1 wk

Presented by ITV, film

| 1986 | 14.1 | Thu 25 Dec 3:10 p.m. | 10 | 1 wk |

In this classic Walt Disney cartoon the little circus elephant with big ears discovers he can fly and finds a friend in a mouse. **Director:** Ben Sharpsteen.

Dummy — 1 wk

ATV, drama

| 1977 | 13.5 | Wed 9 Nov 8:30 p.m. | 17 | 1 wk |

The story of Sandra (Geraldine James), a deaf prostitute. **Writer:** Hugh Whitemore. **Camera:** Chris Menges. **Producer:** Franc Roddam.

Dustbinmen, The — 20 wks

Granada, comedy

Jack Rosenthal's creation of a group of garbage collectors grew out of a single play 'There's a Hole in Your Dustbin, Delilah'. The principal characters were Bloody Delilah (Brian Wilde), Heavy Breathing (Trevor Bannister), Cheese 'n' Egg (Bryan Pringle), Manchester City-mad Winston (Graham Haberfield), Smellie (John Barrett) and Eric (Tim Wylton).

| 1969 | 8.3 | Tue 28 Oct 8:25 p.m. | 1 | 6 wks |

Winston is banned from the City–United derby. **Director:** Les Chatfield. **Producer:** Jack Rosenthal.

| 1970 | 8.0 | Tue 24 Mar 8:25 p.m. | 3 | 14 wks |

Delilah has to leave the depot for a day and leaves Cheese 'n' Egg in charge – but power goes to his head. **Director:** Les Chatfield. **Producer:** Richard Everitt.

Dusty — 3 wks

BBC, music

This series starred Dusty Springfield, who found success with her brother Tom and friend Mike Hurst as the Springfields and went on to solo acclaim in 1963 with 'I Only Want To Be With You'.

| 1967 | 5.6 | Tue 15 Aug 9:05 p.m. | 5 | 3 wks |

Guests: Warren Mitchell with Madeline Bell, Lesley Duncan, Maggie Stredder and the Johnny Pearson orchestra. **Producer:** Stanley Dorfman.

Dutch Girls — 1 wk

LWT, drama

| 1985 | 13.6 | Sun 24 Nov 9:00 p.m. | 8 | 1 wk |

The Strathdonald School hockey team goes to Amsterdam with games master Mr Mole (Bill Paterson). He intends them to train for success and sample the culture of the city. Nothing is further from the boys' minds. Also stars Colin Firth, Timothy Spall and John Wells. **Writer:** William Boyd. **Director:** Giles Foster. **Producer:** Sue Birtwistle. **Executive Producer:** Nick Elliott.

Duty Free				28 wks

YTV, situation comedy

This series by Eric Chappell and Jean Warr dealt with two British couples on holiday in Spain. Keith Barron and Gwen Taylor portrayed David and Amy Pearce; Neil Stacy and Joanna Van Gyseghem played Robert and Linda Cochran. Carlos Douglas was the barman.
Producer: *Vernon Lawrence.*

1984	16.7	Mon 12 Mar 8:00 p.m.	1	14 wks

'Bedroom Farce'
Amy is suspicious when David and Linda go for a midnight swim.

1985	14.2	Wed 7 Aug 8:00 p.m.	2	5 wks

'Snap'
David is appalled when Kev Wilson (Roger Sloman), the man responsible for making him redundant, arrives at the hotel.

1986	17.4	Wed 8 Feb 8:00 p.m.	3	9 wks

'Winter Break'
Unemployed David feels a need to get away from it all.

Dynasty				53 wks

USA presented by BBC, soap

This series, created by Esther Shapiro, began in 1982. Set in Denver, Colorado, it centred on Blake Carrington (John Forsythe), who controlled a vast international oil empire. Other characters in at the beginning included Krystle Jennings (Linda Evans), Blake's ex-secretary who was unsure about marrying him, Blake's daughter Fallon (Pamela Sue Martin, later Emma Samms) and his gay son Steven (Al Corley, later Jack Coleman), who had no love for the oil business. Blake's bitter enemy was Walter Lankershim (Dale Robertson). In subsequent series, important characters included Claudia Blaisdel (Pamela Bellwood), Matthew Blaisdel (Bo Hopkins), Blake's first wife Alexis Carrington (Joan Collins), Nick Toscanini (James Farentino), Jeff Colby (John James), Sammy Jo (Heather Locklear), Dex Dexter (Michael Nader), Alexis's wayward son Adam Carrington (Gordon Thomson), Dominique Devereaux (Diahann Carroll), Prince Michael (Michael Praed), Carress Morell (Kate O'Mara), Alexis's daughter Amanda Carrington (Catherine Oxenberg) and Sable Colby (Stephanie Beacham). Other stars to pass through Denver included George Hamilton, Rock Hudson and Ali McGraw.
Executive Producer: *Aaron Spelling.*

1982	8.2	Sat 14 Aug 9:35 p.m.	18	1 wk

'Witness' by Edward De Blasio.
Evidence mounts against Blake at his murder trial.
Director: *Don Medford.*

1983	9.8	Sat 21 May 10:00 p.m.	19	3 wks

'The Fragment' by Daniel King Benton.
The future of Denver-Carrington is still uncertain.
Director: *Ed Ledding.*

1984	10.8	Sat 14 Jul 9:00 p.m.	8	16 wks

'Reunion in Singapore' by Edward De Blasio.
Blake is delayed at the airport by an angry Alexis. He is hoping to fly East to see his son.
Director: *Gwen Arner.*

1985	13.6	Sat 30 Mar 8:10 p.m.	6	24 wks

'The Mortgage' by Dennis Turner.
Alexis has a murder charge hanging over her, but it does not deflect her from taking Blake for every last cent.
Director: *Jerome Courtland.*

1986	11.8	Fri 11 Apr 8:10 p.m.	8	7 wks

'The Vigil' by Dennis Turner.
Blake Carrington is rushed to hospital with heart failure. His condition is critical.
Director: *Irving Moore.*

1988	8.1	Fri 24 Jun 8:15 p.m.	20	1 wk

'Colorado Roulette' by Edward De Blasio.
The desperate search is on for a missing child.
Director: *Irving Moore.*

1989	8.3	Fri 23 Jun 8:10 p.m.	19	1 wk

'Cache 22' by Samuel J. Pelovitz.
The reconciliation between Blake and Alexis is short-lived, but she may settle her differences with Dex.
Director: *David Paulsen.*

The stars of **Duty Free** pose for a photocall. They are (left to right) Keith Barron, Gwen Taylor, Neil Stacy, Joanna Van Gyseghem and Carlos Douglas.

E

Eagle Has Landed, The — 3 wks

Presented by ITV, film

| 1981 | 14.1 | Thu 3 Sep 7:30 p.m. | 3 | 1 wk |

German intelligence devises a plan to kill Winston Churchill in Suffolk. Stars include Jenny Agutter, Michael Caine, Robert Duvall, Judy Geeson, Larry Hagman, Jean Marsh, Donald Pleasence, Anthony Quayle and Donald Sutherland.
Director: John Sturges.

| 1982 | 10.1 | Sat 11 Sep 7:00 p.m. | 8 | 1 wk |

Repeat showing of the above film.

| 1988 | 11.7 | Tue 27 Dec 9:50 p.m. | 20 | 1 wk |

Repeat showing of the above film on BBC.

Eamonn Andrews Show, The — 26 wks

ABC, chat show

The Irish actor and boxing commentator began his UK career as host of Ignorance Is Bliss on BBC radio in 1951. He became Britain's first personality chat show host with this series presented live from London. The production team included Andy Allan, Roy Bottomley, Tom Brennand, Tom Clegg, Royston Mayoh, Malcolm Morris and Gordon Reece.

1964	4.8	Sun 27 Dec 11:05 p.m.	17	1 wk
1965	6.2	Sun 31 Oct 11:10 p.m.	17	4 wks
1966	5.9	Sun 27 Nov 11:05 p.m.	16	7 wks
1967	6.2	Sun 5 Feb 11:05 p.m.	10	13 wks
1968	5.2	Sun 2 Jun 11:10 p.m.	15	1 wk

Eartha Kitt Show, The — 1 wk

ATV, entertainment

| 1965 | 4.4 | Wed 30 Jun 9:40 p.m. | 18 | 1 wk |

American singer Eartha Kitt stars in her own special. With the Norman Maen dancers and the Jack Parnell orchestra.
Producer: Alan Tarrant.

Earthquake — 4 wks

Presented by ITV, film

| 1981 | 13.5 | Thu 24 Sep 7:30 p.m. | 8 | 1 wk |

A computer predicts a major earthquake in the Los Angeles area. Amongst those looking out for their lives are Ava Gardner and Charlton Heston.
Director: Mark Robson.

1983	10.4	Wed 1 Jun 8:00 p.m.	6	1 wk
1986	12.5	Sun 18 May 7:45 p.m.	5	1 wk
1988	9.1	Wed 22 Jun 8:00 p.m.	14	1 wk

Repeat showings of the above film.

East of Eden — 1 wk

USA presented by ITV, drama

| 1981 | 11.3 | Mon 14 Sep 9:00 p.m. | 16 | 1 wk |

This adaptation of John Steinbeck's story stars Jane Seymour as Cathy. With Timothy Bottoms, Bruce Boxleitner, Lloyd Bridges and Warren Oates.

East Side, West Side — 2 wks

USA presented by BBC, drama

This film series starred George C. Scott as Neil Brock, a social worker dedicated to helping New Yorkers with problems.

| 1964 | 6.8 | Wed 1 Jul 9:25 p.m. | 18 | 2 wks |

'Go Fight City Hall'
Thousands will be affected by plans for a rehousing project. Brock steps in to help just one of those being throttled by red tape.

EastEnders — 616 wks

BBC, soap

This bi-weekly serial had its first transmission on 19 February 1985. The events centred around the people who lived and worked in Albert Square in the fictitious London borough of Walford E20. The original inhabitants of the Square included at 1A Dr Harold Legg (Leonard Fenton), at 1B Ethel Skinner (Gretchen Franklin) and at 1C Lofty Holloway (Tom Watt). Tony and Kelvin Carpenter (Oscar James and Paul J. Medford) lived at No. 3. Mary Smith (Linda Davidson) and her baby Annie occupied the first floor of No. 23 with Ali and Sue Osman (Nejdet Salih and Sandy Ratcliff) and their baby Hassan downstairs. At No. 45 were Pauline and Arthur Fowler (Wendy Richard and Bill Treacher), their children Mark and Michelle (David Scarboro and Susan Tully) and Pauline's mum Lou Beale (Anna Wing). Pauline's brother Pete (Peter Dean), his wife Kathy (Gillian Taylforth) and their son Ian (Adam Woodyatt) lived on the nearby estate. Den Watts (Leslie Grantham) was landlord of the Queen Vic pub where he lived with his wife Angie (Anita Dobson) and daughter Sharon (Letitia Dean). Saeed and Naima Jeffery (Andrew Johnson and Shreela Ghosh) kept the foodstore around the corner. Newcomers Debbie Wilkins (Shirley Cheriton) and Andy O'Brien (Ross Davidson) moved into No. 43 together.

Other principal characters have included Dot Cotton (June Brown), Nick Cotton (John Altman), Barry Clark (Gary Hailes), Colin Russell (Michael Cashman), Simon 'Wicksy' Wicks (Nick Berry), James Willmott-Brown (William Boyde), Frank and Pat Butcher (Mike Reid and Pam St Clement), Hannah Carpenter (Sally Sagoe), Carmel Roberts (Judith Jacob), Mehmet Osman (Haluk Bilginer), Clyde Tavernier (Steven Woodcock) and brothers Phil and Grant Mitchell (Steve McFadden and Ross Kemp).
Producer (1985–90): Julia Smith.

| 1985 | 23.5 | Tue 24 Dec 7:30 p.m.
Thu 26 Dec 7:10 p.m. | 1 | 48 wks |

These episodes were listed together in the ratings.
There's a Christmas Eve knees up at the Vic, and Walford have a home match on Boxing Day.
Writers: Jim Hawkins and Tony McHale. **Director:** Chris Clough.

| 1986 | 27.9 | Tue 23 Dec 7:35 p.m.
Thu 25 Dec 10:00 p.m. | 1 | 51 wks |

These episodes were listed together in the ratings.
Pete Beale displays little sign of holiday spirit. Christmas dinner is served at the Queen Vic.
Writers: Bill Lyons and Tony Holland. **Director:** Nicholas Prosser.

| 1987 | 27.9 | Thu 1 Jan 7:30 p.m. | 1 | 94 wks |

Hangovers abound in Albert Square, but Michelle is working.
Writer: Charlie Humphreys. **Director:** Gareth Tucker.

| 1988 | 24.9 | Tue 19 Jan 7:30 p.m.
Thu 21 Jan 7:30 p.m. | 1 | 107 wks |

These episodes were listed together in the ratings.
Pauline Fowler shows motherly concern for Michelle, whose painful decision stuns Lofty and her family.
Writers: Charlie Humphreys and Tony McHale. **Director:** Tom Kingdon.

| 1989 | 21.6 | Thu 5 Jan 7:30 p.m. | 1 | 106 wks |

Diane (Sophie Lawrence) decides that her brother Ricky (Sid Owen) needs a good talking to. While at the Queen Vic landlord Frank Butcher is finding it hard to attract customers.
Writer: Tony Holland. **Director:** Julia Smith.

| 1990 | 20.8 | Thu 4 Jan 7:30 p.m. | 1 | 104 wks |

Diane is promised the best birthday night ever.
Writer: Tony McHale. **Director:** Darrol Blake. **Producer:** Mike Gibbon.

| 1991 | 22.4 | Thu 7 Nov 7:30 p.m. | 1 | 106 wks |

Frank Butcher and Arthur Fowler are not sleeping in their own beds.
Writer: Helen Millar. **Director:** Richard Holthouse. **Producer:** Corinne Hollingworth.

Easter Surprise Special — 1 wk

LWT, entertainment

| 1991 | 10.5 | Fri 29 Mar 8:55 p.m. | 16 | 1 wk |

Cilla Black is joined by Gordon Burns and Bob Carolgees to present a special edition of SURPRISE SURPRISE.
Producer: Linda Beadle.

Easy Street — 1 wk

Presented by BBC, film

| 1971 | 5.3 | Fri 9 Apr 5:35 p.m. | 20 | 1 wk |

This 1917 short stars its writer and director Charlie Chaplin.

Echo Four-Two — 10 wks

AR, drama

In this police series Eric Lander starred as Detective Inspector Baxter with Geoffrey Russell as Detective Sergeant York. Baxter had been promoted from the rank of Detective Sergeant which he held in NO HIDING PLACE.

| 1961 | 6.8 | Wed 4 Oct 8:55 p.m. | 3 | 10 wks |

'Break Out' by Paddy M. O'Brine.
Baxter is rescued from a tight spot, more by luck than judgement.
Director: Geoffrey Hughes. **Producer:** Richard Mathews.

Echoes in the Darkness — 1 wk

USA presented by BBC, drama

| 1989 | 11.1 | Tue 25 Jul 9:30 p.m. | 7 | 1 wk |
| | | Wed 26 Jul 9:30 p.m. | | |

These episodes were listed together in the ratings.
In this two-part adaptation of Joseph Wambaugh's novel, a Pennsylvania school principal (Robert Loggia) is arrested on suspicion of multiple murder. His colleague Bill Bradfield (Peter Coyote) remains a supporter, but when the body of Susan Reinert (Stockard Channing) is found Bradfield comes under suspicion himself.
Director: Glenn Jordan. **Producer:** Jack Grossbart.

Eddie in August   1 wk

Thames, comedy

| 1970 | 4.5 | Wed 3 Jun 7:00 p.m. | 13 | 1 wk |

A half-hour silent film written by and starring Benny Hill. One day in August, Eddie is suddenly smitten with young love. The dream is a long way from reality and his attempts to win the girl (Nicole Shelby) are all in vain. Eddie is a born loser.
Producer: John Robins.

Educating Rita   1 wk

Presented by BBC, film

| 1986 | 13.9 | Thu 25 Dec 10:40 p.m. | 12 | 1 wk |

Willy Russell's adaptation of his own play stars Julie Walters as a Liverpool hairdresser who tries to better herself at university. Michael Caine portrays her alcoholic tutor. Maureen Lipman and Michael Williams also star.
Director: Lewis Gilbert.

Edward and Mrs Simpson   7 wks

Thames, drama

Adaptation by Simon Raven of the events leading up to the abdication of Edward VIII on 10 December 1936. Edward Fox starred as Edward and Cynthia Harris as Mrs Simpson. Marius Goring played George V, Peggy Ashcroft was Queen Mary and Andrew Ray portrayed the Duke of York, later George VI.

| 1978 | 18.9 | Wed 20 Dec 9:00 p.m. | 9 | 7 wks |

'The Abdication'
The King broadcasts to the nation prior to leaving England to spend the rest of his life in exile.
Director: Waris Hussein. **Producer:** Allan Cameron.

Edward VII   13 wks

ATV, drama

From the biography by Philip Magnus, an adaptation in thirteen parts of the complete life of the heir to Queen Victoria. Most episodes were by David Butler. Produced by Cecil Clarke. The principal characters throughout the series included (in order of appearance) Queen Victoria (Annette Crosbie), Prince Albert (Robert Hardy), the Duchess of Kent (Alison Leggatt), Colonel Bruce (Harry Andrews), Lord Palmerston (André Morell), the young Bertie later Edward VII (Charles Sturridge), Princess Vicky (Felicity Kendal), Bertie (Timothy West), Gladstone (Michael Hordern), Princess Alexandra (Helen Ryan), Princess Dagmar (Jane Lapotaire), Disraeli (John Gielgud), Lillie Langtry (Francesca Annis), Lord Salisbury (Richard Vernon), Lord Coventry (Robert Flemyng), Lady Brooke (Carolyn Seymour), Kaiser Wilhelm (Christopher Neame), Prince Eddy (Charles Dance), Campbell-Bannerman (Geoffrey Bayldon) and H.H. Asquith (Basil Dignam).

| 1975 | 8.8 | Tue 6 May 9:00 p.m. | 1 | 13 wks |

'The Invisible Queen' by David Butler.
Bertie is frustrated the Queen will not give him anything worthwhile to do. Furthermore, she objects to his continual mixing with society.
Designers: Anthony Waller and Henry Graveney. **Director:** John Corrie.

Edward Woodward Hour, The   1 wk

Thames, entertainment

Actor Edward Woodward, a tenor, often guested on other shows in addition to playing musical roles on the stage.

| 1971 | 5.8 | Wed 4 Aug 8:00 p.m. | 5 | 1 wk |

With the Geoff Love concert orchestra and guests Patrick Cargill, Rita Hunter, Nina and Beryl Reid, with Danny Clare, Ann Holloway and Natasha Pyne.
Writers: Johnnie Mortimer and Brian Cooke, Eric Merriman and Peter Robinson. **Producer:** Reginald Collin. **Executive Producer:** Philip Jones.

Edward Woodward Show, The   1 wk

Thames, entertainment

| 1972 | 5.2 | Wed 12 Jul 8:00 p.m. | 12 | 1 wk |

Guests: Dora Bryan, Leslie Phillips and the Geoff Love orchestra.
Writer: Eric Merriman. **Producer:** Keith Beckett.

Eiger Sanction, The   1 wk

Presented by BBC, film

| 1985 | 13.2 | Wed 20 Feb 9:25 p.m. | 18 | 1 wk |

Clint Eastwood directs and stars as Jonathan Hemlock, former hired gun, who is persuaded out of peaceful retirement to kill a man on the north face of the Eiger.

E

El CID — 1 wk

Granada, drama

Blake (Alfred Molina) and Douglas Bromley (John Bird) were private detectives on the Costa del Sol.

1990 11.2 Wed 14 Mar 9:00 p.m. 18 1 wk

'Getting Even' by Paul Anderson.
When Gus Mercer (Kenneth Cranham) went to South America, Blake and Douglas thought they'd seen the last of him. Now he turns up demanding a favour.
Director: Robert Tronson. **Producer:** Matthew Bird. **Executive Producer:** Sally Head.

El Dorado — 1 wk

USA presented by ITV, film

1973 7.1 Thu 27 Dec 6:40 p.m. 3 1 wk

Gun fighters and rival ranchers come to violence in the western town of El Dorado. Starring John Wayne as Cole Thornton, Robert Mitchum as Sheriff J.P. Harrah and James Caan as Mississippi.
Director: Howard Hawks.

Election Special — 2 wks

ITN, news

1970 5.5 Thu 18 Jun 10:00 p.m. 19 1 wk

David Frost and Alastair Burnet host live coverage of the results of the General Election, with the NEWS AT TEN team.

1974 7.4 Thu 28 Feb 10:45 p.m. 9 1 wk

'The Nation Decides'
The polls have closed. Will Edward Heath's three-day working week have damaged the Conservatives sufficiently to allow Harold Wilson to form a Labour government? The reporters are Robert Kee, Peter Snow, Reginald Bosanquet, Andrew Gardner, Julian Haviland and Leonard Parkin.
Producer: David Nicholas.

Electric Horseman, The — 1 wk

Presented by ITV, film

1984 10.4 Thu 12 Apr 7:20 p.m. 20 1 wk

Robert Redford stars as Sonny Steele, five-time world champion cowboy, who kidnaps a horse and disappears into the desert. He is pursued by network newscaster Hallie Martin (Jane Fonda).
Director: Sydney Pollack.

Elizabeth – The First Thirty Years — 1 wk

BBC, documentary

1983 10.3 Sun 29 May 8:45 p.m. 8 1 wk

Ludovic Kennedy narrates this celebration of the reign of Queen Elizabeth II, crowned thirty years ago this week.
Camera: Phillip Bonham-Carter. **Producer:** Jenny Barraclough.

Ellis Island — 1 wk

USA presented by ITV, drama

This six-part drama based on the novel by Fred Mustard Stewart was set in 1907.

1987 8.2 Fri 3 Jul 9:00 p.m. 16 1 wk

A liner crammed with would-be immigrants heads for the clearing centre of US immigration at Ellis Island. Starring Claire Bloom, Judi Bowker, Richard Burton, Faye Dunaway, Alice Krige, Greg Martyn, Milo O'Shea, Peter Riegert, Emma Samms and Ben Vereen.
Director: Jerry London.

Emergency – Ward 10 — 606 wks

ATV, soap

Britain's first twice-weekly serial, created by Tessa Diamond, ran from 1957 to 1967. It was set in a hospital in the fictional town of Oxbridge. The cast endured many changes, but the principal actors included John Alderton as Dr Richard Moone, Jill Browne as Nurse Carole Young, Desmond Carrington as Dr Chris Anderson and Charles Tingwell as Dr Alan Dawson.
Producers included John Cooper (1961–63), Cecil Petty (1964–65) and Jospehine Douglas (1966–67).

1960 6.7 Tue 4 Oct 7:30 p.m. 2 75 wks

There seems to be a hint of romance on the ward, but it must not interfere with the hospital routine.
Writer: Jean Scott Rogers. **Producer:** Anthony Kearey.

1961 6.8 Fri 9 Nov 7:30 p.m. 1 84 wks

Guy Fawkes night has left its usual trail of casualties.
Writer: Michael Ash. **Director:** Geoffrey Stephenson.

1962 6.8 Tue 25 Dec 7:30 p.m. 3 64 wks

The staff present their pantomime ALADDIN.
Writer: Diana Morgan.

1963 7.2 Fri 1 Mar 7:30 p.m. 4 102 wks

Mrs Fitch-Bullen (Edna Landon) continues to be a source of puzzlement. The surgeons pool their diagnoses but are little the wiser.
Writer: Roger Marshall. **Director:** Bill Stewart.

| 1964 | 7.8 | Fri 7 Feb 7:30 p.m. | 2 | 95 wks |

A patient, Mr Fitzgerald (John Arnatt), receives disturbing news about his family affairs. Nurse Carole Young appears to be heading for disaster.
Writer: David Butler. **Director:** Gordon Reed.

| 1965 | 8.0 | Tue 28 Sep 7:30 p.m. | 2 | 103 wks |

Mr Verity (Paul Darrow) appears to be making progress following last week's dinner with Nurse Kwei (Pik-Sen Lim), but he suffers an unexpected setback.
Writer: Basil Dawson. **Director:** Robert D. Cardona.

| 1966 | 7.9 | Fri 25 Feb 7:30 p.m. | 5 | 78 wks |

Following a disaster on an alarming scale with many deaths and injuries the casualty department struggles to cope, in spite of the accident unit not being fully operational.
Writer: Rosemary Anne Sisson. **Director:** Eric Price.

| 1967 | 6.2 | Fri 6 Jan 6:15 p.m. | 13 | 5 wks |

A patient seeks political asylum, presenting tough decisions for Mr Large (John Carlisle).
Writer: Stewart Farrar. **Director:** John Sichel.

Emery
1 wk

BBC, drama

This six-part comedy thriller serial, subtitled 'Legacy of Murder', by John and Steven Singer, starred Dick Emery as Bernie Weinstock of Crimebusters International. He was employed to track down six people who had not been seen for thirty years. Emery also played the parts of Lord Algrave, Joe Galleano, Monica Danvers-Crichton and Mrs Oldfield. Barry Evans, Michael Robbins and Richard Vernon also starred.

| 1982 | 11.3 | Tue 16 Feb 8:00 p.m. | 20 | 1 wk |

'Dying to Meet You'
In a remote part of Haiti, Weinstock is captured by natives in grass skirts, tied to a stake and draped with snakes.
Producer: Harold Snoad.

Emigrants, The
2 wks

BBC (with ABC Australia), drama

In 1975, the Parker family decided to emigrate from Somerset to Australia. Their story was told in four episodes, two made by BBC in England and two by ABC in Australia. The family comprised William (Michael Craig) and his wife May (Sheila Reid), their twenty-two-year-old son Michael (Brian Deacon) and his wife June (Penne Hackforth-Jones), fifteen-year-old son Paul (Simon Gipps-Kent), sixteen-year-old daughter Janice (Lesley Manville) and William Parker Sr (Joe Ritchie).

| 1976 | 7.1 | Tue 23 Nov 9:25 p.m. | 18 | 2 wks |

'13,000 Miles Away' by Peter Kenna.
After three months in a hostel, May has rented a cheap bungalow in the suburbs of Sydney.
Director: Eric Tayler. **Producers:** Frank Hatherley (BBC), Eric Tayler (ABC).

E

Emmerdale Farm
425 wks

YTV, soap

Twice-weekly serial about a farming community in the Yorkshire Dales. The title was shortened to EMMERDALE the week commencing 13 November 1989.
Producers included Michael Glynn (1977–79), Anne W. Gibbons (1980–83), Richard Handford (1984–86) and Stuart Doughty (1989–91). **Executive Producers** included David Cunliffe (1977–79), Michael Glynn (1980–86) and Keith Richardson (1987–90).

| 1977 | 11.9 | Tue 1 Nov 6:30 p.m. | 20 | 1 wk |

Life is full of new dramas for Joe and Annie Sugden (Frazer Hines and Sheila Mercier).
Writer: Andy Baker. **Director:** Darroll Blake.

| 1978 | 15.1 | Wed 8 Mar 5:15 p.m. | 7 | 21 wks |

Joe Sugden is landed with organizing the next meeting of a Young Farmers Club.
Writer: Andy Baker. **Director:** Darroll Blake.

| 1979 | 14.9 | Tue 13 Mar 6:30 p.m. | 8 | 39 wks |

Matt Skilbeck (Frederick Pyne) finds lots of problems on his return to Emmerdale.
Writer: William Humble. **Director:** Michael E. Briant.

| 1980 | 13.7 | Tue 25 Mar 6:30 p.m. | 7 | 19 wks |

Esmareld Eckersley (Debbie Farrington) comes face-to-face with Jack Sugden (Clive Hornby) for the first time since he criticized her book.
Writer: Kevin Laffan. **Director:** Mike Gibbon.

| 1981 | 12.6 | Tue 31 Mar 7:00 p.m. | 16 | 1 wk |

There's a shock in store for Jack Sugden.
Writer: Kevin Laffan. **Director:** Darroll Blake.

| 1983 | 12.5 | Tue 22 Mar 7:05 p.m. | 6 | 34 wks |
| | | Thu 24 Mar 7:05 p.m. | | |

The above episodes were listed together in the ratings.
Alan Turner (Richard Thorp) and Amos Brearly (Ronald Magill) take the problems of Emmerdale onto the golf course.
Writer: Ken Blakeson. **Director:** Chris Baker.

Australian actor Charles Tingwell checks up on the condition of one of his patients in **Emergency – Ward 10.**

1984   **14.1**   **Tue 18 Dec 7:00 p.m.**   **6**   **28 wks**
Thu 20 Dec 7:00 p.m.

The above episodes were listed together in the ratings.
Amos Brearly discovers he may be losing his voice. Joe Sugden rejoins his family for Christmas.
Writer: Michael Russell. **Director:** Darroll Blake.

1985   **14.1**   **Tue 26 Mar 7:00 p.m.**   **2**   **33 wks**

Jackie Merrick (Ian Sharrock) is in money trouble with Jack Sugden.
Writer: Simon Masters. **Director:** William Slater.

1986   **12.9**   **Tue 25 Feb 7:00 p.m.**   **4**   **41 wks**
Thu 27 Feb 7:00 p.m.

These episodes were listed together in the ratings.
Matt goes to the police, making Dolly Skilbeck (Jean Rogers) feel everything will be all right. Amos tries to persuade the customers in the Woolpack to try some fine wines.
Writer: David Angus. **Director:** Richard Handford.

1987   **11.6**   **Tue 24 Nov 7:00 p.m.**   **6**   **28 wks**

Ruth Pennington (Julia Chambers) finds herself in competition for Joe's affection with both another woman and a horse.
Writer and **Producer:** Michael Russell. **Director:** Bob Hird.

1988   **12.7**   **Thu 4 Feb 6:30 p.m.**   **9**   **62 wks**

The wedding reception of Kathy Bates (Malandra Burrows) and Jackie Merrick is held at the farm.
Writer: Tim Vaughan. **Director:** Alister Hallum. **Producer:** Michael Russell.

1989   **12.3**   **Wed 4 Jan 6:30 p.m.**   **10**   **45 wks**

Matt prepares to leave but Dolly has a last surprise for him. Nick Bates (Cy Chadwick) has a guilty secret.
Writer: Peter Dillon. **Director:** Henry Foster.

1990   **11.4**   **Tue 2 Jan 7:00 p.m.**   **9**   **36 wks**

Lynn Whiteley (Fionnuala Ellwood) tells her husband Pete (Jim Millea) she knows about his affair.
Writer: David Joss Buckley. **Director:** Tim Dowd.

1991   **12.5**   **Tue 10 Dec 7:00 p.m.**   **9**   **37 wks**

Seth Armstrong (Stan Richards) tries to trace the whereabouts of Sarah Connolly (Madeleine Howard).
Writer: Rob Gittins. **Director:** Rodney Allison.

Enchanted Isles   **1 wk**

Anglia, documentary

1967   **6.3**   **Tue 5 Dec 8:55 p.m.**   **18**   **1 wk**

A SURVIVAL special, introduced by HRH The Duke of Edinburgh. The film looks at the wildlife of the Galapagos Islands where Charles Darwin devised his theory of evolution in 1835.
Writer: Colin Willock. **Camera:** Alan and Joan Root. **Producer:** Stanley Joseph.

End in Tears   **1 wk**

ATV, drama

1966   **6.4**   **Tue 22 Nov 9:10 p.m.**   **11**   **1 wk**

Four masters in a public school conflict with each other. The consequences are tragic. Stars include Norman Bird, John Castle, Alan MacNaughton and Richard Vernon.
Writer: Gerald Vaughan-Hughes. **Designer:** Alan Pickford. **Director:** John Gorrie. **Producer:** Cecil Clarke.

End of a Street   **1 wk**

Granada, documentary

1964   **7.2**   **Wed 2 Dec 9:40 p.m.**   **6**   **1 wk**

Film about a group of men and women in Oldham whose old homes are being bulldozed and who face a new life somewhere unfamiliar.
Production team: Michael Apted, Alan Price and Richard Sidwell.
Producer: Norman Swallow.

Endurance   **1 wk**

Ulster, documentary

1966   **5.2**   **Wed 17 Aug 9:40 p.m.**   **11**   **1 wk**

James Fisher narrates the story of Ernest Shackleton, whose ship Endurance sailed for the Antarctic on 8 August 1914.
Producer: Ted Emmett. **Executive Producer:** Anthony Finigan.

Enemy at the Door   **1 wk**

LWT, drama

This series by Michael Chapman centred on the Nazi occupation of the Channel Islands. Alfred Burke starred as Major Richter. Music was by Wilfred Josephs.
Director: Bill Bain. **Producer:** Michael Chapman. **Executive Producer:** Tony Wharmby.

1978   **15.1**   **Sat 21 Jan 7:30 p.m.**   **17**   **1 wk**

'By Order of the Führer'
It is the last day of freedom before the occupation of Guernsey.
Designer: Andrew Gardner.

Enforcer, The `1 wk`

Presented by ITV, film

| 1984 | 10.7 | Sat 1 Sep 10:15 p.m. | 7 | 1 wk |

Clint Eastwood stars as San Francisco police Inspector Harry Callahan, whose partner is killed. To his horror, his new partner is a woman, Kate Moor (Tyne Daly).
Director: James Fargo.

Engelbert `6 wks`

ATV, music

This series starred Engelbert Humperdinck, the singer from Leicestershire who adopted the name of the nineteenth-century German composer of the opera 'Hansel und Gretel'. His earlier television appearances had been under the name Gerry Dorsey as a member of Granada's singing team the Granadiers.

| 1967 | 7.0 | Fri 3 Nov 6:30 p.m. | 6 | 6 wks |

Shirley Bassey guests with the Peter Gordeno dancers, the Mike Sammes singers and the Jack Parnell orchestra.
Producer: Colin Clews.

Engelbert Humperdinck Show, The `1 wk`

ATV, music

| 1969 | 5.3 | Fri 26 Dec 8:30 p.m. | 19 | 1 wk |

Guests: Barbara Eden, José Feliciano, Tom Jones, Dionne Warwick. With the Paddy Stone dancers, the Mike Sammes singers and the Jack Parnell orchestra.
Producer: Colin Clews.

Entertainers, The `1 wk`

Granada, documentary

| 1965 | 5.8 | Wed 13 Jan 10:25 p.m. | 19 | 1 wk |

Denis Mitchell follows the lives of some of the many entertainers working the pubs and clubs of the North. Featuring Arlette, Bridgette, Shirley Davis, Johnnie Kennedy, the Marvins and Archie Tower.
Director: John McGrath. **Producer:** Denis Mitchell.

Entertainment Express `2 wks`

Central, entertainment

This series of variety shows was hosted by Mike Reid.

| 1984 | 7.2 | Wed 15 Aug 8:00 p.m. | 19 | 2 wks |

Guests: Frank Carson, Jimmy Logan, Lulu, Mick Miller, Roy Walker and Dax Xenos.
Producer: David Macmahon.

Equalizer, The `34 wks`

USA presented by ITV, drama

Edward Woodward starred as Robert McCall, a former secret agent who ran a one-man security service from his Manhattan apartment. William Zakhai played McCall's music student son Scott.
Created and produced by Michael Sloan.

| 1986 | 13.9 | Wed 12 Nov 9:00 p.m. | 5 | 7 wks |

'Lady Cop'
McCall is asked to help policewoman Sandra Stahl (Karen Young) when she discovers her partner is crooked.

| 1987 | 13.7 | Wed 18 Feb 9:00 p.m. | 7 | 20 wks |

'Out of the Past'
The husband of McCall's former wife is being terrorized by a man just released from prison.

| 1988 | 11.6 | Wed 8 Jun 9:00 p.m. | 7 | 7 wks |

'Hand and Glove'
A wheelchair-bound girl witnesses her father's murder.

Eric and Ernie's Christmas Show `1 wk`

Thames, comedy

| 1983 | 11.2 | Mon 26 Dec 8:45 p.m. | 11 | 1 wk |

Morecambe and Wise welcome Gemma Craven, Nigel Hawthorne, Derek Jacobi, Felicity Kendal, Patrick Mower, Nanette Newman and Peter Skellern. With the Norman Maen dancers and the Harry Rabinowitz orchestra.
Producer: Mark Stuart.

Eric Robinson Presents `1 wk`

BBC, music

Eric Robinson presented popular music programmes with his orchestra throughout the 1950s and 1960s. His best remembered series was MUSIC FOR YOU.

| 1968 | 5.4 | Thu 24 Oct 9:05 p.m. | 20 | 1 wk |

Guests: Enrico Giaconini, Margaret Neville, Semprini, David Toguri and Doreen Wells.
Choreographer: Alfred Rodrigues. **Producer:** Bryan Sears.

Eric Sykes · 25 wks

BBC, situation comedy

Writer and comedian Eric Sykes had several series from the 1950s onwards, always playing the hard-done-by person who lived in cosy semi-detached suburbia. He wrote all his own shows. In this series stalwart support came from Hattie Jacques as his sister, Richard Wattis as a neighbour and Deryck Guyler as an affable policeman.

| 1962 | 6.0 | Tue 27 Feb 8:00 p.m. | 7 | 8 wks |

'Sykes and an Elephant'
The elephant's head, trunk included, hanging in Eric and Hattie's hall turns out to be alive, providing a shock to a visiting aunt. With Joan Hickson and Birma the Elephant from Billy Smart's Circus.
Director: Sydney Lotterby. **Producer:** Dennis Main Wilson.

| 1963 | 7.0 | Thu 4 Apr 8:00 p.m. | 4 | 8 wks |

'Sykes and a Referee'
Eric is the referee in the match between Sebastopol Rangers and Wood Lane Athletic. With Janet Bruce, Thomas Gallagher, Martin Miller and Kenneth Wolstenholme.
Producer: Sydney Lotterby.

| 1964 | 7.6 | Tue 25 Feb 8:00 p.m. | 4 | 8 wks |

'Sykes and a Box'
Eric plays the part of a newspaper reporter. With Ronald Adam, Erik Chitty, Maeve Leslie and Richard Morton.
Producer: Sydney Lotterby.

| 1965 | 5.7 | Tue 9 Nov 7:30 p.m. | 20 | 1 wk |

'Sykes and a Uniform'
Eric and Hattie set out to prove that anyone who gets into a uniform, or even any part of a uniform, becomes a different species from the rest of us. With Pat Coombs, Barney Gilbraith, John Junkin and Bill Treacher.
Director: William G. Stewart. **Producer:** Philip Barker.

Eric Sykes 1990 Show, The · 1 wk

Thames, comedy

| 1982 | 12.3 | Wed 14 Apr 8:00 p.m. | 10 | 1 wk |

Eric Sykes plays the producer of a TOMMY COOPER SHOW with Tommy Cooper, Henry Cooper, Leslie Mitchell, Chic Murray, Dandy Nichols, John Williams and the Band of the Royal Marines.
Writer: Eric Sykes. **Producer:** Dennis Kirkland.

Eric Sykes Show, The · 2 wks

Thames, comedy

| 1977 | 6.7 | Wed 6 Jun 8:00 p.m. | 7 | 1 wk |

With Peter Cook, Eric Delaney, Jimmy Edwards, Irene Handl, Hattie Jacques, John Williams and Dougie Squires' Second Generation. **Musical Director:** Alan Braden. **Producer:** Dennis Kirkland.

| 1978 | 19.6 | Wed 20 Dec 8:00 p.m. | 7 | 1 wk |

Repeat of the above show.

Escapade in Japan · 1 wk

USA presented by BBC, film

| 1964 | 7.2 | Sun 5 Jul 7:50 p.m. | 9 | 1 wk |

Two small boys on the run from the police, one Japanese and the other American, set off on an eventful journey across Japan. Starring Cameron Mitchell, Roger Nakagawa, Jon Provost and Teresa Wright.
Director: Arthur Lubin.

Escape · 5 wks

Granada, drama

This series of six plays by Marc Brandel had a unifying theme of escape, be it from authority, the police or a lynch mob.

| 1967 | 6.0 | Fri 22 Sep 9:00 p.m. | 11 | 5 wks |

'The Kindness of Strangers'
John Castle plays an army deserter. Co-starring Hannah Gordon.
Producer: Cormac (Mike) Newell.

Escape from Sobibor · 1 wk

Central, drama

| 1987 | 13.0 | Sun 10 May 9:00 p.m. | 3 | 1 wk |

This film made for television is Reginald Rose's dramatization of a story by Richard Rashke. Three hundred Jews escape from a Nazi death camp. Starring Alan Arkin, Rutger Hauer and Joanna Pacula. **Director:** Jack Gold. **Producer:** Dennis E. Goty. **Executive Producer:** Martin Starger. (A Zenith production.)

Escape from the Planet of the Apes · 1 wk

Presented by ITV, film

| 1977 | 14.0 | Sat 15 Oct 6:15 p.m. | 6 | 1 wk |

Roddy McDowell, Kim Hunter, Bradford Dillman and Sal Mineo star in the third PLANET OF THE APES film. This time the educated simiens are in modern America.
Director: Don Taylor.

Escape of RD7, The — 5 wks

BBC, drama

This five-part serial by Thomas Clarke starred Barbara Murray as Dr Anna Hastings, a scientist working on large-scale medical research.

| 1961 | 6.7 | Tue 21 Nov 8:30 p.m. | 5 | 5 wks |

'Out of Hand'
Dr Hastings leaves the door of her laboratory unlocked. An intruder is bitten by an animal being used for research and the project to which she has devoted her career is placed in jeopardy.
Producer: James Ormerod.

Escape of the Birdman — 1 wk

Presented by ITV, film

| 1977 | 16.5 | Thu 29 Dec 7:00 p.m. | 2 | 1 wk |

American secret service agent Harry Cook (Doug McClure) smuggles a fellow prisoner out of a Nazi labour camp only to be recaptured and sent to Beckstadt Castle, from where no man has ever escaped.
Director: Philip Leacock.

Escape Route — 1 wk

Presented by ITV, film

| 1962 | 5.1 | Fri 2 Mar 8:20 p.m. | 14 | 1 wk |

Steve Rossi (George Raft) is the production chief of a US aircraft works. He vanishes without trace. He is just the latest in a line of missing scientists.
Directors: Seymour Friedman and Peter Graham Scott.

Escape to Athena — 2 wks

Presented by BBC, film

| 1983 | 11.2 | Sun 3 Apr 7:15 p.m. | 13 | 1 wk |

Second World War prisoners on a Greek island become involved in an art theft. Starring Roger Moore, David Niven and Telly Savalas.
Director: George Pan Cosmatos.

| 1986 | 12.9 | Sat 27 Dec 5:55 p.m. | 18 | 1 wk |

Repeat showing of the above film.

Escape to Victory — 1 wk

Presented by BBC, film

| 1987 | 14.6 | Sun 27 Dec 3:30 p.m. | 10 | 1 wk |

A former soccer star agrees to field a team of his fellow prisoners of war against the German national side. The Germans intend to capitalize on the event for propaganda, whereas the POWs have other plans. Starring Michael Caine, Daniel Massey, Tim Pigott-Smith, Sylvester Stallone, Max Von Sydow and eighteen of the world's top footballers, including Osvaldo Ardiles, Bobby Moore, Pele and Mike Summerbee.
Director: John Huston.

Espionage — 9 wks

ATV, drama

This series of spy stories starring Lee Montague was based on historical incidents and rather gloomy political intrigue.
Producer: George Justin. **Executive Producer:** Herbert Hirschman.

| 1963 | 6.2 | Sat 9 Nov 9:10 p.m. | 12 | 5 wks |

'The Dragon Slayer' by Raymond Bowers and Albert Ruben.
The story of one idealist's grim fight against the tyrannical dictatorship of the Manchu dynasty ruling China towards the end of the last century. Also starring Patrick Cargill, Peter Dyneley, Sam Kydd and Thorley Walters.
Director: William T. Kotcheff.

| 1964 | 6.2 | Sat 11 Jan 10:10 p.m. | 16 | 4 wks |

'Medal for a Turncoat' by Larry Cohen.
A German officer is chosen to fly to England to try to persuade the Allies to sign an armistice on the promise that the regular army will revolt against Hitler. Twenty years later he is forced to face the question – was he hero or traitor? Starring Joseph Furst, Nigel Stock and Fritz Weaver.
Director: David Greene.

E.T. — 1 wk

Presented by BBC, film

| 1990 | 17.5 | Tue 25 Dec 3:05 p.m. | 6 | 1 wk |

A crew member from an alien spacecraft is left behind and befriended by a small boy. Starring Drew Barrymore, Peter Coyote, Robert MacNaughton, K.C. Martel, Henry Thomas and Dee Wallace.
Director: Steven Spielberg.

Europe Without de Gaulle — 1 wk

ITN, news

| 1969 | 5.8 | Mon 28 Apr 10:30 p.m. | 17 | 1 wk |

General Charles de Gaulle resigned the Presidency of France this morning after being defeated in yesterday's referendum. As special riot police take up positions for expected trouble in Paris, Monsieur Alain Poher becomes interim President prior to the election.

European Amateur Ballroom Championships — 1 wk

STV, entertainment

1968 6.8 **Tue 26 Nov 9:00 p.m.** 6 **1 wk**

Bill Tennant introduces the dance competition from Edinburgh.
Producer: Brian Mahoney.

....

European Connections — 1 wk

Central, documentary

This series concerned France as seen through the eyes of Britons who lived there.

1983 6.7 **Thu 11 Aug 9:30 p.m.** 17 **1 wk**

'Alpes Maritimes'
Architect Simon and part-time novelist Marcia live in a farmhouse near Grasse. Marcia was previously married to a Frenchman, and to obtain the custody of her son, was required to remain in France.
Director: Malcolm Feuerstein. **Producer:** Brian Lewis.

....

European Journey, A — 4 wks

Granada, documentary

A series in which René Cutforth and Denis Mitchell travelled through the countries of the Common Market.

1972 6.3 **Mon 6 Mar 8:00 p.m.** 16 **4 wks**

'Back to France'
The team arrives in the Dordogne in time for the grape harvest.
Director: Denis Mitchell. **Executive Producer:** Jeremy Wallington.

....

European Skating Championships, The — 1 wk

BBC, Sport

1969 6.8 **Wed 5 Feb 9:05 p.m.** 11 **1 wk**

Alan Weeks commentates from Garmisch Partenkirchen on the pairs competition in which the defending champions Oleg Protopopov and Ludmilla Belousova will try to retain their title.
Television presentation: West German Television.

....

Eurovision Song Contest, The — 25 wks

Eurovision presented by BBC, music

The Contest began in 1956 and although much derided always attracted huge international viewing figures. After failing to chart in 1987–88 it returned to favour in 1989. Terry Wogan commentated in 1978 and became the regular announcer.

1963 6.0 **Sat 23 Mar 9:00 p.m.** 15 **1 wk**

Catherine Boyle and David Jacobs introduce the show from BBC Television Centre. The UK entry is 'Say Wonderful Things' sung by Ronnie Carroll. (Grethe and Jørgen Ingmann win for Denmark with 'Dansevise'.)
Director: Yvonne Littlewood. **Producer:** Harry Carlisle.

1965 5.6 **Sat 20 Mar 9:00 p.m.** 17 **1 wk**

David Jacobs sets the scene at the RAI Concert Hall in Naples where Kathy Kirby represents Britain singing 'I Belong'. (France Gall wins for Luxembourg with 'Poupée de Cire, Poupée de Son'.)
Production: RAI.

1967 8.9 **Sat 8 Apr 10:00 p.m.** 1 **1 wk**

From the Hofburg, Vienna, Rolf Harris describes the scene where Sandie Shaw sings (and wins) with the UK entry 'Puppet on a String' by Bill Martin and Phil Coulter.
Production: Oesterreichischer Rundfunk-Fernsehen.

1968 9.5 **Sat 6 Apr 10:00 p.m.** 1 **1 wk**

Katie Boyle introduces from the Royal Albert Hall. Cliff Richard represents the UK with 'Congratulations'. (Massiel wins for Spain with 'La, La, La'.)
Producer: Stewart Morris. **Executive Producer:** Tom Sloan.

1969 8.0 **Sat 29 Mar 10:00 p.m.** 1 **1 wk**

David Gell describes the scene from Teatro Real, Madrid, where Lulu represents the United Kingdom with 'Boom Bang-a-Bang' and shares a four-way win. (The other victors are Salome with 'Viva Cantando' for Spain, Lennie Kuhr with 'De Troubadour' for Holland, and Frida Baccara with 'Un Jour, un Enfant' for France.)
Production: Television Español.

1970 9.2 **Sat 21 Mar 10:00 p.m.** 1 **1 wk**

David Gell introduces from the International Congress Centre, Amsterdam. Mary Hopkin sings 'Knock Knock Who's There' for the United Kingdom and Dana sings 'All Kinds of Everything' for Ireland. Julio Iglesias sings for Spain. (Dana wins.)
Producer: Warner Van Kampen.

1971 8.5 **Sat 9 Apr 9:45 p.m.** 1 **1 wk**

From the Gaiety Theatre, Dublin, Dave Lee Travis sets the scene and Clodagh Rodgers sings 'Jack in the Box' for the UK. (Severine wins for Monaco with 'Un Banc, un Arbre, une Rue'.)
Production: Telefis Eirean.

1972 9.1 **Sat 25 Mar 9:30 p.m.** 1 **1 wk**

Moira Shearer introduces from the Usher Hall, Edinburgh, with the New Seekers singing for the UK 'Beg, Steal or Borrow'. (Vicky Leandros wins for Luxembourg with 'Après Toi'.)
Producer: Terry Hughes. **Executive Producer:** Bill Cotton.

1973 9.8 **Sat 7 Apr 9:30 p.m.** 1 **1 wk**

From the New Theatre, Luxembourg, Terry Wogan introduces. Cliff Richard sings the United Kingdom entry, 'Power to All Our Friends'. (The winner is Luxembourg, for the second year running, with 'Tu Te Reconnaitras' sung by Anne-Marie David.)
Production: Radio-Télé-Luxembourg.

1974 8.2 **Sat 6 Apr 9:30 p.m.** 5 **1 wk**

Katie Boyle and David Vine introduce from the Dome, Brighton. The United Kingdom is represented by Olivia Newton-John singing 'Long Live Love'. (The winners are Abba singing 'Waterloo' for Sweden.)
Producer: Michael Hurll. **Executive Producer:** Bill Cotton.

1975 8.0 **Sat 22 Mar 9:00 p.m.** 5 **1 wk**

Pete Murray sets the scene in Stockholm, where the Shadows represent the United Kingdom with 'Let Me Be the One'. (The winner is The Netherlands' 'Ding-a-Dong' by Teach-In.)
Production: Sveriges Radio.

1976 8.6 **Sat 3 Apr 9:00 p.m.** 1 **1 wk**

Michael Aspel commentates from The Hague. The UK entry and contest winner is 'Save Your Kisses For Me' by Brotherhood of Man.
Production: NOS (Dutch Television Service).

1977 9.1 **Sat 7 May 9:00 p.m.** 1 **1 wk**

Angela Rippon introduces from the Wembley Conference Centre. Lynsey de Paul and Mike Moran represent the United Kingdom with 'Rock Bottom'. (Marie Myriam wins for France with 'L'Oiseau et L'enfant'.) Commentator is Pete Murray.
Producer: Stewart Morris.

1978 15.1 **Sat 22 Apr 8:30 p.m.** 6 **1 wk**

Co-Co represent the UK at the Palais Des Congrès, Paris with 'Bad Old Days'. (Izhar Cohen and Alphabeta win for Israel with 'A-Ba-Ni-Bi'. Norway gets no points.) Terry Wogan introduces.
Production: TF1

1979 15.4 **Sat 31 Mar 9:00 p.m.** 10 **1 wk**

John Dunn introduces from the Binyaney Haouma Centre, Jerusalem. Black Lace represent the United Kingdom with 'Mary Ann'. (Israel wins for the second consecutive year with Milk and Honey singing 'Hallelujah'.)
Production: Israel Broadcasting Authority.

1980 14.1 **Sat 19 Apr 8:00 p.m.** 7 **1 wk**

At the Congressgebouw in The Hague, Prima Donna represent the UK with 'Love Enough For Two'. (Johnny Logan wins for Ireland singing 'What's Another Year'.)
Production: Nederlandse Omroep Stichting.

1981 15.3 **Sat 4 Apr 8:00 p.m.** 15 **1 wk**

Bucks Fizz represent the UK at the Royal Dublin Society and win the contest with 'Making Your Mind Up'.
Production: Telefis Eirean.

1982 14.5 **Sat 24 Apr 8:00 p.m.** 8 **1 wk**

Jan Leeming and Ray Moore introduce from the Harrogate Centre. Bardo represent the UK singing 'One Step Further'. (Nicole wins for West Germany with 'Ein Bisschen Friede'.)
Producer: Michael Hurll.

1983 12.5 **Sat 23 Apr 8:00 p.m.** 5 **1 wk**

Sweet Dreams singing 'I'm Never Giving Up' represent the UK at the Rudi-Seldmayr-Halle, Munich. (Corinne Hermes wins for Luxembourg with 'Si La Via est Cadeau'.)
Production: ARD (Germany).

1984 9.8 **Sat 5 May 8:00 p.m.** 12 **1 wk**

Belle and the Devotions represent the UK at the Théâtre Municipal, Luxembourg with 'Love Games'. (The Herreys win for Sweden performing 'Diggi Loo-Diggi Ley'.)
Production: Radio–Télé-Luxembourg.

1985 13.9 **Sat 4 May 8:00 p.m.** 4 **1 wk**

Vikki represents the UK in Gothenburg, Sweden singing 'Love Is'. (The Bobbysocks win for Norway singing 'Let It Swing'.)
Production: Swedish TV Service.

1986 9.8 **Sat 3 May 8:00 p.m.** 17 **1 wk**

The Contest is held in Grieghallen, Norway. Ryder represent the UK with 'Runner in the Night'. (Belgium wins the contest with Sandra Kim singing 'J'aime la Vie'.)
Production: NRK (Norway).

1989 9.5 **Sat 6 May 8:00 p.m.** 19 **1 wk**

From the Palais de Beaulieu, Lausanne, Live Report represent the UK with the song 'Why Do I Always Get It Wrong?'. (Riva wins for Yugoslavia singing 'Rock Me Baby'.)
Production: SSR (Switzerland).

1990 10.2 **Sat 5 May 8:00 p.m.** 8 **1 wk**

From Vatroslav Lisinski Concert Hall, Zagreb. Emma represents the UK with 'Give a Little Love Back to the World'. (Italy wins with Toto Cotugno and 'Altogether 1992'.)
Production: JRT Zagreb.

1991 10.2 **Sat 4 May 8:00 p.m.** 18 **1 wk**

From Cinecitta, Rome, Samantha Janus represents the UK with 'A Message For Your Heart'. (Sweden wins with Carola and 'Captured by a Love Storm'.)
Production: RAI.

Singing 'Congratulations', Cliff Richard represents the United Kingdom in the 1968 **Eurovision Song Contest**.

Ever Decreasing Circles

20 wks

BBC, situation comedy

This series by John Esmonde and Bob Larbey starred Richard Briers as Martin Bryce, a neurotic and obsessively finicky pursuer of law and order and captain of the tennis and cricket club. He manifested insensitivity towards his wife Ann (Penelope Wilton). Next-door neighbour Paul Ryman (Peter Egan) attempted to moderate. The top-rated 1985, 1987 and 1988 programmes were all repeats.
Producer (1986–89): Harold Snoad).

1985	13.0	Mon 30 Sep 8:30 p.m.	8	4 wks

Ann is becoming increasingly bored with her stay-at-home existence. Martin's attempts to get her involved in craft projects fail to spark any enthusiasm.
Producer: Sydney Lotterby.

1986	12.0	Sun 5 Oct 7:15 p.m.	7	5 wks

Ann's interminable suffering at the hands of busybody Martin continues unabated.

1987	14.0	Mon 13 Apr 8:30 p.m.	4	4 wks

Martin wonders why his garden gets molehills and Paul's doesn't.

1988	10.1	Mon 22 Aug 8:30 p.m.	11	6 wks

Martin works up a fiery temper when he and his neighbours are denied access to a public path.

1989	11.7	Sun 24 Dec 7:45 p.m.	17	1 wk

Martin admits for the first time he has too many commitments. He is trying to organize the summer fête and worries how the community would cope without him.

Every Breath You Take

1 wk

Granada, drama

1988	11.1	Sun 10 Apr 9:00 p.m.	16	1 wk

In this play by Nell Dunn a thirteen-year-old boy lives with his divorced mother. He collapses and is rushed to hospital. Starring Connie Booth, Pat Heywood, James Maxwell and Brian Protheroe.
Designer: Alan Price. **Director:** Paul Seed. **Producer:** Roy Roberts.

Every Second Counts

30 wks

BBC, game show

Paul Daniels hosted this game in which couples answered questions to earn seconds on the clock. The pair with the most time went on to use that time to answer questions for prizes.
Directors included Tony Newman (1986–87). **Producer** (1986–87, 1989): David Taylor.

1986	13.6	Sat 15 Feb 7:10 p.m.	11	10 wks
1987	10.9	Fri 2 Jul 7:40 p.m.	7	7 wks
1988	9.7	Fri 17 Jun 7:40 p.m.	10	3 wks

Director: Michael Leggo. **Producer:** Stanley Appel.

1989	11.5	Fri 30 Jun 7:35 p.m.	8	10 wks

Director: John Burrowes.

Every Which Way But Loose

2 wks

Presented by ITV, film

1984	10.5	Sat 25 Aug 9:15 p.m.	3	1 wk

Clint Eastwood stars as Philo Beddoe, the greatest bar-room brawler in history. He is accompanied by an orang-utan. Geoffrey Lewis and Sondra Locke also star.
Director: James Fargo.

1991	14.5	Sat 14 Dec 7:45 p.m.	10	1 wk

The BBC shows the above film.

Everybody's Equal

6 wks

Thames, game show

Chris Tarrant was host to an audience of two hundred people, each of whom held a key pad connected to a computer. Tarrant asked questions and if someone pressed the wrong key they were eliminated. This process continued until only one member of the audience remained as the contestant for the big prize.

1989	9.9	Wed 7 Jun 7:00 p.m.	14	6 wks

Director: Noel D. Greene. **Producer:** Paul Smith. **Executive Producer:** Bob Louise. (A Celador production.)

Exciting Eileen Gourley, The

1 wk

AR, entertainment

1965	5.4	Fri 17 Sep 7:10 p.m.	17	1 wk

This programme showcases the talents of American Singer Eileen Gourley.
Musical Director: Ian McPherson. **Director:** Peter Croft. **Editor:** Barry Cawtheray.

Executive Stress · 8 wks

Thames, situation comedy

This series by George Layton starred Penelope Keith as Caroline Fairchild and Geoffrey Palmer as her husband Donald. Having seen her five children go to university, Caroline was ready for a job. Donald was the sales and marketing director of a publishing house. She became editorial director using the assumed name of Caroline Fielding. They gave no hint of being related.
Producer: John Howard Davies.

| 1986 | 13.1 | Mon 10 Nov 8:00 p.m. | 6 | 7 wks |

Caroline discovers Donald's work ethics fail to meet her expectations.

| 1989 | 8.2 | Mon 31 July 8:00 p.m. | 18 | 1 wk |

Everyone in the office has the wrong idea about everybody else. Anthea Duxbury (Elizabeth Counsell) misunderstands Donald, which amuses Caroline, and Edgar Frankland (Harry Ditson) misreads Caroline. (Repeat.)

Expert, The · 8 wks

BBC, drama

Devised by Gerard Glaister and N.J. Crisp, this series was first shown on BBC2. The police mystery stories featured Marius Goring as pathologist Dr John Hardy.

| 1970 | 5.8 | Tue 16 Apr 8:00 p.m. | 12 | 8 wks |

'Fire Without Smoke' by John Gould.
The tragedy of the death of a small child is compounded by the suspicion that one of the parents may be to blame.
Director: Prudence Fitzgerald. **Producer:** Gerard Glaister.

Explorers of the Deep · 3 wks

Presented by BBC, documentary

This series produced by the Cousteau Society followed the explorations of Jacques Cousteau and other underwater researchers.

| 1979 | 17.2 | Mon 13 Aug 7:15 p.m. | 1 | 3 wks |

'Time Bomb at 50 Fathoms'
A team risked their lives for ten months at a cost of twelve million dollars to remove 300 tons of lethal poison from the hold of a sunken ship.

E

Jacques Cousteau was the foremost of the **Explorers of the Deep**.

FBI Murders, The — 1 wk

Presented by BBC, film

| 1991 | 10.9 | Tue 9 Jul 9:30 p.m. | 7 | 1 wk |

This version of the most violent and bloody shoot-out in FBI history stars Michael Gross and David Soul.
Director: Dick Lowry.

Fabulous Fenella Fielding, The — 1 wk

AR, entertainment

| 1965 | 5.9 | Wed 3 Nov 9:10 p.m. | 20 | 1 wk |

Actress Fenella Fielding sings and dances in her own showcase.
Musical Director: Ian McPherson. **Producer:** Peter Croft.

Facelift — 1 wk

BBC, documentary

| 1981 | 10.5 | Tue 23 Jun 9:25 p.m. | 19 | 1 wk |

A report by Harold Williamson on the cosmetic surgery business.
Producer: Jeremy Bennett.

Falcon Crest — 3 wks

USA presented by ITV, soap

In this saga of the Channing family, large vineyard owners in California's Napa Valley, Jane Wyman was Angie Channing and Robert Foxworth played her nephew Chase Gioberti. He was an airline pilot as well as a grape grower. His mother Jacqueline Perrault was played by Lana Turner. Maggie Gioberti was portrayed by Susan Sullivan.
Created and produced by Earl Hamner.

| 1982 | 13.3 | Thu 18 Feb 8:00 p.m. | 11 | 3 wks |

'In His Father's House'
Chase's mother comes to visit from her home in France.

Fall Guy, The — 30 wks

USA presented by ITV, drama

Lee Majors starred as Colt Seavers, a stuntman who was also a bounty hunter. More than thirty stuntmen appeared in the series. Their leader was Mickey Gilbert, a former rodeo champion who stood in for Majors when required.
Producer: Glen Larson.

| 1982 | 12.5 | Fri 7 May 7:30 p.m. | 11 | 6 wks |

'The Snow Job'
Colt sights a reward as he pursues a gang of criminals.

| 1983 | 12.9 | Fri 14 Jan 7:30 p.m. | 9 | 24 wks |

'The Ives Have It'
Ann Turkel guest stars as identical twins Carla and Kitty Ives, wanted by Colt on suspicion of burglary.

Fallen Hero — 1 wk

Granada, drama

This series by Brian Finch concerned former Rugby League star Gareth Hopkins (Del Henney), prematurely forced out of the game by injury. Wanda Ventham played his wife Dorothy.

| 1979 | 13.5 | Thu 20 Dec 9:00 p.m. | 15 | 1 wk |

As the marriage begins to fail, Gareth's stepson Martin (John Wheatley) faces a murder charge.
Designer: Eugene Ferguson. **Director:** Oliver Horsburgh. **Producer:** June Howson. **Executive Producer:** Michael Cox.

Fame — 25 wks

USA presented by BBC, drama

This series spotlighted students and teachers at New York's dream factory, the High School for the Performing Arts. Debbie Allen starred as Lydia Grant and Gene Anthony Ray as Leroy Johnson.
Director: Robert Scheerer. **Producer:** Stanley C. Rogow.

| 1982 | 11.0 | Wed 22 Sep 8:00 p.m. | 9 | 11 wks |

'Come One, Come All' by Hindi Brooks.
Gwen Verdon guest stars as Melinda MacNeill. Her child, Montgomery (P.R. Paul) is a student at the school and maternal visits are rare. But Melinda's egotistic wants prevent her from noticing her own child's needs.

| 1983 | 10.0 | Thu 19 May 8:00 p.m. | 11 | 14 wks |

'Beginnings' by Ralph Farquhar and Kevin Sullivan.
Romance blossoms between Leroy and a ballet student.

....

Family at War, A — 49 wks

Granada, drama

This series was created by John Finch. It began in middle-class Liverpool in 1938. There were two million unemployed. The series followed the fortunes of the Ashton family: Margaret (Lesley Nunnerley), Freda (Barbara Flynn), Philip (Keith Drinkel), Sheila (Coral Atkins), Edwin (Colin Douglas), David (Colin Campbell) and Jean (Shelagh Fraser).

| 1970 | 7.9 | Tue 14 Apr 9:00 p.m. | 1 | 19 wks |

'The Facts of Life' by John Finch.
Hitler's shadow lengthens over Europe. War appears inevitable.
Director: June Howson. **Producer:** Richard Doubleday.

| 1971 | 8.6 | Wed 3 Feb 9:00 p.m. | 1 | 23 wks |

'Believed Killed' by Alexander Baron.
It is May 1942. David Ashton is disillusioned with marriage and returns to see his illegitimate child, which was born in 1940 to Peggy Drake (Amelia Taylor). Margaret Porter (Lesley Nunnerley) is forced to meet reality face-to-face.
Director: Bob Hird. **Producers:** James Brabazon and Michael Cox.
Executive Producer: Richard Doubleday.

| 1972 | 8.2 | Wed 5 Jan 9:00 p.m. | 2 | 7 wks |
| | | Wed 26 Jan 9:00 p.m. | | |

'The Sensible Thing' by Roy Russell.
It's VE Day, 8 May 1945, time for thoughts of the future and reflections on missed opportunities in the past.
Director: Gerry Mill. **Producer:** Michael Cox. **Executive Producer:** Richard Doubleday.

'A Faint Refrain' by Jonathan Powell.
It is October 1945. The marriage of Margaret Porter is affected by her remembered love for Michael Armstrong (Mark Jones), even though it is more than three years since they said goodbye.
Director: Baz Taylor. **Producer:** Michael Cox.

These two programmes achieved the same viewing figure and chart position.

Family Fortunes — 135 wks

ATV, game show

A game between two families with five members in each team. The programme asked questions of 100 people and contestants tried to guess the most popular answers from the survey. Example: 'Name something you keep in a bathroom cabinet.' Presenters included Bob Monkhouse (1980–83), Max Bygraves (1984–85) and Les Dennis (1987–88, 1990–91).
Directors included Graham C. Williams (1980–82) and Mike Holgate (1987–88). **Producers** included William G. Stewart (1980–82, 1984–85), Tony Wolfe (1987–88) and Dennis Liddington (1990–91).

1980	15.9	Sun 20 Jan 7:15 p.m.	7	13 wks
1981	17.4	Fri 20 Feb 7:00 p.m.	3	23 wks
1982	17.4	Sat 9 Jan 6:45 p.m.	2	25 wks
1983	15.2	Fri 25 Mar 7:00 p.m.	2	36 wks

This celebrity edition features family teams captained by Bernie Clifton and Jack Douglas.
Producer: Graham C. Williams.

| 1984 | 12.2 | Sun 12 Feb 7:15 p.m. | 11 | 7 wks |

Director: David Millard.

| 1985 | 16.1 | Fri 18 Jan 7:30 p.m. | 7 | 12 wks |

Director: Paul Harrison.

1987	10.7	Sat 27 Jun 7:45 p.m.	8	3 wks
1988	11.8	Wed 10 Aug 7:00 p.m.	17	4 wks
1990	12.1	Fri 9 Nov 7:00 p.m.	13	8 wks

Director: Jenny Dodd.

| 1991 | 13.4 | Fri 27 Dec 7:00 p.m. | 13 | 4 wks |

Director: Bob Cousins.

....

Family Fortunes Christmas Show, The — 1 wk

ATV, game show

| 1990 | 12.9 | Fri 21 Dec 7:00 p.m. | 13 | 1 wk |

Using a pantomime theme, Les Dennis pits the Whittington family (Floella Benjamin, Marti Caine, Barry Cryer, Windsor Davies and Linda Lusardi) against the Trot family (Brian Conley, Russell Grant, Bernadette Nolan, Barry McGuigan and Barbara Windsor). Wayne Dobson is the genie.
Director: Jenny Dodd. **Producer:** Tony Wolfe.

Family Plot | 1 wk

Presented by ITV, film

| 1982 | 9.5 | Sat 21 Aug 7:45 p.m. | 10 | 1 wk |

A medium and a taxi driver cross paths with a kidnapper. Starring Karen Black, Bruce Dern, William Devane and Barbara Harris.
Director: Alfred Hitchcock.

Family Solicitor | 20 wks

Granada, drama

These stories centred on the firm of Naylor Freeman and Co. Naylor was played by A.J. Brown and Freeman by Robert Flemyng. Also starred Bernard Horsfall, Mary Kenton and Geoffrey Palmer.

| 1961 | 6.6 | Thu 28 Sep 8:30 p.m. | 3 | 20 wks |

'Conflict of Laws'
Naylor Freeman and Co. had a wealthy client who died intestate. His family stands to inherit until a letter turns up which could reverse matters. With guest star David McCallum.
Director: Christopher McMaster. **Producer:** Jack Williams.

Famine | 1 wk

AR, documentary

| 1967 | 4.9 | Wed 14 Jun 9:40 p.m. | 12 | 1 wk |

Film of the plight of millions of people dying of hunger and disease in Bihar, India, following years of drought.
Camera: Ron Osborne. **Sound:** Don Alton. **Producer:** Jack Gold.

Fancy Wanders | 1 wk

LWT, situation comedy

This series by Sid Green starred Dave King as Fancy and Joe Marcell as his pal Alastair. Both were unemployed tramps.

| 1980 | 12.9 | Fri 24 Oct 7:30 p.m. | 17 | 1 wk |

'With a Little Bit of Luck'
Fancy and Alastair speculate on what the world would be like if they had the power to change it.
Directors: David Crossman and Les Chatfield. **Producers:** Derrick Goodwin and Tony Cornford.

Fans Fans Fans | 1 wk

ATV, documentary

| 1964 | 5.7 | Wed 15 Jul 9:40 p.m. | 7 | 1 wk |

Alan Dell presents an examination of fan worship over five decades, from Mary Pickford, Rudolph Valentino, Clara Bow and Clark Gable to Frank Sinatra, Marilyn Monroe, Elvis Presley and the Beatles.
Writer: Francis Wyndham. **Producer:** Francis Megahy.

Fantasy Island | 2 wks

USA presented by ITV, drama

Mr Roarke (Ricardo Montalban) owned an unusual island where, for a high fee, guests were helped to live out their fantasies.

| 1978 | 13.5 | Tue 24 Oct 7:30 p.m. | 16 | 2 wks |

'Trouble, My Lovely'/'The Common Man'
One visitor dreams of becoming a famous private investigator, while another just seeks a little respect from his family.

Farewell Arabia | 1 wk

AR, documentary

| 1967 | 4.6 | Tue 29 Aug 8:30 p.m. | 20 | 1 wk |

With the newfound wealth derived from oil Sheikh Zaid is steering Abu Dhabi from the old world into the new. Written and narrated by David Holden.
Camera: Ron Osborne. **Sound:** Stan Clarke. **Producer:** Randal Beattie.

Farrington | 2 wks

YTV, situation comedy

This series by Dick Sharples starred Angela Thorne as Harriet Emily Farrington, British Consul General in an obscure Latin-American republic. It also starred Tony Haygarth, John Quayle and Joan Sims.

| 1987 | 9.7 | Wed 10 Jun 8:30 p.m. | 15 | 2 wks |

'In Room 504'
Harriet is the victim of vicious gossip which could harm her career.
Guest star: Elizabeth Sellars.
Producer: Ronnie Baxter.

Fatal Attraction
`1 wk`

Presented by ITV, film

`1991` `15.0` `Sun 22 Sep 9:05 p.m.` `8` `1 wk`

Michael Douglas and Glenn Close star as Dan Gallagher and Alex Forrest. Their brief affair has terrifying consequences.
Director: Adrian Lyne.

....

Father Brown
`3 wks`

ATV, drama

Hugh Leonard's adaptations of G.K. Chesterton's stories of the clerical detective starred Kenneth More in the title role.

`1974` `6.9` `Thu 24 Oct 9:00 p.m.` `7` `3 wks`

'The Key of Apollo'
When Father Brown visits his friend Flambeau (Dennis Burgess) he meets a worshipper of the sun who seeks to advance the causes of women, a practitioner of the occult and exorcism.
Designer: Michael Eve. **Director:** Peter Jefferies. **Producer:** Ian Fordyce.

....

Father Charlie
`1 wk`

Central, situation comedy

This series by Vince Powell starred Anna Quayle as Reverend Mother of the Sisters of St Winifred's Convent. The Bishop (John Savident) appointed eccentric, late-in-life convert Father Charlie (Lionel Jeffries) as their Chaplain.

`1982` `12.3` `Sun 28 Feb 8:15 p.m.` `18` `1 wk`

'The New Chaplain'
Father Charlie arrives to take up his duties at the convent like a lamb to the slaughter.
Producer: Stuart Allen.

....

Father Dear Father
`43 wks`

Thames, comedy

Johnnie Mortimer and Brian Cooke created the Glover family. Patrick Cargill starred as divorced Patrick Glover, trying to bring up his daughters Ann (Natasha Pyne) and Karen (Ann Holloway) while fending off his mother (Joyce Carey), his ex-wife (Ursula Howells) and his housekeeper/nanny (Noël Dyson). A St Bernard named H.G. Wells spent his life asleep on the settee. By the 1969 series, the ex-wife had married Patrick's best friend Bill (Patrick Holt).
Producer: William G. Stewart

`1968` `7.9` `Tue 10 Dec 8:30 p.m.` `2` `6 wks`

'I Should Have Danced All Night'
The family tries to figure out why Patrick has been leaving the house at 8 p.m. each evening and returning with aches and pains.

`1969` `6.6` `Tue 27 May 8:25 p.m.` `2` `6 wks`

'Birthday Surprise'
Patrick has to spend his birthday in bed with a cold.

`1970` `6.4` `Tue 19 May 8:25 p.m.` `3` `6 wks`

'One Dog and His Man'
Mild-mannered Patrick is provoked on the landing and reacts uncharacteristically.

`1971` `7.4` `Mon 18 Oct 8:25 p.m.` `2` `12 wks`

'A Case for Inspector Glover'
Patrick Glover enquires of the police if fingerprints remain in evidence after strangulation. The answer is not quite what he expects. With a guest appearance by Jack Smethurst.

`1972` `7.1` `Tue 20 Jun 8:30 p.m.` `2` `7 wks`

'Brother Dear Brother'
Patrick's mother rings to say his brother Philip (Donald Sinden) is in hospital. What follows causes Patrick to fall out with the lady in the horsemeat shop.

`1973` `7.4` `Tue 6 Feb 7:05 p.m.` `5` `6 wks`

'In All Directions'
Each year the family holds a conference to decide where to go on holiday. Each year it goes to the same place. Will this year be any different?

....

Father Dear Father
`1 wk`

Presented by ITV, film

`1978` `11.9` `Thu 17 Aug 7:45 p.m.` `5` `1 wk`

Feature film version in which Patrick, after a heart-to-heart with a deaf vicar, decides to remarry. By accident he proposes to his charlady. Also starring Joyce Carey, Noël Dyson, Ann Holloway, Ursula Howells, Richard O'Sullivan, Natasha Pyne, Beryl Reid, Donald Sinden and Jack Watling.
Director: William G. Stewart.

Father Dowling Investigates — 3 wks

USA presented by ITV, drama

Tom Bosley starred as Father Frank Dowling, priest to St Michael's parish in Chicago. He engaged in acts of crimebusting in the company of streetwise nun Sister Steve (Tracy Nelson).

| 1991 | 11.3 | Sat 23 Mar 8:10 p.m. | 8 | 3 wks |

'The Mafia Priest Mystery'
Father Dowling attempts to prove that a fellow priest is innocent of murder.

Fawlty Towers — 12 wks

BBC2, situation comedy

This series created and written by John Cleese and Connie Booth was set in a seaside hotel near Torquay. Cleese starred as the manic Basil Fawlty, who ran the hotel with wife Sybil (Prunella Scales). Booth portrayed the always exasperated Polly Sherman. Andrew Sachs was the Spanish waiter Manuel. Only 13 episodes were ever made. The series was first shown on BBC2 and repeated often on both channels.
Director (1979–80, 1988): Bob Spiers. **Producer** (1979–80, 1988): Douglas Argent.

| 1979 | 13.7 | Thu 27 Dec 9:15 p.m. | 18 | 1 wk |

Basil takes an instant dislike to a new guest. Guest stars: Elspet Gray, Nicky Henson and Luan Peters.

| 1980 | 9.6 | Thu 24 Jul 7:55 p.m. | 12 | 1 wk |

Two guests, a psychiatrist and his doctor wife, find Basil's behaviour professionally alarming.

| 1985 | 12.5 | Sun 10 Nov 9:05 p.m. | 12 | 1 wk |

Basil tries to raise the class of the hotel's clientele. (Repeat.)
Producer: John Howard Davies.

| 1988 | 13.1 | Tue 6 Dec 8:00 p.m. | 10 | 9 wks |

Manuel's pet rat gets loose just as the health inspector is about to visit. (Repeat.)

Fear is the Key — 1 wk

ITV, film

| 1977 | 14.5 | Tue 27 Dec 8:30 p.m. | 13 | 1 wk |

Alistair Maclean's story of a man who loses his wife and family in a plane crash and conceives an elaborate plan to track down those responsible stars Barry Newman, Suzy Kendall, Ben Kingsley, Ray McAnally and John Vernon.
Director: Michael Tuchner.

Fellows, The — 6 wks

Granada, drama

This follow-on series from THE MAN IN ROOM SEVENTEEN again starred Richard Vernon and Michael Aldridge as Oldenshaw and Dimmock. They left 'the room' to take up appointments as Research Fellows in Criminology at All Saints College, Cambridge. Mrs Hollinczech (Jill Booty) looked after their research data.

| 1967 | 6.7 | Fri 19 May 9:10 p.m. | 6 | 6 wks |

Episode One:
Within days of starting work the research project receives a posthumous donation.
Writer: Robin Chapman. **Directors:** Bob Hird and Claude Watham.
Producers: Robin Chapman and Peter Plummer.

Fenn Street Gang, The — 31 wks

LWT, comedy

The mob from class 5C in PLEASE SIR went out into the cold world determined to maintain their school friendships and preserve their group identity.
Writers: John Esmonde and Bob Larbey. **Producer:** Mark Stuart.

| 1971 | 7.8 | Fri 12 Nov 7:30 p.m. | 1 | 14 wks |

'The Thin Yellow Line'
When the career of Abbott (David Barry) as a private detective comes to an inglorious end, the army unwittingly opens its arms to a new recruit.
Director: Graham Evans.

| 1972 | 6.8 | Sun 12 Nov 7:25 p.m. | 10 | 13 wks |

'That Sort of Girl'
Eric Duffy (Peter Cleall) needs a new set of ladders but has no money. Sharon (Carol Hawkins) enters a beauty contest to try to win the money for him, but Duffy has his own views on beauty contests.
Director: Mark Stuart.

| 1973 | 7.0 | Sun 7 Jan 7:25 p.m. | 8 | 4 wks |

'Is That a Proposal, Eric?'
Sharon has been Duffy's girlfriend since the third form. The way she sees it, she probably still will be only his girlfriend by the time they collect their pensions. She decides to take drastic steps.
Director: Howard Ross.

Festival of Remembrance, The — 1 wk

BBC, news

This programme presented the annual national homage to the dead of two World Wars.

| 1976 | 6.7 | Sun 14 Nov 10:35 a.m. | 20 | 1 wk |

Her Majesty the Queen leads the mourners at the Cenotaph in Whitehall. The scene is described by Tom Fleming.
Directors: Geraldine Cole and Antony Craxton.

....

Fields of Fire `2 wks`

Central, drama

This two-part story by Miranda Downes and Robert Marchand starred Todd Boyce as Bluey, an Englishman who found a new life in the Queensland outback in the 1930s.

1987	12.7	Sun 3 May 9:00 p.m.	5	2 wks

Part One
Bluey is unprepared for the hostility, the hardships and the heat of Queensland.
Director: Robert Marchand. **Producers:** David Elfick and Steve Knapman. (A Zenith production.)

....

Fifteen Streets, The `2 wks`

Tyne Tees, drama

Rob Bettinson adapted Catherine Cookson's Edwardian story of love and survival in the dockyards of the North East. It starred Ian Bannen, Sean Bean, Clare Holman, Jane Horrocks, Owen Teale, Billie Whitelaw and Frank Windsor.
Director: David Wheatley. **Producer:** Ray Marshall. **Executive Producer:** Geraint Davies.

1989	10.2	Sun 20 Aug 8:15 p.m.	13	1 wk

Episode One

1991	12.1	Sun 9 Jun 7:50 p.m.	7	1 wk

Repeat of the above programme.

....

Fight of the Champions `1 wk`

BBC, sport

1971	6.0	Mon 8 Mar 9:20 p.m.	18	1 wk

Harry Carpenter in New York previews tomorrow's fight in Madison Square Garden between undefeated heavyweights Muhammad Ali and Joe Frazier. This Madison Square Garden bout yields the richest prize to date in the history of sport.
Producer: Bob Duncan.

....

Film Matinee `5 wks`

Presented by BBC, film

1961	4.8	Sun 31 Dec 2:40 p.m.	11	1 wk

'Macao'
Starring William Bendix, Robert Mitchum and Jane Russell in a story of international crime.
Director: Josef Von Sternberg.

1962	5.5	Sun 18 Nov 3:15 p.m.	18	4 wks

'Notorious'
(See separate entry for this film.)

....

Film for Tonight `2 wks`

Presented by BBC, film

1971	7.4	Tue 2 Nov 7:30 p.m.	3	2 wks

'Carry On Cabby'
Starring Sid James and Hattie Jacques with Kenneth Connor, Jim Dale, Liz Fraser, Charles Hawtrey, Renée Houston, Milo O'Shea and Bill Owen.
Director: Gerald Thomas.

....

Film of the Week `4 wks`

Presented by BBC, film

1971	6.5	Sun 6 Jun 7:55 p.m.	1	2 wks

'The Birds'
Alfred Hitchcock's thriller stars Suzanne Pleshette, Jessica Tandy, Rod Taylor and introduces Tippi Hedren.

(Below) Robin Askwith and Leon Vitali of **The Fenn Street Gang** meet their former Teacher John Alderton.

(Bottom) Tippi Hedren is terrorized in 'The Birds', a Number One when shown as **Film of the Week**.

| 1973 | 6.1 | Sun 9 Dec 8:15 p.m. | 19 | 1 wk |

'Heaven Knows, Mr Allison'
During the Second World War a US Marine (Robert Mitchum) is washed ashore on a small Pacific Island inhabited not by the Japanese but by a young nun (Deborah Kerr).
Director: *John Huston.*

| 1976 | 6.6 | Sun 28 Mar 8:15 p.m. | 17 | 1 wk |

'Angels One Five'
The title is the call sign for a squadron of Hurricanes heading towards German aircraft over the Channel in 1940. Starring Michael Denison, Dulcie Gray, Jack Hawkins and John Gregson.
Director: *George More O'Ferrall.*

Film of the Week — 4 wks

Presented by ITV, film

| 1973 | 6.9 | Sun 28 Oct 8:20 p.m. | 7 | 1 wk |

'Operation Cross Eagles'
Richard Conte and Rory Calhoun star in the story of a commando unit in Yugoslavia during the Second World War.
Director: *Richard Conte.*

| 1974 | 5.6 | Sun 1 Sep 8:15 p.m. | 12 | 1 wk |

'The Nun's Story'
A young Belgian girl experiences difficulties facing the principle of unquestioning obedience. Starring Audrey Hepburn with Peggy Ashcroft, Edith Evans, Peter Finch, Dean Jagger and Lionel Jeffries.
Director: *Fred Zinnemann.*

| 1977 | 14.0 | Sun 25 Sep 7:45 p.m. | 4 | 2 wks |

'Hot Rock'
A gang of thieves aims to steal a diamond from the Brooklyn Museum. Starring Robert Redford, George Segal and Zero Mostel.
Director: *Peter Yates.*

Final Countdown, The — 2 wks

Presented by ITV, film

| 1983 | 11.5 | Sun 4 Sep 7:15 p.m. | 2 | 1 wk |

The nuclear-powered aircraft carrier Nimitz suffers serious losses of equipment in a violent Pacific storm. Kirk Douglas and Martin Sheen star.
Director: *Don Taylor.*

| 1985 | 9.3 | Thu 22 Aug 7:30 p.m. | 15 | 1 wk |

Repeat showing of the above film.

Find the Singer — 4 wks

AR, music

Lou Preager introduced contestants competing for five hundred pounds and a recording contract. Jim Dale interviewed the singers.
Producer: *Peter Croft.*

| 1962 | 5.1 | Mon 2 Apr 10:10 p.m. | 11 | 4 wks |

One of the contest heats.

Fine Romance, A — 22 wks

LWT, situation comedy

This series by Bob Larbey starred real-life husband and wife Judi Dench and Michael Williams as Laura and Mike. It followed their on-off-on relationship. Susan Penhaligon and Geoffrey Rose also starred as Helen and Phil.
Producer (1983–85): *Don Leaver.* **Executive Producer:** *Humphrey Barclay.*

| 1982 | 13.5 | Sun 14 Feb 8:15 p.m. | 12 | 3 wks |

Laura decides she and Mike should add a little spice to their lives. Helen and Phil make some suggestions.
Producer: *James Cellan Jones.*

| 1983 | 13.4 | Fri 4 Nov 8:30 p.m. | 5 | 5 wks |

Laura and her parents spend hours waiting for Mike to arrive.

| 1984 | 14.8 | Fri 10 Feb 8:30 p.m. | 3 | 7 wks |

Mike finally proposes, but Laura is uncertain what it is he is actually proposing.

| 1985 | 12.7 | Fri 26 Apr 8:00 p.m. | 7 | 7 wks |

Laura decides she and Mike will give a dinner party for Helen and Phil. (Repeat.)

Fire Crackers — 7 wks

ATV, situation comedy

In this series by Fred Robinson, Alfred Marks starred with Joe Baker and Cardew Robinson. Set in the forgotten village of Cropper's End (population seventy), the stories concerned the village fire service and its beloved engine, Bessie (c. 1907). By a bureaucratic blunder the brigade's existence had been overlooked and, while they drew their pay, they tried to avoid any kind of fire, preferring to ring a neighbouring station if an alarm sounded.

| 1964 | 6.0 | Sat 29 Aug 9:50 p.m. | 7 | 5 wks |

'Semi-Detached'
The village fire department finds fire dodging thirsty work. Just when

they might be needed they're all in the Cropper's Arms.
Director: Josephine Douglas. **Producer:** Alan Tarrant.

1965	5.9	Sat 30 Jan 8:25 p.m.	17	2 wks

'Slap on the Map'
The entire village is thrown into confusion when a group of tourists turns up in Cropper's End.
Director: Josephine Douglas. **Producer:** Alan Tarrant.

....

Fire in the Sky, A — 1 wk

Presented by ITV, film

1979	15.0	Wed 9 May 8:30 p.m.	6	1 wk

Phoenix, Arizona is threatened by a comet on a collision course with Earth.
Director: Jerry Jameson.

....

Firecreek — 1 wk

Presented by ITV, film

1973	5.2	Mon 27 Aug 8:00 p.m.	15	1 wk

Bank Holiday Monday showing of a film set in the 1870s. Violence erupts in the isolated town of Firecreek when a bunch of tough adventurers from the Missouri range wars roll in. Starring Henry Fonda and James Stewart with Ed Begley, Dean Jagger and Inger Stevens.
Director: Vincent McEveety.

....

Firefighters — 1 wk

ATV, documentary

1977	9.5	Wed 3 Aug 9:00 p.m.	20	1 wk

This film follows the progress of Mark Longley, who graduated in chemistry from Bath University and joined the West Midlands Fire Brigade.
Director: David C. Rea. **Producer:** Brian Lewis.

....

Firefox — 1 wk

Presented by ITV, film

1985	13.6	Sat 24 Aug 7:45 p.m.	3	1 wk

Clint Eastwood directs and stars as former Vietnam pilot Mitchell Grant, who accepts a mission to steal Russia's ultimate war plane, Firefox.

First Born — 3 wks

BBC, drama

Ted Whitehead adapted the novel Gorsaga by Maureen Duffy in three parts. Charles Dance starred as scientist Edward Forester who was elated when a hybrid species was born to a gorilla. Also starred Rosemary McHale, Philip Madoc, Julie Peasgood and Peter Tilbury.

1988	15.2	Sun 13 Nov 9:05 p.m.	7	3 wks

Part Three
Gordon (Jamie Foster) is now 18 and doing well at his military academy. But Forester still fears for the future of his hybrid son.
Designer: Humphrey Jaeger. **Director:** Philip Saville. **Producer:** Sally Head.

....

First Great Train Robbery, The — 3 wks

Presented by ITV, film

1982	12.9	Sat 3 Apr 7:45 p.m.	11	1 wk

It is 1855, the time of the Crimean War. A train carrying £25,000 of bullion is travelling from London to Folkestone on its way to the troops. Elegant crook Edward Pierce (Sean Connery) sets his sights on the loot. Lesley-Anne Down, Michael Elphick, Wayne Sleep and Donald Sutherland also star.
Director: Michael Crichton.

1983	9.6	Tue 30 Aug 7:00 p.m.	11	1 wk
1991	10.9	Wed 17 Apr 8:00 p.m.	16	1 wk

Repeat showings of the above film.

....

First In – Last Out — 1 wk

Southern, documentary

1968	5.3	Tue 25 Jun 9:15 p.m.	17	1 wk

Film about the Royal Marine Commandos. Christopher Wain narrates.
Producer: Terry Johnston.

....

First of the Summer Wine — 1 wk

BBC, situation comedy

This series by Roy Clarke took his principal characters from LAST OF THE SUMMER WINE back to their teenage life in Yorkshire in 1939. Peter Sallis played his own character's father, Mr Clegg, with David Fenwick as the eighteen-year-old Norman Clegg. Maggie Ollerenshaw played Mrs Clegg. Paul Wyett was the young Compo, Richard Lumsden the young Foggy and Paul McLain the young Seymour. Helen Patrick was Nora.

| 1988 | 9.2 | Sun 28 Aug 8:35 p.m. | 18 | 1 wk |

Norman Clegg is interested in life with a capital L, but he finds it difficult to find anyone prepared to talk to him about it, or to take him seriously. Anyway he feels that the possibility of war is remote and so concentrates on getting the hang of girls.
Producer: Gareth Gwenlan.

Five Days, Six Hours and Twenty-Six Minutes   1 wk

ITN, news

| 1966 | 5.8 | Wed 17 Aug 9:45 p.m. | 5 | 1 wk |

A police dragnet operation began on Friday 12 August when three plainclothes policemen were shot dead in Braybrook Street near Wormwood Scrubs Common when they stopped their Triumph 2000 Q car to make a chance check on a parked Standard Vanguard. Earlier today one of the two suspects, John Duddy, was arrested in Glasgow and flown to London handcuffed to Detective Inspector Jack Slipper and then taken to Shepherds Bush police station. Police are still hunting Harry Maurice Roberts, who is believed to be carrying three guns.

Flambards   8 wks

YTV, drama

These adaptations of the romantic stories of K.M. Peyton were set in England in the early part of this century.

| 1979 | 16.0 | Fri 16 Mar 8:00 p.m. | 7 | 8 wks |

'Flying High' by Alex Glasgow.
Sandy (Peter Sethelen) loops the loop and becomes the hero of the flying circus.
Director: Michael Ferguson. **Producer:** Leonard Lewis. **Executive Producer:** David Cunliffe.

Flame Trees of Thika, The   4 wks

Thames, drama

John Hawkesworth adapted this series from the novel by Elspeth Hurley. It was filmed entirely on location in Kenya and set in 1913. Holly Aird played the authoress Elspeth with Hayley Mills as her mother Tilly. Ben Cross, Sharon Maughan and David Robb also starred. Produced by Euston Films.

| 1981 | 12.7 | Tue 8 Sep 8:30 p.m. | 7 | 4 wks |

'Hyenas Will Eat Anything'
The family begins to adjust to life in the African bush and the sun-scorched plains.

Director: Roy Ward Baker. **Producers:** John Hawkesworth and Christopher Neame. **Executive Producer:** Verity Lambert.

Flash Gordon   1 wk

Presented by BBC, film

| 1983 | 12.0 | Sat 24 Dec 7:10 p.m. | 11 | 1 wk |

Alex Raymond's comic strip hero Flash Gordon (Sam Jones) is the only man who can prevent energy waves from the planet Mongo causing the moon to crash into the Earth. Stars include Melody Anderson, Brian Blessed, John Osborne, Max Von Sydow and Peter Wyngarde.
Director: Mike Hodges.

Flaxton Boys, The   11 wks

YTV, drama

This series was set in and around Flaxton Hall, somewhere in Yorkshire. Beginning at the turn of the century, it followed the adventures of the Flaxton family through several generations.

| 1971 | 6.5 | Sun 7 Nov 5:35 p.m. | 15 | 11 wks |

'To See a Fine Horse'
It is 1928. Preparations are being made for the forthcoming local horse show.
Writer: Gloria Tors. **Producer:** Robert D. Cardona.

Flight 90, Disaster on the Potomac   1 wk

Presented by ITV, film

| 1987 | 13.9 | Mon 25 May 9:00 p.m. | 3 | 1 wk |

This drama is based on a real-life plane crash that occurred in January 1982. An Air Florida plane crashed through the ice on the Potomac River in Washington. Teams raced to reach survivors before hypothermia killed them. Starring Stephen Macht, Dinah Manoff and Richard Masur.
Director: Robert Lewis.

Flight to Holocaust   1 wk

Presented by ITV, film

| 1977 | 14.3 | Sun 9 Oct 7:45 p.m. | 8 | 1 wk |

An aircraft has crashed into a skyscraper at Los Angeles airport. An attempt is made to rescue the passengers. Desi Arnaz Jr., Sid Caesar, Rory Calhoun, Fawne Harriman, Christopher Mitchum and Patrick Wayne star.
Director: Bernard Kowalski.

....

Floodtide	1 wk

Granada, drama

This series by Roger Marshall followed a cocaine run in England and northern France. Philip Sayer starred as Ramsey, a former doctor who lived in France. A friend of his who had died of cocaine poisoning had once been a cabinet minister. The dead man's daughter Tessa (Gabrielle Dellal) tried to expose the cover-up of his death. Sybil Maas also starred as Dany.

1987	9.7	Sun 26 Jul 9:00 p.m.	14	1 wk

'The Call'
Tessa seeks Ramsey's help.
Designer: Tim Farmer. **Director:** Tom Cotter. **Producer:** Steve Hawes.

....

Fly Me to the Moon	1 wk

ITN, news

1969	6.1	Tue 20 May 11:45 p.m.	7	1 wk

Live pictures of the moon's surface sent to Earth form Apollo 10.

....

Flying Doctors, The	2 wks

Australia presented by BBC, drama

This series about the Royal Flying Doctor Service in the outback town of Cooper's Crossing starred Andrew McFarlane as Dr Tom Callaghan and Liz Burch as Dr Chris Randall.

1988	9.8	Fri 15 Jul 8:10 p.m.	10	2 wks

'Hot Enough For You?' Vince Moran.
A Scottish family with two small children is stranded in the outback during a heatwave.
Director: Arch Nicholson.

....

Flying Lady	2 wks

YTV, drama

This series by Brian Finch starred Frank Windsor as Harry Bradley, who bought a Rolls Royce with his redundancy money. It also starred Gabrielle Daye, Anna Lindup and Anne Stallybrass. Music was by Peter Skellern.

1987	9.3	Sun 21 Jun 7:45 p.m.	16	2 wks

'Great Expectations'
Harry's Aunt Edie (Jean Heywood) was a GI's bride. She has come home to visit old friends.
Designer: Judy Steele. **Director:** Frank Cox. **Producer:** Anne W. Gibbons. **Executive Producer:** Keith Richardson.

....

Flying Machines of Ken Wallis, The	1 wk

BBC, documentary

1980	10.0	Tue 13 May 9:25 p.m.	18	1 wk

The collection of aeroplanes of retired RAF Wing Commander Wallis are often seen at airshows. He pilots his autogyro and shows some of the unusual items he has assembled.
Writer and **Producer:** Brian Johnson.

....

Flying Squad	8 wks

Thames, documentary

This series of programmes recorded the activities of the Metropolitan Police's special unit the Flying Squad.

1989	13.2	Wed 15 Feb 9:00 p.m.	13	8 wks

'Operation Pelican'
The Squad receives information as a result of CRIMEWATCH UK on the identity of a man who has been robbing building societies in South London.
Producer: Robert Fleming. (An Argo production.)

....

Follyfoot	1 wk

YTV, drama

This series aimed at children, was based on an idea by Monica Dickens and set at Follyfoot Farm in Harewood, near Leeds. The principal characters were Dora (Gillian Blake), Steve (Steve Hodson), Slugger (Arthur English), Ron Stryker (Christian Rodska) and the Colonel (Desmond Llewelyn).

1972	5.2	Sun 4 Jun 5:35 p.m.	17	1 wk

'The Debt' by Francis Stevens.
Dora thinks Arthur Wimble (Leslie Dwyer) a nice old man and keeps his horse at Follyfoot. Problems arise when Arthur thinks he needs a younger and stronger horse. Meanwhile, Steve has been searching for his mum and has found her in Liverpool. A debt must be paid.
Director: Claude Watham. **Producer:** Tony Essex.

6

5

1 *Leonard Rossiter achieved his greatest chart success as Rigsby in* **Rising Damp**.

2 ***A Sharp Intake of Breath*** *was David Jason's first series to go to Number One.*

3 *Harry H. Corbett is romantically pursued by June Whitfield in* **The Best Things in Life**.

4 ***Porridge*** *was a Number One in its first month of transmission.*

5 *Frank Spencer (Michael Crawford) and wife Betty (Michele Dotrice) are shown with daughter Jessica (Jessica Forte) in* **Some Mothers Do 'Ave 'Em**.

6 *The Booths and the Reynolds reached Number One in four consecutive years with* **Love Thy Neighbour**.

Football   **118 wks**

Various, sport

1960   **6.2**   **Thu 13 Oct 8:30 p.m.**   **6**   **2 wks**

From Old Trafford, live second-half coverage of Manchester United versus Real Madrid. Commentary by Gerry Loftus. (United lost 2–3.)
Granada television presentation: David Warwick.

1961   **5.6**   **Wed 8 Nov 8:25 p.m.**   **12**   **1 wk**

Live commentary by Gerry Loftus from Old Trafford, Manchester on the match between the Football League and the Italian League. (Welsh international John Charles, of Juventus, inspired the Italian league team to a 2–0 victory.)
Granada television presentation: David Warwick.

1962   **7.4**   **Thu 5 Apr 8:35 p.m.**   **4**   **4 wks**

Live commentary by Gerry Loftus from White Hart Lane on the second half of the second leg of the European Cup semi-final between Tottenham Hotspur and Benfica of Portugal. (Spurs won 2–1, but lost 4–3 on aggregate.)
AR television presentation: Grahame Turner.

1963   **6.9**   **Wed 23 Oct 3:45 p.m.**   **6**   **4 wks**

This England against the Rest of the World match at Wembley was arranged in honour of the Football Association's Centenary Year. Commentary by Gerry Loftus. (England won 2–1.)
AR television presentation: Grahame Turner.

1964   **5.7**   **Wed 18 Nov 8:20 p.m.**   **15**   **1 wk**

From Wembley, live coverage of the second half of the home international, England versus Wales, with Gerry Loftus commentating. (England won 2–1.)
AR television presentation: Grahame Turner.

1965   **5.2**   **Wed 19 May 7:25 p.m.**   **19**   **1 wk**

From Wembley, Kenneth Wolstenholme commentates on the European Cup Winners Cup Final between West Ham United and Munich. (West Ham won 2–0.)
BBC television presentation: Alan Chivers.

1966   **6.8**   **Thu 5 May 7:25 p.m.**   **5**   **5 wks**

From Hampden Park, Glasgow. The European Cup Winners' Cup Final between Liverpool and Borussia Dortmund. Kenneth Wolstenholme commentates. (Borussia Dortmund won 2–1 after extra time.)
BBC television presentation: Bill Stevenson.

1967   **7.4**   **Sat 20 May 3:00 p.m.**   **2**   **2 wks**

David Coleman introduces the FA Cup Final from Wembley in the BBC's CUP FINAL GRANDSTAND. (The match ended Tottenham Hotspur 2 Chelsea 1.)
BBC television presentation: Richard Tilling.

1968   **8.9**   **Wed 29 May 7:05 p.m.**   **1**   **7 wks**

Kenneth Wolstenholme commentates live on the European Cup Final from Wembley between Benfica of Portugal and Manchester United. (Manchester United ran out 4–1 winners (after extra time).)
BBC television presentation: Alec Weeks.

1969   **7.0**   **Sat 10 May 7:00 p.m.**   **1**   **8 wks**

David Coleman commentates from Wembley on the match between England and Scotland, with analysis from Don Revie and Bill Shankly. (England won 4–1.)
BBC television presentation: Alec Weeks.

1970   **6.5**   **Wed 1 Apr 10:30 p.m.**   **13**   **9 wks**

Highlights of tonight's European Cup semi-final between Leeds United and Celtic at Elland Road. (Leeds lost 0–1.)
Television presentation: YTV.

1971   **7.1**   **Fri 21 May 7:25 p.m.**   **2**   **3 wks**

Chelsea meet Real Madrid in the European Cup Winners Cup Final replay in Athens. The teams drew 1–1 the previous Wednesday night. Kenneth Wolstenholme commentates for the BBC. (Chelsea won 2–1.)
Television presentation: Greek Television Service.

1972   **7.8**   **Sat 29 Apr 7:30 p.m.**   **2**   **3 wks**

From Wembley, the first leg of the European Championship quarter-final between England and West Germany with David Coleman commentating. (The Germans crushed England 3–1.)
Analysts: Bobby Charlton, Brian Clough, Don Revie and Bob Wilson.
BBC television presentation: Alec Weeks.

1973   **9.0**   **Wed 17 Oct 10:00 p.m.**   **1**   **8 wks**

From Wembley where England play Poland in a match England must win in order to qualify for next year's World Cup Finals. Commentary by Brian Moore. (The match ended in a 1–1 draw.)
Analysts: Malcolm Allison, Jackie Charlton, Brian Clough and Derek Dougan.
Thames television presentation: Steve Minchin.

1974   **6.6**   **Wed 26 Jun 7:30 p.m.**   **13**   **2 wks**

With Scotland already eliminated from the World Cup in West Germany, and England, Wales and Northern Ireland having failed to qualify, Brian Moore commentates on a Group A match between Holland and Argentina. With analysis from Brian Clough, Jackie Charlton, Derek Dougan, Pat Crerand and Malcolm Allison. (Holland beat Argentina 4–0.)
Television presentation: West German Television Service.

1975   **9.4**   **Wed 28 May 8:00 p.m.**   **1**   **2 wks**

BBC Commentators David Coleman and Don Revie introduce the European Cup Final between Leeds United and Bayern Munich live from the Parc Des Princes, Paris. Match comments from London by Jimmy Hill with Bobby Charlton and Jock Stein. (Munich won 2–0.)
Television presentation: French Television Service.

1976 **7.6** **Wed 12 May 8:00 p.m.** **1** **5 wks**

Dickie Davies introduces the European Cup Final from Hampden Park, Glasgow between Bayern Munich and St Etienne. Brian Moore is the commentator with summaries from Jack Charlton. (Bayern won their third successive European Cup with a 1–0 victory.)
ITV television presentation: Chris Allen.

1977 **16.0** **Wed 16 Nov 7:30 p.m.** **2** **4 wks**

Gerald Sinstadt introduces live coverage from Wembley of England against Italy, a World Cup qualifying match in which England has only an outside chance of reaching the finals in Argentina. Brian Moore is the commentator. (England won 2–0.)
ITV television presentation: Roy Lomas and Steve Minchin.

1978 **19.2** **Wed 10 May 7:00 p.m.** **1** **11 wks**

The European Cup Final from Wembley between Liverpool and Bruges. Brian Moore commentates with summaries from Roger Davies and Kevin Keegan. (Liverpool won 1–0.)
ITV television presentation: Roy Lomas.

1979 **14.8** **Wed 30 May 8:00 p.m.** **1** **1 wk**

Jimmy Hill introduces the European Cup Final between Nottingham Forest and Malmö from the Olympic Stadium, Munich. Barry Davies commentates for the BBC with assessments from Bobby Charlton, Kevin Keegan and Lawrie McMenemy. (Forest won the trophy with a 1–0 victory.)
Television presentation: West German Television Service.

1980 **17.4** **Wed 28 May 7:15 p.m.** **1** **5 wks**

Brian Moore commentates live from Madrid for ITV on the European Cup Final between Nottingham Forest and S.V. Hamburg. (European Footballer of the Year Kevin Keegan played for Hamburg, but couldn't stop Forest winning 1–0.)
Television presentation: Spanish Television Service.

1981 **14.0** **Sat 9 May 3:00 p.m.** **5** **3 wks**

The one hundredth FA Cup Final is contested by Manchester City and Tottenham Hotspur. Commentary is by John Motson with Jimmy Hill and Lawrie McMenemy. (The match ended 1–1, but Spurs went on to win the replay 3–2.)
BBC television presentation: Fred Viner.

1982 **13.2** **Wed 26 May 7:00 p.m.** **5** **3 wks**

From Rotterdam, Dickie Davies introduces the European Cup Final between Aston Villa and Bayern Munich. ITV commentary by Brian Moore and analysis by Brian Clough. (Villa won 1–0.)
Television presentation: Dutch Television Service.

1983 **17.5** **Sat 28 May 7:00 p.m.** **1** **5 wks**

Live from Belfast, Northern Ireland against England in the British Championships. Martin Tyler commentates with Ron Atkinson. (The match finished 0–0.)
ITV television presentation: Bob Gardam.

1984 **14.2** **Wed 30 May 7:05 p.m.** **1** **6 wks**

Steve Rider introduces the European Cup Final between Roma and Liverpool from the Olympic Stadium, Rome. Brian Moore commentates for ITV with Jimmy Greaves, Kevin Keegan and Ian St John. (The match ended in a 1–1 draw (after extra time). For the first time there was a penalty shoot-out to resolve a European Cup Final, and Liverpool won 4–2 on penalties.)
Television presentation: RAI.

1985 **15.0** **Wed 29 May 7:05 p.m.** **1** **3 wks**

Jimmy Hill introduces the European Cup Final between Liverpool and Juventus from the Heysel Stadium in Brussels. Barry Davis commentates for the BBC with Bobby Charlton. (Eighty nations witnessed the shame and agony of soccer hooliganism as television cameras covered the tragic loss of life and appalling injuries sustained in the rioting that preceded the match. The game eventually got underway and several countries decided to opt out of the broadcast. The match was won 1–0 by Juventus.)
Television presentation: Belgian Television Service.

1986 **9.1** **Wed 7 May 7:05 p.m.** **9** **2 wks**

From Seville, Jim Rosenthal introduces the European Cup Final between Barcelona and Steaua Bucharest. Commentators for ITV: Brian Moore and Kevin Keegan. (The match ended 0–0 (after extra time), but Steaua won 2–0 after a penalty shoot-out.)
Television presentation: Spanish Television Service.

1987 **9.2** **Wed 20 May 7:30 p.m.** **20** **2 wks**

Nick Owen and Jimmy Greaves introduce live coverage from Dundee of the UEFA Cup Final second leg between Dundee United and IFK Gothenburg. Martin Tyler and Denis Law commentate. (The match ended 1–1, but Gothenburg won 2–1 on aggregate.)
ITS television presentation: Doug Hammond.

1989 **10.3** **Fri 26 May 8:00 p.m.** **9** **2 wks**

Elton Welsby introduces the First Division game between Liverpool and Arsenal. Brian Moore commentates. (Arsenal's 2–0 victory at Anfield in the last match of the season secured the 1989 First Division championship.)
ITV television presentation: John Watts.

1990 **13.9** **Thu 17 May 7:30 p.m.** **6** **1 wk**

John Motson commentates on the FA Cup Final Replay after the previous Saturday's final between Crystal Palace and Manchester United ended in a 3–3 draw after extra time. (United won this replay 1–0.)
BBC television presentation: John Shrewsbury.

1991 **14.9** **Sat 18 May 3:00 p.m.** **3** **3 wks**

The FA Cup Final between Nottingham Forest and Tottenham Hotspur is introduced from Wembley by Desmond Lynam. John Motson commentates. (Spurs won 2–1 after extra time.)
BBC television presentation: John Shrewsbury, Martin Hopkins.

F

For a Few Dollars More   1 wk

Presented by BBC, film

| 1987 | 12.7 | Mon 5 Jan 9:30 p.m. | 17 | 1 wk |

Clint Eastwood stars as the man with no name in this sequel to A FISTFUL OF DOLLARS. He and fellow bounty hunter Mortimer (Lee Van Cleef) plan to capture a killer in El Paso.
Director: Sergio Leone.

For Adults Only   1 wk

Presented by ITV, film

This series of late evening films was intended for adult audiences.

| 1977 | 5.8 | Mon 18 Jul 10:30 p.m. | 19 | 1 wk |

'Assault'
A sixteen-year-old girl is brutally attacked and raped while taking a short-cut home from school. As she begins to recover from her ordeal another girl is attacked and killed. Starring Lesley-Anne Down, Frank Finlay and Suzy Kendall.
Director: Sidney Hayers.

For Richer, For Poorer   1 wk

Granada, documentary

A five-part enquiry into the economic future of Britain in the wake of Prime Minister Harold Macmillan's late 1950s pronouncement that 'most of our people have never had it so good'.

| 1962 | 5.6 | Wed 18 Apr 9:45 p.m. | 5 | 1 wk |

'Bingo'
Gambling is on the increase as a desperate last resort for many people. Narrator: Robert Holness. Interviewer: Alex Valentine.
Director: Mike Wooller. **Producer:** Tim Hewat.

For the Love of Ada   26 wks

Thames, situation comedy

Created by Vince Powell and Harry Driver. Two seventy-year-olds fall in love and marry. Irene Handl starred as Ada Cresswell and Wilfred Pickles was Walter Bingley. Their neighbourly friends Ruth and Leslie Pollitt were played by Barbara Mitchell and Jack Smethurst.

| 1970 | 7.1 | Mon 5 Oct 9:30 p.m. | 3 | 13 wks |

'Special Day'
Walter decides to make Ada's birthday special by taking her out for dinner. Unfortunately, the Pollitts have other ideas.
Producer: Ronnie Baxter.

| 1971 | 8.0 | Thu 30 Sep 9:00 p.m. | 1 | 13 wks |

'The Christening'
Anthony, the new Pollitt baby, is to be christened, so Walter fetches three crates of brown ale from the Red Lion. Meanwhile, Leslie's mother Nellie (Mollie Sugden) arrives from the North.
Producer: Ronnie Baxter.

For the Term of His Natural Life   1 wk

Australia, presented by BBC, drama

A three-part adaptation of Marcus Clarke's story of Rufus Dawes (Colin Friels) who was transported from England to a life of penal servitude in Australia. The mini-series starred Patrick Macnee and Anthony Perkins with Diane Cilento and Samantha Eggar.

| 1985 | 10.2 | Sun 30 Jun 7:15 p.m. | 17 | 1 wk |

In this final part Rufus attempts a daring escape.
Director: Rob Stewart. **Writer** and **Producer:** Wilton Schiller.

For Whom the Bell Tolls   1 wk

Presented by ITV, film

| 1974 | 7.3 | Mon 15 Apr 8:00 p.m. | 6 | 1 wk |

This version of Ernest Hemingway's story of the Spanish Civil War stars Gary Cooper, Ingrid Bergman and Akim Tamiroff.
Director: Sam Wood.

For Your Eyes Only   3 wks

Presented by ITV, film

| 1986 | 14.7 | Sun 31 Aug 7:15 p.m. | 2 | 1 wk |

James Bond (Roger Moore) searches the Greek islands for a top secret device sunk in a surveillance vehicle. Also starring Jill Bennett, Carole Bouquet, Jack Hedley, Lynn-Holly Johnson, Geoffrey Keen, Lois Maxwell and Topol.
Director: John Glen.

| 1988 | 17.8 | Mon 4 Apr 8:00 p.m. | 2 | 1 wk |
| 1990 | 15.2 | Sat 13 Jan 7:00 p.m. | 8 | 1 wk |

Repeat showings of the above film.

Force 10 from Navarone   2 wks

Presented by ITV, film

| 1982 | 18.9 | Sun 10 Jan 7:15 p.m. | 2 | 2 wks |

Two surviving saboteurs from THE GUNS OF NAVARONE join forces with the US Rangers Force 10 to blow up a dam in order to prevent the Germans slicing Yugoslavia in half. Starring Alan Badel, Harrison Ford, Edward Fox, Franco Nero and Robert Shaw. **Director:** Guy Hamilton.

Foreign Affairs   7 wks

Granada, situation comedy

A fresh setting for the characters BOOTSIE AND SNUDGE, again played by Alfie Bass and Bill Fraser, this time in employment overseas.

1964	6.7	Thu 9 Jan 7:30 p.m.	11	7 wks

Preparing to enter the diplomatic service, Bootsie and Snudge begin their journey to the British Embassy at Bosnik where the Ambassador (Nicholas Phipps) awaits them. Unfortunately Snudge's position in the Foreign Office hierarchy turns out to be less important than he expected. **Writer:** Barry Took. **Director:** Milo Lewis. **Producer:** Peter Eton.

Forever Green   5 wks

LWT, drama

John Alderton and Pauline Collins starred as Jack and Harriet Boult. They moved to live in the country because their daughter Freddy (Daisy Bates) suffered from urban allergies. The show also starred Paola Dionisotti as Lady Patricia Broughall and Wendy Van Der Plank as Hilly.

1989	15.7	Sun 12 Mar 7:45 p.m.	6	5 wks

Jack comes across some horse rustlers and Hilly has some assets that might prove valuable. **Director:** David Giles. **Producer:** Brian Eastman. **Executive Producer:** Nick Elliott. (A Picture Partnership production.)

Forsyte Saga, The   26 wks

BBC, drama

This dramatization in twenty-six parts of John Galsworthy's story was first shown on BBC2 in 1967. BBC1 repeated the series from September 1968 to March 1969. It was produced in black and white by Donald Wilson. Principal characters included Soames Forsyte (Eric Porter), his first wife Irene (Nyree Dawn Porter), his daughter by his second marriage, Fleur (Susan Hampshire), Young Jolyon (Kenneth More), Jon (Martin Jarvis) and Michael Mont (Nicholas Pennell). Other players included Fay Compton, Joseph O'Connor, Lana Morris and Margaret Tyzack. Title music was by Eric Coates.

1968	7.2	Sun 15 Dec 7:25 p.m.	3	17 wks

Part 15: 'To Let' dramatized by Vincent Tylsley. Young Jolyon has been told he has a weak heart. Fleur has discovered the root of the family feud, but she has not told Jon. **Designer:** Sally Hulke. **Director:** James Cellan Jones.

1969	7.4	Sun 2 Mar 7:25 p.m.	4	9 wks

Part 26: 'Swan Song' by Donald Wilson. Jon is having his portrait painted and Fleur is to sit for the same artist. Soames visits Dorset to see the family roots. **Designer:** Spencer Chapman. **Director:** David Giles.

Fossett Saga, The   1 wk

LWT, situation comedy

This series by Dave Freeman starred Jimmy Edwards as James Fossett, an ambitious writer of penny-dreadfuls in late Victorian times. Sam Kydd played Herbert Quince, unpaid manservant to Fossett. June Whitfield played music hall singer Millie Goswick.

1969	6.0	Fri 10 Jan 8:30 p.m.	20	1 wk

Fossett dreams of riches as he plans the expansion of the Empire. **Producer:** David Askey.

Fosters, The   8 wks

LWT, situation comedy

This series concerned the life of a South London immigrant family. Norman Beaton played Samuel and Isabelle Lucas portrayed his wife Pearl. Their children Shirley, Sonny and Benjamin were played respectively by Sharon Rosita, Lenny Henry and Lawrie Mark.

1976	7.3	Fri 9 Apr 7:35 p.m.	9	8 wks

'Sex and the Black Community' by John Elmson and Norman Paul, adapted by Jon Watkins. Mum and Dad are unhappy with sixteen-year-old Shirley going out with a twenty-one-year-old boy. **Producer:** Stuart Allen.

Foundation, The   4 wks

ATV, drama

The story of Davinia Prince (Lynette Davies), the widow of a successful businessman, who brought up her two children Paul and Emma (Andrew Dove and Patsy Kensit) while working as an executive. Bernard Lee played her father-in-law Eddie Prince.

1977	11.4	Fri 19 Aug 9:00 p.m.	15	4 wks

'Love' Davinia mixes business and pleasure with Dutch tycoon Phillippe De Vries (Sandor Elès). **Director:** Robert Tronson. **Producer:** John Cooper.

Wilfred Pickles as Walter Bingley would do anything **For The Love Of Ada** (Irene Handl).

Four of Hearts   2 wks

AR, drama

A quartet of individual plays, each starring Patrick Wymark, with no link other than his involvement with women.

| 1965 | 5.9 | Mon 27 Sep 9:45 p.m. | 19 | 2 wks |

'Tilt' by Michael Watts.
Ernie sees bright romantic prospects when a pretty young blonde walks into his pin-table saloon.
Designer: Fred Pusey. **Director:** Cyril Coke. **Executive Producer:** Antony Kearey.

Four Musketeers, The   1 wk

Presented by ITV, film

| 1980 | 14.2 | Wed 26 Mar 8:00 p.m. | 15 | 1 wk |

The Musketeers are among the troops of Louis XIII fighting the rebels of La Rochelle. Oliver Reed is Athos, Frank Finlay is Porthos, Richard Chamberlain is Aramis and Michael York is D'Artagnon. Also starring Geraldine Chaplin, Faye Dunaway, Charlton Heston, Roy Kinnear, Christopher Lee, Simon Ward and Raquel Welch.
Director: Richard Lester.

Four Seasons of Rosie Carr, The   1 wk

BBC, drama

This cycle of four plays by Ted Willis told the story of a woman at four different stages of her life. June Barry played the title role in the first episode with Jane Hylton in the subsequent three.

| 1964 | 7.4 | Sat 4 Jul 9:45 p.m. | 5 | 1 wk |

'Spring at the Winged Horse'
It is the spring of 1907. Rosie works fourteen hours a day as a barmaid and general skivvy at the Winged Horse. She accepts her life and poverty as the natural order of things, as does her friend Frank the pot boy (James Bolam). Then she meets Tommo (Kenneth J. Warren), a young man who fills her with ideas of green and pleasant lands and fires her dreams to find her own identity and dignity.
Director: Peter Graham Scott. **Producer:** James MacTaggart.

14–18   1 wk

Granada, documentary

| 1963 | 5.8 | Wed 4 Dec 9:40 p.m. | 16 | 1 wk |

This film of the 1914–18 war recreates an appalling chapter in the history of armed conflict. Written by Cecil Saint Laurent, translated by Emile de Harven and adapted for television by Patricia Lagone.
Producer: Jean Aurel.

Foxy Lady   8 wks

Granada, drama

This series by Geoffrey Lancashire starred Diane Keen as Daisy Jackson, the editor of weekly northern newspaper the Ramsden Reminder. The all-male reporting team included Geoffrey Burridge, Alan David, Milton Johns and Patrick Troughton.
Producer: John G. Temple.

| 1982 | 12.4 | Mon 1 Nov 8:00 p.m. | 6 | 2 wks |

Daisy has a bright idea to boost circulation while accountant Joe Prince (Geoffrey Burridge) clamps down on expenses.
Director: Richard Holthouse.

| 1984 | 12.8 | Wed 1 Feb 8:30 p.m. | 11 | 6 wks |

Sports editor Ben Marsh (Milton Johns) has got himself into serious gambling debt and advertises his beloved car for sale.
Director: Malcolm Taylor.

Francis Albert Sinatra   1 wk

USA presented by BBC, music

| 1969 | 5.5 | Thu 8 May 9:05 p.m. | 19 | 1 wk |

This is a one-off special starring Frank Sinatra. (The show was actually the recording of a dress rehearsal that Sinatra liked so much he decided not to proceed with the final performance.)
Guests: Diahann Carroll and the Fifth Dimension.
Director: Clark Jones. **Producers:** Ernest Chambers and Saul Ilson.

Francis Durbridge Presents   8 wks

BBC, drama

The thriller writer introduced his own stories in serial form.

| 1968 | 8.2 | Tue 13 Feb 7:05 p.m. | 2 | 7 wks |

'Bat Out of Hell'
Geoffrey Stewart (Noel Johnson) and his wife Diana (Sylvia Sims) are off on a month's holiday. But Geoffrey is destined not to see the Mediterranean, and Diana embarks on a journey into terror. John Thaw plays Diana's lover Mark and Dudley Foster is Inspector Clay. Serialized in five parts.
Designer: Roy Oxley. **Producer:** Alan Bromley. (First shown on BBC2).

| 1980 | 14.2 | Fri 18 Jan 8:30 p.m. | 20 | 1 wk |

'Breakaway'
Part two of a six-part serial starring Martin Jarvis as Sam Harvey in an extraordinary case involving Scotland Yard.
Designer: Don Giles. **Director:** Paul Ciappessoni. **Producer:** Ken Riddington.

Frank Ifield Show, The   8 wks

ATV, entertainment

The Australian singer settled in England after hitting number one in the charts in 1962 with 'I Remember You'.

1963	5.6	Sun 1 Sep 8:25 p.m.	10	1 wk

Live from the Prince of Wales Theatre, London, with guest star Bob Monkhouse, the Pamela Devis dancers and the Jack Parnell orchestra.
Producer: Albert Locke.

1964	7.6	Wed 26 Feb 9:45 p.m.	5	1 wk

With Des O'Connor, the Pamela Devis dancers and the Jack Parnell orchestra.
Producer: Francis Essex.

1965	7.5	Wed 21 Mar 9:40 p.m.	7	3 wks

With the Countrymen, Vivienne Martin, the Mike Sammes singers, the Pamela Devis dancers and the Jack Parnell orchestra.
Producer: Colin Clews.

1967	7.2	Fri 13 Jan 8:25 p.m.	7	3 wks

With Ted Rogers, the Malcolm Clare dancers and the Peter Knight orchestra.
Producer: Colin Clews.

Frank Ifield Sings   3 wks

ATV, music

1965	7.5	Wed 20 Oct 9:10 p.m.	7	3 wks

One of a new series with old friends the Mike Sammes singers, the Pamela Devis dancers and the Jack Parnell orchestra.
Producer: Jon Scoffield.

Frankie and Bruce   1 wk

Thames, entertainment

1975	6.1	Wed 3 Sep 9:00 p.m.	14	1 wk

Eight years since their last TV special together Frankie Howerd and Bruce Forsyth join forces with assistance from Suzanne Danielle, Marie Gordon-Price and Jenny Lee-Wright.
Writers: Barry Cryer, Sid Green and Dick Hills. **Producer:** David Bell.
Executive Producer: Philip Jones.

Frankie and Bruce Christmas Show, The   2 wks

ABC, entertainment

Frankie Howerd and Bruce Forsyth spent the holiday with friends.
Executive Producer: Philip Jones.

1966	7.0	Sat 24 Dec 9:40 p.m.	6	1 wk

Guests: Cilla Black, Tommy Cooper, Tom Jones, the Kaye Sisters, Aleta Morrison, and the Malcolm Goddard dancers with the ABC Showband.
Writers: Sid Green and Dick Hills. **Producer:** Peter Dulay.

1967	6.5	Sat 23 Dec 9:35 p.m.	8	1 wk

Ninety-minute special with guests Lionel Blair, Tommy Cooper, Anita Harris, Aleta Morrison, the Rockin' Berries, Corin Redgrave and Frankie Vaughan with the Ted Brennan orchestra.
Producer: Peter Frazer-Jones. **Executive Producer:** Philip Jones.

Frankie Howerd   2 wks

BBC, comedy

Comedian Frankie Howerd came to prominence in the late 1940s and was chosen for the Royal Variety Performance of 1950. Although his career had several ups and downs, he was one of the best-loved figures of British show business right up to his death in May 1992. In this series writers Ray Galton and Alan Simpson placed Frankie in unlikely situations.
Producer: Duncan Wood.

1964	4.6	Thu 24 Dec 8:25 p.m.	19	1 wk

With Colin Gordon, Stella Kemball, Len Lowe and Don Smoothey.

1966	5.6	Tue 22 Feb 7:30 p.m.	20	1 wk

With Arthur Mullard, Julian Orchard and Dennis Ramsden.

Frankie Howerd reached Number One in the special subtitled 'The Laughing Stock of Television'. (Overleaf)

Frankie Howerd   1 wk

Thames, comedy

| 1971 | 8.6 | Wed 14 Apr 8:00 p.m. | 1 | 1 wk |

'The Laughing Stock of Television'
A one-off special with guests Arthur English, Pearl Hackney, Hattie Jacques and Carmel McSharry. Written by Barry Took and Marty Feldman, Ray Galton and Alan Simpson, and Talbot Rothwell. **Producer:** John Robins.

Frankie Howerd Hour, The   1 wk

Thames, comedy

| 1971 | 7.2 | Wed 1 Sep 8:00 p.m. | 2 | 1 wk |

A one-hour special with guests Angela Baddeley, Allan Cuthbertson and Jean Kent.
Writers: Ray Galton and Alan Simpson. **Producer:** Peter Frazer-Jones.

Frankie Howerd Meets the Bee Gees   1 wk

Thames, entertainment

| 1968 | 5.0 | Tue 20 Aug 8:55 p.m. | 5 | 1 wk |

Frankie Howerd joins in the music and Barry, Maurice and Robin Gibb try their hands at comedy in this special written by Ray Galton and Alan Simpson.
Producer: Peter Frazer-Jones.

Frankie Howerd Reveals All   1 wk

YTV, comedy

| 1980 | 14.9 | Wed 10 Dec 8:00 p.m. | 11 | 1 wk |

In this special, Howerd explores the class structure of Britain with a little help from Kenneth Connor, Linda Cunningham, Chris Emmett, Henry McGee, Brian Osborne and Sheila Steafel. With special guests the Barron Knights.
Producer: Alan Tarrant.

Frankie Howerd Show, The   8 wks

Thames, entertainment

A series of variety shows with sketches and music.

| 1968 | 7.2 | Wed 25 Sep 9:10 p.m. | 2 | 1 wk |

Guests: Cilla Black, Joe Brown, Diane Cilento, Eric Delaney, Lew Hoad, Bobby Moore, the New Faces and the Ronnie Aldrich orchestra.
Writers: Sid Green and Dick Hills. **Producer:** Peter Frazer-Jones.

| 1971 | 7.0 | Wed 29 Sep 8:00 p.m. | 4 | 1 wk |

Guests: Allan Cuthbertson, Sheila Hancock and boxer Billy Walker.
Writers: Ray Galton and Alan Simpson. **Producer:** Peter Frazer-Jones.

Frankie Howerd Show, The   6 wks

ATV, entertainment

A show with the same format as for Thames.

| | 5.2 | | 16 | |

Guests: Patrick Cargill, Janie Marden and Pan's People, with the Jack Parnell orchestra.
Writers: Sid Green and Dick Hills. **Director:** Milo Lewis. **Producer:** Sid Green.

Frankie Howerd's Titter Time   1 wk

Thames, comedy

A one-off special.

| 1976 | 6.7 | Wed 29 Dec 8:00 p.m. | 11 | 1 wk |

Guests: Hughie Greene and Caterina Valente, with the Ronnie Aldrich orchestra.
Writers: Barry Cryer, Ray Galton and Alan Simpson. **Producer:** Peter Frazer-Jones.

Frankie Vaughan Show, The   2 wks

ATV, entertainment

Frankie Vaughan began making records in 1954 and had a string of hits until 1968. He starred with Marilyn Monroe in the film LET'S MAKE LOVE. He has enjoyed stardom for almost 40 years.

| 1965 | 5.0 | Sat 4 Sep 8:15 p.m. | 16 | 2 wks |

Guests: Clive Dunn, Arthur Haynes and Dermot Kelly.
Musical Director: Ivor Raymonde. **Producer:** Colin Clews.

Fraud Squad   21 wks

ATV, drama

A series of stories involving Scotland Yard's Fraud Squad, starring Patrick O'Connell as Detective Inspector Gamble, Joanna Van Gyseghem as Detective Sergeant Vicky Hicks and Ralph Nossek as Superintendent Proud.

| 1969 | 7.6 | Tue 3 Jun 9:00 p.m. | 1 | 13 wks |

'Last Exit to Liechtenstein' by Robert Holmes.
Rex Lucien (Michael Gambon) is on bail charged with fraud. For reasons best known to himself he decides to go to the police ball.
Designer: Anthony Waller. **Director:** Paul Annith. **Producers:** Robert D. Cardona, Nicholas Palmer.

| 1970 | 6.7 | Sat 7 Nov 9:00 p.m. | 9 | 8 wks |

'Remission – Negative' by Richard Harris.
Gamble receives a complaint from a man whose wife has died following admission to a clinic specializing in nervous diseases. He decides to investigate.
Designer: Anthony Waller. **Director:** John Sichel. **Producer:** Nicholas Palmer.

Freddie Starr Experience, The · 1 wk

LWT, comedy

This outrageous Liverpool comedian, singer and impressionist achieved overnight recognition in the 1970 ROYAL VARIETY PERFORMANCE.

| 1978 | 16.2 | Sun 10 Sep 8:15 p.m. | 3 | 1 wk |

One-hour special with Nicholas Ball, Lewis Collins, Dickie Davies, Lyn Paul, Martin Shaw, Stanley Unwin, Frank Windsor, the Brian Rogers dancers and the Arthur Greenslade orchestra.
Producers: David Macmahon and Maurice Murphy.

Freddie Starr Showcase, The · 1 wk

BBC, entertainment

Freddie Starr hosted a series of talent shows from the Harrogate Centre.

| 1983 | 7.0 | Tue 23 Aug 8:10 p.m. | 20 | 1 wk |

Producer: Alan Walsh.

Freewheelers · 4 wks

Southern, drama

A children's adventure series in six parts. The O'Toole company of young cyclists go on an adventure-packed tour to Spartika with a mysterious load of gas cylinders packed in their luggage. Ronald Leigh-Hunt starred as Colonel Buchan and Valentine Dyall was O'Toole.

| 1970 | 4.5 | Wed 27 May 5:15 p.m. | 15 | 4 wks |

'Merely Players' by Rick Trader Witcombe.
Telephones with gas cylinders hidden inside them are being planted in strategic positions all over Spartika.
Producer: Christopher McMaster.

French Connection, The · 1 wk

Presented by ITV, film

| 1986 | 13.1 | Wed 5 Mar 9:15 p.m. | 9 | 1 wk |

Following the shooting of a French detective, police on both sides of the Atlantic hunt for the French liaison point for a consignment of drugs destined to enter the USA. Gene Hackman, Fernando Rey and Roy Scheider star.
Director: William Friedkin.

French Fields · 7 wks

Thames, situation comedy

John Chapman and Ian Davidson created this sequel to FRESH FIELDS. Hester and William Fields (Julia McKenzie and Anton Rodgers) moved to live in France after he was headhunted for a job there.
Director: Mark Stuart. **Producer:** James Gilbert.

| 1989 | 11.6 | Tue 10 Oct 8:30 p.m. | 10 | 5 wks |

'Le Weekend'
A quiet weekend is disrupted when daughter Emma (Sally Baxter) comes to visit.

| 1990 | 10.3 | Mon 24 Sep 8:00 p.m. | 20 | 1 wk |

'Long Legged Beasties and Things That Go Bump in the Night'
A local farmer causes a sleepless night for the Fields.

| 1991 | 9.6 | Tue 3 Sep 8:30 p.m. | 17 | 1 wk |

'French with Tears'
In spite of her improving Franglais, Hester has trouble understanding French financial affairs.

French Revolution, The · 1 wk

USA presented by AR, documentary

| 1965 | 5.0 | Wed 14 Jul 9:40 p.m. | 19 | 1 wk |

An NBC News special filmed at the actual sites of the storming of the Bastille 176 years ago. Narrator: Michael Redgrave.
Director: George A. Vicas.

The mainstays of Scotland Yard's **Fraud Squad** were Joanna Van Gyseghem and Patrick O'Connell.

Fresh Fields — 21 wks

Thames, situation comedy

This series by John Chapman concerned middle-aged suburban couple Hester and William Fields (Julia McKenzie and Anton Rodgers). Their nosy neighbour Sonia was played by Ann Beach.
Producer: Peter Frazer-Jones.

1984	16.4	Wed 3 Oct 8:30 p.m.	2	11 wks

'Business Contacts'
William is finding it difficult to adjust to Hester acting as his secretary.

1985	17.5	Wed 9 Oct 8:00 p.m.	1	9 wks

'Alarums and Excursions'
Hester has her fortune read by Sonia, who forecasts travel and a secret admirer.

1986	12.0	Mon 8 Dec 8:00 p.m.	12	1 wk

'Business Contacts'
(Repeat.)

Friday Film, The — 1 wk

Presented by ITV, film

1968	5.4	Fri 16 Aug 7:00 p.m.	4	1 wk

'The Pleasure of his Company'
Fred Astaire, Tab Hunter, Lilli Palmer and Debbie Reynolds star in the story of an elderly playboy who, much to his former wife's displeasure, arrives in San Francisco for his daughter's wedding.
Director: George Seaton.

Friday Night Presents — 7 wks

Granada, drama

Another innovative series from the Granada drama department, this featured a resident company of actors as 'The Friday Night Company'. Among their number were Keith Barron, Angela Douglas, Helen Fraser, Alan Rothwell and Brian Wilde. The series consisted of eight original plays about life in the North of England, contemporary in theme and language.
Writers included Jack Rosenthal, Peter Eckersley and Dennis Woolf.
Series Producer: Richard Everitt.

1963	6.8	Fri 29 Nov 9:10 p.m.	11	7 wks

'The Last Big Deal of Dekker Arkwright' by Jim Andrew.
Dekker Arkwright (Keith Barron) is a fast-talking car salesman with an eye for a deal every day of the week. But when there is most at stake, he learns his true values.
Director: Graeme McDonald.

From Here to Eternity — 1 wk

USA presented by ITV, drama

This series picked up where the 1979 BEST SELLERS left off and was concerned with the lives and loves of those caught up in the aftermath of the Japanese attack on Pearl Harbor. Barbara Hershey replaced Natalie Wood. Kim Basinger, William Devane, Don Johnson and Roy Thinnes also starred.

1980	11.2	Sat 21 Jun 8:30 p.m.	8	1 wk

'Re-enlistment Blues'
When Jeff Prewitt (Don Johnson) vows to blow up the military post following the death of his brother, Sgt. Warden (William Devane) issues orders for his arrest. Karen Holmes (Barbara Hershey) tells her husband (Roy Thinnes) she intends to file for divorce.

From Russia with Love — 6 wks

Presented by ITV, film

1976	9.2	Sun 2 May 7:55 p.m.	1	2 wks

Sean Connery stars as James Bond in Ian Fleming's story of Tatiana Romanova (Daniela Bianchi), a clerk in the Russian Embassy in Istanbul who wants to defect with a valuable cipher machine. Also starring Lotte Lenya as Rosa Klebb and Robert Shaw as Red Grant, with Pedro Armendaviz, Eunice Gayson, Bernard Lee and Lois Maxwell.
Director: Terence Young.

1982	14.0	Sun 31 Oct 7:15 p.m.	3	1 wk
1985	17.3	Sun 8 Dec 7:45 p.m.	2	1 wk
1987	10.2	Mon 20 Apr 8:00 p.m.	11	1 wk
1991	12.6	Sat 16 Feb 7:40 p.m.	14	1 wk

Repeat showings of the above film.

Front Page Story — 20 wks

ATV, drama

Innovative drama series about the Daily Globe, a national newspaper based in Shoe Lane, off Fleet Street. Most of the action was shot on location away from the office. The principal players were Roddy McMillan as news editor Alec Ritchie and John Bennett as editor Ray Boscombe. The reporters were played by Derek Godfrey, Patrick Mower, Derek Newark and Harry Towb.

1965	7.2	Tue 9 Feb 9:10 p.m.	6	20 wks

'The Public Interest' by Alan Plater.
Paddy Lucas (Harry Towb) and John Brownhill (Patrick Mower) are given a tough assignment to make a news hero out of 'the little man against the world'. They both pay an odd price for their enterprise.
Editor: Wilfred Greatorex. **Director:** Peter Collinson. **Producer:** Rex Firkin.

Frontier — 4 wks

Thames, drama

This series set in India in the 1880s starred Gary Bond as Lieutenant Russell, Paul Eddington as Lovelace, Fulton Mackay as the adjutant, John Phillips as Lieutenant-Colonel Whitley, Patrick O'Connell as Colour Sergeant O'Brien and James Maxwell as Captain Stoughton.

| 1968 | 4.8 | Wed 11 Sep 9:00 p.m. | 14 | 4 wks |

'Duel of Honour' by Stanley Miller.
The question of honour is raised in gaslit London, five thousand miles away from India, but its effect is felt none the less.
Designer: Patrick Downing. **Director:** Patrick Dromgoole. **Executive Producer:** Lloyd Shirley.

Frost on Sunday — 19 wks

LWT, entertainment

To make this programme David Frost had to cross the Atlantic twice a week, arriving back in London each Friday morning to rehearse with the show's regular team of Ronnie Barker, Ronnie Corbett and Josephine Tewson.

| 1968 | 8.5 | Sun 17 Nov 9:10 p.m. | 2 | 9 wks |

Guests: Stanley Baxter, Ian Carmichael, and Marion Ryan.
Producer: David Askey.

| 1969 | 6.7 | Sun 5 Jan 9:10 p.m. | 11 | 1 wk |

Guests: Billy Eckstine, Nina and Frederik and Topol.
Producer: Philip Casson.

| 1970 | 7.2 | Sun 8 Mar 10:25 p.m. | 10 | 9 wks |

The show usually comes from the studios at Wembley, but this special edition highlights the presentation of the annual British Film and Television Awards from the London Palladium.
Producer: Philip Casson.

Frost Programme, The — 1 wk

AR, documentary

David Frost conducted in-depth interviews. The series included his famous 'trial by television' of fraudster Emil Savundra.

| 1968 | 6.1 | Wed 17 Jan 10:30 p.m. | 17 | 1 wk |

Director: William G. Stewart. **Producer:** Geoffrey Hughes.

Frost Report, The — 21 wks

BBC, comedy

Although David Frost is looked upon today as a serious interviewer, this series featured Frost the satirist. With Ronnie Barker and Ronnie Corbett, John Cleese, Julie Felix, Nicky Henson, Tom Lehrer and Sheila Steafel. Each programme explored a theme through music and sketches.

| 1966 | 6.4 | Thu 14 Apr 9:00 p.m. | 6 | 9 wks |

'The News'
Producer: Duncan Wood.

| 1967 | 6.7 | Thu 4 May 9:05 p.m. | 3 | 12 wks |

'Parliament'
Producer: James Gilbert.

Fugitive, The — 4 wks

USA presented by ITV, drama

This series ran to 120 episodes. Dr Richard Kimble (David Janssen) was on the run from Lieutenant Gerard (Barry Morse), who suspected him of murdering Mrs Kimble. The doctor, innocent, evaded Gerard and pursued the real killer, a one-armed man (Bill Raisch).
Producer: Quinn Martin.

| 1967 | 7.9 | Wed 30 Aug 8:00 p.m. | 1 | 4 wks |

The final episode – Will Gerard finally believe Kimble is innocent?
Director: Don Medford.

Full House — 16 wks

Thames, situation comedy

In this series by Johnnie Mortimer two couples shared a house to ease the mortgage commitments. They were Paul and Marsha Hatfield (Christopher Strauli and Sabina Franklyn) and Murray and Diana McCoy (Brian Capron and Natalie Forbes).

| 1985 | 16.0 | Wed 16 Oct 8:00 p.m. | 3 | 12 wks |

'Baby Talk'
Paul and Marsha contemplate starting a family.
Producer: Peter Frazer-Jones.

| 1986 | 12.4 | Wed 19 Nov 8:30 p.m. | 11 | 4 wks |

'And Baby Makes Five'
With Diana about to give birth, Paul and Marsha try to sell their half of the house.
Producer: Anthony Parker.

Anton Rodgers and Julia McKenzie were happily married in **Fresh Fields**.

Fun and Fancy Free

1 wk

BBC, entertainment

| 1961 | 3.8 | Fri 11 Aug 8:00 p.m. | 17 | 1 wk |

A special performance of the summer revue from the Queen's Theatre, Blackpool starring Al Read with Don Arrol, Allan Bruce, the Two Earls and Yana, with the Ross Taylor dancers, George Mitchell singers and Jack Martin's orchestra.
Television presentation: Barney Colehan.

Fun and Games

4 wks

YTV, game show

Puzzles and brain teasers were solved by mathematics in this series.
Director: Nick Abson. **Producer:** Adam Hart Davis.

| 1987 | 9.6 | Wed 22 Jul 7:00 p.m. | 15 | 2 wks |

Presented by Johnny Ball with Professor of Mathematics Celia Hoyles.
Executive Producer: Duncan Dallas.

| 1988 | 9.0 | Wed 10 Aug 7:00 p.m. | 18 | 2 wks |

Presented by Dr Robert Buckman with Celia Hoyles.
Executive Producer: Simon Welfare.

Fun with Dick and Jane

1 wk

Presented by ITV, film

| 1982 | 11.2 | Thu 23 Sep 7:40 p.m. | 8 | 1 wk |

George Segal and Jane Fonda star as Dick and Jane Harper. When he loses his job she tries for work, but they spiral down the slippery slope to poverty and turn to a life of crime.
Director: Ted Kotcheff.

Funeral of President Kennedy, The

1 wk

BBC/ITV, news

| 1963 | 7.8 | Mon 25 Nov 4:30 p.m. | 5 | 1 wk |

Live coverage via the Telstar Satellite of the funeral in St Matthew's Cathedral, Washington of President John Fitzgerald Kennedy, who was assassinated in Dallas, Texas on Friday 22 November.

Funny Girl Happened to Me on the Way to the Piano

1 wk

AR, music

| 1966 | 6.3 | Wed 13 Apr 9:40 p.m. | 14 | 1 wk |

The Broadway musical FUNNY GIRL opens in London tonight. Bob Monkhouse introduces a tribute to its composer, Jule Styne, starring Millicent Martin and Matt Monro with Brian Davies, Janie Marden, Patsy Ann Noble and Peter Reeves.
Director: Bill Turner. **Executive Producer:** Buddy Bregman.

Funny Side, The

4 wks

Thames, comedy

This series starred Debbie Arnold, Tony Barton, Cherry Gillespie, Derek Griffiths, Aiden J. Harvey and Derek Waring in songs and sketches.

| 1985 | 11.5 | Wed 31 Jul 8:30 p.m. | 7 | 4 wks |

Writer: Eddie Braben. **Choreographer:** Chris Power. **Producer:** Mark Stuart.

Funny Side, The

1 wk

Granada, entertainment

This comedy and music magazine series was presented by Mike Smith with Cheryl Baker and Mick Miller.

| 1988 | 9.4 | Sat 30 Apr 6:15 p.m. | 19 | 1 wk |

Director: Steve Smith. **Producer:** John Longley. **Executive Producer:** David Liddiment.

Futtock's End

1 wk

Presented by BBC, film

| 1979 | 16.3 | Sat 17 Nov 8:00 p.m. | 8 | 1 wk |

Ronnie Barker wrote and starred in various adventures occurring over a weekend in a large country house. With Michael Hordern, Roger Livesey, Julian Orchard and Richard O'Sullivan.
Director: Bob Kellett.

Futureworld

1 wk

Presented by ITV, film

| 1984 | 9.3 | Thu 19 Apr 7:30 p.m. | 20 | 1 wk |

In this sequel to WESTWORLD the robot factory now aims at world domination by reproducing influential people. Starring Yul Brynner and Peter Fonda.
Director: Richard J. Heffron.

G

Gaffer, The — 20 wks

YTV, situation comedy

This series by Graham White starred Bill Maynard as Fred Moffat, proprietor of a small works which was always one step from disaster.
Producer: Alan Tarrant.

| 1981 | 17.0 | Fri 20 Feb 8:30 p.m. | 5 | 6 wks |

'England Exports'
Fred's scheme to boost exports and secure himself a holiday in the South of France lands him in trouble with his staff, the bank and his client.

| 1982 | 15.5 | Fri 26 Feb 8:30 p.m. | 4 | 7 wks |

'Flesh and Blood'
Fred's ever-loathing son Spencer (Chris Langham) hounds him for a job after being kicked out of university.

| 1983 | 10.5 | Tue 7 Jun 8:30 p.m. | 5 | 7 wks |

'Moonlight and Ruses'
In order to secure an order from a new buyer, Fred pretends to be captain of his local golf club.

Gala Opportunity Knocks — 1 wk

ABC, entertainment

| 1967 | 6.5 | Sat 23 Dec 6:35 p.m. | 7 | 1 wk |

Hughie Green presents a selection of the more successful acts from the series over the last four years including Les Dawson, the Doncaster Wheatsheaf Girls Choir, Yvonne Marsh and Ken Wood.
Director: Royston Mayoh. **Producer:** Milo Lewis.

Gala Performance — 1 wk

Granada, entertainment

| 1971 | 6.4 | Sun 27 Jun 7:55 p.m. | 4 | 1 wk |

This event is held at the Empire Theatre, Liverpool to celebrate the opening of the new Mersey Tunnel. Among those appearing in the presence of Her Majesty Queen Elizabeth II are Ken Dodd, Bill Kenwright, Gerry Marsden, Roger McGough, Patricia Routledge, the Scaffold, the Spinners, Jimmy Tarbuck and Frankie Vaughan.
Stage Producer: William Chappell. **Television presentation:** Eric Harrison. **Television Producer:** John Hamp.

Galton and Simpson Comedy, The — 1 wk

LWT, comedy

This series of single light comedies was written by Ray Galton and Alan Simpson, who first found fame as radio writers for Tony Hancock before creating STEPTOE AND SON for television.

| 1969 | 5.0 | Fri 23 May 9:30 p.m. | 20 | 1 wk |

'An Extra Bunch of Daffodils'
Stratford Johns stars as Lawrence Warner, a man looking around for a new wife having buried his well-insured previous five!
Producer: David Askey.

Galton and Simpson Playhouse, The — 10 wks

YTV, comedy

This series of single comedy plays was written by Galton and Simpson.

| 1977 | 7.8 | Thu 19 Feb 9:00 p.m. | 8 | 7 wks |

'Car Along the Pass'
Arthur Lowe stars as a determined British holiday maker on a camping trip to the Alps. He maintains a stiff upper lip in spite of frostbite and an avalanche.
Producer: Vernon Lawrence. **Executive Producer:** Duncan Wood.

| 1978 | 13.3 | Tue 16 May 8:00 p.m. | 5 | 3 wks |

'I Tell You It's Burt Reynolds'
Leonard Rossiter stars as a know-it-all film fan. With Roy Barraclough, Ed Devereaux, Patricia Hayes and Gillian Raine.
Producer: Ronnie Baxter. **Executive Producer:** Duncan Wood.

Gambling City, The — 1 wk

AR, documentary

1967	6.6	Wed 22 Feb 9:45 p.m.	12	1 wk

Robert Kee presents a portrait of Las Vegas in words and images.
Producer: Charlie Squires.

Game for a Laugh — 43 wks

LWT, game show

Contestants performed stunts that invited varying degrees of ridicule. The programme was hosted until 1984 by Jeremy Beadle, Henry Kelly, Matthew Kelly and Sarah Kennedy. In 1985 Beadle was joined by Martin Daniels and Rustie Lee.
Directors: included Phil Bishop and John Longley (1981–83). **Executive Producer:** Alan Boyd.

1981	15.2	Sat 14 Nov 6:10 p.m.	6	10 wks
1982	16.6	Sat 9 Jan 5:45 p.m.	4	15 wks
1983	12.5	Sat 15 Oct 6:30 p.m.	8	11 wks

Directors: John Gorman and Tom Poole. **Producers:** Keith Stewart and Brian Wesley.

1985	17.4	Sun 20 Jan 7:15 p.m.	3	7 wks

Director: Terry Kinane. **Producers:** Phil Bishop and Bob Merrilees.

Gang Show, The — 5 wks

ATV, entertainment

Ralph Reader devised, wrote, produced and presented Boy Scout Gang Shows with scouts from all over the world. He composed their anthem 'Riding Along On The Crest Of A Wave' and was awarded the MBE in 1942 and the CBE in 1957. Reader died on 13 May 1982.

1962	5.5	Wed 19 Dec 9:45 p.m.	14	1 wk

Television presentation: Albert Locke.

1964	7.1	Wed 15 Jan 9:40 p.m.	7	2 wks

Television presentation: Colin Clews.

1965	6.2	Wed 1 Dec 9:40 p.m.	17	1 wk

Television presentation: Albert Locke.

1966	5.6	Wed 14 Dec 9:40 p.m.	18	1 wk

Television presentation: Dicky Leeman.

Gary Cooper Season, A — 3 wks

Presented by BBC, film

1971	5.9	Tue 25 May 7:25 p.m.	15	3 wks

'Garden of Evil'
Gary Cooper plays a former sheriff who agrees to escort Leah (Susan Hayward) through Mexico's dangerous Indian territory where her husband is trapped down a mine.
Director: Henry Hathaway.

Gemini Man — 2 wks

USA presented by BBC, drama

This series starred Ben Murphy as special investigator Sam Casey, who was able to make himself invisible. It also starred Katherine Crawford as Dr Abigail Lawrence and William Sylvester as Leonard Driscoll.
Producer: Leslie Stevens.

1976	6.6	Tue 19 Oct 7:10 p.m.	17	2 wks

'Smithereens'
Casey poses as a truck driver to ensure that a load of new fuel is safely conveyed. However, he is unaware that it has been replaced by a highly dangerous chemical.

General Hospital — 48 wks

ATV, soap

What had failed to chart as a twice-weekly serial in the late afternoon was elevated in 1975 to a Friday evening slot of hour-long episodes.
Series Producer: Royston Morley.

1975	6.5	Fri 12 Sep 6:35 p.m.	9	10 wks

'The Celebration'
An accident-prone doctor, a disastrous engagement party and unexpected guests. Starring David Garth as Dr Armstrong and Carl Rigg as Dr Knight. Also starring Peter Birrel, Nigel Havers, Eleanor Summerfield and Jack Watling.
Writer: Peter Yeldham. **Director:** David Foster.

1976	6.9	Fri 15 Oct 7:30 p.m.	9	16 wks

'Another Time, Another Place'
Consultant Surgeon Guy Waldman (Tom Adams) meets someone from his past.
Writer: Brian Finch. **Director:** David Foster.

1977	15.1	Fri 2 Dec 8:00 p.m.	2	14 wks

'Pound of Flesh'
Midland General Hospital consultant Neville Bywaters (Tony Adams) must decide whether the pains of a mentally disturbed girl are real or imagined.
Writer: Brian Finch. **Director:** Royston Morley.

| 1978 | 16.9 | Fri 10 Feb 8:00 p.m. | 12 | 6 wks |

'Blood and Water'
Sister Holland (Pippa Rowe) faces a decision made difficult by her son's re-appearance.
Writer: Brian Finch. **Director:** Pembroke Duttson.

| 1979 | 14.5 | Fri 5 Jan 8:00 p.m. | 19 | 2 wks |

'The Buck Stops Where?'
A student nurse upsets some of the senior nursing staff.
Writer: Allan Prior. **Director:** Alan Tarrant.

Generation Game, The   160 wks

BBC, game show

The pairs of contestants had to be related and of a different generation. They were required to acquire instant skills from experts and participate in a farcical sketch. This was a vehicle for Bruce Forsyth, whose name formed part of the title for several series – BRUCE FORSYTH'S GENERATION GAME. Anthea Redfern appeared with him between 1972 and 1977. From 1978 to 1981 the programme was hosted by Larry Grayson and was subsequently called LARRY GRAYSON'S GENERATION GAME. His associate was Isla St Clair. Bruce Forsyth returned with Rosemarie Ford in 1990.
Directors included Alan Tarrant (1971–72), Alan Boyd (1974–77).
Producers included James Moir (1971–75), Alan Boyd (1977–79), Marcus Plantin (1980–81) and David Taylor (1990–91).

1971	6.8	Sat 18 Dec 5:45 p.m.	11	7 wks
1972	7.3	Sat 2 Dec 5:55 p.m.	5	11 wks
1973	7.6	Sat 1 Dec 6:25 p.m.	1	18 wks

Director: Terry Henebery.

1974	8.4	Sat 21 Dec 6:15 p.m.	1	20 wks
1975	9.0	Sat 22 Nov 6:10 p.m.	1	2 wks
1976	9.7	Sat 11 Dec 6:50 p.m.	1	18 wks

Producer: Robin Nash.

| 1977 | 20.1 | Sat 10 Dec 6:30 p.m. | 1 | 16 wks |
| 1978 | 17.6 | Sat 11 Nov 6:45 p.m. | 2 | 15 wks |

Director: Marcus Plantin.

| 1979 | 23.9 | Sat 20 Oct 6:40 p.m. | 1 | 17 wks |

Director: K. Paul Jackson.

| 1980 | 18.3 | Sat 22 Nov 6:20 p.m. | 1 | 17 wks |

Director: Keith Stewart.

| 1981 | 13.1 | Sat 1 Oct 6:15 p.m. | 7 | 5 wks |

Director: Marcus Plantin.

| 1990 | 12.5 | Fri 30 Nov 8:00 p.m. | 11 | 12 wks |

Director: Sylvie Boden.

| 1991 | 12.5 | Wed 25 Dec 4:40 p.m. | 19 | 2 wks |

Director: Jòhn Gorman.

Gentle Touch, The   48 wks

LWT, drama

This series created by Brian Finch starred Jill Gascoine as Detective Inspector Maggie Forbes, the widowed mother of a teenager.
Directors included Nic Phillips (1981–83). **Producer** (1981–85): Michael Verney-Elliott. **Executive Producer** (1981–83): Tony Wharmby.

| 1980 | 13.5 | Fri 2 May 9:00 p.m. | 7 | 11 wks |

'Shock' by Brian Finch.
Maggie is assigned to investigate the death of a woman discovered in her 'love nest'.
Producer: Tony Wharmby.

| 1981 | 13.8 | Fri 20 Nov 9:00 p.m. | 13 | 5 wks |

'The Hit' by Terence Feely.
Detective Inspector Forbes has a marksman with a high-powered rifle loose on her patch.

| 1982 | 18.1 | Fri 8 Jan 9:00 p.m. | 4 | 13 wks |

'Black Fox, White Fox' by Jeremy Burnham.
A famous television actress receives death threats.

| 1983 | 13.6 | Fri 14 Jan 9:00 p.m. | 6 | 3 wks |

'Pressures' by Kenneth Ware.
Maggie suffers severe stress when faced with a bloody multiple murder.

| 1984 | 14.1 | Sat 24 Nov 9:15 p.m. | 2 | 15 wks |

'Exit Laughing' by Neil Rudyard.
A minor civil servant is found dead in exotic circumstances. Maggie tries to protect his widow from publicity.
Director: Gerry Mill. **Executive Producer:** Nick Elliott.

| 1985 | 12.3 | Fri 29 Mar 9:00 p.m. | 15 | 1 wk |

'Exit Laughing'
(Repeat.)

George and Mildred — 54 wks

Thames, situation comedy

Johnnie Mortimer and Brian Cooke transported the Ropers (Brian Murphy and Yootha Joyce) from the basement flat of MAN ABOUT THE HOUSE to a modern housing estate for their own series. Mildred took to it like a duck to water but George, working class and proud of it, hated everything about it. His sparring partners in the class war were next-door neighbours Jeffrey and Ann Fourmille (Norman Eshley and Sheila Fearn). While Mildred socially climbed, George lay happily about.
Producer: Peter Frazer-Jones.

| 1976 | 9.4 | Mon 25 Oct 8:00 p.m. | 1 | 10 wks |

'Best Foot Forward'
Having discovered a pub which serves draft gin and tonic, George accuses Jeffrey of attempted murder.

| 1977 | 19.7 | Mon 5 Dec 8:00 p.m. | 1 | 6 wks |

'The Unkindest Cut of All'
George is instructed to be on his best behaviour when Mildred's sister comes for dinner.

| 1978 | 20.8 | Thu 21 Dec 8:00 p.m. | 2 | 27 wks |

'The Mating Game'
Mildred is keen for the dog to have puppies. George is not so keen until he learns there may be money in it.

| 1979 | 16.5 | Tue 13 Nov 8:30 p.m. | 6 | 7 wks |

'The Last Straw'
George thinks neighbours Jeffrey and Ann are toffee-nosed snobs. Mildred agrees, and they wonder whether they should move.

| 1980 | 17.5 | Mon 24 Mar 8:00 p.m. | 3 | 2 wks |

'I Believe in Yesterday'
One of Mildred's old American boyfriends turns up, much to George's disgust.

| 1981 | 13.7 | Tue 13 Jan 8:30 p.m. | 19 | 2 wks |

'You Must Have Showers'
Mildred wants to install a Hollywood-style shower.

George and the Dragon — 24 wks

ATV, situation comedy

This series by Harry Driver and Vince Powell starred Sid James as George Russell and Peggy Mount as Gabrielle Dragon. They were chauffeur and housekeeper respectively to Colonel Maynard (John Le Mesurier). Keith Marsh played the gardener Ralph.
Director: Shaun O'Riordan. **Producer** (1966–67): Alan Tarrant.

| 1966 | 6.4 | Sat 19 Nov 8:30 p.m. | 9 | 6 wks |

'First Day'
Following her visit to an unemployment agency Mrs Gabrielle Dragon arrives to take up her position as housekeeper to Colonel Maynard where she meets George for the first time. Gabrielle warns him to keep his distance since she knows what men are like. George is delighted to oblige.

| 1967 | 5.7 | Sat 3 Jun 8:30 p.m. | 7 | 7 wks |

'The 10.15 Train'
When British Rail cancels the 10.15 to London George and Gabrielle register their protest and all but bring the entire network to a standstill.

| 1968 | 7.4 | Sat 3 Feb 7:00 p.m. | 10 | 11 wks |

'April in Gatwick'
Gabrielle has won a weekend for two in Paris. She decides to take George with her, but the entente is less than cordiale.
Producer: Shaun O'Riordan.

Get Some In — 32 wks

Thames, situation comedy

This series by John Esmonde and Bob Larbey, set in 1955, was about a group of new recruits entering the RAF for their national service. David Janson starred as grammar-school educated Ken Richardson, Robert Lindsay as teddy boy Jakey Smith, Gerald Ryder as vicar's son Matthew Lilley, Brian Pettifer as wide boy Bruce Leckie and Tony Selby as the drill instructor, Corporal Marsh.
Producer: Michael Mills.

| 1975 | 7.4 | Thu 27 Nov 8:30 p.m. | 8 | 7 wks |

Ken, Jakey, Leckie and Lilley go absent without leave. Simon Callow appears in this episode as Wally.

| 1976 | 6.4 | Mon 12 Jul 8:00 p.m. | 3 | 7 wks |

Jakey gets a letter from his mum telling him his parents are about to kick Grandad out of their home. He takes matters into his own hands.

| 1977 | 8.5 | Thu 3 Feb 6:40 p.m. | 4 | 11 wks |

Corporal Marsh and his wife (Lori Wells) are discovering the joys of life in a caravan.

| 1978 | 15.7 | Thu 27 Apr 8:00 p.m. | 5 | 7 wks |

Ken, Jakey, Leckie and Lilley are back from their Malta posting. They join Corporal Marsh on the staff of RAF Hospital Druidswater. Things go missing from the mortuary.

Getaway with Cliff — 1 wk

BBC, music

| 1971 | 5.1 | Mon 30 Aug 7:15 p.m. | 18 | 1 wk |

Bank Holiday special filmed on location in England and France starring Cliff Richard with Marvin, Welch and Farrar, Olivia Newton-John and Severine, with the Norrie Paramor orchestra.
Producer: Michael Hurll.

Ghostbusters — 1 wk

Presented by ITV, film

| 1987 | 16.5 | Sat 26 Dec 7:30 p.m. | 9 | 1 wk |

Dan Aykroyd, Bill Murray and Sigourney Weaver star as a team of ghoul hunters who save New York City from an invasion of the supernatural.
Director: Ivan Reitman.

Ghost Squad — 6 wks

ATV, drama

This series was based on Detective Superintendent John Gosling's book. The real-life 'Ghost Squad' was set up to combat the wave of crime that followed the ending of the Second World War. Donald Wolfit starred as squad chief Sir Andrew Wilson and Michael Quinn played Nick Craig, a member of the Scotland Yard force.

| 1961 | 5.6 | Sat 21 Oct 8:30 p.m. | 12 | 6 wks |

'Still Waters' by Max Marquis.
Craig has to masquerade as a crooked Dutch diamond cutter in order to penetrate a jewel-smuggling gang.
Director: Robert Lynn. **Producer:** Connery Chappell.

Giant — 1 wk

Presented by ITV, film

| 1974 | 5.6 | Tue 1 Jan 7:30 p.m. | 16 | 1 wk |

The story of three people on a Texas cattle ranch: owner Bick Benedict (Rock Hudson), his wife Lesley (Elizabeth Taylor) and surly ranch hand Jeff Rink (James Dean), who worships Lesley and dreams of riches.
Director: George Stevens.

Girl from UNCLE — 1 wk

USA presented by BBC, drama

In this film series Stefanie Powers, as April Dancer, joined the organization dedicated to the fight against worldwide subversion and crime. Leo G. Carroll continued in the role of Mr Waverley first created in THE MAN FROM UNCLE and Noel Harrison played agent Mark Slate.

| 1967 | 5.5 | Thu 25 May 8:00 p.m. | 19 | 1 wk |

'The Catacomb and Dogma Affair'
UNCLE is called in following a series of violations in the Vatican.

Girls About Town — 18 wks

ATV, situation comedy

This series by Adele Rose, watched two housewives trying to overcome the seven-year itch. The series began in 1969 as a one-off comedy starring Anna Quayle as Rosemary and Barbara Mullaney as Sylvia. When it became a series in 1970 there was a complete change of cast. Julie Stevens played Rosemary Pilgrim with Robin Parkinson as her husband George. Denise Coffey played Brenda Liversedge with Peter Baldwin as her husband Harold.

| 1969 | 6.9 | Thu 2 Oct 9:00 p.m. | 5 | 1 wk |

Rosemary and Sylvia are bored with their lives as housewives and decide to become involved with the Elegant Escort agency.
Producer: Ronnie Baxter.

| 1970 | 7.0 | Mon 16 Mar 9:30 p.m. | 10 | 6 wks |

Brenda is upset that her husband has failed to notice something very important and is determined to make him wake up.
Producer: Shaun O'Riordan.

| 1971 | 6.6 | Tue 23 Nov 8:30 p.m. | 16 | 11 wks |

'Charity Ends at Home'
Every year George's mother (Dorothy Reynolds) invites Rosemary and George to her local Conservative Association charity dance. This year Brenda and Harold are going, too. Their problem is finding a prize to contribute to the tombola which will sufficiently impress George's mother without costing too much.
Director: John Scholz Conway. **Producer:** Shaun O'Riordan.

Girls Galore — 1 wk

BBC, entertainment

| 1972 | 6.8 | Fri 7 Apr 9:20 p.m. | 9 | 1 wk |

The search for Miss England, Miss Scotland and Miss Wales is introduced by David Vine and Terry Wogan.
Television presentation: Ian Smith.

George and Mildred was the most successful sit-com of 1976. Brian Murphy and Yootha Joyce starred as the title characters.

Girls in My Life, The
`2 wks`

AR, entertainment

| 1964 | 5.8 | Wed 18 Nov 8:00 p.m. | 14 | 2 wks |

Adam Faith looks back at the girls in his life through conversation and song.
Interviewer: Ronan O'Casey. **Director:** Robert Fleming.

Girls on Top
`5 wks`

Central, situation comedy

Four young women (Dawn French, Jennifer Saunders, Tracey Ullman and Ruby Wax) lodged upstairs in a house owned by Lady Carlton (Joan Greenwood).

| 1985 | 13.8 | Wed 23 Oct 8:30 p.m. | 8 | 5 wks |

'Four-Play'
The four girls get together for the first time.
Producer: Paul Jackson. **Executive Producer:** Allan McKeown.

Give Us a Clue
`108 wks`

Thames, game show

Lionel Blair and Una Stubbs captained opposing teams in this television version of charades. Hosts included Michael Aspel (1979–83) and Michael Parkinson (1984–85).
Producers included David Clark (1980, 1983–84) and Robert Reed (1981–82).

| 1979 | 16.5 | Mon 31 Dec 6:30 p.m. | 5 | 7 wks |

Guests: Davinia Bunyan, Graham Dene, Fenella Fielding, Roy Hudd, Paul Ponting and Libby Morris.
Director: Ian Bolt. **Producer:** Juliet Grimm.

| 1980 | 17.0 | Mon 17 Nov 7:00 p.m. | 4 | 21 wks |

Guests: Ray Alan, Billy Dainty, David Hamilton, Rachel Heyhoe-Flint, Julia McKenzie and Sheila White.

| 1981 | 14.3 | Thu 31 Dec 7:00 p.m. | 5 | 6 wks |

Guests: Patricia Brake, Lonnie Donegan, Gareth Hunt, Nanette Newman, Mollie Sugden and Kenneth Williams.

| 1982 | 14.2 | Tue 13 Apr 7:30 p.m. | 3 | 23 wks |

Guests: Liz Fraser, Denise Nolan, Victoria Wood, Richard O'Sullivan, Lance Percival and Wayne Sleep.

| 1983 | 14.3 | Tue 8 Nov 7:30 p.m. | 2 | 24 wks |

Guests: Rosalind Ayres, Tommy Boyd, Billy Dainty, Martin Jarvis, Isla St Clair and Paula Yates.

| 1984 | 16.1 | Tue 13 Nov 7:30 p.m. | 2 | 21 wks |

Guests: Jane Asher, Floella Benjamin, Les Dennis, Dustin Gee, Judy Loe and Jon Pertwee.

| 1985 | 13.1 | Tue 1 Jan 5:45 p.m. | 8 | 6 wks |

Guests: Bruce Forsyth, Julia McKenzie, Nicola Pagett, Wayne Sleep, Julie Walters and Bernie Winters.
Producer: Keith Beckett.

Glad Rag Ball
`2 wks`

AR (1964) and ATV (1965), music

| 1964 | 7.4 | Wed 25 Nov 9:40 p.m. | 6 | 1 wk |

A charity fancy dress ball from the Empire Pool, Wembley, introduced by Jimmy Savile and Anne Nightingale and featuring the Animals, Long John Baldry, Ginger Johnson and his African drummers, Lorne Lesley, Humphrey Lyttelton and his band, Susan Maughan and the Rolling Stones.
Television presentation: Pat Lumsden.

| 1965 | 6.5 | Wed 8 Dec 9:40 p.m. | 14 | 1 wk |

Jimmy Tarbuck introduces the cabaret from the London Student's Carnival at the Empire Pool, Wembley, featuring Lionel Blair and his Ladies, the Bells, Donovan, the Ted Heath orchestra, Frankie Vaughan and the Who.
Television presentation: Albert Locke.

Gladiator, The
`1 wk`

Presented by BBC, film

| 1989 | 9.2 | Tue 4 Jul 9:30 p.m. | 19 | 1 wk |

A homicidal maniac known as 'The Skull' is terrorizing Los Angeles with his death car. When the younger brother of Rick Benton (Ken Wahl) is killed he converts his pick-up truck into an armoured weapon to seek revenge.
Director: Able Ferrara.

Glen Campbell and Company
`1 wk`

ATV, entertainment

Campbell was one of several entertainers brought across the Atlantic by Lew Grade to make shows at his Elstree studios.

| 1974 | 5.3 | Mon 19 Aug 8:00 p.m. | 16 | 1 wk |

Guests: Burt Reynolds, Sonny and Cher and the Smothers Brothers, with the Jack Parnell orchestra.
Producers: Gary Smith and Dwight Hemion.

Glory Boys, The · 1 wk

YTV, drama

This three-part mini-series starred Anthony Perkins and Rod Steiger in a plot to assassinate a famous nuclear scientist in London. **Designer:** David Crozier. **Director:** Michael Ferguson. **Producer:** Michael Glynn. **Executive Producers:** David Cunliffe and Alan Landsburg.

1984	12.9	Mon 1 Oct 9:00 p.m. Tue 2 Oct 9:00 p.m. Wed 3 Oct 9:00 p.m.	9	1 wk

These three episodes were listed together in the ratings.

Go With Noakes · 2 wks

BBC, documentary

BLUE PETER presenter John Noakes and his dog Shep embarked on voyages of discovery.

1979	13.5	Sun 18 Nov 4:35 p.m.	19	2 wks

'Queensferry to Whitby'
Part five of a six-part journey around the coast of Britain with guest David Bellamy.
Director: Caroline Walmsley. **Producer:** David Brown.

Godfather, The · 1 wk

Presented by BBC, film

1978	11.3	Sun 28 May 9:00 p.m.	15	1 wk

Part 1 of a two-part screening on consecutive nights of Francis Ford Coppola's film of Mario Puzo's novel. Starring Marlon Brando with James Caan, Richard Castellano, Richard Conte, Robert Duvall, Diane Keaton and Al Pacino.

Going My Way · 11 wks

USA presented by BBC, drama

This series was based on the 1940s Bing Crosby film of the same name. Gene Kelly starred as Father Chuck O'Malley and Leo G. Carroll as Father Fitzgibbon with Dick York as Tom Colwell and Nydia Westman as Mrs Featherstone. The stories were was set in the slums of New York City.

1963	6.8	Thu 14 Feb 8:25 p.m.	10	11 wks

'A Dog for Father Fitzgerald'
St Dominic's parish in Manhattan is thrown into disarray on receipt of a gift of a setter puppy. Mrs Featherstone, the housekeeper, threatens to leave if the dog stays. O'Malley is torn between the two sides.

Going Straight · 3 wks

BBC, situation comedy

Dick Clements and Ian La Frenais followed PORRIDGE with this series of life on the outside. Fletcher (Ronnie Barker) and Godber (Richard Beckinsale) had been released from Slade Prison. Ingrid was played by Patricia Brake.

1978	16.5	Fri 24 Mar 8:25 p.m.	7	3 wks

'Going, Going, Gone'
Fletch is released on parole and faces the challenge of how to avoid going back.
Producer: Sydney Lotterby.

Gold · 2 wks

Presented by ITV, film

1980	13.7	Wed 31 Dec 8:00 p.m.	20	1 wk

This adaptation of Wilbur Smith's novel Goldmine stars Roger Moore as Rod Slater, the underground manager of a South African gold mine in which several miners are trapped. Also starring John Gielgud, Ray Milland and Susannah York.
Director: Peter Hunt.

1982	10.5	Thu 21 Oct 7:30 p.m.	19	1 wk

Repeat showing of the above film.

Gold Rush · 1 wk

Presented by BBC, film

1963	5.7	Wed 25 Dec 9:25 p.m.	9	1 wk

Charlie Chaplin stars in his own specially prepared sound version of his classic film in which he wanders through the frozen north meeting gold prospectors, saloon girls, and the inhabitants of a boom town.
Writer, Director, and **Producer:** Charlie Chaplin.

Golden Child, The · 1 wk

Presented by ITV, film

1991	14.5	Wed 28 Aug 8:00 p.m.	6	1 wk

Eddie Murphy stars as a social worker who specializes in finding lost children. When a holy Tibetan child is kidnapped he is called to the rescue. Charles Dance also stars.
Director: Michael Ritchie.

Golden Egg Awards, The · 1 wk

BBC, entertainment

An element of NOEL EDMONDS' LATE LATE BREAKFAST SHOW was given a show of its own.

| 1986 | 16.6 | Fri 28 Mar 8:15 p.m. | 3 | 1 wk |

Noel Edmonds and Mike Smith host.
Producer: Michael Hurll.

Golden Fiddle Awards, The · 1 wk

BBC, music

| 1979 | 11.9 | Fri 10 Aug 6:20 p.m. | 9 | 1 wk |

Every year hundreds of fiddlers converge in Scotland for a week of traditional music. The champion fiddler is named. Kenneth McKellar introduces the proceedings from Kelvin Hall, Glasgow.
Producer: James Hunter.

Golden Moments · 1 wk

BBC, sport

| 1986 | 9.2 | Tue 22 Jul 8:20 p.m. | 15 | 1 wk |

With the opening ceremony of the thirteenth Commonwealth Games in Edinburgh only two evenings away, Desmond Lynam looks back at the highlights of previous Games.

Golden Rendezvous · 2 wks

Presented by ITV, film

| 1982 | 11.4 | Sun 5 Sep 7:15 p.m. | 4 | 1 wk |

Alistair Maclean's story of murder on board a cargo ship which is also used for high stake gambling. Starring Robert Beatty, John Carradine, Richard Harris, Gordon Jackson, David Janssen, Burgess Meredith and Ann Turkel.
Director: Ashley Lazarus.

| 1985 | 10.9 | Thu 1 Aug 7:30 p.m. | 11 | 1 wk |

Repeat showing of the above film.

Golden Shot, The · 38 wks

ATV, entertainment

This show was devised in Germany as Der Goldener Schuss by Hannes and Werner Schmid. The format mixed song and dance with competitive games, the climax featuring a blindfolded contestant guided verbally by his or her partner to fire a bolt from a crossbow at a target. The nearer the bullseye, the greater the prize.

Hosts were Bob Monkhouse (1967–71, 1975), Norman Vaughan (1972) and Charlie Williams (1974). Hostesses, known as Golden Girls, included Carol Dilworth (1967–69) and Anne Aston (1970–75).

| 1967 | 6.5 | Sun 12 Nov 4:50 p.m. | 6 | 14 wks |

Guests: The Bachelors, Norman Chappell and Mark Wynter.
Director: Pembroke Dutson. **Producer:** Colin Clews.

| 1968 | 6.5 | Sun 28 Jan 4:45 p.m. | 12 | 3 wks |

Guests: Shirley Abicair and Frank Ifield.
Director: Anton Bowler. **Producer:** Colin Clews.

| 1969 | 5.4 | Sun 12 Oct 4:45 p.m. | 19 | 2 wks |

Guests: Freddie Davies, Sir Gerald Nabarro and Marty Wilde.
Producer: John Pullen.

| 1970 | 6.5 | Sun 1 Feb 4:45 p.m. | 10 | 10 wks |

Guests: the Baker Twins and David Nixon.
Producer: Edward Joffe.

| 1971 | 6.5 | Sun 24 Oct 4:45 p.m. | 12 | 1 wk |

Guest: Petula Clark. Hostess Anne Aston is joined in this series by a Maid of the Month. In this show it is Chelsea Brown.
Producer: Mike Lloyd.

| 1972 | 6.6 | Sun 6 Feb 4:40 p.m. | 17 | 3 wks |

Guest: Grazina Frame, with Maid of the Month Virginia North.
Director: Paul Stewart-Lang. **Producer:** Les Cocks.

| 1974 | 6.6 | Sun 26 Jan 4:40 p.m. | 15 | 3 wks |

Guest: Judith Durham, with Maid of the Month Jill Stanford.
Producer: Dicky Leeman.

| 1975 | 7.0 | Sun 16 Feb 4:00 p.m. | 17 | 2 wks |

Guests: Clive Lea and Clodagh Rodgers, with Wei Wei Wong as Golden Girl for the Season.
Producer: Dicky Leeman.

Golden Silents · 6 wks

BBC, comedy

Michael Bentine presented this from the National Film Theatre with clips from silent movies illustrating a particular theme.

| 1969 | 6.5 | Fri 28 Nov 8:25 p.m. | 15 | 6 wks |

'A Man's Best Friend'
Scenes in which animals have featured in the films of Buster Keaton, Harry Langdon, Laurel and Hardy, and others.
Producer: Richard Evans.

....

Goldfinger   5 wks

Presented by ITV, film

1976	9.8	Wed 3 Nov 8:00 p.m.	1	1 wk

Ian Fleming's story starring Sean Connery as James Bond with Honor Blackman as Pussy Galore and Gert Frobe as Auric Goldfinger. Also starring Shirley Eaton as Jill Masterson and Harold Sakata as Odd-Job, with Bernard Lee as 'M' and Lois Maxwell as Miss Moneypenny.
Director: Guy Hamilton.

1978	17.5	Sun 12 Mar 7:45 p.m.	3	1 wk
1985	17.0	Sun 21 Apr 7:45 p.m.	1	1 wk
1987	13.9	Tue 27 Jan 8:00 p.m.	4	1 wk
1990	9.5	Sat 1 Sep 7:40 p.m.	18	1 wk

Repeat showings of the film.

....

Goldrobbers, The   13 wks

LWT, drama

In this thirteen-part series Detective Chief-Superintendent Craddock (Peter Vaughan) led the hunt after five and a half million pounds worth of gold ingots were snatched from an airport.

1969	7.5	Fri 29 Aug 9:00 p.m.	2	13 wks

'The Kill' by John Hawkesworth and Martin Hall.
Craddock advances into the robber's own territory in this final episode.
Director: Bill Bain. **Producer:** John Hawkesworth.

....

Goliath Awaits   2 wks

USA presented by ITV, drama

1982	13.4	Thu 10 Jun 8:00 p.m.	1	2 wks

A two-part story in which a group of people were trapped for forty years in the wreck of a liner. Young diver Peter Cabot (Mark Harmon) hears an SOS and then sees the face of a young girl, Lea McKenzie (Emma Samms), at a porthole. Other stars include Eddie Albert, John Carradine, Frank Gorshin, Christopher Lee, John McIntire and Jean Marsh.
Director: Kevin Connor.

Gone With the Wind   1 wk

Presented by BBC, film

1981	14.4	Sat 26 Dec 8:15 p.m.	13	1 wk

Part one of the cinema version of Margaret Mitchell's novel of love and land set during the American Civil War. Clark Gable and Vivien Leigh star as Rhett Butler and Scarlett O'Hara.
Director: Victor Fleming.

....

Good Life, The   29 wks

BBC, situation comedy

Created by John Esmonde and Bob Larbey. Tom and Barbara Good (Richard Briers and Felicity Kendal) decided to opt out of the rat race and so Tom gave up his job as a draftsman. To the consternation of their neighbours Jerry and Margo Ledbetter (Paul Eddington and Penelope Keith), they dug up their suburban garden, installed pigs and hens, sowed and planted and embarked on a life of self-sufficiency in Surbiton. Tom and Jerry had previously been colleagues at work.
Producer: John Howard Davies.

1976	7.8	Fri 15 Oct 8:30 p.m.	7	9 wks

'Whose Fleas are These?'
Margo is horrified when she discovers Tom and Barbara have caught fleas.

1977	7.1	Sun 17 Apr 8:05 p.m.	14	2 wks

'The Green Door'
How do you tell your best friend that his wife is deceiving him?

1978	13.8	Thu 5 Jan 7:40 p.m.	8	4 wks

'Plough Your Own Furrow'
A repeat showing of the episode in which Tom first decides that commuting is no life. He plans independence in Surbiton.

1981	15.5	Thu 1 Jan 7:55 p.m.	11	1 wk

'Silly But It's Fun'
Repeat showing of THE GOOD LIFE CHRISTMAS SPECIAL in which Christmas plans fail to work out for either couple.

1986	13.2	Sat 25 Jan 9:25 p.m.	10	1 wk

'When I'm 65'
A repeat showing of a special edition recorded in June 1978 in the presence of HM The Queen and HRH The Duke of Edinburgh in which both Tom and Jerry are worried about their fitness. Tom's bank manager (George Cole) expresses his worries about Tom's pension scheme.

1989	14.7	Tue 4 Apr 8:00 p.m.	6	12 wks

Repeat showing of **'Whose Fleas Are These?'**.

Having spent her entire life in a sunken ocean liner, Lea McKenzie (Emma Samms) spots a diver outside the porthole in **Goliath Awaits**.

Good Life Christmas Special, The — 1 wk

BBC, comedy

| 1977 | 15.0 | Mon 26 Dec 7:35 p.m. | 10 | 1 wk |

'Silly But It's Fun'
Christmas plans go hopelessly wrong for both couples.
Producer: John Howard Davies.

Good Old Days, The — 23 wks

BBC, entertainment

This series ran for thirty years wallowing in nostalgia for the good old days of music hall. The shows came from one of the few genuine music halls still to survive, the City Varieties in Leeds. The audience dressed up in the fashions of the 1890s and a bawdy atmosphere was encouraged by chairman Leonard Sachs. With members of the Players Theatre Company and the Northern Dance (Radio) Orchestra, conductors Alyn Ainsworth, Bernard Herrmann and Brian Fitzgerald.
Producer: Barney Colehan.

| 1963 | 6.0 | Tue 3 Dec 8:10 p.m. | 15 | 3 wks |

With the King Brothers, Harry Bailey, Betty Jumel, Johnny Stewart and the Tanton Sisters.

| 1966 | 5.6 | Mon 21 Feb 9:50 p.m. | 11 | 3 wks |

With Norman Collier, Ronnie Hilton, Roy Hudd, Sandy Powell and the Two Earls.

| 1967 | 6.2 | Fri 29 Dec 7:30 p.m. | 12 | 2 wks |

With Chantal and Dumont, Kim Cordell, Davy Kaye, Los Rennos and Beryl Reid.

| 1968 | 7.7 | Wed 24 Jan 8:00 p.m. | 4 | 4 wks |

With Ken Dodd, Ray Alan and Lord Charles, Freddie Frinton, Eira Heath and Vince Hill.

| 1970 | 5.8 | Thu 17 Sep 8:15 p.m. | 18 | 2 wks |

With Dora Bryan, Charlie Chester, Ken and Anna Alexis, Paul Dutton, the Kagans and Bertice Reading.

| 1976 | 7.6 | Wed 18 Mar 9:25 p.m. | 5 | 4 wks |

With Hylda Baker, Jan Curry, Val Doonican, Richard Hearne, Robin Hunter and the James Boys.

| 1977 | 8.2 | Thu 6 Jan 9:25 p.m. | 5 | 2 wks |

With Ken Dodd, Beatrice Ashton, John Bouchier and Christine Cartwright.

| 1980 | 9.7 | Wed 6 Aug 9:25 p.m. | 15 | 2 wks |

With Max Wall, Eira Heath, Grace Kennedy and Denny Willis.

| 1981 | 12.6 | Thu 23 Jul 9:25 p.m. | 6 | 1 wk |

With John Inman, Vince Hill, Jan Hunt, Valeria Masterson and Alan Randall.

Good Old Summertime — 1 wk

BBC, drama

| 1966 | 5.6 | Mon 29 Aug 8:00 p.m. | 8 | 1 wk |

Henry and Daphne Pepper (Brian Rix and Joan Sims) and Wilf and Ethel Pearson (Leo Franklyn and Sheila Mercier) are all spending the Bank Holiday at the Bella Vista private hotel. Their pleasure is diminished by the fierce landlady, Mrs Austin (Joan Sanderson).
Director: Wallace Douglas.

Goodbye Again — 1 wk

ATV, entertainment

| 1969 | 4.5 | Sun 3 Aug 7:25 p.m. | 14 | 1 wk |

A special starring Peter Cook and Dudley Moore with their guests Anne Bancroft and Mel Tormé, the Paddy Stone dancers and the Jack Parnell orchestra.
Producers: Gary Smith and Dwight Hemion

Goodies, The — 2 wks

LWT, comedy

Writers and performers Graeme Garden, Tim Brooke-Taylor and Bill Oddie created THE GOODIES for the BBC in the 1970s. They twice won the Silver Rose of Montreux for their farcical comedy. In 1982 LWT revived the show.

| 1982 | 13.6 | Sat 9 Jan 6:45 p.m. | 18 | 2 wks |

When expenses exceed profits, one Goodie must be replaced by automation.
Producer: Bob Spiers. **Executive Producer:** David Bell.

Goodnight and God Bless — 1 wk

Central, situation comedy

This series by Donald Churchill and Joe McGrath starred Churchill as Ronnie Kemp, a one-time stand-up comic now remarried and a successful TV game show host.

| 1983 | 9.6 | Tue 19 Apr 8:30 p.m. | 20 | 1 wk |

'Little Green-Eyed Monster'
Ronnie is away compering a fashion show when he is confronted with evidence that his wife Celia (Judy Loe) is having an affair with the odd-job man Frank (Leslie Grantham).
Producer: Alan Dossor. **Executive Producer:** Joe McGrath.

Goon Show, The				1 wk

Thames, comedy

Legends of radio comedy, the original Goons were conceived in 1947 in the Grafton Arms pub in Victoria. They were Michael Bentine, Spike Milligan, Harry Secombe and Peter Sellers. Bentine left the team in 1954.

1968	5.5	Thu 8 Aug 8:00 p.m.	3	1 wk

Twenty-one years after the birth of the Goons, Sellers, Milligan and Secombe return to character with help from John Cleese, John Hamilton and Christine Pryor.
Writer: Spike Milligan. **Director:** Joe McGrath. **Producer:** Peter Eton.

Goonies, The				1 wk

Presented by ITV, film

1991	13.0	Wed 3 Apr 8:00 p.m.	9	1 wk

Steven Spielberg's story about seven children who find a treasure map to a pirate galleon. As they follow the directions they are followed by a band of incompetent thieves.
Director: Richard Donner.

Goose with Pepper				1 wk

Anglia, drama

1975	5.4	Tue 12 Aug 9:00 p.m.	18	1 wk

Story by Frederick Bradman dramatized by David Ambrose and Tony Marsh. The peaceful retirement of Brigadier Salt Lumley (Kenneth More), 'Pepper' to his pals, is shattered by the uninvited arrival of Company Sergeant Major Goosely (Nigel Davenport). Lumley tries to figure out the reason for the visit and what Goosely's intentions are towards his daughter Pat (Maria Aitken). Also starring Angela Douglas, Clive Morton and Christopher Timothy.
Producer: John Jacobs.

Gosling's Travels				6 wks

Granada, documentary

Series of light roving reports by journalist Ray Gosling.
Director: Philip Trevelyan. **Producer:** Mike Scott.

1974	7.1	Mon 16 Dec 8:30 p.m.	12	1 wk

'A Village for Christmas'
Ray goes in search of the perfect English village – the kind featured on millions of Christmas cards.

1975	6.1	Mon 18 Aug 8:30 p.m.	13	5 wks

'Liverpool Lunchtime'
Ray Gosling explores the alleyways and corners of Liverpool's business district and finds not The Cavern but a topless bar!

Grace Kelly Story, The				1 wk

Presented by ITV, film

1983	10.7	Sun 8 May 7:45 p.m.	12	1 wk

Cheryl Ladd stars as the Hollywood actress who became a princess. Also starring Lloyd Bridges as her father Jack, Diane Ladd as her sister Margaret and Ian McShane as Prince Rainier.
Director: Anthony Page.

Graduate, The				1 wk

Presented by BBC, film

1974	6.2	Mon 23 Dec 9:20 p.m.	11	1 wk

Starring Dustin Hoffman as California graduate Ben Braddock and Anne Bancroft as Mrs Robinson, a family friend. Ben has an affair with Mrs Robinson and then falls for her daughter Elaine (Katharine Ross). Simon and Garfunkel provide several songs.
Director: Mike Nichols.

Grady				1 wk

YTV, drama

This series was created by Edmund Ward. Grady (Anthony Bate), fresh from prison, burst into town to become the labour hero of the shop floor, intent on getting as much money for the workers as possible. A risk taker, he would agitate and make trouble in pursuit of his dream to make the world a better place in which to work. Diana Coupland played his wife Margaret.

1970	6.6	Tue 1 Dec 9:00 p.m.	16	1 wk

'Pieces on a Board'
Confused union politics mean the workers down tools rather than work under supervisors from another union. The management sits tight while an industrial consultant tries to use Grady as a pawn and a scapegoat. Guest stars: Terence Alexander and Wilfred Pickles.
Designer: Vic Symonds. **Director:** Marc Miller. **Producer:** Peter Willes.

Grafters, The — 1 wk

AR, documentary

| 1964 | 5.4 | Wed 18 Nov 9:35 p.m. | 18 | 1 wk |

This film asks if there is a future for street markets.
Director: Charles Squires.

Graham — 1 wk

ATV, documentary

| 1974 | 6.7 | Tue 12 Feb 9:00 p.m. | 16 | 1 wk |

A film portrait of Graham Hill, twice Formula One World Champion who didn't pass his driving test until he was 23! Narrated by Paul Newman, himself a motor racing enthusiast.
Writer and **Producer:** Tony Maylam.

Grand Christmas Circus — 1 wk

ATV, circus

| 1961 | 7.1 | Sun 17 Dec 7:25 p.m. | 2 | 1 wk |

From the Kelvin Hall, Glasgow, Peter Cockburn introduces Circus Knie's Liberty Horses, William Lenz and his chimpanzees and Fossett's Wonder Elephants, with ringmaster A.R. Delboscq.
Television presentation: Bill Ward.

Grand Knockout Tournament, The — 1 wk

BBC, entertainment

| 1987 | 18.3 | Fri 19 Jun 7:40 p.m. | 3 | 1 wk |

From Alton Towers, Stuart Hall introduces a celebrity-studded edition of IT'S A KNOCKOUT with four teams competing for charity. The team captains are HRH The Prince Edward, HRH The Princess Anne, HRH The Duke of York and HRH The Duchess of York.
Games Designer: Stuart Furber. **Director:** Geoffrey Wilson. **Producer:** Alan Walsh.

Grand Larceny — 1 wk

HTV, drama

| 1988 | 12.3 | Sat 9 Apr 8:00 p.m. | 10 | 1 wk |

This play by Peter Stone stars Ian McShane as Flanagan and Marilu Henner as Frederica on the trail of a stolen racehorse.
Director: Jeannot Szwarc. **Producers:** Robert Halmi Jr. and Patrick Deschamps. **Executive Producers:** Robert Halmi Sr. and Patrick Dromgoole.

Grand National, The — 6 wks

BBC, sport

The world's most formidable steeplechase, first run in 1839, always took place at Aintree near Liverpool.

| 1968 | 9.3 | Sat 30 Mar 2:25 p.m. | 1 | 1 wk |

Commentary by Clive Graham, Robert Haynes, Michael O'Hehir, Peter O'Sullevan and Michael Seth-Smith.
Television presentation: Dennis Monger and Ray Lakeland.

| 1983 | 12.9 | Sat 9 Apr 3:20 p.m. | 7 | 1 wk |

Commentary by Peter O'Sullevan and Julian Wilson.
Television presentation: Nick Hunter and Fred Viner.

| 1984 | 10.6 | Sat 31 Mar 3:20 p.m. | 20 | 1 wk |

Commentary by Peter O'Sullevan, Richard Pitman and Julian Wilson.
Television presentation: Nick Hunter, John McNicholas, Richard Tilling and Fred Viner.

| 1986 | 15.4 | Sat 5 Apr 3:20 p.m. | 4 | 1 wk |

Commentary by Peter O'Sullevan, John Hanmer and Julian Wilson.
Television presentation: Fred Viner and Campbell Ferguson.
Editor: John Philips.

| 1987 | 12.2 | Sat 4 Apr 2:45 p.m. | 14 | 1 wk |

Commentary by Peter O'Sullevan, John Hanmer and Julian Wilson.
Television presentation: Fred Viner and Campbell Ferguson.

| 1988 | 14.3 | Sat 9 Apr 3:00 p.m. | 6 | 1 wk |

Commentary by Peter O'Sullevan, John Hanmer and Julian Wilson.
Television presentation: Keith Mackenzie.

Grand Prix — 1 wk

Presented by BBC, film

| 1979 | 13.8 | Mon 20 Aug 8:05 p.m. | 17 | 1 wk |

James Garner, Françoise Hardy, Yves Montand and Eva Marie Saint star in this film about motor racing, set mainly in Monte Carlo.
Director: John Frankenheimer.

Gray Lady Down — 1 wk

Presented by ITV, film

| 1982 | 9.0 | Sat 28 Aug 8:15 p.m. | 15 | 1 wk |

US nuclear submarine Neptune collides with a Norwegian freighter and sinks to a depth of 1450 feet. There is only sufficient oxygen to last forty-eight hours.
Director: David Greene.

Grease | 2 wks

Presented by BBC, film

| 1982 | 10.5 | Tue 28 Dec 6:55 p.m. | 18 | 1 wk |

A musical love affair blooms at a California High School between Australian Sandy Olsson (Olivia Newton-John) and Danny Zucco (John Travolta).
Director: Randal Kleiser.

| 1987 | 11.6 | Sat 25 May 6:50 p.m. | 6 | 1 wk |

Repeat showing of the above film.

Great American Picture Show, The | 2 wks

Presented by BBC, film

| 1976 | 6.2 | Mon 5 Jul 9:25 p.m. | 5 | 2 wks |

'Bonnie and Clyde'
This was screened during a week of special American film presentations to celebrate the Bicentennial of the Declaration of Independence. Bonnie Parker (Faye Dunaway) and Clyde Barrow (Warren Beatty) violently rob their way through America's South in the 1930s. Also starring Gene Hackman, Estelle Parsons, Michael J. Pollard and Gene Wilder.
Director: Arthur Penn.

Great Escape, The | 2 wks

USA presented by BBC, film

| 1971 | 7.1 | Tue 28 Dec 6:30 p.m. | 4 | 1 wk |

This movie set in the 'escape-proof' camp Stalag-Luft North stars Richard Attenborough, Charles Bronson, James Coburn, James Donald, James Garner, Gordon Jackson, John Leyton, David McCallum, Steve McQueen, Donald Pleasence and Nigel Stock.
Director: John Sturges.

| 1983 | 10.1 | Wed 28 Dec 6:00 p.m. | 20 | 1 wk |

Repeat showing of the above film.

Great Fish Muddle, The | 1 wk

BBC, documentary

| 1968 | 5.2 | Tue 24 Sep 9:05 p.m. | 17 | 1 wk |

The fishing industry is going through hard times with trawlers laid up and trawler men laid off. Yet we spend one hundred million pounds each year importing foreign fish.
Producer and **Narrator:** Roger Mills.

Great Outdoors, The | 1 wk

Presented by BBC, film

| 1991 | 12.9 | Fri 27 Dec 8:00 p.m. | 18 | 1 wk |

Dan Aykroyd and John Candy star in this comedy about a quiet holiday ruined by the arrival of loathsome relatives.
Director: Howard Deutch.

Great St Trinian's Train Robbery, The | 1 wk

Presented by BBC, film

| 1971 | 6.5 | Thu 23 Dec 7:30 p.m. | 20 | 1 wk |

Having left a trail of arson behind them in the previous St Trinian's film, the girls move into a new home. However, the Great Train Robbers have left several million pounds under the ballroom floor and plan to retrieve it. Starring Dora Bryan and Frankie Howerd with George Cole, Raymond Huntley, Reg Varney and Richard Wattis.
Director: Frank Launder.

Great Scout and Cathouse Thursday, The | 1 wk

Presented by ITV, film

| 1983 | 7.1 | Sat 6 Aug 9:45 p.m. | 17 | 1 wk |

Robert Culp, Lee Marvin and Oliver Reed star in the story of rough and ready soldiers in Colorado in 1908. They kidnap a group of prostitutes. The women all escape, except for Thursday (Kay Lenz).
Director: Don Taylor.

Great Stars, The | 14 wks

Presented by BBC, film

Series of films featuring some of the greatest stars of Hollywood.

| 1968 | 6.5 | Sun 1 Dec 8:15 p.m. | 2 | 9 wks |

'The Citadel'
King Vidor produced and directed this adaptation of A.J. Cronin's novel, starring Robert Donat, Rex Harrison, Cecil Parker, Ralph Richardson, Rosalind Russell and Emlyn Williams.

G

| 1969 | 6.6 | Sun 2 Feb 8:15 p.m. | 9 | 5 wks |

'How Green was my Valley'
Richard Llewellyn's saga of the life and struggles of a Welsh mining family stars Maureen O'Hara, Walter Pidgeon and Roddy McDowell. **Director:** John Ford.

Great Train Race, The — 1 wk

ATV, documentary

| 1971 | 5.8 | Tue 4 May 9:00 p.m. | 13 | 1 wk |

A look at the world of the commuter. The TV Times billing read: 'A grim and serious business. It frays nerves, can destroy marriages and herds human beings into environments that would not be permitted for cattle.'
Camera: Louis Wolfers. **Producer:** Robin Brown.

Great Waldo Pepper, The — 1 wk

Presented by BBC, film

| 1980 | 14.2 | Mon 7 Apr 7:25 p.m. | 7 | 1 wk |

Easter Monday showing of George Roy Hill's film starring Robert Redford as daredevil aerial stuntman Waldo Pepper. Also starring Margot Kidder, Susan Sarandon and Bo Svenson.

Great Zaire River Expedition, The — 1 wk

Anglia, documentary

| 1975 | 6.2 | Mon 1 Sep 8:00 p.m. | 13 | 1 wk |

Major John Blashford-Snell's team of Royal Marines set out to follow the dangerous route taken by Stanley down the River Congo (Zaire) 100 years ago. The British explorer journalist was on a mission to find Dr Livingstone on behalf of the New York Herald.
Cameras: Jeremy Pass and Erik Rankin. **Producer:** Aubrey Buxton.

Greek Tycoon, The — 1 wk

Presented by ITV, film

| 1983 | 9.5 | Mon 22 Aug 8:00 p.m. | 8 | 1 wk |

Anthony Quinn stars as Theo Tomasis, one of the world's richest men, whose life is changed when he meets American Senator James Cassidy (James Franciscus) and his wife Liz (Jacqueline Bisset). **Director:** J. Lee-Thompson.

Gremlins — 2 wks

Presented by ITV, film

| 1988 | 14.8 | Thu 29 Dec 9:00 p.m. | 6 | 1 wk |

Mogwais are little furry creatures that become very dangerous when wet. Starring Hoyt Axton, Phoebe Cates and Zach Galligan. **Director:** Joe Dante.

| 1990 | 10.7 | Sun 8 Jul 9:00 p.m. | 13 | 1 wk |

Repeat showing of the above film.

Greystoke – the Legend of Tarzan, Lord of the Apes — 1 wk

Presented by BBC, film

| 1987 | 13.5 | Mon 28 Dec 8:30 p.m. | 9 | 1 wk |

Tarzan was the creation of writer Edgar Rice Burroughs. The story begins in 1886 when Lord Clayton and his pregnant wife are shipwrecked off the coast of Africa. Their young son John is reared in the jungle by apes. Starring Christopher Lambert as Tarzan with Cheryl Campbell, Ian Charleson, Nigel Davenport, James Fox, Ian Holm, Andie MacDowell, Ralph Richardson, David Suchet and John Wells.
Director: Hugh Hudson.

Groucho — 2 wks

AR, entertainment

This series of half-hour programmes mixed elements of comedy and quiz. Groucho Marx met the people of Britain and answered their questions, which were put to the star by compere Keith Fordyce.

| 1965 | 4.6 | Thu 8 Jul 7:30 p.m. | 20 | 2 wks |

Producer: Ronald Marriott.

Growing Pains of Adrian Mole, The — 4 wks

Thames, drama

Sue Townsend's sequel to THE SECRET DIARY OF ADRIAN MOLE AGED 13³/₄ again starred Gian Sammarco as Adrian. Lulu portrayed his mother Pauline and Stephen Moore, Beryl Reid and Lindsey Stagg reprised their original roles. Bill Fraser was Adrian's elderly confidant Bert Baxter and Doris Hare played Queenie.

| 1987 | 14.1 | Mon 12 Jan 8:00 p.m. | 6 | 4 wks |

Pauline is pregnant. The Mole family plans a holiday before the birth.
Producer: Peter Sasdy. **Executive Producer:** Lloyd Shirley.

Grumbleweeds Radio Show, The — 4 wks

Granada, comedy

The Yorkshire club group the Grumbleweeds (Albert, Carl, Graham, Maurice and Robin) transferred some of their radio characters to a series of television sketches.
Producer: John Hamp.

1984	8.9	Sat 2 Jun 7:00 p.m.	20	1 wk

Guest: Jimmy Savile.
Director: David Liddiment.

1985	11.8	Sat 27 Apr 6:45 p.m.	16	3 wks

Directors: Dave Warwick and Ian White.

Grundy — 5 wks

Thames, situation comedy

This series by Ken Hoare starred Harry H. Corbett as a newsagent. His marriage had collapsed and he had an eye for the ladies.

1980	12.2	Mon 14 Jul 8:00 p.m.	5	5 wks

Grundy meets Beryl (Lynda Baron) on a tram.
Producer: Robert Reed.

GS 5 — 5 wks

ATV, drama

A ghost squad of secret agents ran international missions. Operators included Peter Clarke (Ray Barrett), Geoffrey Stock (Anthony Marshall) and Tony Miller (Neil Hallett).

1964	6.2	Sat 11 Apr 7:25 p.m.	13	5 wks

'Scorpion Rock' by Guy Morgan.
Tony Miller is sent to the Balearics to investigate the disappearance of another undercover agent. He runs up against Emilio Zafra (Paul Whitsun-Jones), the virtual dictator of the island.
Script Editor: Brian Clemens. **Director:** Bill Stewart. **Producer:** Dennis Vance.

Guinness Book of Records Special, The — 4 wks

Presented by ITV, documentary

In this occasional series David Frost and Norris McWhirter introduced some of the most daring and amazing record breakers. The show was based on the book compiled by Norris and Ross McWhirter. **Director** (1982, 1985): Bruce Gowers. **Executive Producer:** David Frost.

1982	13.7	Sat 23 Jan 5:45 p.m.	14	1 wk

Producer: Marvin Minoff.

1983	13.9	Sat 15 Jan 7:10 p.m.	4	2 wks

Producer: Bruce Gowers.

1985	14.5	Sun 14 Apr 7:45 p.m.	3	1 wk

Producers: Ian Gordon and Carol Rosenstein.

Gunfight at the OK Corral — 1 wk

Presented by ITV, film

1977	13.3	Sun 13 Nov 7:45 p.m.	19	1 wk

Wyatt Earp (Burt Lancaster) and Doc Holliday (Kirk Douglas), whom Earp saved from a lynching, defeat the Clantons. When they return to Dodge City from Fort Griffin, Earp falls in love with gambler Laura Denbow (Rhonda Fleming).
Director: John Sturges.

Guns of Navarone, The — 3 wks

Presented by ITV, film

1976	8.0	Sun 4 Apr 7:25 p.m.	4	1 wk

Two German guns on the Turkish island of Navarone block a vital naval passage to the Allies during the Second World War. In 1943 a sabotage team is sent to destroy them. Starring Stanley Baker, James Darren, Richard Harris, James Robertson Justice, David Niven, Gregory Peck, Anthony Quayle and Anthony Quinn.
Director: J. Lee-Thompson.

1980	12.5	Sun 13 Jul 7:45 p.m.	3	1 wk
1981	10.1	Sat 29 Aug 7:35 p.m.	10	1 wk

These are repeat showings of the above film.

Gunsmoke — 2 wks

USA presented by ITV, western

This classic series began in the USA in 1955 and continued for twenty years starring James Arness as Marshal Matt Dillon. Co-stars included Milburn Stone as 'Doc' Adams, Amanda Blake as Kitty Russell of the Longbranch saloon and, until 1963, Dennis Weaver as the limping deputy Chester Goode.
Executive Producer: John Mantley.

1962	5.4	Fri 27 Apr 9:30 p.m.	6	2 wks

'Cody's Cove'
Cody Durham (Anthony Caruso), a respected Dodge City citizen, harbours a wounded outlaw who has eluded Marshal Dillon. Cody gets bitter reward for his kindness when the outlaw meets his girl.

1

2

3

4

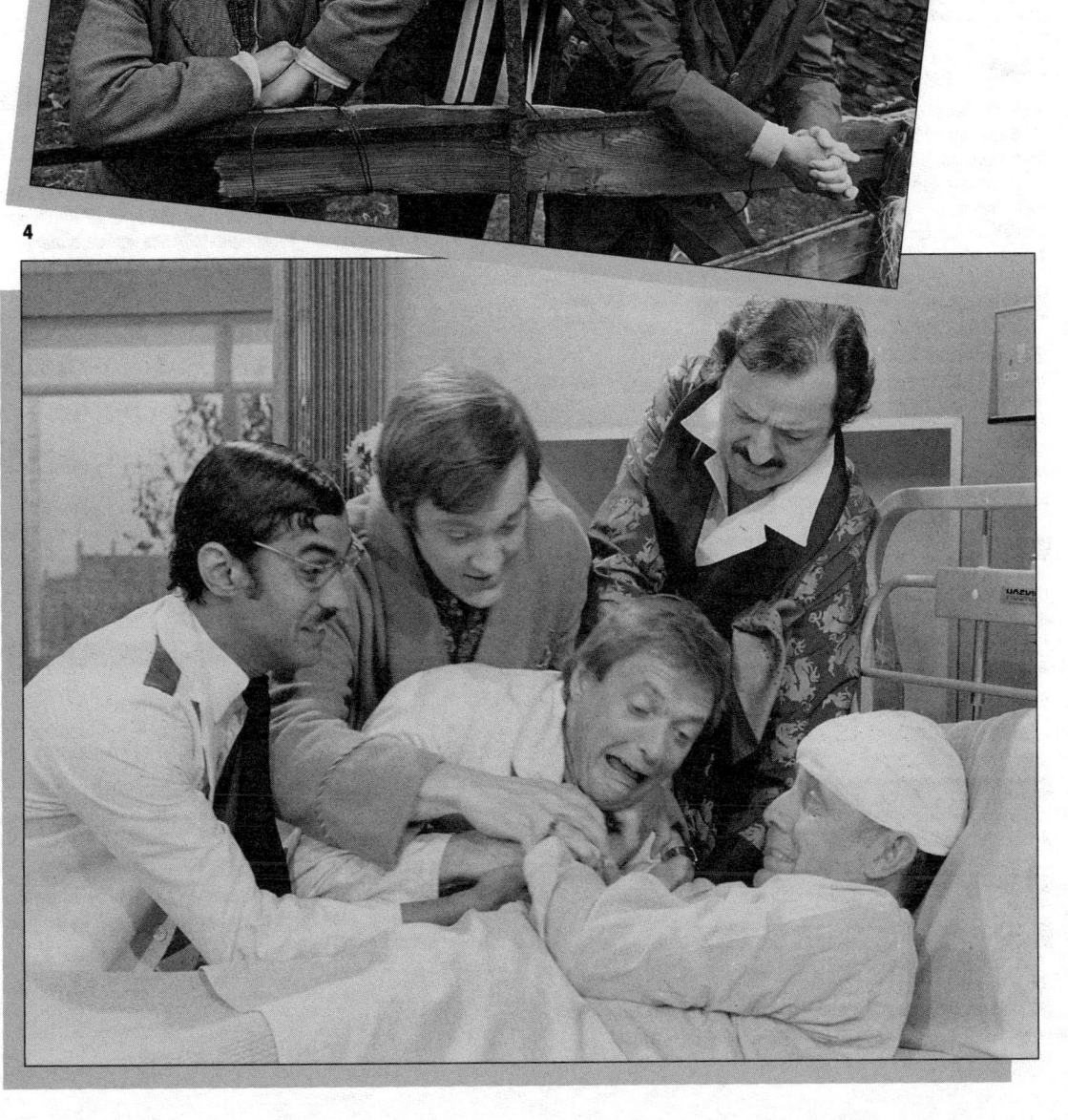

1 *Arkwright (Ronnie Barker) and his assistant Granville (David Jason) ran the corner shop in* **Open All Hours**.

2 *The Boswells prepare to break* **Bread**.

3 *Compo (Bill Owen), Foggy (Brian Wilde) and Clegg (Peter Sallis) first reached Number One in 1980 with* **Last of the Summer Wine**.

4 *Richard Wilson as Thorpe is not amused in* **Only When I Laugh**.

Hadleigh — 30 wks

YTV, drama

This series starred Gerald Harper as James Hadleigh, the Squire of Melford Park, a champion of the underdog who was beset by problems concerning the upkeep of his stately home.

1971 7.9 Fri 19 Feb 9:00 p.m. 5 13 wks

'**Nichola Penn**' by Mervyn Haisman and Henry Lincoln.
Hadleigh met Anne Hepton (Jane Merrow) just three weeks ago, but their relationship has blossomed. When she observes three cups laid for breakfast she is unconcerned – until she sees the beautiful Nichola Penn (Jill Dixon).
Designer: Gordon Livesey. **Director:** Peter Cregeen: **Producer:** Terence Williams.

1973 6.7 Fri 31 Aug 9:00 p.m. 2 12 wks

'**Family Feeling**' by Leslie Sands.
Yorkshire's most eligible bachelor has married Jennifer Caldwell (Hilary Dwyer), an independent girl, wealthy in her own right. Her father Charles Caldwell (Gerald James) comes to visit. A quiet weekend becomes disturbing and threatens to split the family.
Designer: Eric Shedden. **Director:** Michael Ferguson. **Producer:** Jacky Stoller. **Executive Producer:** Peter Willes.

1976 7.0 Fri 16 Apr 9:00 p.m. 9 5 wks

'**Film Story**' by Owen Holder.
Hadleigh leases Melford to a film company. As the staff walk out, the film's leading lady Susan Debray (Stephanie Beacham) walks in.
Designer: Mary Rea. **Director:** Tony Wharmby. **Producer:** Jacky Stoller. **Executive Producer:** David Cunliffe.

Half-Hour Story — 14 wks

AR, drama

Series of half-hour plays with no unifying theme.

1967 6.2 Wed 13 Sep 9:00 p.m. 5 12 wks

'**Bug**' by Peter Draper.
Bob Monkhouse stars as radio ham Q.P. Jakes, who hires seedy private detective R.J. Smellie (Bill Owen) to spy on his wife.
Director: William G. Stewart. **Producer:** Stella Richman.

1968 5.1 Wed 26 Jun 10:30 p.m. 18 2 wks

'**It's Only Us**' by Peter Draper.
Penelope (Jill Bennett) and Martin (John Osborne) spend an afternoon in a seedy hotel.
Director: Gareth Davies. **Producer:** Stella Richman.

Hallelujah — 12 wks

YTV, situation comedy

In this series by Dick Sharples, Salvation Army captain Emily Ridley (Thora Hird) was convinced that the Yorkshire town of Brigthorpe was the last remaining refuge of original sin. She was determined to have the sinners repent. The show also starred David Daker as Brother Benjamin and Patsy Rowlands as Alice Meredith.
Producer: Ronnie Baxter.

1983 10.3 Fri 20 May 7:30 p.m. 9 6 wks

Emily's door-to-door collection to help the poor yields £1.20.

1984 13.9 Fri 21 Dec 7:30 p.m. 8 6 wks

Emily tells her friends the story of Christmas Past, when the Salvation Army fought to save the souls of Ebenezer Dickens (Bryan Pringle) and Ella Scratchit (Joan Sims).

Hammer House of Horror, The — 3 wks

ATV, film

Season of film presentations of the horror stories produced by the Hammer studio.

1980 14.0 Sat 15 Nov 9:15 p.m. 13 3 wks

'**Guardian of the Abyss**'
A chance purchase by an antiques dealer brings a terrifying contact with the Unknown. Starring Rosalyn Landor and Ray Lonnen with John Carson and Paul Darrow.
Director: Don Sharp.

Hancock — 2 wks

ATV, comedy

Tony Hancock, the melancholy, seedy, cunning lad from the fictitious 23 Railway Cuttings, East Cheam, had established HANCOCK'S HALF HOUR (see below) as a hugely successfully radio show in the early 1950s. With script writers Ray Galton and Alan Simpson, he transferred it to BBC television in 1956. Sid James was Tony's sidekick until 1960. In 1963 the star abandoned Galton and Simpson, moved to ATV and soon suffered a decline in fortunes. He died in Sydney, Australia on 25 June 1968.

| 1963 | 7.8 | Thu 3 Jan 8:30 p.m. | 3 | 2 wks |

'The Assistant'
Written by Terry Nation from a story by Ray Whyberd. Hancock has swapped East Cheam, his astrakhan-collared coat and black Homburg for a sheepskin jacket, a soft felt hat and a job in a department store. He accepts the manager's challenge to be polite to the customers in return for the cancellation of his outstanding debt to the shop. With Patrick Cargill, Mario Fabrizi, Kenneth Griffith and Martita Hunt.
Producer: Alan Tarrant.

Hancock's Half Hour — 3 wks

BBC, comedy

A season of repeats of some of the best work of Tony Hancock, written by Ray Galton and Alan Simpson and often co-starring Sid James.

| 1986 | 15.1 | Sun 23 Feb 7:15 p.m. | 7 | 3 wks |

'The Blood Donor'
Recorded in 1961, after the split with Sid James, Hancock goes to give blood. The nurse is June Whitfield, the doctor is Patrick Cargill and the donor patiently waiting to give next is Frank Thornton.
Producer: Duncan Wood.

Hangar 18 — 1 wk

Presented by BBC, film

| 1986 | 8.5 | Sun 3 Aug 7:15 p.m. | 16 | 1 wk |

A UFO crashes in the Arizona desert. It is secretly transported to a remote abandoned hangar in Texas, but two astronauts have already seen the craft destroy a satellite on its way to Earth. Pamela Bellwood, Darren McGavin and Robert Vaughn star.
Director: James L. Conway.

Hannay — 1 wk

Thames, drama

In this six-part spy thriller set in 1912 Richard Hannay, the character created by John Buchan, was played by Robert Powell.

| 1988 | 11.5 | Wed 6 Jan 9:00 p.m. | 19 | 1 wk |

'The Fellowship of the Black Stone' by Michael Robson.
After thirty years in South Africa, Hannay returns to the political cauldron of Europe, where Imperial Germany is on a relentless rise.
Director: David Giles. **Producer:** Richard Bates. **Executive Producer:** Lloyd Shirley.

Hannibal Brooks — 1 wk

Presented by BBC, film

| 1979 | 14.2 | Thu 8 May 7:20 p.m. | 18 | 1 wk |

This film is screened because of the cancellation of A SONG FOR EUROPE due to a walkout by 200 BBC technicians. Oliver Reed stars as a British POW in Germany who escapes across the Alps with an elephant.
Director: Michael Winner.

Hanover Street — 1 wk

Presented by ITV, film

| 1982 | 10.2 | Sun 17 Oct 7:15 p.m. | 17 | 1 wk |

In London in 1943, American bomber pilot David Halloran (Harrison Ford) falls in love with married Red Cross nurse Margaret Sellinger (Lesley-Anne Down). His obsession leads him to withdraw from a dangerous mission. When his replacement is killed, his conscience makes him volunteer for a top secret assignment in occupied France. Patsy Kensit, Alec McCowen, Richard Masur, Christopher Plummer, Michael Sacks and Max Wall also appear.
Director: Peter Hyams.

Happy Apple, The — 6 wks

Thames, situation comedy

Keith Waterhouse adapted Jack Pullman's play into this series about three partners in the small advertising agency Murray, Maine and Spender (respectively played by Nicky Henson, Jeremy Child and John Nettleton).

| 1983 | 9.2 | Mon 1 Aug 8:00 p.m. | 6 | 6 wks |

'Lifetime Guarantee'
The partners are thrown into a panic when they have to come up with a brilliant idea – and quickly.
Producer: Michael Mills.

Happy Birthday Coronation Street — 1 wk

Granada, entertainment

| 1990 | 13.1 | Sun 9 Dec 7:15 p.m. | 11 | 1 wk |

Cilla Black hosts celebrations marking thirty years of the soap. The deputy leader of the Labour Party, Roy Hattersley MP, delivers the opening tribute.
Director: Ian Hamilton. **Producer:** Jane MacNaught.

Happy Ever After — 6 wks

ATV, comedy

A series of unconnected comedy dramas with the unifying requirement that each must have a happy ending.

| 1969 | 7.2 | Tue 30 Dec 9:00 p.m. | 5 | 3 wks |

'The Woman at the Door' by Ian Stuart Black.
Sue Malone (Jennifer Hilary) is bored with her doctor husband (James Kerry) and is on the verge of having an affair with her boss (Keith Barron) when the death of an unknown woman presents her with a painful dilemma.
Designer: Anthony Waller. **Director:** Paul Bernard. **Producer:** John Cooper.

| 1970 | 6.6 | Tue 6 Jan 9:00 p.m. | 15 | 3 wks |

'What's the Matter Darling, Can't You Sleep?' by Alfred Shaughnessy.
Newlyweds Brian and Sarah Grant (John Alkin and Kika Markham) are already under financial strain. What they have comes mostly from her modelling assignments. Brian is a trained architect finding it hard to get on the first rung of the job ladder. He is irritated by his dependence on Sarah. When she lands a job in a TV commercial which requires her to be in bed with the glamorous George Harcourt (Michael Coles), the relationship is strained to its limit. Graham Crowden and Edward Fox have minor roles.
Designer: Trevor Paterson. **Director:** John Nelson Burton. **Producer:** John Cooper.

Happy Ever After — 29 wks

BBC, situation comedy

This series created by John Chapman and Eric Merriman provided a domestic situation for the perennial pairing of Terry Scott and June Whitfield. They played the Fletchers, a suburban couple whose children had flown, leaving them to confront each other without diversion.
Producer: Peter Whitmore.

| 1976 | 7.6 | Thu 14 Oct 7:40 p.m. | 8 | 20 wks |

As Terry and June plan their annual holiday, Terry turns his thoughts to the world's best-known flesh pots.
Writers: John Chapman and Eric Merriman.

| 1977 | 14.6 | Fri 23 Dec 7:55 p.m. | 8 | 7 wks |

June's invitation to her parents for Christmas causes animosity.
Writers: Christopher Bond and Eric Merriman.

| 1979 | 12.8 | Thu 17 May 8:00 p.m. | 6 | 2 wks |

June gets a job and Terry sets about changing his image. (Repeat.)
Writer: Jon Watkins. **Director:** Ray Butt.

Happy Valley, The — 2 wks

Presented by BBC, film

| 1987 | 9.0 | Sun 6 Sep 9:05 p.m. | 20 | 1 wk |

David Reid wrote this film made for television and set it in Kenya in the 1940s. The lives and scandals of British expatriates are observed through the eyes of teenager Juanita Carberry (Holly Aird). Denholm Elliott also stars with Michael Byrne, Cathryn Harrison, Richard Heffer, Amanda Hillwood, Kathryn Pogson and Peter Sands.
Director: Ross Devenish.

| 1989 | 9.0 | Fri 24 Mar 8:15 p.m. | 17 | 1 wk |

Repeat showing of the above film.

Hard to Get — 1 wk

Granada, drama

| 1983 | 6.5 | Tue 19 Jul 9:00 p.m. | 19 | 1 wk |

The second part of Marcella Evaristi's play about sexual politics in Glasgow between 1972 and 1982. Starring David Bannerman, Maureen Beattie, Fay Howard and Derek Thompson.
Designer: Taff Batley. **Director:** Brian Mills. **Producer:** Howard Baker.

Hardcastle and McCormick — 2 wks

USA presented by ITV, drama

Retired judge Hardcastle (Brian Keith) set out to trap criminals who had escaped justice on technicalities. Former prisoner Skid McCormick (Daniel Hugh-Kelly) was paroled to his custody. His prototype supercar helped Hardcastle in his quest.
Director: Roger Young.

| 1983 | 12.7 | Sun 16 Oct 8:45 p.m. | 6 | 2 wks |

Harding Trail, The — 3 wks

BBC, documentary

Comedian and musician Mike Harding embarked on a 1500-mile bicycle ride throughout the Eastern United States.

| 1984 | 8.1 | Mon 16 Jul 8:30 p.m. | 14 | 3 wks |

'Pennsylvania – The Road to Paradise'
In this first programme Harding arrives in Philadelphia, the 'City of Brotherly Love'. He then heads for the Shenandoah River where he must swap pedals for paddles.
Camera: David Jackson. **Sound:** Dennis Cartwright. **Producer:** Cyril Gates.

Harem   1 wk

USA presented by ITV, drama

In this two-part story by Karol Ann Hoeffner, an American heiress en route to Damascus was abducted and taken to a Sultan's harem in Constantinople.

| 1988 | 13.2 | Sun 10 Jan 8:15 p.m. | 10 | 1 wk |

The Sultan's wife Kadin (Ava Gardner) makes life unpleasant for the American arrival Jessica (Nancy Travis). As a result of Kadin's plot, the Sultan (Omar Sharif) sentences Jessica to death. Cherie Lunghi, Art Malik and Sarah Miles also star.

Hark at Barker   6 wks

LWT, comedy

This series starred Ronnie Barker in many guises. The highly opinionated Lord Rustless lived in a stately pile with an uncontrollable staff played by Mary Baxter, Moira Foot, Frank Gatliff, David Jason and Josephine Tewson.

| 1970 | 5.4 | Fri 10 Jul 8:20 p.m. | 14 | 6 wks |

'Rustless on Music'
Ronnie Barker appears as Lord Rustless and also as an onion seller, a psychiatric patient and Abdul the Filthy, among others.
Writers: Peter Caulfield, Bernard McKenna and Gerald Wiley. **Director:** Maurice Murphy. **Producer:** Humphrey Barclay.

Harlech Opening Night   1 wk

HTV, entertainment

| 1968 | 8.1 | Mon 20 May 9:00 p.m. | 1 | 1 wk |

The stars turn out for the opening night of Harlech Television. They include Stanley Baker, Richard Burton, Joan Diener, Osian Ellis, Geraint Evans, Bruce Forsyth, Aleta Morrison, Harry Secombe, Elizabeth Taylor, Julie Wilson and the Bristol Concert Orchestra conducted by Stanley Black.
Choreographer: Irving Davies. **Producer:** Milo Lewis.

Harlem Globetrotters, The   1 wk

BBC, sport

| 1975 | 7.5 | Sat 24 May 5:50 p.m. | 6 | 1 wk |

From the Empire Pool, Wembley, the world's most famous basketball team plays The New York Nationals. In addition, the Globetrotters show off their skills against Bob Wilson's line-up of top goalkeepers including Ray Clemence (Liverpool), Mervyn Day (West Ham), Jim Cumbes (Aston Villa) and Dickie Guy (Wimbledon). Commentary by Alan Weeks.
Television presentation: Douglas Hespe.

Harlem Heatwave   1 wk

AR, music

| 1960 | 5.6 | Thu 19 May 9:35 p.m. | 6 | 1 wk |

A floorshow from the Pigalle night club, London, with Jack Hammer, Mauri Leighton, Meeres and La-Raine, Norma Miller and her Jazzmen, the Woolf Phillips orchestra and the Southlanders.
Choreographer: Lee Sherman. **Director:** Eric Croall.

Harley Street   1 wk

ATV, documentary

| 1965 | 5.3 | Wed 23 Jun 9:40 p.m. | 16 | 1 wk |

A look at the postwar changes in the famous street of medicine, questioning how long it can maintain its prestige and influence over medical practice. Written and narrated by Paul Ferris.
Producer: Colin Clark.

Elizabeth Taylor and Richard Burton were among the stars who turned out for **Harlech Opening Night**.

Harpers West One — 25 wks

ATV, drama

This series of one-hour stories devised by Geoffrey Bellman and John Whitney concerned the staff and customers of a fictitious department store. The principal characters included Edward Cruickshank (Graham Crowden), Mike Gilmore (Tristram Jellineck), Harriett Carr (Jan Holden), Oliver Backhouse (Philip Latham), Philip Nash (Bernard Horsfall), Charlie Pugh (Tenniel Evans) and Frances Peters (Jayne Muir).

| 1961 | 6.6 | Mon 10 Jul 9:35 p.m. | 1 | 13 wks |

Public relations officer Mike Gilmore is a sympathetic man but gets little sympathy in return from his colleagues when a customer makes a serious complaint.
Writer: Owen Holder. **Director:** Philip Dale. **Producer:** Hugh Rennie.

| 1962 | 5.6 | Mon 12 Nov 8:00 p.m. | 16 | 8 wks |

Oliver meets a girl who badly needs a job. When she joins Harpers, tongues begin to wag.
Writers: Geoffrey Bellman and John Whitney. **Director:** Royston Morley. **Producer:** Rex Firkin.

| 1963 | 6.1 | Mon 28 Jan 8:00 p.m. | 11 | 4 wks |

George Pascoe (Patrick McAlinney), Harpers' store detective, finds a young woman apparently shoplifting. He takes her to the manager's office where a series of awkward problems manifest themselves.
Writer: Tudor Gates. **Director:** Phil Brown. **Producer:** Royston Morley.

Harry 'O' — 3 wks

USA presented by BBC, drama

This series starred David Janssen as Harry Orwell, a former policeman who lived in a shack in San Diego. He had been forced to retire after being shot in the back and became a private eye.
Producer: Jerry Thorpe.

| 1974 | 6.4 | Fri 18 Oct 9:25 p.m. | 20 | 1 wk |

'The Admiral's Lady'
It is assumed that the disappearance of a beautiful lady means she has run off with her lover. Her husband (Leif Erickson) assumes otherwise and hires Harry 'O' to find her.

| 1976 | 6.7 | Thu 15 Apr 9:25 p.m. | 12 | 2 wks |

'Forty Reasons to Kill'
In this feature-length episode, Harry investigates the murder of one of his old friends and finds himself caught up in a network of corruption. With guest stars Broderick Crawford, Joanna Pettet, Craig Stevens and Ned Romero.

Harry Secombe Show, The — 2 wks

ATV, entertainment

Swansea-born comedian and singer Secombe made his name on radio, most notably from 1951 when CRAZY PEOPLE with Peter Sellers, Michael Bentine and Spike Milligan became THE GOON SHOW. The tenor became one of Britain's most-loved entertainers and was knighted in 1981.

| 1963 | 6.8 | Sun 7 Apr 8:25 p.m. | 8 | 2 wks |

With guests Terence Alexander, Jill Day, Donald Houston, Janette Scott and David Toguri.
Writers: Sid Green and Dick Hills. **Producer:** Francis Essex.

Harry Secombe Show, The — 11 wks

BBC, entertainment

Producer (1969–72): Terry Hughes.

| 1969 | 5.2 | Sat 5 Apr 7:30 p.m. | 17 | 1 wk |

Guests: Myrna Rose and Frank and Peggy Spencer's Formation Team. Harry also presents a special selection from the musical OLIVER with Lionel Bart, Ron Moody, Peggy Mount, Shani Wallis and Jack Wild. With the Peter Knight orchestra.

| 1970 | 6.1 | Sat 17 Oct 8:15 p.m. | 8 | 2 wks |

Guests: Roy Castle, Mary Hopkin and Julian Orchard, with the Peter Knight orchestra.
Director: James Moir.

| 1971 | 6.2 | Sat 11 Sep 8:30 p.m. | 9 | 1 wk |

Guests: the Roy Budd Trio, Anne Evans, Julian Orchard and Nicol Williamson with the Peter Knight orchestra.

| 1972 | 6.6 | Sat 18 Nov 7:35 p.m. | 16 | 4 wks |

Guests: Gladys Knight and the Pips, Esther Ofarim, Julian Orchard, James Pegler and the Band of the Welsh Guards.

| 1973 | 6.7 | Sat 1 Dec 7:15 p.m. | 16 | 3 wks |

Guests: Dana, Julian Orchard and the Band of the Welsh Guards.
Producer: Colin Charman.

Harry Worth — 4 wks

BBC, situation comedy

This series of comedies written by Ronnie Taylor starred Harry Worth as himself. The dithering comedian began his performing career as a ventriloquist before establishing the character which featured in more than 100 episodes of HERE'S HARRY. He died on 20 July 1989.

| 1967 | 5.4 | Sat 15 Apr 9:30 p.m. | 19 | 2 wks |

'To Be Called For'
The number and variety of excuses that Harry comes up with for his bungling of even the simplest of tasks leaves everyone else speechless. Guests: Edwin Apps and Bryan Pringle. (Repeat.)
Producer: Graeme Muir.

| 1968 | 5.4 | Mon 21 Oct 7:30 p.m. | 20 | 1 wk |

'Private Pimpernel'
Set in 1944. Harry spreads confusion throughout the armed forces at home and abroad. Guests: George Baker, James Beck and John Le Mesurier.
Producer: Duncan Wood.

| 1969 | 5.1 | Wed 28 May 8:20 p.m. | 15 | 1 wk |

Repeat showing of 'Private Pimpernel'.

....

| Harry's Game | | 1 wk |

YTV, drama

A three-part thriller by Gerald Seymour. Ray Lonnen starred as Harry Brown, who was called upon by the British Government to take part in a highly secret manhunt.

| 1982 | 10.6 | Wed 27 Oct 9:00 p.m. | 20 | 1 wk |

Part Three
In this final episode the fears of everyday life in Belfast take their toll.
Designer: Mike Long. **Director:** Lawrence Gordon Clark. **Producer:** Keith Richardson. **Executive Producer:** David Cunliffe.

....

| Hart of the Yard | | 5 wks |

USA presented by ITV, situation comedy

Ron Moody starred as Detective Inspector Hart, an old-fashioned sleuth from Scotland Yard on temporary duty with the San Francisco Police.

| 1980 | 15.2 | Wed 8 Oct 7:00 p.m. | 9 | 5 wks |

'Daddy's Day'
Hart arrives in San Francisco.

....

| Hart to Hart | | 48 wks |

USA presented by ITV, drama

This series starred Robert Wagner as jet set millionaire Jonathan Hart and Stefanie Powers as his journalist wife Jennifer. Lionel Stander was the chauffeur Max.
Executive Producer: Aaron Spelling.

| 1980 | 15.3 | Sun 3 Feb 9:15 p.m. | 2 | 12 wks |

'Hit Jennifer Hart'
Jonathan discovers corruption in America's docklands. He uncovers a major scandal. Then Jennifer has a series of nearly fatal accidents.

| 1981 | 17.4 | Sun 29 Mar 7:45 p.m. | 1 | 13 wks |

'Homemade Murder'
The Harts are held hostage in their own home.

| 1982 | 16.2 | Sun 2 May 7:45 p.m. | 1 | 9 wks |

'Harts and Palms'
The Harts arrive in Hawaii on holiday. Almost immediately their car is nearly forced over a cliff and they are embroiled in a murder plot.

| 1983 | 11.9 | Sun 6 Feb 8:15 p.m. | 13 | 14 wks |

'Rich and Hartless'
Daring criminals hold the Harts hostage for a huge ransom.

....

| Haunted | | 2 wks |

Granada, drama

This series of dramas had a 'haunted' theme.
Producer: Derek Granger.

| 1974 | 7.1 | Mon 30 Dec 9:00 p.m. | 9 | 1 wk |

'Poor Girl' by Elizabeth Taylor, adapted by Robin Chapman. Florence Chasty (Lynne Miller) takes up an appointment as governess to a nine-year-old boy. It is 1907, and Florence enters a house possessed of strange and terrifying forces.
Designer: Colin Grimes. **Director:** Michael Apted.

| 1975 | 7.6 | Thu 11 Dec 9:00 p.m. | 9 | 1 wk |

'The Ferryman' by Kingsley Amis, adapted for television by Julian Bond.
Sheridan Owen (Jeremy Brett) has launched his first best-selling novel. Exhausted, he escapes for a weekend with his wife, Alex (Natasha Parry). The pub where they are staying takes on an increasingly disturbing resemblance to the setting of his novel.
Designer: Colin Rees. **Director:** John Irvin.

....

| Haunting Passion, The | | 1 wk |

Presented by ITV, film

| 1988 | 9.3 | Tue 21 Jun 9:15 p.m. | 11 | 1 wk |

Jane Seymour stars as Julie Evans, who sketches a portrait of a man she has never seen and then meets him.
Director: John Kortz.

Robert Wagner embraces Stefanie Powers who restrains Freeway the dog while Lionel Stander stands by in **Hart to Hart**.

Have a Harry Birthday | 1 wk

YTV, entertainment

1978 | **13.5** | **Wed 11 Oct 8:00 p.m.** | **14** | **1 wk**

Harry Secombe stars in a show of song, dance and comedy about birthdays, with Pat Coombs, Lorna Dallas, Robert Dorning, Fred Evans and the Peter Knight orchestra.
Producer: *Vernon Lawrence.*

Have I Got You . . . Where You Want Me? | 4 wks

Granada, situation comedy

This series by Philip Harland and Paul Harris starred Ian Lavender as dentist Tom and Kim Braden as teacher Valerie. They had shared love and life for ten years, always on the brink of marriage.

1981 | **12.1** | **Wed 17 Jun 8:30 p.m.** | **12** | **4 wks**

'The Exchange'
Valerie has a chance to go to Italy as an exchange teacher. Tom decides to sabotage the idea from the outset.
Director: *Malcolm Taylor.* **Producer:** *Brian Armstrong.*

Having a Lovely Time | 1 wk

BBC, documentary

In this series of six programmes well-known personalities observed the British enjoying their leisure.

1972 | **4.7** | **Thu 31 Aug 8:30 p.m.** | **17** | **1 wk**

'At the Club'
Barry Took spends time at a working men's club in Holmfirth in the West Riding of Yorkshire.
Director: *Michael Rabiger.* **Producer:** *Mike Wooller.*

Hawk the Slayer | 1 wk

Presented by ITV, film

1985 | **13.1** | **Mon 6 May 8:30 p.m.** | **3** | **1 wk**

The story of two brothers, Hawk (John Terry), who is destined for greatness, and Voltan (Jack Palance), the older brother, who is cruel and perverted.
Director: *Terry Marcel.*

Hayley in Disneyland | 1 wk

BBC, entertainment

1962 | **4.6** | **Tue 25 Dec 5:45 p.m.** | **20** | **1 wk**

Christmas special in which Hayley Mills meets Walt Disney in Hollywood and introduces some of her favourite Disney characters.
Producer: *Richard Evans.*

Hazell | 11 wks

Thames, drama

This series was created by former footballer Terry Venables and Gordon Williams and starred Nicholas Ball as James Hazell, ex-policeman turned private detective. He was a reformed alcoholic.

1978 | **17.2** | **Mon 16 Jan 9:00 p.m.** | **5** | **3 wks**

'Hazell Plays Solomon' by Gordon Williams.
Hazell is asked to make some enquiries about a girl who lives with her parents in the East End. Guest stars: Jane Asher, James Faulkner, Roddy McMillan and Barbara Young.
Director: *Jim Goddard.* **Producer:** *June Roberts.*

1979 | **12.6** | **Thu 19 Apr 9:10 p.m.** | **7** | **7 wks**

'Hazell and the Deptford Virgin' by Terry Venables and Gordon Williams.
Hazell disarms a crook but instantly finds three others to fight.
Director: *Mike Vardy.* **Producer:** *Tim Aspinall.*

1980 | **15.9** | **Wed 30 Jan 9:00 p.m.** | **10** | **1 wk**

'Hazell and the Public Enemy' by Murray Smith.
Hazell almost ends up a victim when he tries to extract a confession of murder from a gangster.
Director: *Marek Kanievska.* **Producer:** *Tim Aspinall.*

Hazzard of Hearts, A | 1 wk

Presented by BBC, film

1991 | **9.3** | **Sun 18 Aug 8:35 p.m.** | **14** | **1 wk**

This adaptation of Barbara Cartland's Regency romance stars Helena Bonham Carter as a petulant young virgin. Her father loses her to a lecherous nobleman in a game of cards. Also starring Eileen Atkins, Edward Fox, Fiona Fullerton, Stewart Granger, Anna Massey, Christopher Plummer and Diana Rigg.
Director: *John Hough.*

Headliners | 1 wk

Thames, game show

This game required knowledge of news and was hosted by Derek Jameson, himself once a Fleet Street editor. Different guests joined resident team captains Nigel Dempster and Philippa Kennedy.

| 1988 | 9.8 | Wed 30 Mar 7:00 p.m. | 20 | 1 wk |

Guests: Glenys Kinnock, Koo Stark, Dickie Davies and Jason Connery. **Director:** Terry Yarwood. **Producer:** Brian Klein.

Heart of Show Business, The | 1 wk |

ATV, entertainment

| 1967 | 6.5 | Sun 26 Mar 7:55 p.m. | 8 | 1 wk |

Special Easter Day charity performance from Elstree studios for the benefit of victims of the Aberfan disaster of 21 October 1966, in which 116 children were killed when a coal tip collapsed. Organizers: Stanley Baker, Bernard Delfont, Jimmy Grafton, Donald Houston, Eddie Jarrett and Harry Secombe. Other artists appearing include Lucette Aldous, Shirley Bassey, Georgia Brown, Richard Burton, Sean Connery, Sammy Davis Jr., Clifford Evans, Jessie Evans, John Gilpin, Glyn Houston, Megs Jenkins, Glynis Johns, Tom Jones, Ronald Lewis, Lulu, Millicent Martin, Spike Milligan, Priscilla Morgan, Patricia Mort, Joan Newell, Glyn Owen, the Pendyrus Male Voice Choir, Peter Sellers, Victor Spinetti, Tommy Steele, Elizabeth Taylor, Frankie Vaughan, Emlyn Williams, the Paddy Stone dancers and the Jack Parnell orchestra.
Directors: Jon Scoffield, Alan Tarrant and Dennis Vance. **Producer:** Alan Tarrant. **Executive Producer:** Bill Ward.

Heartland | 1 wk |

ATV, drama

This series about love affairs followed a chain of changing partners, with one central character held over, to the following week.

| 1979 | 9.2 | Fri 3 Aug 9:00 p.m. | 18 | 1 wk |

'Repent at Leisure' by David Cook.
Policeman Geoff Dryden (Cornelius Garrett) is recovering from an unhappy affair. He is transferred to a town in the Black Country where he meets Alice Pearson (Judy Parfitt).
Designer: Tom Carter. **Director:** Gareth Davies. **Producer:** Nicholas Palmer.

Heaven Can Wait | 2 wks |

Presented by ITV, film

| 1983 | 12.2 | Mon 3 Jan 8:00 p.m. | 15 | 1 wk |

Warren Beatty, Julie Christie and James Mason star in the story of a Los Angeles quarterback who arrives in Heaven prematurely after an accident. He returns to Earth in a body belonging to someone else.
Directors: Warren Beatty and Buck Henry.

| 1990 | 10.9 | Sun 15 Jul 8:35 p.m. | 7 | 1 wk |

Repeat showing of the above film.

Hedda Gabler | 1 wk |

BBC with Talent Associates-Paramount and CBS, drama

| 1962 | 4.8 | Fri 28 Dec 9:25 p.m. | 17 | 1 wk |

Henrik Ibsen's classic play adapted for television by Phil Reisman from the translation by Eva Le Galliene. Starring Ingrid Bergman, Trevor Howard, Michael Redgrave and Ralph Richardson, with Dilys Hamlett, Ursula Jeans and Beatrice Varley.
Designer: Fanny Taylor. **Director:** Alex Segal. **Producers:** Norman Rutherford, Lars Schmidt and David Susskind.

Heidi | 4 wks |

BBC, drama

Johanna Spyri's story, translated by Marion Edwards and dramatized in six parts by Martin Worth.

| 1974 | 7.6 | Sun 24 Nov 5:35 p.m. | 8 | 4 wks |

The final episode, in which Heidi (Emma Blake) is happily reunited with her grandfather (Hans Meyer). Flora Robson, Kathleen Byron and Nicholas Lyndhurst also star.
Designer: David Spode. **Director:** June Wyndham-Davies. **Producer:** John McRae.

Helen – A Woman of Today | 12 wks |

LWT, drama

This twelve-part series charted the difficulties of life experienced by Helen and Frank Tulley (Alison Fiske and Martin Shaw) and their two children.

| 1973 | 7.3 | Fri 7 Dec 9:00 p.m. | 5 | 12 wks |

'Stephen' by Alexander Baron.
Helen and Frank are separated. Frank is lonely after girlfriend Carole (Sharon Duce) has walked out. He spies on Helen, who has found emotional comfort in Stephen (Peter Blythe), a colleague at work. The children are fed up with the situation and want their dad back.
Designers: Frank Nerini and Michael Yates. **Director:** Christopher Hodson. **Producer:** Richard Bates.

Hello Cheeky | 1 wk |

YTV, comedy

This was a BBC radio series of comedy sketches transferred to ITV. It was written and performed by Barry Cryer, John Junkin and Tim Brooke-Taylor with the Denis King Trio.

| 1976 | 6.7 | Mon 19 Jan 8:00 p.m. | 20 | 1 wk |

Producer: Len Lurcuck. **Executive Producer:** Duncan Wood.

Hello, Hello Dolly
`1 wk`

AR, music

| 1965 | 8.0 | Wed 1 Dec 9:10 p.m. | 6 | 1 wk |

HELLO DOLLY opens tomorrow at the Theatre Royal, Drury Lane. The songs from the much-heralded musical are previewed by Arlene Dorgan, David Kernan and Take Five.
Producer: Steve Minchin.

Hell's Bells
`1 wk`

BBC, situation comedy

Derek Nimmo starred as Dean Selwyn Makepeace in this series by Jan Butlin. Robert Stephens played Bishop Godfrey Hethercote, Susan Jameson was Emma Hethercote and Phyllida Law was Edith Makepeace.

| 1986 | 8.2 | Mon 23 Jun 8:30 p.m. | 14 | 1 wk |

'Back Page Story'
A homeless couple hear the radical views of the Bishop and, thus encouraged, pitch their tent in the south transept of the cathedral. They want their plight to be publicized. The Dean has other ideas.
Producer: Mike Stephens.

Henderson Hospital
`1 wk`

Granada, documentary

| 1965 | 6.1 | Tue 2 Feb 10:05 p.m. | 14 | 1 wk |

A follow-up to Granada's series INSIDE, examining the work at the hospital which provides an alternative to imprisonment for offenders in need of medical help. Narrated by Bill Grundy.
Producers: Elaine Grand and Mike Grigsby.

Her Majesty's Pleasure
`5 wks`

Granada, situation comedy

This series was set in a prison where the warders felt as trapped as the convicts. The stars were Ken Jones as Prison Officer Mills, John Sharp as Officer Clissit, John Nettleton as Pongo Little, John Normington as Mushy Williams, Tommy Mann as Grizzly Bear Ryan and Neville Smith as Arthur.

| 1969 | 7.0 | Thu 27 Feb 9:00 p.m. | 6 | 5 wks |

'The Bad Seed'
Officer Mills has a skeleton in the cupboard and it turns up in prison.
Writer: Leslie Duxbury. **Director:** June Howson. **Producer:** Peter Eckersley.

Herb Alpert Show, The
`1 wk`

ATV, music

| 1969 | 5.5 | Wed 24 Dec 10:35 p.m. | 16 | 1 wk |

The American trumpet star Herb Alpert and his band the Tijuana Brass in concert from London's Royal Festival Hall.
Producer: Albert Locke. **Executive Producer:** Bill Ward.

Here Come the Girls
`9 wks`

AR, music

Alan Freeman talked to female recording stars of the day.

| 1963 | 6.3 | Wed 23 Oct 9:10 p.m. | 9 | 9 wks |

With Kathy Kirby.
Director: Robert Fleming.

Here Come the Pop Stars
`1 wk`

AR, music

In this series pop singers mimed to their current records.

| 1965 | 7.6 | Wed 8 Dec 9:10 p.m. | 7 | 1 wk |

With Boz, Wilson Pickett, the Small Faces and the Walker Brothers.
Director: Rollo Gamble.

Here Comes Kathy
`1 wk`

ATV, music

| 1967 | 6.5 | Wed 1 Mar 9:40 p.m. | 9 | 1 wk |

Kathy Kirby stars in her own special with guests Tommy Bruce, Clinton Ford and Daniel Remy with the Malcolm Goddard dancers, the Wilfrid Johns singers and the Jack Parnell orchestra.
Producer: Jon Scoffield.

Here Comes Summer
`1 wk`

Granada, entertainment

| 1980 | 12.9 | Wed 25 Jun 8:00 p.m. | 3 | 1 wk |

A mixture of circus and variety with Larry Hagman, Mike Reid, Judy Allen, Charlie Cairoli Jr., the Halfwits, Richard and Lara Jarmain, Tony Monopoly, Marion Montgomery, Showaddywaddy, Stromboli, the Pamela Devis dancers and Jeff Richer's First Edition.
Director: David Liddiment. **Producer:** John Hamp.

Here Comes That Girl | 2 wks

AR, music

| 1966 | 6.6 | Wed 11 May 9:10 p.m. | 7 | 2 wks |

Dodie West sings her favourite country and western songs.
Producer: John P. Hamilton.

....

Here's Harry | 18 wks

BBC, situation comedy

Harry Worth played the mild-mannered twentieth-century knight errant with a trilby for a helmet, glasses for a visor, briefcase for a shield and umbrella for a lance. Oblivious to danger, Harry sallied forth from his semi-detached castle to do battle with the giants and dragons of his time – bureaucracy, red tape and officialdom.
Writers included Vince Powell and Frank Roscoe (1961–64). **Producer** (1961–64): John Ammonds.

| 1961 | 6.7 | Tue 21 Nov 8:00 p.m. | 5 | 5 wks |

'The Plant'
Harry is bitten by the gardening bug, much to the chagrin of the horticultural experts. Guests: Sandra Chalmers, Geoffrey Hibbert and Leonard Williams.
Co-writer: Harry Driver.

| 1962 | 5.8 | Mon 3 Dec 8:00 p.m. | 11 | 7 wks |

'The Handyman'
If there's one thing that Harry isn't, it's a handyman. When he thinks otherwise, then nothing is safe! Guests: Joe Gladwin, Sam Kydd and William Mervyn. (Repeat.)

| 1963 | 7.8 | Fri 22 Nov 7:45 p.m. | 6 | 2 wks |

'The Musician'
The Honorary President of the Woodbridge Orchestra is appalled when Harry asks to join. Guest: Max Jaffa.

| 1964 | 4.9 | Tue 13 Oct 8:00 p.m. | 18 | 1 wk |

'The Golfer'
There is much confusion among the members of the Woodbridge Golf Club when Harry applies to join. Guests: Felix Felton, Jack Smethurst, Geoffrey Sumner and Frank Williams.

| 1966 | 4.8 | Sat 16 Jul 9:20 p.m. | 16 | 3 wks |

'The Dinner Party'
Harry invites some friends to his house for dinner. The result is a shambles. Guests: Sydney Dobson, Dorothy Frere, Ruth Kettlewell, Frank Thornton, Austin Trevor and Valerie Ward. (Repeat.)
Writer: Ronnie Taylor. **Producer:** John Street.

Heroes, The | 2 wks

TVS, drama

This three-part adaptation by Peter Yeldham of the book by Ronald McKie told the true story of Operation Jaywick. This was the plan of Captain Ivan Lyon (Paul Rhys) to raid the Japanese fleet during the Second World War. John Bach, Jason Donovan, John Hargreaves and Bill Kerr also starred.

| 1989 | 15.1 | Sun 2 Apr 9:00 p.m. | 7 | 2 wks |

Episode One
Sumatran villagers flee in panic from Japanese bombing raids. Captain Lyon draws up plans to prevent further raids.
Director: Donald Crombie. **Producer:** Anthony Buckley. **Executive Producers:** Graham Benson and Valery Hardy.

....

Heroes – The Movie | 1 wk

Presented by ITV, film

| 1991 | 8.8 | Fri 28 Jun 8:00 p.m. | 17 | 1 wk |

An abridged TV version of the three-part mini-series THE HEROES in which Captain Ivan Lyon (Paul Rhys) leads 14 starry-eyed young soldiers on a World War Two suicide mission to raid the Japanese fleet in Singapore. Also starring John Bach, Jason Donovan, John Hargreaves and Bill Kerr.
Director: Donald Crombie.

....

Heroes II – The Return | 1 wk

TVS, drama

| 1991 | 11.8 | Sun 15 Dec 7:15 p.m. | 20 | 1 wk |

A two-part sequel to the mini-series THE HEROES tells of Operation Rimau, a second daring raid on the Japanese-occupied Singapore harbour by British and Australian forces during the Second World War. Craig McLachlan and Nathaniel Parker star.
Director: Donald Crombie. **Producer:** Anthony Buckley.

....

Heroes of Telemark, The | 1 wk

Presented by BBC, film

| 1971 | 5.8 | Mon 30 Aug 8:00 p.m. | 7 | 1 wk |

Bank Holiday screening of this wartime film set in occupied Norway in 1942. There is a race against time to keep atomic power from the Germans. Starring Kirk Douglas, Richard Harris, Ulla Jacobsson and Michael Redgrave.
Director: Anthony Mann.

H

Hey Brian! `4 wks`

YTV, entertainment

This series starred comedian Brian Marshall with regular assistance from Gemma Craven and Stu Francis.

1973 5.9 Tue 19 Jun 6:40 p.m. 10 `4 wks`

Guest: Lynsey de Paul.
Director: Roger Cheveley. **Executive Producer:** John Duncan.

....

Hidden Truth, The `8 wks`

AR, drama

This series about the work of forensic scientists starred Alexander Knox as Professor Lazard and James Maxwell as Dr Henry Fox.

1964 6.4 Thu 10 Sep 8:00 p.m. 10 `8 wks`

'Sweets to the Sweet' by Hugh Leonard.
Lazard uses shock tactics on a student caught taking drugs.
Director: Peter Moffatt. **Producer:** Stella Richman.

....

Hi-De-Hi `52 wks`

BBC, situation comedy

Jimmy Perry and David Croft wrote this series, set at Maplin's Holiday Camp in an English resort in the late 1950s. It starred Paul Shane as entertainments manager Ted Bovis, Ruth Madoc as senior 'Yellowcoat' Gladys Pugh, Simon Cadell as camp manager Geoffrey Fairbrother, Su Pollard as chalet maid Peggy and Jeffrey Holland as Spike Dixon.
Director (1981–82): John Kilby. **Producer** (1981–87): David Croft.

1981 16.1 Sun 20 Dec 7:15 p.m. 5 `11 wks`

'On With the Motley'
Ted Bovis is booked to do cabaret at a smart golf club dinner.

1982 14.2 Sun 3 Jan 7:15 p.m. 7 `9 wks`

'Sausages or Limelight'
Spike is in love. His future father-in-law wants him to retire from show business and join his butchery empire.

1983 14.0 Sun 23 Jan 7:15 p.m. 6 `3 wks`

'All Change'
Joe Maplin appoints a new supervisor of all Yellowcoats who takes an immediate dislike to Gladys and demotes her.

1984 15.6 Sat 17 Nov 8:00 p.m. 3 `13 wks`

'Opening day'
Joe Maplin has told the Yellowcoats to meet the first of the new season's campers at the station.

1985 14.0 Wed 25 Dec 6:30 p.m. 16 `1 wk`

'The Great Cat Robbery'
An emerald necklace is hidden somewhere on the camp.

1986 14.2 Sat 8 Nov 7:35 p.m. 5 `9 wks`

'Pigs Might Fly'
Squadron Leader Clive Dempster DFC (David Griffin) is engaged to Gladys. Spike is jealous.

1987 14.6 Sat 26 Dec 6:00 p.m. 12 `1 wk`

'Tell it to the Marines'
Ted challenges the Royal Marines to a race over their assault course.

1988 15.0 Sat 30 Jan 6:20 p.m. 7 `5 wks`

'The Wind of Change'
The Maplin's staff discuss their future plans as the season comes to an end.
Producer: Mike Stephens. **Executive Producer:** David Croft.

....

High Adventure `35 wks`

Presented by BBC, film

A series of film presentations with the unifying theme of adventure.

1966 5.9 Sat 10 Dec 7:00 p.m. 14 `4 wks`

'Reap the Wild Wind'
In 1840, salvagers and less legitimate operators recover ships off the treacherous Florida coast for vast profits. Starring John Wayne with Paulette Goddard, Susan Hayward, Raymond Massey, Ray Milland and Robert Preston.
Director: Cecil B. DeMille.

1967 6.1 Sat 14 Jan 6:40 p.m. 13 `6 wks`

'The Lost World'
Based on the story by Sir Arthur Conan Doyle. Jill St John, Fernando Lamas, Claude Rains and Michael Rennie journey to a prehistoric land peopled with giant monsters.
Director: Irwin Allen.

1969 6.7 Sat 29 Nov 8:15 p.m. 8 `7 wks`

'The Bravados'
A man with a mission to avenge the death of his wife goes on the trail of four outlaws. Starring Gregory Peck, Stephen Boyd and Joan Collins.
Director: Henry King.

1970 7.5 Sat 7 Feb 6:50 p.m. 6 `16 wks`

'The Gunfighter'
Gregory Peck plays a notorious gunman who wants to go straight. Unfortunately he becomes the target for every two-bit sharpshooter out to make a reputation for himself.
Director: Henry King.

| 1973 | 6.6 | Sat 10 Feb 7:00 p.m. | 15 | 1 wk |

'Torpedo Bay'

An Italian submarine attempts to run the blockade of the Mediterranean in 1941. It is relentlessly trailed by a British destroyer into the neutral port of Tangier, where the opposing commanders meet face to face. Starring Gabriele Ferzetti, James Mason and Lilli Palmer. **Director:** Charles Friend.

| 1974 | 6.2 | Sat 11 May 7:30 p.m. | 20 | 1 wk |

'Battle Beneath the Earth'

Computers located at Los Alamos reveal that enemy forces are burrowing a network of tunnels beneath the United States. Starring Kerwin Matthews and Viviane Ventura. **Director:** Montgomery Tully.

....

High Road to China   2 wks

Presented by BBC, film

| 1987 | 12.7 | Thu 24 Dec 8:40 p.m. | 20 | 1 wk |

Tom Selleck stars as Patrick O'Malley, veteran of the First World War and a drunk. He is beseeched by the beautiful Eve Tozer (Bess Armstrong) to help find her father, who has been missing for years. He was last seen in Afghanistan's bandit-infested country. **Director:** Brian G. Hutton.

| 1989 | 13.1 | Fri 24 Mar 8:15 p.m. | 7 | 1 wk |

Repeat showing of the above film.

....

High Society   1 wk

Presented by ITV, film

| 1982 | 11.5 | Thu 16 Sep 7:30 p.m. | 5 | 1 wk |

Cole Porter's musical version of **'The Philadelphia Story'** concerns a rich young woman and her various suitors. Stars include Bing Crosby, Celeste Holm, Grace Kelly, Frank Sinatra and Louis Armstrong. **Director:** Charles Walters.

....

High Street, Mayfair   1 wk

ATV, documentary

| 1967 | 6.5 | Wed 5 Apr 9:40 p.m. | 11 | 1 wk |

The story of London's Bond Street, which was swamp land until it was reclaimed by Sir Thomas Bond in 1686 as a business speculation. **Producer:** Ken Ashton.

Hine   7 wks

ATV, drama

This series was created by Wilfred Greatorex. Joe Hine (Barrie Ingham) was a private arms dealer acting for various international powers, often in competition with huge corporations, in a business with a world turnover in excess of five billion dollars.

| 1971 | 7.1 | Wed 7 Apr 8:00 p.m. | 6 | 7 wks |

'Rifles are Dangerous'

Hine is invited to a party in the Middle East but finds he is far from the only arms dealer present. There is his rival Astor Harris (Paul Eddington), for one. He learns that more than rifles are involved. **Director:** Robert Tronson. **Producer:** Wilfred Greatorex.

....

Hippodrome   20 wks

AR, entertainment

This variety series featured luminaries of circus and vaudeville.

| 1960 | 6.4 | Wed 12 Oct 8:30 p.m. | 7 | 2 wks |

Starring Michael Holliday with The Codrelli Clowns, Freya Josse, Lola Dobritch and the Four Goetschis with the Norrie Paramor orchestra. **Producer:** Bill Turner.

| 1961 | 6.2 | Tue 26 Sep 8:00 p.m. | 7 | 2 wks |

Starring Jeannie Carson with Annel and Brask, Aurelian's Marionettes, Berosini's talking chimps, Los Hellyos and the Peter Knight orchestra. **Producer:** Bill Turner.

| 1962 | 5.2 | Wed 18 Apr 8:00 p.m. | 7 | 8 wks |

Starring the Dagenham Girl Pipers, the Clementi Twins, Dorit Oliver, the Iris Roy Trio, the Two Wallabies and the Trotter Brothers. **Producer:** Alan Morris.

| 1966 | 7.9 | Thu 13 Oct 9:40 p.m. | 3 | 8 wks |

Starring Woody Allen with Michael Allport and Jennifer, Dubsky's Football Dogs, Freddie and the Dreamers, Libby Morris and Roberts Brothers' Boxing Kangaroo with the Peter Knight orchestra. **Director:** Peter Croft. **Producer:** John P. Hamilton.

....

Hippodrome Circus, The   1 wk

BBC, circus

| 1966 | 5.3 | Sat 15 Oct 8:15 p.m. | 15 | 1 wk |

Excerpts from the circus in Great Yarmouth with the Cimarros, Teddy Lorent's Sea Lions, the Michaels, the Rivels and Samson and Delilah. **Circus Director:** Roberto Germains. **Television presentation:** Barrie Edgar.

His and Hers   7 wks

YTV, situation comedy

Probably the first role reversal series in the age of sexual liberation.
The stories were built around Rupert Sherwin (Ronald Lewis), a
freelance journalist with little work who stayed home to run the
house, and his wife Kay (Sue Lloyd), a highly successful accountant
in the city. Written by Ken Hoare and Mike Sharland.

| 1970 | 6.5 | Tue 23 Jun 8:25 p.m. | 4 | 6 wks |

The Sherwins' new neighbours, Toby and Janet Burgess (Tim Brooke-
Taylor and Madelein Smith), consider Rupert and Kay distinctly odd.
Director: David Mallet. **Producer:** Graham Evans. **Executive Pro-
ducer:** John Duncan.

| 1972 | 5.6 | Fri 7 Apr 7:25 p.m. | 20 | 1 wk |

Rupert decides his freelance writing requires a secretary. His new
Girl Friday, Moira (Jennie Linden), finds him very attractive.
Producer: Ian Davidson.

Hit, The   1 wk

Central, drama

| 1986 | 11.1 | Mon 7 Apr 9:30 p.m. | 20 | 1 wk |

Terence Stamp plays Willie Parker, a gangster turned supergrass
hiding out in a remote Spanish village. After ten years, Braddock and
Myron (John Hurt and Tim Roth) arrive to take him to Paris to face the
penalty for betrayal.
Director: Stephen Frears. (A Zenith production.)

HMS Defiant   1 wk

Presented by ITV, film

| 1969 | 5.0 | Mon 7 Apr 8:00 p.m. | 20 | 1 wk |

Easter Monday showing of the story of the strife-torn ship as she
sails against Napoleon's fleet. The stars are Tom Bell, Dirk Bogarde,
Alec Guinness and Anthony Quayle.
Director: Lewis Gilbert.

HMS Paradise   6 wks

AR, situation comedy

This series set aboard a ship of the Royal Navy starred Richard
Caldicott as Captain Turvey, Robin Hunter as Lieutenant Pouter,
Ronald Radd as Chief Petty Officer Banyard and Frank Thornton as
Commander Fairweather.

| 1964 | 4.7 | Thu 20 Aug 7:30 p.m. | 17 | 6 wks |

'It'll All Come Out in the Wash' by Maurice Wiltshire.
The men are given some stirring advice: if there's something you've
never seen in your life before – put a guard on it!
Director: Bill Hitchcock. **Producer:** Sid Colin.

Holding the Fort   5 wks

LWT, situation comedy

This series by Laurence Marks and Maurice Gran followed the
married life of Russell and Penny Milburn (Peter Davison and Patricia
Hodge). He left the brewery to work at home and she returned to work
for the army.

| 1981 | 16.5 | Fri 6 Mar 8:30 p.m. | 5 | 5 wks |

'New Blood'
Russell has taken a dislike to the new neighbours.
Producer: Derrick Goodwin.

Holiday   47 wks

BBC, documentary

The programme was introduced between 1980 and 1986 by Cliff
Michelmore.
Producers: included Clem Vallance (1981–82), Colin Strong (1983–
84) and Patricia Houlihan (1987–89 and 1991). **Producer** (1980 and
1986): Tom Savage and **Executive Producer** (1981–84).

| 1980 | 14.6 | Sun 17 Jan 6:00 p.m. | 11 | 3 wks |

Kieran Prendiville goes horse-trekking around Connemara and Frank
Bough motors through France.

| 1981 | 13.6 | Sun 1 Mar 6:05 p.m. | 17 | 4 wks |

Frank and Nesta Bough continue their Italian journey. Cliff Michelmore
reports from Hong Kong and John Carter explores canals in France.

| 1982 | 12.3 | Sun 14 Mar 6:05 p.m. | 11 | 4 wks |

John Carter is in Sardinia, Cliff Michelmore crosses the Atlantic on
board the QE2 and Paul Hughes climbs mountains in North Wales.

| 1983 | 12.8 | Sun 13 Feb 6:05 p.m. | 10 | 11 wks |

Sarah Kennedy travels to Salisbury for a weekend. Tom Savage looks
at the three basic ways of going to the Mediterranean – motorail,
motorway or minor roads. John Carter samples a weekend package
in London.

| 1984 | 10.4 | Sun 4 Mar 5:55 p.m. | 18 | 1 wk |

Anne Gregg goes on a singles' holiday to Amalfi, Tom Savage tries
sailing in Yugoslavia and Cliff Michelmore visits Jersey.

H

1986	11.4	Tue 15 Apr 7:00 p.m.	16	2 wks

Sarah Kennedy is in the Italian lakes and Cliff Michelmore is in Torquay for a gastronomic weekend.

1987	11.9	Tue 3 Feb 7:00 p.m.	17	7 wks

Frank Bough presents a special report from Majorca, with John Carter and Gillian Reynolds.

1988	13.7	Tue 1 Mar 7:00 p.m.	7	13 wks

Bill Buckley goes island hopping in Britain, Anne Gregg holidays in Corfu and guest reporter Robert Kilroy-Silk visits Bermuda.

1989	10.6	Thu 23 Mar 8:00 p.m.	19	1 wk

Desmond Lynam reports from Tenerife, Gillian Reynolds from Salzburg and Phillip Schofield from Jamaica.

1991	15.4	Tue 22 Jan 7:00 p.m.	9	1 wk

Kathy Tayler reports from Barbados, Anne Gregg explores Budapest and Eamonn Holmes lives on a budget in Majorca.

Holiday Circus Gala — 1 wk

BBC, circus

1966	4.5	Mon 29 Aug 7:00 p.m.	28	1 wk

Keith Fordyce introduces Brian Andro, the Barley Twins, Phil Enos, I Faggioni, the Four Willers, Igor Gridneff, the Herculeans and Susie the Elephant. Ringmaster is Ares De Wit.
Television presentation: Mary David.

Holiday Inn — 1 wk

USA presented by BBC, film

1964	5.0	Thu 24 Dec 8:50 p.m.	14	1 wk

This film introduced the song 'White Christmas'. Starring Fred Astaire and Bing Crosby with music and lyrics by Irving Berlin.
Director: Mark Sandrich.

Holiday on Ice — 1 wk

BBC (with Swiss Television Service), entertainment

1976	6.3	Thu 22 Apr 9:25 p.m.	16	1 wk

Brian Matthew introduces the touring ice show from Lausanne.
Television presentation: Don Sayer.

Holiday on the Buses — 3 wks

Presented by ITV, film

1979	13.7	Mon 7 May 8:00 p.m.	9	1 wk

The ON THE BUSES team star as the transport staff of a holiday camp.
Director: Bryan Izzard.

1981	15.7	Sat 10 Jan 7:35 p.m.	7	1 wk

1986	8.3	Fri 15 Aug 7:30 p.m.	19	1 wk

Repeat showings of the above film.

Holiday Town Parade — 13 wks

ABC, entertainment

This series came from various coastal resorts around Britain.

1962	4.7	Sat 22 Sep 6:15 p.m.	14	13 wks

From the Norbreck Hydro Hotel, Blackpool, Keith Fordyce and Peter Lloyd introduce the twenty-four finalists for the Television Bathing Beauty Queen and the Fashion Queen.
Producer: David Southwood.

Holiday with Strings — 2 wks

YTV, comedy

1974	5.3	Mon 26 Aug 8:00 p.m.	16	2 wks

Special Bank Holiday comedy by Ray Galton and Alan Simpson starring Les Dawson as a package holidaymaker with Frank Thornton as the travel agent, Mollie Sugden as the check-in girl, Patricia Hayes as the air hostess and Roy Barraclough as a fellow holidaymaker.
Producer: Duncan Wood.

Holly — 1 wk

Granada, drama

This six-part series by Robin Chapman was about the marriage of Holly (Brigit Forsyth) and David (Paul Moriarty). Holly was a graduate. David worked for a mail-order firm and was taking an extramural degree in an effort to keep up with her. Gordon (William Gaunt), Holly's friend from university, saw them frequently.

1972	4.7	Fri 1 Sep 9:00 p.m.	17	1 wk

Part One
The three are celebrating Holly and David's second wedding anniversary. Outside a fourth person waits and watches. Tom Prentiss (David Burke) threatens their marriage . . . and their lives.
Director: Gareth Davies. **Producer:** Michael Cox.

Hollywood — 1 wk

USA presented by BBC, entertainment

1963 | **5.4** | Wed 2 Oct 9:10 p.m. | **15** | 1 wk

Henry Fonda introduces a cavalcade of Hollywood's fabulous era, beginning with THE JAZZ SINGER and covering the next thirty-five years up to the epics of the contemporary screen (EL CID, LAWRENCE OF ARABIA and MUTINY ON THE BOUNTY).

Hollywood Greats, The — 1 wk

BBC, documentary

Barry Norman wrote and presented profiles of film legends.

1979 | **9.9** | Fri 10 Aug 9:25 p.m. | **20** | 1 wk

'Groucho Marx'
Director: Sue Mallinson. **Producer:** Barry Brown.

Hollywood Premiere — 3 wks

Presented by BBC, film

Series of movies shown on British television for the first time.

1972 | **6.6** | Sat 8 Jan 7:45 p.m. | **13** | 3 wks

'San Francisco International'
Drama at an international airport with Tab Hunter, Van Johnson and Pernell Roberts.
Director: John Llewellyn Moxey.

Hollywood Wives — 1 wk

USA presented by ITV, drama

This three-part adaptation of Jackie Collins' novel was set among the Hollywood acting fraternity. A killer was on the loose. The mini-series starred Candice Bergen, Joanna Cassidy, Mary Crosby, Angie Dickinson, Steve Forrest, Anthony Hopkins, Roddy McDowall, Stefanie Powers, Suzanne Somers and Robert Stack.

1985 | **18.0** | Mon 28 Oct 9:00 p.m.
Tue 29 Oct 9:00 p.m. | **2** | 1 wk

These programmes were listed together in the ratings. Parts Two and Three were both shown on the Tuesday.

Hombre — 1 wk

Presented by ITV, film

1981 | **14.1** | Thu 15 Oct 7:30 p.m. | **10** | 1 wk

Paul Newman stars with Richard Boone, Diane Cilento, Frederic March and Barbara Rush in the story of an attack on a stagecoach carrying twelve thousand dollars in stolen cash.
Director: Martin Ritt.

Home and Away — 113 wks

Australia presented by ITV, soap

This series told the stories of everyday life in the village of Summer Bay.

1989 | **12.9** | Mon–Fri 11–15 Dec 12:30 p.m.
Mon–Fri 11–15 Dec 5:10 p.m. | **12** | 11 wks

These episodes and late afternoon repeats were listed together in the ratings.
Lance and Martin (Peter Vroom and Craig Thomson) are horrified that Celia (Fiona Spence) has told the newspaper about their benevolent fund. Jeff (Alex Parsons) resigns and decides to leave town. Philip (John Morris) learns that his accident has ruined his chances of becoming a surgeon. Futures are about to be decided on the toss of a coin.

1990 | **13.8** | Mon 31 Dec 12:25 p.m.
Mon 31 Dec 6:00 p.m. | **7** | 52 wks

Al Simpson (Terence Donovan) surrenders to the law. Viv (Mouche Phillips) is restored to her home. Lance and Sally (Kate Ritchie) give Celia the fright of her life.

1991 | **14.2** | Mon–Fri 18–22 Nov 1:20 p.m.
Mon–Fri 18–22 Nov 6:00 p.m. | **7** | 50 wks

These episodes were listed together in the ratings.
Marilyn (Emily Symons) has her first day as a babysitter. Haydn (Andrew Hill) has high hopes for the weekend with his parents away. Patricia (Pam Western) is offered a teaching job in the outback.

Home and Beauty — 1 wk

AR, drama

1966 | **5.3** | Tue 4 Oct 9:15 p.m. | **19** | 1 wk

Somerset Maugham's comedy story adapted for television by Stanley Miller in which a marital mix-up sees a woman trying to dispose of two beaux. Starring Nigel Davenport, Maggie Smith and Robert Stephens with Joan Benham, Alison Leggatt, Reginald Marsh and Brian Oulton.
Designer: John Clements. **Director:** Christopher Hodson. **Executive Producer:** Peter Willes.

Home is the Sailor — 1 wk

ITN, news

| 1967 | 6.4 | Sun 28 May 8:30 p.m. | 7 | 1 wk |

News special to witness the return of Francis Chichester and Gypsy Moth IV as they sail into Plymouth Harbour at 8.56 p.m. after their voyage around the world, a trip of 28,500 miles. (On arrival at Greenwich in London Francis Chichester was knighted by the Queen using Sir Francis Drake's sword.)

Home James — 8 wks

Thames, situation comedy

This series by Geoff McQueen starred Jim Davidson as Jim London, chauffeur to millionaire electronics boss Robert Palmer (George Sewell). Harry Towb played Henry Compton.

| 1987 | 10.5 | Wed 15 Jul 8:00 p.m. | 8 | 6 wks |

'Out of Bounds'
Jim sets out to impress Sarah (Vanessa Knox-Mawer) with his chauffeur's livery.
Producer: Anthony Parker.

| 1990 | 8.5 | Mon 9 Jul 8:00 p.m. | 16 | 2 wks |

'Never Say Die'
Robert is on holiday in Switzerland. While he is away, Jim, Henry and Eleanor (Juliette Grassby) take up healthy eating and keep fit.
Producer: Martin Shardlow. **Executive Producer:** Anthony Parker.

Home to Roost — 19 wks

YTV, situation comedy

This series by Eric Chappell starred John Thaw as divorcee Henry Willows. His eldest son Matthew, played by Reece Dinsdale, destroyed his peace and quiet by coming to live with him.
Director (1985) and **Producer** (1986–87, 1990): David Reynolds.
Producer (1985) and **Executive Producer** (1986): Vernon Lawrence.

| 1985 | 12.3 | Fri 3 May 8:30 p.m. | 9 | 6 wks |

'All You Need is Love'
Matthew brings a girlfriend home. The cleaning lady discovers incriminating evidence in his bedroom.

| 1986 | 11.0 | Fri 17 Oct 8:30 p.m. | 14 | 5 wks |

'Julie'
Matthew's sister Julie (Rebecca Lacey) decides to stay, but Henry and Matthew soon find that three's a crowd.

| 1987 | 12.7 | Sat 21 Nov 8:00 p.m. | 12 | 5 wks |

'Crimewatch'
Henry is paranoid about security and joins the neighbourhood watch.

| 1990 | 13.8 | Fri 19 Jan 8:30 p.m. | 15 | 3 wks |

'Leaving'
Matthew is set to leave for college. Henry is far from sad – he's been looking forward to this day.

Hondo — 1 wk

Presented by BBC, film

| 1976 | 6.8 | Tue 26 Dec 7:55 p.m. | 17 | 1 wk |

Hondo Lane (John Wayne) of the US Cavalry warns Angie (Geraldine Page) and her young son to leave their lonely ranch because of an expected Apache uprising. She refuses. Also starring James Arness and Ward Bond.
Director: John Farrow.

Hooper — 2 wks

Presented by BBC, film

| 1983 | 12.0 | Tue 27 Dec 6:25 p.m. | 4 | 1 wk |

Burt Reynolds stars as Hollywood stuntman Sonny Hooper, who faces a challenge to his supremacy from young rival Ski (Jan-Michael Vincent). Sally Field and Brian Keith also star.
Director: Hal Needham.

| 1987 | 11.3 | Mon 28 Dec 5:20 p.m. | 20 | 1 wk |

Repeat showing of the above film.

Hope and Keen — 4 wks

ATV, entertainment

This series was built around cousins Mike Hope and Albie Keen, the respective sons of former variety stars Syd and Max Harrison.
Producer: Jon Scoffield.

| 1965 | 6.8 | Wed 29 Dec 9:10 p.m. | 7 | 2 wks |

Guests: Peter Elliott, Rex Garner and Clovissa Newcombe with the Square Pegs, the Malcolm Clare dancers and the Jack Parnell orchestra.

| 1966 | 6.3 | Wed 9 Mar 9:10 p.m. | 17 | 2 wks |

Guests: Graham Stark with the Malcolm Clare dancers and the Jack Parnell orchestra.

Hopscotch
1 wk

Presented by ITV, film

| 1985 | 12.4 | Wed 11 Dec 8:00 p.m. | 15 | 1 wk |

Former CIA agent Miles Kendig (Walter Matthau), aided by Isobel Von Schmidt (Glenda Jackson), plans an exposé of the secrets and blunders of international espionage.
Director: Ronald Neame.

Horace
1 wk

YTV, drama

This six-part drama by Roy Minton starred Barry Jackson as the simple-minded Horace. He worked in the local joke factory in a rural Yorkshire town and lived with his elderly mother.

| 1982 | 11.4 | Tue 13 Apr 7:00 p.m. | 17 | 1 wk |

'Horace in the Swim'
Horace spends the afternoon showing off his best jacket.
Director: James Cellan Jones. **Producer:** Keith Richardson. **Executive Producer:** David Cunliffe.

Horne A'Plenty
1 wk

Thames, comedy

One of radio's greatest stars, Kenneth Horne presented this weekly live programme of topical sketches and general comedy.

| 1968 | 6.0 | Wed 4 Dec 9:30 p.m. | 19 | 1 wk |

With Graham Stark and Sheila Steafel.
Director: Peter Frazer-Jones. **Producer:** Barry Took.

Horse of the Year Show, The
1 wk

BBC, sport

The premier event in the British showjumping calendar.

| 1979 | 19.0 | Sat 6 Oct 9:00 p.m. | 19 | 1 wk |

Introduced by David Vine from Wembley Arena. Commentators include Raymond Brooks-Ward (who commentated annually from 1956 until his death on 22 August 1992) and Dorian Williams.
Television presentation: Fred Viner and Johnnie Watherston.

Hostage Tower, The
2 wks

Presented by ITV, film

| 1983 | 11.6 | Thur 10 Nov 7:40 p.m. | 14 | 1 wk |

This film adaptation of Alistair MacLean's story concerns a gang of criminals who plan to seize the Eiffel Tower and imprison a wealthy American woman in it. If thirty million dollars is not paid, they will blow up the Tower and its captive. Starring Maud Adams, Keir Dullea, Britt Ekland, Douglas Fairbanks Jr., Peter Fonda, Celia Johnson, Rachel Roberts and Billy Dee Williams.
Director: Claudio Guzman.

| 1987 | 11.1 | Sat 12 Dec 7:30 p.m. | 17 | 1 wk |

Repeat showing of the above film.

Hotel
4 wks

Presented by ITV, film

| 1983 | 12.4 | Thu 24 Nov 7:45 p.m. | 10 | 4 wks |

In this story by Arthur Hailey, Bette Davis stars as Laura Trent, the owner of the St Gregory Hotel in San Francisco.
Director: Jerry London.

House in Nightmare Park, The
1 wk

Presented by ITV, film

| 1978 | 11.3 | Thu 10 Aug 7:45 p.m. | 7 | 1 wk |

A foggy winter night in London in 1907 reduces the audience to practically nil for the Shakespeare recitation by Foster Twelvetrees (Frankie Howerd). Stewart Henderson (Ray Milland) offers him much needed cash to perform at his stately home where he finds strange goings-on. Also starring Hugh Burden, Rosalie Crutchley, Ruth Dunning and Kenneth Griffith.
Director: Peter Sykes.

House on the Beach, The
1 wk

AR, documentary

| 1965 | 6.2 | Wed 13 Oct 9:45 p.m. | 14 | 1 wk |

The house of the title is at Santa Monica, California and is the headquarters of Synanon, a unit established seven years ago by Chuck Dederich for the unorthodox treatment of drug addicts. The addict coming to the house will be met by no sympathy or compassion. Dederich is an antagonistic operator and his treatment is carried out with no medical supervision whatsoever.
Director: Denis Mitchell. **Executive Producer:** Cyril Bennett.

How to be an Alien
1 wk

AR, comedy

This series written and presented by Frank Muir and Denis Norden, suggested the idea that the English were beginning to accept attitudes and habits previously thought of as suitable only for Americans and Continentals.

| 1964 | 6.4 | Wed 12 Feb 9:10 p.m. | 15 | 1 wk |

'Lithuanians and Letts do it'
With the voices of Ronnie Barker, Peter Goodwright, Gordon Rollings and June Whitfield.
Director: Ian Fordyce. **Producer:** Sid Colin.

....

How to Make a Royal Marines Officer   1 wk

BBC, documentary

| 1989 | 9.9 | Wed 28 Jun 9:30 p.m. | 9 | 1 wk |

The story of twenty-nine young men who arrive at the Commando Training Centre for twelve months of the toughest infantry training in the world.
Writer and **Narrator:** Ian Wooldridge. **Producer:** Michael Begg.

....

Howard's Way   49 wks

BBC, soap

This series created by Gerard Glaister and Allan Prior centred around a boat yard. Principal players included Tony Anholt as Charles Frere, Maurice Colbourne as Tom Howard, Nigel Davenport as Sir Edward Frere, Susan Gilmore as Avril Rolfe, Dulcie Gray as Kate Harvey, Jan Harvey as Jan Howard, Lana Morris as Vanessa Andenberg, Kate O'Mara as Laura Wilde, Glyn Owen as Jack Rolfe, and Stephen Yardley as Ken Masters.
Producer: Gerard Glaister.

| 1985 | 13.7 | Sun 17 Nov 7:45 p.m. | 10 | 10 wks |

Lynne (Tracey Childs) has to come to terms with the fact that what Charles Frere says and does are not necessarily the same thing.
Writer: Raymond Thompson. **Director:** Sarah Hellings.

| 1986 | 14.6 | Sun 23 Nov 8:00 p.m. | 5 | 13 wks |

Avril is resented in the boat yard. It is made clear to her that it takes a lifetime to become a good boatbuilder.
Writer: Jeremy Burnham. **Director:** Keith Washington.

| 1987 | 12.4 | Sun 22 Nov 7:45 p.m. | 8 | 11 wks |

George and Polly Urquhart (Ivor Danvers and Patricia Shakesby) face the problems of their marriage.
Writers: Anthony Osborn and Raymond Thompson. **Director:** Frank W. Smith.

| 1988 | 13.3 | Sun 13 Nov 7:45 p.m. | 10 | 12 wks |

There is a tug of love over a child with accusations of mental cruelty and threats of divorce.
Writer: Mervyn Haisman. **Director:** Alister Hallum.

| 1989 | 10.1 | Sun 17 Sep 7:45 p.m. | 15 | 2 wks |

The power struggle continues at Relton Marine, as Avril sets about undermining Charles Frere's designs on the yard.
Writer: Douglas Watkinson. **Director:** Peter Rose.

| 1990 | 10.1 | Sun 2 Sep 7:45 p.m. | 12 | 1 wk |

Ken Masters returns determined to unseat Laura. Vanessa Andenberg and Charles Frere give Jack Rolfe an ultimatum.
Writer: Mervin Haisman. **Director:** Jeremy Summers.

....

Howerd Confessions, The   1 wk

Thames, comedy

This series starred Frankie Howerd purporting to tell his own home truths. Also starred Joan Sims.
Writer: Dick Hills.

| 1976 | 6.1 | Thu 2 Sep 9:30 p.m. | 13 | 1 wk |

Whatever happened to Godfrey the cat? Who was Mrs Umpleby? What was in the chili con carne? Frankie tells the truth, the whole truth and nothing but the truth.
Producer: Michael Mills.

....

Howerd's Hour   1 wk

ABC, comedy

| 1968 | 9.1 | Sun 12 May 8:25 p.m. | 1 | 1 wk |

Frankie Howerd recalls the intrepid adventures of Grandfather Howerd with the Big Ben Banjo Band, Hattie Jacques, Sandie Shaw, Scott Walker, Patrick Wymark and the Irving Davies dancers, the Mike Sammes singers and the ABC Showband.
Writer: Eric Sykes. **Producer:** Keith Beckett.

Eric Sykes wrote **Howerd's Hour**.

How's Your Father | 12 wks

Granada, situation comedy

The Cropper family included Eddie (Michael Robbins), his wife Doreen (Barbara Young), their children Edward (Nicholas Hoye) and Christine (Georgina Moon), and Eddie's father Ted (Arthur English).
Producer: *Bill Podmore.*

| 1974 | 6.4 | Wed 31 Jul 9:30 p.m. | 4 | 6 wks |

'Excess Baggage'
Doreen and Edward have birthdays on consecutive days and Eddie has problems with the presents.
Writer: *John Stevenson.*

| 1975 | 7.6 | Mon 24 Feb 8:00 p.m. | 6 | 6 wks |

'Last Tango in Laburnum Avenue'
Grandfather Ted contemplates marriage but has a dramatic rethink when confronted with the economic implications.
Writer: *John Stevenson.*

How's Your Father | 5 wks

YTV, situation comedy

This series by Pam Valentine and Michael Ashton starred Harry Worth as Harry, a single-parent father of a teenage son and daughter Martin (Giles Watling) and Shirley (Debby Cumming).
Producer: *Graeme Muir.*

| 1979 | 13.1 | Tue 3 Apr 8:30 p.m. | 20 | 1 wk |

'Wedding Bells'
Harry feels his sixteen-year-old daughter Shirley is too young to get engaged.

| 1980 | 10.7 | Fri 18 Jul 7:30 p.m. | 9 | 4 wks |

'The Disco'
Harry is co-opted on to the school PTA.
Director: *Don Clayton.*

Hugh and I | 3 wks

BBC, situation comedy

This series began in 1962 and starred Hugh Lloyd and Terry Scott as two friends. Hugh was somewhat simple while Terry schemed and plotted. They lived in Lobelia Avenue, Tooting. At the end of the fifth series Hugh won five thousand pounds on the premium bonds.

| 1966 | 6.1 | Tue 29 Nov 7:30 p.m. | 11 | 3 wks |

'Troubled Waters' *by John Chapman.*
Terry and Hugh are on their first night at sea on a luxury cruise paid for by Hugh's premium bond win. Also stars Pat Coombs, Reg Dixon and Glenn Melvyn.
Producer: *David Croft.*

Hughie's Full House | 1 wk

Thames, entertainment

| 1976 | 7.6 | Wed 28 Apr 8:00 p.m. | 6 | 1 wk |

Variety show hosted by Hughie Green with Bernard Bresslaw, Pat Coombs, Renée Houston, Beryl Reid, Eva Reuber-Staier, Rita Webb and the Bob Sharples orchestra.
Producer: *Ronald Fouracre.*

Human Jungle, The | 11 wks

ABC, drama

These were stories from the casebook of psychiatrist Dr Roger Corder MD, DPM, played by Herbert Lom. He was a widower and workaholic. The love of his life was teenage daughter Jennifer (Sally Smith). Corder scorned the psychiatrist's couch, preferring to work with his patients in their own surroundings.
Producers: *Leslie Parkyn and Julian Wintle (An Independent Artists production.)*

| 1963 | 6.0 | Sat 15 Jun 10:10 p.m. | 5 | 4 wks |

'The Two-Edged Sword' *by Bill MacIlwraith.*
Two young mothers ask Dr Corder to help them with entirely different problems. One wants to leave her husband but feels compelled to stay, the other resents her newborn baby and wants to have it adopted. With guests Susan Burnet and Pauline Yates.
Director: *Vernon Sewell.*

| 1965 | 6.3 | Sat 20 Feb 10:05 p.m. | 13 | 7 wks |

'Struggle for a Mind' *by John Kruse.*
A young woman in a state of extreme shock attempts to commit suicide on the London Underground. The doctors' attempts to steer her back towards sanity are hampered by the woman's disturbed and hostile family. With guests Joan Collins, Clifford Evans, Derek Godfrey, Kay Walsh and Margaret Whiting.
Director: *Sidney A. Hayes.*

Hunchback of Notre Dame, The | 1 wk

Presented by ITV, film

| 1982 | 10.4 | Wed 11 Aug 8:00 p.m. | 4 | 1 wk |

Anthony Hopkins stars in the title role. A deformed boy was adopted as a baby in fifteenth-century Paris by Dom Claude Frollo (Derek Jacobi), who named him Quasimodo ('the approximation of a human'). In manhood he is the bell ringer at the cathedral, an activity which has left him deaf. Also starring Lesley-Anne Down as Esmeralda, Robert Powell as Phoebus, John Gielgud as Charmolue, David Suchet as Trouillefou and Gerry Sundquist as Pierre.
Director: Michael Tuchner.

Hunter — 6 wks

USA presented by ITV, drama

Fred Dryer starred as Detective Sergeant Rick Hunter, a mobster's son turned cop whose unorthodox methods posed problems for his boss Captain Lester Cain (Michael Cavanaugh). Hunter's partner Detective Sergeant Dee Dee McCall was played by Stepfanie Kramer.
Producers: Chuck Bowman and Stephen J. Cannell.

| 1985 | 12.6 | Sat 27 Apr 8:30 p.m. | 9 | 6 wks |

Cain hassles Hunter to change his ways.

Hunter's Walk — 34 wks

ATV, drama

This series was based at the local police station in Hunter's Walk in the Midlands town of Broadstone. It was created by Ted Willis and starred Ewan Hooper as Detective Sergeant Smith and Davyd Harries as Sergeant Ridgeway.
Producer: John Cooper.

| 1973 | 6.8 | Mon 4 Jun 9:00 p.m. | 2 | 13 wks |

'Disturbance' by Richard Harris.
The breakdown of the marriage of Dennis and Janet Kenwright (Doug Fisher and Helen Fraser) involves Hunter's Walk police in a hunt for a disturbed and dangerous man.
Designer: Gerry Roberts. **Director:** Robert Tronson.

| 1974 | 7.3 | Mon 13 May 9:00 p.m. | 2 | 13 wks |

'Blind eye' by Brian Finch.
Bert Jackson (Colin Douglas) is a security guard at an establishment which has been robbed. His old friend PC Coombes (Charles Rea) finds himself investigating Bert, who says he neither heard nor saw anything.
Designer: Roger Allen. **Director:** Hugh Munro.

| 1976 | 6.5 | Tue 24 Aug 9:00 p.m. | 3 | 8 wks |

'Kicking and Screaming' by Bob Baker and Dave Martin.
The police find themselves trying to deal with a man who breaks into and wrecks his own home.
Designer: Michael Brammall.

Hunters, The — 1 wk

USA presented by ITV, drama

| 1972 | 6.1 | Mon 29 Aug 8:00 p.m. | 5 | 1 wk |

Two-hour drama produced and directed by Dick Powell, starring Robert Mitchum as jet fighter ace Major Cleve Saville and Robert Wagner as Lieutenant Ed Pell, a hot-headed pilot in a daredevil squadron with a mission that could save hundreds of lives.

Hurricane Higgins — 1 wk

Thames, documentary

| 1972 | 5.1 | Mon 4 Sep 8:00 p.m. | 20 | 1 wk |

A film profile of Alex Higgins, the new World Snooker Champion.
Narrator: John Morgan. **Director:** Chris Goddard. **Producer:** Ian Martin.

Husband of the Year — 9 wks

YTV, game show

In this fifteen-week series hosted by Pete Murray the contestants were quizzed by Marjorie Proops and Leslie Randall and by a pair of married guest celebrities.

| 1976 | 6.8 | Tue 18 May 7:00 p.m. | 6 | 9 wks |

Guests: Gillian Raine, Leonard Rossiter and Frank Thornton.
Director: David Millard. **Producer:** Terry Henebery.

Husbands and Lovers — 2 wks

Granada, drama

Based on the writings of Ferenc Molnar, this three-part series was adapted for television by Julian Mitchell. Molnar was only nineteen years old when he wrote his observations of Budapest society in the early 1900s, presenting it as a hotbed of sex games, intrigue and deception.

| 1970 | 5.2 | Wed 5 Aug 9:00 p.m. | 12 | 2 wks |

Stories of Nicholas (Francis Wallis), a young student in love with a married woman, and Hedwig (Toby Robins), an actress who stole someone's husband and put him in the wardrobe. Then there are Johann (Michael Craig) and Eric (Jonathan Newth), who discover they share similar tastes as they thumb through a book of nudes.
Director: Basil Coleman. **Producer:** Peter Potter.

I, Cassius | 1 wk

BBC, sport

| 1965 | 4.9 | Tue 11 Mar 9:25 p.m. | 13 | 1 wk |

A portrait of boxing champion Cassius Marcellus Clay by Harry Carpenter, filmed in Miami, Florida and Louisville, Kentucky.
Producer: Leslie Ketley.

I Didn't Know You Cared | 5 wks

BBC, situation comedy

This seven-part series was created and written by Peter Tinniswood from his own trilogy of novels of the same title. The Brandon family was North Country in the Andy Capp tradition, phlegmatic and dour. The men played darts in the pub, the women had all the answers. The characters were Mr Brandon (John Comer), Mrs Brandon (Liz Smith), Uncle Mort (Robin Bailey), Carter (Stephen Rea), Pat (Anita Carey) and the three Great Aunts Mona, Maud and Mary (Gabrielle Daye, Beatrix Mackey and Marjorie Sudell).
Producer: Bernard Thompson.

| 1975 | 7.7 | Wed 1 Oct 9:35 p.m. | 3 | 2 wks |

'Large or Small, Big or Tall'
The Great Aunts see danger in the proposed second honeymoon of the Brandons. There is only one answer – and of course Mrs Brandon finds it.

| 1976 | 6.1 | Tue 25 May 9:25 p.m. | 13 | 2 wks |

'Good Wood, God'
Uncle Mort plays bowls and the prize is a fate worse than death.

| 1977 | 5.8 | Tue 28 Jun 9:25 p.m. | 17 | 1 wk |

'A Signal Disaster'
Mr Brandon decides on a mystery trip for the annual works outing. (Repeat.)

I Feel Fine | 1 wk

Granada, entertainment

| 1986 | 9.1 | Sat 12 Jul 7:30 p.m. | 15 | 1 wk |

As the Liverpool Festival of Comedy gets underway, Stan Boardman introduces a programme from the city featuring Tony Christie, Gerry Marsden, Mick Miller, Ringo Starr, Richard Stilgoe, the Royal Liverpool Philharmonic Orchestra and many Merseyside entertainers.
Directors: Noel D. Greene and Tim Sullivan. **Producer:** John Hamp.

I Know My First Name is Steven | 1 wk

Presented by BBC, film

| 1990 | 8.6 | Tue 24 Jul 9:30 p.m. | 13 | 1 wk |
| | | Wed 25 Jul 9:30 p.m. | | |

The two parts of this film, based on a true story, were listed together in the ratings.
A seven-year-old boy was abducted by two men and subjected to seven years of psychological and sexual abuse. He had to re-live this experience in court.
Director: Larry Elikann.

I Look Like This | 1 wk

Granada, documentary

| 1979 | 9.1 | Wed 1 Aug 9:00 p.m. | 19 | 1 wk |

A look at the video dating industry through the personal stories of five lonely people.
Director: Jane Bokova. **Producer:** Norman Swallow.

I Spy | 1 wk

USA presented by ITV, drama

American spies Kelly Robinson (Robert Culp) and Alexander 'Scotty' Scott (Bill Cosby) travelled the world as tennis players.
Producer: Sheldon Leonard.

| 1968 | 4.5 | Wed 14 Aug 8:00 p.m. | 15 | 1 wk |

'Tigers of Heaven'
The Tigers of Heaven are a neo-fascist group in Japan which Kelly and Scotty try to break up, getting themselves into a Samurai sword duel.

I Thought You'd Gone | 4 wks

Central, situation comedy

This series by Peter Jones and Ken Laffan dealt with Gerald and Alice (Peter Jones and Pat Heywood). Their children had left home and they had moved from Croydon to a small house in the country.

| 1984 | 10.1 | Fri 7 Sep 8:30 p.m. | 9 | 4 wks |

Gerald conducts the sale of a boat that has been blocking the garage entrance for far too long.
Director: Paul Harrison. **Producer:** Shaun O'Riordan.

Ice Skating | 3 wks

AR (1963–64) and BBC (1982), sport

| 1963 | 5.4 | Wed 15 May 9:42 p.m. | 14 | 1 wk |

The Championships of the World from the Empire Pool, Wembley. Commentary by Peter Lloyd.
Television presentation: Grahame Turner.

| 1964 | 6.4 | Fri 15 May 9:10 p.m. | 7 | 1 wk |

The World and British Professional Championships from the Empire Pool, Wembley. Commentary by Kent Walton.
Television presentation: John P. Hamilton.

| 1982 | 11.6 | Fri 12 Mar 8:30 p.m. | 17 | 1 wk |

From Copenhagen, Des Lynam introduces Jayne Torvill and Christopher Dean's defence of their World Ice Dance title. Alan Weeks and Robin Cousins commentate.
Television presentation: Danish Television Service.

Ice Station Zebra | 1 wk

Presented by BBC, film

| 1974 | 6.5 | Tue 24 Dec 8:30 p.m. | 9 | 1 wk |

Special Christmas screening of Alistair MacLean's Arctic adventure starring Rock Hudson with Ernest Borgnine and Patrick McGoohan.
Director: John Sturges.

If it's Saturday it Must be Nimmo | 2 wks

BBC, chat show

Derek Nimmo hosted this light chat show series.

| 1970 | 6.3 | Sat 28 Nov 6:15 p.m. | 17 | 2 wks |

Guests: Cilla Black, Billy Graham and Gerry Marsden.
Director: Roger Ordish. **Producer:** Richard Drewett.

If Tomorrow Comes | 2 wks

USA presented by ITV, drama

This four-part mini-series of a Sidney Sheldon story starred Madolyn Smith and Tom Berenger as jewel thieves Tracy and Jeff.

| 1987 | 11.3 | Thu 11 Jun 8:00 p.m. | 7 | 2 wks |

Part Four
Tracy and Jeff plan to flee to South America after one final giant robbery.

If You Go Down to the Woods Today | 1 wk

Thames, comedy

| 1981 | 13.8 | Wed 29 Apr 8:30 p.m. | 10 | 1 wk |

This ninety-minute comedy stars Eric Sykes as Scoutmaster Mr Pangbourne. He takes eight Cubs on a trip to Tangle Woods for a far from peaceful day. Also starring Robin Bailey, Norman Bird, Glyn Houston, Roy Kinnear, Fulton Mackay, Lee Montague, Tony Selby and George Sewell.
Writer and **Director:** Eric Sykes. **Producer:** David Clark.

Illustrated Weekly Hudd, The | 7 wks

BBC, comedy

In this series comedian and music hall impressionist Roy Hudd starred with Marcia Ashton, Doug Fisher and Sheila Steafel with topical gags, songs and sketches.
Writers: Eric Davidson, Dave Freeman and Dick Vosburgh.

| 1966 | 7.0 | Thu 17 Nov 9:05 p.m. | 4 | 6 wks |

Producer: James Gilbert.

| 1967 | 4.8 | Fri 12 May 7:30 p.m. | 19 | 1 wk |

Producer: Michael Hurll.

I'm All Right Jack | 1 wk

Presented by BBC, film

| 1969 | 5.8 | Mon 26 May 9:20 p.m. | 8 | 1 wk |

Bank Holiday presentation of the Boulting Brothers' comedy starring Ian Carmichael as a young and innocent worker who causes a national strike. Peter Sellers plays works union convener Fred Kite. Also starring Richard Attenborough, Liz Fraser, Irene Handl, Sam Kydd, John Le Mesurier, Dennis Price, Margaret Rutherford and Terry-Thomas.
Director: John Boulting. **Producer:** Roy Boulting.

I'm The World's Best Writer — 1 wk

YTV, documentary

1971	5.9	Mon 13 Dec 8:00 p.m.	19	1 wk

Alan Whicker examines the life and lifestyle of the phenomenally wealthy author Harold Robbins.
Camera: Frank Pocklington. **Director:** Peter Robinson. **Executive Producer:** Tony Essex.

Images — 1 wk

Thames, documentary

1972	5.1	Thu 3 Aug 9:15 p.m.	20	1 wk

An examination of those who make the images that enter our lives, the star makers and ad men.
Director: Francis Fuchs. **Producer:** Ian Martin.

Imperial Palace — 1 wk

BBC, drama

This story by Arnold Bennett was dramatized for television in four parts by Michael Voysey. It starred Roy Dotrice as Evelyn Orcham, manager of the Imperial Palace, London's finest luxury hotel. (First shown on BBC2.)

1971	5.9	Sat 3 Apr 9:00 p.m.	20	1 wk

'Declaration'
The final episode. Evelyn goes to Paris on business and has an affair. Monsieur Ceria (George Lambert) proposes to Violet (Anna Cropper), is refused and disappears. All this causes Evelyn to return to London to tie up loose ends.
Designer: Michael Young. **Director:** Paddy Russell. **Producer:** David Conroy.

In at the Deep End — 2 wks

BBC, documentary

Former THAT'S LIFE presenters Paul Heiney and Chris Serle took turns learning a new skill or occupation.
Producer: Nick Handel. **Executive Producer:** Edward Mirzoeff.

1984	11.0	Wed 31 Oct 9:25 p.m.	20	1 wk

Chris Serle is to partner Steve Davis in a snooker doubles match against Alex Higgins and Tony Meo. An audience will watch his efforts. Serle is coached by Terry Griffiths, Ray Reardon and Cliff Thorburn.

1987	9.2	Wed 17 Jun 9:30 p.m.	17	1 wk

Chris Serle, a competent amateur photographer, undergoes six weeks' intense training to work for the Daily Mirror on a Royal assignment in competition with fifty top photographers from Fleet Street and abroad.

In for a Penny — 2 wks

LWT, situation comedy

This series by John Hawkesworth and John Whitney starred Bob Todd as Dan, the Town Hall lavatory attendant of twenty-five years' service.

1972	5.6	Fri 7 Jul 7:25 p.m.	15	2 wks

'Dan and the Housing Problem'
Above is the Town Hall, the awesome monolith of bureaucratic splendour where there are problems to be resolved and below is Dan, with all the answers.
Producer: Mark Stuart.

In Like Flynn — 1 wk

Presented by ITV, film

1986	13.0	Sat 4 Jan 7:45 p.m.	12	1 wk

Jenny Seagrove stars as Terri McLane, researcher for a New York publishing house. Her employers are unaware that she is also the firm's best-selling writer, having created the character Jason Flynn under a pen-name. During a visit to the Caribbean she gets involved in an adventure similar to those she has created for Flynn in her novels.
Director: Richard Lang.

In Loving Memory — 29 wks

Thames (1969) and YTV (1979), situation comedy

Originally a single comedy in 1969, this programme was set in 1929 in the town of Oldshaw, Lancashire. It starred Edward Chapman as undertaker and monumental mason Jeremiah Unsworth and Marjorie Rhodes as his daughter Ivy. Producer Ronnie Baxter resurrected the idea in 1979 with Thora Hird in the role of Ivy. Jeremiah had died by then, and Ivy ran the business with her gormless nephew Billy (Christopher Beeny).
Writer: Dick Sharples.

1969	8.6	Tue 4 Nov 8:25 p.m.	1	1 wk

'In Loving Memory'
Unsworth is asked to handle Oldshaw's biggest and most important funeral.

1979	14.9	Mon 4 Jun 8:00 p.m.	3	7 wks

'Gone Dancing'
Billy finds being an undertaker puts the girls off.

| 1980 | 15.1 | Mon 3 Nov 8:00 p.m. | 11 | 6 wks |

'The Fortune Teller'
Ivy is not a superstitious person, but she is having second thoughts after an unexpected visit from a gypsy.

| 1982 | 12.4 | Tue 12 Oct 8:30 p.m. | 7 | 6 wks |

'The Actress and the Undertaker'
Billy is called to the local music hall when a knife thrower's act goes fatally wrong.

| 1983 | 13.9 | Mon 5 Dec 8:00 p.m. | 5 | 4 wks |

'Trouble at Mill'
When Billy visits a local mill on business, he meets an old flame. Ivy meets an even older flame when she presents the end-of-year prizes at an infants' school.

| 1984 | 15.3 | Mon 23 Jan 8:00 p.m. | 2 | 3 wks |

'Cuckoo in the Nest'
Billy leaves home to find a place of his own. Ivy feels the loneliness.

| 1986 | 10.1 | Mon 23 Jun 8:00 p.m. | 8 | 2 wks |

'Flying Undertaker'
Ivy and Billy go up in the world in more ways than one.

In Private, In Public   1 wk

ITN, documentary

| 1986 | 18.4 | Mon 22 Sep 7:30 p.m. | 2 | 1 wk |

The second programme in Alastair Burnet's two-part profile of the Prince and Princess of Wales.

In Sickness and in Health   40 wks

BBC, situation comedy

Writer Johnny Speight took characters from TILL DEATH US DO PART and gave them a new lease of life. Warren Mitchell still starred as Alf Garnett and Dandy Nichols continued as Else until failing health forced her to leave the series. She died in 1986. Carmel McSharry played Mrs Hollingbery.
Director: Richard Boden. **Producer:** Roger Race.

| 1985 | 16.2 | Thu 26 Dec 8:30 p.m. | 2 | 7 wks |

Although Alf and Else are invited to the church hall for Christmas dinner, Alf is reluctant to miss a free pensioners' knees-up at the pub. He connives with his mate Arthur (Arthur English) to attend both. When daughter Rita (Una Stubbs) comes to look after them, the knees-up takes place in the church hall.

| 1986 | 13.6 | Thu 2 Oct 9:30 p.m. | 4 | 7 wks |

Alf and Arthur find themselves in the money. Rita and Mrs Hollingbery can only look on in amazement.

| 1987 | 13.1 | Fri 25 Dec 10:05 p.m. | 10 | 8 wks |

Alf is to spend Christmas in hospital, where he will undergo a hip replacement operation. Mrs Hollingbery receives his wrath with placid detachment.

| 1988 | 12.2 | Mon 11 Jul 8:30 p.m. | 6 | 6 wks |

Alf falls asleep watching cricket on television. He dreams he is playing for England. (Repeat.)

| 1989 | 12.7 | Thu 19 Oct 8:30 p.m. | 6 | 12 wks |

Alf, Arthur and Mrs Hollingbery are staying with her wealthy brother Ricky (John Bluthal) in Australia. Ricky is a practical joker. The dislike Alf builds up for him turns into open war when they go into the outback.

In Suspicious Circumstances   1 wk

Granada, drama

Edward Woodward presents dramatizations of three true tales of murder and mystery.
Director: Ian White. **Producer:** Sue Durkan.

| 1991 | 9.6 | Mon 3 Jun 9:00 p.m. | 13 | 1 wk |

In the first story, entitled 'Mrs Bravo Regrets', Rory Edwards and Kate Gartside star as Charles and Florence Bravo in a story of a poisoning at a priory. In the second, 'No Smoke Without Fire', Anthony Cairns plays Peter Luckhurst and Olive Pendleton plays Gwendoline Marshall in a story of a murder with a hayfork. In the final part 'The Jewell and the Magpie', Mark Spalding is Tony Maffia and David Ross plays Stephen Jewell in the story of a man framed for a 1960s gangland killing.

In the Heat of the Night   2 wks

USA presented by ITV, drama

This saga of murder and deceit was set in Sparta, a cotton town in Mississippi. Carroll O'Connor played redneck Police Chief Bill Gillespie. Howard Rollins was the black Chief of Detectives, Virgil Tibbs.

| 1988 | 9.4 | Tue 19 Jul 9:00 p.m. | 16 | 2 wks |

A black man is arrested for the murder of a popular local white girl.
Writer: James Lee Barrett. **Director:** David Hemmings.

Marjorie Rhodes was Ivy Unsworth in the original **In Loving Memory**.

In Time of War — 3 wks

Presented by BBC, film

| 1970 | 6.0 | Sun 11 Oct 8:15 p.m. | 13 | 3 wks |

'The Desert Rats'
Richard Burton plays a seasoned British officer commanding inexperienced troops. He earns respect when he refuses to yield to the forces of Rommel (James Mason). Also starring Robert Newton.
Director: Robert Wise.

Incredible Hulk, The — 7 wks

USA presented by ITV, drama

Scientist David Banner (Bill Bixby) conducted experiments on human strength. He was overdosed with gamma rays, turning him into the greenish giant Hulk (Lou Ferrigno) every time he became angry. The series was inspired by Stan Lee and Jack Kirby's comic book character.
Executive Producer: Glen A. Larson.

| 1978 | 13.2 | Sun 23 Jul 7:15 p.m. | 1 | 7 wks |

Banner continues to work for a cure for the affliction that turns him into a monster.

Indiana Jones and the Temple of Doom — 3 wks

Presented by BBC, film

| 1987 | 18.9 | Fri 25 Dec 3:40 p.m. | 6 | 1 wk |

In this prequel to RAIDERS OF THE LOST ARK, Indiana Jones (Harrison Ford) discovers the Sankara Stone.
Director: Steven Spielberg.

| 1989 | 13.8 | Sat 23 Dec 6:00 p.m. | 8 | 1 wk |
| 1991 | 9.8 | Sat 31 Aug 6:20 p.m. | 16 | 1 wk |

Repeat showings of the above film.

Informer, The — 17 wks

AR, drama

This series starred Ian Hendry as Alex Lambert, a disbarred barrister trying to repair his life and marriage as he moved between the worlds of the law and crime as The Informer. Also starring Heather Sears as Janet Lambert and Jean Marsh as Sylvia Parrish.

| 1966 | 7.8 | Wed 7 Sep 8:00 p.m. | 1 | 8 wks |

Part Two of **'Two for Joy'** by Hugh Leonard.
Alex learns the folly of mixing business with pleasure.
Designer: John Clements. **Director:** Richard Doubleday. **Producer:** Peter Collinson.

| 1967 | 7.3 | Wed 27 Sep 8:00 p.m. | 4 | 9 wks |

'Undisclosed Sources' by Alfred Shaughnessy.
The police are challenged in court to produce their witness, but to do so would reveal the identity of The Informer.
Designer: John Clements. **Director:** Christopher Hodson. **Producer:** John Whitney. **Executive Producer:** Stella Richman.

Inheritance — 4 wks

Granada, drama

A series of ten one-hour episodes based on two novels by Phyllis Bentley, adapted by Peter Eckersley and Geoffrey Lancashire. Five programmes were devoted to each story and followed the fortunes of a Yorkshire wool family from 1812 to 1965. Stars included James Bolam, Michael Goodliffe, John Thaw and Thelma Whiteley.

| 1967 | 6.6 | Fri 3 Nov 9:00 p.m. | 9 | 4 wks |

'Misalliance' by Peter Eckersley.
Brigg Oldroyd (Michael Goodliffe) has been rebuffed by his half-cousin, Jamie Smith-Oldroyd (Daphne Heard), who has married Charley Mellor (Royston Tickner) instead. In a fit of pique Brigg marries a country aristocrat Charlotte Stancliffe (Madeleine Christie).
Designer: Alan Price. **Producer:** Howard Baker.

Inheritors, The — 3 wks

HTV, drama

A six-part saga by Wilfred Greatorex about the quest for wealth. The Gethin family in South Wales faced a bill for six million pounds in death duties. The vultures gathered as the estate had to be broken up. Starring Robert Urquhart as Lord Gethin, Peter Egan as Michael Gethin and Bill Maynard as Sefton Garrett.

| 1974 | 5.7 | Thu 29 Aug 8:30 p.m. | 11 | 3 wks |

'Did Machiavelli Have Welsh Blood?'
The castle, the valley and a farm must be sold. Michael is fighting to keep the estate intact, but the odds look hopeless.
Designers: Doug James and Colin Pigott. **Director:** Ian McNaughton. **Producer:** Wilfred Greatorex. **Executive Producer:** Aled Vaughan.

Inside — 2 wks

Granada, documentary

This series of four programmes studied the state of prisons and the prison system.

| 1965 | 6.4 | Tue 19 Jan 10:05 p.m. | 10 | 2 wks |

'Women in Prison'
An enquiry into the conditions of women prisoners, and an investigation into alternative punishments. Narrated by Reginald Marsh.
Producers: Elaine Grand and Mike Grigsby.

Inside George Webley — 3 wks

YTV, situation comedy

This series, created by Keith Waterhouse and Willis Hall, starred Roy Kinnear as the worrying George, and Patsy Rowland as his wife Rosemary, who was quite content eating and sleeping.

1968	6.0	Tue 22 Oct 8:30 p.m.	12	3 wks

'Hold Your Breath and Count To 50'
George has hiccups and tries every suggested cure. With guest stars James Bolam and Frank Thornton.
Producer: Bill Hitchcock.

Inside Story — 1 wk

BBC, documentary

This series tackled a variety of serious subjects.

1989	9.0	Wed 17 May 9:30 p.m.	19	1 wk

'Subway'
An investigation into the 16,000 reported crimes on the London Underground in 1988. They ranged from the picking of pockets to rape, kidnap and murder.
Producer: Christopher Terrill. **Executive Producer:** Paul Hamann.

Inside the Mind of Dave Allen — 1 wk

Thames, comedy

1970	6.2	Wed 8 Jul 8:00 p.m.	6	1 wk

A special hour of comedy and sketches starring Dave Allen with Michael Sharvel-Martin, Nicole Shelby and Bob Todd.
Producer: John Robins.

Inspector Morse — 27 wks

Central, drama

John Thaw starred as an Oxford policeman who loved real ale, was rather mean and filled his brain on the Latin quotations, poetry and theories of his creator Colin Dexter. A ladies man, Morse remained intolerant of intellects lower than his own, especially that of Detective Sergeant Lewis (Kevin Whately).
Producers included Kenny McBain (1987–88) and David Lascelles (1990–91). **Executive Producer:** Ted Childs. (A Zenith production.)

1987	14.8	Tue 20 Jan 8:00 p.m.	3	3 wks

'Service of all the Dead' adapted by Julian Mitchell.
Morse investigates a murder at a quiet country church.
Director: Peter Hammond.

1988	12.2	Tue 22 Mar 8:00 p.m.	10	6 wks

'Last Bus to Woodstock' adapted by Michael Wilcox.
A young secretary is found dead in a pub car park.
Director: Peter Duffell.

1989	15.5	Wed 25 Jan 8:00 p.m.	7	4 wks

'The Secret of Bay 5B' adapted by Alma Cullen.
Morse investigates a baffling murder in a multi-storey car park.
Director: Jim Goddard. **Producer:** Chris Burt.

1990	16.2	Wed 24 Jan 8:00 p.m.	7	8 wks

'Masonic Mysteries' adapted by Julian Mitchell.
Morse is arrested on suspicion of murder. He has to fight to clear his name, putting his own life in danger when he does so.
Director: Danny Boyle.

1991	15.6	Wed 20 Feb 8:15 p.m.	5	6 wks

'Second Time Around' adapted by Daniel Boyle.
Morse comes into contact with an old professional rival, Chief Inspector Dawson (Kenneth Colley), following the mysterious death of a former deputy police commissioner.
Director: Adrian Shergold.

International Cover Girl Contest — 2 wks

AR, entertainment

Models from all over the world competed for a cash prize of £500, a wardrobe of dresses and the chance to be featured on the cover of a magazine.

1966	6.8	Thu 27 Oct 9:40 p.m.	9	1 wk

Keith Fordyce and Huw Thomas introduce the finalists from London's Lyceum Ballroom.
Television presentation: Steve Minchin.

1968	7.0	Tue 30 Jan 9:15 p.m.	13	1 wk

Bob Monkhouse introduces the finalists from the Royal Lancaster Hotel, London.
Television presentation: Steve Minchin and Grahame Turner.

International Ice Gala — 1 wk

BBC, sport

1967	8.0	Tue 12 Dec 9:30 p.m.	5	1 wk

Introduced by Alan Weeks from the Queen's Ice Club, London and starring Bernard Ford, Diane Towler and, from the USA, Gary Visconti.
Television presentation: Richard Tilling.

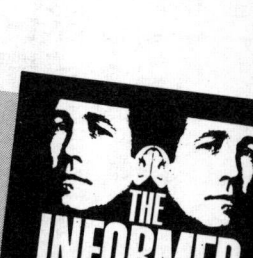

Ian Hendry starred as **The Informer**.

3

4

1 In **All Creatures Great and Small** the animals were as numerous and important as the humans.

2 **Edward VII** (Timothy West) weds Princess Alexandra (Helen Ryan).

3 The Ashtons are about to become a **Family at War**.

4 The last non-soap to reach Number One in the period covered by this book was **The Darling Buds of May**.

International Ice Time — 1 wk

BBC, sport

| 1962 | 5.4 | Tue 27 Mar 8:00 p.m. | 10 | 1 wk |

From the Queen's Club, London, a gala performance of exhibition skating by ice champions of Europe including Alain Calmat, Jacqueline Harboard, Robin Jones and Doris Weinhauser. Commentary by Alan Weeks.
Television presentation: John Vernon.

International Pop Proms, The — 1 wk

Granada, music

This occasional series featured Les Reed with the Pop Proms orchestra and singers.

| 1977 | 6.4 | Wed 13 Jul 8:00 p.m. | 9 | 1 wk |

From the Guild Hall, Preston, with Joe Brown, Emile Ford, Ben E. King, Frankie Laine, Love Machine and Marty Wilde.
Director: Nicholas Ferguson. **Producer:** John Hamp.

International Show Jumping — 1 wk

BBC, sport

| 1979 | 19.0 | Mon–Fri 1–5 Oct 9:25 p.m. Sat 6 Oct 9:00 p.m. | 19 | 1 wk |

These broadcasts were listed together in the ratings.
David Vine introduces the Horse of the Year Show from Wembley Arena. Dorian Williams and Raymond Brooks-Ward commentate.
Television presentation: Fred Viner and Johnnie Watherston.

Into Infinity — 1 wk

BBC, drama

| 1976 | 7.1 | Sat 11 Dec 6:00 p.m. | 18 | 1 wk |

An outer space film odyssey produced by Gerry Anderson. Altares is a prototype spaceship which travels away from the Earth at 186,000 miles a second. Fate takes it beyond its destination into a new universe. Starring Brian Blessed and Joanna Dunham.

Into the Black and Blue Holes — 1 wk

BBC, documentary

| 1987 | 11.2 | Tue 15 Dec 8:30 p.m. | 13 | 1 wk |

A British expedition enters underwater caves in the Bahamas in search of fossils 150 million years old. Andrew Sachs narrates.
Camera: Leo Dickinson and Peter Scoones. **Director:** Robert Palmer. **Producer:** Richard Brock.

Intrigue — 5 wks

ABC, drama

This series of stories from an idea by Tony Williamson starred Edward Judd as Gavin Grant and Caroline Mortimer as Val Spencer. They investigated dirty tricks in big businesses.
Producer: Robert Banks Stewart.

| 1966 | 5.9 | Sat 8 Oct 9:10 p.m. | 13 | 5 wks |

'Big Business' by Anthony Skene.
Industrial espionage is going on right under Grant's nose.
Director: Robert Tronson.

| | | Sat 19 Nov 9:10 p.m. | | |

'50 Million Taste Buds Can't be Wrong' by Robert Holmes.
Grant has confidential information which endangers a man's life.
Director: Bill Bain.
Both these programmes achieved the same viewing figures and chart positions.

Invasion of the Body Snatchers — 1 wk

Presented by ITV, film

| 1982 | 10.2 | Sat 12 Jun 9:15 p.m. | 17 | 1 wk |

Donald Sutherland and Leonard Nimoy star as human beings holding out against the gradual conquest of San Francisco by the 'pod people' from outer space.
Director: Philip Kaufman.

Investiture at Caernarvon — 1 wk

ITV/BBC, news

| 1969 | 5.3 | Tue 1 Jul 7:00 p.m. | 10 | 1 wk |

A recording of the morning's ceremony at Caernarvon Castle performed by Her Majesty The Queen as she invested HRH The Prince Charles as Prince of Wales.

Invitation to a Gunfighter — 1 wk

Presented by Thames for ITV, film

| 1970 | 5.8 | Thu 24 Dec 7:30 p.m. | 17 | 1 wk |

A gunfighter is hired to clear out the last survivor of a New Mexico rebellion. Starring Yul Brunner and George Segal.
Director: Richard Wilson.

....

Island, The				1 wk

HTV, drama

1978	14.3	Sun 30 Apr 9:30 p.m.	13	1 wk

Half-hour adaptation by Robert Fuerst of L.P. Hartley's story about Captain Simmonds (John Hurt), a young British officer in the Second World War who goes to stay at his lover's mansion on a remote island. Also stars Charles Gray as the lover's husband.
Director: Robert Fuerst. **Producer:** William Deneen. **Executive Producer:** Patrick Dromgoole.

....

Island Son				1 wk

USA presented by ITV, drama

Richard Chamberlain starred as Dr Daniel Kulani, who returned to his roots in Hawaii.

1990	9.9	Fri 8 Jun 9:00 p.m.	15	4 wks

'Fathers and Sons'
Daniel tries to reconcile the differences between himself and his son.

....

Istanbul Express				1 wk

Presented by ITV, film

1984	10.8	Fri 20 Apr 8:30 p.m.	10	1 wk

A trans-European express train travels from Paris to Istanbul with spies on board. Gene Barry and Senta Berger star.
Director: Richard Irving.

....

It Ain't Half Hot, Mum				13 wks

BBC, situation comedy

Written and created by Jimmy Perry and David Croft, this series centred on the activities of a concert party platoon in India during the Second World War. Principal characters were Rangi Ram (Michael Bates), Sergeant Major Williams (Windsor Davies), Bombadier Solomons (George Layton), Colonel Reynolds (Donald Hewlett), Captain Ashwood (Michael Knowles) and Gunner Sugden (Don Estelle).
Director (1981–82): John Kilby. **Producer:** David Croft.

1975	5.4	Thu 24 Jul 8:00 p.m.	18	1 wk

'Showing the Flag'
Sergeant Major Williams attempts to train the concert party in the ancient ceremony of lowering the Union Jack at sunset. (Repeat.)

1976	6.9	Tue 7 Dec 8:00 p.m.	17	2 wks

'Flight to Jawani'
The Royal Artillery Concert Party travels to a remote airfield to give a show for a group of RAF men who have not seen any women for two years.
Director: Bob Spiers.

1979	16.9	Fri 17 Aug 7:40 p.m.	4	4 wks

'The Stars Look Down'
An American film unit arrives to make a propaganda film. The concert party players are to be extras. (Repeat.)
Director: Phil Bishop.

1981	13.8	Thu 27 Aug 8:30 p.m.	2	5 wks

'The Long Road Home'
The Royal Artillery Concert party are due for demob.

1982	8.8	Thu 3 Jun 7:45 p.m.	18	1 wk

'Aquastars'
The Concert Party tries to emulate Busby Berkeley and stage a show on the nearby river. (Repeat.)

....

It Happened Like This				3 wks

AR, drama

This series of stories came from between-the-wars thriller writer Sapper, who was actually Lieutenant Colonel H.C. McNeile, the former army officer who created the fictional character Bulldog Drummond.

1962	5.6	Thu 20 Dec 9:45 p.m.	11	2 wks

'A Two-To-One Chance' adapted by Lionel Hale.
The story is introduced by Ralph Michael and stars Dennis Price as rich hypochondriac Sir James Hare who collects rare spiders and harbours suspicions about his wife Grace (Elizabeth Shepherd) and their next-door neighbour Dr Nicholls (Gerald Flood).
Designer: John Emery. **Director:** Ian Fordyce. **Producer:** Norman Marshall.

1963	6.6	Thu 3 Jan 9:45 p.m.	11	1 wk

'Fer de Lance' adapted by Jan Read.
A man who has faked his own disappearance from the world now plans his re-entry. Stars Hugh Burden, Ralph Michael, Derek Waring and Jane Wenham.
Designer: Frank Gillman. **Producer:** Peter Moffatt.

It Shouldn't Happen to a Vet
2 wks

Presented by BBC, film

| 1980 | 16.4 | Sun 21 Dec 7:15 p.m. | 4 | 1 wk |

Alan Plater's screenplay from the stories of James Herriot stars John Alderton as Herriot, Colin Blakely as Siegfried Farnon, and Lisa Harrow as Helen Herriot, with John Barrett, Raymond Francis and Bill Maynard. James is offered a more comfortable and lucrative job in an urban practice.
Director: Eric Till.

| 1985 | 13.3 | Sun 18 Aug 8:00 p.m. | 5 | 1 wk |

Repeat showing of the above film.

Italian Job, The
1 wk

Presented by ITV, film

| 1975 | 8.8 | Sun 25 Jan 7:25 p.m. | 1 | 1 wk |

Troy Kennedy Martin's screenplay for an ingenious plot to hijack four million dollars in gold bullion stars Michael Caine and Noël Coward with Maggie Blye, Rossano Brazzi and Benny Hill.
Director: Peter Collinson.

It'll Be Alright on Christmas Night
1 wk

LWT, comedy

| 1987 | 18.0 | Fri 25 Dec 8:00 p.m. | 7 | 1 wk |

A special Christmas edition of this popular programme.
Writer and **Presenter:** Denis Norden. **Director:** Terry Kinane. **Producer:** Paul Lewis.

It'll Be Alright on the Night
15 wks

LWT, comedy

An anthology of performing cock-ups written and presented by Denis Norden.
Directors included Paul Smith (1984–85) and Terry Kinane (1986, 1988 and 1991). **Producers:** Paul Smith (1977, 1979–83) and Paul Lewis (from 1984).

| 1977 | 16.5 | Sun 18 Sep 7:45 p.m. | 1 | 1 wk |
| 1979 | 17.2 | Sun 7 Jan 8:15 p.m. | 2 | 1 wk |

(Repeat.)

| 1980 | 16.3 | Sun 8 Jun 8:45 p.m. | 1 | 1 wk |

A repeat of the edition first shown in 1979, which went on to win the Silver Rose of Montreux.

| 1981 | 15.7 | Fri 25 Dec 8:30 p.m. | 9 | 1 wk |
| 1982 | 13.7 | Sat 18 Dec 6:10 p.m. | 2 | 1 wk |

(Repeat.)

1983	16.0	Fri 4 Feb 9:00 p.m.	2	1 wk
1984	16.9	Sun 11 Mar 7:15 p.m.	1	2 wks
1985	18.5	Fri 11 Jan 7:15 p.m.	3	1 wk
1986	12.4	Sun 29 Jun 9:15 p.m.	3	2 wks
1988	13.7	Sun 2 May 7:45 p.m.	7	1 wk
1990	17.9	Sun 2 Dec 7:50 p.m.	5	1 wk

Director: Keith Haley.

| 1991 | 15.8 | Sat 14 Dec 6:55 p.m. | 7 | 2 wks |

It's a Celebrity Knockout
3 wks

BBC, game show

Fun and games with celebrities rather than teams in the IT'S A KNOCKOUT format. Commentators: Stuart Hall and Eddie Waring. Referee: Arthur Ellis. Games devised by Stuart Furber.

| 1975 | 6.5 | Fri 11 Jul 8:00 p.m. | 5 | 1 wk |

Two teams, sportsmen and television stars, compete at Craven Cottage football ground.
Director: Geoff Wilson. **Producer:** Barney Colehan.

| 1976 | 5.7 | Fri 9 Jul 8:00 p.m. | 9 | 1 wk |

From Crystal Palace Football Club, the Lord's Taverners compete against the celebrities in the usual knockabout games.
Director: Geoff Wilson. **Producer:** Barney Colehan.

| 1979 | 19.3 | Wed 29 Aug 8:10 p.m. | 2 | 1 wk |

Members of the Lord's Taverners challenge a celebrity team at Loftus Road.
Director: Alan Walsh. **Producer:** Cecil Korer.

It's a Championship Knockout
1 wk

BBC, game show

| 1980 | 8.7 | Sat 2 Aug 7:00 p.m. | 20 | 1 wk |

The eight teams that will represent the UK in the 1980 JEUX SANS FRONTIÈRES compete for the Radio Times trophy at Park Hall, Charnock Richard.
Director: Tony Harrison. **Producer:** Geoff Wilson.

It's a Christmas Knockout — 3 wks

BBC, entertainment

1974 — 6.3 — Mon 23 Dec 6:55 p.m. — 10 — 1 wk

From the Aviemore Centre in Scotland, teams from Belgium, Holland and Italy join the Aviemore team representing the UK in this special IT'S A KNOCKOUT contest. With Stuart Hall, Eddie Waring, Arthur Ellis and international referee Gennaro Olivieri.
Director: Bill Taylor. **Producer:** Barney Colehan.

1980 — 14.3 — Sat 27 Dec 6:00 p.m. — 19 — 1 wk

A special Christmas international from Liège, Belgium with Bristol representing the UK. Introduced by Stuart Hall, Georges Kleinmann, Michael Lemaire, Claudio Leppe and Dick Passchier. Referees: Gennaro Olivieri and Guido Pancaldi.
Producer: Geoff Wilson.

1983 — 10.5 — Tue 27 Dec 5:35 p.m. — 19 — 1 wk

Stuart Hall and Henrik Engberg introduce an Anglo-Swedish competition from the Aviemore Centre in Scotland.
Director: John Rooney. **Producer:** Geoff Wilson.

....

It's a Knockout/Jeux Sans Frontières — 88 wks

BBC/Eurovision, game show

In this roustabout Olympics towns from all over the country competed on greasy poles, up castles and down tubes in all sorts of costumes and settings designed by Stuart Furber. The most successful British team then represented the UK in the Eurovision contests. Initially David Vine hosted (1967–71), but for most years of the series Stuart Hall (1972–82) and Eddie Waring (1967–79), the latter in charge of the mini-marathon, were masters of ceremonies. Former football referee Arthur Ellis supervised the games. The international referees were Genaro Olivieri and Guido Pancaldi.
Director (1975–77, 1979): Geoff Wilson. **Producers** included Barney Colehan (1967–76), Cecil Korer (1977–79) and Geoff Wilson (1980, 1982).

1967 — 6.3 — Wed 6 Sep 9:05 p.m. — 6 — 6 wks

The international final from West Germany is introduced by Camillo Felgen. Cheltenham represents the UK.

1968 — 5.3 — Fri 13 Sep 9:05 p.m. — 7 — 4 wks

The international final from Brussels, introduced by Jean-Claude Menessier and Paule Herreman. Worthing represents the UK.

1969 — 5.0 — Wed 3 Sep 9:05 p.m. — 10 — 2 wks

The international final from Blackpool. Shrewsbury represents the UK.
Director: Philip S. Gilbert.

1970 — 6.9 — Fri 18 Sep 9:20 p.m. — 3 — 10 wks

The international final from Verona, Italy, with hosts Renata Mauro and Giulio Marchetti. Great Yarmouth represents the UK.

1971 — 7.1 — Fri 24 Sep 9:20 p.m. — 4 — 8 wks

International final from Essen, West Germany, in which the UK is represented by the team from Blackpool. Introduced by Camillo Felgen and Tim Elstner.

1972 — 6.1 — Fri 29 Sep 7:45 p.m. — 10 — 9 wks

Jan Hiermayer introduces the international final from Lausanne with Salisbury representing the UK.

1973 — 6.7 — Fri 14 Sep 7:45 p.m. — 4 — 13 wks

The international final from Paris is introduced by Guy Lux and Simone Garnier. Ely represents the UK.

1974 — 6.8 — Fri 20 Sep 7:45 p.m. — 2 — 9 wks

The international final from Leiden, Holland, is introduced by Dick Passchier. Farnham represents the UK.

1975 — 8.3 — Fri 23 May 8:00 p.m. — 1 — 9 wks

Three teams, Falmouth, Redruth and St Ives, compete for the honour of representing the UK in one of the international heats.

1976 — 6.7 — Fri 1 Oct 7:05 p.m. — 16 — 1 wk

The international final from Blackpool with Newbury representing the UK against six other countries.

1977 — 13.2 — Wed 26 Oct 6:50 p.m. — 14 — 5 wks

The seventh international heat comes from Holland with Crawley competing for the UK.

1978 — 13.8 — Fri 5 May 8:00 p.m. — 12 — 5 wks

Teams from Carrickfergus, Dungannon and Londonderry compete for a place in the international final.
Director: Paul Looseley.

1979 — 19.4 — Tue 23 Oct 7:15 p.m. — 3 — 4 wks

The seventh international heat from St Albans with the home team representing the UK.

1980 — 9.8 — Sat 9 Aug 7:10 p.m. — 15 — 2 wks

Guy Lux and Simone Garnier introduce the first international heat from Antibes, France, where Rushcliffe represents the UK.

1982 — 8.8 — Fri 16 Jul 8:10 p.m. — 18 — 1 wk

A domestic heat from Scunthorpe between Scunthorpe, Cleethorpes and Rotherham. Bill Owen and Kathy Staff help Stuart Hall host the proceedings.
Director: John Rooney.

It's a Square World — 3 wks

BBC, comedy

This zany series starred former Goon Michael Bentine. The shows were written by Bentine and John Law.

| 1962 | 4.9 | Thu 1 Nov 8:45 p.m. | 18 | 1 wk |

With Dick Emery, Len Lowe and Frank Thornton.
Producer: John Street.

| 1964 | 6.8 | Thu 2 Jul 9:50 p.m. | 17 | 2 wks |

With Clive Dunn, Freddie Earlle, Joe Gibbons and Frank Thornton.
Producer: John Street.

It's a Woman's World — 3 wks

Granada, drama

This series of plays concerned women of all ages.

| 1964 | 5.7 | Fri 4 Sep 9:10 p.m. | 12 | 3 wks |

'Virginia' by Dennis Woolf.
Virginia is eighteen and boasts that all the boys are after her. The time arrives when she has to prove it. With Julie Samuel as Virginia, Judith Smith as her workmate Honey and Ray Brooks as Casanova.
Designer: Terry Pritchard. **Producer:** Richard Everitt.

It's All in Life — 1 wk

ATV, comedy

| 1972 | 5.3 | Tue 8 Aug 10:30 p.m. | 19 | 1 wk |

A rare television appearance by one of the great stars of radio, Al Read, who sees the funny side of life and current affairs.
Writer: Ronnie Taylor. **Director:** Dennis Wilson. **Producer:** Les Chatfield.

It's Beadle — 1 wk

LWT, comedy

Jeremy Beadle set up stunts for unsuspecting members of the public.

| 1990 | 9.5 | Sat 23 Jun 7:00 p.m. | 14 | 1 wk |

Director: John Gorman. **Producer:** Liz Costalas. **Executive Producer:** Robert Randell.

It's Charlie Williams — 1 wk

Granada, entertainment

Charlie Williams had been a coal miner and a professional footballer before finding fame on THE COMEDIANS.

| 1972 | 5.3 | Sat 22 Jul 6:15 p.m. | 11 | 1 wk |

Guests: Chelsea Brown, Mark Channing and the Pamela Devis dancers.
Musical Director: Derek Hilton. **Director:** Peter Walker. **Producer:** John Hamp.

It's Cliff Richard — 24 wks

BBC, entertainment

The UK's all-time top British pop star appeared in his own series with the Norrie Paramor orchestra.
Producer: Michael Hurll.

| 1970 | 7.5 | Sat 14 Mar 6:15 p.m. | 7 | 10 wks |

With Hank B. Marvin and Una Stubbs. Featuring 'A Song For Europe' sung by Mary Hopkin in the search for Britain's entry to the 1970 EUROVISION SONG CONTEST.
Choreographer: Nita Howard.

| 1971 | 7.3 | Sat 27 Feb 6:15 p.m. | 13 | 8 wks |

With Petula Clark, Hank B. Marvin and Una Stubbs. The winner of A SONG FOR EUROPE, 'Jack in the Box', is sung by Clodagh Rodgers.
Choreographer: Malcolm Clare.

| 1972 | 6.5 | Sat 8 Jan 6:15 p.m. | 15 | 6 wks |

With the Flirtations, Dandy Nichols, Olivia Newton-John and Una Stubbs with the Pamela Devis dancers. The New Seekers sing one of the entries for A SONG FOR EUROPE.
Director: Brian Whitehouse.

It's Dark Outside — 16 wks

Granada, drama

Characters created in Granada's earlier series THE ODD MAN reappeared in this high-powered, frightening and rather tortured series of dramas portraying life in the modern world. William Mervyn starred as Chief Inspector Rose and Keith Barron as Detective Sergeant Swift.

| 1964 | 7.8 | Fri 3 Jan 9:10 p.m. | 5 | 8 wks |

'The Grim World of the Brothers Tulk' by Andrew Hall.
Between four and five on a cold dark winter afternoon a grim-faced crowd gathers around the body of a child lying in the back streets of a dirty city. A horrifying killer is on the loose. With guest stars Jane Barrett, Richard Butler and Aubrey Morris.
Designer: Roy Stonehouse. **Producer:** Derek Bennett.

| 1965 | 6.6 | Fri 2 Apr 9:40 p.m. | 7 | 8 wks |

'The Party' by Marc Brandel.
An elderly pensioner is dying next door. Is it of cancer or poverty? Does anybody care? With guest stars Michael Johnson, Kathlene Michael, Oliver Reed, Sheila Steafel and Barbara Young.
Designer: Roy Stonehouse. **Producer:** Derek Bennett.

It's Lulu   5 wks

BBC, entertainment

Lulu (real name Marie Lawrie) emerged as a teenage star with her recording of 'Shout' in 1964. She soon consolidated her position in the forefront of British entertainment.

| 1973 | 6.3 | Sat 24 Nov 7:15 p.m. | 15 | 5 wks |

Guests: Ronnie Barker (as country and western singer Fat Belly Jones), Roger Kitter, José Luis Moreno, Adrienne Posta and Bill Withers with the Alyn Ainsworth orchestra and the Nigel Lythgoe dancers.
Producer: Vernon Lawrence. **Executive Producer:** John Ammonds.

It's Mike Yarwood   1 wk

Thames, comedy

A one-off special starring Mike Yarwood.

| 1984 | 10.8 | Wed 9 May 8:00 p.m. | 9 | 1 wk |

Guests: Dana, Shakatak and the Ken Warwick dancers.
Writers: Eddie Braben and Eric Merriman. **Producer:** David G. Hillier.

It's Tarbuck   14 wks

ATV, comedy

Jimmy Tarbuck became an overnight star with just one appearance on SUNDAY NIGHT AT THE LONDON PALLADIUM. ATV quickly awarded him his own series. With the Jack Parnell orchestra.

| 1964 | 8.1 | Wed 30 Dec 9:10 p.m. | 3 | 3 wks |

Guests: Amanda Barrie and the King Brothers with the Irving Davies dancers.
Producer: Jon Scoffield.

| 1965 | 7.8 | Wed 13 Jan 9:10 p.m. | 6 | 3 wks |

Guests: Amanda Barrie, Henry McGee and Bob Todd with the Irving Davies dancers.
Producer: Jon Scoffield.

| 1971 | 6.2 | Mon 28 Jun 8:30 p.m. | 5 | 1 wk |

Guest star: Lulu with series regulars Peter Gordeno and Kenny Lynch.
Producer: Albert Locke.

| 1973 | 6.8 | Tue 27 Mar 7:05 p.m. | 9 | 7 wks |

Guests: Gilbert O'Sullivan, Ronald Fletcher, Grazina Frame, Kenny Lynch, Josephine Tewson and Frank Williams with the Mike Sammes singers.
Producer: Albert Locke.

It's the Bachelors   6 wks

ATV, music

The Irish singing group the Bachelors consisted of brothers Con and Dec Cluskey and John Stokes. They first came to prominence in the 1963 pop charts with 'Charmaine'.

| 1969 | 6.5 | Thu 22 May 9:00 p.m. | 6 | 6 wks |

Guests: Freddie Davies and Len Lowe with the Peter Knight orchestra.
Producer: Albert Locke.

It's the Beatles   1 wk

BBC, music

| 1963 | 7.0 | Sat 7 Dec 8:10 p.m. | 10 | 1 wk |

The second of two programmes (see JUKE BOX JURY) from the Empire Theatre, Liverpool, where the Beatles play live to an audience made up entirely of fan club members.
Director: Barney Colehan. **Producer:** Neville Wortman.

It's Young Again   1 wk

Granada, comedy

This British-based series starred American comedian Alan Young, best remembered for his partnership with the talking horse Mr Ed.

| 1963 | 4.1 | Thu 22 Jul 7:30 p.m. | 18 | 1 wk |

Guests: The Avons with the Alyn Ainsworth orchestra.
Director: Milo Lewis.

It's Your Move	2 wks

Thames, comedy

1982	13.7	Mon 18 Oct 8:30 p.m.	4	1 wk

This silent comedy written and directed by Eric Sykes deals with a married couple moving into their first house. The removal men are Tommy Cooper and Eric Sykes. Appearing in cameo roles are Richard Briers, Bernard Cribbins, Jimmy Edwards, Irene Handl, Andrew Sachs, Sylvia Syms and Bob Todd.
Producer: Dennis Kirkland.

1983	11.3	Mon 15 Aug 8:00 p.m.	2	1 wk

Repeat showing of the above.

ITV Playhouse	15 wks

Various, drama

This prestigious presentation of plays was open to productions from all the ITV companies, although in practice most of the slots were filled by the larger ones. Decisions on which plays to show were taken at network programme controllers meetings.

1977	7.5	Tue 26 Apr 9:00 p.m.	5	11 wks

'Blind Love' by V.S. Pritchett.
Adapted for television by James Saunders, Sam Wanamaker stars as Armitage, a blind lawyer whose life changes when he falls in love with his new secretary Helen (Mary Peach). (A Granada production).
Designer: Alan Price. **Director:** Waris Hussein. **Producer:** Michael Dunlop.

1980	10.8	Wed 20 Aug 9:00 p.m.	10	3 wks

'Hands' by Mervyn Watson.
Pam (Rosemary Leach) is given a book entitled A Nationwide Study of Female Sexuality by her twenty-three-year old daughter Linda (Sally Watts). She is unsure how to react. (A Thames production).
Designer: Alex Clarke. **Director:** Alex Marshall. **Producer:** John Bowen.

1982	7.6	Tue 27 Jul 9:00 p.m.	19	1 wk

'Skirmishes' by Catherine Hayes.
An old woman (Anna Wing) lies dying. With her are daughters Rita and Jean (Gwen Taylor and Frances de la Tour). (A Thames production.)
Designer: Martyn Herbert. **Director:** Brian Parker. **Producer:** Joan Rodker.

Ivanhoe	1 wk

Presented by ITV, film

1982	12.5	Sun 26 Sep 7:15 p.m.	4	1 wk

Anthony Andrews stars in the title role of Sir Walter Scott's novel set in twelfth-century England. Also starring Lysette Anthony, Julian Glover, Michael Hordern, Olivia Hussey, James Mason, Sam Neill and Ronald Pickup.
Director: Douglas Camfield.

I've Got a Secret	1 wk

BBC, game show

Tom O'Connor presented this game in which five people or groups offered clues to a celebrity panel. Could the stars guess their secrets?

1986	9.4	Fri 30 May 7:55 p.m.	17	1 wk

Panellists: Angela Gordon, Derek Jameson, Anneka Rice and Alan Titchmarsh.
Director: Peter Fitton. **Producer:** Tim Marshall.

J

Jack and the Beanstalk — 1 wk

Presented by BBC, film

1968 | **5.4** | **Tue 24 Dec 5:00 p.m.** | **20** | **1 wk**

The fantasy of a cartoon giant who threatens a real-life pedlar and his young friend. Produced, directed by and starring Gene Kelly.

Jack the Ripper — 2 wks

Thames, drama

1988 | **14.1** | **Tue 18 Oct 9:00 and 10:35 p.m.** | **8** | **2 wks**

Michael Caine stars as Inspector Frederick Abberline in this retelling of the brutal murders committed by Jack the Ripper in Victorian London. Also starring Armand Assante, Harry Andrews, Lysette Anthony, Lewis Collins, Hugh Fraser, Susan George, Ray McAnally and Jane Seymour.
Writers: Derek Marlowe and David Wickes. **Producer:** David Wickes.
Executive Producer: Lloyd Shirley.

Jacqueline Bouvier Kennedy — 1 wk

USA presented by ITV, drama

1983 | **10.7** | **Mon 2 May 8:00 p.m.** | **12** | **1 wk**

The story of the society girl who became America's First Lady. Jaclyn Smith portrayed her in her adult years. James Franciscus played John F. Kennedy.
Director: Steven Gethers.

Jagged Edge — 1 wk

Presented by BBC, film

1988 | **14.0** | **Sat 24 Dec 9:10 p.m.** | **13** | **1 wk**

Glenn Close stars as lawyer Teddy Barnes. She defends Jack Forrester (Jeff Bridges) on a charge of murdering his wife with a jagged-edged knife.
Director: Richard Marquand.

Jamaica Inn — 1 wk

HTV, drama

Daphne du Maurier's story was dramatized in three parts by Derek Marlowe.

1983 | **11.5** | **Mon 9 May 9:00 p.m.**
Tue 10 May 9:00 p.m.
Tue 10 May 10:30 p.m. | **6** | **1 wk**

All three episodes were counted as one entry in the ratings. Mary Yellan (Jane Seymour) finds herself in a web of intrigue in the lonely inn on Cornwall's Bodmin Moor. It is a notorious meeting place for thieves and smugglers led by her uncle, Joss (Patrick McGoohan). Also starring Trevor Eve, John McEnery, Peter Vaughan and Billie Whitelaw.
Director: Lawrence Gordon Clark. **Producer:** Peter Graham Scott.
Executive Producer: Patrick Dromgoole.

James Bond – The First 21 Years — 1 wk

LWT, documentary

1983 | **10.6** | **Fri 27 May 8:00 p.m.** | **6** | **1 wk**

This tribute includes clips from Bond films and interviews with the stars.
Producer: Charles Brand. **Executive Producer:** Richard Drewett.

James Paul McCartney — 1 wk

ATV, music

1973 | **5.8** | **Thu 10 May 9:00 p.m.** | **18** | **1 wk**

The former Beatle stars with his group Wings on a musical trip involving a pub sing-song, the Hollywood of the 1930s and modern production numbers.
Director: Dwight Hemion. **Producer:** Gary Smith.

James Randi: Psychic Investigator — 2 wks

Granada, documentary

In this series, Canadian James Randi challenged the supernatural powers of healers and psychics. He pitted believers against sceptics and often goaded both into conflict and sometimes hostility.

1991	8.3	Wed 24 Jul 9:00 p.m.	17	2 wks

'Astrology'
The accuracy of horoscopes comes under attack, with help from Jilly Cooper, Stephen Fry, Hugh Laurie and Nina Myskow.
Director: John Birkin. **Producer:** Frankie Glass.

Jane Eyre — 6 wks

BBC, drama

Charlotte Brontë's classic story was dramatized in six parts by Constance Cox with Ann Bell as Jane.

1963	6.4	Sun 12 May 5:45 p.m.	7	6 wks

Episode Six
Jane returns to Thornfield Hall. She finds it is in ruins and Mr Rochester (Richard Leech) has gone.
Designer: Fanny Taylor. **Director:** Rex Tucker. **Producer:** Douglas Allen.

Janet and Company — 2 wks

Thames, comedy

This series starred impressionist and singer Janet Brown.
Writers: Eric Davidson, David Renwick and Laurie Rowley.

1981	13.9	Tue 17 Feb 8:30 p.m.	14	2 wks

Guest: Tim Barrett.
Producer: Keith Beckett.

Jasper Carrott Got This Mole — 1 wk

Granada, comedy

1984	12.5	Sun 23 Dec 5:15 p.m.	16	1 wk

This cartoon written and narrated by Jasper Carrott deals with his efforts to rid the garden of a mole.
Producer: Maurice Pooley. **Executive Producer:** John Starkey.

Jasper Carrott Meets Blackadder — 1 wk

BBC, comedy

1988	15.9	Fri 5 Feb 9:30 p.m.	8	1 wk

For Comic Relief, Carrott gets together with Rowan Atkinson, Warren Clarke, Stephen Fry, Griff Rhys-Jones and Tony Robinson.

Jaws — 5 wks

Presented by ITV, film

1981	23.3	Thu 8 Oct 7:30 p.m.	1	1 wk

The townspeople of Amity won't believe Chief of Police Martin Brody (Roy Scheider) when he tells them a man-eating shark is stalking Long Island. Also stars Richard Dreyfuss and Robert Shaw.
Director: Steven Spielberg.

1982	10.9	Sat 4 Sep 6:45 p.m.	6	1 wk
1984	8.8	Mon 23 Apr 7:40 p.m.	18	1 wk
1986	15.5	Sun 13 Apr 7:45 p.m.	5	1 wk

Repeat showings of the above film.

1987	10.6	Sun 20 Dec 7:50 p.m.	18	1 wk

The above film is shown on BBC.

Jaws II — 4 wks

Presented by ITV, film

1983	15.8	Sun 9 Jan 7:15 p.m.	6	2 wks

The townspeople of Amity still won't believe Brody (Roy Scheider) when he tells them another man-eating shark is stalking Long Island.
Director: Jeannot Szwarc.

1986	14.3	Sun 30 Nov 7:45 p.m.	6	1 wk
1990	8.5	Sat 26 May 8:05 p.m.	19	1 wk

Repeat showings of the above film.

Jaws 3-D — 1 wk

Presented by ITV, film

1987	14.1	Thu 1 Jan 7:45 p.m.	5	1 wk

A big hungry fish feeds on humans at a Florida amusement park. Dennis Quaid, Louis Gossett Jr. and Bess Armstrong try to avoid becoming dinner.
Director: Joe Alves.

Jaws: The Revenge — 1 wk

Presented by BBC, film

1991 | **12.8** | **Sat 30 Nov 7:45 p.m.** | **19** | **1 wk**

Sean Brody (Mitchell Anderson) is now deputy sheriff of Amity, the job held by his late father Martin Brody. His mother Ellen (Lorraine Gray) has rebuilt her life over the years, but out in the sea a shark lurks hungering for revenge. Michael Caine stars as Hoagie, the new love interest in Ellen's life.
Director: Joseph Sargent.

Jayne Torvill and Christopher Dean — 1 wk

ITS, sport

1984 | **11.8** | **Thu 3 May 7:30 p.m.** | **4** | **1 wk**

Dickie Davies and Simon Reed introduce a charity gala night of skating from the Richmond Ice Rink. Torvill and Dean star after having won four World and three European titles plus an Olympic gold.
Producer: John Davis. **Executive Producer:** Bob Burrows.

Jazz Girl — 2 wks

AR, music

In these programmes a different female jazz vocalist was featured each week.

1964 | **5.7** | **Mon 4 May 9:10 p.m.** | **15** | **2 wks**

Starring Joy Marshall with the Tubby Hayes Quintet.
Director: John P. Hamilton.

Jeeves and Wooster — 1 wk

Granada, drama

The stories of P.G. Wodehouse were dramatized by Clive Exton and starred Hugh Laurie as Bertie Wooster and Stephen Fry as Jeeves. (The BBC had produced a version of these stories in the mid-1960s under the title THE WORLD OF WOOSTER, with Ian Carmichael as Wooster and Dennis Price as Jeeves.)

1990 | **8.8** | **Sun 20 May 8:45 p.m.** | **18** | **1 wk**

Jeeves tries to persuade Anatole the cook (John Barrard) to return to Brinkley Court. It seems the only way to restore peace for Aunt Dahlia (Brenda Bruce).
Designer: Eileen Diss. **Director:** Robert Young. **Producer:** Brian Eastman. (A Picture Partnership production.)

Jemima Shore Investigates — 12 wks

Thames, drama

These adaptations of books by Antonia Fraser starred Patricia Hodge as the title character, an investigative television reporter.

1983 | **9.9** | **Wed 24 Aug 9:00 p.m.** | **3** | **12 wks**

'A Little Bit of Wildlife' adapted by Pauline MacAulay.
Jemima discovers that jogging can be both good and bad for the heart.
Director: Neville Green. **Producer:** Tim Aspinall.

Jennie, Lady Randolph Churchill — 7 wks

Thames, drama

This series by Julian Mitchell was launched as part of the centenary celebrations of Sir Winston Churchill, charting the life of his mother, Jennie Jerome, the daughter of an American millionaire. Lee Remick starred as Jennie with Ronald Pickup as Lord Randolph, Rachel Kempson as the Duchess of Marlborough, Jeremy Brett as Count Kinsky, Christopher Cazenove as George Cornwallis-West, Sian Phillips as Mrs Patrick Campbell and Warren Clarke as Winston.

1974 | **7.7** | **Tue 22 Oct 9:00 p.m.** | **2** | **7 wks**

Jennie meets Lord Randolph at a dance on board a ship at Cowes.
Director: James Cellan Jones. **Producer:** Andrew Brown. **Executive Producer:** Stella Richman.

Jenny's War — 4 wks

HTV, drama

Steven Gether's four-part dramatization of the novel by Jack Stonely starred Dyan Cannon as Jenny Baines, a schoolteacher from Bath who was smuggled into wartime Germany to try to find her son Peter. Robert Hardy, Patrick Ryecart, Elke Sommer and Richard Todd also starred.

1985 | **12.5** | **Mon 3 Jun 9:00 p.m.** | **3** | **4 wks**

Episode One Jenny learns that Peter has been shot down over Germany.
Designer: Bruce Grimes. **Director:** Steven Gethers. **Producer:** Peter Graham Scott.

Roy Scheider, Robert Shaw and Richard Dreyfus realize their small boat is no match for **Jaws**.

Jesus of Nazareth | 5 wks

ATV, drama

This dramatization in four parts of the triumphs and trials of Jesus was written by Anthony Burgess, Susan Cecci d'Amico and Franco Zeffirelli. It starred Robert Powell as Jesus. The film was directed by Zeffirelli with music by Maurice Jarre.

The star-studded cast included Anne Bancroft, Ian Bannen, Ernest Borgnine, Claudia Cardinale, Valentina Cortese, Cyril Cusack, James Farentino, Ian Holm, James Earl Jones, Stacy Keach, Ian McShane, James Mason, Lee Montague, Lawrence Olivier, Donald Pleasence, Anthony Quinn, Fernando Rey, Ralph Richardson, Rod Steiger, Oliver Tobias, Peter Ustinov, Yorgo Voyagis and Michael York.

| 1977 | 8.3 | Sun 3 Apr 6:15 p.m. | 6 | 2 wks |

Part One
The story of Jesus is presented from his birth through his escape to Egypt to his return following Herod's death.

| 1979 | 14.2 | Sun 1 Apr 6:10 p.m. | 15 | 3 wks |

Part Two
Jesus is baptized. He preaches in Galilee and starts to perform miracles. (Repeat.)

Jewel of the Nile, The | 1 wk

Presented by ITV, film

| 1989 | 14.3 | Sun 8 Oct 7:45 p.m. | 6 | 1 wk |

Novelist Joan Wilder (Kathleen Turner) has been cruising for six months with her lover Jack Colton (Michael Douglas). She is bored. Just as they decide to part, his yacht blows up.
Director: Lewis Teague.

Jim Davidson Show, The | 16 wks

Thames, comedy

Cockney comedian Jim Davidson enjoyed a successful television career from an early age. His penchant to be naughty and slightly blue evoked memories of the cheeky chappie, Max Miller. Among the many targets of his barbed humour the police had to take more than their share.
Producers included Mark Stuart (1980–82).

| 1980 | 15.1 | Tue 23 Dec 8:00 p.m. | 11 | 4 wks |

Guests: Tim Barrett, Hugh Paddick and Bob Todd. With the Allan Rogers orchestra.

| 1981 | 14.6 | Thu 8 Jan 7:30 p.m. | 15 | 6 wks |

Guests: Tim Barrett, Chas and Dave, Ricardo Montez and Bob Todd. With the Allan Rogers orchestra.

| 1982 | 12.6 | Wed 29 Dec 8:00 p.m. | 5 | 4 wks |

Guests: Debbie Arnold, Chas and Dave, Windsor Davies, Jethro, Burt Kwouk, Stanley Unwin, and Iris Williams. With the Brian Rogers dancers and the Harry Rabinowicz orchestra.

| 1986 | 9.7 | Tue 2 Sep 8:00 p.m. | 16 | 2 wks |

Guests: Susie Blake, Richard Digance, Chris Ellison, Samantha Fox and Raymond Huntley. With the Ray Monk orchestra.
Producer: David Bell.

Jim Davidson's Falklands Special | 1 wk

Thames, comedy

| 1984 | 14.7 | Mon 24 Dec 8:00 p.m. | 17 | 1 wk |

John Mills narrates a film following Davidson around the Falkland Islands, where he entertains men and women of the armed forces.
Director: Stuart Hall. **Producer:** Robert Louis.

Jim Davidson's Special | 7 wks

Thames, comedy

These occasional one-hour shows starred the Cockney comic.
Producer (1983–84): Dennis Kirkland.

| 1979 | 16.3 | Mon 31 Dec 7:00 p.m. | 6 | 1 wk |

Guests: Ernest Clark, the Dooleys and Rudolph Walker join Jim for this New Year's Eve special.
Director: Stuart Hall. **Producer:** John Ammonds.

| 1983 | 11.1 | Wed 28 Dec 8:00 p.m. | 4 | 2 wks |

Guests: Bernie Clifton, Bobby Davro, Gary Glitter, Deryck Guyler, Richard O'Sullivan, Suzi Quatro, Bob Todd, Stanley Unwin and Eli Woods.

| 1984 | 14.1 | Wed 6 Jun 8:00 p.m. | 1 | 2 wks |

Guests: The Brother Lees, Frank Carson, Windsor Davies, Clive Dunn, Melvyn Hayes, Tim Healey, the Krankies, Lindisfarne, Bill Pertwee, Tony Selby and Bob Todd.

| 1985 | 11.0 | Wed 5 Jun 8:00 p.m. | 14 | 2 wks |

Guests: Jim Bowen, Joe Brown, Chas and Dave, Jess Conrad, Anne Diamond, Richard Digance, Georgie Fame, Jimmy Greaves, Hale and Pace, Hank Marvin, Rick Wakeman and Roy Wood.
Director: Stuart Hall. **Producer:** Robert Louis.

Jim'll Fix It | 66 wks

BBC, entertainment

Veteran disc jockey Jimmy Savile (later OBE and eventually Sir James Savile) starred in a long-running series as the man who made dreams come true.
Directors included Peter Campbell (1981–84). **Producer:** Roger Ordish.

1975	6.0	Wed 24 Dec 5:45 p.m.	19	1 wk

Director: Stanley Appel.

1977	14.1	Mon 26 Dec 5:25 p.m.	13	2 wks

Director: Phil Bishop.

1978	15.8	Tue 26 Dec 4:25 p.m.	6	2 wks
1979	15.9	Mon 27 Aug 6:45 p.m.	7	11 wks

Director: Paul Ciani.

1980	19.2	Sat 1 Mar 6:35 p.m.	1	13 wks

Director: Rick Gardner.

1981	14.9	Sat 10 Jan 6:35 p.m.	10	13 wks
1982	14.0	Sat 6 Mar 6:35 p.m.	5	12 wks
1983	12.3	Sat 12 Feb 6:15 p.m.	14	6 wks
1984	12.0	Sat 17 Mar 6:05 p.m.	12	2 wks
1985	13.8	Sat 5 Jan 6:05 p.m.	7	2 wks

Director: Marcus Mortimer.

1988	11.4	Sat 2 Jan 5:45 p.m.	19	1 wk

Director: Tony Newman.

1989	11.3	Sat 18 Mar 6:05 p.m.	20	1 wk

Jimmy Tarbuck Show, The   16 wks

ATV, comedy

The Liverpool comedian hosted his own variety series from ATV's Elstree studios. The Jack Parnell orchestra featured throughout the series.
Producer (1968–70): Colin Clews.

1968	6.9	Fri 15 Nov 9:30 p.m.	4	6 wks

Guests: Arthur Askey, Mireille Mathieu, and the Peter Gordeno dancers.

1969	5.3	Sat 13 Sep 7:00 p.m.	16	1 wk

Guest: Des O'Connor.

1970	7.3	Thu 12 Mar 9:00 p.m.	9	3 wks

Guests: Arthur Askey, Johnny Hackett, and Kathy Kirby, with the Peter Gordeno dancers.

1974	6.4	Thu 4 Jul 6:35 p.m.	4	6 wks

Guests: Georgie Fame, Lesley Goldie and Hugh Paddick, with the Lionel Blair dancers.
Producer: Alan Tarrant.

Jimmy's   1 wk

YTV, documentary

This series told real-life stories from Europe's largest general hospital, St James's in Leeds.

1990	8.5	Sun 29 Jul 7:15 p.m.	16	1 wk

The cameras return to St James's to record actual operations as they take place.
Producer: Irene Cockroft.

Joe Baker Show, The   1 wk

ATV, entertainment

Joe Baker had worked as a double act with Jack Douglas before launching a solo career as a fat, sad-eyed funny man. He subsequently left Britain to settle in California.

1965	4.9	Sat 12 Jun 8:25 p.m.	19	1 wk

Guests: Gerald Harper, Sheila O'Neill, Geoffrey Palmer, John Quayle with the David Toguri dancers, the George Mitchell singers and the Jack Parnell orchestra.
Writers: John Singer and John Warren. **Producer:** Jon Scoffield.

Jim Davidson's Special was most special on 6 June 1984, its sole appearance at Number One.

Over a period of five years **Jim'll Fix It** grew from being a moderate hit to a frequent Number One.

Joe Kidd   1 wk

Presented by BBC, film

| **1983** | **11.3** | **Sat 19 Nov 8:55 p.m.** | **16** | **1 wk** |

Joe Kidd (Clint Eastwood) is willing to serve as a hired gunman in a range war. He goes after a Mexican bandit leader.
Director: *John Sturges.*

Joe Longthorne Entertains   1 wk

Thames, entertainment

A NEW FACES winner, impressionist and singer Longthorne was rewarded with his own series.

| **1987** | **9.4** | **Wed 26 Aug 8:00 p.m.** | **14** | **1 wk** |

Guests: Wayne Dobson and Kate Robbins. With the Alan Braden orchestra.
Producer: *Keith Beckett.*

Joe Longthorne Show, The   5 wks

Central, entertainment

A change of title for Longthorne in 1989, but not a change of format, which remained songs and impressions from the star and his weekly guests.

| **1989** | **9.2** | **Wed 23 Aug 7:00 p.m.** | **16** | **4 wks** |

Guests: Wayne Dobson and Darryl Sivad.
Producer: *Nigel Lythgoe.* **Executive Producer:** *Tony Wolfe.*

| **1991** | **8.5** | **Mon 24 Jun 7:00 p.m.** | **19** | **1 wk** |

Guests: Kelly Monteith and Iris Williams.
Director: *Jon Scoffield.* **Producer:** *Nigel Lythgoe.*

John Browne's Body   7 wks

ATV, situation comedy

In this comedy thriller series by René Basilico Peggy Mount starred as bungling detective Virginia Browne and Naunton Wayne as Fitzroy.

| **1969** | **6.4** | **Thu 3 Apr 9:00 p.m.** | **4** | **7 wks** |

A body rolls out of a funeral car right beside five buskers.
Producer: *Shaun O'Riordan.*

John Davidson Show, The   1 wk

ATV, entertainment

This was a showcase series for American singer Davidson and an opportunity for other variety stars from the USA and elsewhere.

| **1969** | **4.4** | **Sun 24 Aug 7:25 p.m.** | **16** | **1 wk** |

Guests: Phyllis Diller, Rich Little, Aimi Macdonald and Mireille Mathieu, with the Irving Davies dancers, the Mike Sammes singers and the Jack Parnell orchestra.
Director: *Norman Campbell.* **Producer:** *Colin Clews.*

John Denver and the Muppets   1 wk

USA presented by BBC, entertainment

| **1979** | **13.6** | **Sat 15 Dec 8:10 p.m.** | **16** | **1 wk** |

A Christmas festival of songs and sketches.
Director: *Tony Charmoli.* **Producer:** *Bob Finkel.*

Johnny Go Home   1 wk

YTV, documentary

| **1975** | **6.2** | **Tue 22 Jul 9:00 p.m.** | **9** | **1 wk** |

This programme was broadcast from 9:00 p.m. until 11:30 p.m. with a half-hour break for NEWS AT TEN. Nine years after 'Cathy Come Home', the film follows the true stories of Annie, who ran away from home aged ten, and Tommy, who left Glasgow when he was fourteen. They were forced to sleep on the streets. No hostel would accommodate them, as it was an offence to harbour a person under the age of seventeen. Tommy landed in a hostel run by bogus 'Bishop' Roger Gleaves, surrounded by hustlers, burglars and boy prostitutes. Six weeks later, Tommy's pal Bill 'Two-Tone' McPhee's body was found with twenty stab wounds.
Camera: *Frank Pocklington.* **Sound:** *Don Atkinson.* **Producer:** *John Willis.* **Executive Producers:** *Michael Deakin and John Fairley.*

Join Jim Dale   6 wks

ATV, entertainment

This variety series starred the versatile Jim Dale, who had begun his career as a pop star on 6.5 SPECIAL before making several Carry On films and joining the National Theatre. He compered THE LONDON PALLADIUM SHOW, hosted THANK YOUR LUCKY STARS and became a Broadway star in 'Barnum' and 'Me And My Girl'.

| **1969** | **5.0** | **Thu 3 Jul 9:00 p.m.** | **14** | **6 wks** |

With Beryl Reid and the Cyril Stapleton orchestra.
Producer: *Dennis Vance.*

Joint Account
8 wks

BBC, situation comedy

This series by Don Webb spotlighted the reversed roles of Belinda and David Braithwaite (Hannah Gordon and Peter Egan). She was a bank manager while he stayed home to do the housework. **Producer:** Mike Stephens.

| 1989 | 13.3 | Thu 26 Jan 8:30 p.m. | 12 | 3 wks |

To the amazement of their friends, David and Belinda break with all convention.

| 1990 | 10.7 | Mon 2 Apr 8:30 p.m. | 12 | 5 wks |

Action girl Belinda tackles an assault course.

Jonathan Dimbleby in Evidence
1 wk

YTV, documentary

This series of five programmes confronted major world issues.

| 1981 | 10.5 | Mon 7 Sep 8:30 p.m. | 18 | 1 wk |

'The Eagle and the Bear'
An examination of the tension between the USA and USSR. **Director:** Francis Gerard. **Producers:** Michael Deakin and Frank Smith.

Journey to the Centre of the Earth
1 wk

Presented by BBC, film

| 1971 | 5.3 | Sat 4 Sep 6:20 p.m. | 13 | 1 wk |

This adaptation of the Jules Verne story stars James Mason with Diane Baker, Pat Boone and Arlene Dahl. **Director:** Henry Levin.

Jubilee Show, The
1 wk

AR, entertainment

This was a one-off variety show of sketches, singing and dancing.

| 1961 | 5.6 | Wed 1 Nov 8:55 p.m. | 10 | 1 wk |

Nicholas Parsons introduces Elizabeth Larner, Dennis Lotis, Joan Sims, Jimmy Thompson, the George Mitchell singers and the Jubilee dancers. **Choreographer:** Malcolm Goddard. **Producer:** Peter Croft.

Judge Dee
5 wks

Granada, drama

This series was adapted by John Wiles from the novels of Robert Van Gulik. Michael Goodliffe starred as Judge Dee, the Chinese master of deduction who lived AD 630–700.

| 1969 | 5.6 | Tue 22 Apr 9:00 p.m. | 19 | 5 wks |

'The Haunted Pavilion'
A ghost helps Judge Dee to discover who is the truthful witness to a strange death. Guest star appearances by Harold Innocent, David Langton and Rosemary Leach. **Designer:** Peter Phillips. **Producer:** Howard Baker.

Judy and Liza
1 wk

ATV, music

| 1964 | 6.0 | Sun 20 Dec 8:25 p.m. | 14 | 1 wk |

A recording of the midnight concert played by Judy Garland and Liza Minnelli at the London Palladium on 8 November. **Television presentation:** Colin Clews.

Juggernaut
2 wks

Presented by ITV, film

| 1985 | 10.9 | Wed 22 May 8:00 p.m. | 13 | 1 wk |

With the sea too rough to lift passengers off a cruise ship, the bomb squad in London races against the clock to find the detonators of seven bombs on board. Starring Richard Harris, David Hemmings, Ian Holm, Anthony Hopkins, Michael Hordern and Omar Sharif. **Director:** Richard Lester.

| 1988 | 9.8 | Wed 18 May 8:00 p.m. | 9 | 1 wk |

Repeat showing of the above film.

Juke Box Jury
14 wks

BBC, music

In this panel show hosted by David Jacobs celebrity guests judged new record releases 'hits' or 'misses', often unaware that the recording artist was behind a screen listening to their verdict. The programme was devised by Peter Potter.

| 1961 | 4.8 | Sat 2 Dec 6:00 p.m. | 16 | 2 wks |

Panellists: Jill Browne, Harry Fowler, Pete Murray and June Thorburn. **Producer:** Harry Carlisle.

1962   **4.8**   **Sat 27 Jan 6:00 p.m.**   **11**   **5 wks**

Panellists: The Kaye Sisters and John Slater.
Producer: Barney Colehan.

1963   **7.5**   **Sat 7 Dec 6:05 p.m.**   **7**   **1 wk**

This programme was recorded earlier in the afternoon at the Empire Theatre, Liverpool with panel members George Harrison, John Lennon, Paul McCartney and Ringo Starr.
Producer: Neville Wortman.

1964   **7.4**   **Sat 4 Jul 7:10 p.m.**   **5**   **1 wk**

Instead of the usual four panellists, there are five – the Rolling Stones.
Producer: Barry Langford.

1965   **5.5**   **Sat 20 Mar 5:20 p.m.**   **18**   **2 wks**

Panellists include Georgia Brown, Paul Jones and Edmund Purdom.
Producer: Stewart Morris.

1966   **5.0**   **Sat 30 Jul 5:40 p.m.**   **8**   **1 wk**

Panellists: Dave Cash, Susan Hampshire, Joy Marshall and Jackie Stewart.
Producer: Terry Henebery.

1967   **5.1**   **Sat 20 May 5:25 p.m.**   **15**   **1 wk**

Panellists: Leslie Crowther, Kenny Everett, Julie Felix and Shirley Ann Field.
Producer: Colin Charman.

1979   **11.8**   **Sat 11 Aug 6:15 p.m.**   **10**   **1 wk**

The show is revived with Noel Edmonds occupying the chair warmed for so many years by David Jacobs. Panellists: Tina Charles, Kenny Everett, Lesley Judd and Sting.
Director: Bruce Milliard. **Producer:** Roger Ordish.

Julie Andrews Hour, The   1 wk

ATV, entertainment

An occasional series starring Julie Andrews, the child star who became a cinema legend, and whose mother and stepfather Ted and Barbara Andrews had been radio stars.

1972   **5.7**   **Sat 16 Sep 8:25 p.m.**   **18**   **1 wk**

Guest: Rich Little.
Musical Director: Nelson Riddle. **Director:** Bill Davis. **Producer:** Nick Vanoff.

Julie Andrews Show, The   2 wks

USA presented by BBC, entertainment

1965   **5.1**   **Fri 24 Dec 8:00 p.m.**   **16**   **1 wk**

Guests: Gene Kelly and the New Christy Minstrels. With the Irwin Kostal orchestra.
Producer: Alan Handley.

1967   **5.8**   **Sun 31 Dec 7:25 p.m.**   **17**   **1 wk**

A repeat of the above 1965 show.

Julie on Sesame Street   1 wk

ATV, entertainment

1974   **6.2**   **Wed 10 Jul 8:00 p.m.**   **4**   **1 wk**

Julie Andrews stars with Jim Henson's SESAME STREET Muppets and special guest Perry Como.
Choreographer: Paddy Stone. **Producers:** Gary Smith and Dwight Hemion.

Juliet Bravo   63 wks

BBC, drama

This series of fifty-minute dramas concerned a female police inspector in the north of England. Stephanie Turner played Inspector Jean Darblay until 1983 when Anna Carteret took over as Inspector Kate Longton.
Directors included Marc Miller (1984, 1988). **Producer:** Geraint Morris (1983–86 and 1988).

1980   **16.9**   **Sat 29 Nov 7:20 p.m.**   **3**   **14 wks**

'Oscar' by Keith Dewhurst.
Eleven-year-old Janice (Susan Parry) claims she has been told to steal washing from a launderette by a mystery man named Oscar.
Director: Derek Lister. **Producers:** Colin Shindler and Terence Williams.

1981   **13.7**   **Sat 3 Oct 7:10 p.m.**   **7**   **12 wks**

'A Private Place' by Colin Haydn Evans.
Jean senses there is something still to be learned as bulldozers move in on a couple of pensioners who have ignored an eviction order.
Director: Jonathan Alwyn. **Producer:** Terence Williams.

1982   **12.7**   **Sat 27 Nov 7:30 p.m.**   **6**   **12 wks**

'Misunderstandings' by Valerie Georgeson.
An old lady and a young woman share the problem of loneliness with tragic results.
Director: Diarmuid Lawrence. **Producer:** Jonathan Alwyn.

| 1983 | 10.0 | Sat 24 Sep 7:35 p.m. | 12 | 3 wks |

'Solvent Solution' by Wally K. Daly.
Inspector Kate Longton tries to protect children from the deadly habit of glue sniffing.
Director: Sarah Hellings.

| 1984 | 14.2 | Sat 24 Nov 7:10 p.m. | 8 | 10 wks |

'Resolution' by Don Webb.
A man has died after being found unconscious in a police cell.

| 1985 | 13.5 | Sat 30 Nov 7:20 p.m. | 6 | 10 wks |

'Girl Talk' by Wally K. Daly.
Kate investigates the complaints of a schoolgirl's mother.
Director: Roderick Graham.

| 1986 | 9.0 | Tue 19 Aug 8:00 p.m. | 10 | 1 wk |

'Chasing the Dragon' by John Foster.
Kate is called in to help a family facing a serious problem over drugs. (Repeat.)
Director: Frank W. Smith.

| 1988 | 9.9 | Tue 12 Jul 8:00 p.m. | 12 | 1 wk |

'Bad Seed' by John Foster.
A missing doctor's photograph resembles an artist's impression of a wanted man. (Repeat.)

Jumpin' Jack Flash — 1 wk

Presented by ITV, film

| 1991 | 11.9 | Wed 1 May 8:00 p.m. | 10 | 1 |

Whoopi Goldberg stars as bored computer operator Terry Doolittle. She suddenly gets word on her screen from a British spy trapped behind the Iron Curtain. She embarks on a rescue mission.
Director: Penny Marshall.

Jungle Book, The — 1 wk

Presented by BBC, film

| 1980 | 14.7 | Sat 20 Dec 5:55 p.m. | 10 | 1 wk |

Sabu stars as Mowgli in this version of Rudyard Kipling's story of a boy growing up in the jungle with wild animals.
Director: Zoltan Korda. **Producer:** Alexander Korda.

Just Amazing — 12 wks

YTV, entertainment

Kenny Lynch, Barry Sheene and Jan Raven presented daring feats and performances. Suzanne Danielle replaced Raven during the series.

| 1983 | 8.2 | Sat 23 Jul 7:00 p.m. | 10 | 6 wks |

A man takes to the air with a caravan in tow. A Frenchman drives a car through a bus. A deaf child shows an extraordinary gift for music, and a chimpanzee named Jigs is an expert bartender.
Director: Ian Bolt. **Producer:** John Fanshawe.

| 1984 | 11.3 | Sat 2 Jun 7:30 p.m. | 8 | 6 wks |

Among the contributors is a Frenchman who has eaten his way through seven bicycles, two beds, six supermarket trolleys, five televisions and a Cessna light aircraft.
Directors: Phil Bishop and Ian McFarlane. **Producer:** John Fanshawe.

Just Amazing Special — 1 wk

YTV, entertainment

| 1983 | 11.0 | Tue 27 Dec 2:30 p.m. | 17 | 1 wk |

Kenny Lynch, Barrie Sheene and Suzanne Danielle present some of the most dangerous stunts ever attempted.
Directors: Phil Bishop and Ian McFarlane. **Producer:** John Fanshawe.

Just Between Friends — 1 wk

Presented by BBC, film

| 1991 | 10.5 | Sun 31 Mar 8:15 p.m. | 18 | 1 wk |

Holly (Mary Tyler Moore) and Sandy (Christine Lahti) meet by chance and establish a firm friendship. They have several things in common, but neither realizes one of them is Holly's husband Chip (Ted Danson).
Director: Alan Burns.

Just For Laughs — 6 wks

Presented by ITV, comedy

These extracts from classic British film comedies were compiled by producer Gerald Thomas.

1985	10.3	Mon 29 Jul 9:30 p.m.	16	1 wk
1987	9.1	Mon 15 Jun 8:00 p.m.	13	2 wks
1989	9.2	Mon 15 May 8:00 p.m.	17	2 wks
1991	9.4	Mon 5 Aug 8:00 p.m.	17	1 wk

J

Just Good Friends — 32 wks

BBC, situation comedy

This series by John Sullivan starred Paul Nicholas as Vince Pinner and Jan Francis as Penny Warrender. They met at a Rolling Stones concert in Hyde Park. After two years they were to marry, but Vince rode off on his motorbike two days before the wedding. He returned five years later.
Producer: *Ray Butt.*

| 1983 | 11.8 | Thu 3 Nov 9:25 p.m. | 6 | 6 wks |

Penny finally moves into Vince's new flat.

| 1984 | 15.4 | Sun 18 Nov 8:35 p.m. | 3 | 6 wks |

Penny's divorce at last comes through.

| 1985 | 13.7 | Thu 5 Dec 9:25 p.m. | 4 | 10 wks |

Vince cons Penny into going on a goodbye holiday to Portugal.

| 1986 | 20.8 | Thu 25 Dec 6:00 p.m. | 2 | 6 wks |

Vince and Penny prepare for the traditional Christmas.
Director: *Sue Bysh.*

| 1987 | 13.4 | Sun 12 Apr 9.25 p.m. | 7 | 4 wks |

Repeat of the episode in which Penny and Vince meet after five years apart.

Just Good Friends Special — 1 wk

BBC, situation comedy

| 1984 | 15.2 | Tue 25 Dec 7:25 p.m. | 13 | 1 wk |

In this ninety-minute special by John Sullivan, Penny decides that the future with Vince is pointless.
Producer: *Ray Butt.*

Just Jimmy — 1 wk

ABC, situation comedy

Jimmy Clitheroe, the four foot, two inch star of radio's long-running THE CLITHEROE KID, brought the format to television with Mollie Sugden as his mother and Danny Ross as Danny. His catch phrase 'Some mothers do 'ave 'em' was taken up for Michael Crawford's series of the same name. Clitheroe died in 1973.

| 1968 | 5.6 | Sat 27 Apr 5:50 p.m. | 18 | 1 wk |

'The Last Resort'
The annual visit to Blackpool should be simple to organize, that is until Jimmy and Danny cancel out each other's arrangements.
Writer: *Ron McDonnell.* **Producer:** *Ronnie Baxter.*

Just Liz — 6 wks

Thames, situation comedy

This series by John Esmonde and Bob Larbey starred Sandra Payne as Liz Parker, whose fiancé left her to cope while he went to Bahrain to earn enough money so they could get married. Rodney Bewes played her work colleague Reg Last and Gorden Kaye portrayed her neighbour Mr Chatto. Terence Alexander and Avril Angers also starred.

| 1980 | 15.2 | Mon 8 Sep 8:30 p.m. | 4 | 6 wks |

As far as Mr Chatto can see, Reg is keeping too close an eye on Liz.
Producer: *Robert Reed.*

Just One Kid — 1 wk

ATV, documentary

| 1974 | 5.7 | Tue 11 Jun 9:00 p.m. | 13 | 1 wk |

A Jewish tailor returns to his beloved East End of London in search of memories of the struggles of similar Jews in the 1920s and 1930s.
Camera: *Mike Whittaker.* **Producer:** *John Goldschmidt.*

Justice — 38 wks

YTV, drama

This series created by James Mitchell and Edmund Ward starred Margaret Lockwood as Harriet Peterson, a successful barrister.
Producer (1971–73): *James Ormerod.* **Executive Producer:** *Peter Willes.*

| 1971 | 7.3 | Fri 15 Oct 9:00 p.m. | 6 | 11 wks |

'By Order of the Magistrates' by Edmund Ward.
In a child custody case, Harriet comes up against a solicitor with an enviable reputation for winning matrimonial cases.
Director: *Tony Wharmby.*

| 1972 | 6.7 | Fri 14 Jan 9:00 p.m. | 11 | 2 wks |

'A Duty to the Court' by James Mitchell.
Joyce Ramsdell (Barbara Jefford) is accused of poisoning her first husband. Harriet defends her.

| 1973 | 7.2 | Fri 16 Feb 9:00 p.m. | 6 | 12 wks |

'Malicious Damage' by Kevin Laffan.
Harriet finds more than a legal involvement when she comes into contact with a beautiful young wife who is posing for an artist.

| 1974 | 7.2 | Fri 17 May 9:00 p.m. | 1 | 13 wks |

'Trial for Murder' by David Ambrose.

Harriet, defending a woman charged with murder, crosses swords with a barrister new to chambers, James Eliot (Anthony Valentine). **Director:** John Frankau. **Producer:** Jacky Stoller.

....

Justice is a Woman	1 wk

YTV, drama

1969	5.7	Thu 4 Sep 7:30 p.m.	5	1 wk

Single play by Jack Roffey and Ronald Kinnoch adapted for television by Stanley Miller. Margaret Lockwood stars as Julia Stanford, a barrister called to a Scottish court to defend a boy charged with rape and murder. Also starring Allan Cuthbertson, Iain Cuthbertson, Cavan Kendall, David Langton, John Laurie and Roddy McMillan. **Designer:** James Bould. **Director:** Joan Kemp-Welch. **Producer:** Peter Willes.

Margaret Lockwood as Harriet Peterson argues the cause of **Justice**.

Kane and Abel — *1 wk*

USA presented by BBC, drama

In this three-part adaptation by Robert Lenski of Jeffrey Archer's novel, Abel had made a fortune as a hotelier in America and Kane headed the largest bank in the world. The 1929 Wall Street crash heralded a bitter vendetta between them. Peter Strauss starred as Abel Rosnovski and Sam Neill as William Kane. Also starred Christopher Cazenove, David Dukes, Veronica Hamel and Kate McNeil. **Director:** *Buzz Kulik.*

1986	12.6	Tue 3 Jun 8:00 and 9:30 p.m. Thu 5 Jun 8:00 and 9:30 p.m. Fri 6 Jun 8:00 and 9:30 p.m.	3	1 wk

These episodes were listed together in the ratings.

Kangaroo Valley — *1 wk*

ATV, documentary

1967	4.5	Wed 28 Jun 9:40 p.m.	19	1 wk

Up to 50,000 Australians have set up home in the Earl's Court district of London. John Pett takes a look at their lifestyles. **Writer** and **Producer:** *Robin Brown.*

Karate Kid, The — *2 wks*

Presented by ITV, film

1989	14.0	Sat 1 Apr 9:05 p.m.	9	1 wk

Ralph Macchio plays Danny La Russo, a boy from New Jersey who moves to California and joins a karate club. Noriyuki 'Pat' Morita plays his mentor, Mr Miyagi. **Director:** *John G. Avildsen.*

1991	14.1	Sat 9 Nov 9:05 p.m.	12	1 wk

Repeat showing of the above film.

Kate — *31 wks*

YTV, drama

Phyllis Calvert starred in the title role as a widowed mother living in Chelsea with her teenage son. She worked as 'Dear Monica' on the agony column of Heart and Home *magazine, sorting out other people's problems in general and those of her editor in particular.*

1970	8.2	Wed 4 Feb 9:00 p.m.	4	13 wks

'Dance Little Baby, Dance up High' by Alan Falconer.
Kate advises and protects a highly-strung furniture designer from the pressures of commerce and a dominating mother.
   This episode features the first appearance of Philip Lowrie since he left CORONATION STREET. Penelope Keith also appears.
Designer: *Vic Symonds.* **Director:** *Michael Currer-Briggs.* **Producer:** *Peter Mortimer.*

1971	6.9	Fri 1 Oct 9:00 p.m.	4	8 wks

'The Great Female Rebellion' by Fay Weldon.
Heart and Home *is heading for disaster until saved by a women's liberation group.*
Designer: *Gordon Livesey.* **Director:** *June Wyndham Davies.* **Executive Producer:** *Pieter Rogers.*

1972	7.3	Mon 18 Sep 9:00 p.m.	4	10 wks

'People Depend on You' by Susan Pleat.
After an outburst of pilfering, Kate and her secretary Miss Wren (Isabel Dean) have differing views on the proper form of procedure. After thirteen years, there are cracks in their relationship.
Designer: *Gordon Livesey.* **Director:** *Paul Annett.* **Producer:** *Pieter Rogers.*

Kathy Kirby Show, The — *1 wk*

BBC, music

The blonde singer Kathy Kirby reached No. 4 in the pop charts in 1963 with a revival of Doris Day's 1954 hit 'Secret Love'. Television viewers will remember her for her particularly glossy lipstick.

1964	4.6	Fri 16 Oct 9:30 p.m.	20	1 wk

Guests: Bernard Bresslaw, Peter Gordeno and Jessie Matthews, with the George Mitchell singers and the Eric Robinson orchestra. **Producer:** *Ernest Maxin.*

Keep it in the Family   **2 wks**

YTV, situation comedy

The Bannisters each had one parent living with them. James Bannister (Tim Barrett) hosted his mother Norah (Joyce Grant) and Yvonne Bannister (Vivienne Martin) her father Des (Jack Haig). Series by **Writers:** David Nobbs and Peter Vincent.

1971	**6.3**	**Tue 19 Oct 8:30 p.m.**	**17**	**2 wks**

'Happy Event'
Rummaging in the loft, James discovers Norah's old wedding dress. **Director:** Keith Beckett. **Producer:** Ian Davidson.

....

Keep it in the Family   **29 wks**

Thames, situation comedy

This series created by Brian Cooke about the upstairs/downstairs life of two parents and their daughters featured the Rush family: cartoonist father Dudley (Robert Gillespie), mother Muriel (Pauline Yates) and daughters Susan (Stacy Dorning) and Jacqui (Jenny Quayle 1980, Sabina Franklyn 1981–83). Glyn Houston played Dudley's boss, Duncan Thomas. **Producer** (1980–82): Mark Stuart.

1980	**18.1**	**Mon 28 Jan 8:00 p.m.**	**4**	**12 wks**

'The Non-Mechanical Man' by Brian Cooke.
Susan's boyfriend Sid (Mike Grady) is an engineer and consequently useful. Although Susan has had enough of him, Dudley thinks he should stay.

1981	**13.0**	**Thu 29 Sep 7:30 p.m.**	**9**	**6 wks**

'A Matter of Principle' by Alex Shearer.
Susan needs to buy a car, but she must borrow the money from Dudley. (Robbie Coltrane plays the role of Conway.)

1982	**12.3**	**Tue 16 Nov 8:00 p.m.**	**8**	**5 wks**

'Piano Blues' by Dave and Greg Freeman.
The girls form a rock group and Dudley hurts his hand in their piano. He consequently cannot draw his cartoons. Duncan demands two weeks' supply of drawings.

1983	**13.1**	**Wed 12 Oct 8:30 p.m.**	**4**	**6 wks**

'That Old Black Magic' by Dave and Greg Freeman.
Duncan Thomas regrets moving in with the Rushes. It appears his houseplants have similar regrets. **Producer:** Robert Reed.

....

Keeping Up Appearances   **5 wks**

BBC, situation comedy

This series by Roy Clarke starred Patricia Routledge as Mrs Hyacinth Bucket (pronounced 'Bouquet'). She was obsessed with etiquette and social stature, demanding ridiculous standards from her exasperated husband Richard (Clive Swift). Her sisters Daisy (Judy Cornwell) and Rose (Shirley Stelfox, later Mary Millar) caused her much embarrassment, as did her brother-in-law Onslow (Geoffrey Hughes). Josephine Tewson played her unimpressed neighbour Liz and Gerald Sim played the vicar who hid at the first sight of Hyacinth. **Producer:** Harold Snoad.

1990	**13.6**	**Mon 3 Dec 8:30 p.m.**	**8**	**5 wks**

A family christening is fine by Hyacinth, except that it's Daisy's family and they just don't know how to do things properly.

....

Kelly's Heroes   **1 wk**

Presented by ITV, film

1978	**14.3**	**Sat 22 Apr 7:30 p.m.**	**13**	**1 wk**

Private Kelly (Clint Eastwood) leads an American platoon behind enemy lines during the Second World War and accidentally discovers the whereabouts of sixteen million dollars in gold bullion. Also starring Don Rickles, Telly Savalas and Donald Sutherland. **Director:** Brian G. Hutton.

....

Kelvin Hall Circus, The   **5 wks**

ATV (1964–66) and STV (1967), circus

This circus took place annually at Glasgow's Kelvin Hall. The ringmaster was Alfred R. Delbosq. **Television presentation** (1964–66): Francis Essex.

1964	**6.7**	**Wed 11 Mar 9:40 p.m.**	**13**	**1 wk**

Featured: the Berosini Family, the Flying Steeles, Harry Jahn's elephants, Los Onas, the Seven Lukacs and Gloria Smart's ponies.

1965	**6.8**	**Wed 20 Jan 9:45 p.m.**	**12**	**2 wks**

Featured: Ugo Garrido, Jorgen and Conny, Oscar Konyot and the Chimpanzee Rodeo, the Roberts Brothers' Dogs, the Four Rodriguez and the See Hee Troupe.

1966	**6.6**	**Sun 18 Dec 10:05 p.m.**	**9**	**1 wk**

Featured: Les Aratas, the Flying Artons, the Seven Ashtons, Chy-Bao Troupe, the Three Hermanis and the Robert Mariani Trio.

1967	**7.4**	**Sun 24 Dec 4:40 p.m.**	**4**	**1 wk**

Featured: Tibor Alexander and his Dog Revue, the Rudi Lenz Chimpanzees, the Six Kludskys, the Roberts Brothers' Horses and Elephants. **Television presentation:** Bryan Izzard

K

Ken Dodd Christmas Show, The | 3 wks

BBC, entertainment
Producer: Michael Hurll.

| 1965 | 5.8 | Sat 25 Dec 9:30 p.m. | 11 | 1 wk |

Guests: Patricia Hayes, Neville King, John Laurie, David Mahlowe, Graham Stark and Sandie Shaw with the Irving Davies dancers, the Mike Sammes singers and the Ken Jones orchestra.
Producer: Michael Hurll.

| 1966 | 5.5 | Sun 25 Dec 8:00 p.m. | 9 | 1 wk |

Guests: The Bachelors, Patricia Hayes, John Laurie, Graham Stark and Rita Webb, with the Lissa Gray singers, the Bernard Herrmann orchestra and the Diddymen.

| 1967 | 6.5 | Mon 25 Dec 8:40 p.m. | 8 | 1 wk |

Guests: Patricia Hayes, John Laurie, Graham Stark and the Seekers with the Tiller Girls, the Mike Sammes singers and the Peter Knight orchestra.

....

Ken Dodd in 'Funny You Should Say That' | 2 wks

ATV, comedy

| 1972 | 5.8 | Sat 8 Apr 5:45 p.m. | 17 | 2 wks |

With David Hamilton, Jeremy Lloyd, Barbara Mullaney, the Mike Sammes singers and the Jack Parnell orchestra.
Producer: Bill Hitchcock.

....

Ken Dodd Laughter Show, The | 4 wks

Thames, comedy

Songs, sketches and quick-fire gags from Doddy, the 'Squire of Knotty Ash'.

| 1979 | 14.8 | Mon 8 Jan 7:00 p.m. | 12 | 4 wks |

With the series regulars Hilda Fenemore, Talfryn Thomas and the Nigel Lythgoe dancers.
Writers: Norman Beadle and Frank Hughes. **Producer:** Dennis Kirkland.

....

Ken Dodd Show, The | 6 wks

BBC, entertainment

Liverpudlian Ken Dodd rose to television stardom in the mid-1950s. Although known mainly as a comedian he made several hit records, the most successful of which was 'Tears', which held the No. 1 position for 5 weeks in 1965. The shows were written by Eddie Braben and Ken Dodd.

| 1961 | 4.8 | Sat 18 Nov 7:05 p.m. | 17 | 2 wks |

A one-off show from the Empire Theatre, Liverpool. Guests: Rob Murray, Rawicz and Landauer, Lita Roza and the Northern Dance orchestra conducted by Bernard Herrmann with the Irving Davies dancers.
Producer: Barney Colehan.

| 1962 | 5.0 | Sat 27 Oct 7:15 p.m. | 19 | 1 wk |

Guests: The Kaye Sisters and John Slater, with the Irving Davies dancers.
Producer: Barney Colehan.

| 1966 | 5.0 | Sun 24 Jul 8:15 p.m. | 9 | 2 wks |

This show was broadcast live from Blackpool. With guests Wifrid Brambell, Harry H. Corbett, Salena Jones, Graham Stark, the Diddymen, the Bluebell Girls, the Shepherd Singers and the Bernard Herrmann orchestra.
Producer: Duncan Wood.

| 1969 | 5.3 | Sat 21 Jun 7:00 p.m. | 17 | 1 wk |

Guests: the Herculeans, Vince Hill, Nigel Hopkins, Sandy Powell and Luis Alberto de Parana y Trio Los Paraguayos. With series regulars the Diddymen, Dermot Kelly, Ruth Kettlewell, David Mahlowe, Arthur Mullard, the Nita Howard dancers and the Peter Knight orchestra.
Producer: Michael Hurll.

....

Ken Dodd's World of Laughter | 11 wks

BBC, entertainment

| 1974 | 6.8 | Fri 22 Nov 8:15 p.m. | 15 | 5 wks |

Guests: Windsor Davies, Sandy Powell and Bill Tidy with the Young Generation, the Ronnie Hazlehurst orchestra and the Maggie Stredder singers.
Writer: Ken Dodd. **Producer:** Michael Hurll.

| 1975 | 7.7 | Thu 20 Nov 7:45 p.m. | 9 | 6 wks |

Guests: Chris Emmett, Hilda Fenemore, Michael McClain and Talfryn Thomas, with the Dougie Squires Dozen, the Maggie Stredder singers and the Ronnie Hazlehurst orchestra.
Writers: Norman Beadle, Dave Dutton and David McKellar. **Producer:** Michael Hurll.

....

Kennedy | 1 wk

Central, drama

| 1983 | 10.4 | Mon 21 Nov 8:00 p.m.
Tue 22 Nov 8:00 p.m. | 20 | 1 wk |

These two episodes were listed together in the ratings. They are the second and third episodes of a three-part story by Reg Gadney that followed John F. Kennedy from his campaign for the Presidency to his assassination. Martin Sheen starred as JFK and Blair Brown played Jackie. E.G. Marshall was father Joseph and John Shea brother Robert. Vincent Gardenia appeared as J. Edgar Hoover. **Director:** Jim Goddard. **Producer:** Andrew Brown. **Executive Producer:** Margaret Matheson.

Kennedy Shooting, The   1 wk

ITN, news

| 1968 | 5.8 | Wed 5 Jun 10:00 p.m. | 9 | 1 wk |

Robert Kennedy was shot dead in Los Angeles by Sirhan Sirhan after winning the California primary election.

Kenneth More Season, A   5 wks

Presented by BBC, film

This series of famous and not so famous films starred the very British Kenneth More.

| 1970 | 5.5 | Sun 7 Jun 9:10 p.m. | 3 | 5 wks |

'Genevieve'
John Gregson, Kay Kendall, and Dinah Sheridan join Kenneth More in a comedy based on the London to Brighton car run. A 1904 Darracq plays the part of Genevieve.
Director: Henry Cornelius.

Kenny Everett Christmas Show, The   1 wk

BBC, comedy

| 1984 | 15.9 | Thu 27 Dec 7:50 p.m. | 8 | 1 wk |

Guests: Boy George and Culture Club.
Writers: Ray Cameron, Barry Cryer and Kenny Everett. **Director:** David Taylor. **Producer:** Bill Wilson.

Kenny Everett Television Show, The   19 wks

BBC, comedy

The writing trio of THE KENNY EVERETT VIDEO SHOW continued under a new title when they changed channels.

| 1982 | 13.3 | Thu 11 Mar 8:00 p.m. | 7 | 9 wks |

Producer: Bill Wilson. **Executive Producer:** James Moir.

| 1983 | 12.3 | Thu 17 Mar 8:00 p.m. | 8 | 7 wks |

Producer: Bill Wilson.

| 1985 | 13.5 | Sat 13 Apr 8:05 p.m. | 3 | 3 wks |

Producer: John Bishop.

Kenny Everett Video Show, The   11 wks

Thames, comedy

Disc jockey Kenny Everett appeared as a variety of outrageous comedy characters. Raunchy dancers Hot Gossip were choreographed by Arlene Phillips.
Writers: Ray Cameron, Barry Cryer and Kenny Everett. **Producer:** David Mallett.

| 1979 | 14.2 | Mon 19 Feb 7:00 p.m. | 12 | 7 wks |

Guest: David Essex.

| 1980 | 13.8 | Mon 14 Apr 7:00 p.m. | 10 | 4 wks |

Guests: The Police.

Kick Start   2 wks

BBC, sport

This series of motorcycle trials was presented by Dave Lee Travis from Birmingham.

| 1979 | 15.9 | Mon 13 Aug 6:20 p.m. | 8 | 2 wks |

DLT presents eight competitors for a place in next week's final.
Director: Phil Franklin. **Producer:** Derek Smith.

Kids   5 wks

LWT, drama

This 13-part series was set in a Reception and Assessment Centre where children went for juvenile court reports while awaiting adoption or fostering or while their parents could not look after them. James Hazledine played the Centre's superintendent and Caroline Mortimer played his GP wife.

| 1979 | 11.5 | Fri 4 May 9:00 p.m. | 14 | 5 wks |

'Melanie'
The young residents of Kingston House are joined by Granville, a young West Indian, who has offended against the law by stealing a London bus. But who is Melanie? Is she the reason he did it?
Producer: John Frankau. **Executive Producer:** Tony Wharmby.

Killer | 2 wks

STV, drama

This three-part thriller by Glen Chandler introduced Detective Chief Inspector Jim Taggart (Mark McManus), who later featured in his own series of TAGGART.

| 1983 | 10.5 | Tue 20 Sep 9:00 p.m. | 10 | 2 wks |

Episode Three
Taggart is up against a compulsive murderer of young blonde Glaswegian women.
Designer: Marius Van Der Werff. **Director:** Laurence Moody. **Producer:** Robert Love.

Killer | 3 wks

YTV, drama

This trilogy of plays by Robin Chapman and Eric Wendell had a murderous theme.

| 1984 | 11.9 | Fri 24 Feb 9:00 p.m. | 14 | 3 wks |

'Killer Exposed'
Robin Fraser (Anthony Valentine) is fatally fascinated by the outrageously promiscuous Charlie (Molly Radlove).
Designer: David Crozier. **Director:** James Ormerod. **Executive Producer:** David Cunliffe.

Killer Fish | 1 wk

Presented by BBC, film

| 1982 | 9.5 | Tue 15 Jun 7:20 p.m. | 15 | 1 wk |

Stolen emeralds worth millions of dollars are thrown into a Brazilian reservoir. Deadly predator fish guard the treasure. Starring Marisa Berenson, Karen Black, James Franciscus, Margaux Hemingway and Lee Majors.
Director: Anthony M. Dawson.

Killer in the Mirror | 1 wk

Presented by ITV, film

| 1988 | 11.5 | Wed 2 Nov 9:00 p.m. | 16 | 1 wk |

Ann Jillian plays identical twins Samantha and Karen, one of whom is a conniving murderess.
Director: Frank DeFelitta.

Killers | 4 wks

Thames, drama

These reconstructions of actual murder trials were based on original transcripts.

| 1976 | 5.5 | Wed 30 Jun 9:00 p.m. | 14 | 4 wks |

'The Stinie Morrison Case' by Clive Exton.
On New Year's Day, 1911, Leon Beron was clubbed to death on Clapham Common. Stinie Morrison (Stephen Greif) is the accused.
Director: Peter Duguid. **Producer:** Jacqueline Davis.

Killing at Hell's Gate | 1 wk

Presented by BBC, film

| 1986 | 9.8 | Sat 17 May 7:50 p.m. | 15 | 1 wk |

A politician and a lawyer look forward to an exhilarating journey down Oregon's white water rapids. It turns into a nightmare. Paul Burke, Deborah Raffin and Robert Urich star.
Director: Jerry Jameson.

Kind of Loving, A | 6 wks

Granada, drama

Stan Barstow wrote this ten-part adaptation of his own novels. The stories tell of the life and loves of Vic Brown (Clive Wood) in the West Riding of Yorkshire from the 1950s to the 1970s. The series also starred Joanne Whalley as Ingrid Rothwell.

| 1982 | 14.6 | Sun 25 Apr 9:00 p.m. | 2 | 6 wks |

Episode Four 'April–November 1959'.
Vic and the pregnant Ingrid will marry but will have to live with her parents. Vic and Ingrid's mother (Clare Kelly) do not get on at all.
Designers: Chris Truelove and Tim Wilding. **Director:** Gerry Mill. **Producer:** Pauline Shaw.

Kindly Leave the Kerb | 1 wk

LWT, situation comedy

Johnnie Mortimer and Brian Cooke created this series, in which Peter Butterworth as Ernest and Peter Jones as Sidney formed one of the oldest busking teams on the streets of London. This partnership involved Sidney as the manager and spieler for Ernest's escapology act.

| 1971 | 5.5 | Fri 11 Jun 8:25 p.m. | 17 | 1 wk |

'The Wallet'
Ernest can't be a proper escapologist without proper equipment and Sidney can't be a proper manager without cash in his pocket. The queues aren't providing the cash, so some other means must be found.
Producer: Derek Bennett.

King and Castle
1 wk

Thames, drama

This series by Ian Kennedy Martin starred Derek Martin and Nigel Planer as debt collectors Ronald King and David Castle.

| 1988 | 8.8 | Tue 24 May 9:00 p.m. | 17 | 1 wk |

'Hams'
David is given a great recipe for cooking hams, but introducing Hilary (Rowena Roberts) to Carol (Lucy Hancock) is a recipe for disaster. **Director:** Jan Sargent. **Producer:** Peter Duguid. **Executive Producer:** Lloyd Shirley.

King George's Jubilee Trust
1 wk

BBC, documentary

| 1960 | 5.6 | Fri 29 Apr 9:00 p.m. | 9 | 1 wk |

Christopher Chataway MP introduces film of the widely different organizations helped by the Trust. HRH The Duke of Gloucester, Chairman of the Council, speaks about the work of the Trust, founded by his father King George V twenty-five years ago.

King of the River
1 wk

BBC, drama

Bernard Lee starred as Joss King, the skipper of a sailing barge, whose family was determined that his son Saul (Richard James) would not follow him to sea. The series also starred Meg Wynn Owen as Joss's elder daughter Ruth, Geraldine Sherman as younger daughter Susanna, Robert Brown as Uncle Ben and Sandra Dorne as Nel, the landlady of the local pub.

| 1966 | 4.5 | Tue 19 Jul 9:40 p.m. | 16 | 1 wk |

'Shipwreck' by Colin Morris.
Joss is at the wheel of a motor-powered barge in dangerous sea conditions. Saul is on board with him, which has caused a serious rift in the family.
Designer: Roy Stannard. **Producer:** Gerard Glaister.

King's Revolution, A
1 wk

AR for Intertel, documentary

| 1964 | 6.5 | Wed 1 Jan 9:40 p.m. | 12 | 1 wk |

His Majesty The Shah of Iran explains his dramatic plan to transform his ancient and backward land into a progressive industrial nation. Andrew Faulds narrates.
Writer: Paul Johnson. **Director:** Randal Beattie.

Kinvig
2 wks

LWT, situation comedy

This series by Nigel Kneale starred Tony Haygarth as Des Kinvig, an electrical repairman, married to doting wife Netta (Patsy Rowland). His life was changed when he met the mysterious Miss Griffin (Prunella Gee). Prior to her arrival, Kinvig's sole diversion was with his pal Jim Piper (Colin Jeavons), who was obsessed with alien spaceships.

| 1981 | 11.0 | Fri 4 Sep 8:30 p.m. | 14 | 2 wks |

'Contact'
In this opening episode the mysterious Miss Griffin enters Kinvig's repair shop for the first time.
Producer: Les Chatfield.

Kipling
1 wk

BBC, drama

This series of dramatizations of the Indian short stories of Rudyard Kipling starred Joss Ackland as newspaper editor William Stevens and Kenneth Fortescue as James Lockwood, his young assistant.

| 1964 | 7.0 | Sun 5 Jul 9:20 p.m. | 12 | 1 wk |

'A Bank Fraud' adapted by John Maynard.
Stevens and Lockwood become involved in intertwined stories of the rise and fall of Naboth, an Indian sweet-seller, and the short life of Riley, a young man from Yorkshire who works in a local bank. Guest star appearances by Alfred Burke, Barry Letts, Murray Melvin and Ralph Michael.
Designer: Fanny Taylor. **Director:** Shaun Sutton. **Producer:** David Goddard.

Kiss is Just a Kiss, A
1 wk

Anglia, drama

| 1971 | 7.0 | Wed 31 Mar 9:00 p.m. | 10 | 1 wk |

Kit Shaeffer (David Hedison) is a wealthy young lawyer. He has a beautiful wife, Louise (Lelia Goldoni), and a home in the Hollywood hills. He has a life insurance policy and, ominously, goes for a checkup from his best friend Dr Alex Noon (Keir Dullea).
Designer: Barry Learoyd. **Director:** Alvin Rakoff. **Producer:** John Jacobs.

K

Kiss the Girls and Make Them Cry — 2 wks

BBC, drama

This four-part exploration of love by Mike Newling starred Steve Alder as Georgie and Sue Vanner as Wendy.

| 1979 | 17.7 | Tue 13 Nov 8:30 p.m. | 4 | 2 wks |

Episode Three
The ups and downs of a love affair leave George suffering, much against his better instincts. He feels that there is no pleasing his girlfriend Wendy.
Designer: Bernard Lloyd-Jones. **Director:** Richard Stroud. **Producer:** Colin Tucker.

Kit Curran Radio Show, The — 2 wks

Thames, situation comedy

This series by Andy Hamilton starred Denis Lawson as Radio Newtown DJ, Kit Curran. Kit was a conman, a compulsive liar with an all-consuming and passionate interest in himself.

| 1984 | 10.6 | Mon 2 Apr 8:00 p.m. | 14 | 2 wks |

'End of an Era'
Curran is asked to mend his attitude of callous indifference towards his listeners.
Producer: Derrick Goodwin.

Kitty — 1 wk

Presented by BBC, film

| 1964 | 5.3 | Sun 1 Nov 7:50 p.m. | 19 | 1 wk |

This 1945 film stars Paulette Goddard and Ray Milland. The adventures of a beautiful London street urchin in 1783 who, with the help of an aristocrat, rises from the slums to become the city's most beautiful duchess.
Director: Mitchell Leisen.

Knight Errant Ltd. — 21 wks

Granada, drama

Created by Philip Mackie, the firm of Knight Errant Ltd. specialized in solving other people's problems and rescuing damsels in distress. The principal characters were Stephen Drummond (Hugh David), Frances Graham (Wendy Williams), Colonel Cope-Addams (Alan Webb) and Gregory Wilson (Stephen Cartwright).

| 1960 | 6.8 | Thu 17 Nov 8:30 p.m. | 1 | 18 wks |

'Money No Object' by H. V. Kershaw.

A rumbustious Australian millionaire engages Knight Errant Ltd. to investigate a mysterious office break-in during which nothing was stolen. The Australian is in the process of founding a museum and has links with a beautiful secretary and a wartime secret agent.
Director: Derek Bennett. **Producer:** Kitty Black.

| 1961 | 6.6 | Thu 26 Jan 8:30 p.m. | 3 | 3 wks |

'The Genuine Article' by Gerald Savory.
A best-selling authoress finds her long-lost son. She calls in Knight Errant Ltd. to help lose him again.
Director: Roger Jenkins. **Producer:** Kitty Black.

Knight Rider — 22 wks

USA presented by ITV, drama

David Hasselhoff starred as Michael Knight, who was bequeathed an indestructible car named Kitt which could talk. The series was created and produced by Glen Larson.

| 1983 | 12.9 | Tue 10 May 7:30 p.m. | 2 | 15 wks |

'Forget Me Not'
Knight attempts to prevent the killing of a foreign head of state.

| 1984 | 13.1 | Thu 25 Oct 7:30 p.m. | 9 | 7 wks |

'Knight of the Drones'
Knight and Kitt do battle with a high-tech genius.

Knight Rider – The Movie — 1 wk

Presented by ITV, film

| 1988 | 12.0 | Fri 1 Apr 7:00 p.m. | 8 | 1 wk |

David Hasselhoff stars as Michael Long, a Vietnam veteran who has major plastic surgery. He emerges with a new identity, Michael Knight – a fighter for justice.
Director: Dan Haller.

Knock on Any Door — 5 wks

ATV, drama

This anthology of plays based on social realism was created by Ted Willis. He also introduced the series.

| 1965 | 6.1 | Sat 20 Nov 10:05 p.m. | 18 | 4 wks |

'A Houseful of Dreams' by Julian Bond.
An old rundown house is put on the market. An elderly couple still live there, confined to the old servants' quarters. Two couples come to view the property and their lives become inextricably linked with the history of the house. Starring Fay Compton and Ursula Howells.
Designer: Stanley Mills. **Director:** Kevin Shine. **Producer:** Pieter Rogers.

1966	4.8	Sat 4 Jun 10:05 p.m.	18	1 wk

'Dear Ones' by Hugh C. Rae.
All her friends are astonished when Marion Scoullar (Renée Houston) gives up her residence to live in an old folks' home. While there she meets Peter Fisher (John Laurie). The ensuing relationship soon has daughter Sarah (Brenda Bruce) scurrying north of the border from London to check out his intentions towards her mother.
Designer: Brian Bartholomew. **Director:** Cecil Petty. **Producer:** Pieter Rogers.

Knots Landing — 8 wks

USA presented by BBC, soap

David Jacobs, creator of DALLAS, set this series in a small suburban community in southern California. The stories revolved around the families of four couples, Gary and Valene Ewing (Ted Shackleford and Joan Van Ark), Sid and Karen Fairgate (Don Murray and Michele Lee), Richard and Laura Avery (John Pleshette and Constance McCashin) and Kenny and Ginger Ward (James Houghton and Kim Lankford). Gary Ewing was the brother of J.R. and Bobby.

1980	13.3	Sat 26 Apr 9:05 p.m.	7	8 wks

Patrick Duffy guest stars as Bobby Ewing. Lucy Ewing's parents Gary and Valene move into their new home at Knots Landing. They are hoping to make a fresh start, but with Lucy still living at Southfork the family ties may not be so easily broken.
Director: Peter Levin.

Kojak — 39 wks

USA presented by BBC, drama

Theo Kojak (Telly Savalas) was an abrasive New York detective with a distinctive bald head. He wore fancy waistcoats and had a penchant for lollipops. His beat was Manhattan's South Precinct and his aides included Bobby Crocker (Kevin Dobson) and Detective Stavros (George Savalas).
Executive Producer: Matthew Rapf.

1974	6.4	Sat 14 Dec 9:10 p.m.	4	4 wks

'Knockover'
A ring found on the hand of a murder victim turns a routine enquiry into a hunt for a ruthless crime syndicate. Guest star: Alex Rocco.

1975	7.8	Mon 2 Jun 9:35 p.m.	1	13 wks

'Two–Four–Six for Two Hundred'
Kojak knows a robbery is planned and sets up a stake-out. The robbers are alerted and make a getaway. Guest star: Robert Loggia.

1976	8.4	Thu 14 Oct 8:10 p.m.	4	11 wks

'Law Dance'
He may suck lollipops but Kojak is not one to be led a dance by any bunch of criminals. Guest star: David Wilson.

1977	6.4	Sat 16 Apr 8:40 p.m.	11	3 wks

'Monkey on a String'
A young police officer's determination to treat his wife to a fur coat leads him to become the pawn of a gangland boss. Guest star: Joseph Hindy.

1978	15.3	Sat 29 Apr 9:00 p.m.	7	8 wks

'Tears For All Who Loved Her'
Kojak's old friend Carol Austin is suspected of having murdered her mobster husband. Guest star: Sam Jaffe.

Korda Classics — 1 wk

Presented by ITV, film

Series of films produced by Alexander Korda.

1962	5.2	Sun 11 Mar 9:35 p.m.	12	1 wk

'Over The Moon'
Merle Oberon stars as Jane Benson, a girl who inherits eighteen million pounds. She is surrounded by bounty hunters, but the man she really loves is not one of them. Also stars Rex Harrison and Ursula Jeans with Zena Dare, Robert Douglas and Peter Haddon.
Director: Thornton Freeland.

Kramer vs. Kramer — 1 wk

Presented by BBC, film

1984	18.0	Sun 30 Dec 8:35 p.m.	5	1 wk

Dustin Hoffman and Meryl Streep star as estranged parents engaged in a tug-of-love for custody of their child Billy (Justin Henry).
Director: Robert Benton.

Krypton Factor, The — 148 wks

Granada, game show

This series, the ultimate test of both physical strength and mental agility, was devised by Jeremy Fox in 1977. Contestants had to tackle an Army assault course as well as tests of memory and knowledge. The title was inspired by Krypton, the home planet of Jerry Siegel and Joe Shuster's 'Superman'. Gordon Burns hosted.
Director (1984–85): Ian White. **Producers:** Jeremy Fox (1977–79), Stephen Leahy (1980–81), David Jenkins (1983–85), Geoff Moore (1986–87) and Kieran Roberts (1990–91).

1977	12.0	Wed 7 Sep 7:00 p.m.	19	1 wk

Director: Peter Walker.

For once short of a lollipop, **Kojak** (Telly Savalas) licks his finger in anticipation of another New York crime investigation.

1978	13.5	Fri 15 Sep 7:00 p.m.	3	11 wks

The semi-final.
Director: Patricia Pearson.

1979	11.4	Fri 29 Jun 7:00 p.m.	11	7 wks

Director: Nick Abson.

1980	13.9	Mon 29 Dec 7:00 p.m.	2	8 wks

In this special edition all the competitors are world champions. They are Lynn Davies (Olympic long jump gold medallist, 1964), Clare Francis (fastest Transatlantic solo yachtswoman), Jim Fox (Olympic modern pentathlon gold medallist, 1976) and David Wilkie (Olympic breaststroke swimming gold medallist, 1976).
Director: Charles Kitchen.

1981	13.9	Wed 30 Dec 7:00 p.m.	5	15 wks

In this special international edition the winner and runner-up of the first American series challenge their British counterparts.
Director: Mary McMurray.

1982	11.6	Mon 27 Sep 7:00 p.m.	5	12 wks

The final.
Director: Graham C. Williams. **Producer:** Nick Turnbull.

1983	14.0	Mon 17 Oct 7:00 p.m.	2	20 wks

The final.
Director: Brian Lennane.

1984	13.3	Mon 24 Sep 7:00 p.m.	3	17 wks

1985	12.5	Mon 18 Nov 7:00 p.m.	6	7 wks

The final.

1986	11.8	Mon 27 Oct 7:00 p.m.	12	7 wks

Director: Spencer Campbell. **Executive Producer:** Stephen Leahy.

1987	14.2	Mon 28 Dec 7:00 p.m.	7	10 wks

The final.
Director: Rod Natkiel. **Executive Producer:** Stephen Leahy.

1988	12.8	Mon 7 Nov 7:00 p.m.	11	13 wks

Director: Richard Signy. **Producer:** Patricia Pearson.

1989	12.8	Mon 27 Nov 7:00 p.m.	11	10 wks

The final. Steve Coogan and Kathy Staff assist Gordon Burns.
Director: Jonathan Bullen. **Producer:** Rod Natkiel. **Executive Producer:** David Liddiment.

1990	12.1	Mon 26 Nov 7:00 p.m.	16	1 wk

The final. This year guests are invited. They include Keith Chegwin, Derek Griffiths, Matthew Kelly, Barry McGuigan and Gwyneth Strong.
Director: Sue McMahon.

1991	14.8	Mon 25 Nov 7:00 p.m.	10	9 wks

Tony Robinson and Michelle Collins are guests.
Director: Jonathan Glazier.

Krypton Factor International, The   1 wk

Granada, game show

1988	10.5	Mon 28 Mar 7:00 p.m.	15	1 wk

A match between Great Britain, Australia and New Zealand.
Director: Rod Natkiel. **Producer:** Geoff Moore. **Executive Producer:** Stephen Leahy.

Krypton Factor International Special, The   1 wk

Granada, game show

1984	13.3	Mon 31 Dec 7:00 p.m.	18	1 wk

From Cheltenham Gordon Burns introduces contestants from the UK, Australia, New Zealand and the USA.
Director: Graham C. Williams. **Producer:** David Jenkin.

Krypton Factor Special, The   1 wk

Granada, game show

1982	11.5	Thu 30 Dec 7:00 p.m.	10	1 wk

Gordon Burns presents a special edition with jockey Geraldine Rees, film-maker Cindy Buxton, explorer Charles Burton and diver Jonathan Adams.
Director: David Hillier. **Producer:** Nick Turnbull.

Ku Klux Klan – The Invisible Empire   1 wk

ATV, documentary

1965	5.8	Wed 17 Nov 9:40 p.m.	19	1 wk

A consideration of the history and workings of the Klan. For the first time, cameras are allowed to film an initiation ceremony. Officials explain the purpose of their quest for white Protestant supremacy and victims of the Klan's brutality recite their horror stories. Narrated by Charles Kuralt.
Writer and **Producer:** David Lowe. **Executive Producer:** Palmer Williams.

L.A. Law — 3 wks

USA presented by ITV, drama

These stories about a firm of Los Angeles lawyers starred Harry Hamlin as Michael Kuzak, Susan Dey as Grace Van Owen and Amanda Donohoe as C.J. Lamb.

| 1991 | 9.9 | Thu 22 Aug 9:00 p.m. | 14 | 3 wks |

A Christian Science couple are charged with killing their son.

Lace — 2 wks

USA presented by ITV, drama

In this two-part dramatization by Elliott Baker of Shirley Conran's novel, Lili (Phoebe Cates), a Hollywood porn star, claimed to be the long lost daughter of one of three women, Maxine (Arielle Dombasle), Judy (Bess Armstrong) or Pagan (Brooke Adams). Terence Alexander, Honor Blackman, Angela Lansbury, Leigh Lawson, Herbert Lom and Anthony Quayle also starred.
Director: Billy Hale.

| 1984 | 16.2 | Mon 10 Sep 8:00 p.m. | 1 | 2 wks |

Part One
Lili summons her three potential mothers to New York.

Lace II — 1 wk

USA presented by ITV, drama

Shirley Conran's novel was adapted in two parts by Elliott Baker. Lili (Phoebe Cates) had found her mother Judy Hale (Deborah Raffin). Now she looked for her father.
Director: Billy Hale.

| 1985 | 12.0 | Sun 1 Sep 7:45 p.m. | 11 | 1 wk |

Part One
Lili begins to search for the true identity of her father.

Lady in Danger — 1 wk

USA presented by ITV, drama

| 1981 | 12.7 | Sat 11 Jul 7:55 p.m. | 4 | 1 wk |

Lynda Carter stars as a young singer whose husband is killed in strange circumstances. He has left a tape among her cassettes with an incomplete message about toxic waste on farmland. Did he know too much?

Lady Killers — 5 wks

Granada, drama

These plays were taken from real murder cases. Each play was introduced by Robert Morley.

| 1980 | 10.9 | Sun 17 Aug 9:15 p.m. | 8 | 5 wks |

'Don't Let Them Kill Me on Wednesday' by Jeremy Sandford.
Rita Tushingham stars as Charlotte Bryant, an illiterate mother of five living in the 1930s accused of poisoning her husband with arsenic. George Baker also stars as Sir Terence O'Connor QC.
Designer: Vic Symonds. **Director:** Valerie Hanson. **Producer:** Pieter Rogers.

Lady Vanishes, The — 1 wk

Presented by ITV, film

| 1982 | 11.2 | Thu 23 Dec 7:30 p.m. | 11 | 1 wk |

Amanda Kelly (Cybill Shepherd) boards a train in Bavaria in 1939. She joins a compartment occupied by Baroness Kisling (Jean Anderson) and her entourage. Miss Froy (Angela Lansbury) joins them. Amanda falls asleep. When she wakes Miss Froy is gone and the others all deny ever having seen her. Also starring Ian Carmichael, Elliott Gould, Gerald Harper, Herbert Lom and Arthur Lowe.
Director: Anthony Pate.

Lame Ducks — 2 wks

BBC2, situation comedy

This series created by Peter J. Hammond starred John Duttine as Brian Drake. He sold his house after the break-up of his marriage. He intended to use the money to live a hermit's life in the country. He failed to avert a series of disasters and picked up a reformed pyromaniac Tommy (Patric Turner) and a hitchhiker Angie (Lorraine Chase) on the way.
Producer: John B. Hobbs.

1984	11.0	Mon 22 Oct 8:30 p.m.	17	1 wk

In this first episode Drake makes his initial decision to leave suburbia and fulfil his dream of a solitary life. His plans are quickly thrown into disarray.

1986	9.9	Wed 7 May 7:40 p.m.	16	1 wk

BBC1 shows a repeat of the episode in which Brian Drake and Tommy first meet Angie.

Lance at Large — 2 wks

BBC, comedy

Lance Percival graduated from Ned Sherrin's THAT WAS THE WEEK THAT WAS to his own series. It was described in the Radio Times as 'the highly probable adventures of Lance Percival as Alan Day'. The series was written by David Nobbs and Peter Tinniswood and produced by Dennis Main Wilson. The shows made extensive use of film, taking Percival into ordinary situations where an encounter with a stranger turned life topsy-turvy.

1964	5.2	Thu 13 Aug 8:50 p.m.	14	2 wks

A baby in a pram deserves better than to encounter Lance and his guest star Eric Barker.

Land That Time Forgot, The — 2 wks

Presented by BBC, film

1980	14.8	Fri 4 Apr 7:35 p.m.	8	2 wks

Based on a story by Edgar Rice Burroughs. In 1916 the survivors of a British supply ship take over the German submarine which sank them. While heading for a safe port they find themselves in a land with prehistoric beasts and ape men. Starring Doug McClure, John McEnery, Susan Penhaligon and Keith Barron.
Director: Kevin Connor.

Langley Bottom — 1 wk

YTV, situation comedy

This series by Barry Cryer and John Junkin was set in the English village of the title. Bernard Cribbins starred as Seth Raven. Other inhabitants were played by Tim Barrett, Don Crann, Elvi Hale, Barbara Hicks and Rhoda Lewis.

1986	8.1	Mon 14 Jul 8:00 p.m.	18	1 wk

'PC Blues'
PC Wren (Peter Martin) is being transferred after thirty years as Langley Bottom's sole officer of the law.
Producer: Alan Tarrant.

Laramie — 14 wks

USA presented by BBC, western

John Smith and Robert Fuller starred as best friends Slim and Jess, who owned a trading station in Wyoming just after the Civil War. Spring Byington and Dennis Holmes also starred. A succession of passers-by provided them with weekly stories.

1962	6.0	Wed 24 Jul 8:00 p.m.	8	13 wks

'Ladies Day'
Slim and Jess try to adopt an orphan but have problems finding a housekeeper to look after him.

1964	7.0	Sat 4 Jul 7:35 p.m.	12	1 wk

'The Violent Ones'
Some people think they can get whatever they want by using force, threats and violence. But they reckon without Slim and Jess.

Larkins, The — 19 wks

ATV, situation comedy

Created and written by Fred Robinson in the 1950s, the Larkins were a Cockney couple who kept a country pub. Peggy Mount played the battle-axe Ada Larkin and David Kossoff the downtrodden Alf. Hugh Paddick played Osbert Rigby Soames, and Barbara Mitchell portrayed Hetty Prout. The Larkins' son Eddie was played by Shaun O'Riordan and Jeff Rogers by Ronan O'Casey.
Producer: Alan Tarrant.

1960	7.0	Mon 14 Mar 8:00 p.m.	1	6 wks

'Stranger Than Fiction'
Ada finally goes too far driving everyone out of the house following a showdown over her interfering and domineering attitude.

1963	7.5	Sat 9 Nov 8:25 p.m.	7	7 wks

'Café Olé'
The first of a new series in which Alf has been made redundant and the Larkin home has been compulsorily purchased. With the money from both, they've bought a café.

| 1964 | 5.8 | Sat 15 Aug 9:45 p.m. | 9 | 6 wks |

'Dizzy Rich'
Ada proves that there are two sides to every argument – hers and the wrong one – especially where money is concerned.

....

Larry's Christmas Party | 1 wk

ATV, entertainment

| 1972 | 7.3 | Fri 22 Dec 7:30 p.m. | 6 | 1 wk |

Starring Larry Grayson with guests Noele Gordon, Heathmore, Rod Hull and Emu, and Mike and Bernie Winters. With the Lionel Blair dancers and the Jack Parnell orchestra.
Writers: *Bryan Blackburn, Peter Dulay and Bernie Sharp.* **Producer:** *Colin Clews.*

....

Last Frontier, The | 2 wks

USA presented by ITV, drama

This two-part mini-series starred Linda Evans as mother-of-two Kate Hannon, who married Australian ranch-owner Tom Hannon (Tony Bonner). Jason Robards co-starred as Ed Stenning.

| 1987 | 12.4 | Mon 14 Sep 8:00 p.m. | 7 | 2 wks |

Part Two
Kate follows Tom to his ranch in the Australian outback only to learn on arrival that he has been killed in a plane crash.

....

Last Night of the Crazy Gang, The | 1 wk

ATV, entertainment

| 1962 | 7.2 | Sun 20 May 8:25 p.m. | 3 | 1 wk |

A recording of one of the most nostalgic evenings in the history of British entertainment when, last night, Jack Hylton presented the Crazy Gang in the final performance of Young at Heart at London's Victoria Palace. The stars are Bud Flanagan, Jimmy Nervo and Teddy Knox, Charlie Naughton and Jimmy Gold and 'Monsewer' Eddie Gray. There is a surprise appearance by Chesney Allen and Jack Hylton takes the baton as Bud and Ches sing some of their most famous songs.
Show Director: *Charles Henry.* **Choreographer:** *Joan Davis.* **Musical Director:** *Jack Answell.* **Television presentation:** *Bill Ward.*

....

Last Night of the Proms, The | 1 wk

BBC, music

Conductor Henry Wood inaugurated the annual promenade concerts in 1895. The final evening is now a traditional opportunity to combine music with a party.

| 1968 | 5.2 | Sat 14 Sep 8:45 p.m. | 11 | 1 wk |

Richard Baker introduces the concert from the Royal Albert Hall. The conductor is Colin Davis. 'Rule Britannia' is sung by Sybil Michelow.
Television presentation: *Brian Large.*

....

Last of the Baskets, The | 6 wks

Granada, situation comedy

After ninety-three years, the 12th Earl of Clogborough (Richard Hurndall) decided he was ready to abandon his stately pile of decaying bricks and his mounting pile of bills and say farewell to his last remaining servant, Bodkin (Arthur Lowe). First the heir to the title, Clifford Basket (Ken Jones), had to be found. He was living in sublime ignorance with Mrs Basket (Patricia Hayes). Series created by John Stevenson.

| 1971 | 7.0 | Mon 24 May 8:30 p.m. | 3 | 6 wks |

'I Gotta Horse'
Bodkin proposes the theory that a man on horseback has more chance of getting credit from local shopkeepers than one on foot. Clifford's attempts to stay in the saddle are not a total success.
Producer: *Bill Podmore.*

....

Last of the Summer Wine | 82 wks

BBC, situation comedy

This series was written and created by Roy Clarke and set in a village in the West Riding of Yorkshire. Originally the three old school friends living in retirement were Blamire (Michael Bates), Clegg (Peter Sallis) and Compo (Bill Owen). Following the death of Bates, Brian Wilde played the character Foggy, who was temporarily replaced by Seymour (Michael Aldridge). Kathy Staff played Nora Batty, the object of Compo's eternal lust. Other characters included Edie (Thora Hird), Ivy (Jane Freeman), Howard (Robert Fyfe), Marina (Jean Fergusson), Wally (Joe Gladwin), Sid (John Comer) and Pearl (Juliette Kaplan).
Producers *included Sydney Lotterby (1977, 1979, 1980 and 1983) and Alan J.W. Bell (1981–82 and 1984–90).*

| 1975 | 7.5 | Wed 5 Mar 9:35 p.m. | 9 | 2 wks |

'Forked Lightning'
Problems with a bicycle and with Compo's rabbit's foot. Sid tries to evade the dreaded Ivy.
Producer: *Bernard Thompson.*

| 1977 | 6.1 | Tue 31 May 9:25 p.m. | 13 | 1 wk |

'Isometrics and After'
Foggy is concerned that Compo and Clegg are not as physically fit as they ought to be. He sets out to remedy the situation. (Repeat.)

| 1979 | 22.2 | Tue 16 Oct 8:30 p.m. | 2 | 11 wks |

'Earnshaw Strikes Again'
Foggy invokes the wrath of Earnshaw, one of the old Yorkshire gods.

1980 | **13.6** | **Thu 18 Dec 8:00 p.m.** | **1** | **9 wks**

'Small Tune on a Penny Whistle'
Compo proves his undying friendship and loyalty to the others. (Repeat.)

1981 | **17.0** | **Fri 25 Dec 7:15 p.m.** | **2** | **1 wk**

'Whoops!'
Foggy, Clegg and Compo are searching for a Christmas past and visit two old school chums, Chuffer Enright (John Rutland) and Splutter Lippinscale (Arnold Peters).

1982 | **15.3** | **Mon 15 Feb 9:25 p.m.** | **4** | **8 wks**

'From Wellies to Wet Suit'
With Compo's natural aversion to water, Foggy and Clegg are surprised when he expresses a desire to go diving as a frogman.

1983 | **15.9** | **Sun 30 Jan 7:15 p.m.** | **1** | **9 wks**

'The Frozen Turkey Man'
The search is on for Compo's old treacle tin, buried by schoolboys in 1932.

1984 | **15.3** | **Sun 30 Dec 7:15 p.m.** | **3** | **6 wks**

'The Loxley Lozenge'
Compo, Clegg and Foggy offer their expert assistance to Wesley Pegden (Gordon Wharmby), who has made a once-in-a-lifetime discovery.

1985 | **18.8** | **Sun 10 Feb 8:10 p.m.** | **2** | **19 wks**

'The Mysterious Feet of Nora Batty'
Compo is determined to learn the foot size of his innamorata.

1986 | **18.1** | **Wed 1 Jan 8:15 p.m.** | **2** | **2 wks**

'Uncle of the Bride'
This feature length edition centres on the wedding of the daughter of Wesley and Edie. Seymour takes charge of the groom on his stag night – with a little help from Compo and Clegg.

1987 | **13.3** | **Sun 11 Jan 7:15 p.m.** | **11** | **8 wks**

'The Heavily Reinforced Bottom'
Seymour believes that Compo needs to do some canoeing on the canal to get himself fit.

1988 | **17.1** | **Sat 24 Dec 8:00 p.m.** | **5** | **1 wk**

'Crums'
Compo, Clegg and Seymour dress as Father Christmasses to collect for the church social.

1989 | **8.4** | **Thu 25 May 8:00 p.m.** | **18** | **1 wk**

'Dancing Feet'
Wesley takes Compo, Clegg and Seymour for a drive. They end up having to do much walking and pushing, leaving Compo with a pronounced and painful limp.

1990 | **13.1** | **Thu 27 Dec 8:00 p.m.** | **15** | **4 wks**

'What Santa Brought for Nora'
Foggy has a prize Christmas present which just might get Barry (Mike Grady) out of deep trouble.

Last Witness, The | **1 wk**

USA presented by BBC, drama

1962 | **5.5** | **Wed 26 Sep 9:35 p.m.** | **10** | **1 wk**

This short thriller stars Eddie Albert as Max Asher, whose wife has been murdered. Now he is asked to help establish the innocence of the man convicted of the murder.

Late Film, The | **1 wk**

Presented by BBC, film

1986 | **9.1** | **Sat 31 May 10:05 p.m.** | **20** | **1 wk**

'Convoy'
In this movie, inspired by C.W. McCall's hit song, three truckers are caught speeding in Arizona by Sheriff Lyle Wallace (Ernest Borgnine). Using CB radio they gather a huge convoy of trucks and head for the state line, crashing through police blocks on the way. Starring Kris Kristofferson and Ali McGraw.
Director: Sam Peckinpah.

Late Night Film, The | **2 wks**

Presented by BBC, film

1961 | **4.1** | **Fri 1 Sep 9:45 p.m.** | **17** | **2 wks**

'Dangerous Mission'
In this thriller starring William Bendix, Piper Laurie, Victor Mature and Vincent Price, a young girl who has witnessed a murder flees in fear to the Glacier National Park, hotly followed by the murderer and his henchmen.
Director: Louis King.

Laugh Parade | **8 wks**

Presented by BBC, film

A series of comedy films.

| 1970 | 6.8 | Tue 1 Dec 7:30 p.m. | 13 | 5 wks |

'The Square Peg'
Norman (Norman Wisdom) is a road-mender who is accidentally drafted into the Army. He becomes the centre of a plot to impersonate a Nazi General. With Honor Blackman and Edward Chapman.
Director: John Paddy Carstairs.

| 1971 | 6.9 | Tue 5 Jan 7:30 p.m. | 13 | 3 wks |

'Laughter in Paradise'
An eccentric practical joker dies leaving a fortune to each of four relatives, but on ludicrous conditions. Starring Alastair Sim with George Cole, Fay Compton, Hugh Griffith and Guy Middleton. Audrey Hepburn makes her film debut as a cigarette girl in a night club.
Director: Mario Zampi.

Laugh With Hope — 3 wks

Presented by BBC, film

A season of movies starring Bob Hope.

| 1968 | 4.9 | Sun 18 Aug 9:10 p.m. | 10 | 2 wks |

'The Lemon Drop Kid'
A tipster makes frenzied efforts to find ten thousand dollars before Christmas Day.
Director: Sidney Lanfield.

| 1969 | 4.5 | Tue 8 Jul 7:30 p.m. | 19 | 1 wk |

'The Cat and the Canary'
Bob Hope's first major starring role. He is cast opposite Paulette Goddard in this 1939 film set in a spooky house where relatives of a deceased eccentric gather for the reading of the will.
Director: Elliott Nugent.

Laughs from Her Majesty's — 1 wk

LWT, comedy

| 1986 | 11.9 | Sun 21 Dec 8:00 p.m. | 11 | 1 wk |

Jimmy Tarbuck presents comedy highlights from three series of LIVE FROM HER MAJESTY'S.
Director: Alasdair Macmillan. **Producer:** Alan Boyd.

Laughter from the Whitehall — 1 wk

BBC, comedy

| 1963 | 4.7 | Thu 26 Dec 9:05 p.m. | 20 | 1 wk |

Brian Rix presents the Whitehall Company in High Temperature by Avery Hopwood. This farce begins and ends in the bedroom.
Director: Wallace Douglas.

Laughter Show, The — 7 wks

BBC, comedy

Two comedians, Les Dennis and Dustin Gee, joined forces and were rewarded with their own series.

| 1985 | 15.2 | Sat 2 Mar 6:40 p.m. | 3 | 7 wks |

With Harvey and the Wallbangers, Roy Jay and Roy Walker.
Producer: John Bishop.

Laughter USA — 1 wk

USA presented by BBC, film

| 1963 | 7.5 | Thu 7 Feb 8:25 p.m. | 5 | 1 wk |

George Burns introduces classic clips from some of America's great comedy films with contributions from Charlie Chaplin, W.C. Fields, Bob Hope, Buster Keaton, Dean Martin and Jerry Lewis, and the Marx Brothers.

Laughtermakers, The — 1 wk

Presented by ITV, film

Season of British and international comedy films.

| 1968 | 5.3 | Tue 6 Aug 7:00 p.m. | 7 | 1 wk |

'Crooks Anonymous'
The title refers to an organization run by former convicts for those trying to give up a life of crime. Leslie Phillips stars as Danny, a crook who lacks the willpower to give up altogether. With Stanley Baxter, Julie Christie, James Robertson Justice and Wilfrid Hyde White.
Director: Ken Annakin.

Lawrence of Arabia — 2 wks

Presented by ITV, film

| 1975 | 6.1 | Mon 22 Dec 8:00 p.m. | 15 | 2 wks |

Christmas week presentation of David Lean's film. Screenplay by Robert Bolt. Starring Peter O'Toole, Alec Guinness, Anthony Quinn, Omar Sharif, Jack Hawkins, Arthur Kennedy, Claude Rains, José Ferrer and Anthony Quayle.

L

258

1

2

3

4

5

259

6

7

1 For nine chart seasons Dennis Waterman and George Cole found **Minder** a nice little earner.

2 Alfred Burke played an unglamorous detective in **Public Eye**.

3 In one of his early television roles, Windsor Davies played **Probation Officer** Bill Morgan.

4 John Stride starred as solicitor David Main in **The Main Chance**.

5 Hugh David and Wendy Williams jousted for justice in **Knight Errant Ltd.**

6 The French tribunal meets to consider a plea of **Crime of Passion**.

7 Peter Cushing played Conan Doyle's famous sleuth and Nigel Stock was Dr Watson in **Sherlock Holmes**.

LBJ – What Next?   1 wk

ITN, news

| 1968 | 7.1 | Fri 5 Apr 10:30 p.m. | 7 | 1 wk |

Dr Martin Luther King, aged thirty-nine, was assassinated in Memphis, Tennessee on 4 April. The killing provoked turmoil across America and a curfew was imposed in Washington as troops were called to deal with the violence Dr King had preached against for so long. The rhetorical question 'what next?' was addressed to the President of the United States, Lyndon B. Johnson, who swiftly announced that he would not be standing for a further term.

League of Gentlemen, The   1 wk

Presented by BBC, film

| 1967 | 6.3 | Sun 12 Mar 7:25 p.m. | 14 | 1 wk |

Screenplay by Bryan Forbes, adapted from the novel by John Boland, about a group of former officers, headed by an ex-colonel, who plan to steal a million pounds from a bank. Starring Richard Attenborough, Jack Hawkins, Roger Livesey and Nigel Patrick with Terence Alexander, Norman Bird, Robert Coote, Bryan Forbes and Kieron Moore.
Director: Basil Dearden.

Leave it to Charlie   15 wks

Granada, situation comedy

This series by H.V. Kershaw starred David Roper as the disaster-prone Lancastrian Insurance agent Charlie Fisher. Peter Sallis played Charlie's boss, Arthur Simister.
Producer: Eric Prytherch.

| 1978 | 11.2 | Thu 24 Aug 7:15 p.m. | 7 | 6 wks |

'Keep It In The Family'
Charlie thinks anyone would be a better boss than Arthur until he meets his brother Alfie (also played by Peter Sallis).

| 1979 | 15.2 | Wed 7 Mar 8:00 p.m. | 10 | 7 wks |

'Moonlight Becomes You'
Harry (David Ross), the caretaker at Lancastrian Insurance, keeps falling asleep for no reason.

| 1980 | 13.8 | Tue 25 Mar 8:30 p.m. | 16 | 2 wks |

'The Old Flame'
Charlie's former sweetheart Mrs Gloria Murphy (Diana Weston) turns up.

Lena   2 wks

BBC, music

This series starred Lena Zavaroni, the Scottish child-singing star who found fame on OPPORTUNITY KNOCKS in 1973.

| 1981 | 13.4 | Wed 8 Apr 8:30 p.m. | 11 | 2 wks |

Guests: Rod Hull and Emu, and Lulu.
Producer: Stewart Morris.

Lena's Music   2 wks

BBC, music

This series starred Lena Martell, the Scottish singer who had a number one in 1979 with 'One Day at a Time'.

| 1979 | 14.4 | Wed 28 Aug 9:25 p.m. | 15 | 2 wks |

Guests: Dollar, the Shadows and Flick Colby's Ruby Flipper.
Producer: Phil Bishop.

Lenny Henry Show, The   2 wks

BBC, comedy

The former NEW FACES winner graduated to his own series.

| 1987 | 9.1 | Tue 23 Jun 8:30 p.m. | 17 | 2 wks |

Guests: Norman Beaton, Robbie Coltrane, Dawn French and Steve Nallon.
Producer: Geoff Posner.

Les and Dustin's Laughter Show   5 wks

BBC, comedy

This series starred Les Dennis and Dustin Gee.

| 1986 | 13.8 | Sat 1 Feb 6:50 p.m. | 8 | 5 wks |

Guests: Mia Carla and Dan Hartman.
Producer: John Bishop.

Les Dawson Show, The   2 wks

BBC, comedy

| 1984 | 11.2 | Sat 28 Jan 8:00 p.m. | 16 | 2 wks |

Guests: Roy Barraclough, Colin Edwynn, Karen Kay and the Roly Polys.
Producer: Robin Nash.

Les Dennis Laughter Show, The — 1 wk

BBC, entertainment

| 1988 | 9.2 | Sat 4 Jan 8:15 p.m. | 18 | 1 wk |

Guest: Joe Longthorne with Martin P. Daniels, Bella Emberg and Lisa Maxwell.
Director: Michael Leggo. **Producer:** John Bishop.

Les Dennis's Laughter Show — 1 wk

BBC, entertainment

Following the death of his professional partner Dustin Gee in January 1986, Les Dennis carried on the LAUGHTER SHOW as a solo performer.

| 1987 | 10.5 | Sat 13 Jun 7:25 p.m. | 10 | 1 wk |

Guests: Martin P. Daniels, Lisa Maxwell, Joe Longthorne and Shane Richie, with the Jeff Richer dancers and the Alyn Ainsworth orchestra.
Director: Michael Leggo. **Producer:** John Bishop.

Les Sez — 2 wks

YTV, comedy

This comedy series starred Les Dawson, reversing the title and changing the format of his earlier series SEZ LES.

| 1972 | 6.7 | Mon 30 Oct 8:25 p.m. | 13 | 2 wks |

Les peddles his own brand of pessimism assisted by Roy Barraclough, Damaris Hayman, Jenny Lee-Wright and Eli Woods. Guests: Rod Hull and Emu, and Stephen Lewis.
Producers: Peter Dulay and Bill Hitchcock.

Leslie Crowther's Scrapbook — 1 wk

ATV, entertainment

Series of reflective sketches from Crowther's past.

| 1979 | 14.6 | Wed 18 Apr 8:00 p.m. | 6 | 1 wk |

Guests: Anna Dawson, Peter Gordeno, Francis Matthews and Johnny Vyvyan.
Producer: Colin Clews.

Let There Be Love — 6 wks

Thames, situation comedy

This series by Johnnie Mortimer and Brian Cooke starred Paul Eddington as confirmed bachelor Timothy Love. His single status was threatened when he met Judy (Nanette Newman), a widow with three children and a large dog. Henry McGee played the part of Dennis.
Producer: Peter Frazer-Jones.

| 1982 | 15.6 | Mon 4 Jan 8:00 p.m. | 8 | 6 wks |

'Little Things Mean a Lot'
Wedding bells begin to ring, but Timothy starts to discover that the responsibilities of marriage might be more than he bargained for.

Lethal Weapon — 1 wk

Presented by ITV, film

| 1991 | 14.4 | Sat 5 Oct 9:35 p.m. | 8 | 1 wk |

Mel Gibson and Danny Glover star as detectives of opposite character who are teamed to tackle a heroin smuggling operation.
Director: Richard Donner.

Let's Twist on the Riviera — 1 wk

AR, music

| 1962 | 4.0 | Wed 20 Jun 7:00 p.m. | 17 | 1 wk |

From the South of France, David Frost introduces a programme about the dance craze.
Director: Rollo Gamble.

Liars, The — 10 wks

Granada, drama

This series was written by Philip Mackie and Hugh Leonard and revolved around four people whose sole aim was to amuse themselves with short yarns, which they then enacted. The four were Sir Gerald (William Mervyn), Hermione (Nyree Dawn Porter), Sarah (Isla Blair) and Rupert (Ian Ogilvy).

| 1966 | 7.4 | Fri 7 Jun 9:40 p.m. | 6 | 10 wks |

Guests: Judy Child, Fabia Drake, Ronald Elms, Ursula Howells, Frederick Jaeger and Angela Thorne.
Director: David Cunliffe. **Producer:** Philip Mackie.

Liberace Show, The — 7 wks

ATV, music

The American pianist first came to Britain in 1956 to appear in the ROYAL VARIETY PERFORMANCE, which was cancelled on the night because of the Suez crisis. His popularity ensured repeated visits and in 1969 he came over to make his own series.

1969 · 5.4 · **Sun 18 May 7:25 p.m.** · 10 · 7 wks

Guests: Engelbert Humperdinck, Georgina Moon, Terry-Thomas, Dana Valery, Richard Wattis and Jack Wild, with the Irving Davies dancers and the Jack Parnell orchestra.
Director: Norman Campbell. **Producer:** Colin Clews.

Liberace Show, The — 1 wk

USA presented by ITV, entertainment

1978 · 11.4 · **Fri 9 Jun 9:00 p.m.** · 13 · 1 wk

A special from the Hilton Hotel, Las Vegas. Guests: the Chinese Acrobats of Taiwan, Phyllis Diller and Debbie Reynolds.

Liberace's Valentine's Night Special — 1 wk

USA presented by ITV, entertainment

1979 · 15.1 · **Wed 14 Feb 8:00 p.m.** · 13 · 1 wk

A two-part special coming from the Queen Mary, docked at Long Beach in California, and the Hilton Hotel in Las Vegas Nevada. Guest: Sandy Duncan.

License to Thrill — 1 wk

Thames, entertainment

1987 · 10.0 · **Mon 29 Jun 9:00 p.m.** · 8 · 1 wk

This evening THE LIVING DAYLIGHTS starring Timothy Dalton as James Bond has its Royal premiere at the Odeon, Leicester Square, in the presence of the Prince and Princess of Wales. Nick Owen presents a celebration of twenty-five years of Bond films.
Director: Mike Ward. **Producer:** Steve Minchin.

Life and Death of Penelope, The — 3 wks

Thames, drama

In this six-part thriller serial devised and produced by Michael Chapman the body of a girl wearing evening dress was discovered in the River Thames. CID men Det. Chief Supt. Lane (Antony Brown) and Det. Sgt. Fishlock (Matthew Long) set about discovering her identity, the motive and the killer's name.

1976 · 7.2 · **Wed 28 Jan 9:00 p.m.** · 12 · 3 wks

'The Watcher' by Ben Bassett.
Tom Crispin (Richard Heffer) had loved Penelope. Where was he on the night of the murder?
Director: Jonathan Alwyn.

Life Begins at Forty — 11 wks

YTV, situation comedy

This series by Jan Butlin starred Derek Nimmo as the incompetent Chris Bunting and Rosemary Leach as Katy Bunting. The middle class couple learned that they would be parents for the first time at forty years of age.

1978 · 15.7 · **Tue 4 Jul 8:30 p.m.** · 1 · 7 wks

'Foreign Affairs'
Chris persuades Katy she needs an au pair.
Producer: Graeme Muir.

1980 · 15.1 · **Fri 21 Mar 8:00 p.m.** · 10 · 4 wks

'The Christening'
Chris and Katy are still to decide on a name for the baby. Katy's sister, Gertie (Moira Lister), arrives to rock the baby, and everything else! (Repeat.)
Producer: Graeme Muir.

Life for Christine — 1 wk

Granada, drama

1980 · 13.4 · **Tue 2 Dec 8:30 p.m.** · 19 · 1 wk

Play by Fay Weldon, based on a true story. A campaigner for children's rights finds a fourteen-year-old girl serving a life sentence in Holloway Prison. Amanda York plays Christine and Nicholas Ball portrays Colin.
Producer: John Goldsmidt. **Executive Producer:** Gus Macdonald.

Life of Riley, The — 6 wks

Granada, situation comedy

Bill Maynard played widower Frank Riley, an insurance agent with a roving eye and a disapproving God-fearing Welsh-speaking son, Brian (Frank Lincoln).
Producer: Eric Prytherch.

1975 · 8.3 · **Mon 3 Feb 8:00 p.m.** · 3 · 6 wks

'The Visitors'
With Brian on a works outing, Frank has arranged for a lady to visit. His intentions are thwarted by the unexpected arrival of an uncle.
Writer: Brian Finch.

Life with Cooper — 18 wks

ABC, comedy

This series starred Tommy Cooper in a format devised by his agent Miff Ferrie. It placed him in ordinary situations where unlikely and often impossible things would happen. Each episode had a different cast.
Producer: Mark Stuart.

| 1967 | 7.9 | Sat 4 Feb 8:30 p.m. | 4 | 5 wks |

Tommy's troubles are right on his own doorstep when the postman delivers the mail. With Hugh Morton, Bill Oddie and June Whitfield.
Writers: Eric Green, John Muir, John Singer and John Warren.

| 1968 | 8.8 | Sat 16 Mar 7:00 p.m. | 1 | 13 wks |

The Doctor advises Tommy to take up a hobby. With Jack Allen, Judith Furse and Frank Williams.
Writers: Brian Cooke and Johnnie Mortimer.

Life with Cooper — 7 wks

Thames, comedy

The series changed format when Cooper moved to Thames and became a sequence of gags and sketches.

| 1969 | 7.5 | Tue 22 Apr 8:25 p.m. | 2 | 7 wks |

Tommy appears in several guises, including a Shakespeare-inspired prince. With Harry Davis, Cardew Robinson and Bob Todd.
Writers: Derek Collyer, George Evans and Eric Merriman. **Producer:** Milo Lewis.

Life Without George — 2 wks

BBC, situation comedy

This series by Penny Croft starred Simon Cadell as estate agent Larry and Carol Royle as Jenny, who had previously lived for five years with a man named George. Jenny had a dance studio where she employed Mr Chambers (Ronald Fraser). Larry's friend and colleague Ben was played by Michael Thomas. The role of Amanda was played by Rosalind March in the 1988 series and subsequently by Elizabeth Estensen.
Producer: Susan Belbin.

| 1988 | 10.2 | Sun 17 Apr 10:00 p.m. | 16 | 1 wk |

Jenny is pregnant and Larry is expecting problems. Ben encourages him to throw caution to the wind.

| 1989 | 10.5 | Thu 11 May 9:30 p.m. | 15 | 1 wk |

Jenny and Amanda prepare for motherhood.

Lift Off — 1 wk

BBC, comedy

| 1988 | 15.2 | Fri 5 Feb 7:35 p.m. | 10 | 1 wk |

Jim Davidson, Harry Enfield, Lenny Henry, Rod Hull, Griff Rhys-Jones and Jonathan Ross get together for Comic Relief.

Likely Lads, The — 7 wks

BBC, situation comedy

This series created by Dick Clement and Ian La Frenais starred Rodney Bewes as Bob Ferris and James Bolam as Terry Collier, two teenagers from the North East. Terry accepted his lot in society and would always settle for a good time and girls. Bob was his opposite, lacking confidence but with the ambition to climb the class ladder through hard work.

| 1966 | 6.5 | Tue 15 Nov 7:30 p.m. | 11 | 7 wks |

'Love and Marriage'
Marriage seems the unlikeliest possibility for a likely lad, but you can never tell with a girl like Helen (Helen Fraser) around. (Repeat.)
Producer: Dick Clement.

Likely Lads, The — 2 wks

Presented by BBC, film

| 1984 | 7.6 | Fri 17 Aug 7:35 p.m. | 18 | 1 wk |

In this feature film version Bob and Terry embark on a wild holiday trip through the north of England. Also stars Sheila Fearn, Brigit Forsyth, Mary Tamm and Zena Walker.
Director: Michael Tuchner.

| 1989 | 8.0 | Fri 21 Jul 7:30 p.m. | 17 | 1 wk |

Repeat showing of the above film.

(Left) *Chris and Katy Bunting (Derek Nimmo and Rosemary Leach) toast her unexpected pregnancy in* **Life Begins At Forty**.

(Below) *Sheila Hancock finds* **Life With Cooper** *full of surprises.*

Lillie   9 wks

LWT, drama

This thirteen-part life story of Lillie Langtry (Francesca Annis) was written by David Butler and John Gorrie. The society actress became the mistress of the Prince of Wales (later Edward VII) and the toast of America. The series also starred Dennis Lill as Edward, Peter Egan as Oscar Wilde, Don Fellows as Rex Whistler, Anton Rodgers as Lillie's husband Edward Langtry and Derek Smith as King Leopold of the Belgians.
Designers: *Bryan Bagge, Richard Dunn and Roger Hall.* **Producer:** *Jack Williams.* **Executive Producer:** *Tony Wharmby.*

| 1978 | 18.2 | Sun 5 Nov 8:15 p.m. | 3 | 9 wks |

'The Sailor Prince' by John Gorrie.
Lillie is in disgrace because of her indiscretions, but when the Prince of Wales sees her at a soirée all is forgiven.
Director: *John Gorrie.*

Lingalongamax   11 wks

Thames, music

This series starred Max Bygraves with the Tony Mansell singers and the Geoff Love orchestra. Each programme looked back at a particular year – through song, film, fashion and comedy.
Producer: *Royston Mayoh.*

| 1978 | 13.1 | Wed 11 Oct 7:00 p.m. | 16 | 4 wks |

Features 1964.

| 1979 | 12.4 | Mon 21 May 7:00 p.m. | 9 | 6 wks |

Features 1967.

| 1980 | 9.8 | Mon 2 Jun 7:00 p.m. | 20 | 1 wk |

Features 1968.

Little and Large Christmas Show, The   1 wk

BBC, comedy

| 1978 | 15.3 | Sat 23 Dec 6:40 p.m. | 17 | 1 wk |

Guests: Cliff Richard, Berni Flint and Dana Gillespie, with Jeff Richer's First Edition and the Ronnie Hazlehurst orchestra.
Producer: *Michael Hurll.*

Little and Large Show, The   15 wks

BBC, comedy

This long-running series of Saturday night entertainment shows starred Syd Little and Eddie Large with guests and the Ronnie Hazlehurst orchestra.

| 1978 | 13.9 | Sat 30 Sep 8:30 p.m. | 9 | 2 wks |

Guest: Charley Pride, with Jeff Richer's Birds of a Feather.
Producer: *Michael Hurll.*

| 1980 | 18.1 | Sat 1 Mar 8:05 p.m. | 3 | 8 wks |

Guests: Amanda Lear and Foxy Feeling.
Producer: *Michael Hurll.*

| 1982 | 12.5 | Sat 11 Dec 7:05 p.m. | 6 | 1 wk |

Guests: Kenny Ball, Big Daddy, Patrick Moore and the Three Degrees.
Director: *Geoff Posner.* **Producer:** *Brian Penders.*

| 1985 | 13.8 | Sat 5 Jan 6:40 p.m. | 12 | 1 wk |

Guests: Frank Carson, Dudley Doolittle and Jack Jones.
Producer: *Bill Wilson.*

| 1990 | 12.2 | Sat 17 Feb 6:40 p.m. | 17 | 3 wks |

Guests: Curiosity Killed the Cat, Jelly Rolls, Paddy Joyce and Michael Sharvell-Martin.
Producer: *David Taylor.* **Executive Producer:** *Bill Wilson.*

Little and Large Telly Show, The   7 wks

Thames, comedy

Manchester comics Syd Little and Eddie Large began their television career at Thames with this series before they moved to the BBC, where they stayed for many years with THE LITTLE AND LARGE SHOW.

| 1976 | 7.1 | Mon 20 Dec 8:30 p.m. | 13 | 1 wk |

Guests: Ivy Benson's All Girls Band and Tom Shelley.
Producer: *Royston Mayoh.*

| 1977 | 7.6 | Mon 18 Apr 6:45 p.m. | 6 | 6 wks |

Guests: Linda Lewis, Love Machine and Matt Monro.
Producer: *Royston Mayoh.*

Little Big Business, A   4 wks

Granada, situation comedy

David Kossoff starred as Marcus Lieberman, a man teaching his son Simon (Francis Matthews) about the furniture business. Also starred David Conville as Basil, Joyce Marlowe as Miss Stevens, Martin Miller as Lazlo and Billy Russell as Charlie.

| 1963 | 4.6 | Thu 8 Aug 7:30 p.m. | 14 | 1 wk |

In this pilot show the role of Simon Lieberman was played by James Maxwell.
Writer: Paul Jackman. **Director:** Graeme McDonald. **Producer:** Peter Eton.

| 1964 | 6.2 | Thu 27 Feb 7:30 p.m. | 15 | 3 wks |

Despite protests from Marcus, Simon decides to close the workshop.
Writer: Jack Pullman. **Director:** Cliff Owen. **Producer:** Peter Eton.

Little Big Man   1 wk

Presented by BBC, film

| 1980 | 11.4 | Mon 26 May 9:10 p.m. | 11 | 1 wk |

Dustin Hoffman stars as Jack Crabb, an aged storyteller who was the only white survivor of the Battle of Little Bighorn. The character ages from adolescence to 121 years. Faye Dunaway also stars.
Director: Arthur Penn.

Little Bit of Irish, A   1 wk

AR, music

| 1967 | 6.7 | Wed 15 Mar 9:45 p.m. | 12 | 1 wk |

A special starring Bing Crosby with Kathryn Crosby, Siobhan McKenna and Milo O'Shea.
Director: John Robins. **Producers:** Buddy Bregman and Fred O'Donovan.

Little Bit of Wisdom, A   17 wks

ATV, comedy

This series of plays by various writers was specially written to star Norman Wisdom.
Producer (1974–75): John Scholz-Conway.

| 1974 | 7.4 | Tue 9 Apr 6:40 p.m. | 5 | 6 wks |

'The Magic Monkey of Khubla Khan' by John Kane.
Norman buys a brass monkey from a man in a park and starts to win a fortune.

| 1975 | 7.0 | Fri 14 Feb 6:30 p.m. | 16 | 4 wks |

'Norman's Unique Talents' by Lew Schwarz.
A series of accidents launch Norman into the world of art.

| 1976 | 7.8 | Tue 13 Apr 7:00 p.m. | 6 | 7 wks |

'Double Trouble' by John Kane.
A double-glazing company believes it has unbreakable glass – until Norman comes along.
Producer: Les Chatfield.

Little House on the Prairie, The   1 wk

USA presented by BBC, drama

Produced by and starring Michael Landon, this series was based on the novels of Laura Ingalls Wilder and charted the struggles of the Ingalls family, who were homesteaders in Plumb Creek, Minnesota. Karen Grassle and Michael Landon played Caroline and Charles Ingalls. They had three children, Laura, Mary and Carrie, and a dog named Jack.

| 1975 | 7.9 | Tue 27 May 6:50 p.m. | 10 | 1 wk |

'The Plague'
When Laura (Melissa Gilbert) hurts her leg she sees her crippled friend Olga in a new light. Mary (Melissa Sue Anderson) and Carrie (played alternately by twins Lindsay and Sidney Greenbush) help her execute her latest brain wave.

Little Mo   1 wk

Presented by BBC, film

| 1985 | 9.9 | Thu 20 Jun 9:25 p.m. | 18 | 1 wk |

Glynnis O'Connor stars as Maureen Connolly, the youngest tennis player ever to win Wimbledon. She won the tournament at her first attempt aged 17, beating Louise Brough 7–5, 6–3, on 5 July 1952. This made her the youngest champion since Lottie Dod in the last century. She died prematurely on 21 June 1969.
Director: Dan Haller.

Little Moon of Alban   1 wk

Anglia, drama

| 1967 | 5.1 | Thu 18 May 9:40 p.m. | 15 | 1 wk |

After the death of Dennis (Donal McCann), a young Dublin rebel killed by the Black and Tans, his sweetheart Brigid Mary (Valerie Gearon) becomes a nun. She works at a hospital tending wounded English soldiers and falls in love with Lieutenant Kenneth Boyd (David Buck). Father Curran (Liam Redmond) helps her through her crisis.
Designer: James Weatherup. **Writer:** James Costigan. **Producer:** John Jacobs.

Live a Little, Steal a Lot   1 wk

Presented by ITV, film

| 1983 | 10.6 | Fri 30 Dec 7:30 p.m. | 16 | 1 wk |

Two beach bums from Miami (Robert Conrad and Don Stroud) steal precious jewels from New York's Museum of Natural History. **Director:** Marvin Chomsky.

....

Live Aid   1 wk

BBC2, music

Bob Geldof originated the concept of the 'global jukebox' for famine relief. He applied the idea of musical superstars working together, as they had on the multi-million selling single 'Do They Know It's Christmas', to an international day-long fund-raising concert.

| 1985 | 8.7 | Sat 13 Jul 11:50 a.m. | 19 | 1 wk |

The show begins at Wembley and then, after several hours, acts alternate between Wembley and Philadelphia. The American side takes over for good after the Wembley finale shortly after sunset. BBC1 continues the transmission from 10:00 p.m. onwards. Presenters include Mark Ellen, Paul Gambaccini, David Hepworth, Andy Kershaw, Janice Long, Richard Skinner and Mike Smith. (Most of Britain's top rock acts and several American stars participated. The BBC Audience Panel determined that Queen had stolen the show.) **Television presentation:** John Burrowes and Trevor Dann.

....

Live and Let Die   5 wks

Presented by ITV, film

| 1980 | 23.5 | Sun 20 Jan 7:45 p.m. | 1 | 1 wk |

James Bond (Roger Moore) is on the trail of Dr Kananga (Yaphet Kotto), who masterminds a criminal organization which runs from Harlem to New Orleans and on to the island of San Monique. Jane Seymour is Solitaire. **Director:** Guy Hamilton.

1982	13.7	Mon 14 Jun 8:00 p.m.	1	1 wk
1984	15.6	Sun 30 Sep 7:45 p.m.	3	1 wk
1989	13.5	Sat 21 Jan 6:45 p.m.	9	1 wk
1991	13.0	Mon 1 Apr 8:00 p.m.	10	1 wk

Repeat showings of the above film.

....

Live from Her Majesty's   10 wks

LWT, entertainment

This series of variety shows was hosted by Jimmy Tarbuck from Her Majesty's Theatre in London's Haymarket. With the Brian Rogers dancers and the Alyn Ainsworth orchestra. **Director:** Alasdair Macmillan. **Producer:** David Bell.

| 1984 | 13.1 | Sun 1 Apr 7:45 p.m. | 5 | 6 wks |

Guests: Cannon and Ball, the Drifters, Charley Pride, Paul Squire, Shakin' Stevens and Roy Walker.

| 1985 | 12.6 | Sun 20 Oct 8:30 p.m. | 11 | 4 wks |

Guests: Petula Clark, Dana, Bobby Davro and Shakin' Stevens.

....

Live from the Palladium   8 wks

LWT, entertainment

This series of variety shows was hosted by Jimmy Tarbuck from the London Palladium.

| 1987 | 15.2 | Sun 5 Apr 7:45 p.m. | 4 | 7 wks |

Guests: Bob Carolgees, Brian Conley, Five Star, Tom Jones, Stephanie Lawrence and Jennifer Rush, with the Brian Rogers dancers and the Alyn Ainsworth orchestra. **Director:** Alasdair Macmillan. **Producer:** Marcus Plantin.

| 1988 | 11.4 | Sun 27 Nov 7:15 p.m. | 20 | 1 wk |

Guests: Russ Abbot, Bright and Breeze, Bros, Paul Jones, Shahid Malik, Barry Manilow, Billy Pearce, Cliff Richard, Roy Walker and Kim Wilde, with the Alan Harding dancers and the Alyn Ainsworth orchestra. **Producer:** Ian Hamilton. **Executive Producer:** Marcus Plantin.

....

Liver Birds, The   33 wks

BBC, situation comedy

This series created by Carla Lane, Myra Taylor and Lew Schwarz and written by Lane concerned two girls sharing a flat in Liverpool. Originally starring Polly James as Beryl and Nerys Hughes as Sandra, the cast changed over the years, notably with Elizabeth Estensen coming in as Carol after Polly James left the show. **Producers** included Sydney Lotterby (1972–75) and Douglas Argent (1976, 1978).

| 1972 | 6.6 | Fri 7 Apr 7:40 p.m. | 12 | 7 wks |

Sandra would find life tolerable if only her love-life could take an upturn.

| 1973 | 5.7 | Tue 17 Apr 8:30 p.m. | 20 | 1 wk |

Both girls are jobless, the rent is due and the dole seems to offer the only way out. (Repeat.)

| 1974 | 6.4 | Wed 16 Jan 7:40 p.m. | 17 | 3 wks |

'Life is Just a Bowl of Sugar'
Sandra tries to beguile Paul (John Nettles) into marriage, but Mr and Mrs Hutchinson (Ivan Beavis and Mollie Sugden) stick the parental nose in.
Director: Ray Butt.

| 1975 | 7.4 | Fri 10 Oct 8:30 p.m. | 6 | 8 wks |

'The Lily and the Dandelion'
Midway through this series, Beryl leaves, forcing Sandra to find a new flatmate. Carol (Elizabeth Estensen) is far from ideal, but she'll have to do.

| 1976 | 7.0 | Fri 13 Feb 8:00 p.m. | 15 | 5 wks |

'Facing up to Life'
Sandra and Carol are facing up to life, or rather to Mrs Hutchinson.

| 1977 | 14.7 | Fri 23 Dec 8:25 p.m. | 7 | 5 wks |

'Open Your Eyes and it Still Hasn't Gone'
The girls face up to spending Christmas without any men around.
Producer: Roger Race.

| 1978 | 17.4 | Wed 15 Feb 8:30 p.m. | 4 | 4 wks |

'She Dreams a Lot'
Carol moves out when Sandra has a premonition of death. In fact the budgie dies.

Living for Kicks
1 wk

AR, documentary

| 1960 | 5.9 | Wed 2 Mar 8:00 p.m. | 7 | 1 wk |

Daniel Farson investigates the contemporary lives of groups of teenagers living in Brighton, London and Northampton. Comments from the Countess of Albemarle DBE.
Camera: Gilbert Knight. **Producer:** Rollo Gamble.

Living Legends
4 wks

BBC, documentary

Magnus Magnusson introduced this series about legendary characters from folklore.

| 1979 | 15.8 | Thu 19 Apr 8:30 p.m. | 4 | 4 wks |

'Dick Turpin'
England's most celebrated villain, Turpin, was a member of the Gregory Gang and was hanged when he was thirty-three years old.
Editor: Bruce Norman. **Producer:** Nigel Williams.

Living Planet, The
3 wks

BBC, documentary

David Attenborough's twelve-part portrait of the Earth.

| 1984 | 11.6 | Thu 26 Jan 8:05 p.m. | 13 | 3 wks |

'The Frozen World'
This edition examines animals and plants in the frozen wastes of the Arctic and Antarctic.
Producer: Ned Kelly. **Executive Producer:** Richard Brock.

Living with a Giant
1 wk

AR, documentary

| 1962 | 5.3 | Wed 21 Feb 9:45 p.m. | 13 | 1 wk |

Lord Boothby reports on Canada's future and questions whether it will survive as a member of the Commonwealth or whether it will be swallowed up as part of a greater USA.
Writer: Elkan Allan. **Director:** Rollo Gamble. **Producer:** Aidan Crawley.

Lollipop
6 wks

ATV, situation comedy

This was a follow up series to LOLLIPOP LOVES MR MOLE with the title shortened.

| 1972 | 5.7 | Mon 4 Sep 8:25 p.m. | 11 | 6 wks |

'Inspector Hardcastle Investigates'
Reg arrives home too late for his birthday treat. Worse, he's carrying a mysterious green suitcase about which he is secretive. In fact it contains the means to get rid of Bruce and Vi.
Director: David Askey. **Producer:** Shaun O'Riordan.

Lollipop Loves Mr Mole
6 wks

ATV, situation comedy

Jimmy Perry created this series about a marriage of opposites. Hugh Lloyd starred as the ever-obliging Reg (Mr Mole) with Peggy Mount as Maggie (Lollipop), his less obliging spouse. They lived in a cosy cottage in Fulham, London, SW6.

| 1971 | 6.8 | Tue 25 Oct 8:25 p.m. | 10 | 6 wks |

'Home to Roost'
After many years in Africa, Reg's brother Bruce (Rex Garner) and his wife Violet (Pat Coombs) return and spend a few days with Reg and Maggie. When the delivery man (Bill Pertwee) arrives with six cabin trunks, brotherly love wears thin.
Director: David Askey. **Producer:** Shaun O'Riordan.

London Night Out — 33 wks

Thames, entertainment

This series of variety programmes from the New London Theatre was hosted by Tom O'Connor. With the Alan Braden orchestra.
Producers included Paul Stewart Laing (1979–80) and David Clark (1981–83).

1978 15.1 **Wed 5 Jul 8:00 p.m.** 1 **8 wks**

Guests: Tommy Cooper, Champagne, Aiden J. Harvey, the Ladybirds and the Nigel Lythgoe dancers.
Producer: Dennis Kirkland.

1979 15.7 **Wed 28 Nov 8:00 p.m.** 10 **6 wks**

Guests: Dickie Henderson, Gerard Kenny, Johnny Hutch and the Half Wits, with the Ladybirds and the Irving Davies dancers.

1980 17.9 **Wed 19 Nov 8:00 p.m.** 3 **10 wks**

Guests: Petula Clark, Desmond and Marks, Keith Harris, Hot Gossip, Roy Kinnear and Allan Stewart, with the Ladybirds and the Alan Braden orchestra.

1981 17.0 **Wed 16 Dec 8:00 p.m.** 3 **3 wks**

Guests: Aiden J. Harvey, the Kessler Twins, George Schlick, and Stutz Bear Cats, with the Jeff Richer dancers.

1982 17.2 **Wed 13 Jan 8:00 p.m.** 3 **2 wks**

Guests: Dana, Dr Hook, Keith Harris and Chris Langham, with the Jeff Richer dancers and the Alan Braden orchestra.
Director: Paul Smith.

1983 11.6 **Wed 12 Jan 8:00 p.m.** 5 **4 wks**

Guests: Glen Campbell, Chantal and Dumont, Mike Reid and Diane Solomon, with the Jeff Richer dancers.

London Palladium Show, The — 54 wks

ATV, entertainment

SUNDAY NIGHT AT THE LONDON PALLADIUM without the game show 'Beat the Clock'.
Producer: Albert Locke.

1966 9.2 **Sun 27 Nov 10:05 p.m.** 1 **27 wks**

Roger Moore introduces the Bachelors, Arno and Rita van Bolen, Joe Brown, Millicent Martin, Morecambe and Wise, the Tiller Girls and the Paddy Stone dancers.

1967 10.0 **Sun 3 Dec 10:05 p.m.** 1 **23 wks**

Jimmy Tarbuck introduces Shirley Bassey, Rudolf Nureyev and Antoinette Sibley, Mike Yarwood and the Lionel Blair dancers.

1968 6.7 **Sun 28 Jan 10:05 p.m.** 11 **2 wks**

Des O'Connor introduces the Dior Dancers, Tom Jones, Diana Ross and the Supremes with the Pamela Devis dancers.

1969 6.3 **Sun 2 Feb 7:25 p.m.** 14 **2 wks**

Ted Rogers introduces Lena Horne and Engelbert Humperdinck with the Malcolm Goddard dancers.

London v Paris Twist — 1 wk

AR, music

This international competition featured the dance craze which was first introduced to Britain by Chubby Checker late in 1960.

1962 4.7 **Wed 9 May 7:00 p.m.** 19 **1 wk**

Following twist contests in both capitals David Frost introduces the best twisters, who dance for medals.
Producer: Daphne Shadwell.

London's Burning — 30 wks

LWT, drama

A two-hour play by Jack Rosenthal in 1986 spawned this series set in an inner London fire station with the men (and subsequently the women) of Blue Watch B25 Blackwall.
Producer: Paul Knight.

1986 12.5 **Sun 7 Dec 9:00 p.m.** 10 **1 wk**

A replacement fire officer, Josie Ingham (Katharine Rogers) arrives. She is the first woman to enter this previously all-male preserve.
Writer: Jack Rosenthal. **Director:** Les Blair. **Executive Producer:** Linda Agran.

1988 12.6 **Sat 12 Mar 9:20 p.m.** 10 **4 wks**

Station officer Tate (James Marcus) is affected more than usual by a fire made worse by mindless vandalism.
Writer: Anita Bronson. **Director:** Gerry Mill. **Executive Producer:** Linda Agran.

1989 12.8 **Sun 3 Dec 9:10 p.m.** 10 **7 wks**

It's the fifth of November, Guy Fawkes Night, the busiest day of the year for the fire brigade.
Writer: Tony Hoare. **Director:** Gerry Poulson.

1990 13.9 **Sun 18 Nov 9:05 p.m.** 7 **8 wks**

Tate goes for a medical check-up. Malcolm (Rupert Baker) receives an award for bravery.
Writer: David Humphries. **Director:** Keith Washington.

1991 18.9 **Sun 1 Dec 8:45 p.m.** 6 **10 wks**

The fight is on to save Bayleaf (James Hazeldine). Hallam and Recall

(Sean Blowers and Ben Onwukwe) are rushed to hospital.
Writer: *Anita Bronson.* **Director:** *Keith Washington.* **Executive Producer:** *Nick Elliott.*

....

London's Marathon	2 wks

BBC, sport

This event, the brainchild of runner Chris Brasher, began in 1981. Tens of thousands of runners of all ages and vastly contrasting abilities covered the marathon distance of 26 miles and 385 yards through the streets of London. Commentary by David Coleman, Brendan Foster and Ron Pickering.

1982	11.2	Sun 9 May 11:30 a.m.	18	1 wk

The front runners enter the closing stages of the race.
Television presentation: *David Kenning, Richard Tilling and Fred Viner.*

1988	11.0	Sun 17 Apr 9:15 p.m.	13	1 wk

Highlights of this morning's run, in which more than 25,000 people took part.
Television presentation: *Johnnie Watherston and Martin Hopkins.*
Editor: *John Rowlinson.*

....

Lonelyhearts Kid, The	2 wks

Thames, situation comedy

This series by Alex Shearer examined Ken and Judy (Robert Glenister and Deborah Farrington), who had been school sweethearts and lived together for years. But as Judy matured she left Ken behind and they began to drift apart.

1984	9.0	Tue 17 Jul 8:30 p.m.	9	2 wks

'Old Acquaintance'
Ken cries on the shoulder of his sister Ros (Julia Goodman) and vents his frustrations on Ray (George Winter), an old school rival.
Director: *Douglas Argent.* **Producer:** *Anthony Parker.*

....

Loner, The	1 wk

YTV, comedy

This series of comedy plays written by Alan Plater starred Les Dawson in one man's fight against officialdom.

1975	6.7	Wed 7 May 9:30 p.m.	14	1 wk

'Dawson's Complaint'
Dawson believes in taking his complaint right to the top. With Cyril Luckham, George Malpas, Helen Rappaport and Brian Wilde.
Director: *James Ormerod.* **Executive Producer:** *Peter Willes.*

....

Longest Day, The	1 wk

Presented by BBC, film

1975	7.6	Mon 26 May 7:00 p.m.	14	1 wk

Bank Holiday Monday presentation of the story of the Allied invasion of Europe in June 1944. Starring Eddie Albert, Paul Anka, Patrick Barr, Richard Beymer, Richard Burton, Red Buttons, Sean Connery, Fabian, Mel Ferrer, Frank Finlay, Henry Fonda, Steve Forrest, Gert Frobe, Leo Genn, John Gregson, Donald Houston, Jeffrey Hunter, Curt Jurgens, Peter Lawford, Roddy McDowall, Christian Marquand, Michael Medwin, Sal Mineo, Robert Mitchum, Kenneth More, Edmond O'Brien, Leslie Phillips, Sian Phillips, Norman Rossington, Robert Ryan, Tommy Sands, Rod Steiger, Richard Todd, Tom Tryon, Peter Van Eyck, Robert Wagner, John Wayne and Stuart Whitman.
Directors: *Ken Annakin, Andrew Marton and Bernhard Wicki.*

....

Look – Mike Yarwood	23 wks

BBC, comedy

Mike Yarwood was the first British impressionist to become a television star in his own right. His visual and verbal caricatures of politicians, notably Harold Wilson and Edward Heath, and other eccentric personalities like Eddie Waring, Patrick Moore and Eric Morecambe established him in the forefront of light entertainment. He began at ATV, moved to the BBC for his most successful run, and then defected to Thames.
Writer: *Eric Davidson.*

1972	6.4	Fri 26 May 8:30 p.m.	7	6 wks

Guests: Adrienne Posta and Peter Noone.
Producer: *Michael Hurll.*

1973	5.9	Sat 21 Jul 8:50 p.m.	13	8 wks

Guests: Cheryl Kennedy and Peter Noone.
Producer: *James Moir.*

1974	6.3	Sat 4 May 8:20 p.m.	16	2 wks

Guests: Cheryl Kennedy and Cliff Richard.
Producer: *James Moir.* **Executive Producer:** *John Ammonds.*

1975	6.7	Sat 12 Apr 8:30 p.m.	17	4 wks

Guests: Reflections (Dee Eldridge, Tony Kemp, Linda and Gerry Robinson and Sandy Rogers).
Producer: *Michael Hurll.*

1976	6.3	Sat 17 Jan 8:35 p.m.	19	3 wks

Guests: Reflections.
Director: *Alan Boyd.* **Producer:** *John Ammonds.*

Liverpool comedian Tom O'Connor was the host of **London Night Out**.

The Bachelors were among the stars in one of the 13 chart-topping editions of **The London Palladium Show**.

Looks Familiar   1 wk

Thames, entertainment

Denis Norden presented movie memorabilia, usually during the afternoon. The show was based on the radio programme 'Sounds Familiar'.

| 1978 | 16.3 | Wed 22 Feb 8:00 p.m. | 15 | 1 wk |

The hundredth edition of the show is moved to peak time with guests Patricia Hayes and Morecambe and Wise.
Director: Ronald Fouracre. **Producer:** David Clark.

Lorna Doone   2 wks

Presented by BBC, drama

R.D. Blackmore's classic story was dramatized in eleven episodes by Constance Cox from a treatment by A.R. Rawlinson. The cast included Jane Merrow as Lorna Doone (but Fleur Shaw as the young Lorna in Episode One) and Andrew Faulds (Carver Doone), Bill Travers (John Ridd the elder), Jean Anderson (Mrs Ridd) and Nigel Stock (Jeremy Stickles).

| 1963 | 4.7 | Sun 16 Jun 5:45 p.m. | 16 | 2 wks |

Episode One: 'A Boy and a Girl'
A young John Ridd (Vincent Brimble) learns of his father's murder and meets Lorna.
Designer: Desmond Chinn. **Director:** Brandon Acton-Bond. **Producer:** Douglas Allen.

Love Affair, The   31 wks

Presented by BBC, film

This series of films had love affairs as the unifying theme.

| 1966 | 7.0 | Tue 1 Nov 8:00 p.m. | 7 | 20 wks |

'Daisy Kenyon'
Joan Crawford stars as Daisy, a magazine illustrator living with husband Peter (Henry Fonda) in Cape Cod. She is being pursued by her lover Dan (Dana Andrews).
Director: Otto Preminger.

| 1967 | 5.4 | Tue 25 Apr 8:00 p.m. | 12 | 11 wks |

'Female on the Beach'
A woman plunges to her death from a clifftop. Lynn Markham (Joan Crawford) lives next door and meets the man the deceased was with before the accident.
Director: Joseph Pevney.

Love and Hate   2 wks

Canada, presented by BBC, drama

| 1991 | 10.6 | Wed 14 Aug 9:30 p.m. | 11 | 2 wks |

A Canadian story of power and revenge involves a bitter struggle for the custody of children. Kenneth Welsh stars as the outwardly successful and wealthy politician Colin Thatcher. His wife JoAnn (Kate Nelligan) knows him to be brutal and cruel.
Director: Francis Mankiewicz.

Love Bug, The   1 wk

Presented by ITV, film

| 1987 | 16.6 | Thu 1 Jan 5:15 p.m. | 2 | 1 wk |

A Volkswagen belonging to a racing driver assumes a mind of its own. Starring Buddy Hackett, Dean Jones, Michele Lee and David Tomlinson.
Director: Robert Stevenson.

Love of Mike, The   4 wks

AR, situation comedy

In this series Michael Medwin starred as dance band trumpeter Mike Lane. He was eternally broke and forever chasing the girls. Brian Wilde played his flatmate, George Roderick was their neighbour and Carmel McSharry was the charlady.

| 1960 | 4.8 | Mon 27 Jun 8:00 p.m. | 8 | 4 wks |

Producer: Ronald Marriott.

Love on the Dole   1 wk

Granada, drama

| 1967 | 7.1 | Thu 19 Jan 9:40 p.m. | 9 | 1 wk |

This play by Ronald Gow and Walter Greenwood was adapted for television by John Finch. It was set in Hanley Park, Salford in 1933, during the Depression. This was a time of means tests, mass unemployment and love on the dole. The cast includes George A. Cooper, Betty Driver, Martin Shaw, Anne Stallybrass, Malcolm Tierney and Jack Woolgar.
Designer: Peter Caldwell. **Producer:** Derek Bennett.

Love Story   108 wks

ATV, drama

This was a series of light plays with romantic themes.

| 1963 | 6.8 | Mon 9 Sep 8:00 p.m. | 4 | 15 wks |

'Love in a Small Town' by Lewis Greifer.
Tom (Tony Britton) is Deputy Town Clerk of a small town and is encouraged by his ambitious wife (Faith Brook) to apply for the job of Town Clerk when it becomes vacant. One day Pat McKendrick (Judi Dench), a literary agency assistant, walks into his office and revives his hopes of becoming a writer – hopes long ago discouraged by his wife.
Designer: Bill McPherson. **Producer:** Hugh Rennie. **Executive Producer:** Stella Richman.

| 1964 | 7.3 | Tue 14 Apr 9:45 p.m. | 3 | 26 wks |

'The Human Element' by Stan Barstow.
The girl loves the boy but the boy shows more interest in his toy trains, motorbikes and shoes. She despairs, but love is unpredictable. Starring Frances Cuka and Jeremy Kemp with Trevor Bannister, Johnny Briggs and Marjorie Rhodes.
Director: Josephine Douglas. **Producer:** Stella Richman.

| 1965 | 8.4 | Mon 6 Dec 8:00 p.m. | 2 | 19 wks |

'La Musica' by Marguerite Duras.
A dead love affair springs back to life when Anne-Marie and Michel are thrown together for the night after their divorce had been granted earlier in the day. Starring Michael Craig and Vanessa Redgrave.
Designer: Peter Roden. **Director:** John Nelson Burton. **Producer:** Josephine Douglas.

| 1966 | 7.5 | Mon 27 Jun 8:00 p.m. | 1 | 10 wks |

'The Small Hours' by Alfred Shaughnessy.
Jane Kennedy (Hannah Gordon) wins a crossword puzzle competition. Her prize is a night out with film star Richard Page (Patrick Macnee). The date is to change both their lives. Also starring Timothy Bateson and Penelope Keith.
Designer: Eric Shedden. **Director:** Shaun O'Riordan. **Producer:** Pieter Rogers.

| 1967 | 7.5 | Thu 21 Sep 9:00 p.m. | 3 | 11 wks |

'Breach of the Peace' by Jane Gaskell.
The wedding is off. The guests have been sent home and the reception cancelled. Starring Gabrielle Drake and Norman Eshley as Susannah and Edmund, the supposed bride and bridegroom.
Designer: Eric Shedden. **Director:** Valerie Hanson. **Producer:** Pieter Rogers.

| 1968 | 6.3 | Thu 4 Jul 9:00 p.m. | 13 | 4 wks |

'S for Sugar, A for Apple, M for Misery' by Jeri Matos.
All the problems arise over a lost lighter left in a taxi. Starring Barry Foster and Elizabeth Shepherd.
Designer: Richard Lake. **Director:** James Ferman. **Producer:** Rex Firkin.

| 1972 | 7.6 | Tue 14 Mar 9:00 p.m. | 4 | 9 wks |

'Alice' by Jeremy Paul.
Alice (Lois Baxter) comes to London in search of a close friend who is a travelling salesman – but someone else opens the door.
Designer: Richard Lake. **Director:** Ian Fordyce. **Producer:** Henri Safran.

| 1973 | 7.8 | Tue 6 Feb 9:00 p.m. | 2 | 13 wks |

'A Face of Your Own' by John Portman.
Moira (Gwen Watford) has an attractive new lodger (Anton Rodgers). Moira is attractive too – and so is her daughter Sarah (Angharad Rees).
Designer: Michael Bailey. **Director:** Mike Newell. **Producer:** Henri Safran.

| 1974 | 7.0 | Tue 8 Jan 9:00 p.m. | 16 | 1 wk |

'Second Partner' by Noel Robinson.
Alec (Robert Hardy) and his second wife Chris (Angela Browne) live in the country. Chris feels insecure as a result of constant comparison with the first wife. When Lucy (Barbara Jefford), a friend from the former marriage, comes to stay, she is convinced she is under threat.
Designer: Ray White. **Director:** Lionel Harris. **Producer:** Nicholas Palmer.

| Love Thy Neighbour | | | | 57 wks |

Thames, comedy

The first British comedy to face the issues of a multiracial society was created by Vince Powell and Harry Driver. The white couple, Eddie and Joan Booth (Jack Smethurst and Kate Williams), had new black neighbours, Bill and Barbara Reynolds (Rudolph Walker and Nina Baden-Semper). To add to the conflict, Eddie was a staunch socialist while Bill was a true blue Tory.
Producer (1974–76): Anthony Parker.

| 1972 | 8.4 | Thu 25 May 9:00 p.m. | 1 | 13 wks |

Joan decides to make herself more attractive for Eddie, which starts a chain reaction and brings about further conflict between the warring neighbours.
Producer: Stuart Allen.

| 1973 | 8.4 | Wed 12 Dec 8:00 p.m. | 1 | 7 wks |

There is confrontation at the Social Club between Eddie and the new barman, and the house the other side of Eddie is coming up for sale. Eddie fears an immigrant invasion.
Producer: Ronnie Baxter.

| 1974 | 9.6 | Mon 1 Apr 8:00 p.m. | 1 | 18 wks |

Eddie takes delivery of a crate of bananas, a gift for Bill from Trinidad. He quickly finds the crate contains more than bananas.

| 1975 | 9.3 | Thu 30 Jan 8:00 p.m. | 1 | 16 wks |

Eddie decides to trace his family tree, and thinks he may have royal blood.

| 1976 | 7.4 | Thur 15 Jan 8:30 p.m. | 10 | 3 wks |

When the Booths' electricity is cut off, Eddie has to accept neighbourly hospitality.

A fan played by Hannah Gordon won a date with a star in the **Love Story** 'The Small Hours'.

Love Thy Neighbour — 1 wk

Presented by ITV, film

| 1978 | 13.7 | Thu 24 Aug 7:45 p.m. | 2 | 1 wk |

Feature film version in which Joan and Barbara enter a 'Love Thy Neighbour' competition. Their chances are diminished when Eddie and Bill fall out over a union matter. Also starring James Beck, Arthur English, Bill Fraser, Melvyn Hayes, Patricia Hayes and Bill Pertwee. **Director:** John Robins.

Lovejoy — 4 wks

BBC, drama

Ian McShane starred as knowledgeable, but slightly shady, antiques dealer Lovejoy. His assistants were Tinker (Dudley Sutton) and Eric (Chris Jury). Phyllis Logan played Lady Jane Felsham.

| 1991 | 13.1 | Sun 24 Mar 8:15 p.m. | 8 | 4 wks |

'Black Virgin of Vladimir' by Terry Hodgkinson.
An American widow and a Japanese businessman have been swindled out of two million pounds by a crooked antiques dealer. Lovejoy plans an elaborate scheme to get their money back. With guest stars Brian Blessed, James Booth, Linda Gray and Mako.
Director: Francis Megahy. **Producer:** Richard Everitt.

Lovers, The — 10 wks

Granada, comedy

In this series created by Jack Rosenthal, Richard Beckinsale starred as Geoffrey and Paula Wilcox as Beryl. She was trying to hang on to her virginity and he was desperately trying to lose his.

The series was repeated in 1979 in tribute to the late Richard Beckinsale.

| 1970 | 6.3 | Tue 3 Nov 8:25 p.m. | 14 | 1 wk |

Beryl wants to go to the pictures but Geoffrey prefers the idea of the settee – in the dark – and Beryl's mum has gone out! To please her he's ready to give way but she'd be more pleased if he didn't. She'd love him to be a bit more dominant.
Director: Michael Apted. **Writer** and **Producer:** Jack Rosenthal.

| 1971 | 7.8 | Thu 11 Nov 9:00 p.m. | 3 | 7 wks |

Geoffrey suggests a trial marriage as being a good way to test the water at the shallow end before taking the plunge. Beryl counters that the best way to learn to swim is to jump in at the deep end.
Writer: Geoffrey Lancashire. **Producer:** Les Chatfield.

| 1979 | 10.3 | Sun 8 Jul 8:15 p.m. | 15 | 2 wks |

Beryl's mum (Joan Scott) organizes an engagement party for Beryl and Geoffrey.
Writer: Geoffrey Lancashire. **Producer:** Les Chatfield.

Lucy Show, The — 19 wks

USA presented by BBC, situation comedy

After eight years of continuous success with I LOVE LUCY, Lucille Ball and Desi Arnaz divorced in 1960. THE LUCY SHOW had Ball playing Lucy Carmichael, a scatterbrained widow with two children living in Connecticut. Her friend Vivian Bagley, also a widow with a son, was played by I LOVE LUCY co-star Vivian Vance.

| 1963 | 6.3 | Mon 25 Mar 8:00 p.m. | 8 | 19 wks |

Lucy and Vivian become volunteer firemen. With Jimmy Garrett, Ralph Hart, Dick Martin and Candy Moore.

Luke's Kingdom — 9 wks

YTV with Channel 9 (Australia), drama

This thirteen-part series was set in early nineteenth-century Australia. Luke Firbeck (Oliver Tobias) found the land granted to his family had already been settled, so they moved into squatter's territory and fought for their place in the new continent. The family consisted of Luke's brother Samuel (Gerard Maguire), sister Jassy (Elisabeth Crosby) and their retired father, naval lieutenant Jason (James Condon).

| 1976 | 7.0 | Wed 28 Apr 9:10 p.m. | 5 | 9 wks |

'A Woman Waiting' by Donald Bull.
The story of Jack Skelton (David Baxter), a young convict with a wife and child back home in England, who becomes friendly with Jassy.
Director: Peter Hammond. **Executive Producer:** Tony Essex.

Lulu — 1 wk

BBC, music

This series starred Scottish singer Lulu.

| 1969 | 6.4 | Sat 1 Mar 6:25 p.m. | 19 | 1 wk |

Lulu sings the winning song in this year's 'Song For Europe' competition. With Pan's People and the Johnny Harris orchestra.
Producer: Stanley Dorfman.

Lulu's Back in Town — 7 wks

BBC, music

Having first hit the pop charts in 1964 with 'Shout', 19-year-old Lulu was given her own series by the BBC.

| 1968 | 7.4 | Tue 28 May 9:05 p.m. | 2 | 7 wks |

Guests: The Alan Price Set, Peter West with the Ladybirds and the Peter Knight orchestra.
Choreographer: Jo Cook. **Producer:** John Ammonds.

McQ | 1 wk

Presented by ITV, film

1981 | **11.7** | **Sat 12 Dec 9:15 p.m.** | **8** | **1 wk**

John Wayne stars as a police officer who leaves the force to extract vengeance on the villains who killed his pal.
Director: John Sturges.

MacKenna's Gold | 1 wk

Presented by ITV, film

1978 | **13.5** | **Sun 30 Apr 7:15 p.m.** | **15** | **1 wk**

Gregory Peck stars as MacKenna, sheriff in a frontier town in 1872. Numerous attempts are made to find the legendary Valley of Gold, but there are many deaths as a result. Also starring Lee J. Cobb, Raymond Massey, Burgess Meredith, Anthony Quayle, Edward G. Robinson, Telly Savalas and Omar Sharif.
Director: J. Lee-Thompson.

McClain's Law | 3 wks

USA presented by BBC, drama

James Arness starred as tough-guy cop Jim McClain in the hard and seamy Los Angeles waterfront district of San Pedro. Marshall Colt played his partner Harry Gates.

1982 | **10.9** | **Fri 21 May 9:25 p.m.** | **8** | **3 wks**

'From the Mouths of Babes' by Joe Viola.
McClain retired from the force in 1966. When his partner in a fishing venture is killed he faces a tough retraining course to join again.
Director: Bernard McEveety.

Mad Death, The | 3 wks

BBC, drama

This three-part adaptation by Sean Hignett of the novel by Nigel Slater concerned the events that ensued after the first pet cat affected by rabies was smuggled into Britain.

1983 | **8.1** | **Sat 16 Jul 9:40 p.m.** | **11** | **3 wks**

Part One
The spread of the disease goes undetected until the first human victim suffers an agonizing death. Stars include Ed Bishop, Brenda Bruce, Richard Heffer, Barbara Kellerman, Jimmy Logan and Richard Morant.
Designer: Bob Smart. **Director:** Robert Young. **Producer:** Bob McIntosh.

Maggie and Her | 8 wks

LWT, situation comedy

This series by Leonard Webb starred Julia McKenzie as divorced schoolteacher Maggie and Irene Handl as Mrs Perry, her good-natured but nosey neighbour.

1978 | **17.8** | **Fri 10 Feb 7:30 p.m.** | **6** | **7 wks**

'National I Don't Care Week'
Maggie is down in the dumps until she meets Kiddo (Roy Holder), whose carefree attitude is infectious to the point where Mrs Perry is worried.
Producer: David Askey.

1979 | **13.2** | **Sun 29 Apr 7:25 p.m.** | **12** | **1 wk**

'A Holiday For Two'
Maggie's plan to go on holiday with a friend falls through. Mrs Perry lets her know she can be free to step in.
Director: John Reardon. **Producer:** Simon Brett.

Maggie's Place | 1 wk

LWT, entertainment

Maggie Fitzgibbon, Australian-born singer, dancer and actress, was given a nightclub setting for her series of variety shows.

1970 | **5.7** | **Sat 12 Sep 9:15 p.m.** | **14** | **1 wk**

Guests: Mr Acker Bilk and his Paramount Jazz Band, Johnny Hackett and Polly James.
Producer: David Bell.

Magic Circle Festival, The `1 wk`

BBC, entertainment

| 1964 | 5.1 | Thu 22 Oct 9:25 p.m. | 20 | 1 wk |

An excerpt from a week of magic held at the Scala Theatre, London. Magicians include Anna Lou and Maria, Jerry Bergman, Birch and Company, Mr Cox and Alan Shaxon. The compere is Michael Bailey. **Producer:** Barrie Edgar.

Magic Moments `1 wk`

TVS, entertainment

The performers in this series explored various subjects through comedy and song.

| 1986 | 10.4 | Sun 17 Aug 7:45 p.m. | 7 | 1 wk |

Fern Britton, Chris Tarrant and Gary Wilmot dissect love and laughter.
Directors: Vicki Barrass and Bob Collins. **Producer:** John Longley. **Executive Producer:** John Kaye Cooper.

Magnificent Seven, The `1 wk`

Presented by BBC, film

| 1980 | 11.0 | Sun 22 Jun 4:10 p.m. | 12 | 1 wk |

Charles Bronson, Yul Brynner, Horst Buchholz, James Coburn, Brad Dexter, Steve McQueen and Robert Vaughn are a group of professional gunfighters hired by the villagers of Ixcatlan, Mexico. The community is being repeatedly marauded by Calvera (Eli Wallach) and his bandits.
Director: John Sturges.

Magnificent Seven Ride, The `1 wk`

Presented by BBC, film

| 1985 | 10.8 | Sat 3 Aug 6:55 p.m. | 12 | 1 wk |

This fourth film featuring the MAGNIFICENT SEVEN stars Lee Van Cleef and Stefanie Powers in a story of kidnapping and banditry in Mexico.
Director: George McCowan.

Magnificent Showman, The `1 wk`

Presented by ITV, film

| 1977 | 6.1 | Thu 9 Jun 7:00 p.m. | 12 | 1 wk |

The story of Matt Masters (John Wayne), a circus owner at the turn of the century who searches Europe for his former wife. Claudia Cardinale and Rita Hayworth also star.
Director: Henry Hathaway.

Magnum `5 wks`

USA presented by ITV, drama

Tom Selleck starred as carefree, fun-loving private detective Thomas Magnum, who lived on a luxury estate in Hawaii after retiring from naval intelligence. He paid no rent and drove a Ferrari.
The series was created and produced by Donald P. Bellisario and Glen Larson.

| 1981 | 17.6 | Fri 27 Feb 7:30 p.m. | 3 | 5 wks |

'Don't Eat the Snow in Hawaii'
This full-length film introduces the series. Magnum investigates the death of a former Vietnam colleague and finds himself involved with a network of drug dealers.

Magnum Force `2 wks`

Presented by ITV, film

| 1982 | 14.2 | Sat 6 Mar 9:45 p.m. | 6 | 1 wk |

In this sequel to DIRTY HARRY, Inspector Harry Callahan (Clint Eastwood) and his partner Early Smith (Felton Perry) track a wave of underworld killings in San Francisco. It transpires that Smith is the killer.
Director: Ted Post.

| 1985 | 9.9 | Wed 28 Aug 10:30 p.m. | 20 | 1 wk |

Repeat showing of the above film.

Maigret `13 wks`

BBC with Winwell Productions, drama

This series of fifty-minute dramas began in the late 1950s and starred Rupert Davies as George Simenon's Parisian pipe-smoking sleuth. Ewen Solon was Lucas.
Designer: Eileen Diss. **Executive Producer:** Andrew Osborn.

| 1961 | 4.5 | Mon 18 Dec 9:25 p.m. | 14 | 2 wks |

'The Liars' dramatized by Vincent Tilsley.
Based on the novel Maigret à l'école, the Inspector travels to the seaside village of St André to unravel a mystery. His investigations gradually involve him with many local characters – the innkeeper, the postmistress and the schoolmaster.
Producer: Rudolph Cartier.

| 1962 | 7.0 | Mon 29 Oct 9:25 p.m. | 3 | 8 wks |

'Love From Félicie' dramatized by Giles Cooper.
Based on the novel Félicie est là. A miserly old man is discovered shot dead in his bedroom by Félicie (Lana Morris), his pretty young servant. The wardrobe is damaged and suggests she was searching for something. She refuses to answer any of Maigret's questions and the first clues are only found when he reads her diary.
Director: Andrew Osborn.

| 1963 | 5.7 | Tue 1 Oct 9:10 p.m. | 13 | 3 wks |

'Poor Cécile' dramatized by Donald Bull.
Based on the novel Cécile est morte. Cécile (Mary Chester) is a constant visitor to Maigret's waiting room. The simple-minded girl has a crush on the Inspector and has obviously invented tales of a midnight intruder in her aunt's flat. But even Maigret is not infallible, and it becomes apparent that Cécile should have been listened to more carefully.
Director: Michael Hayes.

Maigret · 1 wk

Presented by ITV, film

| 1988 | 9.2 | Sat 21 May 8:00 p.m. | 13 | 1 wk |

Richard Harris stars as Inspector Maigret. His old colleague is murdered on a tram and the body thrown into the River Seine. Also starring Annette André, Ian Ogilvy and Victoria Tennant.
Director: Paul Lynch.

Maigret at Bay · 1 wk

BBC, drama

| 1969 | 6.3 | Sun 9 Feb 8:15 p.m. | 18 | 1 wk |

Rupert Davies returns as Inspector Maigret in a ninety-minute adaptation by Donald Bull of Georges Simenon's novel of the same name. Maigret is accused of attempted rape by a young girl he tried to help.
Designer: Eileen Diss. **Director:** William Slater. **Producer:** Cedric Messina.

Main Attraction, The · 4 wks

BBC, entertainment

This variety series was hosted by a different star each week.

| 1983 | 8.2 | Sat 30 Jul 8:45 p.m. | 9 | 4 wks |

Larry Grayson introduces Anna Dawson, Charlie Drake, Roy Jay, John Junkin, Modern Romance, Elaine Paige, Shakin' Stevens and Brian Rogers' Super Troupers.
Director: John Bishop. **Producer:** John Fisher.

Main Chance, The · 41 wks

YTV, drama

This long-running series created by Edmund Ward starred John Stride as solicitor David Main, a man with a mania for office efficiency. Given to instant and often rash decisions, he would storm in wherever instinct took him, hardly taking time to balance the rights and wrongs of a situation. Kate O'Mara played his wife Julia. Other regular characters included Lady Sarah Radchester (Anna Palk) and Henry and Margaret Castleton (John Wentworth and Margaret Ashcroft).
Director (1969–70, 1972): John Frankau. **Executive Producer** (1969–70, 1972): Peter Willes.

| 1969 | 6.3 | Wed 18 Jun 9:00 p.m. | 5 | 6 wks |

'What About Justice?' by Edmund Ward.
David Main is lured to Yorkshire by Leeds industrialist Charles Arkwright (Leslie Sands) to defend his son Tony (Frederick Danner), who is accused of receiving stolen property.
Designer: Vic Symonds.

| 1970 | 7.5 | Mon 26 Oct 8:30 p.m. | 1 | 13 wks |

'The Best Legal System in the World' by John Malcolm.
Main is approached by the company secretary and several minority shareholders of a company and asked to penetrate the web of its senior management.
Designer: Tom Carter.

| 1972 | 6.9 | Wed 7 Jun 9:00 p.m. | 3 | 11 wks |

'The Killing Ground' by Edmund Ward.
Main finds himself in a life-or-death situation which involves him more than just professionally. His client Richard Nash (Guy Slater) is ill in hospital with a murder charge pending. Helping Main find defence witnesses are Nash's wife Hilary (Estelle Kohler) and her father Harry Selby (Jack Watson).
Designer: Alan Pickford.

| 1975 | 7.3 | Fri 18 Apr 9:00 p.m. | 4 | 11 wks |

'Process' by Edmund Ward.
Lorry driver George Duncan (David Hill) is breathalysed and causes problems for Main and tragedy for himself.
Designer: Malcolm Middleton. **Producer:** Derek Bennett. **Executive Producer:** David Cunliffe.

Mainly Millicent · 4 wks

ATV, entertainment

This series starred Millicent Martin, who came to prominence in BBC's THAT WAS THE WEEK THAT WAS.

| 1964 | 5.3 | Fri 12 Jun 10:05 p.m. | 13 | 4 wks |

Guest: Roy Castle, with the Jack Parnell orchestra.
Producer: Francis Essex.

M

Making of Star Wars, The — 1 wk

USA presented by ITV, documentary

| 1978 | 11.8 | Fri 16 Jun 8:00 p.m. | 12 | 1 wk |

The film's two robots, C-3PO and R2-D2, present a guided tour behind the set and meet the people who made the movie.

Maladjusted Busker, The — 1 wk

BBC, comedy

| 1966 | 6.2 | Thu 3 Mar 9:00 p.m. | 17 | 1 wk |

Frank Muir introduces this thirty-minute film written by John Law. Roy Hudd stars as a Londoner, cut off from his three fellow buskers. He trawls the streets of the City, being drawn each time he hears a snatch of their music.
Director: John Duncan. **Producer:** Dick Clement.

Mallens, The — 10 wks

Granada, drama

Catherine Cookson's story of scandal and passion in nineteenth-century Northumberland was adapted in seven parts by Jack Russell. The Squire of High Bank Hall, ruthless Thomas Mallen (John Hallan), fathered several illegitimate sons, all of whom inherited from him a flash of white hair known as 'The Mallen Streak'. One son, Donald Radlett (John Duttine) reappeared in his father's life with an equally ambitious ruthlessness, and developed a feud with another son, Dick (David Rintoul).

When Thomas faced bankruptcy and lost his estate he shared his life with his young nieces Barbara and Constance Farrington (Pippa Guard and Julia Chambers) and their governess Anna Brigmore (Caroline Blakiston). Dick faced a murder charge, Thomas developed a relationship with Miss Brigmore, Donald married Constance, and Barbara, raped by Thomas, became pregnant and died in childbirth.
Designer: Steven Finereu. **Producer:** Roy Roberts.

| 1979 | 12.0 | Sun 8 Jul 8:45 p.m. | 4 | 4 wks |

Episode Five
Donald Radlett discovers on his wedding night that Constance is not a virgin.
Director: Ronald Wilson.

The second series picked up after several more births, marriages, affairs and deaths. It particularly followed the fortunes of Barbara Farrington's daughter Barbara Mallen (Juliet Stevenson), who had been raised by her mother's governess Anna and Michael Radlett (Gerry Sundquist), the illegitimate son of her Aunt Constance (now played by June Ritchie) and Matthew Radlett, her late brother-in-law.

| 1980 | 13.1 | Thu 29 May 9:00 p.m. | 5 | 6 wks |

Episode One
Barbara and Michael go to the local St Valentine's Day fair.
Director: Mary McMurray.

Man About The House — 69 wks

Thames, situation comedy

In this series created by Johnnie Mortimer and Brian Cooke, Chrissy (Paula Wilcox) shared a flat with Jo (Sally Thomsett). They needed a third girl to share and ended up with Robin Tripp (Richard O'Sullivan), who they found asleep in the bath after a party. His value was as a cook. Landlords Mr and Mrs Roper (Brian Murphy and Yootha Joyce) took a dim view of the arrangement.
Producer: Peter Frazer-Jones.

| 1973 | 7.6 | Tue 11 Sep 8:25 p.m. | 1 | 7 wks |

'It's Only Money'
Jo has no money and the rent is due. She must either sell something or arrange an overdraft.

| 1974 | 8.2 | Wed 13 Feb 8:00 p.m. | 1 | 12 wks |

'Carry Me Back to Old Southampton'
Robin fails his catering examinations and it looks as though he may have to leave London and take a job in Southampton.

| 1975 | 8.8 | Thu 13 Mar 7:55 p.m. | 1 | 22 wks |

'One For The Road'
Chrissy is learning to drive, assisted by Robin. Mr Roper is incensed that the British Legion has increased the price of a pint by one penny, so he starts home brewing.

| 1976 | 9.2 | Wed 7 Apr 8:00 p.m. | 1 | 16 wks |

'Another Bride, Another Groom'
Wedding bells are ringing for Chrissy, but nothing goes according to plan.

| 1977 | 15.8 | Tue 30 Aug 8:30 p.m. | 1 | 11 wks |

Repeat of the above programme.

| 1982 | 10.1 | Tue 6 Jul 7:00 p.m. | 11 | 1 wk |

'Three's a Crowd'
A repeat of the first episode in which the girls discover their new flatmate in the bath.

Man About the House | 1 wk

Presented by ITV, film

| 1981 | 15.2 | Sat 2 Jan 7:40 p.m. | 12 | 1 wk |

In this feature film version of the show a firm of property developers tries to persuade the Ropers to sell the house.
Director: John Robins.

....

Man at the Top | 23 wks

Thames, drama

This series was created by John Braine, the author of ROOM AT THE TOP, which had been a highly popular novel and film. The ambitious and ruthless anti-hero Joe Lampton had made it to the top. This series found him thirteen years on, far from his northern roots, living in Surrey's stockbroker belt. Kenneth Haigh played Joe, Zena Walker portrayed his wife Susan and Avice Landon was Margaret Brown.
Producers (1970–71): George Markstein and Lloyd Shirley.

| 1970 | 6.5 | Mon 21 Dec 8:30 p.m. | 11 | 2 wks |

'It's All Perfectly True' by John Braine.
Joe, a management consultant, is chasing a contract from an important industrialist. Susan begins to suspect his interest extends beyond business when she discovers the industrialist in question is a beautiful woman (Hildegard Neil).
Designers: Patrick Downing and Stan Woodward. **Director:** Mike Vardy.

| 1971 | 8.2 | Mon 22 Feb 9:00 p.m. | 3 | 8 wks |

'Fixtures and Fittings' by Tom Brennand and Roy Bottomley.
Joe has been down but never out. He visits a health farm and considers the possibilities of another job.
Designers: Patrick Downing and David Marshall. **Director:** Dennis Vance.

| 1972 | 7.2 | Mon 3 Jul 9:00 p.m. | 1 | 13 wks |

'A Mug Like Me' by Tom Brennand and Roy Bottomley.
A lorry on the motorway brings tragedy into Joe Lampton's life, but he must get his priorities right and not allow this to affect business.
Designer: Stan Woodward. **Director:** Don Leaver. **Producer:** Jacqueline Davis.

....

Man Called Ironside, A | 71 wks

USA presented by BBC, drama

Raymond Burr played Robert Ironside, San Francisco's chief of detectives. He had been crippled in a shooting incident and was confined to a wheelchair. Also starring Don Galloway as Detective Sergeant Brown, Barbara Anderson as Officer Eve Whitfield and Don Mitchell as Mark Sanger. The series was created by Collier Young.
Producers: Cy Chermak and Joel Rogosin.

| 1968 | 7.4 | Mon 29 Apr 9:05 p.m. | 4 | 3 wks |

'Perfect Crime'
An unsigned note challenges Ironside's conviction that there is no such thing as a perfect crime. Guest stars: Peter Deuel and Brenda Scott.

| 1970 | 6.8 | Sat 21 Mar 9:00 p.m. | 10 | 13 wks |

'The Prophecy'
A fortune-teller with a reputation for being uncannily accurate with her predictions prophesies danger and death for Ironside. Guest star: Martha Scott.

| 1971 | 6.6 | Sat 10 Apr 9:00 p.m. | 3 | 21 wks |

'Beyond a Shadow'
A ruthless television interviewer moves in for a big story when a wealthy widow cleared of her husband's murder tries to kill herself. Guest stars: Mort Sahl and Dana Wynter.

| 1972 | 6.2 | Sat 20 May 9:00 p.m. | 7 | 8 wks |

'This Could Blow Your Mind'
Ironside becomes involved in sessions with a psychologist which develop into a struggle to preserve a vital secret within his subconscious. Guest stars: Bradford Dillman and George Grizzard.

| 1973 | 7.5 | Sat 10 Feb 9:00 p.m. | 5 | 24 wks |

'Achilles Heel'
A ruthless gang boss has been convicted. Although the conviction is only for tax evasion, the judge plans to sentence him to the maximum five years. Gangland makes its own laws, and the judge's son is framed for murder. Guest stars: Rick Lenz and William Windom.

| 1974 | 6.2 | Fri 11 Oct 9:25 p.m. | 13 | 2 wks |

'Mind for Murder'
When a nightclub mind reader tells more than he should know about a fire, Ironside smells arson. Guest stars: John Doucette, Ross Martin and Louie Sorel.

....

Man from Atlantis | 3 wks

USA presented by ITV, drama

Patrick Duffy starred as Mark Harris, believed to be the sole survivor of the legendary lost city. He had gills, which enabled him to breathe under water. He also had a webbed hand. He was co-opted into the US Navy because of his marine skills. Belinda Montgomery played Dr Elizabeth Merrill of the Foundation for Oceanic Research.
Producer: Herb Solow.

| 1977 | 14.7 | Sat 8 Oct 6:15 p.m. | 3 | 3 wks |

'The Death Scouts'
An investigation into the disappearance of three scuba divers brings about the discovery of water-breathing aliens who plan to invade Earth.

Man About the House was the greatest chart success of Richard O'Sullivan's career.

In **Man at the Top** Kenneth Haigh played the character originated by Laurence Harvey in the film Room at the Top.

Man from Haven, The — 1 wk

ATV, drama

This series created by Wilfred Greatorex starred Ian Holm as Jack Byron Lever, an out-of-work businessman who believed he knew how to make one million pounds in one month. Brenda Bruce also starred as Mary Balfour and John Stratton as Ken Durban.

1972	5.3	Fri 21 Jul 9:00 p.m.	12	1 wk

Episode One
Lever discovers the secrets of a few numbered Swiss bank accounts and proposes to use the information to induce the depositors to invest in a new business.
Designer: Stanley Mills. **Director:** Peter Wood. **Producer:** Richard Bates.

Man from UNCLE, The — 45 wks

USA presented by BBC, drama

The outline of this series, initially called SOLO, was drafted by James Bond creator Ian Fleming. When illness prevented his continuing work the producers Norman Felton and Sam Rolfe completed the project.
 In an office behind the secret wall of a New York dry-cleaning and tailoring shop, the men from UNCLE were responsible for countering the attempt by THRUSH to dominate the world. Originally the acronym had no meaning, but in response to fan pressure it was given one, United Network Command for Law Enforcement. Its chief was Alexander Waverly, played by Leo G. Carroll. The UNCLE agents were Napoleon Solo (Robert Vaughn) and Ilya Kuryakin (David McCallum).

1965	6.3	Thu 21 Oct 8:00 p.m.	13	12 wks

'The Green Opal Affair'
Solo encounters a cheater and a cheetah and ends up losing his shirt.

1966	6.7	Thu 24 Mar 8:05 p.m.	8	23 wks

'The Dippy Blonde Affair'
UNCLE agents in Hong Kong discover that THRUSH have an ion machine capable of weakening the human mind.

1967	6.3	Thu 23 Nov 8:00 p.m.	14	9 wks

'The Pieces of Fate Affair'
UNCLE tangles with a village full of villains.

1968	5.7	Fri 5 Jan 7:30 p.m.	19	1 wk

'The Thrush Roulette Affair'
A throw of the dice literally has UNCLE dicing with death.

Man in a Brown Suit, The — 1 wk

Presented by ITV, film

1990	9.6	Mon 23 Apr 9:00 p.m.	16	1 wk

Agatha Christie's story is adapted by Jean Wagner and stars Stephanie Zimbalist as American tourist Anne Beddingfield. She is accused of pushing a man under a car at Cairo airport. She saw a man in a brown suit running away from the scene, but no one else noticed. Also starring Ken Howard, Rue McClanahan, Tony Randall and Edward Woodward.
Director: Alan Grint.

Man in a Suitcase — 12 wks

ATV, drama

Stories of McGill (Richard Bradford), a private intelligence agent for hire.

1968	6.7	Wed 6 Mar 8:00 p.m.	9	12 wks

'Web With Four Spiders' by Edmund Ward.
A set of photographs leads McGill to a Manchester nightclub and to blackmail. Guest star: Ray McAnally.
Director: Robert Tronson. **Producer:** Sidney Cole.

Man in Room 17, The — 31 wks

Granada, drama

Situated somewhere in Whitehall, Room 17 was the centre of operations for the Department of Social Research. The man in Room 17 was Oldenshaw (Richard Vernon) and his partner was Dimmock (Michael Aldridge). Together they pulled the strings of the undercover world and were answerable only to the Prime Minister. Oldenshaw and Dimmock were never seen outside the room, so the series involved a split drama technique in which one team of actors, writers, directors and designers provided the stories inside the room and a second team provided those outside.
Producer: Richard Everitt.

1965	6.3	Fri 11 Jun 9:40 p.m.	4	18 wks

'The Room' by Reed de Rouen.
Designer: Dan Snyder. **Director:** Richard Everitt.

'Tell the Truth' by Robin Chapman.
There is suspicion of serious industrial espionage but Scotland Yard is unable to uncover any leads. The Government calls in the men in Room 17. With Dinsdale Landon, Vladek Sheybal and Meg Wynn Owen.
Designer: Denis Parkin. **Director:** David Boisseau.

1966	7.5	Fri 22 Apr 9:40 p.m.	4	13 wks

'The Room' by John Hawkesworth
Designer: Denis Parkin. **Director:** Claude Watham.

'The Black Witch' by John Hawkesworth
The men in Room 17 are asked to investigate the death of an American found near an old abbey with a devil worship object in his pocket. The cast includes Terence Alexander, Trevor Bannister, Denholm Elliott, Michael Gover and Amber Kammer.
Designer: Michael Grimes. **Director:** Peter Plummer.

Man of the Month
1 wk

ATV, documentary

In this occasional series an individual success story was profiled.

1968	6.4	Tue 3 Dec 9:15 p.m.	15	1 wk

Jack Odell's company, Lesney Products, manufactures five million miniature toy vehicles each week.
Camera: *Charles Stewart.* **Producer:** *Colin Clark.*

Man of the World
4 wks

ATV, drama

A series of fifty-minute adventures with roving photographer Michael Strait (Craig Stevens).

1962	5.8	Sat 10 Nov 7:25 p.m.	15	4 wks

'The Highland Story' *by Lindsay Galloway.*
Strait is assigned to report on the Scottish Clan system. His investigations go deeper than many Clan members would wish. Also starring Ray Barrett, Finlay Currie, John Laurie, Noelle Middleton and Tracy Reed.
Director: *Charles Friend.* **Producer:** *Harry Fine.*

Man on the Moon
2 wks

ITN/LWT, news/music

1969	5.7	Sun 20 Jul 6:00 p.m.	6	2 wks

David Frost presents the latest news from the moon. His guests are Cilla Black, Sammy Davis Jr., Engelbert Humperdinck, Lulu and Cliff Richard. They are all waiting for Neil Armstrong to step from the Apollo 11 lunar module Eagle and set foot on the moon's surface. (Armstrong actually set foot on the Sea of Tranquility at 9:17 p.m. BST.)
For ITN **Director:** *Gordon Hesketh.* **Executive Producer:** *David Nicholas.*
For LWT **Musical Director:** *Harry Rabinowitz.* **Directors:** *David Bell, Terry Hughes and John Philips.* **Producer:** *Geoffrey Hughes.*

Man Outside, The
3 wks

BBC, drama

This series of stories was introduced by Rupert Davies as an outsider looking in on a world of mystery and suspicion.

1972	5.5	Fri 26 May 9:20 p.m.	17	3 wks

'The Birdwatcher' *by Robert Holles.*
Major Grimsby (Peter Barkworth) is harmless if somewhat eccentric until he meets Harry Wichelow (Alec McCowen). The result is murder.

Zena Walker also stars.
Designer: *David Myerscough.* **Director:** *Michael Ferguson.* **Producer:** *Derrick Sherwin.*

Man They Call the Genius, The
1 wk

AR, music

1964	4.7	Wed 26 Aug 9:40 p.m.	19	1 wk

A recording of a concert by singer/pianist Ray Charles.
Television presentation: *Robert Fleming.*

Man Who Would Be King, The
1 wk

Presented by ITV, film

1980	11.1	Mon 25 Aug 8:00 p.m.	7	1 wk

In Rudyard Kipling's story, two late nineteenth-century former British Army sergeants in India, Daniel Dravot (Sean Connery) and Peachy Carnehan (Michael Caine), set off via Afghanistan to seek their fortunes in Kafiristan. Christopher Plummer plays Kipling.
Director: *John Huston.*

Man with the Golden Gun, The
5 wks

Presented by ITV, film

1980	15.3	Thu 25 Dec 6:10 p.m.	9	1 wk

James Bond (Roger Moore) searches for Scaramanga (Christopher Lee) in Hong Kong and Thailand. Britt Ekland is Mary Goodnight.
Director: *Guy Hamilton.*

1983	15.7	Sun 6 Mar 7:15 p.m.	2	1 wk
1988	15.4	Sat 6 Feb 7:15 p.m.	9	1 wk
1989	15.5	Mon 27 Mar 8:00 p.m.	6	1 wk
1991	14.5	Sat 9 Feb 7:40 p.m.	12	1 wk

Repeat showings of the above film.

Manhunt
1 wk

AR, documentary

1968	6.5	Tue 23 Apr 9:15 p.m.	12	1 wk

Peter Williams reports on the hunt for the killer of seven-year-old Christine Darby who was murdered on Cannock Chase, Staffordshire on 19 August 1967.
Director: *Ken Ashton.* **Producer:** *Philip Whitehead.*

Manhunt | 26 wks

LWT, drama

This series was set in Vichy France during the Second World War. RAF Pilot Vincent (Alfred Lynch), resistance leader Jimmy (Peter Barkworth) and Nina (Cyd Hayman) were on the run in occupied territory. Robert Hardy played Abwehr Sergeant Gratz. The series made much play of the mistrust between patrician and communist resistance movements.

| 1970 | 7.0 | Fri 20 Feb 9:00 p.m. | 1 | 26 wks |

'A Different Kind of War' by Jonathan Hales.
It is Christmas Eve and Vincent takes Jimmy and Nina to shelter in a farmhouse. They soon realize they have walked into a sinister situation.
Designer: John Emery. **Producer:** Rex Firkin.

Many Wives of Patrick, The | 3 wks

LWT, situation comedy

This series by Richard Waring starred Patrick Cargill as six-times-married Patrick Woodford.

| 1977 | 6.0 | Sat 18 Jun 9:45 p.m. | 18 | 3 wks |

'Oh What a Lovely Pair!'
Harold (Robin Parkinson) picks up an item in a junk shop. Patrick realizes he once owned an identical item, which would make the pair. He sets about finding it. Also starring Ursula Howells as Elizabeth Woodford.
Producer: William G. Stewart.

March on Washington | 1 wk

ITN, news

| 1963 | 5.6 | Wed 28 Aug 9:15 p.m. | 10 | 1 wk |

Live coverage via Telstar of the conclusion of the historic freedom march. Earlier events of the day are shown in recorded segments. (More than 200,000 freedom marchers, whose goals were racial integration, better housing and improved job opportunities, marched peacefully up Constitution Hill carrying the red-and-white banners of the movement and singing the anthem 'We Shall Overcome'. They converged on the Lincoln Memorial where ten civil rights leaders made speeches. The most significant address came from Dr Martin Luther King, President of the Southern Christian Leadership Conference, who proclaimed 'I Have a Dream').

Margins of the Mind | 3 wks

Granada, documentary

In this series of three programmes Brian Inglis explored the unexplainable.

| 1968 | 6.0 | Tue 7 May 9:15 p.m. | 16 | 3 wks |

'Water Divining'
A look at how diviners are able to find underground water using sticks and stones.
Director: Mark Shivas. **Producer:** Mike Wooller.

Margo Henderson | 1 wk

BBC, entertainment

This Scottish singer, impressionist and pianist had her own series after many guest appearances on other shows.

| 1963 | 4.6 | Wed 25 Sep 9:50 p.m. | 19 | 1 wk |

With musicians Tim Bell (bass), Maurice Placquet (drums), Ronnie Price (piano) and Judd Proctor (guitar).
Producer: Nick Burrell-Davis.

Marilyn Monroe: Ten Years On | 1 wk

USA presented by BBC, documentary

| 1972 | 4.8 | Tue 29 Aug 9:25 p.m. | 16 | 1 wk |

Those who knew her reappraise Marilyn's life and career ten years after her death.

Market in Honey Lane | 13 wks

ATV, drama

This series was created by Louis Marks and set in a fictional market. The hour-long episodes starred John Bennett as Billy Bush, Michael Golden as Sam English, Ray Lonnen as Dave Sampson, Peter Birrel as Jacko Bennet, and Jack Bligh as Jimmy Bentall.

| 1967 | 8.9 | Mon 3 Apr 8:00 p.m. | 1 | 13 wks |

'Nothing's for Nothing' by Louis Marks.
Stallholder Jimmy Bentall has fallen on hard times. He begins to find out who his real friends are.
Designer: Anthony Waller. **Director:** David Reid. **Producer:** John Cooper.

Marti | 1 wk

ATV, entertainment

This one-hour special starred one-time NEW FACES winner Marti Caine.

1977	7.9	Wed 4 May 8:00 p.m.	7	1 wk

Guests: Keith Harris, Gilbert O'Sullivan and the Three Degrees, with the Norman Maen dancers, Tony Mansell singers and Jack Parnell orchestra.
Producer: Peter Harris.

Marti Caine | 1 wk

BBC2, entertainment

Marti starred with regular guest Billy Preston.

1981	12.3	Mon 9 Mar 8:15 p.m.	17	1 wk

Guests: Alfred Marks, Wayne Sleep and Jeff Richer's First Edition.
Producer: Stanley Appel.

Martian Chronicles, The | 1 wk

USA/UK presented by BBC, drama

This three-part adaptation by Richard Matheson of Ray Bradbury's science fiction novel The Silver Locusts starred Rock Hudson as Colonel John Wilder and Gayle Hunnicutt as Ruth Wilder on an exploration of Mars.

1980	9.8	Sat 9 Aug 8:25 p.m.	15	1 wk

Part One 'The Expeditions'
The Zeus Project is the first manned space flight to Mars. It is the fulfilment of Wilder's dream.
Director: Michael Anderson.

Marty | 6 wks

BBC, comedy

Marty Feldman's first solo series. He had been long-known and respected as a comedy scriptwriter, usually in partnership with Barry Took. He was first seen as a performer in 1955 as part of the trio Morris, Marty and Mitch, and in 1967 he appeared with John Cleese in AR's AT LAST THE 1948 SHOW. Feldman died in Mexico City on 2 December 1982.

1968	6.0	Sat 5 Oct 8:15 p.m.	4	6 wks

With Marty are Tim Brooke-Taylor and John Junkin plus guests John Boulter, Dai Francis, Tony Mercer and Les Rawlings from THE BLACK AND WHITE MINSTREL SHOW. (First shown on BBC2).
Producer: Dennis Main Wilson.

Mary Hopkin In . . . | 1 wk

BBC, entertainment

OPPORTUNITY KNOCKS winner and recording star Mary Hopkin appeared in this series with a regular gang of children and a variety of guest stars. Each week they explored a different 'land' whether it be films, legends, books, nursery rhymes, pantomime or the theatre.

1970	7.0	Fri 20 Nov 8:30 p.m.	16	1 wk

'The Land of Theatre'
Guests: Arthur English, David Kernan and Cardew Robinson, with the Mike Sammes singers and the Burt Rhodes orchestra.
Choreographer: Gillian Lynne. **Producer:** Vernon Lawrence.

Mary, Mary | 1 wk

ATV, drama

1974	7.0	Mon 8 Apr 9:00 p.m.	14	1 wk

A play by Susan Pleat about Mary (Lynne Miller), who found herself pregnant by a man she followed to live with in London. He deserted her and she miscarried. She now finds herself in court on a charge of baby snatching.
Designer: Vic Symonds. **Director:** John Nelson Burton. **Producer:** Nicholas Palmer.

Mary Poppins | 1 wk

Presented by BBC, film

1984	17.4	Tue 25 Dec 3:10 p.m.	6	1 wk

Julie Andrews and Dick Van Dyke star in Walt Disney's musical interpretation of the children's tales of P. L. Travers. Glynis Johns and David Tomlinson also star.
Director: Robert Stevenson.

Master of the Game | 2 wks

USA presented by ITV, drama

Sidney Sheldon's story of revenge and power was dramatized in three parts. It starred Dyan Cannon as Kate Blackwell, Ian Charleson as Jamie McGregor, Cherie Lunghi as Margaret Van de Merwe, Donald Pleasence as Solomon Van der Merwe, Jean Marsh as Mrs Talley and Johnny Sekka as Banda. Also starred Leslie Caron, Barry Morse, Angharad Rees, Shane Rimmer and David Suchet.
Directors: Kevin Connor and Harvey Hart. **Producer:** Norman Rosemont.

1988	10.0	Sun 14 Aug 7:45 p.m.	9	2 wks

Part Three
One of the twin daughters of Tony Blackwell (Harry Hamlin) plans to murder the other. (Repeat.)

Mastermind — 81 wks

BBC, game show

In this long-running quiz contestants needed mastery of a specialist subject plus a wide general knowledge. Magnus Magnusson has hosted the show from its beginning. The programme failed to make the charts in 1982 and 1991.
Directors included Peter Massey (1974–76, 1978), Antonia Charlton (1979–81), Laurence Vulliamy (1983–85), David Mitchell (1986–88) and Andrea Conway (1989–90). **Producers** included Bill Wright (1973–80), Roger Mackay (1981–84) and Peter Massey (1985–88, 1990).

1973 | 6.0 | Thu 13 Dec 7:55 p.m. | 19 | 1 wk

From the BBC studios in London.
Director: Martin L. Bell.

1974 | 8.2 | Thu 5 Dec 8:30 p.m. | 1 | 11 wks

A semi-final from the University of Surrey in Guildford.

1975 | 6.2 | Mon 22 Dec 9:15 p.m. | 11 | 1 wk

The 1975 final from the Newman Rooms of the Catholic Chaplaincy in Oxford.

1976 | 7.3 | Tue 30 Nov 8:30 p.m. | 11 | 6 wks

A semi-final from Durham University.

1978 | 15.5 | Thu 16 Nov 8:30 p.m. | 6 | 13 wks

From the University of Hull.

1979 | 22.6 | Wed 17 Oct 8:00 p.m. | 5 | 6 wks

From Aberystwyth University.

1980 | 19.2 | Sun 9 Nov 8:05 p.m. | 3 | 9 wks

From the University of Aberdeen.

1981 | 16.3 | Sun 20 Dec 7:45 p.m. | 5 | 10 wks

A semi-final from Durham University.

1983 | 12.1 | Sun 17 Apr 8:55 p.m. | 8 | 7 wks

From Christchurch College, Canterbury.

1984 | 11.6 | Sun 27 May 7:45 p.m. | 7 | 4 wks

The final from HMS Hermes, Portsmouth

1985 | 13.2 | Sun 27 Jan 8:40 p.m. | 16 | 3 wks

Four contestants from Scotland compete at the Burrell Collection in Glasgow.

1986 | 11.5 | Sun 29 Jun 9:30 p.m. | 3 | 6 wks

The final from the McEwan Hall at the University of Edinburgh.

1987 | 10.7 | Sun 7 Jun 8:50 p.m. | 8 | 1 wk

The final from the Britannia Royal Naval College, Dartmouth.

1988 | 9.7 | Sun 5 Jun 8:35 p.m. | 10 | 1 wk

The final from the University of Stirling.

1989 | 12.1 | Sun 11 Jun 8:40 p.m. | 7 | 1 wk

The final from the University of Warwick.
Producer: David Mitchell.

1990 | 9.9 | Sun 17 Jun 8:35 p.m. | 13 | 1 wk

The final from the City Chambers, Glasgow.

Mastermind International — 1 wk

BBC with ABC (Australia), game show

1981 | 12.7 | Thu 11 Jun 9:25 p.m. | 4 | 1 wk

Introduced by Huw Evans from the Sydney Opera House. Fred Housego represents the UK.

Match of the Decade — 1 wk

BBC, sport

1969 | 4.7 | Sat 7 Jun 10:00 p.m. | 20 | 1 wk

A repeat showing of the 1968 European Cup Final between Manchester United and Benfica in which Manchester United became the first English club to win the competition winning 4–1 at Wembley after extra time. Commentator: Kenneth Wolstenholme.
Television presentation: Alec Weeks.

Mating Machine, The — 1 wk

LWT, comedy

A mechanical matchmaker was the common factor in this series of comedies with a different writer and cast for each episode.

1970 | 6.2 | Fri 16 Oct 8:25 p.m. | 17 | 1 wk

'Flo and Monty and Henry . . . and Henry' by Graeme Garden and Bill Oddie.
After two days without a word from husband Monty (Norman Bird), Flo (Miriam Karlin) decides to take a lover and asks the Mating Machine to find her someone like Steve McQueen. It selects Henry, who is to be met at the Kozy Kat Kaffy. Unfortunately it selects ten Henrys – among whom are Roger Brierley, Adam Kurakin and David Suchet.
Producer: Bill Turner.

Matt Houston   1 wk

USA presented by BBC, drama

Lee Horsley starred in the title role as a Texan millionaire turned private detective. Pamela Hensley played his associate C. J. Parsons. **Director:** Richard Lang. **Producer:** Aaron Spelling.

| 1985 | 9.1 | Thu 30 May 9:25 p.m. | 20 | 1 wk |

'The Ghost of Carter Gault'
An assassination attempt has been made on Gault (William E. Noone) because he knows the truth about a crooked union boss.

Maupassant   11 wks

Granada, drama

This series of dramatizations of Guy de Maupassant's short stories was produced by Philip Mackie. Directors included Silvio Narizzano, Claude Watham, Gordon Flemyng and Derek Bennett.

| 1963 | 5.8 | Fri 25 Oct 9:10 p.m. | 10 | 11 wks |

'Consequences' dramatized by Hugh Leonard.
Three short stories, each self-contained but with a unifying theme demonstrating the consequences of impulsive action: The Arrangement with John Carson and Elizabeth Weaver, A Question of Latin with Colin Campbell, Julia Foster and Edward Jewesbury, and The Olive Grove with Kenneth Colley, André Morell and Doris Rogers. **Director:** Derek Bennett.

Maverick   1 wk

USA presented by ITV, western

This humorous series began in 1957 and starred James Garner as the gambling Bret Maverick and Jack Kelly as his brother Bart. Later Roger Moore appeared as their English cousin Beau Maverick. The name is said to derive from Texas rancher Samuel Maverick, who never branded his cattle. Hence any stray found without a brand was called a maverick.
Producer: Roy Huggins.

| 1960 | 4.6 | Sun 10 Jul 8:00 p.m. | 10 | 1 wk |

'Maverick Springs'
Bret is hired by Kate Dawson (Doris Packer) to extricate her brother Mark (King Donovan) from an undesirable romantic attachment.

Max   25 wks

Thames (1969–72, 1981) and ATV (1974), entertainment

Max Bygraves starred in his own series of half-hour shows with guest artists and pianist Bob Dixon.
Producer (1969, 1970 and 1972): William G. Stewart.

| 1969 | 8.3 | Thu 6 Feb 9:00 p.m. | 1 | 8 wks |

Guests: Anthony Bygraves, and the Cheadle Kingsway School Choir with the Mike Sammes singers and the Geoff Love orchestra.

| 1970 | 8.0 | Thu 26 Feb 9:00 p.m. | 3 | 9 wks |

Guests: Judith Durham and Aimi MacDonald with the Mike Sammes singers and the Geoff Love orchestra.

| 1971 | 6.8 | Wed 12 May 8:00 p.m. | 4 | 1 wk |

Guests: Joe Baker, Aimi MacDonald, Geoff Love, the Pamela Devis dancers with the Mike Sammes singers and the Norrie Paramor orchestra.
Producer: Alan Tarrant.

| 1972 | 7.0 | Thu 6 Apr 9:00 p.m. | 3 | 1 wk |

In this special edition Max takes a trip down Memory Lane recalling some of the great artists he's worked with, including Max Miller and Judy Garland. With the Geoff Love orchestra and the Mike Sammes singers.
Writers: Eric Davidson and Spike Mullins.

| 1974 | 8.3 | Wed 3 Apr 8:30 p.m. | 3 | 5 wks |

Guests: Denise Keene and Happy, the Jack Parnell orchestra and Tony Mansell's Coffee Set.
Producer: Dicky Leeman.

| 1981 | 14.7 | Wed 14 Jan 8:00 p.m. | 10 | 1 wk |

Guests in this one-hour special: Arthur English, Hilda Fenemore, Jon Pertwee and Yootha Joyce, with the Nigel Lythgoe dancers, the Tony Mansell singers and the Geoff Love orchestra.
Writer: Eric Davidson. **Producer:** Dennis Kirkland.

Bygraves first hit Number One with **Max**.

Max Boyce | 1 wk

BBC, entertainment

This was a one-off special from the Welsh entertainer.

| 1981 | 17.1 | Fri 2 Jan 9:15 p.m. | 3 | 1 wk |

Max is in concert from the Grand Theatre, Blackpool. Guests: Therapy.
Producer: Jack Williams.

Max Boyce and Friends | 1 wk

BBC, entertainment

This series spotlighted the Welsh singer and teller of tales, many of them concerning the Welsh National rugby team. It came from the Parc and Dare Theatre, Treorchy.

| 1983 | 9.5 | Wed 27 Apr 9:25 p.m. | 17 | 1 wk |

Guests: Aiden J. Harvey and Ruth Madoc.
Producer: Jack Williams.

Max Bygraves | 1 wk

Granada, entertainment

| 1967 | 7.6 | Tue 7 Nov 9:15 p.m. | 4 | 1 wk |

One-off special in which Max introduces newcomers to television including Amen Corner, the Bonzo Dog Doo Dah Band, Friday Brown and the Grumbleweeds.
Director: David Warwick. **Producer:** John Hamp.

Max Bygraves | 1 wk

Thames, entertainment

| 1970 | 7.8 | Wed 7 Jan 8:00 p.m. | 4 | 1 wk |

This one-hour special features Jim Backus, George Burns, Judith Durham and Geoff Love.
Producer: William G. Stewart.

Max Bygraves at the Royalty | 6 wks

Thames, entertainment

The Royalty Theatre in London is the venue for Max's 1972 series. He shared it with his son Anthony and the Geoff Love orchestra.
Writer: Eric Davidson. **Producer:** Terry Henebery.

| 1972 | 7.1 | Thu 17 Aug 8:00 p.m. | 1 | 6 wks |

Guest: Diana Coupland.

Max Bygraves Hour, The | 1 wk

ATV, entertainment

A one-off special starring Max.

| 1974 | 8.0 | Wed 17 April 8:00 p.m | 3 | 1 wk |

With Anthony Bygraves, Ted Ray and the Jack Parnell orchestra.
Producer: Dicky Leeman.

Max Bygraves Show, The | 2 wks

ATV, entertainment

Max first came to prominence in the late 1940s as a radio star with Peter Brough in EDUCATING ARCHIE. He has remained a popular entertainer for more than four decades. This series featured Anthony Bygraves, Max's son, and the Jack Parnell orchestra.

| 1963 | 8.2 | Wed 6 Nov 9:50 p.m. | 5 | 1 wk |

Producer: Albert Locke.

| 1964 | 7.4 | Wed 12 Feb 9:40 p.m. | 8 | 1 wk |

Producer: Alan Tarrant.

Max Bygraves Show, The | 1 wk

BBC, entertainment

| 1966 | 5.6 | Sat 2 Apr 8:30 p.m. | 19 | 1 wk |

Guests: Alan Freeman and Teresa Kelsey, with the Alyn Ainsworth orchestra.
Producer: Michael Hurll.

Max Bygraves Show, The | 2 wks

Thames, entertainment

| 1971 | 7.3 | Wed 27 Oct 8:00 p.m. | 4 | 1 wk |

A one-hour special with Rodney Bewes, Stephen Lewis, Nina, and the Geoff Love orchestra.
Producer: William G. Stewart.

| 1972 | 6.7 | Wed 17 May 8:00 p.m. | 12 | 1 wk |

A one-hour special with guests Beryl Hall and her dog Ben, Rod Hull and Emu, Manoff's Marionettes and Zsa Zsa the elephant. With Jenny Lee-Wright, the Pamela Devis dancers and the Geoff Love orchestra. **Producer:** Alan Tarrant.

Max in the Roaring Twenties — 1 wk

Thames, entertainment

| 1970 | 6.6 | Wed 25 Nov 8:00 p.m. | 14 | 1 wk |

A one-hour special starring Max Bygraves with Joe Baker, Geoff Love and Aimi MacDonald, with the Pamela Devis dancers, the Mike Sammes singers and the Norrie Paramor orchestra. **Producer:** Alan Tarrant. **Executive Producer:** Philip Jones.

Maxie — 1 wk

Presented by BBC, film

| 1990 | 8.4 | Sun 22 Jul 8:35 p.m. | 14 | 1 wk |

Glenn Close plays the double role of Jan and Maxie in the story of an actress who returned to life sixty years after her death. Ruth Gordon and Mandy Patinkin also star. **Director:** Paul Aaron.

Max's Holiday Hour — 1 wk

Thames, entertainment

A Christmas special starring Max Bygraves.

| 1977 | 14.7 | Tue 27 Dec 7:30 p.m. | 12 | 1 wk |

Guests: Charlie Cairoli and Company, Jim Davidson, Sandra Dickinson, Sharon Hudson, Margaret Powell and Lena Zavaroni, with the Nigel Lythgoe dancers, Tony Mansell singers and Geoff Love orchestra. **Producer:** Mark Stuart.

May to December — 6 wks

BBC, situation comedy

This series by Paul A. Mendelson concerned a romance between an older man, lawyer Alec Callender (Anton Rodgers), and a much younger woman, Zoe Angell (Eve Matheson later Lesley Dunlop). Regulars in the stories included Miss Flood (Frances White), Simone (Carolyn Pickles), Jamie (Paul Venables), Debbie (Chrissie Cotterill) and Hilary (Rebecca Lacey). **Producer** (1989–90): Sydney Lotterby. **Executive Producer:** Verity Lambert. (A Cinema Verity production.)

| 1989 | 11.1 | Sun 2 Apr 8:35 p.m. | 14 | 1 wk |

'It Never Entered My Mind'
In this first episode Alec and Zoe face up to the great age divide.

| 1990 | 13.4 | Thu 1 Feb 8:30 p.m. | 12 | 4 wks |

'There's a Place for Us'
Alec and Zoe decide to live together. They must break the news to their respective families, including Alec's mother (Madeleine Christie).

| 1991 | 9.2 | Tue 2 Jul 9:30 p.m. | 15 | 1 wk |

'I'll See You in My Dreams'
Alec assesses his achievements after twenty-five years with his firm. They don't appear to amount to much. **Producer:** Sharon Bloom.

Me and My Girl — 19 wks

LWT, situation comedy

This series by John Kane starred Richard O'Sullivan as the irresponsible widower Simon Harrap and Joanne Ridley as his teenage daughter Sam. It also featured Tim Brooke-Taylor as Simon's friend Derek Yates and Joan Sanderson as Nell. **Producer:** John Reardon. **Executive Producer:** Humphrey Barclay.

| 1984 | 12.6 | Fri 5 Oct 8:00 p.m. | 5 | 6 wks |

'A Clean Slate'
Simon is not pleased to learn that Sam is in love and is visiting a psychiatrist.

| 1985 | 14.6 | Fri 18 Jan 7:00 p.m. | 10 | 2 wks |

'Love and Kittens'
Simon goes jogging by the canal and falls in.

| 1986 | 8.1 | Fri 27 Jun 6:30 p.m. | 15 | 1 wk |

'Jobs for the Girls'
Simon and Derek think they have won a big advertising contract. Unfortunately all their rival agencies also appear to have won the same contract.

| 1987 | 12.6 | Sat 10 Jan 7:15 p.m. | 12 | 3 wks |

'Love's Young Dream' by Colin Bostock-Smith.
Sam is secretly in love and Nell thinks it is time her son-in-law Simon had a little talk with her.

| 1988 | 12.3 | Fri 30 Sep 7:30 p.m. | 12 | 7 wks |

'My Second Best Friend' by Colin Bostock-Smith.
Simon's French friend Jean-Pierre (Brian Deacon) comes to stay. Sam develops a sudden interest in O-level French.

Anthony Bygraves joins his famous father in a Marx Brothers routine in **Max Bygraves At The Royalty**.

Me Mammy | 2 wks

BBC, situation comedy

This series by Hugh Leonard starred Milo O'Shea as the mother-dominated Bunjy Kennefick and Yootha Joyce as his ever-frustrated fiancée, Miss Argyll. Anna Manahan played Bunjy's mother, Ray McAnally was Father Patrick and David Kelly portrayed Cousin Enda.

| 1970 | 5.6 | Fri 4 Sep 8:20 p.m. | 14 | 2 wks |

'The Night Enda Entered a Convent'
Father Patrick puts on a drama which he has written himself. It creates a problem as it involves Bunjy kissing Chrissie (Rosaleen Linehan). His mammy objects almost as much as Miss Argyll.
Producer: James Gilbert.

Medical Story | 1 wk

USA presented by BBC, drama

This film series of hospital dramas tackled issues of the day. Each story had a separate cast.
Producer: David Gerber.

| 1977 | 12.6 | Wed 31 Aug 9:25 p.m. | 14 | 1 wk |

'Us Against the World'
The trials, tribulations and heartbreak of three medical students, Hope Loring (Christine Belford), Audrey Dale (Donna Mills) and Sunny Wells (Meredith Baxter Birney). Theodore Bikel co-stars as Dr Danziger.

Medusa Touch, The | 1 wk

Presented by ITV, film

| 1982 | 11.9 | Thu 4 Feb 7:30 p.m. | 17 | 1 wk |

Richard Burton stars as John Morlar, who has superhuman powers that can topple buildings, cause planes to crash and make people die. Lee Remick and Lino Ventura also star.
Director: Jack Gold.

Meet Janet Brown | 1 wk

Thames, comedy

Janet Brown had been a top female impressionist since the 1950s. When Margaret Thatcher became Prime Minister on 3 May 1979, she was provided with her most famous subject.

| 1980 | 13.9 | Tue 10 Jun 9:00 p.m. | 3 | 1 wk |

As well as impersonating the Prime Minister, Janet gives her impressions of Esther Rantzen, Cilla Black, Annie Walker of CORONATION STREET and dog trainer Barbara Woodhouse. Guest: Tim Barrett.
Producer: Keith Beckett.

Meet the Wife | 12 wks

BBC, comedy

Like STEPTOE AND SON, this series was developed from a single episode in the COMEDY PLAYHOUSE strand. The stories by Ronald Wolfe and Ronald Chesney were built around the domestic life of the Blacklocks, a couple married for 25 years. They were played by Thora Hird and Freddie Frinton.

| 1964 | 6.7 | Tue 21 Apr 8:00 p.m. | 11 | 9 wks |

'Getting Away'
Thora and Freddie's holiday is dogged by strange experiences. The ultimate holiday experience is not what was planned.
Producer: John Paddy Carstairs.

| 1966 | 5.6 | Mon 5 Dec 7:30 p.m. | 14 | 3 wks |

'Bless 'Em All'
Thora's 27th wedding anniversary coincides with Fred's army reunion parade. He goes to the pub, gets drunk and spends all the money Thora had saved for the anniversary dinner.
Producer: Robin Nash.

Member of the Family, A | 1 wk

ATV, documentary

| 1966 | 5.5 | Wed 9 Mar 9:40 p.m. | 20 | 1 wk |

Six au pair girls present their observations on the British way of life. Their employers talk about the girls. Narrated by Antony Brown.
Director: Tim Aspinall. **Producer:** Elaine Grand.

Men of Action | 1 wk

Presented by BBC, film

Occasional series of feature films.

| 1973 | 5.7 | Sat 29 Sep 8:00 p.m. | 18 | 1 wk |

'The Heroes of Telemark'.
(See separate entry for this film.)

Men of Affairs | 2 wks

HTV, situation comedy

This series starred Warren Mitchell as Sir William, a minister in government, and Brian Rix as Barry Ovis MP, his Parliamentary Private Secretary.

| 1973 | 6.0 | Wed 3 Oct 8:30 p.m. | 13 | 2 wks |

'May We Have Our Ball Back'
The Minister and Ovis accept an invitation to a country weekend at the home of Lord Bledlow (Peter Bland). They hope to raise support for a local by-election.
Writer: Michael Pertwee. **Director:** Derek Clark. **Producer:** Wallace Douglas. **Executive Producer:** Patrick Dromgoole.

Men of Our Time | 2 wks

Granada, documentary

This series of programmes concerned the great men of the century, each programme focusing on one individual.

| 1964 | 7.0 | Wed 20 May 9:40 p.m. | 2 | 2 wks |

The historian A.J.P. Taylor gives his personal analysis of King George V.
Producer: Patricia Lagone.

Menace Unseen | 1 wk

Anglia, drama

This three-part thriller by Alan Seymour was shown on consecutive nights and starred Ian Ogilvy as a computer consultant investigating the mysterious death of a colleague. It also starred Judi Bowker, Brenda Bruce, Cyril Cusack, Clarke Peters, Andrew Ray and John Sessions.

1988	10.0	Tue 3 May 9:00 p.m.	15	1 wk
		Wed 4 May 9:00 p.m.		
		Thu 5 May 9:00 p.m.		

These episodes were listed together in the ratings.
A businessman is killed when his computer terminal blows up. His widow (Judi Bowker) and her aunt (Brenda Bruce) suspect foul play when people begin to show interest in the information stored in his computer. The computer world is exposed as a shadowy world in which big business and the intelligence services wield more power than seems apparent.
Designer: Jon Pusey. **Director:** Paul Annett. **Producer:** John Rosenberg.

Mess Mates | 22 wks

Granada, situation comedy

This series concerned the rather odd crew of the SS Guernsey, known to the Mess Mates as 'The Old Cow'. Captain Biskett (Archie Duncan) commanded the little coastal vessel with Mate 'Tug' Nelson (Victor Maddern) in support. Other mess mates were 'Croaker' Jones (Sam Kydd), Willie McGinnis (Fulton Mackay) and 'Blarney' Finnigan (Dermot Kelly).
Writers: Talbot Rothwell and Lew Schwarz. **Director** (1961–62): Graeme McDonald. **Producer:** Eric Fawcett.

| 1960 | 6.0 | Tue 20 Sep 8:00 p.m. | 4 | 9 wks |

'The New Broom'
Captain Biskett faces problems with his crew when he tries to introduce a few changes on board.
Director: Kenneth Carter.

| 1961 | 6.2 | Tue 26 Sep 8:55 p.m. | 9 | 7 wks |

'One Way Ticket'
This season Captain Biskett has a new command, the MV Continuity, and only 'Croaker' Jones from his former crew has come with him. They are joined by 'Twinkle' Martin (Michael Balfour), 'Fry-up' Dodds (Frank Atkinson) and 'Dapper' Drake (Ronald Hines), who attempts to smuggle an old pal on board for a free trip to Ireland.

| 1962 | 5.0 | Tue 23 Jan 8:55 p.m. | 12 | 6 wks |

'The Black Sheep'
'Croaker' turns up with a previously unheard of twin brother, giving Captain Biskett a double dose of trouble.

Meteor | 2 wks

Presented by ITV, film

| 1982 | 12.6 | Wed 22 Dec 8:00 p.m. | 6 | 1 wk |

A 5-mile-wide meteor, preceded by huge fragments, heads for Earth, forcing the USA and USSR to pool their resources. Starring Sean Connery, Henry Fonda, Trevor Howard, Karl Malden and Natalie Wood.
Director: Ronald Neame.

| 1985 | 10.8 | Sat 3 Aug 9:00 p.m. | 13 | 1 wk |

Repeat showing of the above film.

Miami Drugs War, The | 1 wk

Thames, documentary

| 1981 | 11.8 | Wed 22 Apr 9:00 p.m. | 17 | 1 wk |

Drug smuggling competes with tourism as the main money earner in Miami.
Producer: Michael Houldey.

1

2

3

4

5

6 **7**

1 Celia Johnson starred as **The Dame of Sark** against nasty Nazi Tony Britten.

2 Alfred Lynch, Cyd Hayman and Peter Barkworth evade capture in **Manhunt**.

3 The staff of **Harpers West One** toast their five weeks at Number One in 1961.

4 The cast of **Market in Honey Lane** consider the cost of a cucumber.

5 The most-watched edition of **Armchair Cinema** was 'The Prison', adapted from the story by Georges Simenon.

6 Everyone was shocked when both the wife and landlady of Donald Pleasence disappeared in 'The Cupboard', an edition of **Armchair Theatre**.

7 Although 'A Professional Job' achieved a higher viewing figure, 'Counter Crime' was the only 1968 edition of **Playhouse** to reach Number One.

Miami Vice — 9 wks

USA presented by BBC, drama

This series, created by Anthony Yerkovitch, concerned two under-cover drug squad officers in Miami, Sonny Crockett (Don Johnson), an ex-footballer who lived on a boat with his pet alligator, and Ricardo Tubbs (Philip Michael Thomas), a New Yorker. The series made much use of specially commissioned rock music.
Producer: Michael Mann.

| 1985 | 12.5 | Thu 8 Aug 9:25 p.m. | 5 | 5 wks |

'Lombard'
Crockett is forced to protect the man who murdered his high school girlfriend.

| 1986 | 8.8 | Tue 15 Jul 10:00 p.m. | 11 | 4 wks |

'Yankee Dollar'
Crockett's air hostess girlfriend Sarah dies from an overdose of the cocaine she was smuggling. The trail leads Crockett and Tubbs to a hood who thinks he has kept his hands clean.

Michael Barrymore — 1 wk

Thames, comedy

This was zany comedian Barrymore's first solo series.

| 1983 | 9.5 | Mon 13 Jun 8:00 p.m. | 9 | 1 wk |

Guests: Jade and Nicholas Lyndhurst, with the Ladybirds and the Don Hunt orchestra.
Producer: David Clark.

Michael Barrymore Special, The — 1 wk

Thames, entertainment

| 1987 | 10.3 | Mon 25 May 8:00 p.m. | 10 | 1 wk |

Guests: The Communards, Steve Davis, and Nathalie Enterline, with the Alan Harding dancers and the Don Hunt orchestra.
Producer: Brian Penders. **Executive Producer:** Bob Louis.

Michael Barrymore's Saturday Night Out — 10 wks

BBC, entertainment

This series featured the Bluebell Girls and the Ronnie Hazlehurst orchestra.
Producer: Kevin Bishop.

| 1988 | 9.7 | Sat 23 Jul 7:50 p.m. | 11 | 4 wks |

Guests: June Brown, Keith Harris, Bonnie Langford, Frank Oliver and Greg Rogers.

| 1989 | 9.4 | Sat 26 Aug 7:05 p.m. | 15 | 6 wks |

Guests: Frank Bruno, Gary Lovini, Lulu, Frank Oliver, Elaine Paige and Adrian Walsh.

Michael Winner's True Crimes — 1 wk

ITV, drama/documentary

Film director Michael Winner examined real crime cases through dramatic reconstruction.

| 1991 | 7.5 | Sun 4 Aug 9:05 p.m. | 20 | 1 wk |

'The Golden Rule'
In Spring 1989 a blackmailer implanted razor blades and caustic soda into jars of Heinz baby food to get a £500,000 ransom. The programme looks at how he hatched his plan and why he was finally caught.
Editor: Jeff Pope. **Executive Producer:** Simon Shaps.

Mid-Week Sports Special — 3 wks

ITV, sport

| 1979 | 17.5 | Wed 7 Feb 7:30 p.m. | 3 | 3 wks |

Brian Moore commentates from Wembley on a Group 1 football match from the European Championships. (England beat Northern Ireland 4–0.)
Television presentation: Roy Lomas.

Mike and Bernie — 5 wks

Thames, situation comedy

Mike and Bernie Winters starred in this series by Vince Powell and Harry Driver in which they played themselves, a double act, trying to make headway in show business.
Producer: Stuart Allen.

| 1971 | 6.6 | Tue 21 Dec 8:30 p.m. | 10 | 2 wks |

'Am I My Brother's Keeper?'
Bernie's French girlfriend Tina (Bettina Le Beau) has been two-timing him for Mike, so Bernie sets out to teach them both a lesson. With Billy Dainty and Bill Pertwee.

| 1972 | 6.2 | Tue 11 Jan 8:30 p.m. | 16 | 3 wks |

'A Little Bit on the Side'
Mike and Bernie get a new agent, Lionel Ross (Bernard Spear), the Lew Grade of Lewisham. Lionel is partnered by his wife Gloria (Elizabeth Larner). Billy Dainty makes a guest appearance as himself.

Mike and Bernie's Scene   6 wks

Thames, entertainment

This series of half-hour shows starred the Winters brothers.

| 1970 | 6.4 | Wed 30 Sep 8:00 p.m. | 9 | 6 wks |

'A Tale of Two Winters'
This edition was a special one-hour programme at the end of Mike and Bernie Winters' series of half-hour shows. Guests: Lionel Blair, Joan Collins, Sacha Distel, Peter Jones and Des O'Connor, with the Ronnie Aldrich orchestra.
Writers: Vince Powell and Harry Driver. **Producer:** Peter Frazer-Jones.

Mike and Bernie's Show   20 wks

ABC (1966–67) and Thames (1968–69, 1971–72), entertainment

The double act of brothers Mike and Bernie was first seen on television in the late 1950s on BBC's SIX-FIVE SPECIAL. They enjoyed continued success until the act broke up in 1978.

| 1966 | 5.6 | Sat Aug 8:25 p.m. | 10 | 2 wks |

Guests: Totti Truman Taylor, Sheridan Grant, the Lionel Blair dancers and the ABC Television Showband.
Producer: Keith Beckett.

| 1967 | 6.8 | Sat 30 Dec 6:20 p.m. | 3 | 2 wks |

Guests: Les Dawson, Chris Langford, the New Vaudeville Band and Tanya the elephant. Tanya is presented by Jenda Smaha. With the ABC Television Showband.
Director: Tom Clegg. **Producer:** Pat Johns.

| 1968 | 6.8 | Wed 20 Nov 6:45 p.m. | 6 | 8 wks |

Guests: Joe Church, Frank Ifield and the Spooner Twins, with the Johnnie Harris orchestra.
Producer: Pat Johns.

| 1969 | 5.3 | Mon 7 Jul 6:40 p.m. | 11 | 6 wks |

Guests: Cilla Black and Gil Dova, with the Ronnie Aldrich orchestra.
Producer: Peter Frazer-Jones.

| 1971 | 6.2 | Wed 9 Jun 8:00 p.m. | 3 | 1 wk |

In a one-hour special Mike and Bernie follow in the Hollywood tradition of Al Jolson and Glenn Miller bio-pics as they begin filming the epic Mike and Bernie Story with Lynda Baron, Peter Jones, Garfield Morgan and Bill Pertwee. With the Ronnie Aldrich orchestra.
Writers: Vince Powell and Harry Driver. **Producer:** Alan Tarrant.

| 1972 | 6.0 | Wed 9 Aug 8:00 p.m. | 6 | 1 wk |

Guests: Kenneth Haigh and Barbara Murray with the Lionel Blair dancers and the Ronnie Aldrich orchestra in a one-hour special.
Writer: Eric Merriman. **Producer:** Keith Beckett.

Mike Hammer   6 wks

USA presented by ITV, drama

Stacy Keach starred as Mickey Spillane's private eye Hammer until the series was interrupted when he received a prison sentence for possessing drugs in England. Following his release the series began again in 1986 but failed to have the same impact.
Producers: Jay Bernstein and Lew Gallo.

| 1984 | 11.5 | Mon 20 Feb 9:00 p.m. | 15 | 6 wks |

'Hot Ice'
Mike Hammer has a double goal: to save the life of a beautiful Chinese hostage and return a stolen diamond.

Mike Reid's Mates and Music   2 wks

Central, entertainment

Cockney comedian Mike Reid hosted this variety series. He first found fame on ITV's THE COMEDIANS after calling producer John Hamp at home and auditioning over the phone. Later he played the role of Frank Butcher in EASTENDERS.

| 1984 | 8.2 | Wed 20 Jun 8:00 p.m. | 18 | 2 wks |

Guests: Ray Alan, Sandra Dickinson, Harry Fowler, Kenny Lynch, Duncan Norvelle and Helen Shapiro, with the Alan Harding dancers and the Laurie Holloway orchestra.
Director: Jon Scoffield. **Producer:** Nigel Lythgoe.

Mike Yarwood   1 wk

BBC, entertainment

| 1980 | 11.1 | Thu 12 Jun 7:50 p.m. | 13 | 1 wk |

A repeat of Mike's 1979 Christmas show with Janet Brown and Johnny Mathis.
Director: Stanley Appel. **Producer:** James Moir.

Mike Yarwood Christmas Show, The — 6 wks

BBC (1974, 1976–77, 1979, 1981) and Thames (1982), entertainment

The impressionist starred in several seasonal specials, with guests and the Alan Braden orchestra.
Writers: Eric Davidson and Neil Shand.

1974	6.1	Wed 25 Dec 8:05 p.m.	12	1 wk

Guests: Max Bygraves, with Sue Bond, Larry Martyn and Jacqueline Stanbury.
Producer: John Ammonds.

1976	7.5	Mon 27 Dec 7:55 p.m.	6	1 wk

Guests: the New Seekers, Ballard Berkeley, Raymond Mason, Renée Roberts, Paula Scott and Michael Sharvell Martin.
Producer: John Ammonds.

1977	21.4	Sun 25 Dec 8:20 p.m.	1	1 wk

Guests: Wings and Jenny Lee-Wright.
Director: Alan Boyd. **Producer:** James Moir.

1979	15.7	Tue 25 Dec 7:20 p.m.	4	1 wk

Guests: Janet Brown and Johnny Mathis.
Director: Stanley Appel. **Producer:** James Moir.

1981	14.3	Sat 26 Dec 7:35 p.m.	14	1 wk

Guests: Marti Caine, Suzanne Danielle and Bucks Fizz.
Producer: Peter Whitmore.

1982	13.6	Tue 21 Dec 8:00 p.m.	5	1 wk

Guests: Petula Clark, Suzanne Danielle, the Nolans and Selina Scott, with the Irving Davies dancers and the Alan Braden orchestra.
Producer: Keith Beckett.

Mike Yarwood in Persons — 20 wks

BBC, comedy

This series of 30-minute shows starred Yarwood with guests and the Alan Braden orchestra.
Writers: Eric Davidson and Neil Shand.

1977	8.6	Sat 8 Jan 8:40 p.m.	7	5 wks

Guests: Ruth Kettlewell and Shades.
Director: Alan Boyd. **Producer:** John Ammonds.

1978	16.7	Sat 25 Feb 8:35 p.m.	8	5 wks

Guests: Janet Brown, Tina Charles and Keith James.
Producer: Alan Boyd. **Executive Producer:** John Ammonds.

1979	22.3	Sat 6 Oct 8:30 p.m.	3	6 wks

Guests: Janet Brown and the Nolans with Hilda Fenemore and Michael Stainton.
Director: Stanley Appel. **Producer:** James Moir.

1981	13.6	Sat 3 Oct 8:00 p.m.	7	4 wks

Guest: Suzanne Danielle.
Producer: Peter Whitmore.

Mike Yarwood in Persons — 5 wks

Thames, comedy

1983	13.8	Mon 17 Jan 8:00 p.m.	6	5 wks

Guest: Diane Solomon, with the Irving Davies dancers and the Alan Braden orchestra.
Writers: Barry Cryer, Eric Davidson and David Renwick. **Producer:** Keith Beckett.

Mike Yarwood Show, The — 1 wk

BBC, entertainment

1974	7.5	Fri 15 Nov 8:15 p.m.	10	1 wk

This one-hour special features guests Peters and Lee and Reflections.
Producer: Michael Hurll.

Millicent — 4 wks

ATV, entertainment

This series starred singer, dancer and actress Millicent Martin, who first found fame in THAT WAS THE WEEK THAT WAS.

1966	5.5	Wed 29 Jun 9:10 p.m.	10	4 wks

Guests: Henry McGee, Maggie Jones and the Malcolm Clare dancers.
Writers: Keith Waterhouse and Willis Hall. **Producer:** Jon Scoffield.

Millicent and Roy — 1 wk

AR, entertainment

1966	5.5	Wed 5 Oct 9:45 p.m.	18	1 wk

This special stars Millicent Martin and Roy Castle with the Paddy Stone dancers.
Director: Bill Turner. **Executive Producer:** Buddy Bregman.

Millie in Jamaica
1 wk

AR, documentary

1965	6.7	Wed 6 Jan 9:40 p.m.	9	1 wk

The story of Millie Small who, with 'My Boy Lollipop', came from the slums of Kingston, Jamaica, to the top of the charts in one year. Her story is retraced with the help of fellow Jamaicans Louise Bennett, Jimmy Cliff, Roy Panton and Prince Buster.
Camera: Michael Rhodes. **Director:** Rollo Gamble. **Producer:** Elkan Allan.

Million Dollar Legs
1 wk

Thames, entertainment

This beauty contest was determined by contestants' legs.

1969	5.4	Wed 27 Aug 10:30 p.m.	12	1 wk

From the Royal Lancaster hotel, London, Norman Vaughan introduces the contestants. Cabaret is by Georgie Fame.
Television presentation: Steve Minchin and Grahame Turner.

Mind of Mr J. G. Reader, The
13 wks

Thames, drama

This series was based on the 1920s crime stories of Edgar Wallace. Hugh Burden starred as J. G. Reader, a clerk in the office of the Director of Public Prosecutions. Willoughby Goddard co-starred as Sir Jason Toovey.

1969	7.0	Wed 4 Jun 9:00 p.m.	3	6 wks

'The Troupe' by Malcolm Proctor.
Reader sets a trap to catch international confidence trickster Art Lomer (Patrick Bedford). In the absence of any concrete evidence Sir Jason Toovey pressures Reader to ease up on Lomer.
Designer: Jim Nicholson. **Director:** Robert Tronson. **Producer:** Kim Mills. **Executive Producer:** Lloyd Shirley.

1971	7.1	Mon 26 Apr 9:00 p.m.	6	7 wks

'The Man with a Strange Tattoo' by Gerald Kelsey.
An intruder is accidentally shot by Lady Rothbard (Jane Baxter).
Designer: Peter Le Page. **Director:** Peter Duguid. **Producer:** Robert Love.

Mind Your Language
13 wks

LWT, situation comedy

This series by Vince Powell starred Barry Evans as Jeremy Brown, a long-suffering teacher who taught English to foreign students.

1978	18.2	Fri 10 Feb 7:00 p.m.	2	12 wks

'The Cheating Game'
College principal Miss Courtney (Zara Nutley) decides it is time Brown's class sat a mock exam.
Producer: Stuart Allen.

1982	13.3	Sat 27 Mar 6:15 p.m.	9	1 wk

'Repent at Leisure'
German student Anna Schmidt (Jacki Harding) is advised to marry an Englishman in order to stay in the country. Jeremy Brown looks like a good candidate. (Repeat.)
Producer: Stuart Allen.

Minder
83 wks

Thames, drama

This series, created by Leon Griffiths, was produced by Euston Films. It charted the adventures of self-styled entrepreneur Arthur Daley (George Cole), whose business interests were not always compatible with the law, and Terry McCann (Dennis Waterman), his minder. It gave such phrases as ''er indoors' and 'a nice little earner' to common usage. In 1992 Terry left Arthur's employ and was replaced by new boy Ray (Gary Webster).
Directors included Roy Ward Baker (1984, 1988–89) and Terry Green (1985, 1987). **Producers** included George Taylor (1980, 1982–89); Lloyd Shirley (1980, 1982–87). **Executive Director:** Johnny Goodman.

1980	14.5	Thu 20 Nov 9:00 p.m.	16	3 wks

'Diamonds are a Girl's Worst Enemy' by Paul Wheeler.
A Mercedes entrusted to Terry's care disappears.
Director: Chris King.

1982	15.0	Wed 31 Mar 9:00 p.m.	4	12 wks

'Back in Good Old England' by Andrew Payne.
Terry soon realizes there are a few people around with old scores to settle.
Director: Francis Megahy.

1983	10.5	Mon 25 Apr 9:00 p.m.	4	4 wks

'You Lose Some, You Win Some' by Jeremy Burnham.
Terry and Arthur are delegated to mind a team of gamblers who have received threats from a casino boss.
Director: James Gatward.

1984	17.5	Wed 10 Oct 9:00 p.m.	1	16 wks

'Second-hand Pose' by Tony Hoare.
Terry turns to alternative employment when Arthur leaves him out in the cold.

| 1985 | 15.1 | Wed 27 Nov 9:00 p.m. | 3 | 21 wks |

'If Money be the Food of Love, Play On' by Tony Hoare.
Both Terry and Arthur are in danger of being knocked off their guard by their joint fascination for a young Australian girl (Penny Downie).

| 1986 | 9.2 | Wed 18 Jun 9:00 p.m. | 10 | 2 wks |

'Rembrandt Doesn't Live Here Anymore' by Dave Humphries.
A chance meeting in a club introduces Arthur to the world of fine art.
Director: Tom Clegg.

| 1987 | 10.8 | Wed 22 Jul 9:00 p.m. | 7 | 7 wks |

'Hypnotising Rita' by Alan James.
Arthur takes over a steam-cleaning business.

| 1988 | 11.8 | Mon 26 Jun 8:00 p.m. | 7 | 2 wks |

'An Officer and a Car Salesman' by Tony Hoare.
A ninety-minute special with Arthur running an import/export business in counterfeit goods from his own warehouse. Terry gets a new job in a bid to escape. With guest stars Richard Briers, Mark McManus and Simon Williams.

| 1989 | 14.5 | Mon 2 Jan 8:00 p.m. | 7 | 6 wks |

'It's a Sorry Lorry, Morrie' by Tony Hoare.
Terry leaves fingerprints on a stolen lorry while collecting some stock for Arthur.

| 1991 | 13.4 | Thu 31 Oct 9:00 p.m. | 12 | 10 wks |

'The Greatest Show in Willesden' by Bernard Dempsey and Kevin Sperring.
Arthur has a plan to boost membership of the Winchester Club with a Karaoke machine.
Director: Derek Banham. **Producer:** Ian Toyton.

Miracle of the Scarlet Salmon, The   1 wk

BBC, documentary

| 1988 | 9.9 | Fri 1 Apr 6:15 p.m. | 17 | 1 wk |

Hugh Falkus narrates the incredible journey of two million red salmon, who return after four years of life to the beautiful Adams River near the Canadian Rockies to spawn and then die.
Camera: Rick Rosenthal. **Producer:** Richard Brock.

Mirror Cracked, The   2 wks

Presented by BBC, film

| 1987 | 12.8 | Sun 19 Apr 7:45 p.m. | 7 | 1 wk |

Angela Lansbury stars as Agatha Christie's Miss Marple. Her rural English village is infiltrated by a Hollywood film crew and murder.

Also starring Geraldine Chaplin, Tony Curtis, Edward Fox, Rock Hudson, Kim Novak and Elizabeth Taylor.
Director: Guy Hamilton.

| 1989 | 9.9 | Mon 29 May 8:00 p.m. | 18 | 1 wk |

Repeat showing of the above film.

Misfit, The   5 wks

ATV, situation comedy

This series was created by Roy Clarke and starred Ronald Fraser as Basil 'Badger' Allenby-Johnson who, after half a lifetime in the Far East, returned to London. He found himself bewildered by the aftermath of the swinging sixties and by his trendy son Ted (Simon Ward) and daughter-in-law Alicia (Susan Carpenter).
Producer: Dennis Vance.

| 1970 | 6.5 | Tue 10 Mar 9:00 p.m. | 11 | 2 wks |

'On the Place of Women in the Home'
Badger is totally disenchanted with what he's seen in London and heads north, where further shocks await him.
Director: James Gatward.

| 1971 | 6.7 | Mon 22 Mar 9:00 p.m. | 12 | 3 wks |

'On Superior Persons'
Badger goes in search of a former girlfriend. Guest: Diana Dors.

Misfits   4 wks

YTV, situation comedy

This series by Eric Chappell starred Anne Stallybrass as quiet middle-class Mrs Ridgway, whose life was never the same once Skinner and Oscar (Enn Reitel and Kevin Lloyd) entered it on their way to Katmandu.
Producer: Ronnie Baxter.

| 1981 | 12.6 | Fri 5 Jun 8:30 p.m. | 7 | 4 wks |

'May We Come In?'
Enter Skinner and Oscar, exit a gold cigarette case.

Miss England   8 wks

BBC, entertainment

This annual beauty contest was held at the Lyceum Ballroom, London. The winner went forward to compete in the Miss Universe contest.

Television presentation: Douglas Hespe (1967–71), Ken Griffin (1975–77).

| 1966 | 5.7 | Mon 25 Apr 9:45 p.m. | 15 | 1 wk |

Hosts: Keith Fordyce and Sheila Tracy. Winner: Janice Whiteman.
Television presentation: Robin Scott.

| 1967 | 5.4 | Fri 28 Apr 9:30 p.m. | 14 | 1 wk |

Hosts: Keith Fordyce and Sheila Tracy. Winner: Jennifer Lewis.

| 1968 | 6.0 | Fri 26 Apr 9:05 p.m. | 17 | 1 wk |

Hosts: Keith Fordyce and Sheila Tracy. Winner: Jennifer Summers.

| 1969 | 6.3 | Fri 16 May 9:05 p.m. | 4 | 1 wk |

Hosts: Keith Fordyce and Sheila Tracy. Winner: Myra Van Heck.

| 1970 | 6.6 | Fri 10 Apr 9:10 p.m. | 8 | 1 wk |

Hosts: Michael Aspel and Alex Macintosh. Winner: Yvonne Ormes.

| 1971 | 7.3 | Fri 16 Apr 9:20 p.m. | 4 | 1 wk |

Hosts: Keith Fordyce and Alex Macintosh. Winner: Marilyn Ward.

| 1975 | 6.7 | Fri 21 Mar 9:25 p.m. | 18 | 1 wk |

Hosts: David Vine and Ray Moore. Winner: Vicki Harris.

| 1977 | 7.1 | Fri 18 Mar 9:25 p.m. | 19 | 1 wk |

Hosts: Ray Moore and John Stapleton. Winner: Sarah Long.

Miss England, Miss Scotland, Miss Wales — 1 wk

BBC, entertainment

This was an attempt to amalgamate three contests into one to provide a UK contestant for the Miss Universe competition. This format was abandoned after this first attempt.

| 1973 | 6.8 | Thu 15 Mar 9:25 p.m. | 9 | 1 wk |

Introduced by Terry Wogan and David Vine from the Lyceum Ball-room, London. (The winners were Veronica Cross (England), Caroline Meade (Scotland) and Deirdre Greenland (Wales).)
Television presentation: Ian Smith.

Miss England, Miss Scotland and Miss Wales — 1 wk

Thames, entertainment

This was a more successful attempt to amalgamate the three competitions to produce one contender for the Miss Universe title.

| 1985 | 10.5 | Thu 16 May 8:30 p.m. | 20 | 1 wk |

Presented by Peter Marshall and Anne Diamond. (The winners were Helen Westlake (England), Jackie Hendrie (Scotland) and Barbara Christian (Wales).)
Television presentation: Steve Minchin.

Miss Europe — 1 wk

BBC, entertainment

| 1981 | 12.2 | Tue 9 Jun 9:25 p.m. | 8 | 1 wk |

Simon Cadell and Ray Moore introduce the contestants from The Night Out Restaurant, Birmingham. Cabaret is provided by Marti Caine with Jeff Richer's First Edition and the Arthur Greenslade orchestra. (The winner was Anne Larsen (Denmark).)
Television presentation: Ken Griffin.

Miss Great Britain — 11 wks

Southern (1969) and YTV (1970–78, 1980), entertainment

This beauty pageant was inaugurated in 1945 by the Morecambe and Heysham Borough Council. It was televised from Morecambe in Lancashire between 1970 and 1980 and was hosted until 1977 by Fred Dineage.
Television presentation: Burt Budin (1970–71) and Guy Caplan (1972–80). **Executive Producer** (1970–80): Lawrie Higgins.

| 1969 | 5.6 | Thur 24 Jul 8:45 p.m. | 7 | 1 wk |

From the Locarno Ballroom in Portsmouth. Host: Shaw Taylor. Winner: Wendy Ann George.

| 1970 | 6.5 | Wed 26 Aug 8:00 p.m. | 2 | 1 wk |

Winner: Kathleen Winstanley.

| 1971 | 6.8 | Wed 25 Aug 8:00 p.m. | 4 | 1 wk |

Winner: Carolyn Moore.

| 1972 | 6.0 | Wed 13 Sep 8:00 p.m. | 13 | 1 wk |

Winner: Elizabeth Robinson.

| 1973 | 7.0 | Thu 30 Aug 9:00 p.m. | 5 | 1 wk |

Winner: Gay Spink.

| 1974 | 6.6 | Wed 25 Sep 8:00 p.m. | 6 | 1 wk |

Winner: Marilyn Ward.

| 1975 | 7.1 | Wed 3 Sep 9:10 p.m. | 3 | 1 wk |

Winner: Susan Anne Cuff.

1976	6.6	Wed 29 Sep 8:00 p.m.	17	1 wk

Winner: Dinah May.

1977	14.8	Wed 21 Sep 8:00 p.m.	3	1 wk

Winner: Susan Marcelle Hempel.

1978	12.6	Wed 20 Sep 8:00 p.m.	15	1 wk

Host: Tony Monopoly. Winner: Patricia Morgan.

1980	13.8	Fri 9 May 8:00 p.m.	6	1 wk

Host: Tony Monopoly. Winner: Susan Berger.

Miss Great Britain — 1 wk

BBC, entertainment

After 10 years on Independent Television the competition moved to the BBC.

1981	14.0	Fri 16 Jan 9:25 p.m.	16	1 wk

Hosts: Edward Woodward and Ray Moore from the London International Boat Show. Winner: Michele Hobson.
Television presentation: Ken Griffin.

Miss Jones and Son — 12 wks

Thames, situation comedy

This series by Richard Waring starred Paula Wilcox as Elizabeth Jones, an unmarried mother of a baby son, Roly. Cass Allen played her friend Rose Tucker.
Producer: Peter Frazer-Jones.

1977	9.3	Mon 18 Apr 8:00 p.m.	1	6 wks

'From Here to Maternity'
Elizabeth's parents (Charlotte Mitchell and Norman Bird) are too embarrassed to place a birth announcement in the Daily Telegraph.

1978	18.6	Mon 13 Feb 8:00 p.m.	1	6 wks

'Four Past Harmony'
Neighbour David (David Savile) invites Elizabeth and Roly for a weekend with him and his daughter Penny (Catherine Kirkwood) at his brother's cottage.

Miss Marple — 18 wks

BBC, drama

Joan Hickson starred as Agatha Christie's spinster sleuth from the village of St Mary Mead. She dressed in tweeds with a felt hat and crocodile handbag as befitted the period setting of the 1930s and 40s.
Producer: George Gallaccio.

1985	15.0	Thu 7 Mar 9:25 p.m. / Fri 8 Mar 9:25 p.m.	4	3 wks

'A Pocketful of Rye' dramatized by T. R. Bowen.
This two-part adaptation was listed as one in the ratings. Rex Fortescue (Timothy West) suffered death by poisoning. Who killed him? Peter Davison, Stacy Dorning and Fabia Drake also star.
Designer: Michael Young. **Director:** Guy Slater.

1986	13.3	Thu 25 Dec 8:20 p.m.	9	6 wks

'The Murder at the Vicarage' dramatized by T. R. Bowen.
Miss Marple has five or six suspects in the murder of Colonel Protheroe. Guest stars include Polly Adams, Cheryl Campbell, Paul Eddington and Robert Lang.
Designer: Raymond London. **Director:** Julian Amyes.

1987		Sun 11 Jan 7:45 p.m.		6 wks

'Sleeping Murder' dramatized by Ken Taylor.
In Part One of this two-part drama Giles and Gwenda Reed (John Moulder-Brown and Geraldine Alexander) buy a Victorian villa overlooking a small seaside resort. A series of minor incidents begin to give Gwenda bad feelings about the house.
Designer: Vic Meredith. **Director:** John Davies.

1990	8.8	Sat 25 Aug 8:00 p.m.	17	3 wks

'Nemesis' dramatized by T. R. Bowen.
This repeat is screened as part of a season celebrating Agatha Christie's centenary. She was born in Torquay in 1890, and died in 1976. Miss Marple embarks on a journey around England after receiving a letter from a friend who has subsequently died. Also stars Helen Cherry, Anna Cropper, Valerie Lush and Margaret Tyzack.
Director: David Tucker.

Miss TV Europe — 1 wk

ATV, entertainment

1973	7.8	Thu 4 Jan 8:15 p.m.	3	1 wk

Representatives from television magazines throughout Europe compete for the title. Zoe Spink, Miss TV Times 1972, represents Great Britain. (The Dutch magazine Televizier sent twenty-year-old model Sylvia Kristel as its representative. She won the competition and became a film star the following year in Emmanuelle).
Director: John Scholz-Conway. **Producer:** Steve Minchin.

Miss TV Times — 3 wks

Thames, entertainment

To decide the UK representative for MISS TV EUROPE (see above) heats for Miss TV Times were held by the regional ITV companies in conjunction with their local TV Times editors. Each region produced one finalist for a national competition.

| 1972 | 7.2 | Wed 28 Jun 9:00 p.m. | 1 | 1 wk |

Host: David Hamilton.
Television presentation: Steve Minchin and Grahame Turner.

| 1973 | 6.1 | Thu 28 Jun 9:00 p.m. | 9 | 1 wk |

Host: Pete Murray.
Television presentation: Ken Craig, Steve Minchin and Grahame Turner.

| 1974 | 5.6 | Fri 14 Jun 9:30 p.m. | 15 | 1 wk |

Hosts: Hughie Green and Russell Harty.
Television presentation: Philip Casson.

Miss United Kingdom — 14 wks

BBC, entertainment

This prestigious contest, organized by Eric and Julia Morley in 1958, was presented from Blackpool. The winner went forward to represent the United Kingdom in the MISS WORLD contest.
Television presentation: Philip Lewis (1966–71), Ian Smith (1972–74) and Ken Griffin (1975–79).

| 1966 | 5.7 | Tue 9 Aug 7:30 p.m. | 7 | 1 wk |

Hosts: Simon Dee and Mike Neville. Winner: Jennifer Lowe.

| 1967 | 6.3 | Thu 17 Aug 9:05 p.m. | 3 | 1 wk |

Hosts: Mike Neville and David Symonds. Winner: Jennifer Lewis.

| 1968 | 5.8 | Fri 9 Aug 9:05 p.m. | 2 | 1 wk |

Hosts: Michael Aspel and Dick Norton. Winner: Kathleen Winstanley.

| 1969 | 5.4 | Fri 15 Aug 9:05 p.m. | 7 | 1 wk |

Hosts: Michael Aspel and Keith Fordyce. Winner: Sheena Drummond.

| 1970 | 6.7 | Fri 14 Aug 9:10 p.m. | 3 | 1 wk |

Hosts: Michael Aspel and Keith Fordyce. Winner: Yvonne Ormes.

| 1971 | 6.8 | Fri 20 Aug 9:20 p.m. | 1 | 1 wk |

Hosts: Michael Aspel and David Vine. Winner: Marilyn Ward.

| 1972 | 7.3 | Fri 18 Aug 9:25 p.m. | 1 | 1 wk |

Hosts: David Vine and Terry Wogan. Winner: Jenny McAdam.

| 1973 | 5.4 | Wed 15 Aug 9:25 p.m. | 11 | 1 wk |

Hosts: David Vine and Terry Wogan. Winner: Veronica Cross.

| 1974 | 5.8 | Tue 10 Sep 9:25 p.m. | 15 | 1 wk |

Hosts: Ray Moore and David Vine. Winner: Helen Morgan.

| 1975 | 7.3 | Tue 19 Aug 9:25 p.m. | 2 | 1 wk |

Hosts: Ray Moore and David Vine. Winner: Vicki Harris.

| 1976 | 6.0 | Fri 3 Sep 8:10 p.m. | 17 | 1 wk |

Hosts: Ray Moore and John Stapleton. Winner: Carol Grant.

| 1977 | 12.6 | Fri 2 Sep 8:10 p.m. | 14 | 1 wk |

Hosts: Ray Moore and John Stapleton. Winner: Madeleine Stringer.

| 1978 | 12.1 | Fri 1 Sep 8:10 p.m. | 7 | 1 wk |

Hosts: Ray Moore, Esther Rantzen and Terry Wogan. Winner: Ann Jones.

| 1979 | 18.4 | Fri 31 Aug 8:10 p.m. | 6 | 1 wk |

Hosts: Paul Burnett, Jan Leeming and Ray Moore. Winner: Carolyn Seaward.

Miss Jones and Son were portrayed by Paula Wilcox and Luke Steensil.

Marilyn Ward wins **Miss United Kingdom 1971**.

Miss United Kingdom — 8 wks

Thames, entertainment

Television presentation: Steve Minchin.

| 1980 | 10.8 | Thu 28 Aug 7:45 p.m. | 12 | 1 wk |

From the Brighton Conference Centre. Hosts: Judith Chalmers and Peter Marshall. Winner: Kim Ashfield.

| 1981 | 12.6 | Wed 26 Aug 8:00 p.m. | 4 | 1 wk |

From Grosvenor House, London. Hosts: Judith Chalmers and Peter Marshall. Winner: Michele Donnelly.

| 1982 | 11.8 | Wed 25 Aug 8:00 p.m. | 6 | 1 wk |

From London's Cunard Hotel. Hosts: Judith Chalmers and Peter Marshall. Winner: Della Dolan. (The show was interrupted by animal rights campaigners who protested against the sponsors of the event, Edelson Furs.)

| 1983 | 10.7 | Wed 24 Aug 8:00 p.m. | 2 | 1 wk |

From the Brighton Conference Centre. Hosts: Judith Chalmers and Peter Marshall. Winner: Sarah-Jane Hutt.

| 1984 | 9.9 | Wed 22 Aug 8:00 p.m. | 6 | 1 wk |

From the Brighton Conference Centre. Hosts: Judith Chalmers and Peter Marshall. Winner: Vivienne Rooke.

| 1985 | 10.0 | Wed 21 Aug 8:00 p.m. | 11 | 1 wk |

From Grosvenor House, London. Hosts: Anne Diamond and Peter Marshall. Winner: Mandy Shires.

| 1986 | 9.0 | Wed 20 Aug 8:00 p.m. | 12 | 1 wk |

From Grosvenor House, London. Hosts: Peter Marshall and Mary Stavin. Winner: Alison Slack.

| 1988 | 9.6 | Wed 24 Aug 8:00 p.m. | 15 | 1 wk |

From Grosvenor House, London. Hosts: Peter Marshall and Alexandra Bastedo. Winner: Kirsty Roper.

Miss Universe — 1 wk

USA presented by ITV, entertainment

This was the American equivalent of the MISS WORLD contest.

| 1980 | 10.0 | Sat 12 Jul 7:00 p.m. | 14 | 1 wk |

From Seoul, South Korea. Great Britain is represented by Julie Duckworth (England), Linda Gallagher (Scotland) and Kim Ashfield (Wales). (The contest was won by Shawn Nichols Weatherly (USA).)

Miss World — 19 wks

BBC with Mecca Productions, entertainment

This was an annual beauty contest organized by Eric and Julia Morley. Eric came up with the idea in 1951 as part of the Festival of Britain. The first winner was Miss Sweden, Kiki Haakonson. The success of the event demanded that it become annual. The hosts included David Coleman (1961), Peter West (1961, 64 and 66), Michael Aspel (1964–74), David Jacobs (1965), Simon Dee (1967), Keith Fordyce (1968, 70), Pete Murray (1969), David Vine (1971, 1973–75), Terry Wogan (1972), Ray Moore (1975–77), Patrick Lichfield (1976), Andy Williams (1977), Paul Burnett (1978), Sacha Distel (1978–79) and Esther Rantzen (1979).

The contest was held at the Lyceum Ballroom in London between 1961 and 1964 and then it moved to the Royal Albert Hall. Music was provided by the Joe Loss orchestra until the move in 1964 when the Phil Tate orchestra took over.

Television presentation: Bryan Cowgill (1961–62), Humphrey Fisher (1963), Philip Lewis (1964–75), Michael Begg (1976–78) and Ken Griffin (1979).

| 1961 | 5.9 | Thu 9 Nov 9:25 p.m. | 9 | 1 wk |

Winner: Rosemarie Frankland (UK).

| 1962 | 7.6 | Thu 8 Nov 9:30 p.m. | 3 | 1 wk |

Winner: Catharina Lodders (Holland).

| 1963 | 8.3 | Thu 7 Nov 9:10 p.m. | 4 | 1 wk |

Winner: Carole Crawford (Jamaica).

| 1964 | 7.4 | Thu 12 Nov 9:25 p.m. | 7 | 1 wk |

Winner: Ann Sydney (UK).

| 1965 | 8.0 | Fri 19 Nov 9:25 p.m. | 4 | 1 wk |

Winner: Lesley Langley (UK).

| 1966 | 9.8 | Thu 17 Nov 9:30 p.m. | 1 | 1 wk |

Winner: Reita Faria (India).

| 1967 | 10.1 | Thu 16 Nov 9:05 p.m. | 2 | 1 wk |

Winner: Madeleine Hartog Bel (Peru).

| 1968 | 10.1 | Thu 14 Nov 9:05 p.m. | 1 | 1 wk |

Winner: Penny Plumber (Australia).

| 1969 | 10.6 | Thu 27 Nov 9:10 p.m. | 1 | 1 wk |

Winner: Eva Rueber-Staier (Austria).

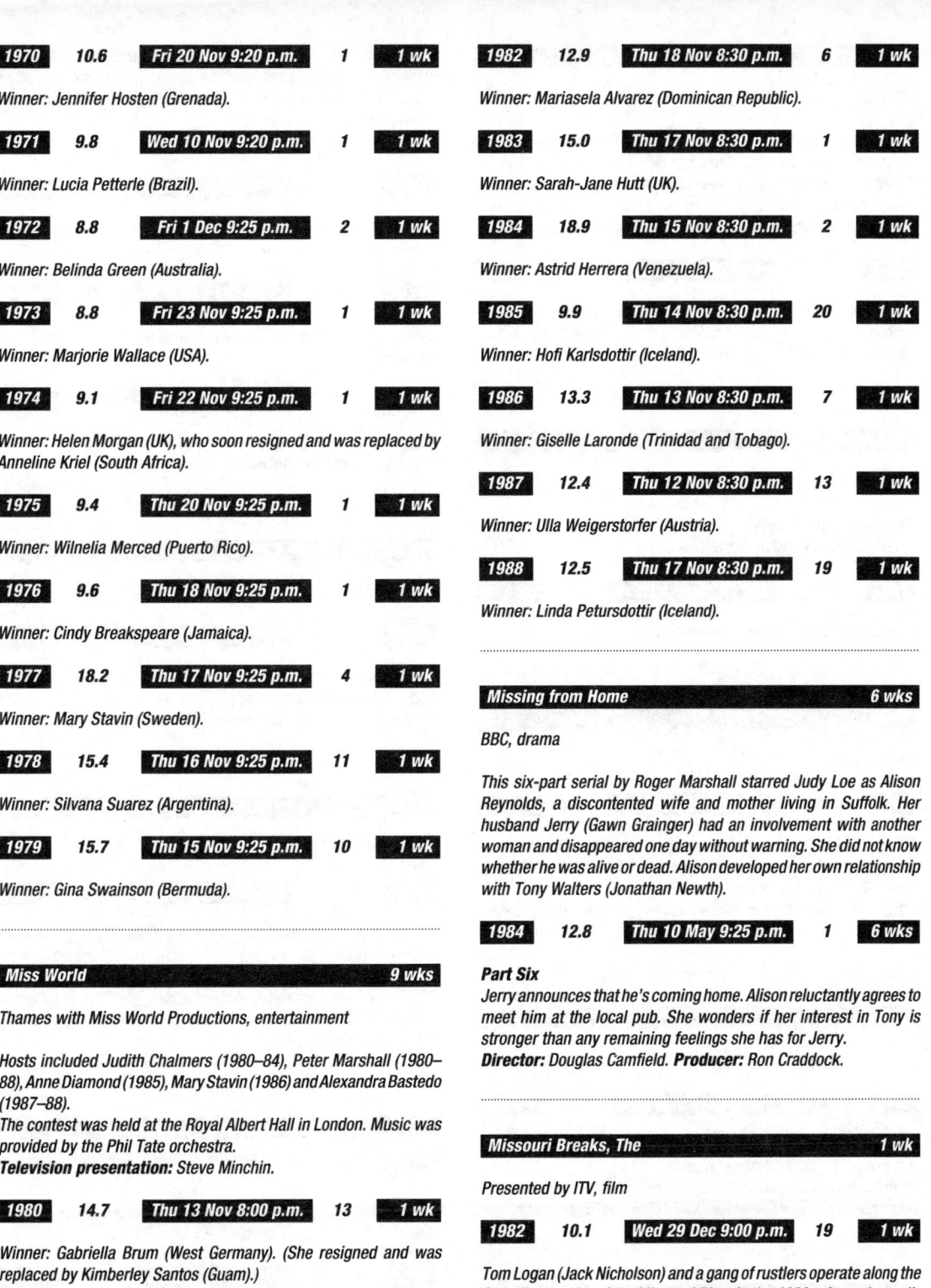

1970 10.6 Fri 20 Nov 9:20 p.m. 1 1 wk
Winner: Jennifer Hosten (Grenada).

1971 9.8 Wed 10 Nov 9:20 p.m. 1 1 wk
Winner: Lucia Petterle (Brazil).

1972 8.8 Fri 1 Dec 9:25 p.m. 2 1 wk
Winner: Belinda Green (Australia).

1973 8.8 Fri 23 Nov 9:25 p.m. 1 1 wk
Winner: Marjorie Wallace (USA).

1974 9.1 Fri 22 Nov 9:25 p.m. 1 1 wk
Winner: Helen Morgan (UK), who soon resigned and was replaced by Anneline Kriel (South Africa).

1975 9.4 Thu 20 Nov 9:25 p.m. 1 1 wk
Winner: Wilnelia Merced (Puerto Rico).

1976 9.6 Thu 18 Nov 9:25 p.m. 1 1 wk
Winner: Cindy Breakspeare (Jamaica).

1977 18.2 Thu 17 Nov 9:25 p.m. 4 1 wk
Winner: Mary Stavin (Sweden).

1978 15.4 Thu 16 Nov 9:25 p.m. 11 1 wk
Winner: Silvana Suarez (Argentina).

1979 15.7 Thu 15 Nov 9:25 p.m. 10 1 wk
Winner: Gina Swainson (Bermuda).

Miss World   9 wks

Thames with Miss World Productions, entertainment

Hosts included Judith Chalmers (1980–84), Peter Marshall (1980–88), Anne Diamond (1985), Mary Stavin (1986) and Alexandra Bastedo (1987–88).
The contest was held at the Royal Albert Hall in London. Music was provided by the Phil Tate orchestra.
Television presentation: Steve Minchin.

1980 14.7 Thu 13 Nov 8:00 p.m. 13 1 wk
Winner: Gabriella Brum (West Germany). (She resigned and was replaced by Kimberley Santos (Guam).)

1981 14.8 Thu 12 Nov 8:30 p.m. 8 1 wk
Winner: Pilin Leon (Venezuela).

1982 12.9 Thu 18 Nov 8:30 p.m. 6 1 wk
Winner: Mariasela Alvarez (Dominican Republic).

1983 15.0 Thu 17 Nov 8:30 p.m. 1 1 wk
Winner: Sarah-Jane Hutt (UK).

1984 18.9 Thu 15 Nov 8:30 p.m. 2 1 wk
Winner: Astrid Herrera (Venezuela).

1985 9.9 Thu 14 Nov 8:30 p.m. 20 1 wk
Winner: Hofi Karlsdottir (Iceland).

1986 13.3 Thu 13 Nov 8:30 p.m. 7 1 wk
Winner: Giselle Laronde (Trinidad and Tobago).

1987 12.4 Thu 12 Nov 8:30 p.m. 13 1 wk
Winner: Ulla Weigerstorfer (Austria).

1988 12.5 Thu 17 Nov 8:30 p.m. 19 1 wk
Winner: Linda Petursdottir (Iceland).

Missing from Home   6 wks

BBC, drama

This six-part serial by Roger Marshall starred Judy Loe as Alison Reynolds, a discontented wife and mother living in Suffolk. Her husband Jerry (Gawn Grainger) had an involvement with another woman and disappeared one day without warning. She did not know whether he was alive or dead. Alison developed her own relationship with Tony Walters (Jonathan Newth).

1984 12.8 Thu 10 May 9:25 p.m. 1 6 wks

Part Six
Jerry announces that he's coming home. Alison reluctantly agrees to meet him at the local pub. She wonders if her interest in Tony is stronger than any remaining feelings she has for Jerry.
Director: Douglas Camfield. **Producer:** Ron Craddock.

Missouri Breaks, The   1 wk

Presented by ITV, film

1982 10.1 Wed 29 Dec 9:00 p.m. 19 1 wk

Tom Logan (Jack Nicholson) and a gang of rustlers operate along the Canadian border of the Missouri River in the 1880s. A rancher calls in a professional, Robert Lee Clayton (Marlon Brando), to apprehend the gang.
Director: Arthur Penn.

Mr Aitch   14 wks

AR, situation comedy

Harry H. Corbett starred in the title role with Norman Chappell and Gordon Gostelow as Albie and Lefty. Mr Aitch owned half an old house on a bomb site in the heart of London. He derived an income from it of £40 per week by turning it into a car park, but would never sell it on principle. Created by Dick Clement and Ian La Frenais.

| 1967 | 7.8 | Thu 5 Jan 8:25 p.m. | 3 | 14 wks |

Mr Aitch will mortgage the site, even dangle it as a carrot for some other deal, but the thought of accepting £150,000 for it offends him. **Director:** Christopher Hodson. **Producer:** Peter Eton.

Mr and Mrs   2 wks

Border, game show

This game tested a couple's knowledge of each other. The host was Derek Batey, assisted by Susan Cuff.

| 1977 | 11.0 | Sat 20 Aug 6:55 p.m. | 17 | 2 wks |

Director: William Cartner. **Producer:** Derek Batey.

Mr Bean   1 wk

Thames, comedy

| 1990 | 13.4 | Mon 1 Jan 8:00 p.m. | 13 | 1 wk |

This almost completely silent film stars Rowan Atkinson as Mr Bean. Also appearing are Paul Bown, Richard Briers, Howard Goodall, Roger Sloman and Rudolph Walker.
Writers: Rowan Atkinson, Richard Curtis and Robin Driscoll. **Producer:** John Howard Davies. (A Tiger Television production.)

Mr Bean Goes to Town   1 wk

Thames, comedy

| 1991 | 14.4 | Tue 15 Oct 8:30 p.m. | 10 | 1 wk |

Rowan Atkinson stars as Mr Bean, whose night out on the town with a date doesn't go according to plan.
Writers: Rowan Atkinson, Richard Curtis and Robin Driscoll. **Producer:** John Howard Davies. (A Tiger Television production.)

Mr Digby Darling   15 wks

YTV, situation comedy

This series by Ken Hoare and Mike Sharland was set in the Rid-O-Rat pesticide company. It starred Peter Jones as Roland Digby, Sheila Hancock as secretary Thelma Teesdale and Michael Bates as Norman Stanhope.
Producer: Christopher Hodson.

| 1969 | 8.3 | Tue 11 Nov 8:25 p.m. | 2 | 12 wks |

Thelma will use any means at her disposal to secure a top job for Mr Digby.

| 1970 | 7.0 | Mon 28 Dec 8:00 | 10 | 1 wk |

Digby and Thelma attempt to stem the tide of a race of super rats on the march.

| 1971 | 6.7 | Mon 25 Jan 9:30 p.m. | 15 | 2 wks |

Digby decides to organize a Miss Rid-O-Rat beauty contest. Thelma organizes a feminist movement to sabotage the idea.

Mr H is Late   1 wk

Thames, comedy

| 1988 | 13.8 | Mon 15 Feb 8:00 p.m. | 7 | 1 wk |

In this silent film many stars play cameo roles as Eric Sykes attempts to get a coffin from a building to a church.
Writer and **Director:** Eric Sykes. **Producer:** Dennis Kirkland.

Mr Music   1 wk

Presented by ITV, film

| 1968 | 4.7 | Fri 9 Aug 7:00 p.m. | 13 | 1 wk |

Paul Merrick (Bing Crosby) is a songwriter whose laziness leads him to work only when he needs the money. His domineering secretary tries hard to motivate him. Also starring Marge and Gower Champion, Charles Coburn, Tom Ewell, Richard Haydn, Ruth Hussey, Dorothy Kirsten, Peggy Lee, Groucho Marx, Nancy Olson and Robert Stack.
Director: Richard Haydn.

Mr Nice Guy – Bernard Manning   1 wk

Granada, comedy

Abrasive comedian Manning, for whom no target or subject was taboo, found fame via Granada's THE COMEDIANS.

| 1977 | 6.7 | Wed 18 May 8:00 p.m. | 16 | 1 wk |

Manning stars in his own one-hour special with Acker Bilk, Elaine Delmar, the Syd Lawrence orchestra, Les Reed and the Three Degrees.
Director: Nicholas Ferguson. **Producer:** John Hamp.

Mr Palfrey of Westminster   2 wks

Thames, drama

This series by George Markstein starred Alec McCowen as Mr Palfrey, a mysterious civil servant involved in non-violent espionage. His nameless boss, known only as The Co-Ordinator, was played by Caroline Blakiston. Clive Wood portrayed Palfrey's minder Blair.

| 1984 | 9.9 | Wed 18 Apr 9:00 p.m. | 15 | 2 wks |

'Once Your Card is Marked'
Mr Palfrey moves into his new office in Dean's Yard at Westminster School, where he was educated.
Designer: David Ferris. **Director:** Christopher Hodson. **Producer:** Michael Chapman. **Executive Producer:** Lloyd Shirley.

Mr Rose   16 wks

Granada, drama

Detective Chief Inspector Rose of THE ODD MAN and IT'S DARK OUTSIDE retired to Eastbourne to write his memoirs but, predictably, events conspired to make his retirement far from relaxed. The series starred William Mervyn as Mr Rose with Gillian Lewis as his secretary Drusilla Lamb and Donald Webster as his manservant John Halifax.

| 1967 | 7.9 | Fri 24 Mar 9:10 p.m. | 2 | 12 wks |

'The Unquiet Ghost' by Robert Holmes.
Mr Rose gets involved in a scandal about a case that never was.
Designer: Peter Phillips. **Director:** Michael Cox. **Producer:** Philip Mackie.

| 1968 | 5.9 | Fri 14 Jun 9:00 p.m. | 11 | 4 wks |

'The Golden Frame' by William Emms.
More than one person is trying to frame Mr Rose.
Designer: Michael Grimes. **Director:** Ian Fordyce. **Producer:** Margaret Morris.

Mrs Amworth   1 wk

HTV, drama

| 1978 | 12.2 | Thu 15 Jun 9:30 p.m. | 8 | 1 wk |

Half-hour adaptation by Hugh Whitmore of a story by E. F. Benson. Mrs Amworth (Glynis Johns) lives in an English village where the inhabitants are gradually being drained of blood. A vampire is suspected.
Director: Alvin Rakoff. **Producer:** William Deneen. **Executive Producer:** Patrick Dromgoole.

Mrs Columbo   1 wk

USA presented by ITV, drama

Kate Mulgrew starred as the detective wife of COLUMBO.

| 1979 | 14.4 | Sun 25 Nov 7:45 p.m. | 12 | 1 wk |

'Caviar With Everything'
Mrs Columbo uncovers a web of greed and jealousy when a caterer dies in a motor accident.

Mistress of Suspense   2 wks

HTV, drama

Mai Zetterling and David Hughes adapted a story by Patricia Highsmith.

| 1990 | 10.1 | Wed 9 May 9:00 p.m. | 10 | 2 wks |

Keeping alive a twenty-year-old memory of a forsaken lover becomes a dangerous obsession for Christopher Waggoner (Ian Holm). Eileen Atkins also stars.
Director: Mai Zetterling. **Producer:** Steven North. **Executive Producer:** Robert Halmi Jr. (A Crossbow Films/Vamp production.)

Mrs Thursday   34 wks

ATV, drama

Created by Ted Willis, this series of one hour light dramas starred Kathleen Harrison as elderly Cockney charlady Alice Thursday who, through inheritance, took over the controlling interest of the Dunrich industrial empire. This, despite George Dunrich's four ex-wives.
Producer: Jack Williams.

| 1966 | 9.6 | Mon 14 Mar 8:00 p.m.
Mon 21 Mar 8:00 p.m. | 1 | 14 wks |

'A Ride in a Rolls Royce' by Ted Willis.
Mrs Thursday is summoned to George Dunrich's bedside.
Director: William G. Stewart.

'Call Me Madam' by Ted Willis.
Mrs Thursday has her first day as head of the Dunrich group.
Director: John Cooper.

These two programmes achieved the same viewing figure and chart position.

| 1967 | 8.6 | Mon 20 Feb 8:00 p.m. | 1 | 20 wks |

'No Tea for the Tallyman' by Robin Smyth.
Mrs Thursday discovers the new tallyman in Fuller Street is not all he should be. She and her right-hand man Richard B. Hunter (Hugh Manning) try to stop his dishonest methods.
Director: William G. Stewart.

Kathleen Harrison as **Mrs Thursday** looks surprised at reaching Number One.

Mitch `1 wk`

LWT, drama

This series by Roger Marshall starred John Thaw in the title role of a crime reporter for a tabloid national newspaper.

| 1984 | 10.6 | Fri 31 Aug 9:00 p.m. | 9 | 1 wk |

'Something Private'
A ten-year-old boy is reported missing from his home in the Cotswolds. His body is found three miles away.
Producer: Peter Cregeen.

Mixed Blessings `13 wks`

LWT, situation comedy

In this series by Sid Green white boy Thomas (Christopher Blake) married black girl Susan (Muriel O'Dunton).
Producer: Derrick Goodwin.

| 1978 | 17.7 | Fri 17 Mar 7:30 p.m. | 4 | 12 wks |

'You Haven't Got Much, Have You?'
Thomas and Susan move into the basement flat of Aunt Dorothy (Joan Sanderson).

| 1980 | 11.2 | Sat 21 Jun 8:00 p.m. | 6 | 1 wk |

'Unto Us a Child'
Thomas and Susan prepare to become parents. (Repeat.)
Director: Pennant Roberts.

Moira Anderson Sings `5 wks`

BBC, music

First seen in Scotland's THE WHITE HEATHER CLUB, Moira Anderson had several series of her own.

| 1968 | 6.8 | Tue 30 Apr 9:05 p.m. | 7 | 5 wks |

Guest star: Russ Conway with the Scottish Radio Orchestra, conductor Iain Sutherland.
Producer: Eddie Fraser.

Monday Film, The `37 wks`

Presented by BBC, film

| 1976 | 6.3 | Mon 26 Jan 9:25 p.m. | 10 | 1 wk |

'They Call Me Mr Tibbs'
Sidney Poitier stars in the sequel to IN THE HEAT OF THE NIGHT. Now a police officer in San Francisco, Tibbs suspects a victim may have been killed by a clergyman.
Director: Gordon Douglas.

| 1977 | 13.4 | Mon 29 Aug 9:05 p.m. | 5 | 2 wks |

'Joe Kidd'
(See separate entry for this film.)
Director: John Sturges.

| 1978 | 11.8 | Mon 15 May 9:25 p.m. | 13 | 5 wks |

'The Legend of Lizzie Borden'
Set in Massachusetts in 1892. Elizabeth Montgomery stars as Lizzie Borden, who was suspected of murdering her parents.
Director: Paul Wendkos

| 1979 | 17.8 | Mon 27 Aug 7:25 p.m. | 7 | 4 wks |

'The Great Escape'
(See separate entry for this film.)

| 1980 | 13.7 | Mon 18 Feb 9:25 p.m. | 5 | 6 wks |

'The Blue Knight'
William Holden plays Bumper Morgan, a tough Los Angeles cop whose methods place him increasingly at odds with his superiors. Lee Remick also stars.
Director: Robert Butler.

| 1981 | 12.2 | Mon 13 Apr 9:25 p.m. | 14 | 2 wks |

'A Fistful of Dollars'
Clint Eastwood stars as a violent stranger in a Mexican town.
Director: Sergio Leone.

| 1982 | 11.7 | Mon 29 Mar 9:25 p.m. | 6 | 5 wks |

'Cagney and Lacey'
(See separate entry for this film.)

| 1983 | 13.2 | Mon 28 Feb 9:25 p.m. | 7 | 7 wks |

'Curse of the Black Widow'
Private detective Mike Higby (Tony Franciosa) suspects the police are trying to cover up several murders. The bodies bear the marks of a spider.
Director: Dan Curtis.

| 1984 | 9.0 | Mon 23 Jul 9:25 p.m. | 6 | 2 wks |

'Tomorrow Never Comes'
Oliver Reed stars as police lieutenant Jim Wilson, whose last day in the force provides the biggest drama of his career. Janie (Susan George), a bar singer, is taken hostage by a former lover. A violent siege ensues. Raymond Burr, John Ireland and Donald Pleasence also star.
Director: Peter Collinson.

| 1985 | 14.9 | Mon 18 Feb 10:05 p.m. | 6 | 1 wk |

'Dirty Harry'
(See separate entry for this film.)

1986	11.5	Mon 15 Sep 10:10 p.m.	11	2 wks

'First Blood'
Sylvester Stallone stars as former Green Beret John Rambo who faces the forces of the Law in a small Californian community.
Director: Ted Kotcheff.

....

Money Pit, The				1 wk

Presented by BBC, film

1990	11.6	Sat 24 Nov 8:15 p.m.	15	1 wk

Walter Fielding and Anna Crowley (Tom Hanks and Shelley Long) buy a cheap house where everything goes wrong. When the floor collapses it reveals a ravenous money pit.
Director: Richard Benjamin.

....

Money with Menaces				1 wk

Anglia, drama

1963	5.8	Fri 20 Dec 9:10 p.m.	18	1 wk

Single drama adapted by Ken Taylor from a story by Patrick Hamilton. If newspaper tycoon Andrew Carruthers (Ronald Lewis) wishes to see his young daughter Jenny (Priscilla Hird) again he must hand over £5,000 to Poland (Philip Madoc).
Designer: Fred Pusey. **Director:** June Howson.

....

Moneychangers, The				1 wk

USA presented by ITV, drama

Adaptation of Arthur Hailey's novel in four parts by Dean Reisner and Stanford Whitmore. Set in the ruthless world of high finance, it starred Kirk Douglas with Anne Baxter, Ralph Bellamy, Timothy Bottoms, Joan Collins, Susan Flannery, Lorne Greene and Christopher Plummer.
Director: Boris Sagal. **Producers:** Ross Hunter and Jacques Mapes.

1978	16.0	Sun 5 Feb 7:45 p.m.	15	1 wk

Episode Three
The First Mercantile Bank tries to discover who is counterfeiting credit cards.

....

Monkees, The				3 wks

USA presented by BBC, music

America's answer to the Beatles starred in this series of zany adventures. The Monkees were Micky Dolenz, Davy Jones, Mike Nesmith and Peter Tork. Created by Bob Rafelson and Bert Schneider.

1967	6.0	Sat 28 Oct 6:45 p.m.	20	3 wks

'Monkee Mother'
The Monkee Mother moves in with the boys. She says 'It's to keep the wolf from the door'.

....

Monroes, The			10 wks

USA presented by BBC, western

In this film series five orphaned children faced the challenge of the new frontiers of Wyoming in the 1870s and fought to hang on to the family homestead. Starring Michael Anderson Jr as Clayton, Barbara Hershey as Kathy, Keith and Kevin Schultz as the twins and Tammy Locke as Amy.
Producer: Frederick Brogger.

1966	6.1	Mon 17 Oct 8:00 p.m.	11	6 wks

'The Intruders'
The Monroe parents drown while saving their five children from the ravages of a turbulent river.

1967	6.5	Mon 16 Jan 8:00 p.m.	12	4 wks

'Gold Fever'
Clayton becomes obsessed with prospecting.

....

Monte Carlo			1 wk

USA presented by ITV, drama

This two-part spy thriller was based on a novel by Stephen Sheppard. It starred Joan Collins as Russian singer Katrina Petrovina and George Hamilton as Harry.

1988	10.3	Sun 10 Jul 8:15 p.m.	8	1 wk

Part One
At the outset of the Second World War, Germany is using the port of Monte Carlo for military purposes. The War Office in London sends Katrina as a spy. Also starring Robert Carradine, Lauren Hutton, Malcolm McDowell and Leslie Phillips.

....

Monte Carlo or Bust			1 wk

Presented by ITV, film

1975	6.3	Wed 1 Jan 2:45 p.m.	19	1 wk

In 1929 Sir Cuthbert Ware-Armitage (Terry-Thomas) inherits half an automobile factory, his father having lost the other half to American gambler Chester Schofield (Tony Curtis). The two enter the Monte Carlo rally, the winner to become the sole owner. Also starring Peter Cook, Susan Hampshire, Jack Hawkins, Dudley Moore and Eric Sykes.
Director: Ken Annakin.

Moody and Pegg — 10 wks

Thames, situation comedy

In this series by Julia Jones and Donald Churchill, Daphne Pegg (Judy Cornwell) and Roland Moody (Derek Waring) came to share a London flat by dint of both appearing to hold a valid lease for the premises.

| 1974 | 6.3 | Mon 2 Sep 9:00 p.m. | 8 | 5 wks |

'He – The Go-Between'
Having returned early from a business trip, next-door neighbour Commander Jeremy Shelby-Gibbs (Terence Alexander) finds a young lady in his flat. When his wife returns unexpectedly, Daphne and Roland become involved in a cover-up.
Director: Jonathan Alwyn. **Producer:** Robert Love.

| 1975 | 6.6 | Thu 14 Aug 9:00 p.m. | 3 | 5 wks |

'Daphne – The Primitive'
Roland invites his daughter Rowena (Lea Dreghorn) to dinner. Daphne labours to emphasize the innocence of their flat sharing.
Director: Baz Taylor. **Producer:** Robert Love.

Moonraker — 5 wks

Presented by ITV, film

| 1982 | 15.5 | Sun 26 Dec 6:30 p.m. | 1 | 1 wk |

James Bond (Roger Moore) travels through Venice, Rio de Janeiro and the upper reaches of the Amazon investigating the disappearance of a space shuttle on a test flight. Also starring Lois Chiles, Michael Lonsdale, Geoffrey Keen, Richard Kiel, Bernard Lee and Lois Maxwell.
Director: Lewis Gilbert.

1984	15.3	Sun 2 Sep 7:45 p.m.	1	1 wk
1985	14.0	Wed 25 Dec 3:05 p.m.	19	1 wk
1988	14.5	Sat 13 Feb 7:15 p.m.	6	1 wk
1991	12.2	Sat 14 Sep 7:25 p.m.	8	1 wk

Repeat showings of the above film.

Moonraker became the first James Bond film to make Number One in two different years.

Moonstrike — 5 wks

BBC, drama

This series of programmes concerned wartime secret agents and the men who flew them to their assignments. The special squadron needed moonlight to fly low into occupied countries. The incidents were factual, the characters fictitious. Created and written by Robert Barr.

| 1963 | 6.2 | Thu 21 Feb 8:25 p.m. | 12 | 5 wks |

'Home by Four'
An agent in enemy-held territory is in danger of arrest. A Lysander pilot flies his tiny machine in a rescue attempt.
Director: James MacTaggart. **Producer:** Gerard Glaister.

Morecambe and Wise at the BBC — 1 wk

BBC, comedy

This series celebrated Eric and Ernie's years with the Corporation.

| 1979 | 15.9 | Thu 11 Jan 8:00 p.m. | 7 | 1 wk |

Repeat showing of an episode of THE MORECAMBE AND WISE SHOW with Eve Blanchard, Arthur Tolcher and Dilys Watling.
Writer: Eddie Braben. **Producer:** Ernest Maxin.

Morecambe and Wise Christmas Show, The — 3 wks

BBC, entertainment

Producer: Ernest Maxin.

| 1975 | 6.5 | Thu 25 Dec 7:40 p.m. | 9 | 1 wk |

Guests: Brenda Arnau, Robin Day, Gordon Jackson, Diana Rigg and Diane Solomon, with Ann Hamilton, Pan's People, Arthur Tolcher and the Peter Knight orchestra.
Writer: Eddie Braben.

| 1976 | 7.0 | Sat 25 Dec 7:45 p.m. | 14 | 1 wk |

Guests: Elton John, Marion Montgomery, The Nolans, Kate O'Mara, John Thaw and Dennis Waterman, with Arthur Tolcher and the Peter Knight orchestra. (Angela Rippon was a surprise guest.)
Writers: Barry Cryer, Mike Craig, Lawrie Kinsley and Ron McDonnell.

| 1977 | 21.3 | Sun 25 Dec 8:55 p.m. | 2 | 1 wk |

Guests: Elton John, Penelope Keith, Francis Matthews, Angharad Rees and Stella Starr, with the Peter Knight orchestra.
Writer: Eddie Braben.

Morecambe and Wise Christmas Show, The — 4 wks

Thames, entertainment

| 1978 | 19.2 | Mon 25 Dec 9:00 p.m. | 1 | 1 wk |

Guests: Frank Finlay, Leonard Rossiter and the Syd Lawrence orchestra.
Writers: Barry Cryer and John Junkin. **Producer:** Keith Beckett.

| 1980 | 14.6 | Thu 25 Dec 8:30 p.m. | 17 | 1 wk |

Guests: Peter Barkworth, Gemma Craven, Peter Cushing, Jill Gascoine, Hannah Gordon, Alec Guinness and Glenda Jackson.
Producer: John Ammonds.

| 1981 | 16.6 | Wed 23 Dec 8:00 p.m. | 5 | 1 wk |

Guests: Suzanne Danielle, Steve Davis, Robert Hardy, Ian Ogilvy, Ralph Richardson, Alvin Stardust and Susannah York.
Writer: Eddie Braben. **Producer:** John Ammonds.

| 1982 | 11.5 | Mon 27 Dec 9:00 p.m. | 10 | 1 wk |

Guests: Diana Dors, Robert Hardy, Denis Healey, Glenda Jackson, Rula Lenska, André Previn, Richard Vernon, Wall Street Crash and Jimmy Young, with the Ken Warwick dancers and Peter Knight orchestra.
Writer: Eddie Braben. **Producer:** John Ammonds.

....

Morecambe and Wise Classics | 1 wk

BBC, comedy

| 1986 | 12.4 | Tue 30 Dec 8:00 p.m. | 13 | 1 wk |

Ernie Wise introduces highlights of THE MORECAMBE AND WISE CHRISTMAS SHOW through the years. (Repeat.)
Producer: Robin Nash.

....

Morecambe and Wise Show, The | 80 wks

ATV, comedy

The first television series to star Britain's favourite double act was RUNNING WILD for the BBC in 1954. It was a critical disaster and the pair remained in the television wilderness until ATV picked them up. They were supported by the Jack Parnell orchestra.
Writers: Sid Green and Dick Hills. **Producer:** Colin Clews.

| 1961 | 5.8 | Thu 30 Nov 8:00 p.m. | 6 | 9 wks |

Guests: Micky Ashman's Ragtime Jazz Band and Valerie Masters.

| 1962 | 6.6 | Sat 15 Sep 9:30 p.m. | 4 | 13 wks |

Guests: The Mike Cotton Jazzmen, Pearl Carr and Teddy Johnson.

| 1963 | 7.0 | Sat 14 Sep 9:30 p.m. | 3 | 15 wks |

Guests: Eric Delaney and his band, Pearl Carr and Teddy Johnson.

| 1964 | 7.3 | Sat 18 Aug 8:25 p.m. | 5 | 12 wks |

Guests: The Beatles.

| 1965 | 5.4 | Sat 14 Aug 8:15 p.m. | 12 | 4 wks |

Guests: The Migil Five and Susan Maughan with the Pamela Devis dancers.

| 1966 | 8.0 | Sat 22 Jan 8:20 p.m. | 5 | 15 wks |

Guests: Lulu, Paul and Barry Ryan.

| 1967 | 8.7 | Sun 12 Nov 10:05 p.m. | 1 | 5 wks |

Guests: The Hollies, Tom Jones and Millicent Martin, the Paddy Stone dancers and the Mike Sammes singers.
Director: Philip Casson.

| 1968 | 8.1 | Sun 17 Mar 10:05 p.m. | 3 | 7 wks |

Guests: Georgie Fame, Millicent Martin and Bobby Vinton, with the Paddy Stone dancers and the Mike Sammes singers.
Director: Philip Casson.

....

Morecambe and Wise Show, The | 50 wks

BBC, comedy

Writers: Sid Green and Dick Hills (1968–69), Eddie Braben (1970–78). **Producers:** John Ammonds (1968–74 and 1977), Ernest Maxin (1976 and 1978).

| 1968 | 6.4 | Sat 28 Dec 7:00 p.m. | 10 | 1 wk |

Eric and Ernie move to the BBC with their second 1968 series. Guests: Acker Bilk and Roy Budd with Sheila Bernette, Bettine Le Beau, Tina Martin, Jenny Russell, Jenny Lee-Wright and the Alyn Ainsworth orchestra.

| 1969 | 7.1 | Sat 8 Feb 7:00 p.m. | 9 | 10 wks |

Guests: Michael Aspel, Kenny Ball's Jazzmen and Chris Langford, with Jimmy Berryman, Lesley Roach, Jenny Lee-Wright and the Alyn Ainsworth orchestra.

| 1970 | 7.3 | Thu 3 Dec 8:15 p.m. | 5 | 10 wks |

This series was first shown on BBC2 with regulars Ann Hamilton, Janet Webb, Jenny Lee-Wright and the Peter Knight orchestra and guest stars Kenny Ball and his Jazzmen, Craig Douglas and Nina.

| 1971 | 6.7 | Tue 16 Mar 8:00 p.m. | 11 | 1 wk |

Guests: Kenny Ball and his Jazzmen, Peter Cushing, William Franklyn, Nina, Eric Porter and Edward Woodward, with Alan Curtis, Ann Hamilton, Rex Rashley, Janet Webb and the Peter Knight orchestra.

| 1972 | 6.8 | Sat 20 May 8:15 p.m. | 7 | 1 wk |

A one-hour special with guest stars Shirley Bassey, Glenda Jackson and André Previn. With Frank Bough, Robert Dougall, Dick Emery, Cliff Michelmore, Patrick Moore, Michael Parkinson, Eddie Waring and the Ernest Maxin dancers. (Repeat.)

| 1973 | 7.9 | Fri 2 Mar 8:15 p.m. | 2 | 13 wks |

Guests: Hannah Gordon, Christopher Neil and Mary Travers, with Raymond Mason, Hatti Riemer, Anthony Sharp, Christine Shaw and the Peter Knight orchestra.

The Morecambe And Wise Christmas Show was a chart cracker for six seasons.

Eric and Ernie in 1967, the first year that The Morecambe and Wise Show reached Number One.

| 1974 | 7.6 | Fri 27 Sep 8:15 p.m. | 1 | 6 wks |

Guests: Magnus Magnusson, Gladys Mills, André Previn, Wilma Reading and Arthur Tolcher, with the Peter Knight orchestra and the Irving Davies dancers.

| 1976 | 8.2 | Wed 7 Jan 8:15 p.m. | 2 | 6 wks |

Guests: Peter O'Sullevan, Gilbert O'Sullivan, the Vernons, Dilys Watling and Arthur Tolcher with the Peter Knight orchestra.

| 1977 | 7.2 | Sat 2 Apr 9:00 p.m | 19 | 1 wk |

A repeat showing of the 1976 MORECAMBE AND WISE CHRISTMAS SHOW to replace THE EUROVISION SONG CONTEST, which is postponed because of a blackout by BBC cameramen.

| 1978 | 12.3 | Wed 7 Jun 7:35 p.m. | 1 | 1 wk |

A shortened repeat of the 1977 MORECAMBE AND WISE CHRISTMAS SHOW after it won the BAFTA award for the Best Light Entertainment Programme.

| **Morecambe and Wise Show, The** | | | | **41 wks** |

Thames, comedy

With the Peter Knight orchestra (1978–82, 1984).
Writer: Eddie Braben. **Producers** included John Ammonds (1981–82 and 1984), and Mark Stuart (1983 and 1985).

| 1978 | 18.7 | Wed 18 Oct 8:00 p.m. | 1 | 1 wk |

The show began its run on Thames with this one-off special. Guests: Peter Cushing, Judi Dench, Derek Griffiths, The Syd Lawrence orchestra, Leonard Sachs and Donald Sinden. With Ann Hamilton and Kenneth Watson.
Producer: Keith Beckett.

| 1979 | 18.3 | Wed 28 Mar 8:00 p.m. | 1 | 1 wk |

A repeat of the 1978 show above.

| 1980 | 14.6 | Wed 8 Oct 8:00 p.m. | 17 | 1 wk |

Guest: Gemma Craven with the Nigel Lythgoe dancers.

| 1981 | 14.5 | Tue 13 Oct 8:00 p.m. | 2 | 8 wks |

Guests: Joanna Lumley and Richard Vernon. With the Carole Todd dancers.

| 1982 | 12.5 | Tue 4 May 8:30 p.m. | 4 | 15 wks |

Guests: Peter Bowles, Faith Brown, Suzanne Danielle. With the Norman Maen dancers.

| 1983 | 14.1 | Wed 19 Oct 8:00 p.m. | 3 | 7 wks |

Guest: Harry Fowler, with Peter Finn and Valerie Minifie, the Nigel Lythgoe dancers and the Harry Rabinowitz orchestra.

| 1984 | 12.3 | Tue 5 Jun 8:30 p.m. | 2 | 7 wks |

Guest: Roy Castle. With Peter Salmon and the Ken Warwick dancers.

| 1985 | 8.0 | Wed 3 Jul 8:30 p.m. | 18 | 1 wk |

Repeat showing of the 1983 show with Harry Fowler.

| **Moscow State Circus** | | | | **3 wks** |

ATV, circus

| 1960 | 6.1 | Sun 21 Aug 9:00 p.m. | 2 | 1 wk |

Excerpts from Tom Arnold's presentation at the Empire Pool, Wembley, including Gosha the Wonder Bear and the Voljansky Family.
Television presentation: Bill Ward.

| 1961 | 5.9 | Sun 4 Jun 8:00 p.m. | 8 | 2 wks |

Ringmaster E. Roushat presents the Kasyanor Troupe, the Mikituk Trio and the Voljansky Family. From the Empire Pool, Wembley.
Television presentation: Bill Ward.

| **Moscow State Circus** | | | | **1 wk** |

BBC, circus

| 1971 | 5.2 | Thu 12 Aug 8:00 p.m. | 20 | 1 wk |

Starring Oleg Popov with Elvina Podchernikova's brown bears, the Arnautov troupe, the Cossack horsemen, Irina Chestua and Vladimir Voljansky.
Television presentation: Alan Mouncer.

| **Moses – the Lawgiver** | | | | **3 wks** |

ATV/RAI Italy, drama

This six-part story of Moses by Anthony Burgess and Vittorio Bonicelli starred Burt Lancaster as Moses and Anthony Quayle as Aaron.

| 1977 | 7.6 | Sun 16 Jan 7:00 p.m. | 17 | 3 wks |

'The Israelites'
In this first episode young Moses is played by William Lancaster.
Director: Gianfranco De Bosio.

Most Beautiful Hotel in the World, The `1 wk`

YTV, documentary

1968 **6.4** **Tue 17 Sep 9:15 p.m.** **3** `1 wk`

Alan Whicker visits Le Touquet, the most fashionable resort of the 1920s.
Director: Richard Loncraine. **Producer:** Michael Blakstad.

....

Most Dangerous Man in the World, The `1 wk`

Presented by ITV, film

1974 **6.5** **Sun 29 Dec 7:55 p.m.** **6** `1 wk`

Suspense film starring Gregory Peck and Anne Heywood. A mission leaves for China to obtain vital information for the West.
Director: J. Lee-Thompson.

....

Most Wanted `1 wk`

USA presented by BBC, drama

Most Wanted was the name of an élite crime squad. The programme starred Robert Stack as Captain Linc Evers, Shelly Novak as Sergeant Charlie Benson and Jo Ann Harris as Sergeant Kate Manners.
Executive Producer: Quinn Martin.

1978 **11.2** **Thu 31 Aug 9:25 p.m.** **14** `1 wk`

'The Two-Dollar Kidnapper'
A gang carries out a series of kidnaps from ordinary families, demanding just a few hundred dollars ransom each time.

....

Motorway `1 wk`

YTV, documentary

1968 **4.8** **Tue 2 Sep 9:15 p.m.** **13** `1 wk`

A film report on the progress of the M62 as it carves its way through the Pennines.
Writer and **director:** Anthony R. Thomas. **Camera:** Mel Davies.
Producer: Tony Essex.

....

Mountbatten `2 wks`

AR/Thames, documentary

The life and times of Lord Louis Mountbatten, 1st Earl Mountbatten of Burma, who was born in 1900, joined the Navy in 1913 and had a distinguished war record, becoming chief of combined operations in 1942. As last Viceroy of India in 1947 he oversaw the transition to independence. He was murdered by the IRA in 1979. This programme was initiated by AR and inherited by Thames.

1969 **6.9** **Wed 1 Jan 10:30 p.m.** **10** `2 wks`

Alec Mango narrates the story of Mountbatten's early years.
Producer: Peter Morley.

....

Movie of the Week `7 wks`

Presented by ITV, film

1977 **17.5** **Sun 30 Oct 7:45 p.m.** **2** `7 wks`

'Skyjacked'
Charlton Heston stars as Captain Hank O'Hara, who takes off from Los Angeles on a routine flight to Minneapolis. Among his passengers is a maniac with a gun.
Director: John Guillermin.

....

Moving Target, The `1 wk`

Presented by BBC, film

1979 **13.8** **Sun 25 Aug 8:05 p.m.** **17** `1 wk`

Paul Newman stars as a private eye hired by a wealthy woman to find her missing husband. He stumbles upon a network of crime and corruption. Also starring Lauren Bacall, Janet Leigh, Robert Wagner and Shelley Winters.
Director: Jack Smight.

....

Muhammad Ali – An Interview With David Frost `1 wk`

Thames, documentary

1972 **6.1** **Mon 18 Dec 8:00 p.m.** **17** `1 wk`

Reflections on Ali's career with selected highlights from his fights.
Producer: Grahame Turner.

....

Mum's Boys `1 wk`

BBC, situation comedy

This series by Jimmy Grafton and Jeremy Lloyd starred Irene Handl as Mum, Mrs Crystal Pallise, an ex-chorus girl and conjuror's assistant. Her boys Leonard Pallise and Robin Fosdyke, products of two marriages, were played by Bernard Bresslaw and Pete Murray.

1968 **5.9** **Wed 3 Apr 8:20 p.m.** **20** `1 wk`

'Cuckoo in the Nest'
In this first episode Robin arrives home. Mum has not seen him since her marriage to the Hon. Bertram Fosdyke was annulled when Robin was just a baby. He was raised by Bertram's parents. The rather simple Leonard is not best pleased at Robin's arrival.
Producer: Eric Fawcett.

M

Muppet Show, The   30 wks

ATV, comedy

Puppeteer Jim Henson first developed his characters, including Kermit the Frog, in the mid-1950s. They appeared regularly on a Washington TV show called 'Sam and Friends'. Henson moved to New York to create a new show called 'Sesame Street', aimed at pre-school children, in which many Muppet characters appeared. When he created 'The Muppet Show' it was rejected by the US networks. ATV's Lew Grade, however, was interested and Henson moved to England to begin work on the shows. The rest is history.

The Muppets were mostly foam rubber glove puppets which were operated by Henson and his colleagues. Henson himself provided the voices for Kermit, Rowlf and Waldorf. Frank Oz was Miss Piggy and Fozzie Bear. Jerry Nelson was Floyd, Robin and Crazy Harry, and Richard Hunt was Scooter, Statler and Sweetums. Dave Goetz was Great Gonzo, Bunsen Honeydew and Zoot. The shows also had an impressive list of human star guests. Henson died in 1990.
Director (1977–79, 1981): *Philip Casson.* **Producer:** *Jim Henson.* **Executive Producer:** *David Lazer.*

| 1977 | 16.5 | Sun 11 Dec 7:15 p.m. | 2 | 13 wks |

Guest: Lou Rawls.

| 1978 | 20.6 | Fri 22 Dec 7:00 p.m. | 5 | 8 wks |

Guests: Rita Coolidge and Kris Kristofferson.

| 1979 | 16.6 | Fri 5 Jan 7:00 p.m. | 4 | 7 wks |

Guest: Harry Belafonte.

| 1980 | 14.7 | Fri 4 Jan 7:00 p.m. | 16 | 1 wk |

Guest: Dizzy Gillespie.
Director: *Peter Harris.*

| 1981 | 13.2 | Sun 25 Jan 5:30 p.m. | 15 | 1 wk |

Guest: Debbie Harry.

Murder   7 wks

Granada, drama

In this series of plays murder was the common theme.

| 1969 | 6.7 | Mon 21 Apr 8:30 p.m. | 5 | 7 wks |

'Mr Buchanan' *by Joseph Green.*
Terence Alexander, Paul Daneman and Ann Firbank star in the story of a dead man's long-estranged son, who refutes the generally held belief that his father was a great man and plans to bury him as the charlatan he believes him to have been.
Director: *Brian Mills.* **Producer:** *Richard Bates.*

Murder in Three Acts   1 wk

Presented by ITV, film

| 1990 | 9.5 | Mon 14 May 9:00 p.m. | 13 | 1 wk |

Agatha Christie's story stars Peter Ustinov as Hercule Poirot, surrounded by death in Acapulco. Tony Curtis and Emma Samms also star.
Director: *Gary Nelson.*

Murder is Easy   2 wks

Presented by ITV, film

| 1982 | 14.2 | Mon 3 May 8:30 p.m. | 2 | 1 wk |

Agatha Christie's story of murder in the sleepy village of Wychwood-under-Ashe stars Helen Hayes as Miss Fullerton. Also starring Bill Bixby, Lesley-Anne Down, Olivia de Havilland, Freddie Jones, Jonathan Pryce, Anthony Valentine and Timothy West.
Director: *Claude Whatham.*

| 1986 | 9.1 | Sun 25 May 7:15 p.m. | 19 | 1 wk |

The BBC shows the film.

Murder, Mystery and Suspense   42 wks

Presented by ITV, film

Series of crime movies.

| 1983 | 14.1 | Tue 18 Jan 7:35 p.m. | 5 | 14 wks |

'Death Cruise'
Three married couples unknown to each other win a cruise in a competition. They find themselves sharing a dining table. One of them disappears. Stars include Edward Albert, Polly Bergen, Celeste Holm, Kate Jackson and Richard Long.
Director: *Ralph Senensky.*

| 1985 | 15.9 | Sun 13 Jan 7:15 p.m. | 4 | 8 wks |

'You'll Never See Me Again'
The title words are uttered by a young wife following a tiff with her husband. As he searches for her, evidence is revealed that appears to implicate him as her murderer.
Director: *Jeanot Szwarc.*

| 1986 | 15.1 | Sun 20 Apr 7:45 p.m. | 4 | 7 wks |

'Ashanti'
(See separate entry for this film.)

| 1987 | 15.3 | Sun 17 May 7:45 p.m. | 3 | 7 wks |

'Murder In Three Acts'
(See separate entry for this film.)

1988	11.1	Sat 26 Mar 8:05 p.m.	13	5 wks

'Detour To Terror'
O. J. Simpson stars as bus driver Lee Hayes and Arte Johnson as tour guide Harry Edwards. On their way to Las Vegas their bus is sabotaged by Jaime (Lorenzo Lamas). **Director:** Michael O'Herlihy.

1990	10.3	Sat 21 Apr 8:10 p.m.	19	1 wk

'Taking Of Flight 847'
TWA flight 847 is hijacked ten minutes after leaving Athens bound for London. The terrorists demand to be flown to Beirut. Senior flight attendant Uli Derickson (Lindsay Wagner) is called to act as interpreter. **Director:** Paul Wendkos.

....

Murder of Quality, A   1 wk

ITV, drama

1991	11.0	Wed 10 Apr 8:00 p.m.	17	1 wk

Denholm Elliott stars as John le Carré's spymaster George Smiley. He goes to the aid of Ailsa Brimley (Glenda Jackson) when she receives a letter predicting death. Too late to save a murder, Smiley sets out to investigate. **Director:** Gavin Millar. **Producer:** Eric Abraham.

....

Murder One   6 wks

BBC, film

A season of films with the theme of murder.

1988	11.3	Tue 30 Aug 9:30 p.m.	15	6 wks

'Chase'
Jennifer O'Neil stars as lawyer Sandy Albright. She is forced to defend the chief suspect in the murder of her own friend. **Director:** Rod Holcomb.

....

Murder Ordained   1 wk

USA presented by BBC, drama

1989	9.9	Tue 11 Jul 9:30 p.m.	10	1 wk
		Wed 12 Jul 9:30 p.m.		

This true case of fatal attraction was shown in two parts on consecutive nights and listed as one entry in the ratings. In a small town in Kansas, Lutheran minister Tom Bird (Terry Kinney) begins a passionate affair with Lorna Anderson (JoBeth Williams). Both are married. Both their spouses are murdered. Keith Carradine also stars. **Director:** Mike Robe. **Producer:** Phil Parslow.

Murder, She Said   1 wk

Presented by BBC, film

1972	5.1	Tue 11 Jul 7:35 p.m.	16	1 wk

Based on Agatha Christie's novel The 4:50 From Paddington, this film is screened as a tribute to Dame Margaret Rutherford, who died on 22 May 1972. She plays the eccentric sleuth Miss Marple, who witnesses a woman being strangled in a passing train. Also starring James Robertson Justice, Arthur Kennedy, Muriel Pavlow, Conrad Phillips, Charles Tingwell and Thorley Walters. (Playing the part of Mrs Kidder was Joan Hickson who, many years later, made the role of **Miss Marple** her own.) **Director:** George Pollock.

....

Murder, She Wrote   22 wks

USA presented by ITV, drama

Angela Lansbury starred as Jessica Fletcher, a widow living in Cabot Cove, Maine. She had always been an avid reader of detective novels and wrote one herself for fun. Her nephew Grady (Michael Horton) got it published and it shot to the top of the best-sellers. Peter Fischer created and produced the series.

1985	12.5	Sun 19 May 8:00 p.m.	5	11 wks

'The Murder of Sherlock Holmes'
Jessica's publisher Preston Giles (Arthur Hill) invites her to a fancy dress party at his weekend estate. The following morning a body is found floating in the swimming pool.

1988	11.3	Sat 17 Dec 7:50 p.m.	16	3 wks

'The Bottom Line is Murder'
A friend of Jessica's is arrested for murder. She investigates.

1989	10.4	Sat 1 Apr 7:45 p.m.	12	2 wks

'Simon Says, Colour Me Dead'
Jessica is invited to a dinner party by painter Simon Thane (Foster Brooks). The next day he is dead and his latest picture is missing.

1990	13.0	Sat 27 Jan 8:00 p.m.	15	6 wks

'Deadpan'
A well-known theatre critic is found murdered.

....

Murder, She Wrote – The Movie   1 wk

Presented by ITV, film

1988	10.0	Sat 2 Jul 8:00 p.m.	10	1 wk

On holiday in Hawaii, Jessica Fletcher (Angela Lansbury) helps private eye Magnum (Tom Selleck) with an investigation. They attend a party where a guest is shot dead. All the evidence points to Magnum.

Murder that Wouldn't Die, The   1 wk

Presented by ITV, film

1981   **12.1**   **Sat 4 Jul 8:10 p.m.**   **7**   **1 wk**

William Conrad stars as Bill Battles in a double murder hunt in Hawaii. Battles is a retired LA cop and the murders that he sets out to investigate took place forty years ago.
Director: Ron Satlof.

Murder with Mirrors   1 wk

Presented by ITV, film

1986   **13.4**   **Mon 1 Sep 8:30 p.m.**   **4**   **1 wk**

Helen Hayes stars as Agatha Christie's Miss Marple. She visits her old school friend Carrie Louise (Bette Davis) at her palatial home, which has been turned into a reform centre for delinquents. While she is there, three murders occur. Also starring Leo McKern, John Mills, Anton Rodgers, Tim Roth, Frances de la Tour, Dorothy Tutin and John Woodvine.
Director: Dick Lowry.

Murphy's Stroke   1 wk

Thames, drama

1980   **11.0**   **Wed 21 May 8:40 p.m.**   **16**   **1 wk**

Based on the true story of Murphy (Niall Tobin) who, in 1974, had the idea to let a good horse romp home at Cartmel races after two favourites had been mysteriously withdrawn. Daily Mail reporter Ewbank Callender (Ray Barron) was suspicious and discovered Murphy's stroke.
Producer: Frank Cvitanovich.

Murphy's War   2 wks

Presented by ITV, film

1976   **5.7**   **Mon 31 May 8:00 p.m.**   **13**   **1 wk**

Murphy (Peter O'Toole) survives a German U-boat torpedo massacre and reaches the Orinoco River. One other survivor is shot by the Germans and Murphy becomes obsessed with revenge. He wants to sink the U-boat. Also starring Sian Phillips with John Hallam, Horst Janson and Philippe Noiret.
Director: Peter Yates.

1978   **17.5**   **Wed 11 Jan 8:00 p.m.**   **6**   **1 wk**

Repeat showing of the above film.

Music Hall   6 wks

ATV, entertainment

This was a series hosted by Americans Tony Sandler and Ralph Young with Judy Carne. Writers Sid Green and Dick Hills took a weekly theme and developed it using comedy and music.
Choreographer: Paddy Stone. **Producer:** Stan Harris.

1969   **6.1**   **Sun 12 Oct 10:20 p.m.**   **13**   **3 wks**

Guests: Kaye Ballard, Jack Haig, Ann Sydney and Terry-Thomas with the Jack Parnell orchestra.

1970   **5.0**   **Wed 22 Jul 9:10 p.m.**   **18**   **3 wks**

Guests: Pat Coombs, Barbara Feldon, Jack Haig and Norman Wisdom with the Jack Parnell orchestra.

Music of Lennon and McCartney, The   1 wk

Granada, music

John Lennon and Paul McCartney introduced their own favourite versions of some of their songs.

1965   **7.9**   **Wed 15 Dec 9:40 p.m.**   **5**   **1 wk**

Guests: The Beatles, Cilla Black, Tony Crombie, Marianne Faithfull, Alan Haven, Billy J. Kramer and the Dakotas, Henry Mancini, Peter and Gordon, Esther Phillips, Dick Rivers, Peter Sellers and Fritz Spiegl with the George Martin orchestra and the Pamela Devis dancers.
Director: Philip Casson. **Producer:** John Hamp.

Music of Morecambe and Wise, The   1 wk

BBC, music

1977   **6.8**   **Mon 6 Jun 7:50 p.m.**   **6**   **1 wk**

Bank Holiday Monday special in which Eric and Ernie chat with Michael Parkinson and introduce some of the musical highlights from their BBC shows over the years. Featuring Vanessa Redgrave, Cliff Richard, Diana Rigg and Angela Rippon.
Producer: Ernest Maxin.

My Brother's Keeper   7 wks

Granada, situation comedy

This series was written by and starred George Layton and Jonathan Lynn as far from identical twin brothers, Brian and Pete Booth, who had far from identical views on life. Brian was a policeman, Pete was a militant student. Also starred Hilary Mason as Mrs Booth and Tenniel Evans as Sergeant Bluett.
Producer: Bill Podmore.

| 1975 | 6.0 | Sun 21 Sep 7:25 p.m. | 19 | 1 wk |

PC Booth is told to clamp down on the spread of pornography in the area. Pete is putting on an end-of-term show for the students, Oh Calcutta!

| 1976 | 6.5 | Mon 10 May 8:00 p.m. | 5 | 6 wks |

Brian wins a weekend for two in Spain and takes Pete with him.

....

My Good Woman   32 wks

ATV, situation comedy

Created by Ronnie Taylor, the series starred Leslie Crowther as Clive Gibbons, a man who firmly believed his own decline and fall was upon him. Sylvia Sims played his wife Sylvia, a champion do-gooder who could not be persuaded that charity should begin at home. Clive's ally was next-door neighbour Philip, played by Keith Barron.

| 1972 | 7.7 | Thu 30 Mar 9:00 p.m. | 3 | 12 wks |

'Room for the Vicar'
The vicar (Richard Wilson) needs alternative lodgings to the vicarage while a new central heating system is installed. Sylvia is happy to oblige.
Producer: Les Chatfield.

| 1973 | 8.1 | Tue 27 Nov 8:25 p.m. | 1 | 11 wks |

'Diary of a Dogsbody'
Sylvia has only two evenings free from her eternal charity work to celebrate her birthday. One is in the distant future and the other on the night of Clive's darts match.
Producer: William G. Stewart.

| 1974 | 7.2 | Tue 1 Oct 8:30 p.m. | 3 | 9 wks |

'Bride to Be'
The most eligible bachelor in town looks to Clive and Sylvia to find him the perfect wife.
Producer: William G. Stewart.

....

My Name is Harry Worth   8 wks

Thames, situation comedy

This series by Ronnie Taylor starred Harry Worth as himself and Lally Bowers as his landlady Mrs Maybury.

| 1974 | 7.5 | Mon 22 Apr 8:00 p.m. | 3 | 8 wks |

Harry moves into his digs.
Producer: William G. Stewart.

....

My Old Man   7 wks

YTV, situation comedy

This series by Gerald Frow starred Clive Dunn as Sam, a crusty old war veteran who was prized from his home by the demolition men. He moved in with daughter Doris (Priscilla Morgan) and son-in-law Arthur (Edward Hardwicke), but life in a flat did not suit him. He needed a garden and his own furniture.

| 1974 | 6.0 | Fri 21 Jun 8:30 p.m. | 7 | 1 wk |

Sam believes it's a grandfather's right to take the children out on their half-term holiday. Neither Doris nor Arthur nor the children agree.
Director: Paddy Russell. **Producer:** John Duncan.

| 1975 | 8.3 | Wed 19 Mar 8:00 p.m. | 2 | 6 wks |

Sam helps an old pal with his problems and gets some of his own.
Producer: Paddy Russell.

....

My Son Reuben   7 wks

Thames, situation comedy

This series was created and written by Vince Powell. Bernard Spear starred as Reuben, who ran a dry-cleaning business. Lila Kaye portrayed his mother, Fay Greenberg. She was an archetypal over-protective Jewish mother who kept Reuben tied to her apron strings.

| 1975 | 7.4 | Mon 13 Oct 8:00 p.m. | 5 | 7 wks |

'Better to Have Loved and Lost'
The routine of the Greenberg home is upset by a letter from one of Fay's old boyfriends. With guest star Milo O'Shea.
Producer: Anthony Parker.

....

Leslie Crowther does not seem particularly pleased with what he's hearing from Sylvia Sims in **My Good Woman**.

My Wife Next Door | 9 wks

BBC, situation comedy

This series created by Brian Clemens and Richard Waring starred John Alderton as George Bassett and Hannah Gordon as Suzi Bassett, a divorced couple who, quite by chance, bought adjoining cottages.
Writer: *Richard Waring.* **Producer:** *Graeme Muir.*

| 1972 | 6.8 | Tue 19 Sep 8:30 p.m. | 9 | 6 wks |

'The Nearness of You'
Following the divorce, George decides to move out of town and into the country. He wonders what his new neighbour will be like.

| 1973 | 6.5 | Thu 13 Sep 10:15 p.m. | 8 | 1 wk |

'Total Separation'
George and Suzi almost get back together until their parents decide to get involved.

| 1980 | 19.3 | Fri 18 Jan 8:00 p.m. | 2 | 2 wks |

'Pregnant Moment'
In this repeat, George has mixed feelings about becoming a family man.

....

Mysterious World of Arthur C. Clarke, The | 8 wks

YTV, documentary

Science fiction writer Arthur C. Clarke, who wrote the book 2001 – A Space Odyssey, *explored the natural curiosities of the world.*

| 1980 | 14.4 | Tue 25 Nov 8:30 p.m. | 14 | 8 wks |

Gordon Honeycombe explains the moving stones of California's Death Valley and questions whether Neanderthal man still lives in Asia.
Directors: *Charles Flynn and Michael Weigall.* **Producer:** *John Fanshawe.* **Series Producer:** *Simon Welfare.* **Executive Producer:** *John Fairley.*

Mystery and Imagination | 12 wks

ABC, drama

Series of plays about the supernatural.

| 1966 | 6.5 | Sun 29 Jan 10:05 p.m. | 14 | 9 wks |

'The Lost Stradivarius' by J. Meade Falkner.
In this adaptation by Owen Holder, David Buck stars as Richard Beckett, a young Victorian to whom things happen. His friend Sir John Maltravers (Jeremy Brett) falls under the evil influence of an old violin.
Designer: *Stan Woodward.* **Director:** *Bill Bain.* **Producer:** *Jonathan Alwyn.*

| 1968 | 6.1 | Mon 18 Nov 8:30 p.m. | 17 | 3 wks |

'Dracula' by Charles Graham.
Denholm Elliott stars as Count Dracula in this adaptation of Bram Stoker's novel, with James Maxwell as Dr Seward, Corin Redgrave as Harker, Suzanne Neve as Mina Harker, Susan George as Lucy Weston, Joan Hickson as Mrs Weston and Bernard Archard as Professor Van Helsing.
Designer: *Davis Marshall.* **Director:** *Patrick Dromgoole.* **Producer:** *Reginald Collins.*

Name That Tune | 37 wks

Thames, game show

This show was given its own half-hour slot after originating as a segment of Thames' WEDNESDAY AT 8. Contestants competed to be first to identify a song. Presented from 1984 by Lionel Blair. With Maggie Moone and the Alan Braden orchestra.
Producer (1983-85): Keith Beckett.

| 1983 | 14.8 | Wed 26 Oct 7:00 p.m. | 2 | 10 wks |

Presented by Tom O'Connor.

1984	15.8	Wed 21 Nov 7:00 p.m.	2	16 wks
1985	16.8	Tue 15 Jan 7:30 p.m.	5	8 wks
1987	10.1	Mon 3 Aug 8:00 p.m.	11	3 wks

Producer: David Clark.

Name That Tune Special | 1 wk

In this seasonal special celebrity guests played for charity.

| 1986 | 11.9 | Tue 30 Dec 7:00 p.m. | 19 | 1 wk |

Hosted by Lionel Blair and Maggie Moone. Guests: Faith Brown and Joe Brown, with the Alan Braden orchestra.
Producer: David Clark.

Nana | 1 wk

BBC, drama

Emile Zola's famous story, dramatized in five parts by Robert Muller. The series was first shown on BBC2.

| 1970 | 6.1 | Fri 13 Nov 9:20 p.m. | 17 | 1 wk |

'The Fall of an Empire'
Count Muffat (Freddie Jones) has again succumbed to the irresistible charms of Nana (Katharine Schofield). She is living in opulence at his expense, but on her terms.
Designer: Susan Spence. **Director:** John Davies. **Producer:** David Couron.

Nancy Wake | 2 wks

Thames, drama

This two-part drama was adapted by Roger Simpson from the book by Russell Braddon. Freelance journalist Nancy Wake (Noni Hazelhurst) was given a wartime assignment in Marseilles in 1939. She played a major part in helping the French Resistance.

| 1988 | 9.4 | Sun 24 Jul 8:15 p.m. | 17 | 2 wks |

Part One
Wealthy businessman Henri Fiocca (John Waters) falls for Nancy in Marseilles and follows her back to Paris. But as Hitler advances through Europe Henri is called up to join the army.
Director: Pino Amenta. **Producers:** Roger Le Mesurier and Roger Simpson.

Nanny | 13 wks

BBC, drama

This series created and written by Terence Brady and Charlotte Bingham starred Wendy Craig as Nanny Barbara Gray. It was set in the 1930s.

| 1981 | 13.7 | Sat 31 Jan 7:10 p.m. | 14 | 3 wks |

'The Magic Island'
The children are falling out because they're stuck indoors while it rains all day every day.
Director: Michael Custance. **Producer:** Guy Slater.

| 1982 | 12.7 | Sat 16 Jan 7:10 p.m. | 18 | 2 wks |

'Comings and Goings'
Barbara sets out for Yorkshire knowing nothing about her prospective employers except that they are cousins of her friend Mr Phipps (Michael Lees) and that they live at Cattisham Hall. Also starring Judy Campbell and Richard Vernon as the Duchess and Duke of Broughton and Celia Johnson as Nanny Broughton.
Director: Christopher Barry. **Producer:** Guy Slater.

| 1983 | 12.4 | Sun 20 Feb 7:45 p.m. | 11 | 8 wks |

'A Journey'
Barbara's visit to her father Donald Gray (Colin Douglas) in Kent has unexpected repercussions. Also starring Geoffrey Chater as Major Fancombe and Allan Cuthbertson as Captain Marsh.
Writer: Julia Jones. **Director:** Peter Cregeen. **Producer:** Bernard Krichefski.

....

Napoleon and Love — 4 wks

Thames, drama

This series by Philip Mackie was about the women in the life of Napoleon Bonaparte. Starring Ian Holm as Napoleon and Billie Whitelaw as Josephine. Also starring Maxine Audley, Stephanie Beacham, Peter Bowles, Karen Dotrice, Janina Faye, Ronald Hines, Peter Jeffrey, T. P. McKenna, Christopher Neame, Nicola Pagett, Diana Quick, and Edward de Souza.

| 1974 | 7.4 | Tue 5 Mar 9:00 p.m. | 10 | 4 wks |

In this first episode, the young Napoleon meets and marries Josephine but leaves for the Italian campaign two days later.
Designers: Patrick Downing and Graham Guest. **Producer:** Reginald Collin.

....

National Salute to the Falklands Task Force, A — 1 wk

LWT, entertainment

| 1982 | 11.3 | Sun 18 Jul 7:45 p.m. | 5 | 1 wk |

Live from the London Coliseum in the presence of HRH The Prince of Wales. Artists include Adam Ant, Michael Aspel, Ronnie Corbett, Leslie Crowther, Billy Dainty, Paul Daniels, Les Dawson, Wayne Eagling, Jill Gascoine, Anita Harris, Dickie Henderson, Danny La Rue, Vera Lynn, Virginia McKenna, Alfred Marks, Peter Morrison, Merle Park, Harry Secombe, Alvin Stardust, Tommy Steele, Jimmy Tarbuck and Kim Wilde.
Stage Director: Robert Nesbitt. **Television Director:** Alan Boyd. **Producer:** David Bell.

Nationwide — 8 wks

BBC, news

This early evening magazine show combined regional news with that of London. It was transmitted most nights of the week with a resident team of reporters including Michael Barrett, Frank Bough, Susanne Hall, Sue Lawley, Bob Wellings and Brian Widlake. A weekly consumer unit was presented by Valerie Singleton and Richard Stilgoe and sport was previewed on Friday evenings by Jimmy Hill, Peter O'Sullevan and others.

| 1975 | 8.2 | Tue 27 May 6:00 p.m. | 7 | 3 wks |

A special featuring a debate on the Common Market referendum.
Editors: Stuart Wilkinson and John Gau.

| 1979 | 19.1 | Wed 17 Oct 6:20 p.m. | 3 | 5 wks |

A special week of programmes from Belfast is presented by Frank Bough, Barry Cowan and Sue Lawley. Glyn Worsnip explores The Ulster Way, a 450-mile footpath.
Editor: Hugh Williams.

....

Nationwide Jubilee Fair — 1 wk

BBC, news

| 1977 | 5.9 | Tue 7 Jun 12:55 p.m. | 18 | 1 wk |

Twenty-five years of Her Majesty The Queen's reign are celebrated at Edinburgh Castle, Chepstow Castle and Buckingham Palace. At 1:15 p.m. members of the Royal Family enter the Great Hall of the Guildhall in London for lunch.
Executive Producer: Antony Craxton.

....

Nationwide Special — 1 wk

BBC, news

| 1981 | 11.2 | Wed 29 Jul 3:30 p.m. | 8 | 1 wk |

On the wedding day of HRH The Prince of Wales and Lady Diana Spencer the NATIONWIDE team presents live coverage. As the bride and bridegroom leave Buckingham Palace in an open carriage for Waterloo Station at the start of their honeymoon, reporters Frank Bough, Richard Kershaw, Sue Lawley and Hugh Scully set the scene. There are also contributions from Arthur Askey, the band of the Welsh Guards, Joe Loss and his orchestra, and the St Pauls choir.
Director: Victor Melleney. **Producers:** John Beveridge and Ian Squires. **Editor:** Hugh Williams.

....

Nature Watch — 15 wks

ATV, documentary

This series was about ordinary people who fell in love with the wonders of nature. Julian Pettifer was the reporter.

1981	13.1	Mon 9 Mar 7:00 p.m.	13	7 wks

Densey Clyne is an Australian housewife turned insect photographer.
Camera: Peter Greenhalgh. **Producer:** Colin Luke.

1982	14.2	Mon 1 Mar 7:00 p.m.	6	8 wks

Ornithologist Carl Jones raises Mauritian kestrel chicks. The species faces extinction.
Camera: Noel Smart. **Producer:** Robin Brown.

Nearest and Dearest — 51 wks

Granada, situation comedy

Brother and sister Eli and Nellie Pledge (Jimmy Jewel and Hylda Baker) ran a Lancashire pickle factory. The series, created by Vince Powell and Harry Driver, also starred Joe Gladwyn as Stan, Madge Hindle as Lily and Edward Malin as Walter.
Producers included Peter Eckersley (1968–69) and Bill Podmore (1970–75).

1968	5.8	Thu 5 Sep 8:00 p.m.	2	6 wks

'Take a Letter'
Eli decides he needs a secretary to help him with the annual reports.
Writers: Tom Brennand and Roy Bottomley. **Director:** June Howson.

1969	7.5	Thu 23 Oct 9:00 p.m.	2	11 wks

'Get Up Them Stairs'
Walter and Lily, the Cary Grant and Ingrid Bergman of Colne, have been together for twenty-four years. It has been one long blissful honeymoon – or so it seems until Lily admits all is not a bed of roses. Then Nellie and Eli become marriage breakers and makers.
Writer: John Stevenson. **Director:** Bill Podmore.

1970	7.6	Thu 24 Dec 7:00 p.m.	4	11 wks

'Compliments of the Season'
It's Christmas and the loved ones are all gathered together – but when they're not much wanted and can't be got rid of, the goodwill soon evaporates.
Writer: John Stevenson.

1971	8.5	Thu 11 Feb 9:00 p.m.	1	8 wks

'X Marks the Spot'
The new works manager Major Lovelace (William Kendall) arrives on the scene. He is a retired army officer. Eli's war record is a closed book and he intends to keep it that way.
Writers: Tom Brennand and Roy Bottomley.

1972	7.2	Thu 1 Jun 9:00 p.m.	1	10 wks

'For Better, For Worse'
Both Nellie and Eli have met someone of the opposite sex and they hear wedding bells – albeit only in the very far distance.
Writer: John Stevenson.

1973	7.6	Thu 11 Jan 8:45 p.m.	4	5 wks

'The French Disconnection'
A Frenchman wishes to market the Pledges' gherkins in France. As Nellie and Eli fly off to Paris they are accused of smuggling drugs inside jars of pickles.
Writer: John Stevenson.

Nearest and Dearest — 1 wk

Presented by ITV, film

1978	12.9	Sun 9 Apr 7:45 p.m.	20	1 wk

Feature film version in which Eli returns after fifteen years to attend his father's funeral. He and his sister Nellie find themselves the owners of the pickle factory.
Director: John Robins.

Needlematch — 3 wks

AR, game show

The pick of new British record releases were pitted against those from the USA.

1962	3.8	Fri 15 Jun 7:00 p.m.	19	3 wks

Referee Keith Fordyce invites Oliver Reed to promote the British releases and David Gell the American releases before an international jury.
Choreographer: Malcolm Clare. **Producer:** John P. Hamilton.

Neighbours — 209 wks

Australia presented by BBC, soap

The dramas of middle-class Australian life made stars of Jason Donovan (Scott) and Kylie Minogue (Charlene). Other performers with popular characters included Anne Charleston (Madge), Alan Dale (Jim Robinson), Ian Smith (Harold Bishop) and Vivean Jones (Mrs Mangel).

1988	18.9	Wed–Fri 28–30 Dec 1:15/5:35 p.m.	3	52 wks

These episodes were listed together in the ratings.
Daphne Clarke (Elaine Smith) finds unexpected problems with motherhood. Henry Ramsey (Craig McLachlan) comes to terms with his relationship with Jane Harris (Annie Jones). Paul Robinson (Stefan Dennis) begins to doubt the loyalty of Gail Robinson (Fiona Corke).

1989	20.1	Mon–Fri 3–7 Apr 1:15/5:35 p.m.	1	53 wks

These episodes were listed together in the ratings.
There's a personal tragedy for Paul and Gail. Charlene meets a Romeo (Nick Carrafa) and takes an instant dislike to her new boss.

N

Jimmy Jewel and Hylda Baker savour their pickle products in **Nearest and Dearest**.

| **1990** | **19.7** | **Mon 1 Jan 1:30/5:20 p.m.**
Tue–Fri 2–5 Jan 1:30/5:35 p.m. | **2** | **53 wks** |

These episodes were listed together in the ratings.
Harold becomes a hero as the search begins to find the cause of a fire. Nick Page (Mark Stevens) is shunned on Ramsay Street. Mike Young (Guy Dey) hopes he can get back with Bronwyn Davies (Rachel Friend).

| **1991** | **18.3** | **Mon–Fri 7–11 Jan 1:30/5:35 p.m.** | **4** | **51 wks** |

These episodes were listed together in the ratings.
Todd and Melissa (Kristian Schmid and Jade Amenta) exchange farewell presents. Matt (Ashley Paske) has his feelings hurt by Bronwyn. Toby Mangel (Finn Greentree Keene) is taken to a haunted house.

....

Nesbitts are Coming, The | 3 wks

YTV, situation comedy

This comedy series by Dick Sharples with music by Laurie Holloway concerned a family of itinerant petty crooks and their battles with the law. Maggie Jones and Clive Swift starred as Mr and Mrs Nesbitt with Deirdre Costello as Marlene, John Price as Len and Christian Rodska as Tom. Ken Jones played Detective Sergeant Nixon and Tony Melody was Station Sergeant Machin.

| **1980** | **13.6** | **Thu 17 Apr 9:00 p.m.** | **11** | **3 wks** |

'Another Town, Another Place'
The least lovable family since the Borgias arrive in town and the local crime statistics go shooting through the roof. There is no rest for the officers of Viaduct Police Station.
Producer: Ronnie Baxter.

....

Never a Cross Word | 1 wk

LWT, situation comedy

Paul Daneman and Nyree Dawn Porter starred as Ronald and Deirdre Baldock, a young married couple living in the London suburbs. Ronald found himself downgraded in his firm's reorganization and, encouraged by Deirdre, resigned. She became the breadwinner, opening up a battle of the sexes.

| **1968** | **6.0** | **Fri 1 Nov 8:30 p.m.** | **14** | **1 wk** |

'Defeat of the Baldocks'
Ronald is informed by his boss that he is no longer required in his present position and that he is to be demoted and receive a lower salary. Guest star: Barbara Windsor.
Writer: Donald Churchill. **Producer:** Stuart Allen.

Never Mind the Quality, Feel the Width | 27 wks

Thames, situation comedy

Vince Powell and Harry Driver created this series about ethnic contrasts, Jewish coat-maker Manny Cohen (John Bluthal) and Irish trouser-maker Patrick Kelly (Joe Lynch). Cohen saw Kelly as a bigoted Catholic and Kelly considered Cohen an ignorant heathen.
Producers: included Ronnie Baxter (1968–70).

| **1968** | **6.4** | **Tue 17 Sep 8:45 p.m.** | **3** | **6 wks** |

'Hello Mother, Hello Father'
Manny discovers that the sins of the child are visited on the parents.

| **1969** | **6.3** | **Thu 21 Aug 9:00 p.m.** | **6** | **6 wks** |

'Old Soldiers Never Die'
Cohen and Kelly start a boasting match on patriotism. Kelly is open-mouthed when Cohen produces a telegram from Moishe Dayan calling him to Israel.

| **1970** | **6.8** | **Thu 9 Jul 9:00 p.m.** | **2** | **5 wks** |

'New Worlds for All'
Manny and Patrick offer the business for sale as a going concern as they plan to emigrate to Australia. With Dick Bentley, Roy Marsden and Bernard Spear.

| **1971** | **7.1** | **Tue 14 Sep 8:30 p.m.** | **2** | **10 wks** |

'Mix Me a Marriage'
All tailoring comes to a halt when Patrick discovers a baby on the doorstep.
Producer: Stuart Allen.

....

Never Mind the Quality, Feel the Width | 1 wk

Thames, film

| **1978** | **11.2** | **Thu 27 Jul 7:45 p.m.** | **4** | **1 wk** |

Feature film version in which Manny and Patrick have a major quarrel after the latter takes a day off to attend a funeral which culminates in a drunken wake.
Director: Ronnie Baxter.

....

Never Say Die | 6 wks

YTV, situation comedy

Created and written by Peter Tinniswood, this series was set in the Emmott Robinson Ward of the Victoria Memorial Hospital, somewhere in Yorkshire (the names of the characters suggest Hebden Bridge). The patients, not there of their own choosing, found they could rarely decide anything. The inmates were Mr Hebden (Reginald Marsh), Mr Oliphant (Patrick Newell), Mr Finucane (Noel Purcell), Mr Bridge (Larry Noble), Mr Corker (Teddy Green) and Mr Albert (Wilfrid Brambell). The staff included Sister Ringstead (Ken Parry), Poniatowski (Hugh Walters) and Nurse Whitethroat (Mary Healey).

| 1970 | 6.0 | Tue 8 Sep 8:25 p.m. | 5 | 6 wks |

'The Gamblers'
The Irish love a gamble and Mr Finucane is no exception. But sedate Mr Bridge has other ideas.
Producer: John Duncan.

| Never Say Never Again | | | | 2 wks |

Presented by ITV, film

| 1987 | 15.0 | Sun 27 Sep 7:45 p.m. | 3 | 1 wk |

Sean Connery returns as James Bond and goes to the Bahamas and the South of France in pursuit of Blofeld (Max Von Sydow), who plans to hold the world to ransom by nuclear terrorism. Also starring Rowan Atkinson, Kim Basinger, Klaus Maria Brandauer, Barbara Carrera, Edward Fox and Alec McCowen.
Director: Irvin Kershner.

| 1988 | 13.4 | Mon 29 Aug 8:00 p.m. | 5 | 1 wk |

Repeat showing of the above film.

| Never the Twain | | | | 43 wks |

Thames, situation comedy

This series created by Johnnie Mortimer dealt with feuding antique dealers Simon Peel (Donald Sinden) and Oliver Smallbridge (Windsor Davies). They failed to patch up their differences even when their children David Peel and Lyn Smallbridge (Robin Kermode and Julia Watson) fell in love, married and subsequently gave them a grandchild.
Producers included Peter Frazer-Jones (1981–87) and Anthony Parker (1988, 1990–91).

| 1981 | 15.1 | Mon 19 Oct 8:00 p.m. | 3 | 6 wks |

'Father of the Groom'
As the wedding day of their children looms, Simon and Oliver try to patch up their differences at a dinner party. Guest star: Honor Blackman.
Writer: Johnnie Mortimer.

| 1982 | 11.7 | Tue 12 Oct 8:00 p.m. | 6 | 6 wks |

'The More We Are Together'
Simon and Oliver prepare to bury the hatchet – in each other!
Writer: Johnnie Mortimer.

| 1983 | 13.9 | Mon 14 Nov 8:00 p.m. | 4 | 6 wks |

'Not on the Same Wavelength'
Simon and Oliver agree to be interviewed on local radio.
Writer: Dick Hills.

| 1984 | 13.7 | Thu 13 Dec 8:30 p.m. | 11 | 3 wks |

'Come Fly with Me'
Simon and Oliver buy 'bucket shop' tickets to visit their children in Canada.
Writer: John Kane. **Director:** Robert Reed.

| 1985 | 10.9 | Tue 16 Jul 7:30 p.m. | 8 | 5 wks |

'As Young as You Feel'
Once again Oliver and Simon fight over Veronica (Honor Blackman). (Repeat.)
Writer: Johnnie Mortimer.

| 1986 | 13.8 | Wed 8 Jan 8:30 p.m. | 10 | 7 wks |

'In Whom We Tryst'
Simon and Oliver's rivalry deepens.
Writer: John Kane. **Director:** Robert Reed.

| 1987 | 13.4 | Thu 15 Jan 8:00 p.m. | 16 | 3 wks |

'Feed a Cold'
Simon is confined to bed and Oliver offers to nurse him. His bedside manner leaves a little to be desired.
Writer: Vince Powell. **Director:** Robert Reed.

| 1988 | 11.9 | Mon 21 Nov 8:00 p.m. | 16 | 3 wks |

'Moving On'
Simon and Oliver worry when Lyn and David suggest they may be about to move again.
Writer: Johnnie Mortimer. **Director:** Douglas Argent.

| 1990 | 10.7 | Wed 10 Oct 7:00 p.m. | 15 | 2 wks |

'A Car by any Other Name'
A ride in the Bentley owned by the Vicar (Jasper Jacob) turns into a disaster.
Writer: Vince Powell. **Director:** Nick Hurran.

| 1991 | 10.9 | Wed 9 Oct 7:00 p.m. | 19 | 2 wks |

'The First in the Queue'
Hoping for a bargain, Simon sleeps out on the street.
Writer: Vince Powell.

| New Ark, The | | | | 1 wk |

Anglia, documentary

| 1962 | 4.8 | Mon 24 Dec 6:30 p.m. | 16 | 1 wk |

HRH The Duke of Edinburgh KG introduces this film which looks at the work being undertaken by the World Wildlife Fund in Africa as it fights to save many species of animal from extinction. Peter Scott narrates.
Writer: Colin Willock. **Producer:** Stanley Joseph.

2

3

1 *James Rockford (James Garner) gives his father Joseph (Noah Beery Jr) an earful in **The Rockford Files**.*

2 ***Rawhide** starring Clint Eastwood was the western with most weeks at Number One.*

3 ***Wagon Train** starring Ward Bond had four separate runs at Number One in 1960.*

4 *In **Lace**, Phoebe Cates (front) uttered the immortal words 'Which one of you bitches is my mother?'*

5 *David Janssen embraces Susan Oliver but keeps one eye open for the one-armed man in **The Fugitive**.*

6 *David Banner (Bill Bixby) seems rather surprised to meet his alter ego The **Incredible Hulk** (Lou Ferrigno).*

New Assistant, The   1 wk

ATV, drama

| 1967 | 4.7 | Thu 29 Jun 9:40 p.m. | 12 | 1 wk |

Single drama by Ronald Harwood. Carvel (Ronald Fraser) applies for a job in a hotel to be near his sick wife (Rachel Kempson). It transpires he may not be telling the truth.
Designer: Peter Roden. **Director:** John Nelson Burton. **Producer:** Cecil Clarke.

....

New Avengers, The   19 wks

ATV, drama

In this series of 26 programmes only John Steed (Patrick Macnee) remained from THE AVENGERS. He was retained as a senior figure, leaving most of the action to his new young assistants, Mike Gambit (Gareth Hunt), a former army major in the Parachute Regiment, and Purdey (Joanna Lumley), a former ballerina trained in the martial art of Panache. Created and produced by Albert Fennell and Brian Clemens.

| 1976 | 7.5 | Fri 19 Nov 8:00 p.m. | 8 | 9 wks |

'Cat Amongst the Pigeons' by Dennis Spooner.
Steed, Gambit and Purdey are sent running for cover – by a bird!
Director: John Hough.

| 977 | 14.1 | Thu 24 Nov 8:00 p.m. | 4 | 10 wks |

'Emily' by Dennis Spooner.
Steed, Purdey and Gambit are on the trail of The Fox, an arch-villain who will use any means to stop them.
Director: Don Thompson.

....

New Christy Minstrels, The   2 wks

Southern, music

This series of musical shows featured American folk singers who based their output and name on a group formed in 1842 by Edwin P. Christy. Although none of the New Christy Minstrels' records made the British charts, a solo single by lead singer Barry McGuire, 'Eve of Destruction', made number 3 in 1965.

| 1965 | 6.0 | Wed 7 Apr 9:10 p.m. | 14 | 2 wks |

....

New Faces   48 wks

ATV (1973–77) and Central (1986–88), entertainment

In this talent show competitors suffered the indignity of having their performance criticized by an often hostile panel. Regular panellists included Clifford Davis, Tony Hatch, Martin Jackson, Nina Myskow

and John Smith. The series was hosted originally by Derek Hobson and then by one-time winner Marti Caine. The artists were accompanied by the Johnny Patrick orchestra (1973–77) and the Harry Rabinowitz orchestra (1986–88).
Directors included Paul Stewart Laing (1973–74), John Pullen (1975–76), and Peter Harris (1986–88). **Producers** included Les Cocks (1973–76) and Richard Holloway (1986–88).

| 1973 | 5.6 | Sat 29 Dec 5:20 p.m. | 14 | 1 wk |

Thirteen winning acts are featured. Tonight's winner will appear on tomorrow night's SUNDAY NIGHT AT THE LONDON PALLADIUM.

| 1974 | 5.8 | Sat 27 Apr 5:20 p.m. | 18 | 2 wks |

Seven acts new to television are featured.

| 1975 | 6.9 | Sat 8 Mar 5:20 p.m. | 18 | 5 wks |

Nicky Martin introduces the all winners show.

| 1976 | 7.4 | Sat 24 Jan 5:30 p.m. | 4 | 27 wks |
| 1977 | 7.8 | Sat 2 Apr 7:00 p.m. | 12 | 3 wks |

Director: Hector Stewart. **Producer:** Albert Stevenson.

| 1986 | 13.5 | Sat 13 Dec 7:45 p.m. | 4 | 6 wks |

The final, from the Birmingham Hippodrome.

| 1987 | 12.9 | Sat 28 Nov 9:05 p.m. | 11 | 3 wks |

The final, from the Birmingham Hippodrome.

| 1988 | 13.6 | Sat 3 Dec 7:50 p.m. | 9 | 1 wk |

The final, from the Birmingham Hippodrome.

....

New Life, A   1 wk

Presented by BBC, film

| 1991 | 9.2 | Sun 11 Aug 8:35 p.m. | 20 | 1 wk |

Alan Alda wrote, directed and stars in this story of a former husband and wife who find themselves single again. Ann-Margret and John Shea also star.

....

New London Palladium Show, The   10 wks

ATV, entertainment

SUNDAY NIGHT AT THE LONDON PALLADIUM under a new name, hosted by Jimmy Tarbuck.

| 1965 | 7.0 | Sun 26 Sep 7:25 p.m. | 8 | 10 wks |

Starring Peter Cook and Dudley Moore, and Peter, Paul and Mary. With Edmund Hockridge, Susan Lane and the Jack Parnell orchestra.
Producer: Colin Clews.

New Lucy Show, The — 1 wk

USA presented by BBC, situation comedy

Lucille Ball starred as Lucy Carmichael with Gale Gordon as Mr Mooney, her boss.

1968	5.4	Sat 26 Oct 6:00 p.m.	20	1 wk

'Lucy the Star Maker'
Lucy thinks she has discovered a brand new star when she comes across singer Frankie Avalon.

New Scotland Yard — 8 wks

LWT, drama

This police series starred John Woodvine as Chief Superintendent Kingdom and John Carlisle as Detective Sergeant Ward.
Producer: Jack Williams. **Executive Producer:** Rex Firkin.

1972	6.6	Fri 20 Oct 9:00 p.m.	11	5 wks

'A Case of Prejudice' by Stuart Douglass.
Kingdom and Ward investigate a murder which has taken place in a theatre club with predominantly black members.
Designer: Roger Hall.

1973	6.1	Sat 15 Sep 9:40 p.m.	13	1 wk

'Pier' by P. J. Hammond.
Kingdom and his wife Angela (Sally Home) have a marriage crisis. She goes away to the seaside for a few days to think. Two days later Kingdom is told to investigate murder – in Margate.
Designer: Rodney Cammish. **Director:** Cyril Coke.

1974	6.3	Sat 27 Apr 8:30 p.m.	19	2 wks

'Death By Misadventure' by Peter Wildeblood.
Detective Sergeant Dexter (Clive Francis) is investigating a burglary and finds a valuable piece of Chinese porcelain is missing. Shortly afterwards, a burglar is found dead.
Designer: Barbara Bates. **Director:** Derrick Goodwin.

Newcomers, The — 3 wks

BBC, soap

In this series devised by Colin Morris, the Cooper family left London for the rural delights of a farm in Angleton. They were Ellis and Vivienne (Alan Browning and Maggie Fitzgibbon), their sons Lance and Philip (Raymond Hunt and Jeremy Bulloch) and Vivienne's mother, Gran Hamilton (Gladys Henson).

1967	6.0	Thu 25 May 7:20 p.m.	11	1 wk

Jeff and Janet Langley (Michael Collins and Sandra Payne) have problems on their farm. Peter and Freda Reilly (John Stratton and Wendy McClure) discuss their future.
Writer: Barry Letts. **Director:** Ronald Wilson. **Producer:** Bill Sellars.

1968	5.8	Thu 31 Oct 7:05 p.m.	17	2 wks

Vivienne makes a decision about her future while Sydney Huxley (Anthony Verner) and Lance investigate a ruined church.
Writer: Bob Stuart. **Director:** Philip Dale. **Producer:** Bill Sellars.

News — 381 wks

BBC, news

1968	4.6	Thu 8 Aug 8:50 p.m.	16	1 wk

ITV has been hit by a strike by the ACTT, the technician's union, since Friday. London's National Heart Hospital confirms that a pig's heart has been used in a failed attempt to save the life of a dying man. Having won the Republican nomination, Richard Nixon names the relatively unknown Spiro Agnew as his running mate. The BBC announces the appointment of Charles Curran to take over from Sir Hugh Greene as Director General. Shirley Bassey announces she will marry Sergio Novak on Monday.

1970	7.3	Tue 29 Dec 9:00 p.m.	4	5 wks

Prolonged blizzards hit the south, and the weathermen warn of a vast snowbelt heading for Britain from Europe. Hundreds of impatient railway travellers risked their lives today as they abandoned their immobile train near Balham and walked along electrified lines.

1971	7.1	Sat 18 Dec 9:59 p.m.	8	12 wks

A hurricane appears to be heading for the South of England. Tension is building in Pakistan, where President Khan is expected to resign soon.

1972	7.5	Wed 18 Oct 9:00 p.m.	2	29 wks

The threat of a go-slow at a power station from tomorrow could black out the whole of Britain. With Northern Ireland on the very brink of civil war, the UDA takes one step back after senior officers meet with British officers to work out a format to unite against the IRA.

1973	7.3	Thu 13 Dec 9:00 p.m.	3	21 wks

An extended edition in which Prime Minister Edward Heath outlines plans for the three day working week following the miners' final rejection of the Coal Board's 16½ per cent pay offer. From 1 January 1974 firms will only be allowed electricity for three days a week. They can continue to trade if they can manage without electric light and heating. From Monday 17 December television will close down at 10:30 p.m. each night.

1974	7.4	Tue 31 Dec 10:15 p.m.	2	21 wks

The jury is out considering its verdicts in the Watergate trials of Ehrlichman, Haldeman, Mitchell and others. Twelve skiers have been killed in an avalanche in the Austrian Alps.

| 1975 | 7.0 | Mon 26 May 9:00 p.m. | 10 | 5 wks |

ITV is off the air today after bosses locked out their employees when they tried to return to work after an ACTT claim which the companies consider unjustified.

This afternoon stuntman Evel Knievel was badly hurt and taken to hospital after attempting to jump over thirteen double decker buses on a motorbike at Wembley Stadium.

| 1976 | 8.2 | Mon 15 Nov 9:00 p.m. | 2 | 26 wks |

THE NINE O'CLOCK NEWS is transmitted between portions of THE ROYAL VARIETY PERFORMANCE, which is being broadcast live for the first time.

Tory MP Ian Sproat names ten Labour MPs in an attack on the 'crypto-Communists' within the Labour party. Three contestants withdraw from the MISS WORLD contest and ten more threaten to quit over the selection of two girls from South Africa, one white, the other black.

| 1977 | 13.2 | Wed 31 Aug 9:00 p.m. | 6 | 2 wks |

George Ward, boss of the Grunwick film processing plant, vows to fight on defiantly, rejecting the recommendations of the Scarman inquiry into the year-long dispute at the factory with the union APEX.

| 1978 | 16.0 | Wed 15 Nov 9:00 p.m. | 8 | 3 wks |

In the wake of yesterday's rejection by the TUC of Chancellor Denis Healey's pact, Tom Jackson of the Post Office workers says he will be putting a 25 per cent claim, adding 'If there's going to be a rat race, we want part of it.' Tommy Docherty's libel case against Granada TV and footballer Willie Morgan is thrown out after Docherty admitted telling a pack of lies to the jury. Costs of £30,000 are awarded against him.

| 1979 | 20.3 | Thu 4 Oct 9:00 p.m. | 2 | 30 wks |

Queens Park Rangers' manager Tommy Docherty was arrested in London and held all day today at a police station in Derby. He was released after nine hours with police saying a report is to be sent to the Director of Public Prosecutions. The investigation centres on the finances of his old club, Derby County.

| 1980 | 14.5 | Wed 17 Dec 9:00 p.m. | 2 | 34 wks |

After 52 days, two of the 37 hunger strikers in the Maze prison are near death. Twenty-six-year-old Sean McKenna is given the last rites. Mrs Thatcher refuses to intervene.

| 1981 | 14.7 | Wed 17 Jan 9:00 p.m. | 5 | 21 wks |

The Cabinet today gave the go ahead for British Rail's £750 million electrification programme. Anthony Wedgwood Benn left hospital after 13 days suffering from polyneuritis vowing to continue his fight for the deputy leadership of the Labour Party.

| 1982 | 14.1 | Thu 27 May 9:00 p.m. | 2 | 24 wks |

Thousands of British troops are sweeping east and south across the Falkland Islands after a six-day build-up of supplies and equipment.

Mrs Thatcher told MPs: 'We have now gone into the islands to do what I believe the islanders wish – to repossess them.'

| 1983 | 11.2 | Mon 3 Jan 5:45 p.m. | 20 | 1 wk |

A row has blown up over a proposal by the Manpower Services Commission to pay young offenders up to £60 per week to repair damage caused by vandalism. Tributes continue to be paid to comedian Dick Emery, who died in King's College hospital last night.

| 1985 | 14.7 | Fri 29 Feb 9:00 p.m. | 3 | 14 wks |

The year-long miners' strike is over and men will return to work on Tuesday. A bloodbath in Ulster is feared as Loyalist terrorists seek reprisals for last night's IRA mortar attack on Newry police station in which nine officers were killed.

| 1986 | 12.4 | Wed 4 Jun 9:00 p.m. | 16 | 11 wks |

British soccer fans were injured today in Mexico City as the World Cup fiesta turned into a riot following Mexico's victory over Belgium in their opening game of the tournament. At home, Joan Collins was besieged by photographers at Royal Ascot.

| 1987 | 13.6 | Sun 6 Dec 9:05 p.m. | 7 | 30 wks |

There have been ugly scenes in Moscow on the eve of President Gorbachev's summit with Mrs Thatcher. KGB men have beaten up scores of Jewish dissidents.

| 1988 | 17.3 | Thu 24 Nov 9:00 p.m. | 5 | 47 wks |

The worst riot scenes in Europe for twenty years happened within sight of the Palace of Westminster. After four hours of confrontation police charged ten thousand students protesting against plans to introduce student loans.

| 1989 | 8.1 | Sat 28 Oct 9:00 p.m. | 19 | 21 wks |

Mrs Thatcher faces the biggest crisis of her political career following the resignation of Chancellor Nigel Lawson after his quarrel with her economic advisor Professor Alan Walters, who also resigned today. John Major is appointed as the new Chancellor. Both Sir Geoffrey Howe and Michael Heseltine have pledged their support.

| 1990 | 16.6 | Tue 25 Dec 9:35 p.m. | 7 | 21 wks |

Her Majesty The Queen today denounced Saddam Hussein and expressed her deep anxiety about the threat of war in the Gulf.

| 1991 | 8.5 | Sun 30 Jun 9:15 p.m. | 18 | 2 wks |

A mobilization of troops is underway in Yugoslavia as fears grow that the federal army is poised to crush the resistance of Slovenia. At home, 114 years of Wimbledon tradition were broken today when the turnstiles opened on the middle Sunday of the championships, usually a rest day for the players, on a first come, first served basis. The organizers had been forced into this plan of action as a result of the delays caused by rain. A carnival atmosphere ensued amid calls for the event to be 're-staged' the following year.

News				1463 wks

ITN, news

1967	7.6	Thu 23 Nov 10:00 p.m.	4	94 wks

President Nasser of Egypt refuses to recognize the State of Israel and prevents her use of the Suez Canal. Has Mr Callaghan made a bid for the leadership of the Labour Party in the wake of last weekend's crisis, which forced a devaluation of the pound from $2.80 to $2.40, and saw the bank base rate raised from 6½ to 8 per cent? Should Harold Wilson resign?

1968	4.6	Fri 12 Apr 10:00 p.m.	16	161 wks

Details have been leaked on this Good Friday that Chancellor Roy Jenkins has approved measures that will mean massive increases in the price of public licenses for sport, music and entertainments.

If your car is towed away by the police it will now cost £4.10s to recover it instead of £2. Judy Garland has charged Thomas Green, the man she was planning to marry, with stealing two rings worth a total of £45,000.

1969	7.7	Tue 18 Feb 10:00 p.m.	1	192 wks

Four Arab terrorists, one female, machine-gunned an Israeli airliner today at Zurich airport wounding six people. A fierce gun battle followed during which airport police killed one of the terrorists and arrested the other three. Also in the news, Lulu and Maurice Gibb marry at St James's Parish Church in Gerrard's Cross.

1970	8.7	Wed 4 Mar 10:00 p.m.	1	159 wks

Raging blizzards bring the South of England to a halt. 700 miners are trapped underground by power cuts and 2000 people are stranded on trains. Euston Station becomes a shelter.

1971	8.0	Wed 3 Feb 10:00 p.m.	2	153 wks

The cabinet is locked in fierce battle over the future of Rolls Royce. More than one hundred Shell, BP and National garages are closed as a result of a strike by tanker drivers.

1972	8.1	Fri 24 Nov 10:00 p.m.	2	133 wks

A gunman holds a stewardess hostage on an airliner at Frankfurt airport, demanding the release of a Czechoslovakian hijacker. An Irish petrol bomb seriously injured three people when it went off in a crowded East End pub. A storm of controversy blew up over the decision by police not to prosecute Princess Anne for speeding on the M1.

1973	7.5	Wed 16 May 10:00 p.m.	2	122 wks

The Watergate hearings begin in the US Senate tomorrow.

1974	8.1	Fri 8 Mar 10:00 p.m.	2	62 wks

Just one week after the election of the new Labour government, the miners win their pay dispute and the three day working week comes to an end. Miners' leader Joe Gormley is triuimphant. The deposed

Miss World, Marjorie Wallace, flies home to the USA. She has been sacked by Eric and Julia Morley after her boyfriend Peter Revson, the racing driver and perfume heir, began to interfere in the business arrangements made by the Morleys. Kathy Anders from Rochdale is the new Miss World.

1975	8.3	Wed 29 Oct 10:00 p.m.	2	76 wks

At 9:25 this evening a bomb went off at the Trattoria Fiori restaurant in South Audley Street, London. Eleven people have been taken to hospital. The IRA is expected to claim responsibility for this outrage. It is twenty-six days since Dutch industrialist Dr Tiede Herrema was kidnapped by Eddie Gallagher and Marion Coyle, who are holding him at gunpoint in the Irish village of Monasterevin. It is hoped they will soon surrender and release their hostage.

1976	7.7	Sun 8 Aug 10:00 p.m.	1	33 wks

A nineteen-year-old soldier in Ulster has been killed by a booby-trapped bicycle. Thirty-four people are being held after a Saturday night battle in Guildford involving a motorcycle group known as The Twists. Fifty-one-year-old Charlie Drake announces he is to marry an eighteen-year-old chorus girl. Twenty-year-old Severiano Ballesteros wins the Dutch Open golf title, earning him £3750.

1977	12.7	Thu 1 Sep 10:00 p.m.	6	33 wks

Tory industry spokesman Sir Keith Joseph launches a savage attack on Lord Justice Scarman's report on the Grunwick affair, calling it 'slipshod, flawed and naive'.

1978	16.4	Fri 22 Dec 10:00 p.m.	2	12 wks

After the BBC strike yesterday spread to radio with a total shutdown for 16,000 workers, the dispute was resolved today with an agreement for a 12½ per cent pay rise. Both radio and television services will be restored tomorrow.

1979	15.5	Wed 21 Mar 10:00 p.m.	7	11 wks

Election fever grows as Prime Minister Callaghan plans to address the nation tomorrow. MPs speculate 26 April or 10 May may be the day of the poll.

1980	14.2	Wed 12 Mar 10:00 p.m.	6	13 wks

Talks break down between British Steel and the Steelworkers Union, whose leader Bill Sirs has led his supporters in an eleven week strike. The back-to-work campaign in defiance of the Union has provoked widespread violence. Steel boss Bob Scholey has said the final offer has been made.

1981	15.3	Thu 8 Jan 10:00 p.m.	7	12 wks

A terrorist bomb exploded without causing a single casualty at RAF Uxbridge on the outskirts of West London.

1982	15.1	Sun 25 Apr 8:45 p.m.	2	66 wks

The Royal Marines today retook South Georgia from the Argentine invaders who had held it for twenty-two days.

1983   **11.8**   **Sun 16 Jan 10:12 p.m.**   **15**   **1 wk**

Controversy rages over the shooting by police of film editor Stephen Waldorf, who was driving in his Mini in London during Friday's rush hour. Police mistook him for escaped prisoner David Martin. In another story, Mrs Thatcher returned from the Falklands to face a sterling crisis.

1984   **12.9**   **Tue 4 Dec 10:00 p.m.**   **18**   **3 wks**

A poison gas cloud has escaped from the Union Carbide chemical plant in the central Indian city of Bhopal. A thousand dead bodies fill the streets and thousands more people have lost their sight.

1985   **14.8**   **Mon–Fri 11–15 Feb 10:00 p.m.**   **9**   **21 wks**

These programmes were listed together in the ratings.
Clive Ponting has been acquitted in the Belgrano secrets trial. Leader of the Opposition Neil Kinnock has accused Mrs Thatcher of lying over her involvement to prosecute Ponting. Ian Botham has been fined £100 for the possession of cannabis.

1986   **12.4**   **Thu 9 Jan 10:00 p.m.**   **16**   **11 wks**

Michael Heseltine sensationally quit the Cabinet today accusing Mrs Thatcher of double-dealing and doctoring Cabinet records in order to get her own way over the Westland helicopter controversy.

1987   **13.4**   **Tue 13 Jan 10:00 p.m.**   **4**   **31 wks**

There have been deaths on the road and rail chaos as a Siberian winter grips Britain. Today's temperature did not rise above –4.4° C. Six hundred people were stranded on a train in Kent for 15 hours with neither heat nor light.

1988   **13.3**   **Sun 29 May 6:45 p.m.**   **6**   **20 wks**

Ronald Reagan today became the first American President to set foot in Russia when he arrived for the Moscow summit with Mr Gorbachev. At home, the first full ITV Telethon gets underway at 7:00 p.m. with Michael Aspel set to host 27 hours of non-stop fund-raising.

1989   **14.2**   **Thu 13 Apr 10:00 p.m.**   **6**   **22 wks**

The Princess of Wales stumbled backwards when a man lunged from the crowd and managed to touch her during a walkabout in Cramlington, Northumberland. The crisis of the marriage between The Princess Royal and Captain Mark Phillips deepened as the Queen's equerry, Commander Timothy Lawrence, accompanied Her Majesty to a charity premiere.

1990   **13.0**   **Sun 2 Dec 8:50 p.m.**   **11**   **15 wks**

Fears are growing that President Bush may be moving towards a deal with Iraq, although he still insists the Iraqis must withdraw from Kuwait.

1991   **16.0**   **Sun 7 Apr 8:50 p.m.**   **5**   **7 wks**

Half a million Kurdish refugees from Iraq head for the Iranian and Turkish borders. Public anger mounts as supplies are failing to reach the refugees. President Bush faces growing criticism for being away on a fishing and golfing holiday at this time. Meanwhile, firefighters today put out the first of 600 blazing oil wells in Kuwait.

News Report – The Embassy Siege   **1 wk**

ITN, news

1980   **11.1**   **Mon 5 May Evening**   **20**   **1 wk**

Several programmes were cancelled to allow live coverage as the SAS stormed the terrorist-occupied Iranian Embassy in London. The BBC also carried live coverage.

Next Voice You See, The   **1 wk**

ATV, drama

1975   **6.2**   **Sat 17 May 9:10 p.m.**   **20**   **1 wk**

Single drama written by Terence Feely from an original story by Brian Clemens. A voice at a party has special significance for blind pianist Stan (Bradford Dillman). It belongs to the man who blinded him and killed his wife.
Designer: Richard Lake. **Director:** Robert Tronson. **Producer:** Ian Fordyce.

Niagara   **1 wk**

Presented by ITV, film

1979   **13.4**   **Sun 29 Aug 7:55 p.m.**   **14**   **1 wk**

Marilyn Monroe stars as Rosie Loomis in the story of a faithless wife who plans to murder her husband at Niagara Falls.
Director: Henry Hathaway.

Nice to Have You Back   **1 wk**

AR, drama

1967   **6.0**   **Thu 26 Jan 9:40 p.m.**   **17**   **1 wk**

Play by Michael Winder starring Kenneth Haigh as Patterson, a British agent held prisoner in the East being released under an exchange agreement. He finds himself just as much a prisoner on release as he has to deal with questioning by his wife (Ann Lynn), an Embassy official (Paul Hardwick), the debriefing officer (Brian Wilde) and an unknown beautiful girl (Suzanne Neve).
Designer: Fred Pusey. **Director:** Christopher Hodson. **Executive Producer:** Peter Willes.

Nice to See You · 1 wk

Thames, entertainment

| 1981 | 14.1 | Mon 21 Dec 8:00 p.m. | 16 | 1 wk |

Bruce Forsyth stars in a special that uses one of his catchphrases as its title. Guests: Lionel Blair, Faith Brown, Marti Webb and the Peter Knight orchestra.
Producer: Keith Beckett.

....

Night of Nights · 1 wk

BBC, entertainment

| 1970 | 7.2 | Sun 22 Nov 8:15 p.m. | 13 | 1 wk |

From the Royal Festival Hall, London, Sir Noël Coward, Bob Hope and Frank Sinatra join forces in a unique gala performance for United World Colleges.
Musical Director: Bill Miller. **Television presentation:** Stanley Dorfman.

....

Night of 100 Stars · 1 wk

ITV, entertainment

| 1977 | 5.6 | Sun 5 Jun 8:00 p.m. | 20 | 1 wk |

A Jubilee Week presentation in the presence of HRH The Princess Alexandra from the Olivier Theatre for The Queen's Silver Jubilee. Stars include Patrick Allen, Moira Anderson, Kenny Ball, Amanda Barrie, Bernard Bresslaw, Jeremy Brett, Dora Bryan, Patrick Cargill, John Clements, John Dankworth, Les Dawson, Wayne Eagling, Geraint Evans, Frank Finlay, Liz Fraser, John Gielgud, Richard Goolden, Stephane Grappelli, Wendy Hiller, Rod Hull, Glenda Jackson, Jimmy Jewel, Penelope Keith, Felicity Kendall, Cleo Laine, Danny La Rue, Humphrey Lyttelton, Jessie Matthews, John Mills, Ron Moody, Kenneth More, Derek Nimmo, David Nixon, Merle Park, Nyree Dawn Porter, Denis Quilley, Beryl Reid, Brian Rix, Helen Ryan, Elaine Stritch, Richard Todd, John Williams, Kenneth Williams, Simon Williams, Barbara Windsor, Edward Woodward and the Jack Parnell orchestra.
Television presentation: Jon Scoffield.

....

Night of 100 Stars · 1 wk

USA presented by BBC, entertainment

| 1985 | 10.0 | Mon 27 May 9:40 p.m. | 16 | 1 wk |

From New York's Radio City Music Hall, Barry Norman sets the scene for an extravaganza that includes George Burns, Charles Bronson, Petula Clark, Joan Collins, Placido Domingo, Dick Van Dyke, Whoopi Goldberg, Dustin Hoffman, Lena Horne, the Pointer Sisters, Kenny Rogers, Mel Tormé, Robert Wagner and Raquel Welch.
Producer: Hildy Parks. **Executive Producer:** Alexander H. Cohen.

Night of 100 Stars · 1 wk

LWT, entertainment

| 1990 | 12.6 | Sat 1 Dec 7:30 p.m. | 14 | 1 wk |

The stars turn out in force to pay tribute to producer David Bell, who recently died. The event becomes a double tribute when Trevor Brown conducts the orchestra that was to have been led by Alyn Ainsworth, who has died after the show has been scheduled.
Stage Director: Norman Maen. **Television Director:** Alasdair Macmillan. **Producer:** John Kaye Cooper.

....

Night Out at the London Casino · 7 wks

Thames, entertainment

This series of variety shows was hosted by Tom O'Connor.

| 1977 | 14.4 | Wed 24 Aug 8:00 p.m. | 1 | 7 wks |

Guests: Champagne, Roger de Courcey, Dukes and Lee, and Tony Monopoly.
Producer: Dennis Kirkland.

....

Night Rider, The · 1 wk

Presented by ITV, film

| 1981 | 11.3 | Sat 19 Sep 9:15 p.m. | 16 | 1 wk |

A masked horseman returns to Virginia City to avenge the murders of his parents and sister, who were killed 15 years earlier. Starring Kim Cattrall, George Grizzard, Anthony Herrera, Percy Rodrigues, Pernell Roberts and David Selby.
Director: Hy Auerback.

....

Norman Wisdom starred in one of the hit editions of **Night Out at the London Casino**.

Night Spot — 2 wks

ATV, entertainment

This series was hosted by Canadian comedian Frank Berry with regular performers Pat O'Hare, Bill Pertwee and Norma Ronald.

1965	5.5	Wed 24 Mar 9:10 p.m.	18	2 wks

Guests: George Meaton and Susan Maughan.
Producer: Albert Locke.

Night They Raided Minsky's, The — 1 wk

Presented by BBC, film

1974	5.1	Thu 15 Aug 9:25 p.m.	20	1 wk

In 1925 Minsky's Burlesque on New York's lower East Side is under attack from both the Society for the Suppression of Vice and the police. Narrated by Rudy Vallee and starring Jason Robards with Harry Andrews, Britt Ekland, Denholm Elliott, Bert Lahr and Norman Wisdom.
Director: William Friedkin.

Night They Took Miss Beautiful Away, The — 1 wk

USA presented by ITV, film

1983	11.6	Sat 26 Mar 8:15 p.m.	11	1 wk

A plane is hijacked on its way to a beauty contest in the Bahamas. Starring Chuck Connors, Sheree North, Phil Silvers and Stella Stevens.
Director: Robert Michael Lewis.

Nightingale's Boys — 2 wks

Granada, drama

Bill Nightingale (Derek Farr) fought in the Spanish Civil War and had been a distinguished school teacher for more than thirty-five years. He attempted to meet up with members of his 'class' of 1949.

1975	7.0	Tue 18 Feb 9:00 p.m.	14	2 wks

'A.J.' by Alexander Baron.
'A.J.' was the nickname of Major Alistair James Cartwright (John Carson), who now meets up with Nightingale during leave.
Designer: Alan Price. **Director:** Roger Tucker. **Producer:** Brian Armstrong.

Nineteenth Hole, The — 2 wks

Central, situation comedy

This series by Johnny Speight starred Eric Sykes as secretary of Prince's Hill Golf Club.

1989	10.3	Mon 5 Jun 8:00 p.m.	13	2 wks

A joker denounces the club and its secretary from atop the flagpole outside the clubhouse.
Producer: William G. Stewart.

Nixon and the Astronauts — 1 wk

ITN, news

1969	4.8	Thu 24 Jul 10:00 p.m.	16	1 wk

Apollo 11 splashed down at 5:44 p.m. BST, thirteen miles off course, thirty seconds late and upside down. President Richard Nixon had flown out to greet them and was waiting on board the aircraft carrier Hornet. When Armstrong, Aldrin and Collins finally came on board, Nixon said 'You look great. This is the greatest week in the world since the creation.' The astronauts were then whisked away to spend three weeks in quarantine.

Nixon at Nine Five — 9 wks

BBC, entertainment

Series with David Nixon and guests.

1967	7.1	Thu 16 Feb 9:05 p.m.	7	9 wks

Guests: the Beverley Sisters with the Harry Rabinowitz orchestra.
Producer: Kenneth Carter.

No Hiding Place — 211 wks

AR, drama

This Scotland Yard mystery series began in 1959 and starred Raymond Francis as Detective Chief Superintendent Lockhart and Eric Lander as Detective Sergeant Baxter.

1960	7.2	Fri 21 Oct 9:35 p.m.	1	27 wks

'Fair Lady' by George Baxt.
Lockhart finds himself in Devon, where his wits are pitted against those of a female crime novelist.
Director: Christopher Hodson. **Producer:** Ray Dicks.

1961	7.7	Fri 17 Feb 9:35 p.m.	1	26 wks

'Man in the Dark' by Bill Strutton.
Lockhart hunts an escaped convict who has a fanatical belief in his own innocence. With guest stars Robert Brown and Paul Massie.
Director: Richard Gilbert. **Producer:** Ray Dicks.

1962	7.1	Tue 4 Sep 8:00 p.m.	3	31 wks

'A Cool Million' by John Kaiser.
Lockhart investigates a case of stolen diamonds.
Director: Mark Lawton. **Producer:** Jonathan Goodman.

1963	7.9	Mon 30 Dec 8:00 p.m.	2	35 wks

'Formula for Death' by Alex Murray.
The secret formula of a dangerous isotope has been leaked. It does not even have to be touched to cause illness.
Producer: Richard West.

1964	8.2	Mon 5 Oct 8:00 p.m.	1	27 wks

'Rogue's Gallery' by Nicholas Jones.
Lockhart and Detective Sergeant Russell (Johnny Briggs) investigate an art theft and a murder. They find a world of fakes, both paintings and people.
Producer: Geoffrey Hughes.

1965	8.5	Mon 22 Feb 8:00 p.m.	2	34 wks
		Mon 1 Mar 8:00 p.m.		

'Pom-Pom' by Jack Trevor Story.
Mr Peters (Jimmy Hanley) is the last person anyone would suspect of anything, but Lockhart is investigating a murder and no one is above suspicion.
Producer: Geoffrey Hughes.

'Bear with a Sore Head' by Martin Worth.
Bill Parkes (Jeffrey Wickham) is a killer on the run. Lockhart leads a nationwide search with a teddy bear as the only clue.
Producer: Ian Fordyce.

These two programmes achieved the same viewing figure and chart position.

1966	8.5	Wed 11 May 8:00 p.m.	1	16 wks

'Ask Me If I Killed Her' by Douglas Livingstone.
A girl's life is at risk if Lockhart makes the wrong decision about whether a man is a murderer or not.
Director: Marc Miller. **Producer:** Geoffrey Hughes.

1967	7.8	Mon 13 Mar 9:10 p.m.	2	15 wks

'It's All Happening' by Alan Falconer and Colin Holder.
Detective Sergeant Gregg (Sean Caffrey) gets himself into a corner trying to help Lockhart prove another policeman is in the wrong.
Director: Marc Miller. **Producer:** Michael Currer-Briggs.

No, Honestly | 9 wks

LWT, situation comedy

This series by Terence Brady and Charlotte Bingham starred John Alderton and Pauline Collins as CD and Clara. In a television innovation, characters would at times speak directly to the camera.

1974	8.4	Sun 17 Nov 9:45 p.m.	1	8 wks

'Now We Are Married'
Just married, CD and Clara are off on honeymoon, but she takes all steps possible to disguise the fact that they are a honeymoon couple.
Director: Bill Turner. **Producer:** Humphrey Barclay.

1975	6.5	Sun 5 Jan 9:45 p.m.	17	1 wk

'Surprise, Surprise'
It's CD and Clara's first wedding anniversary and each is determined to surprise the other.
Director: David Askey. **Producer:** Humphrey Barclay.

No Job for a Lady | 1 wk

Thames, situation comedy

This series by Alex Shearer starred Penelope Keith as Labour backbench MP Jean Price. Her political opponent Godfrey was played by George Baker.

1990	14.4	Wed 7 Feb 8:00 p.m.	9	1 wk

'Who Goes Home'
Newly elected Jean is appalled by the terrible facilities at Westminster and the uncivilized working hours.
Producer: John Howard Davies.

No Place Like Home | 4 wks

BBC, situation comedy

This series by John Watkins starred William Gaunt and Patricia Garwood as Arthur and Beryl Crabtree, parents under siege by their grown-up children, Nigel and his wife Tracy (Martin Clunes and Dee Sadler) and bachelor Paul (Stephen Watson). Friends and neighbours Vera and Trevor Botting were portrayed by Marcia Warren and Michael Sharvell-Martin.
Producer: Robin Nash.

1986	9.5	Fri 8 Aug 7:40 p.m.	10	3 wks

'Don't Tell Mother'
Arthur finally finds an ally when Beryl's mother Lillian (Jean Heywood) comes to stay. (Repeat.)

1988	9.3	Fri 29 Jul 7:40 p.m.	15	1 wk

The local marathon interrupts Arthur's plans for a quiet Sunday.

Real life married couple John Alderton and Pauline Collins lived through the early months of a fictitious marriage in **No, Honestly**.

No Sex Please, We're British   1 wk

Presented by ITV, film

| 1987 | 11.6 | Mon 28 Dec 8:00 p.m. | 18 | 1 wk |

In this cinema version of the West End stage hit an incorrectly addressed package of pornography arrives at a City bank. Starring Ronnie Corbett, Arthur Lowe, Ian Ogilvy, Susan Penhaligon and Beryl Reid.
Director: *Cliff Owen.*

Nobody is Norman Wisdom   6 wks

ATV, comedy

This series created by Watt Nicol and John Sichel starred Norman Wisdom as Nobody, a Walter Mitty-type character with wild dreams. Natalie Kent played his protective and possessive mother and Priscilla Morgan played Grace.

| 1973 | 6.8 | Tue 26 Jun 6:40 p.m. | 4 | 6 wks |

Nobody is determined to shake off his maternal shackles and release his very own somebody.
Producer: *John Sholz-Conway.*

Nobody's Perfect   1 wk

LWT, situation comedy

Bill and Sam Hooper (Elaine Stritch and Richard Griffiths), married for eight years, were each on their second marriage. Kim Braden played Sam's daughter Liz, Ruby Head portrayed the daily help Mrs Whicker and Moray Watson was the neighbour Henry Armstrong.

| 1980 | 12.3 | Sun 28 Sep 8:15 p.m. | 17 | 1 wk |

'Sam's Secret'
Bill is convinced that Sam is hiding something from her and she resolves to get to the bottom of it.
Director: *Christopher Baker.* **Producer:** *Humphrey Barclay.*

Noel Edmonds' Golden Easter Egg Awards, The   1 wk

BBC, entertainment

A segment from the Noel Edmonds' LATE LATE BREAKFAST SHOW was given its own self-contained show.

| 1985 | 12.4 | Sat 6 Apr 6:40 p.m. | 15 | 1 wk |

In this Easter weekend presentation from the Greenwood Theatre in London, Edmonds and Mike Smith show out-takes from television recordings and give prizes to the funniest.
Producer: *Michael Hurll.*

Noel's House Party   1 wk

BBC, entertainment

Noel Edmonds hosted this live show in a studio-built grand house in the fictitious village of Crinkly Bottom. Guests dropped in to relive moments of embarrassment and receive a Gotcha Oscar, to be gunged or to compete with a wind-machine to grab paper money for a viewer within a set time. The programme also featured a visit by hidden mini cameras to the home of an unsuspecting viewer.

| 1991 | 12.2 | Sat 21 Dec 6:10 p.m. | 17 | 1 wk |

Guests: Bernard Cribbins and Leslie Nielsen.
Producer: *Michael Leggo.*

Noel Edmonds' Late Late Breakfast Show   20 wks

BBC, entertainment

The former Radio 1 DJ hosted an evening of games and stunts. He was assisted by Mike Smith and 'Noel's Hit Squad' who turned hidden cameras on an unsuspecting public. Golden Egg Awards for embarrassing out-takes were also featured.
Producer: *Michael Hurll.*

| 1982 | 10.6 | Sat 11 Dec 6:25 p.m. | 19 | 1 wk |

Guests: Abba and Barry Manilow.

| 1983 | 12.1 | Sat 10 Dec 5:55 p.m. | 10 | 5 wks |

Guests: Peter Davison, Sandra Dickinson, Mel Smith and Griff Rhys-Jones and from Los Angeles, via satellite, Rod Stewart.

| 1984 | 13.0 | Sat 15 Dec 5:55 p.m. | 15 | 1 wk |

Guests: Johnny Hart and The Krankies.

| 1985 | 14.4 | Sat 16 Nov 6:15 p.m. | 6 | 7 wks |

Guests: Eddie Kidd and Paul McCartney.

| 1986 | 16.8 | Sat 22 Feb 6:20 p.m. | 3 | 6 wks |

Guests: Boy George and Bob Williamson.

Noel Edmonds' Saturday Road Show   2 wks

BBC, entertainment

Edmonds and his crew travelled all around the country to bring their show of comedy and stunts from different locations.

| 1988 | 12.7 | Sat 17 Dec 6:00 p.m. | 8 | 2 wks |

With Les Dennis, Patrick Moore, and Clarence and Joy Pickles.
Producer: *Michael Leggo.*

Norman — 6 wks

ATV, comedy

This series written by Ray Cooney and John Chapman starred Norman Wisdom as an over-ambitious and under-talented musician trying to forge a career in show business, having given up his safe job at an income tax office.

| 1970 | 7.0 | Thu 2 Apr 9:00 p.m. | 7 | 6 wks |

In this first episode Norman chucks his in-tray out of the window, puts a fist through his hat and tells his boss where to stick the job.
Producer: Alan Tarrant.

....

Norman and Bruce — 1 wk

ATV, entertainment

| 1962 | 5.9 | Wed 26 Dec 9:15 p.m. | 6 | 1 wk |

A repeat showing of the 1960 edition of SUNDAY NIGHT AT THE LONDON PALLADIUM in which Norman Wisdom and Bruce Forsyth took over the whole show.
Producer: Francis Essex.

....

Norman Vaughan Show, The — 1 wk

BBC, entertainment

Following his ATV series A TOUCH OF THE NORMAN VAUGHANS, Vaughan starred for the BBC in a variety format.

| 1966 | 5.8 | Thur 10 Nov 9:05 p.m. | 17 | 1 wk |

Guests: The Karlins, Lauri Lupino Lane, Bill Pertwee and Frankie Vaughan.
Writer: Barry Took. **Producer:** Kenneth Carter.

....

North and South — 2 wks

USA presented by ITV, drama

This adaptation of John Jakes' novel concerned two families in the years leading up to the American Civil War. The Main family were plantation owners from the South and the Hazard family came from the industrial North. The principal characters, Orry Main (Patrick Swayze) and George Hazard (James Read), had different backgrounds and codes of loyalty but were nonetheless friends. The love in Orry's life was Madeline Fabray (Lesley-Anne Down), whose cruel husband Justin (David Carradine) fed her with drugs. The role of Virgilia Hazard was played by Kirstie Alley. Guest stars included Johnny Cash, Robert Guillaume, Olivia de Havilland, Hal Holbrook, Gene Kelly, Robert Mitchum, Jean Simmons, Inga Swenson and Elizabeth Taylor.
Directors: Kevin Connor and Richard Heffron. **Producer:** David Wolper.

| 1986 | 12.6 | Sun 21 Dec 8:00 p.m. | 8 | 2 wks |

Episode Four
The actions of George's militant abolitionist sister Virgilia threaten his friendship with Orry.

....

North and South Book II — 1 wk

USA presented by ITV, drama

This five-part sequel to NORTH AND SOUTH was set in 1861. George Hazard (James Read) was recommissioned into the Union army while his friend Orry Main (Patrick Swayze) became a General in the Confederate forces. Also starring Kirstie Allen, Lloyd Bridges, David Carradine, Linda Evans, Morgan Fairchild, Olivia de Havilland, Wayne Newton, Jean Simmons and James Stewart.
Directors: Kevin Connor and Richard Heffron. **Producer:** David Wolper.

| 1987 | 11.4 | Sun 13 Dec 7:15 p.m. | 14 | 1 wk |

Episode One
Orry finally marries his beloved Madeline and shares a bittersweet reunion with George.

....

North by Northwest — 2 wks

Presented by ITV, film

| 1981 | 10.6 | Sat 22 Aug 7:35 p.m. | 18 | 1 wk |

Cary Grant, Leo G. Carroll, Martin Landau, James Mason and Eva Marie Saint star in Alfred Hitchcock's film account of the events that befall a businessman mistaken for a spy. He becomes a target for enemy agents.

| 1983 | 8.7 | Thu 9 Jun 7:30 p.m. | 13 | 1 wk |

Repeat showing of the above film.

....

North Sea Hijack — 1 wk

Presented by BBC, film

| 1984 | 14.8 | Fri 28 Dec 7:10 p.m. | 16 | 1 wk |

Hundreds of lives and billions of dollars are at stake when explosives are planted on a North Sea oil rig. A ransom is demanded. James Mason, Roger Moore and Anthony Perkins star.
Director: Andrew V. McLaglen.

Northwest Frontier | 2 wks

Presented by BBC, film

| 1970 | 5.6 | Sat 26 Dec 8:05 p.m. | 20 | 1 wk |

BBC's Boxing Day blockbuster. While rescuing a young Indian Prince from a rebellion, an officer in the Indian Army (Kenneth More) leads a party, including the Prince's governess (Lauren Bacall), on a dangerous journey through rebel-held territory. Co-starring Herbert Lom with I. S. Johar and Wilfrid Hyde White.
Director: J. Lee-Thompson.

| 1986 | 7.7 | Sat 5 Jul 6:40 p.m. | 17 | 1 wk |

Repeat showing of the above film.

Not in Front of the Children | 34 wks

BBC, situation comedy

Created and written by Richard Waring, this series was the forerunner of AND MOTHER MAKES THREE. It centred around the lives of the Corner family. Wendy Craig starred as Jennifer and Paul Daneman as Henry. Their children were Trudi (Roberta Tovey), Robin (Hugo Keith-Johnston) and Amanda (Jill Riddick).
Producer: Graeme Muir.

| 1967 | 5.5 | Fri 8 Sep 8:20 p.m. | 10 | 5 wks |

'The Word'
Robin increases his vocabulary in a way that horrifies his parents.

| 1968 | 6.7 | Fri 1 Nov 7:55 p.m. | 5 | 12 wks |

'Look for the Crystal Lining'
On their crystal wedding anniversary Jennifer has forgotten to post the insurance premiums.

| 1969 | 6.9 | Fri 24 Oct 7:55 p.m. | 6 | 15 wks |

'Unemployment Problem'
Henry is out of work so Jennifer decides to try to sell some of his paintings to a local art shop.

| 1970 | 6.4 | Fri 9 Jan 7:55 p.m. | 16 | 2 wks |

'Country Style'
Jennifer tries hard to have her family and their cottage chosen for an advertising campaign.

Not On Your Nellie | 10 wks

LWT, situation comedy

This series by Tom Brennand and Roy Bottomley starred Hylda Baker as Nellie Pickersgill, a lass from Bolton who answered an SOS from her father Jed (John Barrett) to go to Fulham to help him run the Brown Cow public house.
Producer: Bryan Izzard.

| 1974 | 8.0 | Fri 12 Apr 8:30 p.m. | 5 | 7 wks |

'The Apartment'
Nellie needs to keep one step ahead of Jed and the other Brown Cow layabouts, so she goes in search of a flat of her own.

| 1975 | 7.2 | Fri 24 Jan 8:30 p.m. | 15 | 3 wks |

'Brief Encounter'
Life at the Brown Cow is disrupted when Nellie goes shopping.

Not The Nine O'Clock News | 1 wk

BBC, comedy

A series of mild satirical sketches and parodies of politicians, clergymen, other establishment figures and television itself, with Rowan Atkinson, Griff Rhys-Jones, Mel Smith and Pamela Stephenson.

| 1980 | 15.1 | Tue 30 Dec 9:00 p.m. | 13 | 1 wk |

A compilation of highlights from the previous series.
Producers: John Lloyd and Sean Hardie.

Notorious | 2 wks

Presented by BBC, film

| 1961 | 4.3 | Sat 23 Dec 7:15 p.m. | 18 | 1 wk |

Alicia, a young American woman, achieves notoriety when her German father is convicted of treason against the USA. To prove her loyalty she embarks on a secret mission for her country which takes her to Brazil. Complications ensue when she falls in love with her fellow agent. This Alfred Hitchcock film stars Ingrid Bergman, Cary Grant and Claude Rains.

| 1962 | 5.5 | Sun 11 Nov 3:15 p.m. | 18 | 1 wk |

Repeat showing of the above film.

Now and Then | 4 wks

LWT, situation comedy

This series by John Esmonde and Bob Larbey focused on Peter Elston, a 'normal middle-aged Englishman', played as a young man by John Alford and in later years by Bernard Holley. He recalled his own childhood through watching the development of his rebellious son Alan (Marc Gilbey).
Producer: Derrick Goodwin. **Executive Producer:** Humphrey Barclay.

| 1983 | 6.4 | Sun 24 Jul 9:15 p.m. | 20 | 1 wk |

In this first episode Peter recalls the war years. His memories are rosy. He casts his mother (Marcia Warren) as a heroine, his dad (Sam Kelly) and his gran (Liz Smith) as saints and his Uncle Gordon and Aunt Sadie (Barry Stanton and June Brown) as hilarious comedians.

| 1984 | 9.2 | Sun 5 Aug 9:30 p.m. | 12 | 3 wks |

Peter Elston's ambitions to be a concert pianist are halted by the first German doodlebugs to fall on London.

Now Get Out of That | 1 wk

BBC, game show

Bernard Falk presented this series in which teams of amateur adventurers from Britain and America were set the task of rescuing a defecting biochemist from enemy territory in the shortest time. This was a contest of both stamina and teamwork.

| 1984 | 7.8 | Tue 17 Jul 8:30 p.m. | 20 | 1 wk |

The teams have to overcome an enormous setback when they discover that all their canoes have been stolen by the enemy. **Director:** Brian Strachan. **Producer:** Philip Franklin.

Now Who Do You Do? | 3 wks

LWT, comedy

WHO DO YOU DO? with a change of cast.

| 1976 | 6.5 | Sat 13 Mar 6:30 p.m. | 17 | 3 wks |

Guests: Michael Barrymore, Faith Brown, Janet Brown, Les Dennis, Harry Dickman, Dustin Gee, Billy Howard, Franklyn James, Johnny More and Terry Webster.
Producer: Jon Scoffield.

Nurse of the Year | 2 wks

ATV, entertainment

The heats for this competition were held throughout the ITV regions. They were organized by the Department of Health and the Daily Express. A panel of judges looked for ambition, kindliness, efficiency, manner and appearance in the contestants. The winners of each heat went to London for the final. (This competition was previously called the DAILY EXPRESS NURSE OF THE YEAR.)

| 1977 | 7.5 | Wed 11 May 8:00 p.m. | 6 | 1 wk |

Leslie Crowther introduces the national finals.
Director: Hector Stewart. **Producer:** Jean Morton.

| 1979 | 13.9 | Wed 2 May 8:00 p.m. | 8 | 1 wk |

Leslie Crowther introduces the finalists.
Director: Hector Stewart. **Producer:** Jean Morton.

Nurses, The | 2 wks

USA presented by BBC, soap

This was a series about two young nurses and the goings-on at the Alden General Hospital. It starred Shirl Conway as Head Nurse Liz Thorpe and Zina Bethune as the serious-minded Nurse Gail Lucas. **Executive Producer:** Herbert Brodkin.

| 1964 | 7.4 | Thu 2 Jul 8:25 p.m. | 5 | 2 wks |

'The Third Generation'
An elderly nurse, once an inspiration to Liz's and Gail's generation of nurses, causes Liz to take stock of her own future in the profession. Guest star: Cathleen Nesbitt.

Obsession — 1 wk

Presented by ITV, film

| 1981 | 10.5 | Sat 5 Sep 9:15 p.m. | 19 | 1 wk |

Cliff Robertson stars as Michael Courtland, a man whose wife and child were kidnapped and never seen again. Ten years later he meets a woman who is her exact double (Genevieve Bujold).
Director: Brian de Palma.

Octopussy — 2 wks

Presented by ITV, film

| 1988 | 15.9 | Sat 30 Jan 7:15 p.m. | 5 | 1 wk |

James Bond (Roger Moore) tackles an Afghan prince and a beautiful woman who have plans to steal Tsarist treasures. Also starring Maud Adams, Kabir Bedi, Louis Jourdan and Lois Maxwell.
Director: John Glen.

| 1990 | 15.9 | Sat 20 Jan 7:00 p.m. | 7 | 1 wk |

Repeat showing of the above film.

Odd Man, The — 28 wks

Granada, drama

This thriller series created by Edward Boyd starred Edwin Richfield as Chief Inspector Gordon and Sarah Lawson as his wife Judy. Keith Barron played Detective Sergeant Swift. William Mervyn also starred as Inspector Rose.

| 1962 | 5.3 | Fri 18 May 9:15 p.m. | 9 | 8 wks |

'South American Way'
A theatrical agent and his wife are trying to hold their marriage together. They encounter a deaf-mute with a gun for hire and involve themselves in a series of dangerous incidents.
Designer: Roy Stonehouse. **Director:** Derek Bennett. **Producer:** Stuart Latham.

'This Stuff's Thicker Than Water'
The police have closed a case and refuse to re-open it. Jake Justice (James Bolam) is a very determined man, however, and forces the police to think again.
Designer: Michael Bailey. **Director:** Eric Price. **Producer:** Stuart Latham.

| 1964 | 5.4 | Fri 29 May 9:10 p.m. | 12 | 4 wks |

A repeat showing of the above 1963 episode.

Odd Man Out — 1 wk

Thames, situation comedy

This series by Vince Powell starred John Inman as Blackpool fish and chip shop owner Neville Sutcliffe and Josephine Tewson as his step-sister Dorothy. Together they inherited their father's stick-rock factory in Sussex. The series also starred Avril Angers and Peter Butterworth as Ma and Wilf.

| 1977 | 14.0 | Thu 27 Oct 9:00 | 11 | 1 wk |

'A Chip Off The Old Block'
Neville leaves Blackpool for Sussex and receives a cool welcome from Dorothy.
Director: Anthony Parker. **Producer:** Gerald Thomas.

Odd One Out — 5 wks

BBC, game show

Paul Daniels invited contestants to select the odd one out from word, picture or music clues.

| 1983 | 8.7 | Fri 3 Jun 7:30 p.m. | 18 | 3 wks |

Director: John Bishop. **Producer:** Roger Ordish.

| 1984 | 7.5 | Fri 29 Jun 8:30 p.m. | 19 | 1 wk |

Director: David Taylor. **Producer:** John Bishop.

| 1985 | 14.1 | Fri 1 Mar 7:40 p.m. | 9 | 1 wk |

Director: David Taylor. **Producer:** Paul Ciani.

Odessa File, The   1 wk

Presented by BBC, film

| 1980 | 14.4 | Tue 1 Jan 9:05 p.m. | 19 | 1 wk |

Adaptation of Frederick Forsyth's novel about the contents of a diary left by an elderly Jew who committed suicide in Hamburg in 1963. Young journalist Peter Miller (Jon Voight) finds the diary and plans to discover the secrets of the Nazi Odessa organization referred to in it. Also starring Derek Jacobi, Maria Schell, Maximilian Schell and Mary Tamm.
Director: Ronald Neame.

Officer and a Gentleman, An   1 wk

Presented by ITV, film

| 1986 | 16.4 | Mon 31 Mar 9:15 p.m. | 3 | 1 wk |

Richard Gere suffers officer training at the Naval Aviation Candidate School under the ultra-strict Sergeant Foley (Louis Gossett Jr.). Debra Winger plays the newcomer's civilian girlfriend, Paula Pokrifki.
Director: Taylor Hackford.

Oh Boy   4 wks

ATV, music

This was a re-creation of Jack Good's original pop show, which made a star of Cliff Richard in the late 1950s.

| 1979 | 11.2 | Mon 2 Jul 7:00 p.m. | 10 | 4 wks |

With Joe Brown, Les Gray, Bill Hartman, Freddie 'Fingers' Lee, Shakin' Stevens and Johnny Storm.
Producer: Ken O'Neill. **Executive Producer:** Richard Leyland.

Oh Brother   16 wks

BBC, situation comedy

This show had a religious setting, Mountacres Priory. It was written by David Climie and Austin Steele and starred Derek Nimmo as Brother Dominic and Felix Aylmer as Father Anselm, with Geoffrey Hibbert, Patrick McAlinney and Edward Malin.

| 1968 | 6.2 | Fri 18 Oct 7:55 p.m., | 6 | 6 wks |

'Treasures on Earth'
Brother Dominic manages to find disaster among the priceless objects in the monastic and medieval history exhibition.
Producer: Duncan Wood.

| 1969 | 6.5 | Fri 2 May 8:20 p.m. | 4 | 6 wks |

'Behold This Dreamer'
The dreamer in the story is Father Koenig, played by Bernard Archard.
Producer: Harold Snoad.

| 1970 | 6.5 | Fri 6 Feb 7:55 p.m. | 17 | 4 wks |

'A Fool Returneth'
The golf course and Brother Dominic is not a natural partnership. Henry Longhurst makes a guest appearance.
Producer: Johnny Downes. **Executive Producer:** Duncan Wood.

Oh No! It's Selwyn Froggitt   19 wks

YTV, situation comedy

This series was created and written by Alan Plater and starred Bill Maynard in the title role as a handyman with scant knowledge and little ability but a profound belief that he could fix anything.
Producer: Ronnie Baxter.

| 1974 | 6.7 | Mon 30 Sep 8:00 p.m. | 6 | 1 wk |

'Oh No! It's Selwyn Froggitt'
A one-off pilot introducing the character of Froggitt. Also starring Daphne Heard and David Lodge.

| 1976 | 6.7 | Wed 4 Feb 8:30 p.m. | 16 | 3 wks |

'The Master Builder'
Selwyn has extra responsibility in the Public Works Department. He must not just dig the hole but decide where to dig it.

| 1977 | 16.5 | Tue 6 Dec 7:30 p.m. | 1 | 15 wks |

'Sling Along with Selwyn'
Selwyn joins an unusual battle of champions and is quoted at 200–1.
Writer: Bernie Sharp.

Oh yes it's Bill Maynard in **Oh No! It's Selwyn Froggitt**.

Old Bill   1 wk

BBC, documentary

| 1969 | 5.7 | Tue 6 May 7:25 p.m. | 15 | 1 wk |

Billy Cotton died on 25 March 1969. Today would have been his 70th birthday. Cliff Michelmore talks to friends who knew him as a boy, as a soldier, as a racing driver and as a musician and entertainer.
Director: Jim Franklin. **Producer:** Michael Mills.

Oliver `2 wks`

Presented by BBC, film

1978 **14.2** **Sat 30 Dec 6:55 p.m.** **13** `1 wk`

Carol Reed's film of Lionel Bart's musical interpretation of Charles Dicken's Oliver Twist. Mark Lester plays the orphan Oliver, Jack Wild is the Artful Dodger, Ron Moody is Fagin, Oliver Reed plays Bill Sykes, Harry Secombe is Mr Bumble and Shani Wallis portrays Nancy. Also starring Hylda Baker, Kenneth Cranham, Fred Emney, Hugh Griffith, James Hayter, Megs Jenkins, Peggy Mount and Leonard Rossiter.

1986 **12.3** **Sat 20 Dec 5:55 p.m.** **9** `1 wk`

Repeat showing of the above film.

Olympic Challenge `1 wk`

BBC, sport

1984 **8.3** **Thu 26 Jul 9:25 p.m.** **12** `1 wk`

A recording of last month's International Games for the Disabled in New York. Forty-six nations took part and over 1600 athletes competed.
Producer: Jeff Goddard.

Olympic Grandstand `7 wks`

BBC, sport

The Olympic Games (both Summer and Winter) take place every four years. The BBC covered the events since the London Games of 1948.

1968 **5.0** **Sat 12 Oct 5:50 p.m.** **20** `1 wk`

The opening ceremony of the nineteenth Modern Olympic Games in Mexico is screened simultaneously on BBC1 and in colour on BBC2. The scene is described by David Coleman.
Editor: Alan Hart. **Producer:** Bryan Cowgill.

1972 **5.5** **Sun 3 Sep 5:00 p.m.** **4** `1 wk`

Live coverage from Munich of the men's 10,000 metres, the women's 800 metres and the men's 110 metre hurdles. The programme is introduced by Frank Bough and David Vine with commentary by David Coleman, Norris McWhirter and Ron Pickering.
Editors: Alan Chivers, Alan Hart, Sam Leitch and A. P. Wilkinson.
Producer: Bryan Cowgill.

1976 **7.4** **Wed 11 Feb 9:25 p.m.** **11** `2 wks`

From Innsbruck, David Coleman introduces coverage of today's Winter Olympics. John Curry bids to become Britain's first skating gold medallist since Jeanette Altwegg won in Helsinki in 1952. The commentary is by Alan Weeks.
Producer: Brian Venner. **Editors:** Alan Hart and Jonathan Martin.

1980 **15.7** **Tue 19 Feb 6:45 p.m.** **6** `2 wks`
                       Fri 22 Feb 6:45 p.m.

These two programmes achieved the same viewing figure and chart position.

David Coleman introduces coverage of the Winter Olympics from Lake Placid in the United States. Commentators include Tony Gubba, Ron Pickering, David Vine and Alan Weeks.
Editors: Harold Anderson and Jonathan Martin. **Producer:** Martin Hopkins.

1984 **8.7** **Mon 13 Aug 6:15 p.m.** **10** `1 wk`

Desmond Lynam presents a recording of the closing ceremony at the Los Angeles games and highlights of the fortnight. Commentators include David Coleman, Brendan Foster and Ron Pickering.
Editor: Jonathan Martin. **Producer:** Alan Weeks.

Omega Factor, The `1 wk`

BBC, drama

Jack Gerson wrote this series of ten programmes about the psychic research unit of MI5 known as Department 7, which dealt with the unexplained. James Hazeldine starred as Tom Crane, Louise Jameson was Anne Reynolds and John Carlisle portrayed Ray Martindale.

1979 **14.3** **Wed 15 Aug 8:10 p.m.** **16** `1 wk`

'Illusions'
There is a power struggle when Dr Karl Bruckner (John Gabriel) is brought over from East Germany to work in Department 7.
Producer: George Gallaccio.

Omen, The `1 wk`

Presented by ITV, film

1981 **12.6** **Mon 31 Aug 10:00 p.m.** **7** `1 wk`

A series of horrifying happenings follow a child's birthday party. Starring Gregory Peck, Lee Remick, Leo McKern, David Warner and Billie Whitelaw.
Director: Richard Donner.

On Golden Pond `1 wk`

Presented by ITV, film

1985 **12.4** **Sun 15 Dec 7:45 p.m.** **12** `1 wk`

Ethel and Norman Thayer (Katharine Hepburn and Henry Fonda) spend their forty-eighth consecutive summer holiday in New England. Daughter Chelsea (Jane Fonda) brings her new lover and his son to initiate a family conflict which spans three generations.
Director: Mark Rydell.

On Her Majesty's Secret Service 4 wks

Presented by ITV, film

| 1978 | 16.8 | Mon 4 Sep 7:30 p.m. | 1 | 1 wk |

George Lazenby stars as James Bond with Diana Rigg as Tracy. Bond pursues Blofeld (Telly Savalas) who once again threatens the peace of the world. Bernard Lee and Lois Maxwell also star.
Director: Peter Hunt.

1980	12.9	Sat 6 Jun 7:30 p.m.	10	1 wk
1983	14.3	Fri 1 Apr 7:30 p.m.	5	1 wk
1991	9.2	Sat 7 Sep 7:30 p.m.	20	1 wk

Repeat showings of the above film.

On Safari 1 wk

BBC, documentary

Husband and wife team Armand and Michaela Denis were the first television explorers and enjoyed great popularity with their films, which they produced and directed themselves throughout the fifties.

| 1962 | 5.1 | Wed 17 Oct 9:50 p.m. | 18 | 1 wk |

'Kuomboka'
At a time of rapid change in Rhodesia this film follows the journey of Kuomboka, King of the Barotse people, from his low-lying capital to higher grounds safe from the flooding Zambesi.
Camera: Des Bartlett.

On the Buses 68 wks

LWT, situation comedy

This series was created and written initially by Ronald Wolfe and Ronald Chesney about a bus driver for the Luxton Bus Company, his colleagues and family. It starred Reg Varney as Stan Butler, Cicely Courtneidge (later Doris Hare) as his mum, Anna Karen as his sister Olive, Michael Robbins as his miserable brother-in-law Arthur, Bob Grant as Jack the conductor and Stephen Lewis as the woe-begotten, never-smiling Inspector Blakey.
Producers: Stuart Allen (1969–71) and Bryan Izzard (1972–73).

| 1969 | 6.9 | Fri 28 Feb 8:30 p.m. | 12 | 13 wks |

In this opening and untitled programme Stan is scheduled on a new early morning shift which upsets the entire household, especially his mother Mrs Butler.

| 1970 | 8.2 | Fri 4 Dec 8:25 p.m. | 1 | 18 wks |

'The Canteen Girl'
The Inspector is taking out the flighty canteen girl from the depot, much to Stan and Jack's surprise and amusement. When he decides to marry her and retire to rear chickens, they are over the moon. However, the arrival of the new Inspector, Mr Stewart (Alan Curtis), ensures their delight is short-lived.

| 1971 | 8.5 | Sun 21 Feb 7:20 p.m. | 1 | 22 wks |

'Not Tonight'
Stella (Charlotte Howard) is the shapely new waitress in the canteen. When she makes a pass at Stan he's both pleased and surprised.

| 1972 | 8.1 | Sun 5 Mar 7:25 p.m. | 1 | 8 wks |

'Private Hire'
Stan went to the dogs on Friday and lost his week's wages. Mum wants her housekeeping and in desperation Stan borrows £5 from Basher (Maurice Bush) and promises to repay it on Monday. But how?
Writers: Bob Grant and Stephen Lewis.

| 1973 | 6.9 | Sun 4 Mar 7:25 p.m. | 14 | 7 wks |

'The Perfect Clippie'
A financial crisis forces Olive to go to work. Stan grovels to Blakey to get her fixed up as a clippie, not a popular move with the other ticket punchers.
Writers: George Layton and Jonathan Lynn.

On the Buses 1 wk

Presented by ITV, film

| 1976 | 6.6 | Mon 30 Aug 8:30 p.m. | 7 | 1 wk |

Bank Holiday screening of the ninety-five minute feature film version of the show. A shortage of staff means that women are being employed as drivers. Stan and Jack scheme to have the new recruits dismissed.
Director: Harry Booth.

The **On the Buses** team, (left to right) Bob Grant, Reg Varney and Stephen Lewis, enjoyed the full flush of success from 1970 to 1972.

On the House   **7 wks**

YTV, situation comedy

Thomas Clackwood and Sons, builders, tried to construct a bijou estate. Their most formidable opposition came from their own employees. The site foreman, Charlie Cattermole (John Junkin), was pitted against the workers' leader, Gussie (Kenneth Connor). Also working, when they couldn't avoid it, were Peter Atard, Tommy Godfrey, John Normington and Gordon Rollings.
Writer: Sid Colin. **Producer:** David Mallett. **Executive Producer:** John Duncan.

| 1970 | 6.3 | Thu 24 Sep 9:00 p.m. | 8 | 4 wks |

'Let My People Go'
Before the first foundation can be dug in this first episode, Gussie decides the site is not fit for the men and makes major and expensive demands before they will lift a tool.

| 1971 | 5.9 | Thu 27 May 9:00 p.m. | 15 | 3 wks |

'Will the Real Harvey Micklethwaite Please Stand Up?'
Harvey Micklethwaite (Robin Askwith) gets out of his depth when he tries to impress his girlfriend (Paula Wilcox) by telling her he is Clackwood's foreman.

On the Island   **1 wk**

ATV, drama

| 1967 | 6.5 | Thu 5 Jan 9:40 p.m. | 11 | 1 wk |

This play by Jacques Gillies was set on an island off the south coast of South America. The Cosgrove family – Robert, a Nobel Prize winner, Linda and daughter Tess (Marius Goring, Helen Cherry and Michele Dotrice) – find their peaceful life disturbed by the arrival of Colonel Guzzman (Ian Hendry). They are suddenly mixed up in the struggles of a local revolution.
Designer: Vic Symonds. **Director:** Quentin Lawrence. **Producer:** Cecil Clarke.

On the Up   **3 wks**

BBC, situation comedy

Dennis Waterman starred as self-made millionaire Tony Carpenter in this series by Bob Larbey. Judy Buxton played Tony's wife Ruth, who was continually walking out on him and their luxury home. Their faithful servants Sam and Mrs Wembley were played by Sam Kelly and Joan Sims.
Producer: Gareth Gwenlan.

| 1990 | 10.1 | Tue 18 Sep 8:30 p.m. | 13 | 2 wks |

Tony runs into trouble with some Hooray Henrys at the County Show.

| 1991 | 12.3 | Fri 4 Oct 8:30 p.m. | 17 | 1 wk |

While giving his daughter Stephanie (Vanessa Hadaway) a lift back to boarding school, Tony meets the attractive mother of one of his daughter's friends.

Once an Eagle   **4 wks**

USA presented by ITV, drama

Peter S. Fischer dramatized in four parts the Anthony Myrers' story of two US Army officers, Sam Damon (Sam Elliott) and Courtney Massengale (Cliff Potts), in the years between 1918 and the outbreak of the Second World War. Glenn Ford played Major Caldwell, Damon's father-in-law. Ralph Bellamy and Phyllis Thaxter also starred.
Directors: Richard Michaels and E.W. Swackhamer. **Executive Producer:** William Sackheim.

| 1977 | 11.5 | Thu 25 Aug 9:00 p.m. | 17 | 4 wks |

Episode Three
Sam and Tommy Damon (Darlene Carr) fight to repair their marriage. Sam solves a problem in the factory of Ed Caldwell (Ralph Bellamy), but gets into trouble with the foreman (David Huddleston) for his pains. Soldier Joe Brand (Kario Salem) is on trial and the proceedings reveal some truth about racist attitudes within the US Army.

Once Upon a Century – A Very Royal Gala   **1 wk**

ATV, entertainment

| 1977 | 6.5 | Sun 2 Jan 7:25 p.m. | 14 | 1 wk |

Presented by Lew Grade for the St John Ambulance Brigade from the Talk of the Town in the presence of HM The Queen, HRH The Duke of Edinburgh, Princess Anne, Princess Margaret, Princess Alice, The Duke and Duchess of Gloucester, Earl Mountbatten of Burma, King Hussein of Jordan, the King and Queen of Sweden, King Constantine and the Queen of The Hellenes, Princess Margaretha of Sweden, Prince Tomislaw and Princess Katerina of Yugoslavia, Prince and Princess Wilhelm Karl of Prussia, Prince Albert of Monaco and Prince and Princess Guy de Polignac. Among those appearing are Brotherhood of Man, Peter Cook and Dudley Moore, Douglas Fairbanks Jr., Danny La Rue, Daniel Remy, Frankie Vaughan and Andy Williams.
Stage Director: Robert Nesbitt. **Television presentation:** John Pullen. **Producer:** Colin Clews.

One by One   **21 wks**

BBC, drama

This series, based on the stories of a zoo vet by David Taylor, was adapted for television by Johnny Byrne. It starred Rob Heyland as long-suffering zoo vet Donald Turner, Peter Gilmore as Ben Bishop, James Ellis as Paddy Reilly, Sonia Graham as Ethel Ledbetter, Heather James as Maggie Raymond, Andrew Robertson as Jock Drummond and Christina Nagy as Liz Collier.
Designer: John Coleman. **Producer:** Bill Sellars.

| 1985 | 14.9 | Sat 23 Mar 7:15 p.m. | 5 | 8 wks |

'A Close Run Thing'
Lady Ann Pendle's (Catherine Snell) Manford Safari Park prepares to open to the public.
Designer: John Coleman. **Director:** Michael E. Briant.

| 1987 | 13.2 | Sat 7 Mar 7:30 p.m. | 7 | 9 wks |

'Remember the Humble Guinea Pig'
Turner answers a call from Madrid Zoo and encounters a giant panda.
Designer: Raymond Langhorn. **Director:** Andrew Morgan.

| 1988 | 10.0 | Sun 8 May 8:15 p.m. | 14 | 4 wks |

'First Things First'
The head keeper at Bellington Zoo finds that someone is trying to kill his animals. (Repeat.)
Designer: John Coleman. **Director:** Roderick Graham.

One Hour to Doomsday — 1 wk

Presented by ITV, film

| 1977 | 11.8 | Sat 17 Sep 6:15 p.m. | 19 | 1 wk |

When the Earth is theatened by a planetoid the US President orders all the gold in Fort Knox to be shipped to the underground city of Pacifica. Admiral Matthews (Stuart Whitman) is charged with the responsibility of the shipment but, unknown to him, his own brother Brett (Robert Wagner) is involved in a plot to steal the gold. Also starring Richard Basehart, Joseph Cotten, James Darren, Rosemary Forsyth and Sugar Ray Robinson.
Director: Irwin Allen.

One In Every Hundred — 1 wk

AR, documentary

| 1966 | 4.8 | Wed 8 Jun 9:40 p.m. | 19 | 1 wk |

A film report during Mental Health Week about children born with a mental disability.
Director: Maurice Hatton. **Producer:** Richard de la Mer.

One More Train to Rob — 1 wk

Presented by ITV, film

| 1976 | 6.3 | Thu 30 Dec 7:00 p.m. | 15 | 1 wk |

A train is held up by bandits in 1880s California. Starring George Peppard with Diana Muldaur, Frances Nuyen and John Vernon.
Director: Andrew V. McLaglen.

One of the Family — 1 wk

Thames, drama

This play by Terence Brady and Charlotte Bingham was first transmitted in 1975 as part of a trilogy entitled 'Three Comedies of Marriage'. It was given a sudden and unexpected repeat in 1977 when Thames had to withdraw a scheduled episode of ROCK FOLLIES because of a court action.

| 1977 | 5.8 | Wed 1 Jun 9:00 p.m. | 18 | 1 wk |

Susan (Polly Adams) is a fashion conscious young London housewife expecting a baby. Barbara (Valerie Phillips) comes up from Lincolnshire to help around the house, as one of the family. All goes well until they have a misunderstanding at the christening.
Director: Richard Martin. **Producer:** Peter Duguid.

One Step Beyond — 11 wks

AR with ABC America, drama

Some of the most bizarre cases in the annals of psychic phenomena and the supernatural were dramatized in this series created by Merwin Gerard. The stories were all introduced by John Newland.

| 1961 | 6.1 | Wed 27 Dec 8:55 p.m. | 5 | 5 wks |

'The Stranger' by Larry Marcus.
Eleven days after a city is destroyed by an earthquake, three people dying of starvation are found beneath the ruins with the body of an American. The dead man has sustained the others through their ordeal, but fingerprint files prove he died in prison some time ago. Starring Peter Dyneley, Patrick McAlliney, Bill Nagy and Graham Stark.
Director: John Newland. **Producer:** Peter Marriott.

| 1962 | 6.8 | Wed 21 Feb 9:15 p.m. | 3 | 6 wks |

'The Face' by Perry Quinn.
Six-year-old Stephen Bolt (Sean Kelly) has a nightmare from which he remembers the face of a man whom he sees clutching a knife. Years later Stephen finds himself in the Liverpool docks on board a Spanish freighter. One of the crew has the face from the nightmare. (This episode was based on a real incident that took place in the 1880s.)
Producer: Peter Marriot.

1,000 Plane Raid, The — 1 wk

Presented by BBC, film

| 1974 | 5.5 | Tue 2 Jul 7:30 p.m. | 20 | 1 wk |

The story of the biggest airborne armada of the Second World War. Starring Christopher George and Laraine Stephens with J. D. Cannon, Gary Marshall and Ben Murphy.
Director: Boris Sagal.

Onedin Line, The — 1 wk

BBC, drama

This series created in 1972 by Cyril Abraham concerned a nineteenth-century shipping family in Liverpool. Peter Gilmore starred as James Onedin with Anne Stallybrass as his wife Anne. Other important characters included Letty Onedin (Jill Gascoine), Lady Fogarty (Jessica Benton), Captain Baines (Howard Lang), Charlotte Onedin (Laura Hartong), Samuel Onedin (Christopher Douglas), Seth Burgess (Michael Walker) and Sarah Onedin (Mary Webster).

| 1979 | 10.0 | Sun 12 Aug 7:15 p.m. | 18 | 1 wk |

'Dirty Cargo' by Nick McCarty.
James Onedin races halfway around the world to prevent disaster befalling Lady Fogarty.
Producer: Geraint Morris.

Only Fools and Horses — 74 wks

BBC, situation comedy

This series by John Sullivan concerned two brothers living just above the poverty line in South London. David Jason starred as the sharp and ambitious Del Trotter with Nicholas Lyndhurst as the younger and rather dim Rodney. Lennard Pearce played the part of Grandad until his death in 1984. At this point Buster Merryfield entered the show as Uncle Albert.
Director (1988, 1990): Tony Dow. **Producers:** Ray Butt (1983–87) and Gareth Gwenlan (1988–91).

| 1983 | 11.3 | Thu 22 Dec 8:30 p.m. | 12 | 7 wks |

'Who's a Pretty Boy?'
The Trotters embark on a decorating venture.

| 1984 | 11.7 | Mon 6 Aug 8:00 p.m. | 2 | 7 wks |

'Yesterday Never Comes'
Del goes into the antiques business. (Repeat.)

| 1985 | 16.9 | Wed 25 Dec 7:30 p.m. | 2 | 15 wks |

'To Hull and Back'
The Trotters go north on a money-making adventure.

| 1986 | 18.8 | Sun 5 Oct 8:35 p.m. | 2 | 8 wks |

'Who Wants to be a Millionaire?'
Del faces up to the dilemma of the episode title.

| 1987 | 14.5 | Fri 25 Dec 6:25 p.m. | 6 | 9 wks |

Del, Rodney and Uncle Albert are guests at a wedding where Del hears about his mother's buried treasure.

| 1988 | 16.6 | Sun 25 Dec 5:05 p.m. | 7 | 2 wks |

Del and Rodney are flush with cash so they throw a surprise party for Uncle Albert.

| 1989 | 20.1 | Mon 25 Dec 4:05 p.m. | 5 | 16 wks |

'The Jolly Boys Outing'
Del, Rodney and Uncle Albert take a day trip to Margate.

| 1990 | 18.0 | Tue 25 Dec 5:10 p.m. | 3 | 3 wks |

'Rodney Come Home'
Raquel (Tessa Peake-Jones) has moved in with Del. Rodney is having problems with his wife Cassandra (Gwyneth Strong).

| 1991 | 18.9 | Sun 3 Feb 7:15 p.m. | 1 | 7 wks |

'Three Men, a Woman and a Baby'
Rodney and Albert are concerned about the imminent birth of Del's offspring.

Only When I Laugh — 34 wks

YTV, situation comedy

This series by Eric Chappell was set in a hospital ward and starred James Bolam as Figgis, Peter Bowles as Glover and Christopher Strauli as Norman, with Richard Wilson as the long-suffering Dr Gordon Thorpe and Derrick Branch as male nurse Gupte.
Producer: Vernon Lawrence.

| 1979 | 16.9 | Mon 3 Dec 8:00 p.m. | 1 | 7 wks |

'Tangled Web'
Norman is reading a book about a pretty nurse when one actually comes onto the ward.

| 1980 | 17.0 | Tue 6 May 8:30 p.m. | 1 | 7 wks |

'Where There's a Will'
A dirty old farmer comes in as a patient. He is unwelcome until it is realized he is very rich and about to make a will.

| 1981 | 15.4 | Wed 30 Sep 8:00 p.m. | 2 | 13 wks |

'Accident'
Norman has to decide whether to testify against Dr Thorpe about an accident he witnessed.

| 1982 | 11.7 | Mon 20 Dec 8:00 p.m. | 9 | 4 wks |

'Away for Christmas'
The ward is decorated for the holidays. A new patient arrives. (Repeat.)

| 1983 | 13.0 | Wed 6 Apr 8:30 p.m. | 6 | 3 wks |

'The Right Honourable Gentleman'
An MP is admitted for treatment, but he refuses to sign a petition to save the hospital.

Open All Hours | 44 wks

BBC, situation comedy

This series by Roy Clarke was set in a Yorkshire town street and starred Ronnie Barker as Arkwright, the stammering, penny-pinching keeper of the corner shop. David Jason was his overworked assistant and nephew Granville. Arkwright lusted relentlessly after Nurse Gladys Emmanuel, played by Lynda Baron, who lived across the road. Stephanie Cole was Mrs Featherstone.
Producer: Sydney Lotterby.

| 1979 | 12.2 | Fri 4 May 8:30 p.m. | 17 | 1 wk |

Arkwright has some unwelcome visitors – burglars. (First shown on BBC2.)

| 1981 | 16.2 | Sun 1 Mar 7:15 p.m. | 6 | 7 wks |

Gladys blackmails Arkwright into buying her a new washing machine.

| 1982 | 14.5 | Sun 21 Mar 7:15 p.m. | 4 | 5 wks |

Arkwright decides that Granville should learn more of the hard facts of business. His methods, however, bring retribution from some of his customers.

| 1983 | 10.3 | Wed 20 Apr 7:40 p.m. | 16 | 1 wk |

Arkwright's pursuit of Gladys is dampened by the return of one of her old admirers. (Repeat.)

| 1985 | 19.0 | Sun 6 Oct 7:15 p.m. | 1 | 8 wks |

With a ladder and a box of chocolates Arkwright devises a scheme to gain entry to Gladys' boudoir.

| 1986 | 14.2 | Tue 30 Sep 8:00 p.m. | 4 | 6 wks |

A repeat of the first episode in which Arkwright's rudeness causes offence to customers. Gladys and Granville resolve to teach him some manners.

| 1991 | 12.0 | Thu 4 Apr 9:30 p.m. | 7 | 16 wks |

Arkwright is goaded by Gladys into making certain improvements to his business. (Repeat.)

Operation Crossbow | 1 wk

Presented by BBC, film

| 1985 | 11.7 | Sat 11 May 6:45 p.m. | 12 | 1 wk |

A wartime drama in which a group of agents is sent to Germany to destroy the new weapon being developed by the Nazis. Starring Tom Courtenay, John Fraser, Trevor Howard, Richard Johnson, Jeremy Kemp, Sophia Loren, John Mills, Lilli Palmer, George Peppard, Anthony Quayle, Sylvia Syms, Richard Todd, Richard Wattis and Patrick Wymark.
Director: Michael Anderson.

Operation Julie | 1 wk

Tyne Tees, drama

This was a three-part dramatization by Bob Mahoney, Gerry O'Hara and Keith Richardson of the book by Dick Lee and Colin Pratt. It was based on the true story of one of the biggest drug hunts of the 1970s, codenamed Operation Julie. Colin Blakely starred as Detective Inspector Richard Lee and David Swift was Detective Superintendent Gosling.

| 1985 | 12.1 | Mon 4 Nov 9:00 p.m.
Tue 5 Nov 9:00 p.m.
Wed 6 Nov 9:00 p.m. | 18 | 1 wk |

These episodes were listed together in the ratings.
Episode One
The trail begins in Reading when Richard Lee discovers, at first hand, the devastating effects of LSD. He also realizes for the first time that his own patch appears to be the distribution centre.

Episode Two
The undercover work of the police seems to be paying off as one of the ringleaders of the gang has been identified. However, the gang's drug labs have now ceased their production, and the search moves to Switzerland.

Episode Three
With insufficient evidence to secure a conviction the police maintain considerable pressure on Richard Lee to abandon the operation.
Designer: Ashley Wilkinson. **Director:** Bob Mahoney. **Producers:** Malcolm Heyworth and Peter Holmans. **Executive Producer:** Keith Richardson.

Opium Trail, The | 1 wk

ATV, documentary

| 1966 | 6.6 | Wed 14 Sep 9:40 p.m. | 7 | 1 wk |

The film follows the opium from the poppy fields of Burma and Thailand, south to Bangkok and by sea to Hong Kong. The colony is becoming less of an exporter, more a consumer.
Camera: Chris Menges. **Writer, Narrator** and **Producer:** Adrian Cowell.

In the only Number One edition of **Only Fools and Horses** Rodney (Nicholas Lyndhurst) is about to become an uncle.

Opportunity Knocks   397 wks

ABC (1964–65, 1967–69) and Thames (1970–78), entertainment

In this talent show hosted by Hughie Green from 1956 to 1977 viewers voted each week for the best contestant. A winner could reappear until beaten and some significant careers were built on this foundation, notably those of Frank Carson, Les Dawson, Mary Hopkin, Little and Large, Peters and Lee and Lena Zavaroni. The series was briefly revived in the 1980s by the BBC (see BOB SAYS OPPORTUNITY KNOCKS) with Bob Monkhouse as host and Green as consultant.
Director (1977–78): Stuart Hall. **Producers** included Peter Dulay (1964–65, 1977–78), Royston Mayoh (1968, 1971–73), Robert Fleming (1969–70) and Keith Beckett (1974–76).

| 1964 | 6.8 | Sat 3 Oct 7:25 p.m. | 5 | 13 wks |

Director: Ronnie Baxter.

| 1965 | 6.2 | Sat 25 Sep 6:30 p.m. | 10 | 11 wks |

Director: Milo Lewis.

| 1967 | 7.1 | Sat 25 Nov 6:20 p.m. | 8 | 34 wks |

Director: Royston Mayoh. **Producer:** Milo Lewis.

1968	7.5	Sat 16 Mar 6:15 p.m.	2	32 wks
1969	7.5	Mon 3 Feb 6:40 p.m.	3	42 wks
1970	7.9	Mon 2 Mar 6:40 p.m.	3	35 wks

Hughie Green introduces the All Winners Show. Among the finalists are Paul Melba, Gerry Monroe (who will go on to have six hit singles) and comedy vocal group the Black Abbots (whose drummer Russ will become a top comedian in his own right).

1971	7.6	Mon 14 Jun 6:40 p.m.	1	31 wks
1972	8.2	Mon 13 Mar 6:40 p.m.	1	36 wks
1973	7.9	Mon 12 Feb 6:40 p.m.	1	36 wks
1974	8.6	Mon 11 Feb 6:40 p.m.	2	36 wks
1975	8.2	Mon 29 Dec 6:40 p.m.	1	31 wks

The Variety Club Award Show in which all the winning acts from this year's series compete for the award. Previous winners have included Mary Hopkin, Bobby Crush, Millican and Nesbitt and last year's winner Lena Zavaroni.

1976	8.2	Mon 29 Dec 7:00 p.m.	1	25 wks
1977	14.8	Mon 12 Dec 6:45 p.m.	7	24 wks
1978	17.5	Mon 20 Mar 6:40 p.m.	5	11 wks

A special tribute to Hughie Green and the show from those who found success after appearing on it. They include Pam Ayres, Frank Carson, Freddie Davies, Les Dawson, Berni Flint, Mary Hopkin, Little and Large, Tom O'Connor, Peters and Lee, and Lena Zavaroni.

Other 'Arf, The   9 wks

ATV, situation comedy

This series by Terence Howard concerned the romance between upper class MP Charles Latimer (John Standing) and Cockney model Lorraine Watts (Lorraine Chase).
Producer: Tony Charles. **Executive Producer:** Allan McKeown.

| 1980 | 11.8 | Fri 27 Jun 7:30 p.m. | 12 | 5 wks |

'Open to the Public'
The couple visit the estate of Lord Apthorpe (James Villiers).
Director: John Kaye Cooper.

| 1981 | 13.0 | Fri 15 May 8:30 p.m. | 7 | 4 wks |

'A Man of Property'
Charles hits snags when he tries to help a woman being evicted from her home.
Director: Alan Wallis.

Other 'Arf, The   5 wks

Central, situation comedy

| 1984 | 14.0 | Fri 24 Feb 8:30 p.m. | 9 | 5 wks |

Charles is out of politics and Lorraine is out of a job.
Director: Douglas Argent.

Other Man, The   1 wk

Granada, drama

| 1964 | 6.9 | Mon 7 Sep 8:00 p.m. | 6 | 1 wk |

With a duration of 2 hours 25 minutes, this is the longest single play ever shown on ITV in one night. It has a cast of 200 with 60 speaking parts. The plot is complex. Suffice it to say a man and a woman are unaccountably scrambling up a mountainside. What is the deeply disturbing significance of a row of incinerators? Starring Michael

Caine, Sian Phillips and John Thaw with Peter Dyneley, Nigel Green, William Kendall, Godfrey Quigley and Vladek Sheybal. Also appearing are Kenneth Colley, George Layton and John Noakes.
Writer: Giles Cooper. **Designer:** Roy Stonehouse. **Director:** Gordon Flemyng. **Producer:** Gerald Savory.

Our Henry's 50th — 1 wk

BBC, entertainment

| 1984 | 9.3 | Wed 2 May 9:30 p.m. | 15 | 1 wk |

The Variety Club of Great Britain hosts a special birthday party at the London Hilton for Henry Cooper OBE, KSG, who is fifty years old tomorrow.
Director: Simon Betts. **Producer:** Ken Griffin.

Our House — 2 wks

ABC, situation comedy

Many characters lived under the same roof in this series. They were portrayed by, among others, Hylda Baker, Bernard Bresslaw, Charles Hawtrey, Hattie Jacques, Harry Korris, Leigh Maddison and Johnny Vyvyan. Not all the residents appeared in each story.

| 1961 | 5.1 | Sat 11 Nov 7:40 p.m. | 17 | 2 wks |

'Best Man'
Simon (Charles Hawtrey) works himself up into a neurotic state when he agrees to be best man at a friend's wedding.
Writer: Norman Hudis. **Producer:** Ernest Maxin.

Our Kind of Girl — 3 wks

ATV, music

This series starred singer Alma Cogan, billed as 'the girl with a laugh in her voice'. She made her first hit record in 1954 and remained hugely popular until her untimely death from cancer on 26 October, 1966, aged 34.

| 1961 | 5.0 | Thu 28 Sep 8:00 p.m. | 15 | 3 wks |

Guests: The Dallas Boys, Gary Miller and Mike and Bernie Winters with the Alyn Ainsworth orchestra.
Producer: Jo Douglas.

Our Man at Saint Mark's — 43 wks

AR, situation comedy

This series about incidents in the daily life of a country vicar was written and devised by James Kelly and Peter Miller. (In the first series Leslie Phillips starred as Rev. Andrew Parker, but subsequently the Vicar was Rev. Stephen Young played by Donald Sinden. Joan Hickson was the housekeeper, Mrs Peace.
Director (1964–66): Richard Doubleday. **Producer:** Eric Maschwitz.

| 1963 | 7.0 | Wed 27 Nov 9:10 p.m. | 11 | 6 wks |

'The Executive'
An unexpected gift to the old peoples' club lands the Rev. Andrew Parker in some equally unexpected trouble.
Director: Christopher Hodson.

| 1964 | 6.0 | Thu 16 Apr 7:30 p.m. | 5 | 13 wks |

'Quite Nice in Amersham'
The new vicar, Rev. Stephen Young, arrives and immediately finds himself at odds with Mrs Peace.

| 1965 | 7.4 | Mon 21 Jun 9:10 p.m. | 3 | 13 wks |

'Pay Now – Live Later'
With the help of Rev. Young, Mrs Peace decides to take out some insurance.

| 1966 | 6.8 | Mon 12 Sep 9:10 p.m. | 3 | 11 wks |

'My Uncle Oswald'
Rev. Young finds himself in conflict with a patron of his parish who has feudal ideas.

Our Man Flint — 1 wk

Presented by ITV, film

| 1975 | 7.7 | Wed 3 Dec 8:00 p.m. | 8 | 1 wk |

Derek Flint (James Coburn) is a karate champion, a brain surgeon and a nuclear physicist. He is considered the only man capable of outwiting GALAXY, an organization trying to gain control of the world. Also starring Lee J. Cobb.
Director: Daniel Mann.

Ours is a Nice House — 8 wks

LWT, situation comedy

This series was created and written by Harry Littlewood and starred Thora Hird as Thora Parker, landlady of a northcountry boarding house. The boarders came and went from series to series but neighbour Elsie Crabtree (Ruth Holden) begged and borrowed with regularity.
Producer: Stuart Allen.

| 1969 | 6.5 | Fri 14 Nov 7:30 p.m. | 12 | 6 wks |

'Hook, Line and Sinker'
Thora's eccentric Aunt Enid (Nora Nicholson) arrives for a short holiday, but soon it is the Parkers who need the holiday.

| 1970 | 5.0 | Sat 15 Aug 6:45 p.m. | 16 | 2 wks |

'Pretty Bubbles in the Air'
Thora is not pleased when she learns one of her guests is a stripper, Bubbles La Verne (Carmel Cryan). To make matters worse, Bubbles works at the Celebration Club, managed by one of Thora's resident boarders, Dudley Banks Smith (Ray Fell).

....

Out
3 wks

Thames, drama

This six-part serial by Trevor Preston starred Tom Bell as Frank Ross, recently out of prison and back in circulation with the determination to discover who it was who shopped him. Lynn Farleigh also starred as his deranged wife, a patient in a mental hospital.

| 1978 | 11.3 | Mon 14 Aug 9:00 p.m. | 11 | 3 wks |

'A Little Heart to Heart with Miss Bangor'
Frank has his first clue as to who informed on him eight years ago. But, as Detective Inspector Bryce (Norman Rodway) says: 'The way he's going on he'll be back inside or lying in an alleyway with a chalk line drawn around him.'
Director: Jim Goddard. **Producer:** Barry Hanson. **Executive Producer:** Johnny Goodman.

....

Out of this World
3 wks

ABC, drama

Boris Karloff introduced this science-fiction series of one-hour dramas.

| 1962 | 4.6 | Sat 30 Jun 10:00 p.m. | 11 | 3 wks |

'The Yellow Pill' by Rog Phillips, dramatized by Leon Griffiths.
Dr Frame (Nigel Stock) is confronted by a highly unusual case when police bring to him a man suspected of murder (Richard Pasco) who claims to come from another era.
Director: Jonathan Alwyn. **Producer:** Leonard White.

....

Outlaw Josey Wales, The
1 wk

Presented by ITV, film

| 1983 | 10.4 | Mon 29 Aug 9:05 p.m. | 5 | 1 wk |

Josey Wales (Clint Eastwood) vows revenge when Union raiders burn his farm and murder his wife and child.
Director: Clint Eastwood.

Outsider, The
5 wks

YTV, drama

This serial in seven parts by Michael J. Bird was set in the Yorkshire market town of Micklethorpe. John Duttine starred as journalist Frank Scully, who was just passing through visiting old friends – or so he thought.

| 1983 | 10.9 | Fri 21 Oct 9:00 p.m. | 15 | 5 wks |

'Vacant Possession'
A woman is upset when photographs of her as a child are found in the safe of a deceased old man.
Designer: David Crozier. **Director:** Frank W. Smith. **Producer:** Michael Glynn. **Executive Producer:** David Cunliffe.

....

Overboard
1 wk

Presented by BBC, film

| 1991 | 11.6 | Sat 6 Apr 7:40 p.m. | 16 | 1 wk |

A confused and wealthy woman is suffering from amnesia after falling from her yacht. A struggling carpenter sees his chance and claims she is his wife. Goldie Hawn and Kurt Russell star.
Director: Garry Marshall.

....

Overland Trail
5 wks

USA presented by BBC, western

Stage coach driver Kelly (William Bendix) and his young assistant Flip (Doug McClure) slowly headed west with the pioneers.

| 1961 | 5.1 | Sun 5 Nov 5:15 p.m. | 17 | 5 wks |

'All the O'Mara's Horses'
Kelly discovers that his arch rival O'Mara is running a rival stage line.

....

Owner Occupied
1 wk

Thames, drama

| 1977 | 6.3 | Mon 25 Jul 8:00 p.m. | 7 | 1 wk |

This single thirty-minute drama by Robert Banks Stewart is set in the occupied Channel Islands at an hotel where even the presence of the Third Reich fails to interfere with tea and croquet. Starring Hannah Gordon, Robert Hardy and Richard Murdoch.
Designer: David Richens. **Producer:** Robert Reed.

P

P. D. James — 3 wks

Anglia, drama

This series adapted stories by the thriller writer P. D. James.

1991	12.6	Fri 8 Feb 9:00 p.m.	15	3 wks

'Devices and Desires' *dramatized by Thomas Ellice.*
The final episode of this six-part murder mystery stars Roy Marsden as Detective Chief Inspector Adam Dalgliesh on the trail of a murderer who has killed several victims in the north Norfolk countryside. When his chief suspect proves to have an alibi, and he receives a note from someone called 'The Whistler' swearing that he had nothing to do with the killings, Dalgliesh realizes that the killer is still on the loose. Also starring Susannah York as Meg Dennison and Gemma Jones as Alice Mair.
Director: *John Davies.* **Producer:** *John Rosenberg.*

P.O.S.H. — 1 wk

Central, drama

1982	11.9	Mon 5 Apr 8:00 p.m.	14	1 wk

This single drama by Terence Howard subtitled 'A Room with a View' is set on a luxury cruise ship and stars Steve Alder, John Cater, Michael Cashman and Ronald Lacey. P.O.S.H. stands for Port Out, Starboard Home.
Director: *Christopher Baker.* **Producer:** *Tony Charles.* **Executive Producer:** *Allan McKeown.*

Paint Your Wagon — 1 wk

Presented by ITV, film

1980	18.5	Tue 1 Jan 5:15 p.m.	3	1 wk

Western musical by Alan Jay Lerner and Frederick Loewe set in the California Gold Rush and starring Clint Eastwood, Lee Marvin and Jean Seberg.
Director: *Joshua Logan.*

Pale Rider — 2 wks

Presented by ITV, film

1989	12.1	Mon 1 May 9:00 p.m.	7	1 wk

Clint Eastwood directs and stars as Preacher, a lone horseman who during the 1880s rides into a mining camp settlement which has been attacked by raiders.

1991	12.6	Sat 19 Oct 9:05 p.m.	18	1 wk

Repeat showing of the above film.

Panorama — 1 wk

BBC, documentary

BBC's weekly current affairs hour began in the 1950s. Presenters included Malcolm Muggeridge, Richard Dimbleby, Robert Kee and David Dimbleby.

1975	6.7	Mon 19 May 8:10 p.m.	16	1 wk

A special debate on the Common Market with Shirley Williams putting the case for the pro-marketeers and Enoch Powell for the anti-marketeers. The latter would keep foreign goods out of Britain, force people to buy British and get the country out of the Common Market. Introduced by David Dimbleby.
Editor: *Frank Smith.*

Papillon — 1 wk

Presented by BBC, film

1981	15.7	Thu 1 Jan 9:05 p.m.	9	1 wk

Steve McQueen and Dustin Hoffman star in this movie from the novel by Henri Charrière. Imprisoned for life for a murder he did not commit Charrière based the novel on his own experiences. Years of hardship in the jungle of French penal colonies lie between the inmates and freedom.
Director: *Franklin J. Schaffner.*

Parade | 6 wks

Canada presented by ITV, music

This series of special shows were each headlined by a different singer.

| 1962 | 5.3 | Thu 4 Jan 7:30 p.m. | 11 | 6 wks |

American pop star of the 1950s Rosemary Clooney stars with Nelson Riddle and his orchestra.

Paradise Connection, The | 1 wk

USA presented by BBC, film

| 1981 | 10.9 | Sat 18 Jul 7:35 p.m. | 16 | 1 wk |

Buddy Ebsen stars as a Chicago lawyer who goes to Hawaii in search of his son but becomes involved in a mystery of drug smuggling and murder.
Director: Michael Preece.

Paradise Island | 5 wks

Thames, situation comedy

This series starred Bill Maynard as the Rev. Alexander Goodwin and William Franklyn as Cuthbert Fullworthy, a ship's entertainments officer. As the sole survivors of a shipping disaster in the Pacific, they ended up on a desert island.

| 1977 | 7.6 | Thu 21 Apr 7:35 p.m. | 14 | 5 wks |

In this first episode, by Michael Haley, Fullworthy is all for making a raft to head for Australia but Goodwin is quite content where he is.
Producer: Stuart Allen.

Paras, The | 5 wks

BBC, documentary

This series of seven programmes written and presented by Glyn Worsnip followed 41 recruits in the 480 Platoon of the Paratroopers through 22 weeks of the toughest military training in the world.

| 1983 | 12.5 | Thu 7 Apr 8:30 p.m. | 11 | 3 wks |

'Wings'
As the Platoon moves on to parachuting, and the RAF instructors take over from the Army, only 17 of the original 41 recruits remain. They are put on 24-hour standby as reinforcements for the Falkland Islands campaign.
Camera: Dave Gray. **Producer:** Bill Jones. **Executive Producer:** David Harrison.

| 1984 | 8.1 | Thu 2 Aug 8:30 p.m. | 15 | 2 wks |

'Basic Wales'
Enduring the miseries of winter on the Brecon Beacons proves a tough challenge for the remaining 29 recruits. (The 1983 series was repeated in 1984.)

Pardon the Expression | 30 wks

Granada, situation comedy

The first and only character to have a spinoff series from CORONATION STREET was Leonard Swindley (Arthur Lowe), whose conversation often contained the phrase 'If you'll pardon the expression'. Swindley left Gamma Garments where he had worked in 'The Street' and moved up in the world to the post of assistant manager at a branch of Dobson and Hawks, a national chain store. The store manager, Ernest Parbold, was played by Paul Dawkins. Betty Driver portrayed the canteen manageress. The series was written by Harry Driver and Jack Rosenthal.

| 1965 | 6.1 | Wed 16 Jun 7:00 p.m. | 6 | 12 wks |

Mr Swindley plays Solomon while everyone else plays Hamlet.
Director: Walter Butler. **Producer:** Harry Driver. **Executive Producer:** H. V. Kershaw.

| 1966 | 7.0 | Mon 9 Jan 9:10 p.m. | 3 | 18 wks |

'The Sailor Home from the Sea'
Mr Swindley is installed in a new flat which belongs to Dobson and Hawks. When the Brigadier (Anthony Sharpe) comes to inspect he discovers Swindley has been entertaining visitors.
Writer: Christopher Bond. **Director:** Michael Cox. **Producer:** Derek Granger. **Executive Producer:** H. V. Kershaw.

Paris 1900 | 1 wk

Granada, comedy

These six farces by Georges Feydeau were adapted and produced by Philip Mackie and directed by Silvio Narizzano. The regular company of players included Judy Cornwell, Adrienne Corri, Kenneth Griffith, Henry McGee, Alfred Marks and Paul Whitsun-Jones.

| 1964 | 5.3 | Fri 2 Oct 9:50 p.m. | 20 | 1 wk |

'The Ribadier System'
Monsieur Ribadier (Alfred Marks) marries a beautiful widow – but she has learned well from her first husband that all men are deceivers!

Parkinson | 2 wks

BBC, talk show

This series of chat shows was hosted by journalist Michael Parkinson, who began his television career on Granada's local show, SCENE AT 6:30.

| 1980 | 13.9 | Sat 29 Nov 10:00 p.m. | 18 | 1 wk |

Guests: Paul Daniels, Engelbert Humperdinck and Willie Rushton. **Director:** Bruce Milliard. **Producer:** John Fisher.

| 1983 | 6.4 | Sat 30 Jul 10:00 p.m. | 17 | 1 wk |

A 1981 interview with David Niven is repeated following his death yesterday.
Producers: Graham Lindsay and Gill Stribling-Wright. **Executive Producer:** John Fisher.

Parkinson Meets Peter Sellers — 1 wk

BBC, talk show

| 1980 | 11.5 | Sat 26 Jul 9:10 p.m. | 2 | 1 wk |

Michael Parkinson's 1974 interview with Peter Sellers is repeated as a tribute to the actor, who died at 12:30 a.m. at the Middlesex Hospital on Thursday 24 July, aged fifty-four.
Producer: Richard Drewett.

Partners — 5 wks

BBC, situation comedy

This series by Richard Waring starred Derek Waring as Rupert Bannister, chairman of Bannister Bathroom Fittings, and Millicent Martin as his wife Diana.

| 1981 | 15.6 | Thu 26 Feb 8:30 p.m. | 8 | 5 wks |

'Conventional Behaviour'
Bannister takes a trip to a convention in Brighton.
Producer: Harold Snoad.

Partners in Crime — 4 wks

LWT, drama

This series of ten adaptations of Agatha Christie short stories concerned detectives Tommy and Tuppence Beresford (James Warwick and Francesca Annis).

| 1983 | 12.1 | Sun 23 Oct 7:45 p.m. | 11 | 4 wks |

'The House of Lurking Death' adapted by Jonathan Hales.
Three people living in an isolated house become violently ill after eating chocolates.
Designer: John Clements. **Director:** Christopher Hodson. **Producer:** Jack Williams.

Party Political Broadcast — 64 wks

BBC and ITV, politics

Prior to the launch of BBC2, Party Political Broadcasts were shown simultaneously on both channels, affording the viewer no choice of programmes whatsoever.

| 1960 | 7.3 | Wed 30 Nov 9:30 p.m. | 1 | 9 wks |

Broadcast on behalf of the Labour Party entitled **'Homes, Rents, and Pensions'**.

| 1961 | 7.6 | Wed 22 Nov 9:30 p.m. | 1 | 8 wks |

'Relevant and Decisive' was broadcast on behalf of the Conservative and Unionist Party by the Rt. Hon. Iain Macleod MP.

| 1962 | 8.3 | Wed 7 Nov 9:30 p.m. | 2 | 11 wks |

Broadcast on behalf of the Labour Party by the Rt. Hon. James Callaghan MP.

| 1963 | 9.8 | Wed 27 Feb 9:30 p.m. | 1 | 14 wks |

Broadcast by the Leader of the Opposition, the Rt. Hon. Harold Wilson OBE, MP.

| 1964 | 10.4 | Wed 29 Jan 9:30 p.m. | 1 | 18 wks |

'Twelve Wasted Years' was a study of Conservative propaganda broadcast by the Labour Party.

| 1981 | 11.9 | Wed 16 Sep 9:00 p.m. | 14 | 1 wk |

This broadcast on behalf of the Labour Party was shown at this time by ITV.

| 1982 | 13.7 | Wed 17 Mar 9:00 p.m. | 7 | 1 wk |

This broadcast on behalf of the Labour Party was shown at this time by ITV.

| 1983 | 20.6 | Wed 26 Jan 9:00 p.m. | 1 | 2 wks |

This broadcast on behalf of the Labour Party was shown on BBC1, BBC2 and ITV. The viewing figures were totalled and the programme was given a single chart position.

Pass the Buck — 2 wks

Thames, game show

Host George Layton tested couples on their awareness of their partner's general knowledge.

| 1986 | 11.5 | Mon 31 Mar 9:15 p.m. | 15 | 2 wks |

Director: Robert Reed. **Producer:** Malcolm Morris.

The highest rated **Party Political Broadcast** of 1960 was presented on behalf of the Labour Party by Bob Mellish.

Passage, The — 1 wk

Presented by ITV, film

1983 | **8.6** | **Sat 20 Aug 9:30 p.m.** | **10** | **1 wk**

During the Second World War a Basque shepherd guides a scientist and his family through an icy pass in the Pyrenees to Spain. They are pursued by relentless SS officers. Starring Christopher Lee, Malcolm McDowell, James Mason, Patricia Neal and Anthony Quinn.
Director: J. Lee-Thompson.

Passage to India, A — 1 wk

Presented by BBC, film

1988 | **11.9** | **Sun 3 Apr 7:15 p.m.** | **9** | **1 wk**

Easter Sunday showing of David Lean's adaptation of E. M. Forster's novel. Starring Peggy Ashcroft, Victor Banerjee, Judy Davis, James Fox, Alec Guinness, Nigel Havers, Saeed Jaffrey, Art Malik and Richard Wilson.

Passenger, The — 3 wks

BBC, drama

This Francis Durbridge thriller in three parts starred Peter Barkworth as Detective Inspector Denson and Joanna Durham as Sue Denson.

1971 | **7.1** | **Sat 6 Nov 8:55 p.m.** | **9** | **3 wks**

One murder leads to another in this story of infidelity and intrigue.
Designer: Peter Kindred. **Director:** Michael Ferguson. **Producer:** Gerard Glaister.

Passing of Leviathan, The — 1 wk

Anglia, documentary

1975 | **6.0** | **Mon 7 Jul 8:00 p.m.** | **10** | **1 wk**

This film by Des and Jen Bartlett was introduced by Orson Welles. The Bartletts have lived for two years on a remote beach in Patagonia filming whales in danger of extinction.
Producer: Aubrey Buxton.

Patrick, Dear Patrick — 1 wk

Thames, entertainment

1972 | **6.3** | **Wed 26 Jan 8:00 p.m.** | **19** | **1 wk**

An evening with Patrick Cargill and his guests Joyce Carey, Bernard Cribbins, Patrick Macnee, Nina, Beryl Reid, the Geoff Love orchestra and the Mike Sammes singers.
Producer: William G. Stewart.

Paul Daniels' Blackpool Bonanza — 3 wks

Granada, entertainment

This variety series starred magician Paul Daniels with guests.

1978 | **12.8** | **Sat 13 Aug 8:10 p.m.** | **2** | **3 wks**

Guests: Colin Crompton, Ricki Lee, the Konyots, Roy Walker and Arlene Phillips' Night Fever, with the Les Reed orchestra.
Director: Milo Lewis. **Producer:** John Hamp.

Paul Daniels' Golden Rose Show — 1 wk

BBC, magic

1987 | **14.2** | **Sat 21 Feb 7:30 p.m.** | **5** | **1 wk**

A repeat of the show which won the Golden Rose of Montreux in 1985 with Paul, Debbie McGee and guests Tom Noddy and Airjazz, with the Brian Rogers dancers.
Director: David Taylor. **Producer:** John Fisher.

Paul Daniels Magic Christmas Show, The — 2 wks

BBC, magic

1984 | **14.3** | **Tue 25 Dec 6:35 p.m.** | **19** | **1 wk**

Guests: George Carl, Kris Kremo, Robert Maxwell and the Olympiads.
Director: Geoff Miles. **Producer:** John Fisher.

1985 | **13.8** | **Thu 26 Dec 6:20 p.m.** | **20** | **1 wk**

A magical version of Snow White with Debbie McGee as the title character and Fenella Fielding as the Wicked Queen. Other guests include Lance Burton, Matthew Corbett and Sooty, The Jazzy Jumpers, Zhou Shurong and the Brian Rogers dancers.
Director: Geoff Miles. **Producer:** John Fisher.

Paul Daniels' Magical Christmas — 1 wk

BBC, magic

1981 | **16.9** | **Fri 25 Dec 6:35 p.m.** | **3** | **1 wk**

Guests: Pierre Brahma, Les Samurai and Tux.
Director: Bill Wilson. **Producer:** James Moir.

Paul Daniels Magic Show, The   59 wks

BBC, magic

Paul Daniels came from the north-east of England practising his magical skills in working men's clubs, stopping off for a couple of series at Granada in 1977 and 1978, before arriving in London at the BBC and becoming the most successful magician in the history of British television. From 1982 Paul was assisted by Debbie McGee, who was also Mrs Daniels.
Directors included John Hughes (1979–81), John Bishop (1982–83) and Michael Leggo (1986–87). **Producer** (to 1988): John Fisher (himself a member of the Magic Circle).

| 1979 | 15.0 | Sat 22 Dec 7:55 p.m. | 4 | 5 wks |

Guests: Jeffrey Atkins, The Duo Brumbach, Bablu Mallick and Wong Mow Ting.

| 1980 | 16.2 | Sat 18 Oct 8:05 p.m. | 6 | 5 wks |

Guests: Hans Moretti and Geroku.

| 1981 | 14.9 | Sat 10 Oct 8:00 p.m. | 3 | 6 wks |

Guests: Rob Murray, Miss Maty and Karah Khavak with his crocodiles.

| 1982 | 11.8 | Sat 30 Oct 8:20 p.m. | 9 | 9 wks |

Guests: Hans Moretti and Johnny Paul.

| 1983 | 12.1 | Sat 19 Nov 8:00 p.m. | 11 | 8 wks |

Guests: Duban Nickol, Lev Schneider and Fred Trueman.

| 1984 | 13.0 | Sat 6 Oct 8:00 p.m. | 7 | 8 wks |

Guests: Laurence Fanon, Roberto Gasser, George Grimmond and Bernard Price.
Director: Geoff Miles.

| 1985 | 12.4 | Sat 9 Nov 8:30 p.m. | 8 | 3 wks |

Guests: The Boginos, Jeff McBride and Anneka Rice.
Director: David Taylor.

| 1986 | 11.7 | Sat 6 Dec 7:20 p.m. | 16 | 2 wks |

Guests: Lionel Jeffries, John Twomey and Stanley Unwin.

| 1987 | 14.5 | Sat 17 Jan 7:25 p.m. | 4 | 6 wks |

Guests: Topper Martyn and Moy Wright.

| 1988 | 12.7 | Sat 2 Jan 7:25 p.m. | 13 | 3 wks |

Guests: John Gaughan, Mat Pendl and Jamey Turner.
Director: Kevin Bishop.

| 1989 | 13.5 | Sat 18 Feb 7:40 p.m. | 12 | 4 wks |

Guests: Les Foubrac and the Skating Willers.
Producer: Geoff Miles.

Paul Squire Show, The   3 wks

ATV, comedy

Paul Squire found overnight success in the 1980 Royal Variety Performance and was rewarded with his own series in 1981. It was all about making a show. Bobby Knutt played his script-writer, Anna Dawson his producer, Bernard Spear his pianist and Debbie Arnold his secretary.
Producer: Royston Mayoh.

| 1981 | 10.3 | Wed 2 Sep 7:00 p.m. | 20 | 1 wk |

Paul meets his new production team. Guests: Wall Street Crash.

| 1982 | 8.8 | Thu 15 Jul 7:15 p.m. | 18 | 2 wks |

Preparations for the show continue despite the writer turning in useless jokes and the pianist having a broken arm. Guests: Wall Street Crash.

Pearl   1 wk

USA presented by BBC, drama

This three-part mini-series concerned those stationed at Pearl Harbor at the time of the Japanese attack. Starring Alan Arkin, Angie Dickinson, Robert Wagner, Lesley Anne Warren and Dennis Weaver.
Directors: Hy Averback and Alex Singer. **Producer:** Sam Manners.

| 1979 | 13.4 | Mon 19 Nov 9:25 p.m. | 18 | 1 wk |

Part Three
Bombing raids have all but obliterated Pearl Harbor, destroying American planes and the US fleet, and killing thousands of military personnel and civilians. Those who survive try to rebuild their lives. Colonel Forrest (Dennis Weaver) is appointed to organize the reconstruction.

Penmarric   2 wks

BBC, drama

Susan Howatch's story set in late nineteenth-century Cornwall was dramatized in twelve parts.

| 1979 | 20.2 | Fri 12 Oct 8:05 p.m. | 12 | 2 wks |

Part One, dramatized by John Prebble.
Maud Castallack (Angela Scoular), estranged from her husband, calls her eldest son Mark (Martin C. Thurley) to a meeting. Although she abandoned him four years ago, it is time he knew of his inheritance. Also starring Ralph Bates, John Castle, Paul Darrow and Shaughan Seymour.
Designers: Austin Ruddy and Colin Green. **Director:** Tina Wakerell.
Producer: Ron Craddock.

1

2

3

1 *The Bruce Forsyth Show* in 1966 was the entertainer's first Number One since 'Sunday Night At The London Palladium'.

2 In a Number One follow-up to a Number One hit, Dana meets the host in **Bruce and More Girls**.

3 Bruce Forsyth welcomes the Three Degrees to his 1976 special **Bring on the Girls**.

4 *The Generation Game* first reached Number One in 1973 hosted by Bruce Forsyth and Anthea Redfern.

5 *Bruce's Choice* featured the host's favourite clips from 'The Generation Game' with hostess Anthea Redfern.

6 Bruce Forsyth challenges a couple to Beat the Clock in **Sunday Night at the London Palladium**.

People `1 wk`

BBC, documentary

This series about the Great British Public was presented by Derek Jameson.

1988	9.5	Tue 12 Jul 7:00 p.m.	17	1 wk

Among tonight's Great British Public are a Lincolnshire 'supermum', a Punch and Judy man from Llandudno and a survivor of the Zeebrugge disaster. Reporters are Jeni Barnett, Lucy Pilkington and Chris Serle.
Producer: Sarah Caplin. **Series Producer:** Peter Bazalgette.

People Do the Funniest Things `6 wks`

LWT, comedy

Jeremy Beadle hosted this series looking at television's funny moments. He set up hidden cameras to record amusing scenes.
Director: Nick Vaughan-Barratt. **Producer:** Trevor Hopkins.

1986	17.8	Sat 11 Jan 7:45 p.m.	3	3 wks
1987	13.7	Sat 21 Feb 6:45 p.m.	9	3 wks

People in Conflict `1 wk`

BBC, documentary

This series was about groups and individuals for whom society often fails to cater adequately.

1968	6.7	Thu 14 Nov 9:55 p.m.	10	1 wk

Colin Morris talks about the problems of blindness with Harry Minton, a man who suddenly lost his sight.
Director: Simon Wadleigh. **Producer:** Bridget Winter.

People Like Us `1 wk`

LWT, drama

This series was a thirteen-part adaptation by various writers of The Avenue stories by R. F. Delderfield about five London families.

1978	10.2	Fri 23 Jun 9:00 p.m.	19	1 wk

'New Alliances' dramatized by James Saunders.
In this final episode, the Second World War has just started, bringing great changes to every home.
Director: Barry Davis. **Producer:** James Brabazon. **Executive Producer:** Tony Wharmby.

People that Time Forgot, The `1 wk`

Presented by ITV, film

1984	9.7	Sat 18 Aug 8:00 p.m.	5	1 wk

In this sequel to THE LAND THAT TIME FORGOT, from a story by Edgar Rice Burroughs, a canister is found off the coast of Scotland. It contains a message sent by Bowen Tyler (Doug McClure), who was marooned in 1916 on the lost island of Caprona.
Director: Kevin Connor.

Perfect Hero, A `5 wks`

ITV, drama

This wartime drama by Allan Prior was based on the book by Christopher Matthew. Nigel Havers starred as Hugh Fleming and James Fox was surgeon Angus Meikle. Bernard Hepton and Barbara Leigh-Hunt also starred as Hugh's parents Arthur and Iris Fleming. His fiancée, Bunty, was played by Fiona Gilles.

1991	10.3	Fri 17 May 9.00 p.m.	15	5 wks

Fleming and his fellow RAF pilots are waiting to scramble.
Producer: James Cellan Jones.

Permission to Kill `1 wk`

Presented by BBC, film

1983	7.2	Tue 23 Aug 9:25 p.m.	15	1 wk

British agent Alan Curtis (Dirk Bogarde) blackmails five people to help him assassinate an East European liberation leader. Ava Gardner also stars.
Director: Cyril Frankel.

Perry Mason `46 wks`

USA presented by BBC, drama

Raymond Burr played the famous lawyer created by Erle Stanley Gardner. The series ran from 1957 to 1965, during which time he never lost a case. A murder would be investigated by trilby-hatted Lieutenant Arthur Tragg (Ray Collins) who, with District Attorney Hamilton Burger (William Talman), would build a watertight case. The suspect went to Mason, who examined the evidence with his secretary Della Street (Barbara Hale) and private detective Paul Drake (William Hopper). The case would always look beyond hope for Mason's client, but during the trial a witness would crack or last-minute evidence would be turned up by Drake.

1961	5.5	Sat 30 Sep 8:50 p.m.	8	6 wks

'The Case of the Lucky Loser'
Mason is retained by a man to clear his grandson of a hit and run driving charge.

| 1962 | 5.4 | Sat 17 Mar 7:45 p.m. | 10 | 15 wks |

'The Case of the Golden Fraud'
The world's most precious metal attracts the criminal fraternity and presents Mason with a difficult case.

| 1963 | 6.0 | Sun 20 Jan 8:10 p.m. | 13 | 2 wks |

'The Case of the Treacherous Toupée'
A businessman is found murdered with some false hair on his hand. This proves embarrassing for Perry Mason when he learns that his client in the case wears a toupée.

| 1964 | 7.7 | Sat 4 Jul 8:55 p.m. | 3 | 5 wks |

'The Case of the Skeleton's Closet'
A simple case of invasion of privacy turns into a murder trial when the author of a book on life in a small town is found dead.

| 1965 | 6.7 | Mon 4 Jan 9:25 p.m. | 9 | 14 wks |

'The Case of the Garrulous Go-Between'
A young man is arrested for murder after a fortune-teller has warned of impending death.

| 1966 | 5.6 | Mon 21 Jan 9:00 p.m. | 20 | 2 wks |

'The Case of the Twelfth Wildcat'
The disputed ownership of a football team leads to murder.

| 1967 | 6.2 | Fri 7 Jul 9:05 p.m. | 7 | 2 wks |

'The Case of the Crafty Kidnapper'
A child is kidnapped to prevent its parents giving evidence as witnesses to a murder.

Perry Mason Returns   2 wks

USA presented by BBC, drama

| 1987 | 10.7 | Fri 17 Apr 7:35 p.m. | 13 | 2 wks |

Mason (Raymond Burr) is lured out of retirement when his long-time assistant Della Street (Barbara Hale) faces a murder charge. He defends her against seemingly impossible odds.
Writer: Dean Hargrove. **Director:** Ron Satlof. **Producer:** Barry Steinberg.

Person Responsible, The   1 wk

ATV, drama

| 1974 | 6.5 | Tue 17 Sep 10:30 p.m. | 5 | 1 wk |

This play by Ellen Dryden stars Kenneth Haigh as Michael Beasley, a man having daily problems with his wife (Lynn Farleigh). He is anxious to make a success of his new appointment to the headmastership of a comprehensive school. In the absence of support from home, he turns to deputy headmistress Miss Chapman (Gwen Watford).

Designer: Ken Wheatley. **Director:** Don Taylor. **Producer:** Nicholas Palmer.

Person Unknown   1 wk

Anglia, drama

| 1967 | 6.1 | Thu 23 Mar 9:40 p.m. | 13 | 1 wk |

Television adaptation by David Butler of an original story by Olive Chase and Stanley Clayton. A female student disappears from college and is later found murdered. Starring John Gregson and Elizabeth Sellars with Michael Coles, Felicity Kendal, Wendy Varnals and John Wood.
Producer: John Jacobs.

Personal Appearance   2 wks

Granada, entertainment

This was a series of single variety shows with a star and guests.

| 1961 | 4.7 | Tue 31 Oct 9:50 p.m. | 19 | 1 wk |

Starring Victor Borge with Bill Grundy and Leonid Hambro.
Producer: Mark Stuart.

| 1962 | 4.0 | Wed 11 Jul 9:45 p.m. | 20 | 1 wk |

Starring Bing Crosby and Bob Hope with Edie Adams, Gary Crosby, Pete Fountain and the Smothers Brothers. (This USA show was bought in by Granada and transmitted as part of this series).

Persuaders, The   24 wks

ATV, drama

This series starred Roger Moore as Lord Brett Sinclair and Tony Curtis as Danny Wilde, a self-made millionaire from New York. Together they roamed the world fighting corruption.

| 1971 | 8.5 | Thu 14 Oct 8:00 p.m. | 1 | 16 wks |

'Powerswitch' by John Kruse.
The body of a beautiful young girl is found floating in a bay on the Côte d'Azur. Her flatmate Pekoe (Annette André) involves Danny and Brett to determine what happened.
Director: Basil Dearden.

| 1972 | 7.8 | Fri 21 Jan 7:30 p.m. | 4 | 8 wks |

'The Morning After' by Walter Black.
Brett awakes after a night on the booze to find he has a glamorous wife. Is it genuine or has he been tricked?
Director: Leslie Norman. **Producers:** Robert S. Baker and Johnny Goodman.

Tony Curtis and Roger Moore were **The Persuaders**.

Persuaders, The | 1 wk

BBC, documentary

This series explored the worlds of advertising and marketing.

| 1979 | 14.1 | Thu 16 Aug 8:30 p.m. | 20 | 1 wk |

'Rolling the Bandwagon'
As the new Disney film The Black Hole is released, shops stock up on associated merchandise.
Director: Mike Healey. **Producer:** David Martin.

Persuasion | 2 wks

Granada, drama

Jane Austen's story was adapted for television in five parts by Julian Mitchell.

| 1971 | 5.8 | Sun 25 Apr 10:15 p.m. | 14 | 2 wks |

Part Two
Anne Elliot (Ann Firbank) has just met Captain Wentworth (Bryan Marshall) for the first time since she turned down his proposal eight years ago. How does she feel about him now?
Designer: Peter Phillips. **Producer:** Howard Baker.

Petrocelli | 5 wks

USA presented by BBC, drama

Barry Newman starred as Tony Petrocelli, a lawyer in the American Southwest. Susan Howard played his wife Maggie and Albert Salmi portrayed Pete Ritter.
Producers: Edward J. Milkis and Thomas Miller.

| 1978 | 11.5 | Fri 19 May 9:25 p.m. | 20 | 1 wk |

'Edge of Evil'
Petrocelli's old friend is murdered. The man caught running away from the scene asks if he will defend him.

| 1979 | 21.7 | Fri 5 Oct 8:10 p.m. | 8 | 4 wks |

'Survival'
Armed crooks hunt Petrocelli across the desert. His life and half a million dollars are at stake.

Petula Clark | 1 wk

BBC, music

| 1967 | 5.5 | Sat 22 Apr 8:35 p.m. | 17 | 1 wk |

352

Petula Clark stars in this special from the Talk of the Town, London, with the Breakaways and the Harry Rabinowitz orchestra.
Producer: Yvonne Littlewood.

Phantom of the Opera, The | 1 wk

Presented by BBC, film

| 1990 | 8.5 | Sun 26 Aug 8:35 p.m. | 20 | 1 wk |

Charles Dance stars as the Phantom with Burt Lancaster as Gérard Carrière in Gaston Leroux's story of the deformed man who rules the dark world beneath the Paris Opéra. Also starring Andrea Ferreol as Carlotta, Geri Polo as Christine, Ian Richardson as Cholet and Adam Storke as Count Philippe de Chagny.
Director: Tony Richardson.

Piano Smashers of the Golden Sun, The | 1 wk

ATV, drama

| 1974 | 5.6 | Tue 2 Jul 9:00 p.m. | 17 | 1 wk |

This play by Willis Hall was set in a northern pub, The Golden Sun, which is the sole surviving building in an area bulldozed by planners. Now the new flats are going up and the pub's regulars, who've stayed loyal throughout the demolition, decide to celebrate by holding a piano smashing contest.
Designer: Vic Symonds. **Director:** John Nelson Burton. **Producer:** Nicholas Palmer.

Piccadilly Palace | 4 wks

ATV, entertainment

This variety series starred Bruce Forsyth and Millicent Martin with the Paddy Stone dancers and the Jack Parnell orchestra.
Writers: Sid Green and Dick Hills.

| 1968 | 8.0 | Sun 11 Feb 10:05 p.m. | 3 | 4 wks |

Guest: Matt Monro.
Producer: Colin Clews.

Picnic, The | 1 wk

BBC, comedy

| 1976 | 5.4 | Mon 31 May 8:45 p.m. | 20 | 1 wk |

A repeat showing of the silent film which won the Bronze Rose at Montreux in 1976. An elderly General (Ronnie Barker) and his son (Ronnie Corbett) spend a day in the country with their relatives.
Writers: Dave Huggett and Larry Keith. **Producer:** Terry Hughes.

Piece of Cake | 2 wks

Thames, drama

This six-part adaptation by Leon Griffiths of Derek Robinson's novel followed twelve young RAF pilots through the first year of the Second World War.

1988	12.2	Sun 9 Oct 9:00 p.m.	13	2 wks

'Autumn 1939'
The squadron is billeted in an idyllic French château.
Director: Ian Toynton. **Producer:** Andrew Holmes. **Executive Producer:** Linda Agran. (A Holmes Associates production.)

Pied Piper | 1 wk

Granada, drama

1989	11.8	Sun 24 Dec 7:15 p.m.	15	1 wk

This film drama stars Peter O'Toole as John Sidney Howard, the reluctant chaperone to a growing number of children leaving France for England as the Germans advance in 1940.
Director: Norman Stone. **Producer:** Craig McNeil. **Executive Producers:** Michael Cox and Stan Marguiles.

Pig in the Middle | 7 wks

LWT, situation comedy

This series by Terence Brady and Charlotte Bingham about the eternal triangle starred Dinsdale Landon and Joanna Van Gyseghem as Mr and Mrs Barty Wade and Liza Goddard as Nellie Bligh.
Producer: Les Chatfield.

1980	16.9	Sun 27 Jan 8:45 p.m.	5	1 wk

'If Food Be The Music Of Love – Eat On'
Barty is much criticized by his wife for overeating and watching too much television. She is a great giver of parties and Barty likes to talk to people. Enter Nellie Bligh.

1983	11.3	Fri 18 Mar 8:30 p.m.	14	6 wks

'And So . . . To Bed'
Nellie resolves to sort out her tangled relationship with Barty.

Pilger | 3 wks

ATV, documentary

This series of reports from around the world was by television journalist John Pilger.

1975	6.4	Thu 2 Jan 8:30 p.m.	18	1 wk

Pilger reports from Bangladesh on the troubles currently facing that country.
Camera: Ernest Vincze. **Producer:** John Ingram.

1976	7.4	Mon 6 Sep 8:30 p.m.	5	2 wks

One of Pilger's set of reports from the US. Tonight he examines how the abundant food supply of the US is being used as a political weapon.
Camera: Ernest Vincze. **Director:** Richard Marquand. **Producer:** Richard Creasey.

Pink Medicine Show, The | 6 wks

LWT, situation comedy

Doctors Chris Beetles and Robert Buckman wrote this spoof medical show and also took leading parts. Lynda Bellingham, Nickolas Grace and Peter John also starred.

1978	12.0	Fri 7 Jul 7:30 p.m.	9	6 wks

'The Man and the Abdomen'
The surgery is examining the poet Tennyson.
Producer: Paul Smith.

Pink Panther Strikes Again, The | 1 wk

Presented by ITV, film

1983	11.2	Thu 22 Sep 7:30 p.m.	8	1 wk

Following a nervous breakdown, Chief Inspector Dreyfus (Herbert Lom) builds a vast organization dedicated to the extermination of Inspector Clouseau (Peter Sellers). Colin Blakely, Lesley-Anne Down, Burt Kwouk and Leonard Rossiter also star.
Director: Blake Edwards.

Pinky and Perky | 1 wk

BBC, entertainment

These two puppet pigs were created and manipulated by Jan and Vlasta Dalibor.

1966	5.5	Sun 13 Mar 5:55 p.m.	20	1 wk

Assisted by Jimmy Thompson, Pinky and Perky set out to prove that anyone can become Prime Minister.
Writer: Robert Gray. **Producer:** Stan Parkinson.

Pinocchio — 1 wk

Presented by ITV, film

1990 | **11.8** | **Sat 22 Dec 5:35 p.m.** | **17** | **1 wk**

Walt Disney's animated story of the puppet, made by wood carver Gepetto, who becomes a real boy. Dick Jones provides the voice of Pinocchio and Christian Rub that of Gepetto. Former pop star Cliff Edwards is Jiminy Cricket and sings 'When You Wish Upon a Star'.
Directors: Hamilton Luske and Ben Sharpsteen.

....

Pirate, The — 1 wk

USA presented by BBC, drama

This two-part adaptation of Harold Robbins' story about an oil tycoon, known as 'The Pirate', was set against the background of the Arab/Israeli conflict. The Pirate, Baydr Al Fay, was played by Franco Nero. Also starring Anne Archer, James Franciscus, Olivia Hussey, Ian McShane, Christopher Lee and Eli Wallach.
Director: Ken Annakin.

1979 | **15.4** | **Sun 2 Sep 9:00 p.m.** | **16** | **1 wk**

'The Arabian Desert 1933'
The Pirate, who was born a Jew but by a twist of fate raised as a rich Arab ruler, has an indiscreet wife and is hated by his daughter.

....

Place in the Sun, A — 3 wks

YTV, drama

This trilogy of plays set in the South of France starred Odile Versois as Jenny Armstrong and Moray Watson as Martin Armstrong, a property dealer who specialized in villas.

1972 | **7.0** | **Tue 4 Apr 9:00 p.m.** | **3** | **3 wks**

'At the Villa Pandora' by Hugh Whitemore.
The children of former enemies are attracted to each other and Martin finds himself simultaneously facing the past and the future. With guest stars Joyce Carey and Anton Diffring.
Designer: Alan Pickford. **Producer:** John Frankau.

....

Plane Makers, The — 26 wks

ATV, drama

This series created by Wilfred Greatorex dealt with management and union disputes in an aircraft factory, Scott Furlong. After two seasons the action moved to the board room and the title was changed to THE POWER GAME. It starred Patrick Wymark as John Wilder with Barbara Murray as Pamela Wilder and Jack Watling as Don Henderson.
Producer: Rex Firkin.

1963 | **6.3** | **Tue 19 Nov 8:00 p.m.** | **3** | **14 wks**

'The Thing About Auntie' by Raymond Bowers.
Sir Gerald Merle MP (William Devlin) tries to make capital out of gossip surrounding Pamela Wilder and chief test pilot Henry Forbes (Robert Urquhart).
Designer: Eric Shedden. **Director:** Geoffrey Nethercott.

1964 | **7.1** | **Tue 24 Nov 9:10 p.m.** | **5** | **11 wks**

'It's A Free Country – Isn't It?' by Edmund Ward.
The 'Quiet Men' from security call at Scott Furlong and works manager Arthur Sugden (Reginald Marsh) finds himself the subject of their disturbing enquiries.
Designer: Alan Pickford. **Director:** John Cooper.

1965 | **6.7** | **Tue 5 Jan 9:10 p.m.** | **9** | **1 wk**

'A Hoopla of Haloes' by Raymond Bowers.
David Corbett (Alan Dobie) is suspicious of Wilder's continued absence abroad, but when he raises questions he encounters a wall of silence.
Designer: Ray White. **Director:** Eric Price.

....

Planet of the Apes, The — 1 wk

Presented by ITV, film

1977 | **8.2** | **Thu 24 Mar 8.00 p.m.** | **8** | **1 wk**

Charlton Heston stars as George Taylor, one of three astronauts who crash on the planet in a two thousand year time warp. Roddy McDowall and Kim Hunter also star.
Director: Franklin J. Schaffner.

....

Plank, The — 2 wks

Thames, comedy

The brainchild of Eric Sykes, this silent comedy starred him and Arthur Lowe. They made a full day's work out of transporting one plank from a timber yard to a building site. They met many stars along the way. The show was transmitted several times and reached the top twenty twice.
Writer and **Director:** Eric Sykes. **Producer:** David Clark.

1979 | **17.1** | **Mon 17 Dec 8:00 p.m.** | **2** | **1 wk**

1980 | **12.4** | **Wed 4 Feb 7:00 p.m.** | **7** | **1 wk**

(Repeat.)

....

Play for Love, A — 1 wk

YTV, drama

This strand of single plays had a love theme.

1978	13.4	Sun 2 Apr 9:30 p.m.	20	1 wk

'Games' by John Bowen.
Sheila (Barbara Leigh-Hunt) and Donald (Geoffrey Palmer) know what makes their marriage work. To seventeen-year-old Jamie (Ian Sharrock) they are just Mum and Dad until a chance discovery shatters his happy existence.
Designer: Roger Andrews. **Director:** John Glenister. **Executive Producer:** Peter Willes.

....

Play for Today				1 wk

BBC, drama

This series was The Wednesday Play retitled when transmission was moved to Thursdays.

1980	14.5	Thu 3 Jan 9:25 p.m.	17	1 wk

'Chance of a Lifetime' by Robert Holman.
David Daker stars in the story of a school leaver who joins the Army.
Designer: Geoff Powell. **Director:** Giles Foster. **Producer:** Richard Eyre.

....

Play of the Week				147 wks

ITV (various), drama

This long-running strand of single plays was fed by productions from several of the ITV companies.

1960	6.6	Tue 6 Dec 9:35 p.m.	3	23 wks

'The Accomplices' by Paul Lee.
Following the death of Cynthia Hart, all those with information display a reluctance to come forward. Each has his or her own reason for keeping quiet. Starring Renée Asherson, Angela Baddeley, Margot van der Burgh, Iain Cuthbertson, Gareth Davies and Alan MacNaughton.
Designer: Patrick Robertson. **Producer:** Peter Potter. (ATV)

1961	6.4	Tue 11 Apr 9:35 p.m.	2	20 wks

'Midnight Sun' by Claude Spaak, translated by Patricia Moyes.
One man has to make a life-or-death decision when five men are sentenced to death. One, and only one, can be reprieved. Starring David McCallum and Susannah York with Violet Fairbrother, Harold Goldblatt, Olga Lindo and Edward Woodward.
Designer: William Brodie. **Producer:** Julian Amyes. (Granada)

1962	6.8	Tue 11 Dec. 9:15 p.m.	3	23 wks

'Alida' by Paul Lee.
Who is Alida? To seek the answer sets off a sequence of events which can only result in one thing – death! But for whom? And when death comes are seven people responsible, or only one? Starring Jessica Dunning, Jacqueline Ellis, Robin Palmer and Hugh Sinclair.
Designer: Kenneth Mellor. **Producer:** Peter Potter. (ATV)

1963	7.6	Mon 9 Dec 9:10 p.m.	2	41 wks

'The Travelling Man' by Mike Watts.
Nan is the blind teenage daughter of Sam Lynch. Sam has allowed his imagination full rein when describing the scene at a quarry near where they live – a non-existent lakeside landscape with ducks and swans. However, Nan may be able to see again after her next operation. Sam does not want her to regain her sight and learn the hard truth. Starring Nigel Davenport, Vanda Godsell and Maureen Pryor with Coral Atkins, Jim Dale, Pinkie Johnstone and Arthur White.
Designer: John Emery. **Producer:** Michael Currer-Briggs. (AR)

1964	7.5	Mon 16 Mar 9:10 p.m.	5	18 wks

'Shadow of the Sun' by Maurice McGloughlin.
The daughter of a prominent politician is to be expelled from a fashionable girls school in South Africa. However, her father is prepared to go to any lengths, including blackmail, to avoid a public scandal. Starring Anna Neagle.
Designer: Reece Pemberton. **Producer:** George More O'Ferrall. (Anglia)

1965	6.3	Mon 21 Jun 9:40 p.m.	6	13 wks

'The Misunderstanding' adapted by Kitty Black.
An adaptation based on Albert Camus' novel Le Malentendu. After an absence of more than twenty years, Jan returns home to help his mother and sister, but he does not immediately reveal his identity and they plot his murder. Starring Flora Robson with Ewan Hooper, Ruth Meyers, Pauline Munro and Patrick Troughton.
Designer: Roy Stannard. **Director:** Joan Kemp-Welch. **Executive Producer:** Antony Kearey. (AR)

1966	6.5	Mon 2 May 9:40 p.m.	3	9 wks

'The Move After Checkmate' by Harry England.
Superindent Smith (Donald Pleasence) has pursued Sellman (Peter Vaughan) over a period of twenty-seven years. He finally gets him through Sellman's own son. Also starring Dorothy Alison, Robert Brown, John Collin, Michael Crawford, Alan Howard, Philip Latham and Derren Nesbitt.
Designer: Reece Pemberton. **Director:** Alvin Rakoff. **Producer:** John Jacobs. (Anglia)

....

Play Your Cards Right				90 wks

Lwt, game show

This three-stage quiz hosted by Bruce Forsyth required basic general knowledge followed by guesswork to determine the value of certain playing cards. Major prizes were awarded.
Producers: David Bell (1980–82) and Alasdair Macmillan (1983–87).

1980	15.8	Fri 21 Mar 7:30 p.m.	5	26 wks

Director: Ken O'Neill.

1981	16.5	Fri 11 Dec 8:30 p.m.	3	11 wks

Director: Alasdair Macmillan.

| 1982 | 16.9 | Fri 8 Jan 7:00 p.m. | 4 | 16 wks |

Director: Alasdair Macmillan.

1983	11.8	Sun 30 Oct 7:15 p.m.	12	9 wks
1984	14.6	Fri 9 Nov 8:00 p.m.	4	14 wks
1985	12.9	Sun 8 Dec 7:15 p.m.	10	2 wks
1986	12.8	Fri 14 Nov 7:00 p.m.	8	11 wks
1987	10.7	Fri 25 Sep 7:00 p.m.	15	1 wk

Playdate 24 wks

AR, drama

A series of single dramas.

| 1961 | 5.9 | Fri 29 Dec 9:35 p.m. | 6 | 6 wks |

'Salt of the Earth' by Rebecca West.
Jim Pemberton (Cec Linder) is a successful lawyer and his wife Alice (Frances Hyland) is the salt of the earth. She manages to create disruption all around her.
Designer: Murray Laufer. **Director:** George McCowen. **Producer:** Ed Moser.

| 1962 | 6.9 | Mon 22 Jan 8:00 p.m. | 4 | 18 wks |

'Nightmare' by Alfred Harris.
A mother and daughter hear someone trying to enter the house in the middle of the night while father is away on business. The hours that follow see a nightmare unfold. Starring Cec Linder with Tom Harvey and Charmian King.
Designer: Murray Laufer. **Director:** Mel Breen. **Producer:** Ed Moser.

Playhouse 87 wks

ITV (various), drama

ITV's long-running strand of single dramas was produced by several of the companies within the network.

| 1967 | 7.9 | Mon 4 Dec 8:30 p.m. | 4 | 10 wks |

'The Confession' by Maurice McLoughlin.
An apparently innocent man is murdered in strange circumstances. Starring Marie Kean, Ann Lynn, Francis Matthews, Liam Redmond and Leslie Sands.
Designer: Michael Wield. **Producer:** John Jacobs. (Anglia)

| 1968 | 7.7 | Mon 22 Apr 8:30 p.m. | 1 | 26 wks |

'Murder – A Professional Job' by Marc Brandel.
Six men and one woman are enjoying drinks in a hotel suite prior to a convention. One of them is murdered. Starring Michael Bates, Tom Criddle, Jane Downs, Mark Eden, Jimmy Hanley, Robert Urquhart and John Welsh.
Designer: Roy Stonehouse. **Director:** Michael Apted. **Producer:** Marc Brandel. (Granada)

| 1969 | 7.2 | Mon 17 Nov 8:30 p.m. | 6 | 13 wks |

'Suspect' by Mike Hodges.
Rachel Kempson stars as Phyllis Segal, who begins to suspect her husband Mark (Bryan Marshall) is a wanted man. Also starring Michael Coles, Russell Hunter and George Sewell.
Designer: Patrick Downing. **Producer:** Mike Hodges. **Executive Producer:** Lloyd Shirley. (Thames)

| 1970 | 7.0 | Mon 12 Jan 8:30 p.m. | 4 | 13 wks |

'A Man For Loving' by Jeremy Paul.
James Beal (Richard Greene) has lived life as an advertising executive at a hectic pace. It was all too much for his wife Ann (Helen Christie), who left years ago and married Bill (William Fox). James now has a young mistress, Isobel (Lynn Farleigh), who is also tiring of his lifestyle. But James refuses to come to terms with his advancing years.
Designer: Jane Martin. **Director:** James Ormerod. **Executive Producer:** Peter Willes. (YTV)

| 1971 | 6.4 | Tue 23 Mar 9:00 p.m. | 12 | 2 wks |

'The Mosedale Horseshoe' by Arthur Hopcraft.
This play was shot entirely on location. Two unmarried sisters and two bachelors meet each year in the Lake District, the object being to conquer the Mosedale Horseshoe, a spectacular ridge walk across Wasdale. Four times before they have tried but always failed. Is the walk the real reason they return to the Screes Hotel each year? Starring Bernard Hepton, Rosemary Leach, Mary Miller and David Swift.
Director: Michael Apted. **Producer:** Peter Eckersley. (Granada)

| 1972 | 7.0 | Tue 27 Jun 9:00 p.m. | 2 | 5 wks |

'The Substitute' by Barrie Keefe.
A concrete high-rise block is no place for a young lad to grow up. Rod (Adrian Shergold) longs to escape.
Designer: Michael Grimes. **Director:** Les Chatfield. **Producer:** Peter Eckersley. (Granada)

| 1973 | 7.7 | Mon 14 May 9:00 p.m. | 4 | 6 wks |

'The Man in the Wood' based on a story by Edward Hyams.
In the New Forest, a girl begs a lift from an American businessman. His act of kindness leads to murder and threatens his marriage and his life. Starring Isabel Dean, Mark Dignam, David Hedison and Jennifer Hilary.
Designer: James Weatherup. **Director:** Alan Gibson. **Producer:** John Jacobs. (Anglia)

1974	7.4	Tue 19 Feb 9:00 p.m.	1	6 wks

'What Would You Do?' *by Charles Humphreys.*
Derek (Ian McShane) is a successful business and family man devoted to his wife Ann (Helen Cotterill) and their two young children. The future looks nothing but bright until he revisits the city where he spent his bachelor days and realizes the past can never be obliterated.
Designer: *Mike Long.* **Director:** *Marc Muller.* **Executive Producer:** *Peter Willes. (YTV)*

1978	13.3	Tue 23 May 8:45 p.m.	5	3 wks

'Forty Weeks' *by Stephen Fagan.*
Can their marriage survive when Mary Kelly (Pamela Miles) tells husband Barry (Barry Jackson) that the baby she is carrying is not his?
Designer: *Harry Clark.* **Director:** *Waris Hussein.* **Producer:** *Barry Hanson. (Thames)*

1979	12.7	Tue 1 May 9:10 p.m.	14	1 wk

'The Daughters of Albion' *by Willy Russell.*
Girls from the town meet young men from the University at an all-night party.
Executive Producer: *David Cunliffe. (YTV)*

1981	10.6	Sun 19 Jul 10:00 p.m.	19	2 wks

'Singles' *by John Bowen.*
Sophie Baines (Sherrie Hewson) is single and wants a child. She sets about achieving this ambition, but the result is not quite what she intended.
Designer: *Roger Andrews.* **Director:** *Michael Ferguson.* **Producer:** *Pat Sandys.* **Executive Producer:** *David Cunliffe. (YTV)*

Plays for Pleasure | 1 wk

YTV, drama

These six individual plays were about the bright side of relationships.

1981	12.3	Tue 28 Apr 9:00 p.m.	19	1 wk

'The Concubine' *by Clare Higgins.*
George (Bruce Montague) has a wife (Clare Higgins) and a mistress (Judy Parfitt) who both seem to be coping with him reasonably well.
Designer: *Eileen Diss.* **Director:** *Gareth Davies.* **Producer:** *Pat Sandys.* **Executive Producer:** *David Cunliffe.*

Plays of Married Life | 3 wks

Granada, drama

This series of four plays featured different aspects of married life.

1966	6.6	Tue 27 Sep 9:10 p.m.	11	3 wks

'The Bright Side' *by Hugh Forbes.*
Tom Jayson (William Lucas) is the chief reporter on the local newspaper. He and his wife Christine (Colette O'Neill) have two children and seem quite happy until he starts spending the occasional evening with a young reporter, Angela (Judy Parfitt). Also starring Neville Buswell, John Franklyn-Roberts, Moira Graye and Wendy Richard.
Designer: *Peter Caldwell.* **Producer:** *Derek Bennett.*

Plaza Patrol | 1 wk

YTV, situation comedy

Tommy Cannon and Bobby Ball starred as security officers in a shopping plaza.

1991	8.3	Mon 19 Aug 7:00 p.m.	20	1 wk

'The Other Man's Grass'
Both officers have ambitions to broaden their horizons, but in opposite directions.
Writers: *Richard Lewis and Louis Robinson.* **Producer:** *Graham Wetherell.*

Please Sir | 33 wks

LWT, situation comedy

This series was written by John Esmonde and Bob Larbey and set in Fenn Street school. John Alderton starred as Bernard Hedges, a teacher nicknamed 'Privet' by his pupils, most notably those of form 5C. Hedges' fellow teachers were Mr Cromwell (Noel Howlett), Miss Ewell (Joan Sanderson) and Smith (Erik Chitty). Deryck Guyler was Norman Potter, the caretaker.
Producer: *Mark Stuart.*

1968	6.8	Mon 9 Dec 10:30 p.m.	9	3 wks

'Barbarian Librarian'
Hedges lends the library key to 5C, who turn the place into a noisy shambles.

1969	8.0	Sat 8 Nov 7:00 p.m.	3	13 wks

'The Generation Gap'
Class 5C go out to help some old people, but one old codger refuses all help until Craven (Malcolm McFee) gives him a taste of his own medicine.

1970	8.0	Sun 29 Nov 7:20 p.m.	1	13 wks

'The Facts of Life'
When Hedges hears pupil Frankie Abbott (David Barry) give his version of the facts of life, he feels it's time to teach 5C in an adult way. Cromwell, however, does not agree with his version.
Director: *Alan Wallis.*

Sharon Eversleigh (Penny Spencer) seems to be instructing her teacher Mr Hedges (John Alderton) in **Please Sir**.

1971	6.7	Sat 16 Oct 7:05 p.m.	15	4 wks

'David and Goliath'
Hedges has left Fenn Street school and been replaced by Mr Dix (Glynn Edwards). Dix is a tyrant and the staff seek out a young champion to challenge his reign. He arrives in the form of David Ffitchett-Brown (Richard Warwick).
Director: Philip Casson.

Points of View				17 wks

BBC, talk show

Viewers gave their reactions to BBC television programmes. Barry Took was the presenter until 1986.

1982	11.2	Wed 13 Oct 8:45 p.m.	11	7 wks

Producer: Yvonne Hewett.

1983	8.4	Thur 2 Jun 8:50 p.m.	20	1 wk

Producer: Yvonne Hewett.

1985	10.3	Wed 12 Jun 8:50 p.m.	12	3 wks

Producer: Bernard Newnham.

1986	12.7	Tue 1 Apr 8:50 p.m.	8	5 wks

Producer: Penelope Mills.

1989	9.0	Wed 4 Jan 8:50 p.m.	18	1 wk

Presented by Anne Robinson.
Producer: Warwick Cross.

Poirot				12 wks

LWT, drama

David Suchet starred as Hercule Poirot in dramatized versions of Agatha Christie stories.
Director: Edward Bennett (1989–90). **Producer:** Brian Eastman.
Executive Producers: Linda Agran and Nick Elliott.

1989	14.1	Sun 8 Jan 8:45 p.m.	9	4 wks

'The Adventure of the Clapham Cook' dramatized by Clive Exton. Poirot is intrigued to discover the contents of the cook's trunk owned by Ernestine Todd (Brigit Forsyth).

1990	12.2	Sun 21 Jun 8:05 p.m.	16	5 wks

'The Lost Mine' dramatized by Michael Baker and David Renwick. A game of Monopoly leads Poirot to his bank and subsequently to a murder case.

1991	12.5	Sun 13 Jan 8:55 p.m.	16	3 wks

'The Million Dollar Bond Robbery' dramatized by Anthony Horowitz. A shipment of Liberty Bonds from London to New York aboard the Queen Mary provides a case for Hercule Poirot.
Director: Andrew Grieve.

Police				1 wk

BBC, documentary

This fly-on-the-wall series was filmed over nine months inside Thames Valley Constabulary.
Camera: Charles Stewart. **Producers:** Roger Graef and Charles Stewart. **Series Editor:** John Shearer.

1982	11.9	Mon 18 Jan 9:55 p.m.	19	1 wk

'A Complaint of Rape'
With the crime of rape carrying a maximum sentence of life imprisonment, the first thing the police try to establish when a woman makes a complaint is that the offence has actually taken place.

Police Academy				1 wk

Presented by ITV, film

1991	11.4	Mon 15 Apr 9:00 p.m.	11	1 wk

When the female mayor of an American city lifts all restrictions on entry to the police force some unlikely characters enlist at the academy. George Gaynes and Steve Guttenberg star.
Director: Hugh Wilson.

Police Academy 3				1 wk

Presented by ITV, film

1990	10.8	Sat 29 Sep 9:20 p.m.	16	1 wk

There are two academies and the least efficient must be closed. Commandant Manser (Art Metrano) plans to sabotage the academy run by Commandant Lassard (George Gaynes). Steve Guttenberg again stars.
Director: Jerry Paris.

Police Emergency
1 wk

USA presented by BBC, documentary

| 1962 | 5.5 | Tue 28 Aug 9:25 p.m. | 4 | 1 wk |

An NBC crew spent three months filming day and night the real-life duties of two New York cops in their patrol car. The policemen are brothers Mick and Gene Corcoran. Walter Matthau narrates.
Producer: Julian Claman. **Executive Producer:** Irving Gittin.

Police Hour
1 wk

AR, entertainment

| 1960 | 6.2 | Thu 28 Apr 9:35 p.m. | 2 | 1 wk |

Introduced by Hughie Green and starring Jack Hulbert and Cicely Courtneidge, Brian Reece (PC 49), Danny Green and Wee Georgie Wood with Claude Bessy, Ray Powell and members of police forces throughout Britain including their mounted police, dogs, choirs, soloists and pipe bands.
Choreographer: Malcolm Goddard. **Director:** Eric Croall.

Police Woman
6 wks

USA presented by ITV, drama

This series, created by Joseph Wambaugh, starred Angie Dickinson as Sergeant Suzanne 'Pepper' Anderson, an undercover police-woman with the Los Angeles Criminal Conspiracy Department.
Producers: David Gerber and Douglas Benton.

| 1976 | 7.4 | Mon 26 Apr 9:00 p.m. | 9 | 6 wks |

'The Loner'
Pepper seeks a former policeman (Don Meredith) who has been hired to protect the boss of a crime syndicate.

Pop Spot, The
1 wk

ABC, music

In this series of shows top recording stars sang their own choice from their hits.

| 1964 | 6.1 | Sat 10 Oct 9:10 p.m. | 14 | 1 wk |

The Bachelors include 'Diane', 'Ramona' and 'I Wouldn't Trade You For the World'.
Director: Geoff Ramsey. **Producer:** Mark Stuart.

Pop Vintage '38
1 wk

AR, music

| 1961 | 4.5 | Wed 15 Nov 8:55 p.m. | 18 | 1 wk |

The songs of the last year before the Second World War broke out. With Betty Driver, John Hewer, Pat Laurence, Kevin Scott, Stephanie Voss and the Sidney Sax orchestra.
Producer: Peter Croft.

Pope John XXIII
1 wk

ITN, news

| 1963 | 5.1 | Mon 3 Jun Evening | 5 | 1 wk |

ITV programmes were interrupted during the evening to bring news of the Pope's death. He died at 7:40 p.m. BST at the age of 81.

Porridge
43 wks

BBC, situation comedy

Dick Clement and Ian La Frenais created this series set in Slade Prison. The story grew from an earlier play called Prisoner and Escort which starred Ronnie Barker as old lag Norman Fletcher. For the series, Richard Beckinsale was cast as cell-mate Lennie Godber. Another prisoner, Blanco, was played by David Jason. Ken Jones portrayed Ives, Christopher Biggins played Lukewarm and Felix Bowness was Gay Gordon. Fulton Mackay also starred as Chief Prison Officer Mackay and Brian Wilde was Warden Barrowclough.
Producer: Sydney Lotterby.

| 1974 | 7.6 | Thu 26 Sep 8:30 p.m. | 1 | 6 wks |

'A Day Out'
The trip to the outside is eagerly looked forward to – even though it is only to dig drains for the council.

| 1975 | 7.7 | Wed 24 Dec 8:25 p.m. | 1 | 6 wks |

'No Way Out'
Fletch has to call on his reserves of ingenuity when he learns that Christmas has been officially cancelled at Slade prison.

| 1976 | 7.7 | Fri 24 Dec 8:00 p.m. | 8 | 7 wks |

'The Desperate Hours'
Fletch and Godber have been fermenting illicit liquor since last July – to sell to fellow inmates for the festive spirit.

| 1977 | 7.9 | Fri 25 Feb 8:30 p.m. | 12 | 6 wks |

'Poetic Justice'
Fletcher's little domain comes under threat when Officer Mackay proposes the introduction of a third cellmate.

| 1978 | 10.7 | Fri 2 Jun 8:30 p.m. | 19 | 1 wk |

'Men Without Women'
Fletcher gets a new job and responsibility. He is appointed welfare officer. (Repeat.)

| 1979 | 17.5 | Thu 12 Apr 8:30 p.m. | 1 | 2 wks |

As a tribute to Richard Beckinsale, who died on Monday of this week, aged thirty-one, the first episode of PORRIDGE is repeated. Lennie Godber arrives in prison to disturb Fletcher's privacy.

| 1984 | 19.4 | Thu 27 Dec 8:20 p.m. | 1 | 10 wks |

'No Way Out'
(Repeat.)

| 1985 | 13.4 | Sun 15 Dec 6:00 p.m. | 4 | 2 wks |

'Final Stretch'
Godber jeopardizes his chances of parole by getting involved in a fight with another prisoner. (Repeat.)

| 1987 | 9.3 | Mon 22 Jun 8:00 p.m. | 15 | 1 wk |

'Just Desserts'
Just Desserts is repeated in tribute to Fulton Mackay who died earlier this month. To steal on the outside is considered a fair way to make a living, but there is anger on the inside when thefts from fellow inmates are discovered.

| 1990 | 11.7 | Tue 27 Feb 8:00 p.m. | 19 | 2 wks |

'Final Stretch' is repeated again.

Porridge · 2 wks

Presented by BBC, film

| 1982 | 11.5 | Fri 31 Dec 9:15 p.m. | 10 | 1 wk |

In this feature film version a celebrities versus prisoners football match is the cover for an escape plan which unwittingly involves Fletcher and Godber.
Director: Dick Clement.

| 1986 | 11.7 | Sun 7 Dec 7:15 p.m. | 17 | 1 wk |

Repeat of the feature film.

Poseidon Adventure, The · 1 wk

Presented by BBC, film

| 1979 | 19.3 | Sun 23 Dec 7:15 p.m. | 1 | 1 wk |

A freak wave capsizes the luxury liner Poseidon during New Year's Eve celebrations. A small group of survivors fight to escape the sinking ship. Starring Ernest Borgnine, Red Buttons, Gene Hackman, Carol Lynley, Roddy McDowall, Stella Stevens and Shelley Winters. **Director:** Ronald Neame.

Potter · 6 wks

BBC, situation comedy

In a series created by Roy Clarke, Arthur Lowe starred as Redvers Potter, who was intolerant of his own retirement and in search of a new role in life. After Lowe's death the part was assumed by Robin Bailey. Noël Dyson played his wife Aileen, John Barron was the eccentric vicar and John Warner played a character named Tolly. **Producer:** Peter Whitmore.

| 1979 | 14.1 | Thu 29 Mar 8:30 p.m. | 15 | 2 wks |

Potter visits Tolly in his antiques shop and offers his experience as a sweets salesman to the art of selling valuable paintings.

| 1980 | 16.0 | Wed 27 Feb 8:30 p.m. | 7 | 4 wks |

The local vicar's wife is in hospital, so Potter invites himself round to help out at the vicarage.

Power Game, The · 32 wks

ATV, drama

This sequel to THE PLANE MAKERS began where the latter left off. Sir John Wilder had left Scott Furlong and the aviation industry. In return for taking the blame for the unsound financial development of the vertical take-off fighter, he accepted a knighthood and a seat on the board of a merchant bank. But the quiet life began to pall. He started to scheme again and became a rival of tycoon Caswell Bligh (Clifford Evans). The managing director of Bligh's company was his son Kenneth (Peter Barkworth). Patrick Wymark continued as Wilder with Barbara Murray playing his wife Pamela. Jack Watling continued in the role of Don Henderson. Like its predecessor, THE POWER GAME was created by Wilfred Greatorex.

| 1965 | 8.0 | Mon 13 Dec 8:00 p.m. | 3 | 2 wks |

'The New Boy' by Edmund Ward.
Wilder is already bored with the quiet life and starts to cast around for some stimulus.
Designer: Don Fisher. **Director:** Victor Menzies. **Producer:** Rex Firkin.

| 1966 | 7.7 | Mon 17 Jan 8.00 p.m. Mon 14 Feb 8:00 p.m. | 7 | 17 wks |

'Saturday's Women' by Raymond Bowers.
Wilder tries to use civil servant Susan Weldon (Rosemary Leach) to pit Bligh against his son Kenneth.
Designer: Don Fisher. **Director:** John Cooper. **Producer:** Rex Firkin.

'Persons and Papers' by Peter Draper.

Following a shock revelation Wilder is forced into a change of mind over a winding-up operation.

Designer: Trevor Paterson. **Director:** David Reid. **Producer:** Rex Firkin.

These two programmes achieved the same viewing and chart figures.

| 1969 | 8.2 | Tue 18 Feb 9:00 p.m. | 1 | 13 wks |

'Special Envoy – Cat is You, Bird is Me' by Peter Draper.

Wilder is off to Switzerland and not taking Pamela along. He has a pretty good reason – Perpetua Cataline (Felicity Gibson).

Designer: Henry Graveney. **Director:** Robert Tronson. **Producer:** David Reid.

Practice, The · 11 wks

Granada, drama

This series created by Mike Stott centred on life in a modern health centre. It starred John Fraser as Dr Lawrence Golding, Tim Brierley as Dr David Armitage and Brigit Forsyth as Dr Judith Vincent.
Producer: Sita Williams. **Executive Producer:** June Howson.

| 1985 | 16.8 | Fri 18 Jan 8:00 p.m. | 6 | 7 wks |

In this first episode a taxi driver has a bad heart but seeks approval to carry on working, and a patient questions the necessity of a vasectomy.
Designer: Alan Price. **Director:** Sarah Harding.

| 1986 | 9.3 | Fri 23 May 9:00 p.m. | 16 | 4 wks |

Lawrence and Judith are doubtful that the new Dr Clark (Rob Edwards) is going to fit in with either themselves or the patients.
Designer: Stephen Fineren. **Director:** David Richards.

Present for Dickie, A · 5 wks

Thames, situation comedy

Dickie Henderson starred as Dickie in this extension of THE DICKIE HENDERSON SHOW by Jimmy Grafton and Johnny Hayward. For much of the series Dickie's wife Jane (June Laverick) was returning home from Australia on a slow boat, leaving him with his mother-in-law Mrs Upshott-Mainwaring (Fabia Drake). The 'present' in the title came from India in the form of Mini the Elephant. Regulars in the cast were Billy Burden as William, Dennis Ramsden as Parker and Jerry Ram as Abdul the elephant minder.

| 1969 | 6.7 | Tue 30 Dec 8:25 p.m. | 11 | 1 wk |

In this first episode Dickie returns from a cabaret tour of the Far East to learn that Jane is on her way back from Australia, and that a mysterious present is soon to be delivered to him from India.
Producer: Peter Frazer-Jones.

| 1970 | 7.4 | Tue 6 Jan 8:25 p.m. | 6 | 4 wks |

'Things That Go Bump in the Night'

Mini the Elephant has insomnia and the neighbours call the police. Dickie and the elephant minder are locked out of the house while his mother-in-law and Mini are locked inside.
Producer: Peter Frazer-Jones.

Present Laughter · 1 wk

ATV, drama

| 1967 | 5.8 | Thu 2 Mar 9:40 p.m. | 19 | 1 wk |

A special television production of Noël Coward's play about 'theatricals' which he originally entitled Sweet Sorrow. Starring Peter O'Toole as Garry Essendine and Honor Blackman as Liz. Cast also includes Isla Blair, William Dexter, Edward Hardwicke, Avice Landon, Marie Lohr, Tim Preece and Tony Selby.
Designer: Henry Graveney. **Producer:** Gordon Flemyng.

President Kennedy in Europe · 1 wk

ITN, news

| 1961 | 6.2 | Tue 6 Jun 11:05 p.m. | 2 | 1 wk |

President and Mrs Kennedy are now in London for a few days following the Vienna summit conference and the President's visit to West Berlin, cut off from the East of the city by the recently erected wall. He had announced 'I am a Berliner'.

In **The Power Game** Patrick Wymark continued the role of Sir John Wilder from The Plane Makers.

Gene Hackman temporarily rescues Shelley Winters in **The Poseidon Adventure**.

Presley | 1 wk

BBC, documentary

| 1987 | 9.5 | Mon 17 Aug 9:30 p.m. | 10 | 1 wk |

This story of the life and career of Elvis Presley is narrated by Suzi Quatro.
Producer: Ann Frear.

Price is Right, The | 47 wks

Central, game show

Leslie Crowther hosted this American imported format. He induced mass studio hysteria when he invited random audience members to 'come on down' and guess the value of articles. Basic general knowledge or skill was required to win the other prizes.
Producer: William G. Stewart.

| 1984 | 16.0 | Sat 7 Apr 7:00 p.m. | 1 | 10 wks |

Director: David Millard.

| 1985 | 13.6 | Sat 13 Apr 7:10 p.m. | 5 | 15 wks |

Director: Paul Harrison.

| 1986 | 13.9 | Sat 1 Feb 7:00 p.m. | 7 | 19 wks |

Director: Dennis Liddington.

| 1987 | 12.1 | Sat 7 Mar 7:45 p.m. | 13 | 2 wks |

Director: Richard Bradley.

| 1988 | 10.5 | Fri 7 Apr 7:00 p.m. | 18 | 1 wk |

Director: Mike Holgate.

Price of a Record, The | 1 wk

Border/Grampian/Ulster/Westward, documentary

| 1967 | 6.0 | Wed 7 Jun 9:40 p.m. | 8 | 1 wk |

The combined effort of four ITV companies, this film covers the final weeks of 1966 and those at the start of 1967 when Donald Campbell was preparing for his fatal attempt to break the world water speed record on Coniston Water in the Lake District. John Pett talks to Campbell and his wife, Tonia Bern, and to Leo Villa, the chief mechanic, and Ken Norris, the designer of Bluebird.
Camera: Brian Wilson. **Director:** Edward Joffe. **Producer:** Douglas Hurn.

Prime Minister, The | 1 wk

BBC and ITV, news

| 1963 | 9.5 | Wed 30 Jan 9:15 p.m. | 1 | 1 wk |

Prime Minister Harold Macmillan makes an eleven-minute broadcast seen in six European countries following yesterday's wrecking by French President de Gaulle of Britain's bid to join the Common Market.

Prime Suspect | 2 wks

Granada, drama

This two-part thriller by Lynda La Plante starred Helen Mirren as Detective Chief Inspector Jane Tennison. She inherited a murder case complete with suspect. Tom Bell and Zoë Wanamaker also starred.

| 1991 | 14.1 | Mon 8 Apr 9:00 p.m. | 8 | 2 wks |

Part Two
What began as a single and seemingly simple murder enquiry has now developed into a major and complex investigation.
Director: Christopher Menaul. **Producer:** Don Leaver.

Prince and Princess of Wales, The | 1 wk

ITN, documentary

| 1985 | 18.6 | Sun 20 Oct 7:45 p.m. | 1 | 1 wk |

Alastair Burnet is granted the first television interview with The Prince and Princess of Wales since their wedding.
Director: Diana Edwards-Jones. **Editor:** Stewart Purvis.

Prince for Our Time, A | 1 wk

BBC, documentary

| 1981 | 11.5 | Sun 26 Jul 7:15 p.m. | 13 | 1 wk |

Hugh Scully presents a profile of HRH The Prince of Wales.
Producer: Alan Scales.

Prince of Wales Show, The | 1 wk

ATV, entertainment

This variety series was hosted by Jimmy Tarbuck from the Prince of Wales Theatre.

| 1965 | 6.0 | Sun 7 Nov 8:25 p.m. | 15 | 1 wk |

Guests: Adam Faith, Audrey Jeans and Sandie Shaw with the Pamela Devis dancers and the Jack Parnell orchestra.
Producer: Albert Locke.

....

Prince Regent   1 wk

BBC, drama

This eight-part serial starred Peter Egan as George, Prince of Wales (the Prince Regent, later George IV), Nigel Davenport as King George III and Susannah York as Maria Fitzherbert.

| 1979 | 13.7 | Tue 23 Oct 9:25 p.m. | 18 | 1 wk |

'Milk and Honey' by Reg Gadney.
The Regent decides it is time his daughter Princess Charlotte (Cherie Lunghi) married. She has her own opinions on the subject.
Designer: Barry Newbery. **Director:** Michael Simpson. **Producer:** Colin Tucker.

....

Princess Daisy   2 wks

USA presented by ITV, drama

In this two-part dramatization of the novel by Judith Krantz, Daisy and Danielle (both played by Merete Van Kamp) were twin girls. Danielle was born with brain damage and placed in a home by her father (Stacy Keach). Her mother (Lindsay Wagner) believed the child to be dead. Eventually she and Daisy discovered the truth. Ringo Starr and Barbara Bach appeared as trendy fashion designers Robin and Vanessa Valerian.

| 1984 | 14.4 | Mon 17 Sep 8:00 p.m. | 5 | 2 wks |

Part Two
Dani and Daisy's evil half-brother Ram (Rupert Everett) refuses to pay Dani's medical bills. Daisy takes a job with a large cosmetic company to try and raise some money. There she falls in love with Patrick Shannon (Robert Urich) but Ram retains the power to destroy her romance.

....

Prior Commitment, The   1 wk

BBC, Drama

This thriller serial in six-parts by Bill Craig was set on an island in the Firth of Clyde. It starred William Lucas as Eddie Prior, a television reporter searching for the body of his dead wife Helen, and also starred Aubrey Morris as Spinner and Claire Nielson as Helen's sister Liz Elliot.

| 1969 | 5.6 | Tue 6 May 9:55 p.m. | 16 | 1 wk |

Episode Three
An intruder attacks Eddie and escapes with a roll of film. Eddie gives a lift to an ornithologist, Cadwaller (Peter Copley). Later his car is sabotaged.
Music: Andy Park. **Designer:** David McKenzie. **Producer:** Pharic Maclaren.

....

Prison Officer   1 wk

ATV, documentary

| 1960 | 4.7 | Wed 13 Jul 9:35 p.m. | 6 | 1 wk |

The life and work of prison officers filmed at HM Prison Wakefield and at the Officer's Training School. John Neville narrates.
Producer: Michael Redington.

....

Prisoner, The   1 wk

ATV, drama

This cult series was devised by and starred Patrick McGoohan. He was also executive producer, and he directed and partially wrote several episodes. The series was shrouded in mystery, the stories obscure. McGoohan was The Prisoner, a former secret agent captured and brainwashed and held in 'The Village' where he had a cottage with maid service and all modern conveniences. The mountains and sea allowed him no escape. The series was filmed in the Welsh village of Portmeirion.

| 1967 | 5.9 | Sun 3 Dec 7:25 p.m. | 20 | 1 wk |

'Checkmate'
The chess game covers an entire courtyard and the pieces are human beings. The Prisoner takes up his position as the Queen's pawn. Guest appearances by Rosalie Crutchley, Patricia Jessel, Ronald Radd and Peter Wyngarde.
Director: Don Chaffey. **Producer:** David Tomblin.

....

Private Benjamin   3 wks

Presented by ITV, film

| 1984 | 12.8 | Mon 28 May 9:15 p.m. | 3 | 1 wk |

Goldie Hawn stars as a wealthy Jewish widow who joins the US Army.
Director: Howard Zieff.

| 1988 | 10.6 | Mon 1 Aug 9:00 p.m. | 7 | 1 wk |

Repeat showing of the above film.

| 1991 | 10.0 | Sat 10 Aug 8:15 p.m. | 12 | 1 wk |

The BBC shows the above film.

The Prime Minister (Harold Macmillan) made an unscheduled broadcast to the nation in 1963 to explain Britain's rejection from the Common Market.

Prizewinners
1 wk

BBC, all categories

The BBC repeated shows which won awards in festivals and competitions around the world.

| 1970 | 8.0 | Thu 1 Oct 9:20 p.m. | 1 | 1 wk |

'Morecambe and Wise'
Named Best Light Entertainment Performance by the Society of Film and Television Arts. Guest star: Nina. Written by Eddie Braben with 'Trousers' sketch by Sid Green and Dick Hills and Nina's sketch by Mike Craig and Laurie Kinsley.
Producer: John Ammonds.

Probation Officer
47 wks

ATV, drama

This series was created by Julian Bond in the late 1950s. The original stars were Honor Blackman, David Davies and John Paul, who all played probation officers. The stories dealt with cases referred from the Courts to the Probation Service.

| 1960 | 6.4 | Mon 2 May 9:35 p.m. | 3 | 11 wks |

The Chairman of the Bench (Llewellyn Rees) and his fellow magistrates (Esther Lawrence and Dorothy Rundle) have some difficult decisions to make. They seek the help of the Probation Service and its officer Bert Bellman (John Scott).
Writer: Peter Lamola. **Producer:** Antony Kearey.

| 1961 | 7.2 | Mon 29 May 9:35 p.m. | 1 | 17 wks |

Officer Bellman finds himself involved in a divorce case with Sue and Harry Barnett (Miranda Connell and Robert Brown).
Writer: Julian Bond. **Director:** Royston Morley. **Producer:** Antony Kearey.

| 1962 | 6.0 | Mon 16 July 9:15 p.m. | 3 | 19 wks |

Tommy Thomas is a man of low intelligence and the butt of jokes from the factory floor. He tries to win friendship with some stolen cigarettes and lands in trouble with the police. The only person who seems willing to help him is Bill Morgan (Windsor Davies), his probation officer.
Writer: Barbara Waring. **Director:** Royston Morley. **Producer:** Rex Firkin.

Professionals, The
2 wks

Presented by ITV, film

| 1974 | 6.9 | Mon 18 Feb 9:00 | 17 | 1 wk |

A group of adventurers set out from the Nevada desert to rescue a young wife who has been kidnapped by Mexican revolutionaries. Starring Burt Lancaster, Lee Marvin, Robert Ryan, Jack Palance and Claudia Cardinale.

Director: Richard Brooks.

| 1982 | 14.5 | Thu 21 Jan 7.30 p.m. | 4 | 1 wk |

Repeat showing of the above film.

Professionals, The
72 wks

LWT, drama

Executive Producers Brian Clemens and Albert Fennell created this series about CI5, a service which specialized in finishing jobs the police would not know how to start. It starred Lewis Collins as Bodie, Martin Shaw as Doyle and Gordon Jackson as their boss, George Cowley.
Producer: Raymond Menmuir.

| 1978 | 17.4 | Fri 10 Feb 9:00 p.m. | 5 | 14 wks |

'Close Quarters' by Brian Clemens.
Keeping the country clean sometimes calls for dirty tactics.

| 1979 | 15.0 | Sat 10 Nov 9:00 p.m. | 12 | 4 wks |

'Stopover' by John Goldsmith.
Bodie and Doyle come up against a KGB team of killers when a CI5 agent returns from the dead.

| 1980 | 17.6 | Sun 30 Nov 9:00 p.m. | 3 | 10 wks |

'Hijack' by Roger Marshall.
CI5 attempt to prevent a multi-million pound raid which would secure the escape to the West of an East German official.
Director: Martin Campbell.

| 1981 | 14.3 | Sat 10 Jan 9:30 p.m. | 1 | 15 wks |

'The Madness of Mickey Hamilton' by Christopher Wicking.
A medical convention is rigged for a holocaust. CI5 try to find and stop the motiveless slaughterer.
Director: William Brayne.

| 1982 | 13.7 | Sun 2 Nov 9:15 p.m. | 4 | 12 wks |

'Foxhole on the Roof' by Brian Clemens.
Villains prepare a seige with an arsenal of stolen weapons and explosives.
Director: William Brayne.

| 1983 | 13.6 | Sun 9 Jan 9:20 p.m. | 8 | 5 wks |

'Cry Wolf' by Paul Wheeler.
Cowley is asked to investigate a woman whom the police think is wasting their time.
Director: Phil Meheux.

| 1984 | 11.7 | Sun 8 Apr 9:00 p.m. | 4 | 10 wks |

'Discovered in a Graveyard' by Christopher Wicking.
Doyle is wounded by a terrorist bullet.
Director: Anthony Simmons.

| 1987 | 10.1 | Fri 28 Aug 9:00 p.m. | 7 | 2 wks |

'Spy Probe' by Tony Barwick.
Bodie and Doyle investigate why an organization is hiring assassins to exterminate prima-facie nobodies.
Director: Dennis Abey.

Profumo Debate, The | 1 wk

ITN, news

| 1963 | 5.4 | Mon 17 Jun 7:00 p.m. | 8 | 1 wk |

On 22 March of this year John Profumo denied to the House of Commons that he had engaged in any impropriety with Miss Christine Keeler. On 4 June he admitted he had lied to the House and resigned as war minister and MP. Today the government faces a vote of no confidence over the issue. The debate began at 3:30 p.m. this afternoon. In this report Alastair Burnet and Ian Trethowan analyse the events of the day. (The division came shortly after 10:00 p.m. with the government surviving by a smaller-than-hoped-for majority, 321–252. Prime Minister Harold Macmillan left the chamber amid loud calls for his resignation. Both ITN and BBC reported the division.)

Protectors, The | 11 wks

ABC, drama

The motto of the security firm around which the series was written was 'We sell security. Object: To prevent crime'. Stars were Andrew Faulds as Ian Souter, Michael Atkinson as Robert Shoesmith and Ann Morrish as Heather Keys.

| 1964 | 6.7 | Sat 25 Apr 9:10 p.m. | 8 | 11 wks |

'The Loop Men' by Larry Forrester.
An injured railwayman on a remote loop line leads the Protectors to a gang of savage hijackers.
Director: Peter Hammond. **Producer:** Michael Chapman.

Psycho | 1 wk

Presented by BBC, film

| 1968 | 5.9 | Mon 15 Apr 9:30 p.m. | 15 | 1 wk |

Easter Monday showing of Hitchcock's film of murders at the Bates Motel. Starring Anthony Perkins, John Gavin, Janet Leigh, John McIntyre and Vera Miles.

Pub Entertainer of the Year | 1 wk

Thames, entertainment

Performers received awards from licensed victuallers for their talents as seen on the stages of public houses.

| 1977 | 14.0 | Tue 20 Dec 9:00 p.m. | 17 | 1 wk |

Introduced by Frank Carson from the Lakeside Country Club, Frimley Green.
Director: Dave Rogers. **Producer:** Steve Minchin.

Public Eye | 53 wks

Thames, drama

This series starred Alfred Burke as Frank Marker, a rather run-down private detective.

| 1966 | 6.4 | Sat 17 Sep 9:10 p.m. | 8 | 13 wks |

'Twenty Pounds of Heart and Muscle' by Robert Holmes.
Pauline Garrity (Mary Webster) seeks Marker's help to find a missing member of her family.
Director: Piers Haggard. **Producer:** Richard Bates.

| 1969 | 6.7 | Wed 10 Sep 9.00 p.m. | 3 | 7 wks |

'A Fixed Address' by Roger Marshall.
Marker has enjoyed a deepening relationship with his landlady Mrs Mortimer (Pauline Delany) until an unexpected visitor shatters their rapport.
Producer: Kim Mills. **Executive Producer:** Lloyd Shirley.

| 1971 | 7.3 | Wed 1 Sep 9:00 p.m. | 1 | 13 wks |

'The Man Who Didn't Eat Sweets' by Richard Harris.
Mrs Meadows (Marjie Lawrence) leads a happy life running a confectioner's shop. She finds a photograph of a young woman in her husband's (Peter Sallis) pocket and suspects he may be having an affair. She calls in Marker.
Director: James Gatward. **Producer:** Michael Chapman.

| 1972 | 8.2 | Wed 20 Dec 9:00 p.m. | 2 | 6 wks |

'Horse and Carriage' by Richard Harris.
Marker has been hired by Harry (Tony Melody) to check up on his wife Lil (Pat Heywood), whom he suspects of having an affair. Harry is off on one of his own mysterious trips, and Lil has her own suspicions.
Director: Bill Bain. **Producer:** Robert Love.

| 1973 | 8.0 | Wed 10 Jan 9:00 p.m. | 2 | 7 wks |

'The Golden Boy' by Philip Broadley.
A young scholar and sportsman (Eton and Oxford) goes missing without reason. Marker sets out to discover why, encouraged by the boy's former tutor and discouraged by his parents.
Director: Douglas Camfield. **Producer:** Robert Love.

| 1975 | 8.2 | Mon 3 Feb 9:00 p.m. | 4 | 7 wks |

'The Fall Guy' by Brian Finch.
Marker gets a nasty shock in what at first seemed like a straightforward divorce case.
Director: Douglas Camfield. **Producer:** Michael Chapman.

Pull the Other One   3 wks

Central, situation comedy

This domestic series by Michael McStay starred Michael Elphick and Susan Tracy as Sidney and Sadie Mundy. Lila Kaye played Grandma, who lived with them.

1984	**8.4**	**Fri 20 Jul 8:30 p.m.**	**14**	**3 wks**

'Grandma Gets Fit'
Grandma invites all her friends round for a keep-fit class in the front room.
Director: *Peter Ellis.* **Producer:** *Joan Brown.*

Punchlines   49 wks

LWT, game show

Lennie Bennett hosted this show, which teamed contestants with celebrities to use memory and skill to remember 'what they heard and where they heard it'.

1981	**15.3**	**Sat 12 Dec 7:00 p.m.**	**7**	**13 wks**

Director: *Alasdair Macmillan.* **Producer:** *Alan Boyd.*

1983	**13.4**	**Sat 15 Jan 6:40 p.m.**	**5**	**29 wks**

Director: *Noel D. Greene.* **Producer:** *Keith Stewart.* **Executive Producer:** *Alan Boyd.*

1984	**14.1**	**Sat 8 Dec 7:45 p.m.**	**9**	**7 wks**

Director: *Vic Finch.* **Producer:** *Noel D. Greene.* **Executive Producer:** *Alan Boyd.*

Pursuit   1 wk

HTV, drama

1990	**8.4**	**Mon 16 Jul 9:00 p.m.** **Tue 17 Jul 9:00 p.m.**	**15**	**1 wk**

These two episodes were listed together in the ratings. Ben Cross stars in this two-part drama as an SS Officer who has plastic surgery towards the end of the war to avoid prosecution. Other stars include John Glover, Bruce Greenwood, Veronica Hamel, Larry Lamb and Sarah Jessica Parker.
Designer: *Bruce Grimes.* **Director:** *Ian Sharp.* **Executive Producers:** *Henry Plitt and Larry White.*

Putting on the Donegan   5 wks

ATV, music

Lonnie Donegan began his musical career as a banjo player with Chris Barber's Jazz Band. His first record as a vocalist, 'Rock Island Line' was a massive hit on both sides of the Atlantic in 1956. He became the 'King of Skiffle' notching no fewer than 26 British Top Twenty singles. In this TV series he moved towards becoming an all-round entertainer.

1961	**5.9**	**Thu 25 May 8:00 p.m.**	**8**	**1 wk**

Guests: Valerie Masters, Miki and Griff, Trevor Peacock, Shaw Taylor and the Jack Parnell orchestra.
Producer: *Rita Gillespie.*

1962	**3.9**	**Fri 20 Jul 10:10 p.m.**	**13**	**2 wks**

Guests: Billy Baxter, the Kestrels and Miki and Griff, with the Jack Parnell orchestra.
Director: *Rita Gillespie.* **Producer:** *Albert Locke.*

1963	**5.1**	**Sun 25 Aug 8:25 p.m.**	**9**	**1 wk**

From the Queen's Theatre, Blackpool, an extract from Lonnie's summer show with Des O'Connor, Peter Goodwright, the Clark Brothers, the Kestrels and the John Tiller Girls, with the Ken Moule orchestra.
Stage Producer: *Albert J. Knight.* **Television Producer:** *Albert Locke.*

1964	**5.8**	**Fri 3 Apr 10:05 p.m.**	**16**	**1 wk**

A new image for Lonnie in 1964 – exit the wholesome skiffler and enter the all-round entertainer. To this end the series is set in a fictitious cabaret bar called 'Donegan's'.
Guests: The Clark Brothers, the Raindrops and the Jack Parnell band.
Producer: *Francis Essex.*

Pyramid Game, The   13 wks

LWT, game show

This American format was hosted in Britain by Steve Jones. Contestants were paired with celebrities in a game of wit, words and mind reading.
Producer: *Alasdair Macmillan.*

1981	**12.8**	**Sat 14 Nov 5:40 p.m.**	**17**	**2 wks**

Guests: Suzanne Danielle and Paul Gambaccini.

1982	**9.8**	**Sat 18 Dec 5:40 p.m.**	**18**	**1 wk**

Guests: Rob Buckman and Denise Coffey.
Director: *David MacMahon.*

1984	**10.5**	**Fri 18 May 7:00 p.m.**	**9**	**10 wks**

Guests: Nigel Rees and Victoria Wood.
Director: *David MacMahon.*

QED | 4 wks

BBC, documentary

This strand of programmes covered a wide range of subject matter.
Series Editor: David Filkin.

| 1985 | 14.5 | Wed 6 Mar 9:25 p.m. | 6 | 1 wk |

'The Science of Sexual Attraction'
Eleanor Bron and John Fortune explore the factors that draw certain
people together physically.
Producer: Tony Edwards.

| 1986 | 13.7 | Wed 19 Feb 9:30 p.m. | 14 | 2 wks |

'Round Britain Whizz'
Subjects include the view around Britain's coast as seen from an RAF
Hawk flying at five times the speed of Concorde. Patrick Moore
reveals what lies buried beneath Beachy Head. Clay Jones and David
Bellamy provide other reports.
Producer: Laurie John.

| 1989 | 11.5 | Wed 26 Apr 9:30 p.m. | 11 | 1 wk |

'A Case of Spontaneous Human Combustion?'
This programme examines cases in which people have been reduced to ashes without any sign of struggle or panic and where there
is no damage to surrounding materials.
Producer: Teresa Hunt.

Queen, The | 8 wks

BBC (all years) and ITV (1961), news

Her Majesty gives her Christmas Day address to the Commonwealth.

| 1961 | 5.9 | Mon 25 Dec 3:00 p.m. | 6 | 1 wk |

This programme was broadcast simultaneously on BBC and ITV.

1978	15.6	Mon 25 Dec 3:00 p.m.	7	1 wk
1981	13.4	Fri 25 Dec 3:00 p.m.	19	1 wk
1982	12.4	Sat 25 Dec 3:00 p.m.	8	1 wk
1984	18.3	Tue 25 Dec 3:00 p.m.	3	1 wk
1985	17.4	Wed 25 Dec 3:00 p.m.	3	1 wk
1986	16.5	Thu 25 Dec 3:00 p.m.	4	1 wk
1989	15.9	Mon 25 Dec 3:00 p.m.	10	1 wk

Queen Mother at Eighty-five, The | 1 wk

ITN, documentary

| 1985 | 13.5 | Sun 4 Aug 7:45 p.m. | 3 | 1 wk |

Anthony Carthew, ITN's Court correspondent, presents an insight
into the life of Her Majesty.
Director: Diana Edwards-Jones. **Editor:** Stewart Purvis.

Queen Mother – in Person, The | 1 wk

ITN, documentary

| 1990 | 8.9 | Sun 5 Aug 9:05 p.m. | 14 | 1 wk |

Alastair Burnet talks with Her Majesty at the Royal Lodge, Windsor.
The programme is part of her 90th birthday celebrations.
Editor: George Mitchell.

Queenie | 2 wks

USA presented by ITV, drama

This two-part dramatization by Winston Beard and April Smith was
based on Michael Korda's biography of Estelle 'Queenie' Thompson,
who changed her name to Merle Oberon and became a film star. Kate
Emma Davies played her as a girl and Mia Sara as an adult. Also
starring were Joss Ackland, Kirk Douglas, Leigh Lawson, Sarah
Miles and Topol.

| 1988 | 11.1 | Sun 5 Jun 9:00 p.m. | 7 | 2 wks |

Part One
Born of mixed blood in Bombay, Estelle Thompson lived in fear of
being dubbed a half-caste. She sailed from India to America to chase
her movie dream accompanied by her mother (Claire Bloom).
Director: Larry Pearce.

Queenie's Castle — 14 wks

YTV, situation comedy

Keith Waterhouse and Willis Hall forced a northern accent on former Rank starlet Diana Dors, setting her up as 'Queenie' Shepherd, the owner of Buckingham flats. These were her realm. Her courtiers were her three sons, Raymond (Freddie Fletcher), Douglas (Barrie Rutter) and Bunny (Brian Marshall), and brother-in-law Jack (Tony Caunter). The inhabitants of the flats were led by Queenie's arch-enemy Mrs Petty (Lynne Perrie).
Executive Producer: John Duncan.

| 1970 | 6.7 | Thu 12 Nov 9:00 p.m. | 9 | 2 wks |

'The Great Debate'
With the television set broken, Queenie remembers a programme she once saw of a debate from the Oxford Union. She assembles all her courtiers to re-stage that debate.
Producer: Graham Evans.

| 1971 | 6.0 | Thu 17 Jun 9:00 p.m. | 8 | 6 wks |

'The Breadwinner'
Queenie is out of funds. There is nothing to eat and no credit. She apologetically tells the residents that one of them must find a job.
Producer: Ian Davidson.

| 1972 | 5.8 | Tue 5 Sep 8:30 p.m. | 5 | 6 wks |

'The Patter of Tiny Feet'
The boys find their loyalty to Queenie stretched to its limit at the prospect of sharing the lodgings with another member of the Shepherd family.
Producer: Ian Davidson.

Quest, The — 1 wk

USA presented by BBC, western

Brothers Morgan and Quentin Baudine (Kurt Russell and Tim Matheson) searched for their sister Patricia, who had been abducted by the Cheyenne some years previously.
Producers: James H. Brown and Mark Rodgers.

| 1976 | 7.0 | Fri 15 Oct 9:25 p.m. | 17 | 1 wk |

'The Captive'
The brothers join an attack on an Indian camp in the hope of finding Patricia.

Question of Happiness, A — 2 wks

Granada, drama

Four authors, Kingsley Amis, James Hanley, Alan Plater and James Saunders, were each asked to write a play about the same subject – happiness.

| 1964 | 5.9 | Mon 27 Apr 9:10 p.m. | 14 | 2 wks |

'A Question About Hell' by Kingsley Amis.
Bachelor brothers Alfred and Norman Colliver (Patrick Wymark and Richard Johnson) are men of influence throughout the West Indian islands in which they operate. Their rich widowed sister Angela Strachey (Caroline Mortimer) upsets them through her independent behaviour. She sees her brothers in a new light and is shocked to discover their links with the suspicious Lopey (Mike Pratt), who owns a lowdown waterfront bar for undesirables – far removed from their usual Government House circles.
Designer: Terry Pritchard. **Producer:** Claude Watham.

Question of Sport — 79 wks

BBC, game show

This programme began in 1969 and was hosted by David Coleman. Opposing team captains were joined by two current sporting personalities who answered questions on sport in general and their own sport in particular.
Directors included Peter Hayward (1982, 1984), John Tait (1986–87) and Mike Dempsey (1988–89). **Producer:** Mike Adley.

| 1982 | 12.3 | Tue 30 Mar 7:15 p.m. | 16 | 2 wks |

With captains Bill Beaumont and Willie Carson. Guests: Bob Champion, Gareth Edwards, Emlyn Hughes, Clive Lloyd.

| 1984 | 11.8 | Tue 10 Apr 7:40 p.m. | 8 | 10 wks |

With captains Bill Beaumont and Emlyn Hughes. Guests: Jim Aitken, Ian Botham, Kevin Ratcliffe, Liz Sharman.

| 1986 | 14.0 | Thu 17 Apr 8.30 p.m. | 5 | 9 wks |

With captains Bill Beaumont and Emlyn Hughes. Guests: Susan Devoy, Michael Robinson, Charlie Spedding, Willie Thorne.
Director: John Tait.

| 1987 | 19.0 | Thu 5 Feb 8:25 p.m. | 2 | 19 wks |

The two hundredth edition with captains Bill Beaumont and Emlyn Hughes. Guests: HRH The Princess Anne, Linford Christie, Nigel Mansell, John Rutherford.

| 1988 | 12.7 | Tue 9 Feb 8:00 p.m. | 7 | 16 wks |

With captains Bill Beaumont and Emlyn Hughes. Guests: Jeremy Bates, Billy Bonds, Ellery Hanley, Nigel Mansell.

| 1989 | 12.2 | Tue 4 Apr 8:30 p.m. | 10 | 7 wks |

With captains Bill Beaumont and Ian Botham. Guests: Nick Gillingham, Brian McClair, Phil Neale, Dennis Taylor.

| 1990 | 13.3 | Thu 27 Dec 8:30 p.m. | 15 | 8 wks |

The twenty-first birthday of the show is marked by a special edition in which team captains Bill Beaumont and Ian Botham are joined by former team captains Willie Carson, Gareth Edwards, Brendan Foster and Emlyn Hughes.

| 1991 | 11.4 | Tue 2 Apr 8:30 p.m. | 14 | 8 wks |

With captains Bill Beaumont and Ian Botham. Guests: Marcus Armytage, Jonathan Davies, Sally Gunnell and Ray Houghton.

....

| Question of Sport Meets Spitting Image, A | | 1 wk |

BBC, comedy

| 1988 | 16.4 | Fri 5 Feb 8:00 p.m. | 6 | 1 wk |

This meeting between the real and the rubber takes place for Comic Relief. With Mike Gatting, Barry McGuigan, Daley Thompson and David Coleman.

....

| Quincy | | 23 wks |

USA presented by ITV, drama

In this series created and produced by Glen A. Larson, Jack Klugman starred as Quincy, a police pathologist attached to the coroner's office.

| 1981 | 12.9 | Mon 30 Nov 9:00 p.m. | 5 | 9 wks |

'Dead and Alive'
Quincy tries to determine the identity of a charred corpse who may have been involved in a heroin ring.

| 1983 | 9.6 | Tue 26 Apr 9:00 p.m. | 14 | 1 wk |

'No Way to Treat a Flower'
Four mummified old women are discovered in the attic of a boarding house.

| 1984 | 14.2 | Mon 10 Dec 9:00 p.m. | 10 | 8 wks |

'Guilty Until Proven Innocent'
Quincy examines a worker who died in a factory fire. Arson is suspected.

| 1985 | 13.5 | Mon 25 Feb 9:00 p.m. | 15 | 4 wks |

'Sword of Honour, Blade of Death'
Quincy's assistant Sam Fijiyama (Robert Ito) becomes entangled with the Japanese mafia known as the Yakuza.

| 1990 | 11.3 | Fri 14 Dec 8:30 p.m. | 20 | 1 wk |

In this feature length edition Quincy delivers a lecture to pathology students. A girl shows him a thigh bone on which he notices a nick caused by a bullet. The students attempt to identify the victim. **Director:** Alex March.

Q

Race You to the Top — 1 wk

BBC, news

1969   **5.4**   **Sun 11 May 9:40 p.m.**   **20**   **1 wk**

The final stages of the Daily Mail Transatlantic Air Race are in progress. Cliff Michelmore is at London's GPO Tower, Raymond Baxter is at London Airport and Chris Rainbow is at New York's Empire State Building to witness the climax of this race to the top of the two tallest buildings either side of the Atlantic.
Executive Producer: Brian Robins.

Racing Game, The — 4 wks

YTV, drama

This thriller series based on the ideas of Dick Francis starred Mike Gwilym as Sid Halley, a crippled former jockey who set up as an on-course private detective.

1979   **14.2**   **Wed 28 Nov 9:00 p.m.**   **16**   **3 wks**

'Trackdown' by Terence Feely.
Sid Halley uncovers a blackmail and murder plot.
Director: Lawrence Gordon Clark. **Producer:** Jacky Stoller. **Executive Producer:** David Cunliffe.

1980   **13.9**   **Wed 9 Jan 9:00 p.m.**   **19**   **1 wk**

'Needle' by Terence Feely.
Helped by a glamorous biochemist (Meg Davies), Sid discovers that a hypodermic needle is responsible for a trail of sick and dead horses.
Director: Peter Duffell. **Producer:** Jacky Stoller. **Executive Producer:** David Cunliffe.

Raffles — 4 wks

YTV, drama

Philip Mackie adapted stories by E. W. Hornung about gentleman amateur jewel thief Raffles (Anthony Valentine) and his accomplice Bunny (Christopher Strauli) at the turn of the century.

1975   **6.5**   **Wed 10 Sep 9:00 p.m.**   **12**   **1 wk**

'The Amateur Cracksman'
Raffles is invited to a cricket week at the home of the Earl of Milchester (Michael Barrington). He knows that the Dowager Marchioness of Melrose (Margot Lister) will be there - as will her necklace. Also starring James Maxwell as Inspector Mackenzie.
Designer: Roger Andrews. **Producer:** Christopher Hodson. **Executive Producer:** Peter Willes.

1977   **6.7**   **Fri 20 May 9:00 p.m.**   **15**   **3 wks**

'An Old Flame'
Raffles has met his match with the beautiful, rich and determined Lady Paulton (Caroline Blakiston). There appears to be no escape.
Designer: Roger Andrews. **Director:** James Goddard. **Producer:** Jacky Stoller. **Executive Producer:** David Cunliffe.

Rag Trade, The — 13 wks

BBC, situation comedy

This series was created by Ronald Wolfe and Ronald Chesney in the late 1950s and set in a dressmaker's workroom at Fenner Fashions. The women workers took advantage of the bosses on any possible occasion. The original stars were Peter Jones as Mr Fenner, Reg Varney as foreman-cutter Reg, Miriam Karlin as machinist shop steward Paddy and Sheila Hancock as shop treasurer Carole. Esma Cannon played Little Lil, the assistant buttonhole hand and chief tea maker. Paddy's clarion call 'Everybody Out' became a hit catchphrase for the show.
Producer (1961–63): Dennis Main Wilson.

1961   **4.9**   **Fri 8 Dec 8:45 p.m.**   **13**   **1 wk**

Mr Fenner is trying to improve the export trade for the company, but receives little support from the shop floor. Also starring Ann Beach, Judy Carne, Colin Douglas, Toni Palmer, Terry Scott, Rita Smythe and Barbara Windsor.

1962   **5.3**   **Fri 4 May 8:45 p.m.**   **5**   **9 wks**

Mr Fenner struggles to maintain output, pay the workers and make a profit. Paddy and the female brothers of the union defend the sanctity of the tea-break. Also starring Norman Mitchell, Julie Samuel, Vi Stevens, Wanda Ventham, Gwendolyn Watts and Jan Williams.

| 1963 | 6.2 | Sat 9 Mar 8:10 p.m. | 12 | 3 wks |

1963 is National Productivity Year and the girls are keen to do their bit – but not for long. Reg's mum (Irene Handl) joins the staff. Other new workers are played by Carmel Cryan, Claire Davenport, Pat Denys, Sheena Marshe, Amanda Reiss and Stella Tanner, with Esma Cannon and Sheila Hancock having left the series.

The Rag Trade, The   11 wks

LWT, situation comedy

The revived programme had only Peter Jones and Miriam Karlin remaining from the BBC cast.

| 1977 | 15.8 | Sat 19 Nov 7:30 p.m. | 8 | 4 wks |

'The New Girl'
Paddy and the girls want nothing to do with Miss Burleigh (Rachel Davies), who has come straight from college to become Mr Fenner's personal assistant.
Producer: Bryan Izzard.

| 1978 | 14.9 | Fri 13 Oct 7:30 p.m. | 5 | 7 wks |

'Self-Defence'
Paddy hears certain local girls have been molested. She demands self-defence lessons for the workers.
Producer: William G. Stewart.

Rage of Angels   1 wk

USA presented by ITV, drama

This was a two-part adaptation of Sidney Sheldon's novel of ambition and romance.
Director: Buzz Kulik. **Producer:** Richard L. O'Connor.

| 1983 | 10.0 | Sun 22 May 7:45 p.m. | 12 | 1 wk |

Part One
Jennifer Parker (Jaclyn Smith), a judge's daughter, is fired from her job in the New York District Attorney's office. She sets up her own practice. Her first case brings her face to face with Di Silva (Ronald Hunter). He was the man who fired her.

Raging Calm, A   3 wks

Granada, drama

Stan Barstow adapted his own novel of the same title. Four people seemingly lived quiet lives in a West Riding town, but complications set in as the series developed. Starring Alan Badel as Tom Simpkins, Diana Coupland as Norma Moffatt, Michael Williams as Philip Hart and Frances White as Andrea Warner.

| 1974 | 8.0 | Mon 18 Feb 9:00 p.m. | 6 | 3 wks |

'A Vote for Progress'
Shirley Moffatt (Vicky Williams) has discovered Tom Simpkins is her father. Tom and Philip oppose each other in the local elections. Andrea has been having an affair with Philip and now meets his wife Kate (Joanna Craig).
Director: June Howson. **Producer:** Brian Armstrong.

Raiders of the Lost Ark   4 wks

Presented by ITV, film

| 1984 | 19.3 | Tue 25 Dec 8:30 p.m. | 2 | 1 wk |

In the 1930s American archaeologist Indiana Jones (Harrison Ford) races against the Nazis to find a priceless box containing fragments of the stones on which God wrote his laws.
Director: Steven Spielberg.

1986	10.3	Thu 12 Jun 7:15 p.m.	7	1 wk
1987	14.0	Tue 6 Oct 8:00 p.m.	6	1 wk
1989	13.1	Mon 2 Jan 9:00 p.m.	15	1 wk

Repeat showings of the above film.

Rainbow, The   1 wk

BBC, drama

D. H. Lawrence's novel was adapted in three parts by Anne Devlin. It starred Imogen Stubbs as Ursula Brangwen, Tom Bell as Tom Brangwen, Kate Buffery as Winifred Inger, Jon Finch as Uncle Tom and Martin Wenner as Anton Skrebensky.

| 1988 | 11.9 | Sun 4 Dec 9:20 p.m. | 19 | 1 wk |

Part One 'Ghosts'
It is 1899. Ursula lives with her family in the Erewash valley. She is sixteen and haunted by the ghosts of her grandparents.
Director: Stuart Burge. **Producer:** Chris Parr.

Raise the Titanic   2 wks

Presented by ITV, film

| 1983 | 12.7 | Thu 27 Oct 7:30 p.m. | 6 | 1 wk |

The superpowers race to locate the sunken ocean liner. She is rumoured to have been carrying a cargo of byzanium, the ingredient needed to make the ultimate nuclear deterrent. Starring Richard Jordan, Alec Guinness, Jason Robards and David Selby.
Director: Jerry Jameson.

| 1985 | 8.5 | Sat 17 Aug 9:00 p.m. | 20 | 1 wk |

Repeat showing of the above film.

Random Harvest — 1 wk

Presented by BBC, film

| 1967 | 6.8 | Sun 26 Nov 7:55 p.m. | 15 | 1 wk |

Adapted from the novel by James Hilton. Ronald Colman and Greer Garson star in the story of a First World War serviceman who escapes from hospital suffering from amnesia and meets and marries a showgirl. He regains his memory and resumes his former life with no recollection of his marriage.
Director: Mervyn Le Roy.

Raquel — 1 wk

USA presented by BBC, entertainment

| 1970 | 4.5 | Thu 11 Jun 9:10 p.m. | 13 | 1 wk |

Raquel Welch's first television special has her singing and dancing around the world with Bob Hope, Tom Jones and John Wayne.
Director: David Winters.

Rat Catchers, The — 17 wks

AR, drama

A group with no official title were known as The Rat Catchers. Their headquarters were in Whitehall and their orders came from the Prime Minister. They were dedicated to the defence of Britain and the Western Alliance. The series starred Gerald Flood as Peregrine Smith and Glyn Owen as Richard Hurst with Philip Stone as Brigadier Davidson.

| 1966 | 8.5 | Mon 31 Jan 8:00 p.m. | 3 | 14 wks |

'Ticket to Madrid' by Raymond Bowers.
Richard Hurst discovers with surprise and disgust exactly what his new job entails. In this first programme of the series he sets out down a lonely and dangerous road. In Madrid, he and the beautiful Miss Larks (Jan Waters) feel the cold horror of espionage and deception.
Designer: Fred Pusey. **Director:** James Ormerod. **Producer:** Cyril Coke.

| 1967 | 6.2 | Mon 2 Jan 8:00 p.m. | 13 | 3 wks |

'Death in Madeira' by Victor Canning.
Hurst wants to resign for personal reasons. Davidson's plans to prevent this result in some unpleasant violence.
Designer: Barbara Bates. **Director:** Don Gale. **Producer:** Cyril Coke.

Rat Patrol, The — 1 wk

USA presented by BBC, drama

Four commandos, three American and one British, were on a mission to harass the Nazi enemy in the North African desert during the Second World War. The series caused much distress and anger in Britain by apparently understating the role of the British in the North African campaign. Starring Gary Raymond as English Sergeant Jack Moffitt and, as the American rats, Christopher George as Sergeant Sam Troy, Justin Tarr as Private Tully Pettigrew and Lawrence Casey as Private Albert Luckey.

| 1967 | 6.2 | Wed 4 Jan 7:35 p.m. | 12 | 1 wk |

'The Chase of Fire Raid'
The Rats' human enemy is Rommel – but they encounter natural foes in sand, wind, scorching sun and freezing cold nights.

Rawhide — 47 wks

USA presented by ITV, western

The continuing story of a cattle drive ('head 'em up – move 'em out!') from San Antonio, Texas to Sedalia, Kansas. It starred Eric Fleming as Gil Favor and Clint Eastwood as his right-hand man Rowdy Yates. Sheb Wooley appeared as Scout Pete Nolan, Paul Brinegar as Wishbone the cook and James Murdock as Mushy the drover. The title song was sung by Frankie Laine.

| 1960 | 6.5 | Tue 6 Sep 8:30 p.m. | 1 | 22 wks |

'Incident of the Murder Steer'
A steer with the word 'murder' branded on his flanks appears each time a death occurs on the ride. Guest star: James Franciscus.

| 1961 | 5.4 | Wed 27 Dec 8:00 p.m. | 9 | 14 wks |

'Phantom Bugler'
Night prairie winds carry the eerie sounds of a mysterious bugler to the camp. Guest star: Jack Mahoney.
Producer: Endre Bohem.

| 1962 | 6.6 | Fri 2 Feb 8:00 p.m. | 4 | 11 wks |

'Grandma's Money'
Rowdy rides into Indian Springs to collect payment for a herd of cattle. He meets and tries to help an eccentric old lady who almost loses him the contract. Guest star: Josephine Hutchinson.
Producer: Soben Martin.

Ready Steady Go! — 2 wks

AR, music

This weekly pop show was hosted by Keith Fordyce and Cathy McGowan with the slogan 'The Weekend Starts Here'.
Producer: Francis Hitching. **Executive Producer:** Elkan Allan.

| 1963 | 5.1 | Fri 30 Aug 7:00 p.m. | 15 | 1 wk |

Guests: David Gell, Johnny Kidd and the Pirates, and the Springfields.
Director: Bill Turner.

| 1964 | 8.0 | Wed 8 Apr 9:50 p.m. | 5 | 1 wk |

Away from the studio and its usual Friday evening transmission, RSG comes from the Empire Pool Wembley. The Mod Ball has assembled 8000 mods. Keith Fordyce and Cathy McGowan introduce Cilla Black, the Fourmost, Freddie and the Dreamers, Kathy Kirby, Billy J. Kramer and the Dakotas, Kenny Lynch, Manfred Mann, the Merseybeats, the Rolling Stones, the Searchers and Sounds Incorporated.
Director: Peter Croft.

Ready Steady Winner   1 wk

AR, music

The READY STEADY GO team, notably co-editors Francis Hitching and Barry Cawtheray, scoured Britain auditioning would-be hit groups for a week-by-week contest building up to a final with a first prize of £1000 worth of equipment.

| 1964 | 5.8 | Wed 16 Sep 9:40 p.m. | 14 | 1 wk |

The final, introduced by Keith Fordyce and Cathy McGowan. Competing groups include the Bo Street Runners, the Harbour Lights Trio, Jimmy Royal and the Hawks, the Olympics, the Thyrds, and the Toggery 5. The judges include Brian Epstein, Bill Haley and Brian Matthew.
Director: Peter Croft.

Real Charlotte, The   1 wk

Granada, drama

This three-part series by Edith Somerville and Martin Ross was adapted by Bernard Mclaverty. It was shot entirely in Ireland and was set in 1895. The story concerned two cousins, Charlotte and Francie (Jeanette Crowley and Joanna Roth), and their romantic pursuits of Roddy Lambert (Patrick Bergin).

| 1991 | 9.5 | Sun 16 Jun 8:20 p.m. | 19 | 1 wk |

Francie is angry with her cousin Charlotte when she falls for a penniless English officer.
Director: Tony Barry. **Producer:** Nial McCarthy.

Real World, The   1 wk

TVS, documentary

| 1982 | 11.9 | Mon 29 Nov 7:00 p.m. | 13 | 1 wk |

Sue Jay and Michael Rodd examine the science behind bringing 3D to television. (Their examples could be seen by using the special spectacles given away in TV TIMES.)
Director: John Gorman. **Producer:** Peter Kinkead. **Executive Producer:** David Pick.

Rear Window   1 wk

Presented by ITV, film

| 1986 | 9.5 | Wed 23 Jul 8:00 p.m. | 10 | 1 wk |

News photographer 'Jeff' Jeffries (James Stewart) is confined to a wheelchair with a broken leg. As he sits by the rear window of his New York apartment, he is convinced a neighbour has murdered his wife. Raymond Burr and Grace Kelly also star.
Director: Alfred Hitchcock.

Redcap   5 wks

ABC, drama

John Thaw starred as Sergeant Mann of the Special Investigation Branch of the Military Police. The series was created by Jack Bell.

| 1966 | 5.7 | Sat 16 Apr 9:05 p.m. | 13 | 5 wks |

'The Killer' by Troy Kennedy Martin.
Mann goes to Malaysia to investigate a commando unit which has lost a series of men killed by their own side.
Director: Guy Verney. **Producer:** John Bryce.

Reg Varney   8 wks

ATV, entertainment

In this series the star of THE RAG TRADE and ON THE BUSES returned to his solo career as a variety entertainer, joking, singing and playing the piano. With the Jack Parnell orchestra.

| 1973 | 7.1 | Wed 29 Aug 8:00 p.m. | 4 | 7 wks |

Guest: Henry McGee.
Producer: William G. Stewart.

| 1974 | 6.5 | Mon 11 Feb 8:25 p.m. | 19 | 1 wk |

Guests: Henry McGee, Pat Coombs and Tony Selby with the Ladybirds.
Producer: Alan Tarrant.

Reg Varney Christmas Revue, The   1 wk

LWT, entertainment

| 1972 | 6.5 | Sat 23 Dec 6:00 p.m. | 13 | 1 wk |

Guests: George Chisholm, Pat Coombs, Elizabeth Counsell, the Ladybirds, David Lodge, Kenneth McKellar, the Osmonds, Dorothy Squires and Frank Thornton with the Malcolm Clare dancers.
Producer: Bryan Izzard.

1

2

3

4

5

6

7

1 *David Hamilton, in period costume, introduces the swimsuit competition in the 1972* **Miss TV Times**.

2 *One of the youngest winners of* **Opportunity Knocks**, *Neil Reid, went on to have a number two single 'Mother of Mine'.*

3 *Esther Rantzen is flanked by protégés Kieran Prendiville and Glyn Worsnip in* **That's Life**.

4 *Miss India (Reita Faria) is crowned in the first edition of* **Miss World** *to win the chart crown.*

5 *Wings performed 'Mull of Kintyre' on* **The Mike Yarwood Christmas Show** *of 1977.*

6 *Glenda Jackson was one of the victims of the wit of Denis Norden in* **It'll Be Alright on the Nigh**t.

7 *Harry* **Secombe And Friends**, *Shirley Bassey, Jimmy Tarbuck and Dudley Moore make an unusual quartet.*

Reilly – Ace of Spies

1 wk

Thames, drama

This twelve-part series by Troy Kennedy Martin from the book by Robin Bruce-Lockhart celebrated the exploits of the turn of the century British spy Sidney Reilly (Sam Neill). Tom Bell, Kenneth Cranham, Jeananne Crowley, Leo McKern and Norman Rodway also starred.
Executive Producer: Verity Lambert. A Euston Films production.

1983	9.7	Wed 7 Sep 9:00 p.m.	19	1 wk

'Prelude to War'
Reilly is captured by the Russians after his undercover work enabled the Japanese fleet to sink the Russian Pacific Squadron in Port Arthur.
Director: Martin Campbell. **Producer:** Chris Burt.

Relatively Secombe

1 wk

Thames, entertainment

1978	11.8	Wed 28 Jun 8:00 p.m.	13	1 wk

This special stars Harry Secombe with Moira Anderson, Diana Dors and Donald Houston, the Gillian Lynne dancers and the Peter Knight orchestra.
Producer: Keith Beckett.

Reluctant Heroes

1 wk

BBC, comedy

1971	6.4	Sat 3 Apr 7:15 p.m.	14	1 wk

Presented by and starring Brian Rix, this is the twenty-first anniversary production of the famous farce by Colin Morris, recorded before an Army audience at Aldershot. The guests are Tim Barnett, Peter Bland, Anna Dawson, Sandra Duncan, James Grant, Margaret Nolan, John Quayle, Derek Royle and Bill Treacher.
Designer: Rhoda Gray. **Director:** Wallace Douglas.

Remington Steele

1 wk

USA presented by BBC, drama

Stephanie Zimbalist starred as Laura Holt, who started a detective agency called Remington Steele. To her surprise, a man of that very name turned up, a gentleman criminal with a sinister past played by Pierce Brosnan. The series was created by Michael Gleason.

1983	8.1	Sat 3 Sep 9:10 p.m.	18	1 wk

'License to Steele'
Laura is in trouble when one of her clients demands a face-to-face meeting with her non-existent boss.

Remo: Unarmed and Dangerous

1 wk

Presented by BBC, film

1990	9.9	Sun 24 Jun 7:45 p.m.	13	1 wk

Fred Ward stars as New York policeman Remo Williams. He learns the martial art of Sinanju from Korean mystic Chiun (Joel Grey).
Director: Guy Hamilton.

Reporter at Large

1 wk

BBC, documentary

David Dimbleby presented this series of three programmes.

1973	6.8	Thu 1 Mar 8:30 p.m.	15	1 wk

'God Bless Nanny'
David Dimbleby looks at the role of the nanny, both the stern but kindly guardian of the past and Jill Moore, a nanny of today who jets around the world with her charges and their family.
Director: David Gerrard. **Producer:** Frank Smith.

Reporters, The

3 wks

YTV, news

Jonathan Aitken, Stuart Hood, Austin Mitchell, Nicholas Tomlin and Alan Whicker reported on world news.
Executive Producer: Tony Essex.

1968	6.1	Thu 12 Dec 9:30 p.m.	17	2 wks
1969	6.5	Thu 9 Jan 9:30 p.m.	14	1 wk

Return of Captain Nemo, The

1 wk

USA presented by BBC, drama

Jules Verne's character came back in a three-part undersea adventure on the Nautilus. He was freed to overcome an evil professor who held Washington to ransom.
Director: Alex March. **Producer:** Irwin Allen.

1981	11.0	Mon 13 Apr 7:20 p.m.	20	1 wk

Episode One 'Deadly Blackmail'
Two US Navy divers discover the strange craft Nautilus wedged in rocks on the Pacific Ocean bed. They free the ship's captain Nemo (José Ferrer) from suspended animation and enlist his help in overcoming the evil Professor Waldo Cunningham (Burgess Meredith).

Return of Mr Bean, The — 1 wk

Thames, comedy

| 1991 | 12.4 | Wed 13 Feb 9:30 p.m. | 17 | 1 wk |

Mr Bean (Rowan Atkinson) doesn't say very much, even when he goes shopping and meets a Royal.
Writers: Rowan Atkinson, Richard Curtis and Robin Driscoll. **Producer:** John Howard Davies. (A Tiger Television production.)

Return of Shelley, The — 1 wk

Thames, situation comedy

After five years teaching English in the USA and the Arab Emirates, Shelley (Hywel Bennett) returned to discover Yuppie Britain.

| 1988 | 11.2 | Tue 15 Nov 8:30 p.m. | 19 | 1 wk |

'The Big S'
Shelley plays the eloquent teacher to his landlords Carol and Graham (Caroline Langrishe and Andrew Castell). He opens a new world of understanding, freedom of thought and action for Graham. Caroline does not appreciate his good intent.
Writer: Andy Hamilton. **Producer:** Anthony Parker.

Return of Sherlock Holmes, The — 7 wks

Granada, drama

This series was adapted from Conan Doyle's own resurrection of Holmes. Jeremy Brett starred as Holmes with Edward Hardwicke as Dr Watson.
Producer: June Wyndham-Davies. **Executive Producer:** Michael Cox.

| 1986 | 10.4 | Wed 9 Jul 9:00 p.m. | 4 | 5 wks |

'The Empty House' dramatized by John Hawkesworth.
Dr Watson is faced with an unsolved murder three years after Holmes fell to his death from a cliff.
Designer: Margaret Coombes. **Director:** Howard Baker.

| 1988 | 10.3 | Wed 6 Apr 9:00 p.m. | 17 | 2 wks |

'The Devil's Foot' dramatized by Gary Hopkins.
A young Cornish woman is found dead with no visible injuries.
Designer: Michael Grimes. **Director:** June Wyndham-Davies.

Return of the Pink Panther, The — 3 wks

Presented by ITV, film

| 1980 | 14.2 | Sun 14 Sep 7:15 p.m. | 8 | 1 wk |

The Pink Panther diamond is once again stolen, so Inspector Clouseau (Peter Sellers) is called in. David Lodge, Herbert Lom, Christopher Plummer and Graham Stark also star.
Director: Blake Edwards.

| 1981 | 10.8 | Tue 28 Jul 7:00 p.m. | 11 | 1 wk |
| 1983 | 13.2 | Tue 4 Jan 7:00 p.m. | 17 | 1 wk |

Repeat showings of the above film.

Return of the Saint, The — 21 wks

ATV, drama

Ian Ogilvy stepped into Roger Moore's shoes to play Leslie Charteris' character Simon Templar.
Producer: Anthony Spinner. **Executive Producer:** Robert S. Baker.

| 1978 | 15.3 | Sun 26 Nov 7:15 p.m. | 6 | 7 wks |

'Signal Stop' by John Kruse.
A girl on a train leads the Saint to a murder which stems from rape and revenge.
Director: Ray Austin.

| 1979 | 16.0 | Sun 14 Jan 7:15 p.m. | 6 | 10 wks |

'Collision Course' by John Kruse.
The beautiful young Annabel (Gayle Hunnicutt) is widowed when her husband is killed in a power boat race. She involves Templar in a dangerous search for hidden gold.
Director: Cyril Frankel.

| 1980 | 10.7 | Sat 21 Jun 5:30 p.m. | 13 | 4 wks |

'The Village That Sold Its Soul' by John Goldsmith.
The Saint investigates a murder in a remote mountain district of Italy.
Director: Leslie Norman.

Return of the Seven, The — 1 wk

Presented by BBC, film

| 1976 | 7.8 | Sat 18 Dec 6:40 p.m. | 7 | 1 wk |

In this follow-up to THE MAGNIFICENT SEVEN Yul Brynner once again rounds up a small group of fighters. They go to the aid of a small Mexican village where all the men folk have been kidnapped. Also starring Claude Akins, Jordan Christopher, Emilio Fernandez, Robert Fuller, Julian Mateos, Warren Oates and Virgilio Teixera.
Director: Burt Kennedy.

Return to Eden — 11 wks

Australia presented by ITV, drama

In the 1984 three-part mini-series, tennis star Greg Marsden (James Reyne) had one eye on heiress Stephanie Harper (Rebecca Gilling) and the other on her best friend Jilly Stewart (Wendy Hughes). He married Stephanie, but regretted it. Later, in an effort to get rid of her, he threw her into a crocodile swamp with Jilly watching, and they both left her to die. However, she survived, underwent plastic surgery, took a new name, Tara Welles, and started a new career as a model. All the while she nursed revenge on her ex-husband and former friend.

The 13-part series in 1986 took up the story seven years later. Stephanie was then a wealthy and powerful woman. She married her plastic surgeon, Dr Dan Marshall (James Smillie). Greg had died in an air crash and Jilly was in jail for her part in trying to murder Stephanie.

Producers: Hal McElroy and Michael Laurence.

1984	14.8	Tue 25 Sep 9:00 p.m.	7	2 wks

Part Three
When Greg Marsden meets the beautiful Tara Welles he doesn't recognize that she is his former wife. Stephanie's plans for revenge take shape.

1986	13.3	Mon 25 Aug 9:00 p.m.	4	9 wks

Jilly (now played by Peta Toppano) is released from prison and together with Greg's brother, Jake Sanders (Daniel Abinieri), she plans to destroy Stephanie. In a winner-takes-all confrontation Stephanie races her horse, Tara's Pride, in the Melbourne Cup against Jake's horse, Revenge.

Reunion at Fairborough — 1 wk

Presented by ITV, film

1986	13.2	Sun 23 Mar 7:45 p.m.	4	1 wk

Sixty-year-old Carl Hostrup (Robert Mitchum) leaves his elegant Chicago home scarred by two failed marriages and enforced early retirement. He returns to the quiet English village of Fairborough for his Air Force Squadron's fortieth reunion. Red Buttons and Deborah Kerr also star.
Director: Herbert Wise.

Rhodesia — 1 wk

BBC, news

1965	5.7	Thu 11 Nov 9:30 p.m.	20	1 wk

Earlier tonight, the Prime Minister The Rt. Hon. Harold Wilson MP broadcast to the nation on the Unilateral Declaration of Independence proclaimed by Mr Ian Smith's illegal government in Rhodesia following the breakdown of talks between the two men on board HMS Fearless. As Foreign Secretary the Rt. Hon. Michael Stewart MP flies to New York to address the Security Council of the United Nations, the BBC's TWENTY-FOUR HOURS team present an on-the-spot assessment of the situation and the likely effect of sanctions being imposed on Rhodesia. Cliff Michelmore introduces the issues with the BBC's African correspondent Richard Kershaw. Studio guests are the Rt. Hon. Edward Heath MP and the Rt. Hon. Jo Grimond MP.

Rhubarb Rhubarb! — 2 wks

Thames, comedy

1980	14.5	Mon 15 Dec 8:00 p.m.	12	1 wk

Silent except for the title words, Eric Sykes stars as a golf-mad police Inspector. With Charlie Drake, Jimmy Edwards, Bill Fraser, Hattie Jacques, Roy Kinnear, Beryl Reid, Norman Rossington and Bob Todd.
Writer and **Director:** Eric Sykes. **Producer:** David Clark.

1983	10.9	Mon 28 Feb 8:30 p.m.	19	1 wk

Repeat showing of the above programme.

Rich Man, Poor Man — 6 wks

USA presented by ITV, drama

Irwin Shaw's novel was adapted in six parts by Dean Reisner and screened by ITV twice weekly for three weeks. The mini-series traced the fortunes of two brothers, Rudy and Tom Jordache (Peter Strauss and Nick Nolte), from the end of the Second World War until the seventies. As they competed for the same girl, Julie Prescott (Susan Blakely), so their contrasting lives moved towards wealth and success, poverty and failure, concluding with Tom's death. Edward Asner, Dorothy McGuire, Ray Milland and Robert Reed also starred.

1976	6.0	Wed 14 Jul 9:00 p.m.	7	6 wks

Episode One
Rudy rejects Julie and she turns to local playboy Teddy Boylan (Robert Reed).
Director: David Greene.

Rich Tea and Sympathy — 1 wk

YTV, drama

This six-part comedy drama series by David Nobbs starred Patricia Hodge as Julia Merrygrove, divorced mother of two teenagers. She was a local councillor and worked at Rudge Brothers biscuit factory. Denis Quilley starred as her boss, widower George Rudge. The series also starred Jean Alexander as Julia's snooker-crazy mother, Grannie Trellis, and Lionel Jeffries as George's sex-mad father, Grandpa Rudge. Julia's children, John and Samantha were portrayed by Jason Flemyng and Claudia Bryan.

| 1991 | 8.7 | Fri 5 Jul 9:00 p.m. | 17 | 1 wk |

'Sex and Snooker'
Julia and George become enmeshed in more ways than one when their trolleys collide in a supermarket. Very soon Grandma Trellis and Grandpa Rudge are similarly enmeshed.
Producer: *David Reynolds.*

....

Richest Woman in the World, The   1 wk

Presented by ITV, film

| 1991 | 10.9 | Sun 15 Sep 7:45 p.m. | 17 | 1 wk |

Farrah Fawcett stars as Barbara Hutton, the Woolworth heiress.
Director: *Charles Jarrott.*

....

Ride the High Iron   1 wk

Presented by ITV, film

| 1968 | 4.8 | Wed 7 Aug 6:05 p.m. | 10 | 1 wk |

Raymond Burr stars in the story of a public relations man who is led into the seamy side of life by a female client.
Director: *Don Weis.*

....

Ring out the Bells   1 wk

ATV, music

| 1961 | 4.6 | Sun 24 Dec 8:25 p.m. | 11 | 1 wk |

Starring Jo Stafford and Harry Secombe with the children of the Corona Stage School, the choir of Westminster Abbey, the Polka Dots, the Lionel Blair dancers and the Jack Parnell orchestra.
Producer: *Bill Ward.*

....

Rings on Their Fingers   14 wks

BBC, situation comedy

This series by Richard Waring concerned a bright young couple, Sandy and Oliver Pride (Diane Keene and Martin Jarvis) who decided to marry after living together for some time.
Producer: *Harold Snoad.*

| 1978 | 13.6 | Sat 23 Dec 9:50 p.m. | 19 | 2 wks |

'Merry Christmas'
As they prepare for their first Christmas as man and wife, Sandy and Oliver invite both sets of parents for Boxing Day lunch.

| 1979 | 21.1 | Wed 3 Oct 8:30 p.m. | 8 | 5 wks |

'Moving Moments'
Sandy and Oliver prepare to move house. They go through their accumulated bits and pieces trying to decide what to throw out and what to keep.

| 1980 | 16.9 | Thu 23 Oct 8:30 p.m. | 4 | 6 wks |

'It's Not The Thought, It's The Gift'
Oliver ponders what to buy for the girl who has everything, including him!

| 1981 | 11.2 | Thu 16 Jul 8:30 p.m. | 14 | 1 wk |

'And Joybells On Their Toes'
A repeat of the episode in which Oliver tests the reactions of his friends to the news that Sandy is pregnant.

....

Ripper (Five Years of Terror), The   1 wk

YTV, news

| 1981 | 11.3 | Fri 22 May 10:30 p.m. | 19 | 1 wk |

Peter Sutcliffe, known as 'The Yorkshire Ripper', was today found guilty of thirteen murders by the Old Bailey jury. He has been sentenced to life imprisonment. This programme profiles his evil crimes.

....

Rise and Fall of the Third Reich, The   1 wk

BBC (with Wolper-Metromedia), documentary

A documentary in three parts from the book by William Shirer.
Executive Producer: *Mel Stuart.*

| 1969 | 5.0 | Mon 25 Aug 9:40 p.m. | 17 | 1 wk |

Part Three 'Götterdämmerung'
This final programme in the series tells the story of how captive Europeans fared under Hitler, and how his attack on Russia and America's entry into the war sealed his eventual fate.

....

Rising Damp   42 wks

YTV, situation comedy

This series by Eric Chappell was set in a squalid house divided into bedsits. Leonard Rossiter starred as Rigsby, the penny-pinching landlord who lived downstairs with his cat Vienna. The tenants were university administrator Miss Ruth Jones (Frances de la Tour), medical student Alan More (Richard Beckinsale) and mature student Philip Smith (Don Warrington) from Africa.

| 1974 | 6.2 | Mon 2 Sep 8:00 p.m. | 11 | 1 wk |

Rigsby has to swallow his racial prejudice when Philip arrives. He is a friend of Miss Jones and a prince in his own country. He takes over the best room.
Producer: *Ian MacNaughton.*

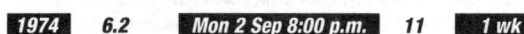

| **1975** | *7.3* | **Fri 12 Dec 7:35 p.m.** | *13* | **8 wks** |

Rigsby's new furniture is much admired by Alan and Philip; who believe that possession is nine-tenths of the law.
Producer: Ronnie Baxter.

| **1976** | *7.2* | **Mon 3 May 8:00 p.m.** | *6* | **4 wks** |

Rigsby accepts a challenge from Alan to fast for 48 hours.
Producer: Ronnie Baxter.

| **1977** | *8.5* | **Tue 26 Apr 8:30 p.m.** | *1* | **7 wks** |

Rigsby gets a sports car and takes Miss Jones for a spin.
Producer: Ronnie Baxter.

| **1978** | *18.6* | **Tue 11 Apr 8:00 p.m.** | *1* | **12 wks** |

Rigsby finds time for repentance when zealous theology student Gwyn (John Clive) moves into the boarding house.
Producer: Vernon Lawrence.

| **1981** | *13.8* | **Tue 1 Dec 8:00 p.m.** | *9* | **5 wks** |

Rigsby terrifies Alan by constantly talking about vampires. (Repeat.)
Director: Len Lurcuck. **Producer:** Ronnie Baxter.

| **1984** | *15.5* | **Mon 17 Dec 8:00 p.m.** | *4* | **5 wks** |

Rigsby places an advertisement in the personal column of a newspaper. This repeat screening is a tribute to Leonard Rossiter, who died on 5 October 1984.

Rising Damp   1 wk

Presented by ITV, film

| **1983** | *12.2* | **Thu 3 Mar 7:45 p.m.** | *12* | **1 wk** |

This feature film version was made after the death of Richard Beckinsale. Rossiter, de la Tour and Warrington are joined by Denholm Elliott and Christopher Strauli.
Director: Joe McGrath.

Rising Stars   2 wks

BBC, entertainment

This talent show hosted by Lennie Bennett came from the ABC Theatre, Blackpool. Teams of judges viewed the acts from BBC centres around the country.

| **1979** | *15.3* | **Sun 11 Nov 5:00 p.m.** | *11* | **2 wks** |

(One of the contestants in this edition was Gary Wilmot.)
Director: Tony Harrison. **Producer:** Barney Colehan.

Risk Business, The   1 wk

BBC, documentary

These programmes examined the financial risks taken in a variety of different businesses.

| **1980** | *12.4* | **Wed 9 Apr 9:25 p.m.** | *19* | **1 wk** |

'The Movie'
Michael Rodd investigates what brings American film producers to make movies in Britain and asks whether, when the price of shooting forces them back home, we will have any film industry left here.
Editor: Michael Blakstad. **Producers:** John Gorman and Andrew Wiseman.

Rivals of Sherlock Holmes, The   19 wks

Thames, drama

This series was based on an anthology by Hugh Greene about other fictional detectives operating in London during the years 1891-1914, when Conan Doyle's Holmes stories were being serialized in Strand magazine.

| **1971** | *6.8* | **Mon 18 Oct 9:00 p.m.** | *11* | **9 wks** |

'The Horse of the Invisible' dramatized by Philip Mackie.
Starring Donald Pleasence as William Hope Hodgson's 'ghost' detective Carnacki, who eerily enters the gas-lit shadows of the Higgins family in search of an invisible horse which haunts them.
Director: Alan Cooke. **Producer:** Jonathan Alwyn. **Executive Producer:** Lloyd Shirley.

| **1973** | *7.4* | **Mon 19 Feb 9:00 p.m.** | *6* | **10 wks** |

'The Secret of the Magnifique' by E. Phillips Oppenheim, dramatized by Gerald Kelsey.
With the aid of two former convicts Detective Laxworthy (Bernard Hepton) secures the safety of the plans for the first torpedo to be used by the French Navy – at great personal profit.
Designer: Peter Le Page. **Director:** Derek Bennett. **Producer:** Reginald Collin.

River, The   1 wk

Presented by BBC, film

| **1989** | *9.3* | **Sun 13 Aug 7:13 p.m.** | *14* | **1 wk** |

The Garvey family has always had a fight on its hands combatting the elements and the river, but now the threat comes from the sinister plans of big business. Mel Gibson and Sissy Spacek star as Tom and Mae Garvey with Scott Glenn as Joe Wade.
Director: Mark Rydell.

Riviera Police — 13 wks

AR, drama

In this series set in Cannes the principal characters were Inspector Legrand (Brian Spink), Lieutenant-Colonel Constant Sorel (Frank Lieberman), Superintendent Adam Hunter (Geoffrey Frederick) and Superintendent Bernie Johnson (Noel Trevarthen).

1965	8.6	Mon 27 Sep 8:00 p.m.	1	13 wks

'Past Indefinite – Future Imperfect' by Anthony Skene. Archaeologists Lady Carteret (Peggy Thorpes-Bates) and her son Derek (Gary Bond) are fascinated by the past – and, in this instance, so too are the police.
Director: Bill Turner. **Producer:** Jordan Lawrence.

Road to Bali — 1 wk

Presented by BBC, film

The 'Road' series of films was developed by the Paramount Studios in Hollywood as a starring vehicle for Bing Crosby, Bob Hope and Dorothy Lamour. It began in 1940 with Road to Singapore and ended in 1952 with this film, the sixth in the series. (A seventh, Road to Hong Kong, was made in a British studio in 1962.)

1965	4.8	Sat 25 Dec 8:00 p.m.	19	1 wk

A Christmas Day showing of the adventure in the South Seas in which Crosby, Hope and Lamour encounter an octopus, a tribe of cannibals and a gorilla who loves crooners.
Director: Hal Walker.

Road to Wigan Pier, The — 1 wk

Thames, documentary

1973	5.5	Tue 16 Oct 9:00 p.m.	19	1 wk

Based on George Orwell's 1936 study of the British working class. Michael Jayston narrates Orwell's words over archive film and stills to present a picture of the North of England in the early 1930s.
Director: Frank Cvitanovich. **Executive Producer:** Ian Martin.

Robe, The — 1 wk

Presented by ITV, film

1975	6.5	Fri 28 Mar 7:30 p.m.	17	1 wk

Good Friday presentation of this epic set in AD33 of the fight for, and the curse of, Christ's robe after his crucifixion. Starring Richard Burton and Jean Simmons with Dawn Addams, Richard Boone, Dean Jagger, Victor Mature and Michael Rennie.
Director: Henry Koster.

Robin of Sherwood — 2 wks

HTV, drama

This series created by Richard Carpenter starred Michael Praed (later Jason Connery) as Robin Hood, John Rhys Davies as King Richard, Nicholas Grace as the Sheriff of Nottingham, Judy Trott as Maid Marian, John Abinieri as Herne the Hunter and Robert Addie as Guy de Gisburne.

1984	10.6	Sat 26 May 6:00 p.m.	15	2 wks

'The King's Fool'
Robin accepts an invitation to fight with King Richard in Normandy, but their relationship soon turns sour.
Director: Ian Sharp. **Producer:** Paul Knight. **Executive Producer:** Patrick Dromgoole.

Robin's Nest — 37 wks

Thames, situation comedy

Johnnie Mortimer and Brian Cooke created this spinoff from MAN ABOUT THE HOUSE. Richard O'Sullivan again starred as Robin Tripp. This time he had a steady girlfriend, Vicky, played by Tessa Wyatt, who became his wife and partner in running a restaurant called 'Robin's Nest'. Tony Britton also starred as Robin's father-in-law.
Producer: Peter Frazer-Jones.

1977	9.2	Tue 18 Jan 8:30 p.m.	2	7 wks

'The Bistro Kids'
Opening day approaches and there are still problems with the Public Health Inspector.
Writers: Johnnie Mortimer and Brian Cooke.

1978	18.7	Mon 27 Nov 8:00 p.m.	1	19 wks

'Day Trippers'
Robin and Vicky seek a peaceful picnic on their day off – but it's not what they get.
Writer: Bernard McKenna.

1980	18.4	Tue 29 Jan 8:30 p.m.	4	11 wks

'Never Look a Gift Horse . . .'
The prospective grandparents are getting more excited about the forthcoming offspring than the parents.
Writer: Adele Rose.

The south of France was the setting for the crime series **Riviera Police**.

Richard O'Sullivan wears an apron promoting his restaurant **Robin's Nest**.

Rock Follies of '77 — 1 wk

Thames, drama

Howard Schuman's sequel to ROCK FOLLIES (which did not make the Top Twenty) starred Charlotte Cornwell, Julie Covington and Rula Lenska as three young women who aspired to be the world's greatest rock group. They were joined by Sue Jones-Davies. The songs were by Schuman and Andy Mackay.

| 1977 | 6.3 | Wed 4 May 9:00 p.m. | 18 | 1 wk |

'The Band Who Wouldn't Die'
This time they're going to win through in spite of the predators in the rock world.
Choreographer: David Toguri. **Director:** Brian Farnham. **Producer:** Andrew Brown.

Rock with Laughter — 1 wk

YTV, comedy

A show of comedy and music from little-known performers.

| 1980 | 11.2 | Sat 21 Jun 6:30 p.m. | 6 | 1 wk |

With Alan J. Bartley, Beano, Ines Burn, Phil Cool, Dave Draper and Robert Shaw, The Druids, Greengage and Terry Webster.
Musical Director: Frank Ricotti. **Director:** Ian Bolt. **Producer:** Mike Goddard.

Rockford Files, The — 6 wks

USA presented by BBC, drama

This series created by Stephen J. Cannell and Roy Huggins starred James Garner as ex-con James Rockford, a California private detective who lived alone in a caravan and kept his gun in a biscuit tin. Rockford took on helpless clients, many of whom could not pay him. Noah Beery Jr. played his father Joseph and Joe Santos was his police chum Sergeant Dennis Becker.
Producer: Roy Huggins.

| 1979 | 19.7 | Mon 22 Oct 7:20 p.m. | 1 | 5 wks |

'Black Mirror'
Jim Rockford gets emotionally involved with a blind client who is under threat from a mysterious assailant.

| 1980 | 9.8 | Sat 2 Aug 8:15 p.m. | 14 | 1 wk |

'Deadlock in Parma'
Jim is on a quiet fishing holiday but finds trouble when he helps a sick friend.

Rocking Horse Winner, The — 1 wk

HTV, drama

| 1977 | 10.2 | Wed 10 Dec 9:00 p.m. | 18 | 1 wk |

Julian Bond's adaptation of D. H. Lawrence's story of a boy whose affinity with his rocking horse leads him to correctly predict winners. Kenneth More stars as Uncle, Angela Thorne as Mother, Peter Cellier as Father and Nigel Rhodes as Paul.
Director: Peter Medak. **Executive Producer:** Patrick Dromgoole.

Rockliffe's Babies — 1 wk

BBC, drama

This series devised by Richard O'Keefe starred Ian Hogg as Detective Sergeant Rockliffe, who headed a team of young police officers. They were PC Adams (Bill Champion), PC Chitty (John Blakey), PC Georgiou (Martyn Ellis), WPC Hargreaves (Alphonsia Emmanuel), PC Hood (Brett Fancy), PC O'Dowd (Joe McGann) and WPC Walsh (Susannah Shelling).

| 1988 | 11.4 | Fri 4 Mar 9:30 p.m. | 20 | 1 wk |

'Black Arrow' by Don Webb.
The two married members of the team have to cancel a dinner engagement. Their night out is very different and risky. Lonnie Donegan plays a cameo role as a character named Ferns.
Director: Clive Fleury. **Producer:** Leonard Lewis.

Rogues, The — 5 wks

USA presented by BBC, drama

This series, created by Collier Young, came from the same stable as THE DICK POWELL THEATRE. A group of upper-class con men headquartered in London saw themselves as modern Robin Hoods. The Rogues' motto was 'Honour Before Honesty'. Starring Charles Boyer, Gladys Cooper, Robert Coote, David Niven and Gig Young.

| 1964 | 6.2 | Thu 8 Oct 8:25 p.m. | 9 | 5 wks |

'The Day They Gave Diamonds Away'
A professor spent years developing a machine to manufacture diamonds. After his death the machine slipped into the hands of the Rogues, who fed in real diamonds for a demonstration that fooled an international diamond merchant into parting with his money.

Rolf Harris Show, The — 34 wks

BBC, entertainment

Australian Rolf Harris carved his own niche in British show business, first as a children's entertainer and then as a recorder of several hit songs, most of them novelties. His television series showed his talents as a cartoonist.
Choreographer (1967–71): Dougie Squires. **Producer** (1967–71): Stewart Morris.

| 1967 | 6.4 | Sat 11 Mar 8:20 p.m. | 10 | 5 wks |

This series features Sandie Shaw singing the entries for 'A Song for Europe' with the Young Generation and the Harry Rabinowitz orchestra. Guests: The Nitwits, Raphael and the Sadri Dancers.

| 1968 | 6.3 | Sat 13 Jan 7:55 p.m. | 20 | 2 wks |

Guests: Janis Ian, the Dudley Moore Trio, Dusty Springfield, the Young Generation and the Harry Rabinowitz orchestra.

| 1969 | 7.2 | Sat 8 Feb 7:30 p.m. | 5 | 14 wks |

Guests: Finn Jon, Abbe Lane and Barry Ryan, with the Young Generation and the Alyn Ainsworth orchestra.

| 1970 | 7.0 | Sat 28 Nov 7:30 p.m. | 9 | 9 wks |

This co-production with ZDF in Germany includes a visit to Heidelberg Castle. Guests: Alice and Ellen Kessler, Esther Ofarim and the Young Generation with the Alyn Ainsworth orchestra.

| 1971 | 6.7 | Sat 2 Jan 7:35 p.m. | 13 | 3 wks |

Guest: Dusty Springfield, with the Young Generation and the Alyn Ainsworth orchestra.

| 1972 | 6.0 | Sat 22 Apr 6:15 p.m. | 20 | 1 wk |

Guests: Johnny Hart, Cleo Laine and Ray Stevens, with the David Toguri dancers and the Harry Rabinowitz orchestra.
Producer: Ronald Fouracre.

Roll Over Beethoven   9 wks

Central/Witzend Productions, situation comedy

This series by Laurence Marks and Maurice Gran starred Liza Goddard as piano teacher Belinda Purcell, who lived a dull life in a small village with her father Oliver, played by Richard Vernon. Nigel Planer played rock legend Nigel Cochrane, who moved into the village and became Belinda's pupil.

| 1985 | 13.6 | Mon 25 Feb 8:00 p.m. | 11 | 9 wks |

Episode One
Oliver believed the world ended when the Beatles received MBEs. Now a rock star is in the village he is horrified.
Director: Derrick Goodwin. **Producer:** Tony Charles. **Executive Producer:** Allan McKeown.

Rollercoaster   2 wks

Presented by ITV, film

| 1981 | 18.9 | Wed 18 Feb 8:00 p.m. | 3 | 1 wk |

A saboteur of amusement parks (Timothy Bottoms) demands $1 million to cease his acts. Safety Inspector Calder (George Segal) and FBI agent Hoyt (Richard Widmark) try to catch him before anyone else is killed.
Director: James Goldstone.

| 1985 | 12.4 | Fri 5 Apr 8:00 p.m. | 15 | 1 wk |

Repeat showing of the above film.

Romance   3 wks

Thames, drama

This series of single dramas had romance as the unifying theme.

| 1977 | 7.3 | Wed 23 Mar 9:00 p.m. | 20 | 3 wks |

'High Noon' by Ruby M. Ayers, dramatized by Julia Jones.
Lynn Farleigh stars as Heather Ashton, who from the age of eighteen brought up her four brothers and sisters after her mother died. In so doing she surrendered the man she loved. Now, in 1935, she feels her future is slipping away.
Director: Barry Davis. **Producer:** Peter Duguid.

Romance   1 wk

YTV, drama

A trilogy of plays.

| 1988 | 10.2 | Fri 2 Sep 7:40 p.m. | 19 | 1 wk |

'Out of the Shadows' dramatized by Michael J. Bird.
Based on the novel by Andrea Davidson, Charles Dance stars as Chief Inspector Michael Hayden, who is in Athens to investigate an art theft. His search turns into a murder enquiry. He is helped in unravelling the mystery by young American Jan Lindsay (Alexandra Paul).
Director: Willi Patterson. **Producer:** Derek Bennett. **Executive Producer:** David Cunliffe.

Romancing the Stone   2 wks

Presented by ITV, film

| 1987 | 14.2 | Thu 10 Sep 8:00 p.m. | 3 | 1 wk |

Michael Douglas, Kathleen Turner and Danny DeVito star in the story of a novelist in search of her kidnapped sister in Colombia.
Director: Robert Zemeckis.

| 1989 | 13.7 | Sun 1 Oct 7:45 p.m. | 6 | 1 wk |

Repeat showing of the above film.

Romany Jones				2 wks

LWT, situation comedy

This series set in a caravan park centred on the Joneses, work-shy Bert (James Beck) and the long-suffering Betty (Jo Rowbottom), living in their leaky, broken-down matrimonial caravan. Living in the adjacent caravan were the Briggs, Wally (Arthur Mullard) and Lily (Queenie Watts).

1973	5.5	Fri 12 Oct 8:25 p.m.	19	1 wk

'Not So Sweet Charity'
Bert is puzzled. Wally and Lily always appear to have money, yet never do any work. It transpires they live on social security. When Bert tries to join the gravy train he discovers it is not so easy to get on board.
Writer: Peter Denyer. **Producer:** Stuart Allen.

1975	5.3	Fri 4 Jul 7:30 p.m.	20	1 wk

'The Washing'
Tempers are frayed in a dispute concerning the use of the communal washing line.
Writers: Ronald Wolfe and Ronald Chesney. **Producer:** Stuart Allen.

Ronn Lucas Show, The				5 wks

Thames, entertainment

American ventriloquist Lucas starred with his dragon dummy Scorch.

1990	12.3	Wed 7 Feb 8:30 p.m.	15	5 wks

Guests: the Clark Brothers, Michael Lanzière, Peter Piper and the John Coleman orchestra.
Director: Brian Penders. **Producer:** Sean Murphy. **Executive Producer:** John Fisher.

Ronnie Corbett's Saturday Special				4 wks

BBC, entertainment

This series of variety shows starred Ronnie Corbett from the BBC Television Theatre and the Skyline Hotel, Heston, London.

1977	8.6	Sat 15 Jan 8:25 p.m.	4	4 wks

Guests: Danny La Rue, Little and Large, Wayne King, the New Seekers and Jeff Richer's New Edition.
Producer: Michael Hurll.

Ronnie Corbett's Thursday Special				3 wks

BBC, entertainment

This variety series was hosted by Ronnie Corbett with guests.

1978	14.7	Thu 6 Apr 9:25 p.m.	10	3 wks

Guests: Madeline Bell, Jimmy Tarbuck, Twiggy and Clive Webb with Jeff Richer's First Edition.
Producer: Michael Hurll.

Roof over Our Mouths, A				1 wk

ATV, drama

1967	6.8	Thu 12 Jan 9:40 p.m.	11	1 wk

This light comedy by Peter Draper concerned matrimonial infidelities and the compulsive need to talk about them. Starring Peter Barkworth, Jennifer Hilary, Moira Redmond and Corin Redgrave.
Designer: Henry Graveney. **Director:** Graham Evans. **Producer:** Cecil Clarke.

Room at the Top				1 wk

Presented by ITV, film

ITV was blacked out by strike action between Wednesday 1 July and early evening Monday 6 July 1964. With regular programmes unavailable ITV gave an unscheduled screening of this Oscar-winning feature film and it went to Number One.

1964	8.3	Tue 7 Jul 9:10 p.m.	1	1 wk

Laurence Harvey stars as Joe Lampton, the ambitious north-country hero of John Braine's novel. Also starring are Hermione Baddeley, Allan Cuthbertson, Donald Houston, Raymond Huntley, Mary Peach, Ambrosine Philpotts, Heather Sears, Simone Signoret, John Westbrook and Donald Wolfit.
Director: Jack Clayton.

Room Down Under				1 wk

AR, documentary

1964	5.2	Wed 5 Aug 9:40 p.m.	10	1 wk

Two million Europeans have flooded into Australia since the end of the Second World War. This film looks at Australia through the eyes of a young female immigrant. James Fleming narrates.
Producer: Dan Klughertz.

Room Service				1 wk

Thames, situation comedy

This series by Jimmy Perry was set in the five-star Prince Henry Hotel in London. It concerned three room-service waiters, Aldo de Vito (Freddie Earlle), Horace Murphy (Chris Gannon) and Mr Spooner (Bryan Pringle).

| 1979 | 15.4 | Tue 2 Jan 8:30 p.m. | 12 | 1 wk |

Episode One
Mr Spooner is convinced Horace is cheating the other waiters out of their share of the tips.
Producer: Michael Mills.

....

Root of All Evil, The   **8 wks**

YTV, drama

In this anthology of plays by various writers money was the unifying theme.
Producer: Peter Willes.

| 1968 | 6.9 | Tue 12 Nov 9:00 p.m. | 8 | 3 wks |

'West of Eden' by Anthony Skene.
Max Huber (Horst Janson), grandson of a Swiss banker, finds himself without money in London. He is swept into a world of weirdos and dolly birds. Also starring Jacqueline Pearce, Christopher Sandford, Eleanor Summerfield and André Van Gyseghem.
Designer: Marilyn Taylor. **Director:** Peter Moffatt.

| 1969 | 7.8 | Mon 8 Dec 8:30 p.m. | 2 | 5 wks |

'What's In It for Me?' by Anthony Skene.
Lord Orme was always considered to be a wealthy industrialist. Now he is dead it appears he has left very little. Where has all the money gone? Stars include Ronald Allen, Frances Bennett, Peter Blythe, Jean Marsh, Anthony Nicholls and George Layton.
Designer: Marilyn Taylor. **Director:** Peter Moffatt.

....

Roots   **1 wk**

ATV, situation comedy

This series by Laurence Marks and Maurice Gran starred Allan Corduner as Melvyn Solomons, a dentist with a promising career in front of him. Joy Shelton and Stanley Meadows played his parents Nettie and Harry.

| 1981 | 10.3 | Fri 11 Sep 8:00 p.m. | 19 | 1 wk |

'The Post Graduate'
Nettie and Harry are horrified when Melvyn decides to become an art student and reduce dentistry to a part-time occupation.
Producer: Keith Farthing.

....

Roots   **3 wks**

USA presented by BBC, drama

Author Alex Haley traced the story of his family from enslavement in the Gambia in 1767 to the years that followed the American Civil War. The stars were John Amos (Kunta Kinte as an adult), LeVar Burton (Kunta Kinte as a young man), Olivia Cole (Matilda), Chuck Connors (Tom Moore), Scatman Crothers (Mingo), Sandy Duncan (Missy Anne), George Hamilton (Stephen Bennett), Lawrence Hilton Jacobs (Noah), Carolyn Jones (Mrs Moore), Robert Reed (Dr William Reynolds), Richard Roundtree (Sam Bennett), John Schuck (Ordell), Madge Sinclair (Bell), Leslie Uggams (Kizzy) and Ben Vereen (Chicken George).
Producer: David Wolper.

| 1977 | 7.0 | Sun 17 Apr 8:35 p.m. | 16 | 3 wks |

Part Four
Kunta Kinte is married to Bell and they have a 16-year-old daughter, Kizzy. Their life seems settled on Dr Reynold's plantation.
Director: Marvin Cromsky.

....

Roots – The Next Generation   **5 wks**

USA presented by BBC, drama

This seven-part continuation of the saga began in 1882 in Henning, Tennessee, where Chicken George (Avon Long) had taken the family. The series brought Alex Haley's search for his roots right up to the 1970s. James Earl Jones played the role of Haley and Marlon Brando had a nine minute Emmy-winning scene as George Lincoln Rockwell.
Producer: David Wolper.

| 1979 | 18.8 | Sun 7 Oct 7:15 p.m. | 4 | 5 wks |

Part Two
It is 1896. Tom Harvey (George Stanford Brown), Chicken George's son, is the pillar of black society. His daughter Elizabeth (Debbie Morgan) is a schoolteacher and his other daughter, Cynthia (Bever-Leigh Banfield), is to marry Will Palmer (Stan Shaw). Will's friend Lee Garnett (Roger E. Mosley) is hunted down and burnt alive by a white mob. Also starring Henry Fonda as Colonel Warner, Olivia de Havilland as Mrs Warner, Slim Galliard as Sam Wesley and Lynne Moody as Irene Harvey.
Director: Charles S. Dubin.

....

Room at the Top was an unscheduled broadcast that went to Number One.

Rosemary Clooney Show, The   1 wk

ATV, music

The American singer had several chart successes in the fifties.

| 1961 | 4.0 | Sat 5 Aug 7:55 p.m. | 17 | 1 wk |

Guests: Dave King, the Malcolm Goddard dancers and the Jack Parnell orchestra.
Producer: Albert Locke.

Rosie   5 wks

BBC, situation comedy

This series by Roy Clarke concerned Police Constables 'Rosie' Penrose and Wilmot (Paul Greenwood and Tony Haygarth).
Producer: Bernard Thompson.

| 1979 | 12.1 | Thu 26 Jun 8:30 p.m. | 6 | 4 wks |

'The Worm That Turns Us All'
Someone is stealing from cars parked down Lover's Lane, where Wilmot just happens to be with Renata (Janet Dale).

| 1981 | 12.0 | Fri 18 Sep 8:15 p.m. | 12 | 1 wk |

'Tune on a Silent Dog Whistle'
Rosie moves in to live with Wilmot.

Route 66   1 wk

Central/Iona Productions, documentary

| 1985 | 11.9 | Tue 22 Oct 9:00 p.m. | 19 | 1 wk |

Route 66 was built in the 1930s and runs 2238 miles across America. It spans eight states and three time zones.
Director: John T. Davis. **Producer:** Malcolm Frazer. **Executive Producers:** Brian Lewis and Alan Wright.

Roy Castle Show, The   2 wks

ATV, entertainment

An accomplished dancer, singer, musician and comedian, Castle began his career as a stooge for the late Jimmy James and was discovered as a solo star at the 1958 ROYAL VARIETY PERFORMANCE at the Coliseum. He was awarded the OBE in 1993.
Writers: Sid Green and Dick Hills. **Producer:** Jon Scoffield.

| 1962 | 5.5 | Sun 16 Dec 8:25 p.m. | 15 | 1 wk |

Guests: Bernard Cribbins, Valerie Masters, Matt Monro, Tommy Reilly, the Tiller Girls and the Jack Parnell orchestra.

| 1963 | 4.8 | Sun 14 Jul 8:25 p.m. | 13 | 1 wk |

Guests: Miriam Karlin, Cleo Laine and Graham Stark with the Pamela Devis dancers and the Jack Parnell orchestra.

Roy Castle Show, The   2 wks

BBC, entertainment

This series was set in a night club, the Castle Room, where Roy was the host. Vince Hill was the resident singer with the Breakaways and the Ronnie Hazlehurst orchestra. Also featured were Berry Cornish, Laura Symonds and Eli Woods.
Choreographer: Nita Howard. **Writer:** Eric Davidson. **Producer:** Michael Hurll.

| 1969 | 4.0 | Sat 9 Aug 7:30 p.m. | 20 | 1 wk |

Guests: Jack Douglas, Jack Haig, Françoise Hardy and Harry Secombe.

| 1970 | 4.9 | Sat 30 May 8:20 p.m. | 11 | 1 wk |

Guests: Shirley Bassey and Ted Rogers.

Roy Hudd Show, The   6 wks

YTV, comedy

Singer and comedian Hudd starred in this series of sketches, songs and impressions of great artists of the Music Hall. Writers included Keith Waterhouse and Willis Hall, David Nobbs, Michael Billington, Richard Ingrams and John Antrobus.

| 1969 | 7.1 | Mon 16 Feb 9:30 p.m. | 10 | 6 wks |

Guests: Frank Abbott, Freddie Jones, Joan Turner and the Dave Lee orchestra.
Director: Ronald Fouracre. **Producer:** John Duncan.

Roy Orbison Show, The   1 wk

ATV, music

| 1964 | 5.1 | Wed 5 Aug 9:40 p.m. | 20 | 1 wk |

This was a one-off special for the only American solo singer to top the UK singles chart in 1964. Guests: Julie Rogers and Daniel Remy, with the Pamela Devis dancers and the Jack Parnell orchestra.
Producer: Albert Locke.

Royal Air Force Association Jubilee Festival, The   1 wk

BBC, entertainment

| 1968 | 6.7 | Sun 31 Mar 8:15 p.m. | 9 | 1 wk |

Live from the stage of the Victoria Palace, London, in the presence of Marshal of the Royal Air Force HRH The Duke of Edinburgh and Air Chief Commandant HRH The Duchess of Gloucester. The show celebrates fifty years of the RAF and the artists are introduced by Richard Burton, Hughie Green, Trevor Howard, Ben Lyon, Kenneth More, Anna Neagle, Ralph Reader and Richard Todd. Among those appearing are the Bachelors, Sam Costa, Jimmy Edwards, Audrey Graham, John Hanson, Kenneth Horne, Roy Hudd, the Kaye Sisters, Terry Lightfoot's Jazzmen, Jimmy Logan, Vera Lynn, Richard Murdoch, Nadia Nerina, Rawicz and Landauer, Raissa Struchkova and Alexander Lapauri of the Bolshoi Ballet, the Tiller Girls, Arthur Worsley and the Central Band of the RAF, the RAF Choir, (Uxbridge), and the Queen's Colour Squadron of the RAF.
Musical Director: Bob Sharples. **Television presentation:** Derek Burrell-Davis.

| **Royal Appointment** | 1 wk |

BBC, entertainment

| 1975 | 7.5 | Thu 11 Dec 8:00 p.m. | 12 | 1 wk |

The initiation of HRH The Prince of Wales as a Companion Rat to the Grand Order of Water Rats is introduced by Ray Moore in the presence of members of the Order.
Television presentation: Douglas Hespe.

| **Royal Birthday Gala, A** | 1 wk |

BBC, entertainment

| 1990 | 9.5 | Sat 4 Aug 7:30 p.m. | 11 | 1 wk |

The ninetieth birthday of Her Majesty Queen Elizabeth, The Queen Mother is celebrated at the London Palladium in her presence and that of HM The Queen, HRH The Duke of Edinburgh and HRH The Princess Margaret. Artists include Peggy Ashcroft, Rowan Atkinson, Richard Attenborough, Lionel Blair, Sarah Brightman, Isobel Buchanan, Darcey Bussell, Simon Cadell, Michael Caine, Christopher Cazenove, Leslie Crowther, Mark Curry, Michael Denison, Placido Domingo, Stephen Fry, James Galway, Jill Gascoine, John Gielgud, Dulcie Gray, Robert Hardy, Anita Harris, Patricia Hodge, Jeffrey Holland, Kiri Te Kanawa, Howard Keel, Bonnie Langford, Vera Lynn, Geraldine McEwan, Robert Meadmore, Hayley Mills, John Mills, Warren Mitchell, Roger Moore, Jonathon Morris, Irek Mukhamedov, Elaine Paige, Angharad Rees, Anneka Rice, Cliff Richard, Eric Roberts, Wayne Sleep, Willard White, Bernie Winters and Jenny Wren.
Stage Director: Norman Maen. **Television Director:** Kevin Bishop.
Executive Producer: Yvonne Littlewood.

| **Royal Celebration of Forty Years of Peace, A** | 1 wk |

LWT, entertainment

| 1985 | 14.8 | Sun 5 May 7:25 p.m. | 2 | 1 wk |

Stars representing each decade of the forty years perform at London's Palace Theatre in the presence of HRH The Princess Anne. Artists include Moira Anderson, Michael Barrymore, The Beverley Sisters, Teresa Brewer, Georgia Brown, Joe Brown, Dora Bryan, Frank Carson, Jess Conrad, Lonnie Donegan, Craig Douglas, Fred Evans, Alan Freeman, Peter Goodwright, Rolf Harris, David Jacobs, Teddy Johnson and Pearl Carr, Paul Jones, Evelyn Laye, Dennis Lotis, Vera Lynn, Pete Murray, Ruby Murray, Alan Randall, Cliff Richard, Lita Roza, Anne Shelton, Topol, Frankie Vaughan, Marti Webb, Marty Wilde and Bernie Winters.
Director: Alan Boyd. **Producer:** David Bell.

| **Royal Day, The** | 1 wk |

ITN, news

| 1986 | 9.2 | Wed 23 Jul 6:45 p.m. | 14 | 1 wk |

Alastair Burnet presents highlights of THE ROYAL WEDDING between HRH Prince Andrew and Miss Sarah Ferguson.
Producer: Mike Townson. **Executive Producer:** Barrie Sales.

| **Royal Engagement, The** | 1 wk |

ITN, news

| 1981 | 13.1 | Tue 24 Feb 10:30 p.m. | 20 | 1 wk |

The engagement was announced today of His Royal Highness The Prince of Wales to Lady Diana Spencer.

| **Royal Family** | 2 wks |

BBC, documentary

| 1969 | 8.1 | Sat 21 Jun 8:00 p.m. | 1 | 2 wks |

Producer Richard Cawston's unprecedented access to the Royal Family has made possible a film of great historical importance. Shooting began on 8 June 1968 and continued for an entire year.

| **Royal Film Performance, The** | 1 wk |

Presented by Thames, entertainment

| 1975 | 7.2 | Mon 17 Mar 10:30 p.m. | 13 | 1 wk |

Her Majesty The Queen attends the screening at the Odeon, Leicester Square of Funny Lady starring Barbra Streisand as Fanny Brice. The film is the sequel to Funny Girl. Pete Murray and John Anthony are in the foyer to interview the stars and introduce the clips.
Director: Jim Pople. **Producers:** Steve Minchin and Bob Service.

Royal Fireworks, The　　　　　　　　　　1 wk

ITV, news

| 1981 | 10.4 | Tue 28 Jul 9:00 p.m. | 18 | 1 wk |

It is the eve of the wedding between HRH The Prince of Wales and Lady Diana Spencer. Alastair Burnet, Andrew Gardner and Selina Scott cover the firework display in Hyde Park and the lighting by Prince Charles of the first beacon in a nationwide chain.
Producers: Stewart Purvis and Mike Ward. **Executive Producer:** Barrie Sales.

....

Royal Fireworks, The　　　　　　　　　　1 wk

BBC, news

| 1981 | 15.1 | Tue 28 Jul 9:25 p.m. | 2 | 1 wk |

Raymond Baxter commentates on the events in Hyde Park.
Television presentation: Peter Hylton Cleaver.

....

Royal Gala, A　　　　　　　　　　1 wk

An ABC/ATV production with contributions from Granada and STV, entertainment

| 1966 | 9.6 | Sun 4 Dec 7:55 p.m. | 1 | 1 wk |

A charity gala held at the London Palladium in the presence of HRH The Duke of Edinburgh with more than sixty stars and the Pipes and Drums of the King's Own Scottish Borderers. Artists include Dave Allen, Eamonn Andrews, Michael Bentine, The Beverley Sisters, Bernard Braden, the Dave Clark Five, Peter Cook and Dudley Moore, the cast of CORONATION STREET, David Frost, Hughie Green, Anita Harris, Frank Ifield, Rosemary Leach, Jimmy Logan, Cathy McGowan, Michael Miles, Bob Monkhouse, Morecambe and Wise, David Nixon, Cliff Richard, Ted Rogers, The Shadows, Sandie Shaw, Jackie Trent, Frankie Vaughan, the Walker Brothers and Patrick Wymark.
Stage director: Albert Locke. **Television presentation:** Colin Clews.

....

Royal Gala, A　　　　　　　　　　2 wks

LWT, entertainment

| 1987 | 12.4 | Sat 19 Dec 8:15 p.m. | 8 | 1 wk |

David Frost and John Ritter introduce the gala from the London Palladium in the presence of The Prince and Princess of Wales in aid of The Prince's Trust. Artists include Rowan Atkinson, Steve Barton, Rory Bremner, Sarah Brightman, Chris de Burgh, Richard Digance, Art Garfunkel, Elton John, Mel Smith and Griff Rhys-Jones, James Taylor, Colm Wilkinson and Robin Williams.
Director: Jeff Margolis. **Producer:** Marcus Plantin. **Executive Producer:** David Frost.

| 1989 | 9.5 | Sun 30 Jul 8:15 p.m. | 11 | 1 wk |

To celebrate twenty-one years of London Weekend Television and to benefit The Prince's Trust, Sean Connery introduces the show from the London Palladium in the presence of HRH The Prince of Wales. Artists appearing include Clive Anderson, Rosanna Arquette, Frank Bruno, Jerry Hall, Nigel Havers, Marie Helvin, Jools Holland, Michael Palin, Trevor Phillips, Jonathan Ross, Terence Stamp, and Daniel J. Travanti. Guest performers include Paula Abdul, Steve Coogan, Peter Cook, Debbie Gibson, Erasure, Dame Edna Everage, Charles Fleischer, French and Saunders, Dame Kiri Te Kanawa, Paul Kozak, Mica Paris, the Pasadenas, Rita Rudner, T'Pau, Then Jerico, Wet Wet Wet and Stephen Wright.
Director: Alasdair Macmillan. **Producer:** Trevor Hopkins. **Executive Producer:** Marcus Plantin.

....

Royal Gala Cabaret　　　　　　　　　　1 wk

ATV, entertainment

| 1970 | 6.6 | Thu 31 Dec 7:30 p.m. | 16 | 1 wk |

An all-star cabaret from London's Talk of the Town in aid of the World Wildlife Fund, attended by Her Majesty The Queen, HRH The Duke of Edinburgh, Prince Charles, Princess Anne, Princess Alexandra, Queen Juliana and Prince Bernhard with Princess Beatrix of the Netherlands, King Constantine and Queen Anne-Marie of Greece, the Grand Duke and Duchess of Luxembourg, the Crown Prince and Princess of Norway, Prince Henrik and the Crown Princess of Denmark, the Prince of Liège, and Prince Don Carlos of Spain. Artists appearing include Glen Campbell, Petula Clark, Rex Harrison, Bob Hope, Engelbert Humperdinck, Tom Jones, George Kirby, Millicent Martin, Rudolf Nureyev, Antoinette Sibley, the Paddy Stone dancers, the Mike Sammes singers and the Jack Parnell orchestra.
Stage Director: Robert Nesbitt. **Television presentation:** Colin Clews. **Executive Producer:** Bill Ward.

....

Royal Gala Performance, A　　　　　　　　　　1 wk

BBC, entertainment

| 1985 | 14.0 | Sun 7 Jul 7:15 p.m. | 2 | 1 wk |

From the Playhouse Theatre, Edinburgh, in the presence of Her Majesty The Queen, HRH The Duke of Edinburgh and HRH The Princess Anne in aid of the XIII Commonwealth Games Appeal Fund. Artists include Moira Anderson, Shirley Bassey, Rory Bremner, Sarah Brightman, Kirk Douglas, Linda Evans, Robert Goulet, Rolf Harris, Aled Jones, Jacques Loussier, Bob Monkhouse, Juliet Prowse and George Segal, with the John Coleman orchestra.
Stage Director: Robert Nesbitt. **Television presentation:** Stewart Morris.

....

Royal Gala Variety Performance, A　　　　　　　　　　1 wk

ATV, entertainment

| 1972 | 5.9 | Sun 28 May 7:55 p.m. | 16 | 1 wk |

A charity performance from the London Palladium in the presence of Her Majesty The Queen and HRH The Duke of Edinburgh. Dan Rowan and Dick Martin introduce: Richard Attenborough, Michael Caine, Phillipe Genty, Larry Grayson, Liza Minnelli, Roger Moore, Des O'Connor, the Osmonds and Lily Tomlin, with the Second Generation, the Mike Sammes singers and the Jack Parnell orchestra.
Stage Director: Albert Locke. **Television Producers:** Gary Smith and Dwight Hemion. **Executive Producer:** Bill Ward.

....

Royal International Horse Show, The — 3 wks

BBC, sport

This event carried the highest prestige in the annual international calendar of the show jumping world.

| 1966 | 4.5 | Wed 20 Jul 9:40 p.m. | 16 | 1 wk |

From White City in the presence of Her Majesty The Queen, Dorian Williams introduces coverage of The King George Vth Gold Cup.
Television presentation: Bill Duncalf.

| 1979 | 9.4 | Tue 17 Jul 9:25 p.m. | 20 | 1 wk |

David Vine introduces coverage from Wembley Arena. The commentary is by Raymond Brooks-Ward and Dorian Williams.
Television presentation: Johnnie Watherston.

| 1980 | 9.7 | Fri 18 Jul 9:25 p.m. | 19 | 1 wk |

From Wembley, David Vine introduces the Grand Prix of Great Britain. The commentary is by Raymond Brooks-Ward and Dorian Williams.
Television presentation: Fred Viner.

....

Royal Night of 100 Stars, A — 1 wk

LWT, entertainment

| 1985 | 17.7 | Sun 31 Mar 7:45 p.m. | 1 | 1 wk |

Jimmy Tarbuck hosts an event in aid of the Save the Children Fund at the National Theatre in the presence of HRH The Princess Anne. Artists include Russ Abbot, Jane Asher, Tim Curry, Fenella Fielding, Bruce Forsyth, Hannah Gordon, Robert Lindsay, Lulu, Emma Thompson, Marti Webb, Gary Wilmot and Lena Zavaroni.
Director: Alan Boyd. **Producer:** David Bell.

....

Royal Romance, A — 1 wk

ITN, documentary

| 1986 | 9.0 | Tue 22 Jul 7:00 p.m. | 18 | 1 wk |

Andrew Gardner and Sue Lawley talk with HRH The Prince Andrew and Miss Sarah Ferguson as they prepare for their forthcoming marriage.
Producer: Jim Pople. **Executive Producer:** Barrie Sales.

Royal Show, The — 1 wk

STV, entertainment

| 1977 | 6.8 | Sun 22 May 8:00 p.m. | 15 | 1 wk |

From the King's Theatre, Glasgow in the presence of Her Majesty The Queen and HRH The Duke of Edinburgh in aid of The Queen's Silver Jubilee Appeal. Artists appearing include Petula Clark, Sydney Devine, the Jacksons, Shari Lewis, Dolly Parton, David Soul, Allan Stewart, Eric Sykes and Hattie Jacques, Lena Zavaroni, the Brian Rogers dancers and the Alyn Ainsworth orchestra.
Director: Chris Allen. **Producer:** David Bell.

....

Royal Television Gala Performance, A — 2 wks

BBC, entertainment

| 1970 | 6.4 | Sun 24 May 8:15 p.m. | 8 | 1 wk |

This gala for the benefit of the British competitors taking part in the British Commonwealth Games in Edinburgh is held at the BBC Television Theatre, Shepherds Bush in the presence of Her Majesty The Queen and HRH The Duke of Edinburgh. Among the artists appearing are Dave Allen, Tony Bennett, Cilla Black, Basil Brush, Vera Lynn, Rod McKuen, Morecambe and Wise, the Young Generation and the casts of DAD'S ARMY and UP POMPEII. With the Alyn Ainsworth orchestra.
Producer: Stewart Morris. **Executive Producer:** Tom Sloan.

| 1973 | 5.4 | Wed 25 Jul 8:00 p.m. | 13 | 1 wk |

A special charity edition of THE HARRY SECOMBE SHOW held in the presence of Her Majesty The Queen and HRH The Duke of Edinburgh. Harry's guests include Jim Bailey, Anna Moffo and Beryl Reid with the Alyn Ainsworth orchestra.
Choreographer: Nigel Lythgoe. **Producer:** Colin Charman.

....

Royal Tournament, The — 2 wks

BBC, entertainment

This annual pageant displayed the skills and courage of the armed forces.
Television presentation: Peter Hylton Cleaver.

| 1982 | 8.1 | Fri 23 Jul 8:00 p.m. | 16 | 1 wk |

From Earl's Court in the presence of HRH The Prince of Wales. Raymond Baxter commentates.

| 1985 | 8.8 | Sat 20 Jul 7:00 p.m. | 20 | 1 wk |

Introduced by Mike Smith from Earl's Court. Robert Hardy commentates.

Jimmy Tarbuck performs for charity in **A Royal Night of 100 Stars**.

BBC/ITV (alternate years), entertainment

The Royal Variety Performance dated back to 1912 but only became an annual event at the suggestion of King George V from 1921. Proceeds of the show went to the Entertainment Artistes' Benevolent Fund and its home, Brinsworth House, in Twickenham. The first Royal Variety Performance to be televised was that of 1960. The impresarios responsible for presenting the show were Bernard Delfont (1961–1978) and Louis Benjamin (1979–85). From 1986 the respective television company assumed the responsibility. The stage directors included Robert Nesbitt (1961–1978) and Norman Maen (1979–1987). The show failed to make the weekly top twenty in 1974. In 1977 it was called THE SILVER JUBILEE VARIETY GALA and in 1990 the show was replaced by A ROYAL BIRTHDAY GALA.

1960   **8.1**   **Sun 22 May 8:00 p.m.**   **1**   **1 wk**

From the Victoria Palace, London, in the presence of Her Majesty The Queen and The Duke of Edinburgh, Jack Hylton presents compere Bruce Forsyth who introduces the guests, including Max Bygraves, Nat 'King' Cole, Russ Conway, Billy Cotton and his Band, the Crazy Gang, Sammy Davis Jr., Lonnie Donegan, Diana Dors, Jimmy Edwards, Adam Faith, Bud Flanagan, Benny Hill, Robert Horton, Frankie Howerd, Hattie Jacques, Liberace, Vera Lynn, Bob Monkhouse, Cliff Richard and the Shadows, the Tiller Girls, Norman Wisdom and Harry Worth.
Stage Director: Charles Henry. **ATV television presentation:** Bill Ward.

1961   **8.4**   **Sun 12 Nov 7:30 p.m.**   **1**   **1 wk**

From the Prince of Wales Theatre in the presence of Her Majesty Queen Elizabeth, The Queen Mother, Bruce Forsyth introduces 'All That Jazz' with the Acker Bilk, Kenny Ball and Temperance Seven bands, Shirley Bassey, Jack Benny and George Burns, Lionel Blair, Max Bygraves, Maurice Chevalier, the Crazy Gang, Sammy Davis Jr., Arthur Haynes, the McGuire Sisters, Morecambe and Wise, Nina and Frederik, Andy Stewart, and Frankie Vaughan.
ATV televeision presentation: Bill Ward.

1962   **9.3**   **Fri 29 Apr 8:00 p.m.**   **1**   **1 wk**

From the London Palladium in the presence of Her Majesty The Queen and HRH The Duke of Edinburgh. Norman Vaughan introduces the Black and White Minstrels, Rudy Cardenas, Rosemary Clooney, Dickie Henderson, Bob Hope and Edie Adams, Frank Ifield, Eartha Kitt, Cleo Laine and Johnny Dankworth, Cliff Richard and the Shadows, Harry Secombe, Andy Stewart, Sophie Tucker and Mike and Bernie Winters.
BBC television presentation: Duncan Wood.

1963   **10.4**   **Sun 10 Nov 7:25 p.m.**   **1**   **1 wk**

From the Prince of Wales Theatre in the presence of Her Majesty Queen Elizabeth, The Queen Mother. Artists appearing include the Beatles, the Clark Brothers, Harry H. Corbett and Wilfrid Brambell, Marlene Dietrich, Michael Flanders and Donald Swann, Buddy Greco, Dickie Henderson, Joe Loss, Susan Maughan, Nadia Nerina, Los Paraguayos, Pinky and Perky, Harry Secombe and the cast from Pickwick, Tommy Steele and the cast from Half a Sixpence, and Eric Sykes and Hattie Jacques.
ATV television presentation: Bill Ward.

1964   **8.4**   **Sun 8 Nov 7:50 p.m.**   **3**   **1 wk**

From the London Palladium in the presence of Her Majesty The Queen the show stars, the Bachelors, Cilla Black, Tommy Cooper, Gil Dova, Gracie Fields, Lena Horne, Kathy Kirby, Brenda Lee, Millicent Martin, Morecambe and Wise, Bob Newhart, Ralph Reader's Gang Show, Cliff Richard and the Shadows, Dennis Spicer, Jimmy Tarbuck and the Tiller Girls.
BBC television presentation: Duncan Wood

1965   **11.0**   **Sun 14 Nov 7:25 p.m.**   **1**   **1 wk**

From the London Palladium in the presence of Her Majesty The Queen and HRH The Duke of Edinburgh. Artists include Shirley Bassey, Tony Bennett, Jack Benny, Max Bygraves, the Carmenas, the Dave Clark Five, Peter Cook and Dudley Moore, Ken Dodd, Johnny Halliday, Arthur Haynes, Hope and Keen, Frank Ifield, the Kaye Sisters, Neville King, Spike Milligan, Peter, Paul and Mary, Peter Sellers, Dusty Springfield and Sylvie Vartan.
ATV television presentation: Bill Ward.

1966   **7.6**   **Sun 20 Nov 7:25 p.m.**   **5**   **1 wk**

From the London Palladium in the presence of Her Majesty Queen Elizabeth The Queen Mother, David Jacobs introduces compere Des O'Connor who presents the Bachelors, the Bal Caron Trio, Gilbert Bécaud, Sammy Davis Jr., Jack Douglas, Hugh Forgie, Christopher Gable and Nadia Nerina, Juliette Greco, Frankie Howerd, Jerry Lewis, Kenneth McKellar, Henry Mancini, Marvo and Dolores, Matt Monro, Wayne Newton, the Peiro Brothers, Gene Pitney and Tommy Steele.
BBC television presentation: Bill Cotton Jr.

1967   **11.6**   **Sun 19 Nov 7:25 p.m.**   **1**   **1 wk**

From the London Palladium in the presence of Her Majesty The Queen and HRH The Duke of Edinburgh. Artists appearing include the Bluebell Girls, Vikki Carr, Tommy Cooper, Ken Dodd, Val Doonican, Rolf Harris, Dickie Henderson, Bob Hope, Tom Jones, Lulu, Mireille Mathieu, the Rockin' Berries, the Rumanian National Dance Company, Harry Secombe, Sandie Shaw and Tanya the elephant.
ATV television presentation: Albert Locke.

1968   **7.6**   **Sun 24 Nov 8:15 p.m.**   **1**   **1 wk**

From the London Palladium in the presence of Her Majesty Queen Elizabeth, The Queen Mother, Des O'Connor introduces Arthur Askey, Lionel Blair, Petula Clark, the Czechoslovakian State Song and Dance Ensemble, Sacha Distel, Val Doonican, Engelbert Humperdinck, the London Irish Girl Pipers, Aimi Macdonald, Ron Moody, Morecambe and Wise, Manitas de Plata, Ted Rogers, Diana Ross and the Supremes, André Tahon, Valente Valente and Mike Yarwood.
BBC television presentation: Stewart Morris.

1969   **9.2**   **Sun 16 Nov 7:25 p.m.**   **1**   **1 wk**

From the London Palladium in the presence of Her Majesty The Queen and HRH The Duke of Edinburgh, Des O'Connor introduces Herb Alpert and the Tijuana Brass, Moira Anderson, Cilla Black, Roy Castle, Ronnie Corbett, Frankie Howerd, Tom Jones, Danny La Rue, Shari Lewis, Mireille Mathieu, the Buddy Rich orchestra, Ginger Rogers and the cast of Mame from Drury Lane, Harry Secombe and the Veterans.
ATV television presentation: Albert Locke.

1970 8.5 **Sun 15 Nov 7:25 p.m.** 1 **1 wk**

From the London Palladium in the presence of Her Majesty Queen Elizabeth, The Queen Mother. Max Bygraves introduces Leslie Crowther, the Pamela Devis dancers, Marty Feldman with Tim Brooke-Taylor, Peter Noone and Herman's Hermits, the Syd Lawrence orchestra, Sandy Powell, Rostal and Schaefer, Freddie Starr, Caterina Valente, Dionne Warwick and Andy Williams.
BBC television presentation: Yvonne Littlewood.

1971 9.1 **Sun 21 Nov 10:30 p.m.** 1 **1 wk**

From the London Palladium in the presence of Her Majesty The Queen. Artists include Shirley Bassey, Norman Collier, Tommy Cooper, Sacha Distel and Stephane Grappelli, Bruce Forsyth, Ken Goodwin, Hughie Green, the Little Angels of Korea, the New Seekers, the Stupids, Lovelace Watkins and the Young Generation.
ATV television presentation: Albert Locke.

1972 7.0 **Sun 5 Nov 7:25 p.m.** 8 **1 wk**

From the London Palladium in the presence of the Queen Mother, Dickie Henderson introduces Carol Channing, Los Diablos Del Bombo, Ken Dodd, Rod Hull and Emu, the Jackson Five, Elton John, Jack Jones, Danny La Rue, Liberace, the cast from TILL DEATH US DO PART and Mike Yarwood.
BBC television presentation: Michael Hurll.

1973 7.5 **Sun 2 Dec 7:25 p.m.** 7 **1 wk**

From the London Palladium in the presence of Her Majesty The Queen and HRH The Duke of Edinburgh. Artists include Ronnie Corbett, Les Dawson, Francis Van Dyke, Duke Ellington and his orchestra, Dick Emery, Philippe Genty, José Luis Moreno, Nana Mouskouri, Rudolf Nureyev and Lynn Seymour, Peters and Lee, Cliff Richard and Dougie Squires' Second Generation.
ATV television presentation: Colin Clews.

1975 10.3 **Sun 16 Nov 9:10 p.m.** 1 **1 wk**

From the London Palladium in the presence of Her Majesty The Queen and HRH The Duke of Edinburgh. Artists include Charles Aznavour, Count Basie and his orchestra, the cast of DAD'S ARMY, Ronnie Dukes and Rikki Lee, Michael Crawford and the cast of Billy, the Kwa Zulu African song and dance company, Kris Kremo, Larry Parker, the Rhos Male Voice Choir, Harry Secombe, Telly Savalas, Ruth Welting and Vera Lynn.
ATV television presentation: John Pullen. **Producer:** Albert Locke.

1976 9.1 **Mon 15 Nov 7:50 p.m.** 3 **1 wk**

The first live broadcast of the annual charity show. From the London Palladium in the presence of Her Majesty Queen Elizabeth, The Queen Mother, Max Bygraves introduces Shirley Bassey, Gilbert Bécaud, the Dance Theatre of Harlem, Dawson Chance, Roger de Courcey, Wayne King, Tom O'Connor, Los Reales del Paraguay, Mike Yarwood and Lena Zavaroni, with the Lionel Blair dancers, the Nigel Lythgoe dancers and the Ronnie Hazlehurst orchestra.
BBC television presentation: Stewart Morris.

1978 15.4 **Mon 13 Nov 7:50 p.m.** 11 **1 wk**

A special tribute show for Her Majesty Queen Elizabeth, The Queen Mother at the London Palladium. David Jacobs introduces Arthur Askey, the Beverley Sisters, Lionel Blair, Max Boyce, Max Bygraves, Marti Caine, Wendy Craig, Leslie Crowther, Bobby Crush, Paul Daniels, Charlie Drake, Cyril Fletcher, Rolf Harris, John Inman, the Kaye Sisters, the Krankies, Danny La Rue, the National Youth Jazz Orchestra with Kenny Ball and Acker Bilk, the Nolan Sisters, Mary O'Hara, Harry Secombe, the Scottish Ballet, Anne Shelton, Showaddywaddy, Wayne Sleep and Lesley Collier, Roger Stevenson's puppets, Andy Stewart, June Whitfield and a surprise appearance by Gracie Fields.
BBC television presentation: Stewart Morris.

1979 17.3 **Sun 2 Dec 7:45 p.m.** 3 **1 wk**

From the Theatre Royal, Drury Lane in the presence of Her Majesty The Queen, with Boney M, Yul Brynner, Red Buttons, Marti Caine, Carol Channing, Bernie Clifton, Gemma Craven, Jim Davidson, Les Dawson, Noel Edmonds, James Galway, Bill Haley and his Comets, Hinge and Bracket, David Kernan, Virginia McKenna, Julia McKenzie, Millicent Martin, Ned Sherrin, Amii Stewart, Elaine Stritch, Vladimir Vasiliev and Ekaterina Maximova, and Elisabeth Welch.
ATV television presentation: David Millard.

1980 17.3 **Sun 23 Nov 7:15 p.m.** 8 **1 wk**

From the London Palladium in the presence of Her Majesty Queen Elizabeth, The Queen Mother and HRH The Prince of Wales, Angela Rippon sets the scene for a two-part tribute to Her Majesty in honour of her 80th birthday. Part one of the show is an all-British presentation with Rowan Atkinson, Lionel Blair, Sheena Easton, Bruce Forsyth, Grace Kennedy, Cleo Laine, Joe Loss, Paul Squire, Una Stubbs, Wall Street Crash and Harry Worth. This section includes a tribute to Music Hall with Chesney Allen, Arthur Askey, Charlie Chester, Billy Dainty, Charlie Drake, Arthur English, Cyril Fletcher, Stanley Holloway (at ninety the oldest performer ever to appear in a Royal show), Roy Hudd, Richard Murdoch, Sandy Powell, Tommy Trinder and Ben Warriss. Part two is a Hollywood tribute hosted by Sammy Davis Jr. and introduced by Lillian Gish, with Victor Borge, Aretha Franklin, Larry Hagman, Danny Kaye, Peggy Lee, Henry Mancini and Mary Martin.
Stage Directors: Norman Maen and Lionel Blair. **BBC television presentation:** Yvonne Littlewood.

1981 16.5 **Sun 29 Nov 7:15 p.m.** 5 **1 wk**

From the Theatre Royal, Drury Lane in the presence of Her Majesty The Queen, Robert Hardy introduces the show, which is compered by Dickie Henderson. Artists include Adam and the Ants, Acker Bilk, Patti Boulaye, the Clark Brothers, Lonnie Donegan, Donovan, Anita Harris, Lenny Henry, John Inman, Stephanie Lawrence, Lulu, Mireille Mathieu, Elaine Paige, Itzhak Perlman, Cliff Richard, the Shadows, Alvin Stardust, Jimmy Tarbuck, Andrew and Julian Lloyd Webber, and Marty Wilde.
ATV television presentation: David Millard.

R

1982   **12.6**   **Sun 14 Nov 7:45 p.m.**   **5**   **1 wk**

From the Theatre Royal, Drury Lane in the presence of Her Majesty Queen Elizabeth, the Queen Mother. In a show celebrating, and entitled 'The Magical World of Musicals', the performers include Moira Anderson, Joe Black, Joyce Blair, Bucks Fizz, Jim Casey, Roy Castle, George Cole, Lesley Collier, Kenneth Connor, Leslie Crowther, Tim Curry, Billy Dainty, Lorna Dallas, Suzanne Danielle, Anna Dawson, Wayne Eagling, Sheena Easton, Helen Gelzer, Peter Glaze, Tommy Godfrey, Billy Gray, John Hanson, Richard Harris, Vince Hill, Roy Hudd, Gloria Hunniford, John Inman, David Jacobs, Jack Jones, Karen Kay, Howard Keel, Bonnie Langford, Chris Langham, Diane Langton, Jan Leeming, Aimi Macdonald, Ruth Madoc, Millicent Martin, Ethel Merman, Pete Murray, Michael Praed, Esther Rantzen, Amanda Redman, Angela Rippon, Liz Robertson, Anton Rodgers, Isla St Clair, Peter Skellern, Don Smoothey, Victor Spinetti, Pamela Stephenson, Richard Stilgoe, Christopher Timothy, Topol, Dennis Waterman, Bernie Winters and Eli Woods.
BBC television presentation: Stewart Morris.

1983   **12.2**   **Sun 13 Nov 7:15 p.m.**   **12**   **1 wk**

From the Theatre Royal, Drury Lane in the presence of Her Majesty The Queen, Gene Kelly hosts the show on the theme 'Gotta Dance'. Artists include Michael Barrymore, George Carl, Gemma Craven, Billy Dainty, Les Dawson, Bob Fosse, Grace Kennedy, Bonnie Langford, Julia McKenzie, Natalia Makarova and Anthony Dowell, Merle Park, Clarke Peters, the Roly Polys, Leslie Sarony, Wayne Sleep, Tommy Tune and Twiggy.
LWT television presentation: Alan Boyd.

1984   **20.6**   **Sun 25 Nov 7:15 p.m.**   **1**   **1 wk**

From the Victoria Palace in the presence of Her Majesty Queen Elizabeth, The Queen Mother. Artists include Eileen Atkins, Simon Callow, Ronnie Corbett, Jimmy Cricket, Leslie Crowther, Billy Dainty, Paul Daniels, Les Dennis and Dustin Gee, Robert Dherry, Charlie Drake, Paul Eddington, Frank Finlay, Tim Flavin, James Galway, Russell Grant, Keith Harris, Harvey and the Wallbangers, Roy Hudd, Howard Keel, the cast of LAST OF THE SUMMER WINE, Robert Lindsay, Henry Mancini, Jean Marsh, Paul Nicholas, Angharad Rees, Emma Thompson, the Tiller Girls and Bernie Winters.
BBC television presentation: Yvonne Littlewood.

1985   **15.9**   **Sun 1 Dec 7:45 p.m.**   **3**   **1 wk**

From the Theatre Royal, Drury Lane in the presence of Her Majesty The Queen and HRH The Duke of Edinburgh, a show celebrating 'The World of Film Musicals'. Artists include Don Ameche, Michael Aspel, Lauren Bacall, Simon Bowman, Sarah Brightman, Geoffrey Burridge, Danielle Carson, Roy Castle, Joan Collins, Patrick Duffy, Alice Faye, Rolf Harris, Russell Harty, Celeste Holm, Michael Howe, Gloria Hunniford, Stephanie Lawrence, Jan Leeming, Rula Lenska, Ron Moody, Anna Neagle, Paul Nicholas, Sarah Payne, Su Pollard, Beryl Reid, Liz Robertson, Martin Shaw, Jean Simmons, Frankie Vaughan and the cast of 42nd Street, Dennis Waterman, Elisabeth Welch, Gary Wilmot and Norman Wisdom.
LWT television presentation: Alan Boyd.

1986   **17.2**   **Sat 29 Nov 7:15 p.m.**   **3**   **1 wk**

From the Theatre Royal, Drury Lane in the presence of Her Majesty Queen Elizabeth, The Queen Mother. Artists include the Bluebells, Victor Borge, Rory Bremner, Max Bygraves, Marti Caine, Frank Carson, Cyd Charisse, Petula Clark, Lesley Collier, Ronnie Corbett, Tyne Daly, Paul Daniels, Ken Dodd, Val Doonican, Sharon Gless, Stephane Grappelli, Simon Howe, the Huddersfield Choral Society, Gloria Hunniford, Aled Jones, Lulu, Vera Lynn, Paul McCartney, Ruth Madoc, Valerie Masterson, Bob Monkhouse, Nana Mouskouri, Paul Nicholas, Nicholas Parsons, Carolyn Pickles, Su Pollard, Alan Randall, Angela Rippon, Peter Ustinov, Marti Webb, Kit and the Widow and Victoria Wood.
BBC television presentation: Yvonne Littlewood.

1987   **14.4**   **Sun 29 Nov 7:15 p.m.**   **9**   **1 wk**

From the London Palladium in the presence of Her Majesty The Queen and HRH The Duke of Edinburgh. Artists include Michael Barrymore, Shirley Bassey, Sarah Brightman, Alan Brind, Cannon and Ball, George Carl, Rosemary Clooney, Bobby Davro, Les Dawson, Five Star, Stephen Fry and Hugh Laurie, James Galway, Evelyn Glennie, Peter Goodwright, Dolores Gray, Hale and Pace, Tom Jones, Eartha Kitt, Johnny Logan, Ronn Lucas, Jessica Martin, the cast of Les Misérables, Anthony Newley, Hilary O'Neil, Vladimir Ovchinikov, Johnnie Ray, the Roly Polys, Harry Secombe, George Shearing, Allan Stewart, Jimmy Tarbuck, Mel Tormé, Gary Wilmot and Mike Yarwood.
LWT television presentation: Alasdair Macmillan.

1988   **18.1**   **Sat 26 Nov 7:30 p.m.**   **4**   **1 wk**

In the presence of Her Majesty Queen Elizabeth, The Queen Mother at the London Palladium, Ronnie Corbett and Bruce Forsyth introduce A-Ha, Russ Abbot with Bella Emberg, Rick Astley, Bananarama, the cast of BREAD, the Chong Qing Troupe, Brian Conley, Paul Daniels with Debbie McGee, Michael Feinstein, the cast of 'The Golden Girls' (Bea Arthur, Estelle Getty, Rue McClanahan and Betty White), Julio Iglesias, Jackie Mason, Ann Miller, Kylie Minogue, Bob Monkhouse, the cast of NEIGHBOURS, Cliff Richard, Mickey Rooney and Mel Smith and Griff Rhys-Jones.
BBC television presentation: Michael Hurll.

1989   **15.5**   **Sat 25 Nov 7:05 p.m.**   **7**   **1 wk**

From the London Palladium in the presence of Her Majesty The Queen and HRH The Duke of Edinburgh. Artists include Michael Ball, Chris de Burgh, Lance Burton, the cast of CORONATION STREET, Wayne Dobson, David Essex, Janet Jackson, Nigel Kennedy, Jerry Lewis, Julian Lloyd Webber, Joe Longthorne, George Marshall, John Mills, Paul Nicholas, the Northern Ballet Theatre, Freddie Starr and Tina Turner.
Stage Director: Brian Rogers. **LWT television presentation:** Ian Hamilton.

1991   **13.1**   **Sat 30 Nov 8:00 p.m.**   **18**   **1 wk**

From the Victoria Palace in the presence of Her Majesty The Queen and HRH The Duke of Edinburgh. Artists include Michael Ball, Simon Bowman, Linda Mae Brewer, Beverley Craven, Jim Dale, Les Dawson, Mike Doyle, Rosemarie Ford, David Frost, Roy Hudd, Gloria Hunniford, Eric Idle, Julia McKenzie, Jackie Mason, Elaine Paige, Billy Pearce, Frances Ruffelle, Lea Salonga, Wayne Sleep and Marti Webb.
Stage Director: Gillian Lynne. **LWT television presentation:** Alasdair Macmillan.

Royal Wedding, The — 6 wks

BBC all and ITV (1986), news

| 1963 | 5.6 | Wed 24 Apr 8:20 p.m. | 11 | 2 wks |

Highlights of the wedding which took place earlier in the day of Her Royal Highness The Princess Alexandra of Kent and The Hon. Angus Ogilvy. The marriage was solemnized by the Archbishop of Canterbury in Westminster Abbey. The commentary was by Richard Dimbleby.
Television presentation: Alan Chivers, Innes Lloyd, Dennis Monger, Alan Rees, John Vernon, Bill Wright. **Producer:** Antony Caxton.

| 1981 | 13.7 | Wed 29 Jul 9:45 a.m. | 3 | 1 wk |

Tom Fleming sets the scene for the wedding at St Paul's Cathedral between HRH The Prince of Wales and Lady Diana Spencer.
Television presentation: Diarmuid Jeffreys. **Editor:** David Lloyd.
Producers: Michael Begg and Michael Lumley.

1986	12.5	Wed 23 Jul 10:00 a.m. (BBC)	3	3 wks
	12.0	Tue 22 Jul 7:00 p.m. (BBC)	4	
	10.2	Tue 22 Jul 6:45 p.m. (ITV)	6	

The Tuesday broadcasts were a rare example of co-operation between the BBC and ITV. HRH Prince Andrew and Miss Sarah Ferguson were interviewed by Sue Lawley (BBC) and Andrew Gardner (ITN) on the eve of their wedding. Both channels then compiled their own pre-wedding programmes based around the interview. David Dimbleby set the scene the next morning for the actual wedding ceremony from Westminster Abbey.

Royal Wedding: A Day to Remember, The — 1 wk

BBC, news

| 1986 | 9.3 | Wed 23 Jul 9:30 p.m. | 12 | 1 wk |

David Dimbleby and Selina Scott present highlights of the day's events.
Producer: Diarmuid Jeffreys. **Editor:** David Lloyd.

Royal Windsor Big Top Show, The — 1 wk

BBC, entertainment

| 1977 | 7.6 | Sun 29 May 7:15 p.m. | 5 | 1 wk |

Hosted by Bruce Forsyth from Billy Smart's Big Top, Windsor in the presence of HM The Queen and HRH The Duke of Edinburgh in aid of the Queen's Silver Jubilee Appeal. Artists include Alan Alan, the Boichanovi Troupe, the Castors, Ronnie Corbett, Les Dawson, the Flying Terrels, Barry Humphries, Elton John, Judy Murton, New Edition, Olivia Newton-John, the Roberts Brothers' Elephants, Leo Sayer, Arthur Scott's Sealions, Eric Sykes, the Veterans and Mike Yarwood.

Circus Producer: David Smart. **Variety Producer:** James Moir. **Television Producer:** Michael Hurll.

Royal Windsor Horse Show, The — 1 wk

ATV, sport

An annual event, this horse show took place at Windsor Great Park.

| 1964 | 5.3 | Fri 13 May 10:10 p.m. | 14 | 1 wk |

The St George of England competition with commentary by Viscount Allenby.
Television presentation: Stephen Wade.

Rugby World Cup — 1 wk

ITV, sport

The finals of this competition lasted five weeks and involved 16 nations who had fought through the qualifying rounds that began as long ago as May 1989.

| 1991 | 13.6 | Sat 2 Nov 1:55 p.m. | 13 | 1 wk |

Frank Bough introduces live coverage from Twickenham of the final of the Rugby Union World Cup between Australia and England. (Australia won 12–6.)
Television presentation: John Watts. **Editor:** John D. Taylor.

Run For Your Life — 5 wks

USA presented by BBC, drama

In this series created by Roy Huggins, Ben Gazzara starred as Paul Bryan, a man given two years to live. He decided to make the most of his time.

| 1968 | 5.7 | Fri 18 Oct 9:05 p.m. | 10 | 3 wks |

'A Game of Violence'
Paul visits Smitty (Sugar Ray Robinson), an old boxing pal, at his training camp. He discovers Smitty has more at stake than the purse and the title.

| 1969 | 6.9 | Fri 22 Feb 9:05 p.m. | 6 | 2 wks |

'Hang Down Your Head and Laugh'
A girl dressed in jeans and cowboy boots and carrying a battered guitar is behaving abnormally.

Run the Gauntlet — 1 wk

Thames, game show

1988	9.3	Wed 25 May 8:00 p.m.	14	1 wk

Martin Shaw introduces a contest of demanding games and races on land, sea and in the air. Teams come from the UK, Holland and Australia/New Zealand. The commentary is by Martin Tyler.
Director: Jim Brown. **Producer:** Julian Grant. **Executive Producer:** Keith Mosedale. (A Creative Action production.)

Russ Abbot Christmas Show, The — 4 wks

BBC, comedy

The Liverpool comedian presented seasonal specials with his regular team of Tom Bright, Les Dennis, Bella Emberg and the Alyn Ainsworth orchestra. Suzy Aitchison appeared from 1986 to 88 and Maggie Moone appeared in 1986 and 1987. Gordon Kennedy joined the team in 1986, as did Paul Shearer in 1987 and Sherrie Hewson in 1988.
Producer: John Bishop.

1986	16.1	Thu 25 Dec 5:25 p.m.	6	1 wk

Choreographer: Tudor Davies.

1987	14.5	Fri 25 Dec 5:45 p.m.	13	1 wk

Choreographer: Dominic Winter.

1988	13.1	Sun 25 Dec 8:30 p.m.	15	1 wk

Guests: Bernard Cribbins, George Malpas and John Nettleton.
Choreographer: Phil Winston.

1989	15.0	Mon 25 Dec 5:35 p.m.	11	1 wk

Guest: Michael Stainton.

Russ Abbot Show, The — 33 wks

BBC, comedy

Abbot starred with his ever-present team Suzy Aitchison, Tom Bright, Les Dennis, Bella Emberg, Maggie Moone and the Alyn Ainsworth orchestra. Paul Shearer featured from 1987 to 1990.
Choreographer: Tudor Davies. **Producer:** John Bishop.

1986	13.0	Sat 25 Oct 7:35 p.m.	7	6 wks
1987	11.4	Sat 10 Oct 7:30 p.m.	13	6 wks
1988	12.2	Sat 10 Sep 7:45 p.m.	7	10 wks
1989	15.0	Thu 8 Jun 8:30 p.m.	7	10 wks

(Repeat.)

1990	10.3	Thu 19 Apr 8:30 p.m.	18	1 wk

(Repeat.)

Russ Abbot's Christmas Madhouse — 2 wks

LWT, comedy

These programmes are Christmas specials from the Madhouse team, with the Alyn Ainsworth orchestra. Featuring Susie Blake, Les Dennis and Dustin Gee, Bella Emberg, Sherrie Hewson and Jeffrey Holland.
Producer: David Bell.

1984	15.7	Sat 22 Dec 6:50 p.m.	3	1 wk
1986	16.1	Fri 19 Dec 7:30 p.m.	6	1 wk

Russ Abbot's Madhouse — 28 wks

LWT, comedy

Russ Abbot starred in this series of sketches with the regular company of Susie Blake, Les Dennis, Bella Emberg, Dustin Gee, Sherrie Hewson and Jeffrey Holland, with the Alyn Ainsworth orchestra. Michael Barrymore featured in the 1982 series.
Producer (1982–84): John Kaye Cooper.

1982	10.6	Sun 7 Nov 7:15 p.m.	6	7 wks
1983	13.1	Sat 19 Nov 7:00 p.m.	7	12 wks
1984	9.2	Sat 21 Jul 7:00 p.m.	8	3 wks
1985	12.6	Sat 31 Aug 7:00 p.m.	5	6 wks

Director: Alasdair Macmillan. **Producer:** David Bell.

Russ Abbot's Saturday Madhouse — 3 wks

LWT, comedy

This was Russ Abbot's first solo series after leaving the comedy cabaret group THE BLACK ABBOTS.

1981	12.8	Sat 11 Jul 7:40 p.m.	12	3 wks

With Michael Barrymore, Susie Blake, Bella Emberg, Dustin Gee, Patti Gold and Jeffrey Holland.
Producer: John Kaye Cooper.

Russ Abbot's Scottish Madhouse — 1 wk

LWT, comedy

| 1984 | 15.6 | Sat 29 Dec 7:00 p.m. | 9 | 1 wk |

A repeat showing of Abbot's special recorded for a previous Hogmanay. He is joined by Michael Barrymore, Susie Blake, Les Dennis, Bella Emberg, Dustin Gee, Sherrie Hewson and Jeffrey Holland. With the Alyn Ainsworth orchestra.
Producer: John Kaye Cooper.

Russ Conway Show, The — 5 wks

ATV, music

Pianist and composer Russ Conway achieved great popularity through his records and his regular appearances on THE BILLY COTTON BAND SHOW.

| 1961 | 7.0 | Thu 26 Jan 8:00 p.m. | 1 | 5 wks |

Guests: Audrey Jeans and Otto Brandenburg.
Producer: Colin Clews.

Russell Harty at the Seaside — 1 wk

BBC, documentary

Former schoolteacher Harty became a television presenter and chat show host, always at his most comfortable when interviewing ordinary people. He died prematurely on 8 June 1988. In this series Harty saw the sights and met the people around Britain's resorts.

| 1982 | 8.8 | Fri 6 Aug 8:30 p.m. | 12 | 1 wk |

Russell visits the Isle of Wight during Cowes week.
Director: Peter Hamilton. **Producer:** Ken Stephinson.

Russian Roulette — 1 wk

Presented by ITV, film

| 1982 | 11.9 | Tue 7 Dec 7:30 p.m. | 12 | 1 wk |

Canadian Mountie Corporal Shaver (George Segal) is assigned to capture Latvian dissident Rudolph Henke (Val Avery) and hold him for the duration of Premier Kosygin's visit to Canada.
Director: Lou Lombardo.

Ruth Rendell Mysteries, The — 21 wks

TVS, drama

George Baker starred as novelist Ruth Rendell's sleuth Detective Chief Inspector Wexford. This quiet, slow-spoken policeman solved complex murder cases around the fictional town of Kingsmarkham. Christopher Ravenscroft also starred as Detective Inspector Burden.
Producer: Neil Zeiger. **Executive Producer:** Graham Benson.

| 1988 | 10.0 | Sun 3 Jul 8:15 p.m. | 9 | 3 wks |

'A Guilty Thing Surprised' dramatized by Clive Exton.
Part three of this three-part adaptation in which Wexford faces a daunting list of suspects. However certain facts come to light which convince him he is on the right track.
Director: Mary McMurray.

| 1989 | 11.6 | Sun 17 Dec 7:15 p.m. | 19 | 1 wk |

'The Veiled One' dramatized by Trevor Preston.
Wexford and Detective Inspector Burden are called to the scene of a brutal murder. Wexford is preoccupied with the knowledge that his daughter Sheila (Deborah Poplett) has been arrested for cutting the perimeter wire fencing at a military base.
Director: Mary McMurray.

| 1990 | 11.3 | Sun 18 Nov 7:45 p.m. | 15 | 6 wks |

'An Unkindness of Ravens' dramatized by Robert Smith.
In this second part of a two-part story Wexford reveals a network of lies and deceit while unravelling a murder.
Director: John Gorrie.

| 1991 | 16.3 | Sun 1 Dec 7:45 p.m. | 7 | 11 wks |

'Means of Evil' dramatized by Peter Berry.
Wexford ponders whether the death of Hannah Kingman was suicide or something more sinister.
Director: Sarah Hellings.

Ryan's Daughter — 1 wk

Presented by ITV, film

| 1980 | 17.0 | Sun 13 Jan 7:45 p.m. | 5 | 1 wk |

Set in Ireland in 1916. Rosy Ryan (Sarah Miles) has a disastrous marriage with Charles Shaughnessy (Robert Mitchum). She falls in love with British officer Major Doryan (Christopher Jones). Also starring Barry Foster, Trevor Howard, Leo McKern and John Mills.
Director: David Lean.

Previously Number One in the pop charts, Britain's favourite pianist was Number One in his only TV chart year with **The Russ Conway Show**.

Sadie It's Cold Outside — 4 wks

Granada, drama

This series by Jack Rosenthal was about a couple questioning their futures after twenty-three years of marriage. Starring Rosemary Leach as Sadie Potter and Bernard Hepton as Norman Potter.

| 1975 | 7.4 | Mon 21 Apr 8:00 p.m. | 3 | 4 wks |

In this opening episode Sadie reflects on life. She feels that there must be more to it than cooking, cleaning, washing and ironing. **Producer:** Les Chatfield.

....

Saga of Saint Trinian's, The — 2 wks

Presented by BBC, film

This was a season of films based on Ronald Searle's academy for young ladies.

| 1970 | 6.9 | Tue 10 Nov 7:30 p.m. | 11 | 2 wks |

'Pure Hell of St Trinian's'
The girls have burned down the school and are on trial at the Old Bailey. Starring Cecil Parker, George Cole and Joyce Grenfell, with Sidney James and Dennis Price.
Director: Frank Launder.

....

Saint, The — 16 wks

ATV, drama

The series began in 1963 and was made in colour for the American market. Roger Moore starred as THE SAINT, Simon Templar. Leslie Charteris created the character in 1928, describing him as 'a roaring adventurer . . . (who) lives for the pursuit of excitement'. He drove a yellow Volvo sportscar with the number plate ST 1.

| 1968 | 7.4 | Fri 17 May 8:00 p.m. | 5 | 16 wks |

'Paper Chase' by Harry W. Junkin.
Simon Templar follows a defecting civil servant who has been tricked into smuggling papers into East Germany.
Director: Leslie Norman. **Producer:** Robert S. Baker.

Saints and Sinners — 1 wk

USA presented by BBC, drama

In this series two city newspaper reporters uncovered human interest stories. Nick Adams starred as Nick Alexander and John Larkin was Mark Grainger.

| 1964 | 4.7 | Fri 21 Aug 9:25 p.m. | 18 | 1 wk |

'All the Hard Young Men'
A veteran policeman is credited with the capture of a notorious criminal. But Nick discovers that a young member of the public was actually responsible and is determined to gain recognition for him. Guest star: Red Buttons.

....

Saki — 6 wks

Granada, drama

The 'Improper Stories' of H. H. Munro were adapted for television by Edward Boyd, Hugh Leonard, Philip Mackie and Gerald Savory. Set in a large country house in the Edwardian era of croquet, billiards and tea on the lawn, Saki's writing reflected his own life. Brought up by a pair of tyrannical aunts who would thrash him regularly, these stories often featured the humiliation of women – perhaps as some sort of revenge for his treatment as a child. The series starred Mark Burns as Clovis, Fenella Fielding as Mary Drakmanton, Rosamund Greenwood as Veronique Brimley-Bomefield, Martita Hunt as Lady Bastable, William Mervyn as Sir Hector and Richard Vernon as the Major.

| 1962 | 4.4 | Fri 20 Jul 9:15 p.m. | 9 | 6 wks |

'The Stampeding of Lady Bastable'
Lady Bastable's servants rush into her bedroom brandishing knives. She believes that her world has come to an end.
Director: Gordon Flemyng. **Producer:** Philip Mackie.

....

Sale of the Century — 140 wks

Anglia, game show

In this series hosted by Nicholas Parsons contestants answered questions in order to earn the right to buy discounted goods. **Producer:** Bill Perry

1974	6.9	Fri 1 Nov 6:30 p.m.	10	10 wks
1975	7.8	Sat 8 Mar 6:20 p.m.	5	25 wks
1976	8.5	Fri 23 Jan 7:35 p.m.	1	36 wks
1977	20.6	Fri 18 Nov 7:00 p.m.	1	32 wks
1978	21.2	Fri 22 Dec 7:30 p.m.	1	20 wks
1979	16.7	Fri 5 Jan 7:30 p.m.	3	10 wks
1980	10.0	Sat 19 Jul 8:00 p.m.	16	2 wks
1981	13.0	Fri 1 May 7:00 p.m.	15	5 wks

Salem's Lot — 1 wk

USA presented by BBC, drama

This two-part dramatization of the novel by Stephen King starred David Soul as writer Ben Mears. He returned through forces he could not comprehend to his home town, Salem's Lot. He became caught up in inexplicable menace and horror. James Mason, Bonnie Bedelia and Lance Kerwin also starred.
Writer: Paul Monash. **Director:** Tobe Hooper. **Producer:** Richard Kobritz.

1985	10.0	Thu 15 Aug 9:25 p.m.	14	1 wk

Part One
Ben is fascinated by the Marsten House and its frighteningly ominous owner Richard Straker (James Mason).

Salzburg Connection, The — 1 wk

Presented by ITV, film

1978	11.6	Thu 20 Jul 7:45 p.m.	7	1 wk

Secret agents from around the world converge on Salzburg in search of a hidden chest containing the names of former Nazi leaders and collaborators. Starring Barry Newman and Anna Karina.
Director: Lee H. Katzin

Sam — 39 wks

Granada, drama

Created and written by John Finch, this series told the story of Sam Wilson. Sam was 10 when his father died and his mother decided that they should return to the Yorkshire village of Skellerton where she was born. The second series saw Sam rebel against the mines, escape to the sea, return to inherit property, sow his wild oats and get work in an engineering factory. By the third and final series, Sam settled in the Yorkshire town of Golwick and married Sarah Corby (Jennifer Hilary) in 1952. They had three children, including a son from Sarah's previous marriage. They had a new Hillman Minx and

Sam had secured a management role in the engineering works.

Sam as a boy was played by Kevin Moreton and as a man by Mark McManus. Other principal characters were Sam's grandparents, Toby Wilson (Frank Mills) and Jack and Polly Barraclough (Michael Goodliffe and Maggie Jones), his Uncle George and Aunt Ethel Barraclough (Ray Smith and Alethea Charlton), Polly's sister May Dakin (Mona Bruce) and May's son Alan (John Price).
Designer: Colin Pocock. **Producer:** Michael Cox.

1973	7.0	Tue 4 Sep 9:00 p.m.	1	13 wks

'Breadwinners'
It is summer, 1938. After a disastrous spell at a charity school, Sam is back at Skellerton, aged fourteen. He sees little prospect of work unless the threat of war in Europe brings the pits back into full production.

1974	7.4	Thu 23 May 8:30 p.m.	1	13 wks

'The Legacy'
Sam is now a grown man. Nine years have passed since he went down the pits at the age of fourteen, just before the outbreak of the Second World War. Now it is the winter of 1947 and Sam's grandfather Toby has died, but he is more concerned with the matrimonial predicament of his Uncle George than with any possible inheritance.
Director: Les Chatfield

1975	6.5	Mon 2 Jun 8:00 p.m.	5	13 wks

'God Sent Sunday'
It is 1960 and Sam is now 35 years old. In the face of his approaching middle age he reflects on the problems facing the future of his family. He remembers the time he had few material trappings and no responsibilities.

Though best-known for his portrayal of the tough Glasgow detective Taggart, Mark McManus reached Number One as **Sam**.

Sam and Janet
2 wks

ATV, situation comedy

This series by David Cumming featured a comfortably-off married couple constantly at war with each other. The show starred John Junkin as Sam Marshall and Joan Sims as Janet Marshall with Harry Locke as Sam's best pal Charlie.

1967	5.2	Tue 27 Jun 9:10 p.m.	10	2 wks

In this first episode it is clear that Sam does the football pools and fancies a pint or six, while Janet wants to discuss the world situation.
Director: Paul Bernard. **Producer:** Alan Tarrant.

Sam Whiskey
2 wks

Presented by BBC, film

1985	10.3	Sat 22 Jun 6:40 p.m.	14	1 wk

Burt Reynolds stars in the title role as an itinerant gambler who is hired to retrieve gold bars from the bed of the Colorado River. Angie Dickinson and Clint Walker also star.
Director: Arnold Laven.

1987	9.6	Sat 18 Jul 7:00 p.m.	17	1 wk

Repeat showing of the above film.

Sammy and Bruce
1 wk

LWT, entertainment

1980	12.6	Sun 21 Sep 8:00 p.m.	17	1 wk

This special stars Sammy Davis Jr. and Bruce Forsyth with the Alyn Ainsworth orchestra.
Producer: David Bell.

Sanctuary
1 wk

AR, drama

This series by Philip Levene focused on a community of nuns and their work in a poor area of London. Fay Compton starred as Sister Juliana, Joanna Dunham as Sister Benedict, Alison Leggatt as Sister Ursula and Peggy Thorpe-Bates as Sister Paul.

1967	6.3	Mon 26 Jun 9:10 p.m.	5	1 wk

'The Mission'
Sister Benedict is recalled from her mission in Tanzania and assigned to parish work in London, where she feels useless. She wonders whether or not she has lost her vocation.
Director: Joan Kemp-Welch. **Producer:** John Harrison.

Sand Pebbles, The
1 wk

Presented by ITV, film

1973	5.4	Mon 28 May 8:30 p.m.	15	1 wk

Bank Holiday presentation of the film starring Richard Attenborough, Candice Bergen, Richard Crenna and Steve McQueen. The Sand Pebbles are the crew of a US gunboat in the Far East in 1926. Chinese students are demanding the expulsion of all foreigners.
Director: Robert Wise.

Sandbaggers, The
2 wks

YTV, drama

This series created by Ian Mackintosh starred Roy Marsden as Neil Burnside, the director of operations of the strong-arm intelligence squad known as the Sandbaggers. Co-starring Richard Vernon with Elizabeth Bennett, Ray Lonnen, Alan MacNaughton, Bob Sherman and Jerome Willis.
Producer: Michael Ferguson. **Executive Producer:** David Cunliffe.

1978	13.1	Mon 23 Oct 9:00 p.m.	20	1 wk

'A Feasible Solution' by Ian Mackintosh.
Danger in Cyprus and hard facts to be faced in London.
Designer: Roger Andrews.

1980	9.7	Mon 30 Jun 9:00 p.m.	19	1 wk

'My Name Is Anna Wiseman' by Gidley Wheeler.
Burnside is handed a document prepared by NATO secretary Anna Wiseman (Carol Gillies) in Brussels stating that by the time he receives it she will already be on trial for offences against the Soviet Union. Burnside becomes involved in a devious game with his superiors, and sends Mike Wallace (Michael Cashman) to Europe on a dangerous mission.
Designer: Jeremy Bear.

Santa Claus –The Movie
1 wk

Presented by BBC, film

1988	15.6	Sun 25 Dec 5:45 p.m.	10	1 wk

A woodcutter turned by elves into Santa Claus goes to New York, where he meets a ruthless toy manufacturer. Starring Dudley Moore with Judy Cornwell, David Huddleston, John Lithgow and Burgess Meredith.
Director: Jeannot Szwarc

Sapphire and Steel
12 wks

HTV, drama

This series by P. J. Hammond starred Joanna Lumley as Sapphire and David McCallum as Steel, agents who travelled through time to put right ancient wrongs.
Producer: Shaun O'Riordan. **Executive Producer:** David Reid.

| 1979 | 11.8 | Tue 10 Jul 7:00 p.m. | 4 | 8 wks |

Episode One
Two children are left alone in a remote country cottage when their parents mysteriously disappear.
Designer: Stanley Mills.

| 1981 | 10.7 | Tue 18 Aug 7:00 p.m. | 15 | 3 wks |

Episode Two by Don Houghton.
A murder takes place in a large house where all the doors and windows are jammed and the phone has been cut.
Designer: Su Chases.

| 1982 | 8.2 | Thu 19 Aug 7:00 p.m. | 18 | 1 wk |

Episode One
Sapphire and Steel discover a service station where the only travellers are from the past.
Designer: Stanley Mills. **Director:** David Foster.

| **Saracen** | | | | 1 wk |

Central, drama

Saracen Systems was a private security firm in London which specialized in protecting VIPs. Its top operatives were David Barber and Tom Duffy (Christian Burgess and Patrick James Clarke).

| 1989 | 9.7 | Sat 16 Sep 9:00 p.m. | 19 | 1 wk |

'Proof of Death' by John Foster.
Barber and Duffy are in a race against time to free a kidnapped TV crew in South America.
Director: Ian Knox. **Producers:** Patrick Harbinson and Deirdre Keir.
Executive Producer: Ted Childs.

| **Saturday Action Film, The** | | | | 2 wks |

Presented by ITV, film

| 1976 | 5.8 | Sat 24 Jul 7:15 p.m. | 12 | 2 wks |

'Dr No'
(See separate entry for this film.)

| **Saturday Crowd, The** | | | | 12 wks |

LWT, entertainment

This series of variety shows was hosted by Leslie Crowther with Lonnie Donegan, Peter Gordeno and Anita Harris. Other regulars throughout the series were Sheila Bernette, Billy Boyle and Dennis Ramsden, with the Peter Gordeno dancers and the Harry Rabinowitz orchestra.
Producer: David Bell.

| 1969 | 6.6 | Sat 11 Jan 6:15 p.m. | 9 | 12 wks |

| **Saturday Film, The** | | | | 28 wks |

Presented by BBC, film

| 1961 | 4.4 | Sat 9 Dec 8:55 p.m. | 19 | 1 wk |

'Impact'
Walter Williams (Brian Donlevy) is almost murdered by his wife's lover. To escape he changes his name and takes a job in a garage owned by a young widow (Ella Raines). Also starring Charles Coburn.
Director: Arthur Lubin.

| 1962 | 5.5 | Sat 17 Mar 8:35 p.m. | 8 | 6 wks |

'My Forbidden Past'
Ava Gardner and Robert Mitchum star in a story of love and pursuit set in New Orleans at the turn of the century.
Director: Robert Stevenson.

| 1963 | 4.7 | Sat 28 Dec 8:05 p.m. | 20 | 1 wk |

'Lost Treasure of the Amazon'
Lon Chaney, Rhonda Fleming and Fernando Lamas star in the story of a dangerous journey into hostile Jivaro Indian country in search of treasure.
Director: Edward Ludwig.

| 1971 | 6.8 | Sat 6 Nov 6:30 p.m. | 11 | 4 wks |

'The Man Who Never Was'
The true story of the deception of the enemy by British Naval Intelligence in the spring of 1943 as the Allies plan the invasion of Europe through Sicily. Starring Stephen Boyd, Gloria Grahame and Clifton Webb.
Director: Ronald Neame.

| 1972 | 6.6 | Sat 11 Nov 7:25 p.m. | 16 | 3 wks |

'The Sheepman'
A story of hatred between cattlemen and sheepmen in Powder Valley, starring Glenn Ford and Shirley MacLaine.
Director: George Marshall.

| 1980 | 14.1 | Sat 13 Dec 9:15 p.m. | 16 | 2 wks |

'Three Days Of The Condor'
Robert Redford stars as Joe Turner, a CIA researcher on the run in New York with just a beautiful photographer (Faye Dunaway) to help him. Also starring Cliff Robertson and Max Von Sydow.
Director: Sydney Pollack.

| 1981 | 12.2 | Sat 28 Mar 7:25 p.m. | 19 | 1 wk |

'The Supercops'
(See separate entry for this film.)

1982 | **11.9** | **Sat 13 Mar 7:40 p.m.** | **10** | **5 wks**

'Last Train From Gun Hill'
The man who raped and murdered the wife of a US marshal turns out to be the son of an old friend. Kirk Douglas and Anthony Quinn star. **Director:** John Sturges.

1983 | **8.2** | **Sat 6 Aug 7:05 p.m.** | **10** | **3 wks**

'El Dorado'
(See separate entry for this film.)

1984 | **9.0** | **Sat 14 July 6:40 p.m.** | | **2 wks**

'Rio Bravo'
This western has John Wayne and Dean Martin holding a town against outlaws. It also stars Ward Bond, Walter Brennan, Angie Dickinson and Ricky Nelson.
Director: Howard Hawks.

Saturday Film, The | **1 wk**

Presented by ITV, film

1968 | **4.4** | **Sat 17 Aug 7:30 p.m.** | **16** | **1 wk**

'The Black Narcissus'
Nuns in the Himalayas face moral dilemmas. Starring Deborah Kerr, Sabu and Jean Simmons. Written and directed by Michael Powell and Emeric Pressburger.

Saturday Gang, The | **1 wk**

LWT, entertainment

This series featured Hale and Pace, Kate Robbins and Gary Wilmot with the Ray Monk orchestra and the Chris Power dancers.

1986 | **13.0** | **Sat 15 Nov 7:15 p.m.** | **10** | **1 wk**

The regular mixture of sketches, songs and comedy.
Director: Vic Finch. **Producer:** Marcus Plantin.

Saturday Night at the Movies | **31 wks**

Presented by BBC, film

1974 | **6.4** | **Sat 5 Oct 6:35 p.m.** | **9** | **3 wks**

'Submarine X-1'
A US submarine embarks on a revenge mission after suffering disastrous casualties in action against the German battleship Lindendorf. Starring James Caan, Rupert Davies and David Sumner.
Director: William Graham.

1975 | **7.4** | **Sat 20 Dec 6:45 p.m.** | **12** | **4 wks**

'The Mosquito Squadron'
Set in 1944. The Allies must destroy the V2 rocket installations the Nazis hold in France. Starring David McCallum, Charles Gray, Suzanne Neve and Dinsdale Landen.
Director: Boris Sagal.

1977 | **6.7** | **Sat 8 Jan 6:55 p.m.** | **20** | **1 wk**

'Kings Of The Sun'
Prince Balam (George Chakiris) succeeds to the throne in the Mayan Kingdom of ancient Mexico. When the nation comes under attack by all-powerful invaders, he sets out to found a new nation. Also starring Yul Brynner and Shirley Ann Field.
Director: J. Lee-Thompson.

1978 | **11.2** | **Sat 2 Sep 6:45 p.m.** | **13** | **1 wk**

'The Sheepman'
(See THE SATURDAY FILM for this film.)

1979 | **19.4** | **Sat 1 Sep 8:15 p.m.** | **1** | **11 wks**

'Black Windmill'
Major John Tarrant (Michael Caine) is a Cold War agent in the Department of Subversive Warfare. His young son is kidnapped by spies. Also stars Joss Ackland, Donald Pleasence and Janet Suzman.
Director: Don Siegel.

1980 | **13.1** | **Sat 14 Jun 7:15 p.m.** | **6** | **10 wks**

'The Vikings'
Tony Curtis and Kirk Douglas star in this ninth-century saga as two half-brothers vying for the love of a captive princess. Also stars Ernest Borgnine, Janet Leigh and Orson Welles as narrator.
Director: Richard Fleischer.

1987 | **9.8** | **Sat 5 Sep 9:10 p.m.** | **13** | **1 wk**

'Risky Business'
Tom Cruise stars as teenager Joel Goodson. When his parents go away for the weekend he takes advantage and, though he emerges relatively unscathed, lives to regret it.
Director: Paul Brickman.

Saturday Night at the Movies | **3 wks**

Presented by ITV, film

1981 | **15.0** | **Sat 7 Feb 7:35 p.m.** | **8** | **3 wks**

'The Golden Gate Murders'
David Janssen stars as a detective and Susannah York as a nun who, together, investigate the death of a priest in San Francisco.
Director: Walter Grauman.

Saturday Night Fever | **1 wk**

Presented by ITV, film

1981	10.8	Wed 29 Jul 7:15 p.m.	11	1 wk

John Travolta stars as Tony Manero, a Brooklyn kid who escapes his job and family for one night a week dancing at the disco. He falls in love with a girl who shows him there are better things in life. With music by the Bee Gees.
Director: John Badham.

Saturday Night Theatre   6 wks

ATV, drama

This was a series of individual plays by various writers, each with its own cast and director.
Executive producer: Cecil Clarke.

1969	4.8	Sat 5 July 9:30 p.m.	14	3 wks

'A Measure of Malice' by Linette Purbi Perry.
Eunice and Lawrence Kellers (Elizabeth Weaver and John Stratton) are routinely married and plodding along in comfort when old flame Erica (Yootha Joyce) lands on the doorstep.
Designer: Eric Shedden. **Director:** Shaun O'Riordan. **Producer:** John Sichel.

1970	5.3	Sat 9 May 10:10 p.m.	13	3 wks

'The Family is a Vicious Circle' by Linette Purbi Perry.
Hilary is the daughter Daddy didn't want – he had hoped for a son. However, like her mother, she's prepared to be his doormat, but before she gets much of a chance he storms off to live with his mistress. Starring Francesca Annis, Basil Henson and Suzanne Neve.
Designer: Peter Roden. **Director:** John Sichel.

Saturday Royal   2 wks

Central, entertainment

This variety series was hosted by Lionel Blair from the Theatre Royal, Nottingham.

1983	8.0	Sat 20 Aug 8:15 p.m.	13	2 wks

Guests: Brian Conley, Talli Halliday, Little Foxes, Duncan Norvelle and Gary Wilmot.
Director: Peter Harris. **Producer:** Nigel Lythgoe.

Saturday Special, The   4 wks

BBC, entertainment

This series of variety shows was hosted by Ronnie Corbett with Jeff Richer's New Edition, the Maggie Stredder singers and the Ronnie Hazlehurst orchestra.

1975	7.5	Sat 29 Nov 8:00 p.m.	13	4 wks

Guests: Tony Blackburn, Dana, Larry Grayson, the Patton Brothers, Ted Rogers and stars from Gerry Cottle's Circus.
Producer: Michael Hurll.

Saturday Stars, The   4 wks

ATV, entertainment

This series showcased a different star each week.

1968	6.1	Sat 9 Nov 9:55 p.m.	10	4 wks

John Hanson sings selections from The Desert Song and The Student Prince with Patricia Michael, Barbara Strathdee and the Paddy Stone dancers.
Musical Director: Harry Rabinowitz. **Producer:** Keith Beckett.

Saturday Thriller, The   67 wks

Presented by BBC, film

1967	7.4	Sat 9 Dec 8:40 p.m.	3	8 wks

'Eye Witness'
A murderer seeks to silence the only witness to his crime. Starring Donald Sinden, Belinda Lee, Muriel Pavlow and Michael Craig.
Director: Muriel Box.

1968	7.3	Sat 14 Dec 8:15 p.m.	2	28 wks

'The List Of Adrian Messenger'
A criminal determined to make a fortune is bent on eliminating eleven people whom he feels are a threat to his plan. His murders always seem to be accidents until Adrian Messenger (John Merivale) gets suspicious. The stars are George C. Scott and Dana Wynter with Clive Brook, Gladys Cooper and Herbert Marshall. On 'The List' in disguise are Tony Curtis, Kirk Douglas, Burt Lancaster, Robert Mitchum and Frank Sinatra.
Director: John Huston.

1969	7.1	Sat 15 Feb 8:20 p.m.	3	22 wks

'Five Fingers'
James Mason, Danielle Darrieux and Michael Rennie star in the true story of Cicero, a Nazi spy during the Second World War.
Director: Joseph L. Mankiewicz.

1970	6.1	Sat 5 Dec 8:20 p.m.	14	4 wks

'See How They Run'
An American agent carrying vital evidence is murdered. His killers begin a ruthless campaign to obtain any evidence that would incriminate them. Starring Senta Berger, John Forsythe and Franchot Tone.
Director: David Lowell Rich.

| 1971 | 6.9 | Sat 13 Feb 8:25 p.m. | 12 | 5 wks |

'Stopover Tokyo'
The CIA get involved when a plot to murder the American High Commissioner in Tokyo is discovered. Starring Joan Collins, Edmond O'Brien and Robert Wagner.
Director: Richard L. Breen.

Saturday Variety | 2 wks

ATV, entertainment

This series of occasional shows had no regular host. The continuity came from the Jack Parnell orchestra, which backed all the featured artists.

| 1972 | 5.6 | Sat 8 Apr 8:25 p.m. | 19 | 2 wks |

Dickie Henderson and Lulu star with Larry Grayson, Shari Lewis, the Pattersons and Dougie Squires' Second Generation.
Producer: Colin Clews.

Saturday Western, The | 11 wks

Presented by BBC, film

| 1971 | 6.8 | Sat 13 Mar 7:00 p.m. | 9 | 10 wks |

'Warlock'
The small town of Warlock is terrorized by a gang of cowpunchers. With a succession of failed sheriffs behind them, the citizens decide to hire a professional gunfighter to be marshal. Henry Fonda, Dorothy Malone, Anthony Quinn and Richard Widmark star.
Director: Edward Dmytryk.

| 1973 | 5.0 | Sat 4 Aug 7:15 p.m. | 20 | 1 wk |

'The Jayhawkers'
It is Kansas in 1859. The territory faces chaos as the governor declares war on outlaw gangs, particularly the Jayhawkers. Jeff Chandler and Fess Parker star.
Director: Melvin Frank.

Scarecrow and Mrs King | 3 wks

USA presented by ITV, drama

This series about an American secret agency starred Bruce Boxleitner as Lee 'Scarecrow' Stetson and Kate Jackson as Amanda King, an ordinary housewife unwittingly involved in the world of espionage.
Producer: Bill McCutchen.

| 1984 | 9.7 | Tue 5 Jun 7:30 p.m. | 13 | 3 wks |

'If Thoughts Could Kill'
Amanda and Lee pursue a killer whose brain is controlled by a doctor bent on vengeance.

Scruples | 3 wks

USA presented by BBC, drama

This three-part adaptation by James Lee of the novel by Judith Krantz starred Lindsay Wagner as Billy Ikehorn with Barry Bostwick, Marie-France Pisier, Connie Stevens, Gene Tierney and Efrem Zimbalist Jr in a saga of sex and crime.
Director: Alan J. Levi. **Producer:** Leonard B. Kaufman.

| 1980 | 12.0 | Thu 31 July 9:25 p.m. | 4 | 3 wks |

Part Three
Billy accepts an invitation to the Cannes Film Festival, where she meets producer Vito Orsini (Nick Mancuso).

Sea Wolves | 1 wk

Presented by ITV, film

| 1983 | 13.3 | Thu 8 Sep 7:30 p.m. | 2 | 1 wk |

German U-boats known as Sea Wolves have been sinking Allied ships in the Indian Ocean in 1943. It is suspected an enemy agent is supplying information to a German ship sheltering in Goa harbour. Stars include Roger Moore, David Niven and Gregory Peck. Also appearing are Patrick Allen, Trevor Howard, Barbara Kellerman and Patrick Macnee.
Director: Andrew V. McLaglen.

Seagull Island | 4 wks

ATV, drama

This mystery serial in five parts was by Agusto Caminito and Jeremy Burnham. Barbara Carey (Prunella Ransome) arrived in Italy in search of her blind sister and was drawn to a small island. Jeremy Brett, Nicky Henson and Gabriele Tinti also starred.

| 1981 | 11.6 | Sat 8 Aug 9:20 p.m. | 6 | 4 wks |

Episode Four
Barbara's friend Martin Foster (Nicky Henson) is worried about her. He visits Seagull Island but sees no sign of her.
Producer: Nestore Ungaro.

Search For A Star | 1 wk

LWT, entertainment

Steve Jones hosted this series of talent shows with voting panels made up of viewers from different areas of the country. The artists were supported by the Brian Rogers dancers and the Alyn Ainsworth orchestra.

| 1979 | 14.4 | Sat 29 Dec 7:15 p.m. | 9 | 1 wk |

Featuring: Greg Bonham, Lee, Marie and Feelings, Tony Peers, the Simmons Brothers and Ann Williamson.
Director: Ken O'Neill. **Producer:** Tony Cornford. **Executive Producer:** David Bell.

Searchline Special | 1 wk

LWT, documentary

| 1990 | 10.3 | Fri 13 Apr 8:00 p.m. | 20 | 1 wk |

SEARCHLINE had been a segment of SURPRISE SURPRISE in which viewers were offered help, live on the air, to find long-lost friends and relatives. On Good Friday, 1990, the segment was given its own show.
Presented by Cilla Black, Gordon Burns and Andy Craig.
Director: Sue McMahon. **Producer:** Linda Beadle.

Seaside Special | 31 wks

BBC, entertainment

This summer season of variety shows from the resorts around the coast of Britain was recorded from 1975 to 1979 in the Big Top of Gerry Cottle's circus. With the Maggie Stredder singers from 1975 to 1979 and the Ronnie Hazlehurst orchestra (1975–79, 1987).
Choreographer (1976–79): Jeff Richer. **Producer:** Michael Hurll.

| 1975 | 6.7 | Sat 16 Aug 8:10 p.m. | 2 | 7 wks |

From Torbay starring Lulu with Abba, Mike Batt, Tony Blackburn, Janet Brown, Daley and Wayne, Roy Hudd, Des Lane, Kenneth McKellar and New Edition.
Choreographer: Mavis Ascott.

| 1976 | 6.2 | Sat 19 Jun 8:30 p.m. | 11 | 3 wks |

From Blackpool starring Ken Dodd, the Goodies (Tim Brooke-Taylor, Graeme Garden and Bill Oddie), the cast of ARE YOU BEING SERVED, Charlie Cairoli and Company, Johnny Hart, Tony Blackburn and Dave Lee Travis, the Daredevils and New Edition.

| 1977 | 12.7 | Sat 27 Aug 8:20 p.m. | 5 | 7 wks |

From Jersey starring Des O'Connor with Jack Douglas, Johnnie and Roy, Roger Kitter, New Edition, Alan Randall, Shades of Love, Brian Taylor and George Truzzi.

| 1978 | 13.4 | Sat 9 Sep 8:20 p.m. | 9 | 5 wks |

From Weymouth starring John Inman with Mike Carter, Norman Collier, Bobby Crush, Dana Gillespie, Lenny Henry, Hope and Keen, and Salena Jones.

| 1979 | 19.2 | Sat 1 Sep 7:25 p.m. | 1 | 8 wks |

From Poole in Dorset starring Roy Castle and Rolf Harris with Candlewick Green, Bernie Clifton, Neil Martin, Peter Powell and Aimi Stewart.

| 1987 | 8.8 | Sat 29 Aug 8:20 p.m. | 19 | 1 wk |

From Jersey, starring Les Dawson, Keith Harris, Joe Longthorne and the Roly Polys. In this series Mike Smith presents a revival of the game show BEAT THE CLOCK, last seen in the 1960s on ATV's SUNDAY NIGHT AT THE LONDON PALLADIUM.
Choreographer: Laura Wynne.

Seasons of the Year | 6 wks

Granada, drama

This was a series of one-hour dramas about 'Seasons', a house in the English countryside which stood for 150 years, and the people and families who lived there.

| 1971 | 6.5 | Mon 14 Jun 9:00 p.m. | 3 | 6 wks |

'The Three Graces' by Anthony Skene.
It is the autumn of 1815, just after the Battle of Waterloo. The house is new and its first family plans a house-warming party. Thora Hird and Dinah Sheridan star.
Designer: Roy Stonehouse. **Director:** Richard Everitt. **Producer:** Peter Potter.

Secombe And Friends | 6 wks

ATV, entertainment

This variety series starred Harry Secombe with various guests and the Jack Parnell orchestra.
Producer: Jon Scoffield.

| 1966 | 9.5 | Sun 13 Nov 10:05 p.m. | 1 | 2 wks |

Friends include Michael Bentine, Tony Hancock, Danny La Rue, Adele Leigh, Jeremy Lloyd and Nora Nicholson.

| 1967 | 8.3 | Sun 15 Oct 10:05 p.m. | 1 | 4 wks |

Friends include Michael Bentine, Billy Burden, John Cleese, Anita Harris, Donald Houston and Mike and Bernie Winters, with the Band of the Welsh Guards, and the choir of the 1st Battalion Welsh Guards.

Roy Castle was one of the guests in the Number One edition of **Seaside Special**.

1

2

3

4

5

6

1 *Julie Andrews rehearses her segment of* **The Silver Jubilee Royal Variety Gala**.

7

8

2 *David Frost, shown here in 1966 with Michael Bentine, hosts* **A Royal Gala** *unaware that he will perform a similar function 21 years later.*
3 *Donny Osmond was one of the star turns in* **The Children's Royal Variety Performance** *that reached Number One in 1984.*
4 *Gretchen Wyler led the cast of 'Sweet Charity' in* **A Special Royal Performance**.
5 *Liberace and Sammy Davis Jr look on as The Queen meets Alfred Marks after* **The Royal Variety Performance** *of 1960.*
6 **The Prince and Princess of Wales** *are interviewed by Alastair Burnet in 1985.*
7 *Prince Charles gives his brother Prince Edward a lesson in stringing the cello in* **Royal Family**.
8 *The Queen and other members of the Royal Family attend one of the bonfires lit to celebrate her* **Silver Jubilee Monday**.

Secombe with Music — 2 wks

YTV, music

These shows starred Harry Secombe concentrating on his Welsh musical upbringing rather than his 'Goon Show' comedy. With the Peter Knight orchestra.
Producer: Vernon Lawrence

1980 | **14.2** | **Wed 17 Dec 8:00 p.m.** | **14** | **1 wk**

Guests: Lorna Dallas, Derek Griffiths and five pianists – Roy Budd, Bobby Crush, John Mills, Semprini and Richard Stilgoe.

1982 | | **Wed 27 Jan 8:00 p.m.** | | **1 wk**

Guests: Larry Adler, Pam Ayres, Bruce Dukov, Instant Sunshine, Lulu and Julia McKenzie.

Second Chance — 1 wk

Presented by BBC, film

1963 | **5.6** | **Sun 27 Jan 3:15 p.m.** | **18** | **1 wk**

A professional killer stalks a gangster's moll in South America. Starring Robert Mitchum, Jack Palance and Linda Darnell.
Director: Rudolph Maté.

Second Chance — 1 wk

YTV, drama

This six part series by Adele Rose dealt with Kate and Chris Hurst (Susannah York and Ralph Bates), who decided to separate after eighteen years of marriage.

1981 | **13.7** | **Fri 6 Feb 9:00 p.m.** | **17** | **1 wk**

'August'
With the marriage ended, Kate takes the children Jill and Martin (Kate Dorning and Mark Eadie) on a camping holiday. She soon discovers that a divorcee is a target for married men.
Designer: Colin Pocock. **Director:** Richard Handford. **Producer:** Keith Richardson. **Executive Producer:** David Cunliffe.

Second City Reports — 1 wk

Granada, drama

These programmes attempted to study the British way of life in a dramatized form. The company of actors included David Battley, Kathleen Breck, Eleanor Bron, David Buck, Gordon Gostelow and Barry Letts. Among the pool of writers were John Bird, Ian Davidson and Michael Frayn.

1964 | **5.7** | **Tue 3 Mar 10:05 p.m.** | **20** | **1 wk**

'Dissent'
An examination of those who are against anything and everything.
Stage Director: John Bird. **Television Director:** David Cunliffe.
Producer: Bernard Sahlins.

Second Thoughts — 7 wks

LWT, situation comedy

This series by Jan Etherington and Gavin Petrie began on BBC Radio 4. Lynda Bellingham and James Bolam starred as divorcees Faith and Bill, who moved in together.

1991 | **10.5** | **Fri 3 May 8:00 p.m.** | **14** | **7 wks**

'Found and Lost'
Faith's teenage children and Bill's ex-wife do not make life easy for them.
Producer: David Askey. **Executive Producer:** Robin Carr.

Second Time Around — 1 wk

BBC, situation comedy

This series by Richard Waring concerned a couple who found love after his divorce. It starred Michael Craig as Harry and Patricia Brake as Vicky, a girl half his age.

1974 | **7.6** | **Wed 23 Oct 9:25 p.m.** | **3** | **1 wk**

'Miss Right'
Just after Harry's fiftieth birthday and ten years after his divorce, he falls head over heels for Vicky, much to the disgust of his friends Ronnie and Maggie (Gerald Flood and Jacqueline Clarke).
Producer: Graeme Muir.

Second Worst of Alright on the Night, The — 2 wks

LWT, comedy

These shows were re-runs of out-takes already featured in IT'LL BE ALRIGHT ON THE NIGHT.

1985 | **14.6** | **Sat 23 Nov 7:00 p.m.** | **4** | **1 wk**

Introduced by Denis Norden with Rory Bremner.
Director: Terry Kinane. **Producer:** Paul Lewis.

1986 | **13.8** | **Sun 7 Dec 7:45 p.m.** | **4** | **1 wk**

Repeat of the above programme.

Secret Army — 12 wks

BBC, drama

This series by various writers concerned 'Lifeline', a wartime secret army which helped the French Resistance in Normandy. Bernard Hepton starred as Albert, Angela Richards was Monique, Clifford Rose played Kessler and Terence Hardiman portrayed Reinhardt.

| 1979 | 22.0 | Sat 13 Oct 7:20 p.m. | 3 | 12 wks |

'A Safe Place' by Allan Prior.
Albert is imprisoned, so Monique takes charge of the line.
Director: Tristan De Vere Cole. **Producer:** Gerard Glaister.

Secret Diary of Adrian Mole Aged 13³/₄, The — 7 wks

Thames, drama

This adaptation by Sue Townsend of her own book starred Gian Sammarco as Adrian Mole, a bespectacled adolescent whose ordeals, aspirations and problems formed the core of the stories. Julie Walters played his mother Pauline, who was separated from his father George (Stephen Moore). Beryl Reid played Grandma Mole and Pandora, the object of Adrian's love, was portrayed by Lindsey Stagg.
Producer: Peter Sasdy. **Executive Producer:** Lloyd Shirley.

| 1985 | 14.0 | Mon 7 Oct 8:00 p.m. | 6 | 6 wks |

Following a school trip to the British Museum, Adrian has anxiety attacks each time he thinks of the M1 or London.

| 1989 | 8.0 | Tue 13 Jun 8:30 p.m. | 20 | 1 wk |

Repeat of the episode in which Adrian has a spell in hospital and his parents try to patch up their marriage.

Secret Hospital, The — 1 wk

YTV, documentary

| 1979 | 11.4 | Tue 22 May 9:00 p.m. | 15 | 1 wk |

This film penetrates the wall of secrecy around Rampton, a top security hospital, where all employees sign the Official Secrets Act. Horrifying conditions are exposed.
Producer: John Willis.

Secret of My Success, The — 1 wk

Presented by BBC, film

| 1991 | 12.1 | Tue 17 Sep 9:30 p.m. | 14 | 1 wk |

Michael J. Fox stars as Brantley Foster, the kid in the mailroom who convinces the boss he is a whiz with radical executive ideas.
Director: Herbert Ross.

Secret of Santa Vittoria, The — 1 wk

Presented by BBC, film

| 1975 | 5.1 | Sun 31 Aug 8:15 p.m. | | 1 wk |

The news of Mussolini's death is followed in the little Italian village of Santa Vittoria by the realization that the Germans are about to occupy the area. The villagers decide to hide a million bottles of wine from the invaders. Starring Anthony Quinn and Anna Magnani with Hardy Kruger and Virna Lisi.
Director: Stanley Kramer.

Secret Place, The — 1 wk

Presented by BBC, film

| 1966 | 6.7 | Tue 22 Feb 8:00 p.m. | 13 | 1 wk |

Belinda Lee, Ronald Lewis and David McCallum star in the story of a young boy who unwittingly finds himself in possession of stolen diamonds.
Director: Clive Donner.

Selwyn — 1 wk

YTV, situation comedy

Bill Maynard, who played the title role in OH NO! IT'S SELWYN FROGGITT, was uprooted from Scarsdale by writers Lawrie Kinsley and Ron McDonnell to broaden his horizons as the entertainments officer at the Paradise Valley holiday camp in a Yorkshire holiday resort.

| 1978 | 12.3 | Tue 26 Sep 8:15 p.m. | 18 | 1 wk |

'Take a Tip from Selwyn'
A simple instruction from the camp manager Mervyn Price (Bernard Gallagher) to dump a load of rubbish results in Selwyn arriving at a nearby stately home.
Producer: Ronnie Baxter.

Sentimental Agent
8 wks

ATV, drama

Carlos Thompson starred as import/export agent Carlos Varela, a character taken from MAN OF THE WORLD. Varela loved to make money but would not hesitate to help someone in trouble. He had two permanent staff, secretary Suzy Carter (Clemence Bettany) and valet Chin (Burt Kwouk).

1963	7.0	Sat 9 Nov 7:15 p.m.	10	8 wks

'A Little Sweetness and Light' by Tudor Gates.
Varela is worried when his trade with the Greek island of Athos ceases and his local representative is reported killed in a road accident. He decides to investigate personally. Guest star: Patrick Allen.
Director: Harold French. **Producer:** Harry Fine.

Sergeant Cork
16 wks

ATV, drama

This series was created by Ted Willis about a Victorian metropolitan policeman played by John Barrie. Cork, a bachelor living close to his Whitehall office, was one of the first to appreciate how science could help fight crime. In the era of opera cloaks, top hats and sweeping skirts, London was in the grip of a crime wave, with murder and violence commonplace. Fingerprints were known but not admissable as evidence. Cork aimed to change things.

1963	5.7	Sat 6 Jul 10:00 p.m.	8	9 wks

'The Case of the Girl Upstairs' by Ted Willis.
Lucy Beasley (Margaret Diamond) is certain a crime is being committed in the Beasley household and she implores Cork to investigate. Is she just a bitter, frustrated woman out to cause trouble, or are her fears justified? With William Gaunt, Mary Kenton, Philip Latham, Meg Ritchie and Carmen Silvera.
Director: Quentin Lawrence. **Producer:** Jack Williams.

1964	5.8	Sat 13 Jun 10:10 p.m.	9	7 wks

'The Case of the Great Pearl Robbery' by Ted Willis.
Monsieur Billot (John Barron), a Parisian diamond merchant, sends valuable pearls in a registered parcel to be collected in London. On its arrival, the pearls are missing.
Director: John Cooper. **Producer:** Jack Williams.

Series of Birds, A
1 wk

BBC, comedy

This series of sketches was written by and stars John Bird and John Fortune.

1967	5.8	Tue 31 Dec 9:05 p.m.	20	1 wk

Producer: Dennis Main Wilson.

Servants, The
1 wk

Tyne Tees, documentary

1967	5.9	Tue 10 Oct 9:15 p.m.	13	1 wk

The servant is a dying occupation in England. This film meets those who have or have had servants and those who serve or served.
Writer: Brian Morris. **Camera:** Fred Thomas. **Director:** Peter Dunbar. **Producer:** Frank Entwistle.

Seven Brides for Seven Brothers
1 wk

Presented by BBC, film

1980	16.9	Sat 16 Feb 7:15 p.m.	4	1 wk

This musical by Johnny Mercer and Gene de Paul stars Howard Keel, Jane Powell, Tommy Rall, Jeff Richards and Russ Tamblyn. Seven brothers in the old west, all of them hard-working ranch men, decide they need wives. With much singing and dancing they collect and choose girls from the surrounding villages.
Director: Stanley Donen.

Seven Deadly Sins
7 wks

AR, drama

A series of seven plays by various writers.

1966	7.1	Mon 13 Jun 9:40 p.m.	2	7 wks

'In The Night' by Anthony Skene.
A blackmailer (Derek Francis) terrorizes one of his victims (Joanna Dunham) while another victim (Adam Faith) is in possession of a gun.
Designer: Fred Pusey. **Director:** Peter Moffatt. **Executive Producer:** Peter Willes.

Seven Deadly Virtues, The
7 wks

AR, drama

This was a follow-up septet to SEVEN DEADLY SINS of plays by various writers with different casts.

1967	6.9	Thu 4 May 9:40 p.m.	8	7 wks

'A Pain in the Neck' by Bill McIlwraith.
Agnes Birling (Liz Fraser) is driven out of her mind by her ultra-understanding husband (Richard Pearson). He works in a casino where the owner (Lee Montague) quickly discovers he is a pain in the neck as far as the underworld is concerned.
Designer: Michael Yates. **Director:** Joan Kemp-Welch. **Executive Producer:** Peter Willes.

Seven Dials Mystery, The — 1 wk

LWT, drama

1981 | **17.6** | **Sun 8 Mar 7:45 p.m.** | **4** | **1 wk**

Pat Sandys adapted Agatha Christie's story in which two Foreign Office employees are murdered. Trying to solve the crimes is Lady Brent (Cheryl Campbell), known as 'Bundle', who follows a trail to the Seven Dials Club. Also starring Terence Alexander, Harry Andrews, John Gielgud, Rula Lenska, Leslie Sands, James Warwick and Brian Wilde.
Designers: Bryan Bagge and Colin Monk. **Producer:** Jack Williams.
Director and Executive Producer: Tony Wharmby.

Seven Faces of Woman — 1 wk

LWT, drama

This series of seven plays examined contemporary woman at seven different ages. It was created by John Hawkesworth and John Whitney. The theme tune 'She' sung by Charles Aznavour reached number one.

1974 | **5.3** | **Sun 2 Jun 10:15 p.m.** | **17** | **1 wk**

'Cherryripe and the Lugworm Digger' by Robert Holles.
Teenager Gaye Kingdom (Julie Peasgood) spends a weekend at a seaside cottage with Colin and Geoff (Tom Chadbon and George Sweeney). To their surprise and disgust she rejects their advances.
Designer: Bryan Bagge. **Director:** Paul Annett. **Producer:** Richard Doubleday.

Seven Weeks of a Summer Season — 1 wk

BBC, documentary

1967 | **5.3** | **Thu 23 Mar 9:30 p.m.** | **20** | **1 wk**

Travelling fairs leave their winter quarters at Easter and travel throughout the summer. They have the seven weeks of the high season in which to make their living. David Mahlowe provides the commentary.
Producer: Don Haworth.

77 Sunset Strip — 2 wks

USA presented by ITV, drama

This series began in the USA in 1958 and featured a firm of private eyes operating from their address on Sunset Boulevard. It starred Efrem Zimbalist Jr. as Stuart Bailey and Roger Smith as Jeff Spencer. Gerald Lloyd Kookson III ('Kookie'), initially a minor character, seized much of the attention. Played by Edward (Edd) Byrnes, 'Kookie' was a parking lot attendant who was constantly combing his hair and speaking his own jive talk. Byrnes recorded a hit duet with Connie Stevens, 'Kookie Kookie (Lend Me Your Comb)'.

1960 | **5.4** | **Sat 17 Sep 9:05 p.m.** | **10** | **2 wks**

'Lovely Alibi'
Stuart Bailey agrees to help his pal Ed Bird (Claude Atkins), a suspended police officer, find the key witness to prove the ruthless Vic Gurney (Steve Brodie) was responsible for an unsolved murder.
Director: George Waggner. **Producer:** Howie Horwitz. **Executive Producer:** William T. Orr.
(Although networked at 9:05 p.m. on Saturday 17 September 1960, different episodes were shown in different regions. This show was the London transmission.)

Sex Game, The — 3 wks

Thames, drama

A series of individual plays.

1968 | **6.5** | **Wed 11 Dec 9:05 p.m.** | **11** | **3 wks**

'Cold Game Pie' by James Brabazon.
Frank Healey (George Cole) is a not very successful architect who comes home one evening to find his wife Dorothy (Rosemary Frankau) gone. She has left a note to tell him there is some cold game pie in the fridge.
Designer: Fred Pusey. **Director:** Bill Bain. **Producer:** Joan Kemp-Welch.

Sexpionage — 1 wk

Presented by ITV, film

1989 | **10.0** | **Wed 21 Jun 9:00 p.m.** | **9** | **1 wk**

Attractive Russian girls are sent to the Institution for American Studies, and not simply to train as interpreters. Sally Kellerman, Linda Hamilton and James Franciscus star.
Director: Don Taylor.

Seychelles – Isles of Love, The — 1 wk

ATV, documentary

1973 | **6.4** | **Mon 8 Jan 8:00 p.m.** | **19** | **1 wk**

A film report on the changes facing the islanders in the wake of the opening of an international airport on 3 July 1971 and the resulting tide of tourism.
Camera: Ernest Vincze. **Sound:** Derek Williams. **Producer:** David Rea.

Sez Les — 21 wks

YTV, comedy

These half-hour comedy programmes starred northern comedian Les Dawson, a one-time OPPORTUNITY KNOCKS winner. Sadly Les Dawson died on 10 June 1993.

1971 6.3 **Mon 16 Aug 8:25 p.m.** 3 **3 wks**

Guests: Manitas de Plata with the Syd Lawrence orchestra, Kevin Kent, the Skylarks and the Denys Palmer dancers.
Producer: David Mallet. **Executive Producer:** John Duncan.

1972 7.6 **Thu 3 Feb 9:00 p.m.** 6 **8 wks**

Guests: The Peddlers with the Syd Lawrence orchestra, Aimi Macdonald and the Denys Palmer dancers.
Producer: David Mallet.

1974 6.8 **Fri 1 Mar 8:25 p.m.** 4 **10 wks**

Guests: John Cleese, Salena Jones, Roy Barraclough and Eli Woods, with the Irving Davies dancers and the Peter Husband orchestra.
Director: David Mallet. **Producer:** Bill Hitchcock.

Sez Les Special — 4 wks

YTV, comedy

These one-hour specials featured Les Dawson and friends.

1976 7.3 **Fri 2 Jan 9:00 p.m.** 6 **4 wks**

Guests: Roy Barraclough, Henry Cooper, Dana, Guys and Dolls, Julian Orchard, Cyril Smith MP and Eli Woods, with the Peter Husband orchestra.
Producer: Vernon Lawrence.

Shabby Tiger — 6 wks

Granada, drama

Geoffrey Lancashire adapted Howard Spring's novel in seven parts. The story took Irish servant girl Anna Fitzgerald (Prunella Gee) and painter Nick Faunt (John Nolan) from their first romantic meeting to their life as bohemians in industrial Manchester.

1973 6.4 **Wed 18 Jul 9:00 p.m.** 5 **6 wks**

'A Jealous Mistress'
Nick and Anna decide to set up house together, but Nick insists there be no emotional ties between them.
Designer: Colin Rees. **Director:** Baz Taylor. **Producer:** Richard Everitt.

Shadow on the Sun, A — 1 wk

LWT, drama

This was a two-part adaptation by Allan Scott of the story of Beryl Markham's (Stefanie Powers) life. She was one of the earliest British travellers to Africa, the first woman to fly solo to America, a famous author and a polo-playing horse trainer. Her private life was just as exciting and controversial, embracing three marriages and numerous affairs. Claire Bloom, Peter Bowles, Trevor Eve, James Fox, Nicola Pagett and Timothy West also starred.
Director: Tony Richardson. **Producer:** Tamara Asseyev. **Executive Producer:** Nick Elliott.

1988 10.1 **Sun 17 Jul 7:45 p.m.** 10 **1 wk**

Part One
The story begins in 1906 when Beryl as a child (Serena McGuinness) gets her first glimpse of Kenya. As an adolescent (Alix Dayken) she grows into the extraordinary life of expatriates in East Africa, and develops her taste for adventure.

Shadows of Fear — 7 wks

Thames, drama

This series of plays had fear as the unifying theme.

1970 5.9 **Wed 17 Jun 9:00 p.m.** 1 **1 wk**

'Did You Lock Up?' by Roger Marshall.
Peter and Moira Astle (Michael Craig and Gwen Watford) are celebrating their wedding anniversary at a hotel. At the same time, burglars are breaking into their home. The couple return to find extensive damage to their property. Peter broods and becomes obsessed with preventing a similar incident recurring.
Designer: Fred Pusey. **Producer:** Kim Mills.

1971 7.7 **Tue 2 Feb 9:00 p.m.** 9 **6 wks**

'Repent at Leisure' by Roger Marshall.
Isabel (Elizabeth Sellars) is recently widowed and totally neurotic. On a Caribbean cruise she meets and then marries Harry (George Sewell), a steward. It is a disaster from the start.
Designer: Peter Le Page. **Producer:** Kim Mills.

Shadows Show, The — 1 wk

ATV, music

With several hit records to their credit in their own right Cliff Richard's backing group were rewarded with their own show.

1962 3.8 **Fri 31 Aug 10:10 p.m.** 17 **1 wk**

Guest: Frank Ifield.
Producer: Dicky Leeman.

Shane | 1 wk

Presented by ITV, film

| 1972 | 5.6 | Mon 28 Aug 8:00 p.m. | 3 | 1 wk |

Bank Holiday presentation of a classic western set in 1890 in Wyoming. Starring Alan Ladd in the title role with Jean Arthur, Van Heflin and Jack Palance.
Director: George Stevens.

Shannon | 1 wk

USA presented by BBC, drama

This series created by Albert Ruben starred Kevin Dobson as policeman Jack Shannon, a single-minded cop and a single parent. Charlie Fields appeared as his son John.
Producer: Alvin Sapinsley.

| 1983 | 6.9 | Fri 15 Jul 9:25 p.m. | 18 | 1 wk |

'Beating the Prime' by Paul F. Edwards.
Shannon's partner Norm White (William Lucking) is totally absorbed in his personal problems, thereby putting several lives at risk.
Director: Richard Colla.

Sharp Intake of Breath, A | 14 wks

ATV, situation comedy

This series by various writers including Kenneth Cope, Leslie Duxbury and Ronnie Taylor was about the problems of a young married couple. Peter and Sheila Barnes (David Jason and Jacqueline Clarke) tried to understand and beat 'the system'. Alun Armstrong also starred as Jack Dyson and Richard Wilson was Dr Condon. The programmes featured cartoons by Mel Calman.

| 1978 | 19.8 | Mon 20 Mar 8:00 p.m. | 1 | 5 wks |

'The Gasman Cometh'
Peter discovers freedom of choice and starts an energy crisis.
Writer: Leslie Duxbury. **Producer:** Les Chatfield.

| 1979 | 16.4 | Mon 26 Mar 8:00 p.m. | 5 | 6 wks |

'What About the Workers?'
Peter becomes entangled in someone else's eternal triangle.
Writer: Ronnie Taylor. **Producer:** Les Chatfield.

| 1981 | 13.0 | Mon 10 Aug 8:00 p.m. | 3 | 3 wks |

'Look Who's Coming For Ever'
Peter's father-in-law Dr Condon decides to stay for a fortnight.
Writer: Ronnie Taylor. **Producer:** Stuart Allen.

Shelley | 22 wks

Thames, situation comedy

This series by Peter Tilbury starred Hywel Bennett as Shelley, a university graduate with a working-class background, who tried with ever decreasing success to improve his social and economic standing in the world. He nonetheless retained his sense of superiority over those less well educated than himself.
Producer: Anthony Parker.

| 1980 | | Mon 29 Dec 8:00 p.m. | 2 | 7 wks |

'Of Mice and Men'
Shelley takes a moral stand against the norms of the advertising world.

| 1981 | 17.3 | Mon 5 Jan 8:00 p.m. | 5 | 6 wks |

'Signing On'
The day of reckoning arrives and Shelley goes to his local DHSS office.

| 1982 | 12.7 | Thu 18 Feb 9:00 p.m. | 11 | 5 wks |

'Unkindest Cuts'
In spite of cutbacks, full time employment at the Foreign Office looms for Shelley.

| 1983 | 11.4 | Thu 8 Dec 8:00 p.m. | | 3 wks |

'It Nearly Always Happens to Someone Else' by Andy Hamilton.
Shelley is made angry by the casual attitude of the police when he reports his toaster has been stolen.

| 1984 | 12.2 | Thu 12 Jan 9:00 p.m. | 17 | 1 wk |

'Brief Encounter'
Shelley's mother (Sylvia Kay) arranges for him to dine with Fran (Belinda Sinclair), who gave him the elbow weeks ago.

Shenandoah | 1 wk

Presented by BBC, film

| 1970 | 5.9 | Sun 27 Dec 8:15 p.m. | 16 | 1 wk |

A special Christmas week presentation of the film starring James Stewart as Charlie Anderson, a peaceful Virginia farmer who is driven to take up arms to re-unite his family.
Director: Andrew V. McLaglen.

Gwen Watford starred in the Number One edition **Shadows of Fear.**

Sherlock Holmes — 16 wks

BBC, drama

This series starred Douglas Wilmer as Sherlock Holmes and Nigel Stock as Dr Watson. In 1968 Peter Cushing played the title role.

1965 | **5.0** | **Sat 8 May 8:30 p.m.** | **19** | **1 wk**

'The Disappearance of Lady Frances Carfax' dramatized by Vincent Tilsley.
When Lady Carfax (Sheila Shand Gibbs) goes missing without explanation Holmes is called in to investigate. Also stars Joss Ackland as the Hon. Philip Green and Ronald Radd as Dr Shlessinger. **Designer:** Roy Oxley. **Director:** Shaun Sutton. **Producer:** David Goddard.

1966 | **4.8** | **Mon 12 Sep 8:00 p.m.** | **20** | **1 wk**

'The Man with the Twisted Lip' dramatized by Jan Read.
Holmes tries to discover how a respectable businessman came to disappear in an East End opium den. Anton Rodgers guest stars as Hugh Boone. **Designer:** Roy Oxley. **Director:** Eric Taylor. **Producer:** David Goddard.

1968 | **7.9** | **Mon 2 Dec 9:05 p.m.** | **1** | **14 wks**

'Shoscombe Old Place' dramatized by Anthony Read.
Holmes tries to fathom the mystery surrounding racehorse trainer Mason (Edward Woodward). One of his horses is a Derby entrant on which much more than money has been staked. **Designer:** Tom Carter. **Director:** Bill Bain. **Producer:** William Sterling.

Sherlock Holmes — 1 wk

Granada, drama

1987 | **12.1** | **Tue 29 Dec 8:00 p.m.** | **15** | **1 wk**

'The Sign of Four' adapted by John Hawkesworth.
This special two-hour presentation marks the centenary of the first appearance of Sherlock Holmes (Jeremy Brett) and Dr Watson (Edward Hardwicke) in Arthur Conan Doyle's first book, A Study in Scarlet, published in 1887. They pursue a murderer and a priceless hoard of Indian treasure. Also starring Emrys James, Ronald Lacey, Jenny Seagrove and John Thaw.
Director: Peter Hammond. **Producer:** June Wyndham Davies. **Executive Producer:** Michael Cox.

Shillingbury Blowers, The — 1 wk

ATV, drama

1980 | **16.2** | **Sun 6 Jan 7:45 p.m.** | **8** | **1 wk**

A single comedy by Francis Essex. The Blowers are the members of a village brass band. They are not very good. When pop musician Peter (Robin Nedwell) arrives in the village and becomes involved with the band, Old Saltie (Trevor Howard), who has been the conductor for years, gets the sack. Also starring Joe Black, Jack Douglas, Diane Keen, Sam Kydd and John Le Mesurier.
Director: Val Guest. **Producer:** Greg Smith.

Shillingbury Tales, The — 2 wks

ATV, situation comedy

This series by Francis Essex developed from THE SHILLINGBURY BLOWERS. Robin Nedwell, Diane Keen, Lionel Jeffries, Bernard Cribbins and Jack Douglas starred.

1981 | **14.4** | **Sun 7 Jun 7:15 p.m.** | **3** | **2 wks**

'The Shillingbury Legend'
A French Major (Jean Pierre Cassel) comes to the village to re-live his war memories. He also brings his beautiful daughter (Diane Stolojan). **Director:** Val Guest. **Producer:** Greg Smith.

Shine on Harvey Moon — 23 wks

Central/Witzend, situation comedy

This series by Laurence Marks and Maurice Gran followed Harvey Moon (Kenneth Cranham) after his demobilization from the RAF in 1946. The former stores clerk had to face postwar austerity.
Director: Baz Taylor. **Producer:** Tony Charles. **Executive Producer:** Allan McKeown.

1982 | **16.4** | **Fri 8 Jan 8:30 p.m.** | **5** | **6 wks**

'Hail the Conquering Hero'
Corporal Harvey Moon arrives back from the war to no home, no wife and no kids.

1984 | **9.3** | **Fri 1 Jun 9:00 p.m.** | **5** | **9 wks**

'Goodnight Sweetheart'
In July 1946 Harvey's home is destroyed by a previously unexploded bomb. He has to move into lodgings.

1985 | **11.6** | **Fri 23 Aug 9:00 p.m.** | **5** | **8 wks**

'Love and Marriage'
It is April 1948, and Harvey has a problem with the Labour Party.

Shirley Bassey — 6 wks

BBC, music

Shirley Bassey became a major star in the 1950s. She made occasional guest appearances on television over the following two decades, but it was not until 1976 that she agreed to star in a series of her own. With the Arthur Greenslade orchestra and the Nigel Lythgoe dancers.
Producer: Stewart Morris.

| 1976 | 7.0 | Sat 30 Oct 8:15 p.m. | 17 | 3 wks |

Guests: Charles Aznavour and the Three Degrees.

| 1979 | 20.4 | Sat 13 Oct 8:15 p.m. | 8 | 3 wks |

Guests: Freddy Cole, Paul Daniels and Tony Monopoly.

....

Shoestring | | | | 22 wks

BBC, drama

This thriller series created and produced by Robert Banks Stewart starred Trevor Eve as Eddie Shoestring, a West Country local radio reporter who tackled mysteries brought his way by listeners and friends. It also featured Michael Medwin as Don Satchley, Doran Godwin as Erica Bayliss and Liz Crowther as Sonia.

| 1979 | 20.7 | Sun 21 Oct 9:15 p.m. | 2 | 10 wks |

'An Uncertain Circle' by Robert Bennett.
Eddie is involved in the search for a missing photographer.
Director: Mike Vardy.

| 1980 | 12.9 | Sun 21 Dec 9:20 p.m. | 20 | 1 wk |

'The Dangerous Game' by Chris Boucher.
Eddie finds that Father Christmas is getting his toys off the back of a lorry. Guest star: Michael Elphick.
Director: Ben Bolt.

| 1981 | 12.2 | Wed 1 Sep 9:25 p.m. | 5 | 4 wks |

'Higher Ground' by Dave Humphries.
Major Hansford (Glyn Houston) is not the sort of man to crack easily, but his strength is tested when his wife rings Shoestring. (Repeat.)
Director: Marek Kanievska.

| 1982 | 12.8 | Thu 25 Feb 9:25 p.m. | 13 | 7 wks |

'Looking For Mr Wright' by Robert Bennett.
There is more than dignity at stake when a dating agency provides a total mismatch. Guest star: Diana Dors. (Repeat.)
Director: Laurence Moody.

....

Shogun | | | | 3 wks

USA presented by BBC, drama

This serial in five parts by James Clavell was inspired by the true story of Will Adams, a sailor in Elizabethan times who became the only non-Japanese Samurai. Richard Chamberlain starred with Alan Badel, Michael Hordern, Toshiro Mifune and Yoko Shimada.
Director: Jerry London. **Producer:** Eric Bercovici. **Executive Producer:** James Clavell.

| 1982 | 10.8 | Sat 27 Nov 9:05 p.m. | 17 | 3 wks |

Episode Two
Having suffered frightening and humiliating experiences in Anjiro, John Blackthorne (Richard Chamberlain) is sent to Osaka's death row prison under orders from Lord Ishido (Nobuo Kaneko). No one sent there has ever survived.

....

Short Circuit | | | | 2 wks

Presented by BBC, film

| 1989 | | Fri 29 Dec 7:25 p.m. | 18 | 1 wk |

A robot goes on the run. Steve Guttenberg and Ally Sheedy star.
Director: John Badham.

| 1991 | 12.1 | Sat 23 Nov 8:05 p.m. | 20 | 1 wk |

Repeat showing of the above film.

....

Shout at the Devil | | | | 2 wks

Presented by ITV, film

| 1981 | 12.5 | Mon 20 Apr 7:30 p.m. | 14 | 1 wk |

Easter Monday showing of this film. Lee Marvin stars as Flynn O'Flynn, based in Portuguese East Africa in 1913 but making raids into German territory to steal ivory and other treasures. Also starring Maurice Denham, Ian Holm, Jean Kent, Roger Moore and Barbara Perkins.
Director: Peter Hunt.

| 1982 | 12.1 | Sun 10 Oct 7:15 p.m. | 7 | 1 wk |

Repeat showing of the above film.

....

Show of My Own, A | | | | 1 wk

YTV, entertainment

| 1977 | 5.9 | Mon 11 Jul 8:00 p.m. | 15 | 1 wk |

This one-off special stars singer and impressionist Dave Evans. Guests: Felix Bowness, Norman Chappell, Lyn Paul and the Ken Jones orchestra.
Producer: Vernon Lawrence.

S

Showdown
`1 wk`

Presented by ITV, film

1978	11.7	Thu 6 Jul 7:45 p.m.	15	1 wk

Set in New Mexico in the late nineteenth century. Sheriff Jarvis (Rock Hudson) is saddened to learn that his lifelong friend Billy Massey (Dean Martin) has been identified as one of a gang of train robbers. **Director:** George Seaton.

....

Showtime
`2 wks`

ATV, entertainment

These occasional one-hour specials featured various entertainers and the Johnny Patrick orchestra.

1978	12.9	Wed 1 Nov 8:00 p.m.	18	1 wk

Starring Patti Boulaye, Peter Cook and Dudley Moore, Derek Griffiths, Mike Lancaster, Diane Langton and Wayne Sleep. With the Irving Davies dancers and the Maggie Stredder singers. **Producer:** Chris Tookey.

1979	11.7	Wed 23 May 8:00 p.m.	12	1 wk

Don Maclean introduces Karen Kay, Mary O'Hara, Wayne Sleep and Frankie Vaughan, with the Ladybirds, the Bob Clarke ensemble, Diana Cousins, Jack Haig and Dave Ismay. **Producer:** Chris Tookey.

....

Shroud for a Nightingale
`5 wks`

Anglia, drama

This P. D. James story was adapted in five parts by Robin Chapman. Adam Dalgliesh (Roy Marsden) of Scotland Yard conducted a murder enquiry in a hospital called Nightingale House. When his principal suspect died suspicion turned on several others, including consultant surgeon Stephen Courtney Briggs (Joss Ackland) and Matron Mary Taylor (Sheila Allen). **Designer:** Jon Pusey. **Director:** John Gorrie. **Producer:** John Rosenberg.

1984	13.6	Fri 6 Apr 8:30 p.m.	6	5 wks

Dalgliesh's young assistant John Massingham (John Vine) is becoming impatient with the case, but there is still insufficient evidence to trap the clever and determined murderer. Time is running out for Dalgliesh, and other lives may be at risk.

....

Shut That Door
`14 wks`

ATV, entertainment

This series starred comedian Larry Grayson. With the Jack Parnell orchestra.
Producer: Colin Clews

1972	6.6	Fri 8 Sep 7:00 p.m.	1	4 wks

Guests: Noele Gordon and Rod Hull and Emu.

1973	7.5	Wed 18 Apr 8:00 p.m.	2	7 wks

Guests: Max Bygraves and the Kaye Sisters.

1974	6.9	Wed 27 Feb 8:25 p.m.	14	1 wk

Guests: Noele Gordon and Rod Hull and Emu.

1975	6.7	Fri 2 May 7:30 p.m.	16	2 wks

Guests: Bob Blackman, David Nixon and Leslie Sarony.

....

Side By Side
`1 wk`

Thames, music

1978	13.9	Wed 8 Nov 8:00 p.m.	20	1 wk

Max Bygraves and Vera Lynn share a show with the Geoff Love orchestra and the Mike Sammes singers.
Director: Keith Beckett. **Producer:** Dave Clark.

....

Silent Evidence
`2 wks`

BBC, drama

This series was created by Evelyn Frazer about the work of police pathologists. Basil Sydney starred as Dr Martin Westlake and Conrad Phillips as Detective Superintendent Evans.

1962	4.6	Wed 29 Aug 9:25 p.m.	11	2 wks

'The Chosen Instrument'
A body is discovered on the Essex marshes. Westlake's findings contradict all the other evidence.
Designer: Stephen Bundy. **Producer:** Patrick Dromgoole.

....

Silver Jubilee Monday
`1 wk`

BBC, entertainment

1977	7.7	Mon 6 Jun 9:50 p.m.	1	1 wk

Raymond Baxter commentates as Her Majesty The Queen lights the first bonfire in a nationwide chain, each one visible to the next until the entire UK is linked to Windsor by beacons. This is followed by a firework display at the castle where the bands of the Royal Horse Guards and Life Guards perform. Max Boyce and the Pendyrus Male Choir sing their toast from Cardiff Castle. The Queen's Own Highlanders play and dance in the Great Hall of Edinburgh Castle, two hundred

children sing at Dunluce Castle in Northern Ireland and there are satellite links to New Zealand and Barbados.
Television presentation: Michael Begg.

Silver Jubilee Thursday | 1 wk

BBC, entertainment

| 1977 | 6.0 | Thu 9 Jun 9:50 p.m. | 13 | 1 wk |

Following a boat journey up the Thames, Her Majesty The Queen and HRH The Duke of Edinburgh watch tonight's Royal River Pageant from the terrace of County Hall. They then tour the newly completed Jubilee Gardens on the site of the 1951 Festival of Britain and witness a firework display. The programme is introduced by Michael Barratt with commentary from Richard Baker and Raymond Baxter.
Executive Producer: Philip S. Gilbert.

Silver Jubilee Variety Gala, The | 1 wk

ATV, entertainment

| 1977 | 21.2 | Sun 4 Dec 7:15 p.m. | 1 | 1 wk |

Replacing THE ROYAL VARIETY PERFORMANCE for one year, Bob Hope introduces Julie Andrews, Paul Anka, Pam Ayres, Harry Belafonte, Brotherhood of Man, Tommy Cooper, Alan King, Cleo Laine with John Dankworth and John Williams, Little and Large, Rich Little, Shirley MacLaine, the Muppets, Rudolf Nureyev and Yoko Morishita.
Stage Director: Robert Nesbitt. **Television presentation:** Gary Smith and Dwight Hemion.

Silver Streak | 3 wks

Presented by ITV, film

| 1982 | 9.6 | Mon 31 May 8:00 p.m. | 11 | 1 wk |

Murder and romance are part of a train journey to Chicago. The train does not stop at the buffers and ploughs into the station. Richard Pryor and Gene Wilder star with Jill Clayburgh and Patrick McGoohan.
Director: Arthur Hiller.

| 1984 | 13.4 | Sat 25 Feb 8:00 p.m. | 11 | 1 wk |
| 1988 | 10.0 | Wed 11 May 8:00 p.m. | 11 | 1 wk |

Repeat showings of the above film.

Simon And Simon | 8 wks

USA presented by ITV, drama

This series was about two brothers who ran a private detective agency in San Diego. It was created and produced by Philip DeGuere.

Jameson Parker and Gerald McRaney portrayed A.J. and Rick Simon.

| 1984 | 10.7 | Fri 1 Jun 7:30 p.m. | 7 | 8 wks |

'Murder Between the Lines'
An author of thrillers is convinced he will be the next victim of a murderer.

Sinbad and the Eye of the Tiger | 1 wk

Presented by ITV, film

| 1982 | 9.5 | Tue 22 Jun 7:00 p.m. | 14 | 1 wk |

Patrick Wayne stars as Sinbad in a story of oriental witchcraft and black magic. He seeks to marry Princess Farah (Jane Seymour).
Director: Sam Wanamaker.

Sing a Song of Emu | 1 wk

BBC, children

This series starred Australian entertainer Rod Hull and his puppet Emu. Broadcast from Manchester, the shows featured the children of local schools.

| 1975 | 6.8 | Sat 24 May 5:05 p.m. | 15 | 1 wk |

Three hundred children sing some of their favourite songs, accompanied by the band of Oulder Hill School, Rochdale.
Producer: Hazel Lewthwaite.

Sing a Song of Sixpence | 13 wks

AR, game show

In this musical game, hosted by Ronan O'Casey and Anne Nightingale, a celebrity panel's knowledge of song lyrics was tested.

| 1965 | 6.6 | Fri 10 Sep 7:00 p.m. | 5 | 13 wks |

The panel includes Hermione Gingold, Jon Pertwee and Jonathan Routh.
Producer: Peter Yolland.

Sing Sing Sing | 2 wks

AR, music

Canadian singer Gino Silvi recorded two programmes with his singers and the Bert Niosi orchestra during his visit to England.

| 1964 | 5.2 | Wed 19 Aug 9:10 p.m. | 14 | 2 wks |

Producer: Norman Sedawie.

Larry Grayson titled the series **Shut that Door** after his personal catch phrase.

Singalongamax
8 wks

ATV, music

This series starred Max Bygraves.

| 1973 | 6.8 | Mon 17 Sep 8:00 p.m. | 6 | 8 wks |

Guests: The Coffee Set and the Kaye Sisters, with the Jack Parnell orchestra.
Producer: Colin Clews.

Singalong Saturday
1 wk

BBC, music

This series was introduced by and starred Val Doonican with the Cliff Adams singers, the Countrymen and the Jack Embloy Quartet. It featured drawings by Tony Hart.

| 1964 | 6.8 | Sat 4 Jul 8:25 p.m. | 17 | 1 wk |

Guest: Anne Shelton.
Producer: Travers Thorneloe.

Singing Years, The
2 wks

BBC, music

BBC's Mr Music during the 1950s and early 60s was Eric Robinson. He selected and presented his favourite tunes of the century for this series.

| 1962 | 4.8 | Wed 17 Jan 8:45 p.m. | 14 | 2 wks |

With Sheila Buxton, Andy Cole, Benny Lee, Dennis Lotis, Stephanie Voss, the George Mitchell Minstrels and the Eric Robinson orchestra.
Choreographer: Douglas Squires. **Producer:** Johnnie Stewart.

Singles
1 wk

YTV, situation comedy

This series by Eric Chappell and Jean Warr focused on two couples who met in a singles bar and became involved in a life of deception and intrigue. It starred Roger Rees as Malcolm, Judy Loe as Pamela, Eamon Boland as Clive and Susie Blake as Jackie.

| 1988 | 11.3 | Wed 27 Jan 8:00 p.m. | 20 | 1 wk |

'Encounters'
The first meeting in the bar.
Producer: Vernon Lawrence.

Sink Or Swim
6 wks

BBC, situation comedy

This series by Alex Shearer starred Peter Davison and Robert Glenister as brothers Brian and Steve Webber. Steve bought a leaky narrow boat in Bristol, on which the two brothers intended to live to escape from the pressures of life ashore.
Director: Roger Race. **Executive Producer:** Gareth Gwenlan.

| 1980 | 14.9 | Thu 11 Dec 8:30 p.m. | 10 | 3 wks |

Brian and his kid brother find romantic problems in bed-sit land.

| 1981 | 16.2 | Thu 15 Jan 8:30 p.m. | 5 | 3 wks |

Brian is unwilling to admit defeat, but the damp and primitive conditions are proving too much for Steve.

Sink the Bismarck
1 wk

Presented by BBC, film

| 1968 | 5.6 | Mon 3 Jun 9:15 p.m. | 15 | 1 wk |

The struggle in May 1941 to sink Hitler's mightiest battleship stars Kenneth More as Captain Shepard with Maurice Denham, Michael Goodliffe, Michael Hordern, Geoffrey Keen, Carl Mohner, Laurence Naismith, Jack Watling and Dana Wynter.
Director: Lewis Gilbert.

Sinners, The
11 wks

Granada, drama

This series of humorous short stories involved life in Ireland.

| 1970 | 6.7 | Wed 9 Sep 9:00 p.m. | 3 | 4 wks |

'In the Bosom of the Country' by Sean O'Faolain.
Adapted by Brian Armstrong, the story concerns retired English Major Frank Keane (John Carson) who lives happily hunting, shooting, fishing and enjoying an affair with Mrs Mohan (Barbara Jefford). He receives a phone call which unwillingly involves him in a campaign being waged by the Monsignor (Cyril Cusack).
Designer: Alan Price. **Director:** Barry Davis. **Producer:** Brian Armstrong. **Executive Producer:** Peter Eckersley.

| 1971 | 7.3 | Mon 6 Sep 9:00 p.m. | 3 | 7 wks |

'The Highwayman and the Saint' by Brian Friel.
Adapted by Brian Armstrong, the story concerns a couple who have been courting for years. The woman will not leave her invalid mother for marriage. Not only that, mother never leaves them alone together downstairs and insists they join in family prayers each evening.
Designer: Alan Price. **Director:** Carol Wilkes. **Producer:** Brian Armstrong.

Sins — 2 wks

USA presented by ITV, drama

A three-part mini-series based on the novel by Judith Gould, adapted for TV by Laurence Heath. Joan Collins starred as Helene Junot, who controlled an empire of fashion magazines based in New York. However, she had scores to settle dating back to her days in Paris during the Second World War. She and her family had fought for the French Resistance and suffered under the Nazis. She hoped to find her long lost brother Edmund (Timothy Dalton) and also to find those responsible for the death of her mother. Her enemies were Major Carl Von Eiderfeld (Steven Berkoff), who had in fact butchered her family, Hubert de Ville (Neil Dickson), whose proposal she turned down, Marcello D'Itri (Giancarlo Giannini) whose magazine she bought, and 'ZZ' Bryant (Lauren Hutton), with whose husband she had an affair. Her friends were fashion editor Luba Tcherina (Marisa Berenson), fashion photographer Jacques Danvers (William Allen Young), her one true love Captain David Westfield (James Farentino), fashion model Odile (Capucine) and Helene's husband Eric Horland (Gene Kelly).
Executive Producers: Joan Collins and Peter Holm.

1987	10.9	Mon 7 Sep 8:00 p.m. Tue 8 Sep 8:00 p.m.	12	2 wks

These episodes were listed together in the ratings.

Sir Arthur Conan Doyle — 3 wks

BBC, drama

Seven stories by the author were adapted for television by John Hawkesworth. First shown on BBC2.

1967	5.0	Mon 14 Aug 9:05 p.m.	10	3 wks

'The Mystery of Cader Ifan'
Philip Hardacre (Michael Latimer) has chosen a quiet inn in the Welsh hills for his holiday pursuing his hobby of lepidoptery. His peace and quiet is short-lived when Julia (Charlotte Rampling) arrives.
Designer: Norman James. **Director:** Peter Sasdy. **Producer:** Henry Moore.

Six Dates with Barker — 3 wks

LWT, comedy

These six comedies by six different writers each starred Ronnie Barker and each with a different supporting cast.

1971	6.8	Fri 8 Jan 8:25 p.m.	14	3 wks

'The Removals Person' by Hugh Leonard.
It is Coronation Day, 1937. The Vaile family is moving house. Mrs Vaile (Joan Benham) goes off to watch the procession, leaving her maid (Josephine Tewson) to supervise the removal man, the very shortsighted Fred (Barker). Before the first piece of furniture is out in the street, romance is in the air.
Director: Maurice Murphy. **Producer:** Humphrey Barclay.

Six Days of Justice — 12 wks

Thames, drama

This series of six stories concerned the everyday cases dealt with by magistrate's courts, fictional but exact in procedural detail.

1972	7.5	Mon 1 May 9:00 p.m.	3	6 wks

'Who Cares' by Roger Parkes.
Fifteen-year-old Karen (Verna Harvey) has been sleeping rough, unwanted by her parents. The authorities ask the magistrates for an order to take her into care. Bernard Hepton plays the Chairman of the Bench.
Director: David Wickes. **Producer:** Reginald Collin.

1973	6.6	Tue 1 May 9:00 p.m.	7	6 wks

'The Counsellor' by Rex Edwards.
Estate agent Richard Price (Ivor Roberts) is accused of stealing an antique silver frame from elderly widow Mrs Winrose (Marjorie Yates). As the case progresses a series of ambiguous relationships are unveiled. John Abinieri plays the Chairman of the Bench.
Producer: Peter Duguid.

Six Million Dollar Man, The — 14 wks

USA presented by ITV, drama

This was created by Henri Simoun from the novel Cyborg by Martin Caidin. Lee Majors played Steve Austin, an astronaut, whose body was all but destroyed in a crash. He was rebuilt with powerful artificial limbs and spare parts at a cost of six million dollars, becoming a 'bionic' spy for the Office of Strategic Operations. There he met fellow agent Jaime Sommers (Lindsay Wagner), who had also been rebuilt after a near fatal accident. She eventually had her own spinoff series, THE BIONIC WOMAN.
Producer: Richard Irving.

1975	7.6	Fri 31 Jan 7:30 p.m.	12	9 wks

'Cross-Country Kidnap'
Steve's attempts to protect a young girl from kidnap are thwarted by the girl herself.

1976	7.2	Sun 12 Dec 7:25 p.m.	17	3 wks

'Wine, Women and War'
In this feature-length episode, with guest stars Britt Ekland and David McCallum, Steve investigates a black market in nuclear weapons.

1977	7.6	Fri 11 Mar 7:30 p.m.	17	2 wks

'The Thunderbird Connection'
Steve plots to save the life of a boy who is heir to the throne of a Middle Eastern country which has been taken over by military force.

Six of the Best | 6 wks

ATV, drama

A series of six comedy plays by six different writers, each with a different cast.

| 1965 | 6.1 | Wed 11 Aug 9:10 p.m. | 6 | 6 wks |

'Annie Doesn't Live Here Any More' by Ray Cooney.
Olive is a piano teacher who moves into a flat previously occupied by a lady of easy virtue. When men come looking for Annie, Olive offers them piano lessons. Starring Dora Bryan with John Alderton, Charles Carson and John Collin.
Designer: Michael Eve. **Director:** Albert Locke. **Producer:** Alan Tarrant.

Six of the Best | 1 wk

BBC, documentary

| 1984 | 14.6 | Fri 23 Nov 9:30 p.m. | 7 | 1 wk |

As part of this evening's CHILDREN IN NEED appeal, Bernard Falk presents a film about the lives of the Walton sextuplets. He wrote and produced the programme.

Six Shades of Black | 5 wks

Granada, drama

In these six one-hour plays, written and produced by Peter Wildeblood, one character from each play is carried over into the next – the hero of one becoming the villain of another.

| 1965 | 6.4 | Fri 21 May 9:40 p.m. | 6 | 5 wks |

'A Loving Disposition'
A psychiatrist falls in love with a patient and quickly discovers he has problems of his own. Starring Frederick Bartman, David Langton, Henry McGee, Nyree Dawn Porter and Frank Thornton.
Designer: Michael Grimes. **Director:** Gordon Flemyng.

633 Squadron | 2 wks

Presented by BBC, film

| 1970 | 8.2 | Tue 17 Nov 7:30 p.m. | 2 | 1 wk |

A crack RAF squadron moves in to destroy a Nazi fuel factory constructed on a fjord near Bergen. Starring George Chakiris and Cliff Robertson with Harry Andrews, Donald Houston and Maria Perschy.
Director: Walter Grauman.

| 1973 | 5.8 | Mon 23 Apr 7:45 p.m. | 14 | 1 wk |

A repeat showing of the above film.

Sixth Form Challenge | 13 wks

Granada, game show

This competition derived from UNIVERSITY CHALLENGE used sixth formers instead of undergraduates.
Director: Peter Mullings. **Producer:** Douglas Terry.

| 1966 | 5.5 | Wed 6 Jul 7:00 p.m. | 10 | 11 wks |

Chris Kelly asks the questions as Malvern College face Alleyn's School.

| 1967 | 5.0 | Fri 16 Jun 10:05 p.m. | 13 | 2 wks |

Chris Kelly introduces teams from Eton College and Benenden School.

Sixty-five Years, The | 1 wk

ITN, documentary

| 1965 | 5.4 | Thu 21 Jan 10:55 p.m. | 19 | 1 wk |

With thirty-five years to go to the year 2000, ITN looks back over the first sixty-five years of this century.

$64,000 Question, The | 10 wks

Central, game show

Bob Monkhouse hosted this game in which contestants answered questions on a chosen subject, the money for each successful answer doubling to a maximum £6400. The title of the show came from the name of an American quiz.
Director: Dennis Liddington. **Producer:** Peter Harris.

| 1990 | 10.9 | Fri 8 Jun 7:30 p.m. | 10 | 8 wks |
| 1991 | 12.3 | Fri 1 Nov 7:00 p.m. | 17 | 2 wks |

Skorpion | 1 wk

BBC, drama

This six-part serial by John Brason was adapted from a story by Arden Winch. It starred Terrence Hardiman as Chief Superintendent Franks. He investigated the curious circumstances surrounding a plane crash on the Scottish Moors.

| 1983 | 11.4 | Wed 12 Jan 9:25 p.m. | 17 | 1 wk |

Episode One
A bomb is planted but fails to kill its intended victim.
Designer: Campbell Gordon. **Director:** Michael Hayes. **Producer:** Gerard Glaister.

Sky Riders — 1 wk

Presented by ITV, film

| 1984 | 12.5 | Fri 13 Apr 8:30 p.m. | 4 | 1 wk |

The family of an American businessman is kidnapped in Athens and held to ransom. A soldier of fortune leads a team of hang gliders to their rescue. Starring Charles Aznavour, James Coburn, Robert Culp and Susannah York.
Director: Douglas Hickox.

Sky's the Limit, The — 65 wks

YTV, game show

This travel game show was piloted by Hughie Green with Monica Rose as hostess and the contestants as passengers.
Director: Royston Mayoh. **Producer:** Peter Holmans.

1971	7.2	Fri 26 Nov 6:35 p.m.	5	30 wks
1972	7.0	Fri 4 Feb 7:00 p.m.	7	23 wks
1973	6.2	Fri 4 May 6:20 p.m.	15	10 wks
1974	5.6	Sat 29 Jun 12:00 p.m.	16	2 wks

Director: Keith Beckett. **Producer:** David Millard.

Slapstick and Old Lace — 6 wks

ATV, comedy

This series starred Charlie Drake with Acker Bilk, Anna Dawson and Henry McGee.

| 1971 | 6.4 | Thu 18 Mar 7:50 p.m. | 15 | 6 wks |

The Slapstick mob join the Scots Guards under Sergeant Major McGee.
Director: John Scholz-Conway. **Producer:** Shaun O'Riordan.

Slight White Paper on Love, A — 1 wk

Granada, documentary

This series of three programmes assessed the state of love and marriage in contemporary society.

| 1965 | 5.2 | Wed 5 May 9:40 p.m. | 18 | 1 wk |

'Can This Be Love?'

In this first programme reporters Peter Eckersley, Michael Parkinson, Denis Pitts and Michael Scott examine contemporary courtship and the rituals of boy meets girl. (One segment of the show involved the then unknown model Julie Goodyear. She was fitted with a microphone hidden in her bra and sat alone at the Locarno Ballroom in Sale. The chat-up lines of the men who approached her were duly filmed and recorded.)
Director: David Cunliffe. **Producers:** Peter Eckersley, Leslie Woodhead and David Plowright.

Small Sacrifices — 1 wk

Presented by BBC, film

| 1990 | 10.5 | Tue 31 Jul 9:30 p.m. Wed 1 Aug 9:30 p.m. | 8 | 1 wk |

This film was shown in two parts which were listed together in the ratings. Diane Downs (Farrah Fawcett) is found outside the local hospital with her three children who have all been shot, one fatally. She becomes the prime suspect. Ryan O'Neal and John Shea also star.
Director: David Greene.

Smashing Day, A — 1 wk

BBC, drama

| 1962 | 3.7 | Fri 17 Aug 9:25 p.m. | 16 | 1 wk |

This single drama by Alan Plater stars Alfred Lynch as Lennie, a bewildered nineteen-year-old youth, who expects everything to turn out wrong for him. John Thaw is cast as his smooth self-confident friend Stan. The girls in Lennie's life are Anne (June Barry) and Liz (Angela Douglas).
Designer: Paul Bernard. **Producer:** Vivian A. Daniels.

Smokey and the Bandit — 2 wks

Presented by ITV, film

| 1982 | 11.9 | Tue 28 Dec 7:00 p.m. | 8 | 1 wk |

Burt Reynolds, Sally Field and Jackie Gleason star in the story of a bootlegger who picks up a damsel in distress and is then chased by her fiancé, who happens to be the sheriff.
Director: Hal Needham.

| 1989 | 8.8 | Tue 27 Jun 8:30 p.m. | 17 | 1 wk |

Repeat showing of the above film.

Smokey and the Bandit Ride Again 3 wks

Presented by ITV, film

| 1984 | 14.0 | Sat 7 Apr 8:00 p.m. | 4 | 1 wk |

Burt Reynolds as 'the Bandit' is hired to steal a crate from the State Governor and transport a pregnant elephant to a political convention. Jackie Gleason, Sally Field, Jerry Reed, Dom DeLuise and Paul Williams also star.
Director: Hal Needham.

| 1985 | 11.9 | Thur 29 Aug 7:30 p.m. | 12 | 1 wk |
| 1986 | 9.1 | Sun 15 Jun 7:45 p.m. | 10 | 1 wk |

Repeat showings of the above film.

Snapshot Hour, The 1 wk

AR, entertainment

| 1960 | 5.1 | Wed 31 Aug 8:30 p.m. | 9 | 1 wk |

Hughie Green introduces a programme of song and dance built around photography and viewers' snapshots with John Charles, Jean Clarke, Jill Day, Cornel Lucas, Libby Morris and Rita Webb.
Choreographer: Malcolm Goddard. **Music:** Steve Race. **Writers:** Sid Green and Dick Hills. **Producer:** Bill Hitchcock.

Snooker 7 wks

Various, sport

| 1981 | 13.1 | Mon 20 Apr 5:00 p.m. | 11 | 2 wks |

David Vine introduces the final session of the Embassy World Professional Snooker Championship from the Crucible Theatre, Sheffield. Commentators include Clive Everton, Jack Karnehm, Ted Lowe, and John Pulman. (Steve Davis beat Doug Montjoy.)
BBC television presentation: Nick Hunter.

| 1982 | 12.1 | Sat 6 Mar 9:00 p.m. | 9 | 2 wks |

Dickie Davies introduces the competition for the Yamaha Organs' Trophy from the Assembly Rooms, Derby. John Pulman and Dennis Taylor commentate. (Steve Davis beat Terry Griffiths.)
Central television presentation: Tony Parker and Sid Kilbey.

| 1984 | 8.9 | Mon 7 May 6:50 p.m. | 20 | 1 wk |

David Vine introduces the final frames of the Embassy World Professional Championship from the Crucible Theatre, Sheffield. Commentators include Clive Everton, Jack Karnehm and Ted Lowe. (Steve Davis beat Jimmy White.)
BBC2 television presentation: Nick Hunter.

| 1985 | 16.4 | Sun 13 Jan 3:15 p.m. | 2 | 2 wks |

Dickie Davies introduces matches in the Mercantile Credit Classic from the Spectrum Arena, Warrington.
ITS television presentation: Eric Harrison and Tim Moores.

Snowtime Special 1 wk

BBC, entertainment

| 1978 | 13.5 | Mon 27 Mar 7:55 p.m. | 18 | 1 wk |

The SEASIDE SPECIAL team go winter sporting in Switzerland. Petula Clark introduces Charles Aznavour, Wolfgang Danne and Jillian, Claude François, Udo Jürgens and Manhattan Transfer, with Jeff Richer's First Edition and the Maggie Stredder singers.
Producer: Michael Hurll.

So Many Children 1 wk

Westward, documentary

| 1967 | 4.7 | Tue 11 Jul 8:45 p.m. | 12 | 1 wk |

There are many mentally handicapped children in Britain. This film looks at the special work of the Downham Training Centre in Plymouth and talks to teachers and parents.
Director: David Scott. **Writer** and **Producer:** John Pett.

So You Think . . . 5 wks

BBC, documentary

In this series Cliff Michelmore and Magnus Magnusson asked viewers to compete with three studio teams on their knowledge of a particular subject.

| 1965 | 4.6 | Tue 24 Aug 9:25 p.m. | 18 | 1 wk |

'. . .You Can Drive?'
Teams are confronted with filmed accidents, road hazards and general motoring quiz questions. Team members include veterans, novices, professionals and family drivers.
Producer: Tim Slessor.

| 1966 | 4.8 | Thu 7 Jul 9:25 p.m. | 20 | 1 wk |

'. . . You Know Your Rights?'
Teams face the problems of buying a house, a car, doing the daily shopping and some general questions on the legal rights of the citizen. Members of the teams include people born in Britain, foreigners resident here and legal practitioners.
Producer: Paul Bonner.

| 1968 | 4.5 | Thu 8 Aug 9:05 p.m. | 18 | 1 wk |

'. . . You Know Fitness?'
The teams of district nurses, sportsmen and sportsmen's wives face questions on healthy living, diet and exercise.
Producer: *John Bird.*

| 1969 | 6.5 | Tue 22 Apr 9:05 p.m. | 7 | 1 wk |

'. . . You Know Children?'
Teams of children, parents and experts (paediatrician, headmistress, psychotherapist and a children's officer) are questioned on the rights and duties of both parents and children.
Director: *Roger Price.* **Producer:** *Patricia Owtram.*

| 1970 | 6.9 | Tue 20 Oct 9:20 p.m. | 7 | 1 wk |

'. . . You're a Good Wife?'
Points are gained for being good company, understanding, practical and tolerant while points are lost for nagging, outbursts of panic or letting the man down in public. Jimmy Young checks up on the wives' shopping abilities. Taking part (with husbands there to ensure no cheating) are Elspet Gray (Brian Rix), Margaret Powell (Albert Powell), Kathy Peters (Martin Peters) and Jean Metcalfe (Cliff Michelmore).
Producer: *Patricia Owtram.*

....

| Soft Touch, A | | 4 wks |

ATV, situation comedy

This series by Connor Fraser starred John Flanagan as Jack Holmes and Maureen Lipman as his wife Alison. Jack dreamed of a show business career but Alison hoped he would find a proper job.

| 1978 | 12.3 | Mon 11 Sep 8:00 p.m. | 9 | 4 wks |

'I Wanna Be Like You'
Jack's latest journey into cloud cuckoo land is to become a model.
Producer: *Les Chatfield.*

....

| Softly, Softly | | 121 wks |

BBC, drama

Originally a spinoff from Z CARS, this series created by Elwyn Jones forged its own identity with Stratford Johns as Detective-Chief Superintendent Barlow, Frank Windsor as Detective Superintendent Watt, Norman Bowler as Detective Inspector Hawkins and Terence Rigby as P C Snow.
Producers: *David E. Rose (1966–67), Leonard Lewis (1968–73) and Geraint Morris (1974–5).*

| 1966 | 5.8 | Wed 23 Nov 8:00 p.m. | 18 | 9 wks |

'Murder Reported' by Elwyn Jones.
Barlow's manpower diplomacy is strongly tested as Detective Superintendent Arthur Jones (Glyn Houston) leads a murder hunt for only the second time in his career.
Director: *Philip Dudley.*

| 1967 | 6.3 | Wed 8 Mar 8:00 p.m. | 13 | 7 wks |

'The Same the Whole World Over' by Alan Plater.
The Regional Crime Squad is on the trail of a gang of robbers.
Director: *Leonard Lewis.*

| 1968 | 6.9 | Thu 7 Mar 8:00 p.m. | 8 | 26 wks |

'Finger of Suspicion' by Allan Prior.
For seven weeks a safe has been blown at the rate of one a week on Barlow's patch.
Director: *Moira Armstrong.*

| 1969 | 6.6 | Thu 4 Dec 8:00 p.m. | 10 | 18 wks |

'Diversion' by Robert Barr.
Routine enquiries into a series of minor break-ins become a major hunt for a dangerous criminal.
Director: *Vere Lorrimer.*

| 1970 | 6.7 | Wed 2 Dec 8:10 p.m. | 10 | 11 wks |

'Do Me A Favour' by Robert Barr.
This story illustrates the dangers of listening to a fast-talking stranger who knocks at the door.
Director: *Brian Parker.*

| 1971 | 7.0 | Wed 6 Jan 8:10 p.m. | 11 | 10 wks |

'Ground Level' by Alan Plater.
The Task Force is sent to investigate theft at a building site.
Director: *David Proudfoot.*

| 1972 | 7.3 | Wed 18 Oct 8:10 p.m. | 5 | 22 wks |

'On The Third Day' by Elwyn Jones.
The tables are turned as Barlow is asked questions in a series of interviews by police assessors.
Director: *Gilchrist Calder.*

| 1973 | 6.7 | Wed 14 Nov 8:10 p.m. | 10 | 9 wks |

'Interrogation' by Robert Barr.
The same gun is used on two different jobs, but there is uncertainty as to whether it was used by the same man on both occasions.
Director: *David Maloney.*

| 1974 | 6.2 | Wed 4 Sep 8:10 p.m. | 11 | 3 wks |

'Alert' by Elwyn Jones.
John Watt tackles a case of attempted plane hijacking.
Director: *David Wickes.*

| 1975 | 6.7 | Wed 8 Oct 8:10 p.m. | 14 | 6 wks |

'And With What Measure?' by Elwyn Jones.
Basil Dignam, Gareth Hunt and Martin Jarvis guest star in the story of a young inexperienced mounted policeman who receives a tip-off from an informer. With Task Force personnel at full stretch decisions have to be made as to the validity of the information.
Director: *Vere Lorrimer.*

Soldier, Soldier — 5 wks

Central, drama

This series about modern life in the British army focused on the officers and men of the King's Fusiliers Infantry Regiment. David Haig starred as Major Tom Kadman with Cathryn Harrison as his wife Laura. Holly Aird, Sean Baker, Robert Glenister, Gary Love and Peter Wingford also starred. The series was originally scheduled for transmission in February but it was delayed because of the Gulf War.

| 1991 | 10.5 | Mon 10 Jun 9:00 p.m. | 11 | 5 wks |

'All the King's Men'
The Regiment returns to its Midlands headquarters following a six-month tour of duty in Northern Ireland.
Director: Laurence Moody. **Producer:** Chris Kelly.

Solo — 7 wks

BBC, situation comedy

This series by Carla Lane starred Felicity Kendal as Gemma Palmer, Stephen Moore as her boyfriend Danny and Elspet Gray as Mrs Palmer. Gemma opted to abandon her job, kick out Danny and lead a solo life following his fling with her friend Gloria. Gemma was fully solo for a second series, Danny having moved away. In that series she was joined by her friend Sebastian, played by Michael Howe.
Producer: Gareth Gwenlan.

| 1981 | 14.8 | Sun 8 Feb 9:10 p.m. | 10 | 4 wks |

Danny has double standards when it comes to sex. He assumes it is a man's right to have the odd one-night stand. Gemma disagrees and once more she goes off alone.

| 1984 | 11.7 | Thu 2 Aug 9:25 p.m. | 2 | 3 wks |

Gemma comforts Sebastian after a painful confrontation with the boyfriend of his latest girl. (Repeat.)

Some Mothers Do 'Ave 'Em — 36 wks

BBC, situation comedy

This series was written by Raymond Allen. Michael Crawford performed dangerous stunts as the simple-minded accident-prone Frank Spencer. Michele Dotrice played his girlfriend and then wife Betty. There were only 13 programmes in the first series and these were repeated many times. In 1978 Crawford returned to the character for a further series.
Producers: Michael Mills (1973, 1974 and the 1980, 1987 and 1990 repeats) and Sydney Lotterby (1978 and the 1979, 1983–84 and 1989 repeats).

| 1973 | 7.9 | Thu 6 Dec 8:30 p.m. | 2 | 11 wks |

Frank tries his hand at public relations – and immediately relations begin to deteriorate. He enrols on a course at the Watson School of Friendship where he causes a total breakdown of the catering services and inspires a fight in the dormitory.

| 1974 | 6.5 | Wed 25 Dec 7:15 p.m. | 7 | 3 wks |

In this special edition Frank and Betty have a baby daughter, Jessica (Emma Ware), who is to be Jesus in the nativity play. Frank plays an angel. Bryan Pringle is Jackson and Cyril Luckham is Father O'Hara.

| 1978 | 20.0 | Sat 11 Nov 8:30 p.m. | 1 | 6 wks |

Frank and Betty have to move house because the council has condemned their home as unfit for habitation despite Frank's DIY efforts. During the move he falls into a barrel of tar.

| 1979 | 20.4 | Fri 5 Oct 7:05 p.m. | 12 | 4 wks |

Frank causes havoc for Dr Mender (Derek Farr) and Detective Sergeant Lang (Bernard Gallagher). (Repeat.)

| 1980 | 13.7 | Mon 29 Dec 6:45 p.m. | 16 | 2 wks |

Repeat of the episode first shown on 25 Dec 1974.

| 1983 | 11.8 | Mon 2 May 6:25 p.m. | 9 | 1 wk |

Repeat of the top 1978 programme.

| 1984 | 11.3 | Sat 17 Mar 6:40 p.m. | 15 | 2 wks |

Frank gets a job as a motorbike courier. (Repeat.)

| 1987 | 11.4 | Tue 15 Dec 8:00 p.m. | 11 | 1 wk |

Frank's harassments rebound, as usual, on the long-suffering Betty. But she remains encouraging. (Repeat.)

| 1989 | 12.6 | Fri 24 Feb 7:35 p.m. | 14 | 3 wks |

Repeat of the top 1984 repeat.

| 1990 | 13.2 | Mon 17 Dec 8:30 p.m. | 10 | 3 wks |

There is a new manager at the Employment Office who refuses to believe that Frank is unemployable. After meeting him, however, he is forced to change his mind. (Repeat.)

Some You Win — 2 wks

Granada, entertainment

This series presented by Lulu, Ted Robbins and Kenneth Williams featured life's winners and losers in interview and through archive footage.

| 1984 | 7.9 | Sat 21 Jul 6:30 p.m. | 18 | 2 wks |

Guests: Lord Denning, Spike Milligan and George Peppard.
Director: Nicholas Ferguson. **Producer:** Geoff Moore. **Executive Producer:** John Hamp.

Somerset Maugham Hour, The | 12 wks

AR, drama

This series of adaptations of W. Somerset Maugham's stories was introduced by Hugh Williams.

| 1960 | 6.6 | Fri 16 Dec 9:35 p.m. | 3 | 8 wks |

'A Man With A Conscience' dramatized by William Woods.
Jean Charvin (David Knight) is driven to crime by his own conscience. Also starring Geraldine McEwan as Marie Louise.
Designer: Fred Pusey. **Director:** Christopher Hodson.

| 1961 | 6.6 | Fri 27 Jan 9:35 p.m. | 3 | 4 wks |

'A Woman of Fifty' dramatized by Stanley Miller.
Laura Green (Jane Barrett) maintains a pleasant serene face. But behind the mask lies a story of tragedy. Also starring Derrick Sherwin and Karel Stepanek.
Designer: Frank Nerini. **Director:** Ronald Marriott. **Producer:** Norman Marshall.

Something in Disguise | 5 wks

Thames, drama

This comedy serial by Elizabeth Jane Howard concerned an eccentric couple, Herbert and May Browne-Lacey, played by Richard Vernon and Ursula Howells. It was a second marriage for both of them. Her children Liz and Oliver (Elizabeth Garvie and David Gwillim) both considered the union a grave mistake, as did his daughter Alice (Clare Clifford), who was married to Leslie Mount (Barry Stanton).

| 1982 | 10.1 | Wed 14 Jul 9:00 p.m. | 11 | 5 wks |

'First Sight'
Liz sets her sights on millionaire John Cole (Anton Rodgers).
Designer: Robin Parker. **Director:** Moira Armstrong. **Executive Producer:** John Frankau.

Somewhere in Time | 1 wk

Presented by ITV, film

| 1984 | 9.8 | Wed 16 May 8:00 p.m. | 17 | 1 wk |

Playwright Richard Collier (Christopher Reeve) experiments with forces beyond his control when he travels back in time to reach an actress whom he had loved in a previous incarnation. Christopher Plummer and Jane Seymour also star.
Director: Jeannot Szwarc.

Somewhere To Run | 1 wk

Thames, drama

| 1989 | 9.3 | Tue 11 Jul 8:30 p.m. | 13 | 1 wk |

This single drama by Matthew Jacobs focuses on fourteen-year-old Sarah (Robin Weaver) and sixteen-year-old Debbie (Victoria Murdock). They are runaways on the streets of London, both victims of neglect and sexual abuse. Michael Jayston, Angela Pleasence, Natasha Pyne and Josette Simon also star.
Designer: Peter Joyce. **Director:** Carol Wiseman. **Producer:** Alan Horrox.

Song for Europe, A | 5 wks

BBC, music

In 1966 Kenneth McKellar sang all five songs competing to be the British entry for The Eurovision Song Contest. In subsequent years artists performed the competing songs within the framework of another series (e. g. THE CLIFF RICHARD SHOW or THE ROLF HARRIS SHOW) on a one song per week basis. However, from 1976 songs and their singers were brought together in a ninety-minute show.
Producer (1976, 1978 and 1981): Stewart Morris.

| 1966 | 6.6 | Thu 27 Jan 9:00 p.m. | 15 | 2 wks |

David Jacobs introduces Kenneth McKellar and the Malcolm Lockyer orchestra, who perform the five competing songs.
Producer: Yvonne Littlewood.

| 1976 | 6.3 | Wed 25 Feb 7:30 p.m. | 18 | 1 wk |

Michael Aspel introduces the singers: Brotherhood of Man, Polly Brown, Champagne, Tony Christie, Co-Co, Hazel Dean, Frank Ifield, Tammy Jones, Sunshine, Sweet Dreams, Joey Valentine and Louisa Jane White with the Alyn Ainsworth orchestra.

| 1978 | 13.7 | Fri 31 Mar 7:30 p.m. | 16 | 1 wk |

Terry Wogan introduces the singers: Babe Rainbow, Brown Sugar, Christian, Co-Co, Ronnie France, the Fruit Eating Bears, Bob James, the Jarvis Brothers, Midnight, Labi Siffre, Jacquie Sullivan and Sunshine with the Alyn Ainsworth orchestra.

| 1981 | 12.4 | Wed 11 Mar 8:05 p.m. | 16 | 1 wk |

Terry Wogan introduces the singers: Gary Benson, Beyond, Bucks Fizz, Leylee Carling, Gem, Headache, Liquid Gold and Unity with the John Coleman orchestra.

Song for Everyone, A | 1 wk

BBC, music

During this series Kenneth McKellar sang the songs bidding to represent the UK in the Eurovision Song Contest 1966. In the last show of the series he reprised the final five in A SONG FOR EUROPE. With the Harry Rabinowitz orchestra.

| 1965 | 5.0 | Thu 23 Dec 9:00 p.m. | 18 | 1 wk |

Producer: Yvonne Littlewood.

....

Sophie Tucker Half Hour, The | 1 wk

ATV, music

American entertainer Sophie Tucker, 'The Last of the Red Hot Mommas', was always popular in Britain. In 1934 she became the first American to appear in a ROYAL VARIETY PERFORMANCE. She died on 10 June 1966.

| 1961 | 5.2 | Wed 6 Sep 8:00 p.m. | 12 | 1 wk |

At the age of seventy-one Sophie is in ATV's Elstree studios with guests Kenny Ball and his Jazzmen, the Tiller Girls and the Jack Parnell orchestra.
Producer: Colin Clews.

....

Sorrell and Son | 6 wks

YTV, drama

Jeremy Paul dramatized this novel by Warwick Deeping in six parts. Richard Pasco starred as Captain Sorrell MC, who emerged from the First World War unemployed, deserted by his wife and left to raise his young son Kit (Paul Critchley) alone. The series also starred Stephanie Beacham, John Shrapnel, Malcolm Terris and Gwen Watford.

| 1984 | 10.0 | Wed 6 Jun 9:00 p.m. | 7 | 6 wks |

In the first episode, Sorrell returns home to emptiness.
Designer: Mike Long. **Producer:** Derek Bennett. **Executive Producer:** David Cunliffe.

....

Sorry | 16 wks

BBC, situation comedy

This series by Ian Davidson and Peter Vincent starred Ronnie Corbett as Timothy Lumsden, a middle-aged man unable to break away from his mother (Barbara Lott). William Moore played his father.
Producer: David Askey.

| 1981 | 16.8 | Thu 9 Apr 8:30 p.m. | 1 | 6 wks |

Chief librarian Tim thinks he might at last break away. He is intent on seeing Gone With the Wind, but fate, his mother and his own mismanagement prevent him.

| 1982 | 11.1 | Thu 28 Oct 8:00 p.m. | 13 | 2 wks |

Tim takes tea with his mother's friend Freddie (Sheila Fearn). She turns out to be nicer than he expected.

| 1984 | 10.8 | Tue 22 May 7:40 p.m. | 14 | 2 wks |

Tim's reputation as a librarian is tarnished and it's all his mother's doing. (Repeat.)

| 1986 | 9.8 | Sat 12 May 7:20 p.m. | 16 | 2 wks |

'Every Clown Wants To Play Hamlet'
Tim is the prompter in the local amateur production of Hamlet.

| 1987 | 12.1 | Mon 22 Jun 8:30 p.m. | 5 | 4 wks |

'Gone But Not Forgotten'
Even though she's away, Mother still dominates Tim's life.

....

Sorry, I'm a Stranger Here Myself | 10 wks

Thames, situation comedy

This series by David Firth and Peter Tilbury starred Robin Bailey as Henry Nunn, whose uncle left him the house in which he had grown up.
Producer: Anthony Parker.

| 1981 | 12.2 | Mon 29 Jun 8:00 p.m. | 6 | 7 wks |

'Arrival'
Henry meets his neighbours, the nosy Tom and Doreen (David Hargreaves and Diana Rayworth) on one side and the curry-cooking Mumtaz (Nadim Sawalha) on the other.

| 1982 | 11.4 | Tue 13 Apr 8:00 p.m. | 17 | 3 wks |

'Whither Henry'
Henry has just about had enough of well-meaning interference from neighbours.

....

Sorry I'm Single | 1 wk

BBC, situation comedy

This series created and written by Ronald Wolfe and Ronald Chesney was set in flatlets in Hampstead. The tenants were David (Derek Nimmo), Brenda (Gwendolyn Watts), Karen (Elizabeth Knight) and Suzy (Pik-Sen Lim).

| 1967 | 4.4 | Tue 1 Aug 7:30 p.m. | 20 | 1 wk |

'Cleaning Up'
Karen is constantly feuding with the recently divorced Brenda while Suzy and the eternal student David saunter placidly onwards.
Producer: John Street.

Sound Barrier, The   1 wk

Presented by BBC, film

| 1968 | 7.2 | Tue 31 Dec 9:05 p.m. | 5 | 1 wk |

David Lean filmed Terrence Rattigan's screenplay of the plane makers and fliers of the Second World War who drove themselves beyond the limits of endurance to conquer the mysteries of supersonic flight. Starring Nigel Patrick, Ralph Richardson and Ann Todd.

Sound of Laughter, The   1 wk

ATV, situation comedy

This series of six single comedy plays, by different writers, used different actors each week.

| 1977 | 5.4 | Thu 28 Jul 6:30 p.m. | 20 | 1 wk |

'Young at Heart' by Ronnie Taylor.
Two doting grandfathers, Albert Sculley (Stratford Johns) and Leonard Jarvis (Richard Pearson), compete for the affections of their little grandson.
Producer: Les Chatfield.

Sound of Motown, The   1 wk

AR, music

| 1965 | 5.3 | Wed 28 Apr 9:40 p.m. | 19 | 1 wk |

Dusty Springfield introduces the stars of the famous Detroit record company: Martha and the Vandellas, Smokey Robinson and the Miracles, the Supremes, the Temptations, Stevie Wonder and the Earl Van Dyke sextet. With the Malcolm Clare dancers.
Director: Rollo Gamble.

Sound of Music, The   1 wk

Presented by BBC, film

| 1978 | 18.5 | Mon 25 Dec 4:20 p.m. | 2 | 1 wk |

The film of the musical by Rodgers and Hammerstein. Julie Andrews and Christopher Plummer star as Maria and Captain von Trapp.
Director: Robert Wise.

Sounds Like Les Dawson   1 wk

YTV, entertainment

| 1974 | 7.2 | Wed 4 Dec 8:00 p.m. | 12 | 1 wk |

This one-hour special stars Les with Roy Barraclough, John Gower, Olivia Newton-John and the Second Generation.
Choreographer: Dougie Squires. **Musical Director:** Peter Husband. **Producer:** Vernon Lawrence.

South America   1 wk

ATV, documentary

| 1962 | 5.3 | Wed 7 Feb 9:45 p.m. | 12 | 1 wk |

On the eve of the Duke of Edinburgh's two-month tour of eleven South American countries, James Morris presents his personal impression of the Andes, the Amazon Jungle, the Rio carnival, gauchos, the land of the Incas and the new city of Brasilia.
Producer: James Bredin.

South Riding   3 wks

YTV, drama

These stories by Winifred Holtby, dramatized by Stan Barstow, were about the lives of people in the fictitious South Riding of Yorkshire. Thirteen one-hour episodes starred Hermione Baddeley as Alderman Mrs Beddows, Nigel Davenport as Councillor Robert Carne and Dorothy Tutin as Sarah Burton, a headmistress.

| 1974 | 6.2 | Mon 23 Sep 9:00 p.m. | 17 | 3 wks |

'A Land of Hope and Glory'
It is August 1932. Sarah Burton, the headmistress of Kipling Girls High School, finds life more difficult than anticipated. There appear to be different rules for the rich and the poor.
Designers: Jane Martin, Chris George, and Gordon Livesey. **Producer:** James Ormerod.

Soviet State Circus, The   2 wks

BBC by arrangement with Central TV of USSR, circus

This was transmitted in two parts.

| 1963 | 6.0 | Sat 30 Nov 8:10 p.m. | 15 | 2 wks |

Part Two
The circus was filmed during performances of the Moscow State Circus, the Georgian State Circus, the Rostov State Circus and the Leningrad State Circus. Starring Oleg Popov with Filatov's bears, Almanuskus Varyakoino's Lithuanian Liberty Pigs, Abdulayev the jug juggling shepherd from Azerbaijan, the Volanski family on the high wire, Ali-Bek and his riders, and the Mikituk trio of foot jugglers.
Television presentation: Gherman Livanov and Derek Burrell-Davis.

Ronnie Corbett and Barbara Lott played a middle-aged man and his possessive mother in **Sorry**.

Space Raiders — 1 wk

Presented by BBC, film

| 1989 | 8.0 | Fri 4 Aug 7:40 p.m. | 20 | 1 wk |

Far in the future a distant planet is raided by pirates from another galaxy.
Director: Howard R. Cohen.

Space Shuttle, The — 2 wks

BBC/ITN, news

| 1981 | 12.9 | Tue 14 Apr 6:55 p.m./BBC 7:00 p.m./ITV | 8 | 2 wks |

(The Space Shuttle Columbia took off from Cape Canaveral in Florida on Sunday 12 April 1981 just after 1:00 p.m. BST for its maiden voyage. It was exactly twenty years to the day since Yuri Gagarin became the first man in space. Astronauts John Young and Bob Crippen manned the craft in space orbit. Soon after the launch it was noticed by Mission Control that a section of silica tiles, used as a heat shield during re-entry, had fallen off the craft.) The world waits in expectation as the Shuttle attempts to withstand temperatures of over 2400°F during re-entry into the earth's atmosphere. Both the BBC and ITV cover this cliff-hanger. Michael Rodd commentates for the BBC and Alastair Burnet for ITV. (In fact Columbia made a perfect landing at Edward's Air Force Base in California at 7:22 p.m. BST after a flight of 2 days 6 hours and 21 minutes. The craft had made 36 orbits of the earth.)

Space Special — 1 wk

ITN, news

| 1969 | 6.7 | Thu 22 May 9:48 p.m. | 2 | 1 wk |

Apollo 10 hit trouble as the lunar module Snoopy headed back to the command module, Charlie Brown, spinning wildly out of control after jettisoning its legs. Normal mode was quickly restored and the mission concluded successfully.

Sparkling Cyanide — 2 wks

USA presented by ITV, drama

| 1984 | 11.3 | Thu 26 Apr 7:40 p.m. | 5 | 1 wk |

Agatha Christie's story of a dinner party at which a rich man's wife is poisoned by cyanide stars Anthony Andrews, Pamela Bellwood and Deborah Raffin.
Director: Robert Lewis.

| 1986 | 13.9 | Sun 30 Mar 7:45 p.m. | 6 | 1 wk |

Repeat showing of this film.

Spate of Speight — 1 wk

Thames, comedy

| 1969 | 6.4 | Mon 5 May 9:10 p.m. | 6 | 1 wk |

This one hour special was written by and starred Johnny Speight, who shares his view on contemporary life with Miriam Karlin, Alfred Marks, Anna Quayle and Eric Sykes.
Producer: Alan Tarrant.

Speaking of Murder — 1 wk

Anglia, drama

| 1971 | 8.7 | Wed 24 Mar 9:00 p.m. | 3 | 1 wk |

This single play by Audrey and William Roos was adapted for television by Brian Phelan. Since Charles Ashton's wife died, her best friend Annabelle has looked after him and his ten-year-old son. One day Charles brings home a lovely young actress as his second wife and the household disintegrates into chaos and jealousy with terrifying results. Starring Jill Bennett, Gwen Ffrangcon-Davies, John Gregson and Jennie Linden.
Designer: Michael Wild. **Director:** Anthony Page. **Producer:** John Jacobs.

Spearhead — 2 wks

Southern, drama

This series created by Simon Theobalds and written by Nick McCarty followed the fortunes of B Company Wessex Rangers, wherever they were posted. Michael Billington starred as Colour Sergeant Jackson with Jacqueline Tong as Mary Jackson, Stafford Gordon as Company Sergeant Major Gilby and Roy Holder as Sergeant Bilinski.

| 1978 | 10.7 | Tue 29 Aug 9:00 p.m. | 20 | 2 wks |

'Truth Games'
Relationships are stretched to breaking point as half the Company goes on adventure training in the Welsh mountains.
Designers: John Dilly and John Shergold. **Producer:** James Omerod. **Executive Producer:** Lewis Rudd.

Special Branch — 58 wks

Thames, drama

These cases involved the security department of Scotland Yard. Derren Nesbitt starred as Detective Inspector Jordan with Fulton Mackay as Detective Superintendent Inman. In later cases George Sewell played Det. Chief Insp. Craven with Patrick Mower as Det. Chief Insp. Haggerty.

1969	7.7	Wed 3 Dec 9:10 p.m.	2	14 wks

'Care Of Her Majesty' by Robert Banks Stewart.
Jordan's methods cause friction in an overseas British Embassy when he goes to investigate the theft of ten thousand pounds.
Director: Jonathan Alwyn. **Producer:** Robert Love.

1970	7.6	Wed 28 Oct 9:00 p.m.	1	13 wks

'Reported Missing' by Louis Marks.
Jordan and Inman go in search of a missing Russian ballerina.
Director: Dennis Vance. **Producer:** Robert Love.

1973	8.0	Wed 16 May 9:00 p.m.	1	12 wks

'Death by Drowning' by John Kershaw.
A body is found floating in the Thames. The dead man is the husband of a junior minister, Pamela Donald (Gwen Watford). Special Branch is called in to determine whether death was caused by murder or suicide.
Director: Dennis Vance. **Producer:** Geoffrey Gilbert. **Executive Producers:** Lloyd Shirley and George Taylor.

1974	8.4	Thu 2 May 8:25 p.m.	2	13 wks

'Diversion' by Peter J. Hammond.
Strand (Paul Eddington) is suddenly drinking heavily. His colleagues begin to wonder if the pressure has finally got to him.
Director: William Brayne. **Producer:** Ted Childs. **Executive Producers:** Lloyd Shirley and George Taylor.

1975	8.0	Thu 15 May 9:00 p.m.	1	6 wks

A repeat showing of 'Death by Drowning' first screened in 1973.

Special Royal Performance, A		1 wk

ATV, entertainment

1968	10.6	Sun 19 May 8:25 p.m.	1	1 wk

From the London Palladium in the presence of Her Majesty the Queen, this show aims to raise money in aid of the British athletes who will compete in the Olympic Games in Mexico. Among those appearing are Long John Baldry, Ronnie Corbett, Bruce Forsyth, Tom Jones, The King Brothers, Danny La Rue, the New Christy Minstrels, Des O'Connor, Esther and Abi Ofarim, Jimmy Tarbuck, Barbara Windsor, Norman Wisdom, Patricia Wymark, Mike Yarwood, the cast of Sweet Charity from the Prince of Wales Theatre, the Paddy Stone dancers, the Mike Sammes singers and the London Palladium orchestra, conducted by Bob Sharples.
Stage director: Albert Locke. **Television presentation:** Colin Clews. **Executive Producer:** Bill Ward.

Specially Selected Canned Carrott		2 wks

BBC, comedy

1991	11.5	Tue 19 Sep 9:30 p.m.	12	2 wks

This compilation from Jasper Carrott's CANNED CARROTT features Hugh Dennis and Steve Punt with special guest Robert Powell.
Producer: Ed Bye. **Executive Producer:** Paul Smith. (A Celador production.)

Spindoe		3 wks

Granada, drama

This six-part series by Robin Chapman starred Ray McAnally as Alec Spindoe, who had just left jail after serving a seven-year sentence for receiving. He had been the boss of a South London gang but he discovered on his release that his number two had taken over not just the gang but his wife as well.

1968	6.7	Fri 19 Apr 9:00 p.m.	5	3 wks

'You Come Out From Nothing'
While a North London gang tries to muscle in on Spindoe's territory the police are happy to sit back in the hope that the villains will eliminate each other.
Designer: Alan Price. **Director:** Mike Newell. **Producer:** Robin Chapman.

Spitting Image		5 wks

Central, comedy

Puppets created by Peter Fluck and Roger Law satirized the famous. The series, which began in 1984, pushed back the boundaries of what was acceptable in terms of comedy targets on television. With scant regard for writs, injunctions and threats of libel actions the team continued to attack members of the Royal Family, Church leaders, politicians and all whom they deemed to have a folly or vice worthy of exposure through ridicule. No one was exempt from their attentions.

1986	14.3	Sun 30 Mar 9:45 p.m.	5	5 wks

With the voices of Chris Barrie, Harry Enfield, Jon Glover, Steve Nallon, John Sessions and others.
Director: Peter Harris. **Producer:** John Lloyd.

Splash		1 wk

Presented by ITV, film

1988	11.9	Sat 16 Apr 8:00 p.m.	7	1 wk

Allen Baner (Tom Hanks) visits Cape Cod on holiday. He falls in love with Madison (Daryl Hannah), a mermaid.
Director: Ron Howard.

Split Ends — 1 wk

Granada, situation comedy

Cath (Anita Dobson) owned a hairdressing salon. There were two men in her life: Clint (Harry Ditson) was an American businessman, David (Peter Blake) a womanizing senior stylist.
Writer: Len Richmond. **Director:** Alan J. W. Bell. **Producer:** James Maw. **Executive Producer:** David Liddiment.

| 1989 | 10.2 | Wed 7 Jun 8:30 p.m. | 14 | 1 wk |

Episode One
Cath gets engaged to Clint, but has a passionate clinch with David at a party.

Spoils of War, The — 1 wk

Granada, drama

Written and created by John Finch, this series dealt with the effects of the Second World War on two Lake District families, the Warringtons and the Haywards, living in the fictitious town of Whitstanton. The Warringtons were father John (David Langton), mother Beth (Colette O'Neill), and their two children Ros (Jane How) and Mark (James Bate), both in their twenties. The Haywards were grandfather Harry (Nat Jackley), his 50-year-old son George (William Lucas), George's wife Helen (Avis Bunnage), and their children Owen (Lesley Schofield) and his wife Jean (Madalaine Newton), Blake (Alan Hunter), Keir (Ian Hastings), Peg (Emily Moore) and Lovett (Gary Carp) aged 13. Owen and Jean had a 12-year-old son, Colin (John Francis Foley).
Producer: Richard Everitt.

| 1980 | 14.8 | Sun 27 Jan 7:45 p.m. | 15 | 1 wk |

'Ends and Beginnings'
It is May 1945. The servicemen return home full of hope for their families' futures.
Designer: Colin Rees.

Spooner's Patch — 3 wks

ATV, situation comedy

This series by Ray Galton and Johnny Speight was set in a corrupt police station headed by Inspector Spooner (Ronald Fraser, later Donald Churchill). The cast also included Peter Cleall, Patricia Hayes, John Lyons and Norman Rossington.
Producer: William G. Stewart.

| 1979 | 10.5 | Mon 16 Jul 8:00 p.m. | 14 | 2 wks |

'The Morning After'
Spooner appears from his flat above the police station wearing his pyjamas and sporting a terrible hangover.

| 1982 | 11.2 | Thu 22 Apr 7:30 p.m. | 19 | 1 wk |

'The Lock-up'
Spooner instructs the staff on how to deal with a knife attacker. Unfortunately he comes to grief himself.

Sporting Triangles — 6 wks

Central, game show

Six sporting personalities were tested on their knowledge of sport. They were divided into three teams, each with a captain.

| 1987 | 14.2 | Wed 14 Jan 8:00 p.m. | 8 | 5 wks |

Nick Owen hosts with captains Willie Carson, Jimmy Greaves and Tessa Sanderson. Guests: Frank Bruno, Terry Griffiths and Harvey Smith.
Director: David Millard. **Producer:** Garry Newbon. **Executive Producer:** Bob Southgate.

| 1989 | 8.6 | Wed 28 Jun 8:00 p.m. | 18 | 1 wk |

Andy Craig hosts with captains Andy Gray, Jimmy Greaves and Emlyn Hughes. Guests: Mark Hughes, Martin Offiah and Steve Smith-Eccles.
Director: David Millard. **Producer:** Jeff Farmer.

Sports Review — 4 wks

BBC, sport

An annual review of the year's major sporting events and achievements, this programme began in the 1950s. Although it always proved popular with sports fans it rarely made the Top Twenty. The BBC SPORTSVIEW Personality of the Year was named on this show.

| 1963 | 5.3 | Thu 19 Dec 9:10 p.m. | 20 | 1 wk |

From the BBC Television Theatre Peter Dimmock recalls the year's highlights before an invited audience of three hundred sports personalities. (Sir Learie Constantine MBE presented the trophy to Personality of the Year Dorothy Hyman.)
Producer: Alec Weeks. **Editors:** Cliff Morgan, Phil Pilley.

| 1966 | 5.9 | Thu 15 Dec 9:30 p.m. | 12 | 1 wk |

Introduced by Frank Bough. David Coleman reviews the year's highlights. (Minister of Sport, Denis Howell MP, presented the trophy to footballer Bobby Moore.)
Producer: Richard Tilling. **Editor:** Alan Hart.

| 1980 | 13.0 | Wed 10 Dec 9:25 p.m. | 20 | 1 wk |

Frank Bough reviews the year's great sporting achievements with Harry Carpenter, David Coleman and Jimmy Hill. (John Arlott presented the trophy to ice skater Robin Cousins.)
Producer: Martin Hopkins. **Editor:** Jonathan Martin.

| 1981 | 13.6 | **Wed 9 Dec 9:30 p.m.** | 18 | **1 wk** |

Introduced by Frank Bough, with the year's events reviewed by Harry Carpenter, David Coleman and Jimmy Hill. (Group Captain Sir Douglas Bader presented the trophy to cricketer Ian Botham.)
Producer: Martin Hopkins. **Editor:** Harold Anderson.

....

| **Sports Special** | | | | **1 wk** |

BBC, sport

| 1983 | 7.3 | **Sat 9 Jul 9:25 p.m.** | 19 | **1 wk** |

Desmond Lynam introduces the programme. David Coleman, Brendan Foster, Ron Pickering and Stuart Storey commentate on athletics from Oslo. Harry Carpenter commentates live from Chicago on the Heavyweight fight between Mike Jameson and Frank Bruno. (Bruno knocked Jameson out in the second round.)
Editor: Mike Murphy.

....

| **Sportsnight** | | | | **5 wks** |

BBC, sport

This was the BBC's regular midweek sports magazine programme.

| 1972 | 6.3 | **Wed 11 Oct 9:55 p.m.** | 14 | **1 wk** |

Featuring international football from Wembley. David Coleman commentates (England and Yugoslavia drew 1–1).
Television presentation: John McGonagle. **Producer:** Jonathan Martin. **Editor:** Sam Leitch.

| 1973 | 6.3 | **Wed 14 Nov 9:25 p.m.** | 19 | **1 wk** |

Introduced by Tony Gubba. With commentary by Barry Davies on the match between Italy and England at Wembley. (Italy won 1–0.) The programme also features the Heavyweight contest between Joe Bugner and Mac Foster, also from Wembley. Commentary is by Harry Carpenter. (Bugner won on points.)
Television presentation: Alec Weeks (football) and Bob Duncan (boxing). **Producer:** Jonathan Martin. **Editor:** Sam Leitch.

| 1974 | 5.9 | **Wed 22 May 9:25 p.m.** | 16 | **1 wk** |

Tony Gubba introduces this programme featuring a variety of sporting events, including coverage of the international between England and Argentina from Wembley. Commentary is by David Coleman and Jimmy Hill, with summaries by Bobby Charlton and Bill Shankly. (The match ended in a 2–2 draw.) There is also boxing from the Empire Pool, Wembley between John Conteh and Chris Finnegan. Commentary is by Harry Carpenter. (Conteh won the fight and took the British, Commonwealth and European Light Heavyweight title.) Also featured is international athletics from Crystal Palace.
Television presentation: Alec Weeks (football), Bob Duncan (boxing) and Alan Mouncer (athletics). **Editor:** Jonathan Martin.

| 1975 | 7.0 | **Wed 1 Oct 8:00 p.m.** | 3 | **1 wk** |

From Manila in the Philippines, Harry Carpenter introduces the third Heavyweight Championship of the World fight between Muhammad Ali and Joe Frazier. (Ali won this time, each boxer having won once before.)
Editor: Jonathan Martin.

| 1990 | 8.4 | **Wed 23 May 10:30 p.m.** | 20 | **1 wk** |

Steve Rider introduces the European Cup Final from Vienna between AC Milan of Italy and Benfica of Portugal. (Milan won 1–0.)
Producer: Vivien Kent. **Editor:** Brian Barwick.

....

| **Sportsnight Special** | | | | **1 wk** |

BBC, sport

| 1978 | 16.9 | **Wed 19 Apr 7:30 p.m.** | 3 | **1 wk** |

International football coverage from Wembley of the England versus Brazil match, with commentary by David Coleman and analysis from Jimmy Hill. (The match ended in a 1–1 draw.)
Television presentation: Alec Weeks. **Editor:** Jonathan Martin.

....

| **Sportsnight with Coleman** | | | | **18 wks** |

BBC, sport

David Coleman presented a weekly sports programme.

| 1968 | 5.3 | **Thu 19 Sep 9:05 p.m.** | 12 | **4 wks** |

Featuring the European Heavyweight championship fight between Henry Cooper and Karl Mildenberger from the Empire Pool, Wembley. (Cooper won.) Also a report on Manchester United as they prepare to leave for the World Club Championship in South America.
Producer: Bob Duncan.

| 1969 | 7.8 | **Thu 13 Mar 9:05 p.m.** | 3 | **3 wks** |

Featuring the European Heavyweight Championship fight from Rome between Henry Cooper, the champion, and Piero Tomasoni, the challenger. (Cooper successfully defended his title.)
Producer: Bob Duncan. **Editor:** Sam Leitch.

| 1970 | 6.3 | **Wed 25 Nov 9:30 p.m.** | 16 | **3 wks** |

An all-round survey of the sporting week, with extended highlights from the England match at Wembley against East Germany. (England won 3–1.)
Television presentation: Alec Weeks. **Producer:** Jonathan Martin. **Editor:** Sam Leitch.

1971 **7.8** **Wed 10 Nov 10:25 p.m.** **2** **7 wks**

Featuring the European Championship qualifier between England and Switzerland at Wembley. (The match ended in a 1-1 draw, leaving both teams on level points with one match still to play.) **Television presentation:** Alec Weeks. **Editor:** Sam Leitch.

1972 **5.7** **Wed 5 Apr 9:20 p.m.** **18** **1 wk**

David Coleman commentates on Tottenham's European Cup tie against AC Milan at White Hart Lane. (Tottenham won 2–1.) Fred Winter looks ahead to the Grand National due to take place next Saturday. **Television presentation:** Alec Weeks. **Producer:** Jonathan Martin. **Editor:** Sam Leitch.

Sportsview 47 wks

BBC, sport

This weekly sports magazine began in 1954 under founding editor Paul Fox.

1962 **5.9** **Wed 26 Sep 9:25 p.m.** **8** **12 wks**

Peter Dimmock introduces the World Heavyweight Championship fight between title holder Floyd Patterson and challenger Sonny Liston, with commentary by Harry Carpenter. (Liston took the title.) **Television presentation:** Bryan Cowgill. **Editors:** Leslie Ketley and Ronnie Noble.

1963 **6.6** **Wed 19 Jun 8:20 p.m.** **4** **1 wk**

Introduced by Peter Dimmock. Harry Carpenter is at ringside for the Heavyweight Championship of Great Britain and the British Empire between Cassius Clay and Henry Cooper. (This was Cooper's greatest moment. He floored Clay in the fourth but Clay was saved by the bell. The fight was stopped in the fifth because of Cooper's cut eye.) **Television presentation:** A. P. Wilkinson.

1964 **7.3** **Wed 1 Jul 8:40 p.m.** **7** **4 wks**

Introduced by Frank Bough and featuring a preview of Friday's Wimbledon Men's Singles Final between Roy Emerson and Fred Stolle, a look at the future of the Grand National following the news that the owner is to sell the 270-acre Aintree course, and a report on the forthcoming Test match between England and Australia. **Television presentation:** Alec Weeks. **Editor:** Cliff Morgan.

1965 **5.4** **Wed 28 Apr 8:50 p.m.** **16** **3 wks**

Frank Bough introduces the race for the Sportsview Greyhound Television Trophy from Wimbledon Stadium, with Harry Carpenter commentating. (The race was won by Lucky Hi There.) Danny Blanchflower looks ahead to Saturday's FA Cup Final between Leeds United and Liverpool. **Television presentation:** Alan Mouncer. **Editor:** Cliff Morgan.

1966 **6.8** **Tue 1 Nov 9:50 p.m.** **10** **4 wks**

Frank Bough introduces a preview of tomorrow night's international between England and Czechoslovakia at Wembley. It is England's first match since winning the World Cup earlier this year, and manager Alf Ramsey has named the same 11 players. **Producer:** Fred Viner. **Editor:** Alan Hart.

1967 **7.5** **Tue 7 Feb 8:00 p.m.** **8** **1 wk**

Introduced by Frank Bough, the programme features highlights of the World Heavyweight Championship fight between Muhammad Ali and Ernie Terrell. (Harry Carpenter commentated on Ali's victory.) **Editor:** Alan Hart.

1968 **7.2** **Tue 5 Mar 9:30 p.m.** **5** **22 wks**

Frank Bough introduces highlights of the Bantamweight fight between Alan Rudkin and Jerry Stokes (won by Rudkin) and of the third Test between the West Indies and England from Bridgetown, Barbados (the match ended in a draw). **Editor:** Alan Hart.

Sportsview Special 1 wk

BBC, sport

1966 **7.4** **Tue 16 Nov 9:05 p.m.** **5** **1 wk**

Frank Bough introduces a recording of the World Heavyweight Championship fight held earlier today at the Houston Astrodome between Cassius Clay and Cleveland Williams. Harry Carpenter and Henry Cooper commentate. (Clay won the fight when the referee stopped the contest in the third round.) **Editor:** Alan Hart.

Sportswide 1 wk

BBC, sport

This sports magazine series was presented by Jimmy Hill and Bob Wilson.

1979 **14.3** **Fri 17 Aug 6:20 p.m.** **16** **1 wk**

The football season, which begins on Saturday, is previewed. **Director:** Mike Moss. **Editor:** Mike Murphy.

Spot the Tune 6 wks

Granada, game show

This series began in 1956. Contestants won cash prizes for their ability to recognize tunes from just a few notes. A weekly jackpot increased in one hundred pound increments until won by a contestant who could identify a song from its opening verse.

| 1960 | 5.5 | Wed 15 Mar 7:55 p.m. | 7 | 4 wks |

Hosted by Jackie Rae and Marion Ryan with Peter Knight and his orchestra.
Producer: Wilfred Fielding.

| 1962 | 3.6 | Fri 17 Aug 7:00 p.m. | 16 | 2 wks |

Hosted by Pete Murray with Marion Ryan and the Peter Knight orchestra.
Director: Philip Casson. **Producer:** John Hamp.

Spotlight — 7 wks

ATV, entertainment

In this occasional variety series different guest stars introduced a series of acts.

| 1967 | 6.8 | Sun 8 Oct 10:05 p.m. | 6 | 3 wks |

Starring Benny Hill with Jack Haig, Noel Harrison, Patricia Hayes, Abbe Lane and Julian Orchard with the Dougie Squires dancers, the Mike Sammes singers and the Jack Parnell orchestra.
Producer: Jon Scoffield.

| 1968 | 6.7 | Sun 24 Mar 10:05 p.m. | 9 | 4 wks |

Starring Eddie Fisher and Connie Stevens with Roy Castle and the Lionel Blair dancers, the Mike Sammes singers and the Jack Parnell orchestra.
Director: Philip Casson. **Producer:** Jon Scoffield.

Spring and Autumn — 17 wks

Thames, situation comedy

This series by Vince Powell and Harry Driver began as a single comedy in 1972. Following Driver's death in early 1973 Powell continued to write the shows alone. Jimmy Jewel starred as cantankerous and awkward 70-year-old widower Tommy, who left his home and his friends to live with his daughter Vera (June Barry) and son-in-law Brian (Larry Martyn) in their high-rise flat. Tommy made a new pal in 12-year-old Charlie Harris (Charlie Hawkins).

| 1972 | 6.8 | Mon 23 Oct 8:25 p.m. | 9 | 1 wk |

Tommy arrives at his new home with nothing but some hand luggage, a stuffed parrot and a chamberpot.
Producer: Stuart Allen.

| 1973 | 6.0 | Mon 20 Aug 8:00 p.m. | 7 | 6 wks |

Tommy decides to pack his bags and head home to Sheffield.
Producer: Ronnie Baxter.

| 1974 | 7.3 | Wed 28 Aug 8:00 p.m. | 1 | 6 wks |

Brian is offered a new job, but it means moving away. Tommy refuses to move and tries every trick to prevent Vera and Brian from accepting the job.
Producer: Mike Vardy.

| 1976 | 6.6 | Thu 7 Sep 8:30 p.m. | 10 | 4 wks |

Tommy and his young friend Charlie visit his father's First World War grave in France.
Producer: Anthony Parker.

Sprout — 1 wk

Thames, comedy

| 1974 | 6.3 | Mon 1 Jul 8:00 p.m. | 6 | 1 wk |

In this single comedy Darwin Sprout (John Alderton) and John Russell (Julian Holloway) are out of work flatmates. Sprout has already failed nine job interviews but is optimistic for the tenth. His only weaknesses are the truth and women. John coaches him for the interview with Mr Barker (Geoffrey Chater) for a job – any job!
Writers: Anthony Matheson and Peter Tilbury. **Producer:** Anthony Parker.

Spy Trap — 1 wk

BBC, drama

Devised by Robert Barr from his own Second World War counter-espionage experiences, this series starred Paul Daneman as Commander Ryan, RN, and Tom Adams as Major Sullivan.

| 1975 | 7.4 | Fri 23 May 9:35 p.m. | 7 | 1 wk |

'The Merrin Memoirs' by Tony Williamson.
NATO security is alerted to the forthcoming memoirs of General Merrin (Robert Flemyng).
Designer: Margaret Peacock. **Director:** Julia Smith. **Producer:** Morris Barry.

Spring and Autumn developed from a one-off play starring Jimmy Jewel as an elderly widower.

Spy Who Loved Me, The — 5 wks

Presented by ITV, film

| 1982 | 22.9 | Sun 28 Mar 7:15 p.m. | 1 | 1 wk |

James Bond (Roger Moore) tracks down a megalomaniac shipping magnate who has an underwater missile base. Curt Jurgens, Barbara Bach, Bernard Lee and Lois Maxwell also star.
Director: Lewis Gilbert.

1983	11.9	Mon 26 Dec 6:30 p.m.	5	1 wk
1986	14.8	Fri 26 Dec 5:15 p.m.	8	1 wk
1990	11.2	Sat 15 Sep 7:40 p.m.	8	1 wk
1991	12.5	Sat 21 Sep 7:15 p.m.	12	1 wk

Repeat showings of the above film.

Spyder's Web — 10 wks

ATV, drama

This thirteen-part comedy thriller concerned 'The Web', an ultra-mysterious organization which handled problems outside the brief of the police or MI5. Patricia Cutts starred as Charlotte Dean, Anthony Ainley as Clive Hawksworth and Veronica Carlson as Wallis Ackroyd.

| 1972 | 7.0 | Fri 4 Feb 9:00 p.m. | 9 | 10 wks |

'Romance on Wheels' by Roy Clarke.
En route to romance in the sun, a couple get carried away – literally.
Designer: Stanley Mills. **Director:** James Gatward. **Producer:** Dennis Vance.

Square Mile of Murder — 1 wk

BBC, drama

Four famous murder cases which took place within one square mile of the city of Glasgow were reconstructed.

| 1980 | 9.7 | Thu 17 Jul 9:25 p.m. | 20 | 1 wk |

'The Trials of Oscar Slater' by Tom Wright.
Andrew Keir introduces the story of Slater (Peter Birrell), whose trial with suppressed evidence disturbed the conscience of Detective John Trench (James Hazeldine). He tried to redress the injustice with the help of journalist William Park (John Bett), lawyer David Cook (Simon Cadell) and writer Sir Arthur Conan Doyle (Simon Lack).
Designer: Guthrie Hutton. **Director:** Bill Bain. **Producer:** Bob Macintosh.

Square Peg, The — 1 wk

Presented by BBC, film

| 1967 | 5.8 | Tue 26 Dec 9:35 p.m. | 17 | 1 wk |

Boxing Day screening of the film starring Norman Wisdom as a road mender who is accidentally drafted and becomes the centre of a plot to impersonate a Nazi General. Honor Blackman and Edward Chapman also star.
Director: John Paddy Carstairs.

Squirrels, The — 15 wks

ATV, situation comedy

This series by Eric Chappell began as a single play in 1974, and was set in the accounts department of International Rentals, a TV hire firm. Bernard Hepton starred as Mr Fletcher, the boss, and Ken Jones played Rex. Alan David was Harry, Ellis Jones played Burke and Patsy Rowland portrayed Susan. The role of the secretary Carol was played in the 1974 play by Susan Tracy and by Karin McCarthy in subsequent series.
Producer: Shaun O'Riordan.

| 1974 | 5.9 | Mon 8 Jul 8:00 p.m. | 8 | 1 wk |

The day begins badly for Rex when he treads on the budgie. Worse awaits him and his boss, Mr Fletcher, who has discovered a deficiency in the accounts.

| 1975 | 7.1 | Fri 15 Aug 8:30 p.m. | 1 | 7 wks |

'The Fiddle'
More problems at International Rentals as the auditors discover a month's supply of crisps is missing from the canteen.

| 1976 | 6.6 | Fri 13 Aug 8:30 p.m. | 2 | 6 wks |

'The Renaissance'
Mr Fletcher's birthday produces an unexpected present.

| 1977 | | Thu 6 Jan 9:00 p.m. | 19 | 1 wk |

'What A Way To Go'
The attraction of a transfer to the Jamaican branch is too much for Mr Fletcher and Rex. Susan is alarmed by their plans.
Writer: Kenneth Cope.

Stand By For Action — 1 wk

Presented by ITV, film

This was a season of adventure films.

| 1968 | 5.3 | Thu 15 Aug 6:30 p.m. | 6 | 1 wk |

'Merrill's Marauders.'

Jeff Chandler as Brigadier General Frank Merrill leads a handful of men through dense jungle as one of the most brutal battles of the Second World War rages in Burma.
Director: Samuel Fuller.

....

Stand Up Jim Davidson				1 wk

Thames, comedy

Jim Davidson starred in a series of adult stand-up comedy shows.
Producer: David Clark.

1990	10.4	Mon 26 Mar 9:30 p.m.	18	1 wk

....

Stanley Baxter Picture Show, The				5 wks

LWT, comedy

Scottish comedian and mimic Stanley Baxter limited his television appearances to specials written by Ken Hoare in which he sent up movies and television alike, playing a variety of different parts.

1972	6.4	Sun 29 Oct 9:30 p.m.	16	2 wks

The last programme in a series of four with Julia McKenzie and the Harry Rabinowitz orchestra. Baxter played pop singer Elfin Nolan, veteran movie-mogul Howard Spitz and 'naughty' TV star Benny Pill.
Producer: David Bell.

1973	6.9	Fri 21 Dec 9:00 p.m.	12	1 wk

Baxter turned Joan Bakewell into Joan Bakelite, Liza Minnelli into Liza Mimammi and Malcolm Muggeridge into Malcolm Gibberidge, with the Harry Rabinowitz orchestra and the Norman Maen dancers.
Producer: David Bell.

1975	6.6	Fri 19 Sep 9:00 p.m.	10	1 wk

Baxter presented the Warner Sisters epic Born to Bitch starring Vicky Lustre, plus a party political broadcast by the Surprise Party. With Denise Coffey, the Norman Maen dancers and the Harry Rabinowitz orchestra.
Producer: Jon Scoffield.

1976	6.6	Sat 3 Apr 6:45 p.m.	19	1 wk

A repeat of the 1975 programme above.

....

Stanley Baxter Show, The				5 wks

BBC, comedy

This comedy series, written by Ken Hoare and Iain MacIntyre, starred Stanley Baxter and was produced in Scotland by David Bell. The shows featured the BBC Scottish Radio orchestra conducted by Iain Sutherland.

1968	5.4	Mon 21 Oct 9:55 p.m.	18	1 wk

Guests: Mark Wynter with Denise Coffey, Bill Henderson, Clare Richards and Lillian Welsh.

1969	5.7	Fri 25 Apr 7:55 p.m.	16	4 wks

Guests: Kenny Lynch with Victor Cariu and Hannah Gordon.

....

Stanley Baxter's Christmas Hamper				1 wk

BBC, comedy

Stanley Baxter finally returned to the BBC after 12 years on the other side.

1985	14.0	Fri 27 Dec 9:20 p.m.	15	1 wk

Baxter portrays an 'old-fashioned girl' in A Raj Too Far, examines the hype of the festive season and delivers The Queen's speech to the Commonwealth. He is assisted by Denise Coffey.
Writer: Ken Hoare. **Producer:** John Bishop.

....

Star				1 wk

Presented by BBC, film

1979	14.2	Mon 13 Aug 8:00 p.m.	19	1 wk

The story of Gertrude Lawrence (Julie Andrews), who ran away from home in 1915 to join the Music Hall and became a star on Broadway and in films. Also starring Michael Craig, Richard Crenna and Daniel Massey as Noël Coward with Jenny Agutter, John Collin, Bruce Forsyth and Beryl Reid.
Director: Robert Wise.

....

The Squirrels want to know who has stolen a month's supply of crisps.

Star Games
8 wks

Thames, sport

Show business and sports stars competed in a variety of disciplines including target golf, rowing, tug-of-war and five-a-side football. The competition was introduced by Michael Aspel.
Commentators: *Alan Pascoe and Gerald Sinstadt.* **Producer:** *Dave Rogers.* **Executive Producer:** *Brian Venner. (Produced in association with Transworld International.)*

| 1978 | 14.1 | Tue 26 Sep 7:30 p.m. | 7 | 4 wks |

From Jesus Green, Cambridge, Rolf Harris captains a team of actors against Jackie Trent's team of variety performers.

| 1979 | 13.8 | Tue 11 Dec 7:00 p.m. | 12 | 1 wk |

From the Harrow Leisure Centre, West London, a team of TV presenters captained by Jimmy Savile faces a team of disc jockeys headed by Ed Stewart. Jenny Hanley interviews the stars.

| 1980 | 13.9 | Tue 18 Nov 7:30 p.m. | 17 | 3 wks |

From The Rye in High Wycombe, Bryan Marshall captains a team of entertainers against Paul Layton's team of minstrels.

Star Trek
7 wks

USA presented by BBC, drama

During the 1960s the crew of the USS Enterprise boldly went where no man had gone before. They finally got into the Top Twenty of the ratings in 1979. This cult series was created by Gene Roddenberry. The Enterprise was the largest starship of the United Federation of Planets, with a crew of 430 aboard her eight decks. Flying at warp factors (warp 1 was the speed of light) the ship had a top speed of warp 8. The Enterprise never landed, so the crew were 'beamed down' by Engineering Officer Montgomery 'Scotty' Scott (James Doohan) to land. The commanding officer of the Enterprise was Captain James T. Kirk (William Shatner), and the first officer, who was half-earthling and half-vulcan with pointed ears and green blood, was Mr Spock (Leonard Nimoy). Other principal characters included Chief Medical Officer Dr Leonard 'Bones' McCoy (DeForrest Kelley), helmsman Sulu (George Takei), navigator Chekov (Walter Koenig) and communications officer Uhura (Nichelle Nichols). The major enemies encountered by the crew on their intergalactic mission to seek out new life forms were the Romulans and the Klingons.

| 1979 | 20.8 | Wed 17 Oct 7:10 p.m. | 8 | 7 wks |

'The Apple'
The landing party from the USS Enterprise encounters problems with the native fruit and the natives themselves. (Repeat.)

Star Trek: The Motion Picture
1 wk

Presented by ITV, film

| 1984 | 10.9 | Mon 3 Sep 7:30 p.m. | 10 | 1 wk |

In the twenty-third century Admiral Kirk again takes command of the USS Enterprise to fight off an alien force. Leonard Nimoy and William Shatner reprise their TV roles.
Director: *Robert Wise.*

Star Trek: The Wrath of Khan
3 wks

Presented by ITV, film

| 1986 | 9.9 | Wed 14 May 8:00 p.m. | 14 | 1 wk |

In the twenty-third century the crew of the USS Enterprise encounter old enemy Khan (Ricardo Montalban) on a distant planet. Leonard Nimoy and William Shatner star.
Director: *Nicholas Meyer.*

| 1987 | 8.5 | Tue 7 Jul 8:00 p.m. | 17 | 1 wk |
| 1990 | 10.5 | Wed 27 Jun 8:00 p.m. | 13 | 1 wk |

Repeat showings of the above film.

Star Trek III: The Search for Spock
1 wk

Presented by BBC, film

| 1989 | 10.8 | Mon 1 May 8:25 p.m. | 10 | 1 wk |

The USS Enterprise has been crippled by an attack. It limps back to Earth with the crew mourning the death of Spock. But his presence is still with them . . . Leonard Nimoy and William Shatner star.
Director: *Leonard Nimoy.*

Star Trek IV: The Voyage Home
1 wk

Presented by ITV, film

| 1990 | 10.9 | Sat 22 Sep 8:00 p.m. | 13 | 1 wk |

The crew of the USS Enterprise is summoned home to a very alien world where they must face trial for mutiny. Leonard Nimoy and William Shatner star.
Director: *Leonard Nimoy.*

Star Wars
2 wks

Presented by ITV, film

| 1982 | 16.1 | Sun 24 Oct 7:15 p.m. | 1 | 1 wk |

Luke Skywalker (Mark Hamill) goes to the aid of a rebel princess (Carrie Fisher) with the help of an intergalactic bounty hunter (Harrison Ford), two robots, and an old warrior (Alec Guinness).
Director: *George Lucas.*

| 1983 | 13.7 | Thu 15 Sep 7:30 p.m. | 2 | 1 wk |

Repeat showing of the above film.

Starburst | 24 wks

ATV (1980–82) and Central (1983), entertainment

This series of variety shows.
Producer (1980–82): David G. Hillier.

| 1980 | 14.5 | Wed 15 Oct 8:00 p.m. | 12 | 2 wks |

Guests: Simon Drake, Sheena Easton, Keith Harris, Grace Kennedy, Don McLean, Johnny More, Peters and Lee, Peter Skellern and Dave Wolfe, with the Nigel Lythgoe dancers and the Jack Parnell orchestra.

| 1981 | 15.6 | Wed 4 Feb 8:00 p.m. | 6 | 8 wks |

Guests: Michael Barrymore, Dave Berry, Gemma Craven, Billy J. Kramer, Brian Marshall, the Merseybeats, Mike Reid and Wall Street Crash, with the Jack Parnell orchestra and the Nigel Lythgoe dancers.

| 1982 | 14.7 | Wed 17 Feb 8:00 p.m. | 5 | 6 wks |

Guests: Jimmy Cricket, Dana, Bonnie Langford, Paul Levent, Mike Reid, Wayne Sleep, Dennis Waterman and Malcolm J. White, with the Nigel Lythgoe dancers and the Harry Rabinowitz orchestra.

| 1983 | 9.7 | Wed 29 Jun 8:00 p.m. | 4 | 8 wks |

Leslie Crowther introduces Bobby Davro, Dollar, Johnny Hackett, George Melly and Dennis Waterman, with the Chris Power dancers and the Harry Rabinowitz orchestra.
Producer: David MacMahon.

Starlight Ballroom, The | 1 wk

Granada, drama

| 1983 | 7.6 | Mon 8 Aug 8:00 p.m. | 10 | 1 wk |

This one-off drama by Oliver Free and Peter Robinson starred Alvin Stardust as Umberto Rossi, a 1940s big band leader and host of the Starlight Ballroom radio show. Rossi's offstage activities led to trauma for his girlfriend Carol (Lynsey de Paul) and the rest of the radio team.
Choreographer: Tudor Davies. **Musical Director:** Kenny Clayton. **Director:** Bryan Izzard. **Producer:** Simon Albury. **Executive Producer:** John Hamp.

Starman | 1 wk

Presented by BBC, film

| 1990 | 10.4 | Sat 24 Mar 7:05 p.m. | 19 | 1 wk |

Jenny Hayden (Karen Allen) hears a spaceship crash. An alien enters her home. He is Starman (Jeff Bridges) and he begins to take on the form of her recently deceased husband.
Director: John Carpenter.

Starring Clint Eastwood | 1 wk

Presented by ITV, film

A season of Clint Eastwood movies.

| 1988 | 8.8 | Sat 6 Aug 9:20 p.m. | 15 | 1 wk |

'The Eiger Sanction'
(See separate entry for this film.)

Starring Robert Redford | 1 wk

Presented by ITV, film.

A season of Robert Redford movies.

| 1988 | 9.1 | Fri 12 Aug 8:00 p.m. | 19 | 1 wk |

'Jeremiah Johnson'
Set during the 1850s, Johnson (Redford) is a former soldier who becomes a mountain trapper.
Director: Sydney Pollack.

Stars and Garters | 30 wks

AR, entertainment

This series was set in a pub, re-kindling memories of the early days of Music Hall. The acts were introduced by Ray Martine.

| 1963 | 7.3 | Wed 4 Dec 9:10 p.m. | 6 | 12 wks |

With: Tommy Bruce, Vince Hill, Kathy Kirby, Debbie Lee, Al Saxon and guests Tony Hume and Safari. With the Alan Braden Band.
Producers: Daphne Shadwell and John P. Hamilton.

| 1964 | 7.8 | Wed 18 Mar 9:45 p.m. | 4 | 7 wks |

With: Tommy Bruce, Vince Hill, Kathy Kirby, Debbie Lee, Al Saxon and guests Rose Brennan, Clinton Ford and Sally Kelly. With the Alan Braden Band.
Producers: Daphne Shadwell and John P. Hamilton.

| 1965 | 7.4 | Mon 15 Feb 9:10 p.m. | 6 | 11 wks |

With: Tommy Bruce, Tsai Chin, Kim Cordell, Susan Maughan and guest Adam Faith. With the Peter Knight orchestra.
Producer: Rollo Gamble.

C3PO (Anthony Daniels) and Princess Leia (Carrie Fisher) seek to save her realm in **Star Wars**.

Stars in Their Eyes — 5 wks

Granada, entertainment

In this series hosted by Leslie Crowther participants impersonated famous singing stars. They had to perform live with the Ray Monk orchestra. The studio audience voted for the winner.
Director: Robert Khodadad. **Producer:** Jane Macnaught. **Executive Producer:** Dianne Nelmes.

| 1990 | 9.2 | Sat 25 Aug 6:50 p.m. | 15 | 1 wk |

The final.

| 1991 | 10.6 | Sat 13 Jul 7:00 p.m. | 8 | 4 wks |

The final.

Stars Look Down, The — 5 wks

Granada, drama

These stories of A. J. Cronin, adapted by Alan Plater, were set in 1910 in the north-east fishing village of Sleescale. Times were tough for Northumbrian fishermen and miners and several of the young men sought to widen their horizons.

| 1975 | 7.2 | Thu 18 Sep 9:00 p.m. | 2 | 5 wks |

'Love'
David and Joe (Ian Hastings and Alun Armstrong) are in the big city of Newcastle. David meets Joe's girlfriend Jenny (Susan Tracy) and falls in love with her. Meanwhile, mine owner Richard Barras (Basil Dignam) has won a new contract.
Director: Roland Joffe. **Producer:** Howard Baker.

Stars on Sunday — 4 wks

YTV, religion

Jess Yates presented viewer requests and attracted many star names to sing songs with a religious slant or read extracts from religious writings. Among those who appeared were Bing Crosby, Gracie Fields and Princess Grace.
Directors: Len Lurcuck and David Millard. **Executive Producer:** Jess Yates.

| 1972 | 6.7 | Sun 6 Feb 6:30 p.m. | 16 | 4 wks |

Featuring the Beverley Sisters, John Gielgud, Howard Keel and Robert Young.

Stars Shine for Jack, The — 1 wk

ATV, entertainment

| 1965 | 7.0 | Sun 30 May 8:25 p.m. | 7 | 1 wk |

A tribute to impresario Jack Hylton is presented by Bernard Delfont in association with Emile Littler and Sir Billy Butlin OBE and introduced by Sir Malcolm Sargeant. The stars include Dora Bryan, Eddie Calvert, Russ Conway, the Crazy Gang, Paul Daneman, Marlene Dietrich, Charlie Drake, Flanagan and Allen, Bruce Forsyth, Eileen Gourlay, 'Monsewer' Eddie Gray, Dickie Henderson, Pat Kirkwood, Elizabeth Larner, Joe Loss, Vera Lynn, Spike Milligan, Nadia Nerina, Peter O'Toole, Al Read, the Tiller Girls, Sophie Tucker and Albert and Les Ward. There is also a special appearance by members of the Grand Order of Water Rats including King Rat Tommy Trinder and Charlie Chester, Cyril Dowler, George Elrick, Ted Ray, Ben Warriss and Georgie Wood.
Stage Director: Alec Shanks. **Television presentation:** Bill Ward.

Starsky and Hutch — 94 wks

USA presented by BBC, drama

This series featured undercover cops Dave Starsky (Paul Michael Glaser) and Ken Hutchinson (David Soul) and their lives of violence and fast cars.

| 1976 | 8.5 | Sat 11 Dec 9:20 p.m. | 1 | 21 wks |

'Nightmare'
Starsky and Hutch arrest two hoodlums for the rape of a nineteen-year-old retarded girl – only to see the case dropped on a technicality.

| 1977 | 16.7 | Sat 10 Dec 9:05 p.m. | 2 | 21 wks |

'The Plague'
A deadly virus is spreading through the city. Starsky and Hutch search for the professional assassin who introduced it. Hutch catches the disease.

| 1978 | 17.1 | Sat 30 Dec 9:15 p.m. | 3 | 15 wks |

'Starsky's Little Brother'
Starsky's younger brother comes to visit. It is soon obvious that he is mixed up in certain criminal activities.

| 1979 | 20.1 | Sat 13 Oct 9:00 p.m. | 9 | 10 wks |

'Starsky Versus Hutch'
Starsky and Hutch fall in love with the same undercover agent.

| 1980 | 14.4 | Fri 3 Dec 9:25 p.m. | 3 | 15 wks |

'Playboy Island'
Starsky and Hutch are on Playboy Island, where they are struggling to unravel the mysteries of a series of deaths surrounding the world's richest recluse. Guest stars: Joan Collins and Samantha Eggar.

| 1981 | 16.7 | Wed 9 Dec 9:30 p.m. | 3 | 3 wks |

'The Trap'
A killer seeking revenge plans to ensnare Starsky and Hutch. (Repeat.)

| **1984** | **9.1** | **Thu 2 Aug 9:55 p.m.** | **6** | **8 wks** |

'The Hostages'
A young security guard is forced to help a gang in a robbery while they hold his pregnant wife hostage. (Repeat.)

| **1985** | **13.4** | **Fri 1 Mar 8:10 p.m.** | **19** | **1 wk** |

'The Velvet Jungle'
The murder of a Mexican draws Starsky and Hutch into a world of illegal immigrants. (Repeat.)

Startime | 12 wks

ATV, entertainment

This was a variety series.

| **1960** | **6.0** | **Wed 21 Dec 8:30 p.m.** | **4** | **3 wks** |

Starring Alma Cogan with the Dallas Boys, Norman Vaughan and the Cyril Stapleton orchestra.
Producer: Colin Clews.

| **1961** | **5.9** | **Wed 7 Jun 8:00 p.m.** | **7** | **1 wk** |

Starring Edmund Hockridge with Russ Conway, the Clyde Valley Stompers, Jack Day, Adele Leigh and the Jack Parnell orchestra.
Producer: Francis Essex.

| **1962** | **5.9** | **Wed 11 Apr 8:00 p.m.** | **6** | **7 wks** |

Starring Helen Shapiro with Charlie Cairoli and Paul, the Clark Brothers, Johnny Hart, Ronnie Hilton, the King Brothers, Dennis Spicer and the Jack Parnell orchestra.
Producer: Josephine Douglas.

| **1963** | **6.2** | **Wed 16 Oct 9:45 p.m.** | **12** | **1 wk** |

Starring Norman Vaughan with Joyce Blair, the Dior Dancers, Jackie Trent, the Pamela Devis dancers and the Jack Parnell orchestra.
Producer: Albert Locke.

State of the Union | 1 wk

ATV, documentary

| **1962** | **4.3** | **Wed 4 Jul 9:45 p.m.** | **13** | **1 wk** |

An assessment of the USA to coincide with Independence Day written by Ian Trethowan and narrated by Frank Duncan.
Producer: James Bredin.

Stay Lucky | 6 wks

YTV, drama

This comedy thriller series by Geoff McQueen starred Jan Francis as Sally, a northern lady, and Dennis Waterman as Thomas, a Cockney wide boy on the run.

| **1989** | **13.1** | **Fri 8 Dec 9:00 p.m.** | **11** | **3 wks** |

'A1 Rain Dancer'
Thomas and Sally meet on the rain-soaked A1.
Designer: Mike Long. **Producer:** David Reynolds. **Executive Producer:** Vernon Lawrence.

| **1990** | **11.2** | **Sat 29 Sep 8:00 p.m.** | **13** | **3 wks** |

'Burning Your Boats'
Thomas is working as a minicab driver in Newcastle and Sally is running a narrowboat charter business in Yorkshire.
Designer: Mike Long. **Director:** David Reynolds. **Producer:** Andrew Benson.

Stay With Me Till Morning | 1 wk

YTV, drama

This trilogy by John Braine was set in the West Riding of Yorkshire. It starred Paul Daneman and Nanette Newman as Clive and Robin Lendrick, the envy of all their friends after twenty years of marriage had brought them everything – or so it appeared on the surface. The series also starred Keith Barron as Stephen Belgard.

| **1981** | **8.9** | **Fri 28 Aug 9:00 p.m.** | **17** | **1 wk** |

'Return of a Travelling Man'
Clive admires the present that Robin has given him on his 47th birthday. But the atmosphere is quickly changed by a telephone call.
Designer: Peter Kindred. **Director:** David Reynolds. **Producer:** Michael Glynn. **Executive Producer:** David Cunliffe.

Steptoe and Son | 107 wks

BBC, situation comedy

The creations of Ray Galton and Alan Simpson, Albert Steptoe (Wilfrid Bramble) and his son Harold (Harry H. Corbett) first appeared on 5 January 1962 in a half-hour play THE OFFER, one of a series of single plays under the umbrella title COMEDY PLAYHOUSE. Such was the impact of the two rag-and-bone men that the subsequent series ran for many years.
Producer (1962–71): Duncan Wood.

| **1962** | **4.5** | **Thu 12 Jul 8:45 p.m.** | **13** | **6 wks** |

'The Holiday'
Harold is tired of holidays at Mrs Clifford's in Bognor Regis and sets his sights on the sun-tanned girls of the Mediterranean.

| 1963 | 8.8 | Thu 14 Feb 7:55 p.m. | 2 | 13 wks |

'Is That Your Horse Outside?'
The horse in question is the faithful Hercules, who is left to comfort the lovesick Harold after he meets ' . . . one of them haughty birds, classy breedin', you know, a cut above the scrubbers I generally knock about with . . .'

| 1964 | 9.8 | Tue 18 Feb 8:00 p.m. | 1 | 13 wks |

'The Lodger'
Albert brings about a crisis in the Steptoe household when he decides to take in a lodger.

| 1965 | 8.0 | Mon 15 Nov 7:30 p.m. | 3 | 7 wks |

'Pilgrim's Progress'
Albert takes a sentimental journey to Flanders, the scene of his oft-recounted triumphs of the First World War. With guests Alan Gifford and Frank Thornton.

| 1966 | 6.4 | Tue 27 Sep 7:30 p.m. | 5 | 7 wks |

A repeat showing of **Pilgrim's Progress.**

| 1967 | 6.9 | Sun 26 Nov 7:25 p.m. | 9 | 13 wks |

'Crossed Swords'
Harold believes he has picked up a valuable piece of Meissen pottery on his rounds. He has identified the manufacturer's crossed blue swords and thinks the sculptor was the famous Johann Kändler. However, the antique shop assistant (Derek Nimmo) and the local auctioneer (Basil Dignam) remain unconvinced.

| 1970 | 8.7 | Fri 6 Mar 7:55 p.m. | 2 | 15 wks |

'A Death in the Family'
Hercules, the faithful old horse, lies dead in the road.

| 1971 | 6.3 | Mon 4 Oct 9:20 p.m. | 11 | 1 wk |

'Steptoe and Son and Son'
After a party some while ago, Harold just about remembers a 'bird' called Daphne. Now she calls him up to say she's pregnant.

| 1972 | 8.4 | Mon 20 Mar 9:20 p.m. | 2 | 7 wks |

'Loathe Story'
Harold's antipathy to Albert reaches new heights. His girlfriend Bunty (Joanna Lumley) persuades him to visit a psychiatrist (Raymond Huntley). Under treatment Harold regresses into childhood and all the reasons for their hostile relationship emerge.
Producer: John Howard Davies.

| 1973 | 7.1 | Wed 28 Nov 9:30 p.m. | 10 | 5 wks |

'Divided We Stand'
Harold decides to redecorate the house. Albert hates his every proposal, with the result that they divide the house in two.
Producer: David Croft.

| 1974 | 7.8 | Wed 4 Sep 9:30 p.m. | 1 | 6 wks |

'Back in Fashion'
Two men discovered prowling in the yard turn out to be a fashion photographer (Roy Holder) and his agent (Peter Birrel). They want to use the lot for a shoot. Harold becomes enthusiastic when he learns that there are models involved, especially Carol (Madeline Smith).
Producer: Douglas Argent.

| 1976 | 6.7 | Fri 5 Mar 8:30 p.m. | 16 | 2 wks |

'Seance in a Wet Rag and Bone Yard'
With guest star Patricia Routledge as fortune-teller Madame Fontana.
Producer: Douglas Argent.

| 1988 | 13.2 | Tue 3 May 8:30 p.m. | 5 | 12 wks |

'Live Now P.A.Y.E. Later'
Despite the fact that the man from the Ministry of Social Security (Edwin Apps) and his assistant (Colin Gordon) insist that Albert is not receiving enough support, Albert is forced to admit to Harold that he has been claiming money for his late wife and a nonexistent daughter. (Repeat.)
Producer: John Howard Davies.

Steptoe and Son | 1 wk

Presented by BBC, film

| 1984 | 12.3 | Sun 23 Dec 8:35 p.m. | 19 | 1 wk |

In this feature film version Harold marries a stripper and Albert accompanies them on honeymoon.
Director: Cliff Owen.

Steptoe and Son Ride Again | 1 wk

Presented by BBC, film

| 1978 | 13.0 | Thu 28 Dec 8:45 p.m. | 20 | 1 wk |

In this second feature film of the series Hercules the horse retires and Albert gives Harold some money to replace him. Harold buys a dud greyhound instead.
Director: Peter Sykes.

Steve McQueen Movie, The | 1 wk

Presented by ITV, film

| 1986 | 9.9 | Sat 12 Jul 9:15 p.m. | 7 | 1 wk |

'Bullitt'
(See separate entry for this film.)

Steve McQueen Season, A — 1 wk

Presented by BBC, film

| 1981 | 13.0 | Mon 25 May 6:50 p.m. | 6 | 1 wk |

'The Great Escape'
(See separate entry for this film.)

Sting, The — 2 wks

Presented by BBC, film

| 1979 | 13.9 | Tue 25 Dec 8:30 p.m. | 15 | 1 wk |

Christmas Day screening of the story of Chicago gangsters in the 1930s, set to the music of Scott Joplin (arranged by Marvin Hamlisch) and starring Paul Newman, Robert Redford and Robert Shaw.
Director: George Roy Hill.

| 1984 | 10.1 | Sat 24 Mar 6:35 p.m. | 20 | 1 wk |

Repeat showing of the above film.

Stories of D. H. Lawrence, The — 6 wks

Granada, drama

This was a series of adaptations of the short stories of D. H. Lawrence written over the twenty years from 1907, depicting the changes in relationships between men and women during that period.

| 1966 | 6.9 | Mon 10 Jan 9:40 p.m. | 14 | 2 wks |

'Daughters of the Vicar' adapted by Peter Eckersley.
A Nottinghamshire mining community vicar (John Walsh) and his wife (Marie Hopps) have two daughters. Mary (Petra Davies) prepares for her approved marriage while her wilful, determined younger sister Louisa (Judi Dench) causes scandal by showing interest in Alfred Durant (William Holmes), a rough but kindly miner.
Designer: Michael Grimes. **Director:** Gerard Dynevor. **Producer:** Margaret Morris.

| 1967 | 5.2 | Thu 8 Jun 9:40 p.m. | 11 | 4 wks |

'Strike Pay' adapted by John Hale.
Set in 1912. The story of two miners, Tom Radford (John Ronane) and Ephraim Wharmby (Bill Kenwright), who set out to walk to the football match between Notts County and Aston Villa, while their wives (Angela Morant and Georgina Hale) wait at home in desperate need of their strike pay.
Designer: Michael Grimes. **Director:** Richard Everitt. **Producer:** Margaret Morris.

Story of The Queen Mary, The — 1 wk

BBC, documentary

| 1967 | 6.4 | Tue 26 Sep 9:05 p.m. | 12 | 1 wk |

Tomorrow The Queen Mary finishes her active life on the seas after thirty-one years. Kenneth More narrates.
Producer: Richard Cawston.

Story of Trad, The — 1 wk

AR, music

| 1962 | 3.5 | Wed 1 Aug 9:45 p.m. | 17 | 1 wk |

Racing driver Stirling Moss discovers the story of traditional jazz with Kenny Ball and his Jazzmen, Lionel Blair, Beryl Bryden, Ken Colyer's Jazzmen, George Melly, the Storeyville Jazzmen, Monty Sunshine's Band and George Webb.
Producer: Geoffrey Hughes.

Storyboard — 2 wks

Thames, drama

This was a series of six single dramas by different writers.

| 1983 | 7.1 | Tue 16 Aug 9:00 p.m. | 18 | 2 wks |

'Woodentop' by Geoff McQueen.
A raw recruit learns all he needs to know in his first twelve hours at an East End police station.
Designer: Philip Blowers. **Director:** Peter Cregeen. **Producer:** Michael Chapman. **Executive Producer:** Lloyd Shirley.

Strangers — 4 wks

Granada, drama

Each episode of this crime series was set in a different part of the country as the Inter-City squad moved into action. Don Henderson starred as Detective Sergeant Bulman with Dennis Blanch as Detective Sergeant Willis, Fiona Mollison as Detective Constable Bennett and Mark McManus as Detective Chief Superintendent Lambie.
Director: William Brayne. **Producer:** Richard Everitt.

| 1980 | 12.7 | Tue 28 Oct 9:00 p.m. | 20 | 1 wk |

'Armed and Dangerous' by Murray Smith.
Bulman and Willis find themselves in Scarborough when a routine job escorting a prisoner turns dangerous.
Designer: Chris Truelove.

| 1982 | 10.7 | Wed 20 Oct 9:00 p.m. | 15 | 3 wks |

'With These Gloves You Can Pass Through Mirrors' by Murray Smith.
An Inter-City squad member is killed trying to arrest a smuggler.
Designer: Tim Farmer.

TAKE YOUR PICK

TAKE YOUR PICK

4

6

1 *A Number One for three consecutive years,* **Sale of the Century** *starring Nicholas Parsons achieved its highest viewing figure on an evening when the BBC was on strike.*

2 *Michael Miles poses on the set of* **Take Your Pick.**

3 *Monica Rose lights Hughie Green's fire in* **Double Your Money.**

4 *Mick has accepted Leslie Crowther's invitation to 'Come on Down' in* **The Price is Right.**

5 *Magnus Magnusson poses with the four finalists in the 1974* **Mastermind** *competition.*

6 *Stuart Hall and Eddie Waring were long-term hosts of* **It's a Knockout.**

7 *Terry Wogan welcomes Michael Parkinson and Russell Harty to the 4 October 1979 edition of* **Blankety Blank.**

Strauss Family, The — 7 wks

ATV, drama

This series of seven programmes told the stories of Austria's great musical family. Music for the series was played by the London Symphony Orchestra.

| 1972 | 8.1 | Thu 19 Dec 9:00 p.m. | 2 | 7 wks |

'Adele' by David Butler.
Johann (Stuart Wilson) marries for the third time. His wife is Adele (Lynn Farleigh). With her inspiration he regains his popularity, which had declined with his advancing years.
Musical Director: Cyril Ornadel. **Designers:** Henry Graveney and Peter Roden. **Producer:** David Reid. **Executive Producer:** Cecil Clarke.

Street Cop — 1 wk

Presented by BBC, film

| 1986 | 11.3 | Tue 5 Aug 9:30 p.m. | 3 | 1 wk |

Karen Valentine stars as Mary Glatzle of the New York Police Department. She is assigned to work undercover to trap a rapist.
Director: Sandor Stern.

Streets Apart — 1 wk

BBC, drama

Adrienne Conway's six-part story focused on cab driver Bernie (James Hazeldine), a widower with two children, and Sylvia (Amanda Redman), a successful literary agent with a busy social life. They both grew up in the same area of London, but she moved away. Eventually she returned.

| 1988 | 12.6 | Mon 28 Nov 8:30 p.m. | 13 | 1 wk |

Part Six
Bernie and Sylvia plan a weekend away, but what is planned is not what happens.
Producer: Sue Bysh.

Streets of San Francisco, The — 2 wks

USA presented by ITV, drama

This series was developed from an original one-off pilot show based on the novel Poor, Poor Ophelia by Carolyn Weston. Karl Malden starred as Mike Stone with Michael Douglas as Steve Keller. Both were San Francisco police detectives. In the final series Douglas was replaced by Richard Hatch.
Producer: Quinn Martin.

| 1977 | 13.0 | Tue 11 Oct 8:00 p.m. | 15 | 2 wks |

'No Place To Hide'
Stefanie Powers guest stars as Rita King, wife of former convict Lou King (Paul Carr). A prison gang leave them no alternative but to get involved in a drug ring.

Strike It Lucky — 69 wks

Thames, game show

Michael Barrymore hosted this game in which couples answered general knowledge questions in the hope of advancing along a bank of TV screens in pursuit of cash and prizes.
Director (1986–89): Brian Penders. **Producer:** Maurice Leonard. **Executive Producer** (1986–89): Robert Louis.

1986	12.2	Wed 26 Nov 8:00 p.m.	10	7 wks
1987	13.0	Thu 12 Nov 8:00 p.m.	5	24 wks
1988	13.2	Thu 7 Jan 8:00 p.m.	10	5 wks
1989	12.4	Tue 3 Jan 7:00 p.m.	19	1 wk
1990	14.6	Mon 26 Feb 8:00 p.m.	7	20 wks

Director: John Birkin.

| 1991 | 14.1 | Mon 4 Nov 8:00 p.m. | 10 | 12 wks |

Director: Paul Kirrage.

Studio '64 — 4 wks

ATV, drama

This strand of single dramas had no unifying theme.

| 1964 | 6.9 | Sun 19 Apr 9:35 p.m. | 12 | 4 wks |

'The Close Prisoner' by Clive Exton.
Harry Hutchins (Bernard Cribbins) has a chest which is impervious to bullets. During the war he was known as 'The Invincible Man'. It all began at the age of fourteen when a rash turned his chest to steel. Norman Bird, Michael Gwynn, Dandy Nichols and Sheila Steafel also star.
Director: Ted Kotcheff. **Executive Producer:** Stuart Burge.

Stunt Challenge — 4 wks

Thames, game show

This was originally titled STUNTMAN CHALLENGE in 1982. Derek Thompson introduced stuntmen and women who risked all as they competed for a silver salver and the winner's title. The contestants judged each other.

Producer: *George Sawford.* **Executive Producer** *(1982–84): Brian Venner.*

1982	12.5	Tue 30 Nov 8:00 p.m.	7	1 wk

Co-presented by Lewis Collins.

1983	10.9	Tue 6 Sep 8:00 p.m.	12	1 wk
1984	10.5	Tue 4 Sep 8:00 p.m.	15	1 wk
1985	10.6	Tue 3 Sep 8:00 p.m.	16	1 wk

Executive Producer: *Don Sayer.*

Sullavan Brothers, The   4 wks

ATV, drama

Created by Ted Willis, this series focused on the good works of the Sullavan family and starred Anthony Bate as Paul Sullavan, Tenniel Evans as John, Mary Kenton as Beth, Hugh Manning as Robert and David Sumner as Patrick.

1964	5.9	Sat 5 Dec 10:05 p.m.	17	4 wks

'A Question of Honour' *by Gerald Kelsey.*
The widow of a magistrate, Mrs Lamorbey (Jean Anderson) asks the Sullavan brothers to help her refute libellous statements about her late husband made by an author in a newly-published book.
Designer: *Vic Symonds.* **Director:** *George More O'Ferrall.* **Producer:** *Jack Williams.*

Summer Holiday   1 wk

Presented by BBC, film

1970	6.4	Fri 6 Mar 7:55 p.m.	15	1 wk

Four young London Transport mechanics take a London bus across Europe to Athens. Starring Cliff Richard with Melvyn Hayes, David Kossoff, Ron Moody, Lauri Peters, the Shadows, Una Stubbs, Teddy Green and Lionel Murton.
Director: *Peter Yates.*

Summer Night Out   2 wks

ITV (various), entertainment

This variety series was presented from different cabaret clubs around the country.

1976	6.1	Wed 21 Jul 8:00 p.m.	3	2 wks

From the Lakeside Country Club in Frimley Green, Tom O'Connor introduces Roger de Courcey, Georgie Fame, Tammy Jones and Des O'Connor, with the Ladybirds and the Lionel Blair dancers.
Producer: *Royston Mayoh.* **Executive Producer:** *Philip Jones (Thames).*

Summer Playhouse   10 wks

ITV, drama

This series of single dramas was produced by various ITV companies.

1967	7.6	Mon 3 Jul 8:30 p.m.	1	10 wks

'The Sleeping Partner' *by Winston Graham, adapted by Patricia Highsmith and Anthony Steven.*
Mike Granville (Keith Michell) comes home from work to find his wife Lynn (Suzy Arthur) is not there. He begins a desperate search. A network of terror tightens around him. Francis Matthews, Peter Jeffrey, Barbara Shelley and William Sylvester also star.
Designer: *Michael Wield.* **Producer:** *John Jacobs (for Anglia).*

Summer Song   2 wks

AR, music

This series of music shows was set outdoors.

1961	4.3	Thur 20 Jul 9:35 p.m.	13	2 wks

The Johnny Dankworth orchestra is joined by Cleo Laine and Dennis Lotis (at Fairoaks Airfield, Chobham), Lyn Cornell and Craig Douglas (at Jupiter House, Surrey), Patricia Lambert (in the City of London), Matt Monro (at Thames Wharf), and Dudley Moore (on the back of a truck). With the Peter Darrell dancers.
Directors: *J. Murray Ashford, Don Gale, John P. Hamilton and Grahame Turner.* **Producer:** *Alan Morris.*

S

Keith Michell was the star of 'The Sleeping Partner', the only Number One edition of **Summer Playhouse.**

Summer Spectacular — 3 wks

ATV, entertainment

This series of variety shows had no resident performers other than the Irving Davies dancers and the Jack Parnell orchestra.

1963	6.0	Sun 7 Jul 8:25 p.m.	4	3 wks

Starring Bob Monkhouse with Diana Dors, Shani Wallis and Mark Wynter.
Writers: Sid Green and Dick Hills. **Producer:** Francis Essex.

Summer Wedding, A — 1 wk

ITN, news

1986	8.5	Fri 18 Jul 7.30 p.m.	14	1 wk

Carol Barnes previews next Wednesday's wedding of HRH The Prince Andrew and Miss Sarah Ferguson.

Summertime Special — 2 wks

BBC, entertainment

This series of variety shows came from around the resorts, with the John Coleman orchestra and the A Team dancers.
Choreographer: Lud. **Producer:** Stewart Morris.

1981	9.6	Sat 8 Aug 8:30 p.m.	16	1 wk

From Brighton come the Bachelors, Rod Hull and Emu, Kaybek and Zari, Maggie Moone, Sheeba and Shakin' Stevens.

1982	8.1	Sat 7 Aug 8:30 p.m.	16	1 wk

From Eastbourne come Bartschelly, the Belle Stars, the Krankies, Tight Fit, Lenny Windsor and Lena Zavaroni.

Summertime Special — 10 wks

TVS, entertainment

This was a series of seaside variety shows with the Nigel Lythgoe dancers and the Alyn Ainsworth orchestra.
Directors: John Kaye Cooper and Nigel Lythgoe. **Producer:** David Bell.

1986	10.0	Sat 16 Aug 7:30 p.m.	6	5 wks

From Bournemouth, Les Dennis introduces Brian Conley, Jim Davidson, Aiden J. Harvey, Grace Kennedy, the Nolans and Iris Williams.

1987	10.4	Sat 8 Aug 8:15 p.m.	6	5 wks

From Bournemouth, Jim Davidson introduces Kevin Devane, Lance Ellington, Nino Firetto, Five Star, Paddy Green, Grace Kennedy, Johnny Logan, Hazel O'Connor and Wayne Sleep.

Sun Television Awards, The — 1 wk

LWT, entertainment

Winners received their votes from readers of the Sun.

1973	5.7	Fri 11 May 10:30 p.m.	19	1 wk

Introduced by Pete Murray with cabaret artists Gladys Knight and the Pips and Freddie Starr.
Producer: Mark Stuart.

Sunday Film, The — 46 wks

Presented by BBC, film

1965	6.2	Sun 7 Nov 7:25 p.m.	9	6 wks

'The Man Who Never Was'
This story of a dead man who went to war and almost certainly saved the lives of thousands of Allied soldiers was based on an actual wartime intelligence operation. Stephen Boyd and Clifton Webb star.
Director: Ronald Neame.

1970	5.9	Sun 26 Apr 7:25 p.m.	1	3 wks

'They Who Dare'
Dirk Bogarde and Denholm Elliott star in the Second World War story of a group of British soldiers on a raiding expedition to Rhodes.
Director: Lewis Milestone.

1977	10.6	Sun 21 Aug 8:05 p.m.	20	1 wk

'Never So Few'
The Japanese attack a band of guerillas in the Burmese jungle during the Second World War. Starring Richard Johnson, Peter Lawford, Gina Lollobrigida, Steve McQueen and Frank Sinatra with Charles Bronson and Dean Jones.
Director: John Sturges.

1978	14.6	Sun 17 Sep 8:05 p.m.	3	5 wks

'The Battle of Britain'
The story of Britain's defence in September 1940 stars Harry Andrews, Michael Caine, Trevor Howard, Curt Jurgens, Ian McShane, Kenneth More, Laurence Olivier, Nigel Patrick, Christopher Plummer, Michael Redgrave, Ralph Richardson, Robert Shaw, Patrick Wymark and Susannah York.
Director: Guy Hamilton.

1979	**19.3**	**Sun 18 Nov 7:15 p.m.**	**1**	**7 wks**

'Juggernaut'
(See separate entry for this film.)

1980	**14.1**	**Sun 14 Dec 7:15 p.m.**	**6**	**5 wks**

'At The Earth's Core'
A prehistoric world is discovered in a vast subterranean cave. Peter Cushing, Doug McClure and Caroline Munro star.
Director: Kevin Connor.

1981	**14.3**	**Sun 26 Apr 7:15 p.m.**	**6**	**7 wks**

'Tora Tora Tora'
The title word means 'tiger' in Japanese and was the code used by the squadron leader to signal success at Pearl Harbor on 7 December 1941. The film stars Joseph Cotten, E. G. Marshall, Tatsuya Mihashi, Jason Robards, Takahiro Tamura and Eijiro Tono.
Director: Richard Fleischer.

1982	**13.5**	**Sun 21 Mar 7:45 p.m.**	**9**	**7 wks**

'Logan's Run'
It is 2274. The world has been destroyed by war and pollution. Logan (Michael York) is a security guard in an enclosed city. He is determined to find a way to the outside. Jenny Agutter, Farrah Fawcett-Majors, Richard Jordan and Peter Ustinov also star.
Director: Michael Anderson.

1983	**11.3**	**Sun 27 Mar 7:15 p.m.**	**12**	**5 wks**

'Berlin Tunnel 21'
Former US Army officer Sandy Mueller (Richard Thomas) leads a group of men who risk all to rescue their loved ones from East Berlin. Horst Buchholz and José Ferrer also star.
Director: Richard Michaels.

Sunday Mystery Theatre				**3 wks**

ATV, drama

This series of single plays had the unifying theme of mystery.

1964	**6.5**	**Sun 12 Jul 9:35 p.m.**	**2**	**3 wks**

'The Primitives' by Brian Clemens.
John and Mary take a quiet holiday to try to repair their disintegrating marriage. Instead they find fear, terror and, ultimately, the truth. Starring Nigel Green, Donald Houston, Glyn Houston and Lana Morris.
Designer: Michael Eve. **Director:** Quentin Lawrence.

Sunday Night at the London Palladium				**181 wks**

ATV, entertainment

A landmark in the annals of British entertainment, this show was first transmitted in the London area alone on 25 September, 1955, when Tommy Trinder was host and the stars were Gracie Fields and Guy Mitchell. There were many subsequent hosts, most notably Bruce Forsyth and Norman Vaughan. But the show was the brainchild of the former 'guv'nor' of the Palladium Val Parnell, and it bore his name as VAL PARNELL'S SUNDAY NIGHT AT THE LONDON PALLADIUM. He left the theatre in 1965 to help Lew Grade and Norman Collins found ATV. Parnell died in September 1972 and the following year the show was revived, but was billed without his name.

This was one of the first programmes to include a game show element. In 'Beat the Clock' couples played games to a time deadline. If time ran out in the middle of a game they were invited back the following week to try again.

1960	**7.5**	**Sun 4 Dec 8:00 p.m.**	**1**	**29 wks**

Don Arrol introduces Bruce Forsyth, Roy Castle, and the George Carden dancers.
Producer: Albert Locke.

1961	**7.9**	**Sun 26 Nov 8:00 p.m.**	**1**	**16 wks**

Bruce Forsyth introduces Billy Dainty, Vera Lynn and Frankie Vaughan.
Producer: Francis Essex.

1962	**7.9**	**Sun 15 Apr 8:25 p.m.**	**2**	**34 wks**

Norman Vaughan introduces Harry Secombe and the Tiller Girls.
Producer: Francis Essex.

1963	**8.0**	**Sun 29 Dec 8:25 p.m.**	**2**	**34 wks**

Bruce Forsyth hosts a special charity edition on behalf of the Stars Organisation For Spastics. With Amanda Barrie, Dora Bryan, Russ Conway, Adam Faith, Sid James, Vera Lynn, Pete Murray, Helen Shapiro and Richard Wattis.
Producer: Jon Scoffield.

1964	**9.7**	**Sun 19 Apr 8:25 p.m.**	**3**	**38 wks**

Bruce Forsyth introduces the Bachelors, Hope and Keen and Frank Ifield, with the Pamela Devis dancers.
Producer: Jon Scoffield.

S

A bomb disposal expert played by Richard Harris seeks to save the 'Juggernaut' in **The Sunday Film**.

| 1965 | 7.4 | Sun 21 Mar 8:00 p.m. | 3 | 21 wks |

Norman Vaughan introduces Morecambe and Wise, Potassy and the Supremes, with the Tiller Girls.
Producer: Colin Clews.

| 1973 | 7.3 | Sun 25 Nov 7:25 p.m. | 4 | 7 wks |

Jim Dale introduces Paul Anka, the Black Theatre of Prague, Pamela Giselle and Larry Grayson, with the Tiller Girls, the Mike Sammes singers and the Jack Parnell orchestra.
Producer: Jon Scoffield.

| 1974 | 6.8 | Sun 20 Jan 7:25 p.m. | 16 | 2 wks |

Jim Dale introduces Max Bygraves and Lorna Luft with the Tiller Girls, the Mike Sammes singers and the Jack Parnell orchestra.
Producer: Jon Scoffield.

Sunday Night at the Prince of Wales — 2 wks

ATV, entertainment

This series of variety shows came from the Prince of Wales Theatre in the West End of London.

| 1963 | 7.3 | Sun 15 Dec 8:25 p.m. | 7 | 2 wks |

Norman Vaughan introduces Gerry and the Pacemakers, Johnny Hart, Shani Wallis and the Jack Parnell orchestra, plus an excerpt from The Boys of Syracuse, currently playing at the Theatre Royal, Drury Lane, and starring Bob Monkhouse, Denis Quilley and Maggie Fitzgibbon.
Producer: Jon Scoffield.

Sunday Night Play, The — 1 wk

BBC, drama

A series of single dramas.

| 1962 | 4.1 | Sun 26 Aug 8:45 p.m. | 16 | 1 wk |

'Dackson's Wharf' by E. V. H. Emmett and Barry Thomas.
Based on the novel A Killing Frost by Eric Burgess. Nick Toberson (Colin Blakeley) is a bargee on the Thames. New manager Mike Russell (Anthony Bate) arrives to take control of Dackson's Wharf and Shipping Company. Nick introduces Mike to his girlfriend Ella (Judy Parfitt) and trouble starts. When a body with a knife in its back is found floating in the river, there are five suspects.
Designer and **Producer:** Hal Burton.

Sunday Night Theatre — 7 wks

ITV, drama

This was a series of single plays.

| 1965 | 5.2 | Sun 28 Mar 10:05 p.m. | 19 | 1 wk |

'The Paper Man' by Peter Evans.
A foreign correspondent is facing a personal crisis which comes to a head with the violent and bizarre death of a wealthy socialite. The event, however, gives him one last chance in life. Starring Harry Andrews, Peter Copley, Ronald Hines, Caroline Mortimer, Nora Nicholson and William Sylvester.
Designer: Sean Kenny. **Director:** John Jacobs. (An Anglia production.)

| 1971 | 5.7 | Sun 20 Jun 10:15 p.m. | 10 | 4 wks |

'The Prize' by John Peacock.
Seventeen-year-old schoolboy Christopher (John Moulder-Brown) seeks the services of a lady of the town, Gribiche (Caroline Blakiston). They develop a fateful relationship.
Designer: Anthony Waller. **Director:** Peter Moffatt. **Executive Producer:** Cecil Clarke. (An ATV production.)

| 1972 | 5.7 | Sun 2 Jul 10:15 p.m. | 12 | 2 wks |

'Madly in Love' by Paul Ableman.
The story of a crazy courtship between shy poet Angus (Richard Beckinsale) and a complex girl, Mary (Madeline Smith). Mary's parents are played by Eleanor Summerfield and Michael Bates.
Designer: Marilyn Taylor. **Producer:** John Jacobs. (An Anglia production.)

Sunday Playhouse — 5 wks

ATV, drama

This was a series of single dramas.

| 1965 | 6.1 | Sun 17 Jan 10:05 p.m. | 13 | 5 wks |

'A Tall Stalwart Lancer' by Gerald Vaughan-Hughes.
Starring James Mason as Torquil Callander, a mysterious character discovered sitting beside several dustbins in a mews.
Designer: Disley Jones. **Director:** John Moxey. **Producer:** Cecil Clarke.

Sunley's Daughter — 1 wk

YTV, documentary

| 1974 | 6.7 | Tue 14 May 9:00 p.m. | 12 | 1 wk |

This film profiles a farming family in the Yorkshire Dales. Joe Sunley breeds Cleveland Bay horses, but he and his wife are now elderly. Their daughter Mary is the only child left at home. They have no electricity and Mary spends six hours each day milking the cows.
Producer: Barry Cockcroft. **Executive Producer:** John Fairley.

Supercops, The | 1 wk

Presented by BBC, film

| 1983 | 6.5 | Wed 10 Aug 7:30 p.m. | 20 | 1 wk |

Two young New York City police recruits soon discover they are fighting corruption not only on the streets but in the police force itself. Starring Ron Liebman and David Selby.
Director: Gordon Parks Jr.

Supergirl | 2 wks

Presented by ITV, film

| 1988 | 12.7 | Sat 9 Jan 7:15 p.m. | 12 | 1 wk |

A Krypton power source falls into the hands of a power-hungry witch. Superman's cousin Supergirl and Lois Lane's sister Lucy become involved. Starring Peter Cook, Faye Dunaway, Mia Farrow, Helen Slater, Peter O'Toole and Simon Ward.
Director: Jeannot Szwarc.

| 1989 | 9.2 | Sat 8 Jul 6:40 p.m. | 20 | 1 wk |

Repeat showing of the above film.

Superman | 2 wks

Presented by ITV, film

| 1983 | 16.0 | Thu 6 Jan 7:25 p.m. | 5 | 2 wks |

Knowing their planet Krypton is about to explode, Jor-El (Marlon Brando) and Lara (Susannah York) send their son Kal-El to Earth in a rocket. He is discovered and raised by the Kents. He has superpowers on his new home planet. Known as Superman, he retains his civilian identity of Clark Kent. Christopher Reeve stars in the double role. Margot Kidder appears as Lois Lane. This film was based on the comic book stories of Jermome Siegel and Joe Schuster.
Director: Richard Donner.

Superman II | 4 wks

Presented by ITV, film

| 1985 | 17.6 | Fri 4 Jan 7:00 p.m. | 4 | 1 wk |

General Zod (Terence Stamp) and his cohorts wreak havoc in the state of Idaho. Christopher Reeve stars as Superman with Gene Hackman as Lex Luthor and Margot Kidder as Lois Lane. Ned Beatty and Susannah York also star.
Director: Richard Lester.

| 1986 | 10.7 | Thu 4 Sep 8:00 p.m. | 12 | 1 wk |

| 1988 | 13.6 | Fri 1 Jan 4:00 p.m. | 8 | 1 wk |
| 1989 | 9.7 | Mon 29 May 8:00 p.m. | 19 | 1 wk |

Repeat showings of the above film.

Superman III | 2 wks

Presented by ITV, film

| 1985 | 15.6 | Thu 5 Sep 7:30 p.m. | 4 | 1 wk |

Gus Gorman (Richard Pryor) provides the means for his boss Ross Webster (Robert Vaughn) to embark on the crime of the century. Only Superman (Christopher Reeve) can stop him.
Director: Richard Lester.

| 1987 | 13.3 | Sat 3 Jan 7:00 p.m. | 7 | 1 wk |

Repeat showing of the above film.

Supermind | 1 wk

BBC, game show

In this bonanza version of MASTERMIND all the contestants were past holders of the title.

| 1976 | 6.8 | Thu 1 Jan 9:30 p.m. | 12 | 1 wk |

Magnus Magnusson asks the questions of the four title holders competing for the SUPERMIND trophy. The contestants are John Hart, Elizabeth Horrocks, Patricia Owen and Nancy Wilkinson.
Director: Peter Massey. **Producer:** Bill Wright.

Supersense | 3 wks

BBC, documentary

This series narrated by Andrew Sachs explored the senses of animals and fish.
Writer and **Producer:** John Downer.

| 1988 | 13.4 | Mon 5 Dec 8:30 p.m. | 7 | 2 wks |

'Sixth Sense'
An investigation into how geese navigate by the sun and the stars, how dolphins use magnetic forces, and how certain mammals can sense body electricity. The programme also illustrates that there are animal meteorologists and even ones that can predict earthquakes.

| 1989 | 9.3 | Sun 9 Jul 7:45 p.m. | 18 | 1 wk |

'Super Scents'
A repeat showing of a programme demonstrating how fish, animals and birds use their sense of smell. Salmon can smell their way to spawning grounds and pigeons navigate by smell, while other animals deter predators by odour.

S

Superstars, The   5 wks

BBC, sport

Top athletes from a whole range of sports competed across a wide range of disciplines in both domestic and European contests. Presenters were David Vine and Ron Pickering.

| 1979 | 14.9 | Fri 16 Feb 7:55 p.m. | 15 | 2 wks |

From Rotterdam. Lynn Davies and Brian Jacks represent Britain in the European Championships.
Director: Pieter Varekamp. **Executive Producer:** Ian Smith.

| 1980 | 16.0 | Fri 18 Jan 7:00 p.m. | 9 | 2 wks |

From the Grangemouth Sports Complex in Scotland. The contestants are Grant Anderson, Steve Assinder, Andy Drzewiecki, Joe Jordan, Alan Minter, Mike Tredgett, J. J. Williams and Terry Yorath.
Television presentation: Peter Hylton Cleaver.

| 1981 | 16.3 | Fri 2 Jan 6:55 p.m. | 6 | 1 wk |

From the Wycombe Sports Centre. The contestants are John Conteh, Tim Crooks, Lynn Davies, Keith Fielding, David Hemery, Brian Jacks, Malcolm Macdonald and John Sherwood.
Television presentation: Peter Hylton Cleaver.

Superteams, The   1 wk

BBC, sport

Teams from individual sports competed over a variety of disciplines including crossbow shooting, basketball, swimming and cycling.

| 1979 | 16.8 | Wed 22 Aug 8:05 p.m. | 3 | 1 wk |

Everton's Mick Lyons' team of footballers face Geoff Capes' team of athletes. Barry Davies and Ron Pickering commentate.
Television presentation: Peter Hylton Cleaver.

Support Your Local Sheriff   1 wk

Presented by BBC, film

| 1977 | 13.6 | Mon 26 Dec 6:05 p.m. | 20 | 1 wk |

James Garner stars as Jason McCullough, lawman in the small town of Calendar where gold is discovered.
Director: Burt Kennedy.

Surgical Spirit   7 wks

Granada, situation comedy

This series by Peter Learmouth starred Nichola McAuliffe as Mrs Sheila Sabatini, a hard-as-nails senior hospital surgeon with a heart of gold. Duncan Preston played Dr Jonathan Haslam with Marji Campi as Joyce Watson. Michael Howarth portrayed Mrs Sabatini's estranged husband Remo.
Director: David Askey. **Producer:** Humphrey Barclay. **Executive Producers:** David Liddiment and Al Mitchell.

| 1990 | 9.6 | Fri 8 Jun 8:00 p.m. | 17 | 4 wks |

'Something in the Air'
Mrs Sabatini and Dr Jonathan Haslam disagree over whether two professional people can form a successful personal relationship.

| 1991 | 13.1 | Fri 8 Feb 8:30 p.m. | 14 | 3 wks |

'The Earth Trembles'
An admirer of Sheila's ends up in hospital following a night out.

Surprise, Surprise   50 wks

LWT, entertainment

Pleasant surprises were provided for members of the public. A segment called SEARCHLINE helped find lost friends and relatives. Cilla Black presented and was assisted by Christopher Biggins in 1984 and by Bob Carolgees and Gordon Burns from 1986 on.
Directors: John Gorman (1984–91), Tom Poole (1984, 1986–87) and Vic Finch (1985–86). **Producers** included Brian Wesley (1985–89) and Linda Beadle (1990–91).

| 1984 | 14.4 | Sun 18 Nov 7:45 p.m. | 7 | 9 wks |

Producer: Bob Merrilees.

1985	12.5	Sun 22 Dec 8:25 p.m.	8	1 wk
1986	16.0	Sun 23 Feb 7:45 p.m.	3	9 wks
1987	14.8	Sun 8 Mar 7:45 p.m.	5	9 wks
1988	13.9	Sun 10 Jan 7:15 p.m.	5	4 wks
1989	11.9	Fri 17 Feb 7:30 p.m.	20	1 wk
1990	13.2	Fri 9 Mar 8:00 p.m.	9	9 wks
1991	12.4	Fri 22 Feb 8:15 p.m.	12	8 wks

Survival   16 wks

Anglia, documentary

This was a long-running wildlife series of half-hour programmes.

| 1966 | 6.7 | Wed 2 Mar 9:40 p.m. | 12 | 1 wk |

'Karamoja'
The African tribes of Karamoja are fierce warriors who find sport in raiding each other for cattle and women. Duncan Carse narrates.
Camera: Alan Root. **Director:** Stanley Joseph.

| 1974 | 7.2 | Wed 30 Oct 7:00 p.m. | 8 | 5 wks |

'The Lake of Flies'
Peter Scott narrates the story of the flies to whom this unusual lake, in Iceland's lava desert, is home.
Camera: Robin Crane. **Writer:** Malcolm Penny. **Producer:** Colin Willock.

| 1976 | 6.3 | Fri 2 Jan 7:05 p.m. | 15 | 1 wk |

'Almost a Dodo'
In the vast swamps of Zambia, the camera tracks down the weirdest bird in the world, the Shrebill or Whale-headed Stork. Kenneth More narrates.
Camera: Lucinda Buxton. **Producer:** Aubrey Buxton.

| 1977 | 13.9 | Tue 6 Sep 8:00 p.m. | 5 | 2 wks |

'Tiger, Tiger'
Kenneth More narrates the story of the threat of extinction to the tigers of India and Nepal, where the jungles are being felled for timber.
Camera: G. Dieter Plage and Mike Price. **Writer** and **Producer:** Colin Willock.

| 1978 | 11.5 | Tue 4 Jul 7:00 p.m. | 15 | 6 wks |

'Tough Near the Top'
An examination of the high altitude life of Sherpas and the fauna in the new national park in the foothills of Everest. Duncan Carse narrates.
Writer: Malcolm Penny. **Camera:** G. Dieter Plage. **Producer:** Colin Willock.

| 1991 | 9.1 | Thu 22 Aug 7:30 p.m. | 16 | 1 wk |

'Killer Mouse'
Brian Blessed narrates this film about the predator mouse of New Zealand. (Repeat.)
Camera: Claude Steelman. **Writer** and **Producer:** Caroline Brett.

....

| **Survival Special** | | | | **7 wks** |

Anglia, documentary

These were extended wildlife specials from the SURVIVAL team.
Series Producer: Colin Willock.

| 1978 | 21.1 | Fri 22 Dec 8:00 p.m. | 2 | 1 wk |

'The Leopard That Changed Its Spots'
David Niven narrates the story of a pet leopard which answered the call of the wild.
Camera: G. Dieter Plage. **Writer** and **Producer:** Colin Willock.

| 1980 | 14.1 | Fri 7 Nov 8:00 p.m. | 17 | 1 wk |

'The Waterhole'
Animals converge on a spring-fed waterhole in Africa's Etosha National Park at the height of the dry season. Alexander John narrates.
Camera: Des and Jean Bartlett. **Writer** and **Producer:** Colin Willock.

| 1982 | 9.6 | Fri 14 May 7:30 p.m. | 20 | 1 wk |

'Stranded on South Georgia'
John Hedges narrates the story of film-maker Cindy Buxton and her assistant Annie Prince. They were filming a programme on King Penguins on a remote part of South Georgia when the Argentinians invaded on 3 April 1982.

| 1983 | 8.3 | Fri 19 Aug 9:00 p.m. | 12 | 1 wk |

'Krakatoa – The Day That Shook The World'
The remote volcanic island of Krakatoa blew up in 1883 and disappeared with the loudest bang the world has ever known. Today, one hundred years later, a new Krakatoa is rising from the sea. It threatens a repeat explosion. John Hedges narrates.
Camera: G. Dieter Plage and Alain Compost. **Writer** and **Producer:** Colin Willock.

| 1984 | 10.1 | Fri 25 May 7:30 p.m. | 11 | 2 wks |

'The Mysterious Journey'
Richard and Julia Kemp follow the migratory pattern of antelope in Southern Sudan. Robert Hardy narrates.

| 1990 | 12.2 | Wed 6 Jun 9:00 p.m. | 7 | 1 wk |

'Here Be Dragons'
Ian Holm narrates this film about the crocodiles of the River Nile.
Camera: Mark Deeble, Alan Root and Victoria Stone. **Writer** and **Producer:** Alan Root.

....

| **Survival Team** | | | | **1 wk** |

BBC, documentary

In these three programmes six ordinary people who had never previously met were taught survival techniques and then left on a remote island to put them into practice.

| 1987 | 9.2 | Mon 3 Aug 9:30 p.m. | 16 | 1 wk |

In this first programme covering the first few days there is nothing to eat but puffballs and mushrooms.
Camera: Jimmy Dibling. **Sound:** Christian Wangler. **Editor:** Liz Thoyts.

Suspense Hour — 5 wks

ATV, drama

This occasional series of single plays had an element of suspense.

| 1965 | 5.7 | Sun 20 Jun 10:05 p.m. | 10 | 5 wks |

'A Question of Disposal' by Gerry Jones.
Peter Evett (George Baker) receives an anonymous note and a phone call, both of which refer to a place inextricably linked with his past. He and his wife Sylvia (Shelagh Fraser) try to determine what connection a man named Ronald Brook (John Standing) may have with them.
Designer: Vic Symonds. **Director:** Graham Evans. **Producer:** Cecil Clarke.

Suspicion — 7 wks

ATV, drama

The plays in this series were based on a partial or unconfirmed belief that something somewhere is wrong and someone is guilty.

| 1971 | 6.5 | Tue 21 Dec 9:00 p.m. | 11 | 3 wks |

'No Case to Answer' by Lewis Greifer.
Lawyer Davyd McGrath (Donald Burton) successfully defends a young driver who killed a schoolboy. The boy's father George Bishop (John Comer) telephones to congratulate McGrath on getting a murderer off. Then McGrath's own son disappears and he and his wife (Barbara Leigh-Hunt) suspect Bishop is taking revenge.
Designer: Don Fisher. **Director:** Henri Safran. **Producer:** Nicholas Palmer.

| 1972 | 8.1 | Tue 4 Jan 9:00 p.m. | 3 | 4 wks |

'Old Man's Hat' by Fay Weldon.
Balding middle-aged Freddo (Ian Hendry) loses his job and finds that he and his wife (Yvonne Mitchell) will have to sell their home to survive. He fears their love may be destroyed in the process.
Designer: Richard Lake. **Director:** Paul Annett. **Producer:** Nicholas Palmer.

Suspicion — 1 wk

HTV, drama

| 1987 | 8.4 | Tue 30 Jun 8:00 p.m. | 14 | 1 wk |

Jonathan Lynn and Barry Levinson adapted Alfred Hitchcock's film story about Lina (Jane Curtin), who believes her husband Johnnie (Anthony Andrews) is a murderer. Betsy Blair, Michael Hordern, Jonathan Lynn and Vivian Pickles also star.
Director: Andrew Grieve. **Producers:** Barry Levinson and Sebastian Robinson.

Sutherland's Law — 3 wks

BBC, drama

This series was created by Lindsay Galloway and set on the West Coast of Scotland. Iain Cuthbertson starred as John Sutherland, a procurator fiscal. Harriet Buchan as Gail Munro and Martin Cochrane as David Drummond also starred.

| 1974 | 6.4 | Tue 3 Sep 8:10 p.m. | 6 | 1 wk |

'Just a Little Death' by Nick McCarty.
A small boy dies from poisoning. Sutherland must act quickly in order to prevent further deaths.
Designers: David McKenzie and Helen Rae. **Director:** Gilchrist Calder. **Producer:** Frank Cox.

| 1975 | 7.8 | Tue 27 May 8:10 p.m. | 9 | 2 wks |

'In At The Deep End' by Lindsay Galloway.
Sutherland has a new assistant, Helen Matheson (Virginia Stark). Her first case involves the whereabouts of a Mrs Shaw. James Shaw (Michael Gough) booked into the Oban Hotel alone.
Designer: Archie Clark. **Director:** Don Leaver. **Producer:** Frank Cox.

Swarm, The — 2 wks

Presented by BBC, film

| 1984 | 10.1 | Fri 23 Mar 7:05 p.m. | 20 | 1 wk |

Michael Caine stars as entomologist Brad Crane, who is assigned to arrest the progress of a plague of killer bees heading for Houston. Richard Chamberlain, José Ferrer, Henry Fonda, Olivia de Havilland, Ben Johnson, Fred MacMurray, Katharine Ross and Richard Widmark also star.
Director: Irwin Allen.

| 1986 | 12.7 | Sat 4 Jan 9:15 p.m. | 18 | 1 wk |

Repeat showing of the above film.

Sweeney, The — 72 wks

Thames/Euston films, drama

This series developed from a TV movie, REGAN. The title came from 'Sweeney Todd', the Cockney rhyming slang for the Flying Squad. Rough and often violent, the cops womanized, drank and used bad language, but they got their villains. John Thaw starred as Detective Inspector Regan and Dennis Waterman as Detective Sergeant Carter.
Producer: Ted Childs. **Executive Producers:** Lloyd Shirley and George Taylor.

| 1975 | 8.8 | Mon 13 Oct 9:00 p.m. | 1 | 25 wks |

'Golden Fleece' by Roger Marshall.
Two young Australians develop the golden touch for fleecing people.
Director: David Wickes.

| 1976 | 9.4 | Mon 8 Nov 9:00 p.m. | 1 | 15 wks |

'Sweet Smell of Succession' by Peter Hill.
One of London's biggest villains, Joe Castle, has an heir, Steven (Hywel Bennett) – a fact which only emerges at Joe's funeral.
Director: William Brayne.

| 1977 | 16.2 | Mon 5 Dec 9:00 p.m. | 2 | 9 wks |

'Supersnout' by Ranald Graham.
Regan has to work with informers from time to time but he never likes them – especially Strickley (John Tordoff).
Director: Tom Clegg.

| 1978 | 19.1 | Thu 21 Dec 9:00 p.m. | 3 | 16 wks |

'Selected Target' by Troy Kennedy Martin.
A quarrel inside a prison appears to involve a criminal on the outside who is Regan's current target for investigation. He and Carter become involved in a dangerous case against Kibber (Lee Montague) and Oates (Ronald Fraser). Mrs Smedley (Maureen Lipman), a housewife, is innocently caught up in the action. (Repeat.)
Director: Tom Clegg.

| 1981 | 13.4 | Mon 2 Feb 9:00 p.m. | 13 | 7 wks |

Repeat of the top 1976 episode.

Sweeney | 1 wk

Presented by ITV, film

| 1980 | 14.8 | Mon 22 Dec 9:00 p.m. | 15 | 1 wk |

In this full-length feature film version Regan and Carter find them-
'ves accidentally involved against the British government during
'on-based conference of oil-producing countries. John Thaw
and Dennis Waterman star with Ian Bannen, Michael Coles, Barry Foster, Joe Melia and Colin Welland.
Director: David Wickes.

Sweeney II | 1 wk

Presented by ITV, film

| 1981 | 16.1 | Mon 21 Dec 9:15 p.m. | 8 | 1 wk |

A series of bank robberies involves the Flying Squad in violent investigations. They discover that the culprits are expatriates re-turned from Malta. John Thaw and Dennis Waterman star with David Casey, Denholm Elliott, John Flanagan, Nigel Hawthorne and Barry Stanton.
Director: Tom Clegg.

Sweepstakes Game, The | 3 wks

LWT, game show

A studio audience placed bets on which celebrities could answer questions put to them by Bernard Braden. A computer then worked out the odds on each celebrity coming up with a correct answer. Contestants then placed their bets based on these odds.

| 1976 | 5.7 | Sat 7 Aug 6:45 p.m. | 15 | 3 wks |

Celebrity panel: Michael Aspel, Jim Davidson, Vicky Harris, Monty Modlyn, Carmen Munro and Freddie Trueman.
Producer: Bruce Gowers.

Sweet Nothing's | 1 wk

BBC, drama

This four-part love story by Ted Whitehead starred Tom Bell as Tom and Lynn Farleigh as Mary. The title was taken from Brenda Lee's hit record of 1960.

| 1980 | 12.6 | Thu 6 Mar 8:25 p.m. | 20 | 1 wk |

Part Three
Tom is obsessed with Mary and builds his love on the lyrics of the teenage ballads of the sixties. Mary finds it increasingly difficult to handle his obsession.
Designer: David McKenzie. **Director:** Martyn Friend. **Producer:** Colin Tucker.

Sweet Revenge | 1 wk

Presented by ITV, film

| 1989 | 9.5 | Wed 14 Jun 9:00 p.m. | 10 | 1 wk |

Kevin Dobson and Kelly McGillis star in the story of a senior army officer who tries to pass the blame for a girl's death on to a young lieutenant.
Director: David Greene.

Switching Channels | 1 wk

Presented by BBC, film

| 1991 | 9.2 | Sun 25 Aug 8:35 p.m. | 15 | 1 wk |

Christopher Reeve, Burt Reynolds and Kathleen Turner star in a story of the high-pressure world of television news.
Director: Ted Kotcheff.

S

Sword of Justice — 5 wks

USA presented by BBC, drama

Dack Rambo starred as Jack Cole, recently released from prison after serving a sentence for a crime he did not commit. While in prison he learned criminal skills which he used to exact his revenge on those responsible. The series also featured Alex Courtney as Arthur Woods and Bert Rosario as Hector Ramirez.
Creator and **Producer:** Glen Larson.

| 1979 | 14.3 | Sat 11 Aug 9:15 p.m. | 4 | 5 wks |

'Blackjack'
Jack devises a method of marking the cards to recover embezzled union money from a Las Vegas casino.

Sykes — 18 wks

BBC, comedy

This series starred Eric Sykes and Hattie Jacques as a brother and sister who shared a house. Deryck Guyler and Richard Wattis also starred.
Writer: Eric Sykes. **Producer:** Roger Race.

| 1972 | 6.0 | Thu 21 Dec 8:00 p.m. | 12 | 5 wks |

'Lodger'
Mr Brown (Richard Wattis) has the decorators in and decides to stay next door with Eric and Hattie.

| 1975 | 8.6 | Tue 27 May 7:40 p.m. | 4 | 3 wks |

'Haunting'
Eric's Uncle Edouardo has died leaving a legacy. Eric and Hattie look forward to a bit of the good life.

| 1976 | 7.1 | Thu 30 Dec 7:40 p.m. | 10 | 4 wks |

'Bath'
While their own bathroom is being redecorated Eric and Hattie arrange to use their neighbour's facilities.

| 1979 | 22.4 | Fri 19 Oct 7:35 p.m. | 6 | 6 wks |

'The Stay At Home Holiday'
Having been abroad last year, Eric and Hattie plan this year's holiday in the West Country.

Sykes and a Big, Big Show — 1 wk

BBC, comedy

This series was written by and starred Eric Sykes as the originator of fantastic ideas for spectacular television shows with a cast of thousands and elephants galore. His counterpart was Hattie Jacques, who reassured everybody that the ideas were all in his mind. The regular guest star was Ian Wallace, who was called upon to sing a song every time one of Sykes's ideas fell apart – which was very often.

| 1971 | 6.6 | Fri 5 Mar 8:30 p.m. | 18 | 1 wk |

Sykes imagines a show with himself as a Roman general leading a huge army. With Christopher Holmes, Tony Melody, Leslie Noyes, Billy Russell, Winifred Sabine, the George Mitchell singers and the Ken Jones orchestra.
Director: Dougles Argent. **Producer:** Dennis Main Wilson.

Sykes With The Lid Off — 1 wk

Thames, entertainment

| 1971 | 5.1 | Wed 7 Jul 8:00 p.m. | 14 | 1 wk |

This one-hour special with sketches and music stars Eric Sykes with Philip Gilbert, Hattie Jacques, Leslie Noyes and Dilys Watling with the Ronnie Aldrich orchestra and the Johnny Greenland dancers.
Producer: David Bell.

Sykes Versus ITV — 1 wk

ABC, comedy

| 1967 | 7.1 | Sun 26 Nov 10:05 p.m. | 8 | 1 wk |

Eric Sykes pleads his case in court as to why he should now be given a series on ITV. He receives help from Bernard Bresslaw, Tommy Cooper, Irving Davies, Robert Dorning, John Hanson and the ABC Showband.
Producer: Keith Beckett.

System, The — 1 wk

Granada, drama

This series of individual plays was produced by John Finch.

| 1968 | 5.2 | Tue 10 Sep 9:00 p.m. | 9 | 1 wk |

'Victims' by John Finch.
Anthony Bate and Libby Glen star as Stephen and Katherine, a couple who desperately need to talk but do not find it easy.
Designer: Peter Caldwell. **Director:** Michael Apted. **Executive Producer:** H. V. Kershaw.

T

Taggart | 35 wks

STV, drama

Mark McManus starred as the tough Glasgow cop who was first seen in KILLER. The series was peopled by a variety of Glaswegian characters created by writer Glenn Chandler.
Designer (1985–88): Marius Van Der Werff. **Director** (1986–87): Haldane Duncan. **Executive Producer:** Robert Love.

| 1985 | 10.2 | Tue 23 Jul 9:00 p.m. | 10 | 5 wks |

'Murder in Season'
When Eleanor Samson (Isla Blair) tries for a reconciliation with her husband, his new girlfriend is burned to death. Eleanor is suspected of murder.
Director: Peter Barber-Fleming.

| 1986 | 14.0 | Mon 10 Mar 9:00 p.m. | 3 | 6 wks |

'Knife Edge'
Three severed female legs have been found on a golf course.

| 1987 | 12.0 | Wed 29 Apr 9:00 p.m. | 7 | 9 wks |

'The Killing Philosophy'
In this final episode of a three-part story, Taggart and Detective Sergeant Livingstone (Neil Duncan) follow a pattern of murders and try to prevent further killings.

| 1988 | 13.3 | Wed 12 Oct 9:00 p.m. | 8 | 6 wks |

'Root of Evil'
In this final episode of a three-part story, a man has been axed to death – just like his brother before him.
Producer: Peter Barber-Fleming.

| 1989 | 10.6 | Tue 5 Sep 9:00 p.m. | 15 | 2 wks |

'Flesh and Blood'
This first episode in a three-part story concerns the murder of a social worker, crushed to death by a car driven by an unknown assailant.
Designer: Ann Gooch. **Director:** Alan Macmillan.

| 1990 | 12.9 | Mon 17 Dec 9:00 p.m. | 10 | 7 wks |

'Death Comes Softly' by Julian Jones
This first episode in a three-part story begins when a mummified body is discovered in an attic.
Director: Laurence Moody. **Producer:** Murray Ferguson.

Taggart – The Movie | 2 wks

Presented by ITV, film

| 1990 | 10.4 | Sat 12 May 9:10 p.m. | 17 | 2 wks |

'Cold Blood' by Glenn Chandler.
A woman shoots her husband through the windscreen of his car. The findings of the police surgeon complicate the matter.
Director: Haldane Duncan. **Producer:** Robert Love.

Take a Letter | 84 wks

Granada, game show

This game of crossword and spelling was hosted by Bob Holness. Contestants played for small amounts of money.

| 1962 | 6.1 | Wed 7 Nov 7:00 p.m. | 4 | 44 wks |

Director: Wilfred Fielding. **Producer:** John Hamp.

| 1963 | 6.2 | Wed 13 Feb 7:00 p.m. | 5 | 40 wks |

Director: Wilfred Fielding. **Producer:** Max Morgan-Witts.

Take a Letter Mr Jones | 1 wk

Southern, situation comedy

This series by Ronald Wolfe and Ronald Chesney concerned role reversal in business. It starred Rula Lenska as boss Mrs Warner and John Inman as secretary Graham Jones.

| 1981 | 11.7 | Sat 10 Oct 7:35 p.m. | 20 | 1 wk |

'Business Before Pleasure'
Mrs Warner is host to a visiting American executive.
Producer: Bryan Izzard.

Take It From Us — 1 wk

Southern, documentary

| 1967 | 4.8 | Tue 8 Aug 8:40 p.m. | 16 | 1 wk |

Hidden cameras prove the apathy of the general public to crime. Policemen act as criminals in two staged crimes: the violent abduction of a schoolgirl and a daylight raid on a jeweller's shop. Eyewitnesses refuse to get involved. Peter Clark narrates.
Producer: Terry Johnston.

Take Me Home — 3 wks

BBC, drama

This three-part story by Tony Marchant set in the Midlands new town of Woodleigh Abbots began when taxi driver Tom (Keith Barron) was driving home one winter's night. He was waved down by a young woman, Kathy (Maggie O'Neill), who was in distress after a row with her husband. Their affair began slowly. The pair's respective spouses, Liz and Martin, were played by Annette Crosbie and Reece Dinsdale.

| 1989 | 10.4 | Tue 16 May 9:30 p.m. | 9 | 3 wks |

Part Three
Kathy's affair with Tom has been discovered by her husband.
Designer: Marjorie Pratt. **Director:** Jane Howell. **Producer:** David Snodin.

Take My Wife — 4 wks

Granada, situation comedy

This series by Anthony Couch starred Duggie Brown as struggling comedian Harvey Hill and Victor Spinetti as his agent Maurice Watkins.

| 1979 | 15.2 | Wed 7 Mar 8:30 p.m. | 9 | 4 wks |

Harvey turns songwriter and plans to make a record. His wife Josie (Elisabeth Sladen) remains unimpressed.
Director: Gordon Flemyng. **Producer:** John G. Temple.

Take Three Girls — 1 wk

BBC, situation comedy

Charlotte Bingham and Terence Brady created the three girls. Victoria (Liza Goddard), Kate (Susan Jameson) and Avril (Angela Down) shared a flat.

| 1970 | 6.8 | Mon 2 Feb 9:10 p.m. | 15 | 1 wk |

'Gloria For First Offence'
Victoria is upset by the hostile attitude of her family. She discovers an outrageous solution to the problem and develops a new ability to cope with life.
Director: Mark Cullingham. **Producer:** Michael Hayes.

Take Your Pick — 304 wks

AR, game show

This show, hosted by 'Your Quiz Inquisitor' Michael Miles, began in 1955 and ran for almost twenty years. Contestants faced simple general-knowledge questions and a Yes-No interlude in which Miles asked quick-fire questions, each of which invited a yes or no response. Should a contestant use either word, nod or shake their head, they would be gonged out. The week's survivor would select a numbered key to a mystery box. Miles would offer increasing cash temptations for the key if the contestant answered his questions correctly, with the audience rising to fever pitch chants of 'take the money' or 'open the box'. The box could contain anything from a car to a clothes peg. Bob Danvers-Walker was the voice behind the boxes, Harold Smart the organist and Alec Dane the gong holder.
Director: Audrey Starrett.

1960	7.5	Fri 25 Nov 8:30 p.m.	1	32 wks
1961	6.9	Fri 17 Feb 8:30 p.m.	1	28 wks
1962	7.2	Fri 23 Nov 7:00 p.m.	1	40 wks
1963	8.0	Fri 13 Dec 7:00 p.m.	2	38 wks
1964	8.4	Fri 27 Nov 7:00 p.m.	2	39 wks
1965	8.8	Fri 26 Nov 7:00 p.m.	1	38 wks
1966	8.8	Fri 2 Dec 7:00 p.m.	1	25 wks
1967	8.8	Fri 20 Jan 7:00 p.m.	1	33 wks
1968	7.9	Fri 26 Jan 6:30 p.m.	1	31 wks

Tales of Mystery — 15 wks

AR, drama

This series of dramatizations of stories by Algernon Blackwood dealt with the unexplained or supernatural. John Laurie introduced each story in the guise of Blackwood himself.
Producer: Peter Graham Scott.

| 1961 | 6.4 | Wed 29 Mar 8:50 p.m. | 3 | 4 wks |

'The Terror of the Twins' adapted by Giles Cooper.
Sir George Fletton (Malcolm Russell) has long yearned for a son and heir. However, when he becomes the father of twin boys his paternal feelings change into an unnatural hatred bordering on madness.
Director: Geoffrey Hughes.

| 1962 | 6.1 | Wed 11 Jul 9:15 p.m. | 3 | 10 wks |

'Chinese Magic' adapted by Giles Cooper.
The life of an Orientalist, Edward Farque (Hugh Burden), is believed by him to be enchanted through his study of magic. This theory is

derided by his brain specialist friend Owen Francis (Peter Williams). Francis is soon forced to think again.
Director: John Frankau.

| 1963 | 5.9 | Thu 7 Feb 9:45 p.m. | 17 | 1 wk |

'The Second Generation' adapted by Owen Holder.
Maybe George Smith (Tenniel Evans) has a very ordinary name; maybe he is a very ordinary person. This does not preclude him being involved in some extraordinary circumstances which lead to an unexpected and frightening conclusion.
Director: John Frankau.

Tales of the Unexpected   39 wks

Anglia, drama

This series of plays had sardonic themes. Many of which were introduced by Roald Dahl.
Producer (1980–82, 1985–88): John Rosenberg. **Executive Producer:** John Woolf.

| 1980 | 10.4 | Sat 23 Aug 9:45 p.m. | 12 | 4 wks |

'Proof of Guilt' by Bill Pronzini dramatized by Johnny Byrne.
George Stamford (Jeremy Clyde) is a murder suspect. Chief Inspector Walters (Roy Marsden) still lacks one vital clue when another suspect, Miss Tower (Elizabeth Richardson), provides bizarre new evidence.
Designer: James Weatherup. **Director:** Chris Lovett.

| 1981 | 13.5 | Sun 19 Jul 9:15 p.m. | 3 | 3 wks |

'A Glowing Future' by Ruth Rendell dramatized by Ross Thomas.
Betsy (Joanna Pettet) is angry and dangerous because she has been deceived and ridiculed by her unfaithful lover Jack (John Beck).
Designer: Michael Bailey. **Director:** John Peyser.

| 1982 | 11.8 | Sun 2 May 10:00 p.m. | 14 | 6 wks |

'The Eavesdropper' by Ruth Wissmann dramatized by Robin Chapman.
Moira (Dorothy Tutin) does not intentionally overhear the conversation at the next table, but what she does hear almost drives her insane. Michael Craig and Sheila Ruskin also star.
Designer: Marilyn Taylor. **Director:** John Gorrie.

| 1983 | 10.0 | Sat 7 May 9:30 p.m. | 3 | 5 wks |

'Heir Presumptuous' by C. B. Clifford dramatized by Ross Thomas.
Twin nephews Donald and David (both played by David Cassidy) are prime suspects in the murder of their rich uncle.
Designer: Jim Shanahan. **Director:** Philip Leacock. **Producer:** Norma Lloyd.

| 1984 | 13.5 | Sun 16 Sep 9:30 p.m. | 4 | 3 wks |

'The Reconciliation' by Nicholas Monsarrat dramatized by Roy Russell.

James Howgill (Roger Rees) employs a private detective to trail his wife Caroline (Meg Davies) after she has refused him a divorce.
Designer: Michael Bailey. **Director:** John Jacobs. **Producer:** Graham Williams.

| 1985 | 11.7 | Sat 22 Jun 9:45 p.m. | 6 | 2 wks |

'Royal Jelly' by Roald Dahl dramatized by Robin Chapman.
Susan George stars as Mabel and Timothy West as her bee-keeper husband Albert.
Designer: Eileen Diss. **Director:** Herbert Wise.

| 1986 | 11.6 | Fri 22 Aug 9:30 p.m. | 3 | 4 wks |

'The Boy Who Talked With Animals' by Roald Dahl, dramatized by Robin Chapman.
Nine-year-old David (Paul Spurrier) has special powers with animals. While on holiday in Jamaica he has an adventure which changes the lives of all the people around him, including a total stranger.
Designer: Leo Austin. **Director:** Alan Gibson.

| 1987 | 10.9 | Sat 15 Aug 9:30 p.m. | 6 | 1 wk |

'Vicious Circle' by Donald Honig, dramatized by Robin Chapman.
Small-time criminal Rex Tobin (Patrick Field) is given a chance to start afresh thanks to Mrs Grady (Siobhan McKenna).
Designer: Leo Austin. **Director:** Philip Dudley.

| 1988 | 13.5 | Sun 20 Nov 9:30 p.m. | 9 | 11 wks |

'The Orderly World of Mr Appleby' by Stanley Ellin dramatized by Robin Chapman.
Arthur Appleby (Robert Lang) has already buried three wealthy wives by the time he meets Martha (Elizabeth Spriggs).
Designer: John Wood. **Director:** John Gorrie.

Tanamera, Lion of Singapore   6 wks

Central, drama

This six-part adaptation by Peter Gibbs from the novel by Noel Barber followed the changing history of Singapore, from the days of British Imperial rule through Japanese invasion to the struggle against Communism and Singapore's ultimate emergence as a free nation. The story followed two powerful families, the Dexters and the Soongs, rivals in business and in love. The gulf between the families came to a head when Julie Soong (Khym Lam), scheduled to marry her cousin Keow Tak (Kay Tong Lim), fell in love with John Dexter (Christopher Bowen). Other principal characters included Grandpa Jack (Ed Devereaux), Papa Jack (Lewis Fiander), Mama Jack (Penne Hackforth-Jones), Chalfont (Bryan Marshall), Natasha (Tushka Bergen), P. P. Soong (Tony Yeow) and Irene Bradshaw (Anne Louise Lambert).
Director: Kevin Dobson. **Producers:** David Lee and Jan Bladier. **Executive Producer:** Ted Childs. (A Grundy production.)

| 1989 | 14.5 | Sun 9 Apr 9:00 p.m. | 7 | 6 wks |

In this first episode John and Julie begin to test the unwritten laws that separate them. Their childhood friendship has grown into love, but both are bound by strict social taboos.

Tarbuck at the Prince of Wales | 5 wks

ATV, entertainment

This variety series was hosted by Jimmy Tarbuck from the Prince of Wales Theatre in London's West End.

| 1966 | 7.1 | Sun 22 May 10:05 p.m. | 5 | 5 wks |

Guest: Woody Allen. With the Pamela Devis dancers, the Mike Sammes singers and the Peter Knight orchestra.
Producer: Dicky Leeman.

Tarbuck's Back | 7 wks

ATV, entertainment

This variety series starred Jimmy Tarbuck. With the Jack Parnell orchestra.

| 1968 | 5.9 | Wed 1 May 10:30 p.m. | 19 | 3 wks |

Guests: Audrey Jeans and the Shadows.
Writer: Bryan Blackburn. **Producer:** Colin Clews.

| 1969 | 5.0 | Fri 29 Aug 7:05 p.m. | 14 | 4 wks |

Guests: Russ Conway, Jack Douglas, Audrey Jeans and Kenny Lynch.
Writer: Bryan Blackburn. **Producer:** Colin Clews.

Tarbuck's Luck | 1 wk

BBC, entertainment

This series starred Jimmy Tarbuck and was set in a 4th floor flat at the BBC's Television Centre.
Writers: Mike Craig, Lawrie Kinsley and Ron McDonnell.

| 1972 | 5.7 | Sat 8 Apr 8:30 p.m. | 18 | 1 wk |

Guests: Clodagh Rodgers and June Whitfield. With Gretchen Franklin, Clovissa Newcombe, Daphne Oxenford, the Norman Maen dancers and the Ronnie Hazlehurst orchestra.
Producers: Freddie Carpenter and James Moir.

Tarby and Friends | 4 wks

LWT, entertainment

This chat and performance show starred Jimmy Tarbuck. With the Brian Rogers dancers and the Alyn Ainsworth orchestra.
Director: Alasdair Macmillan. **Producer:** David Bell.

| 1984 | 14.6 | Sat 8 Dec 7:00 p.m. | 7 | 2 wks |

Guests: Michael Barrymore, Shirley Bassey, David Copperfield, Matt Monro and Shakin' Stevens.

| 1986 | 11.7 | Sat 12 Apr 8:30 p.m. | 17 | 2 wks |

Guests: Shirley Bassey, Samantha Fox and Aiden J. Harvey.

Tarby and New Year Friends | 1 wk

LWT, entertainment

| 1985 | 13.4 | Sat 5 Jan 7:45 p.m. | 12 | 1 wk |

Last weekend's show, which was partially blacked out by power failure, is repeated. Jimmy Tarbuck's guests include Cilla Black, Foster Brooks, Gloria Hunniford, Michael Parkinson and Gary Wilmot.
Director: Alasdair Macmillan. **Producer:** David Bell.

Tarby's Frame Game | 6 wks

YTV, game show

In this game hosted by Jimmy Tarbuck, contestants had to find missing words to win prizes.
Producer: Graham Wetherell.

| 1987 | 9.9 | Sun 26 Jul 7:15 p.m. | 12 | 5 wks |
| 1988 | 9.4 | Sat 16 Jul 7:30 p.m. | 19 | 1 wk |

Target | 1 wk

BBC, drama

This police series starred Patrick Mower as Steven Hackett, a detective superintendent with a regional crime squad. Philip Madoc (Detective Chief Superintendent Tate), Brendan Price (Detective Sergeant Frank Bonney) and Vivien Heilbron (Detective Sergeant Louise Colbert) also starred.

| 1977 | 12.4 | Fri 16 Sep 9:25 p.m. | 9 | 1 wk |

'Blow Out' by David Agnew.
A nasty accident leads Hackett towards a gang of jewel thieves.
Director: Douglas Camfield. **Producer:** Philip Hinchcliffe.

Tarzan | 2 wks

USA presented by ITV, drama

This series starred Ron Ely as Tarzan.
Producer: Sy Weintraub.

| 1967 | 6.5 | Wed 8 Nov 6:10 p.m. | 12 | 2 wks |

'Three Faces of Death'
The daughter of a dead chief is about to assume the leadership of her tribe until challenged by a giant warrior. Tarzan becomes her champion and must undergo three tests of supreme courage before she may be declared leader.

....

Task Force South	4 wks

BBC, documentary

Brian Hanrahan, who reported from the scene during the fighting, narrated this series of eight programmes documenting the war for the Falkland Islands.

1982	8.5	Thu 12 Aug 9:25 p.m.	13	4 wks

'The Final Assault'
In this last programme of the series, it is bitterly cold on the islands in the middle of June. British troops wait in the bunkers and foxholes for the order to be given to descend on Port Stanley. Suddenly a white flag is waved and Argentinian troops are seen to be retreating.
Producer: Gordon Carr.

....

Taxi	4 wks

USA presented by BBC, situation comedy

Set mainly in a New York cab shelter, this series created by James L. Brooks starred Judd Hirsch as Alex Rieger with Randall Carver as John Burns, Jeff Conaway as Bobby Wheeler, Tony Danza as Tony Banta and Danny De Vito as Louie de Palma.
Producers: Glen and Les Charles.

1980	11.2	Thu 19 Jun 8:05 p.m.	8	1 wk

'Blind Date' by Michael Leeson.
A sexy voice on the answering service sets off Alex's romantic instincts.
Director: James Burrows.

1982	11.3	Wed 28 Apr 9:25 p.m.	5	3 wks

'Tony's Sister and Jim' by Michael Leeson.
Tony's divorced sister Monica (Julie Kavner) turns up. He tries to fix her up with Alex, but she has set her sights on Reverend Jim (Christopher Lloyd).
Director: James Burrows.

....

Teen Wolf	1 wk

Presented by BBC, film

1989	13.0	Sun 30 Dec 8:00 p.m.	14	1 wk

Michael J. Fox stars as high-school student Scott Howard, whose basketball playing is helped when he becomes a teenage werewolf.
Director: Rod Daniel.

Telefon	1 wk

Presented by ITV, film

1984	10.9	Sun 12 Feb 7:45 p.m.	18	1 wk

A group of Stalinists aims to force the USSR and USA away from détente and towards warlike postures. Starring Charles Bronson, Alan Badel, Tyne Daly, Donald Pleasence and Lee Remick.
Director: Don Siegel.

....

Telethon	3 wks

ITV, charity

Michael Aspel hosts twenty-seven hours of non-stop fund-raising events involving every ITV company from the Shetlands to the Channel Islands. The network segments come from LWT, with each individual company hosting its own events.
Producer: Gill Stribling-Wright. **Executive Producer:** Alan Boyd.

1988	13.4	Sun 29 May	4	1 wk
1990	10.7	Sun 27 May Mon 28 May	11	2 wks

....

Television Playhouse	61 wks

ITV, drama

This series of single plays was produced by various ITV companies.

1960	6.5	Thu 13 Oct 9:35 p.m.	3	15 wks

'Murder Stamp' by Geoffrey Bellman and John Whitney.
Jango Smith (Robert Urquhart) is Professor of Criminology at Nairobi University and is on temporary attachment to Scotland Yard. On arrival he learns that a murder suspect from six years ago is leaving for Australia. He re-examines the case.
Designer: Frank Nerini. **Director:** Jonathan Alwyn. (AR.)

1961	6.5	Thu 2 Feb 9:35 p.m.	3	19 wks

'Witness – The Night' by J. H. B. Peel.
When police investigate a hit and run accident their inquiries threaten to destroy the lives of both the guilty and the innocent. Starring Maxine Audley, Joanna Dunham, Cyril Raymond and Peter Vaughan.
Designer: John Clements. **Producer:** Ian Fordyce. (ATV.)

1962	6.2	Fri 26 Oct 9:45 p.m.	9	7 wks

'A Free Weekend' by Anne Piper.
Laura (Moyra Fraser) is bored and arranges a weekend in Paris with her friend Harry (John Stratton). Domesticity, a husband, three children and the family pets intervene in her plans. Also starring Francesca Annis, Georgina Cookson and Richard Vernon.
Designer: Stephen Doncaster. **Director:** John Hale. (ATV.)

T

| **1963** | **6.9** | **Fri 15 Feb 9:15 p.m.** | **5** | **20 wks** |

'A Builder by Trade' by Pamela Gems.
Two sisters, May Vine (Vanda Godsell) and Louie Robbins (Pauline Letts), take in Reg Beech (Harry Locke) as a lodger. May is an attractive, plump and cheerful widow. Louie is a severe, thin and miserable spinster. Reg is a builder by trade. May's son Charlie (Michael Williams) has just married, much to Louie's disgust, which is why they have found it necessary to take in a lodger. But when Reg shows an interest in gardening, Louie begins to warm to him.
Designer: Roy Stannard. **Director:** Ian Fordyce. (ATV.)

458

Telford's Change | 1 wk

BBC, drama

In this ten-part series by Brian Clark, Peter Barkworth starred as Mark Telford, a high-flying banker who chose to return to life as a provincial bank manager. His wife Sylvia (Hannah Gordon) opted to remain in London to pursue a show-business career. The series also starred Keith Barron as Tim Hart, Colin Douglas as Maddox and Zena Walker as Helen Santon. It was produced by Mark Shivas with original music by Johnny Dankworth.

| **1980** | **10.9** | **Sat 2 Aug 9:45 p.m.** | **11** | **1 wk** |

Episode Ten
Mark faces crucial decisions. Should he accept the new job in the International Division and should he confront Tim Hart, who threatens his marriage?
Director: Barry Davis.

Tell the Truth | 7 wks

ATV, game show

A celebrity panel tried to discover which of three contestants claiming to be the same individual was the actual person.

| **1961** | **4.6** | **Wed 6 Sep 7:00 p.m.** | **13** | **7 wks** |

Chairman: Shaw Taylor. Panellists: Frankie Day, Ruth Dunning, Keith Fordyce and Jack Good.
Producer: Rita Gillespie.

Telly Addicts | 2 wks

BBC, game show

Noel Edmonds hosted this game in which family teams answered questions about television programmes of the past and present.

| **1985** | **15.6** | **Tue 24 Dec 7:00 p.m.** | **8** | **1 wk** |

In this special edition, 1985 champions the Pain family take on a professional team of Michael Grade, Larry Grayson, Nina Myskow and Barry Took.
Director: Juliet May. **Producer:** John King.

| **1989** | **11.0** | **Mon 11 Dec 8:00 p.m.** | **20** | **1 wk** |

The Whiteway family take on the Rossiter family.
Director: Nick Hurran. **Producer:** Richard L. Lewis.

Telstar | 1 wk

ITN and BBC, news

| **1962** | **5.3** | **Mon 23 Jul 10.45 p.m.** | **6** | **1 wk** |

Following the launch of the first communications satellite this is the initial transmission of television pictures from across the world. Telstar orbits low and can link the hemispheres for 22 minutes at a time. Included in this link-up are a stampeding herd of buffalo, a live excerpt from Tosca in Rome and a visit to President Kennedy's regular news conference.

10 | 1 wk

Presented by ITV, film

| **1983** | **10.3** | **Mon 4 Apr 9:45 p.m.** | **18** | **1 wk** |

Dudley Moore stars as songwriter George, depressed by the onset of middle age and liberated by the vision of a beautiful young woman (Bo Derek). Julie Andrews plays his suffering girlfriend.
Director: Blake Edwards.

Ten Commandments, The | 6 wks

YTV, drama

Executive Producer Peter Willes co-ordinated a series on THE SEVEN DEADLY SINS while at Thames and set this up after his move to Yorkshire. Each play was one hour in length.

| **1971** | **6.9** | **Tue 6 Apr 9:00 p.m.** | **7** | **6 wks** |

'The Nineteenth Hole' by Bill MacIlwraith.
Willy (Paul Eddington) is a prosperous Doctor and a first class amateur golfer. When his friend Gerry (Peter Sallis) suggests proposing him for membership of his golf club, it all seems straightforward. But what follows means life will never be the same again. Willy begins to see through the mask worn by the pipe-smoking Major (Donald Sinden), president of the club. He hopes it will not be too late to avert tragedy.
Designer: Roger Andrews. **Director:** James Ormerod.

Ten Years of It'll Be Alright on the Night — 1 wk

LWT, comedy

| 1989 | 13.2 | Sun 24 Sep 7:15 p.m. | 6 | 1 wk |

Denis Norden celebrates ten years of his occasional series of amusing moments lost on the cutting room floor.
Director: Chris Fox. **Producer:** Paul Lewis.

....

Tenderfoot — 8 wks

USA presented by BBC, western

Will Hutchins starred as Tom Brewster, a young cowboy adventurer who was also a law student.

| 1962 | 5.3 | Sun 18 Mar 5:25 p.m. | 12 | 8 wks |

'A Noose for Nora'
Tom defends a woman on a murder charge even though he witnessed her commit the crime.

....

Tenko — 27 wks

BBC, drama

These three ten-part series were created by Lavinia Warner and told of the ordeals suffered by European women interned by the Japanese during the Second World War. They starred Jean Anderson, Reneé Asherson, Stephanie Beacham, Ann Bell, Jeananne Crowley, Joanna Hole, Burt Kwouk, Claire Oberman and Wendy Williams.
Producer: Ken Riddington.

| 1981 | 15.0 | Thu 3 Dec 9:25 p.m. | 9 | 8 wks |

Part Seven
As the hour approaches for Sally Markham (Joanna Hole) to have her baby, she finds herself increasingly reliant on Nellie Keene (Jeananne Crowley).
Writer: Jill Hyem. **Designer:** Colin Shaw. **Director:** David Askey.

| 1982 | 13.5 | Thur 9 Dec 9:25 p.m. | 4 | 9 wks |

Part Eight
The Japanese are out in the jungle searching for a missing prisoner. The atmosphere in the camp becomes tense when gunshots are heard.
Writer: Anne Valery. **Designer:** Paul Munting. **Director:** Jeremy Summers. **Producer:** Vere Lorimer.

| 1984 | 16.8 | Sun 16 Dec 8:50 p.m. | 2 | 10 wks |

Part Ten
The days leading up to the departure for home are fraught with anxiety.
Writer: Anne Valery. **Designer:** Ken Ledsham. **Director:** Michael Owen Morris.

Tennessee Ernie Ford Show, The — 1 wk

ATV, entertainment

| 1969 | 6.1 | Wed 31 Dec 8:00 p.m. | 17 | 1 wk |

The American singing star of the mid-1950s gets his own New Year's Eve special with guests Davy Jones, Harry Secombe, Terry-Thomas and Norman Wisdom. Also appearing are the Irving Davies dancers, the Mike Sammes singers and the Jack Parnell orchestra.
Director: Albert Locke. **Producers:** Digby Wolfe and Bob Wynn.

....

Terminator, The — 1 wk

Presented by BBC, film

| 1991 | 9.1 | Sat 17 Aug 11:15 p.m. | 17 | 1 wk |

Arnold Schwarzenegger stars in this sci-fi thriller. In the not so very distant future, machines rule the Earth. A killing machine is sent back to the present day on a mission of extermination.
Director: James Cameron.

....

Terry and June — 19 wks

BBC, situation comedy

Terry Scott and June Whitfield starred as Terry and June Medford, a middle-class suburban couple. Reginald Marsh played Terry's boss Sir Dennis Hodge and Joanna Henderson played their secretary Miss Fennel. Terry's immediate boss was played variously by Terence Alexander, Tim Barrett and John Quayle. Neighbour Beattie was portrayed by Rosemary Frankau.
Producers included Peter Whitmore (1980, 1981, 1983) and Robin Nash (1986–87).

| 1980 | 13.8 | Fri 10 Oct 8:20 p.m. | 10 | 5 wks |

'Only Two Can Play' by Jon Watkins.
June takes up the cello.

| 1981 | 13.2 | Fri 27 Nov 7:30 p.m. | 10 | 3 wks |

'It's A Knockout' by John Kane.
Nephew Alan (Roger Martin) has acquired some old costumes from IT'S A KNOCKOUT. Terry is wearing an outrageous example when Company Chairman Sir Dennis Hodge arrives for dinner.

| 1982 | 13.0 | Tue 12 Jan 8:00 p.m. | 15 | 2 wks |

'Snookered' by Terry Ravenscroft.
Terry finds he is no match for Joe Davis (Jack Haig) and advertises his snooker table for sale.
Producer: John B. Hobbs.

| 1983 | 10.7 | Mon 21 Nov 6:50 p.m. | 17 | 1 wk |

'The Barbecue' by John Kane.
Terry and June discover all the permutations of things that can go wrong with summertime outdoor cooking.

1985 | **11.4** | **Sat 27 Apr 6:10 p.m.** | **19** | **1 wk**

'**Break In**' by John Kane.
An ordinary day has a peculiar ending with Terry and June burgling a friend's house. (Repeat.)

1986 | **7.7** | **Tue 17 Jun 7:00 p.m.** | **19** | **1 wk**

'**Terry in Court**' by John Chapman and Eric Merriman.
Following an incident with a corporation dustcart, Terry decides to defend June in Court. (Repeat.)
Director: Martin Shardlow.

1987 | **11.6** | **Mon 27 Jul 8:30 p.m.** | **5** | **6 wks**

'**The Fire Extinguisher**' by David Grigson.
Terry's boss is far from amused when plans for a revolutionary talking fire extinguisher go missing.
Director: Martin Shardlow.

***

Terry Scott on Christmas | **1 wk**

BBC, comedy

1969 | **6.0** | **Tue 23 Dec 8:00 p.m.** | **12** | **1 wk**

This special features Peter Butterworth, Robin Hunter, Henry McGee, George Moon, June Whitfield and the Rita Williams singers.
Writer: Bryan Blackburn. **Choreographer:** Bob Stevenson. **Producer:** Kenneth Carter.

***

Thank Your Lucky Stars | **118 wks**

ABC, music

On this pop show from Birmingham recording stars mimed to their records and a panel judged the new releases. The most famous panellist was Janice Nicholls, whose 'Oi'll give it foive' in a Brummie accent became a catch phrase.
Producer (1961–63): Philip Jones.

1961 | **4.2** | **Sat 30 Dec 5:50 p.m.** | **20** | **1 wk**

Brian Matthew hosts a special year-end edition featuring some of the biggest hits of the year with Chubby Checker, Billy Fury, Cliff Richard, the Shadows and Helen Shapiro.

1962 | **5.9** | **Sat 29 Dec 5:50 p.m.** | **5** | **4 wks**

Brian Matthew introduces the 'Hit Parade of '62' with Kenny Ball and his Jazzmen, Ronnie Carroll, Petula Clark, the Karl Denver Trio, Craig Douglas, Frank Ifield, Cliff Richard, the Shadows and Helen Shapiro.

1963 | **7.4** | **Sat 9 Nov 5:50 p.m.** | **4** | **32 wks**

Brian Matthew introduces Joe Brown, Freddie and the Dreamers, Johnny Kidd and the Pirates, Billy J. Kramer, Dion DiMucci, the Viscounts and Timi Yuro.

1964 | **6.8** | **Sat 14 Mar 5:50 p.m.** | **7** | **44 wks**

Brian Matthew introduces the Applejacks, the Brumbeats, the Dave Clark Five, Linda Doll, the Overlanders, Peter and Gordon and Gene Pitney. With guest disc jockey Henry Mancini.
Producer: Helen Standage.

1965 | **5.8** | **Sat 13 Nov 6:15 p.m.** | **2** | **35 wks**

Jim Dale introduces Winifred Atwell, the Caesars, Carol Deene, Gerry and the Pacemakers, Brian Poole and the Tremeloes, and Danny Williams with the Jo Cook dancers.
Producer: Keith Beckett.

1966 | **5.7** | **Sat 26 Feb 5:50 p.m.** | **19** | **2 wks**

Jim Dale introduces Cliff Bennett and the Rebel Rousers, Kiki Dee, Tom Jones, Paddy, Klaus and Gibson, Patsy Ann Noble, Gene Pitney, and The Yardbirds.
Producer: Milo Lewis.

***

That Beryl Marston . . .! | **6 wks**

Southern, situation comedy

This series by Jan Butlin was about Georgie Bodley (Julia McKenzie), proprietress of a Brighton curiosity shop, and her husband Gerry (Gareth Hunt), a company executive. Their lives were one big success, with the exception of their marriage. Their differences were brought to a head by Gerry's affair with Beryl Marston, sex goddess of East Sussex. (She was never seen in the series.) Georgie and Gerry were kept from coming to blows by their friends Harvey and Phil (Peter John and Jonathon Morris), a gay couple who ran a health food shop.

1981 | **12.5** | **Fri 24 Jul 8:30 p.m.** | **6** | **6 wks**

Gerry begins his affair with Beryl.
Producer: Bryan Izzard.

***

That Lucky Touch | **2 wks**

Presented by ITV, film

1980 | **11.3** | **Sun 7 Sep 7:15 p.m.** | **14** | **1 wk**

Roger Moore stars as Michael Scott, an international arms dealer living in Brussels who falls in love with crusading journalist Julia Richardson (Susannah York). Lee J. Cobb, Donald Sinden, Raf Vallone and Shelley Winters also star.
Director: Christopher Miles.

1982 | **11.5** | **Tue 8 Jun 7:30 p.m.** | **7** | **1 wk**

Repeat showing of the above film.

That Old Black Magic | 1 wk

AR, drama

| 1967 | 6.6 | Thu 2 Feb 9:40 p.m. | 11 | 1 wk |

This play by Paul Jones touches on the problems of racial integration. The Cockburns (George Cole and Joan Sims) take in a black lodger, medical student Ambrose (Johnny Sekka). The Cockburns' efforts to show how liberal-minded they are towards blacks causes extreme embarrassment to their daughter Cherry (Julia Foster) and is sorely tested when she and Ambrose develop a romantic attachment. **Designer:** Michael Wild. **Director:** Peter Moffatt. **Executive Producer:** Peter Willes.

That's Carry On | 1 wk

Thames, film

| 1981 | 11.4 | Mon 25 May 7:00 p.m. | 15 | 1 wk |

Bank Holiday compilation of clips from CARRY ON films. **Director:** Gerald Thomas.

That's Life | 174 wks

BBC, entertainment

This long-running series was hosted and for the most part produced or edited by Esther Rantzen. This magazine format show blended serious issues with comedy, songs and unusual performances. The supporting cast began in 1975 with Cyril Fletcher, Kieran Prendiville and Glyn Worsnip. The latter two were replaced in 1978 by Chris Serle and Paul Heiney. This pair and Fletcher continued until 1981. Other billed regulars included Bill Buckley (1982–85), Gavin Campbell (1982–90), Doc Cox (1982–84, 1986–90), Michael Groth (1982–85), Joanna Munro (1982–84), Grant Baynham (1986–89) and Adrian Mills (1986–90). **Directors** included Pieter Morpurgo (1976–77) and Bob Marsland (1981, 1983–87) and Robert Bexter (1988–89). **Producers** included Henry Murray (1979, 1981). **Editors** included John Morrell (1975–77, 1985–88), Peter Chafer (1978–79), and Gordon Watts (1982–84).

| 1975 | 5.5 | Sat 12 Jul 10:00 p.m. | 17 | 2 wks |

Song of the week from Lois Lane. **Director:** Mike Catherwood.

| 1976 | 6.9 | Sun 15 Feb 9:50 p.m. | 9 | 8 wks |

Song of the week from Fivepenny Piece.

| 1977 | 8.0 | Sat 21 May 9:55 p.m. | 3 | 6 wks |

Song of the week from Catherine Howe.

| 1978 | 13.6 | Sun 16 Jul 9:40 p.m. | 1 | 7 wks |
| 1979 | 16.4 | Sun 18 Mar 9:45 p.m. | 5 | 12 wks |

| 1981 | 15.1 | Sun 26 Apr 9:35 p.m. | 5 | 16 wks |

Editor: Ronald Neil.

| 1982 | 10.2 | Sun 17 Oct 9:20 p.m. | 13 | 3 wks |

Director: Chris Fox.

1983	12.6	Sun 8 May 9:40 p.m.	2	10 wks
1984	13.5	Sun 15 Jul 9:30 p.m.	1	19 wks
1985	18.4	Sun 17 Feb 9:20 p.m.	2	24 wks

With Maev Alexander and John Gould.

| 1986 | 14.3 | Sun 9 Feb 9:25 p.m. | 3 | 20 wks |

With actress Mollie Sugden.

| 1987 | 13.6 | Sun 11 Jan 9:25 p.m. | 6 | 16 wks |
| 1988 | 15.9 | Sun 28 Feb 9:15 p.m. | 4 | 20 wks |

Producer: Bryher Scudamore.

| 1989 | 12.2 | Sun 5 Feb 9:30 p.m. | 8 | 8 wks |

Producer: Richard Woolfe. **Editor:** Bryher Scudamore.

| 1990 | 9.2 | Sun 24 Jun 9:45 p.m. | 16 | 3 wks |

With Howard Leader and Simon Fanshawe. **Editor:** Shaun Woodward.

That's Life Compilation | 1 wk

BBC, documentary

| 1984 | 8.6 | Tue 28 Aug 7:45 p.m. | 19 | 1 wk |

This special edition features some of the most requested items from the recent season of programmes. **Director:** Bob Marsland. **Producer:** Esther Rantzen. **Editor:** Gordon Watts.

That's Life Report | 4 wks

BBC, documentary

This series of special investigations was by Esther Rantzen and the THAT'S LIFE team.

| 1980 | 12.0 | Thu 22 May 8:30 p.m. | 8 | 4 wks |

Esther Rantzen and Nick Ross follow up their previous investigations into cases of people persuaded to confess to crimes they did not commit while being held in police custody. **Producers:** Esther Rantzen and Henry Murray.

That's My Boy — 22 wks

YTV, situation comedy

This series by Pam Valentine and Michael Ashton starred Christopher Blake as young Dr Robert Price. He was torn between his adoptive mother Mrs Price (Clare Richards) and his real mother Ida Willis (Mollie Sugden). Jennifer Lonsdale played Robert's wife Angie. **Producer:** Graeme Muir.

| 1981 | 14.4 | Fri 23 Oct 8:30 p.m. | 8 | 6 wks |

'Live As Family'
Real mother Ida Willis installs herself in Robert and Angie's flat as housekeeper.

| 1983 | 14.1 | Fri 14 Jan 8:30 p.m. | 3 | 9 wks |

'Wakey Wakey'
Ida agrees to take part in a sponsored 'wake' in aid of distressed gentlewomen.

| 1984 | 12.0 | Fri 1 Jun 8:30 p.m. | 6 | 7 wks |

'Dirty Linen'
Ida finds a crumpled note in Robert's jacket which provokes a family crisis.

That's Television Entertainment — 1 wk

BBC, entertainment

| 1986 | 13.9 | Sat 1 Nov 7:35 p.m. | 6 | 1 wk |

This three-hour selection of archive segments celebrates fifty years of BBC television. The show begins with the original opening announcement from Alexandra Palace in 1936 with Adèle Dixon. This is followed by a selection of clips from the entertainment archives spanning the half century.
Compiler and **Producer:** Colin Strong.

Theatre '60 — 1 wk

ATV, drama

This was a series of single plays.

| 1960 | 4.3 | Sun 31 Jul 10:00 p.m. | 10 | 1 wk |

'The Devil Makes Sunday' by Bruce Stewart.
Set in 1840 in an Australian penal colony. Clay (Alfred Burke) leads a revolt in his quest for freedom. His enemy is the Governor, Major Childs (André Morell).
Designer: Anthony Waller. **Producer:** Christopher Morahan.

There was a Crooked Man — 1 wk

Presented by ITV, film

| 1982 | 9.5 | Sat 14 Aug 7:45 p.m. | 10 | 1 wk |

Paris Pitman Jr. (Kirk Douglas) enters prison in 1833 convicted of theft. He is determined to escape. Henry Fonda also stars.
Director: Joseph L. Mankiewicz.

They Disappear When You Lie Down — 1 wk

ATV, drama

| 1974 | 5.4 | Tue 11 Jun 10:30 p.m. | 20 | 1 wk |

There is no love lost between sisters Susie and Morag (Virginia Clarke and Sally Grace), who use skill and sex appeal to put off male opposition in the college table tennis finals. The crunch comes when they face each other in the mixed doubles.
Designer: James Weatherup. **Director:** Graham Evans. **Producer:** Nicholas Palmer.

They Don't Make Summers Like They Used To — 1 wk

Anglia, drama

This single play was by David Bernstein.

| 1963 | 6.2 | Fri 27 Dec 9:10 p.m. | 7 | 1 wk |

For years a person will follow a routine. Then some incident may set off a deviation. The trigger for Stan (John Meillon) is a bus strike which induces him to retrieve his old tandem from the loft. His wife Alice (Carmel McSharry) refuses to ride with him. When he gives a lift to Sally (Frances White), summer love blossoms.
Director: June Howson.

They've Sold a Million — 11 wks

AR, music

Each programme in this series of interviews and music featured a pop star or group who had literally sold a million records or more.

| 1963 | 8.2 | Wed 30 Oct 9:10 p.m. | 4 | 1 wk |

Alan Freeman meets Gerry and the Pacemakers.
Director: Robert Fleming.

| 1964 | 7.1 | Wed 15 Apr 9:10 p.m. | 6 | 9 wks |

Gordon Williams talks to Freddie and the Dreamers.
Director: Peter Croft.

| 1965 | 6.5 | Wed 10 Feb 9:10 p.m. | 12 | 1 wk |

Alan Freeman talks to Cilla Black.
Director: Peter Croft.

Thick as Thieves | 1 wk

LWT, situation comedy

This series by Dick Clement and Ian La Frenais starred Bob Hoskins as Dobbs, who came out of prison to find his wife Annie (Pat Ashton) living with his best mate Stan (John Thaw). They settled into a ménage à trois.

| 1974 | 5.2 | Sat 22 Jun 8:30 p.m. | 19 | 1 wk |

'Two Men in My Life'
Dobbs and Stan are in Annie's bad books and she goes off to stay with cousins. The house rapidly becomes a tip, especially when Tommy (Trevor Peacock), a mate of Dobbs, escapes from prison and insists on staying with them.
Director: Mike Gibbon. **Producer:** Derrick Goodwin.

Thicker Than Water | 1 wk

YTV, situation comedy

This series by Dick Sharples dealt with widower Joseph Lockwood (Joss Ackland) and his bachelor sons Alan and Malcolm (Colin Farrell and Peter Denyer).

| 1981 | 13.1 | Tue 28 Apr 8:30 p.m. | 14 | 1 wk |

'Yes Sir That's My Baby'
Malcolm is the bass player in his brother's band, Al Lockwood's Syncopated Serenaders. He decides to quit the band and settle down.
Producer: Graeme Muir.

Third Time Lucky | 2 wks

YTV, situation comedy

This series by Jan Butlin starred Derek Nimmo as George Hutchenson, who was married to Beth Jenkins (Nerys Hughes) for eleven years. George subsequently married Millie (Angela Douglas) and Beth married Bruce (Clifford Earl). Neither marriage worked, so George and Beth planned to wed each other again.

| 1982 | 8.7 | Fri 27 Aug 8:30 p.m. | 18 | 2 wks |

'All in a Day's Work'
George's firm is under new Japanese ownership. There are several surprise changes in store.
Producer: Graeme Muir.

Thirteen at Dinner | 2 wks

Presented by ITV, film

| 1986 | 9.7 | Sun 8 Jun 7:45 p.m. | 10 | 1 wk |

Peter Ustinov stars as Hercule Poirot in this adaptation of Agatha Christie's book Lord Edgware Dies. Faye Dunaway also stars.
Director: Lou Antonio.

| 1987 | 11.5 | Wed 16 Dec 9:00 p.m. | 10 | 1 wk |

Repeat showing of the above film.

Thirty Minute Theatre | 2 wks

Southern, drama

This was a series of self-contained half-hour plays.

| 1962 | 5.6 | Wed 14 Mar 9:15 p.m. | 7 | 2 wks |

'The Little Goldmine' by Ted Willis.
Ruth Dunning stars as a widow who keeps a corner shop. She has her work cut out to avoid becoming easy prey for parasites.
Director: Stuart Burge.

Thirty Minutes' Worth | 19 wks

Thames, comedy

Harry Worth starred as himself in this series of sketches set in the past and the present.

| 1972 | 6.9 | Tue 31 Oct 7:00 p.m. | 9 | 8 wks |

Harry loses a string of sausages and the people in the lost property office nearly lose their minds. John J. Carney, Dennis Chinnery, David Hamilton, Harry Littlewood, William Maxwell, Paula Wilcox and Paul Williamson also appear.
Writers: Mike Craig, Lawrie Kinsley, Ron McDonnell and Frank Roscoe. **Producer:** Les Chatfield.

| 1973 | 7.0 | Wed 18 Jul 8:00 p.m. | 1 | 11 wks |

Harry fumbles his way through an identity crisis causing mayhem to others on the way. Pamela Cundell, Glyn Houston, Tony Melody, Rose Power, Robert Raglan and and Bill Wallis also appear.
Writers: Maurice Sellar and Roy Tuvey. **Producer:** William G. Stewart.

After waiting for many years Harry Worth enjoyed his first and only three weeks at Number One in July 1973 with **Thirty Minutes Worth**.

2

1 *1981 was a Number One year for* **The Professionals.**

2 **No Hiding Place** *was the top drama series of the early 1960s.*

3 *John Thaw and Dennis Waterman were members of the Flying Squad in* **The Sweeney.**

4 *Paul Michael Glaser and David Soul were American police partners* **Starsky and Hutch.**

5 *The security department of Scotland Yard was the subject matter of* **Special Branch.**

Thirty Years After — 1 wk

AR, documentary

| 1961 | 3.6 | Wed 26 Jul 9:35 p.m. | 20 | 1 wk |

Adrienne Corri introduces film clips and discussion to consider the changes in society over the last thirty years. With Lord Boothby, Colin Clark, Sir Bernard Lovell, Beverley Nichols, Fred Perry, Donald Pleasence, Andrew Shonfield and Sybil Thorndyke.
Director: Peter Robinson. **Producer:** Aidan Crawley.

35 Up — 1 wk

Granada, documentary

| 1991 | 8.8 | Wed 22 May 8:00 p.m. | 18 | 1 wk |

In 1964, WORLD IN ACTION team member Michael Apted filmed fourteen children aged seven in a programme entitled 7 Up. He has continued to follow their lives every seven years since. They are now all 35 years old.

Thirty-Nine Steps, The — 1 wk

Presented by ITV, film

| 1982 | 11.5 | Thu 30 Sep 7:40 p.m. | 6 | 1 wk |

Robert Powell stars as Richard Hannay, who discovers the secret of the thirty-nine steps in this remake of Alfred Hitchcock's 1935 film. George Baker, Karen Dotrice, John Mills, Ronald Pickup, Eric Porter, David Warner and Timothy West also star.
Director: Don Sharp.

This England — 11 wks

Granada, documentary

This series of half-hour films masterminded by Executive Producer Norman Swallow focused on a broad cross-section of contemporary English life.

| 1966 | 5.8 | Tue 9 Aug 10:05 p.m. | 6 | 7 wks |

'Model Couple'
Bill Grundy narrates the story of twenty-year-old model Debbie and her fashion photographer husband David, who live in a fashionable suburb of Manchester. (The couple subsequently divorced and Debbie moved to London, where she founded the Pineapple dance studios.)
Director: Francis Megahy.

| 1977 | 17.8 | Mon 5 Dec 8:30 p.m. | 5 | 3 wks |

'Home from Home'
Granny Charlotte Wynter has been going on holiday from Peterborough to Blackpool for thirty consecutive years.
Director: John Irvin.

| 1978 | 12.0 | Mon 11 Sep 6:30 p.m. | 18 | 1 wk |

'Green Tables'
A look at the increasingly popular game of snooker, with young professionals Jim Meadowcroft, David Taylor and John Virgo.
Producer: Denis Mitchell.

This is Petula Clark — 8 wks

BBC, music

Singer Petula Clark hosted this series in which she and her guests sang with the Harry Rabinowitz orchestra.
Producer: Yvonne Littlewood.

| 1966 | 7.9 | Thu 7 Jul 9:00 p.m. | 4 | 3 wks |

Guest: Fred Bongusto.

| 1967 | 8.2 | Tue 12 Dec 9:05 p.m. | 4 | 2 wks |

Guest: Anthony Newley.

| 1968 | 7.9 | Tue 9 Jan 9:05 p.m. | 4 | 3 wks |

Guest: Sacha Distel.

This is Sinatra — 1 wk

ABC, music

| 1962 | 5.1 | Sat 2 Jun 8:25 p.m. | 9 | 1 wk |

David Jacobs introduces from the Royal Festival Hall. Frank Sinatra sings with the Bill Miller Sextet in the presence of HRH The Princess Margaret and The Earl of Snowdon.
Television presentation: Philip Jones.

This is Tom Jones — 5 wks

ATV, entertainment

This expensive series made by ATV was affordable as it was pre-sold for networking in the USA during the same week as the British transmissions.

| 1969 | 6.6 | Sun 9 Feb 7:25 p.m. | 13 | 4 wks |

Guests: Joey Heatherton, Mary Hopkin, The Moody Blues, Richard Pryor and Peter Sellers, with the Mike Sammes singers and the Jack Parnell orchestra.
Producer: Jon Scoffield.

| 1970 | 6.9 | Tue 3 Feb 9:00 p.m. | 19 | 1 wk |

Guests: Victor Borge, Paula Kelly and Harry Secombe with the Mike Sammes singers and the Johnnie Spence orchestra. **Director:** Philip Casson. **Producer:** Jon Scoffield.

This is Your Life | 11 wks

BBC, documentary

This series was devised in the USA by Ralph Edwards and presented in Britain by Eamonn Andrews from the mid-1950s. The first British show, in 1956, was hosted by Edwards with Andrews as the subject.

| 1962 | 5.6 | Tue 16 Oct 7:00 p.m. | 8 | 6 wks |

Subject: Canon Sydney MacEwan.
Director: Vere Lorrimer.

| 1963 | 6.7 | Tue 26 Mar 7:55 p.m. | 5 | 5 wks |

Subject: Zena Dare.
Director: T. Leslie Jackson.

This is Your Life | 528 wks

Thames, documentary

Eamonn Andrews presented until his death in 1987. He was succeeded by Michael Aspel.
Directors included Margery Baker (1969–73), Royston Mayoh (1974, 1976–79) and Terry Yarwood (1977–87), Paul Stewart Laing (1982–83), Michael D. Kent (1984–87), and the team of David Clark and Brian Klein (1988–89). **Producers:** Robert Tyrrel (1969–71), Malcolm Morris (1972–1974, 1983–91) and Jack Crawshaw (1975–82). Regular contributors to the series as consultants were Tom Brennand and Roy Bottomley.

| 1969 | | Wed 3 Dec 7:00 p.m. | 1 | 6 wks |

Subject: Harry Driver.

| 1970 | 8.9 | Wed 1 Apr 7:00 p.m. | 1 | 27 wks |

Subject: Ronnie Corbett.

| 1971 | 8.8 | Wed 24 Mar 7:00 p.m. | 1 | 26 wks |

Subject: Clive Dunn.

| 1972 | 8.9 | Wed 2 Feb 7:00 p.m. | 1 | 26 wks |

Subject: Charlie Williams.

| 1973 | 9.1 | Wed 28 Feb 7:00 p.m. | 1 | 25 wks |

Subject: Diana Coupland.

| 1974 | 9.9 | Wed 13 Feb 7:00 p.m. | 1 | 31 wks |

Subject: Patrick Moore.

| 1975 | 9.3 | Wed 29 Jan 7:00 p.m. | 1 | 27 wks |

Subject: Charles Harry Johnson.

| 1976 | 9.0 | Wed 3 Mar 7:00 p.m. | 1 | 28 wks |

Subject: Vince Hill.

| 1977 | 17.7 | Wed 23 Nov 7:00 p.m. | 1 | 23 wks |

Subject: Richard Beckinsale.

| 1978 | 20.8 | Wed 20 Dec 7:00 p.m. | 1 | 30 wks |

Subject: David Bellamy.

| 1979 | 19.3 | Wed 14 Feb 7:00 p.m. | 1 | 21 wks |

Subject: Kevin Keegan.

| 1980 | 19.8 | Wed 2 Jan 7:00 p.m. | 1 | 32 wks |

Subject: Andrew Sachs.

| 1981 | 19.7 | Wed 18 Feb 7:00 p.m. | 1 | 25 wks |

Subject: Tim Brooke-Taylor.

| 1982 | 19.3 | Wed 6 Jan 7:00 p.m. | 1 | 24 wks |

Subject: Anita Harris.

| 1983 | 16.6 | Wed 5 Jan 7:00 p.m. | 1 | 23 wks |

Subject: Stan Stennett.

| 1984 | 16.1 | Wed 18 Jan 8:00 p.m. | 2 | 16 wks |

Subject: Liza Goddard.

| 1985 | 16.1 | Wed 16 Jan 8:00 p.m. | 2 | 21 wks |

Subject: Bob Geldof.

| 1986 | 14.7 | Wed 8 Jan 7:00 p.m. | 4 | 24 wks |

Subject: Oliver Reed.

| 1987 | 14.1 | Wed 25 Feb 7:00 p.m. | 5 | 15 wks |

Subject: Christopher Cazenove.

| 1988 | 14.8 | Wed 26 Oct 7:00 p.m. | 6 | 14 wks |

Subject: Phil Collins.

| 1989 | 15.1 | Wed 22 Feb 7:00 p.m. | 6 | 20 wks |

Subject: Nigel Mansell.

T

Eamonn Andrews and **This Is Your Life** achieved the longest number of consecutive years in which a programme reached Number One.

1990 **15.7** **Wed 10 Jan 7:00 p.m.** **7** **22 wks**

Subject: Elizabeth Dawn.
Directors: Brian Kline and Paul Kirrage.

1991 **14.5** **Wed 4 Dec 7:00 p.m.** **7** **22 wks**

Subject: Liz McColgan.

....

This is Your Life Extra **1 wk**

Thames, entertainment

A special edition on Election Night.

1974 **7.1** **Thu 28 Feb 10:15 p.m.** **13** **1 wk**

Subject: Dr Gordon Ostlere who wrote the famous 'Doctor' books under the name of Richard Gordon.
Director: Peter Webb. **Producer:** Malcolm Morris.

....

This is Your Life Special **2 wks**

Thames, entertainment

These were special one hour long extended editions.

1977 **10.1** **Wed 27 Apr 7:00 p.m.** **1** **1 wk**

Subject: Lord Mountbatten.
Director: Terry Yarwood. **Producer:** Jack Crawshaw.

1983 **14.5** **Wed 26 Oct 9:00 p.m.** **3** **1 wk**

Subject: Sir John Mills.
Directors: Michael D. Kent and Terry Yarwood. **Producer:** Malcolm Morris.

....

This Week **264 wks**

AR (1961–68) and Thames (1968–77), news/documentary

This current affairs series began in 1956. Each season featured a reporting team; individual reports would be filed by individual reporters. They did not all appear each week. Over the years a number of distinguished reporters, producers and editors served the programme.
Producers included Jeremy Isaacs (1963–65) and David Elstein (1975–77).

1961 **5.1** **Fri 15 Sep 8:00 p.m.** **14** **5 wks**

A report on nuclear disarmament, introduced by Brian Connell. Reporters: Judith Jackson, Peter Duval Smith and Desmond Wilcox.
Producer: Peter Morley. **Editors:** Elkan Allan and Cyril Bennett.

1962 **6.5** **Thu 15 Nov 9:15 p.m.** **4** **29 wks**

A report on unemployment, introduced by Brian Connell. Reporters: Paul Johnson, Bryan Magee, Russell Spurr and Desmond Wilcox, plus contributions from James Cameron and Al Capp.
Producer: Peter Morley. **Editor:** Cyril Bennett.

1963 **8.0** **Thu 31 Oct 9:10 p.m.** **2** **20 wks**

A report on the Kinross by-election. Reporters: James Cameron, George Ffitch, Paul Johnson, Bryan Magee, Russell Spurr, and Desmond Wilcox.

1964 **7.6** **Thu 9 Sep 9:10 p.m.** **5** **23 wks**

A report on mental illness with the reporting team from 1963.
Director: James Butler.

1965 **8.4** **Thu 22 Apr 9:10 p.m.** **2** **44 wks**

A report called 'Der Gastarbeiter', on immigrant workers in West Germany. Reporters: James Cameron, George Ffitch, Robert Kee, Bryan Magee, and Desmond Wilcox.
Director: Peter Robinson.

1966 **7.2** **Thu 29 Sep 9:10 p.m.** **3** **38 wks**

A report on accidents, 'The Price of Carelessness'. Reporters: James Cameron, George Ffitch, Llew Gardner and George Scott.
Director: Peter Robinson. **Producer:** Cliff Morgan.

1967 **6.1** **Thu 6 Apr 9:10 p.m.** **13** **20 wks**

A report on housing in Glasgow ,'A National Disgrace'. Reporters: George Ffitch, Llew Gardner, Geoffrey Hodgson and Peter Williams.
Director: Terry Yarwood. **Producer:** James Butto.

1968 **6.2** **Thu 9 May 8:30 p.m.** **11** **13 wks**

A report on 'Race – Parliament and Public Opinion'. Reporters: Llew Gardner, Geoffrey Hodgson, Robert Kee, John Morgan and Peter Williams.
Director: Terry Yarwood. **Producer:** Phillip Whitehead.

1969 **6.9** **Thu 30 Jan 9:30 p.m.** **6** **22 wks**

A report called 'Football – Nice Managers Get Sacked'. Reporters: John Edwards, Llew Gardner, John Morgan, and Peter Williams.
Directors: Arnold Bulka and David Elstein. **Producer:** Philip Whitehead.

1970 **6.8** **Thu 5 Mar 9:30 p.m.** **5** **19 wks**

A report on 'Nixon – The Big Gamble'. Guest Reporter: Anthony Howard. Reporters: Charles Douglas-Home, John Edwards, Llew Gardner, Robert Kee, John Morgan and Peter Williams.
Directors: Chris Goddard and Jolyon Wimhurst. **Producer:** Jo Menell.

1971 **7.0** **Thu 18 Feb 9:30 p.m.** **10** **16 wks**

A report on the post office strike. Reporters: Alastair Burnet, John Edwards, Robert Kee, John Morgan and Peter Williams.
Directors: Udi Eichler, David Elstein, David Gill and Jolyon Wimhurst.
Editor: Ian Martin.

| 1972 | 6.5 | Thu 18 May 9.30 p.m. | 13 | 5 wks |

A report called 'Safe As Houses' investigates property speculation. Reporters: Jonathan Dimbleby, Peter Taylor, Denis Tuohy and Peter Williams.
Directors: David Gill, Vanya Kewley, Peter Tiffin and Terry Yarwood. **Producer:** John Edwards.

| 1974 | 6.2 | Thu 16 May 9:30 p.m. | 18 | 1 wk |

A report on 'Section 99 – How to Beat the System'. Reporters: Jonathan Dimbleby, John Fielding, Peter Taylor and Peter Williams. **Directors:** David Elstein, David Gill, Peter Tiffin and Terry Yarwood. **Producer:** Arnold Bulka.

| 1975 | 7.6 | Thu 6 Mar 8:30 p.m. | 8 | 7 wks |

A report titled 'Killer – The Black Panther', a report on the investigation into Lesley Whittle's murder, led by Det. Chief Supt Booth. With the same reporting team as 1974.
Directors: Ian Stuttard, Martin Smith, Terry Yarwood, Ken Craig and Norman Fenton.

| 1976 | 5.4 | Thu 26 Aug 9:25 p.m. | 18 | 1 wk |

A report on drink titled 'Have Another One, Jimmy'. With the same reporting team as 1974–75.
Directors: Ken Craig, Norman Fenton, Martin Smith, Ian Stuttard and Peter Tiffin.

| 1977 | 5.2 | Thu 30 Jun 9:30 p.m. | 20 | 1 wk |

A report titled 'Intelligence – Don't Call Me A Spy' (Part Four of a four-part investigation). With the same reporting team as 1974–76.
Directors: Ken Craig, Mike Dormer, Norman Fenton and Peter Tiffin.

....

| This Year, Next Year | | | | 12 wks |

Granada, drama

This thirteen-part drama by John Finch centred on the life of Harry Shaw (Ronald Hines), who moved from his home in the Yorkshire Dales to London in the 1950s. His brother Jack (Michael Elphick) remained in the Dales. Twenty years later, with a wife (Virginia Stride) and three children, he had all the trappings of success and the affluent society. Suddenly his world and security collapsed and he faced starting again in his mid forties. He returned to the Dales.

| 1977 | 8.0 | Tue 19 Apr 9:00 p.m. | 8 | 12 wks |

'Full Circle'
In this final episode Harry's family wait anxiously in London to hear if he will return or stay in Yorkshire.
Designer: Colin Pocock. **Director:** Alan Grint. **Producer:** Howard Baker. **Executive Producer:** Mike Cox.

| Thomas and Sarah | | 6 wks |

LWT, drama

This spinoff series featured two characters from UPSTAIRS DOWNSTAIRS. Thomas the chauffeur (John Alderton) and Sarah the parlourmaid (Pauline Collins) had both left the Bellamy household in 1911 to live in the country.

| 1979 | 16.7 | Sun 28 Jan 8:15 p.m. | 5 | 6 wks |

'The Vanishing Lady' by Jeremy Paul.
Sarah goes missing and Thomas goes in search of her.
Producer: Christopher Hodson. **Executive Producer:** Tony Wharmby.

....

| Thorn Birds, The | | 5 wks |

USA presented by BBC, drama

Carmen Culver's five-part adaptation of Colleen McCullough's novel concerned the church, love, ambition and desire over fifty years and two continents. It starred Richard Chamberlain as Ralph de Bricassart, Richard Kiley as Paddy Cleary, Piper Laurie as Anne Mueller, Christopher Plummer as Contini-Verchese, Jean Simmons as Fiona Cleary, Barbara Stanwyck as Mary Carson, and Rachel Ward as Meggie Cleary with Philip Anglim as Dane and Ken Howard as Rainer. **Producers:** Stan Margulies and David Wolper. **Director:** Daryl Duke.

| 1984 | 15.6 | Sun 22 Jan 7:45 p.m. | 3 | 3 wks |

Part Five
After seven years training, Dane is to be ordained in Rome. The Cleary family and Cardinal de Bricassart are justly proud, although Meggie refuses to attend the ceremony.

| 1986 | 10.5 | Tue 12 Aug 9:30 p.m. | 6 | 2 wks |

A repeat of Part Three in which Ralph is made a bishop, and Meggie begins a new but unsuccessful life in Queensland.

....

| Those Fellers | | 1 wk |

ABC, comedy

Sid Green and Dick Hills, having written for so many people, most notably Morecambe and Wise, were rewarded with their own series as performers.

| 1967 | 4.6 | Thu 1 Jun 8:25 p.m. | 16 | 1 wk |

Sid and Dick wanted to book Dan Leno for the show but discovered he was not available on account of being deceased. They've settled for the next best thing, Ted Ray.
Producer: Keith Beckett.

Three Amigos | 1 wk

Presented by BBC, film

| 1991 | 8.8 | Sun 14 Jul 8:35 p.m. | 17 | 1 wk |

Chevy Chase, Steve Martin and Martin Short star as the Amigos who are fearless silent screen heroes. Off screen they are quite the reverse.
Director: John Landis.

Three Comedies of Marriage | 3 wks

Thames, drama

This trilogy of plays dealt with the subject of marriage.

| 1975 | 6.4 | Thu 10 Jul 9:00 p.m. | 6 | 3 wks |

'Feeling His Way' by Donald Churchill.
When a mistress walks out, a wife is invited for lunch. Starring Michael Bryant, Sandra Dickinson, Wendy Gifford and Geoffrey Palmer.
Designer: Mike Hall. **Producer:** Peter Duguid.

Three Great Stars | 2 wks

Presented by BBC, film

This was a season of films starring either Clark Gable, Tyrone Power or Spencer Tracy.

| 1969 | 5.6 | Sat 18 Oct 8:15 p.m. | 15 | 2 wks |

'The Homecoming'
Clark Gable stars as a wartime doctor who finds the stress of battle causes him to reconsider his values, especially after he meets Lieutenant Jane McCall (Lana Turner).
Director: Mervyn Leroy.

Three Live Wires | 24 wks

AR, situation comedy

Michael Medwin starred as the Cockney foreman of a television sales and repair shop. Also in the series were Bernard Fox, Deryck Guyler and George Roderick, all of whom had been with Medwin in THE LOVE OF MIKE.

| 1961 | 6.6 | Mon 15 May 8:00 p.m. | 2 | 24 wks |

'French Cleaner' by James Kelly and Peter Miller.
Cockney leers and parlez-vous chat-up lines to the new shop cleaner (Marie France) get the lads into trouble with the manager and the law.
Producer: Christopher Hodson.

Three of a Kind | 5 wks

BBC, comedy

This series was devised in the late 1960s as a showcase for developing talents Ray Fell, Lulu and Mike Yarwood. They performed sketches, comedy, songs and impressions – both solo and collectively. Lulu and Yarwood became long-serving stalwarts of BBC light entertainment and Fell went on to become a headlining comedian in Las Vegas. The format was revived in 1982 as a vehicle for promising talents David Copperfield, Lenny Henry and Tracey Ullman.
Producer: Paul Jackson.

| 1982 | 12.1 | Sat 11 Dec 7:45 p.m. | 10 | 2 wks |

Guests: Toto Coelo.

| 1983 | 10.0 | Mon 2 May 8:45 p.m. | 16 | 3 wks |

Guest: Phil Collins.

3-2-1 | 121 wks

YTV, game show

This long-running game show was hosted by London comedian Ted Rogers, assisted by the booby prize – a mechanical toy named Dusty Bin. Contestants played for prizes and were required to use simple powers of deduction to interpret clues in order to eliminate red herring prizes and go for the jackpot.
Producer (1979–80) and **Executive Producer** (1981–87): Alan Tarrant.

| 1978 | 16.5 | Fri 15 Sep 8:00 p.m. | 1 | 13 wks |

Director: David Millard. **Producer:** Derek Burrell-Davis.

| 1979 | 16.1 | Fri 21 Dec 7:30 p.m. | 4 | 10 wks |

Director: Paddy Russell.

| 1980 | 15.2 | Fri 4 Jan 7:30 p.m. | 11 | 3 wks |
| 1981 | 16.7 | Sat 21 Mar 6:35 p. m | 4 | 10 wks |

Director: Ian Bolt. **Producer:** Mike Goddard.

| 1982 | 15.0 | Sat 27 Mar 6:45 p.m. | 4 | 15 wks |

Producer: Ian Bolt.

| 1983 | 14.6 | Sat 12 Feb 7:10 p.m. | 2 | 18 wks |

Director: Don Clayton. **Producer:** Ian Bolt.

| 1984 | 15.5 | Sat 25 Feb 7:00 p.m. | 3 | 20 wks |

Director: Graham Wetherell. **Producer:** Terry Henebery.

| 1985 | 12.7 | Sat 26 Oct 7:45 p.m. | 9 | 14 wks |

Producer: *Terry Henebery.*

| 1986 | 12.1 | Sat 27 Sep 7:45 p.m. | 8 | 11 wks |

Producer: *Graham Wetherell.*

| 1987 | 12.0 | Sat 21 Nov 5:45 p.m. | 14 | 7 wks |

Producer: *Graham Wetherell.*

3-2-1 Christmas Show, The   2 wks

YTV, game show

Ted Rogers presented seasonal celebrity editions of his popular game show.

| 1986 | 12.9 | Sun 21 Dec 5:00 p.m. | 6 | 1 wk |

A celebrity edition for charity with John Boulter, Kenneth Connor, Anna Dawson, Lance Percival, Bill Pertwee and Tony Selby, with the Brian Rogers dancers.
Producer: *Don Clayton.* **Executive Producer:** *Alan Tarrant.*

| 1987 | 12.5 | Sat 19 Dec 6:25 p.m. | 7 | 1 wk |

Couples from three soap operas compete for charity: Vera and Jack from CORONATION STREET (Liz Dawn and Bill Tarmey), Sheila and Bobby from BROOKSIDE (Sue Johnston and Ricky Tomlinson), and Dolly and Matt from EMMERDALE FARM (Jean Rogers and Frederick Pyne). Other guests include Bob Champion, Norman Collier, Pat Coombes, Sharon Davies, Gareth Hunt, Denis Law, Jan Leeming, Bernie Winters and Eli Woods.
Producer: *Graham Wetherell.* **Executive Producer:** *Alan Tarrant.*

Three Up, Two Down   31 wks

BBC, situation comedy

This series by Richard Ommanney starred Michael Elphick and Angela Thorne as Sam and Daphne, Dad and Mum respectively of the recently married Nick (Ray Burdis) and Angie (Lysette Anthony). Their opinions clashed regularly on grounds of class and, when the time came, over their relative importance to their new grandchild. The series explored the possibility of true romance between ageing Cockney oik Sam and stuck-up Cheltenham snob Daphne.

| 1985 | 13.6 | Mon 20 May 8:30 p.m. | 2 | 6 wks |

Daphne reaches the end of her tether with Sam.
Director: *Mandie Fletcher.* **Producer:** *David Askey.*

| 1986 | 15.8 | Mon 7 Apr 8:30 p.m. | 3 | 8 wks |

Daphne hopes her new neighbour will be better company than Sam's penguin.
Producer: *John B. Hobbs.*

| 1987 | 15.6 | Mon 23 Feb 8:30 p.m. | 3 | 12 wks |

Daphne receives good and bad news. For Sam it is the reverse. Her good news is his bad news, and her bad news seems good to him. (Repeat.)
Producer: *John B. Hobbs.*

| 1988 | 9.8 | Tue 3 May 7:00 p.m. | 13 | 5 wks |

Angie remains unemployed while the career of Nick seems to be ready to take off. (Repeat.)
Producer: *John B. Hobbs.*

Thriller   7 wks

ATV, drama

This series of plays was created by Brian Clemens.

| 1974 | 6.8 | Sat 26 Jan 9:00 p.m. | 16 | 3 wks |

'Only a Scream Away' adapted by Terence Feely.
On the wedding day of Samantha and Robert (Hayley Mills and David Warbeck), an unidentified person throws red paint over the bride's dress. This is just the first in a series of menacing incidents.
Designer: *Stanley Mills.* **Director:** *Peter Jeffries.* **Producer:** *John Sichel.*

| 1976 | 6.5 | Sat 24 Apr 9:15 p.m. | 13 | 4 wks |

'Nightmare for a Nightingale' by Brian Clemens.
Famous American opera singer Anna Cartell (Susan Flannery) is making her London debut and about to embark on a new marriage when her first husband turns up, ten years after his supposed death. Keith Baxter, Stuart Damon, Ronald Leigh-Hunt and Sydney Tafler also star.
Designer: *Lewis Logan.* **Director:** *John Scholz-Conway.* **Producer:** *Ian Fordyce.*

Through the Keyhole   26 wks

YTV, game show

In this game show hosted by David Frost, Loyd Grossman visited the homes of well-known people and gave clues to their identity. A celebrity panel then tried to guess the owners of the residences.
Producer: *Ian Bolt.* **Executive Producer:** *Kevin Sim.*

| 1987 | 10.0 | Fri 1 May 7:00 p.m. | 13 | 3 wks |

Panellists: Patrick Lichfield, Nina Myskow and Chris Tarrant. The cameras visit the homes of Bryan Robson and Beryl Reid.

| 1988 | 10.0 | Fri 22 Apr 7:00 p.m. | 12 | 5 wks |

Panellists: Pattie Coldwell, Patrick Lichfield and Eve Pollard. The cameras visit the homes of Yuri Geller and Bob Carolgees.

Dusty Bin and his assistant Ted Rogers presented **3-2-1**.

| 1990 | 11.9 | Fri 23 Mar 7:00 p.m. | 12 | 10 wks |

Panellists: Pattie Coldwell, Mike Read and Willie Rushton. The cameras visit the homes of Barry McGuigan and Barbara Castle.

| 1991 | 9.9 | Fri 21 Jun 7:00 p.m. | 13 | 8 wks |

Panellists: Andrew O'Connor, Molly Parkin and Nigel Rees. The cameras visit the homes of Duncan Norvelle and Rabbi Lionel Blue.

Thunderball — 4 wks

Presented by ITV, film

| 1977 | 8.6 | Sat 26 Feb 8:00 p.m. | 7 | 1 wk |

Sean Connery stars as James Bond on the trail of SPECTRE, the crime syndicate planning to steal two atomic bombs during a NATO training mission. Bernard Lee and Lois Maxwell also star.
Director: Terence Young.

1978	12.5	Mon 29 May 7:30 p.m.	6	1 wk
1984	16.6	Mon 2 Jan 7:00 p.m.	1	1 wk
1989	12.8	Sat 7 Jan 6:45 p.m.	17	1 wk

Repeat showings of the above film.

Thursday Adventure Film, The — 1 wk

Presented by ITV, film

| 1976 | 6.6 | Thu 20 May 8:30 p.m. | 2 | 1 wk |

'Those Magnificent Men in Their Flying Machines'
Ken Annakin's star-studded comedy of the 1910 air race from London to Paris stars Eric Barker, Fred Emney, James Fox, Gert Frobe, Tony Hancock, Benny Hill, Gordon Jackson, John Le Mesurier, Zena Marshall, Sarah Miles, Robert Morley, Flora Robson, Norman Rossington, Red Skelton, Eric Sykes, Terry-Thomas, Sam Wanamaker and Stuart Whitman.

Thursday Movie, The — 5 wks

Presented by ITV

| 1986 | 11.9 | Thu 9 Oct 8:00 p.m. | 8 | 5 wks |

'The Runaway Train'
A train leaves a ski resort headed for Jackson City when engineer Holly Gibson (Ben Johnson) discovers the brakes have frozen.
Director: David Lowell Rich.

Till Closing Time Us Do Part — 1 wk

BBC, situation comedy

| 1967 | 6.6 | Mon 27 Mar 8:20 p.m. | 5 | 1 wk |

A Bank Holiday knees-up with the Garnetts from TILL DEATH US DO PART and some of their friends, Ray Barrett, Dermot Kelly, Kenny Lynch, Arthur Mullard, Joan Sims, Jimmy Tarbuck and Rita Webb.
Writer: Johnny Speight. **Producer:** Dennis Main Wilson.

Till Death Us Do Part — 52 wks

BBC, situation comedy

Johnny Speight's creation of the monstrous Alf Garnett (Warren Mitchell) and his long-suffering wife Else (Dandy Nichols), daughter (Una Stubbs) and son-in-law Mike (Anthony Booth) began as a single COMEDY PLAYHOUSE. Subjects previously taboo were the norm, including race, religion, politics, royalty and all minorities, not forgetting West Ham United.
Producer: Dennis Main Wilson.

| 1966 | 7.0 | Sat 1 Oct 9:00 p.m. | 7 | 7 wks |

'Claustrophobia'
According to Alf, the house isn't big enough for four.
Director: Douglas Argent.

| 1967 | 5.7 | Mon 27 Feb 7:30 p.m. | 4 | 15 wks |

'Cleaning Up TV'
Alf is suffering from gastro-enteritis. While confined to bed he reads a book by Mary Whitehouse and gives her ideas and opinions his patriotic approval.

| 1968 | 8.4 | Sat 21 Dec 10:05 p.m. | 1 | 13 wks |

'Peace and Goodwill'
Alf offers peace and goodwill to nearly all men. Wally the milkman (John Junkin) joins in the Christmas spirit.

| 1969 | 8.2 | Sat 4 Jan 9:45 p.m. | 1 | 4 wks |

'In Sickness and in Health'
Alf proves to be one of the world's worst patients. Guest stars: Mark Eden, Tommy Godfrey, Valerie Murray and Graham Stark.
(Repeat.)

| 1972 | 8.3 | Wed 18 Oct 9:25 p.m. | 1 | 7 wks |

'Up the 'Ammers'
Alf has plans for his grandson to play for West Ham United and introduces him to his heroes. But son-in-law Mike is a Liverpool fan, and is suitably disgusted.
Guest stars: Alan Ball, Bobby Moore, Martin Peters and Joan Sims.

| 1974 | 8.0 | Tue 31 Dec 10:25 p.m. | 2 | 4 wks |

'Outback Bound'
Else's sister in Australia is ill and she wants to visit her.

| 1975 | 6.7 | Wed 17 Dec 9:40 p.m. | 19 | 1 wk |

'Marital Bliss'
Next-door-neighbours Bert and Min (Alfie Bass and Patricia Hayes) have had a row, so Bert brings his dinner round to the Garnetts'.

| 1986 | 12.5 | Thu 13 Feb 10:00 p.m. | 19 | 1 wk |

'Three-day Week'
Prime Minister Edward Heath has put the nation's workforce onto a three-day working week. Else decides she'll join them, cleaning, washing and cooking only three days out of seven.

This 1974 episode is repeated as a tribute to Dandy Nichols, who died a few days ago.

Time Gentlemen Please · 1 wk

AR, entertainment

| 1962 | 5.8 | Wed 5 Dec 9:45 p.m. | 15 | 1 wk |

Daniel Farson conducts a pub crawl around London to meet the pub entertainers. Starring Ida Barr and Marie Kendall with Kim Cordell, Mike McKenzie, Tommy Pudding and Queenie Watts.
Producer: Rollo Gamble.

Time of Your Life, The · 6 wks

BBC, entertainment

Noel Edmonds helped recreate a magical moment in the life of a famous person with the help of friends, family and colleagues.
Producer: Henry Murray.

| 1983 | 11.1 | Fri 29 Apr 8:00 p.m. | 6 | 4 wks |

Irene Handl remembers February 1937.
Director: Peter Morpurgo.

| 1984 | 8.5 | Fri 22 Jun 8:20 p.m. | 14 | 1 wk |

Gary Glitter relives June 1972.

| 1985 | 10.7 | Tue 20 Aug 7:30 p.m. | 8 | 1 wk |

Dame Kiri Te Kanawa relives December 1971.

Tin Pan Alice · 1 wk

Granada, comedy

This one-off comedy was written by Peter Coke.

| 1963 | 4.2 | Thu 15 Aug 7:30 p.m. | 19 | 1 wk |

Athene Seyler starred as Alice, a publisher of classical music, who wrote a pop song that became a hit. Carole Carr, Warren Mitchell and Steve Race lso starred.
Director: Eric Fawcett. **Producer:** Peter Eton.

Titanic · 1 wk

TVS, documentary

| 1986 | 10.5 | Sun 31 Aug 9:50 p.m. | 17 | 1 wk |

Dr Robert Ballard made an expedition to the sunken liner. He took a series of remarkable photographs two and a half miles beneath the surface of the North Atlantic.
Camera: Paul Houlson. **Sound:** Maurice Hillier. **Producer:** Graham Hurley. **Executive Producer:** Peter Williams.

T. J. Hooker · 28 wks

USA presented by ITV, drama

William Shatner starred as Detective Sergeant Hooker.
Executive Producer: Aaron Spelling.

| 1983 | 13.0 | Sat 9 Apr 8:15 p.m. | 2 | 12 wks |

'King On The Hill'
Hooker believes an old friend has been wrongfully arrested while chasing a gang of supermarket thieves who use their loot to finance the reconstruction of racing cars.

| 1984 | 14.0 | Sat 24 Mar 8:00 p.m. | 5 | 15 wks |

'Raw Deal'
A group of compulsive gamblers have been forced into making drug deliveries as a result of their debts.

| 1985 | 12.4 | Sat 12 Jan 7:45 p.m. | 19 | 1 wk |

'Walk A Straight Line'
A drunken officer puts lives in danger while Hooker is staking out a crime.

To Catch a Thief | 2 wks

Presented by BBC, film

| 1979 | 14.6 | Sun 12 Aug 8:05 p.m. | 3 | 1 wk |

This special screening is a tribute to Alfred Hitchcock on his 80th birthday. Cary Grant stars as John Robie, a jewel thief enjoying the proceeds of his crimes on the French Riviera, who falls in love with Frances Stevens, played by Grace Kelly.

| 1986 | 8.4 | Wed 4 Jun 8:00 p.m. | 20 | 1 wk |

Repeat showing of the above film.

To Live Till You Die | 1 wk

AR, documentary

| 1965 | 4.7 | Wed 28 Jul 9:40 p.m. | 18 | 1 wk |

In Britain the old age pension book is considered a passport to loneliness and neglect. This film looks at the elderly in Italy, where the old still have their place in society, and in Sweden, where one of the world's most advanced welfare states is working out a new deal for its senior citizens.
Director: Robert Morgan. **Writer** and **Producer:** J. C. Sheers.

To the Manor Born | 21 wks

BBC, situation comedy

Penelope Keith starred as Audrey fforbes-Hamilton, whose reduced circumstances had forced her to sell her stately home to Richard De Vere (Peter Bowles), a nouveau-riche grocery tycoon. Audrey moved to a small lodge near the gate of her former estate and embarked on a love-hate relationship with Richard. The series also starred Daphne Heard as Richard's mother Mrs Polouvicka and Angela Thorne as Audrey's old school friend Marjory Frobisher. The series was created by Peter Spence.
Producer: Gareth Gwenlan.

| 1979 | 24.0 | Sun 7 Oct 8:45 p.m. | 1 | 8 wks |

Audrey moves out of Grantleigh Manor.
Writer: Peter Spence.

| 1980 | 21.6 | Sun 9 Nov 8:35 p.m. | 1 | 6 wks |

The first programme of the second series finds Richard becoming increasingly attracted to Audrey.
Writer: Peter Spence.

| 1981 | 17.8 | Sun 29 Nov 7:45 p.m. | 1 | 7 wks |

Will Audrey and Richard marry in this last programme of the series?
Writer: Christopher Bond.

Today at the Commonwealth Games | 1 wk

BBC, sport

| 1974 | 6.8 | Thu 31 Jan 6:45 p.m. | 14 | 1 wk |

From Christchurch, New Zealand. Events include the final stages of the marathon, run through the streets of Christchurch, the women's 100 metre hurdles final and the men's pole vault and discus finals. The commentary is by David Coleman and Ron Pickering.
Television presentation: Alan Mouncer, Richard Tilling, Fred Viner. **Producer:** Brian Venner. **Editors:** Alan Hart and A. P. Wilkinson

Tokyo '64 | 1 wk

ATV, sport

Coverage of the 1964 Olympics was daily for the two weeks of their duration.

| 1964 | 5.7 | Fri 23 Oct 10:20 p.m. | 1 wk |

This transmission features the highlights of the second Friday. Pictures are sent by satellite from Japan across the Pacific to the USA, then by radio link to Canada and chartered plane to Europe.
Producer (in London): Grahame Turner. **Executive Producer** (in Tokyo): Bill Ward.

Tom and Jerry | 1 wk

USA presented by BBC, cartoon

| 1982 | 15.5 | Sat 24 Apr 10:13 p.m. | 3 | 1 wk |

This cartoon is inserted into the schedule following THE EUROVISION SONG CONTEST and preceding NEWS AND SPORT. (TOM AND JERRY outrated both of them, drawing a million more viewers than THE EUROVISION SONG CONTEST.)

Tom Brown's Schooldays | 1 wk

BBC, drama

Anthony Steven dramatized Thomas Hughes' novel in five parts.

| 1971 | 6.3 | Sun 12 Dec 5:20 p.m. | 18 | 1 wk |

Part Five
Flashman (Richard Morant) has finally triumphed by having Tom (Anthony Murphy) wrongly accused of poaching and publicly flogged by Dr Arnold (Iain Cuthbertson).
Designer: Paul Allen. **Director:** Gareth Davies. **Producer:** John McRae.

Tom, Dick and Harriet — 8 wks

Thames, situation comedy

This series by Johnnie Mortimer and Brian Cooke dealt with the Madison household: father Tom (Lionel Jeffries); son Dick (Ian Ogilvy); and daughter-in-law Harriet (Brigit Forsyth). **Producer:** Michael Mills.

| 1982 | 13.8 | Mon 18 Oct 8:00 p.m. | 3 | 6 wks |

'Paternal Triangle'
Tom behaves badly at a very important dinner party.

| 1983 | 14.6 | Thu 17 Feb 7:30 p.m. | 4 | 2 wks |

'Get Out and Get Under'
Tom acquires an old banger.

Tom Jones — 9 wks

ATV, music

The Welsh singer starred in his own series of half-hour shows before leaving Britain to find greater fortune in the USA in 1968.

| 1966 | 7.4 | Wed 14 Sep 9:10 p.m. | 5 | 6 wks |

Guests: Salena Jones, Mike Yarwood, the Pamela Devis dancers and the Jack Parnell orchestra. **Producer:** Colin Clews.

| 1967 | 5.7 | Thu 2 May 6:30 p.m. | 14 | 3 wks |

This year's series gives musical interpretations to weekly themes. This week Tom considers money with the help of Hattie Jacques, the Malcolm Clare dancers, the Mike Sammes singers and the Jack Parnell orchestra. **Producer:** Alan Tarrant.

Tom O'Connor — 6 wks

Thames, comedy

This series starred the former Liverpool schoolteacher who emerged from THE COMEDIANS.

| 1977 | 8.7 | Tue 1 Mar 8:30 p.m. | 4 | 6 wks |

Guest: Mahogany.
Writers: Pat Finan, Dick Hills and Spike Mullins. **Producer:** William G. Stewart.

Tommy Cooper — 1 wk

Thames, documentary

| 1984 | 11.6 | Wed 13 Jun 8:00 p.m. | 3 | 1 wk |

This programme pays tribute to the entertainer who died 15 April 1984 after collapsing on stage during the television show LIVE FROM HER MAJESTY'S. Eric Sykes and Richard Briers host the tribute with special contributions from Janet Brown, Jimmy Tarbuck, Ernie Wise and Mike Yarwood.
Producers: Dennis Kirkland, Bridget Moore and Terry Yarwood.

Tommy Cooper Hour, The — 9 wks

Thames, comedy

This occasional series of light entertainment specials starred Cooper with guests and the Ronnie Aldrich orchestra.

| 1973 | 7.1 | Wed 31 Oct 8:00 p.m. | 6 | 1 wk |

Guests: Allan Cuthbertson, Dana, Peters and Lee, and Springfield Revival.
Writers: Johnnie Mortimer and Brian Cooke. **Producer:** Peter Frazer-Jones.

| 1974 | 8.7 | Wed 2 Jan 8:00 p.m. | 1 | 3 wks |

Guests: Acker Bilk and his Paramount Jazz Band, Richard Davies, Design, Anita Harris, Hugh Paddick, Anthony Sharp and Sheila Steafel. With the Lionel Blair dancers.
Writers: Johnnie Mortimer and Brian Cooke. **Producer:** Terry Henebery.

| 1975 | 8.7 | Wed 26 Apr 8:00 p.m. | 1 | 3 wks |

Guests: Anne-Marie David, Design, Robert Dorning, Hugh Paddick, Sheila Steafel, Frank Thornton and the Alex Welsh Band, with the Lionel Blair dancers and the Coffee Set.
Writers: Johnnie Mortimer and Brian Cooke. **Producer:** Terry Henebery.

| 1976 | 6.9 | Tue 18 May 7:30 p.m. | 4 | 2 wks |

Guests: The Black Theatre of Prague, Allan Cuthbertson, Georgie Fame, Tommy Godfrey, Vince Hill, Jenny Lee-Wright, Ireen Sheer and the voice of Kenny Everett. With the Johnny Greenland dancers.
Writer: Dick Hills. **Producer:** Royston Mayoh.

Tommy Cooper Show, The — 1 wk

Thames, comedy

| 1975 | 8.4 | Wed 26 Feb 8:00 p.m. | 3 | 1 wk |

One-hour special with Allan Cuthbertson, Tommy Godfrey, Lena Martell and Jenny Lee-Wright with the Tony Mansell singers and the Ronnie Aldrich orchestra.
Producer: Royston Mayoh. **Executive Producer:** Philip Jones.

T

Audrey fforbes-Hamilton (Penelope Keith) was **To the Manor Born**.

Britain's best-loved magician was Number one in two consecutive years with **The Tommy Cooper Hour**.

Tommy Steele and a Show `1 wk`

Thames, entertainment

`1977` `14.1` `Wed 28 Sep 8:00 p.m.` `6` `1 wk`

This one-hour special celebrates 21 years in show business for Britain's first rock 'n' roller. With the Irving Davies dancers, the Mike Sammes singers and the Peter Knight orchestra.
Writer: Eric Merriman. **Producer:** Keith Beckett. **Executive Producer:** Philip Jones.

Tommy Steele Hour, The `1 wk`

LWT, entertainment

`1972` `7.7` `Sun 14 May 7:55 p.m.` `3` `1 wk`

This special stars Steele with the Irving Davies dancers, the Mike Sammes singers and the Peter Knight orchestra.
Producer: David Bell.

Tommy Steele Show, The `1 wk`

ATV, entertainment

`1962` `4.7` `Sun 23 Dec 8:25 p.m.` `18` `1 wk`

'Quincy's Quest' by Eric Merriman from an original story by Tommy Steele. This Christmas musical for children stars Tommy Steele as Quincy with Pat Coombs, Peter Hawkins, Henry McGee, Hugh Paddick, Una Stubbs and the Jack Parnell orchestra.
Choreographer: Pamela Devis. **Producer:** Francis Essex.

Tomorrow's Ireland `1 wk`

BBC, documentary

`1975` `8.0` `Thu 29 May 6:45 p.m.` `9` `1 wk`

The TOMORROW'S WORLD team report from Dublin Castle on the revolution in Irish science and technology.
Editor: Michael Blakstad.

Tomorrow's World `28 wks`

BBC, documentary

This long-running series of programmes examined the ever-changing world of science, medicine and technology. The presenters changed over the years.

`1967` `5.4` `Wed 12 Apr 7:05 p.m.` `15` `3 wks`

Raymond Baxter introduces reports on new safety devices for lorries and a new type of window from America.
Editor: Max Morgan-Witts.

`1972` `5.4` `Tue 15 Feb 7:05 p.m.` `18` `1 wk`

Raymond Baxter and James Burke introduce reports on a sleeping bag which can be used in sub-zero temperatures, and a new carbon fibre for use in an RB211 engine. With Michael Rodd and William Woollard.
Producers: Brian Johnson and Andrew Wiseman. **Editor:** Lawrence Wade.

`1974` `6.1` `Mon 23 Dec 5:40 p.m.` `12` `1 wk`

Raymond Baxter introduce some 'magic moments in science' with Michael Rodd and William Woollard.
Director: Hilary Henson. **Producer:** Michael Blakstad.

`1979` `14.0` `Thu 27 Dec 6:50 p.m.` `13` `1 wk`

Judith Hann, Kieran Prendiville and Michael Rodd take a reflective look at the scientific advances of the 1970s.
Director: John Gorman. **Producers:** Alan Dobson and Andrew Wiseman. **Editor:** Michael Blakstad.

`1980` `13.0` `Thu 14 Feb 7:40 p.m.` `20` `1 wk`

Judith Hann, Su Ingle, Kieran Prendiville and Michael Rodd conduct a St Valentine's Day enquiry into how technology can aid romance.
Director: John Gorman. **Producers:** John Groom, Laurie John and Andrew Wiseman. **Editor:** David Filkin.

`1982` `11.4` `Thu 11 Mar 7:00 p.m.` `20` `1 wk`

A new method of heating is particularly suited to public houses. With Judith Hann, Peter Macann and Kieran Prendiville.
Director: Martin Mortimore. **Producers:** Cynthia Page, Dana Purvis and Richard Reisz. **Editor:** David Filkin.

`1986` `12.4` `Thu 17 Apr 8:00 p.m.` `11` `5 wks`

After the waterwheel, hydro-electricity and wave power comes the water windbag. With Judith Hann, Peter Macann, Maggie Philbin and Howard Stableford.
Director: Julie Harrup. **Producers:** Martin Freeth, Martin Mortimore, Cynthia Page and Dana Purvis. **Editor:** Richard Reisz.

`1987` `12.2` `Thu 26 Feb 8:00 p.m.` `5` `14 wks`

With Judith Hann, Peter Macann, Maggie Philbin and Howard Stableford looking at the airliners of the future.
Director: Tom Wragg. **Producers:** Viv King, Martin Mortimore, Cynthia Page and Dana Purvis. **Editor:** Richard Reisz.

`1988` `9.7` `Thu 9 Jun 8:00 p.m.` `15` `1 wk`

Judith Hann introduces the programme with HRH The Prince of Wales presenting the Award for Industrial Innovation and Production.
Director: Tom Wragg. **Producer:** Cynthia Page. **Editor:** Richard Reisz.

Tomorrow's World at Large
1 wk

BBC, documentary

| 1986 | 10.2 | Thu 22 May 8:00 p.m. | 11 | 1 wk |

'On the Trail of the Big Cat'
Judith Hann investigates sightings in Britain of large and ferocious wild cats.
Producer: Martin Hughes-Games. **Series Producer:** Richard Reisz.

Tomorrow's World Christmas Quiz
1 wk

BBC, game show

| 1986 | 12.6 | Thu 18 Dec 8:00 p.m. | 7 | 1 wk |

With presenters Judith Hann, Peter Macann, Maggie Philbin and Howard Stableford.
Director: Stuart McDonald. **Producer:** Cynthia Page. **Editor:** Richard Reisz.

Tonight with Dave Allen
5 wks

ATV, comedy

This series starred Irish comedian Allen in solo performance.

| 1967 | 5.8 | Sun 1 Oct 11:05 p.m. | 15 | 5 wks |

Producer: Gordon Reece.

Tony Hatch and All Kinds of Music
1 wk

ATV, music

| 1978 | 12.1 | Wed 30 Aug 8:00 p.m. | 7 | 1 wk |

This special stars prolific composer Tony Hatch with Moira Anderson, the Brighouse and Rastrick Brass Band, the Dooleys, Buddy Greco and George Hamilton IV, with the Jack Parnell orchestra.
Producer: Colin Clews.

Tootsie
1 wk

Presented by BBC, film

| 1986 | 14.0 | Sun 28 Dec 7:50 p.m. | 11 | 1 wk |

Dustin Hoffman stars as actor Michael Dorsey. The struggling thespian passes himself off as actress Dorothy Michaels in order to get work in a television soap opera. Jessica Lange and Bill Murray also star.
Director: Sydney Pollack.

Top Gun
1 wk

Presented by ITV, film

| 1990 | 12.3 | Sat 6 Oct 9:20 p.m. | 10 | 1 wk |

Tom Cruise stars as Pete 'Maverick' Mitchell, a fighter pilot at the US Navy's elite air combat training school. Anthony Edwards, Val Kilmer, Kelly McGillis, Meg Ryan and Tom Skerritt also star.
Director: Tony Scott.

Top of the Pops
192 wks

BBC, music

This series began in 1963. Sticking rigidly to the Top 40 singles the programme was the country's most successful weekly pop music show. Following the Musician's Union 1966 ban on artists miming to records the show featured the Top of the Pops orchestra directed by Johnny Pearson from 1967 to 1979. Choreographer Flick Colby provided dancers Pan's People (1972–76) and Legs and Co (1978–82). A succession of presenters and producers were employed. The format was slightly modified in 1991.
Producers included Johnnie Stewart (1963–67, 1972–73), Robin Nash (1975–76), Brian Whitehouse (1978, 1986–87) and Michael Hurll (1981–85).

| 1964 | 6.9 | Wed 1 Jul 7:35 p.m. | 9 | 16 wks |

Introduced by Alan Freeman.

| 1965 | 6.2 | Thu 28 Oct 7:30 p.m. | 15 | 18 wks |

Introduced by David Jacobs.

| 1966 | 5.8 | Thu 24 Mar 7:30 p.m. | 14 | 10 wks |

Introduced by Pete Murray.

| 1967 | 6.0 | Thu 28 Dec 7:30 p.m. | 14 | 4 wks |

A review of the year's hits, introduced by Pete Murray. With music by Long John Baldry, the Beatles, the Bee Gees, Dave Dee, Dozy, Beaky, Mick and Tich, Engelbert Humperdinck, Lulu, Scott McKenzie, the Monkees, Procol Harum, Diana Ross and the Supremes, and Traffic.

| 1968 | 6.3 | Thu 21 Mar 7:30 p.m. | 10 | 15 wks |

Introduced by Pete Murray.
Director: Mel Cornish. **Producer:** Colin Charman.

| 1969 | 5.4 | Thu 9 Oct 7:05 p.m. | 20 | 3 wks |

Introduced by Pete Murray.
Producer: Mel Cornish.

| 1972 | 5.7 | Thu 31 Aug 7:30 p.m. | 15 | 2 wks |

Introduced by Noel Edmonds.

| 1973 | 6.9 | Thu 1 Mar 6:45 p.m. | 12 | 4 wks |

Introduced by Tony Blackburn.

| 1975 | 8.6 | Thu 29 May 7:10 p.m. | 4 | 2 wks |

Introduced by Dave Lee Travis.

| 1976 | 6.4 | Thu 8 Jan 7:10 p.m. | 17 | 2 wks |

Introduced by Noel Edmonds.

| 1978 | 13.9 | Thu 2 Nov 7:20 p.m. | 9 | 2 wks |

Introduced by Dave Lee Travis.

| 1979 | 19.7 | Thu 11 Oct 7:20 p.m. | 6 | 22 wks |

Introduced by Andy Peebles.
Producer: David G. Hillier.

| 1980 | 13.6 | Thu 23 Oct 7:20 p.m. | 14 | 4 wks |

Introduced by Dave Lee Travis.
Producer: Stanley Appel.

| 1981 | 15.9 | Thu 3 Dec 7:20 p.m. | 9 | 21 wks |

Introduced by David Jensen.

| 1982 | 13.6 | Thu 11 Mar 7:25 p.m. | 5 | 28 wks |

Introduced by Simon Bates.

| 1983 | 11.5 | Thu 17 Mar 7:25 p.m. | 11 | 21 wks |

Introduced by Tony Blackburn and Gary Davies.

| 1984 | 10.5 | Thu 22 Mar 7:30 p.m. | 12 | 5 wks |

Introduced by Peter Powell and Janice Long.

| 1986 | 9.0 | Wed 11 Jun 7:40 p.m. | 12 | 2 wks |

Introduced by Mike Smith.

| 1987 | 9.2 | Fri 5 Jun 7:40 p.m. | 20 | 1 wk |

Introduced by Gary Davies.

| 1988 | 11.7 | Thu 10 Mar 7:00 p.m. | 11 | 10 wks |

Introduced by Mike Smith and Steve Wright.
Producer: Paul Ciani.

Top of the Pops' Christmas Party | 2 wks

BBC, music

These extended editions reviewed the Number One hits of their years.

| 1985 | 14.7 | Wed 25 Dec 2:00 p.m. | 11 | 1 wk |

The Christmas Party is presented by Gary Davies, Jonathan King, Janice Long, Dixie Peach, John Peel and Steve Wright.
Producer: Michael Hurll.

| 1986 | 12.8 | Thu 25 Dec 2:00 p.m. | 19 | 1 wk |

Presented by Simon Bates, Gary Davies, Janice Long and Peter Powell.
Producer: Michael Hurll.

Top Sailing | 2 wks

BBC, documentary

This series covered all aspects of sailing for the enthusiast and for newcomers to the pastime.

| 1979 | 14.3 | Thu 16 Aug 6:20 p.m. | 16 | 2 wks |

Martin Muncaster follows the crew of the Island Cruising Clubs schooner Hoshi to France and the Channel Islands.
Producer: Jeremy Pallant.

Top Secret | 26 wks

AR, drama

In these stories of international intrigue in South America, William Franklyn starred as Peter Dallas, Patrick Cargill as Garetta and Alan Rothwell as Mike.

| 1961 | 6.9 | Fri 10 Nov 9:35 p.m. | 1 | 14 wks |

'Festival of the Year' by John Warwick.
Dallas, Garetta and Mike answer an appeal for help from a justifiably terrified harlequin. They arrive in Brazil at the height of carnival in Rio.
Director: Mark Lawton. **Producer:** Jordan Lawrence.

| 1962 | 6.6 | Wed 16 May 8:00 p.m. | 3 | 12 wks |

'The Man from Carataz' by Jordan Lawrence.
When Don Enrique Broca arrives from Carataz, a sinister discovery suggests that he has some well-informed enemies. In his search to find them Peter Dallas meets a beautiful girl and narrowly misses a bullet. Based on a story by Lewis Davidson.
Producer: Jordan Lawrence.

Topaz
1 wk

Presented by ITV, film

| 1975 | 7.1 | Wed 1 Jan 8:00 p.m. | 10 | 1 wk |

Alfred Hitchcock's reconstruction of an espionage case in Copenhagen in 1962 is based on the novel by Leon Uris. Starring Karin Dor, John Forsythe, Dany Robin, Frederick Stafford and John Vernon.

Tormentors, The
1 wk

ATV, drama

| 1966 | 6.1 | Tue 29 Nov 9:10 p.m. | 11 | 1 wk |

This drama by Brian Phelan stars Stanley Baker as John Ellis, a patient in a prison hospital, and James Mason as psychiatrist Bernard Sholto.
Designer: Vic Symonds. **Director:** John Moxey. **Producer:** Cecil Clarke.

Touch of the Norman Vaughan's, A
11 wks

ATV, entertainment

Norman Vaughan achieved instant television fame as compere of SUNDAY NIGHT AT THE LONDON PALLADIUM, succeeding Bruce Forsyth. His catch phrases 'Swinging' (with thumbs up) and 'Dodgy' (with thumbs down) quickly caught on. He was rewarded with his own ATV series.

| 1964 | 7.3 | Fri 3 Jan 10:10 p.m. | 5 | 11 wks |

Guest star Millicent Martin, with Bill Pertwee, the Irving Davies dancers and the Jack Parnell orchestra.
Writer: Eric Merriman. **Director:** Colin Clews. **Producer:** Alan Tarrant.

Towering Inferno, The
2 wks

Presented by BBC, film

| 1980 | 17.7 | Fri 26 Dec 8:15 p.m. | 4 | 1 wk |

A night of terror is in prospect for the inhabitants of the 138-storey San Francisco 'Glass Tower'. Starring Steve McQueen and Paul Newman with Fred Astaire, Richard Chamberlain, Faye Dunaway, William Holden, Jennifer Jones, O. J. Simpson, Robert Vaughn and Robert Wagner.
Director: John Guillermin.

| 1984 | 11.1 | Sun 2 Jan 7:45 p.m. | 16 | 1 wk |

Repeat showing of the above film.

Town Like Alice, A
4 wks

Australia presented by BBC, drama

Rosemary Anne Sisson and Tom Hegarty adapted Nevil Shute's novel in four parts. A group of women were taken prisoner by the Japanese just before the fall of Singapore. A love story began which was fulfilled years later in the town of Alice Springs. The series starred Dorothy Alison, Bryan Brown, Gordon Jackson, Helen Morse, Yuki Shimoda and Anna Volska.
Director: David Stevens. **Producer:** Henry Crawford.

| 1981 | 16.2 | Wed 17 June 9:25 p.m. | 2 | 3 wks |

Part One
Jean Paget (Helen Morse) is taken prisoner, and with other women and children is forced to walk the length of Malaya with little food and no medical supplies. Joe Harman (Bryan Brown), an Australian, does his best to ease their conditions.

| 1984 | 10.0 | Tue 7 Aug 9:25 p.m. | 3 | 1 wk |

A repeat of the final episode in which Joe Harman and Jean Paget escort an injured man through creeks of rapidly rising water.

Town on Trial
1 wk

Presented by BBC, film

| 1967 | 5.9 | Sun 29 Jan 7:25 p.m. | 20 | 1 wk |

Superintendent Mike Halloran (John Mills) investigates the death of a young girl in a country town. Barbara Bates, Charles Coburn, Fay Compton, Derek Farr, Raymond Huntley, Geoffrey Keen, Alec McCowen and Elizabeth Seal also star.
Director: John Guillermin.

T. R. Sloane of the Secret Service
1 wk

USA presented by ITV, drama

Thomas Remington Sloane (Robert Logan) was the top agent for UNIT, a counter-espionage team assigned to dangerous missions. The series also starred Ji-Tu Cumbuka as Torque, Clive Revill as Eric Clawson and Ann Turkel as Sabrina Dorffman. The series was created by Philip Saltzman.
Producers: Quinn Martin and Cliff Gould.

| 1980 | 16.6 | Thur 3 Jan 7:15 p.m. | 4 | 1 wk |

In this feature-length introductory film a team of arms dealers aiming for world power has stolen a machine which can dehydrate people.

Patrick Cargill adventured in South America in **Top Secret**.

Trading Places — 2 wks

Presented by ITV, film

| 1988 | 11.8 | Mon 15 Aug 9:00 p.m. | 7 | 1 wk |

As a bet between two rich businessmen (Don Ameche and Ralph Bellamy), a stockbroker (Dan Aykroyd) swaps places with a con man (Eddie Murphy). James Belushi, Jamie Lee Curtis and Denholm Elliott also star.
Director: John Landis.

| 1990 | 10.4 | Mon 7 May 9:30 p.m. | 18 | 1 wk |

Repeat showing of the above film.

Train Robbers, The — 1 wk

Presented by ITV, film

| 1978 | 11.9 | Thu 13 Jul 7:45 p.m. | 7 | 1 wk |

John Wayne, Ann-Margret and Rod Taylor star in the story of adventurers in search of stolen gold who are pursued by a posse and a stranger smoking a cigar.
Director: Burt Kennedy.

Trainer — 1 wk

BBC, drama

This series concerned racehorse trainer Mike Hardy (Mark Greenstreet) and his adventures in the racing world. Nigel Davenport, David McCallum and Susannah York also starred.

| 1991 | 9.3 | Sun 1 Sep 8:15 p.m. | 19 | 1 wk |

'A Racing Certainty' by Christopher Green.
Mike is out to prove that he can be a success.
Director: Jeremy Summers. **Producer:** Gerard Glaister.

Trapped — 5 wks

ATV, drama

Series of single dramas.

| 1967 | 6.1 | Sat 3 Jun 10:05 p.m. | 3 | 5 wks |

'Goodnight Mrs Dill' by Fay Weldon.
Daisy (Frances Cuka) is happily married to Stephen (Andrew Ray) until Dr Matilda Dove (Petra Davies) breaks her leg and has to stay with them. Next-door neighbour Ivy Searle (Renee Houston) is disgusted by the carryings on.
Designer: Eric Sheddon. **Director:** June Howson. **Producer:** Anthony Firth.

Travelling Man — 5 wks

Granada, drama

This series by Roger Marshall starred Leigh Lawson as former Detective Inspector Lomax, who had just been released following a two-year prison sentence. He returned to his narrow boat Harmony and cruised the canals of northern England searching for the man who framed him and looking for his own runaway son.

| 1984 | 13.2 | Wed 21 Nov 9:00 p.m. | 14 | 5 wks |

'The Watcher'
Lomax follows a lead to a remote Welsh village. When a child goes missing he becomes the number one suspect.
Director: Laurence Moody. **Producer:** Brian Armstrong.

Trial and Error of Colonel Winchip, The — 1 wk

Granada, drama

| 1967 | 6.1 | Thu 1 Jun 9:40 p.m. | 5 | 1 wk |

This one-off play by Manus Hardy stars Donald Houston as Abel Winchip, Ursula Howells as Margot Winchip and Ray Brooks as Private Thomas. Winchip finds both his authority and his marriage are in jeopardy when Private Thomas becomes his temporary batman.
Designer: Peter Caldwell. **Producer:** Derek Bennett.

Trials of Life, The — 6 wks

BBC, documentary

This history of animal behaviour was written and presented by David Attenborough.

| 1990 | 12.8 | Wed 24 Oct 8:00 p.m. | 9 | 6 wks |

'Hunting and Escaping'
Stories of ambush, camouflage and life-and-death struggles on land and underwater. The programme features unforgettable scenes of a killer whale attacking sea lion pups off a beach in Patagonia.
Producer: Keenan Smart. **Executive Producer:** Peter Jones.

Triangle — 4 wks

Granada, drama

In this innovative drama series masterminded by Philip Mackie, a chosen theme was explored by three different writers forming a triangle of playlets each week. The series ran for seven weeks.

| 1964 | 5.3 | Fri 17 Jul 9:10 p.m. | 10 | 4 wks |

'Courtship' by Robin Chapman, Michael Hastings and Hugh Leonard.
Three views, comic, tragic and ironic, of the process by which a man and a woman move towards love and marriage. Starring John

Abineri, Clive Elliott, Philippa Gale, Barrie Gosney, Murray Hayne, Peter Jeffrey, Ann Kennedy, James Kerry, Madeleine Newbury, Henry Soskin and Veronica Strong.
Designer: Terry Pritchard. **Director:** Derek Bennett. **Producer:** Philip Mackie.

....

Tribute to Bernard Youens, A — 1 wk

Granada, news

| 1984 | 9.6 | Wed 29 Aug 7:30 p.m. | 13 | 1 wk |

The actor who played Stan Ogden in CORONATION STREET died on Monday of this week.

....

Tribute to Bevan — 1 wk

ITN, news

| 1960 | 4.9 | Wed 6 Jul 9:25 p.m. | 7 | 1 wk |

Aneurin Bevan, born in 1897, died at his Chiltern home at 4:10 p.m. this afternoon. Son of a Welsh miner and a miner himself at the age of thirteen, he was Member of Parliament for Ebbw Vale from 1929 until his death. As Minister of Health (1945–51) he inaugurated the National Health Service. A radical socialist, he led the Welsh miners in the 1926 strike and was a noted orator.

....

Tribute to Eddie Cantor — 1 wk

AR, news

| 1964 | 7.0 | No record of broadcast | 5 | 1 wk |

The Broadway and Hollywood star died on 10 October. Because the programme was necessarily unscheduled and AR no longer exists, there is no printed evidence of the precise date or time of the show. However, it was shown during the week commencing 12 Oct.

....

Tribute to Ingrid Bergman, A — 1 wk

ITN, news

| 1982 | 10.9 | Wed 1 Sep 8:00 p.m. | 6 | 1 wk |

The star of CASABLANCA and many other films died on 29 August.

....

Tribute to Jack Howarth, A — 1 wk

Granada, news

| 1984 | 14.5 | Mon 2 Apr 7:30 p.m. | 3 | 1 wk |

The actor who played Albert Tatlock in CORONATION STREET died yesterday.

Tribute to Kenneth More, A — 1 wk

Presented by ITV, film

| 1982 | 10.7 | Thu 15 Jul 8:00 p.m. | 8 | 1 wk |

The comedy film 'Genevieve' is shown as a tribute to the actor Kenneth More, who died three days ago.
See A KENNETH MORE SEASON for details of this film.

....

Tribute to Pat Phoenix, A — 1 wk

Granada, news

| 1986 | 11.9 | Wed 17 Sep 8:00 p.m. | 8 | 1 wk |

A celebration of the actress who played Elsie Tanner in CORONATION STREET. She died at 8:45 this morning.

....

Tribute to President Kennedy — 1 wk

BBC, news

| 1963 | 6.1 | Sat 23 Nov throughout the day | 17 | 1 wk |

The day following the assassination of President Kennedy the BBC pays tribute to the man and his work. The programme is presented by Kenneth Allsop, Richard Dimbleby, Cliff Michelmore and Ian Trethowan. (The previous evening both ITV and BBC had been thrown into unprecedented confusion by the assassination. Both were severely criticized. The announcement of the President's death came just after 7:00 p.m. ITV made the announcement and went straight back to EMERGENCY WARD TEN for ten minutes before cutting out and playing solemn music. The BBC on the other hand played solemn music immediately after the announcement but at 7:50 p.m. showed an episode of the comedy show HERE'S HARRY.)

....

Tribute to Tony Hancock, A — 1 wk

BBC, news

| 1968 | 6.1 | Wed 26 Jun 9:30 p.m. | 9 | 1 wk |

Tony Hancock was found dead in his Sydney apartment on Tuesday 25 June. BBC's Head of Light Entertainment Tom Sloan pays tribute to him and introduces an extract from his 1961 recording THE RADIO HAM.

....

Tribute to Violet Carson, A — 1 wk

Granada, news

| 1983 | 13.2 | Wed 28 Dec 7:30 p.m. | 2 | 1 wk |

The actress who played Ena Sharples in CORONATION STREET died on 26 December.

Tripper's Day — 4 wks

Thames, situation comedy

This series by Brian Cooke starred Leonard Rossiter as Norman Tripper, manager of the Supafare Supermarket.

| 1984 | 15.6 | Mon 24 Sep 8:00 p.m. | 4 | 4 wks |

'Special Offers'
As a devoted fan of American TV police series, Tripper briefs his staff in the manner of a Chief of Police.
Producer: Anthony Parker.

Tropic — 2 wks

ATV, drama

This six-part serial by Leslie Thomas was based on his book Tropic of Ruislip about life on the executive housing estate of Plummer's Park. It starred Ronald Pickup as Andrew Maiby, Hilary Tindall as his wife Audrey, John Clive as Rev. Ivor Boon, Ronald Lacey as Geoffrey Turvey and George Maplas as Hercules.

| 1979 | 9.5 | Sun 29 Jul 9:00 p.m. | 16 | 2 wks |

Chapter One 'Monday's Child'
Andrew starts work on a novel, Rev. Boon crusades in vain and Audrey wonders where life is heading.
Producer: Matthew Robinson. **Executive Producer:** Greg Smith.

Trouble with Men, The — 1 wk

Granada, documentary

| 1962 | 5.2 | Wed 13 Jun 9:45 p.m. | 5 | 1 wk |

A panel of women chaired by cook Fanny Craddock appraises and discusses contemporary men.
Director: Joan Kemp-Welch. **Producer:** Elaine Grand.

Trouble with Women, The — 1 wk

Granada, documentary

| 1962 | 5.3 | Wed 18 Jul 9:45 p.m. | 6 | 1 wk |

A panel of men chaired by Brian Inglis discusses modern woman. With Kingsley Amis, Bernard Levin and Malcolm Muggeridge.
Director: Claude Watham. **Producer:** Philip Mackie.

Troubleshooters, The — 7 wks

BBC, drama

This long-running series by John Elliot about an oil company was also known as MOGUL, its overseas title. The principal players were Ray Barrett as Peter Thornton, Robert Hardy as Alec Stewart, Geoffrey Keen as Brian Stead and Philip Latham as the financial wizard Willy Izzard. Originally produced by Peter Graham Scott.

| 1969 | 5.4 | Mon 19 May 9:05 p.m. | 15 | 6 wks |

'Lord, What a Tangled Web' by John Lucarotti.
Mogul is drilling for oil in Berlin, scene of a wartime incident involving Stead and now dragged up twenty-four years later to discredit him.
Designer: Barrie Dobbins. **Director:** Lennie Mayne. **Producer:** Anthony Read.

| 1970 | 4.6 | Mon 27 Jul 9:10 p.m. | 18 | 1 wk |

'A Truly Exotic Development' by John Elliot.
The Stewarts return to the Caribbean, where Mogul's drilling rig has been sabotaged. Stead sends Alec's old rival Thornton to investigate.
Designer: Richard Hunt. **Director:** Paul Ciappessoni. **Producer:** Anthony Read.

True Grit — 1 wk

Presented by BBC, film

| 1979 | 13.0 | Sun 24 Jun 8:05 p.m. | 3 | 1 wk |

John Wayne stars as a hard-drinking old marshal who helps a young girl avenge the murder of her father. Glen Campbell, Robert Duvall and Dennis Hopper also star.
Director: Henry Hathaway.

Tuesday Documentary, The — 3 wks

ATV, documentary

This series of films tackled a wide range of serious subjects.

| 1970 | 6.3 | Tue 13 Jan 10:30 p.m. | 18 | 2 wks |

'The Violent Earth'
A study of volcanologists at work. Haroun Tazieff and his team spend their lives searching out the secrets of volcanoes and trying to learn more about their unpredictable behaviour. Graham Lines narrates. (A Ciné-Documents Tazieff production.)

| 1971 | 6.1 | Tue 25 May 10:30 p.m. | 11 | 1 wk |

'The Most Powerful Briton in America'
A film profile of theatre critic Clive Barnes of the New York Times, a man whose review can decide whether a show runs or folds. Bernard Levin narrates.
Camera: Ernest Vincze. **Director:** Charles Mapleston, **Producer:** Brigid Segrave.

Tuesday Film, The — 12 wks

Presented by BBC, film

| 1968 | 5.2 | Tue 13 Aug 7:00 p.m. | 7 | 2 wks |

'The Malta Story'
The true story of the George Cross Island during the Second World War and the RAF officers who defended it. Jack Hawkins and Anthony Steel star with Renée Asherson, Peter Bull, Rosalie Crutchley, Jerry Desmonde, Michael Medwin, Muriel Pavlow, Flora Robson and Nigel Stock.
Director: Brian Desmond Hurst.

| 1979 | 16.7 | Tue 14 Aug 7:30 p.m. | 5 | 4 wks |

'South of Algiers'
Thieves and archaeologists search the Sahara for a mask contained in a long lost tomb. Starring Van Heflin, Eric Portman and Wanda Hendrix.
Director: Jack Lee.

| 1980 | 12.5 | Tue 21 Oct 6:55 p.m. | 19 | 2 wks |

'Donovan's Reef'
John Wayne, Dorothy Lamour and Lee Marvin star in a story of war veterans who settle on a South Pacific island.
Director: John Ford.

| 1981 | 10.9 | Tue 30 Jun 7:45 p.m. | 15 | 3 wks |

'Horror at 37,000 Feet'
An ancient English abbey is being freighted to America. A lady on board warns of the dire consequences of moving the abbey. A sequence of events convinces the crew and passengers that she may be right.
Director: David Lowell Rich.

| 1984 | 10.3 | Tue 23 Jul 7:25 p.m. | 5 | 1 wk |

'Carry On Doctor'
(See separate entry for this film.)

....

Tuesday Movie, The — 2 wks

Presented by ITV, film

| 1977 | 8.2 | Tue 4 Jan 7:30 p.m. | 3 | 2 wks |

'Beyond the Bermuda Triangle'
Fred MacMurray stars as Harry Ballanger, a retired and wealthy man living in southern Florida. He owns a luxury yacht and sets out in search of friends missing without trace in the notorious waters known as the Bermuda Triangle.
Director: William A. Graham.

Tuesday's Documentary — 4 wks

BBC, documentary

This series presented a wide spectrum of films on serious subjects.

| 1971 | 6.1 | Tue 14 Sep 9:20 p.m. | 11 | 2 wks |

'When Fire Fell from the Skies'
Group Captain Peter Townsend introduces a film made by West German Television examining the reasons for the defeat of Hitler's Luftwaffe in World War Two's battle for the skies. Michael Wolf narrates.
Producer: Rudolf Woller.

| 1974 | 6.2 | Tue 21 May 9:25 p.m. | 13 | 1 wk |

'Cross Your Heart and Hope to Live'
An investigation into heart disease and the vulnerability of different categories of people. Richard Leech narrates.
Producer: Karl Sabbagh.

| 1975 | 7.4 | Tue 27 May 9:35 p.m. | 16 | 1 wk |

'Chastity, Poverty and Obedience'
An examination of the inner world of nuns and what happens when a woman answers a compulsive call to serve God.
Camera: Roy Henman. **Producer:** Hugh Burnett.

....

Tully — 1 wk

Thames/Euston films, drama

| 1975 | 7.2 | Wed 26 Nov 8:30 p.m. | 18 | 1 wk |

In this single play Anthony Valentine stars as insurance agent Tully, who follows the trail of some stolen antiques to Australia. Once there he dodges sharks, bullets and beautiful decoy girls to secure his 10 per cent commission on finding items.
Writer: Ian Stuart Black. **Producer:** James Gatward. **Executive Producers:** Lloyd Shirley and George Taylor. (A Euston Films Production.)

....

Tumbledown — 1 wk

BBC, drama

| 1988 | 10.5 | Tue 31 May 9:30 p.m. | 9 | 1 wk |

This film drama tells the story of Robert Lawrence (Colin Firth), who sailed to the Falkland Islands as a 22-year-old officer with the British task force in 1982. He was wounded just hours before the Argentinian surrender. His real battle began when he returned home.
Writer: Charles Wood. **Designer:** Geoff Powell. **Producer:** Richard Broke. **Director:** Richard Eyre.

Turn out the Lights | 6 wks

Granada, situation comedy

This was the second spinoff series for the character of Leonard Swindley as played by Arthur Lowe, first in CORONATION STREET and then in PARDON THE EXPRESSION. Swindley and Walter Hunt (Robert Dorning) were unceremoniously sacked from Dobson and Hawks in July, 1966, at the end of the latter series. They were now amateur ghost hunters, sleuths for a world of spooks and spirits.

| 1967 | 7.3 | Fri 6 Jan 9:10 p.m. | 8 | 6 wks |

'The Boyhood Haunt'
Walter confesses that he is under the influence of his own star sign, Aries the Ram. Swindley scoffs, but when he meets Mr Merlin (Peter Wyngarde), a famous astrologer, his life is poised for change.
Writers: Peter Eckersley and Kenneth Cope. **Producer:** Derek Granger.

TV Eye | 4 wks

Thames, documentary

This replacement for the long-running AR/Thames programme THIS WEEK was little different, so little it resumed the title THIS WEEK in 1986.
Editor: Mike Townson.

| 1978 | 18.4 | Thu 21 Dec 8:30 p.m. | 10 | 1 wk |

Reporters: Jonathan Dimbleby, Llew Gardner, Vanya Kewley, Julian Manyon, Peter Taylor and Peter Williams.
Producer: Ken Craig.

| 1980 | 11.9 | Thu 24 Apr 8:30 p.m. | 14 | 1 wk |

Reporters: Llew Gardner, Peter Gill, Bryan Gould, Vanya Kewley, Julian Manyon, Robert Southgate and Denis Tuohy.

| 1982 | 9.1 | Thu 15 Jul 9:30 p.m. | 16 | 1 wk |

Reporters: Llew Gardner, Peter Gill, Bryan Gould, Julian Manyon and Denis Tuohy.

| 1984 | 10.5 | Thu 5 Apr 9:30 p.m. | 19 | 1 wk |

Reporters: Alastair Burnet, Peter Gill, Julian Manyon, Peter Prendergast and Denis Tuohy.

TV Times Top Ten Awards, The | 12 wks

Thames, entertainment

TV Times *readers voted for their favourite shows and personalities. The winners of the various categories were presented with their awards by the editor of the magazine.*
Producers included David Clark (1976, 1986–89), Steve Minchin (1979–80) and Malcolm Morris (1981–84).

| 1976 | 8.4 | Wed 14 Apr 8:00 p.m. | 2 | 1 wk |

Hosted by Richard O'Sullivan.
Director: Daphne Shadwell.

| 1977 | 8.1 | Thu 14 Apr 7:35 p.m. | 4 | 1 wk |

Hosted by Richard O'Sullivan.
Producer: Stuart Hall.

| 1978 | 14.9 | Tue 23 May 8:00 p.m. | 1 | 1 wk |

Hosted by Richard O'Sullivan.
Producer: Dennis Kirkland.

| 1979 | 16.8 | Wed 9 May 8:00 p.m. | 2 | 1 wk |

Hosted by Richard O'Sullivan.

| 1980 | 15.1 | Wed 21 May 8:00 p.m. | 2 | 1 wk |

Hosted by David Hamilton.

| 1981 | 14.1 | Wed 29 Apr 8:00 p.m. | 9 | 1 wk |

Hosted by David Hamilton.

| 1982 | 14.0 | Wed 28 Apr 8:00 p.m. | 6 | 1 wk |

Hosted by Michael Aspel and Joan Collins.

| 1984 | 11.8 | Tue 31 Jan 7:30 p.m. | 13 | 1 wk |

Hosted by Bruce Forsyth and Nanette Newman.

| 1986 | 13.9 | Wed 26 Feb 8:00 p.m. | 4 | 1 wk |

Hosted by Peter Bowles.

| 1987 | 12.1 | Tue 3 Mar 8:00 p.m. | 13 | 1 wk |

Hosted by Anneka Rice.

| 1988 | 12.4 | Wed 20 Jan 8:00 p.m. | 14 | 1 wk |

Hosted by Nigel Havers.

| 1989 | 12.8 | Wed 15 Feb 8:00 p.m. | 18 | 1 wk |

Hosted by Michael Barrymore.
Director: Ian Hamilton.

Twenty Questions | 10 wks

AR, game show

This long-running radio format was brought to television not by the BBC but by ITV. The chairman was Stewart MacPherson. The BBC had tried it on TV in the 1950s.
Producer: Tig Roe.

1960	4.9	Fri 17 Jun 8:00 p.m.	7	2 wks

Panellists: Isobel Barnett, Frankie Howerd, Stephen Potter and Muriel Young.

1961	4.9	Tue 5 Sep 8:00 p.m.	10	8 wks

Panellists: Isobel Barnett, John Blythe, Kenneth Pearson and Nancy Spain.

Twenty Thousand Leagues under the Sea — 1 wk

Presented by BBC, film

1982	9.9	Fri 24 Dec 6:35 p.m.	18	1 wk

Walt Disney's film of Jules Verne's story, set in 1868, about a terrifying monster that attacked ships in the Pacific. Starring Kirk Douglas and James Mason.
Director: Richard Fleischer.

Twenty Years of the Two Ronnies — 22 wks

BBC, comedy

The twentieth anniversary of the pairing of Corbett and Barker provided the BBC with a reason to repeat some of the highlights of the past two decades.

1986	15.4	Sun 26 Oct 7:15 p.m.	3	13 wks

With John Scott-Martin, Claire Nielson, John Rutland, Joan Sims and April Walker.
Writers: David Nobbs, Spike Milligan, Spike Mullins, David Renwick and Gerald Wiley.

1987	14.7	Fri 4 Dec 8:15 p.m.	5	9 wks

A repeat showing of the above programme.

---

24 Carrott Gold — 1 wk

BBC, comedy

1991		Tue 25 Jun 9:30 p.m.	13	1 wk

A repeat of a 50-minute recording of Jasper Carrott on his British tour of 1990, with new monologues and some of his timeless classic stories.
Producer: Paul Smith. (A Celador production.)

Twenty-Four Hours — 4 wks

BBC, news

This nightly current affairs show was anchored by Kenneth Allsop, Ludovic Kennedy and Cliff Michelmore with a distinguished team of reporters including Michael Barratt, Robin Day, David Lomax, Robert McKenzie, Leonard Parkin, Michael Parkinson, Julian Pettifer, Fyfe Robertson, Philip Tibenham and Ian Trethowan.
Editor (1967–68): Anthony Whitby.

1966	5.8	Tue 15 Nov 10:25 p.m.	18	2 wks

Editor: Derrick Amoore.

1967	6.9	Thu 16 Nov 10:00 p.m.	11	1 wk

1968	5.3	Tue 23 Jul 9:30 p.m.	6	1 wk

---

21 Years of Laughter — 3 wks

LWT, comedy

1989	9.4	Sat 29 Jul 8:10 p.m.	12	1 wk

Denis Norden presents comedy selections from variety shows made by London Weekend Television during its 21 years of broadcasting.
Director: John Gorman. **Producer:** Paul Lewis.

1990	13.3	Sat 22 Dec 8:10 p.m.	9	2 wks

Repeat of the 1989 show above.

Twenty-Two Years of the Two Ronnies — 1 wk

BBC, comedy

1988	10.5	Fri 16 Sep 8:15 p.m.	15	1 wk

Ronnie Barker and Ronnie Corbett celebrate their 22-year association with their personal selection of favourite moments.

Geraldine McEwan was voted 1978 actress of the year in **The TV Times Top Ten Awards**.

Two in Clover | 12 wks

Thames, situation comedy

This series was written by Vince Powell and Harry Driver about two former City clerks, Sid Turner (Sid James) and Vic Evans (Victor Spinetti), who decided to buy and run a farm.
Producer: Alan Tarrant.

| 1969 | 7.8 | Tue 18 Feb 8:25 p.m. | 2 | 6 wks |

Sid and Vic are knee deep in Fresian cows.

| 1970 | 7.4 | Tue 17 Mar 8:25 p.m. | 8 | 6 wks |

Sid's sporting activities are usually confined to the indoor type – preferably after dark. Vic tricks him into playing cricket for the vicar's eleven. Guests: Jan Butlin, Graham Crowden, John Inman, Anthony Sagar and Fred Trueman.
Producer: Alan Tarrant.

Two of a Kind | 1 wk

Thames, documentary

| 1982 | 13.3 | Wed 3 Feb 8:00 p.m. | 13 | 1 wk |

Eric Morecambe and Ernie Wise are in conversation with Alan Whicker. They select film clips of their own favourite double acts of the past.
Producer: David Clark.

Two of Us, The | 24 wks

LWT, situation comedy

In this series by Alex Shearer young lovers Elaine and Ashley (Janet Dibley and Nicholas Lyndhurst) lived together in spite of their opposing outlooks on life.
Directors: John Gorman (1986, 1988) and Terry Kinane (1989, 1991). **Producers:** Marcus Plantin (1986, 1988) and Robin Carr (1987, 1989–91). **Executive Producer** (1987, 1989): Marcus Plantin.

| 1986 | 11.7 | Fri 30 Oct 8:30 p.m. | 13 | 2 wks |

'Proposals'
Elaine rejects Ashley's proposal of marriage. She is quite content with the status quo.

| 1987 | 11.2 | Fri 11 Sep 8:30 p.m. | 12 | 1 wk |

'The Vital Spark'
Elaine returns after six months in India.

| 1988 | 11.9 | Sat 9 Apr 7:30 p.m. | 12 | 9 wks |

Repeat showing of the top 1986 episode.

| 1989 | 13.2 | Fri 17 Feb 8:30 p.m. | 13 | 6 wks |

'Say It With . . .'
A friend tells Ashley he should buy Elaine a few romantic presents He gets her a cactus and a jar of chutney.

| 1990 | 12.0 | Sun 11 Feb 7:15 p.m. | 17 | 3 wks |

'At Last'
Ashley and Elaine finally decide to get married.

| 1991 | 8.9 | Sat 13 Jul 7:40 p.m. | 14 | 3 wks |

'No Deposit – No Return'
Ashley and Elaine adopt a green life style.

Two Ronnies, The | 92 wks

BBC, comedy

The most durable of pairings, Ronnie Barker and Ronnie Corbett were first brought together in the 1960s on THE FROST REPORT. As THE TWO RONNIES they made an annual series for the BBC as well as occasional specials for more than 20 years until Barker's retirement. The show's format hardly changed over the years with a 'news' summary at the opening and closing, sketches, playlets, songs and parodies. There was always a lot of dressing up, and each show featured a monologue from Corbett delivered from a chair. Ronnie Barker contributed much of the writing supported by many eminent names over the years, including Barry Cryer, Eric Idle, Spike Mullins, David Nobbs, Gerald Wiley (a pseudonym for Barker himself), John Cleese, Ian Davidson, David Renwick, John Sullivan, Peter Vincent, Bryan Blackburn and Laurie Rowley.
Director (1985, 1987): Marcus Mortimer. **Producers** included Terry Hughes (1971–76), Peter Whitmore (1977–78), Paul Jackson (1980–82, billed K. Paul Jackson 1980), and Marcus Plantin (1983–84). **Executive Producer** (1980–85) and **Producer** (1987): Michael Hurll.

| 1971 | 6.5 | Sat 15 May 8:10 p.m. | 8 | 8 wks |

Guests: Tina Charles, New World and Madeline Smith.
Executive Producer: James Gilbert.

| 1972 | 6.2 | Sat 7 Oct 7:25 p.m. | 14 | 5 wks |

Guests: Georgie Fame and Alan Price, Thelma Houston and Sue Lloyd.

| 1974 | 5.5 | Sat 13 Jul 8:35 p.m. | 19 | 1 wk |

Guests: Finn Jon, Noël Dyson and Claire Nielson. (This programme was first shown on BBC2.)

1975	8.8	Thu 9 Oct 7:45 p.m.	1	9 wks

Guests: Cyd Hayman, Michel Legrand and Swingle II. (This programme was first shown on BBC2.)

1976	8.4	Sat 23 Oct 8:15 p.m.	2	9 wks

Guests: The Caledonian Highlanders, Barbara Dickson and the Metropolitan Police Band.

1977	17.8	Sat 10 Dec 8:20 p.m.	2	6 wks

Guests: The Nolan Sisters.

1978	17.6	Sat 7 Jan 8:15 p.m.	5	3 wks

Guests: The Nolan Sisters.

1979	18.4	Sat 6 Jan 8:30 p.m.	1	9 wks

Guests: Manhattan Transfer.
Producer: Brian Penders.

1980	18.6	Sat 29 Nov 8:10 p.m.	2	10 wks

Guests: Elkie Brooks, Jenny Logan and Raymond Mason.

1981	16.9	Sat 5 Dec 8:00 p.m.	3	5 wks

Guests: Kiki Dee and Elizabeth Larner.

1982	16.4	Sat 9 Jan 8:05 p.m.	5	6 wks

Guests: Patricia Brake, Elkie Brooks, Jenny Logan and Claire Nielson.

1983	13.9	Sat 10 Dec 8:10 p.m.	6	3 wks

Guests: Leslie Ash, Elaine Paige and Robin Parkinson.

1984	13.6	Sat 14 Jan 8:00 p.m.	4	6 wks

Guests: Helen Cotterill, Barbara Dickson and Dilys Watling.

1985	18.5	Wed 25 Dec 9:00 p.m.	2	11 wks

Guests: John Blythe, Phil Collins, Paul McDowell and Janet Mahoney.

1987	9.8	Thu 11 Jun 9:15 p.m.	13	1 wk

A repeat of the top 1985 show.

··

Two Ronnies' Christmas Show, The				1 wk

1982	11.1	Sat 25 Dec 7:30 p.m.	12	1 wk

Guests: David Essex and Brigit Forsyth.
Producer: Paul Jackson. **Executive Producer:** Michael Hurll.

··

Two's Company				3 wks

LWT, situation comedy

This series created by Bill Macllwraith starred Elaine Stritch as Dorothy McNab, a best-selling American author living in London, and Donald Sinden as Robert, her butler.

1978	17.3	Sun 5 Feb 9:15 p.m.	2	3 wks

'The Pet'
Dorothy brings home a little dog. Guest star: Beryl Reid.
Director: John Reardon. **Producer:** Humphrey Barclay.

*Long-running partners Corbett and Barker were **The Two Ronnies**.*

UK Ballroom Dancing Championships 〔1 wk〕

BBC, entertainment

| 1969 | 5.6 | Fri 24 Apr 9:55 p.m. | 19 | 1 wk |

From the Lyceum, Peter West introduces the finals of the amateur Latin American and Modern Championships. Judith Chalmers and Peggy Spencer commentate.
Television presentation: Douglas Hespe.

Ultra Quiz 〔14 wks〕

TVS, game show

Two thousand contestants began a globetrotting quiz that involved general knowledge and stunt work. Many were eliminated each week until only five remained to compete for the £10,000 first prize.
Producer: Tony McLaren.

| 1983 | 8.4 | Sat 9 Jul 7:45 p.m. | 8 | 5 wks |

Michael Aspel hosts. Sally James and Jonathan King assist. The two thousand contestants gather on Brighton sea front for the first round.
Director: Phil Bishop. **Executive Producer:** Jeremy Fox.

| 1984 | 9.4 | Sat 18 Aug 7:30 p.m. | 6 | 7 wks |

David Frost, assisted by William Rushton, introduces the five remaining contestants in the final from Hawaii.
Director: Dave Heather.

| 1985 | 9.4 | Sat 17 Aug 7:45 p.m. | 13 | 2 wks |

Stu Francis and Sara Hollamby introduce the final from Bournemouth. Only five contestants are still in the competition. Guests: Wayne Dobson, Larry Parker and Wall Street Crash.
Director: Ian Hamilton. **Executive Producer:** John Kaye Cooper.

Uncrowned Jewels, The 〔1 wk〕

BBC, documentary

| 1987 | 12.9 | Mon 30 Mar 8:00 p.m. | 11 | 1 wk |

This is the final opportunity to see the entire £5 million collection of jewels which belonged to the Duke and Duchess of Windsor. The collection goes under the hammer in Geneva on Thursday.
Producers: Martyn Gregory and Elaine Thomas.

Undefeated, The 〔1 wk〕

Presented by ITV, film

| 1982 | 10.5 | Sat 23 Oct 7:05 p.m. | 19 | 1 wk |

John Wayne and Rock Hudson star as colonels from opposite sides in the wake of the Civil War. They meet on the Rio Grande.
Director: Andrew V. McLaglen.

Undersea World of Jacques Cousteau, The 〔5 wks〕

Presented by BBC, documentary

This series of films found teams led by the world-famous diver Jacques Cousteau in the seas and oceans of the world. Produced by the Cousteau Society with Metromedia Producers Corporation.

| 1975 | 8.4 | Wed 29 May 8:10 p.m. | 6 | 5 wks |

'The Sleeping Sharks of Yucatan'
The sleeping sharks of Yucatan are studied in their haunts in caverns off the coast of Mexico.

Union Castle 〔3 wks〕

Granada, situation comedy

Stratford Johns starred as Lord Mountainash, a trade unionist elevated to the peerage. He bought a castle in Wales.

| 1982 | 11.8 | Mon 19 Apr 8:00 p.m. | 11 | 3 wks |

In this first episode Mountainash discovers the castle did not come with vacant possession.
Director: Douglas Argent. **Producer:** Eric Prytherch.

United! — 3 wks

BBC, soap

This series about the fortunes of a football team and its followers was created by Brian Hayles, with stories by Tom Brennand, Roy Bottomley and Nick McCarty. Jimmy Hill provided technical advice.

| 1967 | 6.2 | Mon 27 Feb 7:05 p.m. | 14 | 3 wks |

John Lennington (Jeremy Mason) has an important appointment with Mark Wilson (Ronald Allen).
Director: Mike Bowen. **Producer:** John McRae.

United Kingdom Disco Dancing Championships — 1 wk

Thames, entertainment

| 1980 | 12.7 | Tue 14 Oct 7:30 p.m. | 19 | 1 wk |

Peter Gordeno introduces the competitors with Darts and the Ray McVay orchestra.
Producer: Steve Minchin.

University Challenge — 137 wks

Granada, quiz

In this general knowledge quiz, Bamber Gascoigne as question master presided over university teams. The series was based on the American show COLLEGE BOWL.
Director: Peter Mullings. **Producers** (1964–68): Douglas Terry.

| 1963 | 5.8 | Tue 26 Nov 7:00 p.m. | 10 | 13 wks |

Producer: Patricia Owtram.

1964	5.8	Wed 30 Dec 7:00 p.m.	17	2 wks
1965	6.9	Wed 17 Nov 7:00 p.m.	6	39 wks
1966	7.2	Wed 30 Nov 7:00 p.m.	6	40 wks
1967	7.2	Wed 11 Jan 7:00 p.m.	7	34 wks
1968	6.3	Wed 31 Jan 9:00 p.m.	11	9 wks

Unmarried Mothers — 1 wk

Granada, documentary

| 1963 | 5.3 | Wed 31 Jul 9:45 p.m. | 3 | 1 wk |

A special report on unwed mothers is written and narrated by Douglas Keay.
Director: Michael Grigsby. **Producer:** Elaine Grand.

Unnatural Causes — 1 wk

Central, drama

This series of seven plays concerned death by unnatural causes.

| 1986 | 11.3 | Sat 8 Nov 9:00 p.m. | 18 | 1 wk |

'Home Cooking' by Paula Milne.
A murder takes place in a private hotel run by Judith and Vic (Prunella Scales and Brian Cox). The establishment is famous for its home cooking.
Designer: Jeff Pessler. **Director:** Tim King. **Producer:** Nicholas Palmer.

Untouchables, The — 1 wk

Presented by BBC, film

| 1991 | 11.9 | Mon 6 May 9:20 p.m. | 8 | 1 wk |

The Untouchables were Federal investigators who were prepared to risk everything to end Al Capone's violent reign of terror in Prohibition era Chicago. Sean Connery, Kevin Costner, Robert De Niro and Andy Garcia star.
Director: Brian De Palma

Up Pompeii — 8 wks

BBC, comedy

Frankie Howerd starred as Lurcio, the Roman slave who master-minded the household of his master Ludicrus Sextus (Max Adrian). Other characters included Nausius (Kerry Gardner), Ammonia (Elizabeth Larner), Erotica (Georgina Moon), Plautus (Walter Horsbrugh, later William Rushton), Ambrosia (Lynda Baron), Flavia (Mollie Sugden), Prodigus (David Kernan) and Odius (John Junkin).

| 1969 | 5.4 | Wed 17 Sep 9:10 p.m. | 20 | 1 wk |

An introductory episode to the works of Plautus as presented by Lurcio.
Writer: Talbot Rothwell. **Producer:** Michael Mills.

| 1970 | 6.1 | Mon 11 May 9:10 p.m. | 13 | 2 wks |

In this final episode of the series Lurcio is called upon to defend his master's bad behaviour and is anxious to please Lusha (Tricia Noble).
Writer: Talbot Rothwell. **Producer:** David Croft.

| 1971 | 6.5 | Sat 6 Nov 9:40 p.m. | 12 | 5 wks |

Money is tight and one or two luxuries will have to be given up – like Lurcio, for instance.
Writers: Talbot Rothwell and Sid Colin. **Producer:** Sydney Lotterby.

U

Up the Elephant and Round the Castle				13 wks

Thames, situation comedy

This series starred Jim Davidson as first time homeowner Jim London in the Elephant and Castle. His aunt Mini had died and left him her terraced house.
Producer: Anthony Parker.

1983	14.9	Wed 7 Dec 8:30 p.m.	3	4 wks

'May the Best Man Win'
Jim's old pal Arnold (Christopher Ellison) invites him to be best man at his wedding.
Writer: Jim Eldridge.

1984	13.8	Wed 11 Jan 8:30 p.m.	7	2 wks

'Every Two Minutes'
Jim learns there is a break-in in London every two minutes. Now it's his turn.
Writer: Tony Hoare.

1985	13.7	Tue 9 Apr 8:00 p.m.	10	7 wks

Repeat of the 1984 episode above.

Up the Polls				1 wk

BBC, comedy

1970	5.0	Thu 18 Jun 10:05 p.m.	9	1 wk

This one-off twenty-minute comedy interrupted the serious coverage of election night as Cliff Michelmore and the experts awaited results. Written by Johnny Speight, it starred Eric Sykes as the foreman, Warren Mitchell as Alf Garnett and Spike Milligan as Paki-Paddy. The three meet to discuss the election in a public bar.
Producer: Dennis Main Wilson.

Up the Sandbox				1 wk

Presented by BBC, film

1980	10.1	Thu 28 Aug 9:25 p.m.	20	1 wk

Barbra Streisand stars as Margaret, a young New Yorker with an identity crisis. She is married with two children and pregnant. Husband Paul (David Selby) shows more concern for history than their matrimonial predicament.
Director: Irwin Kershner.

Up the Workers				11 wks

ATV, comedy

This series by Tom Brennand and Roy Bottomley was based on an idea by Lance Percival. It was set in the Midlands factory of Cocker's Components Ltd. and starred Henry McGee as managing director Dicky Bligh, Lance Percival as labour-relations officer Bernard Peck and Norman Bird as shop steward Sid Stubbins.

1974	7.7	Wed 1 May 8:30 p.m.	4	7 wks

'Grapevine'
A shop-floor apprentice starts a rumour that could cost Bligh his job.
Producer: John Scholz-Conway.

1976	7.9	Wed 7 Apr 8:30 p.m.	4	4 wks

'A Fishy Business'
Mr Bligh has obviously found a new interest in life. The workers think it's the ladies, but machinist Fred Hamflitt (Victor Maddern) discovers the truth – it's angling.
Producer: Alan Tarrant.

Upchat Line, The				7 wks

Thames, situation comedy

This series by Keith Waterhouse concerned Mike Upchat (John Alderton), the pen name of a little-known author better known for chatting up every pretty woman in sight. The music was by Mike Batt.

1977	15.3	Mon 26 Sep 8:00 p.m.	2	7 wks

'Pulling'
Upchat's current home is a luggage locker at Marylebone Station. His problem of where to sleep is solved at a party for liberated ladies. Alexandra Dane, Dennis Lill and Wanda Ventham also star.
Producer: Robert Reed.

Upper Hand, The				21 wks

Central, situation comedy

In this series by Greg Freeman, Joe McGann played former football star Charlie Burrows. He kept house for female executive Caroline Wheatley (Diana Weston). Honor Blackman appeared as Laura West.
Producer: Christopher Walker.

1990	11.3	Tue 29 May 8:30 p.m.	7	11 wks

'Caroline's First Fight'
Caroline disapproves of Charlie's attitude towards the children.
Director: Martin Dennis.

1991	11.6	Mon 11 Mar 8:00 p.m.	10	10 wks

'Wedding Bells'
Everyone converges on Cannes for the wedding of Laura's ex-husband.
Director: Martin Dennis.

Upstairs Downstairs   58 wks

LWT, drama

The Bellamy family and their domestic servants lived in Eaton Square, London. The series chronicled their lives from 1903, just after the death of Queen Victoria, until 1930. The idea was by Eileen Atkins and Jean Marsh.

The principal players were Angela Baddeley as Mrs Bridges, Gordon Jackson as Hudson, David Langton as Richard Bellamy, Jean Marsh as Rose and Simon Williams as James Bellamy. Other principal characters included Lady Marjorie Bellamy (Rachel Gurney), Elizabeth Bellamy, later Kirbridge (Nicola Pagett), Sarah (Pauline Collins), Thomas (John Alderton), Roberts (Patsy Smart), Ruby (Jenny Tomasin), Edward (Christopher Beeny), Lawrence Kirbridge (Ian Ogilvy), Sir Geoffrey Dillon (Raymond Huntley), Hazel Forrest (Meg Wynn Owen), Georgina Worsley (Lesley-Anne Down), Lady Prudence Fairfax (Joan Benham), Daisy (Jacqueline Tong), Frederick (Gareth Hunt) and Virginia Bellamy (Hannah Gordon).
Script Editor: Alfred Shaughnessy. **Director** (1972, 1974–5, 1982): Bill Bain. **Producer:** John Hawkesworth. **Executive Producer:** Rex Firkin.

| 1971 | 6.8 | Sun 14 Nov 10:15 p.m. | 12 | 3 wks |

'A Cry for Help' by Julian Bond.
It is October, 1906. Richard Bellamy is alone in the house working on a book. He finds the housemaid Mary (Susan Penhaligon) crying as she lays the fire in the library. He learns her troubles and unwisely promises help in a step which could endanger his career.
Designer: John Clements. **Director:** Derek Bennett.

| 1972 | 8.4 | Fri 17 Nov 7:55 p.m. | 1 | 12 wks |

'Guest of Honour' by Alfred Shaughnessy.
King Edward VII is coming to dinner at Eaton Place.
Designer: John Clements.

| 1973 | 7.6 | Fri 19 Jan 9:00 p.m. | 3 | 13 wks |

'A Family Gathering' by Alfred Shaughnessy.
Elizabeth breaks off a relationship. James returns from India with a fiancée who causes a stir both upstairs and down.
Designer: John Clements. **Director:** Raymond Menmuir.

| 1974 | 7.4 | Sat 12 Jan 8:25 p.m. | 8 | 14 wks |

'Distant Thunder' by Alfred Shaughnessy.
Hazel Bellamy is in bed having just lost her first baby. James consoles himself by escorting Georgina to a ball, causing high tension throughout the house.
Designer: John Emery.

| 1975 | 8.5 | Sun 23 Nov 7:55 p.m. | 3 | 15 wks |

'Will Ye No' Come Back Again?' by Rosemary Anne Sisson.
James's feelings for Georgina are brought to a head when Richard Bellamy borrows a fishing lodge in the Highlands.
Designer: John Emery.

| 1982 | 10.4 | Sat 12 Jun 8:00 p.m. | 14 | 1 wk |

Repeat of the top 1982 episode.

....

Uri Geller – Is Seeing Believing?   1 wk

Thames, documentary

| 1974 | 8.1 | Tue 15 Jan 7:30 p.m. | 3 | 1 wk |

The spoon-bending Geller is filmed in New York, both in performance and under scientific investigation, after a series of tests have been performed on metals bent by him.
Producer: Terry Dixon.

Nicola Pagett and Jean Marsh bridge the class barrier in A Special Mischief, the episode of **Upstairs, Downstairs** that reached Number One at Christmas 1972.

V

V	1 wk

USA presented by ITV, drama

In this five part mini-series, aliens in UFOs invaded 31 cities throughout the world.
Director: Richard Heffron. **Producer:** Kenneth Johnson.

1984	10.0	Mon 30 Jul 9:00 p.m.	7	1 wk

The aliens arrive in Los Angeles, ostensibly on a peace mission. As they go about occupying California their true intentions become clear.

Val Doonican Music Show, The | 21 wks

BBC, music

Doonican returned to the BBC in the late 1970s following several years on ITV. The shows were broadcast live from the BBC Television Theatre in Shepherd's Bush, London. He was supported by the Ronnie Hazlehurst orchestra.
Producer: Yvonne Littlewood.

1977	7.1	Sat 23 Apr 7:55 p.m.	18	2 wks

Guests: George Hamilton IV, Vera Lynn, Lynsey de Paul and Mike Moran.

1978	13.3	Sat 29 Apr 8:15 p.m.	17	1 wk

Guests: James Galway and Tom Paxton.

1979	13.4	Sat 7 Apr 8:15 p.m.	12	6 wks

Guests: David Attenborough, Nana Mouskouri and the Cambridge Buskers.

1980	15.0	Sat 5 Apr 7:50 p.m.	6	8 wks

Guests: Roy Clark and Nana Mouskouri.

1981	13.4	Sat 11 Apr 8:25 p.m.	11	1 wk

Guests: Vic Damone and Barbara Dickson.

1982	10.7	Sat 26 Jun 8:45 p.m.	6	2 wks

A special show filmed in Ireland features Mary O'Hara, Stockton's Wing and Robert White.

1983	9.7	Sat 28 May 9:30 p.m.	13	1 wk

Guests: Rita Coolidge, Ronnie Milsap and Harry Secombe.

Val Doonican Show, The | 42 wks

BBC, music

The Irish singer, noted for his sweaters and rocking chair, hosted his own series. He first came to England as a member of the close harmony group The Ramblers.
Producer: John Ammonds.

1965	6.4	Thu 9 Dec 9:00 p.m.	13	8 wks

Guests: Dave Allen and Johnny Pearson, with the Cliff Adams singers, the Jo Cook dancers and the Ken Thorne orchestra.

1966	6.4	Sat 10 Dec 9:00 p.m.	9	9 wks

Guests: Dave Allen, Jeannie Carson, David and Marianne Dalmour with the Gojos, the Cliff Adams singers and the Ken Thorne orchestra.

1967	7.2	Sat 25 Nov 7:55 p.m.	3	11 wks

Guests: Julie Felix, Ted Ray and the Shadows, with the Gojos, the Cliff Adams singers and the Peter Knight orchestra.

1968	7.5	Sat 16 Nov 7:30 p.m.	2	13 wks

Guests: Moira Anderson, Des O'Connor and Trio Athenee, with the Gojos, the Cliff Adams singers and the Peter Knight orchestra.

1969	5.2	Sat 24 May 7:30 p.m.	18	1 wk

Guests: Ray Barrett, Roy Castle and the Dagestan Dance Company from the USSR, with the Cliff Adams singers and the Peter Knight orchestra.

Val Doonican Show, The 30 wks

ATV (1970) and Thames (1971–72, 1974–75), music

After five years with the BBC Val Doonican moved to ITV. With the Kenny Woodman orchestra (1971–72, 1974–75).

| 1970 | 7.6 | Wed 18 Nov 8:00 p.m. | 8 | 11 wks |

Guests: Arthur Askey, Patricia Cahill, André Tahon's puppets and Roger Whittaker, with the Mike Sammes singers, the Malcolm Clare dancers and the Jack Parnell orchestra.
Director: Ian Fordyce. **Producer:** Les Cocks.

| 1971 | 7.1 | Wed 3 Nov 8:00 p.m. | 9 | 4 wks |

Guests: Hylda Baker, Friday Brown, Peter Goodwright and Norman Vaughan.
Producer: John Robins.

| 1972 | 6.5 | Sat 1 Apr 9:00 p.m. | 12 | 2 wks |

Guests: Harry Secombe and John Williams.
Producer: John Robins.

| 1974 | 8.6 | Tue 12 Feb 7:10 p.m. | 1 | 9 wks |

Guests: Basil Brush and Fabric.
Producer: Alan Tarrant.

| 1975 | 8.3 | Tue 28 Jan 6:40 p.m. | 4 | 4 wks |

Guest: Paul Melba.
Producer: Keith Beckett.

Valley of the Dolls, The 1 wk

Presented by ITV, film

| 1975 | 7.5 | Wed 26 Feb 9:00 p.m. | 10 | 1 wk |

This film version of Jacqueline Susann's novel of a small-town girl caught up in the hard, bitchy world of New York show business stars Paul Burke, Patty Duke, Lee Grant, Susan Hayward, Barbara Perkins and Sharon Tate.
Director: Mark Robson.

Van der Valk 18 wks

Thames, drama

Barry Foster starred as Van der Valk, the Dutch detective created by Nicholas Freeling.

| 1973 | 7.8 | Wed 5 Sep 9:00 p.m. | 1 | 6 wks |

'A Man of No Importance' by Arden Winch.
The body of a man wearing only pyjama bottoms is found on a canal barge. The bargee is lost for explanation. A crowd has gathered as Van der Valk chances by and decides to investigate.
Director: Douglas Camfield. **Producer:** Robert Love. **Executive Producer:** Lloyd Shirley.

| 1977 | 14.5 | Mon 26 Sep 9:00 p.m. | 4 | 9 wks |

'Wolf' by Philip Broadley.
A young German is murdered. In his apartment Van der Valk finds many clues – in fact, one too many.
Director: Mike Vardy. **Producer:** Geoffrey Gilbert. **Executive Producers:** Lloyd Shirley and George Taylor.

| 1991 | 13.0 | Wed 16 Jan 8:00 p.m. | 13 | 3 wks |

'Doctor Hoffman's Children' by Jonathan Hales.
It is fourteen years since the last series and Van der Valk now heads the Amsterdam murder squad. He tries to find a connection between the murders of a businessman and an ageing prostitute.
Director: Anthony Simmons. **Producer:** Chris Burt. (An Elmgate production.)

Variety Club Tribute Dinner to Morecambe and Wise 1 wk

ATV, entertainment

| 1978 | 13.2 | Tue 12 Dec 8:30 p.m. | 20 | 1 wk |

Terry Wogan introduces the proceedings from the Albany Hotel, Birmingham.
Television presentation: John Pullen.

Barry Foster was Dutch detective **Van der Valk**.

Basil Brush is a guest in the all-time top-rated edition of **The Val Doonican Show**.

Variety Parade — 1 wk

ATV, entertainment

| 1967 | 6.5 | Tue 19 Dec 9:15 p.m. | 8 | 1 wk |

Guests: Kathy Kirby, Ted Rogers, Trio Athenee and the Ukranian Cossacks.
Producer: Philip Casson.

Variety Show, The — 4 wks

Granada, entertainment

This series presented international performers.

| 1960 | 6.2 | Thu 12 May 9:35 p.m. | 2 | 4 wks |

Starring Diahann Carroll with Ted Lune, Italo Medini, the Smeed Trio, and the Tony Osborne orchestra.
Producer: David Warwick.

Variety Years, The — 1 wk

Thames, documentary

| 1975 | 7.1 | Wed 30 Apr 8:00 p.m. | 15 | 1 wk |

Denis Norden wrote and introduces this programme. It reflects on the years of the Variety theatres and their performers with the help of Arthur Askey, Jimmy Jewel, Sandy Powell, Ted Ray and archive clips.
Producer: John Robins.

Vegas — 1 wk

USA presented by ITV, drama

This series about private investigators in Las Vegas stared Robert Urich as Dan Tanna and Tony Curtis as Phil Roth.
Executive Producer: Aaron Spelling.

| 1978 | 17.9 | Fri 22 Dec 9:00 p.m. | 11 | 1 wk |

'Yes My Darling Daughter'
A supposedly dead man appears at his daughter's wedding.

Vendetta — 4 wks

BBC, drama

This series created by Brian Degas and Tudor Gates starred Stelio Candelli and Neil McCallum as Danny Scipio and Angelo James, international agents, whose pursuit of the Mafia took them across continents.

| 1968 | 4.9 | Mon 19 Aug 9:05 p.m. | 7 | 4 wks |

'The Blackfoot Man' by David Hodson and Robert Schlitt.
Kieron Moore joins the cast as Mike Hammond, an American District Attorney also in pursuit of mafiosi.
Designer: John Hurst. **Director:** Viktors Ritelis. **Producer:** Anthony Coburn.

Verdict is Yours, The — 4 wks

Granada, drama

This series began in 1958 under the executive control of Denis Forman. Actors, only a few with any legal experience, pleaded unscripted cases before retired judge Mr Justice David Ensor and a jury recruited from Granada viewers. Professional writers prepared the scenario for each case and handed the actors a dossier of events and participants.

| 1962 | 5.4 | Mon 17 Sep 9:15 p.m. | 6 | 4 wks |

'Regina v Zyrawska'
A girl is in trouble with the French police. Her parents blame their Polish paying guest and go to Court to seek an injunction to stop him seeing her. Case devised by Hugh Forbes.
Director: Eric Price. **Producer:** Peter Wildeblood.

Very Big Very Soon — 1 wk

Central, situation comedy

This series by Daniel Peacock starred Paul Shane as Harry James, a poor theatrical agent with a bunch of no-hopers on his books.

| 1991 | 7.8 | Fri 19 Jul 7:00 p.m. | 20 | 1 wk |

'Ladies Night'
Ernie Chester (Tim Wylton) loses his job as a bingo caller. Harry tries to team him up with another turn to do a double act at a Ladies Night.
Director: Paul Harrison. **Producer:** Glen Cardno.

Victoria Wood — 5 wks

BBC, comedy

This series was written by and starred the former NEW FACES winner.

| 1989 | 13.9 | Thu 7 Dec 8:30 p.m. | 9 | 4 wks |

'We'd Quite Like to Apologise'
Susie Blake, Celia Imrie, Philip Lowrie, Una Stubbs and Julie Walters all star with Victoria in this story of a top script writer who has previously served 16 years in prison for armed robbery.
Director: Kevin Bishop. **Producer:** Geoff Posner.

| 1990 | 8.6 | Thur 5 Jul 9:30 p.m. | 20 | 1 wk |

'We'd Quite Like to Apologise'
(Repeat.)

Victorians, The   7 wks

Granada, drama

This anthology of nineteenth-century plays was produced by Philip Mackie.

| 1963 | 6.0 | Fri 28 Jun 9:15 p.m. | 5 | 7 wks |

'Two Roses' by James Albery.
Set in Kent in the 1860s. Digby Grant is a charlatan and a bit of a rogue, though his two daughters love him dearly. When he comes into an unexpected fortune he becomes an egocentric snob and cuts them off from the two young men they love. Starring Geoffrey Bayldon, Patricia Garwood, Ingrid Hafner, Joan Hickson, Barrie Ingham and John Wood.
Designer: Roy Stonehouse. **Director:** Richard Everitt.

Video Entertainers, The   14 wks

Granada, entertainment

This series, hosted and produced by John Hamp, featured modern entertainers recommended by club owners, record companies, journalists and television producers. The artists were accompanied by the Derek Hilton orchestra.

| 1981 | 13.0 | Wed 17 Jun 8:00 p.m. | 5 | 6 wks |

Guests: Madeline Bell, Stan Boardman, Tammy Cline, Greengage, Aiden J. Harvey and Elaine Paige.
Directors: Ian Hamilton and Dave Warwick.

| 1982 | 8.5 | Tue 6 Jul 7:30 p.m. | 18 | 1 wk |

Guests: Aiden J. Harvey, Richard Kerr, Bobby Knutt, Sunny Leslie and Lisa Stansfield, with the Brian Rogers dancers.
Director: Ian Hamilton.

| 1983 | 7.3 | Tue 16 Aug 7:00 p.m. | 16 | 7 wks |

Guests: Gloria Gaynor, Bizzy Line, Michael Praed, Prelude and Sheila Steafel, with the Alan Harding dancers.
Director: Peter Walker. **Producer:** Jon Plowman. **Executive Producer:** John Hamp.

View to a Kill, A   2 wks

Presented by ITV, film

| 1990 | 16.9 | Wed 31 Jan 8:00 p.m. | 7 | 1 wk |

James Bond (Roger Moore) finds himself up against a ruthless international industrialist. Also starring Fiona Fullerton, Grace Jones, Patrick Macnee and Christopher Walken.
Director: John Glen.

| 1991 | 12.3 | Sat 31 Aug 8:15 p.m. | 9 | 1 wk |

Repeat showing of the above film.

Village Earth   7 wks

Central, documentary

This series of thirteen programmes was devoted to individuals who worked to preserve and develop remote cultures.

| 1983 | 7.3 | Mon 7 Mar 7:00 p.m. | 16 | 7 wks |

'In the Footsteps of the Incas'
English engineer Martin Ede helps the Aymaran Indians with an irrigation scheme.
Producer: David Wright. **Series Producer:** Peter Coulson.

Village Hall   7 wks

Granada, drama

The plays in this series were set in the same village hall with different writers and cast for each play.

| 1974 | 6.8 | Tue 30 Jul 9:00 p.m. | 1 | 7 wks |

'There'll Almost Always be an England' by Jack Rosenthal.
Fourteen friends, neighbours and enemies have to spend the night together in the village hall. Starring Bernard Hepton, Dilys Laye and Norman Rossington.
Designer: Colin Rees. **Director:** Quentin Lawrence. **Producer:** Michael Dunlop.

*Though not the top-rated episode, Mr Ellis Versus the People starring Ron Moody and Brian Miller was the only Number One edition of **Village Hall**.*

Villains | 1 wk

LWT, drama

Thirteen-part series about villains of all ages and types.

| 1972 | 5.0 | Sat 22 Jul 9:30 p.m. | 16 | 1 wk |

'George' by Ray Jenkins.
David Daker stars as George, the leader of a gang known as 'The Bog Robbers' en route from prison to the appeal court. An escape is planned.
Designer: Frank Nerini. **Director:** Tony Wharmby. **Producer:** Andrew Brown.

....

Villains, The | 21 wks

Granada, drama

This series presented detailed character studies of the criminal elements in northern society.

| 1964 | 7.2 | Fri 11 Dec 9:10 p.m. | 4 | 13 wks |

'Bent' by Jack Rosenthal.
A policeman with great social principles is a great asset to the community, but as his beliefs become warped he turns into a liability. Bryan Mosley stars.
Designer: Terry Pritchard. **Director:** Michael Beckham. **Producer:** Howard Baker.

| 1965 | 7.3 | Fri 15 Jan 9:10 p.m. | 6 | 8 wks |

'Three to a Cell' by Alan Plater.
One partner in crime is rather resentful and does not subscribe to the equal sharing of the profits of the partnership. Starring Jerry Desmonde, Dudley Foster, Victor Henry and Jack Smethurst.
Designer: Terry Pritchard. **Director:** Howard Baker. **Producer:** Royston Morley.

....

Virginian, The | 5 wks

USA presented by BBC, western

This series set in the 1880s was based on a novel by Owen Wister. The Virginian (James Drury) was the silent foreman of the Shiloh Ranch in Medicine Bow, Wyoming, owned by Judge Henry Garth (Lee J. Cobb). Doug McClure played Trampas, the Virginian's assistant. Gary Clarke played Trampas' friend Steve and Roberta Shore portrayed Judge Garth's teenage daughter Betsy.
Executive Producer: Norman MacDonnell.

| 1968 | 6.2 | Wed 3 Jan 7:30 p.m. | 15 | 3 wks |

'The Executioners'
Betsy's fifteenth birthday party is in full swing when a stranger named Paul Taylor (Hugh O'Brian) arrives at Shiloh. He claims to be a cowhand and is offered a job by the Viginian. Only Sheriff Brandon (John Larch) is apprehensive. His caution proves justified.

| 1969 | 5.6 | Fri 2 May 6:40 p.m. | 19 | 2 wks |

'Two Men Named Laredo'
Guest star Fabian plays Eddie Laredo, a quiet poetry-loving cowboy, who, to Judge Garth's mystification, is accused of murder. The Judge embarks on a strange series of investigations.

....

Virus X | 1 wk

BBC, drama

| 1962 | 3.8 | Mon 25 Jun 9:25 p.m. | 18 | 1 wk |

This suspense drama by Evelyn Frazer is set in a hospital where a mystery virus threatens. The cast includes Jean Alexander, A. J. Brown, Gilbert Davis, Leslie Dwyer, Anne Hudson, Brenda Kaye, Richard Leech, Wally Patch and Rosemary Rogers.
Designer: Barry Learoyd. **Producer:** Stephen Harrison.

....

Visit, The | 2 wks

BBC, documentary

This series written and produced by Desmond Wilcox featured significant and perhaps dramatic journeys.

| 1983 | 8.1 | Tue 7 Jun 9:50 p.m. | 15 | 1 wk |

'The Boy David'
The face of a Peruvian Indian boy has been reconstructed by Scottish plastic surgeon Ian Jackson. David is nine years old and has at least 50 operations behind him and another 50 to go. When Jackson and his wife Marjorie, whom David calls Dad and Mum, first found him he was 18 months old and abandoned in a pauper's hospital in Peru. The centre of his face had been destroyed by a malignant disease.
Camera: Andrew Dunn. **Director:** Alex McCall. **Executive Producer:** Neil Fraser. (The following night, Wed 8 June, there was a follow-up programme tracking Marjorie's attempts to adopt David legally even though he had no papers and no official identity.)

| 1987 | 11.6 | Wed 2 Dec 9:30 p.m. | 16 | 1 wk |

'Coma: Towards Light'
Connie Taylor is an 11-year-old victim of a road accident who is fighting her way back from a long coma.
Director: Alex McCall.

Visit of President Reagan, The 1 wk

BBC, news

| 1982 | 10.2 | Tue 8 Jun 9:35 p.m. | 17 | 1 wk |

David Dimbleby reports from St George's Hall, Windsor, where Her Majesty the Queen is giving a banquet in honour of the President of the United States.
Television presentation: Michael Lumley.

Volcano 1 wk

Presented by ITV, film

| 1982 | 10.2 | Sat 9 Oct 7:00 p.m. | 19 | 1 wk |

In 1883 Captain Chris Hanson (Maximilian Schell) sails in search of treasure near the volcanic island of Krakatoa. Thirty convicts on board attempt a mutiny.
Director: Bernard L. Kowalski.

Von Ryan's Express 3 wks

Presented by ITV, film

| 1973 | 6.0 | Tue 25 Dec 9:05 p.m. | 9 | 1 wk |

Christmas Day offering starring Frank Sinatra and Trevor Howard. Colonel Joseph Ryan is dubbed Von Ryan by his fellow prisoners at War Camp 202 in Italy when he gives away the secrets of their escape tunnel. It is when they are being transferred to Berlin by train that he launches his scheme.
Director: Mark Robson.

| 1978 | 18.8 | Wed 4 Jan 8:00 p.m. | 2 | 1 wk |
| 1981 | 12.0 | Sat 4 Apr 7:35 p.m. | 19 | 1 wk |

Repeat showings of the above film.

Voyage into England 1 wk

BBC, documentary

In this series of six programmes Macdonald Hastings hitch-hiked his way through 500 miles of inland waterways from Bristol via the Midlands and the North to Little Venice in London.

| 1964 | 5.0 | Mon 6 Jul 7:00 p.m. | 14 | 1 wk |

'The Key to the Cut'
Hastings takes a slow boat to Birmingham, meeting the people and seeing the places on the way.
Director: Kenneth Savidge. **Producer:** Peter Bale.

Voyage of the Damned 2 wks

Presented by ITV, film

| 1984 | 10.4 | Sun 5 Aug 7:45 p.m. | 4 | 2 wks |

Jewish refugees bound for Cuba. Cuba refuses to take them. Starring Faye Dunaway, Ben Gazzara, Malcolm McDowell, James Mason, Katharine Ross, Max Von Sydow, Sam Wanamaker, Orson Welles and Oscar Werner.
Director: Stuart Rosenberg.
This film was screened on two successive Sundays.

V

1

2

3

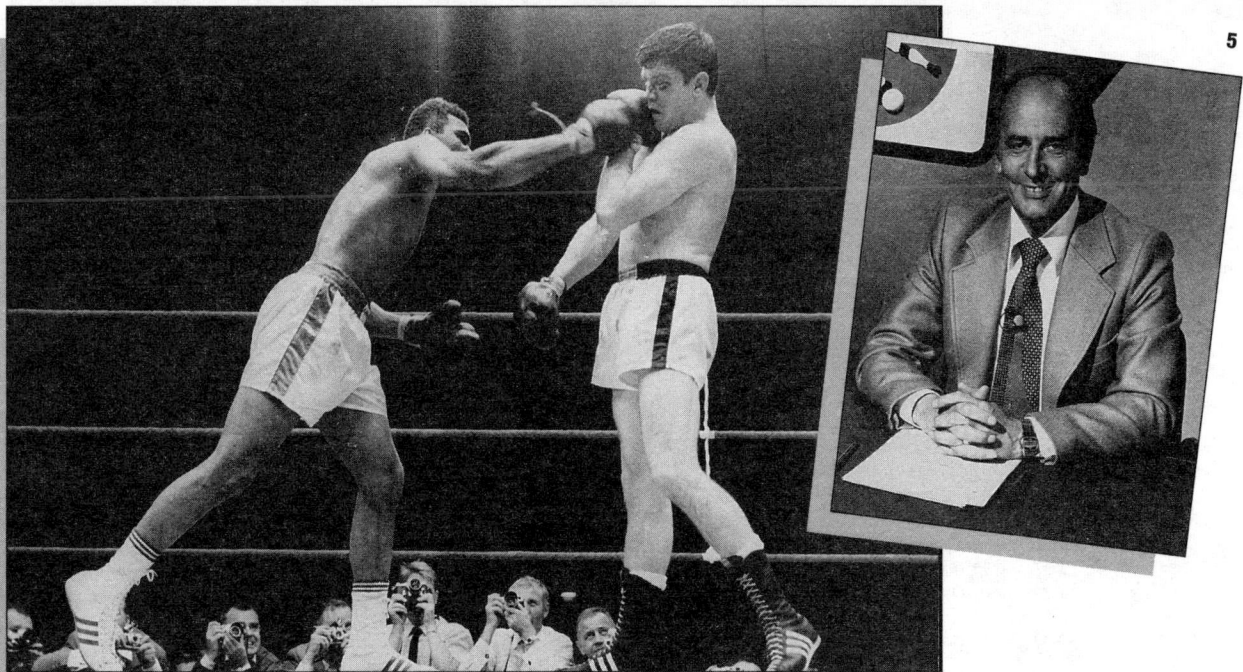

1 *George Best watches David Sadler lift the European Cup for Manchester United in 1968 in the first Number One* **Football** *match.*

2 *Brian Fletcher rode Red Alligator to victory in the 1968* **Grand National**.

3 *The camera captures the action of the 1966* **World Cup**.

4 *In the first Number One* **Boxing** *match, world heavyweight champion Cassius Clay lands a right on challenger Karl Mildenberger.*

5 *Brian Moore was the commentator on the highest rated edition of* **Midweek Sports Special**.

6 *Alastair Burnet and Reginald Bosanquet were two of the mainstays of Independent Television* **News**.

Wackers, The — 6 wks

Thames, situation comedy

This series by Vince Powell about a Liverpudlian family starred Ken Jones and Sheila Fay as Billy and Mary Clarkson. They had three children: Tony (David Casey), Bernadette (Alison Steadman) and Raymond (Keith Chegwin). There was one grandparent from each side of the family, Maggie Clarkson (Pearl Hackney) and Joe Farrell (Joe Gladwin). Half the family was Catholic, the other half Protestant. Half supported Liverpool, and the rest supported Everton.

| 1975 | 7.5 | Wed 19 Mar 9:30 p.m. | 11 | 6 wks |

'Out of the Frying Pan'
In this first episode Billy returns home after two years away at sea.
Producer: *Anthony Parker.*

Wagon Train — 36 wks

USA presented by ITV (1960–61) and BBC (1962–63), western

This series was based on the 1950 John Ford film WAGONMASTER. The WAGON TRAIN began to roll in the USA in 1957 on its journey west from Missouri to California. Ward Bond starred as Major Seth Adams and Robert Horton as Flint McCullough, the scout. Regular members of the train were Chuck Wooster (Frank McGrath), Duke (Dennis Miller) and Hawks (Terry Wilson). In each episode the trek encountered new characters. In 1960, Ward Bond died on location after a heart attack, aged 57. He was replaced by John McIntire as new trail boss Chris Hale. Horton also left the show, to be replaced by Robert Fuller.

| 1960 | 7.2 | Mon 25 Apr 8:30 p.m. | 1 | 19 wks |

'The Dick Jarvis Story'
Major Adams befriends two youngsters, crippled boy Dick Jarvis (Tommy Nolan) and orphan Joey (Bobby Diamond). Mrs Jarvis (Vivi Janiss) resents Joey's efforts to help her son to walk and she keeps the boys apart. Her interference almost costs Dick his life.

| 1961 | 4.1 | Mon 28 Aug 8:30 p.m. | 16 | 5 wks |

'The Chalice'
Duke and Hawks come across a couple in a lone wagon abandoned by an earlier train. Marcello and his wife Lisa agree to go back with them, but there is soon trouble. The wagoners see they have a strongbox and suspect it contains treasure.

| 1962 | 5.7 | Sun 23 Dec 5:25 p.m. | 10 | 1 wk |

'The Dr Denker Story'
Dr Denker (Theodore Bikel), a new and well-liked member of the train, purports to be a Doctor of Musicology. However, the instruments on his wagon are found to be of a different kind.

| 1963 | 6.8 | Sun 24 Feb 5:20 p.m. | 4 | 11 wks |

'Clyde'
Wooster's pet buffalo has an unhappy knack of upsetting things as well as people and creates a situation which Chris Hale finds difficult to solve.

Wallenberg – The Lost Hero — 2 wks

USA presented by ITV, drama

This two-part story by Gerald Green starred Richard Chamberlain as Raoul Wallenberg, a Swedish diplomat who, in 1944, saved hundreds of Hungarian Jews from the Nazis. He was eventually imprisoned by the Russians and never seen again. Kenneth Colley, Jimmy Nail and Olaf Pooley also starred.
Director: *Lamont Johnson.*

| 1985 | 12.9 | Sun 28 Apr 7:45 p.m. | 5 | 2 wks |

Part One
Having lived through the war with his family in neutral Sweden, Raoul is revolted by the systematic extermination of Europe's Jews and decides to take action.

Walt Disney — 2 wks

Thames, documentary

| 1977 | 7.6 | Wed 20 Apr 9:10 p.m. | 14 | 2 wks |

A two-part biography of Disney with contributions from those who knew and worked with him. Excerpts from his films are included.
Producer: *Terence Dixon.*

War and Remembrance
1 wk

USA presented by ITV, drama

This epic sequel to WINDS OF WAR was also based on a novel by Herman Wouk. It began in the days following the Japanese attack on Pearl Harbor, and tracked the lives of those who lived through its aftermath. Robert Mitchum continued his role as Victor 'Pug' Henry. Other principal characters included Natalie Henry (Jane Seymour), Byron Henry (Hart Bochner), Pamela Tudsbury (Victoria Tennant), Leslie Slote (David Dukes), Rhoda Henry (Polly Bergen), Warren Henry (Michael Woods), Janice Henry (Sharon Stone), Alistair Tudsbury (Robert Morley), Avram Rabinovitz (Sami Frey), Berel Jastrow (Topol), Philip Rule (Ian McShane), Brigadier von Roon (Jeremy Kemp), Adolf Hitler (Steven Berkoff), Winston Churchill (Robert Hardy), Franklin D. Roosevelt (Ralph Bellamy) and Aaron Jastrow (John Gielgud).

| 1989 | 11.6 | Sun 3 Sep 8:15 p.m. | 9 | 1 wk |

Episode One
Captain 'Pug' Henry takes command of the cruiser Northampton, while his wife Rhoda resumes her affair in Singapore. Pamela meets an old love – journalist Phil Rule. Avram Rabinovitz organizes an escape exodus from Italy to Palestine.

War – Both Sides
1 wk

AR, documentary

| 1967 | 5.1 | Thu 8 Jun Evening | 15 | 1 wk |

Israel was fighting what would prove to be the six-day war against Egypt, Syria and Jordan. This unscheduled programme presents the case for both sides.

War Games
1 wk

Presented by BBC, film

| 1987 | 11.9 | Mon 20 Apr 8:10 p.m. | 5 | 1 wk |

Matthew Broderick stars as computer whiz David Lightman. He breaks into computer systems hundreds of miles away and starts World War III.
Director: John Badham.

War of Darkie Pilbeam, The
3 wks

Granada, drama

This trilogy of plays by Tony Warren featured a wartime black marketeer spiv in the north of England.

| 1968 | 6.2 | Fri 12 Jul 9:00 p.m. | 6 | 3 wks |

It is 1939, and the first effects of the war begin to be felt by the Pilbeam family. Trevor Bannister stars as Darkie with Alan Browning, John Collin, Gabrielle Daye, Maggie Don, Caroline Dowdeswell, Terry Gilligan, Julie Goodyear, Christine Hargreaves and Rhoda Lewis.
Producer: Richard Everitt.

War of the Running Dogs, The
1 wk

Anglia, documentary

| 1974 | 5.5 | Tue 9 Jul 9:00 p.m. | 19 | 1 wk |

This film traces the political background of Malaya since the country's liberation from Japan in 1945. The writer, narrator and producer is Paul Honeyman.
Director: Harry Aldous.

War of the Worlds
1 wk

Presented by ITV, film

| 1970 | 5.2 | Mon 31 Aug 8:00 p.m. | 16 | 1 wk |

Bank Holiday Monday screening of H. G. Wells' classic story. Aliens invade Earth through midwest America. Gene Barry stars.
Director: Byron Haskin.

War Wagon, The
1 wk

Presented by BBC, film

| 1972 | 5.9 | Sat 23 Dec 8:10 p.m. | 20 | 1 wk |

A man seeks revenge and hunts down the person responsible for putting him in prison. Kirk Douglas, Howard Keel and John Wayne star.
Director: Burt Kennedy.

Warhol
1 wk

ATV, documentary

| 1973 | 7.3 | Tue 27 Mar 10:30 p.m. | 6 | 1 wk |

Genius or joker? This film explores the weird and wonderful world of artist and film maker Andy Warhol.
Camera: Ernest Vincze. **Sound:** Derek Williams. **Producer:** David Bailey. **Executive Producer:** Verity Lambert.

Warning Shot — 1 wk

Presented by BBC, film

| 1985 | 9.3 | Sat 20 Jul 8:30 p.m. | 19 | 1 wk |

Detective Sergeant Tom Valens (David Janssen) kills a man in self-defence. When the victim is found to be unarmed, Valens faces a murder charge. Steve Allen, Ed Begley, Joan Collins, Lillian Gish, Eleanor Parker, Walter Pidgeon, Stefanie Powers, George Sanders and Sam Wanamaker also star.
Director: Buzz Kulik.

Warship Eagle — 1 wk

AR, documentary

| 1966 | 5.5 | Wed 13 Jul 9:40 p.m. | 8 | 1 wk |

The aircraft carrier HMS Eagle is the biggest ship in the Royal Navy at 44,000 tons. The film shows her on a six-week voyage from Aden to Singapore. Ludovic Kennedy narrates.
Camera: Tony Mander, Chris Menges. **Sound:** Basil Rootes, Gordon Temple. **Director:** Charlie Squires. **Producer:** Richard De La Mer.

Watch on the Mekong — 1 wk

AR, documentary

| 1962 | 3.5 | Wed 8 Aug 9:45 p.m. | 17 | 1 wk |

Earlier this year Thailand called in the US Marines and Air Force to help protect its frontiers against Communist moves from Laos. Now rival forces keep an uneasy watch on the banks of the river Mekong.
Camera: Harry Hart. **Sound:** Freddie Slade. **Writer** and **producer:** Peter Hunt. **Director:** Bill Morton.

Watch This Space — 2 wks

BBC, situation comedy

This series by Ronald Wolfe and Ronald Chesney concerned a team of workers in an advertising agency. It starred Christopher Biggins as Brian, Peter Blake as Bob, Liza Goddard as Claire, Leo Dolan as Jonathan and Gillian Taylforth as Brenda.

| 1980 | 13.8 | Thur 7 Feb 8:30 p.m. | 18 | 2 wks |

'Crackly Delight'
The team takes a scientific approach towards promoting a new washing-up liquid. Guest star: Magnus Pyke.
Producer: Roger Race.

Watcher in the Woods, The — 1 wk

Presented by BBC, film

| 1985 | 9.4 | Sun 25 Aug 7:15 p.m. | 13 | 1 wk |

A series of weird and frightening events occur in an isolated country house owned by Mrs Aylwood (Bette Davis). Carroll Baker and David McCallum also star.
Director: John Hough.

Watching — 22 wks

Granada, situation comedy

Jim Hitchmough's creation starred Emma Wray as Brenda Wilson and Paul Bown as ornithologist Malcolm Stoneway. Liza Tarbuck played Brenda's sister Pamela and John Bowler was David Lynch.
Director: Les Chatfield. **Producer** (1988–89) and **Executive Producer** (1990–91): David Liddiment.

| 1988 | 11.2 | Fri 1 Apr 8:30 p.m. | 10 | 1 wk |

'Moving'
Brenda has a job, but only for a couple of days.

| 1989 | 12.6 | Fri 8 Dec 8:00 p.m. | 15 | 6 wks |

'Pairing'
There is shock and horror when the au pair takes the baby on a motorbike.

| 1990 | 14.8 | Fri 19 Jan 8:00 p.m. | 10 | 8 wks |

'Floating'
Malcolm and Brenda go to Hoylake for the day.

| 1991 | 16.4 | Fri 8 Feb 8:00 p.m. | 7 | 7 wks |

'Bonding'
Malcolm's wedding-day nerves persist in spite of reassurances from David that nothing can go wrong.

Watership Down — 1 wk

Presented by BBC, film

| 1985 | 14.0 | Sat 28 Dec 7:15 p.m. | 17 | 1 wk |

The animated film of the Richard Adams novel about a colony of rabbits features the voices of Joss Ackland, Harry Andrews, Richard Briers, Simon Cadell, Denholm Elliott, Lyn Farleigh, Hannah Gordon, Nigel Hawthorne, Michael Hordern, John Hurt, Roy Kinnear, Zero Mostel and Ralph Richardson. Art Garfunkel sings the theme tune 'Bright Eyes'.
Director: Martin Rosen.

Wayne and Shuster Show, The — 1 wk

USA presented by ITV, comedy

Johnny Wayne and Frank Shuster were Canadian comedians made famous in the US by frequent appearances on 'The Ed Sullivan Show'.

| 1964 | 5.6 | Fri 27 Mar 9:10 p.m. | 14 | 1 wk |

Guests: Don Gilles and Shirley Harmer.
Producer: Don Hudson.

....

Wayne Dobson – A Kind Of Magic | 1 wk

Central, magic

The comedy magician was given his own series after several years of guesting on other shows.
Producer: Nigel Lythgoe. **Executive Producer:** Tony Wolfe.

| 1990 | 9.3 | Sat 19 May 6:55 p.m. | 14 | 1 wk |

On location in Greece Dobson presents illusions and magic skills.
Guests: Richard Coombs and Linda Lusardi.

....

We Got It Made | 1 wk

USA presented by BBC, situation comedy

A live-in maid was employed by two New York bachelors. The series starred Teri Copley as Mickey, Matt McCoy as David, Tom Villard as Jay, Bonnie Urseth as Beth and Stepfanie Kramer as Claudia.

| 1984 | 9.0 | Thu 10 May 8:35 p.m. | 19 | 1 wk |

'Mickey Gets Married'
Having just married Claudia's rich Uncle Victor (Alejandro Ray), Mickey finds herself a widow, the mother of a grown man and president of an international company, all on her wedding day.
Writers: Chick Mitchell and Geoffrey Neigher. **Director:** Alan Rafkin.

....

We Love TV | 11 wks

LWT, game show

A team of viewers pitted their knowledge of popular television programmes against that of a team of celebrities. It was hosted by Gloria Hunniford.

| 1984 | 12.7 | Fri 26 Oct 8:30 p.m. | 12 | 6 wks |

Guests: Judy Geeson and Brian Murphy.
Director: John Gorman. **Producer:** Brian Wesley. **Executive Producer:** Alan Boyd.

| 1986 | 9.4 | Sat 16 Aug 7:00 p.m. | 11 | 5 wks |

Guests: Anita Dobson and Paul Shane.
Director: Nick Vaughan-Barratt. **Producer:** Trevor Hopkins.

Weaver's Green | 20 wks

Anglia, soap

This twice-weekly serial set in an English village was created by Peter and Betty Lambda. The stories centred on two vets, Alan Armstrong (Grant Taylor) and his younger partner Geoffrey Toms (Eric Flynn), and their wives. Dotty Armstrong was played by Megs Jenkins and Celia Toms by Georgina Ward.

| 1966 | 7.0 | Thu 7 Apr 6:05 p.m. | 6 | 20 wks |

Celia is a city girl finding it difficult to settle in the country.
Director: June Howson. **Producer:** John Jacobs.

....

Wedding of a Princess, The | 1 wk

ITN, news

| 1973 | 6.7 | Wed 14 Nov 10:00 p.m. | 9 | 1 wk |

An extended edition of NEWS AT TEN with highlights of this morning's wedding, solemnized by the Archbishop of Canterbury in Westminster Abbey, between HRH The Princess Anne and Captain Mark Phillips.

....

Wedding of the Year | 1 wk

Thames, documentary

| 1973 | 6.3 | Mon 12 Nov 8:00 p.m. | 19 | 1 wk |

Just two days before their wedding, HRH The Princess Anne and Captain Mark Phillips talk at Buckingham Palace to Alastair Burnet and Andrew Gardner about themselves and the wedding.
Producer: Stuart Hall. **Executive Producers:** Grahame Turner and Ian Martin.

....

Wedding on Saturday | 1 wk

Granada, documentary

| 1964 | 5.8 | Wed 1 Apr 9:40 p.m. | 16 | 1 wk |

An award-winning film about a wedding in the parish church of South Elmsall, in the heart of the South Yorkshire coalfield. Pamela Stanton, the girl from the local post office, marries Donald Forshaw, a miner. Producer Norman Swallow uses the occasion to look at the village and its life.

Wednesday at 8 — 18 wks

Thames, entertainment

This was an occasional variety series. During 1977 and 1978 the game show NAME THAT TUNE was introduced as a section of the programme.

| 1976 | 8.2 | Wed 22 Dec 8:00 p.m. | 3 | 7 wks |

Tom O'Connor introduces John Inman, Roger Kitter, Little and Large, David Nixon and Sheila White, with the Alan Braden orchestra and the Lionel Blair dancers.
Producer: Dennis Kirkland.

| 1977 | 18.0 | Wed 14 Dec 8:00 p.m. | 3 | 1 wk |

Tom O'Connor introduces Ray Alan, Champagne, Cyd Charisse, Tony Martin and Mike Reid, with the Nigel Lythgoe dancers, the Ladybirds and the Alan Braden orchestra.
Producer: Dennis Kirkland.

| 1978 | 17.5 | Wed 29 Nov 8:00 p.m. | 4 | 5 wks |

Tom O'Connor introduces Ray Alan and Lord Charles, Cilla Black, Tony Christie and Bob Rosetti, with the Nigel Lythgoe dancers, the Ladybirds and the Alan Braden orchestra.
Producer: Paul Stewart Laing.

| 1988 | 10.6 | Wed 23 Mar 8:00 p.m. | 17 | 5 wks |

Jim Davidson introduces Ed Alonzo, Chas and Dave, Richard Digance, the Temptations and Mark Walker with the Brian Rogers dancers and Alyn Ainsworth orchestra.
Producer: John Kaye Cooper.

....

Wednesday Film, The — 5 wks

Presented by BBC, film

| 1975 | 7.9 | Wed 28 May 6:45 p.m. | 10 | 1 wk |

'Challenge To Lassie'
Lassie goes on trial for her life when her rightful ownership is questioned. Starring Geraldine Brooks, Donald Crisp and Edmund Gwen.
Director: Richard Thorpe.

| 1981 | 15.1 | Wed 25 Feb 7:30 p.m. | 11 | 1 wk |

'Doctor in the House'
(see separate entry for this film.)

| 1982 | 9.8 | Wed 23 Jun 7:25 p.m. | 11 | 3 wks |

'The Pistolero of Red River'
Although Marshal Dan Blaine (Glenn Ford) wants to hang up his gun and retire, a showdown is inevitable when Lot McGuire (Chad Everett) arrives determined to test his reputation as the best gunman in the land. Also starring Angie Dickinson as Lisa Denton.
Director: Richard Thorpe.

Wednesday Play, The — 11 wks

BBC, drama

This series of single plays pulled no punches and allowed writers to say what they had to say about the world. The original producers were Tony Garnett, James MacTaggart, Roger Smith and Kennith Trodd. The 1965 season included Neil Dunn's memorable UP THE JUNCTION and 1966 brought the award-winning CATHY COME HOME by Jeremy Sandford, which starred Carol White and Ray Brooks, and was first transmitted on 16 November. However, neither of these two plays scored the highest viewing figures of their seasons.

| 1965 | 4.8 | Wed 22 Dec 9:00 p.m. | 19 | 1 wk |

'The Coming Out Party' by James O'Connor.
A little boy begins a sad search in Notting Hill just before Christmas. It leads him into trouble, but on the way there is much festivity and comedy.
Designer: Michael Wield. **Director:** Kenneth Loach. **Producer:** James MacTaggart.

| 1966 | 6.7 | Wed 16 Mar 9:25 p.m. | 10 | 6 wks |

'Boy in the Smoke' by Patrick Galvin.
Sean Caffrey stars as Paddy, an Irish immigrant recently arrived at Paddington station with a large hangover and without his wallet. He makes friends with Billy Carey (Raymond Hunt), to whom Paddington is home.
Designer: Roy Oxley. **Director:** William Slater. **Producer:** Peter Luke.

| 1967 | 6.1 | Wed 4 Jan 9:05 p.m. | 15 | 3 wks |

'Person to Person' by Joan Henry.
The story of divorced journalist Julia (Elizabeth Sellers), her lover Mark (Robin Bailey) and young student Alan (Michael Standing), to whom Julia speaks. As they talk, the nature of their relationship changes.
Designer: Eileen Diss. **Director:** Raymond Menmuir. **Producer:** Lionel Harris.

| 1968 | 4.5 | Wed 21 Aug 9:05 p.m. | 14 | 1 wk |

'Mrs Lawrence Will Look After It' by Tony Parker.
Mrs Lawrence (Constance Chapman) is a kind-hearted woman who takes on the responsibility of caring about other people's children. Also starring Nina Baden-Semper, Pauline Collins, Barry Jackson, Mary Miller and Ray Smith.
Designer: Keith Harris. **Director:** John Mackenzie. **Producer:** Irene Shubik.

....

Wednesday Thriller, The — 2 wks

BBC, drama

During the summer break for THE WEDNESDAY PLAY a series of single thrillers was shown.

1965 6.0 | Wed 22 Sep 9:00 p.m. | 15 | 2 wks

'The Cellar' by Patricia Highsmith.
Ursula Howells stars in a murder mystery underground. Also starring Gilbert Davis, Scott Forbes, Jeanette Roach and Terry Scully.
Designer: Michael Wield. **Director:** George R. Foa. **Producer:** Bernard Hepton.

....

Weekend of Terror | 1 wk

USA presented by LWT, drama

1972 7.5 | Sun 14 May 9:00 p.m. | 5 | 1 wk

This movie made for television tells the story of a kidnapping, a resultant death and the imprisonment of three nuns in a cellar. Starring Robert Conrad and Lee Majors with Carol Lynley, Lois Nettleton and Jane Wyatt as the nuns.
Director: Jud Taylor.

....

We'll Meet Again | 13 wks

LWT, drama

This series created by David Butler dealt with the arrival of the 525th Bomb Group of the US 8th Air Force with two thousand men in the small Suffolk market town of Market Wetherby. Susannah York starred as Helen Dereham, with Michael J. Shannon as Major Jim Kiley, June Barry as Vera Mundy, Ronald Hines as Ronald Dereham, Patrick O'Connell as Jack Blair and Ray Smith as Albert Mundy.

1982 15.0 | Fri 19 Feb 8:30 p.m. | 3 | 13 wks

'All Day and Every Day'
In this first episode, the Group arrives in the unprepared village.
Designers: John Clements, John Emery and Colin Monk. **Writer:** David Crane. **Producer:** Tony Wharmby.

....

We'll Think of Something | 2 wks

Thames, situation comedy

Sam Kelly and Marcia Warren starred as Les and Maureen Brooks. His pride would not allow him to sign on the dole.

1986 10.9 | Mon 8 Sep 8:00 p.m. | 11 | 2 wks

'You Know Who Your Friends Are' by Geoff Rowley.
Les decides to be a scrap metal merchant.
Producer: John Howard Davies.

Wells Fargo | 1 wk

USA presented by BBC, western

This series about the famous Wells Fargo stagecoach company was set in the days of the California gold rush. Dale Robertson starred as Jim Hardie.

1962 3.6 | Mon 6 Aug 6:20 p.m. | 16 | 1 wk

'Relay Station'
Jim is sent to tend the station after the death of a Wells Fargo agent. On the way he meets a boy who has been mysteriously wounded.

....

West End Tales | 5 wks

ATV, situation comedy

This seven-part series by Keith Waterhouse looked at Soho life through the eyes of Fiddler (Robin Nedwell) and his two pals the Bishop (Garfield Morgan) and Checkie (Larry Martyn). It also starred Toni Palmer as Ma, Peter Childs as Sergeant Dobbs and Susan Skipper as Tina.
Director: James Gatward. **Producers:** Colin Frewin and Keith Beckett.

1981 13.7 | Mon 16 Feb 8:00 p.m. | 16 | 5 wks

'Some You Lose'
The three go to the races prepared to take a huge gamble.

....

Western, The | 18 wks

Presented by BBC, film

This was a series of western films.

1965 6.8 | Sat 11 Dec 7:25 p.m. | 9 | 7 wks

'Jesse James'
Tyrone Power and Henry Fonda star in the story of the West's most notorious outlaw and his gang.
Director: Henry King.

1966 6.4 | Sat 15 Jan 7:00 p.m. | 8 | 11 wks

'Tension at Table Rock'
Angie Dickinson, Richard Egan, Dorothy Malone and Cameron Mitchell star in the story of a man branded a coward who is terrified by a group of marauding trail-herders.
Director: Charles Marquis Warren.

What a Carry On — 1 wk

ATV, comedy

1973 **6.3** **Thu 4 Oct 9:00 p.m.** **10** **1 wk**

Cameras join the stars for an excerpt from tonight's opening night of the Carry On team's first stage revue at the Victoria Palace, London. Shaw Taylor introduces stars Bernard Bresslaw, Peter Butterworth, Kenneth Connor, Jack Douglas, Sid James and Barbara Windsor. **Writers:** Talbot Rothwell, Dave Freeman and Eric Merriman. **Theatre Producer:** Albert Knight. **Choreographer:** Tommy Shaw. **Musical Director:** Richard Holmes. **Television presentation:** Alan Tarrant.

What a Carry On — 3 wks

Presented by BBC, film

An occasional season of CARRY ON films.

1975 **6.7** **Wed 22 Oct 6:40 p.m.** **16** **1 wk**

'Carry On Doctor'
(see separate entry for this film.)

1979 **20.6** **Fri 21 Sep 7:25 p.m.** **6** **2 wks**

'Carry On Doctor'
(Repeat.)

What a Carry On — 4 wks

BBC, comedy

1987 **12.3** **Thu 16 Jul 8:00 p.m.** **4** **4 wks**

A compilation of clips from the CARRY ON films. **Director:** Gerald Thomas. **Producer:** Peter Rogers.

What Would You Do? — 3 wks

YTV, drama

The plays in this series involved situations in which anyone might question what he or she would do in similar circumstances.

1975 **6.8** **Thu 26 Jun 9:00 p.m.** **3** **3 wks**

'Love Me to Death' by David Ambrose.
What would you do to avoid paying tax and escape with two million pounds? Starring Robin Bailey, Susan Penhaligon, Anthony Valentine and Gwen Watford.
Designer: Alan Pickford. **Director:** Marc Miller. **Executive Producer:** Peter Willes.

Whatever Happened to the Likely Lads? — 5 wks

BBC, situation comedy

Dick Clement and Ian La Frenais, creators of THE LIKELY LADS, aged their characters four and a half years before viewers met them again. Terry (James Bolam) had spent the intervening years in the army, playing around with girls in foreign lands and marrying one. Bob (Rodney Bewes) had worked to better himself, acquiring a house and car, and holidays on the Costa Brava. At the point where Terry returned, expecting to pick up more or less where he and Bob had left off, Bob was planning marriage – to Thelma (Brigit Forsyth), daughter of his boss. They married. The 26 episodes that ensued exploited the class war between Bob and Terry.

1973 **6.6** **Tue 27 Feb 8:30 p.m.** **16** **1 wk**

'Guess Who's Coming to Dinner?'
Bob thinks Terry needs some new friends but invites disaster by taking him to a trendy dinner party.
Producer: James Gilbert.

1974 **7.3** **Tue 5 Feb 8:30 p.m.** **2** **2 wks**

'The Great Race'
Bob and Terry challenge each other to a cross-country cycle race.
Producer: Bernard Thompson.

1975 **6.9** **Mon 26 May 6:30 p.m.** **18** **1 wk**

'Between Ourselves'
Thelma is home with her mother, leaving Terry and Bob alone to look after each other.
Producer: Bernard Thompson.

1985 **11.9** **Sun 17 Nov 6:00 p.m.** **20** **1 wk**

'No Hiding Place'
The lads do not want to know the result of a football match, a recording of which is about to be shown on television.
Producer: James Gilbert.
(Repeat.)

Whatever Happened to the Likely Lads Christmas Special — 1 wk

BBC, situation comedy

James Bolam and Rodney Bewes starred in an hour-long Christmas edition as Terry and Bob, the Likely Lads.

1974 **7.3** **Tue 24 Dec 7:45 p.m.** **2** **1 wk**

Bob and Thelma (Brigit Forsyth) are all set to enjoy the festivities to the full until Terry gets everything off on the wrong foot.
Writers: Dick Clement and Ian La Frenais. **Producer:** Bernard Thompson.

Whatever Next   8 wks

BBC, game show

In this series hosted by Noel Edmonds contestants were invited to watch a piece of film and then determine 'what happened next'. **Producer:** Michael Hurll.

| 1987 | 12.5 | Mon 19 Oct 8:30 p.m. | 12 | 8 wks |

What's My Line   20 wks

Thames, game show

The most famous panel game of all time was created in the USA by the undisputed kings of the genre, Mark Goodson and Bill Todman. It began in the UK on BBC in 1951. Chairman Eamonn Andrews invited members of the public to 'sign in, please' and do a brief mime of their job. The panel then tried to determine the nature of the job before Andrews logged ten 'no' answers to their questions. The most regular panel members through the 1950s were Isobel Barnett, Gilbert Harding, Barbara Kelly and David Nixon. When Thames revived the format in 1984 Eamonn was still in the chair but Barbara Kelly was the only surviving member of the original panel. The original producer was T. Leslie Jackson. **Producer:** Maurice Leonard. **Executive Producer:** Malcolm Morris.

| 1984 | 12.5 | Mon 16 Apr 7:00 p.m. | 4 | 12 wks |

Panellists: Jilly Cooper, George Gale, Barbara Kelly, Patrick Mower and Ernie Wise.

| 1986 | 11.4 | Mon 14 Apr 8:00 p.m. | 9 | 7 wks |

Panellists: Jilly Cooper, George Gale, Barbara Kelly, Barry Sheene and Ernie Wise.
Director: Stuart Hall.

| 1987 | 10.0 | Mon 18 May 8:00 p.m. | 11 | 1 wk |

Panellists: Jilly Cooper, George Gale, Barbara Kelly and Ernie Wise.
Director: Stuart Hall.

What's On Next?   14 wks

Thames, comedy

This series of comedy sketches was presided over by William Franklyn, with Pam Ayres, Barry Cryer, Jim Davidson, Anna Dawson, Sandra Dickinson, Andonia Katsaros and Bob Todd.
Producer: Mark Stuart.

| 1976 | 5.9 | Mon 16 Aug 6:45 p.m. | 13 | 2 wks |

Guests: Hinge and Bracket.

| 1977 | 7.4 | Mon 13 Jun 8:00 p.m. | 3 | 4 wks |

Guests: Hinge and Bracket.

| 1978 | 13.4 | Wed 25 Oct 8:00 p.m. | 5 | 8 wks |

Guests: Linda Lou Allen and Anne Bruzac.

What's On Wogan?   2 wks

BBC, talk show

Terry Wogan hosted a live chat show, the forerunner of WOGAN.

| 1980 | 11.4 | Sat 31 May 6:15 p.m. | 14 | 2 wks |

Guests: Captain and Tennille, Fran and Anna, Albert Saveen, Barbara Woodhouse.
Director: Brian Penders. **Producer:** Alan Boyd.

Wheel of Fortune   11 wks

STV, game show

This general knowledge game show was hosted by Nicky Campbell. The financial value of correct answers was determined by a spin of the wheel.

| 1988 | 11.7 | Tue 27 Sep 7:30 p.m. | 12 | 8 wks |

Director: Anne Mason. **Producer:** Stephen Leahy. **Executive Producer:** Sandy Ross.

| 1991 | 9.3 | Thu 8 Aug 8:30 p.m. | 15 | 3 wks |

Director: John Frame. **Producer:** Anne Mason.

Wheels   5 wks

USA presented by ITV, drama

Millard Lampbell and Hank Searls dramatized in five parts Arthur Hailey's novel about the American car industry. Rock Hudson starred as senior executive Adam Trenton and Lee Remick played his wife Erica.
Director: Jerry London. **Producer:** Roy Huggins.

| 1978 | 12.9 | Thu 15 Jun 7:45 p.m. | 4 | 5 wks |

Episode Three
Erica returns to Adam after the death of her lover. Adam ends his affair with Barbara (Blair Brown).

Wheeltappers and Shunters Club, The · 2 wks

Granada, entertainment

This series set in a studio-built working men's club starred Colin Crompton as the concert chairman and Bernard Manning as the heckling compere. Derek Hilton provided the music. The series was created and produced by John Hamp.
Director: David Warwick.

| 1974 | 6.2 | Sat 20 Apr 9:30 p.m. | 15 | 1 wk |

Guests: Bill Haley and his Comets, Brandy di Franck and the Grumbleweeds.

| 1975 | 6.1 | Sat 5 Apr 8:45 p.m. | 19 | 1 wk |

Compere Bernard Manning moves into the star spot with supporting performances from Mike Carter, Itojo Kumano and Jerry Stevens.

When Comedy Was King · 1 wk

USA presented by BBC, comedy

| 1966 | 5.6 | Mon 26 Dec 3:45 p.m. | 14 | 1 wk |

A pageant of Hollywood's most famous laughter makers narrated by Dwight Weist. Clips feature Charlie Chaplin, Buster Keaton, Laurel and Hardy, Harry Langdon, Fatty Arbuckle and Wallace Beery. Written and compiled by Robert Youngson.

When Day Is Done · 1 wk

Thames, drama

| 1975 | 7.0 | Tue 7 Jan 8:25 p.m. | 18 | 1 wk |

Edward Woodward stars as Phil Warne, who dreams of singing with his own big band. Also starring Rosemary Leach as his wife, who suffers his endlessly singing along to records.
Writer: John Kershaw. **Producer:** Reginald Collin. **Executive Producers:** Lloyd Shirley and George Taylor.

When the Boat Comes In · 9 wks

BBC, drama

This series created by James Mitchell was set on Tyneside during the 1930s Depression. The stories revolved around Jack Ford (James Bolam), a fitter in the shipyards determined to fight his way out of the hopeless environment into which he was born, and the Seaton family: mother Bella (Jean Heywood), father Bill (James Garbutt), sons Billy and Tom (Edward Wilson and John Nightingale) and daughter Jessie (Susan Jameson).

| 1976 | 7.2 | Thu 25 Mar 8:10 p.m. | 11 | 9 wks |

'Heads You Win, Tails I Lose' by Sid Chaplin.
Jessie raises her objections to the men, whose answer to everything is to put up their fists.
Producer: Leonard Lewis.

When the North Wind Blows · 1 wk

Presented by BBC, film

| 1980 | 15.9 | Tue 30 Dec 6:55 p.m. | 8 | 1 wk |

An Alaskan trapper has killed a Siberian snow tiger and finds himself fighting for survival in frozen wastes inhabited by its mate. The stars are Henry Brandon, Dan Haggerty and Herbert Nelson.
Director: Stewart Raffill.

When Time Ran Out · 2 wks

Presented by ITV, film

| 1983 | 13.6 | Mon 30 May 8:00 p.m. | 1 | 1 wk |

A volcano erupts on a Pacific island which has become a rich man's playground. The guests at a luxury hotel attempt to escape the path of molten lava. Starring Paul Newman and Jacqueline Bisset with Edward Albert, Ernest Borgnine, Red Buttons, James Franciscus, William Holden and Burgess Meredith.
Director: James Goldstone.

| 1986 | 15.1 | Sun 12 Jan 7:45 p.m. | 7 | 1 wk |

Repeat showing of the above film.

When Worlds Collide · 1 wk

Presented by ITV, film

| 1968 | 4.2 | Mon 12 Aug 6:05 p.m. | 19 | 1 wk |

Richard Derr and Barbara Rush star in this science-fiction story. A planet is on a collision course with Earth.
Director: Rudolph Maté.

Where Are They Now? · 1 wk

BBC, entertainment

David Jacobs presented this series, in which celebrities from yesteryear revealed their modern activities.

1979	14.7	Wed 29 Aug 7:10 p.m.	16	2 wks

With Reita Faria (Miss World 1966), Sir Alec Rose (who once sailed around the world) and Gerald Campion (Billy Bunter in the 1950s TV series).
Director: Pieter Morpurgo. **Producer:** Shirley Fisher.

Where Eagles Dare 4 wks

Presented by BBC, film

1979	17.5	Wed 26 Dec 7:10 p.m.	2	1 wk

This film of an Alistair MacLean novel stars Richard Burton as Major John Smith and Clint Eastwood as Lieutenant Morris Schaffer. Seven paratroopers are sent on a mission to penetrate the Nazi stronghold known as 'Castle of the Eagles'.
Director: Brian G. Hutton.

1981	16.8	Wed 29 Apr 7:00 p.m.	2	1 wk
1983	12.7	Sat 28 May 6:55 p.m.	4	1 wk
1985	10.4	Sat 25 May 10:05 p.m.	19	1 wk

Repeat showings of the above film.

Where There's Brass 1 wk

YTV, comedy

1980	13.8	Sun 16 Mar 8:45 p.m.	20	1 wk

Joe Lockwood (Derek Smith) is a captain of industry. He has two errant sons and he's also the conductor of the Brigthorpe Brass Band.
Writer: Dick Sharples. **Producer:** Ronnie Baxter.

Where There's Life 71 wks

YTV, documentary

In this series Doctors Robert Buckman and Miriam Stoppard presented the latest developments in the world of medicine.
Director (1981–85): Ian McFarlane. **Executive Producer:** Duncan Dallas.

1981	13.0	Wed 29 Apr 7:00 p.m.	7	12 wks

An examination of everyday worry and stress.
Producers: John Fanshawe and David Taylor.

1982	13.8	Wed 31 Mar 7:00 p.m.	6	23 wks

Rob Buckman reports on medical lore in the Far East. Miriam

Stoppard meets a young girl in Texas with Hodgkinson's disease – and a great sense of humour.
Co-director: Peter Jones.

1983	12.2	Wed 20 Apr 7:00 p.m.	4	22 wks

People describe their own experiences of sickness, proving that there is more drama than most people imagine in the average person's life.
Producer: Derek Goodall.

1984	11.0	Wed 19 Sep 7:00 p.m.	9	6 wks

Miriam Stoppard reports from America on jogging following the death of 52-year-old Jim Fixx, one of the sport's prime advocates.
Producer: John Fanshawe.

1985	9.9	Wed 7 Aug 7:00 p.m.	17	2 wks

An examination from New York of American cosmetic surgeon Dr Felix Schiffman and his methods.
Director: Nick Abson. **Producer:** Irene Garrow.

1986	8.9	Wed 4 Jun 7:00 p.m.	15	4 wks

Tonight's topic is how much parents should influence their children.
Director: Nick Abson. **Producer:** Anne Pivcevic.

1987	8.4	Wed 8 Jul 7:00 p.m.	18	1 wk

A report examining the difficulties of fighting back to health faced by the victims of serious road accidents. Tonight the guest is Bucks Fizz star Mike Nolan, himself such a victim in 1984.
Producer: David Poyser.

1988	8.4	Wed 25 May 7:00 p.m.	19	1 wk

An examination of the ways of coming to grips with pain without resorting to drugs.
Director: Nick Abson. **Producer:** Paul Bader. **Editor:** Petrina Rance.

Whicker in Europe 4 wks

YTV, documentary

In this series of seven programmes Alan Whicker travelled the continent meeting people.

1970	7.3	Thu 5 Feb 9:30 p.m.	9	4 wks

'Miss Bluebell'
Whicker is in Paris to meet Miss Bluebell, Margaret Kelly, who was born in Dublin but adopted by a family in Liverpool, where she was brought up. She has been the iron hand behind the Bluebell girls since 1934.
Director: Fred Burnley. **Executive Producer:** Tony Essex.

Paul Newman and Jacqueline Bisset take their time fleeing the lava in **When Time Ran Out**.

Whicker Way Out West — 6 wks

YTV, documentary

In this series Alan Whicker explored the whackier eccentricities of California and its people.

1973 7.3 **Wed 3 Oct 7:00 p.m.** 2 **6 wks**

Alan Whicker meets Dr Kurt Wagner, a plastic surgeon who makes more than a million dollars a year out of the narcissism business. He talks with his patients before, during and after their reconstructions. Mrs Wagner boasts that if her husband ever goes off her, he can always change her. He already has in many ways.
Camera: Frank Pocklington. **Director:** Michael Deakin.

Whicker's New World — 6 wks

YTV, documentary

Alan Whicker looked at aspects of American life which had yet to be found in Britain.

1969 6.4 **Mon 2 Jun 8:00 p.m.** 6 **6 wks**

'Immortality Inc.'
Die now, live later is the prediction of a Michigan professor who sees the start of a multi-billion dollar industry in preservation.
Director: Peter Batty. **Executive Producer:** Tony Essex.

Whicker's Orient — 2 wks

YTV, documentary

In this series Alan Whicker explored the Far East.

1972 6.7 **Tue 8 Feb 8:30 p.m.** 7 **2 wks**

'Thai Tycoons and the Executive Street'
Whicker looks at the role of women in the Thai business world.
Camera: Frank Pocklington. **Director:** Ian McFarlane. **Producer:** John Fairley. **Executive Producer:** Tony Essex.

Whicker's South Seas — 6 wks

YTV, documentary

In this series Alan Whicker explored and met the people of the South Seas.

1973 7.7 **Tue 6 Mar 7:05 p.m.** 2 **6 wks**

'The Only Compliment – She's a Good Sport'
Whicker meets the women of New Zealand. They claim the only compliment they've ever been paid by men is 'She's a good sport!'
Camera: Frank Pocklington. **Director:** Fred Burnley. **Executive Producer:** John Fairley.

Whicker's Walkabout — 7 wks

YTV, documentary

In this series of seven programmes Alan Whicker explored the continent of Australia.

1970 7.1 **Mon 14 Sep 8:00 p.m.** 1 **7 wks**

'They're Dishing Out Money Here – For Nothing'
Alan Whicker is in Kalgoorlie, the Klondyke of the 1970s. Earlier this year three Aborigines sold their claim to a piece of the desert for £50. Six weeks later it was valued on the stock market at £80 million.
Camera: Brian Wilson. **Director:** Michael Blakstad. **Executive Producer:** Tony Essex.

Whicker's World — 11 wks

BBC, documentary

1967 5.5 **Mon 14 Aug 8:00 p.m.** 7 **2 wks**

'The Quest for Beauty'
Alan Whicker examines the extent to which some people endure pain and spend money to improve on nature. (First shown on BBC2.)
Producer: David C. Rea.

1985 12.5 **Sun 3 Nov 9:05 p.m.** 9 **5 wks**

'Living with Uncle Sam'
The last of ten programmes in which Alan Whicker meets British people who live and work in the USA.
Camera: Mike Fox. **Sound:** John Parker and Keith Rodgerson. **Producer:** Jonathan Steadall.

1988 12.6 **Sun 31 Jan 8:10 p.m.** 12 **4 wks**

'Living with Waltzing Matilda'
The fourth of ten programmes in Australia's bicentennial year finds Whicker in northern Queensland, where crocodiles continue to take their toll of human life.
Camera: Ray Henman. **Sound:** Keith Rodgerson. **Producer:** Roger Mills.

Whicker's World — 19 wks

YTV, documentary

1975 7.8 **Tue 4 Mar 9:00 p.m.** 5 **5 wks**

'Where the Great Dream Still Lies'
Alan Whicker samples the life and lifestyle of Vancouver, Canada.
Camera: Frank Pocklington. **Director:** Fred Burnley. **Executive Producer:** John Fairley.

1976 6.4 **Tue 14 Sep 9:10 p.m.** 11 **6 wks**

'Penang'
Whicker reports from the Pearl of the Orient and the Gateway to the East.

Camera: Dick Dodd. *Director:* Michael Deakin. *Executive Producer:* John Fairley.

| 1977 | 14.1 | Wed 28 Sep 9:00 p.m. | 5 | 4 wks |

'Salt Lake City, Utah'
Whicker reaches 'the city of saints' on his journey across America.
Camera: Frank Pocklington. *Director:* Peter Batty. *Producer:* Nigel Turner. *Executive Producer:* John Fairley.

| 1980 | 14.7 | Wed 23 Apr 9:00 p.m. | 3 | 4 wks |

'I Feel Trapped in Paradise Here'
Alan Whicker explores Sunset Boulevard, meeting Britt Ekland and Sherry Lansing on the way and attending a birthday party for dogs.
Camera: Allan Pyrah. *Producer:* David Green. *Executive Producer:* Frank Smith.

White Christmas   1 wk

Presented by BBC, film

| 1969 | 6.3 | Sun 21 Dec 8:15 p.m. | 19 | 1 wk |

Seasonal screening for the film starring Bing Crosby, Rosemary Clooney, Danny Kaye and Vera-Ellen.
Director: Michael Curtiz.

White Wedding   1 wk

AR, entertainment

| 1963 | 5.8 | Wed 16 Jan 9:45 p.m. | 16 | 1 wk |

Hughie Green invites international skaters to present an ice extravaganza in celebration of the wedding of skating stars Sue Park and Douglas Breniser, who will themselves dance the love duet from Snow White.
Television presentation: John P. Hamilton.

Who Dares Wins   1 wk

Presented by ITV, film

| 1985 | 14.6 | Thu 26 Dec 9:00 p.m. | 12 | 1 wk |

A British government undercover agent is assassinated during a CND march in London. The Special Air Services (SAS – motto 'Who Dares Wins') infiltrates a gang of terrorists who have plans to take over the American Embassy. Starring Patrick Allen, Lewis Collins, Judy Davis, Ingrid Pitt, Robert Webber, Richard Widmark and Edward Woodward. This film is also known as The Final Option.
Director: Ian Sharp.

Who Do You Do?   3 wks

LWT, entertainment

This series featured various impressionists, sometimes performing solo, sometimes as a team, with quick-fire gags and visual caricatures.

| 1972 | 5.6 | Sat 12 Aug 5:45 p.m. | 8 | 3 wks |

The impressionists include Janet Brown, Dailey and Wayne, Peter Goodwright, Len Lowe, Johnny More and Freddie Starr.
Producer: Jon Scoffield.

Who Do You Do? (Christmas Special)   1 wk

| 1974 | 6.4 | Sun 29 Dec 7:25 p.m. | 8 | 1 wk |

Impressionists include Janet Brown, Peter Goodwright, Aiden J. Harvey, Johnny More and Freddie Starr.
Producer: Jon Scoffield.

Who Is Sylvia?   4 wks

ATV, situation comedy

This comedy love story in three parts was devised by and starred Charlie Drake with Kathleen Byron as Mrs Proudpiece, the secretary of a marriage bureau who tried to find the perfect mate for him.

| 1967 | 7.8 | Sat 11 Feb 8:30 p.m. | 6 | 4 wks |

'The Great Lover'
In this first episode Charles Rameses Drake visits Mrs Proudpiece to introduce himself.
Director: Sean O'Riordan. *Producer:* Alan Tarrant.

Who-Dun-It?   13 wks

ATV, drama

This series of single mystery plays was produced by Jack Williams.

| 1969 | 7.4 | Tue 9 Sep 9:00 p.m. | 1 | 13 wks |

'Fall of a Goddess' by Bryan Cooper.
Trisha Noble stars as a Hollywood film star murdered on a transatlantic liner. Eric Barker also stars.
Designer: Anthony Weller. *Director:* Ian Fordyce. *Producer:* Jack Williams.

Television's most famous globetrotter pauses for tea on **Whicker's Walkabout**.

Radio star Eric Barker scaled the television heights in **Who-Dun-It?**

Whodunit – Murder In Space?　　　　1 wk

Central, drama

1985　**10.4**　**Tue 13 Aug 8:30 p.m.**　**11**　**1 wk**

Four astronauts on a mission to Mars die in violent and mysterious circumstances. Five survivors make a desperate attempt to return to Earth knowing that one of their number is a killer.
Writer: Wesley Ferguson. **Director:** Steven Hilliard Stern. **Producer:** Robert Cooper. (A Zenith production.)

Whodunnit?　　　　37 wks

Thames, game show

In this series introduced by Edward Woodward (Jon Pertwee from 1974) a fictional crime drama would be enacted on film and a panel of amateur sleuths in the studio would examine the evidence and try to deduce who had committed the offence.
Writers: Jeremy Lloyd and Lance Percival.

1973　**6.3**　**Mon 16 Jul 6:40 p.m.**　**5**　**6 wks**

'Did He Fall Or Was He Pushed?'
Guest panel Kingsley Amis, Peter Byrne, Russell Hunter and Moira Lister watch the drama unfurl as a managing director is found dead at the foot of a three-storey building.
Director: Robert Reed. **Producer:** Malcolm Morris.

1974　**6.8**　**Mon 22 Jul 6:40 p.m.**　**3**　**6 wks**

'The Art of Theft'
Panellists Kingsley Amis, Jackie Collins, Arthur Mullard, and Emperor Rosko decide who stole a famous painting.
Director: Robert Reed. **Producer:** Malcolm Morris.

1975　**6.4**　**Mon 15 Sep 6:45 p.m.**　**15**　**8 wks**

'Beware – Wet Paint'
Anouska Hempel, Nerys Hughes, Jimmy Jewel and Patrick Mower attempt to solve the riddle of how a dead body managed to cross a freshly painted floor without leaving any traces.
Producers: Robert Reed and Dennis Kirkland.

1976　**5.6**　**Mon 19 Jul 6:45 p.m.**　**4**　**4 wks**

'Final Verdict'
Honor Blackman, Norman Bowler and Richard O'Sullivan must decide who poisoned the unsuspecting victim.
Producer: Robert Reed.

1977　**6.4**　**Mon 25 Jul 6:45 p.m.**　**5**　**3 wks**

'Last Tango in Tooting'
Anouska Hempel, Stratford Johns and Roy Plomley look for a criminal reason why a couple should score zero in the finals of a chemical works dancing competition.
Producers: Anthony Parker and Leon Thau.

1978　**15.8**　**Mon 3 Apr 6:45 p.m.**　**6**　**10 wks**

'All Part of The Service'
With Diana Coupland, Liza Goddard, Alfred Marks and Patrick Mower attempting to deduce the criminal elements that evolve from a deadly game of tennis.
Producers: Anthony Parker and Robert Reed.

Whole Lotta Shakin' Goin' On　　　　1 wk

Granada, music

1964　**5.6**　**Wed 30 Sep 9:50 p.m.**　**17**　**1 wk**

Jerry Lee Lewis gives an unrehearsed and unscripted performance in Granada's Studio 6. With the Animals and Gene Vincent. (The audience was so worked up by the star that the cameras had to fight for pictures.)
Director: Philip Casson. **Producer:** John Hamp.

Whoops Baghdad!　　　　1 wk

BBC, situation comedy

Frankie Howerd played Ali Oopla, the bondservant to the Wazir of Baghdad (Derek Francis). All the Wazir's troubles stemmed from women. He either had too few or too many. The series was written by Sid Colin, David McKellar and David Nobbs.

1973　**7.2**　**Thu 25 Jan 10:15 p.m.**　**7**　**1 wk**

In the first episode of the series Ali tries to find a new wife for the Wazir, who is plagued by his troublesome daughters Saccharine (Hilary Pritchard) and Boobiana (Anna Brett). Josephine Tewson plays the part of Fatima, favourite for the role of the Wazir's wife.
Producer: John Howard Davies.

Who's The Greatest?　　　　1 wk

Thames, documentary

1987　**9.9**　**Wed 29 Apr 8:30 p.m.**　**15**　**1 wk**

Brian Moore chairs the comparison between snooker players Joe Davis and Steve Davis. Alfred Marks makes the case for Joe, Lennie Bennett for Steve.
Director: Ian Little-Smith. **Producer:** John D. Taylor.

Why Didn't They Ask Evans?　　　　1 wk

LWT, drama

| 1980 | 15.6 | Sun 30 Mar 7:45 p.m. | 9 | 1 wk |

The first television adaptation of an Agatha Christie novel is set in the 1930s. Vicar's son Bobby Jones (James Warwick) and Lady Frances Derwent (Francesca Annis) become amateur sleuths unravelling clues to what looks like murder. Connie Booth, Raymond Francis, John Gielgud, Doris Hare, Joan Hickson, Leigh Lawson, Bernard Miles, Eric Porter and Madeline Smith also star.
Designers: Bryan Bagge and Frank Nerini. **Directors:** John Davies and Tony Wharmby. **Producer:** Jack Williams.

Widows   11 wks

Thames, drama

This series by Lynda La Plante starred Debby Bishop as Bella, Ann Mitchell as Dolly, Maureen O'Farrell as Linda and Fiona Hendley as Shirley. The four were widowed when their husbands died attempting a raid on a security van. The quartet decided to carry out the next robbery themselves. (A Euston Films production.)

| 1983 | 12.8 | Wed 6 Apr 9:00 p.m. | 4 | 6 wks |

The plans are almost complete. The police are keeping a close eye on all the women, but have so far come up with nothing to suggest they have criminal intent.
Director: Ian Toynton. **Producer:** Linda Agran. **Executive Producer:** Verity Lambert.

| 1985 | 13.8 | Wed 10 Apr 9:00 p.m. | 2 | 5 wks |

After successfully pulling off a raid, the widows arrive in Rio to start a new life. However, Dolly's husband Harry (Maurice O'Connell) was not killed after all, and is in pursuit of the loot.
Director: Paul Annett. **Producer:** Irving Teitelbaum. **Executive Producers:** Linda Agran and Johnny Goodman.

Wild Geese, The   2 wks

Presented by ITV, film

| 1981 | 15.6 | Sat 24 Oct 9:25 p.m. | 4 | 1 wk |

A force of fifty mercenaries named 'The Wild Geese' embark on a mission to rescue an African leader held hostage in his own country. Starring Richard Burton, Stewart Granger, Richard Harris, Hardy Kruger and Roger Moore.
Director: Andrew V. McLaglen.

| 1985 | 12.5 | Tue 25 Jun 9:00 p.m. | 3 | 1 wk |

Repeat showing of the above film.

Wildcats   2 wks

Presented by ITV, film

| 1990 | 13.0 | Mon 16 Apr 8:30 p.m. | 7 | 1 wk |

Goldie Hawn stars as Molly, who gets a job as football coach to one of Chicago's toughest schools.
Director: Michael Ritchie.

| 1991 | 13.6 | Mon 12 Aug 8:00 p.m. | 7 | 1 wk |

Repeat showing of the above film.

Wildcats of St Trinian's, The   1 wk

Presented by BBC, film

| 1983 | 10.9 | Fri 9 Dec 7:20 p.m. | 17 | 1 wk |

Sheila Hancock stars as headmistress of the uncontrollable schoolgirls who have a total disregard for all authority. Michael Hordern, Maureen Lipman and Joe Melia also star.
Director: Frank Launder.

Wilde Alliance, The   13 wks

YTV, drama

This comedy thriller series was based on the eventful lives of detective story writer Rupert Wilde (John Stride) and his wife Amy (Julia Foster).

| 1978 | 16.6 | Tue 7 Feb 9:00 p.m. | 4 | 13 wks |

'Things That Go Bump in the Night' by Philip Broadley.
An old house contains more than the fixtures and fittings listed on the contract.
Designer: Peter Caldwell. **Director:** Marc Miller. **Producer:** Ian Mackintosh. **Executive Producer:** David Cunliffe.

Wilderness Road   1 wk

BBC, situation comedy

This series by Richard Cottan and Bob Goody was set around the Sun, a London pub, and its adjoining off-licence and tenants. Leslie Sands played the publican Arch, with Robin Driscoll as Moon, Peter Jonfield as Alan, Gary Olsen as Keith, Veronica Quilligan as Nancy and David Sibley as Cage.

| 1986 | 8.2 | Mon 28 Jul 8:30 p.m. | 17 | 1 wk |

'In Between Days'
Cage, Moon and Nancy are installed in the off-licence.
Director: Susan Belbin. **Producer:** John Kilby.

Wildlife on One
19 wks

BBC, documentary

This long-running and highly respected series of natural history programmes was introduced and narrated by David Attenborough. **Series Producers:** Peter Bale (1979, 1982–3) and Dilys Breese (1988–9).

| 1979 | 12.0 | Thu 31 May 8:05 p.m. | 7 | 3 wks |

'Squirrel on My Shoulder'
The story of a baby squirrel found abandoned in Oxfordshire. **Camera** and **Producer:** John Paling.

| 1982 | 12.7 | Thu 14 Jan 8:00 p.m. | 18 | 3 wks |

'The Great Hedgehog Mystery'
The incredible story of a mammal which has been around for fifteen million years.
Camera: Owen Newman. **Writer** and **Producer:** Dilys Breese.

| 1983 | 12.3 | Thur 17 Feb 8:00 p.m. | 15 | 3 wks |

'A Touch of the Butterflies'
A film about the life cycles of butterflies – both in the jungles of Malaysia and in an exotic hothouse just off the M4.
Camera: Owen Newman. **Writer** and **Producer:** John Downer.

| 1988 | 12.5 | Tue 29 Mar 8:30 p.m. | 6 | 1 wk |

'Trivial Pursuit? The Natural Mystery of Play'
A film considering the quirks present in animals' play – like why kittens will always play with a ball of wool.
Writer: Dilys Breese.

| 1989 | 11.6 | Mon 24 Apr 8:30 p.m. | 10 | 7 wks |

'Under the Weather'
An examination into how animals react to weather and if they can predict it with any more accuracy than humans.
Writer and **Producer:** Pelham Aldrich-Blake.

| 1991 | 13.1 | Mon 7 Jan 8:30 p.m. | 13 | 2 wks |

'Devilfish'
The story of the giant octopus of the North Atlantic.
Writers and **Producers:** Mark Deeble and Victoria Stone.

Will the Real Mike Yarwood Stand Up
4 wks

ATV, comedy

With the election of Harold Wilson as Prime Minister in 1964 and the appointment of Edward Heath as leader of the Conservative Party in 1965 impressionist Yarwood was presented with his two most famous subjects for mimicry. He fully exploited their comic value in this series.

| 1969 | 6.8 | Tue 4 Feb 8:25 p.m. | 7 | 4 wks |

Guests: Joe 'Mr. Piano' Henderson, Norman Vaughan and Dilys Watling.
Writers: Eric Davidson and Tony Hawes. **Producer:** Bill Hitchcock.

Wilt
1 wk

Presented by ITV, film

| 1991 | 11.1 | Sat 12 Oct 9:15 p.m. | 18 | 1 wk |

This adaptation of Tom Sharpe's best-seller stars Griff Rhys Jones as Henry Wilt, the polytechnic lecturer who blurs fantasy and reality in his life. Also starring Mel Smith as Inspector Flint, Alison Steadman as Eva Wilt and Diana Quick as Sally.
Director: Michael Tuchner.

Wimbledon Grandstand
8 wks

BBC, sport

The first Wimbledon tennis championships were held in 1877. Although the first filmed broadcast was on 21 June 1937, regular TV coverage was first provided by the BBC from 1950, when the commentators were Richard Dimbleby, Freddie Grisewood and Raymond Glendenning. In 1967 the championships were opened to both amateurs and professionals and provided the location for the first colour broadcast in the United Kingdom. For several decades commentator Dan Maskell was regarded as the voice of tennis. Other commentators included Fred Perry, Jack Kramer, Peter West, John Barrett, Mark Cox, Bill Threlfall, David Lloyd, Gerald Williams, Christine Janes, Anne Jones and Virginia Wade. The programmes were introduced for many years by Harry Carpenter, Desmond Lynam and David Vine.

| 1981 | 12.7 | Sat 4 Jul 2:00 p.m. | 3 | 1 wk |

In the men's final John McEnroe plays Bjorn Borg who has won the title for the last five years. (McEnroe won 4–6, 7–6, 7–6, 6–4.)
Television presentation: Jonathan Martin, John Philips, Jim Reside, Fred Viner and Johnnie Watherston.

| 1982 | 11.3 | Sat 3 Jul 2:00 p.m. | 3 | 1 wk |

The Ladies' Singles final is between Martina Navratilova and Chris Evert-Lloyd. (Navratilova won 6–1, 3–6, 6–2.)
Television presentation: Fred Viner and John Watherson. **Editor:** Harold Anderson.

| 1983 | 7.9 | Sun 3 Jul 2:00 p.m. | 19 | 1 wk |

The unpredictable genius John McEnroe competes again for the Men's Singles title, this time against New Zealand's Chris Lewis. (McEnroe won 6–2, 6–2, 6–2.)
Television presentation: Fred Viner and Johnnie Watherston. **Editor:** Harold Anderson.

1984	8.9	Sun 8 Jul 2:00 p.m.	6	1 wk

As expected McEnroe is through to the Men's Singles final to play fellow-American Jimmy Connors. (Again McEnroe won, this time 6–1, 6–1, 6–2.)
Television presentation: Fred Viner, Johnnie Watherston and Jim Reside. **Editor:** John Philips.

1987	8.2	Sun 5 Jul 2:00 p.m.	18	1 wk

Australian heart-throb Pat Cash Faces the icy-cool Ivan Lendl in the Men's final. (Cash won 7–6, 6–2, 7–5. He thrilled the viewing audience by climbing up the stands and throwing his arms around his father in celebration of his victory.)
Television presentation: John Rowlinson. **Editor:** John Philips.

1988	9.7	Sat 2 Jul 2:00 p.m.	11	1 wk

The Ladies' Singles final is between Germany's Steffi Graf and eight times champion Martina Navratilova. (Graf won 5–7, 6–2, 6–1.)
Television presentation: Fred Viner, Johnnie Watherston, Alastair Scott and Wendy Sheppard.

1989	11.7	Sun 9 Jul 2:00 p.m.	6	1 wk

The powerful Boris Becker faces the defending champion Stefan Edberg from Sweden in the Men's final. (Becker won 6–0, 7–6, 6–4.)
Television presentation: Johnnie Watherston, Alastair Scott and Wendy Sheppard.

1991	8.1	Sun 7 Jul 2:00 p.m.	19	1 wk

Despite all the predictions the Men's final is an all-German affair between Boris Becker and the unfancied Michael Stich. (In one of the biggest upsets in tennis history Stich won 6–4, 7–6, 6–4.)

Wind and the Lion, The — 1 wk

Presented by ITV, film

1980	13.0	Wed 11 Jun 7:50 p.m.	7	1 wk

It is Morocco, 1914. Mrs Pedecaris (Candice Bergen) and her two children are kidnapped by the rebel leader Mulay El Raisuli (Sean Connery). He demands a ransom to help his outlawed people. In the USA, Secretary of State John Hay (John Huston) urges President Theodore Roosevelt (Brian Keith) to send warships towards Morocco.
Director: John Milius.

Winds of War — 5 wks

USA presented by ITV, drama

This epic eight-part saga by Herman Wouk traced the lives of an American family during the years 1939 to 1941. Robert Mitchum starred as Commander 'Pug' Henry of the US Navy, sent to Europe to meet the wartime leaders of both sides on behalf of President Roosevelt (Ralph Bellamy). Polly Bergen played Pug's wife Rhoda who during his absence fell in love with Palmer Kirby (Peter Graves). His naval pilot son Warren was played by Ben Murphy, while his other son Byron was played by Jan Michael Vincent. Lisa Eilbacher played his daughter Madeline, a student in Washington. Pug wandered through Europe on his quest, met and fell in love with Natalie Jastrow (Ali MacGraw), with whom he was trapped by events in Poland. Also starred Anton Diffring, Jeremy Kemp, Edmund Purdom, Victoria Tennant and Topol.
Producer: Dan Curtis.

1983	14.1	Mon 3 Oct 8:00 p.m.	2	5 wks

In this final episode Rhoda writes to Pug telling him that their marriage is finished. The world, already ravaged by war, is split further apart by the Japanese air-raid on Pearl Harbor.

Winner Takes All — 133 wks

YTV, game show

This game was devised by Geoffrey Wheeler and hosted by Jimmy Tarbuck. Contestants were given six possible answers to a question with varying odds quoted for each answer. The object was to accumulate as much money as possible.
Producers included Guy Caplan (1976, 1978–79), Ian Bolt (1980–82), Don Clayton (1982–83), Terry Henebery (1984–86) and Graham Wetherell (1985–86). **Producer** (1977) and **Executive Producer** (1976, 1978–79): Lawrie Higgins.

1976	6.7	Fri 11 Jun 7:00 p.m.	11	3 wks
1977	14.5	Fri 9 Sep 7:00 p.m.	3	12 wks
1978	15.8	Fri 14 Apr 7:00 p.m.	1	12 wks
1979	15.1	Fri 16 Mar 7:30 p.m.	3	19 wks
1980	12.6	Fri 27 Jun 7:00 p.m.	5	15 wks
1981	12.1	Fri 7 Aug 7:00 p.m.	3	11 wks
1982	11.7	Fri 11 Jun 7:00 p.m.	4	13 wks
1983	13.5	Fri 30 Sep 7:00 p.m.	3	15 wks
1984	11.2	Fri 1 Jun 7:00 p.m.	4	14 wks
1985	11.4	Sun 11 Aug 7:15 p.m.	7	11 wks
1986	9.9	Sun 10 Aug 7:15 p.m.	6	8 wks

W

Jimmy Tarbuck smiles as **Winner Takes All**.

Winning Widows — 9 wks

ATV, situation comedy

Widowed sisters Martha (Peggy Mount) and Mildred (Avice Landon) lived in the same house. The series was created and written by Sid Green and Dick Hills.
Producer: Alan Tarrant.

| 1961 | 5.6 | Sat 21 Oct 9:30 p.m. | 12 | 4 wks |

A young niece arrives unexpectedly and leads Martha and Mildred into a world of beatniks and coffee bars.
Director: Dicky Leeman.

| 1962 | 6.0 | Fri 26 Oct 9:15 p.m. | 10 | 5 wks |

The traffic authorities have problems as Mildred and Martha start driving lessons.

Wish Me Luck — 6 wks

LWT, drama

This series created by Jill Hyem and Lavinia Warner centred on the secret army of men and women who went into German-occupied France as spies during the Second World War. If caught they could expect torture and certain death. The series followed two women, Liz Grainger (Kate Buffery) and Matty Firman (Suzanna Hamilton). Julian Glover played the head of the spy network in France, Colonel James Cadogan, and Jane Asher played his assistant Faith Ashley.

| 1988 | 13.2 | Sun 6 Mar 8:15 p.m. | 11 | 5 wks |

In this final episode of the first series Matty is in the hands of the Gestapo. Liz is back in France with Kit Vanston (Michael J. Jackson) and does not yet know that Matty was betrayed by Claudine de Valois (Shelagh McLeod).
Writer: Kevin Clarke. **Director:** Gordon Flemyng. **Producers:** Colin Shindler and Lavinia Warner. **Executive Producer:** Nick Elliott.

| 1989 | 13.7 | Sun 19 Feb 7:45 p.m. | 10 | 1 wk |

In episode seven of the second series, Vivien (Lynn Farleigh) and her daughter are in German hands. The agents of Area 7 must decide between their own freedom and the lives of Vivien and her daughter.
Writer: Terry Hodgkinson. **Designers:** Brian Bagge and Rodney Cammish. **Director:** Bill Hays. **Producer:** Michael Chaplin. **Executive Producer:** Nick Elliott.

Wish Upon A Star — 1 wk

AR, entertainment

| 1965 | 5.7 | Wed 17 Mar 9:40 p.m. | 15 | 1 wk |

Part of the prize for the winner of ITV's SEARCH FOR A STAR 1964, Judi Johnson, is this show built around her. Support comes from Madeline Bell, Rupert Davies, Keith Finlayson, Keith Fordyce, Gerry and the Pacemakers, Vince Hill, the Mike Sammes singers, and the Lennie Mayne dancers.
Director: Joan Kemp-Welch. **Executive Producer:** Elkan Allan.

Wish You Were Here — 126 wks

Thames, documentary

Television presenters served as holiday guides around the world.
Producer: Christopher Palmer.

| 1982 | 15.5 | Mon 8 Feb 7:00 p.m. | 4 | 7 wks |

Judith Chalmers, Chris Kelly and Ed Stewart are in Germany, the Scottish Highlands and Orlando respectively.

| 1983 | 14.8 | Mon 28 Feb 7:00 p.m. | 4 | 13 wks |

Judith Chalmers and Chris Kelly report from Singapore and Northumberland respectively.

| 1984 | 14.7 | Mon 20 Feb 7:00 p.m. | 3 | 11 wks |

Judith Chalmers is in Egypt and Chris Kelly is in the Yorkshire Dales.

| 1985 | 19.0 | Wed 2 Jan 7:00 p.m. | 1 | 13 wks |

The New Year holiday programme begins with Judith Chalmers in St Lucia and Chris Kelly in the Canary Islands. Guest reporters Mr and Mrs Ted Moult take a coach tour of the Scottish Highlands.

| 1986 | 14.3 | Mon 17 Feb 7:00 p.m. | 6 | 11 wks |

Judith Chalmers introduces from the studio with Peter Marshall in Menorca and Anneka Rice travelling Europe by train.

| 1987 | 14.8 | Mon 12 Jan 7:00 p.m. | 4 | 14 wks |

Judith Chalmers, Chris Kelly and Anneka Rice report from Bermuda, Orlando and Malta respectively.

| 1988 | 14.6 | Mon 18 Jan 7:00 p.m. | 5 | 12 wks |

John Carter is studio bound while Judith Chalmers is in Salzburg and Anneka Rice samples Caribbean cruises.

| 1989 | 13.6 | Mon 13 Feb 7:00 p.m. | 6 | 15 wks |

John Carter and Judith Chalmers report from Acapulco while Anne Davies assesses the accessibility of Paris for disabled travellers.

| 1990 | 15.9 | Mon 22 Jan 7:00 p.m. | 7 | 15 wks |

Judith Chalmers visits battlefields in Holland and John Carter goes to Amalfi.

1991	14.3	Mon 7 Jan 7:00 p.m.	8	15 wks

Judith Chalmers launches a new international award scheme for 'green' tourist destinations.

Witches – New Fashion, Old Religion   1 wk

Thames, documentary

1972	6.8	Thu 6 Jan 9:15 p.m.	12	1 wk

A presentation of the facts surrounding the modern revival of witchcraft with meetings in back rooms, healers, summoners of fairies and naked dancers. John Stapleton narrates.
Camera: Frank Hodge. **Director:** Maurice Hatton. **Executive Producer:** Jeremy Isaacs.

With Hilarious Consequences   1 wk

Thames, comedy

1988	12.1	Tue 27 Dec 6:00 p.m.	16	1 wk

Denis Norden selects clips from twenty-one years of Thames' situation comedies.
Director: David Clark. **Producer:** Malcolm Morris.

Within These Walls   25 wks

LWT, drama

Set in Stone Park prison for women, this series originally starred Googie Withers as Governor Faye Boswell. Successive governors were played by Katharine Blake and Sarah Lawson.

1974	8.4	Fri 8 Mar 9:00 p.m.	4	13 wks

'Guessing Game' by P. J. Hammond.
The relationship between young inmate Anne French (Angharad Rees) and her cellmate Rowena Patterson (Rosalind Ayres) poses problems for Faye.
Designer: Bryan Bagge. **Director:** Bill Bain. **Producer:** Jack Williams. **Executive Producer:** Rex Firkin.

1975	7.7	Fri 11 Apr 9:00 p.m.	6	12 wks

'For Life' by David Butler.
Officers Spencer and Berryman (Elaine Wells and Diana Rayworth) have problems with a mentally disturbed patient. Faye realizes the value of stepping outside the walls after a shift and returning to normal life.
Designer: Bryan Bagge. **Director:** Philip Casson. **Producer:** Jack Williams. **Executive Producer:** Rex Firkin.

Witness   1 wk

Presented by BBC, film

1988	9.6	Tue 6 Sep 9:30 p.m.	19	1 wk

Harrison Ford stars as Philadelphia policeman John Book, assigned to protect the reclusive Rachel Lapp (Kelly McGillis), whose son has witnessed a murder. All three are forced to run for their lives.
Director: Peter Weir.

Witness for the Prosecution   2 wks

Presented by BBC, film

1985	11.3	Mon 26 Aug 8:10 p.m.	16	1 wk

Barrister Sir Wilfred Robarts (Ralph Richardson) battles to save Leonard Vole (Beau Bridges) from the gallows even though all the evidence points to his being a murderer and his own wife Christine (Diana Rigg) gives evidence against him. Also starring Wendy Hiller, Deborah Kerr, David Langton, Donald Pleasence, Peter Sallis and Richard Vernon.
Director: Alan Gibson.

1987	9.5	Sun 23 Aug 7:15 p.m.	11	1 wk

Repeat showing of the above film.

Wodehouse Playhouse   1 wk

BBC, drama

This series featured the short stories of P. G. Wodehouse, adapted for television by David Climie. Each was introduced by Wodehouse. John Alderton and Pauline Collins starred in all.

1975	6.5	Wed 28 May 10:15 p.m.	19	1 wk

'Rodney Fails to Qualify'
The relationship between William Bates (John Alderton) and Jill Packard (Pauline Collins) is threatened by Rodney Spelvin (Geoffrey Whitehead). He is not only a poet but, to the horror of the golf club's oldest member (William Mervyn), a non-golfer. Also starring Andrew Downie and Josephine Tewson.
Designer: Daphne Shortman. **Producer:** David Askey.

Wish You Were Here with Judith Chalmers was the only travel show to reach Number One.

Wogan — 5 wks

BBC, talk show

The former Radio 2 DJ Terry Wogan hosted his own programme. The series began on Saturday nights but moved to three times a week (Mon, Wed, Fri) in 1985.
Series Producer: Frances Whittaker.

1983	10.7	Sat 2 Apr 10:00 p.m.	17	1 wk

Guests: Eamonn Andrews and Jerry Lee Lewis.
Director: Stanley Appel. **Producer:** Marcus Plantin.

1984	10.4	Sat 7 Apr 9:50 p.m.	19	2 wks

Guests: Val Doonican, the Flying Pickets and Peter O'Toole.
Director: David Taylor. **Producer:** Marcus Plantin.

1985	12.0	Mon 9 Dec 7:00 p.m.	16	2 wks

Guests: John Cleese, Gretchen Franklin, Whitney Houston, Delia Smith.
Director: Bruce Millar. **Producer:** Jon Plowman.

Wogan's Women — 1 wk

BBC, talk show

1984	12.8	Sat 22 Dec 9:05 p.m.	14	1 wk

Terry Wogan and Felicity Kendal review some of the outstanding appearances by women in the recent series of WOGAN. Those featured include Bo Derek, Grace Jones, Sophia Loren, Beryl Reid and Raquel Welch.
Director: Kevin Bishop. **Producer:** Geoff Posner.

Wojeck — 3 wks

Canada presented by BBC, drama

John Vernon starred as Dr Steve Wojeck, a tough coroner who fought for his principles. Patricia Collins played his wife Marty.

1969	5.2	Thu 11 Sep 9:10 p.m.	13	3 wks

'You've Been Very Kind'
An emotionally disturbed woman commits suicide. Wojeck seeks answers as to why the help she required was not forthcoming to prevent the tragedy.
Writer: Lindsay Galloway. **Director:** René Bonnière.

Wolcott — 1 wk

ATV, drama

This three-part series by Patrick Carroll and Barry Wasserman was about East End policeman Winston Churchill Wolcott (George William Harris), the first black law officer in Hackney.

1981	14.0	Tue 13 Jan 9:00 p.m.	16	1 wk

Episode One
Winston moves from the uniformed branch to the CID. He is immediately faced with the problems of a dead woman, a boy on a bicycle and a pushy journalist.
Designer: Mike Porter. **Director:** Colin Bucksey. **Producer:** Jacky Stoller. **Executive Producer:** Barry Hanson.

Wolf to the Slaughter — 3 wks

TVS, drama

This serial, based on the novel by Ruth Rendell, was dramatized in four parts by Clive Exton. It starred George Baker as Detective Chief Inspector Wexford. Other stars included Donald Hewlett, Jean Heywood, Russell Hunter, Carmel McSharry and Christopher Ravenscroft.
Designer: Christine Ruscoe. **Producer:** John Davies. **Executive Producer:** Graham Benson.

1987	10.6	Sun 2 Aug 7:45 p.m.	7	3 wks

Episode One
Investigating the murder of a girl called Ann, Wexford receives an anonymous note saying 'The man who done it is small, dark and young and has a black car. Name of Geoff Smith'.

Women In Prison — 1 wk

AR, documentary

1964	5.9	Wed 12 Aug 9:40 p.m.	8	1 wk

Andrew Faulds introduces the first British documentary to be made about women prisoners. The prison population of the country is 28,000, but only 900 of these are women.
Writer: Martin Worth. **Director:** Stephen Peet.

Wonder Woman — 14 wks

USA presented by BBC, drama

Charles Moulton's comic book creation from the 1940s was transferred to television with Lynda Carter in the title role. Lyle Waggoner played her love interest Steve Trevor.

| 1980 | 16.1 | Sat 9 Feb 5:50 p.m. | 6 | 14 wks |

'Gault's Brain'
During an investigation into outbreaks of arson at a giant industrial complex, Wonder Woman (alias Diana Prince) finds she needs all her powers to foil an evil transplant plot.
Director: Gordon Hessler.

....

| Wonderful World of Disney, The | | | | 6 wks |

USA presented by BBC, film

| 1973 | 6.1 | Sat 10 Nov 5:40 p.m. | 20 | 1 wk |

'The City Fox'
Rusty the fox cub escapes down river from a pack of hounds and meets many animals on his subsequent adventures.

| 1974 | 6.7 | Fri 15 Nov 7:00 p.m. | 18 | 3 wks |

'Chandor, The Black Leopard Of Ceylon'
Dasa (Esram Jayasinghe) befriends a leopard, whom he saves from danger outside the ruined temple in which he was born.

| 1975 | 7.2 | Fri 23 May 7:15 p.m. | 11 | 1 wk |

'Carlo, The Sierra Coyote'
Driven from his den, Carlo heads for the mountains and forms a very strange friendship.

| 1979 | 13.6 | Wed 22 Aug 6:20 p.m. | 19 | 1 wk |

'Johnny Shiloh'
The story of a young drummer boy who is determined to join the Blue Raiders in the American Civil War.

....

| Wood, Walters . . . and Wise | | | | 1 wk |

BBC, comedy

| 1988 | 16.6 | Fri 5 Feb 8:30 p.m. | 4 | 1 wk |

Victoria Wood, Julie Walters and Ernie Wise unite for Comic Relief.

....

| Worker, The | | | | 22 wks |

ATV, situation comedy

Charlie Drake starred in the title role as a worker in a different trade each week. He also wrote the series with Lew Schwarz.

| 1965 | 6.9 | Sat 20 Mar 8:25 p.m. | 6 | 12 wks |

'No Automation Without Representation'
Charlie has never held a job for more than two days. Mr Whittaker (Percy Herbert), the clerk at the Labour Exchange, has found him 980 jobs over 20 years. But Charlie does not like the sound of the 981st. With Leslie Dwyer, John Glyn-Jones, Reginald Marsh and Wanda Ventham.
Director: Shaun O'Riordan. **Producer:** Alan Tarrant.

| 1969 | 6.8 | Mon 29 Dec 9:30 p.m. | 9 | 1 wk |

'Hallo Cobbler'
Mr Pugh (Henry McGee) of the Labour Exchange thought he'd seen the last of Charlie after disappearing more than three years ago. Suddenly, there he is again, asking for another job!
Director: Paul Annett. **Producer:** Shaun O'Riordan.

| 1970 | 7.7 | Mon 12 Jan 9:30 p.m. | 4 | 9 wks |

'The Siege of Kidney Street'
Police are called to a house in Kidney Street where a demolition worker is reported to have gone berserk.
Director: Paul Annett. **Producer:** Shaun O'Riordan.

....

| World at War, The | | | | 12 wks |

Thames, documentary

This series masterminded by Jeremy Isaacs had several leading producer/directors contributing programmes. The twenty-six part series, narrated by Laurence Olivier, used film gathered from all over the world, much of it never before seen. Eyewitnesses described events from Hitler's pre-war Germany to Hiroshima.

| 1973 | 6.3 | Wed 19 Dec 9:00 p.m. | 19 | 1 wk |

'The Desert 1940–1943'
The story of the struggle between the 8th Army and Rommel's Afrika Korps. The tide finally turns with a great British victory at El Alamein.
Producer: Peter Batty.

| 1974 | 7.5 | Wed 27 Feb 9:00 p.m. | 8 | 11 wks |

'Morning'
From 6 June 1944 (D-Day) to August 1944 and the victims of German oppression dare to hope again.
Producer: John Pett.

World Cup — 70 wks

BBC (1966, 1970, 1978 and 1990) and ITV (1974, 1978, 1982 and 1986), sport

| 1966 | 7.1 | Wed 20 Jul 7:00 p.m. | 1 | 11 wks |

David Coleman introduces the final match in Group 1 from Wembley. (England beat France 2-0 and gained a place in the quarter final.) Commentator: Kenneth Wolstenholme.

| 1970 | 7.2 | Sun 14 Jun 6:25 p.m. | 6 | 5 wks |

This is the quarter final match between England and West Germany from Leon in Mexico. (Bobby Charlton was substituted to keep him fresh for the semi-final with England 2–0 in front. But West Germany came from behind to win 3–2.)

| 1974 | 5.8 | Wed 26 Jun 7:00 p.m. | 13 | 4 wks |

From Gelsenkirchen in West Germany. Brian Moore commentates on the Group A match between Holland and Argentina. (Holland won 4–0.)

| 1978 | 14.3 | Wed 21 Jun 6:30 p.m. | 2 | 9 wks |

The last match in Group A is between Holland and Italy. The winners will earn a place in the final. (Holland won 2–1.)

| 1982 | 13.7 | Sun 11 Jul 6:15 p.m. | 1 | 14 wks |

The final from the Bernabeu Stadium in Madrid between Italy and West Germany. Brian Moore commentates. (Italy won 3–1 to become World Champions.)

| 1986 | 11.7 | Sun 29 Jun 6:30 p.m. | 4 | 5 wks |

The World Cup final between Argentina and West Germany is played at the Aztec Stadium in Mexico City. Brian Moore commentates, (Argentina won 3–2.)

| 1990 | 16.7 | Wed 4 Jul 6:35 p.m. | 2 | 22 wks |

John Motson commentates on the semi-final between England and West Germany in Turin. (The match ended in a 1–1 draw, but England went out after an agonizing penalty shoot-out as Stuart Pearce and Chris Waddle both missed their kicks.)

World Disco Dancing Championships — 2 wks

Thames, entertainment

Competitors from around the World assembled to writhe and gyrate for the World Championship title at the Empire Ballroom in Leicester Square, London. With the Ray McVay orchestra.
Producer: Steve Minchin.

| 1978 | 14.0 | Tue 12 Dec 7:30 p.m. | 13 | 1 wk |

Introduced by David Hamilton.

| 1980 | 14.2 | Tue 16 Dec 7:30 p.m. | 14 | 1 wk |

Introduced by Peter Gordeno.

World Figure Skating Championships, The — 2 wks

BBC, sport

| 1966 | 6.8 | Fri 25 Feb 9:25 p.m. | 10 | 1 wk |

From Davos, Switzerland, Alan Weeks introduces the men's free skating final.
Television presentation: Don Sayer and Ian Smith.

| 1967 | 6.4 | Thu 2 Mar 9:05 p.m. | 11 | 1 wk |

From the Vienna Ice Club Alan Weeks introduces the pairs competition where reigning Russian champions Oleg Protopopov and Ljudmila Belousova are expected to retain their title.
Television presentation: Ian Smith.

World in Action — 316 wks

Granada, documentary

This pioneer series of investigative reports was launched by Tim Hewat in 1963. Among its notable producers were David Plowright, Jeremy Wallington, Leslie Woodhead, Gus McDonald, Denis Mitchell, Mike Wooller, Michael Apted, John Birt, Ray Fitzwalter. Alex Valentine and Brian Lapping.

1963	5.4	Mon 23 Dec 10:05 p.m.	11	1 wk
1964	6.6	Tue 24 Nov 10:05 p.m.	11	17 wks
1965	6.0	Tue 9 Feb 10:05 p.m.	10	14 wks
1967	8.1	Mon 30 Oct 8:00 p.m.	3	21 wks
1968	8.2	Mon 5 Feb 8:00 p.m.	2	42 wks
1969	7.2	Mon 17 Feb 8:00 p.m.	5	34 wks
1970	7.4	Mon 23 Mar 8:00 p.m.	6	33 wks
1971	7.2	Mon 26 Apr 8:00 p.m.	6	32 wks
1972	7.2	Mon 2 Oct 8:00 p.m.	4	24 wks

1973	7.3	Mon 14 May 8:30 p.m.	6	18 wks
1974	7.8	Mon 11 Mar 8:30 p.m.	9	25 wks
1975	6.9	Mon 13 Oct 8:30 p.m.	9	10 wks
1976	6.9	Mon 1 Nov 8:30 p.m.	17	4 wks
1977	12.7	Mon 26 Sep 8:30 p.m.	3	14 wks
1978	16.8	Mon 20 Feb 8:30 p.m.	11	4 wks
1979	12.6	Mon 9 Apr 8:30 p.m.	11	4 wks
1980	15.0	Mon 22 Dec 8:30 p.m.	8	5 wks
1981	10.6	Mon 29 Jun 8:30 p.m.	12	4 wks
1982	12.2	Mon 29 Mar 8:30 p.m.	12	3 wks
1983	9.8	Mon 31 Oct 8:30 p.m.	11	3 wks
1984	12.9	Mon 23 Jan 8:30 p.m.	8	4 wks

World of Bob Hope, The — 1 wk

BBC, entertainment

1970	6.0	Thu 8 Oct 9:20 p.m.	16	1 wk

A record of Bob Hope's annual tour of North America with guests Jack Benny, Cary Grant, David Janssen, Arnold Palmer and Gregory Peck. **Producer:** Denis Pitts.

World of Hugh Hefner, The — 1 wk

YTV, documentary

1974	7.6	Tue 29 Jan 9:00 p.m.	7	1 wk

The story of Hugh Hefner, founder of Playboy, who borrowed $600 to start his empire and in 1974 was thought to be worth $200 million. **Director:** Tony Palmer. **Producers:** Sheridan Dufferin and Tom Richter.

World of Pam Ayres, The — 10 wks

LWT, comedy

This series starred Oxford poet and OPPORTUNITY KNOCKS winner Pam Ayres, with Henry McGee, Ken Hollow, Paul Aylett and Shambles the puppet dog, the Tony Mansell singers and the Laurie Holloway orchestra.

1977	15.0	Fri 25 Nov 7:30 p.m.	3	10 wks

Producer: Keith Beckett.

World of Television, The — 1 wk

YTV, documentary

This series of six programmes examined the television industry. It was written and produced by Peter Batty, with Nigel Pegram narrating.

1975	5.7	Wed 4 Jun 9:30 p.m.	18	1 wk

'Hollywood – The Beautiful Business'
Television series are bought and sold by the yard in the production factories of Tinseltown for distribution to more than 300 million homes around the world.

World of Whicker, The — 11 wks

YTV, documentary

Television's roving reporter Alan Whicker presented more travelogues.

1971	7.5	Thu 11 Feb 9:30 p.m.	5	11 wks

'Papa Doc – The Black Sheep'
One of Whicker's more dangerous assignments takes him to Haiti. He reports on the island's sinister leader Papa Doc (Dr François Duvalier) and the murderous gang known as the Ton-Ton Macoute. **Camera:** Frank Pocklington. **Sound:** Terry Ricketts. **Producer:** Michael Blakstad. **Executive Producer:** Tony Essex.

World on a Knife Edge, The — 1 wk

ATV, documentary

1965	4.7	Wed 11 Aug 9:40 p.m.	18	1 wk

A look at the future of Hong Kong and its three and three-quarter million inhabitants. Robert Beatty narrates. **Writer** and **Producer:** Gordon Bradley. **Executive Producer:** Viscount Furness.

World Superstars — 2 wks

BBC with Transworld International and Candid Productions, sport

International stars of sport competed in a variety of disciplines. **Television presentation:** Peter Hylton Cleaver.

1980	12.5	Mon 26 May 7:00 p.m.	7	1 wk

Ron Pickering and David Vine introduce this Spring Bank Holiday edition from the Bahamas. Britain's Brian Jacks defends his title of International Superstars' Champion.

W

1982   **12.2**   **Fri 9 Apr 8:40 p.m.**   **12**   **1 wk**

From Key Biscayne, Florida, David Vine and Ron Pickering commentate, with Brian Hooper and Alan Lerwill representing Britain.

World Tomorrow, The   12 wks

Granada, documentary

The WORLD IN ACTION team, under Tim Hewat, developed this series, which considered issues relevant to the future of the world.

1966   **6.9**   **Tue 4 Jan 10:05 p.m.**   **9**   **11 wks**

A study of world famine, with reports from London, New York, Tokyo, Rome and Paris.
Executive Producer: *Tim Hewat.*

1967   **6.1**   **Wed 8 Feb 9:40 p.m.**   **15**   **1 wk**

A special report on LSD (lysergic acid diethylamide) which is used by more than ten million Americans. Commentators Bill Grundy and Chris Kelly hear those who say it expands the mind and those who condemn its use.
Producer: *John Macdonald.* ***Executive Producer:*** *David Plowright.*

World Tonight, The   9 wks

Granada, news

The brainchild of Tim Hewat, this series had reporters in capital cities throughout the world.

1965   **6.9**   **Tue 19 Oct 10:05 p.m.**   **9**   **9 wks**

In Mexico City this week athletes from eight nations are taking part in a series of tests to determine if it is safe to hold the 1968 Olympic Games in Mexico, where the air is thin and low in oxygen. Reporters tonight are in London, New York, Mexico City, Paris, Rome and Tokyo.
Studio Director: *Eric Harrison.* ***Executive Producer:*** *Tim Hewat.*

World War III   2 wks

Presented by ITV, film

1983   **9.8**   **Mon 11 Apr 9:00 p.m.**   **16**   **2 wks**

Set in 1987–88. Starving Russians riot in Moscow as an American grain embargo bites deep. A Russian military group lands in Alaska to seize the oil pipeline. The world comes to the brink of nuclear holocaust. Starring Rock Hudson, Brian Keith and David Soul.
Director: *David Greene.*

World's Strongest Man, The   2 wks

ITV, sport

This international contest involved feats of power and strength.

1980   **15.3**   **Tue 23 Dec 7:00 p.m.**   **9**   **1 wk**

Derek Hobson introduces the event with Henry Cooper from the Country Club Playboy Resort, New Jersey. Geoff Capes represents Britain.
Producer: *George Sawford.* ***Executive Producer:*** *Brian Venner.*

1981   **14.8**   **Tue 8 Dec 7:30 p.m.**   **11**   **1 wk**

Mike Adamle introduces the programme from the Country Club Playboy Resort, New Jersey. Geoff Capes again represents Britain.
Producer: *George Sawford.* ***Executive Producer:*** *Brian Venner.*

World's Strongest Man, The   2 wks

BBC, sport

The programme moved to the BBC, keeping the same format.

1982   **10.7**   **Thu 9 Dec 8:00 p.m.**   **17**   **1 wk**

Donny MacLeod introduces from Magic Mountain, California with Geoff Capes representing Britain.
Producer: *Peter Hylton Cleaver.*

1985   **13.3**   **Mon 30 Dec 6:00 p.m.**   **9**   **1 wk**

Archie Macpherson introduces the competition from Cascais, Portugal, with Geoff Capes representing Britain.
Producer: *Simon Betts.*

Worst of It'll be Alright On The Night, The   1 wk

LWT, comedy

1980   **14.8**   **Sun 21 Sep 7:15 p.m.**   **8**   **1 wk**

Denis Norden introduces clips old and new in which things fail to go according to plan.
Producer: *Paul Smith.*

Worst Witch, The   1 wk

Central, drama

1986   **11.3**   **Sat 1 Nov 5:15 p.m.**   **17**   **1 wk**

A comedy fantasy for Halloween by Jill Murphy and Pleshette Willis. Mildred Hubble (Fairuza Balk) is struggling in her first term at the

International Academy for Witches run by Miss Cackle (Charlotte Rae). She is terrified of her form mistress Miss Hardbroom (Diana Rigg) and tormented by the nasty Ethel (Anna Kipling). Miss Cackle's evil twin sister tries to turn staff and pupils into toads. Tim Curry portrays the Grand Wizard and Sabina Franklyn plays Miss Spellbinder.
Designer: Giovanni Guarino. **Director:** Robert Young. **Producer:** Colin Shindler. **Executive Producers:** Hilary Heath and Lewis Rudd.

....

Wrecking Crew, The | 1 wk

Presented by ITV, film

| 1974 | 5.5 | Mon 27 May 8:00 p.m. | 16 | 1 wk |

Bank Holiday presentation starring Dean Martin as Matt Helm on the trail of one million dollars worth of bullion hijacked in Denmark. Also starring Nancy Kwan, Elke Sommer and Sharon Tate.
Director: Phil Karlson.

....

Wrestlers, The | 1 wk

Granada, documentary

| 1967 | 6.2 | Tue 5 Sep 8:45 p.m. | 7 | 1 wk |

This film goes behind the scenes to discover the true characters of the top wrestlers once they climb out of the ring. Featuring Roy 'Bull' Davies, Johnny Eagles, Vic Faulkner, Abe Ginzberg and Les Kellett.
Camera: David Wood. **Director:** Michael Elster. **Executive Producer:** Denis Mitchell.

....

Wrestling | 31 wks

ATV (1962, 1964–65, 1967–68) and AR (1963), sport

Television built up a large following for professional wrestlers in the 1960s. Canadian Kent Walton commentated and became the voice of wrestling.

| 1962 | 5.1 | Sat 17 Nov 4:05 p.m. | 18 | 3 wks |

From Lime Grove Baths, London. Ernie Riley against Eric Leiderman, Arthur Ricardo against Steve Bell and Alan Dennison against John Foley.
Television presentation: Stephen Wade.

| 1963 | 5.6 | Wed 22 May 8:00 p.m. | 12 | 2 wks |

From the Royal Albert Hall, in the presence of HRH The Duke of Edinburgh, Peter Cockburn introduces John Da Silva (New Zealand) versus Tibor Szakacs (Hungary) and Mick McManus (England) against Lindy Caulder (West Indies). The proceeds of the evening are going to the Duke's Awards Scheme.
Television presentation: Grahame Turner.

| 1964 | 5.6 | Wed 30 Dec 10:25 p.m. | 12 | 9 wks |

From the Fairfield Hall, Croydon. Featuring Seamus Donlevy versus Rana Singh and Johnny Yearsley versus Tibor Szakacs.
Television presentation: Stephen Wade.

| 1965 | 7.3 | Wed 13 Jan 9:40 p.m. | 9 | 15 wks |

From Wryton Stadium, Bolton. Featuring Roy 'Bull' Davies versus Billy Howes and Johnny Eagles versus Ken Cadman.
Television presentation: David Southwood.

| 1967 | 4.4 | Wed 9 Aug 10:30 p.m. | 20 | 1 wk |

From the Floral Hall, Southport. Featuring Les Kellett versus Honey Boy Zimba and Johnny Eagles versus Colin Joynson.
Television presentation: David Southwood.

| 1968 | 6.4 | Thu 8 Jul 9:00 p.m. | 4 | 1 wk |

A gala night from the Royal Albert Hall in the presence of HRH The Duke of Edinburgh in aid of the St John's Ambulance Brigade. The bouts include Mick McManus against Gil Cesca and Jackie Pallo against Jean Corne.
Television presentation: Jim Pople.

....

Wrong Arm of the Law, The

Presented by BBC, film

| 1968 | 6.5 | Fri 27 Dec 6:30 p.m. | 8 | 1 wk |

Peter Sellers stars in the story of a gang of phoney policemen who hijack a gang of crooks and make off with their spoils. Also starring Bernard Cribbins, Ed Devereaux, Vanda Godsell, Lionel Jeffries, Davy Kaye, Dermot Kelly, Bill Kerr, John Le Mesurier, Arthur Mullard, Nanette Newman and Graham Stark.
Writers: Ray Galton, Alan Simpson and John Antrobus. **Director:** Cliff Owen.

X Y Z

XYY Man, The   4 wks

Granada, drama

This series starred Stephen Yardley as Spider Scott, a former cat burglar trying to go straight but hampered by the XYY chromosome in his genetic make-up. Vivienne McKee and Don Henderson also starred as Maggie Parsons and Detective Sergeant Bulman, respectively.

| 1977 | 9.8 | Mon 8 Aug 9:00 p.m. | 12 | 4 wks |

'Whisper Who Dares' by Murray Smith.
Spider confronts a multiple murderer. One or both of them could die.
Designer: Jack Robinson. **Director:** Carol Wilkes. **Producer:** Richard Everitt.

Yanks   2 wks

Presented by ITV, film

| 1984 | 13.8 | Sun 19 Feb 7:45 p.m. | 6 | 1 wk |

A division of the American Army is based in a Lancashire town during the Second World War. Some of the GIs find romance. Richard Gere and Vanessa Redgrave star with William Devane, Lisa Eichhorn, Joan Hickson and Rachel Roberts.
Director: John Schlesinger.

| 1985 | 15.5 | Tue 31 Dec 9:00 p.m. | 5 | 1 wk |

Repeat showing of the above film.

Yanks Go Home   8 wks

Granada, drama

This series was set on a US Air Force base in Lancashire in 1942. The cast included Norman Bird, Bruce Boa, Stuart Damon, Meg Johnson, Alan MacNaughton, Lionel Murton and David Ross.

| 1976 | 7.5 | Mon 22 Nov 8:00 p.m. | 14 | 3 wks |

'**Somewhere in England**' by Michael Carter.
The first wave of American troops arrives at the airfield.
Producer: Eric Prytherch.

| 1977 | 13.2 | Mon 19 Sep 8:30 p.m. | 12 | 5 wks |

'**The First of the GI Brides**' by H. V. Kershaw.
Corporal Pasquale (Freddie Earlle) begins a desperate search for the relevant regulations when Private Tutt (Jay Benedict) decides to marry a local girl.
Director: Roger Cheveley. **Producer:** Eric Prytherch.

Yarwood In Town   2 wks

Thames, entertainment

| 1982 | 9.4 | Wed 8 Sep 8:00 p.m. | 13 | 1 wk |

Mike Yarwood's first special for ITV features guests Gilbert O'Sullivan and Elaine Paige, with the Brian Rogers dancers and the Alan Braden orchestra.
Writers: Barry Cryer, Eric Davidson, and David Renwick. **Producer:** Keith Beckett.

| 1983 | 9.8 | Wed 17 Aug 8:00 p.m. | 5 | 1 wk |

A repeat of the 1982 programme.

Yeah, Yeah, Yeah (New York Meets the Beatles)   1 wk

Granada, documentary

| 1964 | 7.2 | Wed 12 Feb 10:25 p.m. | 10 | 1 wk |

The Beatles visit New York City. Scenes of pandemonium and mass hysteria meet them at the airport.
Producer: Dick Fontaine.

Year of the Wildebeest, The — 1 wk

Anglia, documentary

| 1974 | 6.4 | Tue 15 Oct 9:00 p.m. | 20 | 1 wk |

Film by Alan and Joan Root, who spent three years filming the annual migration of half a million wildebeest on the Serengeti plains.

Yellow Cab — 1 wk

BBC, documentary

| 1978 | 11.5 | Tue 13 Jun 9:25 p.m. | 13 | 1 wk |

Two New York plain clothes detectives cruise Harlem's 28th Precinct in a yellow cab. They are Frank Grimes and Tom McGoldrick. Their shift is six at night until two in the morning.
Producer: Christopher Jeans.

Yellowthread Street — 1 wk

YTV, drama

This series was set in Hong Kong, where the police battled furiously with the thugs and extortionists who ruled the streets with fear and terror. The principal law officers were Vale (Ray Lonnen), Brady (Mark McGann), Kelly (Catherine Neilson), Eden (Bruce Payne), Pak (Tzi Ma), Marenta (Robert Taylor) and Jackie (Doreen Chan).

| 1990 | 12.1 | Sat 13 Jan 9:25 p.m. | 20 | 1 wk |

'Power Play' by David Wilks.
Eden throws away the rule book when an extortionist tries to ply his trade with the police. Adapted from the novel by William Marshall.
Director: Ian Stuttard. **Producer:** Ranald Graham.

Yes Minister — 3 wks

BBC, situation comedy

This series by Anthony Jay and Jonathan Lynn made the most of the foolishness of certain aspects of parliamentary practice. Paul Eddington starred as Jim Hacker MP and Nigel Hawthorne played senior civil servant Sir Humphrey Appleby. Derek Fowlds portrayed his personal private secretary Bernard Woolley.

| 1980 | 12.2 | Thu 11 Sep 8:30 p.m. | 14 | 2 wks |

'The Official Visit'
Hacker turns his responsibilities over the official visit of the President of Buranda (Thomas Baptiste) to party political advantage. (First shown on BBC2.)
Producer: Sydney Lotterby.

| 1985 | 12.9 | Mon 30 Dec 9:10 p.m. | 13 | 1 wk |

'Party Games'
The Christmas festivities are dampened by rumours of a Cabinet reshuffle. (First shown on BBC2.)
Producer: Peter Whitmore.

You Bet — 27 wks

LWT, game show

Celebrities sponsored skilled people to perform a task in a set time. If the effort failed, the celebrity suffered a forfeit. The audience bet on the outcome for the benefit of charity. Bruce Forsyth was the original host, with Matthew Kelly his successor in 1991. The format came from Holland.
Director (1990–91): John Gorman. **Producer** (1990–91): Linda Beadle. **Executive Producer** (1988–90): Marcus Plantin.

| 1988 | 13.8 | Sat 20 Feb 7:05 p.m. | 8 | 6 wks |

Guests: Dickie Davies, Richard Digance and Kate Robbins.
Director: Noel D. Greene. **Producer:** Richard Hearsey.

| 1989 | 11.5 | Sat 1 Apr 6:45 p.m. | 12 | 2 wks |

Guests: Bruno Brooks, Geoff Capes, Helen Shapiro and Ellis Ward.
Producer: Alasdair Macmillan.

| 1990 | 12.8 | Sat 3 Mar 7:10 p.m. | 8 | 8 wks |

Guests: Fern Britton, Sylvester McCoy, Gary Stretch and Ellis Ward.

| 1991 | 12.3 | Sat 16 Feb 6:40 p.m. | 9 | 11 wks |

Guests: Brian Glover, Vicki Michele and Nick Skelton.
Director: Bob Wild.

You Can't Sleep Here — 1 wk

Presented by BBC, film

| 1967 | 6.1 | Sun 8 Jan 7:25 p.m. | 15 | 1 wk |

A lieutenant in the US Women's Army Corps encounters red tape when she is recalled to the USA after marrying a French Army Officer. Starring Cary Grant and Ann Sheridan.
Director: Howard Hawks.

You Can't Win   7 wks

Granada, drama

In this seven-part series by Roy Madron adapted William Cooper's stories Scenes From Provincial Life and Scenes From Married Life, set between 1939 and 1949. Ian McShane starred as Joe Lunn, a science teacher working on a novel. Patricia Garwood played his wife Myrtle.

1966	5.7	**Fri 8 Jul 9:40 p.m.**	9	**7 wks**

'Who's For America?'
Joe's friends Robert and Tom (John Humphry and Peter Birrel) are planning to emigrate to America. Joe is reluctant to join them because of Myrtle.
Director: Howard Baker. **Producer:** Margaret Morris.

You Must Be the Husband   2 wks

BBC, situation comedy

This series by Colin Bostock-Smith concerned the married life of Tom and Alice (Tim Brooke-Taylor and Diane Keen). The show also starred Sheila Steafel and Garfield Morgan as their friends Miranda and Gerald.

1988	11.7	**Mon 28 Mar 8:30 p.m.**	11	**2 wks**

'A Bit Prickly in the Morning'
Alice realizes the heartwarming truth about her husband – whatever she does Tom will immediately misunderstand.
Director: Richard Boden. **Producer:** John Kilby.

You Only Live Twice   5 wks

Presented by ITV, film

1977	20.8	**Sun 20 Nov 7:45 p.m.**	1	**1 wk**

SPECTRE tries to provoke World War III by intercepting American and Russian space capsules in orbit. Starring Sean Connery as James Bond and Donald Pleasence as Blofeld. With Charles Grey, Mie Hama, Bernard Lee, Lois Maxwell, Tetsuro Tamba and Akiko Wakabayashi. **Director:** Lewis Gilbert.

1979	15.6	**Mon 16 Apr 8:00 p.m.**	5	**1 wk**
1984	10.5	**Sun 8 Jan 7:45 p.m.**	19	**1 wk**
1986	17.3	**Tue 7 Jan 8:00 p.m.**	6	**1 wk**
1989	12.2	**Sat 14 Jan 6:45 p.m.**	17	**1 wk**
1991	12.4	**Mon 26 Aug 8:00 p.m.**	8	**1 wk**

Repeat showings of the above film.

You Rang M'Lord   2 wks

BBC, situation comedy

This series by Jimmy Perry and David Croft was set in a large house in an Upstairs Downstairs milieu. The principal characters downstairs were Alf (Paul Shane), Ivy (Su Pollard), James (Jeffrey Holland), Mrs Lipton (Brenda Cowlind), Henry (Perry Benson) and Mabel (Barbara New), with P. C. Wilson (Bill Pertwee) a regular visitor to the kitchen. Those upstairs were Lord Meldrum (Donald Hewlett), the Hon. Teddy (Michael Knowles), Cissy (Catherine Rabett), Poppy (Susie Brann), Lady Lavender (Mavis Pugh), Sir Ralph (John Horsley) and Lady Agatha (Angela Scoular).

1990	12.3	**Sun 4 Feb 7:15 p.m.**	19	**2 wks**

'Fair Shares'
Ivy wonders whether she should tell Sir Ralph she saw his wife in bed with Lord Meldrum.
Producer: David Croft.

You'll Never See Me Again   1 wk

HTV, drama

1986	12.1	**Mon 24 Mar 9:00 p.m.**	17	**1 wk**

In this short story by William Irish adapted for television by Terence Feeley Detective Superintendent Weston (Leslie Phillips) investigates the disappearance of 17-year-old Margaret Alden (Georgina Slowe). Also starring Yves Beneyton, Diana Coupland, Peter Gilmore and Wanda Ventham.
Producer: Terry Miller. **Executive Producer:** Patrick Dromgoole.

You'll Never Walk Alone   1 wk

YTV, drama

1974	6.0	**Mon 9 Sep 8:00 p.m.**	9	**1 wk**

In this single comedy Maurice and Marjorie (Brian Glover and Maureen Lipman) and their friend Trevor (Gordon Rollings) are fanatical Leeds United supporters travelling by train to the Cup Final. They meet three fellow citizens of Leeds (Norman Chappell, Peter Jones and Paul McDowell) who are not fans and are not even going to the match. They set about converting them.
Writers: Ray Galton and Alan Simpson. **Producer:** Vernon Lawrence.

Young Adults, The   1 wk

BBC, documentary

1965	4.7	Tue 20 Jul 9:25 p.m.	19	1 wk

Michael Schofield, author of a report published this week entitled 'The Sexual Behaviour of Young People', examines the sexual mores of teenagers.
Director: Patrick Dowling. **Producer:** Lorna Pegram.

Young At Heart — 11 wks

ATV, situation comedy

This series by Vince Powell starred John Mills as Albert Collyer who faced the problem of retirement in Stoke-on-Trent with his wife Ethel (Megs Jenkins).
Producer: Stuart Allen.

1980	14.4	Mon 14 Apr 8:00 p.m.	6	5 wks

'Pastures Green and New'
Albert worked in the local pottery for fifty years. Now he is home all day he is getting under Ethel's feet.

1981	12.0	Thu 25 Jun 8:00 p.m.	10	4 wks

'Love Is'
Norman (David Neilson) is on the receiving end of Albert's advice on women.

1982	10.4	Fri 8 Oct 8:30 p.m.	17	2 wks

'Wish You Were Here'
Albert and Ethel and a few pesetas fly off to Majorca.

Young Offenders, The — 1 wk

ATV, documentary

1962	4.4	Wed 2 May 9:45 p.m.	14	1 wk

This programme examines why twenty-five per cent of the country's crime is committed by boys and girls between the ages of twelve and fifteen. Antony Brown narrates.
Producer: Philip Barker.

Younger Generation, The — 6 wks

Granada, drama

This was television's first repertory company and was the brainchild of Peter Wildeblood. The team of young writers included Tim Aspinall, Maureen Duffy, Patrick Garland, Robert Holles and Adrian Mitchell. Among the actors were Johnny Briggs, Judy Cornwell, Ronald Lacey, Reginald Marsh, Mary Miller and John Thaw.

1961	5.2	Fri 11 Aug 9:35 p.m.	4	6 wks

'Josie' by Maureen Duffy.
Josie (Karal Gardner) is envious of her friend Rita (Judy Cornwell) because she has no family ties. But the more Josie struggles to break away from her own family, the more she finds she needs them.
Designer: Terry Pritchard. **Director:** Claude Watham. **Producer:** Peter Wildeblood.

Your Life In Their Hands — 2 wks

BBC, documentary

This long-running series about practical medicine and British hospitals showed actual surgical operations and treatments.

1963	5.8	Wed 20 Mar 9:45 p.m.	17	2 wks

'Caesarean Section'
The programme explains why normal childbirth is not always possible and shows two babies being delivered by Caesarean section.
Producer: Peter Bruce. **Executive Producer:** Humphrey Fisher.

You're Never Too Old — 1 wk

ATV, entertainment

1977	6.8	Wed 1 Jun 8:00 p.m.	6	1 wks

With the benefit of make-up the stars are seen as they might be in their dotage. Starring the Bachelors, Frank Carson, Hope and Keen and Lena Zavaroni with the Norman Maen dancers.
Writer: Bryan Blackburn. **Producer:** Colin Clews.

Television's Number Ones end not with a bang but with a Bond – **You Only Live Twice**.

You're On Your Own — 1 wk

BBC, drama

This series created by N. J. Crisp and Gerard Glaister starred Denis Quilley as Ryder, a one-time cop who left the force for uncertain reasons. Alone with his personal and ethical problems he worked to make a lot of money fast. June Ritchie co-starred as his girlfriend Kathy.

1975 | 7.4 | Wed 5 Mar 8:10 p.m. | 11 | 1 wk

'Value for Money'
Ryder has resigned and is on his own with burning ambitions to beat the police at their own game. Also starring Gerald Case, Diane Keen and Shane Rimmer.
Designer: Ken Sharp. **Director:** Simon Langton. **Producer:** Peter Cregeen.

You're Only Young Twice — 6 wks

ATV, situation comedy

This series was created and written by Jack Trevor Story and set in Twilight Lodge, an old people's home where the residents were very much alive.

1971 | 5.6 | Mon 9 Aug 8:25 p.m. | 10 | 6 wks

'Collapse of Stout Party'
The residents have secret plans to take Matron (Adrienne Corri) and the staff on holiday. The scheme goes sadly wrong.
Director: David Askey. **Producer:** Shaun O'Riordan.

You're Only Young Twice — 17 wks

YTV, situation comedy

This series by Pam Valentine and Michael Ashton was set in Paradise Lodge, a home for elderly ladies. It starred Peggy Mount as Flora Petty, Pat Coombs as Cissie Lupin, Lally Bowers as Dolly Love, Charmian May as Miss Milton, Diana King as Mildred Fanshawe and Peggy Ledger as Katy O'Rourke.
Producer: Graeme Muir.

1977 | 14.3 | Tue 4 Oct 7:30 p.m. | 8 | 6 wks

'Flora's Birthday'
It's Flora Petty's birthday, and she's determined to make it an occasion.

1978 | 11.9 | Mon 12 Jun 8:00 p.m. | 10 | 7 wks

'The Windfall'
Cissie returns from a funeral in a very good mood. Flora soon discovers why.

1979 | 11.7 | Wed 4 Jul 8:00 p.m. | 8 | 4 wks

'Cissie's Last Chance'
Cissie tells Flora she is not going to church with her.

You're On Your Own — 1 wk

AR, entertainment

This occasional series featured a different performer in each show.

1965 | 5.7 | Wed 5 May 9:10 p.m. | 14 | 1 wk

Starring Tsai Chin, who became a star on the London stage in The World of Suzie Wong.
Musical Director: Harry Robinson. **Producer:** Peter Croft.

You've Been Framed — 12 wks

Granada, comedy

Jeremy Beadle presented amusing home videos sent in by viewers.

1990 | 12.0 | Sat 14 Apr 6:10 p.m. | 11 | 3 wks

Director: Robert Khodadad. **Producer:** Jane Macnaught.

1991 | 17.8 | Sun 10 Feb 8:10 p.m. | 6 | 9 wks

Director: Wendy J. Dyer. **Producer:** Kieran Roberts.

You've Gotta Have Heart — 1 wk

YTV, documentary

1986 | 7.9 | Tue 24 Jun 8:00 p.m. | 16 | 1 wk

Dr Miriam Stoppard prescribes doses of music and comedy to help explain the nature and treatment of heart disease. Entertainers include Keith Barron, James Bolam, Instant Sunshine, David Kernan and Andrew Sachs.
Producer: Duncan Dallas.

Yus M'Dear — 5 wks

LWT, situation comedy

This spin-off series by Ronald Wolfe and Ronald Chesney, transported Wally and Lilly Briggs (Arthur Mullard and Queenie Watts) from their caravan site in ROMANY JONES to the comfort of a house.

| 1976 | 7.3 | Sat 10 Jan 6:30 p.m. | 13 | 5 wks |

'Brother Benny'
Wally is earning good money working on a building site. His brother Benny (Mike Reid) tries to get his hands on it before Lilly can get hers on it.
Producer: Stuart Allen.

....

| Z Cars | | | | 109 wks |

BBC, drama

This series devised by Troy Kennedy Martin and Elwyn Jones was set in Newtown, a fictitious area of Merseyside. Between 1960 and 1978, 667 episodes were transmitted. The distinguished list of writers included Robert Barr, John Hopkins, Troy Kennedy Martin, Alan Plater and Allan Prior. The characters became household names including Inspector Barlow (Stratford Johns), Detective Sergeant Watt (Frank Windsor), Detective Inspector Dunn (Dudley Foster), P. C. Jock Weir (Joseph Brady), Bert Lynch (James Ellis), Bob Steele (Jeremy Kemp), PC Sweet (Terence Edmond), 'Fancy' Smith (Brian Blessed) and Dave Graham (Colin Welland).

Only one Z car remained for the 1967 series, that of Jock Weir. The police had new crime-fighting vehicles, Panda cars. Bert Lynch was elevated to Sergeant and two new CID members joined, Detective Inspector Sam Hudson (John Barrie) and Detective Sergeant Tom Stone (John Slater).

| 1962 | 6.3 | Tue 27 Mar 8:25 p.m. | 5 | 29 wks |

'Sudden Death' by Troy Kennedy Martin.
Lynch and Steele are first on the scene as Barlow organizes a murder hunt.
Director: James Ormerod. **Producer:** David E. Rose.

| 1963 | 6.8 | Wed 18 Nov 9:50 p.m. | 6 | 28 wks |

'Running Milligan' by Keith Dewhurst.
Freddy Milligan is serving a prison sentence for robbery with violence. With six weeks of his sentence to run he is given compassionate parole to attend his wife's funeral. He fails to report back and the Newtown police have the job of bringing him in.
Director: Robin Midgley. **Producer:** David E. Rose.

| 1964 | 6.6 | Wed 13 May 9:40 p.m. | 5 | 7 wks |

'Centre of Disturbance' by John Hopkins.
A brutal mid-afternoon shooting in the middle of a shopping area leaves a store full of people dumbfounded and the Newtown police force shaking its head in disbelief.
Director: Terence Dudley. **Producer:** David E. Rose.

| 1965 | 6.6 | Wed 19 May 9:30 p.m. | 4 | 1 wk |

'Checkmate' by Robert Barr.
Unwelcome visitors arrive in Newtown and get special treatment from the police.
Director: Peter Cregeen. **Producer:** David E. Rose.

| 1967 | 8.2 | Mon 6 Mar 7:05 p.m. | 2 | 15 wks |

'I Don't Want Evidence' by Harry Green.
A fire has killed an entire family and it wasn't started accidentally.
Director: Douglas Camfield. **Producer:** Colin Morris.

| 1968 | 6.3 | Mon 8 Jan 7:05 p.m. | 16 | 7 wks |

'You Can't Win 'Em All' by David Ellis.
Det. Insp. Todd (Joss Ackland) wants answers – and quickly.
Director: Christopher Barry. **Producer:** Ronald Travers.

| 1969 | 6.1 | Tue 11 Mar 7:00 p.m. | 13 | 7 wks |

'Special Duty' by Rex Edwards.
Part Two of a two-part story. A police officer is on special duty as a decoy, but is more like a sitting duck.
Director: Hugh David. **Producer:** Richard Benyon.

| 1970 | 7.1 | Tue 17 Nov 7:05 p.m. | 14 | 6 wks |

'A Very High Rocket' by Rex Edwards.
Part Two of a two-part story involving the threat of explosives.
Director: Noel Lidiard White. **Producer:** Ron Craddock.

| 1971 | 6.7 | Tue 5 Jan 7:05 p.m. | 15 | 7 wks |

'Prevention' by Tony Holland.
Part Two of a two-part story. Detective Sergeant Bickford (Barry Jackson) infiltrates a gang of villains and gets a job – as a murderer.
Director: Tina Wakerell. **Producer:** Ron Craddock.

| 1973 | 7.0 | Thu 1 Mar 7:15 p.m. | 2 | 1 wk |

'Operation Watchdog' by Len Rush.
The force is facing an outbreak of vandalism.
Director: Joan Craft. **Producer:** Ron Craddock.

| 1978 | 12.5 | Wed 6 Sep 8:15 p.m. | 20 | 1 wk |

'Prey' by P. J. Hammond.
A woman who cried wolf to the police once too often is dead.
Director: Alan Gibson. **Producer:** Ron Craddock.

....

| Zero One | | | | 11 wks |

BBC in association with MGM TV, drama

Zero One was the call sign of International Air Security, a firm of aviation investigators. Nigel Patrick starred as airline detective Alan Garnett.

1962 **6.6** **Wed 31 Oct 9:25 p.m.** **6** **6 wks**

'Donovan's Disaster' by Lewis Davidson.
A faint SOS comes over the radio from an emergency landing field in a remote part of Ireland. The field is officially non-operative because of a dispute between its manager and local villagers led by Captain Donovan (Patrick McAlinney).
Director: Pennington Richards. **Producer:** Lawrence P. Bachmann.

1963 **5.7** **Wed 20 Feb 9:25 p.m.** **12** **5 wks**

'Discord' by John Briley.
A famous pianist from behind the Iron Curtain seeks political asylum at London Airport. Is he genuine or is he a spy? With Harry H. Corbett and Willoughby Goddard.
Director: Peter Graham Scott. **Producer:** Lawrence P. Bachmann.

Zodiac **2 wks**

Thames, drama

This light-hearted thriller series starred Anouska Hempel as Esther Jones, an astrologer who helped solve crimes using the stars. Anton Rodgers played David Gradley, a sceptical policeman.

1974 **7.5** **Mon 25 Feb 9:00 p.m.** **9** **2 wks**

'Death of a Crab' by Roger Marshall.
If Harry Parker (Peter Childs) had read his Sunday horoscope, his whole future might have been different.
Designer: Bill Palmer. **Director:** Raymond Menmuir. **Producer:** Jacqueline Davis. **Executive Producer:** Kim Mills.

Zoo Gang, The **4 wks**

ATV, drama

The Zoo Gang was the name of a French Resistance group whose members were known by animal code names. Thirty years on, 'Elephant' Tommy Devon (John Mills) recognized a top Nazi officer in the South of France. He contacted the others and the Zoo Gang was back in business. Members included Leopard, Manouche Roget (Lili Palmer), Fox, Stephen Halliday (Brian Keith) and Tiger, Alec Marlow (Barry Morse).

1974 **7.4** **Fri 12 Apr 7:30 p.m.** **8** **4 wks**

'Mindless Murder' by Howard Dinsdale.
The motiveless murders of three girls on the Riviera baffle the police. The Zoo Gang expose a widespread extortion racket.
Director: John Hough. **Producer:** Peter Hirschman.

THE NUMBER ONES

The following chart is a list of all the programmes that have reached Number One since the first regular weekly chart (7 March 1960). The dates shown are the 'week commencing' dates.

An '=' indicates that two shows achieved the same leading figure that week. When runs at number one are accumulated by soaps that have several broadcasts per week, the actual day of transmission sometimes varies (for example, if *Coronation Street* is number one for a Wednesday programme one week and a Monday show the next, this list will merely show *Coronation Street* as being Number One for two consecutive weeks). The eagle-eyed reader will note that on a couple of occasions the spread between weeks is not seven days. This is because on these occasions the chart compilers changed the day of the week they used for their 'week commencing' date.

1960

Mar 7	The Larkins (ATV)		2 wks
21	Wagon Train (ITV)		2 wks
Apr 4	The Budget (all channels)		1 wk
11	Wagon Train (ITV)		1 wk
18	Armchair Theatre (ABC)		1 wk
25	Wagon Train (ITV)		3 wks
May 16	The Royal Variety Performance (ATV)		1 wk
23	Wagon Train (ITV)		2 wks
Jun 6	Sunday Night at the London Palladium (ATV)		2 wks
20	No Hiding Place (AR)		2 wks
Jul 4	Rawhide (ITV)		8 wks
Aug 28	No Hiding Place (AR)		1 wk
Sep 4	Rawhide (ITV)		1 wk
11	No Hiding Place (AR)		2 wks
25	The Army Game (Granada)		1 wk

Oct 2	No Hiding Place (AR)		1 wk
9	Bootsie and Snudge (Granada)=		1 wk
	No Hiding Place (AR)		
16	No Hiding Place (AR)		1 wk
23	Take Your Pick (AR)		1 wk
30	Bootsie and Snudge (Granada)		1 wk
Nov 6	Bootsie and Snudge (Granada)=		1 wk
	Conservative Party Political Broadcast (all channels)		
13	Bootsie and Snudge (Granada)		1 wk
20	Take Your Pick (AR)		1 wk
27	Labour Party Political Broadcast (all channels)		1 wk
Dec 4	Armchair Theatre (ABC)		1 wk
11	The Army Game (Granada)=		1 wk
	Bootsie and Snudge (Granada)		
18	Knight Errant (Granada)		1 wk
25	The Arthur Haynes Show (ATV)=		1 wk
	Bootsie and Snudge (Granada)		

1961

Jan	1	The Russ Conway Show (ATV)	1 wk
	8	Emergency Ward 10 (ATV)=	1 wk
		Sunday Night at the London Palladium (ATV)	
	15	Sunday Night at the London Palladium (ATV)	1 wk
	22	The Russ Conway Show (ATV)=	1 wk
		Bootsie and Snudge (Granada)	
	29	No Hiding Place (AR)	4 wks
Feb	26	The Army Game (Granada)=	1 wk
		Bootsie and Snudge (Granada)	
Mar	5	No Hiding Place (AR)	1 wk
	12	Bootsie and Snudge (Granada)=	1 wk
		The Dickie Henderson Show (AR)	
	19	No Hiding Place (AR)	1 wk
	26	The Dickie Henderson Show (AR)	1 wk
Apr	2	No Hiding Place (AR)	1 wk
	9	Labour Party Political Broadcast (all channels)	1 wk
	16	The Budget (all channels)	1 wk
	23	Bootsie and Snudge (Granada)	1 wk
	30	No Hiding Place (AR)	2 wks
May	14	Bootsie and Snudge (Granada)	2 wks
	28	Probation Officer (ATV)	1 wk
Jun	4	No Hiding Place (AR)	1 wk
	11	Probation Officer (ATV)	1 wk
	18	No Hiding Place (AR)	1 wk
	25	Harpers West One (ATV)	2 wks
Jul	9	Labour Party Political Broadcast (all channels)	1 wk
	16	Harpers West One (ATV)	1 wk
	23	No Hiding Place (AR)	1 wk
	30	Harpers West One (ATV)=	1 wk
		No Hiding Place (AR)	
Aug	6	Top Secret (AR)	1 wk
	13	Harpers West One (ATV)	1 wk
	20	Coronation Street (Granada)	1 wk
	27	Blackpool Tower Circus (ATV)	1 wk
Sep	3	Sunday Night at the London Palladium (ATV)	1 wk
	10	Coronation Street (Granada)	1 wk
	17	Coronation Street (Granada)=	1 wk
		Take Your Pick (AR)	
	24	Coronation Street (Granada)	1 wk
Oct	1	Coronation Street (Granada)=	1 wk
		Sunday Night at the London Palladium (ATV)	
	8	Sunday Night at the London Palladium (ATV)	2 wks
	22	Coronation Street (Granada)	2 wks
Nov	5	The Royal Variety Performance (ATV)	1 wk
	12	Coronation Street (Granada)	1 wk
	19	Sunday Night at the London Palladium (ATV)	1 wk
	26	Coronation Street (Granada)=	1 wk
		Sunday Night at the London Palladium (ATV)	
Dec	3	Coronation Street (Granada)=	1 wk
		Sunday Night at the London Palladium (ATV)	
	10	Coronation Street (Granada)	3 wks

1962

Jan	1	Coronation Street (Granada)	14 wks
Apr	9	The Budget (all channels)	1 wk
	16	Coronation Street (Granada)	28 wks
Oct	29	The Royal Variety Performance (BBC)	1 wk
Nov	5	Coronation Street (Granada)	7 wks
Dec	24	Coronation Street (Granada)=	1 wk
		Take Your Pick (AR)	
	31	Coronation Street (Granada)	1 wk

1963

Jan	7	Coronation Street (Granada)	3 wks
	28	The Prime Minister (all channels)	1 wk
Feb	4	Coronation Street (Granada)	3 wks
	25	Labour Party Political Broadcast (all channels)	1 wk
Mar	4	Coronation Street (Granada)	2 wks
	18	Conservative Party Political Broadcast (all channels)	1 wk

	25	Coronation Street (Granada)	1 wk
Apr	1	The Budget (all channels)	1 wk
	8	Coronation Street (Granada)	2 wks
	22	Labour Party Political Broadcast (all channels)	1 wk
	29	Conservative Party Political Broadcast (all channels)	1 wk
May	6	Labour Party Political Broadcast (all channels)	1 wk
	13	Liberal Party Political Broadcast (all channels)	1 wk
	20	Conservative Party Political Broadcast (all channels)	1 wk
	27	Coronation Street (Granada)	3 wks
Jun	17	Conservative Party Political Broadcast (all channels)	1 wk
	24	Coronation Street (Granada)	19 wks
Nov	4	The Royal Variety Performance (ATV)	1 wk
	11	Coronation Street (Granada)	1 wk
	18	Conservative Party Political Broadcast (all channels)	1 wk
	25	Coronation Street (Granada)	6 wks

1964

Jan	6	Steptoe and Son (BBC)	3 wks
	27	Labour Party Political Broadcast (all channels)	1 wk
Feb	3	Steptoe and Son (BBC)	3 wks
	24	Labour Party Political Broadcast (all channels)	1 wk
Mar	2	Coronation Street (Granada)	2 wks
	16	Conservative Party Political Broadcast (all channels)	1 wk
	23	Coronation Street (Granada)	2 wks
Apr	6	Labour Party Political Broadcast (all channels)	1 wk
	13	The Budget (all channels)	1 wk
	20	Liberal Party Political Broadcast (all channels)	1 wk
	27	Coronation Street (Granada)	1 wk
May	4	Conservative Party Political Broadcast (all channels)	2 wks

	18	Coronation Street (Granada)	6 wks
Jun	29	Club Night (BBC)	1 wk
Jul	6	Room at the Top (ITV)	1 wk
	13	Labour Party Political Broadcast (all channels)	1 wk
	20	Conservative Party Political Broadcast (all channels)	1 wk
	27	Coronation Street (Granada)	3 wks
Aug	17	Conservative Party Political Broadcast (all channels)	1 wk
	24	Labour Party Political Broadcast (all channels)	1 wk
	31	No Hiding Place (AR)	1 wk
Sep	7	Conservative Party Political Broadcast (all channels)	1 wk
	14	Coronation Street (Granada)	16 wks

1965

Jan	4	Coronation Street (Granada)	30 wks
Aug	2	Riviera Police (AR)	2 wks
	16	Coronation Street (Granada)= Riviera Police (AR)	1 wk
	23	Coronation Street (Granada)	11 wks
Nov	8	The Royal Variety Performance (ATV)	1 wk
	15	Coronation Street (Granada)= Take Your Pick (AR)	1 wk
	22	Take Your Pick (AR)	1 wk
	29	Coronation Street (Granada)	5 wks

1966

Jan	3	Take Your Pick (AR)	3 wks
	24	Coronation Street (Granada)= Double Your Money (AR)	1 wk
	31	Coronation Street (Granada)	3 wks
Feb	21	Double Your Money (AR)	2 wks
Mar	7	Coronation Street (Granada)	1 wk
	14	Mrs Thursday (ATV)	4 wks
Apr	11	Coronation Street (Granada)	1 wk
	18	Mrs Thursday (ATV)	2 wks

May	2	Coronation Street (Granada)	1 wk
	9	No Hiding Place (AR)	2 wks
	23	Coronation Street (Granada)=	1 wk
		No Hiding Place (AR)	
	30	Coronation Street (Granada)	1 wk
Jun	6	Mrs Thursday (ATV)	1 wk
	13	The Blackpool Show (ABC)	1 wk
	20	Coronation Street (Granada)	1 wk
	27	Love Story (ATV)	1 wk
Jul	4	The Blackpool Show (ABC)	2 wks
	18	The Blackpool Show (ABC)=	1 wk
		World Cup Grandstand (BBC)	
	25	No Hiding Place (AR)=	1 wk
		World Cup Grandstand (BBC)	
Aug	1	The Informer (AR)	1 wk
	8	Coronation Street (Granada)	1 wk
	15	The Bruce Forsyth Show (ABC)	1 wk
	22	Coronation Street (Granada)	2 wks
Sep	5	Boxing (BBC)	1 wk
	12	Coronation Street (Granada)	1 wk
	19	The London Palladium Show (ATV)	2 wks
Oct	3	Coronation Street (Granada)	5 wks
Nov	7	Secombe and Friends (ATV)	1 wk
	14	Miss World (BBC)	1 wk
	21	The London Palladium Show (ATV)	1 wk
	28	A Royal Gala (ATV)	1 wk
Dec	5	Coronation Street (Granada)=	1 wk
		The London Palladium Show (ATV)	
	12	Coronation Street (Granada)	3 wks

1967

Jan	2	Take Your Pick (AR)	2 wks
	16	The London Palladium Show (ATV)	1 wk
	23	Take Your Pick (AR)	1 wk
	30	The London Palladium Show (ATV)	2 wks
Feb	13	Take Your Pick (AR)	1 wk
	20	Mrs Thursday (ATV)	3 wks
Mar	13	Take Your Pick (AR)	1 wk

	20	Mrs Thursday (ATV)	1 wk
	27	The London Palladium Show (ATV)	1 wk
Apr	3	Market in Honey Lane (ATV)	2 wks
	17	The London Palladium Show (ATV)	3 wks
May	8	Coronation Street (Granada)	3 wks
	29	The London Palladium Show (ATV)	1 wk
Jun	5	Coronation Street (Granada)	9 wks
Aug	7	Summer Playhouse (AR)	1 wk
	14	Coronation Street (Granada)	2 wks
	28	The Fugitive (ITV)	1 wk
Sep	4	Coronation Street (Granada)	3 wks
	25	The Morecambe and Wise Show (ATV)	1 wk
Oct	2	Coronation Street (Granada)	5 wks
Nov	6	The Morecambe and Wise Show (ATV)	1 wk
	13	The Royal Variety Performance (ATV)	1 wk
	20	Coronation Street (Granada)	1 wk
	27	The London Palladium Show (ATV)	1 wk
Dec	4	Coronation Street (Granada)	4 wks

1968

Jan	1	Till Death Us Do Part (BBC)	1 wk
	8	Coronation Street (Granada)	2 wks
	22	Coronation Street (Granada)=	1 wk
		Take Your Pick (AR)	
		Till Death Us Do Part (BBC)	
	29	Coronation Street (Granada)	7 wks
Mar	11	Life With Cooper (ABC)	1 wk
	18	Coronation Street (Granada)=	1 wk
		Life With Cooper (ABC)	
	25	The Grand National (BBC)	1 wk
Apr	1	The Eurovision Song Contest (BBC)	1 wk
	8	Coronation Street (Granada)	1 wk
	15	The Big Show (ATV)	1 wk
	22	The Des O'Connor Show (ATV)	2 wks
May	6	Howerd's Hour (ABC)	1 wk
	13	A Special Royal Performance (ATV)	1 wk
	20	Harlech Opening Night (Harlech)	1 wk

27	European Cup Final (BBC)	1 wk

Jun	3	International Football (BBC)	1 wk
	10	Cinema (Granada)	1 wk
	17	Life With Cooper (ABC)	1 wk
	24	Coronation Street (Granada)	1 wk

Jul	1	News at Ten (ITN)	2 wks
	15	Coronation Street (Granada)	1 wk
	22	Playhouse (Anglia)	1 wk
	29	No chart published	

Aug	5	Coronation Street (Granada)	14 wks

Nov	11	Miss World (BBC)	1 wk
	18	The Royal Variety Performance (BBC)	1 wk
	25	Coronation Street (Granada)	2 wks

Dec	9	Till Death Us Do Part (BBC)	1 wk
	16	Sherlock Holmes (BBC)	1 wk
	23	Till Death Us Do Part (BBC)	1 wk
	30	Coronation Street (Granada)	1 wk

1969

Jan	6	Coronation Street (Granada)=	1 wk
		Till Death Us Do Part (BBC)	
	13	Max (Thames)	1 wk
	20	Coronation Street (Granada)	1 wk
	27	Max (Thames)	2 wks

Feb	10	Coronation Street (Granada)=	1 wk
		Max (Thames)	
	17	The Power Game (ATV)	1 wk
	24	Coronation Street (Granada)	1 wk

Mar	3	The Power Game (ATV)	1 wk
	10	Coronation Street (Granada)	2 wks
	24	The Eurovision Song Contest (BBC)	1 wk
	31	Coronation Street (Granada)	1 wk

Apr	7	Max (Thames)	1 wk
	14	Callan (Thames)	1 wk
	21	Coronation Street (Granada)	2 wks

May	5	Football (BBC)	1 wk
	12	Coronation Street (Granada)	1 wk
	19	Fraud Squad (ATV)	2 wks

Jun	2	News at Ten (ITN)	1 wk
	9	Fraud Squad (ATV)	1 wk
	16	Royal Family (BBC)	1 wk
	23	Coronation Street (Granada)=	1 wk
		Fraud Squad (ATV)	
	30	Fraud Squad (ATV)=	1 wk
		News at Ten (ITN)	

Jul	7	Fraud Squad (ATV)	1 wk
	14	News at Ten (ITN)	1 wk
	21	Fraud Squad (ATV)	2 wks

Aug	4	News at Ten (ITN)	1 wk
	11	Fraud Squad (ATV)	1 wk
	18	Who-Dun-It (ATV)	1 wk
	25	News at Ten (ITN)	1 wk

Sep	1	Who-Dun-It (ATV)	2 wks
	15	The Best Things in Life (ATV)	1 wk
	22	The Dustbin Men (Granada)	6 wks

Nov	3	In Loving Memory (Thames)	1 wk
	10	The Royal Variety Performance (ATV)	1 wk
	17	The Benny Hill Show (Thames)	1 wk
	24	Miss World (BBC)	1 wk

Dec	1	Coronation Street (Granada)	3 wks
	22	Carry on Christmas (Thames)	1 wk
	29	This is Your Life (Thames)	1 wk

1970

Jan	5	Coronation Street (Granada)	1 wk
	12	Coronation Street (Granada)=	1 wk
		This is Your Life (Thames)	
	19	This is Your Life (Thames)	2 wks

Feb	2	Coronation Street (Granada)	1 wk
	9	This is Your Life (Thames)	1 wk
	16	Coronation Street (Granada)	2 wks

Mar	2	This is Your Life (Thames)	1 wk
	9	The Benny Hill Show (Thames)	1 wk
	16	The Eurovision Song Contest (BBC)	1 wk
	23	Coronation Street (Granada)	1 wk
	30	This is Your Life (Thames)	4 wks

Apr 27	Coronation Street (Granada)	1 wk
May 4	This is Your Life (Thames)	2 wks
18	Coronation Street (Granada)	1 wk
25	Callan (Thames)=	1 wk
	The Sunday Film (BBC)	
Jun 1	Manhunt (LWT)	1 wk
8	World Cup Grandstand (BBC)	1 wk
15	Shadows of Fear (Thames)	1 wk
22	Coronation Street (Granada)	6 wks
Aug 3	A Family at War (Granada)	1 wk
10	Whicker's Walkabout (YTV)	1 wk
17	Coronation Street (Granada)	4 wks
Sep 14	The Main Chance (YTV)=	1 wk
	Whicker's Walkabout (YTV)	
21	Special Branch (Thames)	1 wk
28	Prizewinners (The Morecambe and Wise Show) (BBC)	1 wk
Oct 5	Coronation Street (Granada)	4 wks
Nov 2	Please Sir (LWT)	1 wk
9	The Royal Variety Performance (BBC)	1 wk
16	Miss World (BBC)	1 wk
23	Please Sir (LWT)	1 wk
30	On the Buses (LWT)	1 wk
Dec 7	On the Buses (LWT)=	1 wk
	Please Sir (LWT)	
14	News at Ten (ITN)	1 wk
21	This is Your Life (Thames)	1 wk
28	Coronation Street (Granada)	1 wk

1971

Jan 4	This is Your Life (Thames)	1 wk
11	Nearest and Dearest (Granada)	1 wk
18	Coronation Street (Granada)	1 wk
25	Coronation Street (Granada)=	1 wk
	A Family at War (Granada)	
Feb 1	Coronation Street (Granada)	2 wks
15	On the Buses (LWT)	1 wk
22	Coronation Street (Granada)=	1 wk
	This is Your Life (Thames)	

Mar 1	This is Your Life (Thames)	1 wk
8	Boxing (BBC)	1 wk
15	This is Your Life (Thames)	1 wk
22	The Benny Hill Show (Thames)	1 wk
29	The Eurovision Song Contest (BBC)	1 wk
Apr 5	This is Your Life (Thames)	1 wk
12	Frankie Howerd (Thames)	1 wk
19	Coronation Street (Granada)	6 wks
May 31	The Black and White Minstrel Show (BBC)=	1 wk
	Film of the Week (BBC)	
Jun 7	Coronation Street (Granada)=	1 wk
	Opportunity Knocks (Thames)	
14	Coronation Street (Granada)	4 wks
Jul 12	Public Eye (Thames)	1 wk
19	Coronation Street (Granada)=	1 wk
	Crime of Passion (ATV)	
26	Coronation Street (Granada)	3 wks
Aug 16	Miss United Kingdom (BBC)	1 wk
23	Public Eye (Thames)	2 wks
Sep 6	For the Love of Ada (Thames)	2 wks
20	The Fenn Street Gang (LWT)=	1 wk
	For the Love of Ada (Thames)	
	The Persuaders (ATV)	
27	For the Love of Ada (Thames)	1 wk
Oct 4	The Fenn Street Gang (LWT)=	1 wk
	The Persuaders (ATV)	
11	The Persuaders (ATV)	2 wks
25	A Family at War (Granada)	1 wk
Nov 1	Coronation Street (Granada)	1 wk
8	Miss World (BBC)	1 wk
15	The Royal Variety Performance (BBC)	1 wk
22	This is Your Life (Thames)	4 wks
Dec 20	The Benny Hill Show (Thames)	1 wk
27	This is Your Life (Thames)	1 wk

1972

Jan 3	This is Your Life (Thames)	6 wks

Feb 14	On the Buses (LWT)	1 wk	
21	This is Your Life (Thames)	1 wk	
28	On the Buses (LWT)=	1 wk	
	This is Your Life (Thames)		
Mar 6	This is Your Life (Thames)	2 wks	
20	The Eurovision Song Contest (BBC)	1 wk	
27	This is Your Life (Thames)	7 wks	
May 15	Love Thy Neighbour (Thames)	2 wks	
29	Nearest and Dearest (Granada)	1 wk	
Jun 5	Crime of Passion (ATV)	2 wks	
19	Danny La Rue at the Palace (Thames)	1 wk	
26	Miss TV Times (Thames)	1 wk	
Jul 3	Man at the Top (Thames)	1 wk	
10	Crime of Passion (ATV)	5 wks	
Aug 14	Miss United Kingdom (BBC)	1 wk	
21	Man at the Top (Thames)	1 wk	
28	Max Bygraves at the Royalty (Thames)	1 wk	
Sep 4	Shut That Door! (ATV)	1 wk	
11	Till Death Us Do Part (BBC)	3 wks	
Oct 2	Love Thy Neighbour (Thames)	1 wk	
9	Love Thy Neighbour (Thames)=	1 wk	
	Till Death Us Do Part (BBC)		
16	Till Death Us Do Part (BBC)	1 wk	
23	The Benny Hill Show (Thames)	1 wk	
30	Opportunity Knocks (Thames)	2 wks	
Nov 13	This is Your Life (Thames)	6 wks	
Dec 25	Upstairs Downstairs (LWT)	1 wk	

1973

Jan 1	This is Your Life (Thames)	11 wks	
Mar 19	Love Thy Neighbour (Thames)	1 wk	
26	This is Your Life (Thames)	1 wk	
Apr 2	The Eurovision Song Contest (BBC)	1 wk	
9	This is Your Life (Thames)	3 wks	
30	Bless This House (Thames)	1 wk	
May 7	This is Your Life (Thames)	1 wk	
14	Bless This House (Thames)	1 wk	

21	And Mother Makes Three (Thames)	2 wks	
Jun 4	Special Branch (Thames)	1 wk	
11	And Mother Makes Three (Thames)	2 wks	
25	Special Branch (Thames)	1 wk	
Jul 2	Thirty Minutes' Worth (Thames)	3 wks	
23	Coronation Street (Granada)	1 wk	
30	Coronation Street (Granada)=	1 wk	
	Sam (Granada)		
Aug 6	Coronation Street (Granada)	4 wks	
Sep 3	Van der Valk (Thames)	1 wk	
10	Cannon (BBC)	1 wk	
17	Man About the House (Thames)	1 wk	
24	Van der Valk (Thames)	1 wk	
Oct 1	Coronation Street (Granada)	1 wk	
8	Van der Valk (Thames)	1 wk	
15	World Cup Football (ITV)	1 wk	
22	Opportunity Knocks (Thames)	2 wks	
Nov 5	The Generation Game (BBC)	1 wk	
12	Opportunity Knocks (Thames)	1 wk	
19	Miss World (BBC)	1 wk	
26	My Good Woman (ATV)	1 wk	
Dec 3	The Benny Hill Show (Thames)	1 wk	
10	Love Thy Neighbour (Thames)	1 wk	
17	This is Your Life (Thames)	1 wk	
24	The Benny Hill Show (Thames)	1 wk	
31	This is Your Life (Thames)	1 wk	

1974

Jan 7	This is Your Life (Thames)	1 wk	
14	The Val Doonican Show (ATV)	1 wk	
21	This is Your Life (Thames)	4 wks	
Feb 18	Love Thy Neighbour (Thames)	1 wk	
25	This is Your Life (Thames)	2 wks	
Mar 11	Love Thy Neighbour (Thames)	5 wks	
Apr 15	This is Your Life (Thames)	1 wk	
22	The Tommy Cooper Hour (Thames)	1 wk	
29	And Mother Makes Five (Thames)=	1 wk	
	This is Your Life (Thames)		

May 6	This is Your Life (Thames)	2 wks
20	Sam (Granada)	1 wk
27	Armchair Cinema (Thames)	1 wk
Jun 3	Justice (YTV)	1 wk
10	Coronation Street (Granada)	1 wk
17	Playhouse (Anglia)	1 wk
24	Coronation Street (Granada)	3 wks
Jul 15	Village Hall (Granada)	1 wk
22	Coronation Street (Granada)	1 wk
29	Spring and Autumn (Thames)	3 wks
Aug 19	Love Thy Neighbour (Thames)	1 wk
26	Spring and Autumn (Thames)	1 wk
Sep 2	Steptoe and Son (BBC)	1 wk
9	The Battle of Britain (BBC)	1 wk
16	Steptoe and Son (BBC)	1 wk
23	The Morecambe and Wise Show (BBC)	1 wk
30	Porridge (BBC)	1 wk
Oct 7	Man About the House (Thames)	1 wk
14	Bless This House (Thames)	4 wks
Nov 11	No, Honestly (LWT)=	1 wk
	This is Your Life (Thames)	
18	Miss World (BBC)	1 wk
25	Bless This House (Thames)	3 wks
Dec 16	The Generation Game (BBC)	1 wk
23	Mastermind (BBC)	1 wk
30	Love Thy Neighbour (Thames)	1 wk

1975

Jan 6	Love Thy Neighbour (Thames)	2 wks
20	This is Your Life (Thames)	2 wks
Feb 3	Love Thy Neighbour (Thames)	3 wks
24	This is Your Life (Thames)	1 wk
Mar 3	Man About the House (Thames)	1 wk
10	The Benny Hill Show (Thames)	1 wk
17	This is Your Life (Thames)	4 wks
Apr 14	Love Thy Neighbour (Thames)	1 wk
21	Edward VII (ATV)	1 wk

28	Love Thy Neighbour (Thames)	1 wk
May 5	Edward VII (ATV)	1 wk
12	Special Branch (Thames)	1 wk
19	It's a Knockout (BBC)	1 wk
26	European Cup Final (BBC)	1 wk
Jun 2	Kojak (BBC)	1 wk
9	Edward VII (ATV)	4 wks
Jul 7	Coronation Street (Granada)	2 wks
21	Down the Gate (ATV)	1 wk
28	Man About the House (Thames)	2 wks
Aug 11	The Squirrels (ATV)	1 wk
18	Man About the House (Thames)	1 wk
25	The Dick Emery Show (BBC)	1 wk
Sep 1	Man About the House (Thames)	2 wks
15	The Two Ronnies (BBC)=	1 wk
	Man About the House (Thames)	
22	Man About the House (Thames)	1 wk
29	The Two Ronnies (BBC)	1 wk
Oct 6	The Sweeney (Thames)	2 wks
20	The Two Ronnies (BBC)	1 wk
27	Dr No (ITV)	1 wk
Nov 3	The Generation Game (BBC)	1 wk
10	The Royal Variety Performance (BBC)	1 wk
17	Miss World (BBC)	1 wk
24	The Generation Game (BBC)	2 wks
Dec 8	This is Your Life (Thames)	1 wk
15	The Benny Hill Show (Thames)	1 wk
22	Porridge (BBC)	1 wk
29	Opportunity Knocks (Thames)	1 wk

1976

Jan 5	This is Your Life (Thames)	2 wks
19	The Italian Job (ITV)	1 wk
26	Sale of the Century (Anglia)	1 wk
Feb 2	This is Your Life (Thames)	2 wks
16	The Benny Hill Show (Thames)	1 wk
23	This is Your Life (Thames)	4 wks
Mar 22	The Benny Hill Show (Thames)	1 wk

	29	The Eurovision Song Contest (BBC)	1 wk
Apr	5	Man About the House (Thames)	1 wk
	12	This is Your Life (Thames)	1 wk
	19	The Benny Hill Show (Thames)	1 wk
	26	From Russia with Love (ITV)	1 wk
May	3	This is Your Life (Thames)	1 wk
	10	European Cup Final (ITV)	1 wk
	17	Crossroads (ATV)	4 wks
Jun	14	Coronation Street (Granada)	1 wk
	21	Crossroads (ATV)	1 wk
	28	The Bionic Woman (ITV)	1 wk
Jul	5	News at Ten (ITN)	1 wk
	12	The Bionic Woman (ITV)	1 wk
	19	News at Ten (ITN)	1 wk
	26	Bring on the Girls (Thames)	1 wk
Aug	2	News at Ten (ITN)	3 wks
	23	Starsky and Hutch (BBC)	1 wk
	30	Crossroads (ATV)	1 wk
Sep	6	George and Mildred (Thames)	5 wks
Oct	11	The Generation Game (BBC)	2 wks
	25	George and Mildred (Thames)	1 wk
Nov	1	Goldfinger (ITV)	1 wk
	8	The Sweeney (Thames)	1 wk
	15	Miss World (BBC)	1 wk
	22	The Generation Game (BBC)	4 wks
Dec	20	This is Your Life (Thames)	1 wk
	27	The Dame of Sark (Anglia)	1 wk

1977

Jan	3	This is Your Life (Thames)	9 wks
Mar	7	Oh No It's Selwyn Froggitt (YTV)	2 wks
	21	The Benny Hill Show (Thames)	1 wk
	28	Coronation Street (Granada)	1 wk
Apr	4	Oh No It's Selwyn Froggitt (YTV)	1 wk
	11	Bruce and More Girls (Thames)	1 wk
	18	Coronation Street (Granada)	1 wk
	25	This is Your Life Special (Thames)	1 wk

539

May	2	The Eurovision Song Contest (BBC)	1 wk
	9	Coronation Street (Granada)	2 wks
	23	Rising Damp (YTV)	1 wk
	30	Coronation Street (Granada)	1 wk
Jun	6	Silver Jubilee (BBC)	1 wk
	13	Coronation Street (Granada)	3 wks
Jul	4	Sale of the Century (Anglia)	1 wk
	11	News at Ten (ITN)	1 wk
	18	Night Out at the London Casino (Thames)	1 wk
	25	Coronation Street (Granada)	1 wk
Aug	1	Man About the House (Thames)	3 wks
	22	Night Out at the London Casino (Thames)	1 wk
	29	Man About the House (Thames)	1 wk
Sep	5	The Generation Game (BBC)	6 wks
Oct	17	Bruce's Choice (BBC)	1 wk
	24	The Generation Game (BBC)	1 wk
	31	The Benny Hill Show (Thames)	1 wk
Nov	7	The Generation Game (BBC)	1 wk
	14	You Only Live Twice (ITV)	1 wk
	21	The Generation Game (BBC)	1 wk
	28	The Silver Jubilee Royal Variety Gala (BBC)	1 wk
Dec	5	The Generation Game (BBC)	1 wk
	12	The Generation Game (BBC)= George and Mildred (Thames)	1 wk
	19	The Mike Yarwood Christmas Show (BBC)	1 wk
	26	This is Your Life (Thames)	1 wk

1978

Jan	2	Coronation Street (Granada)	2 wks
	16	This is Your Life (Thames)	4 wks
Feb	13	Miss Jones and Son (Thames)	1 wk
	20	A Sharp Intake of Breath (ATV)	1 wk
	27	This is Your Life (Thames)	1 wk
Mar	6	A Sharp Intake of Breath (ATV)	3 wks
	27	This is Your Life (Thames)	2 wks
Apr	10	Rising Damp (YTV)	4 wks
May	1	Armchair Thriller (Thames)	1 wk

	8	European Cup Final (ITV)	1 wk
	15	Armchair Thriller (Thames)	1 wk
	22	The TV Times Top Ten Awards (Thames)	1 wk
	29	Best Sellers (ITV)	1 wk
Jun	5	Winner Takes All (YTV)	1 wk
	12	Life Begins at Forty (YTV)	1 wk
	19	Winner Takes All (YTV)	1 wk
	26	Life Begins at Forty (YTV)	2 wks
Jul	10	That's Life (BBC)	1 wk
	17	The Incredible Hulk (ITV)	1 wk
	24	Life Begins at Forty (YTV)	1 wk
	31	London Night Out (Thames)	4 wks
Aug	28	Bless This House (ITV)	1 wk
Sep	4	On Her Majesty's Secret Service (ITV)	1 wk
	11	3-2-1 (YTV)	2 wks
	25	All Creatures Great and Small (BBC)	1 wk
Oct	2	Coronation Street (Granada)	2 wks
	16	The Morecambe and Wise Show (Thames)	1 wk
	23	Coronation Street (Granada)	2 wks
Nov	6	Some Mothers Do 'Ave 'Em (BBC)	2 wks
	20	Coronation Street (Granada)	1 wk
	27	Robin's Nest (Thames)	1 wk
Dec	4	Coronation Street (Granada)	2 wks
	18	Sale of the Century (Anglia)	1 wk
	25	The Morecambe and Wise Christmas Show (Thames)	1 wk

1979

Jan	1	The Two Ronnies (BBC)	1 wk
	8	This is Your Life (Thames)	4 wks
Feb	5	Coronation Street (Granada)	1 wk
	12	This is Your Life (Thames)	4 wks
Mar	12	The Benny Hill Show (Thames)	1 wk
	19	Dirty Money (ITV)	1 wk
	26	Coronation Street (Granada)= The Morecambe and Wise Show (Thames)	1 wk
Apr	2	This is Your Life (Thames)	1 wk
	9	Porridge (BBC)	1 wk

	16	Coronation Street (Granada)	1 wk
	23	The Benny Hill Show (Thames)	1 wk
	30	Coronation Street (Granada)	1 wk
May	7	Blankety Blank (BBC)	1 wk
	14	Coronation Street (Granada)	2 wks
	28	European Cup Final (BBC)	1 wk
Jun	4	Dick Emery Comedy Hour (Thames)	1 wk
	11	Midweek Sports Special (ITV)	1 wk
	18	The Benny Hill Show (Thames)	1 wk
	25	Coronation Street (Granada)	4 wks
Jul	23	Explorers of the Deep (BBC)	1 wk
	30	The Benny Hill Show (Thames)	1 wk
Aug	6	Explorers of the Deep (BBC)	2 wks
	20	Seaside Special (BBC)	1 wk
	27	Saturday Night at the Movies (BBC)	1 wk

The industrial dispute beginning the week commencing 13 August 1979 took all ITV programmes off the air until 5:45 p.m. on Wednesday 24 October. No charts were published for the weeks 3 and 10 September.

Sep	17	Blankety Blank (BBC)	1 wk
	24	To the Manor Born (BBC)	4 wks
Oct	22	The Rockford Files (BBC)	1 wk
	29	To the Manor Born (BBC)	2 wks
Nov	12	The Sunday Film (BBC)	1 wk
	19	The Generation Game (BBC)	1 wk
	26	Coronation Street (Granada)	2 wks
Dec	10	Only When I Laugh (YTV)	1 wk
	17	The Poseidon Adventure (BBC)	1 wk
	24	To the Manor Born (BBC)	1 wk
	31	This is Your Life (Thames)	1 wk

1980

Jan	7	This is Your Life (Thames)	1 wk
	14	Live and Let Die (ITV)	1 wk
	21	Jim'll Fix It (BBC)	1 wk
	28	All Creatures Great and Small (BBC)	1 wk
Feb	4	Jim'll Fix It (BBC)	1 wk

11	All Creatures Great and Small (BBC)	1 wk
18	Jim'll Fix It (BBC)	4 wks
Mar 17	All Creatures Great and Small (BBC)	1 wk
24	This is Your Life (Thames)	2 wks
Apr 7	Dallas (BBC)	1 wk
14	This is Your Life (Thames)	1 wk
21	Coronation Street (Granada)	1 wk
28	Only When I Laugh (YTV)	3 wks
May 19	Coronation Street (Granada)	1 wk
26	European Cup Final (Thames)	1 wk
Jun 2	It'll be Alright on the Night (LWT)	1 wk
9	European Championship Football (ITV)	1 wk
16	Coronation Street (Granada)	5 wks
Jul 21	Last of the Summer Wine (BBC)	1 wk
28	Coronation Street (Granada)	2 wks
Aug 11	Last of the Summer Wine (BBC)	1 wk
18	Coronation Street (Granada)	1 wk
25	The Generation Game (BBC)	1 wk
Sep 1	The Morecambe and Wise Show (Thames)	3 wks
22	The Generation Game (BBC)	1 wk
29	To the Manor Born (BBC)	1 wk
Oct 6	The Morecambe and Wise Show (Thames)	1 wk
13	To the Manor Born (BBC)	4 wks
Nov 10	Dallas (BBC)	3 wks
Dec 1	Coronation Street (Granada)	3 wks
22	Blankety Blank (BBC)	1 wk
29	Coronation Street (Granada)	1 wk

1981

Jan 5	The Benny Hill Show (Thames)	1 wk
12	Coronation Street (Granada)	1 wk
19	This is Your Life (Thames)	4 wks
Feb 16	Coronation Street (Granada)	2 wks
Mar 2	This is Your Life (Thames)	1 wk
9	Diamonds are Forever (ITV)	1 wk
16	Coronation Street (Granada)	2 wks

30	Hart to Hart (ITV)	1 wk
Apr 6	Coronation Street (Granada)	1 wk
13	Sorry! (BBC)	1 wk
20	Coronation Street (Granada)	5 wks
May 25	The Professionals (LWT)	1 wk
Jun 1	Hart to Hart (ITV)	1 wk
8	Coronation Street (Granada)	16 wks
Sep 28	The Benny Hill Show (Thames)	1 wk
Oct 5	Jaws (ITV)	1 wk
12	Coronation Street (Granada)	2 wks
26	To the Manor Born (BBC)	2 wks
Nov 9	Coronation Street (Granada)	1 wk
16	To the Manor Born (BBC)	2 wks
30	Bergerac (BBC)	1 wk
Dec 7	Coronation Street (Granada)	4 wks

1982

Jan 4	This is Your Life (Thames)	1 wk
11	Coronation Street (Granada)	1 wk
18	This is Your Life (Thames)	1 wk
25	Coronation Street (Granada)	1 wk
Feb 1	This is Your Life (Thames)	2 wks
15	Coronation Street (Granada)	1 wk
22	This is Your Life (Thames)	4 wks
Mar 22	The Spy Who Loved Me (ITV)	1 wk
29	This is Your Life (Thames)	1 wk
Apr 5	Coronation Street (Granada)	2 wks
19	The News (ITN)	1 wk
26	Hart to Hart (ITV)	1 wk
May 3	Coronation Street (Granada)	5 wks
Jun 7	Goliath Awaits (ITV)	1 wk
14	Live and Let Die (ITV)	1 wk
21	Coronation Street (Granada)	2 wks
Jul 5	World Cup (ITV)	1 wk
12	Coronation Street (Granada)	6 wks

Aug	23	Best Sellers (ITV)	1 wk
	30	Coronation Street (Granada)	7 wks
Oct	18	Star Wars (ITV)	1 wk
	25	Coronation Street (Granada)	3 wks
Nov	15	This is Your Life (Thames)	1 wk
	22	Coronation Street (Granada)	5 wks
Dec	27	Moonraker (ITV)	1 wk

1983

Jan	3	Coronation Street (Granada)	3 wks
	24	Labour Party Political Broadcast (all channels)	1 wk
	31	Coronation Street (Granada)	8 wks
Mar	28	Labour Party Political Broadcast (all channels)	1 wk
Apr	4	This is Your Life (Thames)	1 wk
	11	Coronation Street (Granada)	6 wks
May	23	FA Cup Final Replay (BBC1 and ITV)	1 wk
	30	When Time Ran Out (ITV)	1 wk
Jun	6	Coronation Street (Granada)	23 wks
Nov	14	Miss World (BBC)	1 wk
	21	This is Your Life (Thames)	2 wks
Dec	5	Coronation Street (Granada)	3 wks
	26	Last of the Summer Wine (BBC)	1 wk

1984

Jan	2	Thunderball (ITV)	1 wk
	9	Coronation Street (Granada)	8 wks
Mar	5	It'll be Alright on the Night (LWT)	1 wk
	12	Duty Free (YTV)	1 wk
	19	Coronation Street (Granada)	1 wk
	26	Duty Free (YTV)	1 wk
Apr	2	The Price is Right (Central)	1 wk
	9	Coronation Street (Granada)	7 wks
May	28	News at Ten (ITN)	1 wk
Jun	4	Jim Davidson's Special (Thames)	1 wk

	11	Coronation Street (Granada)	1 wk
	18	The Children's Royal Variety Performance (LWT)	1 wk
	25	Coronation Street (Granada)	2 wks
Jul	9	That's Life (BBC)	1 wk
	16	Coronation Street (Granada)	5 wks
Aug	20	Porridge (BBC)	1 wk
	27	Moonraker (ITV)	1 wk
Sep	3	Minder (Thames)	1 wk
	10	Lace (ITV)	1 wk
	17	Minder (Thames)	1 wk
	24	Coronation Street (Granada)	2 wks
Oct	8	Minder (Thames)	1 wk
	15	Coronation Street (Granada)	5 wks
Nov	19	The Royal Variety Performance (BBC)	1 wk
	26	Coronation Street (Granada)	4 wks
Dec	24	Porridge (BBC)	1 wk
	31	Wish You Were Here (Thames)	1 wk

1985

Jan	7	Coronation Street (Granada)	11 wks
Mar	25	A Royal Night of 100 Stars (LWT)	1 wk
Apr	1	Coronation Street (Granada)	2 wks
	15	Goldfinger (ITV)	1 wk
	22	Coronation Street (Granada)	5 wks
May	27	European Cup Final (BBC)	1 wk
Jun	3	Boxing (BBC)	1 wk
	10	Coronation Street (Granada)	5 wks
Jul	15	Dallas (BBC)	1 wk
	22	Coronation Street (Granada)	2 wks
Aug	5	Eastenders (BBC)	2 wks
	19	Coronation Street (Granada)	1 wk
	26	Open All Hours (BBC)	1 wk
Sep	2	Fresh Fields (Thames)	1 wk
	9	Open All Hours (BBC)	5 wks

| Oct | 14 | The Prince and Princess of Wales (ITN) | 1 wk |
| | 21 | Eastenders (BBC) | 11 wks |

1986

| Jan | 6 | Eastenders (BBC) | 52 wks |

1987

Jan	5	Eastenders (BBC)	50 wks
Dec	21	Coronation Street (Granada)	1 wk
	28	Eastenders (BBC)	1 wk

1988

Jan	4	Eastenders (BBC)	42 wks
Oct	24	Bread (BBC)	1 wk
	31	Eastenders (BBC)	9 wks

1989

Jan	2	Eastenders (BBC)	2 wks
	16	Coronation Street (Granada)	28 wks
Jul	31	Neighbours (BBC)	2 wks
Aug	14	Coronation Street (Granada)	19 wks
Dec	25	Crocodile Dundee (BBC)	1 wk

1990

Jan	1	Coronation Street (Granada)	13 wks
Apr	2	Eastenders (BBC)	1 wk
	9	Coronation Street (Granada)	23 wks
Sep	17	Eastenders (BBC)	1 wk
	24	Coronation Street (Granada)	4 wks
Oct	22	Eastenders (BBC)	2 wks
Nov	5	Coronation Street (Granada)	1 wk
	12	Eastenders (BBC)	1 wk
	19	Coronation Street (Granada)	4 wks
Dec	17	Eastenders (BBC)	3 wks

1991

Jan	7	Coronation Street (Granada)	1 wk
	14	Eastenders (BBC)	2 wks
	28	Only Fools and Horses (BBC)	1 wk
Feb	4	Eastenders (BBC)	3 wks
	25	Coronation Street (Granada)	1 wk
Mar	4	Eastenders (BBC)	3 wks
	25	Coronation Street (Granada)	1 wk
Apr	1	Eastenders (BBC)	2 wks
	15	The Darling Buds of May (YTV)	4 wks
May	13	Eastenders (BBC)	3 wks
Jun	3	Coronation Street (Granada)	2 wks
	17	Eastenders (BBC)	2 wks
Jul	1	Coronation Street (Granada)	6 wks
Aug	12	Eastenders (BBC)	1 wk
	19	Coronation Street (Granada)	3 wks
Sep	9	Eastenders (BBC)	2 wks
	23	Coronation Street (Granada)	1 wk
	30	Eastenders (BBC)	2 wks
Oct	14	Coronation Street (Granada)	3 wks
Nov	4	Eastenders (BBC)	4 wks
Dec	2	Coronation Street (Granada)	2 wks
	16	Eastenders (BBC)	3 wks

PICTURE CREDITS

544

BBC Books would like to thank the following for providing photographs and for permission to reproduce copyright material. While every effort has been made to trace and acknowledge all copyright holders, we would like to apologise should there have been any errors or omissions: Anglia Television; ITC Enterprises; BBC; British Film Institute; Central Independent Television; Granada Television; Independent Television Commission; Independent Television News; London Weekend Television; Thames Television; Yorkshire Television.

Other pictures: Aquarius Picture Library 39 (above), 47, 215, 223, 263 (right), 318 (2) (3), 351, 381 (above), 467; Camera Press 201, 475 (below); Hulton Deutsch Collection 374 (4); 498 (1) (2); 499 (4); Kobal Collection 85 (5); The Labour Party 345; Pictorial Press 23 (below), 479; Popperfoto 319 (5); 404 (1); 499 (5); Press Association 405 (8); Redferns 404 (3); Rex Features 53 (above), 157, 297 (below); Scope Features 179, 319 (4), 517; Universal Pictorial Press 227 (above), 485.

We would also like to acknowledge the following: Columbia Pictures Television; Grundy International Distribution; MCA Television International; Romulus Films Ltd; Twentieth Century Fox; United International Pictures; Viacom Entertainment; World Vision Enterprises.